Praise for the Reformation Commentary on Scripture

"Protestant reformers were fundamentally exegetes as much as theologians, yet (except for figures like Luther and Calvin) their commentaries and sermons have been neglected because these writings are not available in modern editions or languages. That makes this new series of Reformation Commentary on Scripture most welcome as a way to provide access to some of the wealth of biblical exposition of the sixteenth and seventeenth centuries. The editor's introduction explains the nature of the sources and the selection process; the intended audience of modern pastors and students of the Bible has led to a focus on theological and practical comments. Although it will be of use to students of the Reformation, this series is far from being an esoteric study of largely forgotten voices; this collection of reforming comments, comprehending every verse and provided with topical headings, will serve contemporary pastors and preachers very well."

Elsie Anne McKee, *Archibald Alexander Professor of Reformation Studies and the History of Worship, Princeton Theological Seminary*

"This series provides an excellent introduction to the history of biblical exegesis in the Reformation period. The introductions are accurate, clear and informative, and the passages intelligently chosen to give the reader a good idea of methods deployed and issues at stake. It puts precritical exegesis in its context and so presents it in its correct light. Highly recommended as reference book, course book and general reading for students and all interested lay and clerical readers."

Irena Backus, *Professeure Ordinaire, Institut d'histoire de la Réformation, Université de Genève*

"The Reformation Commentary on Scripture is a major publishing event—for those with historical interest in the founding convictions of Protestantism, but even more for those who care about understanding the Bible. As with IVP Academic's earlier Ancient Christian Commentary on Scripture, this effort brings flesh and blood to 'the communion of saints' by letting believers of our day look over the shoulders of giants from the past. By connecting the past with the present, and by doing so with the Bible at the center, the editors of this series perform a great service for the church. The series deserves the widest possible support."

Mark A. Noll, *Francis A. McAnaney Professor of History, University of Notre Dame*

"For those who preach and teach Scripture in the church, the Reformation Commentary on Scripture is a significant publishing event. Pastors and other church leaders will find delightful surprises, challenging enigmas and edifying insights in this series, as many Reformational voices are newly translated into English. The lively conversation in these pages can ignite today's pastoral imagination for fresh and faithful expositions of Scripture."

J. Todd Billings, *Gordon H. Girod Research Professor of Reformed Theology, Western Theological Seminary*

"The reformers discerned rightly what the church desperately needed in the sixteenth century—the bold proclamation of the Word based on careful study of the sacred Scriptures. We need not only to hear that same call again for our own day but also to learn from the Reformation how to do it. This commentary series is a godsend!"

Richard J. Mouw, *President Emeritus, Fuller Theological Seminary*

"Like the Ancient Christian Commentary on Scripture, the Reformation Commentary on Scripture does a masterful job of offering excellent selections from well-known and not-so-well-known exegetes. The editor's introductory survey is, by itself, worth the price of the book. It is easy to forget that there were more hands, hearts and minds involved in the Reformation than Luther and Calvin. Furthermore, encounters even with these figures are often limited to familiar quotes on familiar topics. However, the Reformation Commentary helps us to recognize the breadth and depth of exegetical interests and skill that fueled and continue to fuel faithful meditation on God's Word. I heartily recommend this series as a tremendous resource not only for ministry but for personal edification."

Michael S. Horton, *J. G. Machen Professor of Systematic Theology and Apologetics,*
Westminster Seminary, California

"The Reformation was ignited by a fresh reading of Scripture. In this series of commentaries, we contemporary interpreters are allowed to feel some of the excitement, surprise and wonder of our spiritual forebears. Luther, Calvin and their fellow revolutionaries were masterful interpreters of the Word. Now, in this remarkable series, some of our very best Reformation scholars open up the riches of the Reformation's reading of the Scripture."

William H. Willimon, *Professor of the Practice of Christian Ministry, Duke Divinity School*

"The Reformation Scripture principle set the entirety of Christian life and thought under the governance of the divine Word, and pressed the church to renew its exegetical labors. This series promises to place before the contemporary church the fruit of those labors, and so to exemplify life under the Word."

John Webster, *Professor of Divinity, University of St Andrews*

"Since Gerhard Ebeling's pioneering work on Luther's exegesis seventy years ago, the history of biblical interpretation has occupied many Reformation scholars and become a vital part of study of the period. The Reformation Commentary on Scripture provides fresh materials for students of Reformation-era biblical interpretation and for twenty-first-century preachers to mine the rich stores of insights from leading reformers of the sixteenth century into both the text of Scripture itself and its application in sixteenth-century contexts. This series will strengthen our understanding of the period of the Reformation and enable us to apply its insights to our own days and its challenges to the church."

Robert Kolb, *Professor Emeritus, Concordia Theological Seminary*

"The multivolume Ancient Christian Commentary on Scripture is a valuable resource for those who wish to know how the Fathers interpreted a passage of Scripture but who lack the time or the opportunity to search through the many individual works. This new Reformation Commentary on Scripture will do the same for the reformers and is to be warmly welcomed. It will provide much easier access to the exegetical treasures of the Reformation and will hopefully encourage readers to go back to some of the original works themselves."

Anthony N. S. Lane, *Professor of Historical Theology and Director of Research, London School of Theology*

"This volume of the RCS project is an invaluable source for pastors and the historically/biblically interested that provides unparalleled access not only to commentaries of the leading Protestant reformers but also to a host of nowadays unknown commentaters on Galatians and Ephesians. The RCS is sure to enhance and enliven contemporary exegesis. With its wide scope, the collection will enrich our understanding of the variety of Reformation thought and biblical exegesis."

Sigrun Haude, *Associate Professor of Reformation and Early Modern European History, University of Cincinnati*

"The Reformation Commentary on Scripture series promises to be an 'open sesame' to the biblical exegesis, exposition and application of the Bible that was the hallmark of the Reformation. While comparisons can be odious, the difference between Reformation commentary and exposition and much that both preceded and followed it is laid bare in these pages: whereas others write about the Bible from the outside, Reformation exposition carries with it the atmosphere of men who spoke and wrote from inside the Bible, experiencing the power of biblical teaching even as they expounded it. . . . This grand project sets before scholars, pastors, teachers, students and growing Christians an experience that can only be likened to stumbling into a group Bible study only to discover that your fellow participants include some of the most significant Christians of the Reformation and post-Reformation (for that matter, of any) era. Here the Word of God is explained in a variety of accents: German, Swiss, French, Dutch, English, Scottish and more. Each one vibrates with a thrilling sense of the living nature of God's Word and its power to transform individuals, churches and even whole communities. Here is a series to anticipate, enjoy and treasure."

Sinclair Ferguson, *Senior Minister, First Presbyterian Church, Columbia, South Carolina*

"I strongly endorse the Reformation Commentary on Scripture. Introducing how the Bible was interpreted during the age of the Reformation, these volumes will not only renew contemporary preaching, but they will also help us understand more fully how reading and meditating on Scripture can, in fact, change our lives!"

Lois Malcolm, *Associate Professor of Systematic Theology, Luther Seminary*

"Discerning the true significance of movements in theology requires acquaintance with their biblical exegesis. This is supremely so with the Reformation, which was essentially a biblical revival. The Reformation Commentary on Scripture will fill a yawning gap, just as the Ancient Christian Commentary did before it, and the first volume gets the series off to a fine start, whetting the appetite for more. Most heartily do I welcome and commend this long overdue project."

J. I. Packer, *Retired Board of Governors Professor of Theology, Regent College*

"There is no telling the benefits to emerge from the publication of this magnificent Reformation Commentary on Scripture series! Now exegetical and theological treasures from Reformation era commentators will be at our fingertips, providing new insights from old sources to give light for the present and future. This series is a gift to scholars and to the church; a wonderful resource to enhance our study of the written Word of God for generations to come!"

Donald K. McKim, *Executive Editor of Theology and Reference, Westminster John Knox Press*

"Why was this not done before? The publication of the Reformation Commentary on Scripture should be greeted with enthusiasm by every believing Christian—but especially by those who will preach and teach the Word of God. This commentary series brings the very best of the Reformation heritage to the task of exegesis and exposition, and each volume in this series represents a veritable feast that takes us back to the sixteenth century to enrich the preaching and teaching of God's Word in our own time."

R. Albert Mohler Jr., *President, The Southern Baptist Theological Seminary*

"Today more than ever, the Christian past is the church's future. InterVarsity Press has already brought the voice of the ancients to our ears. Now, in the Reformation Commentary on Scripture, we hear a timely word from the first Protestants as well."

Bryan Litfin, *Professor of Theology, Moody Bible Institute*

"I am delighted to see the Reformation Commentary on Scripture. The editors of this series have done us all a service by gleaning from these rich fields of biblical reflection. May God use this new life for these old words to give him glory and to build his church."

Mark Dever, *Senior Pastor, Capitol Hill Baptist Church, and President of 9Marks.org Ministries*

"Monumental and magisterial, the Reformation Commentary on Scripture, edited by Timothy George, is a remarkably bold and visionary undertaking. Bringing together a wealth of resources, these volumes will provide historians, theologians, biblical scholars, pastors and students with a fresh look at the exegetical insights of those who shaped and influenced the sixteenth-century Reformation. With this marvelous publication, InterVarsity Press has reached yet another plateau of excellence. We pray that this superb series will be used of God to strengthen both church and academy."

David S. Dockery, *President, Trinity International University*

"Detached from her roots, the church cannot reach the world as God intends. While every generation must steward the scriptural insights God grants it, only arrogance or ignorance causes leaders to ignore the contributions of those faithful leaders before us. The Reformation Commentary on Scripture roots our thought in great insights of faithful leaders of the Reformation to further biblical preaching and teaching in this generation."

Bryan Chapell, *chancellor and professor of practical theology, Covenant Theological Seminary*

"After reading several volumes of the Reformation Commentary on Scripture, I exclaimed, 'Hey, this is just what the doctor ordered—I mean Doctor Martinus Lutherus!' The church of today bearing his name needs a strong dose of the medicine this doctor prescribed for the ailing church of the sixteenth century. The reforming fire of Christ-centered preaching that Luther ignited is the only hope to reclaim the impact of the gospel to keep the Reformation going, not for its own sake but to further the renewal of the worldwide church of Christ today. This series of commentaries will equip preachers to step into their pulpits with confidence in the same living Word that inspired the witness of Luther and Calvin and many other lesser-known Reformers."

Carl E. Braaten, *cofounder of the Center for Catholic and Evangelical Theology*

REFORMATION COMMENTARY ON SCRIPTURE

NEW TESTAMENT
III

LUKE

EDITED BY
BETH KREITZER

GENERAL EDITOR
TIMOTHY GEORGE

ASSOCIATE GENERAL EDITOR
SCOTT M. MANETSCH

IVP Academic

An imprint of InterVarsity Press
Downers Grove, Illinois

InterVarsity Press
P.O. Box 1400, Downers Grove, IL 60515-1426
World Wide Web: www.ivpress.com
E-mail: email@ivpress.com

InterVarsity Press® is the book-publishing division of InterVarsity Christian Fellowship/USA®, a movement of students and faculty active on campus at hundreds of universities, colleges and schools of nursing in the United States of America, and a member movement of the International Fellowship of Evangelical Students. For information about local and regional activities, write Public Relations Dept., InterVarsity Christian Fellowship/USA, 6400 Schroeder Rd., P.O. Box 7895, Madison, WI 537077895, or visit the IVCF website at <www.intervarsity.org>.

Excerpts from The Writings of Dirk Philips, 1504-1568, edited and translated by Cornelius J. Dyck, William E. Keeney and Alvin J. Beachy, are copyright © 1992 by Herald Press, Scottdale, PA 15683. Used by permission.

Excerpts from Paraphrase on Luke 11–24, translated and edited by Jane E. Phillips, are copyright © 2003 by University of Toronto Press. www.utpress.utoronto.ca. Reprinted with permission of the publisher.

Excerpts from Luther's Works, vol. 75, Church Postil I, are copyright © 2013 by Concordia Publishing House, cph.org. Used by permission. All rights reserved.

Excerpts from Luther's Works, vol. 76, Church Postil II, are copyright © 2013 by Concordia Publishing House, cph.org. Used by permission. All rights reserved.

Excerpts from Catharina Regina von Greiffenberg reprinted with permission from Catharina Regina von Greiffenberg, from Meditations on the Incarnation, Passion, and Death of Jesus Christ, edited and translated by Lynne Tatlock, The Other Voice in Early Modern Europe, copyright © University of Chicago Press, Chicago, 2009. All rights reserved.

Excerpts from Katharina Schütz Zell reprinted with permission from Katharina Schütz Zell, from Church Mother: The Writings of a Protestant Reformer in Sixteenth-Century Germany, edited and translated by Elsie McKee, The Other Voice in Early Modern Europe, copyright © University of Chicago Press, Chicago, 2006. All rights reserved.

Excerpts from Thomas More, "A Treatice vpon the Passion of Chryste" (1534), The Complete Works of St. Thomas More 13, edited by Garry E. Haupt, 1-188, are copyright © Yale University Press, New Haven, 1976. Used by permission.

Excerpts from Thomas More. De Tristitia Christi, The Complete Works of St. Thomas More 14,1, edited and translated by Clarence H. Miller, are copyright © Yale University Press, New Haven, 1976. Used by permission.

Excerpts from John Calvin, Institutes of the Christian Religion (1559), edited by John T. McNeill, translated by Ford Lewis Battles, Library of Christian Classics 20-21, are copyright © Westminster Press, Philadelphia, 1960. Used by permission.

Excerpts from Denck, Hans, The Spiritual Legacy of Hans Denck: Interpretation and Translation of Key Texts, edited by Clarence Bauman, are copyright © Brill, Leiden, 1991. Used by permission of Koninklijke BRILL NV.

Design: Cindy Kiple
Images: Wooden cross: iStockphoto
The Protestant Church in Lyon: The Protestant Church in Lyon, called "The Paradise" at Bibliotheque Publique et Universitaire, Geneva, Switzerland, Erich Lessing/Art Resource, NY.
Image of Jesus' Baptism in Jacques Lefèvre d'Étaples, Commentarii Initiatorii in Quatuor Evangelia (Nuremberg: Petreius, 1526), 201v; Bayerische StaatsBibliothek digital.

ISBN 978-0-8308-2966-8 (print)
ISBN 978-0-8308-6480-5 (digital)

Printed in the United States of America ∞

Library of Congress Cataloging-in-Publication Data
Luke / edited by Beth Kreitzer.
       pages cm. — (Reformation commentary on Scripture. New
Testament ; Volume 3)
    Includes bibliographical references and index.
    ISBN 978-0-8308-2966-8 (hardcover : alk. paper)
    1. Bible. Luke—Commentaries. I. Kreitzer, Beth, editor.
    BS2595.53.L864 2014
    226.4'0709031—dc23
                                      2014034431

| P | 28 | 27 | 26 | 25 | 24 | 23 | 22 | 21 | 20 | 19 | 18 | 17 | 16 | 15 | 14 | 13 | 12 | 11 | 10 | 9 | 8 | 7 | 6 | 5 | 4 | 3 | 2 | 1 |
| Y | 39 | 38 | 37 | 36 | 35 | 34 | 33 | 32 | 31 | 30 | 29 | 28 | 27 | 26 | 25 | 24 | 23 | 22 | 21 | 20 | 19 | 18 | 17 | 16 | 15 |

For Lucas

Reformation Commentary on Scripture
Project Staff

Project Editor
David W. McNutt

---

*Managing Editor and
Production Manager*
Benjamin M. McCoy

Copyeditor
Linda Triemstra

Assistant Project Editor
Todd R. Hains

Editorial Assistant
Ethan McCarthy

Assistants to the General Editors
Le-Ann Little
Jason Odom

Design
Cindy Kiple

Design Assistant
Beth McGill

Content Production
Richard Chung
Kirsten Pott
Maureen G. Tobey
Jeanna L. Wiggins

Proofreaders
Ashley Davila
Ethan McCarthy

Print Coordinator
Jim Erhart

InterVarsity Press

Publisher
Robert A. Fryling

Associate Publisher, Editorial
Andrew T. Le Peau

Senior Editor
Daniel G. Reid

Production Director
Anne Gerth

CONTENTS

ACKNOWLEDGMENTS

Like Luke, I appreciate that "many have undertaken to compile a narrative of the things that have been accomplished" (Lk 1:1) and that this volume follows other, greater witnesses to and ministers of the Word. My own work rests on the efforts of so many others that it is difficult to recognize and thank them all. My first and greatest debt is to all those reformers and theologians, men and women of faith of the early modern period, who thought, wrote and preached about the Gospel of Luke, allowing me to come to a greater understanding not only of the Reformation but also of the Bible itself and its meaning(s) in the great tradition of the church. Theophilus may have received his confirmation through the "orderly account" provided by Luke, but my own confirmation comes through the faithful wrestling with the text by my colleagues of the past and present.

I would like to thank Timothy George and Scott Manetsch, General Editor and Associate General Editor of the Reformation Commentary Series, both for their leadership and for inviting me to participate in the project. The project editors, Joel Scandrett, Michael Gibson, Brannon Ellis, Dan Reid and David McNutt, have provided invaluable feedback, help in finding sources, and continued encouragement throughout the process. I would like to give a special thanks to Todd Hains for help in finding new sources, which was one of the most challenging aspects of this project.

David Steinmetz was my initial guide into the history of scriptural exegesis, and a role model for life as a Christian, a theologian and a member of the academy—he has my great esteem and deserves my thanks as well. Many of my fellow editors, and dear friends, are also former students of David, and I would like to note my appreciation and affection for them here. John Thompson deserves the recognition (or the blame) for introducing this series to me and asking me to participate. He, Mickey Mattox and Craig Farmer have been particularly helpful whenever I had questions, Latin or otherwise, related to the project or to life in general.

I should also recognize here the anonymous armies who have worked to digitize sources from the early modern period and have provided them on websites such as the Post-Reformation Digital Library and the Münchener DigitalisierungsZentrum Digitale Bibliothek, both of which (along with World Cat) are stored under "Popular" on my laptop. Without the countless hours these folks spent digitizing and storing documents for public use, I would not have been able to complete this project.

Finally, I would like to thank my family, especially my husband, Lucas Lamadrid; my children Claire, Grace and Jack; and my parents, John and Sonja (who were always willing to take the kids off my hands). For some years of collecting, reading, translating and writing, I was a full-time parent and only a part-time academic, so my children grew up along with the book and are now also almost ready to be released into the world. Without them, I might well have finished this book sooner, but my life would have been immeasurably diminished, for they are far more important than any book on a shelf.

Beth Kreitzer

ABBREVIATIONS

ACCS   Ancient Christian Commentary on Scripture. 29 vols. Edited by Thomas C. Oden. Downers Grove, IL: InterVarsity Press, 1998–2009.

ANF   The Ante-Nicene Fathers. 10 vols. Edited by Alexander Roberts and James Donaldson. Buffalo, NY: Christian Literature, 1885–1896. Available online at www.ccel.org.

BCP 1549   The Book of Common Prayer (1549). In The Two Liturgies, A.D. 1549 and A.D. 1552. Edited by Joseph Ketley, 9-158. Cambridge: Cambridge University Press, 1844.

BoC   The Book of Concord: The Confessions of the Evangelical Lutheran Church. Edited by Robert Kolb and Timothy J. Wengert. Translated by Charles Arand, et al. Minneapolis: Fortress, 2000.

BRN   Bibliotheca Reformatoria Neederlandica. 10 vols. Edited by S. Cramer and F. Pijper. The Hague: Martinus Nijhoff, 1903–1914. Digital copies online at babel.hathitrust.org.

BSLK   Die Bekenntnisschriften der evangelisch-lutherischen Kirche. 12th ed. Göttingen: Vandenhoeck & Ruprecht, 1998.

CHB   Cambridge History of the Bible. 3 vols. Cambridge: Cambridge University Press, 1963-1970.

CO   Ioannis Calvini Opera quae supersunt omnia. 59 vols. Corpus Reformatorum 29-88. Edited by G. Baum, E. Cunitz and E. Reuss. Brunswick and Berlin: C. A. Schwetschke, 1863–1900. Digital copy online at archive-ouverte.unige.ch/unige:650.

CRR   Classics of the Radical Reformation. 12 vols. Waterloo, ON, and Scottdale, PA: Herald Press, 1973–2010.

CS   Corpus Schwenckfeldianorum. 19 vols. Edited by Chester David Hartranft. Leipzig: Breitkopf and Härtel, 1907–1961. Digital copies online at babel.hathitrust.org.

CTS   Calvin Translation Society edition of Calvin's commentaries. 46 vols. Edinburgh, 1843–1855. Several reprints, but variously bound; volume numbers (when cited) are relative to specific commentaries and not to the entire set. Available online at www.ccel.org.

CWE   Collected Works of Erasmus. 86 vols. projected. Toronto: University of Toronto Press, 1969–.

CWM	*The Complete Works of St. Thomas More.* 15 vols. New Haven, CT: Yale University Press, 1963–1997.
DMBI	*Dictionary of Major Biblical Interpreters.* Edited by Donald K. McKim. Downers Grove, IL: InterVarsity Press, 2007.
E²	*Dr. Martin Luther's sämmtliche Werke.* 2nd ed. 26 vols. Frankfurt and Erlangen: Heyder & Zimmer, 1862–1885. Digital copies online at babel.hathitrust.org.
EEBO	Early English Books Online. Subscription database, eebo.chadwyck.com.
FC	Fathers of the Church: A New Translation. Washington, DC: Catholic University of America Press, 1947–.
LB	*Desderii Erasmi Roterodami Opera Omnia.* 10 vols. Edited by Jean LeClerc. Leiden: Van der Aa, 1704–1706; reprint, Hildesheim: Georg Olms, 1961–1962. Digital copies online at babel.hathitrust.org.
LCC	Library of Christian Classics. 26 vols. Edited by John Baillie, et al. Philadelphia: Westminster Press, 1953–1966.
LEA	*D. Martin Luthers Evangelien-Auslegung.* 5 vols. Edited by Erwin Mülhaupt. Göttingen: Vandenhoeck & Ruprecht, 1961. Digital copies online at digi20.digitale-sammlungen.de.
LW	*Luther's Works* [*American edition*]. 82 vols. projected. St. Louis: Concordia; Philadelphia: Fortress, 1955–1986; 2009–.
MO	*Philippi Melanthonis Opera quae supersunt omnia.* 28 vols. Corpus Reformatorum 1-28. Edited by C. G. Bretschneider. Halle: C. A. Schwetschke, 1834–1860. Digital copies online at archive.org and books.google.com
mss.	Manuscripts
OER	*Oxford Encyclopedia of the Reformation.* 4 vols. Edited by Hans J. Hillerbrand. New York: Oxford University Press, 1996.
NPNF	A Select Library of the Nicene and Post-Nicene Fathers of the Christian Church. 28 vols. in two series, denoted as NPNF and NPNF². Edited by Philip Schaff, et al. Buffalo, NY: Christian Literature, 1887–1894. Several reprints; also available online at www.ccel.org.
QGT	Quellen zur Geschichte der Täufer. 18 vols. Leipzig: M. Heinsius; Gütersloh: Gerd Mohn, 1930–. The first two volumes are under the series title Quellen zur Geschichte der Wiedertäufer.
PG	Patrologia cursus completus. Series Graeca. 161 vols. Edited by J.-P. Migne. Paris, 1857–1866.
PL	Patrologia cursus completus. Series Latina. 221 vols. Edited by J.-P. Migne. Paris: Migne, 1844–1864.
r, v	Some early books are numbered not by page but by folio (leaf). Front and back sides (pages) of a numbered folio are indicated by *recto* (r) and *verso* (v), respectively.
RCS	Reformation Commentary on Scripture. 28 vols. projected. Edited by Timothy

George and Scott M. Manetsch. Downers Grove, IL: IVP Academic, 2011–.

WA   *D. Martin Luthers Werke, Kritische Gesamtausgabe: [Schriften].* 73 vols. Weimar: Hermann Böhlaus Nachfolger, 1883–2009. Digital copies online at archive.org.

WABr *D. Martin Luthers Werke, Kritische Gesamtausgabe: Briefwechsel.* 18 vols. Weimar: Hermann Böhlaus Nachfolger, 1930–1983.

WADB *D. Martin Luthers Werke, Kritische Gesamtausgabe: Deutsche Bibel.* 12 vols. Weimar: Böhlaus Nachfolger, 1906–1961.

WATR *D. Martin Luthers Werke, Kritische Gesamtausgabe: Tischreden.* 6 vols. Weimar: Hermann Böhlaus Nachfolger, 1912–1921. Digital copies online at archive.org.

ZO   *Huldrici Zuinglii Opera.* 8 vols. Edited by Johann Melchior Schuler and Johannes Schulthess. Zurich: F. Schulthess, 1828–1842. Digital copies online at babel .hathitrust.org.

ZSW   *Huldreich Zwinglis Sämtliche Werke.* 14 vols. Corpus Reformatorum 88-101. Edited by E. Egli, et al. Berlin: C. A. Schwetschke, 1905–1959; reprint Zürich: Theologischer Verlag Zürich, 1983. Digital access via Institut für Schweizerische Reformationsgeschichte.

BIBLE TRANSLATIONS

DV	Douay-Rheims Version
ESV	English Standard Version
KJV	King James Version
LXX	Septuagint
NKJV	New King James Version
RSV	Revised Standard Version
Vg	Vulgate

A GUIDE TO USING THIS COMMENTARY

Several features have been incorporated into the design of this commentary. The following comments are intended to assist readers in making full use of this volume.

Pericopes of Scripture

The scriptural text has been divided into pericopes, or passages, usually several verses in length. Each of these pericopes is given a heading, which appears at the beginning of the pericope. For example, the first pericope in the commentary on Luke is "1:1-4 The Prologue." This heading is followed by the Scripture passage quoted in the English Standard Version (ESV). The Scripture passage is provided for the convenience of readers, but it is also in keeping with Reformation-era commentaries, which often followed the patristic and medieval commentary tradition, in which the citations of the reformers were arranged according to the text of Scripture.

Overviews

Following each pericope of text is an overview of the Reformation authors' comments on that pericope. The format of this overview varies among the volumes of this series, depending on the requirements of the specific book(s) of Scripture. The function of the overview is to identify succinctly the key exegetical, theological and pastoral concerns of the Reformation writers arising from the pericope, providing the reader with an orientation to Reformation-era approaches and emphases. It tracks a reasonably cohesive thread of argument among reformers' comments, even though they are derived from diverse sources and generations. Thus, the summaries do not proceed chronologically or by verse sequence. Rather, they seek to rehearse the overall course of the reformers' comments on that pericope.

We do not assume that the commentators themselves anticipated or expressed a formally received cohesive argument but rather that the various arguments tend to flow in a plausible, recognizable pattern. Modern readers can thus glimpse aspects of continuity in the flow of diverse exegetical traditions representing various generations and geographical locations.

Topical Headings

An abundance of varied Reformation-era comment is available for each pericope. For this reason we have broken the pericopes into two levels. First is the verse with its topical heading. The reformers' comments are then focused on aspects of each verse, with topical headings summarizing the essence of the individual comment by evoking a key phrase, metaphor or idea. This feature provides a bridge by which modern readers can enter into the heart of the Reformation-era comment.

Identifying the Reformation Authors, Texts and Events

Following the topical heading of each section of comment, the name of the Reformation commentator is given. An English translation (where needed) of the reformer's comment is then provided. This is immediately followed by the title of the original work rendered in English.

Readers who wish to pursue a deeper investigation of the reformers' works cited in this commentary will find full bibliographic detail for each reformation title provided in the bibliography at the back of the volume. Information on English translations (where available) and standard original-language editions and critical editions of the works cited is found in the bibliography. The Biographical Sketches section provides brief overviews of the life and work of each commentator, and each confession or collaborative work, appearing in the present volume (as well as in any previous volumes). Finally, a Timeline of the Reformation offers broader context for people, places and events relevant to the commentators and their works.

Footnotes and Back Matter

To aid the reader in exploring the background and texts in further detail, this commentary utilizes footnotes. The use and content of footnotes may vary among the volumes in this series. Where footnotes appear, a footnote number directs the reader to a note at the bottom of the page, where one will find annotations (clarifications or biblical cross references), information on English translations (where available) or standard original-language editions of the work cited.

Where original-language texts have remained untranslated into English, we provide new translations. Where there is any serious ambiguity or textual problem in the selection, we have tried to reflect the best available textual tradition. Wherever current English translations are already well rendered, they are utilized, but where necessary they are stylistically updated. A single asterisk (*) indicates that a previous English translation has been updated to modern English or amended for easier reading. We have standardized spellings and made grammatical variables uniform so that our English references will not reflect the linguistic oddities of the older English translations. For ease of reading we have in some cases removed superfluous conjunctions.

GENERAL INTRODUCTION

The Reformation Commentary on Scripture (RCS) is a twenty-eight-volume series of exegetical comment covering the entire Bible and gathered from the writings of sixteenth-century preachers, scholars and reformers. The RCS is intended as a sequel to the highly acclaimed Ancient Christian Commentary on Scripture (ACCS), and as such its overall concept, method, format and audience are similar to the earlier series. Both series are committed to the renewal of the church through careful study and meditative reflection on the Old and New Testaments, the charter documents of Christianity, read in the context of the worshiping, believing community of faith across the centuries. However, the patristic and Reformation eras are separated by nearly a millennium, and the challenges of reading Scripture with the reformers require special attention to their context, resources and assumptions. The purpose of this general introduction is to present an overview of the context and process of biblical interpretation in the age of the Reformation.

Goals

The Reformation Commentary on Scripture seeks to introduce its readers to the depth and richness of exegetical ferment that defined the Reformation era. The RCS has four goals: the enrichment of contemporary biblical interpretation through exposure to Reformation-era biblical exegesis; the renewal of contemporary preaching through exposure to the biblical insights of the Reformation writers; a deeper understanding of the Reformation itself and the breadth of perspectives represented within it; and a recovery of the profound integration of the life of faith and the life of the mind that should characterize Christian scholarship. Each of these goals requires a brief comment.

Renewing contemporary biblical interpretation. During the past half-century, biblical hermeneutics has become a major growth industry in the academic world. One of the consequences of the historical-critical hegemony of biblical studies has been the privileging of contemporary philosophies and ideologies at the expense of a commitment to the Christian church as the primary reading community within which and for which biblical exegesis is done. Reading Scripture with the church fathers and the reformers is a corrective to all such imperialism of the present. One of the greatest skills required for a fruitful interpretation of the Bible is the ability to listen. We rightly emphasize the importance of listening to the voices of contextual theologies today, but in doing so we often marginalize or ignore another crucial context—the community of believing Christians through the centuries. The serious study of Scripture requires more than the latest

Bible translation in one hand and the latest commentary (or niche study Bible) in the other. John L. Thompson has called on Christians today to practice the art of "reading the Bible with the dead."[1] The RCS presents carefully selected comments from the extant commentaries of the Reformation as an encouragement to more in-depth study of this important epoch in the history of biblical interpretation.

Strengthening contemporary preaching. The Protestant reformers identified the public preaching of the Word of God as an indispensible means of grace and a sure sign of the true church. Through the words of the preacher, the living voice of the gospel (*viva vox evangelii*) is heard. Luther famously said that the church is not a "pen house" but a "mouth house."[2] The Reformation in Switzerland began when Huldrych Zwingli entered the pulpit of the Grossmünster in Zurich on January 1, 1519, and began to preach a series of expositional sermons chapter by chapter from the Gospel of Matthew. In the following years he extended this homiletical approach to other books of the Old and New Testaments. Calvin followed a similar pattern in Geneva. Many of the commentaries represented in this series were either originally presented as sermons or were written to support the regular preaching ministry of local church pastors. Luther said that the preacher should be a *bonus textualis*—a good one with a text—well-versed in the Scriptures. Preachers in the Reformation traditions preached not only about the Bible but also from it, and this required more than a passing acquaintance with its contents. Those who have been charged with the office of preaching in the church today can find wisdom and insight—and fresh perspectives—in the sermons of the Reformation and the biblical commentaries read and studied by preachers of the sixteenth century.

Deepening understanding of the Reformation. Some scholars of the sixteenth century prefer to speak of the period they study in the plural, the European Reformations, to indicate that many diverse impulses for reform were at work in this turbulent age of transition from medieval to modern times.[3] While this point is well taken, the RCS follows the time-honored tradition of using Reformation in the singular form to indicate not only a major moment in the history of Christianity in the West but also, as Hans J. Hillerbrand has put it, "an essential cohesiveness in the heterogeneous pursuits of religious reform in the sixteenth century."[4] At the same time, in developing guidelines to assist the volume editors in making judicious selections from the vast amount of commentary material available in this period, we have stressed the multifaceted character of the Reformation across many confessions, theological orientations and political settings.

Advancing Christian scholarship. By assembling and disseminating numerous voices from such a signal period as the Reformation, the RCS aims to make a significant contribution to the ever-growing stream of Christian scholarship. The post-Enlightenment split between the study

---

[1]John L. Thompson, *Reading the Bible with the Dead* (Grand Rapids: Eerdmans, 2007).
[2]WA 10,2:48.
[3]See Carter Lindberg, *The European Reformations*, 2nd ed. (Malden, MA: Wiley-Blackwell, 2010).
[4]Hans J. Hillerbrand, *The Division of Christendom* (Louisville, KY: Westminster John Knox, 2007), x. Hillerbrand has also edited the standard reference work in Reformation studies, *OER*. See also Diarmaid MacCulloch, *The Reformation* (New York: Viking, 2003), and Patrick Collinson, *The Reformation: A History* (New York: Random House, 2004).

of the Bible as an academic discipline and the reading of the Bible as spiritual nurture was foreign to the reformers. For them the study of the Bible was transformative at the most basic level of the human person: *coram deo*.

The reformers all repudiated the idea that the Bible could be studied and understood with dispassionate objectivity, as a cold artifact from antiquity. Luther's famous Reformation break-through triggered by his laborious study of the Psalms and Paul's letter to the Romans is well known, but the experience of Cambridge scholar Thomas Bilney was perhaps more typical. When Erasmus's critical edition of the Greek New Testament was published in 1516, it was accompanied by a new translation in elegant Latin. Attracted by the classical beauty of Erasmus's Latin, Bilney came across this statement in 1 Timothy 1:15: "Christ Jesus came into the world to save sinners." In the Greek this sentence is described as *pistos ho logos*, which the Vulgate had rendered *fidelis sermo*, "a faithful saying." Erasmus chose a different word for the Greek *pistos—certus*, "sure, cer-tain." When Bilney grasped the meaning of this word applied to the announcement of salvation in Christ, he tells us that "Immediately, I felt a marvellous comfort and quietness, insomuch as 'my bruised bones leaped for joy.'"[5]

Luther described the way the Bible was meant to function in the minds and hearts of believ-ers when he reproached himself and others for studying the nativity narrative with such cool unconcern:

> I hate myself because when I see Christ laid in the manger or in the lap of his mother and hear the angels sing, my heart does not leap into flame. With what good reason should we all despise ourselves that we remain so cold when this word is spoken to us, over which everyone should dance and leap and burn for joy! We act as though it were a frigid historical fact that does not smite our hearts, as if someone were merely relating that the sultan has a crown of gold.[6]

It was a core conviction of the Reformation that the careful study and meditative listening to the Scriptures, what the monks called *lectio divina*, could yield transformative results for *all* of life. The value of such a rich commentary, therefore, lies not only in the impressive volume of Reforma-tion-era voices that are presented throughout the course of the series but in the many particular fields for which their respective lives and ministries are relevant. The Reformation is consequen-tial for historical studies, both church as well as secular history. Biblical and theological studies, to say nothing of pastoral and spiritual studies, also stand to benefit and progress immensely from renewed engagement today, as mediated through the RCS, with the reformers of yesteryear.

Perspectives

In setting forth the perspectives and parameters of the RCS, the following considerations have proved helpful.

---

[5]John Foxe, *The Acts and Monuments of John Foxe: A New and Complete Edition*, 8 vols., ed. Stephen Reed Cattley (London: R. B. Seeley & W. Burnside, 1837), 4:635; quoting Ps 51:8; cited in A. G. Dickens, *The English Reformation*, 2nd ed. (University Park, PA: The Pennsylvannia State University Press, 1991), 102.
[6]WA 49:176-77, quoted in Roland Bainton, "The Bible in the Reformation," in *CHB*, 3:23.

Chronology. When did the Reformation begin, and how long did it last? In some traditional accounts, the answer was clear: the Reformation began with the posting of Luther's Ninety-five Theses at Wittenberg in 1517 and ended with the death of Calvin in Geneva in 1564. Apart from reducing the Reformation to a largely German event with a side trip to Switzerland, this perspective fails to do justice to the important events that led up to Luther's break with Rome and its many reverberations throughout Europe and beyond. In choosing commentary selections for the RCS, we have adopted the concept of the long sixteenth century, say, from the late 1400s to the mid-seventeenth century. Thus we have included commentary selections from early or pre-Reformation writers such as John Colet and Jacques Lefèvre d'Étaples to seventeenth-century figures such as Henry Ainsworth and Johann Gerhard.

Confession. The RCS concentrates primarily, though not exclusively, on the exegetical writings of the Protestant reformers. While the ACCS provided a compendium of key consensual exegetes of the early Christian centuries, the Catholic/Protestant confessional divide in the sixteenth century tested the very idea of consensus, especially with reference to ecclesiology and soteriology. While many able and worthy exegetes faithful to the Roman Catholic Church were active during this period, this project has chosen to include primarily those figures that represent perspectives within the Protestant Reformation. For this reason we have not included comments on the apocryphal or deuterocanonical writings.

We recognize that "Protestant" and "Catholic" as contradistinctive labels are anachronistic terms for the early decades of the sixteenth century before the hardening of confessional identities surrounding the Council of Trent (1545–1563). Protestant figures such as Philipp Melanchthon, Johannes Oecolampadius and John Calvin were all products of the revival of sacred letters known as biblical humanism. They shared an approach to biblical interpretation that owed much to Desiderius Erasmus and other scholars who remained loyal to the Church of Rome. Careful comparative studies of Protestant and Catholic exegesis in the sixteenth century have shown surprising areas of agreement when the focus was the study of a particular biblical text rather than the standard confessional debates.

At the same time, exegetical differences among the various Protestant groups could become strident and church-dividing. The most famous example of this is the interpretive impasse between Luther and Zwingli over the meaning of "This is my body" (Mt 26:26) in the words of institution. Their disagreement at the Colloquy of Marburg in 1529 had important christological and pastoral implications, as well as social and political consequences. Luther refused fellowship with Zwingli and his party at the end of the colloquy; in no small measure this bitter division led to the separate trajectories pursued by Lutheran and Reformed Protestantism to this day. In Elizabethan England, Puritans and Anglicans agreed that "Holy Scripture containeth all things necessary to salvation: so that whatsoever is not read therein, nor may be proved thereby, is not to be required of any man" (article 6 of the Thirty-nine Articles of Religion), yet on the basis of their differing interpretations of the Bible they fought bitterly over the structures of the church, the clothing of the clergy and the ways of worship. On the matter of infant baptism, Catholics and

Protestants alike agreed on its propriety, though there were various theories as to how a practice not mentioned in the Bible could be justified biblically. The Anabaptists were outliers on this subject. They rejected infant baptism altogether. They appealed to the example of the baptism of Jesus and to his final words as recorded in the Gospel of Matthew (Mt 28:19-20), "Go therefore, and make disciples of all nations, baptizing them in the name of the Father, and of the Son, and of the Holy Spirit, teaching them to observe all that I have commanded you." New Testament Christians, they argued, are to follow not only the commands of Jesus in the Great Commission, but also the exact order in which they were given: evangelize, baptize, catechize.

These and many other differences of interpretation among the various Protestant groups are reflected in their many sermons, commentaries and public disputations. In the RCS, the volume editor's introduction to each volume is intended to help the reader understand the nature and significance of doctrinal conversations and disputes that resulted in particular, and frequently clashing, interpretations. Footnotes throughout the text will be provided to explain obscure references, unusual expressions and other matters that require special comment. Volume editors have chosen comments on the Bible across a wide range of sixteenth-century confessions and schools of interpretation: biblical humanists, Lutheran, Reformed, Anglican, Puritan and Anabaptist. We have not pursued passages from post-Tridentine Catholic authors or from radical spiritualists and antitrinitarian writers, though sufficient material is available from these sources to justify another series.

Format. The design of the RCS is intended to offer reader-friendly access to these classic texts. The availability of digital resources has given access to a huge residual database of sixteenth-century exegetical comment hitherto available only in major research universities and rare book collections. The RCS has benefited greatly from online databases such as Alexander Street Press's Digital Library of Classical Protestant Texts (DLCPT) as well as freely accessible databases like the Post-Reformation Digital Library (prdl.org). Through the help of RCS editorial advisor Herman Selderhuis, we have also had access to the special Reformation collections of the Johannes a Lasco Bibliothek in Emden, Germany. In addition, modern critical editions and translations of Reformation sources have been published over the past generation. Original translations of Reformation sources are given unless an acceptable translation already exists.

Each volume in the RCS will include an introduction by the volume editor placing that portion of the canon within the historical context of the Protestant Reformation and presenting a summary of the theological themes, interpretive issues and reception of the particular book(s). The commentary itself consists of particular pericopes identified by a pericope heading; the biblical text in the English Standard Version (ESV), with significant textual variants registered in the footnotes; an overview of the pericope in which principal exegetical and theological concerns of the Reformation writers are succinctly noted; and excerpts from the Reformation writers identified by name according to the conventions of the *Oxford Encyclopedia of the Reformation*. Each volume will also include a bibliography of sources cited, as well as an appendix of authors and source works.

The Reformation era was a time of verbal as well as physical violence, and this fact has presented a challenge for this project. Without unduly sanitizing the texts, where they contain anti-Semitic, sexist or inordinately polemical rhetoric, we have not felt obliged to parade such comments either. We have noted the abridgement of texts with ellipses and an explanatory footnote. While this procedure would not be valid in the critical edition of such a text, we have deemed it appropriate in a series whose primary purpose is pastoral and devotional. When translating *homo* or similar terms that refer to the human race as a whole or to individual persons without reference to gender, we have used alternative English expressions to the word *man* (or derivative constructions that formerly were used generically to signify humanity at large), whenever such substitutions can be made without producing an awkward or artificial construction.

As is true in the ACCS, we have made a special effort where possible to include the voices of women, though we acknowledge the difficulty of doing so for the early modern period when for a variety of social and cultural reasons few theological and biblical works were published by women. However, recent scholarship has focused on a number of female leaders whose literary remains show us how they understood and interpreted the Bible. Women who made significant contributions to the Reformation include Marguerite d'Angoulême, sister of King Francis I, who supported French reformist evangelicals including Calvin and who published a religious poem influenced by Luther's theology, *The Mirror of the Sinful Soul*; Argula von Grumbach, a Bavarian noblewoman who defended the teachings of Luther and Melanchthon before the theologians of the University of Ingolstadt; Katharina Schütz Zell, the wife of a former priest, Matthias Zell, and a remarkable reformer in her own right—she conducted funerals, compiled hymnbooks, defended the downtrodden and published a defense of clerical marriage as well as composing works of consolation on divine comfort and pleas for the toleration of Anabaptists and Catholics alike; and Anne Askew, a Protestant martyr put to death in 1546 after demonstrating remarkable biblical prowess in her examinations by church officials. Other echoes of faithful women in the age of the Reformation are found in their letters, translations, poems, hymns, court depositions and martyr records.

Lay culture, learned culture. In recent decades, much attention has been given to what is called "reforming from below," that is, the expressions of religious beliefs and churchly life that characterized the popular culture of the majority of the population in the era of the Reformation. Social historians have taught us to examine the diverse pieties of townspeople and city folk, of rural religion and village life, the emergence of lay theologies and the experiences of women in the religious tumults of Reformation Europe.[7] Formal commentaries by their nature are artifacts of learned culture. Almost all of them were written in Latin, the lingua franca of learned discourse well past the age of the Reformation. Biblical commentaries were certainly not the primary means by which the Protestant Reformation spread so rapidly across wide sectors of sixteenth-century society. Small pamphlets and broadsheets, later called *Flugschriften* ("flying writings"), with their graphic woodcuts and cartoon-like depictions of Reformation personalities and events, became the means of choice for mass communication in the early age of printing. Sermons and works of

---

[7]See Peter Matheson, ed., *Reformation Christianity* (Minneapolis: Fortress, 2007).

---

devotion were also printed with appealing visual aids. Luther's early writings were often accompanied by drawings and sketches from Lucas Cranach and other artists. This was done "above all for the sake of children and simple folk," as Luther put it, "who are more easily moved by pictures and images to recall divine history than through mere words or doctrines."[8]

We should be cautious, however, in drawing too sharp a distinction between learned and lay culture in this period. The phenomenon of preaching was a kind of verbal bridge between scholars at their desks and the thousands of illiterate or semi-literate listeners whose views were shaped by the results of Reformation exegesis. According to contemporary witness, more than one thousand people were crowding into Geneva to hear Calvin expound the Scriptures every day.[9] An example of how learned theological works by Reformation scholars were received across divisions of class and social status comes from Lazare Drilhon, an apothecary of Toulon. He was accused of heresy in May 1545 when a cache of prohibited books was found hidden in his garden shed. In addition to devotional works, the French New Testament and a copy of Calvin's Genevan liturgy, there was found a series of biblical commentaries, translated from the Latin into French: Martin Bucer's on Matthew, François Lambert's on the Apocalypse and one by Oecolampadius on 1 John.[10] Biblical exegesis in the sixteenth century was not limited to the kind of full-length commentaries found in Drilhon's shed. Citations from the Bible and expositions of its meaning permeate the extant literature of sermons, letters, court depositions, doctrinal treatises, records of public disputations and even last wills and testaments. While most of the selections in the RCS will be drawn from formal commentary literature, other sources of biblical reflection will also be considered.

Historical Context

The medieval legacy. On October 18, 1512, the degree *Doctor in Biblia* was conferred on Martin Luther, and he began his career as a professor in the University of Wittenberg. As is well known, Luther was also a monk who had taken solemn vows in the Augustinian Order of Hermits at Erfurt. These two settings—the university and the monastery—both deeply rooted in the Middle Ages, form the background not only for Luther's personal vocation as a reformer but also for the history of the biblical commentary in the age of the Reformation. Since the time of the Venerable Bede (d. 735), sometimes called "the last of the Fathers," serious study of the Bible had taken place primarily in the context of cloistered monasteries. The Rule of St. Benedict brought together *lectio* and *meditatio*, the knowledge of letters and the life of prayer. The liturgy was the medium through which the daily reading of the Bible, especially the Psalms, and the sayings of the church fathers came together in the spiritual formation of the monks.[11] Essential to this understanding

---

[8]Martin Luther, "Personal Prayer Book," LW 43:42-43* (WA 10,2:458); quoted in R. W. Scribner, *For the Sake of Simple Folk: Popular Propaganda for the German Reformation* (Cambridge: Cambridge University Press, 1981), xi.

[9]Letter of De Beaulieu to Guillaume Farel (1561) in J. W. Baum, ed., *Theodor Beza nach handschriftlichen und anderen gleichzeitigen Quellen* (Leipzig: Weidmann, 1851) 2:92.

[10]Francis Higman, "A Heretic's Library: The Drilhon Inventory" (1545), in Francis Higman, *Lire et Découvire: la circulation des idées au temps de la Réforme* (Geneva: Droz, 1998), 65-85.

[11]See the classic study by Jean Leclercq, *The Love of Learning and the Desire for God* (New York: Fordham University Press, 1961).

was a belief in the unity of the people of God throughout time as well as space, and an awareness that life in this world was a preparation for the beatific vision in the next.

The source of theology was the study of the sacred page (*sacra pagina*); its object was the accumulation of knowledge not for its own sake but for the obtaining of eternal life. For these monks, the Bible had God for its author, salvation for its end and unadulterated truth for its matter, though they would not have expressed it in such an Aristotelian way. The medieval method of interpreting the Bible owed much to Augustine's *On Christian Doctrine*. In addition to setting forth a series of rules (drawn from an earlier work by Tyconius), Augustine stressed the importance of distinguishing the literal and spiritual or allegorical senses of Scripture. While the literal sense was not disparaged, the allegorical was valued because it enabled the believer to obtain spiritual benefit from the obscure places in the Bible, especially in the Old Testament. For Augustine, as for the monks who followed him, the goal of scriptural exegesis was freighted with eschatological meaning; its purpose was to induce faith, hope and love and so to advance in one's pilgrimage toward that city with foundations (see Heb 11:10).

Building on the work of Augustine and other church fathers going back to Origen, medieval exegetes came to understand Scripture as possessed of four possible meanings, the famous *quadriga*. The literal meaning was retained, of course, but the spiritual meaning was now subdivided into three senses: the allegorical, the moral and the anagogical. Medieval exegetes often referred to the four meanings of Scripture in a popular rhyme:

> The letter shows us what God and our fathers did;
> The allegory shows us where our faith is hid;
> The moral meaning gives us rules of daily life;
> The anagogy shows us where we end our strife.[12]

In this schema, the three spiritual meanings of the text correspond to the three theological virtues: faith (allegory), hope (anagogy) and love (the moral meaning). It should be noted that this way of approaching the Bible assumed a high doctrine of scriptural inspiration: the multiple meanings inherent in the text had been placed there by the Holy Spirit for the benefit of the people of God. The biblical justification for this method went back to the apostle Paul, who had used the words *allegory* and *type* when applying Old Testament events to believers in Christ (Gal 4:21-31; 1 Cor 10:1-11). The problem with this approach was knowing how to relate each of the four senses to one another and how to prevent Scripture from becoming a nose of wax turned this way and that by various interpreters. As G. R. Evans explains, "Any interpretation which could be put upon the text and was in keeping with the faith and edifying, had the warrant of God himself, for no human reader had the ingenuity to find more than God had put there."[13]

With the rise of the universities in the eleventh century, theology and the study of Scripture moved from the cloister into the classroom. Scripture and the Fathers were still important, but they came to function more as footnotes to the theological questions debated in the schools and

---

[12]Robert M. Grant, *A Short History of the Interpretation of the Bible* (New York: Macmillan, 1963), 119. A translation of the well-known Latin quatrain: *Littera gesta docet/Quid credas allegoria/Moralis quid agas/Quo tendas anagogia.*

[13]G. R. Evans, *The Language and Logic of the Bible: The Road to Reformation* (Cambridge: Cambridge University Press, 1985), 42.

brought together in an impressive systematic way in works such as Peter Lombard's *Books of Sentences* (the standard theology textbook of the Middle Ages) and the great scholastic *summae* of the thirteenth century. Indispensible to the study of the Bible in the later Middle Ages was the *Glossa ordinaria*, a collection of exegetical opinions by the church fathers and other commentators. Heiko Oberman summarized the transition from devotion to dialectic this way: "When, due to the scientific revolution of the twelfth century, Scripture became the *object* of study rather than the *subject* through which God speaks to the student, the difference between the two modes of speaking was investigated in terms of the texts themselves rather than in their relation to the recipients."[14] It was possible, of course, to be both a scholastic theologian and a master of the spiritual life. Meister Eckhart, for example, wrote commentaries on the Old Testament in Latin and works of mystical theology in German, reflecting what had come to be seen as a division of labor between the two.

An increasing focus on the text of Scripture led to a revival of interest in its literal sense. The two key figures in this development were Thomas Aquinas (d. 1274) and Nicholas of Lyra (d. 1340). Thomas is best remembered for his *Summa Theologiae*, but he was also a prolific commentator on the Bible. Thomas did not abandon the multiple senses of Scripture but declared that all the senses were founded on one—the literal—and this sense eclipsed allegory as the basis of sacred doctrine. Nicholas of Lyra was a Franciscan scholar who made use of the Hebrew text of the Old Testament and quoted liberally from works of Jewish scholars, especially the learned French rabbi Salomon Rashi (d. 1105). After Aquinas, Lyra was the strongest defender of the literal, historical meaning of Scripture as the primary basis of theological disputation. His *Postilla*, as his notes were called—the abbreviated form of *post illa verba textus* meaning "after these words from Scripture"—were widely circulated in the late Middle Ages and became the first biblical commentary to be printed in the fifteenth century. More than any other commentator from the period of high scholasticism, Lyra and his work were greatly valued by the early reformers. According to an old Latin pun, *Nisi Lyra lyrasset, Lutherus non saltasset*, "If Lyra had not played his lyre, Luther would not have danced."[15] While Luther was never an uncritical disciple of any teacher, he did praise Lyra as a good Hebraist and quoted him more than one hundred times in his lectures on Genesis, where he declared, "I prefer him to almost all other interpreters of Scripture."[16]

Sacred philology. The sixteenth century has been called a golden age of biblical interpretation, and it is a fact that the age of the Reformation witnessed an explosion of commentary writing unparalleled in the history of the Christian church. Kenneth Hagen has cataloged forty-five commentaries on Hebrews between 1516 (Erasmus) and 1598 (Beza).[17] During the sixteenth century, more than seventy new commentaries on Romans were published, five of them by Melanchthon alone, and nearly one hundred commentaries on the Bible's prayer book, the Psalms.[18] There were

---

[14]Heiko Oberman, *Forerunners of the Reformation* (Philadelphia: Fortress, 1966), 284.

[15]Nicholas of Lyra, *The Postilla of Nicolas of Lyra on the Song of Songs*, trans. and ed. James George Kiecker (Milwaukee: Marquette University Press, 1998), 19.

[16]LW 2:164 (WA 42:377).

[17]Kenneth Hagen, *Hebrews Commenting from Erasmus to Bèze, 1516-1598* (Tübingen: Mohr, 1981).

[18]R. Gerald Hobbs, "Biblical Commentaries," *OER* 1:167-71. See in general David C. Steinmetz, ed., *The Bible in the Sixteenth Century* (Durham: Duke University Press, 1990).

two developments in the fifteenth century that presaged this development and without which it could not have taken place: the invention of printing and the rediscovery of a vast store of ancient learning hitherto unknown or unavailable to scholars in the West.

It is now commonplace to say that what the computer has become in our generation, the printing press was to the world of Erasmus, Luther and other leaders of the Reformation. Johannes Gutenberg, a goldsmith by trade, developed a metal alloy suitable for type and a machine that would allow printed characters to be cast with relative ease, placed in even lines of composition and then manipulated again and again making possible the mass production of an unbelievable number of texts. In 1455, the Gutenberg Bible, the masterpiece of the typographical revolution, was published at Mainz in double columns in gothic type. Forty-seven copies of the beautiful Gutenberg Bible are still extant, each consisting of more than one thousand colorfully illuminated and impeccably printed pages. What began at Gutenberg's print shop in Mainz on the Rhine River soon spread, like McDonald's or Starbucks in our day, into every nook and cranny of the known world. Printing presses sprang up in Rome (1464), Venice (1469), Paris (1470), the Netherlands (1471), Switzerland (1472), Spain (1474), England (1476), Sweden (1483) and Constantinople (1490). By 1500, these and other presses across Europe had published some twenty-seven thousand titles, most of them in Latin. Erasmus once compared himself with an obscure preacher whose sermons were heard by only a few people in one or two churches while his books were read in every country in the world. Erasmus was not known for his humility, but in this case he was simply telling the truth.[19]

The Italian humanist Lorenzo Valla (d. 1457) died in the early dawn of the age of printing, but his critical and philological studies would be taken up by others who believed that genuine reform in church and society could come about only by returning to the wellsprings of ancient learning and wisdom—*ad fontes*, "back to the sources!" Valla is best remembered for undermining a major claim made by defenders of the papacy when he proved by philological research that the so-called Donation of Constantine, which had bolstered papal assertions of temporal sovereignty, was a forgery. But it was Valla's *Collatio Novi Testamenti* of 1444 that would have such a great effect on the renewal of biblical studies in the next century. Erasmus discovered the manuscript of this work while rummaging through an old library in Belgium and published it at Paris in 1505. In the preface to his edition of Valla, Erasmus gave the rationale that would guide his own labors in textual criticism. Just as Jerome had translated the Latin Vulgate from older versions and copies of the Scriptures in his day, so now Jerome's own text must be subjected to careful scrutiny and correction. Erasmus would be *Hieronymus redivivus*, a new Jerome come back to life to advance the cause of sacred philology. The restoration of the Scriptures and the writings of the church fathers would usher in what Erasmus believed would be a golden age of peace and learning. In 1516, the Basel publisher Froben brought out Erasmus's *Novum Instrumentum*, the first published edition of the Greek New Testament. Eras-

---

[19]E. Harris Harbison, *The Christian Scholar in the Age of the Reformation* (New York: Charles Scribner's Sons, 1956), 80.

---

mus's Greek New Testament would go through five editions in his lifetime, each one with new emendations to the text and a growing section of annotations that expanded to include not only technical notes about the text but also theological comment. The influence of Erasmus's Greek New Testament was enormous. It formed the basis for Robert Estienne's *Novum Testamentum Graece* of 1550, which in turn was used to establish the Greek *Textus Receptus* for a number of late Reformation translations including the King James Version of 1611.

For all his expertise in Greek, Erasmus was a poor student of Hebrew and only published commentaries on several of the psalms. However, the renaissance of Hebrew letters was part of the wider program of biblical humanism as reflected in the establishment of trilingual colleges devoted to the study of Hebrew, Greek and Latin (the three languages written on the *titulus* of Jesus' cross [Jn 19:20]) at Alcalá in Spain, Wittenberg in Germany, Louvain in Belgium and Paris in France. While it is true that some medieval commentators, especially Nicholas of Lyra, had been informed by the study of Hebrew and rabbinics in their biblical work, it was the publication of Johannes Reuchlin's *De rudimentis hebraicis* (1506), a combined grammar and dictionary, that led to the recovery of *veritas Hebraica*, as Jerome had referred to the true voice of the Hebrew Scriptures. The pursuit of Hebrew studies was carried forward in the Reformation by two great scholars, Konrad Pellikan and Sebastian Münster. Pellikan was a former Franciscan friar who embraced the Protestant cause and played a major role in the Zurich reformation. He had published a Hebrew grammar even prior to Reuchlin and produced a commentary on nearly the entire Bible that appeared in seven volumes between 1532 and 1539. Münster was Pellikan's student and taught Hebrew at the University of Heidelberg before taking up a similar position in Basel. Like his mentor, Münster was a great collector of Hebraica and published a series of excellent grammars, dictionaries and rabbinic texts. Münster did for the Hebrew Old Testament what Erasmus had done for the Greek New Testament. His *Hebraica Biblia* offered a fresh Latin translation of the Old Testament with annotations from medieval rabbinic exegesis.

Luther first learned Hebrew with Reuchlin's grammar in hand but took advantage of other published resources, such as the four-volume Hebrew Bible published at Venice by Daniel Bomberg in 1516 to 1517. He also gathered his own circle of Hebrew experts, his *sanhedrin* he called it, who helped him with his German translation of the Old Testament. We do not know where William Tyndale learned Hebrew, though perhaps it was in Worms, where there was a thriving rabbinical school during his stay there. In any event, he had sufficiently mastered the language to bring out a freshly translated Pentateuch that was published at Antwerp in 1530. By the time the English separatist scholar Henry Ainsworth published his prolix commentaries on the Pentateuch in 1616, the knowledge of Hebrew, as well as Greek, was taken for granted by every serious scholar of the Bible. In the preface to his commentary on Genesis, Ainsworth explained that "the literal sense of Moses's Hebrew (which is the tongue wherein he wrote the law), is the ground of all interpretation, and that language hath figures and properties of speech, different from ours: These therefore in the first place are to be opened that the natural meaning of the Scripture, being known, the mysteries of godliness therein implied, may be better discerned."[20]

The restoration of the biblical text in the original languages made possible the revival of scriptural exposition reflected in the floodtide of sermon literature and commentary work. Of even more far-reaching import was the steady stream of vernacular Bibles in the sixteenth century. In the introduction to his 1516 edition of the New Testament, Erasmus had expressed his desire that the Scriptures be translated into all languages so that "the lowliest women" could read the Gospels and the Pauline epistles and "the farmer sing some portion of them at the plow, the weaver hum some parts of them to the movement of his shuttle, the traveler lighten the weariness of the journey with stories of this kind."[21] Like Erasmus, Tyndale wanted the Bible to be available in the language of the common people. He once said to a learned divine that if God spared his life he would cause the boy who drives the plow to know more of the Scriptures than he did![22] The project of allowing the Bible to speak in the language of the mother in the house, the children in the street and the cheesemonger in the marketplace was met with stiff opposition by certain Catholic polemists such as Johann Eck, Luther's antagonist at the Leipzig Debate of 1519. In his *Enchiridion* (1525), Eck derided the "inky theologians" whose translations paraded the Bible before "the untutored crowd" and subjected it to the judgment of "laymen and crazy old women."[23] In fact, some fourteen German Bibles had already been published prior to Luther's September Testament of 1522, which he translated from Erasmus's Greek New Testament in less than three months' time while sequestered in the Wartburg. Luther's German New Testament became the first best-seller in the world, appearing in forty-three distinct editions between 1522 and 1525 with upwards of one hundred thousand copies issued in these three years. It is estimated that five percent of the German population may have been literate at this time, but this rate increased as the century wore on due in no small part to the unmitigated success of vernacular Bibles.[24]

Luther's German Bible (inclusive of the Old Testament from 1534) was the most successful venture of its kind, but it was not alone in the field. Hans Denck and Ludwig Hätzer, leaders in the early Anabaptist movement, translated the prophetic books of the Old Testament from Hebrew into German in 1527. This work influenced the Swiss-German Bible of 1531 published by Leo Jud and other pastors in Zurich. Tyndale's influence on the English language rivaled that of Luther on German. At a time when English was regarded as "that obscure and remote dialect of German spoken in an off-shore island," Tyndale, with his remarkable linguistic ability (he was fluent in eight languages), "made a language for England," as his modern editor David Daniell has put it.[25]

[20]Henry Ainsworth, *Annotations Upon the First Book of Moses Called Genesis* (Amsterdam, 1616), preface (unpaginated).

[21]John C. Olin, *Christian Humanism and the Reformation* (New York: Fordham University Press, 1987), 101.

[22]This famous statement of Tyndale was quoted by John Foxe in his *Acts and Monuments of Matters Happening in the Church* (London, 1563). See Henry Wansbrough, "Tyndale," in Richard Griffith, ed., *The Bible in the Renaissance* (Aldershot, UK: Ashgate, 2001), 124.

[23]John Eck, *Enchiridion of Commonplaces*, trans. Ford Lewis Battles (Grand Rapids: Baker, 1979), 47-49.

[24]The effect of printing on the spread of the Reformation has been much debated. See the classic study by Elizabeth L. Eisenstein, *The Printing Press as an Agent of Change* (Cambridge: Cambridge University Press, 1979). More recent studies include Mark U. Edwards Jr., *Printing, Propaganda and Martin Luther* (Minneapolis: Fortress, 1994), and Andrew Pettegree and Matthew Hall, "The Reformation and the Book: A Reconsideration," *Historical Journal* 47 (2004): 1-24.

[25]David Daniell, *William Tyndale: A Biography* (New Haven: Yale University Press, 1994), 3.

Tyndale was imprisoned and executed near Brussels in 1536, but the influence of his biblical work among the common people of England was already being felt. There is no reason to doubt the authenticity of John Foxe's recollection of how Tyndale's New Testament was received in England during the 1520s and 1530s:

> The fervent zeal of those Christian days seemed much superior to these our days and times; as manifestly may appear by their sitting up all night in reading and hearing; also by their expenses and charges in buying of books in English, of whom some gave five marks, some more, some less, for a book: some gave a load of hay for a few chapters of St. James, or of St. Paul in English.[26]

Calvin helped to revise and contributed three prefaces to the French Bible translated by his cousin Pierre Robert Olivétan and originally published at Neuchâtel in 1535. Clément Marot and Beza provided a fresh translation of the Psalms with each psalm rendered in poetic form and accompanied by monophonic musical settings for congregational singing. The Bay Psalter, the first book printed in America, was an English adaptation of this work. Geneva also provided the provenance of the most influential Italian Bible published by Giovanni Diodati in 1607. The flowering of biblical humanism in vernacular Bibles resulted in new translations in all of the major language groups of Europe: Spanish (1569), Portuguese (1681), Dutch (New Testament, 1523; Old Testament, 1527), Danish (1550), Czech (1579–1593/94), Hungarian (New Testament, 1541; complete Bible, 1590), Polish (1563), Swedish (1541) and even Arabic (1591).[27]

Patterns of Reformation

Once the text of the Bible had been placed in the hands of the people, in cheap and easily available editions, what further need was there of published expositions such as commentaries? Given the Protestant doctrine of the priesthood of all believers, was there any longer a need for learned clergy and their bookish religion? Some radical reformers thought not. Sebastian Franck searched for the true church of the Spirit "scattered among the heathen and the weeds" but could not find it in any of the institutional structures of his time. *Veritas non potest scribi, aut exprimi*, he said, "truth can neither be spoken nor written."[28] Kaspar von Schwenckfeld so emphasized religious inwardness that he suspended external observance of the Lord's Supper and downplayed the readable, audible Scriptures in favor of the word within. This trajectory would lead to the rise of the Quakers in the next century, but it was pursued neither by the mainline reformers nor by most of the Anabaptists. Article 7 of the Augsburg Confession (1530) declared the one holy Christian church to be "the assembly of all believers among whom the Gospel is purely preached and the holy sacraments are administered according to the Gospel."[29]

Historians of the nineteenth century referred to the material and formal principles of the

---

[26]Foxe, *Acts and Monuments*, 4:218.

[27]On vernacular translations of the Bible, see *CHB* 3:94-140 and Jaroslav Pelikan, *The Reformation of the Bible/The Bible of the Reformation* (New Haven: Yale University Press, 1996), 41-62.

[28]Sebastian Franck, *280 Paradoxes or Wondrous Sayings*, trans. E. J. Furcha (Lewiston, NY: Edwin Mellen Press, 1986), 10, 212.

[29]BoC 42 (BSLK 61).

Reformation. In this construal, the matter at stake was the meaning of the Christian gospel: the liberating insight that helpless sinners are graciously justified by the gift of faith alone, apart from any works or merits of their own, entirely on the basis of Christ's atoning work on the cross. For Luther especially, justification by faith alone became the criterion by which all other doctrines and practices of the church were to be judged. The cross proves everything, he said at the Heidelberg disputation in 1518. The distinction between law and gospel thus became the primary hermeneutical key that unlocked the true meaning of Scripture.

The formal principle of the Reformation, *sola Scriptura*, was closely bound up with proper distinctions between Scripture and tradition. "Scripture alone," said Luther, "is the true lord and master of all writings and doctrine on earth. If that is not granted, what is Scripture good for? The more we reject it, the more we become satisfied with human books and human teachers."[30] On the basis of this principle, the reformers challenged the structures and institutions of the medieval Catholic Church. Even a simple layperson, they asserted, armed with Scripture should be believed above a pope or a council without it. But, however boldly asserted, the doctrine of the primacy of Scripture did not absolve the reformers from dealing with a host of hermeneutical issues that became matters of contention both between Rome and the Reformation and within each of these two communities: the extent of the biblical canon, the validity of critical study of the Bible, the perspicuity of Scripture and its relation to preaching and the retention of devotional and liturgical practices such as holy days, incense, the burning of candles, the sprinkling of holy water, church art and musical instruments. Zwingli, the Puritans and the radicals dismissed such things as a rubbish heap of ceremonials that amounted to nothing but tomfoolery, while Lutherans and Anglicans retained most of them as consonant with Scripture and valuable aids to worship.

It is important to note that while the mainline reformers differed among themselves on many matters, overwhelmingly they saw themselves as part of the ongoing Catholic tradition, indeed as the legitimate bearers of it. This was seen in numerous ways including their sense of continuity with the church of the preceding centuries; their embrace of the ecumenical orthodoxy of the early church; and their desire to read the Bible in dialogue with the exegetical tradition of the church.

In their biblical commentaries, the reformers of the sixteenth century revealed a close familiarity with the preceding exegetical tradition, and they used it respectfully as well as critically in their own expositions of the sacred text. For them, *sola Scriptura* was not *nuda Scriptura*. Rather, the Scriptures were seen as the book given to the church, gathered and guided by the Holy Spirit. In his restatement of the Vincentian canon, Calvin defined the church as "a society of all the saints, a society which, spread over the whole world, and existing in all ages, and bound together by the one doctrine and the one spirit of Christ, cultivates and observes unity of faith and brotherly concord. With this church we deny that we have any disagreement. Nay, rather, as we revere her as our mother, so we desire to remain in her bosom." Defined thus, the church has a real, albeit relative and circumscribed, authority since, as Calvin admits, "We cannot fly without

---

[30]LW 32:11-12* (WA 7:317).

wings."[31] While the reformers could not agree with the Council of Trent (though some recent Catholic theologians have challenged this interpretation) that Scripture and tradition were two separate and equable sources of divine revelation, they did believe in the coinherence of Scripture and tradition. This conviction shaped the way they read and interpreted the Bible.[32]

Schools of Exegesis

The reformers were passionate about biblical exegesis, but they showed little concern for herme-neutics as a separate field of inquiry. Niels Hemmingsen, a Lutheran theologian in Denmark, did write a treatise, *De methodis* (1555), in which he offered a philosophical and theological framework for the interpretation of Scripture. This was followed by the *Clavis Scripturae Sacrae* (1567) of Matthias Flacius Illyricus, which contains some fifty rules for studying the Bible drawn from Scripture itself.[33] However, hermeneutics as we know it came of age only in the Enlightenment and should not be backloaded into the Reformation. It is also true that the word *commentary* did not mean in the sixteenth century what it means for us today. Erasmus provided both annota-tions and paraphrases on the New Testament, the former a series of critical notes on the text but also containing points of doctrinal substance, the latter a theological overview and brief exposi-tion. Most of Calvin's commentaries began as sermons or lectures presented in the course of his pastoral ministry. In the dedication to his 1519 study of Galatians, Luther declared that his work was "not so much a commentary as a testimony of my faith in Christ."[34] The exegetical work of the reformers was embodied in a wide variety of forms and genres, and the RCS has worked with this broader concept in setting the guidelines for this compendium.

The Protestant reformers shared in common a number of key interpretive principles such as the priority of the grammatical-historical sense of Scripture and the christological centeredness of the en-tire Bible, but they also developed a number of distinct approaches and schools of exegesis.[35] For the purposes of the RCS, we note the following key figures and families of interpretation in this period.

Biblical humanism. The key figure is Erasmus, whose importance is hard to exaggerate for Catholic and Protestant exegetes alike. His annotated Greek New Testament and fresh Latin translation challenged the hegemony of the Vulgate tradition and was doubtless a factor in the decision of the Council of Trent to establish the Vulgate edition as authentic and normative. Erasmus believed that the wide distribution of the Scriptures would contribute to personal spiri-tual renewal and the reform of society. In 1547, the English translation of Erasmus's *Paraphrases*

---

[31]John C. Olin, ed., *John Calvin and Jacopo Sadoleto: A Reformation Debate* (New York: Harper Torchbooks, 1966), 61-62, 77.

[32]See Timothy George, "An Evangelical Reflection on Scripture and Tradition," *Pro Ecclesia* 9 (2000): 184-207.

[33]See Kenneth G. Hagen, "'De Exegetica Methodo': Niels Hemmingsen's *De Methodis* (1555)," in *The Bible in the Sixteenth Century*, ed. David C. Steinmetz (Durham: Duke University Press, 1990), 181-96.

[34]LW 27:159 (WA 2:449). See Kenneth Hagen, "What Did the Term *Commentarius* Mean to Sixteenth-Century Theologians?" in Irena Backus and Francis M. Higman, eds., *Théorie et pratique de l'exégèse* (Geneva: Droz, 1990), 13-38.

[35]I follow here the sketch of Irena Backus, "Biblical Hermeneutics and Exegesis," *OER* 1:152-58. In this work, Backus confines herself to Continental developments, whereas we have noted the exegetical contribution of the English Reformation as well. For more comprehensive listings of sixteenth-century commentators, see Gerald Bray, *Biblical Interpretation* (Downers Grove, IL: Inter-Varsity Press, 1996), 165-212; and Richard A. Muller, "Biblical Interpretation in the Sixteenth and Seventeenth Centuries," *DMBI* 22-44.

was ordered to be placed in every parish church in England. John Colet first encouraged Erasmus to learn Greek, though he never took up the language himself. Colet's lectures on Paul's epistles at Oxford are reflected in his commentaries on Romans and 1 Corinthians.

Jacques Lefèvre d'Étaples has been called the "French Erasmus" because of his great learning and support for early reform movements in his native land. He published a major edition of the Psalter, as well as commentaries on the Pauline Epistles (1512), the Gospels (1522) and the General Epistles (1527). Guillaume Farel, the early reformer of Geneva, was a disciple of Lefèvre, and the young Calvin also came within his sphere of influence.

Among pre-Tridentine Catholic reformers, special attention should be given to Thomas de Vio, better known as Cajetan. He is best remembered for confronting Martin Luther on behalf of the pope in 1518, but his biblical commentaries (on nearly every book of the Bible) are virtually free of polemic. Like Erasmus, he dared to criticize the Vulgate on linguistic grounds. His commentary on Romans supported the doctrine of justification by grace applied by faith based on the "alien righteousness" of God in Christ. Jared Wicks sums up Cajetan's significance in this way: "Cajetan's combination of passion for pristine biblical meaning with his fully developed theological horizon of understanding indicates, in an intriguing manner, something of the breadth of possibilities open to Roman Catholics before a more restrictive settlement came to exercise its hold on many Catholic interpreters in the wake of the Council of Trent."[36] Girolamo Seripando, like Cajetan, was a cardinal in the Catholic Church, though he belonged to the Augustinian rather than the Dominican order. He was an outstanding classical scholar and published commentaries on Romans and Galatians. Also important is Jacopo Sadoleto, another cardinal, best known for his 1539 letter to the people of Geneva beseeching them to return to the church of Rome, to which Calvin replied with a manifesto of his own. Sadoleto published a commentary on Romans in 1535. Bucer once commended Sadoleto's teaching on justification as approximating that of the reformers, while others saw him tilting away from the Augustinian tradition toward Pelagianism.[37]

Luther and the Wittenberg School. It was in the name of the Word of God, and specifically as a doctor of Scripture, that Luther challenged the church of his day and inaugurated the Reformation. Though Luther renounced his monastic vows, he never lost that sense of intimacy with *sacra pagina* he first acquired as a young monk. Luther provided three rules for reading the Bible: prayer, meditation and struggle (*tentatio*). His exegetical output was enormous. In the American edition of Luther's works, thirty out of the fifty-five volumes are devoted to his biblical studies, and additional translations are planned. Many of his commentaries originated as sermons or lecture notes presented to his students at the university and to his parishioners at Wittenberg's parish church of St. Mary. Luther referred to Galatians as his bride: "The Epistle to the Galatians is my dear epistle. I have betrothed myself to it. It is my Käthe von Bora."[38] He considered his

---

[36]Jared Wicks, "Tommaso de Vio Cajetan (1469-1534)," *DMBI* 283-87, here 286.

[37]See the discussion by Bernard Roussel, "Martin Bucer et Jacques Sadolet: la concorde possible," *Bulletin de la Société de l'histoire du protestantisme français* (1976): 525-50, and T. H. L. Parker, *Commentaries on the Epistle to the Romans, 1532-1542* (Edinburgh: T&T Clark, 1986), 25-34.

[38]WATR 1:69 #146; cf. LW 54:20 #146. I have followed Rörer's variant on Dietrich's notes.

1535 commentary on Galatians his greatest exegetical work, although his massive commentary on Genesis (eight volumes in LW), which he worked on for ten years (1535–1545), must be considered his crowning work. Luther's principles of biblical interpretation are found in his *Open Letter on Translating* and in the prefaces he wrote to all the books of the Bible.

Philipp Melanchthon was brought to Wittenberg to teach Greek in 1518 and proved to be an able associate to Luther in the reform of the church. A set of his lecture notes on Romans was published without his knowledge in 1522. This was revised and expanded many times until his large commentary of 1556. Melanchthon also commented on other New Testament books including Matthew, John, Galatians and the Petrine Epistles, as well as Proverbs, Daniel and Ecclesiastes. Though he was well trained in the humanist disciplines, Melanchthon devoted little attention to critical and textual matters in his commentaries. Rather, he followed the primary argument of the biblical writer and gathered from this exposition a series of doctrinal topics for special consideration. This method lay behind Melanchthon's *Loci communes* (1521), the first Protestant theology textbook to be published. Another Wittenberger was Johannes Bugenhagen of Pomerania, a prolific commentator on both the Old and New Testaments. His commentary on the Psalms (1524), translated into German by Bucer, applied Luther's teaching on justification to the Psalter. He also wrote a commentary on Job and annotations on many of the books in the Bible. The Lutheran exegetical tradition was shaped by many other scholar-reformers including Andreas Osiander, Johannes Brenz, Caspar Cruciger, Erasmus Sarcerius, Georg Maior, Jacob Andreae, Nikolaus Selnecker and Johann Gerhard.

The Strasbourg-Basel tradition. Bucer, the son of a shoemaker in Alsace, became the leader of the Reformation in Strasbourg. A former Dominican, he was early on influenced by Erasmus and continued to share his passion for Christian unity. Bucer was the most ecumenical of the Protestant reformers seeking rapprochement with Catholics on justification and an armistice between Luther and Zwingli in their strife over the Lord's Supper. Bucer also had a decisive influence on Calvin, though the latter characterized his biblical commentaries as longwinded and repetitious.[39] In his exegetical work, Bucer made ample use of patristic and medieval sources, though he criticized the abuse and overuse of allegory as "the most blatant insult to the Holy Spirit."[40] He declared that the purpose of his commentaries was "to help inexperienced brethren [perhaps like the apothecary Drilhon, who owned a French translation of Bucer's *Commentary on Matthew*] to understand each of the words and actions of Christ, and in their proper order as far as possible, and to retain an explanation of them in their natural meaning, so that they will not distort God's Word through age-old aberrations or by inept interpretation, but rather with a faithful comprehension of everything as written by the Spirit of God, they may expound to all the churches in their firm upbuilding in faith and love."[41] In addition to writing commentaries on all four Gospels, Bucer published

---

[39]CNTC 8:3 (CO 10:404).

[40]*DMBI* 249; P. Scherding and F. Wendel, eds., "Un Traité d'exégèse pratique de Bucer," *Revue d'histoire et de philosophie religieuses* 26 (1946): 32-75, here 56.

[41]Martin Bucer, *Enarrationes perpetuae in sacra quatuor evangelia*, 2nd. ed. (Strasbourg: Georg Ulrich Andlanus, 1530), 10r; quoted in D. F. Wright, "Martin Bucer," *DMBI* 290.

commentaries on Judges, the Psalms, Zephaniah, Romans and Ephesians. In the early years of the Reformation, there was a great deal of back and forth between Strasbourg and Basel, and both were centers of a lively publishing trade. Wolfgang Capito, Bucer's associate at Strasbourg, was a notable Hebraist and composed commentaries on Hosea (1529) and Habakkuk (1527).

At Basel, the great Sebastian Münster defended the use of Jewish sources in the Christian study of the Old Testament and published, in addition to his famous Hebrew grammar, an annotated version of the Gospel of Matthew translated from Greek into Hebrew. Oecolampadius, Basel's chief reformer, had been a proofreader in Froben's publishing house and worked with Erasmus on his Greek New Testament and his critical edition of Jerome. From 1523 he was both a preacher and professor of Holy Scripture at Basel. He defended Zwingli's eucharistic theology at the Colloquy of Marburg and published commentaries on 1 John (1524), Romans (1525) and Haggai-Malachi (1525). Oecolampadius was succeeded by Simon Grynaeus, a classical scholar who taught Greek and supported Bucer's efforts to bring Lutherans and Zwinglians together. More in line with Erasmus was Sebastian Castellio, who came to Basel after his expulsion from Geneva in 1545. He is best remembered for questioning the canonicity of the Song of Songs and for his annotations and French translation of the Bible.

The Zurich group. Biblical exegesis in Zurich was centered on the distinctive institution of the *Prophezei*, which began on June 19, 1525. On five days a week, at seven o'clock in the morning, all of the ministers and theological students in Zurich gathered into the choir of the Grossmünster to engage in a period of intense exegesis and interpretation of Scripture. After Zwingli had opened the meeting with prayer, the text of the day was read in Latin, Greek and Hebrew, followed by appropriate textual or exegetical comments. One of the ministers then delivered a sermon on the passage in German that was heard by many of Zurich's citizens who stopped by the cathedral on their way to work. This institute for advanced biblical studies had an enormous influence as a model for Reformed academies and seminaries throughout Europe. It was also the seedbed for sermon series in Zurich's churches and the extensive exegetical publications of Zwingli, Leo Jud, Konrad Pellikan, Heinrich Bullinger, Oswald Myconius and Rudolf Gwalther. Zwingli had memorized in Greek all of the Pauline epistles, and this bore fruit in his powerful expository preaching and biblical exegesis. He took seriously the role of grammar, rhetoric and historical research in explaining the biblical text. For example, he disagreed with Bucer on the value of the Septuagint, regarding it as a trustworthy witness to a proto-Hebrew version earlier than the Masoretic text.

Zwingli's work was carried forward by his successor Bullinger, one of the most formidable scholars and networkers among the reformers. He composed commentaries on Daniel (1565), the Gospels (1542–1546), the Epistles (1537), Acts (1533) and Revelation (1557). He collaborated with Calvin to produce the *Consensus Tigurinus* (1549), a Reformed accord on the nature of the Lord's Supper, and produced a series of fifty sermons on Christian doctrine, known as *Decades*, which became required reading in Elizabethan England. As the *Antistes* ("overseer") of the Zurich church for forty-four years, Bullinger faced opposition from nascent Anabaptism on the one hand and resurgent Catholicism on the other. The need for a well-trained clergy and scholarly resources, including Scripture commentaries, arose from the fact that the Bible was "difficult or obscure to the unlearned, unskillful, unexercised, and malicious or corrupted wills." While for-swearing papal claims to infallibility, Bullinger and other leaders of the magisterial Reformation saw the need for a kind of Protestant magisterium as a check against the tendency to read the Bible in "such sense as everyone shall be persuaded in himself to be most convenient."[42]

Two other commentators can be treated in connection with the Zurich group, though each of them had a wide-ranging ministry across the Reformation fronts. A former Benedictine monk, Wolfgang Musculus, embraced the Reformation in the 1520s and served briefly as the secretary to Bucer in Strasbourg. He shared Bucer's desire for Protestant unity and served for seventeen years (1531–1548) as a pastor and reformer in Augsburg. After a brief time in Zurich, where he came under the influence of Bullinger, Musculus was called to Bern, where he taught the Scriptures and published commentaries on the Psalms, the Decalogue, Genesis, Romans, Isaiah, 1 and 2 Cor-inthians, Galatians and Ephesians, Philippians, Colossians, 1 and 2 Thessalonians and 1 Timothy. Drawing on his exegetical writings, Musculus also produced a compendium of Protestant theol-ogy that was translated into English in 1563 as *Commonplaces of Christian Religion*.

Peter Martyr Vermigli was a Florentine-born scholar and Augustinian friar who embraced the Reformation and fled to Switzerland in 1542. Over the next twenty years, he would gain an inter-national reputation as a prolific scholar and leading theologian within the Reformed community. He lectured on the Old Testament at Strasbourg, was made regius professor at Oxford, corre-sponded with the Italian refugee church in Geneva and spent the last years of his life as professor of Hebrew at Zurich. Vermigli published commentaries on 1 Corinthians, Romans and Judges during his lifetime. His biblical lectures on Genesis, Lamentations, 1 and 2 Samuel and 1 and 2 Kings were published posthumously. The most influential of his writings was the *Loci communes* (*Commonplaces*), a theological compendium drawn from his exegetical writings.

The Genevan Reformers. What Zwingli and Bullinger were to Zurich, Calvin and Beza were to Geneva. Calvin has been called "the father of modern biblical scholarship," and his exegetical work is without parallel in the Reformation. Because of the success of his *Institutes of the Christian Religion* Calvin has sometimes been thought of as a man of one book, but he always intended the *Institutes*, which went through eight editions in Latin and five in French during his lifetime, to serve as a guide to the study of the Bible, to show the reader "what he ought especially to seek in Scripture and to what end he ought to relate its contents." Jacob Arminius, who modified several principles of Calvin's theology, recommended his commentaries next to the Bible, for, as he said, Calvin "is incomparable in the interpretation of Scripture."[43] Drawing on his superb knowledge of Greek and Hebrew and his thorough training in humanist rhetoric, Calvin produced commentar-ies on all of the New Testament books except 2 and 3 John and Revelation. Calvin's Old Testament

---

[42]Euan Cameron, *The European Reformation* (Oxford: Oxford University Press, 1991), 120.

[43]Letter to Sebastian Egbert (May 3, 1607), in *Praestantium ac eruditorum virorum epistolae ecclesiasticae et theologicae varii argumenti*, ed. Christiaan Hartsoeker (Amsterdam: Henricus Dendrinus, 1660), 236-37. Quoted in A. M. Hunter, *The Teaching of Calvin* (London: James Clarke, 1950), 20.

commentaries originated as sermon and lecture series and include Genesis, Psalms, Hosea, Isaiah, minor prophets, Daniel, Jeremiah and Lamentations, a harmony of the last four books of Moses, Ezekiel 1–20 and Joshua. Calvin sought for brevity and clarity in all of his exegetical work. He emphasized the illumination of the Holy Spirit as essential to a proper understanding of the text. Calvin underscored the continuity between the two Testaments (one covenant in two dispensations) and sought to apply the plain or natural sense of the text to the church of his day. In the preface to his own influential commentary on Romans, Karl Barth described how Calvin worked to recover the mind of Paul and make the apostle's message relevant to his day:

> How energetically Calvin goes to work, first scientifically establishing the text ('what stands there?'), then following along the footsteps of its thought; that is to say, he conducts a discussion with it until the wall between the first and the sixteenth centuries becomes transparent, and until there in the first century Paul speaks and here the man of the sixteenth century hears, until indeed the conversation between document and reader becomes concentrated upon the substance (which must be the same now as then).[44]

Beza was elected moderator of Geneva's Company of Pastors after Calvin's death in 1564 and guided the Genevan Reformation over the next four decades. His annotated Latin translation of the Greek New Testament (1556) and his further revisions of the Greek text established his reputation as the leading textual critic of the sixteenth century after Erasmus. Beza completed the translation of Marot's metrical Psalter, which became a centerpiece of Huguenot piety and Reformed church life. Though known for his polemical writings on grace, free will and predestination, Beza's work is marked by a strong pastoral orientation and concern for a Scripture-based spirituality.

Robert Estienne (Stephanus) was a printer-scholar who had served the royal household in Paris. After his conversion to Protestantism, in 1550 he moved to Geneva, where he published a series of notable editions and translations of the Bible. He also produced sermons and commentaries on Job, Ecclesiastes, the Song of Songs, Romans and Hebrews, as well as dictionaries, concordances and a thesaurus of biblical terms. He also published the first editions of the Bible with chapters divided into verses, an innovation that quickly became universally accepted.

The British Reformation. Commentary writing in England and Scotland lagged behind the continental Reformation for several reasons. In 1500, there were only three publishing houses in England compared with more than two hundred on the Continent. A 1408 statute against publishing or reading the Bible in English, stemming from the days of Lollardy, stifled the free flow of ideas, as was seen in the fate of Tyndale. Moreover, the nature of the English Reformation from Henry through Elizabeth provided little stability for the flourishing of biblical scholarship. In the sixteenth century, many "hot-gospel" Protestants in England were edified by the English translations of commentaries and theological writings by the Continental reformers.

---

[44]Karl Barth, *Die Römerbrief* (Zurich: TVZ, 1940), II, translated by T. H. L. Parker as the epigraph to *Calvin's New Testament Commentaries*, 2nd ed. (Louisville, KY: Westminster John Knox, 1993).

The influence of Calvin and Beza was felt especially in the Geneva Bible with its "Protestant glosses" of theological notes and references.

During the later Elizabethan and Stuart church, however, the indigenous English commentary came into its own. Both Anglicans and Puritans contributed to this outpouring of biblical studies. The sermons of Lancelot Andrewes and John Donne are replete with exegetical insights based on a close study of the Greek and Hebrew texts. Among the Reformed authors in England, none was more influential than William Perkins, the greatest of the early Puritan theologians, who published commentaries on Galatians, Jude, Revelation and the Sermon on the Mount (Mt 5–7). John Cotton, one of his students, wrote commentaries on the Song of Songs, Ecclesiastes and Revelation before departing for New England in 1633. The separatist pastor Henry Ainsworth was an outstanding scholar of Hebrew and wrote major commentaries on the Pentateuch, the Psalms and the Song of Songs. In Scotland, Robert Rollock, the first principal of Edinburgh University (1585), wrote numerous commentaries including those on the Psalms, Ephesians, Daniel, Romans, 1 and 2 Thessalonians, John, Colossians and Hebrews. Joseph Mede and Thomas Brightman were leading authorities on Revelation and contributed to the apocalyptic thought of the seventeenth century. Mention should also be made of Archbishop James Ussher, whose *Annals of the Old Testament* was published in 1650. Ussher developed a keen interest in biblical chronology and calculated that the creation of the world had taken place on October 26, 4004 B.C. As late as 1945, the Scofield Reference Bible still retained this date next to Genesis 1:1, but later editions omitted it because of the lack of evidence on which to fix such dates.[45]

Anabaptism. Irena Backus has noted that there was no school of "dissident" exegesis during the Reformation, and the reasons are not hard to find. The radical Reformation was an ill-defined movement that existed on the margins of official church life in the sixteenth century. The denial of infant baptism and the refusal to swear an oath marked radicals as a seditious element in society, and they were persecuted by Protestants and Catholics alike. However, in the RCS we have made an attempt to include some voices of the radical Reformation, especially among the Anabaptists. While the Anabaptists published few commentaries in the sixteenth century, they were avid readers and quoters of the Bible. Numerous exegetical gems can be found in their letters, treatises, martyr acts (especially *The Martyrs' Mirror*), hymns and histories. They placed a strong emphasis on the memorizing of Scripture and quoted liberally from vernacular translations of the Bible. George H. Williams has noted that "many an Anabaptist theological tract was really a beautiful mosaic of Scripture texts."[46] In general, most Anabaptists accepted the apocryphal books as canonical, contrasted outer word and inner spirit with relative degrees of strictness and saw the New Testament as normative for church life and social ethics (witness their pacifism, nonswearing, emphasis on believers' baptism and congregational discipline).

We have noted the Old Testament translation of Ludwig Hätzer, who became an antitrinitarian, and Hans Denck that they published at Worms in 1527. Denck also wrote a notable commentary

---

[45]*The New Scofield Reference Bible* (New York: Oxford University Press, 1967), vi.
[46]George H. Williams, *The Radical Reformation*, 3rd ed. (Kirksville, MO: Sixteenth Century Journal Publishers, 1992), 1247.

on Micah. Conrad Grebel belonged to a Greek reading circle in Zurich and came to his Anabaptist convictions while poring over the text of Erasmus's New Testament. The only Anabaptist leader with university credentials was Balthasar Hubmaier, who was made a doctor of theology (Ingolstadt, 1512) in the same year as Luther. His reflections on the Bible are found in his numerous writings, which include the first catechism of the Reformation (1526), a two-part treatise on the freedom of the will and a major work (On the Sword) setting forth positive attitudes toward the role of government and the Christian's place in society. Melchior Hoffman was an apocalyptic seer who wrote commentaries on Romans, Revelation and Daniel 12. He predicted that Christ would return in 1533. More temperate was Pilgram Marpeck, a mining engineer who embraced Anabaptism and traveled widely throughout Switzerland and south Germany, from Strasbourg to Augsburg. His "Admonition of 1542" is the longest published defense of Anabaptist views on baptism and the Lord's Supper. He also wrote many letters that functioned as theological tracts for the congregations he had founded dealing with topics such as the fruits of repentance, the lowliness of Christ and the unity of the church. Menno Simons, a former Catholic priest, became the most outstanding leader of the Dutch Anabaptist movement. His masterpiece was the *Foundation of Christian Doctrine* published in 1540. His other writings include *Meditation on the Twenty-fifth Psalm* (1537); *A Personal Exegesis of Psalm Twenty-five* modeled on the style of Augustine's *Confessions*; *Confession of the Triune God* (1550), directed against Adam Pastor, a former disciple of Menno who came to doubt the divinity of Christ; *Meditations and Prayers for Mealtime* (1557); and the *Cross of the Saints* (1554), an exhortation to faithfulness in the face of persecution. Like many other Anabaptists, Menno emphasized the centrality of discipleship *(Nachfolge)* as a deliberate repudiation of the old life and a radical commitment to follow Jesus as Lord.

Reading Scripture with the Reformers

In 1947, Gerhard Ebeling set forth his thesis that the history of the Christian church is the history of the interpretation of Scripture. Since that time, the place of the Bible in the story of the church has been investigated from many angles. A better understanding of the history of exegesis has been aided by new critical editions and scholarly discussions of the primary sources. The *Cambridge History of the Bible*, published in three volumes (1963–1970), remains a standard reference work in the field. The ACCS built on, and itself contributed to, the recovery of patristic biblical wisdom of both East and West. Beryl Smalley's *The Study of the Bible in the Middle Ages* (1940) and Henri de Lubac's *Medieval Exegesis: The Four Senses of Scripture* (1959) are essential reading for understanding the monastic and scholastic settings of commentary work between Augustine and Luther. The Reformation took place during what has been called "le grand siècle de la Bible."[47] Aided by the tools of Renaissance humanism and the dynamic impetus of Reformation theology (including permutations and reactions against it), the sixteenth century produced an unprecedented number of commentaries on every book in the Bible. Drawing from this vast storehouse of exegetical treasures, the RCS allows us to read

---

[47]J-R. Aarmogathe, ed., *Bible de tous les temps*, 8 vols.; vol. 6, *Le grand siècle de la Bible* (Paris: Beauchesne, 1989).

Scripture along with the reformers. In doing so, it serves as a practical homiletic and devotional guide to some of the greatest masters of biblical interpretation in the history of the church.

The RCS gladly acknowledges its affinity with and dependence on recent scholarly investigations of Reformation-era exegesis. Between 1976 and 1990, three international colloquia on the history of biblical exegesis in the sixteenth century took place in Geneva and in Durham, North Carolina.[48] Among those participating in these three gatherings were a number of scholars who have produced groundbreaking works in the study of biblical interpretation in the Reformation. These include Elsie McKee, Irena Backus, Kenneth Hagen, Scott H. Hendrix, Richard A. Muller, Guy Bedouelle, Gerald Hobbs, John B. Payne, Bernard Roussel, Pierre Fraenkel and David C. Steinmetz. Among other scholars whose works are indispensable for the study of this field are Heinrich Bornkamm, Jaroslav Pelikan, Heiko A. Oberman, James S. Preus, T. H. L. Parker, David F. Wright, Tony Lane, John L. Thompson, Frank A. James and Timothy J. Wengert.[49] Among these scholars no one has had a greater influence on the study of Reformation exegesis than David C. Steinmetz. A student of Oberman, he has emphasized the importance of understanding the Reformation in medieval perspective. In addition to important studies on Luther and Staupitz, he has pioneered the method of comparative exegesis showing both continuity and discontinuity between major Reformation figures and the preceding exegetical traditions (see his *Luther in Context* and *Calvin in Context*). From his base at Duke University, he has spawned what might be called a Steinmetz school, a cadre of students and scholars whose work on the Bible in the Reformation era continues to shape the field. Steinmetz serves on the RCS Board of Editorial Advisors, and a number of our volume editors have pursued doctoral studies under his supervision.

In 1980, Steinmetz published "The Superiority of Pre-critical Exegesis," a seminal essay that not only placed Reformation exegesis in the context of the preceding fifteen centuries of the church's study of the Bible but also challenged certain assumptions underlying the hegemony of historical-critical exegesis of the post-Enlightenment academy.[50] Steinmetz helps us to approach the reformers and other precritical interpreters of the Bible on their own terms as faithful witnesses to the church's apostolic tradition. For them, a specific book or pericope had to be understood within the scope of the consensus of the canon. Thus the reformers, no less than the Fathers and the schoolmen, interpreted the hymn of the Johannine prologue about the preexistent Christ in consonance with the creation narrative of Genesis 1. In the same way, Psalm 22, Isaiah 53 and Daniel 7 are seen as part of an overarching storyline that finds ultimate fulfillment in Jesus

---

[48]Olivier Fatio and Pierre Fraenkel, eds., *Histoire de l'exégèse au XVIe siècle: texts du colloque international tenu à Genève en 1976* (Geneva: Droz, 1978); David C. Steinmetz, ed., *The Bible in the Sixteenth Century* [Second International Colloquy on the History of Biblical Exegesis in the Sixteenth Century] (Durham: Duke University Press, 1990); Irena Backus and Francis M. Higman, eds., *Théorie et pratique de l'exégèse. Actes du troisième colloque international sur l'histoire de l'exégèse biblique au XVIe siècle, Genève, 31 aôut-2 septembre 1988* (Geneva: Droz, 1990); see also Guy Bedouelle and Bernard Roussel, eds., *Bible de tous les temps*, 8 vols.; vol. 5, *Le temps des Réformes et la Bible* (Paris: Beauchesne, 1989).

[49]For bibliographical references and evaluation of these and other contributors to the scholarly study of Reformation-era exegesis, see Richard A. Muller, "Biblical Interpretation in the Era of the Reformation: The View From the Middle Ages," in *Biblical Interpretation in the Era of the Reformation: Essays Presented to David C. Steinmetz in Honor of His Sixtieth Birthday*, ed. Richard A. Muller and John L. Thompson (Grand Rapids: Eerdmans, 1996), 3-22.

[50]David C. Steinmetz, "The Superiority of Pre-Critical Exegesis," *Theology Today* 37 (1980): 27-38.

Christ. Reading the Bible with the resources of the new learning, the reformers challenged the exegetical conclusions of their medieval predecessors at many points. However, unlike Alexander Campbell in the nineteenth century, their aim was not to "open the New Testament as if mortal man had never seen it before."[51] Rather, they wanted to do their biblical work as part of an interpretive conversation within the family of the people of God. In the reformers' emphatic turn to the literal sense, which prompted their many blasts against the unrestrained use of allegory, their work was an extension of a similar impulse made by Thomas Aquinas and Nicholas of Lyra.

This is not to discount the radically new insights gained by the reformers in their dynamic engagement with the text of Scripture; nor should we dismiss in a reactionary way the light shed on the meaning of the Bible by the scholarly accomplishments of the past two centuries. However, it is to acknowledge that the church's exegetical tradition is an indispensible aid for the proper interpretation of Scripture. And this means, as Richard Muller has said, that "while it is often appropriate to recognize that traditionary readings of the text are erroneous on the grounds offered by the historical-critical method, we ought also to recognize that the conclusions offered by historical-critical exegesis may themselves be quite erroneous on the grounds provided by the exegesis of the patristic, medieval, and reformation periods."[52] The RCS wishes to commend the exegetical work of the Reformation era as a program of retrieval for the sake of renewal—spiritual réssourcement for believers committed to the life of faith today.

George Herbert was an English pastor and poet who reaped the benefits of the renewal of biblical studies in the age of the Reformation. He referred to the Scriptures as a book of infinite sweetness, "a mass of strange delights," a book with secrets to make the life of anyone good. In describing the various means pastors require to be fully furnished in the work of their calling, Herbert provided a rationale for the history of exegesis and for the Reformation Commentary on Scripture:

> The fourth means are commenters and Fathers, who have handled the places controverted, which the parson by no means refuseth. As he doth not so study others as to neglect the grace of God in himself and what the Holy Spirit teacheth him, so doth he assure himself that God in all ages hath had his servants to whom he hath revealed his Truth, as well as to him; and that as one country doth not bear all things that there may be a commerce, so neither hath God opened or will open all to one, that there may be a traffic in knowledge between the servants of God for the planting both of love and humility. Wherefore he hath one comment[ary] at least upon every book of Scripture, and ploughing with this, and his own meditations, he enters into the secrets of God treasured in the holy Scripture.[53]

Timothy George
General Editor

---

[51]Alexander Campbell, *Memoirs of Alexander Campbell*, ed. Robert Richardson (Cincinnati: Standard Publishing Company, 1872), 97.

[52]Richard A. Muller and John L. Thompson, "The Significance of Precritical Exegesis: Retrospect and Prospect," in *Biblical Interpretation in the Era of the Reformation: Essays Presented to David C. Steinmetz in Honor of His Sixtieth Birthday*, ed. Richard A. Muller and John L. Thompson (Grand Rapids: Eerdmans, 1996), 342.

[53]George Herbert, *The Complete English Poems* (London: Penguin, 1991), 205.

INTRODUCTION TO LUKE

The Gospel of Luke in the Reformation

Today, most but not all Scripture scholars accept the Synoptic source hypothesis, which suggests that Mark is the oldest Gospel and was a primary source for both Matthew and Luke (both written later). These three Gospels together are called the Synoptics, from the Greek for "seen together," because of their many similarities and clearly overlapping passages. Matthew and Luke also appear to share another, otherwise unknown sayings source, labeled Q in contemporary discussion.[1] Each of these Gospels likewise had various sources separate from their common sources, thus explaining the differences between them.[2]

Scripture scholars of earlier eras also had theories about the authorship, dating and relationship between the Gospels, although these were perhaps not considered the most important matters in interpreting them. Generally people assumed that Matthew was the earliest Gospel—its place of primacy in the canon gave weight to that assumption—and Luke was assumed to have had access to both Matthew and Mark in the composition of his text. He may well also have known other noncanonical Gospels, as some commentators note in interpretations of his preface. Because Matthew was assumed to be the primary Gospel of the Synoptics, there are few Reformation commentaries that focus on the Gospel of Luke independently. Most either address the Synoptics together, as John Calvin does in his *Harmony of the Gospels* (which largely follows the structure of the Matthean text), or they take up Luke after writing commentary on Matthew and refer to that text when common passages are reached.[3]

In addition to those reformers who wrote formal commentaries and annotations on Luke (e.g., Heinrich Bullinger), others published paraphrases (e.g., Desiderius Erasmus). However,

---

[1]For the meaning of Q, see Lou H. Silberman, "Whence Siglum Q: A Conjecture," *Journal of Biblical Literature* 98, no. 2 (1979): 287-88, and John J. Schmitt, "In Search of the Origin of the Siglum Q," *Journal of Biblical Literature* 100, no. 4 (1981): 609-11.

[2]See A. D. Baum, "Synoptic Problem," in *Dictionary of Jesus and the Gospels*, 2nd ed., ed. Joel B. Green, Jeannine K. Brown and Nicholas Perrin (Downers Grove, IL: IVP Academic, 2013), 911-19.

[3]One benefit of this approach is that authors often discuss the varied presentations of the same event in the different Gospels. For example, in the comments on Jesus' genealogy in Luke 3, many authors note that there are differences between Matthew and Luke on this point, and these differences reflect the authors' varied purposes and intentions. John Lightfoot suggests that Matthew was writing to a Jewish audience and wanted to convey that Jesus was the promised Son of David; therefore he followed Joseph's line back to David and Abraham. Luke, however, wanted to show that Jesus fulfilled the prophecy of Genesis 3:15 as the "seed of the woman" who would defeat the serpent; thus he followed the line of Mary's ancestry and traced his descent from Adam. The key hermeneutical principle that guided these discussions is that there were no accidental omissions or errors in the text—differences between the Gospels must always be based on a good reason and could usually be explained.

many reformers—such as Martin Luther—never wrote a commentary on Luke but regularly preached from it. Despite his preference for the Gospel of John, Luther had plenty to say on many passages in Luke, though that was largely in sermons and in more topical writings.[4] And along with sermons, Luther (and many others) penned a Passional—a popular genre dedicated to Jesus' passion and death as told in the four Gospels. Such texts were not so much traditional commentary on pericope or verse as they were meditations on Jesus' death and sacrifice, as well as its universal implications.

In short, then, the majority of comments on Luke's Gospel from the sixteenth and early seventeenth centuries that are useful for a book such as this one, intended to provide reflection on and interpretation of the text, come from sermons. Of course, as Timothy George notes, many commentaries from this period had their origins in sermons, and Protestants believed that "through the words of the preacher, the living voice of the gospel (*viva vox evangelii*) is heard."[5] The gospel itself, according to Luther, is not so much the texts written by Matthew, Mark, Luke and John but "a sermon about Christ, Son of God and of David, true God and human being, who by his death and resurrection has overcome for us the sin, death and hell of all human beings who believe in him."[6] Sermons, then, have a direct connection to God's Word, both in interpreting the written text of the Bible for listeners (and readers) and in that they are, in themselves, the gospel or the good news about Jesus.

The text of published sermons is, in many cases, different from what was preached. Luther and many other preachers did not preach from a written text but rather only from an outline, while students and colleagues (or, in Calvin's case, a paid stenographer) took notes in the congregation. These notes were then occasionally prepared for publication, sometimes with the original preacher's input, and sometimes by the hand of another editor or editors.[7] Some sermons were written as "model" sermons and published in sermon collections or postils arranged around the lectionary, which is the standard set of Scripture readings for Sundays and holidays throughout the church year.[8] These postils were likely not preached by their authors in the exact format published (if at all) but were very influential and widely used by many preachers.[9] Luther's *Church* and *House*

[4]Martin Luther, "Preface to the New Testament," LW 35:362 (WADB 6:10; cf. p. 11); after 1537 Luther elided this section from his preface (see LW 35:358 n. 5). Luther famously commented that "John's Gospel . . . is far, far to be preferred over the other three and placed high above them," for John stressed Jesus' preaching, while the other three stressed the works of Jesus.

[5]See the General Introduction in this volume, p. xxii. Andrew Pettegree notes that it was a common practice among Reformation preachers to move sequentially through the biblical texts, preaching expository sermons which would then lend themselves to eventual compilation as a commentary. See Pettegree, *Reformation and the Culture of Persuasion* (Cambridge: Cambridge University Press, 2005), esp. chap. 2.

[6]"Preface to the New Testament," LW 35:360* (WADB 6:7; cf. p. 6).

[7]See the chapter on "Preaching" in Pettegree, *Reformation and the Culture of Persuasion*, esp. pp. 18-25.

[8]Most Western churches that use a lectionary cycle for their readings today follow a three-year cycle, but that was not the case in the early modern period, when a one-year cycle was followed. For the one-year lectionary, see WADB 7:536-44; the most common lectionaries used today are the Roman Catholic Mass Lectionary (catholic-resources.org, and, for the daily lectionary, www.usccb .org) and the Revised Common Lectionary (lectionary.library.vanderbilt.edu).

[9]Model sermon collections were a popular genre in late medieval Europe, and many popular pre-Reformation texts have survived. For information on preaching and sermons prior to and during the Reformation, see Anne T. Thayer, *Penitence, Preaching and the Coming of the Reformation* (Aldershot, UK: Ashgate, 2002) and John Frymire, *The Primacy of the Postils: Catholics, Protestants and the Dissemination of Ideas in Early Modern Germany* (Leiden: Brill, 2009).

Postils and Bullinger's *Decades* were model sermon collections that became international bestsellers, popular reading for ministers and literate lay readers alike.[10]

Despite the challenges in recovering the spoken word through the written word (a challenge to students of the Bible itself), there are many benefits to approaching the message of the reformers through their sermons. These sermons reflect pastoral concerns rather than merely academic ones, and, as in the (mostly homiletic) scriptural exegesis of the church fathers, we are reminded that "the gospel is always heard and interpreted within a worshipping community."[11] The purpose of the authors whose texts are included in this volume is always to preach the gospel; like Luke himself, they worked and preached so that their listeners and readers might be confirmed in what they had been taught.

Themes in the Gospel of Luke

In discussions of Luke's Gospel, it is frequently noted that Luke was a Greek speaker, writing to other Greeks, and although there is some debate about whether he was writing largely to a Jewish or to a Gentile community, there is a strong theme of *acceptance of Gentiles as true believers* running throughout the text. Luke's genealogy traces Jesus' lineage back to Abraham, and even further to Adam, suggesting that he is related to all of us, and not only to the children of Israel. It also firmly connects Jesus to the prophecy in Genesis 3:15, often called the *protevangelium*, the first prophecy of the Messiah in the Old Testament, for he is the "seed of the woman" (Mary, but also of Eve through Adam, his father). Although Luke here connects Jesus to the Old Testament messianic prophecies, he frequently stresses that his own people will not accept him, but that he will be welcomed more faithfully by Gentiles and foreigners. In Luke 11:29-32, we read of the "sign of Jonah," and the queen of the South and the Ninevites who will "rise up at the judgment with this generation and condemn it." While these foreigners accepted God's Word, many of Jesus' own people did not accept him as the Messiah.

We might expect that this theme would lead the reformers to stress the legitimacy of the Gentiles inheriting the kingdom over against a rejection of the Jews, but that was not the general tendency. While there were criticisms of the Jews and anti-Semitic comments in some of these texts, it is far more common to find criticisms directed at the Pharisees, the scribes and the other leaders of the Jewish community, and not Jews as a whole. These leaders thought themselves especially holy and worthy, largely based on their observance of laws and religious rituals, but as Jesus points out, they refused to recognize and repent their sin, thus allowing God's grace to penetrate their hearts. Early modern commentators were well aware that the first Christians were

---

[10]See Bodo Nischan, "Demarcating Boundaries: Lutheran Pericopic Sermons in the Age of Confessionalization," *Archiv für Reformationsgeschichte* 88 (1997): 199-216, esp. pp. 202-3. The Gospel portions from Luther's Christmas postil can be found in English translation in LW 52. Concordia Publishing House is preparing an additional eight volumes of Luther's postils. Volumes 75-79 will contain the *Christmas, Advent, Lenten* and *Summer Postils*, while volumes 80-82 will contain the *House Postil*. For Bullinger's work in English, see *The Decades of Henry Bullinger*, 5 vols., trans. H. I., ed. Thomas Harding (Cambridge: Cambridge University Press, 1849–1852).

[11]ACCS NT 3:xvii.

Jews, and the commentators were able to make a distinction between Jews who rejected Jesus and Jews who accepted him. Instead they stressed the fact that salvation comes through faith in Christ rather than one's family background—or, for that matter, through adherence to the law, or religious rituals or even kinship to Jesus. Thus, salvation is for all—Jews and Gentiles—in Jesus the Savior and Son of God.

A second theme of Luke's Gospel commonly noted in modern scholarship is *its focus on women*. At all stages of Jesus' life, Luke notes the women who were close to him. In fact, tradition suggests that Luke was a confidant of Jesus' mother, Mary, because he recorded so many details of the angel's annunciation, her pregnancy, her visit to Elizabeth and Zechariah, and the birth of Jesus. Beyond Mary's appearances in the text, Luke also records a number of female disciples who followed Jesus (Lk 8:2-3) and Jesus' interactions with women, such as the widow of Nain (Lk 7:11-17), the "sinful" woman who anointed his feet (Lk 7:36-50), his close friends Mary and Martha (Lk 10:38-42) and the women who were present at his death (Lk 23:27-31), burial (Lk 23:55-56) and resurrection (Lk 24:1-12).[12] We can perhaps compare these mentions of women to the emphasis on the acceptance of and even occasional preference for Gentiles that Luke portrays, and suggest that women were in a similar category—as second-class citizens, the weaker sex, the fact that Jesus socialized with women and included them in his company was out of the ordinary. The reformers did not often focus on this theme but on occasion were forced to address what appeared to them to be cultural oddities: how could it be appropriate that Jesus would travel with female disciples, and even be supported financially by them? Visiting Mary and Martha in their home (in the company of their brother, Lazarus, no doubt) was one thing, but accepting charity from wealthy women, especially those who had been healed of demon possession—that was a challenge to explain. But these women were "good soil," as the parable of the sower suggests (Lk 8:8), and Jesus came to heal the sick (that is, sinners), not the healthy. Jesus did not choose to associate with only those the world deemed worthy, and that included his female followers. But these same followers, as Catharina von Greiffenberg pointedly notes, were more loyal and courageous in following Jesus to his death and to his tomb than any of the men.

A third theme common to Luke is that of *Jesus' mercy and compassion*. He frequently shows compassion to others—the poor and downtrodden, the sick (whom he regularly healed), those who were possessed by demons, the hungry and forsaken—and insists that those who follow him also show such compassion. He seeks out those who were disregarded or avoided, such as demoniacs or public sinners like Zacchaeus and Matthew. He speaks to women and embraces children, he touches the unclean, and he does all these things in the face of the disapproving Pharisees, who cannot see beyond the fact that Jesus frequently breaks ritual laws, especially the law about working on a sabbath. And yet the irony, noted by many reform-minded exegetes, is that it is

---

[12]In his second book, the Acts of the Apostles, Luke also notes the presence of the Virgin Mary and other female disciples in the earliest Christian community gathered in Jerusalem after Jesus' ascension (see Acts 1:14). Church tradition suggests that at least Mary was present at Pentecost when the Spirit rested on them (see Acts 2:1-4, which notes that "they were all together in one place").

precisely in his obedience to the law that Jesus shows his greatest compassion. He was obedient to the law in his circumcision and presentation in the temple—these events revealed not only his parents' obedience but also his own. And in his obedience to the law (despite the fact that he had no sin and so was exempt from the law's requirements)—in returning home with his parents after remaining behind in the temple (Lk 2:41-52), in his regular attendance at synagogue services, even in his baptism—he shows his deep compassion for us. For he did not obey the law for his own sake, but rather for ours. It was because he perfectly fulfilled the law that we are freed from its punishment. His obedience on our behalf even extended to the cross, for he who was utterly innocent took on himself the punishment reserved for all of us—eternal death and separation from God—and paid our debt, so that we might become children of God instead. This sacrifice on the cross was in fact the main purpose which Jesus as the Messiah came to fulfill. He was the despised and suffering servant rather than a powerful king, and it was just this point that was so difficult for his own disciples to comprehend and accept.

As Jesus' primary position toward us is one of compassion, our position, according to Luke's Gospel, should be one of **repentance**. In Luther's dialectic, the law and the gospel, while opposites in a way, also function together. The law serves to break down our pride and self-reliance, and when it has done its work, the gospel shows us what God gives to us quite apart from anything we might try to do or earn. The law, then, has the function of leading us to repentance, which is the necessary companion of faith in the gospel message. And this was the aspect of the law that the Pharisees could never seem to comprehend. They thought that following the law—fulfilling every requirement and observing every ritual—was what made them good, holy and righteous. But in Luke's Gospel, Jesus constantly affirms that they were sinners like everyone else and just as much in need of repentance. That is the message of the parable of the Pharisee and the tax collector (Lk 18:9-14), which shows two sinners—one repents of his sins and begs for forgiveness, but the other is grateful to God only because he believes that he is not a sinner but a good man, a holy state which he believes he has achieved all on his own. Jesus' conclusion—that only the tax collector went home justified—shows that the saving effect of the law must take place within the heart. It is there that repentance must bloom, for it is only there that faith can grow.

Reformation Controversies in Luke

As Scripture was, for the reformers, the center and the highest authority for all Christian belief and practice, it is logical that interpretation of the scriptural text in just about any context could provide a forum for theological debate and assertions. Exegesis of Luke is no different, and even if perhaps more debate can be found in Latin commentary literature and (naturally) polemical writings, the often vernacular sermons still addressed issues contested in the sixteenth and seventeenth centuries. One example is orthodox Christology, which was defended by the majority of reformers in discussions of Jesus' conception. Luther notes that in the promise of the angel we see Christ's true nature confirmed: he is a true, human son of Mary, and the true, eternal King, "united in the single Word."[13] Calvin agrees that the orthodox formulation of Christ's two natures in one person is affirmed in Luke and critiques Michael Servetus (the Spanish theologian deemed a heretic by many) for reading the text "He shall be called the Son of the Most High" (Lk 1:32) to promote the idea that Jesus only became the Son of God when he took flesh—a resurrection of some sort of adoptionist heresy.

While the text of the annunciation was taken (by most) as affirming traditional orthodox belief of the incarnation, it was not read in a way supportive of a Roman Catholic perspective on the Virgin Mary. When the angel greets her as "full of grace," that does not mean that she in any way earned such a recognition or was so full of grace that she could now, as a queenly figure, deign to portion out such grace to others. Instead, Luke's word for "full of grace," *kecharitōmenē*, has a more passive sense and should be translated as "beloved," one who is chosen by God's grace.[14] She is not called to be the mother of the Son of God because of her humility, but in spite of it. Mary receives her share of criticism in some of these Gospel stories, particularly when her reaction to finding Jesus in the temple is discussed, but in general it is her deep faith that is noted as her most important characteristic and the element that should lead every generation to call her blessed. It is her faith in God's Word that leads her to accept and believe the angel's statement that she would bear a child, although she was a virgin (not, of course, that she had vowed to remain a virgin), and that this child would be God's Son.[15] And she accepts this word, Luther stresses, purely from faith alone—that is, from a trust in God's truthfulness and strength. She could not have accepted the angel's statement based on human reason or experience, for such a thing had never happened in the world before. Despite the evidence of her reason and the devil's attempts to derail her, "she believed, and closed her eyes . . . her heart clung alone to the Word."[16]

John's baptism is likewise an important locus for discussions about the sacrament. Anabaptists, proponents of believers' baptism who rejected the baptism of infants, claim John's example as authority for the notion that a water baptism should be given only to those who first believe and then repent. John himself first taught the people, encouraging them to repent and change their lives, and only then baptized them. This process could not have included little children, they insist, for children cannot believe in a trinitarian God, nor can they comprehend anything about the sign of water—even Christ was not baptized until he was thirty years old. The majority of Protestants agreed with medieval Catholicism that it is right and fitting to baptize infants, affirming that in this event water and Word, human and divine, are brought together, visibly granting the

---

[13]*LEA* 1:79 (cf. *WA* 17,1:154).

[14]See, for example, Huldrych Zwingli's comment on the angelic greeting (Lk 1:26-29). For a further discussion of interpretation of the Ave Maria, see Beth Kreitzer, *Reforming Mary: Changing Images of the Virgin Mary in Lutheran Sermons of the Sixteenth Century* (Oxford: Oxford University Press, 2004), esp. pp. 32-36.

[15]In general, most early Protestant theologians, and many later ones as well, accepted the notion of Mary's perpetual virginity but rejected the idea that she, like a nun, had somehow vowed her life to virginity. Instead they stressed that the fact that she married and bore a child affirmed marriage and family life for women, not avowed chastity in a convent. See Kreitzer, *Reforming Mary*, esp. pp. 134-36.

[16]*LEA* 1:66 (cf. *WA* 12:458).

promise of salvation in Christ.[17] And Jesus himself, although he did not specify the acceptability of infant baptism, also did not reject it when it was practiced by Jews and presumably by the earliest Christians. Jesus' example shows that baptism is not merely an event that follows and affirms repentance, for Jesus had nothing of which to repent. Instead in his baptism he bound himself to us in the water, thereby taking up the cross on our behalf.

The theme of wealth and its problems is raised a number of times in the Gospel—from the story of Zacchaeus to the phrase about the camel and the eye of the needle, the perils of money are frequently noted by Jesus in Luke's Gospel. In the Beatitudes he preaches that the poor are blessed and will inherit the kingdom. And unlike in Matthew's Gospel, Luke also records a corresponding "woe" to the rich, for they have "received their consolation" (Lk 6:20, 24). The dividing line in this controversy is again the majority of reformers over against the Anabaptists, particularly those Anabaptists like the Hutterites who practiced communal ownership of goods. Peter Walpot, a Hutterite leader and bishop, argued that Jesus' words must be taken in their most literal sense—it is those who own no possessions who are blessed.[18] Others, such as Philipp Melanchthon, suggest that this reading is not correct, for poverty is more of a scourge than a blessing. He insists that poverty is not the blessing meant here; rather the kingdom of heaven is—all those who suffer their lot in life with humility and gratitude to God are destined for the kingdom. Huldrych Zwingli is ready to concede in his discussion of the destruction of the herd of pigs (Lk 8:32-33) that sharing goods in common was God's original plan for creation and that it was only because of sin and selfishness that human beings invented private property. However, because we are all sinners, there is no way to revert to that original plan for Paradise. It is far more important to remember that everything we have belongs to God, and we use it only as stewards, so we should be grateful and remember that we will have to answer for our use of these goods.

A further debate between Anabaptists and nearly everyone else has to do with the use of "the Sword": that is, the use of physical force or violence for the purposes of protecting or forwarding the gospel, or even more broadly, in conducting the business of a government. While some early Anabaptists embraced violent struggle to establish the kingdom on earth (Thomas Müntzer is one example represented here), the majority, especially after the kingdom of Münster's fall in 1535, were pacifists. While they believed that Christians could not protect themselves or their church communities by any violent means but should be ready to sacrifice themselves for the gospel, they also asserted that no Christian should ever wield the sword. The larger implication of that belief is that no Christian could be a soldier, an executioner, even a judge or magistrate, for all those duties require the sword in some way. When Peter wields the sword before Jesus' arrest (Lk 22:50-51), Jesus rebukes him—a sign, pacifists argued, that he desires that none of his followers ever take up

---

[17]There is great diversity among the magisterial reformers' baptismal theology. For further detail and nuance, see "Baptism," *OER* 1:115-20 (cf. "Sacraments," *OER* 3:463-67); and Timothy George, *Theology of the Reformers*, rev. ed. (Nashville: B & H Academic, 2013).

[18]Interestingly, even Walpot makes a distinction in his exegesis, for "blessed are the poor" could not include the unworthy poor, those who are lazy and corrupt. Instead Jesus could only have meant those who embrace poverty through the Holy Spirit—that is, those who live in a community such as his own.

a sword again. Zwingli suggests, however, that Jesus is condemning only Peter's presumption and his rebellion against authority. Only those who are properly ordained by God to wield the sword have the right to do so. Legitimate rule includes the power of physical force (but never its abuse), and because legitimate governments are ordained by God, then it is acceptable for Christians who are so designated to participate in them.

Not all disputes were between various reform movements, of course, and the Gospel of Luke provided at least some arguments against Roman Catholic practices. Fasting, ceremonies and ascetic practices were easily compared with the practices of the hypocritical Pharisees and thus condemned. External observance of laws, especially laws that were only human requirements, was seen as an attempt to earn salvation through building up merit. The reformers utterly rejected the notion that observing rituals or laws could earn a person anything—external practice without internal change was empty and led to hypocrisy. Fasting, for example, could be terribly harmful if people believed that in itself it was a mark of righteousness or that the bare practice of it was pleasing to God. But Jesus fasted, and recommended fasting at the appropriate time—that is, when the "bridegroom" is taken away (Lk 5:35). Spiritual discipline such as fasting is, in fact, a sign of repentance and change of heart. It should accompany and encourage such a change but can never serve as a substitute for it.

Another important element of Catholic practice rejected by Protestants was clerical celibacy, and a number of passages in Luke supported the idea that ministers do not need to give up spouses or families, homes or possessions, but only those things that would hinder their service. Levi (or Matthew) was called by Jesus and got up and left everything behind (Lk 5:28), but then he returned to his home and gave a great banquet for Jesus. What he "left behind" clearly did not include his home. Likewise Peter had a mother-in-law (which implies a wife) and a home (Lk 4:38), and while his ministry frequently called him away from his home, it did not mean that he forsook them. Luke's Gospel provides much useful information for ministers, regarding how they should behave, how they should be chosen and trained, how they should dedicate themselves faithfully to the task—and be paid a salary (Lk 10:7)—but, according to these exegetes, it does not require them to take impossible vows for human requirements such as celibacy.

Probably the most significant controversy to find expression through the Gospel of Luke was over the Lord's Supper. This controversy involved Christians of all stripes—all Protestants rejected aspects of Catholic teaching, but the various reformers also disagreed with each other to such an extent that unification (both political and ecclesiastical) between Lutheran, Zwinglian and Calvinist groups became impossible.[19] Luther and his followers, although they rejected transubstantiation (the doctrine that in the sacrament the substances of bread and wine are changed to the body and blood of Christ, while the "accidents," the taste, smell, shape, consistency of the bread and wine remain the same), were accused of being too Roman because they held tightly

---

[19]This was most evident in the disagreements between Luther and Zwingli at the Colloquy of Marburg (1529) and the subsequent Diet of Augsburg (1530), where Protestants presented three different confessions to Charles V. See further, Amy Nelson Burnett, *Karlstadt and the Origins of the Eucharistic Controversy: A Study in the Circulation of Ideas* (Oxford: Oxford University Press, 2011).

to the idea that Christ is truly, even physically present in the elements of bread and wine. Zwingli and his followers rejected the idea that there was any physical presence of Christ, especially not in chunks of bread or cups of wine. Zwingli's watchword was John 6:63: "The Spirit gives life, but the flesh profits nothing." If the "flesh profits nothing," and Jesus' body is in heaven, then there could be no physical presence in bread and wine, nor would it benefit us. The sacrament is instead symbolic, bringing Christ's Spirit into the community gathered in worship. Calvin attempted to find the middle ground, insisting that we truly receive Christ in communion but that his human body is in heaven (if it is a real body, it cannot be multiplied), so we must be lifted up through the mediation of the Holy Spirit so that our souls may receive that spiritual food, even as our bodies receive bread and wine. The text that we find in Luke 22:14-20 is central to the debate, because here we read that Jesus took bread and gave it to his disciples, saying, "This is my body" (stressed in the literal sense by Luther but seen as a metaphor by Zwingli), but he also said, "Do this in remembrance of me" (stressed by Zwingli, in that the sacrament is established to remember his sacrifice, not somehow recreate it).

A Note on Sources

There is, quite intentionally, a large variety of sources used in this volume. The authors represent almost every corner of sixteenth- and seventeenth-century Christianity imaginable. The greater lights are here: Luther, Zwingli, Calvin, Erasmus (who was both a reformer and a lifelong Roman Catholic), even Kaspar von Schwenckfeld, a uniquely "spiritual" voice among Protestants. Their followers and imitators are here, too, and some who mostly re-presented the sermons and other writings of their teachers, as did Johannes Spangenberg with the teachings of Luther and Konrad Pellikan with Erasmus. Lesser lights, including a number of little-known English churchmen, also have their say. These texts may not have been widely read, but they must have been considered exceptional in some way to be published, and they show not only the attempts of more "average" preachers to struggle with Luke's Gospel but also reveal the influence of the wider tradition on them. Even the writings of several Anabaptists are included, although they are largely statements or confessions of faith rather than sermons or commentaries.

A note should be added about the texts of the French Protestant Augustine Marlorat (c. 1506–1562), who edited a collection of books similar to those in this series. Marlorat sampled authoritative writings by a number of reformers, including Calvin (first and foremost), Melanchthon, Brenz, Bucer, Zwingli, Bullinger, and even his own comments as well. Some of his "commentaries" were translated into English after his death by several other editors. The layers of editorial activity (and Marlorat's own tendency to translate according to his own beliefs) should suggest that we read his version of Melanchthon et al. with care, but while these selections might not be exactly the same as in the original versions, they are in fact what was distributed to and read by many people, and thus they had a great influence of their own.[20]

A final word should be said about women authors. As Timothy George notes in his general

---

[20]For example, there was one quotation by Marlorat, a selection of Melanchthon on the Lord's Supper, which I decided not to use, because it seemed to be modified to reflect an entirely Calvinist viewpoint.

introduction, there are few texts authored by women which were published in the sixteenth and seventeenth centuries. Very few women had the education, the authority or the opportunity to speak in the public sphere in such a way. This is not to suggest that women were not interested in the Bible, in reading it, talking about it, even writing and teaching others about it, but that their efforts rarely made it into print. However, some exceptions exist, and I made a concerted effort to include the voices of women, where appropriate, in these comments on the Gospel of Luke. Most notable are the writings of Katharina Schütz Zell (c. 1498–1562), wife of the Rev. Matthias Zell of Strasbourg, which include letters, meditations and even sermons (which she preached), and those of Catharina Regina von Greiffenberg (1633–1694), an Austrian noblewoman and Lutheran who is noted as a mystic and a poet. Her meditations on the birth and death of Christ in particular portray her perspective as a woman, and a sensitivity to the women in Jesus' life.

For Luther, Luke 2:11 is a summary of the entire form and content of Scripture and the gospel. He preached on this verse and its Old Testament referent (Is 9:6) several times a year. In this sermon from the *Church Postil* he notes that "to you is born a Savior" is the gospel in a nutshell:

> See here what the gospel is, namely, a joyful sermon about Christ our Savior. Whoever preaches him rightly preaches the gospel and pure joy. How can a heart hear of greater joy than that Christ is given to him as his own? He not only says that Christ is born, but he also makes his birth our own by saying "your Savior." Therefore, the gospel not only teaches the history and events of Christ but also makes him our own and gives him to all who believe it.[21]

For Luther, and the other reformers as well, the gospel is not merely history, but even more importantly it is God's good news *for us*.

The Gospels are often read as historical accounts of Jesus' birth, life, ministry, death and resurrection. In the recent past (and even today), some have uncritically accepted every word as historically true and accurate, while others have applied contemporary knowledge about the reality of the world and its physical forces and declared that some of the events recorded in these texts could not have happened. Therefore, they argue, the Gospels are not history at all and thus not true. Faith in God's Word is closely tied to the specific words, and whether they can be verified or documented as true or false. But such a static view of the biblical text seems to be a particularly modern phenomenon—one good reason why reading scriptural exegesis (that is, interpretation or analysis of the Bible) from earlier eras is a beneficial activity. The word *gospel*, from the old English *godspel* or "good story," is the English version of the Greek *evangelion*, or "good news." The Gospels tell the "good news" of Jesus the Christ, the Messiah or "Anointed One" of God, and its use *for us*. They are not, or at least not just, histories of a man, Jesus of Nazareth.

Luke's Gospel, the only one to include an address or preface, quite specifically notes that its

---

[21] LW 75:220* (WA 10,1.1:79; E² 10:149 cf. LW 52:20); citing Lk 2:11.

author was neither an actor in nor an eyewitness of the events he recorded. Instead, he was a historian (and writing about history always includes a large dose of interpretation), certainly an ethnographer and most definitely a believer. He suggests that he is writing this "orderly account" for Theophilus—perhaps a specific person or perhaps any "friend of God"—so that "you may know the truth concerning the things about which you have been instructed" (Lk 1:3-4). He gives the sense of wanting to collect and write down stories and sayings both to preserve them and to place them in a certain order—an order that would help to confirm the truth for someone who has already received instruction in the faith. This Gospel was written, then, according to the stated intention of the author, to convey the truth about Jesus, to convey God's Word through words, to confirm and deepen the faith of its readers. The Gospel of Luke may also do many other things—the stated intention of an author is never the only factor in a text's interpretation (it may not even be the author's only intention)—but we should remember that it is first and foremost the good news of Jesus Christ and the salvation that he brings *for us.*

Beth Kreitzer

COMMENTARY ON LUKE

OVERVIEW: In order to read and hear Scripture, for the reformers it is essential that we know and understand the gospel—who Jesus is, what he has done for us and what he continues to do for us. This is especially true of the Gospel genre, which seems to sound like the sole proprietor of the gospel. But it is not. Therefore, before wading into the comment proper, the reformers fix their attention on the question, What is the gospel? Every discourse that presents the history and benefit of God's Son is the gospel. This is the promised salvation foretold in the Hebrew Scriptures (the Law, the Prophets and the Writings). The triune God's resounding Yes to all human beings is divulged in the one man Jesus of Nazareth, who through his birth, life, death, resurrection and ascension is both gift and example to us by the mediation of the Holy Spirit. Luke the Evangelist has recorded his own version of this redemptive story for every Theophilus, every lover of God.

Prolegomena

WHAT DOES "GOSPEL" MEAN? JOHN CALVIN: In order to read with profit the history of the gospel, it is of great importance to understand the meaning of the word *gospel*. We will thus be able to grasp the specific intention these divinely inspired witnesses had in writing, and what the purpose of these events that they related is. (Others did not impose this name on their histories, but the authors themselves inscribed them thus, as Mark demonstrates who explicitly says that he relates "the beginning of the gospel of Jesus Christ.") A clear and certain definition of the word *gospel* can be determined from a passage of Paul, where he states that the gospel was "promised by God in the Scriptures through the prophets concerning his Son who was begotten from the seed of David and revealed as God's Son with power according to the Spirit of holiness by his resurrection from the dead."

First, this passage shows that the gospel is a testimony of the revealed salvation which had been formerly promised to the ancestors through the continuous succession of generations. It also points out a distinction between the promises which kept the hope of the faithful in suspense and this joyful message, by which God declares that he has accomplished those things which he had formerly required them to hope for. In the same manner he states a little afterwards, that in the gospel the righteousness of God is openly manifested, which was testified by the Law and the Prophets. The same apostle calls it, in another passage, an embassy by which the reconciliation of the world to God, once accomplished by the death of Christ, is daily offered to human beings.

Second, Paul means not only that Christ is the pledge of all the blessings that God has ever promised but also that we have in him a full and complete exhibition of them, as he elsewhere declares that "all God's promises in him are Yes and Amen." And, indeed, the freely bestowed adoption, by which we are made children of God, as it proceeds from the good pleasure which the Father had from eternity, so it has been revealed to us that Christ (who alone is the Son of God by nature) has clothed himself with our flesh and received us as his brothers. That satisfaction by which sins are blotted out, so that we are no longer under the curse and the judgment of death, is to be found nowhere else than in the sacrifice of his death. Righteousness and salvation and perfect happiness have been established in his resurrection.

The gospel, therefore, is the promulgation of the Son of God manifested in the flesh, to renew a ruined world and to restore human beings from death to life. It is justly called a good and joyful message; in it perfect happiness is obtained. Its goal is to establish the kingdom of God in us, destroying the corruption of the flesh and reviving us by the Sprit, in order to draw us into heavenly glory. For this reason it is often called the kingdom of heaven, and the renewal to a blessed life, which is brought to us by Christ, is sometimes called the kingdom of God. COMMENTARY ON A HARMONY OF THE GOSPELS: THE ARGUMENT.[1]

THE GOSPEL IS NOT A BOOK BUT CHRIST AS GIFT AND EXAMPLE. MARTIN LUTHER: People are strongly accustomed to count the Gospels according to their books and to say, "There are four Gospels." That is why people do not know what Paul and Peter say in their epistles, and why their doctrine is regarded only as an appendix to the doctrine of the Gospels. . . . It is a still worse custom that people regard the Gospels and Epistles as law books in which we are taught what we are to do, and the works of Christ are described in no other way than as examples for us. Where these two erroneous opinions remain in people's hearts, they can read neither the Gospels nor the Epistles in a useful and Christian way; they remain mere heathen as before.

Therefore, we should know that there is only one gospel—though written by many apostles.

Each epistle of Paul and Peter, along with Luke's Acts, is a gospel, even though they do not report all the works and words of Christ, but one has it shorter and less than another. There is not one of the four great Gospels which includes all the words and works of Christ, nor is that necessary. The gospel is and should be nothing else than a conversation or history about Christ. . . .

Thus the gospel should be and is nothing else than a chronicle, history and legend about who Christ is, what he has done, said and experienced, which some write short, some long, some this way, some another way. Most briefly, the gospel is a conversation about Christ that he is God's Son who became a human being for us, died, rose again and was made Lord over all things. . . . Second, you should not make a Moses out of Christ, as if he did no more than teach and set an example, as the other saints do, as if the gospel were a book of doctrine or law.

Therefore, you should grasp Christ—his Word, works and suffering—in two ways. One way is as an example that you should follow and act like. . . . As you see him pray, fast, help people and show love, so you should also do for yourself and for your neighbor. But that is the least part of the gospel—by which alone it cannot even be called "gospel," for in this way Christ is of no more use to you than any other saint. His life remains with him and does not help you at all. In short, this way does not make any Christians but only hypocrites. You must go much higher than this—though now for a long time this has been regarded as the best way, even an extraordinary way to preach.

The main point and basis of the gospel is that before you grasp Christ as an example, you first receive and know him as a gift and present given to you by God to be your own. When you see or hear that he has done something or suffered something, do not doubt that Christ himself with his deeds and suffering is yours. You can rely on him no less than if you had done it—indeed, as if you were Christ. See, that's truly knowing the gospel, that is the superabundant goodness of God, which no prophet, no apostle, no angel has ever fully

---

[1]CTS 31:xxxv-xxxvii* (CO 45:1-2); citing Mk 1:1; Rom 1:2-4; 3:21; 2 Cor 5:20; 1:20; 1 Tim 3:16.

expressed, which no heart can ever sufficiently be amazed at and comprehend. That is the great fire of God's love for us by which the heart and conscience become happy, certain and at peace. That is what preaching Christian faith means. SHORT INSTRUCTION: WHAT SHOULD BE SOUGHT AND EXPECTED IN THE GOSPELS.[2]

WHO IS LUKE? THE ENGLISH ANNOTATIONS: This sacred history was dictated by the Holy Spirit whose penman was Luke. Luke was from Antioch in Syria, a physician by profession. He was a follower and faithful assistant of Paul and thus became also a physician of the soul. But who was the first ministerial means of his conversion is not certain. Some think he was one of the seventy disciples—the other unnamed disciple who with Cleopas went to Emmaus after Christ's resurrection. If so, he had had Christ, the best teacher. But others think Paul converted him at Thebes. But Luke himself shows best in his preface what instruction he had: "those who from the beginning were eyewitnesses and ministers of the same gospel." From this it is evident that some of the apostles

instructed him in the mysteries of salvation through Christ and faithfully related to him this whole story.

Matthew, it seems, wrote to the Hebrews, and the other three Evangelists wrote to the Gentiles in the Greek language, in which Luke in an elegant style dedicates two excellent pieces (this Gospel and the Acts of the Apostles) to Theophilus, an honorable person. And in Theophilus Luke dedicates these two pieces to all the faithful who are lovers of God. ANNOTATIONS UPON THE GOSPEL ACCORDING TO SAINT LUKE: THE ARGUMENT.[3]

HEAL OUR SOULS. BOOK OF COMMON PRAYER (1549): Almighty God, who called Luke the physician—whose praise is in his Gospel—to be a physician of the soul: may it please you by the wholesome medicine of his holy doctrine to heal all the diseases of our soul: through your Son Jesus Christ our Lord. COLLECT ON THE FEAST OF SAINT LUKE THE EVANGELIST.[4]

---

[2]LW 75:7-9* (WA 10,1.1:8-12; E² 7:6-8; cf. LW 35:117-19).

[3]Downame, ed., *Annotations*, Rr4r*; citing Acts 1:1; Jn 20:30-31; Col 4:14; 2 Tim 4:11; Lk 24:18; 1:2.
[4]BCP 1549, 74*.

1:1-4 THE PROLOGUE

Inasmuch as many have undertaken to compile a narrative of the things that have been accomplished among us, ²just as those who from the beginning were eyewitnesses and ministers of the word have delivered them to us, ³it seemed good to me also, having followed all things closely for some time past, to write an orderly account for you, most excellent Theophilus, ⁴that you may have certainty concerning the things you have been taught.

OVERVIEW: The prologue to Luke's Gospel brings up an issue over which Protestants fought among themselves. The question was through what means the Spirit would bring God's message into people's hearts. Because Paul stated that it is the Spirit rather than the letter that saves, the reformers argued over the relationship between the two, especially when approaching the literal words of Scripture. As Luke explains to his friend Theophilus, the lover of God, he is writing this text to set down an "orderly account" of things that Theophilus already knows and believes, in order to help with his certainty. So, does God work always or sometimes through the written word, or are these words really unnecessary, because it is the Spirit who brings life? While some reformers such as Thomas Müntzer and Kaspar von Schwenckfeld, often denigrated as "enthusiasts," believed that God's Spirit was not captive to a text, and that direct communion with the divine was a much higher religious experience, most of the reformers stressed the centrality of the written word—the Word comes through the word, and it is where God chooses to meet us. Thus, Word and Spirit are not to be divorced, let alone opposed against one another; they are harmonious and trustworthy witnesses to God's acts.

LUKE ASSERTS THE AUTHORITY OF HIS GOSPEL. THE ENGLISH ANNOTATIONS: It seems that Matthew and Mark did not write before Luke, for if they had, he would have spoken more reverently concerning them. Whether he means by "many" those counterfeit pieces under the titles of the Gospel of Nicodemus, Thomas, according to the Egyptians or according to the Twelve is uncertain, because he names neither these nor others like them. But in affirming a full assurance of what he writes (along with the other holy Evangelists), he seems modestly to deny that others had such assurance. ANNOTATIONS UPON THE GOSPEL ACCORDING TO SAINT LUKE 1:1.[1]

DANGERS FACING THE GOSPEL WRITER. JOHN CALVIN: Luke is the only Evangelist who gives a preface to his Gospel, for the purpose of explaining briefly the motive which induced him to write. By addressing a single individual he may appear to be foolish, when it was his duty to sound the trumpet aloud and to call all people to faith. . . . But it is not less true that Paul's teaching pertains to everyone, although some of his epistles were addressed to certain cities and others to certain people. On the contrary, we must acknowledge, if we take into account the state of those times, that Luke adopted a conscientious and prudent course. There were tyrants on all sides who, by terror and alarm, would hinder the progress of sound teaching. This gave occasion to Satan and his servants to spread abroad the clouds of error, by which the pure light would be obscured. Now, as most people cared little about maintaining the purity of the gospel, and few reflected attentively on the inventions of Satan or the amount of danger that lurked under such disguises, every one who excelled others by uncommon faith, or by extraordinary gifts of the Spirit, was the more strongly bound to do his utmost, by care and industry, to preserve the

---

[1]Downame, ed., *Annotations*, Rr4v*.

doctrine of piety pure and uncontaminated from every corruption. Such persons were chosen by God to be the sacred keepers of the law, to hand down to posterity in good faith this deposit of heavenly teaching. With this in view, Luke dedicates his Gospel to Theophilus, that he might undertake its faithful preservation; it is the same duty that Paul enjoins and recommends to Timothy. COMMENTARY ON A HARMONY OF THE GOSPELS: PROLEGOMENA TO LUKE.[2]

WHAT DOES "MOST EXCELLENT" THEOPHILUS MEAN? DESIDERIUS ERASMUS: I am bewildered as to why Lyra suspected Theophilus to be some great person or prince, because Luke added the epithet "most excellent." So should we not call nobles "most excellent," or is it then specific to only them to be "most excellent"? True, Lyra had read in some other gloss that it was possible to read it in this way, since, because of ignorance, he was not able to understand the Greek language. For among the Greeks *kratos* sounds like "strength" or "rule." And *kratein* is "to conquer" or "to be in control"—thus, Paul in the Acts of the Apostles calls Festus *kratiston*, as if you would say "very powerful." . . . Lyra rejects Origen's homilies in Luke which note that *kratistos* means "most excellent" or "most powerful."[3]

Theophilus sounds like "lover of God" or "pleasing to God"—whether it is a special name or an epithet to the pious reader others dispute. I myself think it is a person's proper name. ANNOTATIONS ON LUKE 1:3.[4]

WHAT LUKE HAS WRITTEN CONFIRMS WHAT WAS TAUGHT ORALLY. DESIDERIUS ERASMUS: Now Theophylactus notes that it is not said *hina gnōs*, that is, "so you might discover" [*cognoscas*], but *ipignōs*, "so you might acknowledge" [*agnoscas*]. For we discover [*cognoscimus*] when we learn something earlier unknown to us; we acknowledge [*agnoscimus*] when we are already familiar with something, as when we recognize someone's face we saw years ago. Long ago, those who were newly baptized were given the mysteries of the Christian faith by word of mouth without writing, according to the manner of the old priests among the Egyptians and the Druids among the French. To be newly instructed in the mysteries was called by Paul and Luke in Greek *gatechein*; for *echein* signifies to sound with the voice. From this word came *catechein*, which signifies to teach and instruct by word of mouth those things which one does not want to leave in writing. So those who were taught were called *catechoumenoi*, or *catechetoi*, this is, not yet entered into the church, and those who taught them were called *catechetai*, that is, teachers. Therefore this is the sense and meaning of Luke: "That you might more fully and certainly know now, by writing, those things which you learned earlier by word of mouth at your entry into the church." And so we learn that we must read Luke to this end, that we might be without all fear and secure in his narration, not doubting whether or not he may be trusted but assuring ourselves that we have a true and most certain narration. AN ECCLESIASTICALL EXPOSITION UPON SAINT LUKE 1:4.[5]

---

[2]CTS 31:3-4* (CO 45:5-6); alluding to 2 Tim 1:14; 3:14.
[3]See ACCS NT 3:4 (FC 94:8-9).
[4]LB 6:219-20; citing Acts 26:25. For Nicolas of Lyra's comment, see *Biblia Sacra: Cum Glossa Oridinaria et Nicolai Lyrani Expositionibus, Literali et Morali*, 6 vols. (Lyon: Vincent, 1545), 5:122v. Contemporary scholarship continues to wrestle with the impact of "most excellent"; most reject Theophilus as a type for every Christian but also note that *kratistos* "does not constrain one to assume that Theophilus was a high-ranking official" (François

---

Bovon, *Luke 1: A Commentary on the Gospel of Luke 1:1–9:50*, trans. Christine M. Thomas, ed. Helmut Koester [Minneapolis: Fortress, 2002], 22-23, here 23). See also Bruce J. Malina and Richard L. Rohrbaugh, *Social-Science Commentary on the Synoptic Gospels* (Minneapolis: Fortress, 1992), 283.
[5]Marlorat, ed., *Catholike and Ecclesiasticall Exposition of the Holy Gospell After S. Marke and Luke*, 5-6* (cf. LB 6:220).

1:5-25 THE ANNOUNCEMENT OF JOHN'S BIRTH

⁵In the days of Herod, king of Judea, there was a priest named Zechariah,ᵃ of the division of Abijah. And he had a wife from the daughters of Aaron, and her name was Elizabeth. ⁶And they were both righteous before God, walking blamelessly in all the commandments and statutes of the Lord. ⁷But they had no child, because Elizabeth was barren, and both were advanced in years.

⁸Now while he was serving as priest before God when his division was on duty, ⁹according to the custom of the priesthood, he was chosen by lot to enter the temple of the Lord and burn incense. ¹⁰And the whole multitude of the people were praying outside at the hour of incense. ¹¹And there appeared to him an angel of the Lord standing on the right side of the altar of incense. ¹²And Zechariah was troubled when he saw him, and fear fell upon him. ¹³But the angel said to him, "Do not be afraid, Zechariah, for your prayer has been heard, and your wife Elizabeth will bear you a son, and you shall call his name John. ¹⁴And you will have joy and gladness, and many will rejoice at his birth, ¹⁵for he will be great before the Lord. And he must not drink wine or strong drink, and he will be filled with the Holy Spirit, even from his mother's womb. ¹⁶And he will turn many of the children of Israel to the Lord their God, ¹⁷and he will go before him in the spirit and power of Elijah, to turn the hearts of the fathers to the children, and the disobedient to the wisdom of the just, to make ready for the Lord a people prepared."

¹⁸And Zechariah said to the angel, "How shall I know this? For I am an old man, and my wife is advanced in years." ¹⁹And the angel answered him, "I am Gabriel. I stand in the presence of God, and I was sent to speak to you and to bring you this good news. ²⁰And behold, you will be silent and unable to speak until the day that these things take place, because you did not believe my words, which will be fulfilled in their time." ²¹And the people were waiting for Zechariah, and they were wondering at his delay in the temple. ²²And when he came out, he was unable to speak to them, and they realized that he had seen a vision in the temple. And he kept making signs to them and remained mute. ²³And when his time of service was ended, he went to his home.

²⁴After these days his wife Elizabeth conceived, and for five months she kept herself hidden, saying, ²⁵"Thus the Lord has done for me in the days when he looked on me, to take away my reproach among people."

ᵃ Greek Zacharias

OVERVIEW: This pericope introduces a new character to the story of salvation—John, the prophet and forerunner of Jesus. The story of his parentage, conception and birth makes clear that he has been especially chosen and appointed by God. John himself, the great preacher of repentence, serves as an excellent example and type for ministers—his role or office is to convert souls, spread the gospel and prepare the way for the Messiah. In a nod to criticisms that Protestants were teaching new ideas and new doctrine, Luther repeats the common refrain that in fact the reformers were only returning to the Bible and to the ancient teaching of the church; likewise, John was not preaching a new doctrine but rather the Messiah already foretold long ago by the prophets.

But John's parents are the main characters of this selection: Luke tells us that they were both "upright in the sight of God" and followed the law "blamelessly" (Lk 1:6). Human righteousness and works were a major point of contention for Protestants, and many writers are quick to point out that while Elizabeth and Zechariah are wonderful examples for Christians in how to be good and law-abiding (especially in following God's law rather than one they made up themselves), they still cannot achieve divine or salvific righteousness on their own; it is not their works but their faith in God's grace that shows them to be saved. When challenged by the prophecy of the angel, Zechariah reveals his limitations—in following human reason, he questions God's power. His punishment of having his power of speech removed leaves open the question of why Mary is not likewise punished later for asking a similar question. However, Zechariah's example proves for these writers that God is both far greater and far more gracious than we can comprehend.

1:5-7 The Parents and Background of the Baptist

A QUICK HISTORY OF HEROD. JOHN LIGHT-FOOT: Herod the Great, an Edomite by descent, was placed by the Romans as the king of Judea (compare Gen 27:40). Among the many plagues of his uneven and rocky reign, he had slain the Sanhedrin, and to patch up the business again, by the counsel of Bava ben Bara he had repaired the temple and made it incomparably more sumptuous than it was before.[1] He began this work in the eighteenth year of his reign, and it took him eight years to finish it. So this new building was but eight or nine years old at this year that we are upon. THE HARMONY OF THE NEW TESTAMENT, SECTION 3.[2]

JOHN'S GOOD PARENTAGE LENDS AUTHORITY TO HIS WITNESS TO CHRIST. JOHANNES BRENZ: Luke is preparing to describe the nativity of Christ, and because John the Baptist is his forerunner, sent before him to testify to all Israel that he was the promised Messiah; therefore Luke first of all describes the conception and birth of John. And because a witness has no credit, especially in matters of great weight, unless he is very honest and of good reputation, Luke first of all

describes John by the honesty of his stock and parents. Then he describes the miracles which do not so much adorn John's nativity as they give authority to and commend the testimony which he was going to give concerning Christ. AN ECCLESI-ASTICALL EXPOSITION UPON SAINT LUKE 1.[3]

JOHN'S PARENTS PROVIDE A GOOD EXAMPLE OF VIRTUE. HULDRYCH ZWINGLI: The prophet commends John's parents for their holiness and righteousness, not for riches, power or that sort of thing, on which people of that time prided themselves but which abandon them after death; he commends them for holiness and righteousness, which follow people after death and make them famous and worthy of praise. It is silly to commend a person on account of his works, for he produces nothing himself either desirable or imitable for the human mind. But virtue in itself is truly commendable to the human soul, and the human mind will be led to desire it eagerly [when it is praised], just as people are inflamed with desire for earthly pleasures after they hear about them. In itself, virtue is certainly more sacred than our minds might be able to discern, but when we see it in others, it is now made even more praiseworthy to us. Thus many have examples of influence for imitation, if they should be applied to virtue. The example of Moses encourages more to faith and gentleness, if it is put forward simply. A singular example moves and teaches more than a thousand words which are beautiful, good and honest, as the leaders expect. The work was nothing to God, that it would have led him to count Zechariah as just, for to him nothing is hidden. These things are truly found in the written Word of God for our sake, to give us examples which we might follow, for otherwise no one would be considered just before God. A noble birth is true and commendable only if it is attached to a holy life, virtue and righteous-ness. IN THE GOSPEL OF LUKE 1.[4]

---

[1]Josephus, *Antiquities of the Jews* 14-15.
[2]Lightfoot, *Harmony, Chronicle and Order of the New Testament*, 2*.
[3]Marlorat, ed., *Catholike and Ecclesiasticall Exposition of the Holy Gospell After S. Marke and Luke*, 8*.
[4]*D. Hvldrichi Zvinglii in Plerosqve Novi Testamenti Libros*, 183.

Zechariah and Elizabeth Suffered from Sterility but Were Granted a Miracle.
Konrad Pellikan: The newness of the birth, and that it was by a miracle from an elderly, sterile woman should bring forth admiration of John in the human heart. For certainly the people should expect something from him who was born by benefit of the heavens, rather than in the regular course of common human nature. The saints had had too few happy things at that time for them to fit in happily with the rest of the world. Although it was wonderful how the couple always lived in marital happiness, the sterility was the first point of shame for them, and it was one of the particular evils of life that these holy people were not able to be enriched by any child. This was a serious matter which disturbed the minds of them both, but especially Elizabeth, who was now called by the common and shameful name of sterile. Old age had increased the desperation of them both for a child, but while nature would not allow it, the goodness of God granted it. Often, however, the sterility of an upright woman, or of upright wives, is maintained so that the glory of God might be greatly spread abroad when they finally give birth miraculously. Commentary in Luke 1:7.[5]

1:8-17 Zechariah in the Temple and Gabriel's Prophecy

The Priestly Work Follows the Example of David. Johann Agricola: Concerning the arrangement of the ministers of the temple according to the law of David, read 1 Chronicles 24. Because David similarly was a model when he was a guide in the mountains, he composed the series of instrumental songs and sacrifices that they might serve through the priests in the temple. And when it was the eighth hour, it fell to the lot of Zechariah to go into the temple to perform the religious rites; by a miracle and the apparition of the angel, he learned he should stay for the great benefit of Judah. Thus you will observe all laws, festival days, the new moon, the sabbath, which are a shadow of the things to come. The *sōma*, however, is the thing which signifies Christ, that is, it is about Christ after John says in a clear voice, "He must become greater, I must become less." Annotations in the Gospel of Luke 1.[6]

As Priest, Zechariah Prayed for Himself and the People. Konrad Pellikan: Zechariah entered on the sabbath not into the Holy of Holies but into the holy place, that is, the first part of the temple, where every day the lamps were prepared and the incense was placed at the hour of regular sacrifice. He was the priest over all duties for his period, and those things were presided over by another high priest who once in the year entered into the Holy of Holies, on the Feast of the Atonement, when the blood of goats and young bulls was burned for the sins of the people. By the time of the second temple, it can be seen that much had changed, and not for the better.[7] Otherwise, no one was admitted into the holy place except only for priests. They were served by a Levite in the atrium, before which the people were standing in their rows—he prayed outside, wishing to be secluded. Meanwhile they were praying for the health and prosperity of all the people, while the burnt sacrifice and incense were offered up on the altar, so that God might deem it worthy to accept. Having accomplished the sacrifice, the priest would go forth to the atrium, and he would finish up with the remaining duties which applied to the ceremony of legitimate sacrifices. He did not only pray for the people but before all for himself according to the rule of the law, and because he was mortal himself, he was, without doubt, liable to human errors and faults. Therefore at that time Zechariah

---

[5]Pellikan, *In Sacrosancta Quatuor Evangelia et Apostolorum Acta*, 6 (cf. LB 7:285). Pellikan's New Testament commentary follows Erasmus's *Paraphrase* very closely, often verbatim. For that reason, each time Pellikan appears in this volume, the corresponding passage from Erasmus is cross-referenced.

[6]Agricola, *In Evangelium Lucae Annotationes*, 19r-v; citing Col 2:16-17; Jn 3:30. *Sōma* is translated in the ESV as "substance" (Col 2:17), see Calvin's comments in RCS NT 11:200-201.
[7]For the original instructions for the Day of Atonement (Yom Kippur), see Lev 16.

grew weary of repeatedly praying to God for a son, among other prayers, and for the redemption of the people, so long expected by many generations of saints. The prayer of a pious priest had penetrated all the way to God, the angels having revealed to no one that they were this time bringing back a response. Meanwhile the people in fact, as it was said, were standing outside at the time of sacrifice and burning of incense and praying together. COMMENTARY IN LUKE 1:8-9.[8]

THE INCENSE IS THE PRAYERS OF THE PEOPLE OFFERED BY CHRIST. THE ENGLISH ANNOTATIONS: "The time of incense," that is, while the priest, according to the law, burned incense within. This incense was to be offered morning and evening by the priest, when he dressed the lamps. This was not without a singular mystery, for the lamps signified the light of God's Word, and the incense signified the prayers of God's people to be joined with it, for these prayers are a sweet spiritual incense acceptable to him. They are presented by Christ, our high priest, ministering in the true tabernacle which the Lord erected; he appears in God's presence for us, offering incense in the golden censer of the angel of the covenant, Christ. These prayers, as that incense offered morning and evening, ought to be continual, as our high priest "ever lives to make intercession for us." ANNOTATIONS UPON THE GOSPEL ACCORDING TO SAINT LUKE 1:11.[9]

ZECHARIAH IS FLESH AND DOES NOT BELIEVE. FRANÇOIS LAMBERT: Of all the fables and useless questions, Luke considers here what many want to know, that is, why this man, from the priestly order of Abijah, whose wife was Elizabeth, was called to be the father of John, and why the angel Gabriel was sent to Zechariah. Not to make a vain comparison, he is the greatest of all the angels, or at least of the seraphim. Likewise, why

did the angel bring the news to Zechariah while he was occupied in the priestly office in God's temple, with the incense burning and the people outside praying? These things, they say, give glory, although they are the most trivial details, as if those deeds which Gabriel announced to the Blessed Virgin would not be much more excellent, although he appeared outside of the temple. Therefore, getting rid of those useless details, it can be seen in this passage that once Zechariah had seen the angel, the greatest fear rushed on him. But what would an angel be, except for a messenger from God? First he frightens Zechariah, but then he speaks wonderful words of consolation, so that one might give close attention to what is announced from the mouth of God. All of God's words concerning his will which are announced to us likewise through the mouth of a true evangelist first frighten the flesh, which is now mortified through the Spirit of Christ—this is "more desirable than gold" and many precious stones, and sweeter and more pleasant than honey from the comb.

Zechariah was terrified by the messenger of God as long as he did not believe him. For then he was flesh, and flesh does not grasp those things which are of God, and so it is unable to believe them. But when the Father Most High draws one, and through him immoral flesh is mortified and crucified, afterwards one is made faithful and spiritual. It would be enough to say that a great peace in the soul and consolation come to the one who is tested. COMMENTARY IN LUKE 1:8-11.[10]

THE NAME JOHN SHOWS HE IS CHOSEN TO PREACH GOD'S GRACE. MARTIN BUCER: Frequently in ancient times God gave names to those whom he chose to do great things, agreeing to the same, as we may see in Abram, in Sarai and in Jacob. And so our Lord had the name of Jesus given to him, and he himself afterward changed the name of his more special apostles. In this passage John also had his name given to him by God before he was born, as his office was to preach Christ's

---

[8]Pellikan, *In Sacrosancta Quatuor Evangelia*, 6 (cf. LB 7:285).
[9]Downame, ed., *Annotations*, Rr4v*; citing Ex 30:7-8; Ps 141:2; Heb 8:2; 9:24; Rev 8:3-4; Heb 7:25; 1 Thess 5:17.

[10]Lambert, *In Divi Lucae*, B4v-B5r; citing Ps 19:10.

presence to the world and to point toward him. His office was to be a preacher of grace and mercy, and therefore he received his name through grace. For him whom we call John, the Hebrews call Iohanan, from the Hebrew verb which signifies to gratify, to endue, to give freely. Therefore Iohanan, or John, signifies gracious and accepted, who indeed was most acceptable, who indeed God had chosen to so notable an office of the gospel with so many great miracles. But really he was called gracious and acceptable because he was a preacher of the grace of God through Christ. AN ECCLESIASTICALL EXPOSITION UPON SAINT LUKE I.[11]

ABSTINENCE FROM ALCOHOL IS NOT A DIVINE COMMAND. JOHN CALVIN: "He will drink neither wine nor strong drink" must not be understood to mean that John's abstemiousness was a singular virtue but that God wanted to distinguish his servant by this visible sign, by which the world would acknowledge him to be a lifelong Nazarite. The priests also abstained from wine and strong drink while they were performing their duties in the temple. The same abstinence was enjoined on the Nazarites until their vow was fulfilled. God showed by an extraordinary token that John was dedicated to him to be a Nazarite for his whole life, as we learn was also the case with Samson. But we must not on this ground imagine that the worship of God consists in abstinence from wine, as imitators select some part of the actions of the ancestors to copy. Let all practice moderation: let those who suffer ill effects from drinking wine abstain of their own accord, and let those who have none endure the lack with equanimity. COMMENTARY ON A HARMONY OF THE GOSPELS.[12]

PREACHING FOR REPENTANCE IS THE PRIEST'S OFFICE. MARTIN LUTHER: This is about the office of John and also concerns us. By God's command, the angel makes John into a priest while

still in the womb. Because of this office, it is laid on him that "he will convert." That is service to the Word. He will be such a priest that he will not just preach into the wind but "will convert many." And there is a great need for preaching. The noblest office in the world is the preaching office. And therefore we also celebrate, because John's office is one that helps people against sin, the world and Satan, and leads them to the kingdom of God. Therefore it is the most glorious office. For even if someone is a king above kings, that is not going to help him against Satan. SERMON ON SAINT JOHN'S DAY (1529).[13]

JOHN FULFILLS THE OLD TESTAMENT PROPHECIES. JOHANNES BRENZ: When in his time true religion was defiled with the idolatrous worship of Baal and the children of the patriarchs followed another kind of religion than the patriarchs themselves had followed, Elijah so restored true religion that he reformed the religion of the patriarchs among their children, and reformed the religion of the children by the religion of the patriarchs, and the unbelieving children followed the wisdom (that is to say, the faith) of the righteous patriarchs. They are called righteous because they believed the promise made to Abraham: "Abram believed the Lord, and he credited it to him as righteousness." Moreover, there was great controversy and dissension concerning religion: the greatest part of the people in the kingdom of Israel followed the religion of Baal; very few observed the true religion of the God who was worshiped in Jerusalem. So it came to pass that some parents followed Baal and the children the true God, and some children were idolaters and the parents true worshipers of God; so that, not only in one city but in one house also, and even in one bed, diverse religions were found.

Therefore, when he had overcome the prophets of Baal by the miracle of the sacrifice which was consumed by fire from heaven, Elijah turned the hearts of the parents toward their children; that is

---

[11]Marlorat, ed., *Catholike and Ecclesiasticall Exposition of the Holy Gospell After S. Marke and Luke*, 14-15*.
[12]CTS 31:17* (CO 45:14); alluding to Lev 10:9; Num 6:3; Judg 13:3-4.

[13]LEA 1:55 (cf. WA 29:420-21).

to say, he restored among the parents and their children one and the same uniform religion. So the children of Israel who were then alive cast aside the wicked worship of Baal and followed the pure religion of the true God, who had been loved by their ancestors. So by the ministry of Elijah, the children of Israel were converted to the faith of the righteous who were godly and wise judges of religion. John also began to make such a binding and union of parents with their children, and Christ at the last finished it. So when Malachi speaks of turning, he gives us to understand that the state of the church will be rent and torn at the coming of the other Elijah. And so it was indeed, as the histories plainly record. AN ECCLESIASTI-CALL EXPOSITION UPON SAINT LUKE 1.[14]

1:18-20 *Zechariah's Doubt and Punishment*

JUST PUNISHMENT FOR ZECHARIAH'S LACK OF FAITH. JOHN CALVIN: Next follows the doubt of Zechariah, and the punishment which the Lord inflicted on his lack of faith. He had prayed that he might obtain offspring, and now that it is promised, he is distrustful, as if he had forgotten his own prayers and faith. It might, at first sight, appear harsh that God is so offended by his reply. He brings forward his old age as an objection. Abraham did the same, and yet his faith is so highly applauded that Paul declares he "considered not his own body now dead, neither yet the deadness of Sarah's womb" but unhesitatingly relied on the truth and power of God. Zechariah inquires how, or by what proof, he might become more certain. But Gideon was not blamed, although he asked twice for a sign. In fact, shortly after this we are informed of Mary's objection, "How shall this be, since I know not a man?" which the angel ignores as if there was no fault in it. Why then does God punish Zechariah so severely, as if he had been

guilty of a very grave sin? I would say that, if the words alone are considered, either all were equally guilty or Zechariah did nothing wrong. But as human actions and words must be judged from the state of the heart, we must abide by the judgment of God, to whom the hidden secrets of the heart are open.

Unquestionably, the Lord saw in Zechariah something worse than his words reveal, and therefore God's anger was kindled against him for rejecting the promised grace with distrust. We have no right, indeed, to lay down a law to God which would not leave him free to punish in one the fault which he pardons in others. But it is very evident that the case of Zechariah was widely different from that of Abraham or Gideon or Mary. This does not appear in the words, and therefore the knowledge of it must be left to God, whose eyes pierce the depths of the heart. Thus God distinguishes between Sarah's laugh and Abraham's, though the one apparently does not differ from the other. The reason why Zechariah doubted was that stopping at the ordinary course of nature, he ascribed less than he ought to have done to the power of God. Those who believe that God will do no more than what seems probable in nature take a narrow and disparaging view of the works of God, as if his hand were limited by our human senses or confined to earthly means. COMMENTARY ON A HARMONY OF THE GOSPELS.[15]

GABRIEL'S AUTHORITY SHOULD HAVE CONVINCED ZECHARIAH. MARTIN BUCER: This is contrary to what Abraham did, when Zechariah considered his body now to be dead and Elizabeth's womb dead also, for they were not even as advanced in years as Abraham and Sarah were. It was on account of this that he doubted the promises presented by the angel, and thus he was made mute; if we should dwell on these things, it makes sense that faith would be weak. But if one keeps in mind God's power and goodness, then

---

[14]Marlorat, ed., *Catholike and Ecclesiasticall Exposition of the Holy Gospell After S. Marke and Luke,* 19-20*; quoting Gen 15:6; alluding to Mal 4:5-6.

[15]CTS 31:23-24* (CO 45:18-19); quoting Rom 4:19; alluding to Judg 6:17, 37, 39; Heb 4:13; Gen 18:12; 17:17.

nothing is too difficult to believe. Because Zechariah gets caught up in worrying about his age and that of his wife, he provokes the angel, who replies, "I am Gabriel, who stands in the sight of God, and I have been sent to speak to you." It is as if he said, "Why do you consider your age and that of your wife, instead of considering who I am announcing this to you, and by whom I was sent? I am an angel, that is, a messenger of God; I stand in the sight of God, and I have been sent to announce these glad tidings to you. Therefore, the things I announce cannot be in vain, or that would mean something is impossible for God. And that you might rouse yourself to greater hope, I am Gabriel, the mighty captain of God, who once foretold many things about the future to Daniel; surely therefore you will not doubt that what you have heard from me will happen. But whoever does not have faith at once in my words will not be able to speak until those things come to pass which I have foretold." Commentary on the Gospel According to Luke 1.[16]

Only Believers Can Speak Words of Divine Truth. François Lambert: Rightly, because he did not believe, he was deprived of words. The language of truth is abundantly delivered only to those who believe. We see in Psalm 116: "I believed, even when I said 'I am greatly afflicted.'" For no one is able to speak the truth unless he has already believed, and in whose heart the Holy Spirit has already written the truth. But if someone is unbelieving or impious and proclaims the eloquence of truth with an impure heart (by which he lives), then he does not speak the words of God, but rather he touches on the most indifferent human fabrications. Finally, it is impossible that a person who never had real truth in his heart could speak the words of truth, without mixing them with lies. Commentary in Luke 1:20.[17]

1:21-23 Zechariah Leaves the Temple

Zechariah's Muteness Prepares the People for God's Greater Work. Heinrich Bullinger: With this passage the story is finished. But there are three chief points that we can see. The first is the truth, consistency and certainty of divine prophecies. Just as of course the angel foretold that Zechariah would be mute, so all the things he said came to pass. The second is that we can see how much power there is for corrupt people sometimes in discipline, obedience and patience. When the priest comes out much later than usual, they wait in a calm and orderly manner, with the calmest feelings; today, however, whatever the priests do in holy meetings seems to take too long. Finally, an unexpected miracle or sign appears from the Lord to this new crowd; he wanted to support and prepare the mind of the people for an even greater thing, that each one might think for himself what a great wonder and prodigy this child is going to be. Afterwards, Luke calls the temple holy, the part of the temple for the whole thing. But the Israelites understood when they saw Zechariah's face, as his face and whole body showed some aspect of the divine, and because he communicated through nodding, just as if he would praise the greatness of the works of God. Meanwhile he remains mute, so that none of the words of God should be forgotten. Commentary on Luke 1:21-23.[18]

Zechariah Could Still Serve in the Temple. John Trapp: Although Zechariah ceased to speak, he did not cease to minister. For although he could not speak, he was not lame—he could make the sacrifice, and so he made it. We may not whenever we please take occasions of withdrawing ourselves from the divine services. A Commentary upon the Gospel According to Saint Luke 1.[19]

---

[16]Bucer, *In Sacra Quatuor Evangelia*, 533.
[17]Lambert, *In Divi Lucae*, C5r-v; citing Ps 116:10.
[18]Bullinger, *In Luculentum et Sacrosanctum Evangelium Secundum Lucam Commentariorum*, 10v.
[19]Trapp, *Commentary or Exposition*, 373*.

1:24-25 Elizabeth's Pregnancy

GOD'S PROMISE IS FULFILLED DESPITE ZECHARIAH'S DOUBT. JOHANNES BRENZ: Behold here the fruit and power of the Word of God! A wonderful son was promised to Zechariah by the word of God, although he did not receive this promise in faith in the beginning. Despite this, the Lord is so faithful and just that he fulfilled what he had promised, and he brought it to pass that the wife of Zechariah, although she was both by nature and by old age highly unlikely to conceive, conceived her promised son. AN ECCLESIASTICALL EXPOSITION UPON SAINT LUKE 1.[20]

ELIZABETH CONCEALS HER CONDITION FOR THE SAKE OF OTHERS. JOHN CALVIN: Her words show clearly that her hope was not doubtful or uncertain. By saying "thus the Lord has done to me," she clearly and calmly announces that his grace was known. There were, however, two possible reasons for this to be concealed. The first is that, before this miracle of God became visible, it would have exposed it to the diverse opinions of people, for the world is often accustomed to chatter indiscreetly and dishonorably about the works of God. The second is that when people would have suddenly discovered that she was pregnant, it would more greatly encourage them to praise God. For when the works of God gradually emerge over time, they are often of little value to us. So Elizabeth did not conceal it for her own sake but rather with a greater regard for others. COMMENTARY ON A HARMONY OF THE GOSPELS.[21]

THE LORD LOOKS ON ELIZABETH AND SHOWS HER FAVOR. AUGUSTIN MARLORAT: By these words, "he looked on me," Elizabeth notes that the grace and benefit which had happened to her were in fact undeserved by her. The opposite of this is to be turned around and looking another way. Here we can read what the prophet David says: "Though the Lord is on high, he looks on the lowly, but the proud he knows from afar." That is to say, the Lord has compassion on the lowly but not so on the proud. And the word does not differ much from the word *mercy*, except that "looks on" signifies the gesture of him who has compassion, and "mercy" is the affection of God's good will toward us. Elizabeth therefore considered it a singular benefit of God that she was great with child, and not without cause. AN ECCLESIASTICALL EXPOSITION UPON SAINT LUKE 1.[22]

LIKE ELIZABETH, WE SHOULD DELIGHT IN CHILDBIRTH. MARTIN LUTHER: The Jews highly esteemed childbirth. . . . (In the comedies we see that the Greeks delighted in their offspring, too.) Among the Jews it was not only a disgrace not to have children, but it was even feared to be the wrath of God. Thus, Elizabeth considered it such a great thing that this disgrace—that she was barren—had been taken away from her. TABLE TALK (1542).[23]

---

[20]Marlorat, ed., *Catholike and Ecclesiasticall Exposition of the Holy Gospell After S. Marke and Luke*, 27*.
[21]CO 45:23 (cf. CTS 31:29-30).

[22]Marlorat, ed., *Catholike and Ecclesiasticall Exposition of the Holy Gospell After S. Marke and Luke*, 28*; citing Ps 138:6.
[23]WATR 5:165 no. 5458 (cf. Ewald Plass, ed., *What Luther Says: An Anthology*, 3 vols. [St. Louis: Concordia, 1959], 1:137]. Luther was amazed by what he considered the high office of childbirth, so much so, in fact, he believed that "if you were not a woman, you should wish . . . on account of this work alone, that you were a woman" (WABr 7:363-64).

1:26-38 THE ANNUNCIATION TO MARY AND JESUS' CONCEPTION

²⁶*In the sixth month the angel Gabriel was sent from God to a city of Galilee named Nazareth,* ²⁷*to a virgin betrothed*^a *to a man whose name was Joseph, of the house of David. And the virgin's name was Mary.* ²⁸*And he came to her and said, "Greetings, O favored one, the Lord is with you!"*^b ²⁹*But she was greatly troubled at the saying, and tried to discern what sort of greeting this might be.* ³⁰*And the angel said to her, "Do not be afraid, Mary, for you have found favor with God.* ³¹*And behold, you will conceive in your womb and bear a son, and you shall call his name Jesus.* ³²*He will be great and will be called the Son of the Most High. And the Lord God will give to him the throne of his father David,* ³³*and he will reign over the house of Jacob forever, and of his kingdom there will be no end."*

³⁴*And Mary said to the angel, "How will this be, since I am a virgin?"*^c

³⁵*And the angel answered her, "The Holy Spirit will come upon you, and the power of the Most High will overshadow you; therefore the child to be born*^d *will be called holy—the Son of God.* ³⁶*And behold, your relative Elizabeth in her old age has also conceived a son, and this is the sixth month with her who was called barren.* ³⁷*For nothing will be impossible with God."* ³⁸*And Mary said, "Behold, I am the servant*^e *of the Lord; let it be to me according to your word." And the angel departed from her.*

a That is, legally pledged to be married b Some manuscripts add *Blessed are you among women!* c Greek *since I do not know a man* d Some manuscripts add *of you* e Greek *bondservant*; also verse 48

OVERVIEW: This portion of the text provides the reformers with an opportunity to discuss the differences between worldly expectations and the divine way of doing things. The world would expect a savior to come with loud, blaring trumpets to the rich and powerful, and human reason cannot comprehend a meek and lowly, truly human beginning for the divine Son of God; but God has his own plans. The angel is sent to a poor, insignificant girl, engaged but not yet married, to announce that she will be the mother of the Messiah. And even Mary asks, How? But when Gabriel clarifies God's plan, she does not doubt but believes, and that is the true miracle and the reason why Mary stands with the greatest saints as an example of faith. She accepts what many in the church's history could not—that Jesus would be both truly human, her son, and truly divine, the Son of God. The mystery of the incarnation is incomprehensible to human reason, and so it is also a perennial topic for Protestant thinkers, divided between those who accept the Chalcedonian formulation and those (such as Michael Servetus) who cannot accept either Christ's full humanity or his full divinity.

The story of the annunciation to Mary also allowed Protestants to give voice to how their views were different from a traditional Roman Catholic perspective. What did it mean to say that Mary was "full of grace," as the angel said? Why was she the one chosen to be the mother of the Savior, or the "Mother of God," as the traditional title *Theotokos* upholds?[1] What did her virginity, and then her marriage, mean for average Christians? The texts in this section are an important locus for Protestants concerned to distance themselves from what they considered to be inappropriate and superstitious beliefs about Mary but yet honor her as the one whom "all generations will call blessed." Protestants still struggle with this dilemma.

---

[1] Literally "Bearer of God."

1:26-29 *The Angelic Greeting*

The Humble Maid Was Predestined to This Honor. Catharina Regina von Greiffenberg:

The highest God above all the heavens sent an ambassador, one of the most glorious angels, down to earth, to Galilee, a poor, obscure spot on the way to Nazareth, an unimportant little hamlet, to a virgin who was the most insignificant and lowliest of maidens, the betrothed of a simple, common carpenter. In this simplicity, however, the divine Trinity showed its greatest wisdom in that it knew both how to find in the greatest lowliness capacity for virtue and how to impart the capacity for divine things to the most wretched incapacity. It shows its omnipotence in its ability to exalt a little speck of earth to heavenly spectacles and splendid miracles. It displays its goodness by electing the most miserable things for the purpose of its elevation, and it displays its freedom by turning with its grace there where, at the beginning, one—and all the rest of the world—would not have expected it.

Who would believe that the King of kings, the Lord of all the potentates, would dispatch an angel as an ambassador to a poor maiden or the wife of an artisan? What is more absurd before the world and yet better disposed for the dispensation of heaven? Poverty and lowliness are no hindrance to divine calling: as little as they could take from her the right of inheritance of her royal birth from the house of David and still less the gracious election by God, whose piercing eyes see through all the mountains of misery the small flash of the metal of virtue that his hand has placed within them. He selected her from the very beginning of eternity for this high honor and from that same beginning made her fit for it. And so he therefore suffered her to be called to it too. For all divine calling has its roots and foundation in eternal Providence. Meditation on the Incarnation of Christ.[2]

The Preached Word Brings About Faith.

Martin Luther: The office of a true preacher is demonstrated by the angel. God does not want to make the Virgin pregnant without sending the Word to her beforehand. Otherwise he could have conveyed the message to her secretly in her heart, so that she would simply have felt it: "You are going to bear a child." But he does not want to do that, for first he has her spoken to with a physical voice. She must be called beforehand. This passage shows how both the office of preaching and the preacher should be. God sets up his kingdom so that the Word must be preached. He does not want anyone to run around aimlessly without the Word or to despise it. Faith needs a Word. Therefore God has ordained that the gospel be recorded. No one should begin on their own to make themselves pious through their own reason and work but should hear the Word and then believe, and so be justified. You see, the message that the angel brings is exactly the sermon that is written in the whole gospel. There you have the entire mystery of Christianity: the Word and faith. Sermon on the Annunciation to Mary (1521).[3]

What Does It Mean to Say "Full of Grace"? Huldrych Zwingli:

After the angel came inside to her, he greeted her with the following words: "God greets you, you who are full of grace! The Lord is with you. You are highly praised among women." Here you should notice that the phrase "full of grace" is the translation of the Greek word *kecharitōmenē*, which means "beloved" or "filled with grace" or "favored one."[4] We learn from this that the phrase "full of grace" should not be understood in the sense that she was full of grace from herself but that all the grace with which

---

[2]Greiffenberg, *Meditations on the Incarnation, Passion and Death of Jesus Christ,* 165-66.

[3]*LEA* 1:69 (cf. WA 9:624-25).

[4]After the publication of Erasmus's critical edition of the Greek New Testament in 1516, many humanists and reformers scrutinized individual biblical words and phrases, both to critique the Vulgate and Roman Catholic theology often dependent on such terms and to retranslate and reinterpret contested passages such as this one. In this case, Zwingli (along with Luther and others) points out that the Greek verb *kecharitōmenē* is in passive voice, which is not conveyed by the Vulgate's *gratia plena.*

she was richly filled came from God. For to be "full of grace" means nothing else than to be the most beloved of God, to be made worthy and to be chosen from among all other women. For grace is the good will of God alone. And if I say, "God gave much grace to someone," all that means is, "God has granted him much and given him many blessings." Although we usually say, "Blessed are you among women," to avoid confusion over the meaning of the word *blessed*, I have said, "You are highly praised among women," for the Greek word *eulogēmenē* means "highly praised" more than "blessed." However, I am not going to discard the word *blessed*, but we need to understand "blessed are you" in the sense of "highly praised are you." And this is the end of the angelic greeting.[5] SERMON ON MARY, THE PURE MOTHER OF GOD.[6]

THE ANGEL'S MESSAGE REASSURED MARY.
MARTIN LUTHER: She thought he was a suitor and took what he said as inappropriate speech, as if she would reply, "It's too much!" And she did not accept his greeting, because she thought herself inferior. Nevertheless she did not contradict his words. There has never been anything like it in the world, how she was afraid, but then he brought her to listen to his sermon and message. It is a fine thing, when the message is rightly preached and then believed! It is as if the angel wanted to say: "I won't hurt you; I'm bringing you a message that will make you happy." Those are beautiful and golden words. SERMON ON THE ANNUNCIATION TO MARY (1525).[7]

1:30-33 Mary's Child Is the Son of the Most High

THE ANGEL COMFORTS MARY BY REVEALING

THE MESSIAH. HEINRICH BULLINGER: Although the Virgin did not answer a word to the angel, he nevertheless perceived by her countenance and behavior that she was somewhat afraid. Therefore he kindly explained to her in full the salutation, which was a remedy for her fear, and thereby he briefly and exactly declared the scope and purpose of his message. And first he said, "Fear not, Mary, for all those things which you are fearing are in safety, and so that you may plainly understand, I will tell you the reason for my salutation, and why I am coming to you as a messenger from God." . . .

The angel very diligently shows how great and who this Jesus would be, speaking of the glory and the eternity of his kingdom. He does not explain his entire office but considers it sufficient to declare him to be the Messiah and the Redeemer promised in the Law and the Prophets. He says that he shall be great. AN ECCLESIASTICALL EXPOSITION UPON SAINT LUKE 1.[8]

MARY FOUND FAVOR WITH GOD OUT OF HIS COMPASSION. HULDRYCH ZWINGLI: This is a confirmation of what the angel said before, "Greetings, you who are highly favored!" We have the same kind of speech in the books of Moses: "You have found favor with me"; also, "And the Lord said to Moses, 'I will do the very thing you have asked, because I am pleased with you and I know you by name.'" By this manner of speech, the Jews declare that God is the cause and wellspring of grace, and he pours his grace into us freely without our merit but rather bestows his benefits on us out of his pure liberality and goodness. For a person is not said to find grace when he seeks it, but rather it is offered to him without him seeking it. Thus we read that Noah found favor in the sight of the Lord. It is as if the Scripture had said, "God had compassion on Noah; he loved Noah and blessed him." Therefore Mary found favor with the Lord, that is to say, the Lord out of his goodness and ready good will had compassion on her and poured

---

[5]In the medieval period, the *Ave Maria* was also known as the *angelica salutatio*, or angelic greeting; the first half of the prayer comes from this scriptural passage and was in use from at least the twelfth century. For more information on the prayer and its uses, see Anne Winston-Allen, *Stories of the Rose: The Making of the Rosary in the Middle Ages* (University Park: Pennsylvania State University Press, 1997).
[6]ZO 1:92.
[7]LEA 1:77 (cf. WA 17,1:153).

---

[8]Marlorat, ed., *Catholike and Ecclesiasticall Exposition of the Holy Gospell After S. Marke and Luke*, 32-33*.

his grace and gifts into her, loved her and ordained her to great honor. AN ECCLESIASTICALL EXPOSITION UPON SAINT LUKE 1.[9]

MARY IS THE VIRGIN OF ISAIAH'S PROPHECY. CATHARINA REGINA VON GREIFFENBERG: Behold, just consider what an unimaginable miracle I must announce to you. You will conceive in the womb! Conceive—you who are the epitome of chastity, for your thoughts and actions are well known to me through divine concession. You will not alter your heart and life, and yet what I say will come to pass. You will not give up your chaste being and yet you will be pregnant. You will not become pregnant in the sense of lofty thoughts or the fruit of the intellect. No! Instead [you will become pregnant] in your womb with a son who will be in the form of other human children and will be discovered to conduct himself like a human. [To understand] that this is, however, a great thing, devised by God long ago, then learn and think back and remember what the prophet Isaiah prophesied many hundreds of years ago concerning it: "Behold, a virgin shall conceive and bear a son." You who love God and his word doubtless must have often read and contemplated these words. Now you yourself are this virgin who was in God's word and mind long, long ago. In you will be fulfilled what has been hoped for so ardently for several thousand years. In you the one promised in Paradise will begin to be what he is not, even if he is everything! MEDITATION ON THE INCARNATION OF CHRIST.[10]

THE INCARNATION AND THE RESURRECTION ARE BOUND TOGETHER. MARTIN LUTHER: The person himself . . . will possess the kingdom in which David will rule, "and of his kingdom there will be no end." That is the true central point of the gospel, and it does nothing else but preach of the kingdom of Christ. Whoever knows that is a good

Christian. Out of this text, everything follows together wonderfully: she would become pregnant with her own child and he was mortal, she a normal woman and he her real son, both mortal—and the man so born should be king eternally and his person should not change. How does that make sense? To be eternal does not reconcile with being a mortal human being. It is all united in the single Word. Christ would die, and afterwards rise up again from the dead. If he is to live eternally, he must rise up from the dead. There is a great deal one can say about these words, but it has already often been said. And it is for this that we have Romans 4: "who was willing to be given up for our sins and raised for our justification." Human reason does not understand these words at all, that a mortal man should reign forever. For "mortal" and "eternal" cannot exist at the same time, it says, so how could it be? But God allowed him to die and raised him again so that he lives eternally; his kingdom began there, he sent the Holy Spirit, and he reigns even now, bringing life through the Word and the Holy Spirit and freeing us from sin, and beginning in us also eternal life. He begins from the outside with just a single point. This text proves that Christ will rise up from the dead and begin his reign. The article of the creed is also based on this: I believe in the resurrection of the dead. And his rule is constant over those who belong to his kingdom. We all live in his presence, whether we are living or dead. Reason does not understand such words. But in his presence all things hold together. For now it's still hidden. SERMON ON THE ANNUNCIATION TO MARY (1525).[11]

CHRIST IS THE TRUE SON OF GOD. JOHN CALVIN: Christ is the only Son, the only-begotten of the Father. The future tense of the verb ["he shall be called the Son of the Most High"] is tortured by that filthy dog Servetus to prove that Christ is not the eternal Son of God but began to be considered so when he took our flesh on

---

[9]Marlorat, ed., *Catholike and Ecclesiasticall Exposition of the Holy Gospell After S. Marke and Luke*, 32-33*; quoting Ex 33:12, 17; citing Gen 6:8.
[10]Greiffenberg, *Meditations on the Incarnation, Passion and Death of Jesus Christ*, 176-77; citing Is 7:14.

[11]LEA 1:78-80 (cf. WA 17,1:154); quoting Lk 1:33; Rom 4:25; alluding to Col 1:15-20.

himself.[12] This is a gross misrepresentation. He argues that Christ was not the Son of God before he appeared in the world clothed with flesh, because the angel says, "He shall be called." But on the contrary, I take it that the words of the angel mean nothing more than that he, who had been the Son of God from eternity, would be manifested as such in the flesh, for "to be called" denotes clear knowledge. There is a great difference between these two statements—that Christ began to be the Son of God, which he was not before—and that he was manifested among people, so that that they might know him to be the one who had been formerly promised. Certainly, in every age God has been addressed by his people as a Father, and hence it follows that there was a Son in heaven, from whom and through whom that fatherhood would remain with humanity. For people claim too much for themselves if they dare to boast of being the children of God in any other respect than as members of the only-begotten Son. COMMENTARY ON A HARMONY OF THE GOSPELS.[13]

CHRIST FULFILLS THE LORD'S COVENANT WITH DAVID. EDWIN SANDYS: Now as David did, so the children of David after him fulfilled their days and fell asleep: the throne of David was not established in them forever. But of Christ the angel of the Lord said, "The Lord shall give to him the throne of his father David, and he shall reign over the house of Jacob forever, and of his kingdom there shall be no end." Wherefore in Christ this covenant with David is fulfilled. The mercies which were promised to David are the benefits and, as the apostle calls them, "the holy things" which we receive by Christ Jesus. This covenant is everlasting. . . . The covenant made with David is made with us: his mercies are our mercies, if we perform what here is required of us. If we hearken diligently

to him who cries, "Come to the waters," if we cleave fast to his truth, if we embrace his promises with joy, eating what is good, shunning and loathing what is evil, surely his hand shall be established with us as with David; his arm shall be our strength. The enemy shall not oppress us, neither shall the wicked do us harm, but God shall destroy all our enemies before us and plague them that hate us. He shall keep his mercies toward us forever, his covenant shall stand fast with us, our souls shall live and he shall make an everlasting covenant with us, even the sure mercies of David. A SERMON MADE IN SAINT PAUL'S, ON THE DAY OF CHRIST'S NATIVITY.[14]

1:34-35 Gabriel Clarifies God's Plan

THE SPIRIT WILL ACCOMPLISH GOD'S PLAN WITHIN MARY. HEINRICH BULLINGER: It is as if he should say, "That pure and Holy Spirit shall cover you in such a way that no one shall doubt or suspect any uncleanness. For God is a consuming fire, incoporeal, without affection and corruption. This pure Spirit of God, I say, shall extend his divine power over you, and shall make you fruitful without the seed of a man and shall bring it about that from your bodily substance, the Son of God shall take the substance of his true and human body, differing from other human beings in no way except for sin." These words, "come on you," contain great emphasis and force and signify that the work shall be extraordinary where the natural means are lacking. It is as if he should say, "The Son shall not only descend from heaven into you but also shall come on you with great power, that he may work effectually in you." The Spirit of God has been said to have descended on Samson and the prophets in this way. It is as if Scripture had said, "The Spirit of God moved Samson and the prophets, and was effectual in them and brought those things to pass which it desired to accomplish with great might." AN ECCLESIASTICALL EXPOSITION UPON SAINT LUKE I.[15]

---

[12]Michael Servetus (Miguel Servet) was a Spanish humanist highly trained in many fields, particularly theology and medicine. In the course of his career he developed a nontrinitarian theology that led church leaders of all stripes to label him a heretic. He was eventually burned for heresy in Geneva in 1553. [13]CO 45:27-28 (cf. CTS 31:37); citing Jn 1:14; 1 Tim 3:16; Jn 1:18.

[14]Sandys, *Sermons*, 32-33*; quoting Acts 13:34.
[15]Marlorat, ed., *Catholike and Ecclesiasticall Exposition of the Holy Gospell After S. Marke and Luke*, 38*.

MARY GIVES BOTH DWELLING PLACE AND MATERIAL TO CHRIST. KASPAR VON SCHWENCKFELD: In short, God the heavenly Father sent his Word and gave and decreed the Holy Spirit to the construction of the temple of Jesus Christ, his only begotten Son (from which God the Father, as the chief builder, could certainly not be far away). And he had in Mary, one might say, the green wood and choice material, that is, a pure, holy flesh born from God, founded for the building, and from it, taken in speedy skillfullness, whatever and however much he would and should. Thus Mary did not only give residence to the soul of Christ but also the Word, and in her virginal service offered to the Builder, the Holy Spirit, what would be enough for the soul, the Word and the flesh, that the whole Christ might be born from her. ON THE FLESH OF CHRIST (1584).[16]

THE INCARNATION BRINGS GREAT BLESSINGS TO US. PHILIPP MELANCHTHON: God wanted Christ to be born without the joining together of a man and a woman, that it might be a conception without sin, but still of the seed of Abraham and David. The body, sanctified by the Holy Spirit out of the Virgin, was taken up. The Son assumed that body and united it to himself in a personal union. But we are not able to say a great deal about these sacred mysteries. Let us consider the reasons why the Son of God was sent, and think about God's wrath against sin. Let us think about the forgiveness of sins, the renewal of human nature because of our union with Christ, the restoration of justice, the daily preservation of the church. Let us exercise this faith in invocation, in order that we might make progress in knowledge, because this is not able to be learned without some effort, without invocation, as it is repeated nearby: "How much more will your heavenly Father give the Holy Spirit to those who ask him?" Also: "Ask and it shall be given to you." Also: "Whoever has, will be given more." If we do not want to exercise this gift, it will be lost. You will often hear this: excite your heart

to prayer by these meditations, ask that these meditations might bring light to you and give thanks for those great blessings and for all the other blessings to everyone. GOSPEL ON THE DAY OF THE ANNUNCIATION TO MARY.[17]

IN MARY, FAITH OVERCOMES REASON. MARTIN LUTHER: This is a joyous Gospel, in which faith is held up for us. And in the whole we find both teaching and exhortation. This virgin had a faith of which there is no equal in the entire Bible. One can see here how reason is able to accomplish nothing at all—it fails completely, for faith cannot tolerate reason.

First the angel is sent to the Virgin, [to announce] that she would become a mother. That is nothing so great and lofty to be amazed at, for it is natural that a virgin should become a wife. But it is a lofty thing that she should ask, "How can that be, since I do not know a man?" That is the first thing that occupied her, that she should become a mother without a husband. For she is alone: never before has there been an example of such a thing. Reason certainly could have quarreled with her here: why should something totally new be starting with you? If she were guided by her reason, she would come to accept it only with great difficulty, for nature and all living creatures oppose [such a conception]. And so also does the devil assail faith at the moment of death: "My dear, do you really think that God wants to begin something totally new with you and sanctify you without any merit, when he has otherwise condemned the whole great crowd?" Mary could have thought likewise here. But what did she do instead? She believed, and closed her eyes, although reason and all creatures were against it: her heart clung alone to the Word. So the devil focuses diligently on this point and produces all the natural things and events that are against the Word of faith, so that he can force people away from the Word and make a person restless: then the devil has already won. Whoever struggles in faith will soon find that the things to

---

[16]CS 7:321.

[17]MO 24:572; quoting Lk 11:13, 9; Mt 13:12.

which the Word is opposed will all collapse. But faith abandons all creatures, all earthly visible things, and even itself, and clings only to the Word of God. And so it must happen, my dear fellow: faith relies on nothing, grasps after nothing in order to be certain—and that is how it is maintained. Sermon on the Annunciation to Mary (1522).[18]

1:36-38 The Sign of Elizabeth's Pregnancy and Mary's Faithful Response

The Miracle of Elizabeth's Pregnancy Is Proof of God's Power. Johannes Brenz: It is as if the angel should say, "Elizabeth has up until now suffered the reproach and ignominy of barrenness among all people. And this is now the sixth month since her conception of a son in her old age. Therefore, if it is possible for God to make an old woman far advanced in age to be with child, how much more possible is it for him to make a virgin conceive a child without a man's seed? And so therefore there is no cause, Mary, why you should worry so much about the usual means of conception, seeing that you have before you in Elizabeth so manifest a proof of God's divine power." An Ecclesiasticall Exposition upon Saint Luke 1.[19]

All Effective Things Are Possible with God, the Creator of All. Catharina Regina von Greiffenberg: Every impossible thing that can be imagined is possible with God. What is more impossible than walking through the sea? Still he made it come to pass. Than a rock giving forth water? Still he made it flow forth. Than to stop the sun? Still he made it stand still, indeed, made it go back to where he wanted it to be.[20] Nature can have nothing and the sharpest mind think of nothing that would be impossible for God. He who set limits to nature holds sway in

complete freedom outside of the bounds of nature. Nothing is impossible for him except finding something impossible for him.

One could of course say that in him there is the impossibility of doing evil. But evil is not a power but instead a weakness and does not belong to the things of nature but is the corruption of Satan, of which thing the Divinity is of course incapable. But nothing is impossible for God in any effective thing that can be imagined or invented. He could make the mountains into pearls, the stars into tinsel; in contrast, sand into stars and the sea into flames. He could make jewels grow on trees and in mussels, cherries. He could make it so the rocks gave forth oil and the grain bore ore. He could make nature turn around or create a new such thing in which what is now unnatural would be natural. Meditation on the Incarnation of Christ.[21]

Mary Believed the Angel's Message. Georg Spindler: She believed this great, peculiar and supernatural, indescribable miracle. Saint Bernard took this faith also as a great miraculous sign and was completely amazed that dear Mary should have believed so strongly, as also the aged Elizabeth was amazed and called Mary's faith "blessed." And as soon as the Virgin believed, she became pregnant through the Holy Spirit and the power of the Most High and conceived the Savior of the world, whom she bore after forty weeks in Bethlehem. On the Day of Mary's Annunciation.[22]

The Church's Womb Holds the Infinite Lord. John Donne:

> Salvation to all that will is nigh;
> That All, which always is All every where,
> Which cannot sinne, and yet all sinnes must beare,
> Which cannot die, yet cannot chuse but die,
> Loe, faithfull Virgin, yeelds himselfe to lye

---

[18]LEA 1:65-66 (cf. WA 12:457-58).
[19]Marlorat, ed., Catholike and Ecclesiasticall Exposition of the Holy Gospell After S. Marke and Luke, 40*.
[20]For these examples, see Ex 14:22-31; 17:6; Josh 10:12-14.

[21]Greiffenberg, Meditations on the Incarnation, Passion and Death of Jesus Christ, 186.
[22]Spindler, Postilla, PPPP2r.

In prison, in thy wombe; and though he there
Can take no sinne, nor thou give, yet he will weare
Taken from thence, flesh, which death's force may trie.
Ere by the spheares time was created, thou
Wast in his minde, who is thy Sonne and Brother;

Whom thou conceiv'st, conceiv'd; yea thou art now
Thy Maker's maker, and thy Father's mother;
Thou hast light in darke; and shutst in little roome,
Immensity cloystered in thy deare wombe.

LA CORONA.[23]

---

[23]Donne, *Poems of John Donne*, 319.

1:39-45 THE VISITATION

³⁹*In those days Mary arose and went with haste into the hill country, to a town in Judah, ⁴⁰and she entered the house of Zechariah and greeted Elizabeth. ⁴¹And when Elizabeth heard the greeting of Mary, the baby leaped in her womb. And Elizabeth was filled with the Holy Spirit, ⁴²and she exclaimed with a loud cry, "Blessed are you among women, and blessed is the fruit of your womb! ⁴³And why is this granted to me that the mother of my Lord should come to me? ⁴⁴For behold, when the sound of your greeting came to my ears, the baby in my womb leaped for joy. ⁴⁵And blessed is she who believed that there would be*ᵃ *a fulfillment of what was spoken to her from the Lord."*

a Or believed, for there will be

OVERVIEW: Mary's visit to Elizabeth was a traditional Sunday pericope, which provided many preachers with the regular opportunity of worrying about why such a young woman went out traveling unprotected and unsupervised, and how they should preach it to their congregations without providing unsuitable ideas to their female listeners. They focus on the inspiration for this trip—the Holy Spirit—and its purpose—sharing the good news and helping Elizabeth. In these terms, Mary can still be a pious, modest and chaste example for women to emulate. But of course this Gospel is about much more, and we also witness in the meeting of these two women the beginning of the church: it is the first preaching of the gospel, by Elizabeth, who recognizes Mary as the "mother of my Lord." The Savior of the world is now present, and all those who hear the good news are saved by their faith in him—including Mary, who, these preachers are at pains to point out, is saved by her faith in her son, not by being his mother.

1:39-40 Mary Journeys to Visit Elizabeth

THE SPIRIT OF CHRIST LEADS MARY TO VISIT ELIZABETH. MARTIN BUCER: This proverb is always true: Like will to like. And God always brings like to like in God's matters. And this is just as true among people who are sincere and sound, for they are capable only of sincere, sound and just friendship. That is why the Blessed Virgin, the chosen vessel of God who is blessed among women, when she heard that Elizabeth was blessed, went out from Nazareth into Judah. She did this to celebrate with her cousin and bring her the joyful news of the blessing announced to her, even though she was a virgin and undoubtedly not accustomed to travel. So the ones whom the Spirit of Christ possesses, these he joins together not only in body but also in mind. We see an example in the apostle Paul, who had such an earnest and frequent desire to see his brothers, and so often wrote to them. But today we have great cause to fear that many who reckon themselves among the chief maintainers of the gospel are in fact very little possessed with the Spirit of Christ, because they have so small a consideration of the friendship and connection which they ought to have with their brothers. Whoever rightly knows Christ does not choose, but in fact must go wherever his brothers in Christ are; that is to say, all those who confess his name with their mouths and do not deny him with their deeds. Let us therefore behold the fervent desire of Mary, who went quickly, not in order to satisfy her own pleasure but rather was carried by a godly zeal. And she did not consider what she might have if she had been ambitious: "Why should she not rather come and see me?" For Elizabeth was her elder, and close to her time of delivery. It is becoming for the faithful to do their duty toward one another and support each other in doing the same, which Mary did in visiting her cousin. And this visit which Luke mentions testifies that the faith of Mary was not gone, because the promise of God did not vanish along with the angel, but it rested still in her mind. AN ECCLESIASTICALL EXPOSITION UPON SAINT LUKE 1.[1]

MARY WAS QUICK TO MAKE HER VISIT. JOHANN WIGAND: "Quickly": with this word the Evangelist reveals the disposition of the Virgin. She did not wander around or linger out on the road, but rather she hurried along the way, so that she might come sooner to her dear relative. For the faith was ardent and fervent within her, through which she longed and desired both to hear what was happening with Elizabeth, as well as at the same time to bring the report of what had happened to them to other people, and give them joy with such a happy message and good news. . . .

The house of Zechariah was the goal or object of Mary's trip, and she went so that she might be able to greet Elizabeth there. But now the Evangelist is getting closer to the great miracle which has taken place so especially with Elizabeth. From this we should learn how Mary is obedient to God's order and command. For when she had received the command, she did not put it aside or ignore the deadline but came herself immediately, without refusal or delay. She spared no pains and feared no danger but was happy both to teach and learn. Today, unfortunately, there is a great lack of diligence among the people, who have such easy access to the Word and yet do not hear it, while the Virgin had to walk twenty miles just so that she could hear Zechariah and Elizabeth. Mary's trip is also an image and representation of the Lord Christ, for just as Mary traveled over the fields with her sweet little infant, still inside his mother's body and not yet born, so Christ also later traveled through the land of Canaan, spreading the Word

of the heavenly Father far and wide. So also the Christian church travels like Mary the stranger and pilgrim, for the Virgin Mary is an image of the Christian church, which is bound to no place. And it is a gentle Virgin who stands in great trouble, but nevertheless God lifts her up and protects her. The gates of hell will never overcome her. GOSPEL ON THE DAY OF MARY'S VISITATION.[2]

1:41 *The Babe Leaped in Her Womb*

JOHN LEAPS, ELIZABETH PREACHES. MARTIN LUTHER: When Mary lets her voice be heard and speaks with Elizabeth, [John] feels it within the womb and is made aware by the Spirit even before his mother, Elizabeth. Then his mother thinks, what does this mean, that the child who is so newly living within me stirs? And through this the Holy Spirit enlightens the matron Elizabeth so that she begins to speak, full of joy and the Spirit. And what does she say? Listen how she receives her guest! She doesn't thank her and say, "You are most welcome, my dear Mary"—as one is wont to say quite cheerfully. Out of an even greater joy she forgets the normal greeting and does not even recognize Mary as herself but rather as the blessed mother. And this even though Christ had only been conceived hardly four days before! But even if it had been half or even a whole month, how is it possible that Elizabeth could have felt it, how could she have guessed? Mary was still young, and no one could see from her figure that she was pregnant. It is the highest recognition that she praises Mary as a mother and as one who carries the child who is above all others. And she places her above all women for eternity. For, she says, you carry a son who is a Lord of us all. "And how does it happen to me, that the mother of my Lord comes to me?" That is the first sermon on earth, that Mary is the mother of the Lord, and it comes from the aged, honorable matron. Jesus is hardly a month in the womb, and even so Elizabeth calls her "Mother" and "Mother of the Lord." "Lord" is

[1]Marlorat, ed., *Catholike and Ecclesiasticall Exposition of the Holy Gospell After S. Marke and Luke*, 40*.

[2]Wigand, *Postilla*, 104-5; citing Mt 16:18.

the name of the true God. It is an exalted word, which has never before resounded in the world. Elizabeth did not hear it from anyone but rather spoke it through the prompting of the Holy Spirit. SERMON ON THE VISITATION (1535).[3]

1:42-45 Elizabeth's Blessing and Response

THE PROPER WAY TO VIEW MARY AS BLESSED. EDWARD LEIGH: We do acknowledge that the Virgin Mary was blessed among women, as here, and a blessed woman, as in Luke 1:28 and Luke 1:48. Yet as Augustine said, she is more blessed in receiving the faith than in conceiving the flesh of Christ.[4] We count her holy, meek and humble; we praise God for her, that he made her the instrument of Christ coming into the world; and we desire to imitate those virtues and excellencies that were in her. ANNOTATIONS UPON SAINT LUKE 2.[5]

ELIZABETH SPEAKS PRAISE THROUGH HUMILITY. MARTIN LUTHER: What Elizabeth sings of Christ has never been sung of anyone. All those born of women are children of wrath, which was swiftly decreed over us in Paradise. Only this child alone is blessed, and there is nothing in him to punish, but only pure blessing and grace and mercy. She said this to glorify the one whom Mary carried. The Holy Spirit spoke to her heart and told her why this child had come, that he might redeem the human race. I am a poor, miserable, despised woman, she thinks, why should this honor come to me? Why did you not go to the wife of Annas or Caiphas, but rather to a wrinkled old woman who was barren and lived in disgrace? And she forgets about Mary's royal lineage and just calls her mother, and Mother of the Lord. That is a woman, she thinks, the Mother of the Lord! There the humility of the one finds that of the other. Mary abases herself and Elizabeth thinks that she is unworthy of Mary's visit to her. She is made

happy by this and is very pleased that Mary has come. This is certainly done through the Holy Spirit. SERMON ON THE VISITATION (1535).[6]

JOHN SHOWED HIS JOY IN CHRIST THROUGH MOVEMENT. CATHARINA REGINA VON GREIFFENBERG: My helpless little boy appears to confirm my offer of service by receiving his Lord and Master with a leap of joy. As soon as I heard your voice greet me, he stirred and leaped for joy, because he does not yet have a voice to speak and cannot offer his service in any other way than through movement. The presence of Jesus always kindles joy, even when it is hidden and is with hidden things. Jesus, hidden in his mother's womb, gladdens John, who is likewise lying beneath his mother's heart. This shows that no darkness or seclusion, no invisibility or concealment, neither flesh nor blood, nor corporeal or natural thing—nothing—can impede joy in Jesus.

This joy in Jesus penetrates all obstacles, illuminates all darkness, enters through all locks, grants in the midst of prison the most pleasant freedom, makes visible within invisibility the gleam of its beams, and in the deepest obscurity does not conceal itself before those who love him; it employs flesh and blood, which to be sure are by nature incapable of this, as a tool of its operation; it makes even of unborn children an instrument for its music. And since the child as yet has no little mouth with which to speak, thus must its entire body be the tongue that reveals the presence of joy in Jesus through its movement. MEDITATION ON THE PREGNANCY OF MARY.[7]

MARY IS BLESSED FOR ACCEPTING GOD'S WORD AND EXPRESSING HER FAITH. JOHANN BAUMGART (POMARIUS): The Virgin Mary and her cousin Elizabeth remind us with their examples of fine Christian and honorable virtues, to which we should devote ourselves.

---

[3]LEA 1:93-94 (cf. WA 41:353-54).
[4]Augustine, De Virginitate 3 (NPNF 3:418).
[5]Leigh, Annotations upon All the New Testament Philologicall and Theologicall, 98*.

[6]LEA 1:95 (cf. WA 41:354-55).
[7]Greiffenberg, Meditations on the Incarnation, Passion and Death of Jesus Christ, 212-13.

First, we see that Mary was praised by Elizabeth as blessed because she believed, even though the idea of the conception and incarnation of the Son of God is against all reason and is incomprehensible. Therefore we should also in this concept and in other articles of faith take our reason captive under obedience to Christ.

Second, this faith in Mary did not remain hidden, but it expressed itself and burst forth, and in order to confirm and increase it, and to prove it by fruits, she set out with special earnestness and zeal and traveled through the holy land, over the mountains, into the city of Judea to the house of Zechariah. Likewise, Christians should testify and confess their faith and our dear Lord Jesus, whom we receive in our hearts. We should love all Christian gatherings where people discuss God and his Word, for that is the holy land, the city of Judea and the house of Zechariah, where God established his own and the remembrance of his name. This is where we acknowledge him, where we sing and speak of him, teach and learn, and where we deal with his Word and sacraments according to his will and establishment. GOSPEL ON THE DAY OF MARY'S VISITATION. [8]

---

[8]Baumgart, *Postilla*, 424r.

1:46-56 THE MAGNIFICAT

⁴⁶*And Mary said,*

"My soul magnifies the Lord,
    ⁴⁷*and my spirit rejoices in God my Savior,*
⁴⁸*for he has looked on the humble estate of his*
    servant.
    For behold, from now on all generations will
    call me blessed;
⁴⁹*for he who is mighty has done great things for*
    me,
    and holy is his name.
⁵⁰*And his mercy is for those who fear him*
    from generation to generation.
⁵¹*He has shown strength with his arm;*

he has scattered the proud in the thoughts of
    their hearts;
⁵²*he has brought down the mighty from their*
    thrones
    and exalted those of humble estate;
⁵³*he has filled the hungry with good things,*
    and the rich he has sent away empty.
⁵⁴*He has helped his servant Israel,*
    in remembrance of his mercy,
⁵⁵*as he spoke to our fathers,*
    to Abraham and to his offspring forever."

⁵⁶*And Mary remained with her about three*
months and returned to her home.

OVERVIEW: The song of Mary solidifies her role as one of the foremost teachers of the Christian faith. For Protestant interpreters, she lays out the key elements of the relationship between God and human beings: God is in charge, while we are lowly and unworthy.[1] Neither the rich nor the world's rulers hold any power in and of themselves but rather are subject to God's providence and justice. Mary knows that she herself is subject to God, unworthy of his notice yet chosen through his mercy and grace. She should not be praised for the virtue of humility, but rather she reveals God's mercy in that he chose her in spite of her humility, now translated as lowness or abjectness. And in her faithful acceptance of God's grace, she becomes a true model of hope for all, who are equally unworthy of salvation.

1:46-49 Mary Gives Praise to God

MARY PRAISES GOD FROM HER HEART.
DESIDERIUS ERASMUS: For "soul" and "spirit," the Scriptures oftentimes use the word *heart*, and these are phrases of speech very common with the Hebrews, especially in the Psalms: "Praise the Lord, O my soul," also, "Say to my soul, I am your salvation." There is great force in these phrases of speech, and much more is expressed then if it simply said, "Praise the Lord," "I magnify the Lord," or "Say to me, I am your salvation." By this we are taught that if we truly want to praise God, we must praise him from our heart; if the heart is not moved, the Lord rejects and abhors our praise. Therefore the true foundation of thanksgiving is the inward affection of the mind. By these speeches we may see the difference between the spirit of truth and hypocrisy, which praises God with the mouth and lips only. "The Lord" is a word of power, by which Mary preaches the power of God, with which he effected in her works surpassing nature. Moreover, she claims none of these benefits for herself because she is the Mother of God, or because she was blessed among women or because she behaved modestly. She claims nothing for herself but turns a joyful and merry heart toward God. She acknowledges receiving everything from him and praises his holy name. Thus we also ought

---

[1]Since the early church, the Magnificat, Zechariah's Benedictus and Simeon's Nunc Dimittis have been used in worship for evening prayer (vespers), morning prayer (matins) and night prayer (compline), respectively.

to lean only on God, and not on any creatures or on our own gifts. An Ecclesiasticall Exposition upon Saint Luke 1.[2]

Mary Believed in Her Own Low Estate.
John Calvin: She explains the reason why the joy of her heart had its foundation in God—it is because, of course, he regarded her out of pure grace. By calling herself humble she renounces all worthiness and ascribes every opportunity for boasting to the gracious goodness of God. For *humilitas* here does not—as some ignorant and uncivilized people have stupidly imagined—signify submission, or modesty or a habit of the mind, but rather it means a mean and abject condition. Therefore the sense is this: "I was insignificant and despised, but that did not prevent God from turning his eyes toward me." But if the humility of Mary is compared with excellence, we see—as the matter itself proclaims and as is apparent from the Greek—that Mary completely empties herself and praises God alone. But this was not the public proclamation of a false humility. Rather it was her simple and natural confession of the conviction that was engraved in her mind, for she was of no value before the world, and she esteemed herself no more than that. Commentary on a Harmony of the Gospels.[3]

Mary's Sorrow and Her Glory. Martin Luther: So what do Annas's and Caiphas's daughters have for all their renown? But people will never forget this one [Mary], as she herself sings: "Behold, from now on all generations will call me blessed." That means, he has regarded that I am only a poor little girl, and on account of that regard, he has made me into the Mother of God. This song will be sung of God, and people will say: she was a poor Cinderella that nobody wanted to regard, but God has done it, and now she will be called blessed by friend and foe, by angels and devils. "From now

on I will be called blessed" means I will never be forgotten, not for the sake of my humility, but because God has worked his miracle in me and made me into the mother of the Savior. This song will be sung unceasingly; from the cradle on children will be taught this confession of faith: "conceived by the Holy Spirit, born of the Virgin Mary"—that she who is called the Virgin Mary is also a mother. So no one should be afraid, if he had tough times growing up or is miserable and despised. It is not a bad omen. Look at Mary's example. And look at what God made out of her! From the time she had her son, the misery never ended. She suffered so much! And at the end, he was crucified before her eyes. And even after he was gone, she endured further suffering! How much hatred and jealousy did she bear, when she heard from Christ how he was slandered while he preached! What he suffered, she also suffered. . . . And despite [her misery] he regarded her, the one who is not merely an emperor but God, and so regarded her that she became the mother of his Son. "From this time on all generations will call me blessed": that means from now on the whole world forever and ever will exalt me. It is synecdoche,[4] which means that even though the Jews and some of the heathen do the opposite, her renown and her honor will remain among many until the end of the world: for no one can preach Christ without speaking of his mother. When she is so highly praised by the Son, then others will also say: Blessed is she who bore him, nursed him and raised him. "But it is not my glory," says Mary, "but [it belongs to] the one who regarded me." Afternoon Sermon on the Visitation (1535).[5]

God's Name and Works Are Holy and Wonderful. Johannes Brenz: And the name of God is taken for his power, and oftentimes for God himself, as he manifests himself to us. As we

---

[2]Marlorat, ed., *Catholike and Ecclesiasticall Exposition of the Holy Gospell After S. Marke and Luke*, 47-48*; quoting Ps 103:1; 35:3. [3]CO 45:37-38 (cf. CTS 31:53-54).

[4]Synecdoche is a figure of speech in which the part takes the place of the whole ("a set of wheels," meaning a car) or the whole takes the place of a part (one might say "Use your head!" for "Use your brain!"). [5]*LEA* 1:106-7 (cf. WA 41:362-63).

read in Matthew, "Our Father in heaven, hallowed be your name." That also is properly called holy which is separated from the profane and common use of things. What is separated is kept in secret, and so what is holy is also called hidden. God therefore is called holy because his works are hidden far from human reason and are so wonderful that human wisdom cannot comprehend them. For God works glory by disgrace, joy by sorrow, happiness by misery and life by death. What manner of working can be said to be more wonderful than this? And this wonderful manner of working was also shown forth in Mary. Moreover, the name of God is called holy because it deserves the highest reverence, so that as often as mention is made of God, we must always remember his awesome majesty. AN ECCLESIASTICALL EXPOSITION UPON SAINT LUKE 1.[6]

1:50-55 Mary Praises God's Might and Mercy

ONLY THOSE WHO FEAR GOD WILL RECEIVE MERCY. THOMAS MÜNTZER: O, how highly necessary fear is for us! For as little as one can happily serve two masters, so little can one happily reverence both God and his creatures. Nor can God have mercy on us (as the Mother of Christ our Lord says), unless we fear him with our whole heart. Therefore God says: If I be your Father, where is my honor? If I be your Lord, where then is my fear? SERMON BEFORE THE PRINCES.[7]

GOD IS MERCIFUL TO THOSE WHO TRUST HIM. AUGUSTIN MARLORAT: This is spoken so that the wicked might not be made proud by the pretense of the name [of Christian]. For they are puffed up with vain security, as the apostle Paul says, "and brag about their relationship with God." That bragging is evil. The prophet David speaks to the same purpose: "The Lord's love is with those

who fear him, and his righteousness with their children's children—with those who keep his covenant and remember to obey his precepts." Therefore God is merciful to the children of the saints forever according to his promise, but despite this he gives no occasion for hypocrites to have vain trust. Those who are degenerate children of the saints and have forsaken their godliness and faith boast in vain that God is their Father. So by this exception their vanity and boasting are reproved, which are puffed up by false pretense and rely on the grace of God without any faith. It is true that God made a general covenant of salvation with the children of Abraham, but just as the stones are not softened by rain showers, so the obstinacy and hardness of heart of the unbelievers will keep the promised righteouness and salvation from entering into them. All godliness and religion are comprehended under the fear of God, which cannot stand without faith. AN ECCLESIASTICALL EXPOSITION UPON SAINT LUKE 1.[8]

GOD'S STRENGTH DEFEATS ALL THE PLANS OF HUMAN PRIDE. CATHARINA REGINA VON GREIFFENBERG: He shows strength with his arm, he who created the world and strength. The origin of all strength—shall he not exercise what he is himself and make it bubble up and flow like a spring forever and ever? He shows it as a master his art, as a king his authority—a cause whose success cannot fail to happen. He has shown it from the beginning of the world and will show it to its end, indeed, in infinity. His strength has the same confines as does his wisdom, namely, endlessness. What miracles will yet emerge? Oh! Who could regard and contemplate them sufficiently?

O adorable strength of God! What manner of miracle will you not yet work? Almighty arm of God! What more will you yet effect, especially against the proud? For you scatter them in the imagination of their hearts. When they have

---

[6]Marlorat, ed., *Catholike and Ecclesiasticall Exposition of the Holy Gospell After S. Marke and Luke*, 50-51*; quoting Mt 6:9.
[7]LCC 25:53-54*; citing Mt 6:24; Mal 1:6.

[8]Marlorat, ed., *Catholike and Ecclesiasticall Exposition of the Holy Gospell After S. Marke and Luke*, 51-52*; quoting Rom 2:17; Ps 103:17-18.

gathered their spirits and forces like stone and lime mortar and erect a great Babel in their imagination, you scatter them by not assenting to its completion; when they have set mountain upon mountain, like the giants, to storm heavenward, so much they perish in the sea of your might and wisdom.[9] When, like ants, they have assembled their mountains of pillage and smoke, he customarily spreads them out and scatters them with the staff of his mouth so, like those ants, they must run off and hide in a thousand places. MEDITATION ON THE PREGNANCY OF MARY.[10]

ALL RULERS MUST BE HUMBLE BEFORE GOD. EDWIN SANDYS: He that raises up can likewise cast down. For "he has cast down the mighty from their seat." And what he has done once, he can do again. The highest place is not the sweetest or the safest place: much authority is weighed down with many cares. Such as have entered into a great responsibility must also enter into a great accounting. And they have greater cause to fear their reckoning than to be proud of their ruling. The more that God has lifted you up, the more you ought to humble yourself before him, lest he cast you down eternally. A SERMON PREACHED BEFORE THE QUEEN.[11]

BEARING THE CHRIST CHILD IS A GREATER HONOR THAN ANY KING HAS. JOHN LAWSON: "He hath put down the mighty from their seat." In comparison with Mary and the honor which she has by bearing this Savior, kings and their honor are, as it were, no honor, as a candle light is no light where the sun shines. The honor which comes by suffering for Christ is a greater honor than what comes by ruling a kingdom. The honor of Paul and the other martyrs of Christ is a greater honor than

that of Alexander, who conquered the world. Who would not be in the apostle's shoes, rather than in the shoes of Alexander the Great? GLEANINGS AND EXPOSITIONS OF SOME PLACES OF SCRIPTURES.[12]

MARY'S WORDS TEACH BOTH RULERS AND SUBJECTS. RUDOLF HOSPINIAN: The example of the Virgin Mary particularly serves here, for she was a simple, poor, disregarded girl, but she was raised up to the highest honor and dignity in that she should carry his Son in her body and should bear him, a true human being, for this world. . . . To sum up, all histories are full of the same sort of example, and daily experience is enough for us to understand that God holds all kings and princes, yes, even cruel tyrants and maniacs, under his rule and in his power. He may take a while to punish the wicked world, but in the end he knocks them down also with great dishonor, disgrace and shame.

In the first place we learn in the record that all kings, emperors, princes, rulers, and those in authority have their power from nobody else but from God alone. And all those who are subjects now learn from this that they should be obedient to those in authority, because they are put in place and ordered by God. They should not oppose them rebelliously. But likewise, all rulers and authorities should be reminded by their offices that they should place God's honor before all other things, because he alone lifted them up into great honor and dignity, and he can also easily pull them down again and bring them to ruin. . . .

Third, these words of the Blessed Virgin Mary also serve as a lovely comfort for all poor, simple, oppressed and troubled people, against all temptations and vexations of the flesh. For because they are scorned and despised by the world and have no better than the others, they have such a hard time that they might also believe they will be abandoned by God and that he takes no notice of them, and so will not ask them how it goes with them on earth. But here they hear from the Virgin Mary that God has a good estimation of poor, despised and

---

[9]Lynne Tatlock notes that "In Greek mythology, the Aloadai giants attempt to storm the home of the gods in the sky by piling Mount Ossa on top of Mount Olympus and Mount Pelion on top of Mount Ossa" (p. 234 n. 149).
[10]Greiffenberg, *Meditations on the Incarnation, Passion and Death of Jesus Christ*, 234.
[11]Sandys, *Sermons*, 142*.

[12]Lawson, *Gleanings and Expositions*, 23*.

troubled simple folk and is so far from forgetting them that he even at times lifts them up to the highest honor and glory. And in fact, he considers in such a fatherly way in temporal things that they should not doubt that he has a much greater estimation of their souls. THE FIFTH SERMON.[13]

THE "HUNGRY," OR POOR CHRISTIANS, WILL BE FILLED WITH GOOD THINGS. SIMON MUSAEUS: With these words, Mary leaves the city hall and worldly government and turns to the governance of the home, for now she speaks of those people of wealth who will be empty and the hungry who will be satisfied, all of which belong to the governance of the home. Now, the Lord can certainly suffer the wealthy with their riches, just as he suffers the powerful on their seats, because it is all his gift and blessing, as Solomon said: "The blessing of the Lord makes rich." But Mary shows that the majority misuse their riches against God and his Son, by neglecting his word, by capitulating under persecution, and with stinginess, usury and cheating. Therefore Mary threatens such servants of godless mammon and those enslaved to their own bellies with the curse of the Lord, that God will send them away empty, which can happen when they lose their riches through sudden bad luck, theft or robbery, fire or shipwreck. These things can quickly turn a rich man into a beggar. However, even if a person still has and maintains his wealth, if he is stingy or is weighed down by cares, depression or sickness, he cannot be happy or live a balanced life, and finally he will end up with wicked and irresponsible heirs. . . .

But Mary comforts the hungry—that is, poor Christians who seek the kingdom of God before everything else for the sake of God's Word. The "hungry" are those who will risk everything of this world and who act justly and honestly, so that they would never bring any sort of derision on God. They will be filled richly, not with many tons of gold or silver but with something that is much

better, namely, with "good things." These "good things" are the blessed means of sustenance, whether great or small, that they along with their children and heirs receive, that they might use and enjoy these blessings with happy consciences and healthy bodies, to the welfare of the body and the benefit of the soul. As David says in Psalm 37: "The little that a righteous person has is better than the greatest possessions of many wicked." Why is it better? Answer: It is blessed by God, and he allows them to enjoy it, as Saint Paul explains when he says, "God . . . richly provides us with everything to enjoy," for it is not like the false appearance of the cursed possessions of the wicked, which they cannot enjoy. Therefore one should take these words of Mary, "He fills the hungry with good things," and write them with justice on the door of every house and treasury, in order to comfort poor, hungry Christians. They should take comfort, despite their poverty, in the inexhaustible blessings of God. But these words will bring terror to the wicked, rich folk who serve their bellies—they should not take comfort in their many piles of things, for the curse of the Lord can comprehend everything and cut it all away. EXPOSITION OF THE GOSPEL ON THE DAY OF MARY'S VISITATION.[14]

GOD IMPOVERISHES THOSE WHO MISUSE THEIR WEALTH. MARTIN LUTHER: Possessions produce courage, courage pride, pride poverty, and poverty causes pain.[15] But the hungry he fills with good things, so they have food and drink. She speaks of the rich. The "rich" are not those who have possessions but those who love them. David also had possessions, pious kings and emperors have had wisdom and power but did not put their trust in them. Therefore [the Bible] says: those who trust in them are the idolators, those who will not use their goods to honor God and to benefit their neighbors. God can humble them and turn

---

[13]Hospinian, *Lobgesang der Heiligen Hochgelobten Reinen Jungfrauwen Maria*, 80-84.

[14]Musaeus, *Außlegung der Episteln vnd Euangelien* (Festpostil), 111v-112r; quoting Prov 10:22; Ps 37:16; 1 Tim 6:17.
[15]*Gut macht Mut, Mut Hochmut, Hochmut Armut, Armut wehe tut.* See Emmanuel Strauss, *Dictionary of European Proverbs*, 3 vols. (London: Routledge, 1994), 1:56; 2:1094.

them into beggars. As the proverb says, the third heir never enjoys ill-gotten gains.[16] If they already romp and carouse as long as they live, the third heir doesn't have anything left. And these are the three arrogant ones: first, the saints and the clever, then worldly authority, and finally riches. They are all proud over against God and other people.... Of the wealthiest families of sixty years ago, today the heirs are all beggars, because they did not fear God and misused their wisdom, power and riches. And in turn God has lifted up the humble, the insignificant and the hungry. And he carries out this work throughout the whole world. AFTERNOON SERMON ON THE VISITATION (1535).[17]

THE RICH ARE THOSE WHO THINK THEY DESERVE GOD'S GRACE. HANS DENCK: You say: We come therefore and seek Christ in order to find and learn such [truth] from him, but you hold [that] one should have it beforehand. How does that fit together? Response: The Word of God is with you before you seek it; gives to you before you ask; opens up for you before you knock. No one comes of himself to Christ except the Father draw him, which he then in his goodness truly does. But, whoever is not drawn by the mind of [Christ] and wants to come on his own initiative presumes to give God something which he has not received from him. He wishes to be deserving of God without needing to thank him for his grace. Abraham rejoiced in the day of Christ before he had seen it. Cornelius was a spiritual and God-fearing man long before he acknowledged Christ. Paul had a righteous and divine zeal for the law of God before the revelation of Christ. The disciples of Christ left house and home without delay, wife and child for Christ's sake, and did not yet know who he was. All the elect rejoice and seek, not knowing what and why, all of which is without detriment to the gospel of Christ. For such work has not gone forth

from human beings but from God, from whom everything derives which may be truly identified as significant, as the gospel also bears witness. Therefore, no one can vaunt his works or faith before God as though they were [acquired] from himself. For he who boasts of himself in himself, being satisfied with himself, is one of the rich whom God leaves empty and unsatisfied. WHETHER GOD IS THE CAUSE OF EVIL.[18]

GOD IS MERCIFUL TO ISRAEL IN REMEMBER-ING HIS PROMISES. RUDOLF HOSPINIAN: First in part, in this word *Israel*, she understood the Jewish people, as those who were born of Israel or Jacob. By the offering of God's hand, she understood his comfort, protection and shelter, help and salvation. Therefore she wants to say that God is come to comfort and help the people through his Son, our Lord Christ. Through these words she points to the miserable, lamentable condition of the entire Jewish people at that time, relative to both spiritual and to worldly matters. The religion and the external worship of God were everywhere under the control of the Pharisees, who had invented all sorts of human statutes with which they led away the simple people from the hope of their ancestors, and the promised Messiah, our Lord Christ. Instead they were led to focus on sacrifices, donations and other works, which had made the temple into a shopping mall, and public worship everywhere into a trading and retail market. Outside of the kingdom and their authority, what is relevant is that about sixty years prior to this time, the Roman hero Pompey oppressed them, and they were brought under Roman rule. The Romans finally set Herod over them, who was a cruel tyrant and born of their ancient enemies, the Idumeans.... And now the holy Virgin Mary says, "God has offered his hand to the poor, oppressed, leaderless people; that is, he sends comfort and help to them through the real, true Savior and Redeemer, whom he has now sent."

---

[16]A famous proverb of Juvenal, a Roman poet active in the late first/early second century.
[17]*LEA* 1:111 (cf. WA 41:367).

[18]Denck, *Spiritual Legacy*, 110*; alluding to Jn 8:56; Acts 2; Phil 3:4-6; Mt 19:27; Eph 2:8.

And here we can see how we will soon have a clearer understanding of the current situation, because the time was now at hand, that God would allow his Son, the promised Messiah, our Lord Christ, to be born a true human being. . . .

But no one should presume that the Jews had been rewarded by God because they had somehow merited such a thing, and ascribe the great benefit of all humankind to such a thing. That is why the Virgin Mary relates the reason and cause why such a thing is done by God, and for whose sake. She said, "God did this to keep in mind his mercy, as he promised to our ancestors, namely, to Abraham and his seed forever." As if she would say, "God wants at this time to send the true and real Messiah, or Savior and Redeemer, to his oppressed and long-suffering people, not because they have in some way earned such a thing from him but because he considers his promise to their ancestors and before that to Abraham long ago to be lasting and permanent, which was said and promised out of his pure grace and mercy." THE SIXTH SERMON.[19]

THE PROMISE OF GRACE WAS GIVEN TO ISRAEL. MARTIN LUTHER: By this all merit and presumption are laid low, and the pure grace and mercy of God are exalted. For God did not accept Israel on account of its merits but because of his own promise. Out of pure grace he made the promise, and out of pure grace he fulfilled it. Therefore Saint Paul says in Galatians 3 that God gave the promise to Abraham four hundred years before he gave the law to Moses, that no one might boast or say that he had earned or achieved such grace and promise through the law or the works of the law. And so the Mother of God praises and exalts this promise above everything and ascribes this work of the incarnation of God to the divine, gracious, unearned promise alone, which he gave to Abraham. THE MAGNIFICAT.[20]

1:56 *Mary Helps Elizabeth, Then Returns Home*

MARY HELPED ELIZABETH AND ENJOYED THE PIOUS SOCIETY. PHILIPP MELANCHTHON: It is said several times, however, that Mary remained with Elizabeth for three months. The question is, what did she do there during that time? Did she approve of dances? I would respond, about parties: certainly she approved of the society of respectable people, and Elizabeth, too. But it is one thing to attend a respectable party, and another to long for dances. The elderly woman did not go to a dance; she was around one hundred years old and was all danced out. They visited holy women. Mary did all domestic or economic duties after having those delightful conversations. But foremost there were prayers and thanksgiving. They criticized the errors of the Pharisees, spoke about matters of worship, confirming each other. Elizabeth said: "This is how it is usually done." The church is a society, in which people should unite in the duty of prayer and consolation. Likewise it is said: "and after you have turned back, confirm your brothers."

The temple was the place where the honest matrons and virgins met. This place was called the "Mirror of Women," that is, the school of women. . . . Mary was also in this gathering, and they had many very pleasant discussions among themselves. The pure enjoy great consolation. SERMON ON THE DAY OF MARY'S VISITATION.[21]

MARY IS AN EXAMPLE ESPECIALLY FOR WOMEN. GEORG SPINDLER: Accordingly all females should especially consider dear Mary, for she is held up as a mirror to all women and virgins, that they might see in her an example of all feminine virtues and piety. The Holy Spirit praises especially her excellent faith here, that she assiduously followed God's Word, heard it, embraced it, remembered and confessed it, and sincerely called on God and thanked him for his blessings.

---

[19]Hospinian, *Lobgesang der Heiligen Hochgelobten Reinen Jungfrauwen Maria*, 102-7.
[20]*LEA* 1:160 (cf. WA 7:597; LW 21:351-52); alluding to Gal 3:17.

[21]MO 25:156-58; quoting Lk 22:32.

After these things, the Spirit praises the beautiful virtues which follow from such a faith: that she was a modest, quiet, secluded, humble and pious virgin, who did not lord it over anyone because she was born into a royal lineage or because she became the mother of the eternal Son of God and was the greatest and most honored female on earth. Rather, she remained humble and traveled to visit her elderly relative. ON THE DAY OF MARY'S VISITATION.[22]

---

[22]Spindler, *Postilla*, CCCCC6v.

1:57-66 THE BIRTH AND CIRCUMCISION OF JOHN

[57]*Now the time came for Elizabeth to give birth, and she bore a son.* [58]*And her neighbors and relatives heard that the Lord had shown great mercy to her, and they rejoiced with her.* [59]*And on the eighth day they came to circumcise the child. And they would have called him Zechariah after his father,* [60]*but his mother answered, "No; he shall be called John."* [61]*And they said to her, "None of your relatives is called by this name."* [62]*And they made signs to his father, inquiring what he wanted him to be called.* [63]*And he asked for a writing tablet and wrote, "His name is John." And they all wondered.* [64]*And immediately his mouth was opened and his tongue loosed, and he spoke, blessing God.* [65]*And fear came on all their neighbors. And all these things were talked about through all the hill country of Judea,* [66]*and all who heard them laid them up in their hearts, saying, "What then will this child be?" For the hand of the Lord was with him.*

OVERVIEW: The birth of John, and his attendant naming, shine an even greater light on the miraculous events about to happen surrounding Jesus' birth. For our interpreters they reveal to all that this child is special and has an important future ahead of him. Most prominent among these passages is the naming of John and the subsequent healing of Zechariah. Zechariah reveals once again the merciful but all-powerful hand of God. The birth of John is an event that signifies a changing of the guard, a shift from the old to the new—from the law, in a way, to the gospel. John appears to be the pivotal figure. His circumcision is still required by the law, but he is the last prophet, born just before the Christ, and unlike Zechariah (a priest under the old law), John represents and ushers in the new covenant as the one who prepares the way of the Lord.

1:57-58 Elizabeth Delivers a Son

CHILDREN ARE A GREAT, GOD-GIVEN BLESSING. CHRISTOPHER HOOKE: The Lord granted her to bring forth a child, a male child, and such a child who would be filled with the Holy Spirit, even from his mother's womb, to be the prophet of the Most High and to go before him in the spirit and power of Elijah—this is the sum and perfec-

tion of all benefits. And even in ordinary births, bringing forth the child makes all the sorrows of labor to be forgotten. Women know this to be true by their own experience. And our Savior Christ, from whom no thing is hidden, teaches us the same thing, saying: "When a woman is giving birth, she has sorrow because her hour has come, but when she has delivered the baby, she no longer remembers the anguish, for joy that a 'man' has been born into the world." By "man" he means the female child as well as the male child, because both are great blessings of the Lord, although in some respects the male child is preferred to the female, because it is by the male that the family name continues longest in remembrance, which people (and even godly people) desire most of all earthly blessings. . . . Thus we see what a blessing it was to Elizabeth that she was made fruitful and brought forth a son, and also how generally the fruit of the womb is an inheritance and blessing that comes from the Lord. And this is a most necessary doctrine to be taught these days, particularly to two sorts of people. One sort thinks that children are a drag and a drain, and therefore if they can choose, they would rather be without them than have them. These people are very far from the knowledge of God's truth in this matter, for he teaches us that children are a blessing, an inheritance, a reward and a crown for us from the Lord. . . . The other sort for whom the knowledge of this doctrine is necessary are those who take the greatest possible delight in their children but do not appreciate the depth of this blessing. They perceive it not to be a blessing from the Lord, but rather they take it as a natural and ordinary work of nature. In doing so they not only rob the Lord of the honor and thanks that are due to him, but they also deprive themselves of that inward joy that the godly experience when they realize that the Lord has a special regard for them. THE CHILD-BIRTH OR WOMAN'S LECTURE.[1]

A GREAT CROWD GATHERED TO CELEBRATE. JOHN CALVIN: It may be doubted whether these people appreciated the wonderful blessing of God just because she bore a child, or whether they had previously heard that an angel appeared to Zechariah and promised a son to him. This was certainly no ordinary divine favor, that, outside of the course of nature, a barren woman of an advanced age had brought forth a child. It is possible that, on this ground alone, they praised the great goodness of God. Next, on the eighth day, from a sense of duty or from courtesy, as is customary on such occasions, some people assemble; but God uses this occasion to make them witnesses and spectators of his power and glory. There can be no doubt but the extraordinary birth brought a greater crowd of people. They had considered it a strange wonder to see an old and barren woman suddenly become pregnant; and now that the child is born, their astonishment is renewed and increased. We gather from the words of Luke that, although they circumcised their children at home, they usually did it with a large company and assembly of people. This was right, for it was a common sacrament of the church, and it was not proper to administer it in a secret or private manner. COMMENTARY ON A HARMONY OF THE GOSPELS.[2]

1:59-63 The Circumcision and Naming of John

CIRCUMCISION IS THE SEAL OF THE COVENANT BETWEEN ABRAHAM AND GOD. JOHANNES BRENZ: The Lord chose Abraham that he might set up the Lord's kingdom and worship in the land of Canaan through his posterity, but also so that through his descendants would come Christ, in whom all nations might obtain the blessing. And so the Lord commanded this circumcision by which, as by a public seal, he might testify and declare the covenant made with Abraham and with his seed and might confirm the faith of everyone who was circumcised according to the divine institution, because the covenant of God also applies to them and brings salvation to them. When John was born, the law of Moses was in effect, and there was never any time closer to the time when Christ should be born, who was promised to the seed of Abraham. And there was no other person who should give more evident testimony concerning Christ, his ascension into heaven and the sending of the Holy Spirit after he was glorified, than John. Therefore none ought more justly and necessarily to be circumcised than John. AN ECCLESIASTICALL EXPOSITION UPON SAINT LUKE 1.[3]

THE NAMING OF JOHN IS INSPIRED BY THE SPIRIT. MARTIN LUTHER: Was it at the prompting of the Holy Spirit that the mother said, "He should be called not Zechariah, but John"? Saint Ambrose said that she was impelled to name him thus by the Holy Spirit, and not her husband, because he had been struck dumb. Mark this well, that it came from the Holy Spirit that she named him John. It is a very good name, but one that many scoundrels also bear, just like the excellent name of Christ. He is called Christ who is anointed with the Holy Spirit; there is no greater name on earth and therefore there is no greater

---

[1]Hooke, *Child-birth or Womans Lecture*, B3r-B4v*; citing Jn 16:21; Ps 127:3; Prov 17:6.
[2]CO 45:43-44 (cf. CTS 31:63-64).

[3]Marlorat, ed., *Catholike and Ecclesiasticall Exposition of the Holy Gospell After S. Marke and Luke*, 58-59*.

villainy than has come about under this name of Christ. The greater the name, the greater the scoundrel using it. But it is obvious that she called him that in order to praise God, the way that people used to honor the saints by giving the name Erasmus.[4] She was moved to it by the Holy Spirit, was filled with the Spirit and wanted to name her son John as a sign that she was giving thanks to God; the child should have a name with which she could always be giving thanks to the Lord. It is clear that she gave him the name through the promptings of the Holy Spirit. And afterwards her husband gave his approval, as if he wanted to say: he is truly a child given out of mercy and favor. SERMON ON SAINT JOHN'S DAY (1529).[5]

ZECHARIAH REPRESENTS THE OLD LAW, JOHN THE NEW. RICHARD TAVERNER: But Elizabeth his mother said he should not be called Zechariah, but that John should be his name. She did not learn this name from her husband, who at the time lacked speech, but by the inspiration of the Holy Spirit, signifying that he who was born should be the town crier or messenger of the new law, which would abrogate the old traditions and turn carnal worship into a spiritual grace. For in Hebrew, Zechariah means "a rememberer of God," while John means "the grace of God." The justice of the law stood in appointed works; the justice of the gospel stands by faith through grace and favor. Nevertheless, the kinsfolk would not be ruled by the mother who wanted to give him this strange name, because there was no one in all of their family who was called John, and so they wanted to call him Zechariah after his father. Even so, today there are some who are better pleased with the name Zechariah than with the name of John—these are the ones who cannot

suffer that the ceremonies of the old law should be abolished, so in effect they cry that they will have none of this new name of John but will stick with the old Zechariah. And so, because the child's mother and the rest of the family could not agree on the name, it was necessary that the authority of the father should be called on to break up the argument. Unfortunately, he still did not have the use of his tongue, although he was now called on to speak. Therefore they used signs to ask him what name he desired for his child to have. He realized that the situation called for him to use a writing tablet, so that by dumb letters he could declare the thing which he could not bring forth with a lively voice. When the tablet was brought, he wrote, "His name is John." Now came the time for the law of Moses to speak, for before it could only describe with figures, after a fashion, the grace of the gospel. The time was now come that the mouth which unfaithfulness had locked should now be opened by faith. ON THE DAY OF SAINT JOHN THE BAPTIST.[6]

1:64-66 Zechariah Speaks

ZECHARIAH'S POWER OF SPEECH RETURNS. JOHN CALVIN: God brings honor on the birth of his prophet by restoring speech to his father: for there can be no doubt that this benefit was delayed until that day with the end and design of turning people's eyes toward John. Zechariah spoke, blessing God, not only for the purpose of testifying his gratitude but also so that his relatives and neighbors would know that this punishment had been inflicted on him because he had been too slow to believe: for he was not ashamed to connect his own dishonor to the praises of the glory of God. Thus it became universally known that the birth of the child was not an accidental or ordinary event but had

---

[4]The name John is of Hebrew origin and means "the Lord is gracious." Erasmus is of Greek origin and has the meaning "beloved." Saint Erasmus or Elmo, a martyr of the early church, was also thought to be a bishop and is counted one of the Fourteen Holy Helpers, saints venerated for their reported healing powers. [5]LEA 1:64 (cf. WA 29:430-31).

[6]Taverner, *On Saynt Andrewes Day*, 19v-20r*. Taverner translated many important continental Reformation works into English, but sometimes he presented these translations as his own work (most notably, Calvin's 1536 catechism). His postils might be based on Erasmus Sarcerius's.

been promised by an announcement from heaven. COMMENTARY ON A HARMONY OF THE GOSPELS.[7]

THE MIRACLES SURROUNDING JOHN'S BIRTH CAUSED THE PEOPLE TO WONDER. MARTIN BUCER:

Because the people saw the mighty power of the Lord, which was shown in various miracles concerning the child, there was cause for why they should look for great things concerning him, and should be, as it were, frightened by the clearly present majesty of the Lord. For this is how human hearts are constructed, that the more they see the Lord's outstretched arm and power, the more they fear God. And so therefore all signs and wonders which manifestly declare the power of God terrify people greatly. AN ECCLESIASTICALL EXPOSITION UPON SAINT LUKE 1.[8]

MANY CAN SPEAK TO THE NATURE AND ROLE OF JOHN. PETER HAUSTED:

"What then will this child become?" To whom is this question directed? I perceive that there are many who are able to answer it. If you ask the child himself, just wait a while until he learns to speak, and he will quote you a prophet concerning himself and tell you that he is "the voice of one crying out in the wilderness, 'Make straight the way of the Lord.'" If you ask his father, if we will have patience until the Lord gives him his speech again, which was taken from him because of his unbelief, or if you will not stay so long, give him a tablet and he will write it, that "he shall be called the prophet of the Most High." And you, child, will be called "the prophet of the Most High, for you will go before the Lord to prepare his ways." If you ask David this question, behold, he stands ready to give you an answer in Psalm 85 and calls him by a high name indeed—no less than "justice" or "righteousness" in the last verse of the psalm: *Iustitia ante eum ambulabit*, Justice or "righteousness will walk before him." Or ask the prophet Malachi what manner of child this will be, and in his third chapter he will tell you of an angel: "Behold, I send my angel (or my messenger), and he will prepare the way before me." Or if you will not content yourselves with human answers, inquire of the angel Gabriel, and he will instruct you that "he will be great in the sight of the Lord." Or if you would rather go to the oracle itself, ask our Savior and hear what account he gives of John in the eleventh chapter of Saint Matthew: "Truly, I say to you, among those born of women there has arisen no one greater than John the Baptist." THE FOURTH SERMON, PREACHED UPON SAINT JOHN THE BAPTIST'S DAY.[9]

---

[7]CTS 31:65* (CO 45:44).
[8]Marlorat, ed., *Catholike and Ecclesiasticall Exposition of the Holy Gospell After S. Marke and Luke*, 61-62*.

[9]Hausted, *Ten Sermons*, 69-70*; quoting Jn 1:23 (which cites Is 40:3); Ps 85:13; Lk 1:76; Mal 3:1; Lk 1:15; Mt 11:11.

1:67-80 THE BENEDICTUS

⁶⁷And his father Zechariah was filled with the Holy Spirit and prophesied, saying,

⁶⁸"Blessed be the Lord God of Israel,
   for he has visited and redeemed his people
⁶⁹and has raised up a horn of salvation for us
   in the house of his servant David,
⁷⁰as he spoke by the mouth of his holy prophets
   from of old,
⁷¹that we should be saved from our enemies
   and from the hand of all who hate us;
⁷²to show the mercy promised to our fathers
   and to remember his holy covenant,
⁷³the oath that he swore to our father Abraham,
   to grant us
⁷⁴that we, being delivered from the hand of
   our enemies,
might serve him without fear,

⁷⁵in holiness and righteousness before him
   all our days.
⁷⁶And you, child, will be called the prophet of
   the Most High;
   for you will go before the Lord to prepare
   his ways,
⁷⁷to give knowledge of salvation to his people
   in the forgiveness of their sins,
⁷⁸because of the tender mercy of our God,
   whereby the sunrise shall visit usᵃ from on
   high
⁷⁹to give light to those who sit in darkness and
   in the shadow of death,
   to guide our feet into the way of peace."

⁸⁰And the child grew and became strong in spirit, and he was in the wilderness until the day of his public appearance to Israel.

a Or *when the sunrise shall dawn upon us*; some manuscripts *since the sunrise has visited us*

OVERVIEW: Zechariah's prophecy concerning his son broaches a number of central themes in the reformers' theology.[1] John's arrival signifies that the kingdom of God has begun on earth, and the promise made in the covenant with Israel is now to be fulfilled. The texts stress God's mercy and grace in sending the promised Messiah but also the responsibility that God's people have to live rightly and serve the Lord. The righteousness given through forgiveness of sins—not anyone's merits—means not only that Christians can stand righteous before God but also that Christians must work at reforming their lives. John's message to the people of Israel is one of repentance—his listeners must recognize their sinfulness and rely only on God's mercy for salvation.

1:67 Zechariah Prophesies

ONLY THE HOLY SPIRIT OPENS THE TEXT OF SCRIPTURE. MARTIN LUTHER: We see in this song how to distinguish between those who read Scripture according to reason without faith and the Spirit, and those who have the Spirit. Luke says that after John was born and circumcised, it happened that his father's mouth was opened and he continued to praise God—thus he prophesied. See, he ought to have a very different understanding now than at first. At first, he too read the prophet's passages, but he did not understand them as he does now. . . . Not only does Zechariah read the prophets, but he understands them and will thus become a prophet himself. Not only are they prophets who prophesy like Isaiah, but also they interpret correctly. Such people must have the Holy Spirit; otherwise they are unable to interpret correctly. If it is from reason—that is, whoever interprets holy Scripture from his own mind—it is not prophecy (as in 2 Peter 1). Therefore whoever

---

[1]On the Benedictus, see p. 26 n. 1.

wants to understand prophecy must have the energy and power of the Holy Spirit. The Holy Spirit has been poured over all the earth, as Zechariah says.

We charge into holy Scripture with our reason. I don't want to make a [wax] nose out of Scripture; instead it must shape me. So because the lawyers at any time have heard four senses of Scripture, holy Scripture is a wax nose—someone can twist it to the right, to the left, up, down, because each person approaches ineptly with his own interpretation and twists Scripture according to his own understanding; another according to his. When it's twisted in this way, holy Scripture remains tightly closed shut—it will not allow itself to be twisted. You cannot twist it, because Scripture does not allow opposing or varying opinions; instead your understanding should agree with Scripture, not Scripture with your understanding. . . . You are making a wax nose out of yourself, not Scripture. . . .

"Do not read *into* but read *from* holy Scripture!"[2] I should study in such a way that the Holy Spirit illuminates me and I obtain true understanding—which the Holy Spirit willingly grants. Christ says: "I will send prophets, wise people, scribes." He gives apostles, prophets, evangelists. The church must have these people. Where there is no prophecy of the Holy Spirit—who illuminates apostles—there is no Christian church. For we pray and confess: I believe in the Holy Spirit. Much less is there a holy church unless it is ruled by the Holy Spirit—as even the pope admits! . . . When we interpret holy Scripture according to our own will, those are thoughts which sprout from our own minds and only obscure holy Scripture.

Therefore such people are false teachers. Thus, Scripture is said to be a wax nose. But it has a single, fixed meaning—that and no other—without which there are no other senses. Before, Zechariah read holy Scripture but did not

understand. But now the Holy Spirit makes him a prophet. From this passage the fanatics say: "You see there that the spoken Word is nothing; instead the Holy Spirit must come first and then we will understand Scripture." So Thomas Müntzer cast aside the Bible: "Refuse to listen to the spoken Word!" And thus they abandoned the gospel and the sacraments. The enthusiasts want to be filled with the Holy Spirit first; then they form holy Scripture according to their own understanding— they then make fanatics. Zechariah did not obtain the Holy Spirit without the Word: he read even though he did not understand. Now pay attention to these lessons. In his time the Holy Spirit comes and reminds you, as Christ said, "and he will remind you what I have said to you." Zechariah does not say "I knew that," but through this the living Lord speaks, like on Easter day, "And they remembered." They did not import meaning into the Word, but instead through the Word that they had already heard they were illuminated. Therefore we never accept the Holy Spirit apart from the Word. SERMON ON THE FEAST OF MARY'S VISITATION (1538).[3]

1:68-75 God Remembers His Covenant with Israel

ISRAEL IS THOSE WHO HAVE FAITH IN JESUS CHRIST. JOHANNES BRENZ: The Lord is not only the God of Israel but also of the Gentiles and of all creatures, for the whole world is subject to his dominion. However, he is said to be particularly the God of Israel because, first, by a public covenant he bound himself to the people of Israel, as we can see in Genesis 17; second, because he had given patriarchs, prophets, the law, the worship of God and the promises of the coming Christ to this people; and last, because Christ was to be born of this people after the flesh. But after Christ had come, this Israel after the flesh was no longer the true Israel; rather, the true Israel is those who have

---

[2]Hilary, *On the Trinity* 1.18 (NPNF[2] 9:45). "For the best student does not read his thoughts into the book but lets it reveal its own; draws from it its sense and does not import his own into it, or force on its words a meaning which he had determined was the right one before he opened its pages."

[3]WA 46:464-67; citing Gen 22:16; 17:5; 22:18; 2 Pet 1:21; Jer 31:34; Mt 23:34; 1 Cor 12:28; Jn 14:26; Lk 24:8; Wis 7:27; Jn 4:42.

faith in Christ Jesus. So although the Lord is the Lord of all nations by his power and government, yet he is properly said to be the God of the faithful in Jesus Christ, because he acknowledges these alone to be the heirs of his heavenly kingdom. Therefore in respect to the covenant he is specially called the God of that nation. But for this reason he is not called the God of Adam, the God of Abel or of others, namely, that he would always have his covenant be remembered and will be acknowledged to be the one who he manifests himself to be. We should not seek for anything more, nor should we imagine any uncertain thing of him, and suggest that he is this or that; rather, we should simply embrace him as he reveals himself to us. An Ecclesiasticall Exposition upon Saint Luke 1.[4]

The Horn of Salvation Brings Life to Christians. Martin Luther: "He has raised it up in the house of his servant David," namely, through the Word and the Holy Spirit. That is a wonderful thing: it is a kingdom on earth, but still a kingdom of salvation. It brings the two things together! The "house of David" means the lineage and family of David, and he was a human being. Zechariah does not also speak of a kingdom of angels, for this kingdom is placed among people, in the house of David. And a "house" is people who are altogether mortal. How does such honor come into shame, such salvation into wretchedness, such life into death? People who are mortal shall not die; those who are the devil's shall be God's! You have to patch these things together: people, who die, are nevertheless immortal in this kingdom. A Christian who comes into this kingdom does not die and cannot die. For Christ has defeated death so that we do not have to die, has taken our sin onto himself so that we do not have to bear it and has overcome the devil so that a Christian will never be enslaved to him or to sin. This text must be true: "He has raised up a horn of salvation in the house

of his servant David." And therefore a Christian is living, without sin, and never enslaved to the devil. Sermon on Saint John's Day (1525).[5]

The Word That Ministers Preach Is God's Word, Not Their Own. John Jewel: For it is not a human being but God who speaks, as Christ tells the apostles, "It is not you that speaks, but the Spirit of your Father which speaks in you." And the prophet Zechariah says, "He spoke by the mouth of his holy prophets, which have been since the world began." The prophets and apostles and holy men of God were merely instruments. It was God who gave his Holy Spirit, which gave them tongues to speak and words to utter. Therefore Christ said, "I will give you a mouth, and wisdom, against which all your adversaries shall not be able to speak nor resist." Although people are simple, the word they deliver is mighty; although they are mortal, the word of the Lord endures forever.

Where this word is received, it is a fire which burns; it is a hammer which breaks the hardness of the heart; it is mighty in operation; it cleanses the inner person; it opens the conscience; it is the fragrance of life; it is the means of salvation. One who receives this word and believes shall be saved. This is the word of reconciliation. God has committed it to us. A Treatise of the Sacraments: On Holy Orders.[6]

God's Gift and Our Duty. Edwin Sandys: The greater and better part of holy Scripture either sets forth God's goodness toward us or our duty toward him. In these few but most pithy words of Zechariah both are comprehended. The great benefit we receive from God is our redemption in Christ. The duty which we owe to him again is to serve him continually in holiness and righteousness of life. He treats our redemption in one word but explicates in many words the duty which we owe

---

[4]Marlorat, ed., *Catholike and Ecclesiasticall Exposition of the Holy Gospell After S. Marke and Luke*, 63*.

[5]*LEA* 1:175 (cf. WA 17,1:293-94).
[6]Jewel, *Works*, 2:1130*; quoting Mt 10:20; Lk 21:15; citing 2 Cor 2:16.

for it to our Redeemer; giving us hereby secretly to understand that people are easily taught to know but only with difficulty brought to do their master's will. We are rich in all speech and understanding, but in deeds full poor and barren. A SERMON PREACHED AT HIS FIRST COMING TO YORK.[7]

GOD PROMISED SALVATION THROUGH GRACE ALONE. MARTIN LUTHER: Not only will he set us free from spiritual and physical enemies—for when many evils fall on a Christian, they also eventually fall away again—but he will also show mercy, as he promised to our ancestors. The prophets are happy to look back and speak of the promises God made to our ancestors. But our ancestors are now dead: how should God demonstrate his mercy to them? And the prophets who announced this are also dead. That means that not only God's truth must be proven but also his mercy, which we have not earned. God promised Abraham that he would bless the entire world, that is, that through Christ a sermon would go out that would bless everyone. This promise was long delayed, as it is with all promises, but still he delivered what he promised to our father Abraham. If then such mercy was promised and sworn to the ancestors, it is clear that God is not merciful and gracious to us because of our merits but solely out of grace. Those are pure thunderbolts against our merits. For I cannot boast of my own strength when the text says, "you promised it a thousand years before I was born." And who would have asked God about it before that time? Already long before this he had decided that he wanted to do it. By doing so he shuts up our mouths: "See how you stand in grace and in the kingdom of mercy, and you can't give yourself any credit for it, for I had already promised it before you knew anything about it." And so we have to say, it's true! It is pure grace and blessing. AFTERNOON SERMON ON SAINT JOHN'S DAY (1525).[8]

GOD FULFILLS THE COVENANT WITH ABRAHAM THROUGH CHRIST. JOHANNES BRENZ: Here we see how true and just God is in keeping his promises. He does not only observe those promises which he made through the prophets but also observes the covenants which he made with the patriarchs, and especially with Abraham and David, which he also confirmed with an oath. This is the testament or covenant which God made with Abraham and his seed: "I will bless those who bless you, and whoever curses you I will curse"; and again, "Your descendants will take possession of the cities of their enemies, and through your offspring all nations on earth will be blessed." These promises made to Abraham and David concerning victory over their enemies, security and tranquility of life and the endurance of a most happy kingdom seem to be eternal blessings only as that applies to fulfillment in this world. However, by this verse of Zechariah (which is like a paraphrase of all the promises which God made to Abraham and David) we may plainly understand that these promises did especially relate to spiritual blessings.

Zechariah explains that these things are to be understood of those enemies who were overcome by Christ Jesus and of that tranquility and felicity of life which is purchased for us by Christ. For Christ did not conquer the Egyptians, or the Babylonians or even the Romans by the external preparation of war, but he overcame those enemies and delivered his people from all those things of which Paul speaks. The chief of these enemies is Satan, while the second is sin, into which Satan cast Adam by suggestion, and finally, death and hell. Furthermore, Christ restored his people, not to that security by which they might worship according to the levitical law in Jerusalem (that was only a civil worship and a preparation for Christ), but he forgave them their sins. By this remission the conscience is made so quiet through faith, that it no longer fears Satan, sin or even death and hell. AN ECCLESIASTICALL EXPOSITION UPON SAINT LUKE I.[9]

---

[7]Sandys, *Sermons*, 177*.
[8]*LEA* 1:179 (cf. WA 17,1:302-304).

[9]Marlorat, ed., *Catholike and Ecclesiasticall Exposition of the Holy Gospell After S. Marke and Luke*, 68-69*; quoting Gen 12:3; 22:17-18.

THE GOSPEL TEACHES US TO LIVE RIGHTLY.
JOHN JEWEL: The gospel that Christ left us is not a song to delight our ears, it is not a harmony to content and please our hearing; but it is a measure by which to direct our lives, a rule by which to frame all our doings. Saint Paul said, "To this end the grace of God that brings salvation has appeared to us, that we should deny ungodliness and worldly lusts and that we should live discreetly, righteously and godly in this world." Therefore God has given us his gospel, therefore he has given us his Word, that we should according to it live a sober, discreet and modest life, he says. And in another place: "That we by the same gospel may serve and please him in newness of life."[10] And so Zechariah, that holy father, being with the Holy Spirit, said, "That we, being delivered our of the hands of our enemies, might serve him all the days of our life in such holiness and righteousness as is accepted before him." For as our profession is, so should our lives be. If we profess the name of Christ, we should live like Christians; if we profess God, we should live in a way that is becoming to the servants of God. SERMON ON PSALM 67:3-4.[11]

SERVING THE LORD IS TRUE CHRISTIAN FREEDOM. HEINRICH BULLINGER: Zechariah, the priest and father of John the Baptist, in his hymn of thanksgiving in Luke 1 declares the truth and goodness of God in performing for us what he promised to our ancestors, to wit, "That we, being delivered out of the hands of our enemies, might serve him without fear in holiness and righteousness before him all the days of our life." In this testimony of his we have true liberty; that freedom, I mean, wherein we, being delivered by the Lord from all our enemies, both visible and invisible, should no longer serve them with fear but serve our God in joy and gladness. There is added also the manner and order of how to serve him: "in holiness and righteousness." Holiness cuts off and

casts away all uncleanness and intemperance; righteousness gives to everyone what is due, that is, the things which we of duty owe to each person—it unites both freedom and benevolence. And in this kind of service they who are made free serve the Lord their God, not for a day or two, or a certain few years, but all the days of their life. Therefore true Christian liberty is the perpetual service with which we serve God. SERMON 9: ON CHRISTIAN LIBERTY AND SCANDAL.[12]

1:76-79 *John Is a Prophet to the Lord's People*

JOHN IS CHOSEN EVEN FROM HIS BIRTH.
THOMAS BASTARD: We have first the tender herb or blade, "And you, my child." From this we learn that God begins and continues his work of sanctification from our infancy, until he discloses his power and virtue in our full growth. For he who wrought wondrously in John the Baptist when he was a man, wrought secretly in him yet as a child, that we may learn to ascribe our beginning, our middle, our end and all to God. For does the sun, which ripens the fruit, leave it forsaken and destitute of virtue in the seed? Therefore as the fruits of the earth grow to perfection from littleness and contemptibleness, so do God's elect rise from their littleness to further height and perfection, as is here said, "The child grew and waxed strong in spirit." THE MARIGOLD AND THE SUNNE.[13]

GOD SENDS A PROPHET TO PREPARE THE WAY.
HEINRICH BULLINGER: The father Zechariah rejoices over his infant, because he knows the excellence of his office, and, as it were, prophesies about it. A prophet is, in a sense, the interpreter of the oracles of God, a teacher also, and a preacher in the church, by whom the Lord speaks to the church and reveals his will, which the following words of Zechariah give us to understand. We also

---

[10]From Rom 6:4; this phrase is found in several Anglican and Scottish Communion services.
[11]Jewel, *Works*, 2:1055*; quoting Tit 2:11-12.

[12]Bullinger, *Decades*, 3:306*.
[13]Bastard, *Five Sermons*, 2*.

see it in the words of Matthew, where John the Baptist is said to be preaching in the wilderness of Judea, saying, "Repent, for the kingdom of heaven is near." It is a most certain argument for God's clemency when he sends his prophets to any people, for the people cannot stand without prophets. For all things pass and slide away, which can be seen today where the gospel is not preached. In these places there may be many godly people who are displeased with ungodliness, but none of them dare to speak against the wicked or resist them. But where there are faithful prophets, they step forth and disclose wickedness, openly declaring it without ceasing. These prophets lift up their voices as if they were trumpets and show the people their sins, reproving and condemning them, so that the wicked might be ashamed and known and might be driven with fear, to increase the love of righteousness among the people. But could not God, who can do all things and whose will no one can resist, illuminate the hearts of the people with his spirit, so that they might acknowledge and receive the Son when he came to be the savior? But God provides this answer: he first sends his prophet, who by his preaching may prepare the way of the Lord. AN ECCLESIASTICALL EXPOSITION UPON SAINT LUKE 1.[14]

JOHN'S ROLE IS TO GIVE KNOWLEDGE OF SALVATION. JOHN CALVIN: Zechariah now touches the chief point of the gospel when he teaches that the knowledge of salvation consists in the forgiveness of sins. As we are all born the children of wrath, it follows that we are by nature condemned and ruined: and the cause of our condemnation is that we are guilty of unrighteousness. There is, therefore, no other provision for escaping death except by God reconciling us to himself, not imputing our sins to us. That this is the only righteousness which remains to us before God may be readily gathered from the words of Zechariah. For whence comes salvation, but from

righteousness? But if the children of God have no other way to know salvation except through the forgiveness of sins, it follows that righteousness must not be sought anywhere else. Thus righteousness, which proud people forge and manufacture out of the merits of good works, is nothing other than the imputation of righteousness, when God, out of free grace, acquits us from our offenses. It ought to be observed here that Zechariah is not speaking of outsiders but of the people of God. Hence it follows, that not only does the beginning of righteousness depend on the forgiveness of sins, but it is by imputation that believers are righteous before God to the very end: for they cannot endure before his tribunal in any other way than by bringing themselves daily to a free reconciliation. COMMENTARY ON A HARMONY OF THE GOSPELS.[15]

CHRIST IS THE RISING SUN WHO COMES TO US FROM HEAVEN. HEINRICH BULLINGER: And Zechariah calls Christ the Dayspring from on high, in respect to his divinity, by which he was and is above all creatures. Where there is nothing but only height itself, there is Christ in his divinity, even as the "dayspring" or the sun rising. For he proceeds from the Father even as beams of light proceed from the sun. Thus Christ speaks of himself, "No one has ever gone into heaven except the one who came from heaven." For he does not have his origin from the earth, where he was conceived and born. In like manner he says, "I came from the Father and entered the world." This Son of God, says Zechariah, has visited us, coming to us on the earth, and has given remission of sins to us miserable, damned sinners. . . . As the sun gives light to our bodies, so Christ gives light to our minds. And with this, Zechariah shows why he calls Christ the "Dayspring": namely, because he will lighten those who sit in darkness and in the shadow of death. By these words we are taught that there is no lifegiving light in the world without Christ, but that without him all things are covered

---

[14]Marlorat, ed., *Catholike and Ecclesiasticall Exposition of the Holy Gospell After S. Marke and Luke*, 71-72*; quoting Mt 3:1-2.

[15]CTS 31:76-77* (CO 45:51); citing Eph 2:3; 2 Cor 5:19; Eph 2:12.

with the horrible darkness of death. AN ECCLESI-ASTICALL EXPOSITION UPON SAINT LUKE 1.[16]

THE SHADOW OF DEATH IS A STATE OF SIN AND IGNORANCE. HENRY HAMMOND: The meaning of this figurative speech, "the shadow of death," will be best conjectured by comparing it with Psalm 23:4, "though I walk through the valley of the shadow of death." Making God his shepherd in verse 1, the psalmist compares himself with a sheep, which feeds sometimes on a hill, sometimes in a valley, sometimes in danger from wolves, or else free from that danger. The hills, being the highest, have all the light and warmth of the sun on them. The valleys, contrariwise, that are shaded by the hills, have much less of that warmth or light and are also more subject to incursion of wolves than the hills were (where their coming would be more discernible). This, then, is the meaning of "the valley of the shadow of death": it is a gloomy vale of danger of the utmost evil. So proportionately here (in a spiritual sense), the "shadow of death" is a state of sin and ignorance, a want of light or knowledge and want of warmth or grace. This is a description of the state under the law, which afforded neither of these in any proportion to what is now done by Christ, and so left people in a dangerous condition until Christ was pleased to shine on them and thereby to rescue them out of it. ANNOTATIONS ON SAINT LUKE 1.[17]

HE GUIDES US IN THE WAY OF PEACE. JOHANN BAUMGART (POMARIUS): This is also comforting, because our life and our ways here are a bothersome pilgrimage and wandering, and this world is a dangerous labyrinth, full of wrong ways and side roads. Yes, we have all gone too far and down the wrong paths, and our feet only hurry off to evil. There is nothing that we need more greatly as a guide than to have the Lord as our companion, for he wants to direct our feet onto the way of peace,

so that we have peace with God, and so that we travel in the Lord's ways and worthily in the gospel of peace. Finally, when our short and difficult pilgrimage is accomplished, we will "depart in peace" with the beloved Simeon, and be received by our Lord into eternal peace and joy. A SECOND SERMON ON ZECHARIAH'S SONG OF PRAISE.[18]

1:80 *John Spends His Youth in the Wilderness*

JOHN GROWS IN THE SPIRIT, PREPARING FOR HIS COMING WORK. HEINRICH BULLINGER: Luke touches only very briefly on the adolescence and youth of John. It was enough for him to mention the fortitude and moderation of the young man, and that he prepared himself in the best possible way for the contests and other things that lay ahead. Young people justly deserve praise if they train themselves with enthusiasm in similar things or other excellent works. However, Luke indicates that the author and preserver of this fortitude and moderation is the Holy Spirit, the author and preserver of all good things. We see that John followed the practice of the Nazirites in his life. He was on very careful guard lest the filth of the world should pollute him, so that he might later on scold with even greater authority against the corruption of the world. For this reason young people should learn fortitude and moderation. Parents should learn how to educate their children conscientiously, and as much as possible to preserve them from the contagion of the world. John lived in the desert but was not a stranger to all human society and only keeping company with wild animals. Otherwise the people to whom he later preached would not recognize him, but that part of Judea was called "the desert" where he lived a very austere life...But to return to the point, for his age he conducted himself very modestly, and moreover it was right that at this time he might be strengthened by the Spirit and furnished with the most splendid gifts,

---

[16]Marlorat, ed., *Catholike and Ecclesiasticall Exposition of the Holy Gospell After S. Marke and Luke*, 74*; quoting Jn 3:13; 16:28.
[17]Hammond, *Paraphrase and Annotations*, 192*.

[18]Baumgart, *Postilla*, 413v-414r; alluding to Ps 14; Is 59:8; Rom 5:1; Acts 16; Lk 2:29-30; Mt 25.

although he certainly did not try to take over any function within the church before the proper time. And so God is truly pleased for the servant to prepare the way for Christ himself. He goes ahead, for there is need of the service of a most faithful prophet. . . . But this is where Luke breaks off the history of John, which he will not return to again until chapter three. COMMENTARY ON LUKE 1:76-80.[19]

---

[19]Bullinger, *In Luculentum et Sacrosanctum Evangelium Secundum Lucam Commentariorum*, 24v-25r, 25v.

2:1-20 THE BIRTH OF JESUS

In those days a decree went out from Caesar Augustus that all the world should be registered. ²This was the first registration when^a Quirinius was governor of Syria. ³And all went to be registered, each to his own town. ⁴And Joseph also went up from Galilee, from the town of Nazareth, to Judea, to the city of David, which is called Bethlehem, because he was of the house and lineage of David, ⁵to be registered with Mary, his betrothed,^b who was with child. ⁶And while they were there, the time came for her to give birth. ⁷And she gave birth to her firstborn son and wrapped him in swaddling cloths and laid him in a manger, because there was no place for them in the inn.

⁸And in the same region there were shepherds out in the field, keeping watch over their flock by night. ⁹And an angel of the Lord appeared to them, and the glory of the Lord shone around them, and they were filled with great fear. ¹⁰And the angel said to them, "Fear not, for behold, I bring you good news of great joy that will be for all the people. ¹¹For unto you is born this day in the city of David a Savior, who is Christ the Lord. ¹²And this will be a sign for you: you will find a baby wrapped in swaddling cloths and lying in a manger." ¹³And suddenly there was with the angel a multitude of the heavenly host praising God and saying,

¹⁴"Glory to God in the highest,
    and on earth peace among those with whom
        he is pleased!"^c

¹⁵When the angels went away from them into heaven, the shepherds said to one another, "Let us go over to Bethlehem and see this thing that has happened, which the Lord has made known to us." ¹⁶And they went with haste and found Mary and Joseph, and the baby lying in a manger. ¹⁷And when they saw it, they made known the saying that had been told them concerning this child. ¹⁸And all who heard it wondered at what the shepherds told them. ¹⁹But Mary treasured up all these things, pondering them in her heart. ²⁰And the shepherds returned, glorifying and praising God for all they had heard and seen, as it had been told them.

a Or This was the registration before   b That is, one legally pledged to be married   c Some manuscripts peace, good will among men

---

OVERVIEW: Jesus' birth narrative gave Protestants an opportunity to stress some of their favorite themes but also to prove their orthodoxy to the ancient faith of the church. It was God's providence that brought Mary and Joseph to Bethlehem, where Jesus' birth could fulfill the biblical prophecies, but it also brought many hardships for the young couple, whose baby was born in a smelly cattle stall. The disparity between the wretched situation of Mary birthing her first child in a dirty animal pen and the divine significance of the event, heralded by throngs of angels singing beautiful praises to God, was not lost on these interpreters— God does not work on human timetables or according to human reason. Even the shepherds, humble people themselves, were not expecting such a miserable situation for the promised Savior, and yet their faith, like Mary's, was strong. Christ's desperately humble beginnings should show us all the extent to which Jesus humbled himself for our sakes, taking on this "temporary lodging" so that we might have permanent homes in heaven.

These writers take this opportunity to stress their orthodoxy regarding the incarnation—while some individuals might have questioned Jesus' full divinity or full humanity (as Calvin accused Servetus of doing), most accepted that Christ was truly human and divine. They also generally agreed that Mary was a virgin, before, during and after the birth; by stressing that Mary gave birth to God, they in essence assert the traditional title of *Theotokos* for Mary—the God-bearer.[1]

2:1-5 *The Roman Census*

GOD CAN USE EVEN A TYRANT TO ACCOMPLISH HIS PLANS. JOHN CALVIN: Thus we see that the holy servants of God, even though they sometimes wander about, not knowing where they are going, still keep the right path, because God directs their steps. Nor is the providence of God less wonderful in employing the command of a tyrant to draw Mary from home, that the prophecy may be fulfilled. God had marked out by his prophet—as we shall afterwards see—the place where his son should be born. If Mary had not been compelled by the requirement, she would have decided to give birth at home. Augustus orders a census to be conducted in Judea, and each person to give his or her name, that they might afterwards pay an annual tax, which they were formerly accustomed to pay to God. Thus an ungodly man seizes and carries off what God was accustomed to collect from his people. It was, in effect, just as if he had prohibited the Jews from choosing for themselves to be considered the people of God. COMMENTARY ON A HARMONY OF THE GOSPELS.[2]

MARY WAS DESPISED, WHEN SHE SHOULD HAVE BEEN HONORED. MARTIN LUTHER: See how plainly and simply things happen on earth, and yet how high they are regarded in heaven. On earth it happens this way: Here is a young woman, Mary of Nazareth, regarded as nothing at all and thought of as one of the least citizens of the city. No one is aware of the great miracle she carries; she is silent, does not think of herself and regards herself as the least in the city. She starts out with her husband, Joseph; very likely they had no servant,

so he is master and servant, and she is mistress and maid. They abandoned their home or entrusted it to others.

Now they may have had a donkey on which Mary sat, though the Gospel does not mention it, and it is probable that she went on foot with Joseph. Imagine how she was despised at the inns along the way, though she was worthy of being brought there in a golden carriage and all pomp. How many wives and daughters of prominent men at that time lived in comfort and respect, while this woman, the Mother of God, takes a journey in midwinter on foot while pregnant! How unfairly things happen! Now it was more than a day's journey from Nazareth in Galilee to Bethelehem in the land of Judea. THE CHURCH POSTIL (1540): CHRISTMAS DAY.[3]

CHRIST IS A KING IN THE LINEAGE OF DAVID. KASPAR VON SCHWENCKFELD: When the Evangelist Luke writes that Joseph was of the house and lineage of David, he also wants to include Mary in that description, for a married couple according to the law must be from the same lineage. The splendor of the royal line of David's lineage was faded and in decline at the time when Christ took his humanity from the Virgin Mary, to indicate that although he would be a king, he would not be the sort of king that this world expects, with pomp and wealth. That is why, when Pilate asked him if he were a king, he answered, "You say that I am a king," and before that, "My kingdom is not of this world." But rather he would be an eternal, spiritual king, who would have no

---

[1]The Formula of Concord explicitly names Mary the "Mother of God"—the traditional Latin rendering (*mater dei*) of the Greek *Theotokos*. See Article 8, "The Person of Christ," BoC 508-14, 616-35, esp. 510, 620 (BSLK 804-12, 1017-49, esp. 806, 1024).
[2]CTS 33:109* (CO 45:71).

[3]LW 75:210-11* (WA 10,1.1:62-63; E² 10:136; cf. LW 52:9). Most scholars connect the Church Postil to its original publication in 1522 after Luther's time at the Wartburg. However, the new *Luther's Works* (vols. 75-79) emphasize the final form of this publication and therefore cite the publication dates as 1540–1544 (the Advent to Easter portion edited by Luther himself, 1540; the Easter to Advent portion edited by Caspar Cruciger, 1544). Still, for most of the passages there is no difference—let alone any substantial differences—in the German base text of 1522 and 1540. Most of the 1540 edits are inserted section titles for clarity. For a detailed discussion of the Church Postil's bibliographic-critical issues, see LW 75:xiii-xxxi.

successor but would set up an everlasting kingdom in which he would reign forever.

It was promised to Abraham and David that the Christ should be born from their seed, from the lineage of the holy fathers and from the fruit of the lands of David. However, it would otherwise have been forgotten, but the Holy Spirit showed and proved it in the Gospels, so that we should be certain that Jesus, who was born from Mary, was the promised Messiah and Christ our Lord. The prophet David witnesses to this promise when he says, "I will sing of the grace of the Lord forever, and proclaim his truth with my mouth forever and ever." INTERPRETATION OF THE GOSPEL: LUKE 2 (1547).[4]

2:6-7 The Birth of Jesus

GOD ALMIGHTY BECOMES ALL WEAKNESS FOR US. JOHN DONNE:

Immensitie cloystered in thy dear wombe,
Now leaves his welbelov'd imprisonment,
There he hath made himselfe to his intent
Weake enough, now into our world to come;
But Oh, for thee, for him, hath th'Inne no
    roome?
Yet lay him in this stall, and from the Orient,
Starres and wisemen will travell to prevent
Th'effect of Herod's jealous generall doome.
Seest thou, my Soule, with thy faith's eyes,
    how he
Which fils all place, yet none holds him, doth
    lye?
Was not his pity towards thee wondrous high,
That would have need to be pittied by thee?
Kisse him, and with him into Egypt goe,
With his kinde mother, who partakes thy woe.

LA CORONA.[5]

CHRIST IS TRULY HUMAN AND DIVINE. JOHANN WIGAND: The first point is that the Lord Christ was born naturally. Therefore the text says,

"the time came for the baby to be born." Christ was carried in his mother's body just like any other child; that is, he is a true and natural human being that did not develop suddenly but over time and grew within Mary. So he is no false apparition, with only the appearance of life, as certain heretics have falsely and perversely imagined, asserted and insulted. But he was a true human being, with body and soul, just like other children, only without sin. "And then Mary brought forth her firstborn son." The history is very short, for it is enough that we know that Christ was born. However, the Christian church believes and holds as certain that Mary remained a virgin both during and after the birth. Human reason cannot discover, establish or explain this secret, and likewise with one other thing—that Mary is the bearer and Mother of God. That is, Mary did not only give birth to a true human being but also God, for the wonderful, incomprehensible joining of the two natures took place within her body. Indeed, the divinity is solely from the Father, but the humanity is from Mary. The divinity did not begin in Mary's body but has been from eternity. But the humanity began right there. Now because these natures were indivisibly united within Mary, therefore she gave birth to God and a human being, that is, the person of Jesus Christ. This miracle far exceeds our understanding—reason cannot grasp it, and it can only be seized by faith. GOSPEL ON HOLY CHRISTMAS DAY.[6]

CHRIST IS THE FIRST AND ONLY BEGOTTEN SON OF MARY. MARTIN BUCER: He is called the first begotten son whose parents had no other sons prior to him, even if there were never any born after him either. And Luke did not say "his first begotten," but "her first begotten son," and because he said "her son," as Epiphanius noted, he leads us to understand that he was born of her after the flesh.[7] The same one who is here called her first

---

[6]Wigand, Postilla (Festpostille), 67.
[7]See, for example, Epiphanius, Panarion 78. The question of Mary's perpetual virginity was a common discussion point in the early church, with this verse serving as one rallying point. One important tract on the matter was Jerome's Against Helvidius (ca. 383).

---

[4]CS 10:228-29; quoting Jn 18:36-37; Ps 89:1.
[5]Donne, Poems of John Donne, 319.

begotten was also called the first begotten of all creatures, not joined to any creature but begotten before any creature was. He is also called the first begotten among many brethren, not in a fleshly sense, as though Mary bore other sons, but he is so called among those who are worthy to receive adoption as children of God through him. He is called both the first begotten and the Son of Mary, not because she had other sons, for he is called a similar name also in his first, divine generation before his coming in the flesh. For he who is indeed the first begotten Son of his heavenly Father, before all creatures, is not called the first begotten because others were begotten after him of the Father (he has no second brother but is the *only* begotten Son); so also the case stands of his coming into the flesh. For he is the son and the first begotten of Mary but at the same time is also the *only* begotten Son of Mary, having no second brother. AN ECCLESIASTICALL EXPOSITION UPON SAINT LUKE 2.[8]

HE HUMBLED HIMSELF IN SWADDLING CLOTHES FOR US.

JOHANN BAUMGART (POMARIUS): He who is glorious and splendid, who is clothed with light as with a robe, was wrapped in poor rags and diapers, that he might cover and conceal our sins from his Father's eyes. Yes, he just pulls on a sack and lets himself lie in dust and earth, in a stinking, filthy cow stall, to make amends for the improper desires of our parents, which led them astray in Paradise, and to acquire for us the "first robe"—that lost honor and lordly robe, that wedding garment.[9] He does penance in sackcloth and ashes for our arrogance and the lazy smoke and smell of sins, and to purify us from the slime and mud, the muck and manure of sins, so that we should not in the end smell of the sulphurus smoke of hell and the odor of the devil's dung.

He voluntarily let himself be tied and bound to free us from the power and shackles of sin, death and the devil, to make amends and pay for what Adam and Eve were guilty of in their freedom, with their hands reaching out for the forbidden fruit, so that we would not be eternally constrained by the devil and bound by the fastenings and bands of hell and the chains of darkness.

Although he is over all heaven, he did not grasp after heaven but let himself yield and bend into a narrow little cradle as if into a prisoner's stocks. And the Lord of lords humbled himself so deeply that he let himself be laid next to the cattle in the surrounding stalls, in order to save us from our prisoners' stocks and to gain for us the heavenly rooms for a living space. He made amends for our pride, through which we became cattle and beasts, and lifts us up to heavenly glory with him, so that we might also be revealed with him in glory and carry the likeness of heavenly people, just as here we carried the earthly likeness. GOSPEL ON CHRISTMAS DAY.[10]

CHRIST'S BIRTH IS THE TRUE EPIPHANY.

JOHN DONNE: The whole life of Christ was a continual passion; others die martyrs, but Christ was born a martyr. He found a Golgotha (where he was crucified) even in Bethlehem, where he was born; for to his tenderness then the straws were almost as sharp as the thorns after, and the manger as uneasy at first as his cross at last. His birth and his death were but one continual act, and his Christmas Day and his Good Friday are but the evening and morning of one and the same day. And as even his birth is his death, so every action and passage that manifests Christ to us is his birth, for Epiphany is manifestation; and therefore, though the church does now call Twelfth Day Epiphany, because on that day Christ was manifested to the Gentiles in those wise men who came then to worship him, yet the ancient church called this day (the day of Christ's birth) the Epiphany, because this day Christ was manifested to the world, by

---

[8]Marlorat, ed., *Catholike and Ecclesiasticall Exposition of the Holy Gospell After S. Marke and Luke*, 80-81*; for first begotten, see Rom 8:29; Col 1:15.

[9]The *stolam primam* is the robe which the prodigal's father urges the servant to fetch for his son; see Lk 15:22. For the wedding robe, see Mt 22:11-14.

[10]Baumgart, *Postilla*, 25v.

being born this day. Every manifestation of Christ to the world, to the church, to a particular soul, is an Epiphany, a Christmas Day. SERMON 4, PREACHED AT SAINT PAUL'S ON CHRISTMAS DAY (1626).[11]

2:8-15 The Shepherds and the Angels

CHRIST IS EVERYWHERE IN SCRIPTURE. MARTIN LUTHER: In all of Scripture there is nothing other than Christ—either in open or veiled words. . . . Therefore, the angel wants Christ to be seen everywhere in Scripture. Who would have been able to say this? That Christ is signified everywhere in Scripture?! If the prophets themselves had come to the manger, they would have hesitated, unless the Spirit of the Lord illuminated them. For this reason, a new light was necessary; the angel announced it after he led them into the Scripture. In this way, Christ is found through the gospel; he is revealed by the Holy Spirit. Following this sign, it is Scripture so long as we find nothing other in Scripture than what presents Christ. SERMON ON SAINT STEPHEN'S FEAST (1523).[12]

THE SHEPHERDS WATCH, FULFILLING THEIR DUTIES. HUGH LATIMER: But let us consider, to whom was the nativity of Christ first announced? To the bishops or the great lords who were in Bethlehem at that time? Or to those fine damsels in their hoopskirts, with their petticoats and fine jewelry? No, no: they had so many reasons to dress up and bedeck themselves with finery that they could have no time to hear of the nativity of Christ—their minds were so occupied with other things that they were not allowed to hear of it. But his nativity was revealed first to the shepherds, and it was revealed to them at night, when everybody else was asleep. It was then that they heard the joyful tidings of the Savior of the world, for these shepherds were watching their sheep at night to protect them from wolves, foxes and other beasts.

The sheep in that region lamb twice a year, and so it was necessary for the sheep to have a shepherd to protect them. And here we should note the diligence of these shepherds, for whether the sheep were their own or whether they were servants, I cannot tell—it is not expressed in the book—but it is most likely that they were servants, and their masters had entrusted them with the care of the sheep. Now, if those shepherds had been deceitful fellows, then when their masters had entrusted them with the care of the sheep, they would have instead been drinking in a bar all night, as some of our servants do nowadays. And then the angels would not have appeared to them to tell them of this great joy and glad tidings. . . .

Now these shepherds, as I said, watch the whole night—they are attentive to their vocation. They act according to their calling, and protect the sheep. They do not run around, spending their time in silliness or vain pursuits, neglecting their responsibilities and their calling. No, that is not what they did. Everyone can learn to attend to their responsibilities and callings from these shepherds. I wish that all clergy—the curates, parsons, vicars, bishops and all spiritual persons—would learn this lesson from these poor shepherds: to abide by their flocks and by their sheep, to be present among them and to be careful over them. They should not run around pursuing their own pleasure but should be present in their benefices and feed their sheep with the food of God's word, and keep hospitality, and so feed them both soul and body. A SERMON ON SAINT JOHN THE EVANGELIST'S DAY (1552).[13]

THE ANGEL REVEALED THE GLORY OF THE LORD. THE ENGLISH ANNOTATIONS: It was such a heavenly brightness and light that the amazed shepherds might by such unusual glory perceive that he was the angel of the Lord. Thus God adorned his messenger, to the end that the message by him sent might deeply affect their minds and be received no otherwise than as if it came from the

---

[11]Donne, *Works*, 1:57-58*.
[12]WA 11:223.
[13]Latimer, *Sermons and Remains*, 118-20*.

mouth of the Lord. Had the angel appeared with less majesty and authority (as sometimes angels appeared), perhaps this great mystery would not have been so readily believed. We more easily credit what we believe comes from heaven. This glory was necessary here for the confirmation of the faith of these witnesses, who were going to find the Messiah in so low an estate of humiliation. ANNOTATIONS UPON THE GOSPEL ACCORDING TO SAINT LUKE 2:9.[14]

THE GOSPEL IS THAT CHRIST IS BORN FOR Us. MARTIN LUTHER: With these words the angel demonstrates the gospel most clearly and that nothing else is to be preached in Christendom. He takes on himself the office and words that conform to the gospel and says, *evangelizo*. He does not say, "I preach to you," but rather, "I speak gospel to you; I am an evangelist; my word is gospel." Thus the word *gospel* (as said above during Advent) means a good, joyful message which is the proclamation of the new covenant.[15] What does the gospel say? Listen. He says: "I bring you good news of great joy; my gospel speaks of great joy." Where is it? Listen again. "To you is born a Savior, Christ the Lord, today in Bethlehem in the city of David."

See here what the gospel is, namely, a joyful sermon about Christ our Savior. Whoever preaches him rightly preaches the gospel and pure joy. How can a heart hear of greater joy than that Christ is given to him as his own? He not only says that Christ is born, but he also makes his birth our own by saying "your Savior." Therefore, the gospel not only teaches the history and events of Christ but also makes him our own and gives him to all who believe it, which is the true and proper nature of the gospel (as we said above).[16] What would it help me if Christ had been born a thousand times and it were sung daily in a most lovely manner, if I were never to hear that he was born for me and was to be my very own?! If the voice makes a sound,

no matter how quiet and awful it sounds, my heart listens with joy; it penetrates through and indeed sounds sincere. Now if there were something else to be preached, the evangelical angel and angelic Evangelist would have touched on it. THE CHURCH POSTIL (1540): CHRISTMAS DAY.[17]

JESUS, OUR SAVIOR, FULFILLS ALL THE BIBLICAL PROPHECIES. EDWIN SANDYS: His birth, foretold so long ago by the heavenly prophet [Isaiah], was in fullness of time accomplished, as this day, in Bethlehem, a city of David, according to the testimony of that angel sent from heaven to proclaim the birth of the Son of God at the same time, saying: "Behold, I bring you tidings of great joy, that shall be to all the people; because this day is born to you a Savior, which is Christ our Lord, in the city of David." This is that Seed of the woman which breaks the serpent's head, that meek Abel murdered by his brother for our sin, that true Isaac whom his father offered up to be a sacrifice of pacification and atonement between him and us. This is that Melchisedek, both a king and a priest, who lives forever, without father or mother, beginning or ending. This is Joseph who was sold for thirty pieces of money. This is that Samson full of strength and courage, who, to save his people and destroy his enemies, willingly brought death on his own head. This is that Lord and Son of David, to whom the Lord said, "Sit at my right hand." This is that Bridegroom in the Canticle, whose heart is so inflamed with heavenly love toward his dear spouse, which is his church. This is he whom holy Simeon embracing prophesied that he should be "a light to the Gentiles and a glory to his people Israel"; he on whom the Holy Spirit descended and of whom the Father testified from heaven, "This is my well-beloved Son." This is that Lamb of God, pointed at by John and sent to "take away the sins of the world," to redeem us from thraldom, not with gold or silver but with the inestimable price of his precious blood; to be made our wisdom, justification, sanctification and

---

[14]Downame, ed., *Annotations*, Ss2r*.
[15]See LW 75:29, 39, 145-46 (WA 10,I.2:23-24, 34-35, 158-59; E² 10:5, 18-19, 95-97).
[16]See LW 75:216 (WA 10,I.1:72-73; E² 10:143-44; cf. LW 52:15-16).

[17]LW 75:220* (WA 10,I.1:78-80; E² 10:148-49; cf. LW 52:20-21).

redemption. This is the Child who is born for us, the Son who is given for our cause, the King whose rule is on his shoulders, whose name is Marvelous, the Giver of Counsel, the Mighty God, the Everlasting Father, the Prince of Peace; the same Messiah who was foreshadowed in the ceremonies and sacrifices of old, who was prefigured in the law, and is presented in the gospel and has been proved to the world by signs and wonders, by so clear evidence as cannot be either dissembled or denied. Let us therefore embrace this babe with joy, let us kiss the Son, let us, with the angels of heaven, praise the Lord; let us sing their psalm to the honor of his name, "Glory be to God on high, and on earth peace." A Sermon Made in Saint Paul's, on the Day of Christ's Nativity.[18]

Christ Is Our Lord and King. Augustin Marlorat: Note here how Luke teaches the office of Christ, or the Messiah whom they looked for: namely, that he should save. And it is declared in another place from what he should save them, where it is said, "because he will save his people from their sins." The angel gives the name of Lord to Christ because he is to have governance over everything, that he might exercise his dominion or rule here. For as God frequently announced through the prophets that he alone is our Lord, King and Lawgiver, even so, when he manifested his Son in the flesh, he declared him to be the same, in whom he would reign and govern. And so we have one God from whom we and all things exist. Christ is thus declared not only to be a master and a teacher, to whom we must pay attention when he teaches, but also a prince to whose government we must be subject and whose commandment we must obey. For the Father has given to him in his house the dignity of the first begotten, that he might have superiority over his brothers with power and might order and dispose the riches of the

inheritance. An Ecclesiasticall Exposition upon Saint Luke 2.[19]

The Shepherds Are Given a Sign. Heinrich Bullinger: Lest the shepherds should doubt these new and wonderful tidings, the angel helps them out by giving them a sign, saying "Experience it yourselves, and the truth of the matter will prove to you that I have told nothing but the truth. Go on over to Bethlehem, and seek the newborn child whom I have proclaimed to be Christ the Lord. You will find him wrapped in swaddling cloths and lying in a manger." Here the angel is imitating common human practice, for it is quite common for us in great and doubtful matters to join signs with our words. And so we see the goodness of God shining through, in that he frames himself to our infirmities. . . . However, the sign which is given to the shepherds is not agreeable to human sense but in fact is quite contrary to the wisdom of the flesh. The shepherds had to look on and consider one thing, and in their minds to comprehend something else. According to his own ways, God does not set glorious things before us, in order that he might confound and overthrow human reason. An Ecclesiasticall Exposition upon Saint Luke 2.[20]

A True Picture of an Angel. Martin Luther: We can learn from this song what kind of creatures the angels are. Do not consider what earthly philosophers dream about them. Here they have all been painted in such a way that they could not be painted better, so that even their heart and thoughts may be known. First, when they sing glory to God with joy, they show how full of light and fire they are. They acknowledge that all things are God's alone, attributing nothing to themselves; instead with great fervor they give the glory only to him to whom it belongs. Therefore if you want to think of a humble, pure, obedient and joyful heart

---

[18]Sandys, *Sermons*, 7-8*; quoting Ps 90:1; Lk 2:32; Mt 3:6, 17; Jn 1:29; Is 4:6; Lk 2:14.

[19]Marlorat, ed., *Catholike and Ecclesiasticall Exposition of the Holy Gospell After S. Marke and Luke*, 86*; quoting Mt 1:21.
[20]Marlorat, ed., *Catholike and Ecclesiasticall Exposition of the Holy Gospell After S. Marke and Luke*, 87*.

praising God, think of the angels. This is the first part of their walk before God.

The second part is their love for us. . . Here you see what great and gracious friends they are for us. They favor us no less than themselves; they rejoice in our salvation almost as if it were their own, so that in this song they give us a comforting inducement to wish the best for them as for the best of friends. See, in this way you rightly understand the angels, not according to their substance, as earthly philosophers fruitlessly deal with them but according to their inner heart, spirit and mind, so that I don't know what they are but rather what their chief desire and constant work is. By this we see into their heart. THE CHURCH POSTIL (1540): CHRISTMAS DAY.[21]

THIS BABY IS OUR PRINCE OF PEACE. HEINRICH SALMUTH: The angels preach in this song of the blessings of this newborn baby, the Lord Christ, when they say, "Peace on earth," and they show by it that the Lord Christ will bring peace to the earth, and that as the angel says, he will be our Savior. . . .

Through these words it is made clear that the Savior of the world is born, but he does not bring a worldly peace (as it is often said), but rather a spiritual and eternal peace. And by this peace he makes us free who were slaves to sin, and he delivered our inheritance to our beloved God and our own Lord and Creator, who created us for eternal life and brought the ransom for us in that he accomplished enough divine righteousness and achieved salvation for us.

We were poor and pitiful sinners, and on account of our sin we should have been eternally rejected by God, because sin divides us from him. But this newborn baby became our Prince of Peace, in that he gained for us peace, life and salvation through his obedience and satisfied the righteousness of God, so that our beloved God wants to be gracious and reconciled to us and forgive our sins, on account of the blood and death of his beloved

Son, Jesus Christ. THE FOURTH SERMON ON THE INCARNATION AND BIRTH OF CHRIST.[22]

THE ANGELS REVEAL GOD'S GOODNESS TO THE WORLD. HUGH LATIMER: The angel bade them go to Bethlehem to search for the child, and then a great many angels came together rejoicing, singing and praising God, that for our sake the Redeemer of all humankind was born into the world. Without him, nothing else will avail in the sight of God the Father. Without him, no one can praise God, for it has pleased God to be favorable and loving toward humankind only for the sake of his Son and to receive only the prayers which are made to him in the name of Christ our Savior. Therefore all those who come without him before God will be rejected as people who are rebellious against God and his constitutions. For God's will, pleasure and counsel is only to receive those who come to him in the name of his Son, our Savior—those who know themselves, lament their own sins, confess their own sinfulness and wickedness and put their whole trust and confidence only in the Son of God, the Redeemer of humankind—the angels testify to this.

We should note that in this Gospel there was singing and rejoicing over the unspeakable goodness and mercy of almighty God the Father, who decided to redeem humankind through the death of his only, natural and most dearly beloved Son, our Savior and Redeemer, Jesus Christ. He was true God and true man, the Son of God after his divinity and the Son of Mary after his humanity. He took human nature on himself for our sake, to redeem and deliver us from all misery, to bring us to unity with God, the Father, and finally to bring us to everlasting life. A SERMON MADE ON CHRISTMAS DAY (1522).[23]

OUR FAITH DRAWS US TOWARD THE WORKS AND KNOWLEDGE OF GOD. MARTIN BUCER: Thus we see [in the example of the shepherds] that

---

[21]LW 75:227-28* (WA 10,1.1:92-93; E² 10:159-60; cf. LW 52:29-30); alluding to Lk 15:10.

[22]Salmuth, *Weihenacht Predigten*, 60r-v.
[23]Latimer, *Sermons and Remains*, 85*.

faith draws us to God and brings to pass that we bend ourselves with all our strength toward where we know Christ to be; that is to say, where we know that those works are, which are approved and accepted by God. As the shepherds said, "Let's go to Bethlehem and see this thing that has happened," or "and see how this thing which the Lord has told us about is fulfilled." For they correctly ascribe to the Lord what they heard only from the angel, and to him whom they consider to be the servant of the Lord, they give as much authority as if he were the Lord himself. Because of this, the Lord calls us to him, lest the majesty of his word might be considered vile in the sight of humankind. And so let us also acknowledge today, that whatever we have heard up to now concerning the birth of the Messiah is the word and work of the Lord God. An Ecclesiasticall Exposition upon Saint Luke 2.[24]

2:16-20 *The Visit and Witness of the Shepherds*

The Shepherds Took No Offense at Christ's Poverty. Hugh Latimer: Here we see proven the faith of the shepherds: they heard a voice from heaven which promised them a Savior, and now when they arrive, they find nothing but a poor infant lying in a manger. This could have been a big problem for them, for they thought they would find him in a position in keeping with his title, that is, like a Savior, but they found instead a poor child who, according to human perception, was not able to help himself. However, they had conceived such a strong and hearty faith that this faith preserved them from all outward challenges and offenses. In this we can learn from these shepherds not to be offended by the poor kingdom that our Savior kept in this world, for we can see that it is very common for the rich and wealthy of this world to despise and scorn the Word of God. So let us also be despised in this world with

Christ, our King, that we may have with him afterward everlasting life, while those proud and sturdy fellows will be thrust into everlasting fire. These shepherds were not offended by the poverty of our Savior, and therefore did not stay and meddle any further but went forth and preached and talked of it to other folks. And they could not do this without danger to their own lives, for the Pharisees and spiritual leaders were so stubborn that they would not allow any doctrine to be taught except for their own fantasies. This became apparent later, when they killed Christ himself, and after him a great number of the apostles. Yet for all that, these shepherds were content to lose their lives in God's fight. A Sermon Made on Christmas Day (1522).[25]

The Shepherds Spread the Good News They Saw and Heard. Martin Bucer: That the shepherds published abroad those things which they saw, we may gather from the following verse, "and all who heard it were amazed at what the shepherds said to them." We may understand from this that true faith does not exist without confession and that it desires that the truth which it has truly conceived may be known to others. Faith wants to communicate that truth to others as a most excellent and incomparable treasure. Whoever does otherwise boasts in vain of having faith.

Moreover, the shepherds did not publish only those things which they saw but also those things which they heard from the angels. This shows us that, above all things, the fruit and purpose of works is to be incorporated into the preaching of the gospel. For while some only set forth the history that the Lord is born, the angel taught the shepherds that he was born for the salvation of his faithful people. Furthermore, we must note that they preached nothing but those things which were true and manifest, which they themselves had heard and seen. By this example, ministers of the Word should learn to set nothing but the Word of God before the flock committed

---

[24]Marlorat, ed., *Catholike and Ecclesiasticall Exposition of the Holy Gospell After S. Marke and Luke*, 91*.

[25]Latimer, *Sermons and Remains*, 91-92*.

to their charge. God has no need of invented lies. That is why John says, "What was from the beginning, which we have heard, which we have seen with our eyes, which we have looked at and our hands have touched—this we proclaim concerning the Word of life." And those things which those shepherds heard and saw, and surely also all the apostles, must be preached by the ministers of Christ to the people of God, and not their own dreams, for those things are most sure and certain. AN ECCLESIASTICALL EXPOSITION UPON SAINT LUKE 2.[26]

MARY'S FAITH IS CONSTANT. JOHANNES BRENZ: As we wondered before at the simple faith of the shepherds which could not be shaken by any offense [to human reason], so now we must commend the modest constancy of faith in the Virgin Mary, who gathered up certain principles of her faith out of all those things which were done concerning her child. She was well assured that although the Lord our God begins his works in a lowly way, he ends them with great honor. She learned from the shepherds what the angel revealed and what the heavenly company sang, and yet she held her peace, keeping in her mind and diligently considering in her heart all those things which had happened before and at the present time. She reserved in secret the mystery of her virginal conception until a more proper time; she did not boast to others of her felicity. She had offered and still offers herself to be a handmaid to the work and the will of the Lord: she saw in herself a new way by which the Lord intended to work concerning the salvation of humankind. She considers that all things are full of new miracles. AN ECCLESIASTICALL EXPOSITION UPON SAINT LUKE 2.[27]

---

[26]Marlorat, ed., *Catholike and Ecclesiasticall Exposition of the Holy Gospell After S. Marke and Luke*, 92-93*; quoting 1 Jn 1:1.

[27]Marlorat, ed., *Catholike and Ecclesiasticall Exposition of the Holy Gospell After S. Marke and Luke*, 94*.

2:21-40 JESUS' CIRCUMCISION AND PRESENTATION IN THE TEMPLE

²¹*And at the end of eight days, when he was circumcised, he was called Jesus, the name given by the angel before he was conceived in the womb.* ²²*And when the time came for their purification according to the Law of Moses, they brought him up to Jerusalem to present him to the Lord* ²³*(as it is written in the Law of the Lord, "Every male who first opens the womb shall be called holy to the Lord")* ²⁴*and to offer a sacrifice according to what is said in the Law of the Lord, "a pair of turtledoves, or two young pigeons."* ²⁵*Now there was a man in Jerusalem, whose name was Simeon, and this man was righteous and devout, waiting for the consolation of Israel, and the Holy Spirit was upon him.* ²⁶*And it had been revealed to him by the Holy Spirit that he would not see death before he had seen the Lord's Christ.* ²⁷*And he came in the Spirit into the temple, and when the parents brought in the child Jesus, to do for him according to the custom of the Law,* ²⁸*he took him up in his arms and blessed God and said,*

²⁹*"Lord, now you are letting your servant*ᵃ
depart in peace,
according to your word;
³⁰*for my eyes have seen your salvation*

³¹*that you have prepared in the presence of all peoples,*
³²*a light for revelation to the Gentiles, and for glory to your people Israel."*

³³*And his father and his mother marveled at what was said about him.* ³⁴*And Simeon blessed them and said to Mary his mother, "Behold, this child is appointed for the fall and rising of many in Israel, and for a sign that is opposed* ³⁵*(and a sword will pierce through your own soul also), so that thoughts from many hearts may be revealed."*

³⁶*And there was a prophetess, Anna, the daughter of Phanuel, of the tribe of Asher. She was advanced in years, having lived with her husband seven years from when she was a virgin,* ³⁷*and then as a widow until she was eighty-four.*ᵇ *She did not depart from the temple, worshiping with fasting and prayer night and day.* ³⁸*And coming up at that very hour she began to give thanks to God and to speak of him to all who were waiting for the redemption of Jerusalem.*

³⁹*And when they had performed everything according to the Law of the Lord, they returned into Galilee, to their own town of Nazareth.* ⁴⁰*And the child grew and became strong, filled with wisdom. And the favor of God was upon him.*

a Greek *bondservant*   b Or *as a widow for eighty-four years*

OVERVIEW: This next section of the chapter is about the law and examples of people who are obedient to it through faith. The circumcision of Jesus shows Mary and Joseph but especially Jesus accepting the law and living under its demands, despite not really needing to—that is, Jesus, because he had no sin, was exempt from the law's requirements and yet was obedient to it for our sake. Luther and others mention the parallel between circumcision and baptism—that baptism is the sacrament of the new covenant, while circumcision is of the old—but this was not a particularly important locus for arguments about baptism. Rather, what is stressed here are the examples of obedience to the law and faith in the promised Messiah. Simeon and Anna, as elderly prophets, represent the faithful Jews who were still waiting for the Messiah—living good, moral lives, filled with prayer and service to God. Simeon in his song points to Jesus as the Messiah who would bring division—some would reject him (and still do today), while some would accept him in faith. Anna, the widow who lived a life of prayer and fasting, was an important example (especially for women) whose interior faith and piety were lived out in her actions. Finally, Jesus' parents, but especially Mary, who "kept all these things in her heart," fulfilled the demands of the law but also faithfully accepted these signs and prophecies about their son.

2:21 *The Circumcision and Naming of Jesus*

WHY CIRCUMCISION? MARTIN LUTHER: First, let us ask the sophist, Lady Jezebel,[1] natural reason: Is it not a foolish, ridiculous, useless command when God demands circumcision? Could he find no other member of the body than that? If Abraham had here followed reason, he would not have believed that it was God who demanded this of him. In our eyes it is such a foolish thing that there can scarcely be anything more foolish. In addition, the Jews had to endure great humiliation and disgrace, were despised by all the world because of it and were regarded as an abomination. Besides, there is no use in it. What benefit is it if the body is damaged? The person is made no better for it; everything depends on the soul.

But all of God's commandments and works are and should be this way. In our eyes they appear most foolish, most contemptible and most useless, in order that haughty reason, which thinks itself clever and wise, may be put to shame and blinded and may surrender its opinion and submit to God, give him honor and believe that whatever he asserts is most useful, most honorable and most wise, though it does not see it and thinks quite differently. If God had given a sign which would have been suitable to it and useful, wise and honorable in its opinion, it would have remained in its old skin, would not have subordinated its

haughtiness, would have continued in its custom of seeking only honor, gain and wisdom, and living on earth—and so would have become ever more deeply rooted in worldly, temporal things. But now that God places before reason foolish, useless and shameful things, he tears it away from the quest for gain, honor and wisdom and teaches it to look only to the invisible, divine wisdom, honor and gain—and therefore gladly to suffer the lack of temporal honor, gain and wisdom. Be a fool, a beggar and a good-for-nothing; despised for God's sake! Therefore, God was not concerned about circumcision but about the humiliation of proud nature and reason.

In the same way we have baptism in the new covenant, in order that we should surrender ourselves under the water and believe that we are there cleansed from sin and saved. Likewise, Christ's body is in the bread of the altar. Likewise, we worship the crucified man as Lord and God. All this is immeasurably far above and against reason. So all the works and words of God are against reason, and reason, too, is contrary to God and kicks against "the sign of contradiction." . . . In all this God seeks nothing more than humility, so that human beings surrender their reason into captivity and are subject to divine truth. THE CHURCH POSTIL (1540): NEW YEAR'S DAY.[2]

CHRIST PLACES HIMSELF UNDER THE LAW TO REDEEM US FROM IT. MARTIN BUCER: The equity of the law is what binds all people to keep it and which curses and condemns all those that transgress it. But there is no one and never has been one so holy that he has fully satisfied and kept the whole law. For we are all of the flesh, conceived and born in sin, and enslaved to sin. That is why Christ came into the world and made himself subject to the law by circumcision, for as Paul says,

---

[1] Luther also uses the epithet *Frau Hulda* to refer to human reason, implying its unfaithful "whoring" after anything but its Creator.

[2] LW 76:39-40* (WA 10, 1.1:505-6; E² 10:319-20; cf. LW 52:149-50); alluding to Gen 17:1-14; quoting Lk 2:34. For more on Reformation exegesis and the sign of circumcision, see John L. Thompson, "'So Ridiculous a Sign': Men, Women, and the Lessons of Circumcision in Sixteenth-Century Exegesis," *Archiv für Reformationsgeschichte* 86 (1995): 236-56, esp. 250-52.

"every man who lets himself be circumcised is obligated to obey the whole law." But Christ has perfectly fulfilled the law, so that all those who believe in him might be redeemed from this heavy yoke of the law and that the law might henceforth have no power to curse or condemn them. The law requires perfect righteousness and holiness, but all those who believe in Christ do not have their sins imputed to them but are counted as just and holy through Christ. And those who are accepted as just and holy already have what the law requires, namely, righteousness and holiness. They have these, not by the merit of their works but by faith through Christ, who by sin condemned sin in the flesh, that the righteousness of the law might be fulfilled in us, and who is the end of the law to the justifying of everyone who believes. Therefore Paul writes that "Christ redeemed us from the curse of the law by becoming a curse for us." An Ecclesiasticall Exposition upon Saint Luke 2.[3]

The Name of Jesus Means Salvation.

Lucas Lossius: The name Jesus comprises all the benefits of the Son of God. It signifies "Savior," as the angel expounds in Matthew 1, adding on the purpose of the name, lest he be ridiculed for having a name without also including its content, as can often happen with other titles, when he said to Joseph: "And you will call his name Jesus, and he will save his people from their sins." This is the chief benefit of Christ, that he frees his people, that is, the church, or those who believe in him, from sins. However, those who he frees from sins, he also frees from the payment and punishment of sinners, which are the wrath of God, eternal death and other disasters by which humankind, on account of sin, is oppressed. Just as Paul said in Romans 6: "The wages of sin is death, but the gift of God is life eternal through Jesus Christ our Lord." But Christ does not save everyone, but only those who believe in him, or, as the angel said, "his people," and that he

does freely, that is, without any merits of their own, or fulfilling the law. This happens first because no one can fulfill the law, because of the corruption of human nature. That is why Saint Paul said in Ephesians 2: "By grace you have been saved, through faith—and this not from yourselves, it is the gift of God . . . so that no one can boast." But it would not be by grace but by obligation, if it were through the merit of works. Second, he says it so that we should not doubt the promise of God, as if it depends on the condition of the law being fulfilled. Thus the same apostle said in Romans 4: "Therefore the inheritance was given through faith, that according to grace the promise might be guaranteed to his entire offspring." Annotations in the Gospel According to Luke 2.[4]

2:22-24 Joseph and Mary Present Jesus in the Temple

External Sacrifices Must Be Accompanied by an Interior Change.

Huldrych Zwingli: Christ was made under the law, although he owed nothing to the law, that he might redeem us who were under the law; in all things he wanted to be like his brothers. The sacrifices of the Old Testament signify truly that they cleansed from sins. Therefore, just as beasts were sacrificed and their blood was poured out, so the sinner himself declared this sacrifice to be true and that he was pricked to the soul and as it were mortified to the level of death; it is true that, unless he came near to faith in the promised seed, this brought nothing but desperation. Therefore the blood of goats and bulls could not cleanse him from sins, and for that reason the sacrifices were repeated daily. And there were very many among the Jews who, although they offered the external sacrifices, were only a little bit pricked on the inside; for how could they testify to interior change by an exterior sacrifice of beasts, unless they were hypocrites?

---

[3]Marlorat, ed., Catholike and Ecclesiasticall Exposition of the Holy Gospell After S. Marke and Luke, 95-96*; citing Gal 5:3; Rom 8:3-4; 10:4; Gal 3:13.

[4]Lossius, Novum Testamentum de Jesu Christo Nazreno . . . Annotationibus, 47; quoting Mt 1:21 (see also Ps 130:8); Rom 6:23; Eph 2:8-9; Rom 4:16.

And along with these things, the avarice of the priests led them to claim that the sacrifice of riches also could help cleanse the people of their sins, and that was the worst of all. Thus many who started out and at first were established in goodness, in time were corrupted and made bad by this abuse. The sacrifices did signify, however, that someone was coming whose blood could make amends for sin. IN THE GOSPEL OF LUKE 2.[5]

THE FIRSTBORN WERE HOLY TO THE LORD.
THOMAS BECON: This Gospel presents the history of how the child Jesus was presented in the temple after the time of his mother's lying-in. And after the manner of the law, the Evangelist calls the whole time of her lying-in the "days of purification." The same term is used by Moses. This was not the law of nature, which is why the Gentiles did not use it. God constituted this law among his people for a particular purpose, so that the mother, if she brought forth a male, would come to the temple after thirty-three days, but if it were a female, after sixty-six days. . . .

It was especially commanded in the law that the first begotten, after the aforementioned time was expired, must be presented and dedicated to the Lord. It is written in the law of Moses that every child that opens the mother's womb should be called holy to the Lord. And that was true not only of human beings but also of animals. All those were called the Lord's, and were the Lord's. And this was the origin of the prerogative and special interest of the eldest sons or first begotten, who were then preferred in the priesthood and in other things. However, with such a large number of people, these would have grown to an infinite multitude if all the firstborn would have remained in the temple to serve the Lord. Therefore God permitted parents to redeem their children by paying a price, either by a one-year-old lamb or by a pair of turtle doves, according to each one's ability

to pay. And so the child was restored to his parents and yet was called the child of the Lord. Here it appears that Mary did not have much wealth, for she offered only a pair of turtle doves, which was the gift of poorer folks. By this gift she redeemed her son and so also confessed that, although she was his true mother, yet he was not her son alone, but the Son of God as well as her own. For he was the first begotten. . . .

And in all these things there is no great thing for us to learn, except what we discussed already concerning Christ's circumcision: that is, that Christ is under the law, although there was no right that kept him subject or bound to it. THE PURIFICATION OF MARY.[6]

MARY AND JOSEPH FOLLOW THE COMMANDS OF GOD'S LAW. JOHN CALVIN: This was another obligation of piety which Joseph and Mary performed. The Lord commanded that all the males should be dedicated to him, in remembrance of their deliverance, because when the angel killed all the firstborn of Egypt, he had spared the firstborn of Israel. They were afterwards permitted to redeem their firstborn at a certain price. That was the ancient ceremony: and, because the Lord is the common Redeemer of all, he has a right to claim us as his own, from the least to the greatest. Nor is it a mistake that Luke so frequently repeats that Joseph and Mary did what was written in the law of the Lord. For these words teach us that we must not, on our own judgment, attempt anything in the worship of God but must obediently follow what he enjoins in his Word. COMMENTARY ON A HARMONY OF THE GOSPELS.[7]

2:25-27 Simeon the Righteous

CONSOLATION IS GIVEN TO THOSE WHO EAGERLY AWAITED THE CHRIST. MARTIN BUCER: For the consolation of Mary, Joseph and

---

[5]*D. Hvldrichi Zvinglii in Plerosqve Novi Testamenti Libros*, 193; citing Gal 4:4—this last phrase is repeated in his comment on Lk 2:40.

[6]Becon, *New Postil*, 128v-129v*; citing Lev 12:6; Ex 13:1-2; Num 8:14-19.
[7]CTS 31:140* (CO 45:88); alluding to Ex 12:29; Num 3:13.

others among the elect, the Lord wants to make Christ's birth clear in a number of ways. Also, from the expectations of Simeon, it is clear that at the time Christ was born, his coming had long been desired by the pious. For example, the greater part of the prophets describe that the scepter would not depart from Judah, Daniel's "sevens," and other things referring to this time. At the least they confess everything which they believe and are not able to hold themselves back. They desired the good for as many as possible, so there is no doubt that at the time of the coming of Christ, there would be many holy people like Simeon who would be admonishing the people. But because no one who seeks after carnal things values Christ, they would be preaching his coming to the deaf. There were not very many left among the people who acknowledged God, but rather, because of their blindness, they turned toward destruction. It is certainly true that Simeon is praised for his virtue in awaiting the consolation of Israel as if he were an exception, like Joseph of Arimathea, who we see also praised by name. Now the consolation of Israel was in this kingdom of God, which Simeon awaited. Most of those left among the people were not concerned about the kingdom of God and Christ, and whence the consolation of Israel would come, as if a person among worldly things cannot savor the spiritual. But Paul promised the crown of righteousness to those who longed for the advent of Christ and his kingdom. For surely God is worshiped most highly where his grace is highly valued and the redemption which he promises is eagerly awaited. This is how Simeon eagerly awaited the coming of Christ, and so at the time which the prophets indicated, the Lord wanted to console him, first by seeing the promised Savior and then also by holding him up. THE GOSPEL ACCORDING TO LUKE 2.[8]

SIMEON RECEIVED A GREAT BLESSING.

JOHANNES BRENZ: The way Christ's life proceeds agrees with the way it began. As Christ was born in misery and poverty, so now he is acknowledged only by poor and abject people. He is not visited by kings but by shepherds; he is not worshiped by Pharisees but by magi, who, although they were men of great renown in their own country, were condemned and despised among the Jews. So these lowly beginnings agree with what the Evangelist now describes. As yet, the priests did not know the child offered in the temple, the high priests did not salute him, kings did not honor him, but only a certain old man named Simeon, a citizen of Jerusalem, famous neither for his riches, his dignity nor his office, comes to salute and embrace the child. It is probable that people thought he was out of his wits, but whatever other people thought of him, Scripture commends him highly, saying that he was "righteous and devout."

And he was given a revelation through the Holy Spirit "that he would not die before he had seen the Lord's Christ." Behold here what an excellent gift was given to Simeon beyond all the patriarchs and prophets. Christ was promised to the patriarchs, and his coming was revealed to the prophets. However it was not promised to any of these that they would see Christ in this world with their physical eyes, although they greatly desired it. But both of these things happened to Simeon. "Blessed are your eyes," says Christ, "because they see, and your ears because they hear. For I tell you the truth, many prophets and righteous men longed to see what you see but did not see it." And there is no doubt but that this revelation was made to Simeon alone, that from him a general confirmation might come to all the godly. AN ECCLESIASTICALL EXPOSITION UPON SAINT LUKE 2.[9]

SIMEON WAS GIVEN THE SPIRIT OF PROPHECY.

JOHN DONNE: Simeon was a man who had the Holy Spirit on him, the Gospel says. The testimony given before—that he was *justus* and *timoratus*, righteous and fearing God—was

---

[8]Bucer, *In Sacra Quatuor Evangelia*, 545; citing Gen 49:10; Dan 9:24; 2 Tim 4:8.

[9]Marlorat, ed., *Catholike and Ecclesiasticall Exposition of the Holy Gospell After S. Marke and Luke*, 100-102*; quoting Mt 13:16-17.

evidence enough that the Holy Spirit was on him. This addition is a testimony to a more particular presence and operation of the Holy Spirit in a certain way, and everyone has agreed that the way is *in dono prophetiae*, that is, the Holy Spirit was on him in the gift of prophecy, so at that time he was made into a prophet. We are all prophets to ourselves when we come to holy Communion—we are able to foretell and to pronounce on ourselves what we will be forever. . . .

At this time, our Savior Christ was presented to God in the temple, according to the law by which all the firstborn were to be presented to God in the temple at a certain time after their birth, and there he was acknowledged to belong to God and then bought back from him again by his parents at the price prescribed by the law. A lord could not exhibit his son to his tenants and say, "This is your landlord"; a king could not show his son to his subjects and say, "This is your prince," until first he had been offered to God, for they were all his. If a child is not God's first, he is not truly his king's, or even his own. And God does not sell him back again to his parents at an inflated price. He sells a lord or a king back again to the world as cheaply as a pauper: he takes one and the same price for all. God made all humankind of one blood; and with one blood, the blood of his Son, he bought us all back again. He has delivered everything to the world at one price, and on the same conditions. SERMON 4, PREACHED AT SAINT PAUL'S ON CHRISTMAS DAY (1626).[10]

2:28-32 Simeon's Song: The Nunc Dimittis[11]

A RIGHTEOUS MAN HAS A PEACEFUL DEATH. MARTIN LUTHER: Now Simeon's heart became young again. His heart was prepared: "I have the child in my arms!" It would have been no surprise if he had died in his joy, because he did not only

see the child, but took him in his arms. Therefore he sings this happy song of praise: "I will die now with joy in my heart, and death will seem sweet to me, for my eyes have seen your Savior." That is the treasure that makes death sweet and dear. Whoever can see and recognize this young Lord who became subject to the law for us, his heart will be made happy against all adversity. See what kind of heart this venerable man had: "I am ready to depart in peace." It is a great word that he speaks: he will be happy and die in peace. Take a look at how people usually die: there is no joy in their hearts, but the heart beats and throbs, the body shakes and trembles, the mind goes blank. Death is too powerful. . . . But this man gives praise that he now can die as if there were no death. He doesn't even say "death," but "let [me] depart." He calls it a gentle departure. How can I learn to see death as a sweet sleep, when it is usually so terrifying? In this case, the law, sin and Satan were all removed from his heart. He didn't know anything about these things, or even about death. Where sin and an evil conscience are, there death is bitter. But if you want death to be a peaceful sleep, you have to have a clear conscience, and Moses and his law must be far away. A SERMON FROM FEBRUARY 2, 1526.[12]

SIMEON SAW WHAT GOD HAD PROMISED HE WOULD SEE. JOHN DONNE: *Viderunt oculi*, his eyes had seen that salvation, for that was the accomplishment and fulfilling of God's Word: "according to your Word." Everything that God had said would be done was done, for, as it is said in verse 26, it was revealed to him by the Holy Spirit that he would not see death before he had seen the Lord's Christ; and now his eyes had seen that salvation. Abraham saw this earlier, but only with the eyes of faith, and yet he rejoiced to see it—he was glad even of that. Simeon saw it before this time, then—when he was enlightened with that revelation he saw it—but only with the eyes of hope. Abraham had no cause for such hope; he had no particular hope, no promise, that he would see

---

[10]Donne, *Works*, 1:60, 68*.

[11]On the Nunc Dimittis, see p. 26 n. 1. Since the sixteenth-century many Lutherans have sung this as the post-communion canticle.

[12]LEA 1:252-53 (cf. WA 20:254-56).

the Messiah in his time. Simeon had, and yet he waited, he attended God's leisure. But hope deferred makes the heart sick, says Solomon, but when the desire is fulfilled, it is a tree of life. His desire was come; he saw his salvation. . . . He saw it, according to God's Word: that is, to the extent that God had promised he would see it. He did not see how God, who was in this child and was this child, was the Son of God. He did not see the manner of that eternal generation. He did not see how this Son of God became human in a virgin's womb, who did not know a man; he did not see the manner of this incarnation, for this eternal generation and this miraculous incarnation did not fall within that *secundum verbum*, "according to your Word." God had promised Simeon nothing concerning those mysteries, but Simeon saw the *Christum Domini*, the Lord's Salvation, and his own salvation, that is, the person who was all those things (and this is all that was in the word and the promise)—and he saw it with his bodily eyes. SERMON 4, PREACHED AT SAINT PAUL'S ON CHRISTMAS DAY (1626).[13]

THE CHILD COMES TO SAVE BOTH JEWS AND GENTILES. THOMAS BECON: This child is the salvation over death and sin that allows Simeon to "depart in peace." But moved by the consideration of this saving health, he opens up for all others the purpose for which God has prepared this salvation through giving a glowing commendation of it. "This salvation," he says, "is not only ordained for my sake, for many belong to the fellowship and fruition of this saving health. God has prepared this salvation in the presence of all people, so this child is not only my Savior, nor just his mother's, but the Savior and salvation of all people." Simeon's saying is significant and great. He pronounces the child to be the Savior of all nations, as well as of the Jews, notwithstanding that there was a great difference between them, on account of Moses' law and the divine ceremonies. But when he considers this child, he sees no difference. For all have the

same need for salvation in order that they might be delivered from death and sin. Even the observation of the law does not prevail in delivering from sin and death.[14] It is only by this Savior that all salvation is prepared. And this Savior is not the sort that comes for some and not for others. "God has prepared," he says, "this salvation, not before the face of certain people only, but before the face of all people." This sentence is one with the promise made to Abraham, where God promises blessing to all nations in his seed. And the Jews also cannot be excluded from all tribes and from all people, but those who are blessed were not blessed before but lived under God's curse. Therefore, the meaning of this cannot be taken otherwise than that, if this brings the salvation of all people, then there are none who can be saved who lack this salvation. And this is a central thing: Simeon makes everyone equal, pronouncing that the Jews as well as the Gentiles will be damned for their sins, unless they obtain salvation through this saving health. THE SERMON OF SIMEON IN THE TEMPLE.[15]

CHRIST BRINGS LIGHT TO THE GENTILES FOR THEIR SALVATION. DESIDERIUS ERASMUS: In this last verse, Simeon declares the reason why God revealed Christ before all people. It was in order to enlighten the Gentiles, who before were in darkness, and to be the glory of the people Israel. A "light to lighten the Gentiles" means that he will give light to the Gentiles and expel all the darkness out of their minds. So Christ testifies of himself, "I am the light of the world. Whoever follows me will never walk in darkness but will have the light of life." He compares darkness with light, and the Gentiles were in this darkness. Whatever good thing is accomplished without Christ is darkness, and so is the wisdom of the world, the wisdom of the flesh, and all manner of sins of which the apostle speaks in various places, which help with the interpretation of this place, such as Colossians 3:5, Ephesians 5:3 and 1 Corinthians 6:9. We can

---

[13]Donne, *Works*, 1:72-73*; quoting Prov 13:12.

[14]Becon points to Abraham's faith in Gen 22 as an example.
[15]Becon, *New Postil*, 140v-141r*.

also understand better by these words of Christ to Paul: "I have appeared to you to appoint you as a servant and as a witness of what you have seen of me and what I will show you. I will rescue you from your own people and from the Gentiles. I am sending you to them to open their eyes and turn them from darkness to light, and from the power of Satan to God, so that they may receive forgiveness of sins and a place among those who are sanctified by faith in me." Therefore the revelation of the Gentiles is their illumination and the opening of their eyes by which they see that they are in the darkness of sin, and that they must flee to Christ for remission of sins and newness of life. AN ECCLESIASTICALL EXPOSITION UPON SAINT LUKE 2.[16]

2:33-35 Simeon's Prophecy

MARY AND JOSEPH DID NOT DOUBT BUT EMBRACED THE NEWS. JOHANNES BRENZ: It may seem strange that Mary and Joseph marveled at these words of Simeon, because they had already received so many testimonies that this infant was the true Messiah and Savior of the world. Hadn't Mary learned from the angel Gabriel that she would be the mother of the Messiah, the Son of the Highest? Wasn't Joseph told by the angel that his wife had conceived the Savior of the world through the Holy Spirit? Did they not see the magi worship and acknowledge him to be the Most High King? What then had happened to them that they now wondered at the words of Simeon? Might it be that they were offended by Christ's humility, and so now believed none of the things which they had seen and heard? God forbid! Luke does not mean that they wondered as if this were a new thing, but rather that they reverently considered and embraced with admiration this prophecy of the Spirit uttered by Simeon, that they might profit more and more in the knowledge of Christ.

Therefore they wondered, not because they didn't believe but because they *did* believe. For those who do not believe do not wonder but rather condemn and scorn. Those who do believe, the more they hear excellent testimonies of Christ and the more plainly they know Christ, the more their admiration increases. And that is why the name of the Lord is called "Wonderful," and his works also: not because they are not believed but because the godly hear them with great admiration of faith. AN ECCLESIASTICALL EXPOSITION UPON SAINT LUKE 2.[17]

UNBELIEVERS ARE ENEMIES OF CHRIST AND THE GOSPEL. JOHN CALVIN: Therefore it did not take away from the main point that Simeon prophesied that Christ was "set for the ruin of many in Israel." What it means is that he was divinely ordained to throw down and destroy many. But it should be noted that this ruin happens because unbelievers push against him. This is expressed a little later, when Simeon calls Christ "a sign that is opposed." Therefore, because unbelievers are rebels against Christ, they dash themselves against him, which causes their ruin. This metaphor is based on the target at which shooters aim, as if Simeon had said, "Here the evil of human beings is perceived—the deepest depravity of all human nature—that, as if they had made a great conspiracy, they all roar and cry out against the Son of God." The world would not have reached such a consensus to oppose the gospel if there was not a certain natural disagreement between the Son of God and those people. Their ambition or fury pushes them in different directions, so that factions are split into different parties and a great variety of superstitions separate the idolaters from each other. But even if these enemies of the gospel disagree among themselves, nevertheless they all agree that they oppose the Son of God. For this reason it is truly said that the fact that people speak against Christ everywhere is obvious proof of

---

[16]Marlorat, ed., *Catholike and Ecclesiasticall Exposition of the Holy Gospell After S. Marke and Luke*, 103-4*; quoting Jn 8:12; Acts 26:16.

[17]Marlorat, ed., *Catholike and Ecclesiasticall Exposition of the Holy Gospell After S. Marke and Luke*, 105*; citing Is 9:6.

human depravity. It is a terrible sign that the world should thus rise up against its creator, but Scripture predicted that this would happen in the future. The reason for it appears to be well known: people who are once alienated from God through sin naturally flee from him. So examples of this should not confuse us, but rather our faith, furnished with this armor, should be prepared to fight against the opposition of the world. COMMENTARY ON A HARMONY OF THE GOSPELS.[18]

JESUS WAS OPPOSED BY THE UNFAITHFUL, JUST LIKE TODAY'S CHRISTIANS. RICHARD TAVERNER: Then, through the Spirit of God speaking in him, Simeon said of the child what had not been shown to Mary and Joseph before, that is, that he would be destined for the falling and rising up again of many in Israel. For surely Christ our Savior is he who brings the ruin and loss of all the infidels in Israel who did not believe in his word. On the other hand, he was the raising up, the resurrection and health of the faithful who believed in his word and followed his doctrine. Simeon says moreover that he was to be a sign or a mark whom many would oppose, that is, the scribes and Pharisees, the bishops and priests of the old law, who were always against him and in his face, even as today the heretical, wicked and unfaithful people speak against true and catholic Christians. There is no doubt that all those who earnestly follow Christ and cleave to his word will have to bear their crosses and suffer affliction and trouble in this world, inasmuch as there is no servant who is greater than his lord or master. THE GOSPEL ON THE SUNDAY AFTER CHRISTMAS.[19]

CHRIST WILL REVEAL HIDDEN HEARTS. THOMAS BECON: And as we can see in this case, it is according to what Simeon said to Mary. The Son will convict the world of great crimes—of theft, of manslaughter, of murdering their parents—even those who are now almost counted for gods will be

convicted. He will open them up, along with their hearts, so that they will declare with full evidence that they are extreme enemies of God. We now have to suffer that hypocrisy in which the outward appearance hides great offenses, but that will not continue long. When Christ comes along with his gospel, it will be evident that the whole world is full of immoral people, the enemies of God and thieves and robbers. They cannot patiently put up with being called these things, but before God they cannot pretend to be innocent of these crimes. For although their outward living is upright, they still have the fault that there is such great ungodliness in them that they cannot bear God's Word, which is what can make God's name agreeable to all people. It only takes a small thing, and some occasion, to drive the tongue and the hands to slaughter, if the heart is already full of slaughter. This vice, which otherwise no one would know or believe, is revealed by the gospel. THE SUNDAY BEFORE NEW YEAR'S DAY.[20]

THE SWORD COULD NOT OVERCOME MARY'S FAITH. HULDRYCH ZWINGLI: This is a very sure example of a firm faith, which Mary had toward God, that she was not terrified by Simeon's horrible prophecy into abandoning the baby Jesus, when he said to her: "A sword will pierce your own soul, so that the thoughts of many hearts will be revealed." With this comment Simeon suggested that she would see the misery of her child's shameful death on the cross, and that would wound her heart as painfully as if she herself had died. And she would feel the death of her child within herself, and it would increase her own pain so much that she, who before had either been a true follower of Christ or had certainly wished him well, would leave him, abandon him and even abuse and disparage him. That is just how it happens with all those fickle people, those who flatter and agree with those who teach the pure truth, as long as things are going well, so that others think they are also pious. But as soon as the teachers

---

[18]CO 45:92-93 (cf. CTS 31:148).
[19]Taverner, *Epistles and Gospelles (Wynter Parte)*, 30v-31r*.

[20]Becon, *New Postil*, 55r-v*.

bring the truth out even more strongly, so that the falsity and darkness of human minds can't stand it, they begin to persecute the teachers, and then the fickle hearts will be revealed. From that moment on they run away from and defame those whom they had formerly held in honor, saying, "I don't like his teaching either," and "I'm surprised that people have put up with him for so long!" . . . But with Mary, her inner faith, which the Spirit of God maintained in her heart, did not allow any doubt or estrangement to grow within her. Therefore she could witness the death of her own child bravely,[21] if with great pain, without falling away from or abandoning her faith, even though she saw all the people raging against him. SERMON ON MARY, THE PURE MOTHER OF GOD.[22]

2:36-38 Anna the Prophet

GOOD WORKS PROCEED FROM A GOOD PERSON. MARTIN LUTHER: Here someone might say: In this Anna you see that good works are exalted, such as fasting and praying and going to church; therefore, they must not be rejected. Answer: Who has ever rejected good works? We only reject the false, glittering good works. Fasting, praying and going to church are good works when they occur correctly. But the trouble is that these blind heads fall on Scripture, tromp in blindly with boots and spurs, look only at the works and examples of the dear saints and immediately want to teach and imitate them. Thus they become nothing but apes and hypocrites, for they do not perceive that Scripture speaks more of the person than of the works.[23]

Scripture praises Abel's sacrifice and works, but first praises the person much more. They, however, disregard the person and only make use of the example. Thus they grasp at the works and miss the faith. They eat the bran and spill the flour. Likewise, the prophet Hosea says that they turn to other gods and love the grapeskins more than the grapes. If you want to fast and pray with this holy Anna, well and good; but take care first that you imitate the person and then the works. First become an Anna. But let us see what Luke says of her works and her person, so that we may correctly understand her example.

He says that she was a prophetess and undoubtedly a holy, godly prophetess. Most assuredly the Holy Spirit was in her and consequently the person, without any works, was good and righteous. Therefore the works which she produced were also good and righteous. So you see that Saint Luke does not mean that she became godly and a prophetess through her works but that she was a godly prophetess first, and then her works also become good. Why would you cut up and contort this example and the gospel? Reading first and only the works, while Luke describes first the person and not only the works? THE CHURCH POSTIL (1540): SUNDAY AFTER CHRISTMAS.[24]

ANNA IS A SPECIAL EXAMPLE FOR VIRGINS, WIVES AND WIDOWS. JOHANN BAUMGART (POMARIUS): The God-fearing matron, Anna, reminds all females—virgins, wives and widows— of their necessary virtues, in that she came as a virgin to her husband in marriage, lived with him in marriage for seven years and then lived in her condition as a widow uninterruptedly, until she had been a widow for eighty-two years. Likewise virgins should protect their virginal chastity as their best treasure, next to God and his Word, and should not let the little garland turn into flowers, as Dinah did.[25] Wives are also reminded by Anna

---

[21]The term Zwingli uses is *mannlich* ("manly"), which was a term commonly used even in quite early texts to describe Mary's bravery under the cross. The irony is that it was primarily the women who stayed with Jesus until the end.

[22]ZO 1:99-100.

[23]This person-works distinction resonates with Luther's gift-example distinction concerning Christ and the gospel; see "Short Instruction: What Should Be Sought and Expected in the Gospels," LW 75:7-12 (WA 10,1.1:8-18; E² 7:8-13; cf. LW 35:113-24).

[24]LW 75:415* (WA 10,1.1:410-11; E² 10:287-88; cf. LW 52:122-23); alluding to Gen 4:4; Hos 3:1.

[25]The *Kränzelein*, or little garland or wreath, is a common image used in morality books of the period, with the different blooms representing different virtues. Here "blooming" has a sexual connotation.

that they should not live in conflict with their husbands but should be of one mind with them, and should not live with or tie themselves to any other, or live alone or keep house in separation or abandonment of their husbands. Likewise the widows also should not be frivolous, lascivious and unchaste, or live for the pleasures of the flesh, but rather should live a retired life in the fear of God. GOSPEL ON THE SUNDAY AFTER CHRISTMAS.[26]

ANNA LABORED IN PRAYER. HEINRICH BULLINGER: The Lord commands us to pray always; that is to say, as often as we conveniently may, at all times and in all places, to be of an upright heart toward God in all things, we should always wait for good things at God's hand, should give him thanks for benefits received and should also continually ask for his favor. Such an endeavor is commended to us in Anna, the daughter of Phanuel, of whom Luke makes mention, that she "departed not from the temple, but night and day served the Lord with fasting and prayers." Not that she did nothing else, having no regard to her body, nor did at any time eat, drink or sleep; but because that was her continual and chief business. Speaking in the same manner today, we say that the worker labors without ceasing, and the student reads night and day, but everyone understands that by this kind of speech is signified a continual and exceedingly great diligence in work and reading. SERMON 5, OF PRAYER.[27]

A PROPER FAST IS BENEFICIAL TO THE SOUL. WILLIAM PERKINS: There are four proper reasons for a religious fast. The first is to subdue the flesh, that is, to bring the body and bodily lusts into subjection to the will and Word of God.... The second is to stir up our devotion and to confirm the attention of our minds in hearing and in prayer. To this purpose in the Scripture, fasting and prayer are for the most part, if not always, joined together, because when the stomach is full,

the body and mind are less able to do any good duty; but when abstinence is used, the heart is lighter, the affections in better order, the whole person quicker and more lively in the service of God. For this very cause Anna is said "to worship God night and day with fasting and prayer." The intent there of the Holy Spirit is to commend her for the fervency of her prayer; she testified that by such exercises, she stirred up and increased the attention of her mind.

The third reason is to testify to the humility and contrition of our hearts, that is to say, our inward sorrow and grief for sin, and our repentance and effectual turning toward God. Without this purpose, the fast is but a vain ceremony....

The fourth reason for a fast is to admonish us of our guiltiness before the Lord and to put us in mind of the acknowledgment of our sins, which make us unworthy of any blessing, gift or mercy, even unworthy to walk on the ground, to breathe in the air, to eat, drink, sleep or enjoy any other benefit. In a word, it reminds us that we have deserved by our sins all the plagues and punishments threatened in the law against sinners. THE WHOLE TREATISE OF THE CASES OF CONSCIENCE.[28]

PEOPLE THOUGHT SHE WAS A CRAZY OLD LADY. JOHANN SPANGENBERG: What does Anna then say to Jerusalem? She says that the little child would be the Savior of the world, the Messiah, whom they had so long awaited and looked forward to. Did they then believe her? Not all of them. Most of the crowd thought that she was a crazy old lady for certain, because she was saying such outrageous and unheard-of things about a little baby. Indeed, who knows how it went afterwards with the pious Anna and the priest Simeon. If their age was not respected, then they did not of course remain alive, and then certainly what was done to other prophets was done to them. GOSPEL ON THE SUNDAY AFTER CHRISTMAS.[29]

[26]Baumgart, *Postilla*, 31r; alluding to Gen 34; 1 Tim 5.
[27]Bullinger, *Decades*, 5:182*.
[28]Perkins, *Whole Treatise of the Cases of Conscience*, 103*.
[29]Spangenberg, *Postilla* (1582), XXXIIr.

2:39-40 *Jesus Grows in Grace and Wisdom*

They Observed the Law, Then Went Home. John Trapp: It is often recorded of them in this chapter that they observed the law exactly, to their singular commendation. The law is to be kept as the apple of one's eye, and we must consider nothing that the Lord commands to be unimportant. It is just as much treason to counterfeit pence as a twenty-shilling piece. A Commentary upon the Gospel According to Saint Luke 2.[30]

The Incarnate Christ Must Be Properly Understood. Huldrych Zwingli: "And the boy grew" like other people, you may be sure; he certainly wanted to be like his brothers in everything. He grew in wisdom and in spirit. His spirit, which was perfect from eternity, grew up more and more within the human Christ. For God was not within Christ like a soul, but the created, intellectual soul which he received in his body made progress from day to day, for he did not know everything from the beginning. Thus in another place Christ said that the Son of Man does not know that day; that is to say, he is true man, for it is lawful that God knows all things. For example, if a certain senator knew the actions of another senator which were outside the senate, and he should be questioned, he would say that he did not know the private man. Then we might imagine two men in one person, or we might consider the same person to be twofold. Therefore these matters are accepted by us, not as if we wanted to separate the natures in Christ, for God and man are one Christ, but that we desire to distinguish justly between the two works and properties of each nature, that they might not be mingled. In the Gospel of Luke 2.[31]

"And the Grace of God Was on Him." John Trapp: It was on him without measure, so that of his overflow we have all received "grace on grace." He had a fullness that not only filled him up, but overflowed also; it was a fullness not only of plenty but also of bounty, not only of abundance but also of redundancy. He was anointed with the oil of gladness, not only above but also for his companions. A Commentary upon the Gospel According to Saint Luke 2.[32]

---

[30]Trapp, *Commentary or Exposition*, 381*; citing Prov 7:2.

[31]*D. Hvldrichi Zvinglii in Plerosqve Novi Testamenti Libros*, 194; citing Mk 13:32. Reformed theologians tended to emphasize the distinction of Christ's human and divine natures, while Lutheran theologians tended to emphasize their union—which often caused misunderstanding and disagreement, especially regarding Christ's presence in the Eucharist.

[32]Trapp, *Commentary or Exposition*, 381*; quoting Jn 1:16; citing Ps 45:7; Heb 1:9.

2:41-52 THE TWELVE-YEAR-OLD JESUS IN THE TEMPLE

⁴¹*Now his parents went to Jerusalem every year at the Feast of the Passover.* ⁴²*And when he was twelve years old, they went up according to custom.* ⁴³*And when the feast was ended, as they were returning, the boy Jesus stayed behind in Jerusalem. His parents did not know it,* ⁴⁴*but supposing him to be in the group they went a day's journey, but then they began to search for him among their relatives and acquaintances,* ⁴⁵*and when they did not find him, they returned to Jerusalem, searching for him.* ⁴⁶*After three days they found him in the temple, sitting among the teachers, listening to them and asking them questions.* ⁴⁷*And all who heard him were amazed at his understanding and his answers.* ⁴⁸*And when his parents[a] saw him, they were astonished. And his mother said to him, "Son, why have you treated us so? Behold, your father and I have been searching for you in great distress."* ⁴⁹*And he said to them, "Why were you looking for me? Did you not know that I must be in my Father's house?"[b]* ⁵⁰*And they did not understand the saying that he spoke to them.* ⁵¹*And he went down with them and came to Nazareth and was submissive to them. And his mother treasured up all these things in her heart.*

⁵²*And Jesus increased in wisdom and in stature[c] and in favor with God and man.*

a Greek *they* b Or *about my Father's business* c Or *years*

OVERVIEW: The Gospel of Luke is filled with challenging, complicated stories—passages that can be difficult to understand and interpret. This story of Jesus at twelve years old is the only canonical tale recounting his childhood, so all Scripture readers know that it retells an event of special significance— and yet how should we interpret a story that presents a child who runs away from his loving, law-abiding parents? Mary and Joseph are praised by Protestants as obedient and pious people who take their son on a long trip to the temple—faithful believers who were happy to praise and worship God in religious services and festivals. And yet Jesus, despite his youth, could not possibly be at fault here in his actions, for the presupposition is that he is entirely sinless. This passage gives a quick glimpse of the divine nature otherwise mostly hidden in a normal child. Jesus here reveals who his true Father is and previews his coming role as the Messiah but then returns home with his parents. Likewise, Mary and Joseph act in what seems to be a normal way—panicking when Jesus is not found, returning quickly to the city, searching for him frantically, and then, when he is finally found, safe and well in the temple, chastising him for causing them such worry. But because Jesus cannot be at fault, then his parents—more specifically, his mother—must be. She presumed too much and spoke out of her emotions, forgetting who her son was. But the real question is, how does this situation apply to us? When is it acceptable for a child to disobey his or her parents? Rarely, according to these interpreters! Only in matters of religion, when the parents are denying the child the true practice of or instruction in religion—one can imagine situations where a youth was attracted to the reform movement but parents were opposed. That was, everyone agreed, the main or perhaps only acceptable reason for a child to disobey his or her parents, as Jesus did here.

2:41-45 Jesus Is Lost in Jerusalem During the Passover

JESUS' PARENTS WERE DILIGENT IN WORSHIPING GOD. JOHANN WIGAND: The parents of

Christ attended and celebrated this festival, established by God and commanded in his law. The reasons were that, first, they also needed some instruction; second, they wanted to be members of this church; third, they understood that it was not yet the time for such laws to be suspended, because the Messiah was still a sweet little child and had not yet accomplished everything. He had not yet sacrificed himself for our sins, nor had he publicly abolished these ceremonies. They also wanted to avoid giving any offense to the elders. So they took Christ with them and headed off toward Jerusalem. They did this, first, so that he, as a human being, would be taught and instructed, and raised and made accustomed to attending the worship service of the people of God diligently; second, so that more testimony of the Messiah might unceasingly be sent out; and third, so that they might present him in his own foreordained place. GOSPEL ON THE FIRST SUNDAY AFTER EPIPHANY.[1]

CHRIST WAS ALSO OBEDIENT TO THE LAW.
RICHARD TAVERNER: It is good to consider further why Christ also went with them into Jerusalem. It is sure that Christ came to be the spiritual king and even to set up the spiritual kingdom, but by the law he was not subject to the law, for he was no unrighteous sinner, as it were. Instead, he was the one promised by the mouths of the prophets to be the abrogator and defeater of Moses' law. And yet we see that in all things and by all means he subjected himself to the law. Concerning this subjection of Christ, various doctors have suggested various causes. Some say that Christ our Savior submitted himself to the obedience of the law because he was the truth, and so he might finish and bring to an end all figures, and there might be no excuse left for those who should have believed. Others, including the holy Bede, say that Christ wanted to be subject to the law because by his example he would declare to us the virtue of obedience, and his intent was that through his compassion he would help those who were under the law but could not bear its burden. Now,

while these things are true, considering this question we should understand that according to Saint Paul's teaching, our Savior Christ was subject to the law for this chief reason: he wanted to redeem those who were under the law and in danger from it, so that we might all receive the title and name of the children of God through adoption. It was suitable for Christ to make himself subject to the law, because he was the promised fulfiller of the law. He recorded concerning himself that he came not to break the law but to fulfill it. By this we should perceive that he calls it his office to fulfill the law. We should diligently consider then that the final cause for why Christ, although he was free, wanted to be under and subject to the law is that he did it for our sakes, so that he might deliver us from the curse of the law and freely purify us through faith in him, as Saint Paul says. ON THE SECOND SUNDAY AFTER THE TWELFTH DAY OF CHRISTMAS.[2]

MARY AND JOSEPH GLADLY STAYED FOR THE WHOLE RELIGIOUS CELEBRATION. JOHN BOYS: "And when they had fulfilled the days," that is, the whole seven days, according to the custom. They came with the first and went home with the last. Now, for their honor, worldly men will ride post to the court to be knighted with the first; they will be first with their profit at the mill and market; for their pleasure they will be first at play; they will be first at hunting and at any merry get-together; but as for the church, they think they come too early and stay too long. Winter days are too short for hunting, and summer days are too short for hawking, yet one hour out of seven days that is spent in God's worship is thought long. As one wit said, "Long sa[l]mons and short sermons please best."[3] Yet if we look not with the spectacles of the world, but with the eyes of faith, and discern things properly, we shall find

---

[1]Wigand, *Postilla*, 151.

[2]Taverner, *Epistles and Gospelles (Wynter Parte)*, 43r-v*; citing Gal 4:5; Mt 5:17.
[3]Boys's reference is "Anton. Guevara. Epist." The *Epistolas Familiares* (1539–1545), sometimes called the Golden Letters, were a popular work of the Spanish bishop and man of letters Antonio de Guevara (1481–1545).

that there is no such honor as to be God's servant, no such gain as godliness and no such pleasure as a good conscience. THE FIRST SUNDAY AFTER THE EPIPHANIE.[4]

JESUS MEANT TO TEACH HIS PARENTS AND US. NIELS HEMMINGSEN: The first reason for the situation is announced in these words, "The child Jesus stayed behind in Jerusalem." You might want to say, "Why didn't he just inform his parents of it?" The first reason is that with this act he wanted to let everyone know that he was not only Mary's son but also God's, which is even more significant. So he pays no less attention to God the eternal Father than to Mary his mother. Second, he wants to teach children with his example that they should not ask for advice from their parents in matters where a person should be obedient to God. For a person owes more obedience to God than to his parents. Third, he wanted to encourage his parents to greater care and diligence, as well as generally to encourage everyone who has children to take much greater care of them, for they are a valuable pledge entrusted to them by God. Fourth, that by godly discipline and earnest reflection, both Joseph and Mary would be reminded what kind of poor people they were in their human natures, that is, lazy, slothful and idle, which is why they would not always perform their job as parents well in every way. ON THE FIRST SUNDAY AFTER EPIPHANY.[5]

JESUS SHOWS A RARE BUT ACCEPTABLE DISOBEDIENCE. PHILIPP MELANCHTHON: When is it acceptable for the son to reject the authority of his parents? I would say that the command of God takes priority over the will of the parents, as Christ says: "If anyone loves his father or mother more than me, he is not worthy of me." This applies when parents prohibit the study of true doctrine, the confession of faith, or marriage. On the other hand, outside of these cases, one

should be obedient to his parents. That is why here Christ returns home with his parents, in perfect duty to his vocation. THE FIRST SUNDAY AFTER EPIPHANY.[6]

MANY LEAVE CHRIST BEHIND AT CHURCH AND DO NOT WORRY. JOHANN BAUMGART (POMARIUS): The parents of Christ lost their twelve-year-old son Jesus at the holy Passover festival in the temple at Jerusalem, both through lack of attention and a confident (but false) impression that they would find him quite well in the evening, and he would be among their companions and relatives. But he was missing for three full days, and it caused them unspeakable heartache and pain. When they found him again on the third day in the temple among the learned men, they were filled with joy. This situation reminds us how easily one can lose or misplace the noble treasure of Christ, and it is quite right to say, "It is no less of an achievement to keep a possession than it is to acquire it."[7] That can just as commonly happen from attractive causes as from a lack of attention, because some head home from the temple (or church) on Sundays and holidays and do not make sure and consider whether they also have brought Christ home with them in their hearts. Oftentimes they leave him behind and return home without him. These people often have the confidence, along with their desire to procrastinate, that when they realize that they have lost Christ, they do not see the need to worry much, for they think that they will find him soon enough—if not right now, then certainly in the evening, when the sun goes down, and the light of life will be extinguished. Then he will stand among the companions and relatives, among the good friends, the confessors and the spiritual advisors around the dying—he will certainly be found there and brought forth again. Such confidence and lack of attention deceive some and will bring about earnest prayers and grief, fear and wailing, anxious calling and seeking

---

[4]Boys, *Exposition of the Dominical Epistles and Gospels*, 1:123*; alluding to Ex 23:15.
[5]Hemmingsen, *Postilla*, 151.

[6]MO 14:202; quoting Mt 10:37.
[7]Ovid, *Ars Amatoria* 2.l.13.

and the scorn of the devil and the world. It will cause much crying and heartfelt pain, which will not be extinguished or quieted until Christ is found again. GOSPEL ON THE FIRST SUNDAY AFTER EPIPHANY.[8]

MARY HAD GREAT JOY BUT ALSO GREAT SUFFERING. MARTIN LUTHER: So this Gospel first presents the Mother of Christ as an example of the cross and great suffering which God allows to happen to his saints. Although the holy Virgin was greatly blessed with all grace and was a beautiful temple of the Holy Spirit, chosen above all for the great honor of being the Mother of the Son of God—and without a doubt also had the greatest pleasure and joy in her child, more than any mother as it naturally had to be—yet God so ordained that she had to have not pure paradise but great distress, pain and sorrow because of him. The first misery which happened to her was that she had to give birth in Bethlehem, in a strange place, where she along with her child did not have a place to rest other than to lay down in a public stable. The second misery was that after six weeks she had to flee with the child into a foreign country, until he was seven years old. Without a doubt she had much more misery which is not described.

One of these miseries, and not the least, is this one which he hung around her neck: when he separated himself from her in the temple and let her search so long and not find him. He made her so terrified and distressed that she could have despaired, as she also confesses and says, "Your father and I searched for you in distress." Let us reflect for a bit how she must have felt in heart and mind! Every father and mother understands the misery and sorrow when a child they love leaves them unexpectedly, and they know nothing but that the child is lost. If it lasts only an hour, how great is the sorrow, crying and lamenting—there is no comfort, no eating, drinking, sleeping or resting—and such misery that they would rather be dead. How much greater is it when it lasts a whole day and night, or even longer, when each hour is not one hour but a hundred years?! THE CHURCH POSTIL (1540): FIRST SUNDAY AFTER EPIPHANY.[9]

2:46-50 His Parents Find Jesus in the Temple

WISDOM IS JUSTIFIED BY HER CHILD(REN). JOHN DONNE:

> With his kind mother who partakes thy woe,
> Ioseph turne back; see where your child doth sit,
> Blowing, yea blowing out those sparks of wit,
> Which himselfe on the Doctors did bestow;
> The Word but lately could not speak and low,
> It sodenly speakes wonders, whence comes it,
> That all which was, and all which should be writ,
> A shallow seeming child, should deeply know?
> His Godhead was not soule to his manhood,
> Nor had time mellowed him to this ripenesse,
> But as for one which hath a long task, 'tis good,
> With Sunne to beginne his business,
> He in his ages morning thus began
> By miracles exceeding power of man.

LA CORONA.[10]

JESUS TEACHES HIS WISDOM AMONG THE WISEST RABBIS. JOHN LIGHTFOOT: At these times then, the school learning [of the Sanhedrin] was come to the very height, Hillel and Shammai having promoted it to a pitch incomparably transcendent above what it had been before.[11] And accordingly now began the titles of Rabban and Rabbi, Rabban Simeon the son of Hillel being the first president of the Sanhedrin that carried a title. Until these times their great and learned men had been called only by their bare proper names.

---

[8]Baumgart, *Postilla*, 41r.

[9]LW 76:193-94* (WA 17,2:17-18; E² 11:17-18); alluding to Lk 2:7; Mt 2:13-15.
[10]Donne, *Poems of John Donne*, 320.
[11]Hillel and Shammai were founders of two of the most important schools of Rabbinic Judaism, particularly associated with the development of the Mishnah and the Talmud. Both were living during the reign of Herod.

So now in a double appropriateness, Christ the divine wisdom appears and sits among them, at twelve years old beginning, and all the time of his ministry after, going on to show them wisdom fully, and his own word and doctrine the divine oracles of wisdom. The Harmony of the New Testament, Section 8.[12]

Christ Is Found in the Temple, That Is, God's Word. Martin Luther: See, he rebukes his parents for running around and seeking him in earthly and human things and affairs, among acquaintances and friends, and not thinking that he must be in what is his Father's. By this he wants to show that his government and the whole Christian life exists only in the Word and in faith, not in other external things . . . or in temporal, worldly life or government. In short, he will not let himself be found among friends or acquaintances, or in anything outside of the office of the Word. He does not want to be worldly or to be in what is worldly, but in what is his Father's, as he has always demonstrated throughout his life, ever since his birth. He was certainly in the world but did not cling to the world, as he said to Pilate: "My kingdom is not of this world." He was with friends and acquaintances and whomever he came to, but he did not take an interest in any of that whole worldly life, except that he traveled as a guest through it and used it for the necessities of his body. He attended only to what is his Father's (that is, the Word's). There he lets himself be found. There he must be sought by whoever wants to meet him truly. The Church Postil (1540): First Sunday After Epiphany.[13]

The Light of the Gospel Astonishes Everyone. Bernard Gilpin: They found him in the temple, not idly occupied as many are, and not mumbling things which he did not understand—*sine mente sonum*—a confused sound without knowledge.[14] But they found him occupied in the business of the Father of heaven, as all people should be in the temple, either in speaking to God by humble and heartfelt prayer or in hearing God speak to them in his most blessed Word. Christ was occupied among learned men, sitting with them. By this he teaches us always to be as glad to learn as to teach. It is probable that he opened to them the Scriptures which spoke of the Messiah, a matter which was then in controversy. But whatever the matter was, the Evangelist says, "He astonished them all with his understanding and answers." So the glory of his Godhead began to shine even then. Through this we may note the wonderful power of the gospel: even the hard-hearted, who will not receive it, will be astonished by the bright beams of the truth shining in it. It also causes the godly to marvel, as we see with Mary and Joseph, but their admiration always ends with joy. A Sermon Preached in the Court at Greenwich.[15]

In Her Grief, Mary Thinks of Herself More Than of God. John Calvin: Those who think that the holy Virgin spoke in this manner for the purpose of showing her authority are, in my opinion, mistaken. It is even possible that it was not till they were apart, and the witnesses had withdrawn, that she began to expostulate with her son, after they had left the assembly. However that may be, this complaint was not the result of ambition but was the expression of grief, which had lasted three days. Yet the manner of her complaint, as if she had received an injury, shows how ready we are by nature to defend our own rights, even if it means neglecting God. The holy Virgin would a thousand times rather have died than deliberately preferred herself to God, but in the indulgence of a mother's grief, she falls into it without thinking. And undoubtedly this example warns us that we ought to be suspicious of all the affections of the flesh and should certainly beware

---

[12]Lightfoot, *Harmony, Chronicle and Order of the New Testament,* 7-8*.
[13]LW 76:200* (cf. WA 17,2:24; E² 11:26-27); quoting Jn 18:36.

[14]Vergil, *The Aeneid* 10.639.
[15]Gilpin, *Godly Sermon,* 7-8*; citing Acts 4:13-16.

that, by grasping after our rights and what we want for ourselves more than is proper, we might defraud God of his honor. COMMENTARY ON A HARMONY OF THE GOSPELS.[16]

CHRIST LIVED IN PERFECT OBEDIENCE TO THE FATHER. BERNARD GILPIN: Mary seems to charge him with breaking the fourth commandment, in that he had not treated his parents well. But Christ so shapes his answer that he takes away her whole complaint. In this way he teaches us how the precepts of the second table [of the Ten Commandments] may not be understood as in any way a hindrance to the first. "Did you not know that I must go about my Father's business?" Where our duty and service to God are concerned, all human service and obedience which might be a hindrance to it must stand back and give place, no matter to whom it is, father or mother, king or emperor. Besides this, he teaches us here a most necessary lesson that we should all learn and take with us: his whole life and death were nothing else but perfect obedience to the will of his heavenly Father, and he was always fully occupied in that task. He teaches us that if we look to be children and co-heirs by adoption along with Christ of his Father's kingdom, we must also along with our Master and Lord yield ourselves up wholly to the will of our heavenly Father and always be occupied in his business. "*Exemplum dedi vobis:* I have given you an example, that you also should do as I have done to you." A SERMON PREACHED IN THE COURT AT GREENEWITCH.[17]

HIS PARENTS DID NOT KNOW EVERYTHING, BUT ENOUGH TO BE THANKFUL TO GOD. MARTIN BUCER: Mary and Joseph knew that he was Christ, but as of yet they did not know how he should begin his office or yet the condition of those things which were done by him. Therefore they were kept still with a certain admiration for him and those things which he did, but especially when the spirit of God revealed itself more manifestly in him. And they were not even a bit unhappy because they did not know many of those things. For it is sufficient for everyone to know enough of the works of God that he might love him above all things and conform himself wholly to God's will. So it was enough for Mary and Joseph to know that they had Christ present with them, that they might diligently attend on him and might be thankful to the Father with their whole hearts, who had bestowed so great a grace on the world and especially on the Jews. As for the other things which were to be revealed to them, they were deferred until another time.

Therefore the godly think it sufficient to know the good will of God toward them in Christ, and how they are to be thankful to God for it. . . . The wicked omit these things and try to search out the secrets of God. And that is why it has come to pass that there are so many arguments and disputations about vain things among them. AN ECCLESIASTICALL EXPOSITION UPON SAINT LUKE 2.[18]

2:51-52 Jesus Obeys His Parents and Returns Home

JESUS TEACHES THAT OBEDIENCE TO SUPERIORS IS A VIRTUE. JOHN BOYS: As the former part of this gospel is a pattern for parents in how they should instruct their children, so this latter part is a mirror for children in how they should obey their parents: *omnis enim actio Christi, instructio Christiani*, for every action of Christ is a lesson for a Christian.[19] The Lord of all submitted himself to the government of his supposed father and under him his mother, as Jerome notes: "He venerated the mother of whom he himself was the Father; he respected the foster father whom he himself had fostered."[20] In fulfilling filial and economic duties in their house for the space of thirty years, what

---

[16]CTS 31:170* (CO 45:106).
[17]Gilpin, *Godly Sermon*, 8-9*; quoting Jn 13:15.
[18]Marlorat, ed., *Catholike and Ecclesiasticall Exposition of the Holy Gospell After S. Marke and Luke*, 119*.
[19]Innocent III, Sermon 22 de tempore; cited by Thomas in the *Summa* (IIIa.37.1).
[20]Jerome, *Epistle* 117, NPNF[2] 6:215-20, here 216.

does he teach except obedience to superiors? He teaches especially that children should honor father and mother, no matter how poor, for this subjection is a virtue, not a weakness.[21]

If parents demand things which are unlawful and contrary to Scripture, then, as commentators on this text frequently note, we must prefer our Father in heaven before our parents on earth and say with Christ, "How did it happen that you came looking for me? Did you not know that I must go about God's business?" Otherwise we should not offend them with so much as a look. For this, see the fifth commandment. The First Sunday After the Epiphanie.[22]

Like Mary, We Should Imprint These Words in Our Hearts. Martin Luther: It is to be noted that the Evangelist says: "His mother kept all these words in her heart." This, too, is said for our admonition, so that we also endeavor to treasure God's Word in our hearts, as the dear Virgin did. When she saw that she had erred and had not understood, because she had learned her lesson, she became all the more diligent to impress on and treasure in her heart what she heard from Christ. Again, she gives us an example that we indeed should cling to the Word above all things and not let it out of our hearts but always focus on it, and learn to strengthen, comfort and grow

ourselves in it, which is very necessary. When things become serious and we are assailed or tested, then it is soon forgotten or lost, even among those who are diligent. The Church Postil (1540): First Sunday After Epiphany.[23]

Christ Made Manual Labor Holy. Johann Spangenberg: After this, what did he do from when he was twelve years old to when he was thirty? The Evangelists do not report anything special, other than that he was obedient to his parents, and so of course he helped to support them. He did not attend school as a child, for in John 7 the people said, "How does this man know the Scripture, when he has never studied?" He certainly was never idle, for he also had the Father's command: "In the sweat of your brow you will earn your bread." He passed the time working, framing and building houses. That is why the people said in Mark 6, "Isn't that the carpenter Jesus, Mary's son?" And now Christ, through the touch of his holy body, has made water, the cross and all suffering holy and beneficial. He has also made holy all crafts and all honest labor, so that whoever practices and conducts them in faith practices a holy work and receives through it God's blessing, and, finally, eternal life, Amen. Gospel on the First Sunday After Epiphany.[24]

---

[21]*Non infirmitatis sed pietatis.* Ambrose, *Expositio Evangelii Secundum Lucam* 2.2.

[22]Boys, *Exposition of the Dominical Epistles and Gospels,* 1:127*.

[23]LW 76:207* (WA 17,2:31-32; E² 11:36-37); quoting Lk 2:51.

[24]Spangenberg, *Postilla* (1582), XLVIr-v; quoting Jn 7:15; Gen 3:19; Mk 6:3.

3:1-20 THE MINISTRY OF JOHN THE BAPTIST

In the fifteenth year of the reign of Tiberius Caesar, Pontius Pilate being governor of Judea, and Herod being tetrarch of Galilee, and his brother Philip tetrarch of the region of Ituraea and Trachonitis, and Lysanias tetrarch of Abilene, ²during the high priesthood of Annas and Caiaphas, the word of God came to John the son of Zechariah in the wilderness. ³And he went into all the region around the Jordan, proclaiming a baptism of repentance for the forgiveness of sins. ⁴As it is written in the book of the words of Isaiah the prophet,

"The voice of one crying in the wilderness:
'Prepare the way of the Lord,ᵃ
  make his paths straight.
⁵Every valley shall be filled,
  and every mountain and hill shall be made low,
and the crooked shall become straight,
  and the rough places shall become level ways,
⁶and all flesh shall see the salvation of God.'"

⁷He said therefore to the crowds that came out to be baptized by him, "You brood of vipers! Who warned you to flee from the wrath to come? ⁸Bear fruits in keeping with repentance. And do not begin to say to yourselves, 'We have Abraham as our father.' For I tell you, God is able from these stones to raise up children for Abraham. ⁹Even now the axe is laid to the root of the trees. Every tree therefore that does not bear good fruit is cut down and thrown into the fire."

¹⁰And the crowds asked him, "What then shall we do?" ¹¹And he answered them, "Whoever has two tunicsᵇ is to share with him who has none, and whoever has food is to do likewise." ¹²Tax collectors also came to be baptized and said to him, "Teacher, what shall we do?" ¹³And he said to them, "Collect no more than you are authorized to do." ¹⁴Soldiers also asked him, "And we, what shall we do?" And he said to them, "Do not extort money from anyone by threats or by false accusation, and be content with your wages."

¹⁵As the people were in expectation, and all were questioning in their hearts concerning John, whether he might be the Christ, ¹⁶John answered them all, saying, "I baptize you with water, but he who is mightier than I is coming, the strap of whose sandals I am not worthy to untie. He will baptize you with the Holy Spirit and fire. ¹⁷His winnowing fork is in his hand, to clear his threshing floor and to gather the wheat into his barn, but the chaff he will burn with unquenchable fire."

¹⁸So with many other exhortations he preached good news to the people. ¹⁹But Herod the tetrarch, who had been reproved by him for Herodias, his brother's wife, and for all the evil things that Herod had done, ²⁰added this to them all, that he locked up John in prison.

a Or *crying, Prepare in the wilderness the way of the Lord*   b Greek *chiton*, a long garment worn under the cloak next to the skin

OVERVIEW: John is a transitional figure—an Old Testament-style prophet who also knew and preached Jesus, not just a long-awaited but still distant Messiah. Apart from Jesus, John is arguably the most important model for preachers in the New Testament. He lived an austere lifestyle, insisted on true repentance and real piety in his listeners (both internal and external) and offered baptism to those who believed. Not surprisingly, it is the baptism he offered that receives a great deal of attention here. Anabaptists see in John's example a central bulwark in their belief that a water baptism can be given only to those who first believe and repent—he taught the people, corrected them, called them to repentance and only then baptized them. Such actions, men like Peter Walpot claim, could not have included children, for they could not believe in the message or understand the sign.

Even Jesus was not baptized until he reached adulthood. But the alternate viewpoint is also represented here, although not always as obviously—John's water baptism was meant to prepare people for the coming baptism of the Spirit, not signal that it had already come. It was a humanly administered sign, as both Zwingli and Erasmus emphasize, to which the promise of Christ's grace was attached. The proponents of infant baptism do not defend it here (they do that in the following section, as well as elsewhere); instead they focus on John's message of repentance. Repentance always brings fruit: humility, holiness of life, works of charity. When the heart is turned back to God, people's lives are transformed. But when John said to share our clothes and food with others, did he mean that we should hold our goods in common? When he told the soldiers to be content with their wages and not to extort money, was he condemning war and the legitimate use of weapons? Not at all, say those concerned to counteract what they saw as the excesses of Anabaptism. John's message of repentance did not imply that Christians had to become extremists but rather that they should share with, help and protect others.

3:1-2 *The Historical Context of John's Ministry*

CHRISTIANITY BEGAN LONG BEFORE THE LIFE OF JESUS. JOHN WOOLTON: Eusebius Pamphilus, commending Christian faith and religion to the world, extols it not only for the reverend majesty which the name carries but also for its antiquity and ancientness, as having always been since the creation of the world, and through which alone all holy people have pleased God and attained to everlasting felicity.[1] His sentence and judgment might appear strange to some simple and unlearned persons, who carry that vain opinion that the Christian religion first began in the days of Tiberius Caesar. They are likely moved to that opinion by Saint Luke's Gospel, where it is written

that John the Baptist began to preach in the fifteenth year of Tiberius, and because histories generally consent that Jesus Christ, the Savior of the world, was crucified in the eighteenth year of the same emperor.

It cannot truly be denied that all prophecies were complete and true salvation perfected in that time. And it must be granted that Christ's most precious treasures were then opened and communicated to the world more plainly and plentifully than ever before. Yet the same salvation was shadowed long before by the prophets and promised to the ancestors in Christ Jesus. It came to pass that they foresaw in their spirit the Christ to come, and, as we now do, put their whole trust and confidence in him only. Indeed, these things are proposed, offered and exhibited most absolutely and clearly to us in the New Testament, and in the time of grace, which they under the law had in hope, and that certain, although somewhat more obscurely than we now have, and looked for it with most constant and ardent minds. THE CHRISTIAN MANUAL (1576).[2]

WHY ARE THERE TWO HIGH PRIESTS? THE ENGLISH ANNOTATIONS: There were three degrees of ministers under the law: priests, Levites and *nethinim*.[3] Over these the high priest was chief, and that office was successively tied to the line of Aaron's firstborn—all the rest of his posterity were priests. But there was to be only one high priest, after whose death another was to succeed. That two are here named high priests together, some think is due to the Grecian kings who at their pleasure made high priests to officiate by the year, not for life. . . . Others impute this disorder and violation of God's law concerning the perpetuity of this office in one man during life to the power and covetousness of the Romans. But for a better resolution we must consider that the high priest

---

[1]Eusebius, *Ecclesiastical History* 1.4. 4.

[2]Woolton, *Christian Manual*, 16r-v*; citing Is 9; 1 Pet 1.
[3]This Hebrew word was usually transliterated rather than translated until the publication of the RSV, which rendered it as "temple servants"—subsequently followed by all major English translations except the NKJV. It literally means "dedicated ones."

also had his suffragan . . . who in the case of the high priest's pollution performed his office. (Such was Zephaniah, Jer 52:24.) . . . Here Caiaphas was the suffragan to Annas his father-in-law, who was the high priest. ANNOTATIONS UPON THE GOSPEL ACCORDING TO SAINT LUKE.[4]

THE AUTHORITY OF JOHN'S OFFICE AND COMMISSION.

JOHN CALVIN: Before relating, as the other Evangelists do, that John entered his teaching office, Luke asserts that he was divinely called to that office—demonstrating that his ministry has authority. Why interpreters have preferred to translate *upon* John rather than *to* John, I do not understand. Nevertheless because its meaning is not in the least ambiguous—clearly this commission was entrusted to him and he was given the command to preach—I have followed the received version.[5] From this, understand that there are no true teachers except those God has anointed with an office. Nor is it sufficient to have the Word of God, unless a special calling is added to it also. COMMENTARY ON A HARMONY OF THE GOSPELS.[6]

3:3-9 *John the Prophet Preaches Repentance*

JOHN'S LIFE AND WORDS INSPIRED OTHERS TO REPENTANCE AND BAPTISM.

KONRAD PELLIKAN: So up till now, John was concealed among the wild animals and passed his life in unusual austerity, hidden in clothing woven from camel's hair with a leather belt around his waist, living on wild honey and locusts, certainly never touching wine or strong drink, that he might be fit to be a preacher of repentance. He wanted first to teach by his life, and then by his words, so that he might be free from all accusations and have great liberty to rebuke the sins of others. Inspired and urged by the Spirit of God, he went forth from his hermit's refuge, but he did not head for the temple, which is the place given to Christ, but into all those regions which border on the river Jordan. Here there was plenty of water provided so that he might baptize. And so he preached the coming of the kingdom of heaven, encouraging them by the coming blessings that they might first prepare by repentance of life and baptism by water, which he gave as a forerunner so that they might be rendered suitable for the baptism of the spirit, which would be given by the one whose coming was imminent. COMMENTARY IN LUKE 3:3-6.[7]

JOHN WOULD NOT BAPTIZE CHILDREN.

PETER WALPOT: Children are not able to believe in God, the creator of heaven and earth, nor in Jesus Christ his Son, nor in the Holy Spirit. They have no knowledge of [Christ's] suffering, death, resurrection or his ascension, nor of eternal life, nor of the forgiveness of sins. They know nothing of the testament of God, the Gospels, baptism, the communion of saints, the Last Judgment, or even of the love of God or the neighbor, or of the will of God.

Whoever can teach an infant can also baptize him. But if you cannot teach him, so you also cannot baptize him. For baptism is "the washing of water with the word." . . . John the Baptist teaches the people he is going to baptize and does not allow anyone to be baptized unless he can testify that he believes in the forgiveness of sins. On account of his office, he did not allow any child to be baptized, for he baptized with the baptism of repentance, and he told the people that they should believe in the one who came after him, namely, in Christ, and that is something that children could not do. And not only in John's, but also in Christ's baptism, both word and external sign appear, through which God moves, frightens and cheers up the heart through faith—this happens when one hears the word and sees the sign. So neither John's nor Christ's baptism is appropriate for children,

---

[4]Downame, ed., *Annotations*, Ss3v*; citing 1 Chron 9:2; 2 Kings 22:8; 25:18; Jer 52:24; Jn 18:24, 13.
[5]That is, the Vulgate.
[6]CTS 31:177-78* (CO 45:111).

[7]Pellikan, *In Sacrosancta Quatuor Evangelia*, 42 (cf. LB 7:309); on rebuking sins, cf. Mt 3:4; Lk 1:15.

since they could not believe the word nor see the sign. For if John had not preached ahead of time, he would have had to pour out a great deal of water before he would have prepared the way of the Lord. For it is the recognition of sin, not the poured water, that drives us to Christ, since he is the way, the truth and the life.

Christ himself, our model, only first received baptism when he was thirty years old and was beginning his ministry. He did this as an example that we should not be baptized as children, until we come to a certain maturity and a good understanding and can set about [doing] God's will. THE GREAT ARTICLE BOOK: ON BAPTISM.[8]

THE PROPHECY OF ISAIAH IS FULFILLED.

MARTIN BUCER: In this passage, Isaiah prophesies of the preaching of the gospel, which would be begun by John but not finished. The prophet includes this under the type of the deliverance made by Cyrus. And so he writes, "Comfort, comfort my people, says your God. Speak tenderly to Jerusalem, and proclaim to her that her hard service has been completed, that her sin has been paid for. . . . A voice of one calling: 'In the desert prepare the way for the Lord; make straight in the wilderness a highway for our God.'" The sense and meaning of the words of the prophet are this: O chosen and true Israelites, he shall give the command to his preachers to preach a new consolation and the gospel of grace, that your hearts may be filled with courage and be joyful. He shall command them also to shout forth with a loud voice that the time is fulfilled in which he must fight with all kinds of evil, that iniquity is forgiven and pardoned, after he has received sufficient correction for all his sins. And shortly, the voice which is the proclaimer of felicity shall be

heard crying out in the wilderness, that is to say, among the people of Israel who are devoid of all piety. It shall exhort all people to prepare the way of the Lord and to make the path straight for our God; that is to say, they should put away all false religion and other sins, and all ridiculous trust in the law and in human reason, and receive the obedience of the Word of God and faith in Christ. By these means every valley shall be exalted and every hill brought low; that is to say, whatever shall be inconvenient or in the Lord's way will be removed. Human traditions which are against the Word of God will be condemned, trust in works will fail, pride in reason will be forsaken, the flesh with its vices and concupiscence will be crucified and people will repent and be renewed. Then the glory of the Lord will be revealed by the gospel throughout the whole world, and all flesh, that is to say, all mortal beings, will see, acknowledging by true faith that the mouth of the Lord has spoken the truth. They will see the Messiah offered to them by whom God has appointed salvation for all humankind. AN ECCLESIASTICALL EXPOSITION UPON SAINT LUKE 3.[9]

JOHN DEMANDS TRUE REPENTANCE, WHICH SHOWS IN THE FRUITS.

DESIDERIUS ERASMUS: "You generation of vipers," John says, "most vicious and corrupt children of most vicious and corrupt ancestors, from whence have you perceived that the vengeance of God hangs over you, unless you amend your lives at the right time? Who has given you warning that you should flee from the immediate, severe judgment of God, who shall show mercy to no generation, no nation, or any person of high or low status? Just as the remedy is offered to everyone who will yield himself to be cured, so punishment remains for all those without exception who refuse to change from their former ways. Why did the love of God not draw you before, where now the fear of punishment drags you? Your hearts are not yet changed. But

[8]QGT 12:62-63; quoting Eph 5:26; alluding to Jn 14:6. Walpot says a little later that "children have not committed any real sins, therefore they do not need the baptism of repentance, nor any improvement" (76). Most Anabaptists agreed with Walpot that children were not accountable for their sin until it was "intentional." See further Thomas N. Finger, *A Contemporary Anabaptist Theology: Biblical, Historical, Constructive* (Downers Grove, IL: InterVarsity Press, 2004), 160-70, esp. 168-69.

[9]Marlorat, ed., *Catholike and Ecclesiasticall Exposition of the Holy Gospell After S. Marke and Luke*, 123-24*; quoting Is 40:1-3.

after this, if you truly repent of your past life and take up other habits, then you will declare by these deeds that your lives have been reformed. Up until now like the wild trees in a forest, you have brought forth the sour and deadly fruits of evil works: pride, wrathfulness, greed, jealousy, hypocrisy and contention. Now if you have truly transformed into good trees, bring forth the good fruits, that they may testify that your hearts have changed to a better state. It is not necessary to change your clothes or the kind of food you eat, but you must change the improper passions of your hearts. This is the root of the tree, which if it has bitter and noxious sap, will produce evil fruit from its branches; but if contrary to this, the root fills the tree with sweet and healthy sap, the fruits of the spirit that are worthy of God will grow on its branches: instead of hatred, there will be love; instead of bitterness, gladness; instead of discord, peace; instead of aggressiveness, tolerance; instead of greed, beneficence; instead of immodesty, chastity; instead of deceitfulness, candor; instead of arrogance, modesty; instead of superstition, true piety." PARAPHRASE ON THE GOSPEL OF LUKE 3:7-8.[10]

THE SPIRIT SEPARATES THE BAD FROM THE GOOD, CONDEMNING THE BAD. FRANÇOIS LAMBERT: The trees are people—the good trees are believers and the bad are unbelievers. The ax is the Spirit of God, which is the most penetrating of Scripture, but also has unchanging judgment. The ax stands at the root of the trees that it might separate out the bad, because they do not believe the truth which is revealed through Christ, and so he reveals most plainly that the eternal judgment will be death for the accused. The good trees, however, he leaves, that they might produce fruit. He directs those who are faithful and true, that they might always produce plentifully the desired fruits of eternal welfare. To be sure, the Spirit, through unchanging judgment and the Word of God, rejects the impious and unbelievers, just as

the roots are broken off and separated by the ax. COMMENTARY IN LUKE 3:9.[11]

3:10-14 *John Teaches the People*

JOHN DEMANDS CHARITY RATHER THAN CEREMONIES. JOHN CALVIN: A true feeling of repentance produces an anxiety that causes the sinner to seek eagerly after what it is that God desires and commands. But John's reply briefly explains the fruits worthy of repentance; for the world always desires to discharge its duty toward God with ceremonies, and everyone is inclined to give fictitious worship to God, whenever he invites us to repentance. But what fruits does the Baptist here recommend? The duties of charity and the second table of the law: not that God does not attend to the external profession of piety and worship of him, but because this is a more certain sign of distinction and less often leads to error. The hypocrites trouble themselves excessively to prove themselves to God through the performance of ceremonies, but they forget about caring for true justice, for they are either cruel to their neighbors or addicted to deceit and robbery. That is why it is necessary to submit them to a more simplistic test and see whether they practice honesty toward others, or come to the aid of the poor, or show mercy to the wretched, or share generously what the Lord bestowed on them. For this reason, Christ particularly names "justice, mercy" and truth as the main points of the law, and Scripture recommends justice and judgment throughout.[12] We should first notice here that the duties of charity are named, not because they are better than the worship of God but because they testify to people's piety, in that they detect the pretense of those who brag with their mouths about things that are far away from their hearts. COMMENTARY ON A HARMONY OF THE GOSPELS.[13]

---

[10]Erasmus, *In Evangelivm Lvce Paraphrasis*, e7r-v (LB 7:310-11).

[11]Lambert, *In Divi Lucae*, I7r-v.
[12]Calvin here replaces the Matthean "faith" for "truth."
[13]CO 45:119 (cf. CTS 31:192-93); alluding to Mt 23:23.

THE SLAVE TO FASHION OPPOSES CHRISTIAN DOCTRINE. WILLIAM PERKINS: Vain and curious people are not competent judges of this matter, but rather we must regard the judgment and example of modest, grave and frugal persons in every order and estate, who by experience and knowledge are best able to determine what is necessary and what is not. Again, although we must not seek for more than necessary apparel, if God out of his goodness gives us the ability to have and maintain more, we must thankfully receive it and use it well to the good example of others.

But some will say, "It seems that we ought not to have much, although God gives the ability, because we may not have more than one coat. For John gives this rule: Let him that has two coats give to him that has none." Answer: John's meaning must be this: he that has not only necessary raiment, but more than necessary, must give of his abundance to those in need. For otherwise his rule should not agree with Christ's own practice, who himself had two coats, an inner and an upper garment, which he kept and wore, nor with Saint Paul's, who had both a cloak and a coat.

This rule exposes the common sinful practice of many people in the world. The greater sort of people are exceedingly careful, by all means and ways, to follow the fashion and to take up every newfangled attire, whenever it comes abroad. This is a course completely contrary to Christ's doctrine, which commands an honest care only for necessary ornaments, and condemns the contrary. This is for good reason, as inordinate and affected care is commonly a great pickpocket. It fills people's heads and hearts with vain and foolish thoughts; it makes them wastefully abuse the blessing God has given to them, whereby they are disabled from helping others who are in need. Rather, the first and principal care ought to be for the adorning of the soul with grace and putting on the Lord Jesus: this will yield more comfort to the mind and conscience than any external consideration to the outward state of humanity. WHAT IS THE RIGHT, LAWFUL AND HOLY USE OF APPAREL?[14]

COMMON OWNERSHIP OF GOODS IS NOT REQUIRED FOR CHRISTIANS. JOHNANNES BRENZ: John did not appoint here that people's goods should be held in common, as the Anabaptists teach and the seditious desire, neither does he take away the civil division of things, ordained by public laws. For although riches are sometimes spoken against because of the evil abuse of them, in themselves they are part of God's good creation and are God's gift. The blessing of the Lord, says Solomon, brings wealth. And in Job it is said, "And the Lord made him prosperous again and gave him twice as much as he had before." And the Lord also said to Solomon, "I will give you what you have not asked for—both riches and honor—so that in your lifetime you will have no equal among kings." Thus you see by the testimony of God's Word that riches are the gift of God. Anyone who denies it to be lawful for a Christian to have and to possess the gifts of God is lacking in shame, for the earth is the Lord's and everything in it. And Christians also belong to the Lord. Why is it, then, that they should not lawfully possess the gifts of the Lord their God? Moreover, we must remember what is written in the law, "You shall not steal." This commandment undoubtedly confirms the division of things, and superiority. But if it were ungodly for a person to possess his own goods, then there would be no need to label anything wicked theft; just as he who uses the air does not commit theft, because by natural right the air is common to everyone. . . . And so in this sermon, John does not teach a new law but expounds and interprets the old and natural law, not only to the Jews but also to the Gentiles. For the natural law is this: "So in everything, do to others what you would have them do to you." AN ECCLESIASTICALL EXPOSITION UPON SAINT LUKE 3.[15]

FAITH WITHOUT CHARITY AND EQUITY IS DEAD. THE ENGLISH ANNOTATIONS: Here John criticizes the unjust exactions whereby such men

---

[14]Perkins, *Whole Treatise of the Cases of Conscience*, 134-35*.

[15]Marlorat, ed., *Catholike and Ecclesiasticall Exposition of the Holy Gospell After S. Marke and Luke*, 126-27*; citing Prov 10:22; Job 42:10; 1 Kings 3:13; Ps 24:1; 1 Cor 10:26; Ex 20:15; Mt 7:12.

commonly grieve the people. Therefore in Luke 19:8, Zaccheus in his conversion proclaims restitution, without which (where there is any ability) there can be no true repentance. It is not that the office [of tax collector] was unlawful, but rather that oppression and religion are inconsistent. Therefore of the many sins for which John the Baptist might have admonished them, he noted only this one to which they were commonly given and which cannot stand with charity and equity, without which faith is dead and all religion counterfeit. ANNOTATIONS UPON THE GOSPEL ACCORDING TO SAINT LUKE 3:14.[16]

WAR IS NOT IN ITSELF WRONG, ONLY THE MISUSE OF IT. MARTIN LUTHER: There are some who misuse this office, and slaughter and kill needlessly, from sheer maliciousness, but that is the fault of those people, not of the office. After all, is there any office, type of work or anything so good that malicious, bad people do not misuse or abuse it? They are just like crazy doctors, who would cut off a perfectly good hand, not because the person needed it removed but simply because they felt like it. They are part of that universal unrest and lack of peace which must be restrained by legitimate war and the sword, and forced into peace. It always happens, and always has happened, that those who begin war unnecessarily are defeated, for in the end they cannot escape God's judgment, that is, his sword. He finds them and strikes them in the end, which is what happened to the peasants in the rebellion.[17]

To confirm this, we have the greatest preacher and teacher after Christ, namely, John the Baptist. When soldiers came to him and asked what they should do, he did not condemn their occupation or tell them to give it up, but he rather confirmed

it even more and said, "Be content with your wages, and commit no violence or wrong against anyone." And so he himself praised the office of soldier, but at the same time he restrained and forbade the misuse of it. For the abuse does not have to do with the office. Thus Christ, when he stood before Pilate, acknowledged that war was not wrong, for he said, "If I were the king of this world, my servants would fight to keep me from being handed over to the Jews." Here we also remember all the stories of war in the Old Testament, the stories of Abraham, Moses, Joshua, the judges, Samuel, David and all of the kings of the people of Israel. If war or the profession of soldier was in itself wrong and displeasing to God, we would have to condemn Abraham, Moses, Joshua, David and all the other holy fathers, kings and princes who served God in this occupation and whose works are well-known and celebrated in Scripture. WHETHER SOLDIERS TOO CAN BE SAVED (1526).[18]

A TRUE LOVER OF GOD CANNOT COMMIT VIOLENCE. HANS DENCK: For it is the nature of love not to intend or desire to be harmful to anyone but to serve for the betterment of all as much as he is able. Let one who is father of a family deal with his wife and child, servant and maid, as he would have God deal with him—to which love does not object. And, insofar as it is possible for a government to act in similar fashion, it also might well be Christian in its realm. But, since the world will never tolerate this, a friend of God therefore should and must not advance into but rather out of government if he wishes to have Christ as his Lord and Master. He who loves the Lord loves him whatever his profession may be, but he should not forget what befits a true lover, namely, that he should renounce all violence for the Lord's sake and should not oppose being subject to others '"as to the Lord." But someone may say: Even so, John the Baptist did not abrogate and repudiate the vocation of the soldiers

---

[16]Downame, ed., *Annotations*, Ss3v*.

[17]Although Luther initially supported the demands of peasants for better treatment in the uprisings of the mid-1520s, his views changed when the revolts became violent and, in his eyes, opposed to legitimate rule. His role in the "revolution of the common man" is still debated. See, for example, Peter Blickle, *The Revolution of 1525: The German Peasants' War from a New Perspective* (Baltimore: Johns Hopkins University Press, 1985).

[18]WA 19:627 (LW 46:97-98); citing Jn 18:36.

when they asked him what they should do. Response: The Law and the Prophets continued until John. But John did not come to annul the law, for it belongs only to the Light itself to do this insofar and inasmuch as it should happen. For John was not that Light but only a witness to the Light. The One who takes away sin may also take away the Law; that is the Lamb of God, Jesus Christ, to whom John pointed. He proclaimed the wrath of God on all who do not abide in the words of the Law in order that they be converted. But Christ first proclaimed and freely offered grace to these in order that they might live without reproach according to God's good pleasure. CONCERNING TRUE LOVE (1527).[19]

3:15-18 *John Is Not the Coming Messiah*

JOHN'S SACRAMENT DOES NOT GIVE THE SPIRIT. HULDRYCH ZWINGLI: It is as if John should say: "I am not the one who you have assumed me to be. I am only a servant and minister of outward signs and sacraments, not one who can provide you with grace and the Spirit. Strictly speaking, I pour water onto the body—I cannot change a mind or a heart. I bathe the body with outward water, and I admonish through teaching and the word, but I am not truly able to illuminate and confirm by the Spirit internally. After me comes one who baptizes with the Spirit, that is, who strengthens the heart and washes clean and purifies by the water of grace." Therefore ministers of the Word and sacraments employ external things and administer them according to the precepts of the Lord, but within the soul they do no work. However, the Word and sacraments are employed in vain externally, unless the heart is pulled and illuminated through the Spirit internally. It is the Spirit alone who writes the law of God in human hearts. Sacraments are external signs of an invisible and spiritual thing—they do not give grace, and they do not strengthen faith.[20] Rather, they serve the weakness of the flesh and the senses in obedience of faith. We have two sacraments in the church of Christ: baptism, by which we are received into the church and the people of Christ; and the Eucharist, by which we give thanks to the Lord for his death on our behalf. IN THE GOSPEL OF LUKE 3.[21]

JOHN ACKNOWLEDGES THAT HIS BAPTISM CANNOT CONVEY THE SPIRIT WITHOUT CHRIST. DESIDERIUS ERASMUS: Here John makes Christ the author of spiritual baptism, but also a minister of the external thing. He seems here to prevent beforehand, secretly, a question that might be raised as an objection: that is, to what end and purpose did the baptism which he received serve? This was no small trifle, that he brought a new and unusual thing into the church of God that is especially designed for a new kind of beginning, and that should be more perfect and better than the law of God. Therefore he answers that he has done nothing rashly, and that although he was a minister of the outward sign, yet he did nothing at all to diminish the virtue and power of God. And so we may easily gather that it was not part of his meaning to distinguish and make a difference between his baptism and what Christ commanded his disciples to use, and which use he would also have continually established in the church. He also did not compare the visible sign with the invisible, but, comparing the persons of the servant and the lord together, he teaches what is proper. Pertaining to the servant, he also teaches what is due and right that he should render to the lord. Out of this we can gather a general doctrine, that is to say, what is the human part in baptism and what is properly the part of the Son of God. We see that the

---

[19]Denck, *Spiritual Legacy*, 201*; alluding to Lk 3:14; Mt 11:13; Jn 1:8, 29, 36.

[20]Here Zwingli subverts the dominant medieval understanding of a sacrament as an outward and visible sign of inward and spiritual grace; for him a sacrament is merely a sign like the insignia on a soldier's uniform and nothing more (see ZSW 4:216-17; cf. LCC 24:130-31). For the reaffirmation of the Catholic view, see *The Catechism of the Council of Trent*, trans. J. Donovan (Baltimore: F. Lucas, 1829), 99-101, 109-12.

[21]*D. Hvldrichi Zvinglii in Plerosqve Novi Testamenti Libros*, 201-2.

administration of the outward and visible sign is only what is committed to human beings, while the truth itself remains only in Christ. AN ECCLESIASTICALL EXPOSITION UPON SAINT MATHEWE 3.[22]

CHRIST WIELDS THE WINNOWING FORK OF THE GOSPEL. JOHN CALVIN: In the previous verse, John preached about the grace of Christ, so that the people might give themselves up to him to be renewed; now, however, he discusses judgment, so that he might cause fear in those despisers. For since there are always many hypocrites who proudly reject the grace of Christ offered to them, likewise it is necessary that they be warned about the vengeance which waits for them. For this reason John describes Christ here as a severe judge against unbelievers. And this is a sequence that should be maintained by us in our teaching, so that hypocrites might know that those who reject Christ are not going to go away unpunished. Then, in stirring up their sluggishness, they might begin to be afraid of the one who avenges, whom they rejected as the author of salvation.

Next, I do not doubt that John also wanted to teach what Christ was going to bring about through his gospel. Therefore, the preaching of the gospel is the winnowing fork, or fan, since before the Lord sifts us, all the world is disabled by confusion, each one seeks out his own pleasure and the good is mixed in with the bad—in short, it is absolutely necessary to blow out the chaff. But when Christ brings forth his gospel to the public, when he proves consciences guilty and summons them to God's tribunal, the chaff which had covered the threshing floor is blown away. Although the gospel also purges away the chaff for each one of us, here John compares the reprobate with chaff and the faithful with wheat. Consequently the "threshing floor" is not taken to mean the world, as some people like to think, but the church, which we can see if we take into account the people to whom he is speaking. The people were puffed up with the mere title [of the people of God], but John warns them that they are foolish to be proud simply because for the time being they might occupy God's church. Soon they will be thrown out just as chaff is blown away from the threshing floor. In this way he touches on the corrupt character of the church at the time, since it was crowded with husks, dirt and other junk, but it would soon be purged by the living breeze of the gospel. But how is Christ said to separate the chaff from the wheat, when there is nothing but chaff in every human being? The response is easy: the elect are to be formed into wheat, so that, freed from chaff, they may be collected into the storehouse. Christ began this other cleansing and daily accomplishes it; nevertheless the process will not be complete until the Last Day. That is why John brings it to our attention. But let us remember: today, the faithful enter through hope into God's storehouse, which they will finally have in reality as their eternal home; likewise the reprobate now experience truly in guilt the burning of that fire whose actual burning they will feel on the Last Day. COMMENTARY ON A HARMONY OF THE GOSPELS.[23]

3:19-20 Herod Imprisons John

JOHN RISKED HIS LIFE TO SPEAK THE TRUTH TO HEROD. ERASMUS SARCERIUS: John did not only preach to common folks but also to princes, and especially to Herod, the tetrarch of Galilee, who was also named Antipas, of whom Mark writes: "Herod feared John and protected him, knowing him to be a righteous and holy man. When Herod heard John, he was greatly puzzled, yet he liked to listen to him." Moreover, John did not only preach faith and the fruits of faith to Herod but also, not fearing the cruelty and power of the wicked king but using the holy liberty of preaching and Christian fortitude, reproved his wickedness, first his incestuous marriage, then his other wicked acts. For there is no doubt that

---

[22]Marlorat, ed., *Catholike and Ecclesiasticall Exposition of the Holy Gospell After S. Mathewe,* 50*.

[23]CO 45:123-24 (cf. CTS 31:199-200).

Herod used tyranny, bullied the miserable people and oppressed the liberty of God's people. He set all things for sale in his kingdom and consumed all his money with luxury, excessive meat and drink and filthy pleasures.

So here the ministers of the church should learn not to dissemble or to hold their tongue at the wickedness of princes. For otherwise the Lord of justice will demand a payment for the blood of those that perish from that "dumb dog" that cannot bark, or that will not bark, his mouth being stopped up with fear. An Ecclesiasticall Exposition upon Saint Luke 3.[24]

Herod Imprisons John for Telling the Truth. François Lambert: You see that Herod is most wicked, and that above the rest of his crimes he is charged with seizing John and throwing him into prison. He would not endure patiently with the word of truth from John but imprisoned him, and for no more serious a crime than that John opposed him with the word of truth and the Holy Spirit. Commentary in Luke 3:20.[25]

---

[24]Marlorat, ed., *Catholike and Ecclesiasticall Exposition of the Holy*

Gospell After S. Marke and Luke, 131*; citing Mk 6:20.
[25]Lambert, *In Divi Lucae*, K2v.

3:21-38 THE BAPTISM AND GENEALOGY OF JESUS

²¹Now when all the people were baptized, and when Jesus also had been baptized and was praying, the heavens were opened, ²²and the Holy Spirit descended on him in bodily form, like a dove; and a voice came from heaven, "You are my beloved Son;ᵃ with you I am well pleased."ᵇ

²³Jesus, when he began his ministry, was about thirty years of age, being the son (as was supposed) of Joseph, the son of Heli, ²⁴the son of Matthat, the son of Levi, the son of Melchi, the son of Jannai, the son of Joseph, ²⁵the son of Mattathias, the son of Amos, the son of Nahum, the son of Esli, the son of Naggai, ²⁶the son of Maath, the son of Mattathias, the son of Semein, the son of Josech, the son of Joda, ²⁷the son of Joanan, the son of Rhesa, the son of Zerubbabel, the son of Shealtiel,ᶜ the son of Neri, ²⁸the son of Melchi, the son of Addi, the son of Cosam, the son of Elmadam, the son of Er, ²⁹the son of Joshua, the son of Eliezer, the son of Jorim, the son of Matthat, the son of Levi, ³⁰the son of Simeon, the son of Judah, the son of Joseph, the son of Jonam, the son of Eliakim, ³¹the son of Melea, the son of Menna, the son of Mattatha, the son of Nathan, the son of David, ³²the son of Jesse, the son of Obed, the son of Boaz, the son of Sala, the son of Nahshon, ³³the son of Amminadab, the son of Admin, the son of Arni, the son of Hezron, the son of Perez, the son of Judah, ³⁴the son of Jacob, the son of Isaac, the son of Abraham, the son of Terah, the son of Nahor, ³⁵the son of Serug, the son of Reu, the son of Peleg, the son of Eber, the son of Shelah, ³⁶the son of Cainan, the son of Arphaxad, the son of Shem, the son of Noah, the son of Lamech, ³⁷the son of Methuselah, the son of Enoch, the son of Jared, the son of Mahalaleel, the son of Cainan, ³⁸the son of Enos, the son of Seth, the son of Adam, the son of God.

a Or my Son, my (or the) Beloved   b Some manuscripts beloved Son; today I have begotten you   c Greek Salathiel

OVERVIEW: In this section on Jesus' baptism, some support is provided for infant baptism: because we know from historical sources (Maimonides) that Jews baptized both little children and adults, we know that it was a common practice in Jesus' day to baptize infants. For some interpreters, the fact that Jesus did not specifically address and condemn the practice means that he accepted it and wanted it to continue. But the question concerning the baptism of infants was by no means the only, or even the most important, matter to address when looking at Jesus' baptism. Why did Jesus present himself for baptism when he had no sin? What would have been the purpose of a "baptism of repentance" for someone who had nothing to repent? This sacramental moment between Jesus and John was highly significant in that the sinless Jesus chose to be baptized to connect himself with us—his baptism represented, in a sense, his taking up the cross on our behalf. By binding himself to us, he took our sins on himself and accepted his role as our Savior. He also, not surprisingly, revealed himself to his witnesses as the beloved of the divine—the Son of God. The presence of the Father (through the heavenly voice), the Son and the Spirit (as a dove) affirmed, as it had for the fathers of the church, the nature of God as a Trinity of persons but a unity of Godhead.

The genealogy of Jesus, as presented by Luke, led these writers to consider both the broader questions of Jesus' identity and the differences between Matthew's and Luke's presentations of Jesus' background. Why is it that different ancestors are mentioned by Matthew and Luke, and why does Matthew record back only to Abraham, while Luke uncovers Jesus' ancestry all the way back to Adam and then to God? Everyone agrees that Matthew and Luke had different purposes in composing their lists (no one suggests that they had access to different sources on these points). Matthew, of a Jewish background writing to Jews, showed Jesus to be descended of David through the royal line (more appropriate for the Jewish Messiah). Likewise, Abraham as the father of the Jewish nation was the appropriate terminal point for a genealogy written for a Jewish audience. Luke, however, was a Gentile, and writing to help convert Gentiles to the faith. Thus he stresses that Jesus shares a background with all of us, as he is a son of Adam, descended of Gentiles. Luke reveals Jesus as the "seed of the woman," promised to Adam, sent to destroy Satan by the Word, and it is thus appropriate that the genealogy stands not in the birth narrative but at the beginning of his ministry.

In a broader sense, Luke's genealogy reveals Jesus not only as the Jewish Messiah, the Son of David, and not even only as the son of Adam, an "everyman" for a Gentile audience, but as the Son of God. By extension, then, Luke's Gospel underlines the union of Jesus' divine and human natures and emphasizes that it is through our relationship with him that we too become sons and daughters of God.

3:21-22 The Baptism of Jesus

Baptizing Infants Was the Common Practice of Jesus' Day. John Lightfoot: Baptism had been in long and common use among the Jews many generations before John the Baptist came, using it for admission of proselytes into their church and baptizing men, women and children for that end. . . . As we read in Maimonides, "An Israelite who takes a little heathen child, or who finds a heathen infant, and baptizes him as a proselyte, behold, that makes him a proselyte."[1]

Hence a ready reason may be given why there is so little mention of baptizing infants in the New Testament, and why there is neither plain precept nor example for it, which is the argument some make against it: the reason is that no such mention was needed, as the baptizing of infants was as ordinarily used among the Jews as it ever has been in the Christian church. It was enough to mention that Christ established baptism as an ordinance under the gospel, and then who it was who should be baptized was well enough known by the use of this ordinance of old. Therefore it is a good argument to make, that because there is no clear forbidding of the baptizing of infants in the gospel, ergo they are to be baptized. For because it was in common use among the Jews, that infants as well as men and women should be baptized, our Savior would have given some special prohibition if he intended that they should have been excluded. Silence in this case necessarily brings us to the conclusion that he approved that the practice which had been long in use should be continued. Harmony of the New Testament, section 9.[2]

Baptism Bound Christ to His Salvific Work for Sinners. William Cowper: But now let us come and see why Jesus is baptized, seeing that he had neither sin to be forgiven nor nature to be renewed. The reasons are many, but we will especially speak of three, the first of which he gave himself: when John refused to baptize him, suggesting that he had more need to be baptized by Jesus, he received this answer, "Let it be so now, for it is proper for us to fulfill all righteousness."

As for the righteousness of the moral law, he had fulfilled it perfectly from his youth, for he was the innocent Lamb of God, without spot or blemish, and guile was never found in his mouth. But now he wants to say, "There is more required of me than just the performance of that common law given to everyone; there is the singular law of the redeemer, which I have yet to fulfill." This law was

---

[1]Maimonides' Code, Avadim 8. Maimonides was one of the most significant Torah scholars and rabbis of the medieval period, conveying the thought of Aristotle (along with the Muslim Averroës) to the west.

[2]Lightfoot, *Harmony, Chronicle and Order of the New Testament*, 10*.

never imposed on any angel or person but only on the Son of God, Christ Jesus, by which he was so bound to love his Father that it was fitting for him to vindicate the glory both of his justice and of his mercy, and so bound to love his brothers and sisters that it was fitting for him to take the debt of their sins on him, to satisfy his Father's justice for them. "This is that high point of righteousness," our Savior wants to say, "which I have yet to fulfill and for which I must be baptized. For in receiving baptism, I become obliged to do for my brothers and sisters what they could not do for themselves." For just as when a man received circumcision, by that very same deed he became bound to fulfill the whole law, so when a person receives baptism, that one is obliged to every condition of that covenant of which baptism is a seal. THE BAPTISM OF CHRIST.[3]

JOHN TESTIFIES THAT JESUS IS THE ONE WHO BAPTIZES WITH THE SPIRIT.

PHILIPP MELANCHTHON: This opening of the heavens that is specified here signifies that this man is the one who would come from heaven and would teach heavenly things, that is, he would show the will of his Father to heavenly people. Furthermore it signifies that he is the one who by his incarnation and blood would make unity between human things and heavenly things, as Saint Paul wrote to the Ephesians and the Colossians. Third, it signifies that he is that same Christ who made for us free passage and recourse to the throne of his grace, because he broke open the gates of heaven for us. In short, what was revealed to Jacob in his vision of the opening of the heavens and of the ladder which reached from the earth up to heaven is declared from above by this inauguration and celebration of Christ.

And John himself said in another place, "I did not know him, but he that sent me to baptize with water said to me: 'The one on whom you shall see the Spirit descend and stay on him, he is the one who baptizes with the Holy Spirit.' I have seen

and I testify that this is the Son of God." AN ECCLESIASTICALL EXPOSITION UPON SAINT MATHEWE 3.[4]

CHRIST'S BAPTISM PROVES A TRINITARIAN GOD.

THOMAS BECON: When it was time to create human beings, God the Father said to the Son and to the Holy Spirit, "Let us make man like unto our own similitude and image." In these two words, us and our, is declared the plurality of persons; and in these two words, similitude and image, is expressed the unity or singularity of the Godhead in the Trinity of persons. The holy Scripture testifies that Abraham saw three and worshiped one: that is to say, three in the propriety of persons, and one in the unity of the divine substance. The prophet Isaiah heard seraphim crying: "Holy, holy, holy, the Lord God of hosts." By the thrice repetition of this word *holy*, the three persons in the Trinity are expressed to us, but by the denomination of God, one Deity or one only divine substance of those three persons is declared to us. Likewise, as by the one naming of the Lord of hosts, the lordship, kingdom, majesty, power and authority of this one God is understood to be all one and the same. The psalmist also writes in this manner: "By the Word of the Lord the heavens were made sure, and with the Spirit of his mouth all the power of them." Here likewise is set forth for us that there are three persons in the Godhead. The Father is called the Lord, the Son the Word and the Holy Spirit the Spirit. In the evangelical history we read that when Christ was baptized, the Father from heaven was heard saying, "This is my well-beloved Son, in whom I have great delight." We read also that the Holy Spirit came down from heaven in the likeness of a dove and rested on Christ. Here it is most evident that in that most blessed, glorious and everlasting Godhead there are three persons, the Father, the Son and the Holy Spirit. THE SECOND PART OF THE CATECHISM. OF FAITH.[5]

---

[3]Cowper, *Three Heavenly Treatises*, 62-64*; citing Mt 3:15; 1 Pet 1:19; Is 53:9; Gal 5:3.

[4]Marlorat, ed., *Catholike and Ecclesiasticall Exposition of the Holy Gospell After S. Mathewe*, 54*; citing Eph 1; Col 1; Jn 1:31, 33-34.
[5]Becon, *Catechism*, 16-17*; citing Gen 1; 18; Is 6; Ps 33.

UNIFIED WITNESS OF THE TRINITY. PILGRAM MARPECK: The Son taught the physical words, which he himself was as the Word of the Father, and revealed the Father. Thus he was glorified before humanity as true God. The Holy Spirit, in the visible form of a dove, testified to the Son that God, the Creator of heaven and earth, was his Father. He also appeared as tongues of fire to the apostles. Although God is and remains a Spirit in three persons—Father, Word and Spirit—an eternally invisible heavenly unity, Father, Son and Holy Spirit nevertheless witnessed before humanity on earth in visible, physical form. KUNSTBUCH: CONCERNING THE LOWLINESS OF CHRIST.[6]

3:23-38 The Genealogy of Jesus

CHRIST IS THE TRUE SON OF GOD AND OF MAN. MARTIN BUCER: Now Luke shows the age of our Savior Christ at which he came not only to the office of teaching but also to the perfecting of salvation. Epiphanius calculates the years of his age diligently, disputing against the heresy number 51. Among other things, he says, "He was actually twenty-nine years and ten months old when he came to be baptized, so just about but not quite thirty years."[7] . . . He does not say that Joseph was his father, for he was only supposed to be the father of Christ. His true father was God, of whom he had his eternal and everlasting birth.

And so that all people might manifestly behold that this Jesus, the Son of the eternal God, is also the Son of Man, that as he is true God, so is he true man, Luke brings the genealogy of the Lord from Joseph to Zerubbabel, from him to David, from David to Abraham, from Abraham to Noah, from Noah to Adam, and yes, even to God himself,

the creator of Adam. AN ECCLESIASTICALL EXPOSITION UPON SAINT LUKE 3.[8]

DIFFERENCES IN JESUS' GENEALOGIES ARE BASED ON THEIR PURPOSES. JOHN LIGHTFOOT: Because Matthew's genealogy and this in Luke display a different lineage, so they also have different purposes. Matthew intends to show that Jesus Christ was the Son promised to David. Luke shows him to be the seed of the woman promised to Adam, who in the following section begins to break the head of the serpent. Therefore when that promise to Adam begins to take place in Christ entering on his ministry and in his being sealed as the Messiah by the Holy Spirit, this genealogy is divinely woven into the text.

Matthew derives his line by the pedigree of Joseph his supposed father and draws it from Solomon. Luke follows the pedigree of Mary his mother and draws it from Nathan. For as the Jews looked on him as the Son of David, they would regard the masculine and royal line as central; therefore Matthew gives it at his birth. But looked on as the seed promised to Adam, the seed of the woman, he was to be looked after by the line of his mother. And whereas the seed of the woman was to destroy the power of Satan by the word of truth, as Satan has destroyed humankind by words of falsehood, Luke properly draws his line up to Adam and includes it at this point when he is to begin to preach the Word. HARMONY OF THE NEW TESTAMENT, SECTION 10.[9]

JESUS AND ADAM ARE A PAIR, ALIKE AND DIFFERENT. JACQUES LEFÈVRE D'ÉTAPLES: This genealogy can be arranged in groups of fifteen as follows [see figure 1].

This diagram, drawn from Luke, appears in five groups of fifteen. Now, in each group of fifteen there is contained a group of seven and eight. And [Jesus] is at the top of the diagram when read from the new

---

[6]CRR 12:607-8 (QGT 17:583); citing 1 Jn 5:7; Jn 17:4; Mt 3:16-17; Mk 1:10; Lk 3:22; Jn 1:32; Acts 2:3.
[7]Epiphanius, *Panarion/Adversus Haereses*. Epiphanius (ca. 320-ca. 403), the bishop of Salamis in Cyprus, was involved in the Origenist controversies and became a friend of Jerome. He wrote this three-volume work cataloguing eighty heresies. It is translated into English as *The Panarion of Epiphanius of Salamis*, trans. by Frank Williams, Nag Hammadi Studies 35-36 (Leiden: Brill, 1987, 1994).
[8]Marlorat, ed., *Catholike and Ecclesiasticall Exposition of the Holy Gospell After S. Marke and Luke*, 132*.
[9]Lightfoot, *Harmony, Chronicle and Order of the New Testament*, 11*; citing Gen 3:15.

α JESUS

1	Joseph	Joseph	Matthat	Sala	Eber
2	Heli	Joda	Levi	Nahshon	Shelah
3	Matthat	Joanan	Simeon	Amminadab	Cainan
4	Levi	Rhesa	Judah	Aram	Arphaxad
5	Melchi	Zerubbabel	Joseph	Hezron	Shem
6	Jannai	Shealtiel	Jonam	Perez	Noah
7	Joseph	Neri	Eliakim	Judah	Lamech
8	Mattathias	Melchi	Melea	Jacob	Methuselah
9	Amos	Addi	Menna	Isaac	Enoch
10	Nahum	Cosam	Mattatha	Abraam	Jared
11	Esli	Elmadam	Nathan	Terah	Mahalaleel
12	Naggai	Er	David	Nahor	Cainan
13	Maath	Joshua	Jesse	Serug	Enos
14	Mattathias	Eliezer	Obed	Reu	Seth
15	Semein	Jorim	Boaz	Peleg	Adam

ω GOD

Figure 1.

to the old. Now if you add a group of seven and eight, a group of fifteen results. It is important that the first and the last names [that is, Jesus and God] are not contained in the sequence, but they precede and follow every number, and they are the beginning and end of all things—as is made clear in the first diagram.

When this genealogy is portrayed as a quadrangle [see figure 2], you can see how the beginning is joined to its end, and how Jesus and Adam have God as the source of their close relationship: Jesus by nature, Adam by creation. Both are the nearest to God, but Jesus is the greatest. Adam is related to God indirectly, Jesus properly; the one is transitory, the other eternal; the one has substance out of nothing, the other has substance of God. Both are of God, but Jesus, who is the Christ, is of God and at the same time is God. Adam is of God, but he himself is nothing, and yet he is not of himself but of God. If anyone is of himself and not of God, he is sin and is nothing. Christ is everything in truth; Adam is everything in likeness. Christ creates

everything, is capable of everything and is incapable of nothing. Adam creates nothing and is able to sin, but in that sense he is not able not to sin, and so the power to be able not to sin is withdrawn. And thus they answer in opposition: Christ, who is the second Adam, and Adam who is the first Adam, just like truth and its footprint, the artist and the work, light and shadow. In fact every person is a shadow, for only Christ is the light who unites the lowest and the highest, the one who is exalted over every creature. In the series of generations, which is from God the Father who is without beginning, Christ takes up the beginning, leading back to God the Father. To him, through him, in the Holy Spirit, be honor, glory and might, throughout all ages, Amen! IN THE GOSPEL OF LUKE 3.[10]

---

[10]Lefèvre d'Étaples, *Commentarii Initiatorii in Quatuor Evangelia*, 2:24v, 25v. Here Lefèvre—along with most of the reformers—follows the Majority text which harmonizes v. 33 with Mt 1:3. Thus it differs slightly from modern Bibles, which have Admin and Arni in place of Aram.

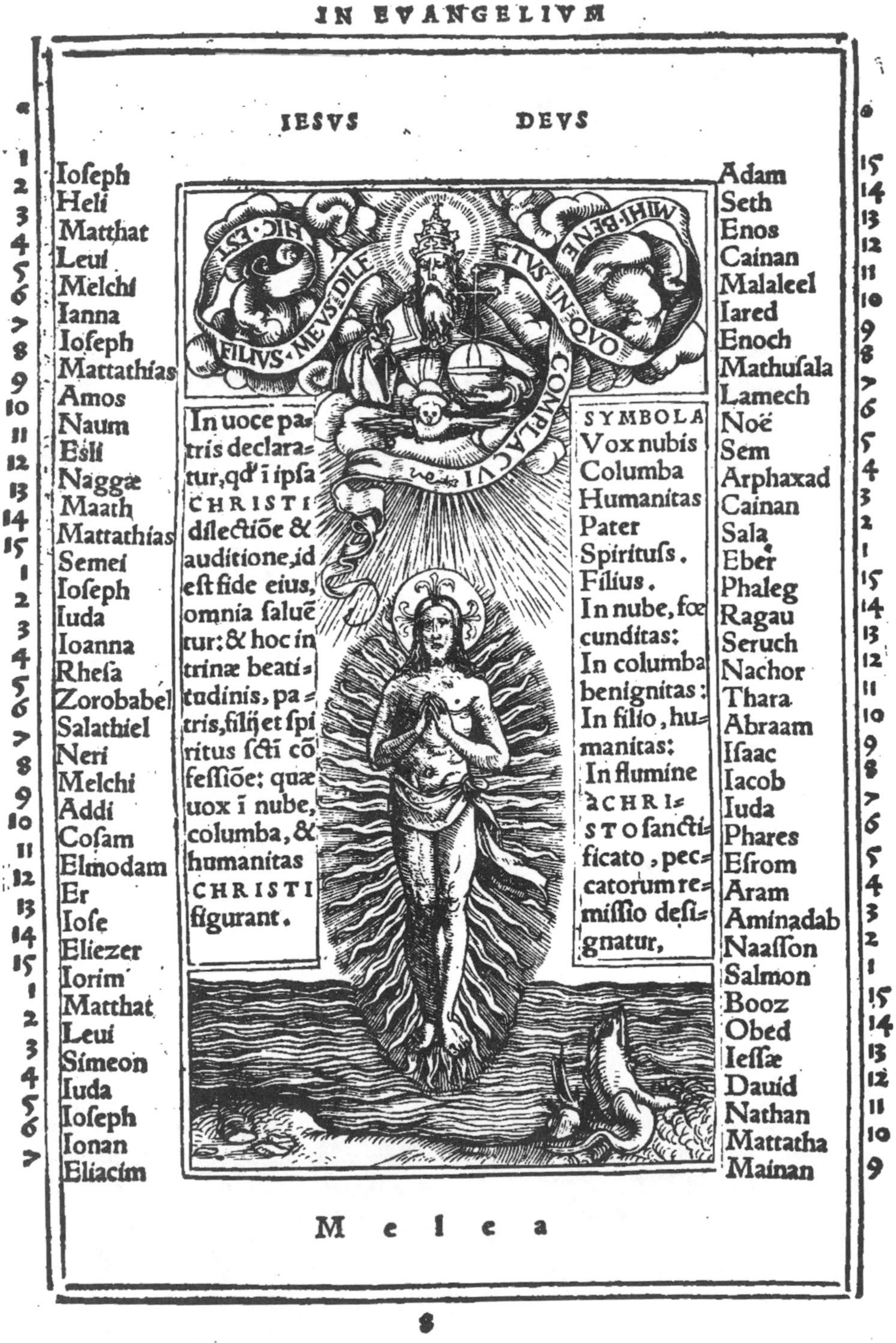
IN EVANGELIVM

IESVS DEVS

1 Ioſeph
2 Heli
3 Matthat
4 Leui
5 Melchi
6 Ianna
7 Ioſeph
8 Mattathias
9 Amos
10 Naum
11 Eſli
12 Naggæ
13 Maath
14 Mattathias
15 Semei
1 Ioſeph
2 Iuda
3 Ioanna
4 Rheſa
5 Zorobabel
6 Salathiel
7 Neri
8 Melchi
9 Addi
10 Coſam
11 Elmodam
12 Er
13 Ioſe
14 Eliezer
15 Iorim
1 Matthat
2 Leui
3 Simeon
4 Iuda
5 Ioſeph
6 Ionan
7 Eliacim

HIC EST FILIVS MEVS DILECTVS IN QVO MIHI BENE COMPLACVI

In uoce pa-
tris declara-
tur, qđ ĩ ipſa
CHRISTI
dilectiõe &
auditione, id
eſt fide eius,
omnia ſaluẽ
tur: & hoc in
trinæ beati-
tudinis, pa-
tris, filij et ſpi
ritus ſcti cõ
feſſiõe: quæ
uox ĩ nube,
columba, &
humanitas
CHRISTI
figurant.

SYMBOLA
Vox nubis
Columba
Humanitas
Pater
Spiritusſ.
Filius.
In nube, fœ-
cunditas:
In columba
benignitas:
In filio, hu-
manitas:
In flumine
à CHRI-
STO ſancti-
ficato, pec-
catorum re-
miſſio deſi-
gnatur,

Adam 15
Seth 14
Enos 13
Cainan 12
Malaleel 11
Iared 10
Enoch 9
Mathuſala 8
Lamech 7
Noë 6
Sem 5
Arphaxad 4
Cainan 3
Sala 2
Eber 1
Phaleg 15
Ragau 14
Seruch 13
Nachor 12
Thara 11
Abraam 10
Iſaac 9
Iacob 8
Iuda 7
Phares 6
Eſrom 5
Aram 4
Aminadab 3
Naaſſon 2
Salmon 1
Booz 15
Obed 14
Ieſſæ 13
Dauid 12
Nathan 11
Mattatha 10
Mainan 9

M e l e a

Figure 2. Image from Lefèvre's commentary on the Gospels (1526).

CHRIST DESCENDS FROM THE FAITHFUL OLD TESTAMENT BELIEVERS. RICHARD TAVERNER: Now Christ is called here the "son of David," and you must understand that he descended lineally from David according to the flesh, as Saint Paul declares in the beginning of his epistle to the Romans, so that we will not run into the errors of certain heretics who say that Christ was nothing else but a man and not the Son of God, but merely the son of David.[11] Christ discussed this error himself when he proposed this question to the Pharisees: "And what do you think of the Christ? Whose son is he?" And when they answered, "The son of David," he asked them, "Then why did David in the spirit call him 'Lord,' saying, 'The Lord said to my Lord, "Sit at my right hand?"'" By this he meant that Christ was above David, and not only a man but also God. So you must understand him to be the son or issue of David according to the flesh but not according to his Godhead. And you should also note that he is called the son of David after the manner of speaking of the Hebrews, because he came of the proper line of David. For the Hebrews call all nephews and nieces (no matter how distantly related) sons and daughters. Christ's whole pedigree is here drawn and conveyed from his ancestors, and it only includes those who were partakers of the promise which was made of Christ. Therefore you must mark out two different lines of people, which when they are well marked will show of whom Christ would be and was born. For although the promise of Christ was made to Adam, yet Christ's pedigree is not conveyed through Cain, his son. So there is one line, of the members of the true church, from which Christ's lineage is derived— that is, from the holy fathers and mothers who were partakers of the promise. And there is another line which contains the children who did not follow in their parents' footsteps and therefore are not partakers of the promise. If you diligently trace these two lines throughout the Old Testament, you will see that Christ proceeds from the faithful stock and not from that line which deviated, whose members include Cain, Esau and their offspring. And it was appropriate for Christ, the head of the church, to come from the members of the true church. ON THE DAY OF OUR LADY'S CONCEPTION.[12]

LUKE'S GENEALOGY EXTENDS TO ADAM FOR THE SAKE OF GENTILES. WILLIAM COWPER: The first group, then, is from Adam to Noah, and it contains ten fathers: Adam, Seth, Enoch, Kenan, Mahalaleel, Jared, Enoch, Methusaleh, Lamech and Noah. This is only from Saint Luke's reckoning, because Matthew goes no higher than Abraham. The reason for this diversity is that Saint Matthew in his writing had a special desire to move the Jews to accept the gospel and therefore begins it in a manner most plausible to them: "The book of the generation of Jesus Christ, the son of David, the son of Abraham." It was commonly believed by everyone at that time that the Messiah would be the son of David. But Saint Luke was, as Eusebius testifies, a Gentile by birth, born in Antioch, learned in medicine and now a proselyte, himself converted.[13] And so he writes his Gospel to convert others, and, especially for the comfort of believing Gentiles, he draws the lineage of Christ twenty degrees higher than Saint Matthew does, the one teaching us to seek the Savior of the world in the lineage of Abraham and David, the other again teaching how all believing people have their interest in Christ—not only those who are of Abraham's posterity but also those of Adam's. THE GENEALOGY OF CHRIST.[14]

---

[11]See Rom 1:3-4. A number of heresies in the early church questioned the true divinity of Christ, including the Ebionites and the Arians.

[12]Taverner, *On Saynt Andrewes Day*, 3v-4r*; quoting Mt 22:42-44 (citing Ps 110:1).
[13]See Eusebius, *Church History* 3.4.6. Paul refers to a Luke as a physician in Col 4:14.
[14]Cowper, *Three Heavenly Treatises*, 6-8*.

4:1-13 THE TEMPTATION OF JESUS

And Jesus, full of the Holy Spirit, returned from the Jordan and was led by the Spirit in the wilderness ²for forty days, being tempted by the devil. And he ate nothing during those days. And when they were ended, he was hungry. ³The devil said to him, "If you are the Son of God, command this stone to become bread." ⁴And Jesus answered him, "It is written, 'Man shall not live by bread alone.'" ⁵And the devil took him up and showed him all the kingdoms of the world in a moment of time, ⁶and said to him, "To you I will give all this authority and their glory, for it has been delivered to me, and I give it to whom I will. ⁷If you, then, will worship me, it will all be yours." ⁸And Jesus answered him, "It is written,

> *"'You shall worship the Lord your God,*
> *and him only shall you serve.'"*

⁹And he took him to Jerusalem and set him on the pinnacle of the temple and said to him, "If you are the Son of God, throw yourself down from here, ¹⁰for it is written,

> *"'He will command his angels concerning you,*
> *to guard you,'*

¹¹and

> *"'On their hands they will bear you up,*
> *lest you strike your foot against a stone.'"*

¹²And Jesus answered him, "It is said, 'You shall not put the Lord your God to the test.'" ¹³And when the devil had ended every temptation, he departed from him until an opportune time.

OVERVIEW: For Reformation interpreters, the temptation of Jesus in the desert contains a twofold revelation: first, we see Jesus, post-baptism, preparing to begin his ministry with forty days of fasting and prayer, in parallel to his Old Testament precursors, Moses and Elijah; second, he contends with Satan in a battle of wits and wills. Both of these purposes reveal Jesus as the Son of God—Jesus is the second Moses, come to bring a new "law" and fulfill the old, and the Savior who can defeat the ancient enemy of humankind. Satan, who hated the God-man from the beginning for elevating the human race above the angels by uniting God to humanity, tests Christ to be certain that he is the Son of God. Our faith in Jesus as God's Son is confirmed by his miraculous fasting in the desert and his masterful defeat of Satan. By his example he also teaches us how to combat and, with God's help, defeat the devil—a figure of terrifying reality for Protestants of this time period. Satan attacks us at our weakest places—for Jesus, who was hungry, it was an offering of food, but was also tempted by power and authority. Unlike

us, Christ never places self before God, and he is able continually to answer Satan with Scripture, placing the power of the Word of God over the devil. We ourselves should turn to God's Word, these commentators contend, whenever we are beset by temptations, and have faith that God (who allows these temptations only to try and strengthen us) will never see us tempted beyond what we can bear.

4:1-2 Jesus Is Led by the Spirit into the Desert

JESUS PREPARES FOR HIS MINISTRY THROUGH FASTING AND TEMPTATION IN THE DESERT. DESIDERIUS ERASMUS: At Jesus' baptism, the dove had landed on his head, and this was not an empty sign for he was now filled with the Holy Spirit. But before he would undertake the service of preaching the gospel, and in order that he would be proved and tested in all things, he left the Jordan. In this he teaches that after baptism, a person should strive to reach the greatest heights of religious devotion. He withdrew himself from the crowds he usually associated with, because close association can often corrupt a man and decrease the authority of his teaching. And through the Spirit, by whom he was completely seized and carried off, he was led into the desert (the same desert out of which John also came to begin his ministry) as it were to provoke that enemy of the human race, that he might get all his arts and schemes in order. Doubtless this was to show to us that he who had been up until now the conquerer of the human race could at the same time be conquered, and to point out to us the way to defeat him. Satan eagerly watched for an opportunity that would be suitable for the temptations, and it was offered by means of Jesus' hunger. For Moses, before he received the law, fasted for forty days, and now Jesus, who presents a parallel figure, also fasted for forty days before he brought forth the new, evangelical law for the world. In all this time he touched no food, but he spent the entire time in holy prayer to God, giving praise, glory and continual thanks to him. This was a sign of an individual of rare virtue. PARAPHRASE ON THE GOSPEL OF LUKE 4:1-2.[1]

GOD SENDS TEMPTATIONS TO INSTRUCT AND TEST US. JOHN BOYS: Saint James said a person may not say when he is tempted, "I am tempted by God," for God can neither be tempted with evil nor tempt any to evil. So how then could the Spirit lead Christ to be tempted? An answer is made by Saint Augustine in his epistle [120] to Consentius: *Alia tentatio deceptionis, alia probationis*: There are two sorts of temptations, one to test, another to deceive us. Now God only tempts in order to try us, but Satan to destroy us. God tempts to make people better, and therefore David said, "Prove me, O Lord, and try me." Also, Saint James said, "Count it all joy, my brothers, when you meet trials of various kinds, for you know that the testing of your faith produces steadfastness." But Satan tempts to make people worse, as in 1 Corinthians 7:5 and

1 Thessalonians 3:5. *Diabolus tentat ut subruat, Deus ut coronet*: The devil tempts us to destroy, but God tempts us for our instruction.[2]

But some will object: If Christ were led by the Spirit to be tempted by the devil, does that make the almighty God the author of evil? In answering this, we must understand that in some respects God may be said to be *actor in malo* but not *author mali*, that is, a worker in temptation and yet free from sin. First, God may be said immediately to tempt by offering occasions and objects to try whether someone will sin or not. A master who suspects his servant lays a purse of money in his way to test if he will steal it; if he steals it, then the master has found a secret thief by watching him, and so will prevent him from deceiving any longer. Now this sort of test is no fault in the master, but this stealing is a sin in the servant. In like manner, God tempts his servants in order to test them: "You shall not listen to the words of that prophet or that dreamer of dreams. For the Lord your God is testing you, to know whether you love the Lord your God with all your heart and with all your soul." THE FIRST SUNDAY IN LENT.[3]

FASTING AND PRAYER STRENGTHEN EACH OTHER. WILLIAM COWPER: Our Savior undertook this fasting, partly for our instruction and partly for confirmation to us of his calling. First, for our instruction, he would teach us that a spiritual life, wherein God may be honored and our own salvation and the salvation of others may be procured, can neither be begun nor continued without abstinence and prayer. By these, the godly have obtained at the hand of God the knowledge of great mysteries, as you may see in Daniel; by these they have confounded the conspiracies of their enemies, as you may see in Esther. These have always been the most effective armor of the church to divert evil, to draw down good, to confound their enemies, to confirm themselves—and the one of

---

[1]Erasmus, *In Evangelivm Lvce Paraphrasis*, g r-v (LB 7:318).

[2]Ambrose, *De Abraham* 1.8.
[3]Boys, *Exposition of the Dominical Epistles and Gospels*, 2:27-28*; citing Jas 1:13; Ps 26:2; Jas 1:2-3; Deut 13:3.

these strengthens the other. "Prayer obtained strength to fast, fasting obtains grace to pray; fasting strengthens prayer, prayer sanctifies fasting."[4]

But because this fasting of our Lord was miraculous, we may see that he also undertook it for the end for which he wrought the rest of his miracles: namely, to confirm his calling and doctrine to us. As Moses fasted forty days at the giving of the law, and as Elijah fasted forty days at the restoring of the law, so the Lord Jesus fasts for forty days at his coming to preach the gospel. He did this partly so that he might correspond to these former exemplars, because they prefigured what he was to do, and partly, as I said, to confirm to us the certainty of his calling. THE COMBAT OF CHRIST WITH SATAN.[5]

4:3-4 The First Temptation: Stones into Bread

SATAN HATES THE SON OF GOD OUT OF ENVY.
EDWARD LEIGH: The opinion of many theologians is that it is probable that the devil's sin at first was this: when God revealed to him that the Son of God should assume human nature and commanded him to submit himself to the man Christ, he envied Christ that, although he was a man, he was preferred before himself, a glorious angel. He was angry that the human nature should be assumed into a hypostatic union with the second person of the Trinity; therefore he rebelled against God and Christ. When he perceived that Jesus was called the Son of God by the Father and John the Baptist, he decided to test to see if he was the true Son of God, so that he might pour out on him his ancient envy, anger and indignation. Therefore it is probable that the devil did not at first abruptly say to him, "If you are the Son of God, command these stones to become bread," but rather at first he courteously saluted him and ingratiated himself to

him with fair speeches, saying, "My lord, what are you doing here alone? What are you musing on? I saw you baptized in the Jordan and heard a voice from heaven saying 'This is my Son,' so I desire to know whether you truly are the Son of God by nature, or only his adopted Son by grace? I see also that since you have been fasting for forty days, you are very hungry; so, if you are the Son of God, satisfy your hunger and turn these stones into bread, for it will be very easy for you to do it." ANNOTATIONS UPON SAINT LUKE 4.[6]

WE LIVE BY GOD'S DECISION, NOT BY BREAD.
PHILIPP MELANCHTHON: By this word *bread*, he understands all manner of food whatsoever that we use in order to sustain our body (look in the sixth chapter following). Some subvert this testimony of Moses quite falsely, as if it had been said that human lives were not nourished with visible bread but with the word of God. In some respects this is true, but Moses also respected another thing. For when they had no other bread at hand, he showed his people that manna was an extraordinary food, so that by this record it might be witnessed forever that the life of human beings is not bound up in bread but that it depends rather on the will and pleasure of God. The word *bread* in this passage, therefore, is not taken for doctrine but for the decree which God published in order to defend the order of nature and for the nourishing of his creatures. He does not reject the people who are the work of his hands, but he pours life into them so that, once it is given, he may daily sustain them. The word is the virtue and power of God, by which we are sustained as well with meat as without it: whether he provides any other thing in the place of meat, such as the manna which he gave to our forebears, or even nothing, as he kept and preserved Moses, Elijah and Christ for so many days. AN ECCLESIASTICALL EXPOSITION UPON SAINT MATHEWE 3.[7]

---

[4]Bernard of Clairvaux, *In Quadragesima*, sermon 4.2. See Bernard of Clairvaux, *Sermons for Lent and the Easter Season*, trans. Irene Edmonds, ed. Mark A. Scott, Cistercian Fathers Series 52 (Collegeville, MN: Liturgical Press, 2013), 40.
[5]Cowper, *Three Heavenly Treatises*, 147-50*; alluding to Exod 24:18; 34:28; 1 Kings 19:8.

[6]Leigh, *Annotations upon All the New Testament Philologicall and Theologicall*, 104*.
[7]Marlorat, ed., *Catholike and Ecclesiasticall Exposition of the Holy Gospell After S. Mathewe*, 61*.

4:5-8 The Second Temptation: Authority over Earthly Kingdoms

CHRIST WILL NOT COMMIT IDOLATRY.
JOHANN SPANGENBERG: How does the devil tempt him with power and authority? The devil takes Jesus with him to the top of a high mountain, and shows him all the kingdoms of the world and their magnificence and says to him: "I will give all of this to you, if you fall down and worship me." It is as if he would say: "Why would you want to be despised and rejected any longer in this world? Follow me, and I will make you a ruler over all the kingdoms of this world—just fall down and worship me." And what does Christ do with this temptation? Because the devil maliciously pushes Christ toward idolatry, he rejects him out of hand and says: "Get yourself away from me, Satan, for it is written: 'You should worship the Lord your God, and serve him alone.'" GOSPEL ON THE FIRST SUNDAY IN LENT.[8]

CHRIST TEACHES US TO USE SCRIPTURE AGAINST THE DEVIL. RICHARD TAVERNER: The devil would gladly have enticed Christ to tempt God by letting himself fall down from the temple without any necessity for it. He even used Scripture for this purpose, attempting by this means to see whether he could overcome Christ, who seemed in outward appearance to be of great simplicity and clothed in sheepskin garments, and whether he might move him to attempt anything against God's word. Here we should note that the devil has more ways than one to assault us silly [i.e., poor] mortal men and women. He knows what is our weakest part, and if he happens to fail of his purpose in one way, he tries another way, for he takes great pleasure in our destruction and condemnation. Although he could not entice Christ by the needs of his belly, he hoped to strike him through by this dart, with which he would move him to tempt God through vainglory. He set him on top of the temple, saying: "If you really are

the Son of God, jump down, for he has given a command to his angels concerning you, that they should take you up into their hands, lest you should stumble against any stone with your feet." But why do you think that the devil skipped that part of the psalm, "to guard you in all your ways"? Surely it was because it was opposed to his purpose. And therefore Christ answered him: "It is written, 'You shall not tempt the Lord your God.'" It is as if he would say, "God strongly defends his faithful children and does not leave them in any distress. He did not command his angels to take charge of me alone, but also of all the faithful and chosen people, that they may make this journey without any disturbance or grief. But God does not want us to despise the means by which he helps us and works. Why should I cast myself into the water if I have a bridge or a ship to convey me over it? In like manner, why should I here cast myself down from the temple if I have stairs by which I can descend? Whoever loves peril will fall into it." So Christ again bears the victory in the battle against the devil, and he teaches us how, with strong and pithy objections taken out of Scripture, we should in like manner make war with the devil. THE GOSPEL ON THE FIRST SUNDAY IN LENT.[9]

4:9-12 The Third Temptation: Testing God's Love

SATAN CAN ONLY TEMPT, NOT DESTROY.
PHILIPP MELANCHTHON: It is as if Satan had said, "You depend on your Father's providence. Now since you are quite hungry and in extreme need, do not doubt but that he will sustain you. All is well! Now cast yourself down headlong, that you may show even more that you depend on his providence, for no danger will come to you." But why did Satan not throw Christ down himself, rather than try to persuade him that he should throw himself down headlong? The answer is this: No one tempts God who does not willingly and without necessity

---

[8]Spangenberg, *Postilla* (1582), LXXXIVv.

[9]Taverner, *Epistles and Gospelles (Wynter Parte)*, 89r-90r*; citing Ps 91:12; Deut 6:16.

throw himself into danger, but is brought into it against his will; furthermore, the providence of God takes care not of those who love danger but of those who are in peril against their wills. Therefore, when Satan tempted the children of God, he did not attempt to throw them down by force or violence into destruction but rather that they themselves should willingly throw themselves down headlong into mischief. Furthermore, it is not in his power to constrain the children of God by violence. It is permitted that he should tempt but not destroy. So it comes to pass that he does not drown the desperate against their wills, or hang them or cut their throats, but that by his temptations he causes that they do such violence to themselves. AN ECCLESIASTICALL EXPOSITION UPON SAINT MATHEWE 3.[10]

THIS "THEOLOGICAL" TEMPTATION IS FOR POWER AND PRESTIGE. JOHANNES MATHESIUS: When Satan figures out that the Lord Christ could not be overcome through the cross or through want, the crafty traitor turns around and, because his adversary relies on the Word as his authority and finds great gifts and virtues in it, he attacks by means of these gifts and says: "You are a great and learned man—you act like a bishop and bring the news that something new and wonderful is beginning and blazing a new trail. What are you doing here in this desert? Try out something new and unique—be bold and try something completely unheard of, so that you will become well-known and preferred, and will receive honors, respect, and other such things. Therefore, now while you are standing at the pinnacle or spire of the temple, go ahead and throw yourself down— take a leap! You do not need to worry about or fear that any danger or injury will happen. Scripture is a support and bridge for you and stands with you, for it says, 'He has commanded his angels concerning you, that they will bear you in their hands.' Then you will see that God is with you and that

the dear angels serve you." Now this is a very quick, crafty, dangerous and indeed truly almost a theological temptation, or at least one that is common to great theologians and learned people and to powerful and arrogant rulers. Yes, it is certainly a very devilish and hellish temptation. That is why few people recognize it, for the devil attacks the great leaders and thinkers and over-throws them with splendor, ambition and arro-gance, so that some presume to undertake some-thing new, and they desire to break out, to be entitled, to become well-known and to oppress others. THE THIRD SERMON FROM THE GOSPEL, MATTHEW 4.[11]

SATAN ALSO ATTACKS US BY OUR PRIDE. JOHANN BAUMGART (POMARIUS): Satan attacks you with pride, presumption and audacity, con-vincing you that you have risen up through your own abilities. But what you should especially understand is that Jesus answers him, "You should not test the Lord your God" but should instead walk in his ways, since then the angels have the command to guard and protect you. Say, "I do not want to approach God's grace and gifts with maliciousness, or to love danger, so that I do not destroy them. Rather, I will humble myself under the powerful hand of God, and even if I am the greatest, I will rather be the least." GOSPEL ON INVOCAVIT SUNDAY.[12]

4:13 The Devil Leaves, for a While

LIKE CHRIST, WE WILL ALWAYS SUFFER TEMPTATION. MARTIN BUCER: If you cleave to the Word of God, Satan cannot prevail against you but eventually will depart. As long as we are in the world where Satan is prince, we are subject to his temptations. But at the same time, the God of consolation will not cease ministering comfort to us, and when he has put away the devils from us,

---

[10]Marlorat, ed., *Catholike and Ecclesiasticall Exposition of the Holy Gospell After S. Mathewe*, 63*.

[11]Mathesius, *Postilla Symbolica*, 93v-94r; quoting Ps 91:11-12.
[12]Baumgart, *Postilla*, 78v-79r; citing Deut 6:16; Ps 91; Sir 3:18-20; 1 Pet 5:6-10; Mt 10:19-20.

he will send his angels to bear us up, as Matthew writes of Christ at the end of this temptation.

But note that the devil did not make an end to his temptation of Christ until he had used up all his power and had spent all of his armor and strength, even as a willful warrior does not cease to provoke his enemy until he is laid on the ground. Therefore, following the example of Christ, we must prepare ourselves to bear diverse temptations. It is not sufficient that we have repulsed him, unless we have overcome him. And we see that Satan cannot do as much as he would like, for Luke says, "And when all the temptation was ended."

Satan never lacks the will, but the Lord has bound him so that he cannot exercise his subtleties as he desires. Furthermore, we have a promise, "He will not suffer you to be tempted above what you are able to bear." Satan did not go away permanently, that Christ might lead the rest of his life without trouble. If therefore it happens that we are so tempted, let us not think that an end is made to it by and by, but let us prepare ourselves for new conflicts. AN ECCLESIASTICALL EXPOSITION UPON SAINT LUKE 4.[13]

---

[13]Marlorat, ed., *Catholike and Ecclesiasticall Exposition of the Holy Gospell After S. Marke and Luke*, 134*; quoting 1 Cor 10:13.

4:14-30 JESUS' MINISTRY BEGINS IN GALILEE AND NAZARETH

[14]*And Jesus returned in the power of the Spirit to Galilee, and a report about him went out through all the surrounding country.* [15]*And he taught in their synagogues, being glorified by all.*

[16]*And he came to Nazareth, where he had been brought up. And as was his custom, he went to the synagogue on the Sabbath day, and he stood up to read.* [17]*And the scroll of the prophet Isaiah was given to him. He unrolled the scroll and found the place where it was written,*

[18]*"The Spirit of the Lord is upon me,*
because he has anointed me
to proclaim good news to the poor.
He has sent me to proclaim liberty to the
captives
and recovering of sight to the blind,
to set at liberty those who are oppressed,
[19]*to proclaim the year of the Lord's favor."*

[20]*And he rolled up the scroll and gave it back to the attendant and sat down. And the eyes of all in the synagogue were fixed on him.* [21]*And he began to say to them, "Today this Scripture has been fulfilled in your hearing."* [22]*And all spoke well of him and marveled at the gracious words that were coming from his mouth. And they said, "Is not this Joseph's son?"* [23]*And he said to them, "Doubtless you will quote to me this proverb, 'Physician, heal yourself.' What we have heard you did at Capernaum, do here in your hometown as well."* [24]*And he said, "Truly, I say to you, no prophet is acceptable in his hometown.* [25]*But in truth, I tell you, there were many widows in Israel in the days of Elijah, when the heavens were shut up three years and six months, and a great famine came over all the land,* [26]*and Elijah was sent to none of them but only to Za-rephath, in the land of Sidon, to a woman who was a widow.* [27]*And there were many lepers[a] in Israel in the time of the prophet Elisha, and none of them was cleansed, but only Naaman the Syrian."* [28]*When they heard these things, all in the synagogue were filled with wrath.* [29]*And they rose up and drove him out of the town and brought him to the brow of the hill on which their town was built, so that they could throw him down the cliff.* [30]*But passing through their midst, he went away.*

a *Leprosy* was a term for several skin diseases; see Leviticus 13

OVERVIEW: This pericope, like most others in the Gospels according to the reformers, is designed to teach us what we should know and believe about Christ and thus how we should live. In this passage, our commentators remind us, we learn that although Christ was free from obligation to the law, still he regularly attended the synagogue services. Therefore we have no excuse and should attend church services every week. Likewise, the people in attendance were totally attentive to Christ, not sleeping or being distracted by others—the lesson is obvious. And we see lessons for how not to behave or think: the people were attentive but were not true believers, for they doubted his words ("Isn't this Joseph's son?") and sought miracles to confirm his claim. They were ungrateful, even though God allowed his own Son to be raised in their town, and they expected God's grace and miracles to come to them because of their ancestry. But Christ gives the lie to their expectations through his words: the prophets were sent to foreigners to show that God's grace and mercy are given to whom he wills, and Christ (to whom this prophecy applied) was sent to preach the gospel to the poor, the afflicted and oppressed, but not to those who believe they have no need for repentance. The people were, naturally, enraged by Christ's words and sought to destroy him; ministers of the Word who try to improve and correct their parishioners will be treated in the same way. The swine trample the pearls underfoot, but the reformers emphasize that the gospel must still be preached, for there are true sheep who need to hear the voice of their Shepherd. And so we learn, too, that Jesus is that Good Shepherd who fulfills the Old Testament prophecies, who has the fullness of the Spirit's gifts and who came to make satisfaction for our sins, to redeem us and to restore us to Paradise.

4:14-15 *The Spirit Leads Jesus to the Synagogues of Galilee*

CHRIST, WITH THE POWER OF THE SPIRIT, DEFEATS SATAN'S TEMPTING. ERASMUS SARCERIUS: When Luke says that Christ returned by the power of the Spirit into Galilee, he was considering what had happened before: his purpose is to show that in these conflicts, Christ escaped the power of the Conquerer not by human power but by the power of the Holy Spirit. Not that Christ, because he was God, needed the grace of the Spirit or to be helped by another; but when he was tempted, because he was a man, it was necessary that his human nature should be strengthened by the grace of the Holy Spirit, that he might have the victory. This is clearly spoken for the consolation of the godly. For as Christ mastered Satan, helped by the grace of the Holy Spirit, even so shall we have victory by the power of the same Spirit. And we must note that we should not have reaped such great fruit or so much consolation if he had only repeated the history and not the reason and manner of the victory, which is also set before us. Paul declares this sufficiently, saying, "But if the Spirit of him who raised up Jesus from the dead dwells in you, he who raised up Christ from the dead shall also give life to your mortal bodies, because his Spirit dwells in

you." If he had said that Christ had raised himself up, it would have been true, but it would not have provided nearly so much consolation to the faithful. AN ECCLESIASTICALL EXPOSITION UPON SAINT LUKE 4.[1]

CHRIST OBEYED THE SABBATH CUSTOM BY ENTERING THE SYNAGOGUE. PHILIPP MELANCHTHON: We should consider what the custom of the sabbath was among the Jews: Christ observed this usage diligently, as we may plainly see in Luke, which says that he, according to his custom, went into the synagogue every sabbath day. Therefore if the Jews practiced the reading of Moses with such great diligence on the sabbath, what should we do in these days when not Moses but one far exceeding him speaks, when certain ceremonies and external observations are not used, but only the kingdom of God and its mysteries are used and preached? If Christ observed the sabbath in this manner and entered into the synagogue, when he himself had no need of the reading of Moses, what excuse will those have today who, either by contempt or disdain, neglect and utterly refuse to come to church on the sabbath, in which not the observance of the Law but the doctrine of life is set forth? Can we not see here that Christ himself obeyed this custom by his presence? AN ECCLESIASTICALL EXPOSITION UPON SAINT MATHEWE 13.[2]

HIS DIVINE POWER WAS EVIDENT FROM THE BEGINNING. JOHN CALVIN: This is explicitly recorded by Luke so that we might understand that, from the very beginning, the divine power glowed in Christ, which brought together the people not yet infected by the wicked enthusiasm of contradiction in admiration of him. COMMENTARY ON A HARMONY OF THE GOSPELS.[3]

---

[1]Marlorat, ed., *Catholike and Ecclesiasticall Exposition of the Holy Gospell after S. Marke and Luke*, 134-35*; quoting Rom 8:11.
[2]Marlorat, ed., *Catholike and Ecclesiasticall Exposition of the Holy Gospell After S. Mathewe*, 302*.
[3]CO 45:139 (cf. CTS 31:226).

4:16-21 *Jesus Reveals That He Fulfills the Prophecies*

The Lord Was Well-known in the Nazareth Synagogue. Jacques Lefèvre d'Étaples: And returning to Galilee, he taught in the Galilean synagogues: and they made much of his teaching, valuing it highly, especially in those places where neither he nor his parents were known. But when he came into the city of Nazareth, it turned out differently. He and his parents were well-known there, because he was nursed there after the presentation in the temple, although he was beginning to wean by that time, and then he was raised there after his return from Egypt all the way up to his thirtieth year. Therefore he entered the synagogue in Nazareth according to his custom on the sabbath day: according to his custom, it says, for it was a habit for him. Although it was right that he was above the law, nevertheless he observed the law, but the spirit of the law, not the superstitions of pharisaical blindness. In the synagogue, however, according to the significance of the day, someone was accustomed to stand up. When he received the book from the minister of the synagogue, being considered appropriate for that office, he explained the sacred text to the people who were there to hear, as time permitted. And so from the middle of the group, the Lord stood up, so that he might do that. In the Gospel of Luke 4.[4]

Jesus Is Truly Indicated by This Passage, So John Changes Plural to Singular. John Calvin: There is no doubt that Christ chose this passage with deliberation. Some think it was presented to him by divine inspiration, but because freedom of choice was given to him, I prefer to say that it was his decision to choose this passage over others. Isaiah promises that after the Babylonian exile there would still be some witnesses to God's grace who would gather the people together from

ruin and the shadows of death and renew by a spiritual power a church so afflicted by disasters. But because that redemption was to be promulgated alone by the name and authority of Christ, he speaks in the singular here, and in this way indicates the person of Christ, by which he would more effectively encourage the hearts of the pious in strong faith. It is certain that what is related here belongs properly to Christ alone for two reasons: first, because he alone was given the fullness of the Spirit, so that he would be our witness and the representative of our reconciliation with God (which is the reason why Paul assigns especially to him what is common to all ministers of the gospel, namely, that "in coming, he announced peace to those who were far off, and to those who were near"); and second, because he alone, by the power of his Spirit, brings about and performs all the good things promised here. Commentary on a Harmony of the Gospels.[5]

Christ's Work of Salvation Is Through God's Power. Erasmus Sarcerius: Therefore he said that the Spirit of the Lord was on him, to the end that we might know that Christ does no human or private work, either in himself or in his ministers, but that he is sent from above to restore salvation to the church. He testifies that he does nothing by human instinct or counsel but by the moderation of the Spirit of God, that the faith of the godly might be founded on the authority and the power of God. An Ecclesiasticall Exposition upon Saint Luke 4.[6]

Unlike Others, Christ Received the Fullness of the Spirit. Johannes Brenz: And we note what we touched on before, that the fullness of the Spirit was given to Christ alone. For the Spirit (or gifts of the Spirit) was given to others, in part and with limits.

To Moses was given the spirit of wisdom and of

---

[4]Lefèvre d'Étaples, *Commentarii Initiatorii in Quatuor Evangelia*, 2:28r.

[5]CTS 31:227-28* (CO 45:140-41); alluding to Jn 3:34; Eph 2:17.
[6]Marlorat, ed., *Catholike and Ecclesiasticall Exposition of the Holy Gospell After S. Marke and Luke*, 137*.

working miracles; to Samson was given the spirit of fortitude; to Solomon, the spirit of wisdom; to the prophets, the spirit of knowledge and understanding of God's mysteries; but to Christ was given the fullness of the Spirit, and all the gifts of the Spirit were poured on him. . . . Saint John says, "God gives the spirit to him without limit." Similarly, Paul writes, "In him dwells all the fullness of God bodily." Wherefore, when the prophet [Isaiah] says that the Spirit of the Lord is on Christ, he means that all the fullness and all the gifts of the Spirit are on him. AN ECCLESIASTICALL EXPOSITION UPON SAINT LUKE 4.[7]

CHRIST REDEEMS US THROUGH A SPIRITUAL JUBILEE YEAR. JOHANNES BRENZ: The prophet [Isaiah] alludes to the year of Jubilee, of which mention is made by Moses. During this year two things were especially observed: all servants were freed, and all lands which had had to be sold were restored to their former owners or else to their heirs. This civil law was very suitable for the land of Canaan and necessary for the government of Israel. In that year all quarrels, contentions, brawls, debts, legal actions, covenants, laws, letters and seals were ended. In that year, there was a public composition and pacification of all civil controversies.

Now, as to the external observation of the year of Jubilee according to the law of Moses, we have nothing to do with that, but only with the matter which is signified by the year of Jubilee. This "spiritual" Jubilee began first when Christ started preaching the gospel and continued not for a year only but forever. For the Lord says, "He has sent me to preach;" that is to say, that I should sound forth with the trumpet of the gospel the acceptable year of the Lord. For if we take a good look at ourselves, we shall find that we were made servants and captives of Satan through sin, and that by eating the forbidden fruit we "sold" and lost the possession of Paradise and the inheritance of all heavenly blessings. But now Christ is come and has made satisfaction

for our sins. He has redeemed us from the power of Satan and has restored to us our former possession of Paradise and to the inheritance of heavenly graces. All these things he openly proclaims by the preaching of his gospel. AN ECCLESIASTICALL EXPOSITION UPON SAINT LUKE 4.[8]

THEY NEEDED TO HEAR TO BELIEVE. JOHN CALVIN: There is little need for Christ to say these few words, for he proved by the actual event that the time was now at hand when God wanted to restore the ruined church. He wanted the explanation of the prophecies to be clearly established for his hearers; in the same way, interpreters handle the Scriptures rightly and in proper order when they apply it to current circumstances. He says "fulfilled in their hearing," rather than "in their sight," because merely seeing it would not be effective, but teaching must hold the first place. COMMENTARY ON A HARMONY OF THE GOSPELS.[9]

4:22 The People of Nazareth Are Amazed

THE PEOPLE KNEW HIS POOR BACKGROUND. KONRAD PELLIKAN: Most of the people here looked up to Jesus as having the highest authority, and yet at the same time a different sort of gentleness. They admired his speech, which was quite different from that of the Pharisees. He spoke mildly, gently, in a friendly way with many hidden graces, never being superior or stern or arrogant, but at the same time not speaking to them as one who lacks authority. Because the words of the Pharisees flowed out of their hearts, they had the same ambition, avarice, envy, and all the other corrupt evil passions which could be found in their source. But the rest of the speech which came from the mouth of Jesus, because it flowed from his heart, was filled with the heavenly Spirit, friendly to all good things and effective toward well-being. . . .

---

[7]Marlorat, ed., *Catholike and Ecclesiasticall Exposition of the Holy Gospell After S. Marke and Luke*, 137*; citing Jn 3:34; Col 2:9.

[8]Marlorat, ed., *Catholike and Ecclesiasticall Exposition of the Holy Gospell After S. Marke and Luke*, 140*.
[9]CO 45:142 (cf. CTS 31:230).

They were now among those to whom the humbleness of his family and background might have diminished somewhat the authority of his heavenly teaching. Up to this point everyone believed him to be the son of Joseph and Mary, and the poverty of both his parents and his relatives was not unknown in the neighborhood. They knew that from his childhood for many years he had only learned the trade of his father and could not spend his time at the discussions of the Pharisees and the experts in the law, who teach the mysteries of the sacred scrolls with great arrogance. And so they were amazed that he spoke with such eloquence and authority. Commentary in Luke 4:22.[10]

4:23-27 Jesus Speaks of Their Refusal to Accept Him

The People Are Offended at Jesus' Lowliness. Erasmus Sarcerius: It is as if Jesus should say, "Seeing that you are now so offended with the lowliness of my person, I perceive that you will quote this proverb to me." With his words, Christ prevents the thoughts of the Nazareans, which otherwise they would have spoken in words, if Christ had not prevented them. For the people, being offended at the lowliness of his person, cannot help but doubt both the doctrine and the offices of Christ and will now require external things for the confirmation both of doctrine and of his office. But see what happens to those who are offended by the lowliness of persons. First of all, they hear the word with their ears only; second, they testify to it with their mouth only; third, they only wonder at the word of grace and do not truly believe it; and fourth, they are wholly offended at a person's lowly status, and if they despise that, they also despise that person's doctrine and office. An Ecclesiasticall Exposition upon Saint Luke 4.[11]

"Prove Yourself to Us!" Erasmus Sarcerius: It is as if they should say, "It is commonly said to the physician or doctor who professes that he can heal others and is himself full of sores, 'Physician, heal yourself.' Why then should we not say that to you? For if you are the one who heals those who are broken in heart, who delivers all people from their unhappiness and makes them happy, why do you not first of all and especially show your power to your own townspeople and kinfolk?" An Ecclesiasticall Exposition upon Saint Luke 4.[12]

Christ Does Not Perform Miracles Among Unbelievers. John Calvin: He reproaches them, for it was their fault that he did not reveal his power in miracles to them, as he did in other places: people's unbelief obstructs God's appearance, and he does not work as it might be wished for their salvation (as in Matthew 13; Mark 6). Therefore Jesus was not able to perform any signs among them, because they did not believe in him. Not that it is within human power to tie up God's hands, but that he denies the benefits of his works to those who are found to be unworthy because of their unbelief. Likewise, it is as if Christ answered them, "If you wish to have a share in miracles, why do you not give place to God? Or rather, why do you proudly reject the minister of his power? Therefore you receive a just reward for your contempt, when, passing you by, I show by miracles elsewhere that I am the Messiah of God, to whom is appointed the restoration of the church." And certainly this ingratitude was hardly to be borne, when God had desired that his Son should be brought up in their city, and then they scorned such a foster son. Justly, therefore, he withdrew his hand, that it might not be the object of derision to such impious despisers. But here we learn how much God values his Word, in that in order to punish those who despise it, he takes from their midst those gifts which are testimonies

---

[10]Pellikan, *In Sacrosancta Quatuor Evangelia*, 61 (cf. LB 7:326-27).
[11]Marlorat, ed., *Catholike and Ecclesiasticall Exposition of the Holy Gospell After S. Marke and Luke*, 142-43*.

[12]Marlorat, ed., *Catholike and Ecclesiasticall Exposition of the Holy Gospell After S. Marke and Luke*, 143*.

to its presence. COMMENTARY ON A HARMONY OF THE GOSPELS.[13]

THESE EXAMPLES WERE MEANT TO TEACH THE PEOPLE ABOUT GRACE. FRANÇOIS LAMBERT: This foreign widow was from outside of Israel, naturally, from Zarephath in Sidon. Likewise Naaman was a Syrian, but they both experienced God's highest mercy. For that reason the most excellent Savior chose them, that he might show to those impious people of Nazareth that it is often the decision of God to reveal his greatness to foreigners. In contrast to them, the people of Nazareth demand that he give them some signs in his own country. But he makes clear in this example that with God, one's nationality, or even flesh and blood, do not *make* anything happen. To be sure, the benefits of God are bestowed on no one on account of their nationality or familial relationship. It is certain that everything originates from his benevolence, just as he decreed in eternity. Now we have to look more diligently at Paul, for in Romans 11[:28], he seems to claim that God would do something for the children because of the parents, because he says, "According to election they are beloved on account of their ancestors." But it is certainly still true that God bequeathed nothing to the ancestors, or to the children, unless he did it by grace. And if it is by grace, then it is not by merit. And nevertheless it is also certain of those who are elect on account of their ancestors, or other servants of God, that God himself will often give generously to their children and others, if they pray to him on their behalf. Truly it is not because of their merits but because of his glory, and because it is the highest good, he deems it worthy to hear them who fear his will. Pay attention also, for he said these things of the widow and of Naaman so that the pride of these people would be destroyed, for they suggested that everything was owed to themselves, and not to the nations. COMMENTARY IN LUKE 4:24-27.[14]

4:28-29 The People Attempt to Kill Jesus

LIKE CHRIST, PREACHERS ARE ENDANGERED FOR THE SAKE OF THE WORD. JOHANNES BRENZ: Because he pointed out their ingratitude and unbelief in his sermon, the people are so angry and outraged against him that they seek to destroy him, and not only as a simple heretic but also as the author of all impiety and as a horrible monster, hated by God and people.

Here in the example of the Nazareans we can see what will happen to the ministers of God's Word among wicked people. For even as Christ was derided by his fellow citizens and carried off to his death because he preached the gospel out of Isaiah and words of threat and punishment out of the Law, even so all the ministers of God's Word, if they preach Christ and the magnificent promises of the gospel, and place their hearers in the kingdom of heaven and in everlasting felicity, their reward at the hands of the wicked is to be laughed to scorn and to be disdained as a babbler. And if they preach the Law and its threats, and cry out against the sins of people and deliver them up to Satan for the destruction of the flesh so that their soul may be saved in the Day of the Lord Jesus, then they are called railing knaves, traitors, seditious persons, and unworthy to live on the earth. And they are carried off to death as if they were the most wicked of all people. For it usually happens that when pearls are cast before swine and what is holy is given to dogs, the ones will tread the pearls under their feet, and the others will turn on their benefactors to tear them to pieces. What then? Should we not go out and preach the Word of God? Yes, of course it must be preached! For even if there are many who will condemn and persecute them, nevertheless the Lord always has sheep who hear the voice of the shepherd; and although the preacher of the Word may be in many dangers, not one of his enemies can hurt the least hair of his head without it being the will of God. AN ECCLE-SIASTICALL EXPOSITION UPON SAINT LUKE 4.[15]

---

[13]CTS 31:232-33* (CO 45:143-44); alluding to Mt 13:58; Mk 6:5; Jn 12:37.
[14]Lambert, *In Divi Lucae*, L4v-L5r; alluding to Rom 11:6.

[15]Marlorat, ed., *Catholike and Ecclesiasticall Exposition of the Holy*

4:30 *Jesus Goes on His Way*

HIS TIME HAD NOT YET COME. JOHANN AGRICOLA: Here you can see that this pertains to what Christ said to the Jews in Luke 22: "Have you come out as against a robber with swords and clubs? When I was with you every day in the temple you did not lay hands on me. But this is your hour, and the power of darkness," that is, "You would have had no authority over me, if it had not been allowed to you." Likewise we see in the prophecies that Jerusalem is the place where Jesus should die, not Nazareth. Therefore the evil intentions of the people were not able to harm Jesus here, because that time had not yet come. ANNOTATIONS IN THE GOSPEL OF LUKE, CHAP. 4.[16]

Gospell After S. Marke and Luke, 146*; citing Mt 7:6; Lk 21:17-18.

[16]Agricola, *In Evangelium Lucae Annotationes*, 69v; citing Lk 22:52-53 (see also Jn 19:11); Mt 23:37; Lk 13:34; 18:31.

4:31-44 TEACHING AND HEALING IN CAPERNAUM

[31]And he went down to Capernaum, a city of Galilee. And he was teaching them on the Sabbath, [32]and they were astonished at his teaching, for his word possessed authority. [33]And in the synagogue there was a man who had the spirit of an unclean demon, and he cried out with a loud voice, [34]"Ha![a] What have you to do with us, Jesus of Nazareth? Have you come to destroy us? I know who you are—the Holy One of God." [35]But Jesus rebuked him, saying, "Be silent and come out of him!" And when the demon had thrown him down in their midst, he came out of him, having done him no harm. [36]And they were all amazed and said to one another, "What is this word? For with authority and power he commands the unclean spirits, and they come out!" [37]And reports about him went out into every place in the surrounding region.

[38]And he arose and left the synagogue and entered Simon's house. Now Simon's mother-in-law was ill with a high fever, and they appealed to him on her behalf. [39]And he stood over her and rebuked the fever, and it left her, and immediately she rose and began to serve them.

[40]Now when the sun was setting, all those who had any who were sick with various diseases brought them to him, and he laid his hands on every one of them and healed them. [41]And demons also came out of many, crying, "You are the Son of God!" But he rebuked them and would not allow them to speak, because they knew that he was the Christ.

[42]And when it was day, he departed and went into a desolate place. And the people sought him and came to him, and would have kept him from leaving them, [43]but he said to them, "I must preach the good news of the kingdom of God to the other towns as well; for I was sent for this purpose." [44]And he was preaching in the synagogues of Judea.[b]

a Or *Leave us alone* b Some manuscripts *Galilee*

OVERVIEW: One of the more significant and troubling questions this passage raised for early modern people related to Satan: What was the devil's role in causing illness? In the sixteenth and the seventeenth centuries, the majority of people believed in the physical reality of the devil and demonic possession. Demons were believed to cause illness, bad luck, even death, and often through the mediation of another person (a witch or sorcerer, which the Pharisees might have assumed Jesus was). The fact that Jesus healed demon-possessed people was believable, and quite comforting. If demons were able to cause us harm or illness, we needed an even more powerful exorcist on our side—and Jesus could drive out demons and heal the damage they caused with only a word. For the reformers, his miraculous exorcism of the demons was a sign that what he preached was true, but it also showed that the Word of God had power over Satan and his minions. God allowed Satan to work in the world, to test people and even to harm them, but only to a certain point. His providential plan was always in control.

The story of Peter's sick, poor and elderly mother-in-law depicts a disease not caused by a demon or by sin (another common putative cause of illness) but simply part of being human. In fact, for these interpreters, it is shameful and uncharitable (and thus sinful) to neglect or condemn those who are sick or elderly, as many do, and this miraculous healing reveals Jesus' sympathy for the poor and ill and God's concern and love for them. But while charitable acts and neighborly concern are a necessity, it is not always necessary to remain where contagion is present; if "charity and faith" are not injured, then flight (from the plague especially) is acceptable. But this miracle, for our interpreters, also reveals another centrally important fact: the apostles were not expected to give up their homes and families or avoid their wives. Peter's involvement with his family was an important sign for Protestants that ministers could, and even should, have homes, wives, children, possessions and familial responsibilities. The Catholic requirement of clerical celibacy, according to them, was counter to the apostolic example.

4:31-37 Jesus' Authority Is Shown Through Words and Driving Out Evil Spirits

CHRIST DID NOT REVENGE HIMSELF ON THE PEOPLE BUT FOLLOWED HIS CALLING.

JOHANNES BRENZ: This is the vengeance which Christ takes on his fellow citizens: he does not command fire to come down from heaven, he does not raise up a flood of waters, he does not make their fields barren, neither does he send a plague or pestilence on them, but only follows his own calling. And what calling is that? First, in relation to the abasing and emptying of himself, his calling was not to revenge himself but to leave vengeance to the Lord God his Father, for according to Scripture, "Vengeance is mine, and I will repay." Therefore Christ, obeying this command, so resigned vengeance to God that he did not harm one hair of the heads of his fellow citizens for the injury they did to him. Second, relating to his ministry, he was called to preach the gospel, as we have heard out of the prophet [Isaiah]. Therefore, because he did not seek vengeance but rather the fulfilling of his calling, he went to Capernaum, a city of Galilee. AN ECCLESIASTICALL EXPOSITION UPON SAINT LUKE 4.[17]

HE IMPRESSED THEM BY SPEAKING WITH AUTHORITY. JOHN CALVIN: The Evangelists signify that the power of the Spirit shone in the words of Christ, so that even his impious and indifferent listeners were compelled to admire him. Luke says that his words were "with authority," that is, full of majesty. Mark speaks more fully by adding an antithesis: "it was different from the words of the scribes." They were false interpreters of Scripture, and so their teaching was literal and dead, breathed nothing of the efficacy of the Spirit and had no majesty at all in it. . . . In short, the Evangelists mean that the way of teaching at that time was so inferior and corrupted that it did not touch human minds with the reverence of God. But the divine power of the Spirit was conspicuous in the words of Christ, which gained him their confidence. This is the power, or rather the dignity and authority, at which the people were astounded. COMMENTARY ON A HARMONY OF THE GOSPELS.[18]

CHRIST'S EXORCISM IS A SEAL ON WHAT HE HAD PREACHED. JOHANNES BRENZ: Christ commanded the devil to hold his peace that he might now confirm the gospel, which he had hitherto preached in words, by a miracle as by a certain seal. He preached that he was sent by God to bring deliverance to captives and give sight to the blind, that is to say, that he would deliver people from sin and from the power of Satan. Therefore when one possessed by a devil was shown to him in the synagogue, he commanded the devil to hold his peace, and he was silent. He commanded him to go out of the man, and the devil threw the man down in the midst of everyone but did him no harm, and by and by went out of him. Christ did this miracle in the demoniac to confirm by an external seal that power was given to him over Satan, and that it was true what he had preached, that he was sent to deliver all those that believe in him from their sins and from death, and to restore them to perfect felicity. For to this end Christ worked his miracles, that they might be sure seals of the gospel and public testimonies of the doctrine of remission of sins by faith in Christ. By

---

[17]Marlorat, ed., *Catholike and Ecclesiasticall Exposition of the Holy Gospel After S. Marke and Luke*, 147*; quoting Deut 32:35.

[18]CO 45:153 (cf. CTS 31:247-48); quoting Mk 1:22.

these words, "when the devil had thrown him," we have to understand that the nature of Satan is such that he raises up great tumults against the gospel of Christ and against the faithful. But if one stands fast in the word of Christ, Satan will do no harm at all to him. AN ECCLESIASTICALL EXPOSITION UPON SAINT LUKE 4.[19]

4:38-41 Jesus Heals Simon's Mother-in-Law and Many Others

THE APOSTLES' MINISTRY DID NOT MEAN NO HOMES OR FAMILIES. MARTIN BUCER: The apostles clearly did not forsake all things and never use them again: they gave themselves and all that they had, yes, they committed their souls and lives into the hands of the Lord, being ready for his sake to forgo everything, if necessity and occasion should demand it. But in the meantime, they used those things as far as it was lawful and as long as their ministry and office would give them leave. They did not rashly forsake their parents, their wives, their children and families, but they cared for them as faithfully and diligently as they could. This story sufficiently proves that fact, as it witnesses that Peter, although he had been called to the ministry of the Word, had a house even a long time after that and took the necessary care of it. Also, after Christ had died, Peter said to Thomas, Nathaniel, the two sons of Zebedee and two of the other disciples, "I will go fishing," and they said to him, "We will also go with you." But we know that they truly forsook all things in that they gave themselves wholly to his will and calling and first sought to fulfill whatever pertained to that. AN ECCLESIASTICALL EXPOSITION UPON SAINT MATHEWE 8.[20]

JESUS SHOWS CONCERN FOR THE SICK AND THE POOR. JOHANNES BRENZ: In this passage we must note the great humility of Christ. Now that

he is in the famous city of Capernaum, where he was held in great esteem on account of his miracles, he did not go to stay with rich people and famous Pharisees, whose favor he might have gotten with one word (because they were still his friends at this point). But instead he lodged in the poor cottage of a fisherman, where there was a sick old woman lying in bed.

Christ did this not in order to teach us that rich people and nobles are to be quite rejected by God, for God is no respecter of persons. But rather he comes to this poor cottage to show that poverty and sickness are not as neglected and condemned by God as they are by human beings. For in this world there is nothing more abject than poor people, and no one less regarded than those who are sick. But Christ comes to these and shows that of everyone he cares the most for them. Therefore, those who are oppressed with poverty and afflicted by sickness should not faint or be discouraged, neither should they think that because of their poverty and sickness they are rejected by God. But let them be sure that the more they are pressed down with afflictions, the more they are beloved and regarded by God. AN ECCLESIASTICALL EXPOSITION UPON SAINT LUKE 4.[21]

OLD AGE IS A GIFT FROM GOD. AUGUSTIN MARLORAT: The piety of Simon Peter's family is set before us to be imitated. They nourish their mother-in-law, who was a bother for them both on account of her old age and because of her sickness, and besides this they also pray to Christ to restore her health. Many people today are quite different from this, for many disdain elderly women, and when they are sick would rather that the devil would fetch them away than that they might be restored to health. What could be more beastly and cruel? Old age is considered to be honorable among wild and barbarous people, and yet some modern folks consider it to be a curse to have to care for an elderly woman.

[19]Marlorat, ed., *Catholike and Ecclesiasticall Exposition of the Holy Gospell After S. Marke and Luke*, 148*.
[20]Marlorat, ed., *Catholike and Ecclesiasticall Exposition of the Holy Gospell After S. Mathewe*, 160*; quoting Jn 21:2-3.

[21]Marlorat, ed., *Catholike and Ecclesiasticall Exposition of the Holy Gospell After S. Marke and Luke*, 149*; alluding to Rom 2:11.

Among the gifts of God, old age is not the least! So what kind of madness is it to curse an old body for the gift of God? But it commonly happens, by the just judgment of God, that those scoundrels who despise this gift of God are not allowed to participate in it themselves. AN ECCLESIASTICALL EXPOSITION UPON SAINT LUKE 4.[22]

GOD USES HARDSHIPS ACCORDING TO HIS WILL. JOHN CALVIN: Such a manner of speaking might seem harsh to those readers not sufficiently experienced in the Scriptures, but there is a good reason for it. Fevers and other diseases, famine, pestilence and hardships of all kinds are God's servants, through whom his justice is carried out. Therefore just as he is said to send out such messengers by his command and will, so also he restrains and withdraws them when it seems right. COMMENTARY ON A HARMONY OF THE GOSPELS.[23]

WHEN IS IT ACCEPTABLE TO FLEE THE PLAGUE? HULDRYCH ZWINGLI: This indicates perfect health. It teaches, meanwhile, that after being sick, we might be restored to even better health and that we should serve our neighbors in charity. One might ask here whether it is appropriate to flee illness and contagion. Above all, the pious should take care that they might thus live where they do not experience any disease, which is what happens if they return to God through his grace. Often, therefore, we see that sins are the cause of disease. To be sure, when God punishes evil people, the pious should pay attention and take care to be on their guard, so that they might prevent the wrath of God. The pious are allowed sometimes to consider fleeing in order to avoid the plague or other contagious diseases. They are allowed to seek remedy for disease and to try to escape or avoid death, as long as it would not bring faith and charity to any harm. For if faith or charity are injured, the one who flees sins. Therefore we

should fix this rule in everything which we attempt, and everyone should stamp this on their conscience. IN THE GOSPEL OF LUKE 4.[24]

JESUS ANTICIPATES THE DEMONS' TREACHERY. THE ENGLISH ANNOTATIONS: The devils confessed him in hope thereby to bring him into suspicion with the multitude. Therefore, Christ forbade them to testify concerning him. As Tertullian says, Christ wants human beings, not unclean spirits, to acknowledge him to be the Son of God. He had sent those before him who were to reveal him—they were more worthy preachers. ANNOTATIONS UPON THE GOSPEL ACCORDING TO SAINT LUKE 4:41.[25]

4:42-44 Jesus Must Continue Traveling to Preach the Kingdom

JESUS CAME NOT TO IMPRESS THE CROWDS BUT TO HEAL SOULS. DESIDERIUS ERASMUS: Truly Jesus did not come to heal the body but the soul, and he did not come to one city only, but to all countries of the whole world. He had performed miracles in Capernaum and began spreading the good seed of evangelical philosophy there by wholesome doctrine, but the crowds marveled at his deeds and sought healing of the body rather than that of the soul. So before these crowds could gather around him again, he left the city at dawn and retreated to the desert, as if to flee their great commotion. By this example he teaches us that he did not perform miracles simply to show off or at the whim of the people, but he did it insofar as they were useful for people's health and to the glory of God, always avoiding the suspicion that they were to gain him any kind of empty attention or praise. That he healed everyone was an example of being ready to be kind-hearted to all people. When he withdrew secretly, it was an example of modesty, in that he was fleeing any sort of fame and

---

[22]Marlorat, ed., *Catholike and Ecclesiasticall Exposition of the Holy Gospell After S. Marke and Luke*, 149*.
[23]CO 45:155 (cf. CTS 31:250-51).

[24]*D. Hvldrichi Zvinglii in Plerosqve Novi Testamenti Libros*, 207.
[25]Downame, ed., *Annotations*, Ttɪr*; citing Tertullian, *Against Marcion* 4.8 (ANF 3:354-55).

showiness. Now, when day came, all sorts of people poured in, drawn by the greatness of the things done the day before. When they realized that Jesus had gone, many of them followed him. On finding him, they attempted to detain him, so that he would not leave their city but take up a permanent residence among them. Their affection toward Jesus was not ungodly, but even more blessed are those who do not allow the Lord Jesus to cut off his residence in their hearts, and, when he prepares to go, call him back by many prayers. PARAPHRASE IN THE GOSPEL OF LUKE 4:42.[26]

CHRIST TRAVELED WIDELY TO AWAKEN THE MINDS OF MANY. JOHN CALVIN: It is noteworthy that he says that he was sent or came out for this purpose, because his words testify that it was his intent to fulfill his duty. But one might ask, is it better that the ministers of the gospel run about here and there so that God's teaching is enjoyed only in small bits and meagerly in each place, or should they stay in one spot, to give thorough instruction to genuine listeners? I respond: Christ's plan, which is mentioned here, was agreeable to the order and calling of the Father and was founded on the best reasons. For Christ was going to travel throughout Judea in a short amount of time, that the minds of the people in many places might be awakened to the hearing of the gospel as if by the sound of a trumpet. COMMENTARY ON A HARMONY OF THE GOSPELS.[27]

---

[26]Erasmus, *In Evangelivm Lvce Paraphrasis*, i4r-v (LB 7:333).

[27]CO 45:156 (cf. CTS 31:252-53).

5:1-11 THE CALLING OF THE FIRST DISCIPLES

On one occasion, while the crowd was pressing in on him to hear the word of God, he was standing by the lake of Gennesaret, ²and he saw two boats by the lake, but the fishermen had gone out of them and were washing their nets. ³Getting into one of the boats, which was Simon's, he asked him to put out a little from the land. And he sat down and taught the people from the boat. ⁴And when he had finished speaking, he said to Simon, "Put out into the deep and let down your nets for a catch." ⁵And Simon answered, "Master, we toiled all night and took nothing! But at your word I will let down the nets." ⁶And when they had done this, they enclosed a large number of fish, and their nets were breaking. ⁷They signaled to their partners in the other boat to come and help them. And they came and filled both the boats, so that they began to sink. ⁸But when Simon Peter saw it, he fell down at Jesus' knees, saying, "Depart from me, for I am a sinful man, O Lord." ⁹For he and all who were with him were astonished at the catch of fish that they had taken, ¹⁰and so also were James and John, sons of Zebedee, who were partners with Simon. And Jesus said to Simon, "Do not be afraid; from now on you will be catching men." ¹¹And when they had brought their boats to land, they left everything and followed him.

OVERVIEW: Luther was famously critical of the (ab)use of allegory by medieval and contemporary preachers, but we should not assume that Protestants never found abstract symbolism in Bible stories. Several commentators here see in the boat, the nets and the fishermen important symbols for the Christian life and faith. But it was more common to see historical, doctrinal and practical lessons in Scripture stories. For example, while Simon's boat could be seen as a symbol of the visible church, more commonly it was seen as the means for Jesus' preaching—because of the crowd of people, Jesus asked Simon to push the boat out a little ways, so that he could better address his audience. Simon, despite being busy with his work, was ready to serve; when Jesus told him to put out to deeper water and let down his nets, he willingly obeyed, despite the fact that it was counter to his experience and knowledge as a fisherman. The point here was not merely to pay Simon with fish, but rather by this miracle to reveal Christ's divinity and to encourage these men to follow him. And Peter is appropriately afraid and overwhelmed— how could he, a simple (and sinful) fisherman, possibly serve Christ and share his message with others? He knew he was not worthy to receive God's attention and to be given a divine calling. But Jesus comforted him, as he does all sinners, by acknowledging what we lack and showing that God will give us what we need. It is Christ who will make them fishers of people and the word itself that will give the power to preach it. They were fearful and unlearned, but the Spirit led the word straight to their hearts, and they were so enflamed by this pearl of great price that they gave up everything and followed him.

5:1-3 Jesus Preaches by the Lake

THE CROWD THRONGS AROUND JESUS, WHO SEEKS THE LOST SHEEP. CASPAR HUBERINUS: Saint Luke shows us here how the common Jewish folk feel about Jesus and what they think about his salutary teaching. Namely, he shows that the people thronged around Christ. This pressing in on him shows the true zeal and great desire which the people had toward Christ and the gospel. For it is out of all proportion how the people are moved by godly zeal and set on fire by God's Word, and give themselves so earnestly to the gospel. However, when the love toward God's

Word grows cold, and the zeal decreases and the listeners become fervent toward false teaching and error, then things go badly. It is an especially terrible plague and punishment when the common crowd turns enemy to correct doctrine, does not want to hear it anymore, despises it and becomes bored with it. Then they become curious about false teachings, and lust after only what is new and seldom listen to the old. Their curiosity pushes them toward various sects, to listen to the false teaching and to embrace it. Then Satan has won the game and conquered that place and authority again which he had previously been driven out of by the gospel. . . .

And we should also observe here the great diligence, pains, trouble and work which Christ took on himself for our sakes. Here he has begun his wide-ranging travels across the whole land of the Jews to reveal his godly teachings and to show us the way to holiness. Now he preaches in the towns, then in another spot, now at the sea, then in the desert, diligently seeking everywhere he goes for the straying and lost sheep. ON THE FIFTH SUNDAY AFTER TRINITY.[1]

THE NETS ARE THE WORD, WHICH CATCHES SOULS. KASPAR VON SCHWENCKFELD: The nets, or the yarn, of the fishermen means the Word of God and the salutary pure teaching by which the soul of its own free will and for its own benefit is caught. This proves itself in that just as the net is made and woven together with criss-crossing threads, so also each part in the teaching must agree with the rest, not to explain disagreeable or changeable things but because with the unanimous holy Scripture everything in Christ will be well-covered. Consciences should likewise be properly edified in the way of grace. The Lord talks about this in the Gospel: "Therefore every scribe who has been trained for the kingdom of heaven is like a master of a house, who brings out of his treasure what is new and what is old." And just as the fish that is caught is held in the net, so also

Christ will not lightly part from that one who is caught in his grace through the word of faith, even if the net should tear beneath him: "Everything that my Father gives me comes to me," says the Lord, and "Whoever comes to me, I will not throw him out."

So the fishermen wash the nets when the preacher or minister of Christ grows in the Word of life or in the grace of God. When the minister is watered more and more from above with the gospel, he improves in understanding and gains in the gifts of the Holy Spirit. The preacher as well as the congregation should grow in the gifts, strength, Spirit and grace of God, because he also is alive. He should not only study and care for others but also for himself, if it otherwise stands properly between him and the congregation, and he should go forward piously with the harvest. INTERPRETATION OF THE GOSPEL, LUKE 5, ON THE FIFTH SUNDAY AFTER TRINITY.[2]

CHRIST MAKES THE SHIP HIS PULPIT. JOHN BOYS: It is a very common note that Simon's ship is a type of the church militant, floating in the waves of this troublesome world. The politicians accuse it of folly, the superstitious of heresy, the schismatic of idolatry, the Jews jest at it, the Separatists run out of it, the Turks despise it. In this ship, Christ is tossed, but the people stand on the shore. The pastor is exposed to greater peril than his parishioners, if any tempest arises. Interpreting literally, Christ taught in the wilderness and the city, sometimes conferring with one person and sometimes instructing multitudes, in the synagogue, in the streets, on the land and in the water. In every place where he traveled it was his food and drink to do the will of his Father. Therefore being pressed on here and oppressed with troops of listeners, he makes a ship his pulpit, that he might teach them with greater convenience. Everyone should therefore labor in his respective vocation and office to follow Christ's example, doing as much good as he can at

---

[1] Huberinus, *Postilla Teütsch*, 2:c5v-c6r, c7r-v.

[2] CS 10:481; quoting Mt 13:52; Jn 6:39.

all times and in all places. THE FIFTH SUNDAY AFTER TRINITY.[3]

5:4-7 The Miraculous Catch of Fish

BY JESUS' POWER, PREACHING THE GOSPEL BRINGS IN A LARGE CATCH. HEINRICH BULLINGER: By these words Jesus teaches how vain a thing it is to teach or command anything without his commandment and power. But when the Word is preached with his commandment and name, an infinite number are taken with the net of the gospel. Matthew compares the preaching of the gospel with fishing, because just as a net cast into the sea takes in diverse fishes, so also the gospel being preached in the world brings diverse people into the church of God. But Christ's purpose in this miracle was not so much to signify what would come to pass but more to inspire these men to follow him, despite him being poor, and only a little before having been cast out by all his neighbors and acquaintances and threatened with death. AN ECCLESIASTICALL EXPOSITION UPON SAINT LUKE 5.[4]

PETER ACCEPTS CHRIST'S WORD, DESPITE HIS IGNORANCE OF FISHING. THOMAS BECON: It should be especially marked in Peter's example that he would suffer nothing to hinder him but cast away from himself the contrariness of the unbelievers and went wholly to God's Word. And so that we may understand how great this faith is in Peter, we see that he is not irritated by what is God's common practice in all his works (and that he uses also in this situation), that is, that he points out what should first be done, but in a seemingly ignorant way. For it is common that fishermen do not look for any great catch out of the water at midday. The night is more appropriate for that sort of gain. And those who are fishing rarely fish in the open water but stay close to the banks. Christ

disregards this common practice of fishermen and commands Peter to launch out into the deep water, even though they had caught nothing there all night. Now at midday he bids them to lower their nets for a catch. This seems to be an absurd and foolish thing to Peter, and he sees that Christ is not familiar with the usual practices of fishermen, and yet he answers very politely: "Lord," he says, " we have labored all night long and have taken nothing. If we followed the usual practices of our profession, we would have no great hope of a catch, but I will accept your word. If it does not help, we have only lost our labor." If Peter had not been showing reverence to Christ, he might have spoken to him more rudely, because of the ignorance which he displayed. How can this man presume to take on himself to teach a fisherman his craft, of which he is ignorant? Why should he put his oar into another's boat?[5] A teacher and a fisherman are not the same thing—when Christ teaches, he should be heard, but when he teaches how to fish, why should anyone listen to him? This is the way in which we might answer Christ, for this is our usual sort of response. We think we are wiser than Christ. But Peter is wiser than us, for he lays aside all such thoughts and thinks instead: "Whatever my skill happens to be, I will not despise this word." And so he embraces it with all his heart and lets go of both his knowledge and his reason. THE FIFTH SUNDAY AFTER TRINITY SUNDAY.[6]

ALL THE BLESSINGS FROM OUR WORK COME FROM THE LORD. JOHANNES BRENZ: By this miracle, the fact is also proven that Christ is Lord not only of the earth but also of the sea and all things which are in it. For if he were not Lord of the fishes in the sea, how could it happen that at his word so great a multitude of fishes should be caught? This also teaches us from whence the blessing, increase or gain of our labor comes. It also teaches that nothing happens for our prosperity and happiness but what has been commanded by

---

[3]Boys, *Exposition of the Dominical Epistles and Gospels*, 3:129-30*; citing Job 4:3.

[4]Marlorat, ed., *Catholike and Ecclesiasticall Exposition of the Holy Gospell After S. Marke and Luke*, 152*; alluding to Mt 13:47.

---

[5]In other words, why should he meddle in another's affairs?
[6]Becon, *New Postil*, 39v-40r*.

the Lord. So unless the Word of God teaches us otherwise, let us do all things liberally, doubting nothing but believing that everything we do pleases God as long as we remain within the limits of our calling. We will wait and attend to what the Lord commands, never straying from his commandments or Word. And we must note that even if we do not see the blessing and increase of our daily labor, despite this we will keep on working. For Christ said, "Put out into deep water, and let down the nets for a catch." He commands the fishermen here to put down their nets, and in the same way also he commands all people to follow their calling and labor, not to forsake their office and their work and give themselves over to idleness. AN ECCLESIASTICALL EXPOSITION UPON SAINT LUKE 5.[7]

THE MIRACLE WAS MEANT TO SHOW CHRIST'S DIVINE GLORY. JOHN CALVIN: Certainly the purpose of the miracle was that Christ's divinity would be recognized, and that Peter and the others would dedicate themselves to him as disciples. Generally, however, this example teaches that we should not be at all afraid that our labor will not be given the blessing of God and a desirable outcome, if we apply ourselves to the work by the order and guidance of Christ's hand. For there was such an abundance of fish that the ships were sinking, and the minds of the viewers were lifted up in admiration. It was proper, therefore, that the divine glory of Christ was manifested by this miracle, and that his authority was fully established. COMMENTARY ON A HARMONY OF THE GOSPELS.[8]

5:8-11 *Simon's Confession and Jesus' Commission*

PETER HAD FEAR EVEN IN THE FACE OF CHRIST'S MERCY. PHILIPP MELANCHTHON: Peter's fear had many benefits: he judged himself

unworthy to be in the presence of God, but also there was a great and unexpected benefit in that he saw himself not according to his labor but as grasping the benefits of God. This is an example of how everybody might be affected when they experience that God is not angry but rather is merciful. Whether the human mind fears the wrath of God or sees his mercy, whichever it may be, it flees them both. Therefore this thought clings in every soul, that we might be worthy of punishment, but we are definitely unworthy of mercy. Therefore it is as necessary for us as it was for Peter to hear the voice of Christ, "Do not fear," as if he said, "Because you are a sinner and terrified of your unworthiness, I want you to have hope in my mercy and goodness, and take comfort. Therefore have confidence, and not so much in that you will see the benefits in this thing, but in that I will make you a fisher of men, that is, an apostle and teacher in my kingdom." THE FIFTH SUNDAY AFTER TRINITY.[9]

GOD GIVES THE POWER TO BECOME PREACHERS. THE ENGLISH ANNOTATIONS: To comfort them, he declares what the effect of his presence will be: that they should thereby be enabled by preaching the gospel, that great fishing net of God's kingdom, to draw people out of the bitter floods of sin to life everlasting. And Christ has enabled them as he promised: "all our sufficiency is of God," who therefore called all ignorant people to an effectual and powerful ministry of the Word to save souls. Whoever he calls thus, he miraculously makes able ministers of the New Testament. If the false apostles who pretend to an extraordinary calling can make apparent that God has wrought this miracle in them, we shall believe that they are indeed called to preach the gospel. One thing is certain: Christ never called any idiot or unlearned person to this office to leave him thus, but to show a miraculous power in enabling him to that to which he called him. And although Christ said this to Peter (who out of a deeper sense of his own sins and the majesty of Christ shining in this miracle

---

[7]Marlorat, ed., *Catholike and Ecclesiasticall Exposition of the Holy Gospell After S. Marke and Luke*, 152-53*.
[8]CO 45:149 (cf. CTS 31:241).

[9]MO 14:325.

begged Christ to depart from him), it was a common grace promised to them all, and so no prerogative of Peter, although Christ addressed this comfort by name to Peter whom he saw to be most afraid. Annotations upon the Gospel According to Saint Luke 5:10.[10]

Christ Called Them to Be Fishers of People. Johann Spangenberg: What does Jesus say to him? "Do not be afraid, from now on you will catch people." With these words, Christ leads these disciples from fear to joy, from hell to heaven, from condemnation into eternal life. It is as if he said: "Dear Simon, you shall not die because of your sins, nor shall you be condemned. You shall live a long life and become a fisher, not of fish but of people. And not you alone, but the others with you. I will not only absolve all of you from your sins, but I will also give you the power to absolve the sins of others." And what did Peter, Andrew, John and James do when they heard these words? They brought the ship to land and, leaving everything, followed after him. And how was God's word so powerful? Christ did not of course only speak to them in their ears but also in their hearts. To leave father and mother, house and hearth, and everything on account of God is not such a small work that a person could do it all on his own. It is a work of the Holy Spirit. But we know that the word of Christ is spirit and life, so it is good to believe that the calling of the apostles did not only come into their ears but also into their hearts; otherwise they would not have given up father and mother and everything else so quickly and followed Christ. Gospel on the Fifth Sunday After Trinity.[11]

The Gospel Contains the Pearl of Great Price. Johannes Brenz: In every promise in the gospel there are comprehended and set forth such divine and heavenly graces that he who considers and tastes just the least part of them by faith cannot stop himself, but he must wholly submit himself and cleave only to Christ. The kingdom of heaven, says the Lord, is like a treasure hidden in a field. When a person finds it, he hides it, and in great joy goes, sells all he has and buys that field. And again he says, the kingdom of heaven is like a merchant who was seeking fine pearls. When he found one precious pearl, he went and sold all he had and bought it.

This precious pearl signifies heavenly joy and the perfect happiness which lies hidden in the shell of the gospel. One who finds this pearl in the gospel by faith would rather forsake everything than leave the gospel. These fishermen found such treasure, such riches and such great happiness in this gospel that they chose to forsake everything else rather than give up Christ who had called them. An Ecclesiasticall Exposition upon Saint Luke 5.[12]

---

[10]Downame, ed., *Annotations*, Ttir*; alluding to Mt 13:47; 4:18; 2 Cor 3:5, 6.

[11]Spangenberg, *Postilla . . . von Ostern biß auffs Aduent*, XCIIv; alluding to Jn 6:63.

[12]Marlorat, ed., *Catholike and Ecclesiasticall Exposition of the Holy Gospell After S. Marke and Luke*, 154*; alluding to Mt 13:44-45.

5:12-16 JESUS HEALS THE MAN WITH LEPROSY

¹²While he was in one of the cities, there came a man full of leprosy.ᵃ And when he saw Jesus, he fell on his face and begged him, "Lord, if you will, you can make me clean." ¹³And Jesusᵇ stretched out his hand and touched him, saying, "I will; be clean." And immediately the leprosy left him. ¹⁴And he charged him to tell no one, but "go and show yourself to the priest, and make an offering for your cleansing, as Moses commanded, for a proof to them." ¹⁵But now even more the report about him went abroad, and great crowds gathered to hear him and to be healed of their infirmities.¹⁶But he would withdraw to desolate places and pray.

a *Leprosy was a term for several skin diseases; see Leviticus 13*　b *Greek he*

OVERVIEW: This particular healing story shows again an oblique criticism of the Pharisees and thus anyone who was committed to external observance of the law without interior change. Lepers were kept far away from people and communities, and this leper ran a risk by approaching Jesus. But his faith moved him to come to Christ, for he believed Christ could help him, if only he would. Indeed Christ did will to help him, healing him with a mere command. But Christ can heal not only body but soul as well, and this man's soul was already filled with faith, thus making him a far better person than those who focused on external perfection. But because Jesus was willing to speak with an "untouchable" did not mean that he wanted to disregard the Law altogether. When he had healed this man, he sent him to be inspected by a priest, according to the levitical rule. Christ came to fulfill the Law, but that does not mean that we are free to do as we please, as some early in the Reformation assumed. His instructions to this man are taken as confirmation of the importance of rules and authority. The man would not be allowed to resume his life in the community without the approbation of the priest, so it was (practically as well as morally) right that he go immediately for a priestly inspection. As he often did, Jesus instructed this man to say nothing to anyone, implying that the preaching office is not given to all. Jesus himself was always willing, however, to share his message and healing with everyone, but there are times when even he needed to withdraw from the crowds. The end of this passage shows Jesus taking some time—not to pamper himself but instead to communicate more directly with his Father. This example teaches us that it is through the help of the Father that he pursues his course. His ministry and work are completed according to God's plan and with the support of the Holy Spirit.

5:12-13 *The Leper Asks Jesus to Heal Him*

THE LEPER WAS HEALED BECAUSE OF REPENTANCE AND FAITH. DESIDERIUS ERASMUS: Jesus provided this example to show that there is no fault so horrible or deadly that it cannot be forgiven, if only the person who has it acknowledges his disease and, through faith in the gospel, begs for the remedy from Jesus, the heavenly physician. So it happened that there was a certain man in a certain place who was seriously affected by leprosy, and his entire body was covered with the most foul and disgusting scabs. This sort of person was considered abominable by the Jews, and they were banished from any association with others and removed to a distance. The law forbade them from touching anyone because of the immediate threat of contagion. But much more foul and abhorrent than leprosy of the body is leprosy of the mind and soul. And the Jews, who overflowed with many internal vices themselves, greatly detested Gentiles, tax collectors, and others who were known to be sinners. When it would happen that they would have to speak to anyone like this, they would return home and wash their bodies from head to toe, just as if they might contract some disease from being near them. But Christ wanted his disciples to stay far, far away from this sort of presumptuous cleanliness. Paraphrase on the Gospel of Luke 5:12.[1]

The Leper Trusted That Christ Was the Savior. Hugh Latimer: The leper took Christ to be a savior, and so he came to him for help. So we should also come to him, for he is the Savior of humankind, and he is the only helper who can nourish both our bodies and our souls. He saves our souls by his word, if when we hear it we believe it. The salvation of our bodies will occur at the Last Day, when body and soul will come together and there will be rewarded—that is, if the soul is saved, the body will be saved, for soul and body will go together—and so he saves both our bodies and our souls. And pay attention here also to the behavior of the leper, for not even the greatest doctor of theology should be ashamed to learn from his example: in him a marvelous, strong faith and a firm confidence in Christ appears. He did not doubt at all that Christ was able to help him, and he trusted fully in his goodness and mercy. Therefore his faith moved him to come to Christ and to seek his help. A Sermon on the Third Sunday After Epiphany (1552).[2]

Christ Is the Good Doctor. John Boys: Now I come to the physician, in whom two things are observable: first, his mercy, because he so readily helps; second, his might, because he could so easily cure such an incurable leprosy. . . . He granted cheerfully what the leper so earnestly

desired. The leper said, "If you will," and Christ answered, "I will," and "as I will, I say, be clean! And as I say, I do." The man's leprosy was immediately healed—Christ spoke the word and it was done; he commanded and it was effected, even with only a little movement of his lips and a touch of his finger.

Here there is comfort for the distressed soul: the leper calls, and Christ heals him; the centurion comes, and Christ helps him. Other physicians are often deceived themselves, and often deceive others, and therefore we take a big risk when we trust them a little. The best medicine, as someone once said, is to take no medicine. But if we commit our cause to this heavenly doctor, our venture is without any peradventure or doubt, for he cures all who call on him, and he eases everyone who comes to him. The Third Sunday After Epiphany.[3]

5:14-15 Jesus Instructs the Healed Man

Jesus Did Not Want to Take Away from What Is Right. Johann Spangenberg: How does he demonstrate his love toward the priest? He said: "Look, don't tell anyone, but go and show yourself to the priest, and offer the gifts that Moses commanded, as a testimony to you." It was required, according to Leviticus 14, that the priest had to inspect the leper and see whether he was clean or unclean. Now he did not want that the man should diminish his righteousness; as also no one takes anything away from the gospel but gives more to it. What should we learn from this? That we should not do good for anyone who would harm another person, which is what people have been doing for years when they have built churches and cloisters with stolen, plundered and usurious goods. And now there are many who take the gospel to be only for worldly freedom, to do and to allow whatever they please. Now, why does he say, "Tell no one"? He did not want for one person to entrust the preaching office to each one, and by this he gives us an example, that in God's work we

[1]Erasmus, *In Evangelivm Lvce Paraphrasis*, kr-v (LB 336-37).
[2]Latimer, *Sermons and Remains*, 168-69*.

[3]Boys, *Exposition of the Dominical Epistles and Gospels*, 1:165-66*.

should not look for our own honor and glory but for God's honor alone. GOSPEL ON THE THIRD SUNDAY AFTER EPIPHANY.[4]

5:16 *Jesus Retreats for Prayer*

CHRIST SHARES HIS MESSAGE WITH EVERYONE. JOHANN AGRICOLA: Christ is always one and the same, revealing his office readily and openly to everyone, so that he might suffer none of his longed-for work whatsoever to pass away. Now he will separate himself from the crowd, indeed from the entire multitude of people, withdrawing into solitude, to seek a place for conversation with his Father, to whom he assigns everything, not even sustaining the person by himself. He does this indeed to teach the same truth by the example of his life, to show that through the help of the Father he takes it on himself to save the body and soul. Meanwhile he lives in the sight of the people, that the gentler souls might be rescued and return to him. For a time he employs human customs, so that uniting them with benefits and with gentleness they might love and worship him. He frees Mary Magdalene from the demons, saves the adulterous woman from stoning, saves the thief on the cross and socializes with tax collectors. However, he allows Peter to sink and David to fall into murder and adultery, that we might learn that what Paul said is true: "Whoever stands should watch out so that he does not fall." ANNOTATIONS IN THE GOSPEL OF LUKE 5.[5]

LIKE CHRIST, WE NEED TO SPEND TIME IN PRAYER TO OUR FATHER. JOHANNES BRENZ: Again Christ shuns the multitude and goes into a deserted place, lest in gathering many people around himself, he might seem to be vainglorious or else to be promoting rebellion against the civil authority. Also, he went off on his own to rest himself from his work for a little while, from preaching the gospel and healing the sick. But we must note here how Christ relaxed and spent his time in his solitude: he spent this time in prayer, giving thanks to God the Father for the benefits which he gave to people through himself, God's Son. What can be sweeter than prayer by which we talk with the Lord our God and discuss things with him with regular conversation? For God is our Father, our Savior, our Redeemer and our happiness. AN ECCLESIASTICALL EXPOSITION UPON SAINT LUKE 5.[6]

---

[4]Spangenberg, *Postilla* (1582), LIIIIv; citing Lev 14:2-3.

[5]Agricola, *In Evangelium Lucae Annotationes*, 73r-v; quoting 1 Cor 10:12.

[6]Marlorat, ed., *Catholike and Ecclesiasticall Exposition of the Holy Gospell After S. Marke and Luke*, 154*.

5:17-26 JESUS HEALS THE PARALYTIC BEFORE THE PHARISEES

[17]On one of those days, as he was teaching, Pharisees and teachers of the law were sitting there, who had come from every village of Galilee and Judea and from Jerusalem. And the power of the Lord was with him to heal.[a] [18]And behold, some men were bringing on a bed a man who was paralyzed, and they were seeking to bring him in and lay him before Jesus, [19]but finding no way to bring him in, because of the crowd, they went up on the roof and let him down with his bed through the tiles into the midst before Jesus. [20]And when he saw their faith, he said, "Man, your sins are forgiven you." [21]And the scribes and the Pharisees began to question, saying, "Who is this who speaks blasphemies? Who can forgive sins but God alone?" [22]When Jesus perceived their thoughts, he answered them, "Why do you question in your hearts? [23]Which is easier, to say, 'Your sins are forgiven you,' or to say, 'Rise and walk'? [24]But that you may know that the Son of Man has authority on earth to forgive sins"—he said to the man who was paralyzed—"I say to you, rise, pick up your bed and go home." [25]And immediately he rose up before them and picked up what he had been lying on and went home, glorifying God. [26]And amazement seized them all, and they glorified God and were filled with awe, saying, "We have seen extraordinary things today."

a Some manuscripts *was present to heal them*

OVERVIEW: In this pericope our commentators highlight the contrast between the Pharisees' understanding of righteousness and Jesus'. The Pharisees agreed with Jesus that only God can forgive sin, but they trusted in their own works and service as meriting their salvation, not God's gracious and undeserved mercy. But, the reformers assert, no one's good works can earn salvation, any more than the actions of the paralytic's friends could assure his healing. Salvation is in Christ alone by faith alone. Truly good works follow—but do not precede—such salvation.

5:17 Jesus Preaches and Has the Power to Heal

JESUS FIRST HEALED THEIR SOULS. KONRAD PELLIKAN: And because he was the source of all healing, Jesus aspired to nothing other than a certain divine power for the healing of people, for which purpose he came by grace to earth. And in truth the first part is preferable to the people, that he laid claim to their care, and by his words he healed the diseases of souls. Thus first he taught, while seated, in justice a doctor by his authority laying claim to his benefit. He was more than capable of warding off physical disease, and because he was exposed to all eyes, he also did that to add to their faith by both greater delight and virtue, but not so that they all carried it equally in their souls. Here we can see a ready truth training natural capacity. COMMENTARY IN LUKE 5:17.[1]

5:18-20 Friends Bring the Paralytic for Healing

BOTH THE FRIENDS AND THE MAN DISPLAYED GREAT FAITH. JOHN BOYS: In these porters and attendants we observe unfeigned love to their friend and a lively faith in Christ: in being "feet to the lame," we see great love. In their bringing him to Christ, and in the strange manner which Saint Mark reports, "they removed the roof above him, and when they had made an opening,

---

[1]Pellikan, *In Sacrosancta Quatuor Evangelia*, 74 (cf. LB 7:339).

they let down the bed on which the paralytic lay," and when he was so brought to Christ holding it sufficient to present *miserum ante misericordem*, an object of misery to the father of mercy, they showed even greater faith.[2] Others would have instead poured out a long prayer with many words to Christ, or have brought in a long petition in writing on behalf of their friend; but they were well-assured, as Erasmus elegantly states, that the distressed on his bed "spoke more eloquently to the mercy of the doctor because he could not speak." Therefore the text says in the next clause that Jesus "saw their faith." As God, he saw their faith as he saw the thoughts of the scribes, and as a man, he saw their faith by their works. He saw the faith of the porters in bringing and of the paralyzed man in allowing himself to be brought in such a manner; and therefore Christ, the "consolation of Israel," affords him comfort instantly both in word and in deed. He tells him to be of good cheer, for whoever believes in Christ "has the right to become children of God." If you are God's child, you may very well be of good cheer, for your Father in heaven knows your wants and provides all things necessary for you. Indeed, Jesus first healed his sins and then his sores. THE NINETEENTH SUNDAY AFTER TRINITY.[3]

THE PARALYTIC AND HIS FRIENDS BOTH BELIEVED. FRANÇOIS LAMBERT: Through the faith of others, he speaks a wonderful word to the sick man, "Your sins are forgiven," although the fact that he also had faith should not be doubted. Anyone can say what he wants of the paralytic, but I would understand this, where Luke says "their faith," to mean not so much just those letting down the sick man through the roof, but he also understood the faith of the sick man himself. For just as by their faith they lowered him through the roof,

so by his faith he wanted to be lowered down into the midst of the people. Therefore Jesus regarded both the faith of the sick man and of those who carried him, which was pleasing to him.

Let us not deny the truth that the faith of one person is able to help another. For even if one's own faith is necessary if one is to be justified, a person's faith can bring about faith in another, who afterwards would be justified. But the one who brings a brother or sister to Christ does not merit anything at all. For first in the believing Christ has the merit, because in pleading on behalf of the brother he was heard. And second therefore also Christ merits to himself the one he gained. Therefore all merit is of Christ alone. COMMENTARY IN LUKE 5:18-20.[4]

5:21-23 *Jesus and the Pharisees Disagree*

JESUS' CRITICS DID NOT UNDERSTAND THAT HE WAS GOD. MARTIN BUCER: The thing which is honey to the bee is gall to the spider; just so, nothing can be so well done or spoken which will not be judged evil by evil and wicked people. There was a great multitude of people who glorified God for such a great miracle, but the scribes and Pharisees found something to complain about and criticize. So the first are last, and the last first, and every tree brings forth its fruit. . . . They did not understand that Christ was God. But despite this, these scribes and Pharisees were more holy and religious than a great many today, namely, those who affirm that they can absolve sins and that by indulgences they can forgive sins, for these claims blaspheme the name of the Lord. Only the Lord remits and forgives sins; the minister of the Lord only announces out of the Word and the mouth of God that God has forgiven and will forgive sins. For all power is the Lord's forever, and ministers only have the administration of it. AN ECCLESIASTICALL EXPOSITION UPON SAINT MATHEWE 9.[5]

---

[2] The reference is to Thomas Beauxamis, *Commentarii in Evangelicam Harmoniam*, 4 vols. (Paris: Chaudiere, 1583). Beauxamis (1524–1589) was a Carmelite theologian and polemicist in Paris.

[3] Boys, *Exposition of the Dominical Epistles and Gospels*, 4:138-39*; citing Job 29:15; LB 7:339 (Erasmus); Lk 2:25; Jn 1:12; Mt 6:8, 33.

[4] Lambert, *In Divi Lucae*, M3v-M4r.

[5] Marlorat, ed., *Catholike and Ecclesiasticall Exposition of the Holy Gospell After S. Mathewe*, 174-75*.

CHRIST AFFIRMS THIS MIRACLE WITH TWO MORE MIRACLES. JOHANN SPANGENBERG: What do the Pharisees say to this? They say among themselves: "How can this man speak such blasphemy? Who can forgive sins except for God?" Here we can see the poisonous evil of the Pharisees, who scold Christ as a blasphemer, because he, a man, forgave sins. And yet they themselves set the forgiveness of sins in their human work and service, that is, their fasting, praying and other ceremonies. What is that besides stealing God's honor and ascribing divinity to themselves? They saw a splinter in someone else's eye and did not notice the log in their own eyes.

And what does Christ do? He witnesses to this miracle with two more miracles. First, he answers their thoughts, which only God is able to do, saying: "Why do you think such evil things in your hearts? What is easier to say, 'Your sins are forgiven,' or to say, 'Stand up and walk?'" Second, he also heals this paralyzed man, not only so that he can stand up and walk but also can take up his bed onto his shoulders and carry it home. GOSPEL ON THE NINETEENTH SUNDAY AFTER TRINITY.[6]

BOTH ARE EQUALLY DIFFICULT. HULDRYCH ZWINGLI: "Which is easier?" Certainly, if you want to judge rightly, they both are difficult. In fact, you promise the remission of sin through human misery, but wrongly, to be sure, through your own sacrifice. However, you are not able to cleanse anyone by this. He sees in this their avarice and hypocrisy, for they were imitating others who were justified, just as they make priests and popes who are released from sin by themselves, even though they might be the most unclean themselves, then they promise purification to others. "And although you wish to be seen by me as having power over this thing, you will learn that in something equally difficult, suddenly and by my command alone, I will raise up this man who was lying down, and I will make him able to walk, when he had to be

carried here by others." And right when he said these things, he ordered the man to get up. IN THE GOSPEL OF LUKE 5.[7]

5:24-26 *The Healing of the Paralytic Displays Jesus' Power*

CHRIST'S BENEFITS ARE GREATER THAN MERELY HEALING THE BODY. CASPAR HUBERINUS: In this Gospel we see that our Lord Jesus Christ demonstrates a threefold benefit. Here we can recognize and take from it his sympathetic will, true heart and dear and abundant benefits, which he first teaches in his lovely, comforting sermon. Preaching the Word of God reveals the will of our Father in heaven and praises his mercy, and it provides one of the highest benefits, namely, to liberate the people from Satan's kingdom, which is a kingdom of darkness, to comfort sinners and to reconcile them with God. The second benefit is that Christ allows himself to be easily importuned and persuaded to make this sick man healthy in body, and not this man alone but many more sick people. The third benefit is that he forgives the sins of this poor man and finally even dies for him, and in fact dies willingly for all of us. He calls him his son, for Christ in his office is called an everlasting father. From there the fresh water flows, that is, from the delightful spring which cleanses from sin and impurity. It is the Lord who forgives our sins. ON THE NINETEENTH SUNDAY AFTER TRINITY.[8]

THE PALSY IS LIKE SIN—IT PREVENTS US FROM ACCOMPLISHING GOOD. THOMAS BECON: Now let us briefly touch on the story. The man who is sick with palsy is an example of all sinners, for the property of the disease is that the members of the body cannot do their proper functions. When a palsied person tries to draw his feet or hands to him, they fall farther away from him. That is why Aristotle in his *Ethics* compared such a

---

[6]Spangenberg, *Postilla . . . von Ostern biß auffs Aduent*, CLVIr; alluding to Mt 7:3.

[7]*D. Hvldrichi Zvinglii in Plerosqve Novi Testamenti Libros*, 209.
[8]Huberinus, *Postilla Teütsch*, 2:Aa7r-v; alluding to Mk 2:2; Mt 8:1-17; Is 9:6; Zech 13:1; Is 43:25.

person with wild and fierce youth, which can be tamed by no means. But whoever wants to understand this disease well must understand that it is spoken of hypocrites who want to be justified by their works. The more that they labor to draw closer to God and to pacify him, the farther they are cast from him. And when they think that they give him the most pleasure, that is when they displease him the most—for they have no faith. Therefore whoever desires to be rid of this evil should come to this man, Christ, who delivers relief when he says, "My son, be of good comfort, for your sins are forgiven." By such a word is strength restored to the bodily members so that they may work together. For wherever there is remission of sins, there real and true good works will ensue, for sin is taken away. This is what Christ especially meant with that one who was sick with the palsy. He lay sick in his bed, for his disease would not allow him to do otherwise—he was like a slaughtered animal, for his body would not serve him. But when Christ commanded him to rise, he rose up and was strong and happy, and where he used to be carried from his home, now he carried his own bed back to his home. THE NINETEENTH SUNDAY AFTER TRINITY SUNDAY.[9]

THE PEOPLE GIVE AN EXCELLENT EXAMPLE IN PRAISING GOD. JOHANN BAUMGART (POMARIUS): We should also learn from the people in this story always to bless and thank God, as we also give an appropriate thanks and say a prayer to the Lord when he helps us or those near to us in body or soul, or in both together. For God demands both when he says, "Call on me in your need, and I will deliver you, and you shall glorify me." Saint Paul also admonishes us and wants that not only all of our prayers and entreaties but also our thanksgiving would be made known to God.

Consequently we should also offer the Lord "young bulls" with our lips and say with the beloved David, "I will bless the Lord at all times, his praise shall always be in my mouth. My soul makes its boast in the Lord, that the wretched hear and are glad. Praise the Lord with me, and let us together exalt his name! When I sought the Lord, he answered me, and saved me from all of my fears." Likewise he says, "Bless the Lord, my soul, and do not forget all of his benefits to you, who forgives all of your sins and heals all of your infirmities." GOSPEL ON THE NINETEENTH SUNDAY AFTER TRINITY.[10]

---

[9]Becon, New Postil, 146v-147r*.

[10]Baumgart, Postilla, 241r-v; citing Ps 50:15; Phil 4:6; Ps 34:1-4; 103:2-3.

5:27-39 LEVI'S CALL AND BANQUET

[27] After this he went out and saw a tax collector named Levi, sitting at the tax booth. And he said to him, "Follow me." [28] And leaving everything, he rose and followed him.

[29] And Levi made him a great feast in his house, and there was a large company of tax collectors and others reclining at table with them. [30] And the Pharisees and their scribes grumbled at his disciples, saying, "Why do you eat and drink with tax collectors and sinners?" [31] And Jesus answered them, "Those who are well have no need of a physician, but those who are sick. [32] I have not come to call the righteous but sinners to repentance."

[33] And they said to him, "The disciples of John fast often and offer prayers, and so do the disciples of the Pharisees, but yours eat and drink." [34] And Jesus said to them, "Can you make wedding guests fast while the bridegroom is with them? [35] The days will come when the bridegroom is taken away from them, and then they will fast in those days." [36] He also told them a parable: "No one tears a piece from a new garment and puts it on an old garment. If he does, he will tear the new, and the piece from the new will not match the old. [37] And no one puts new wine into old wineskins. If he does, the new wine will burst the skins and it will be spilled, and the skins will be destroyed. [38] But new wine must be put into fresh wineskins. [39] And no one after drinking old wine desires new, for he says, 'The old is good.'"[a]

a Some manuscripts better

Overview: Some commentators see in this story an even greater miracle than the first, for turning a rich tax collector away from the love of his ill-gotten gains is even harder than healing a man so he can walk again. So, what is the message? *Anyone* can be called—anyone, no matter how sinful or how opposed to Christ and the gospel. God's love and forgiveness can be offered to anyone, and God's call has great power. It convinced Matthew, who did not think or second guess but immediately rose up and followed Jesus. And it did not matter to Jesus that Matthew had been a "great sinner," he called him anyway to preach the gospel, showing the other apostles (and the Pharisees) that anyone who accepts Jesus' call can preach. What does it mean to accept the call? One must repent and reform one's life. But Matthew did not abandon everything, only his sinful life—the things that impeded his service of Jesus and the gospel. He maintained his home and family and even offered a great banquet for Jesus to celebrate—an important example for Protestant ministers who

now had wives, families, homes and the attendant responsibilities.

The second element of this story follows: what is better—feast or famine? How is one to live a moral Christian life? Does it mean spiritual discipline, fasting and restraint? Or is it feasting and celebrating? The Pharisees were quite critical of Jesus' feasting with his disciples—and he even included tax collectors and sinners at the event—instead of insisting on ritual fasting. This was an important question for Protestant ministers, because they were often critical of Roman Catholic religious practices that focused on empty rituals (like the Pharisees) but did not change the heart or serve others. Yet the Christian life is not all feasting and celebration; even Christ says here that once the bridegroom is gone, there will be time for fasting. But how is this work of fasting supposed to be incorporated, because good works do not gain salvation? Clearly fasting should not be seen as meritorious but should instead be part of that repentance and change of heart that was so instantaneous in Matthew. Fasting, along with prayer, is an appropriate response to catastrophes and afflictions, whether individual or community-wide. But such spiritual discipline cannot be imposed, especially on those who are still weak as Jesus' disciples were, or it will not have the desired effect. Instead of bringing the heart to repentance, it will only create hypocrisy.

5:27-28 *Jesus Calls Levi*

JESUS CALLS MATTHEW (OR LEVI) THE TAX COLLECTOR. DESIDERIUS ERASMUS: After he had finished teaching by the pool, Jesus left that place, teaching meanwhile that the seed of evangelical conversation is to be sown in all places without exception. As he was passing by, he noticed a certain tax collector by the name of Matthew, who was also called Levi, the son of Alphaeus, sitting in the customs office. This did not happen by chance, but in the noticing, Matthew was chosen. And he chose a tax collector for the fellowship of the apostles that he might teach them that no sort of person is to be rejected from the profession of the gospel, provided that they eagerly forsake their former life and dedicate themselves completely to piety. Jesus then said to him, "Follow me." And when he heard the voice of Jesus, as if a powerful enchantment had transformed him into another man, he rose and, just as he was, followed the Lord, leaving everything behind. Now this was a singular miracle, that a man dedicated to amassing disreputable profits and wrapped up in complicated business affairs suddenly trans-formed into another sort of man altogether; that is a more extraordinary miracle than to restore the muscles of a paralyzed man. And this very thing was now a great annoyance to the Phari-sees, that, despising them, Jesus admitted tax collectors, whom the Jews felt defiled them when-ever they had dealings with them. PARAPHRASE ON THE GOSPEL OF LUKE 5:27-28.[1]

THIS EXAMPLE LIKEWISE TEACHES GOD'S FORGIVENESS FOR THE FAITHFUL. HEINRICH BULLINGER: Now the Evangelist teaches by a new example that the Lord forgives the sins of those who obey and believe in him. For the chief point of our faith ought to be shown frequently and clearly by many plain examples. And clearly this example differs very little from the previous story, for in that example he taught that the sins of the faithful are truly and fully remitted. He teaches the same thing in this example, but he adds that Christ draws us away from the habit of sinning, which is a certain special grace of God, and, being received into grace and favor, he defends us against all the malicious lies of hypocrites. The example is that of the Evangelist Matthew himself. Christ drew Matthew to him with his secret power and strength, touching his heart inwardly, but outwardly he moved him with his word: what effected his calling were Christ's words, "Follow me." In those words he said to Matthew, "Follow me, cleave to me, hear me, behold me, do what I command, and wholly frame yourself according to my example, that you may serve me in the ministry of the Word." AN ECCLESIASTICALL EXPOSITION UPON SAINT MATHEWE 9.[2]

MATTHEW'S CALLING SHOWS CHRIST'S POWER. PHILIPP MELANCHTHON: Two things should be noted here. The first is that the divine calling of God is of great force and power. The other is that this is an example of true and perfect obedience. For we see in such ready obedience the efficacy of the word of Christ, not that all who hear these words have the same operation in their hearts, but Christ meant to show in this man a singular sign that we might know that he was not called by flesh and blood. He does not question how he will live, but he rises up from all his profits, forsaking everything, and follows Christ with nothing. Furthermore, he does not stand there reasoning with Christ about whether or not he should go, but without delay and all things set apart, he follows

---

[1]Erasmus, *In Evangelivm Lvce Paraphrasis*, k6v (LB 7:341).

[2]Marlorat, ed., *Catholike and Ecclesiasticall Exposition of the Holy Gospell After S. Mathewe*, 177*.

Christ. Likewise when Abraham was called, he went out of his father's house, not knowing where he should go. Third, he does not weigh or consider that he is following a man whom the leaders and rulers of the people persecute. It would have been an easy matter to follow someone whom everyone held in reverence and high estimation. And no one would delay or tarry who was called out of the pit of misery into continual happiness. And so truly the power of Christ appeared more clearly in the conversion of Zacchaeus than in calling Peter the fisherman; also this calling of Matthew sets forth the power of Christ more clearly than the calling of Peter. It is as hard for a camel to go through the eye of a needle as it is for a rich person to enter the kingdom of heaven. And so from this example we may gather that we should despair of no rich person, because the grace of God is available to everyone. And our Savior Christ says, what is impossible with people is possible with God. Instead, if we see a rich person who will not follow Christ, let us pray that Christ will deign to draw him with his power and the Holy Spirit. AN ECCLESIASTICALL EXPOSITION UPON SAINT MATHEWE 9.[3]

5:29-32 The Banquet and Its Critics

MATTHEW DID NOT GIVE UP HIS HOME AND FAMILY, ALTHOUGH HE FOLLOWED CHRIST. AUGUSTIN MARLORAT: And Levi made a great feast for him in his house. This seems to disagree with what was spoken before, which said that he forsook all and followed Jesus. But it may safely be answered that, setting aside all impediments and obstacles, he gave himself wholly to Christ, yet not so that he could not reserve for himself something pertaining to his household. Using the example of soldiers, Paul exhorts the ministers of the Word to keep themselves free from all impediments that might hinder the work of the church, saying, "No soldier gets entangled in civilian pursuits." But in saying this, he does not mean that any man who

goes to war should divorce his wife, forsake his children and renounce his house, that he may devote himself entirely to war. Likewise, nothing held Matthew back from following Christ no matter where he was called, although he maintained an interest in his house and his other abilities, so far as his calling would allow him. The feast is called "great" not so much in reference to the multitude of guests as it is to the abundance and cost of the food and drink. For we should note that Christ did not maintain such austerity that he would give up attending feasts given by rich people just to avoid luxury. But there is no doubt that, because he himself was a singular example of temperance, he must have exhorted those he was with to avoid excess and to receive only moderate amounts of food and drink. AN ECCLESIASTICALL EXPOSITION UPON SAINT MATHEWE 9.[4]

WHO WERE THE SINNERS AT MATTHEW'S FEAST? PHILIPP MELANCHTHON: These two, publicans and sinners, are often joined together, as when it is said, "a friend of publicans and sinners." And "publicans and sinners" came to Jesus, whereby it appears that their orders of life were diverse. Some think that this text refers to those sinners who were excommunicated by the Jews as notorious offenders in some public crime. It could also be those who, being of a more dissolute life, had familiarity with every Gentile and publican, which was considered by the Pharisees to be a heinous offense. It is likely that, because the Gentiles dwelled among the Jews, they had many Jews with whom they associated and kept company, not regarding the rites and ceremonies of the law or the institutions of the ancestors. This behavior caused these people to receive the public and common reproach of other sinners. AN ECCLESIASTICALL EXPOSITION UPON SAINT MATHEWE 9.[5]

THESE COMPLAINING HYPOCRITES SHOULD

---

[3]Marlorat, ed., *Catholike and Ecclesiasticall Exposition of the Holy Gospell After S. Mathewe*, 178*; citing Mt 19:24; Lk 18:27.

[4]Marlorat, ed., *Catholike and Ecclesiasticall Exposition of the Holy Gospell After S. Mathewe*, 178*; quoting 2 Tim 2:4.
[5]Marlorat, ed., *Catholike and Ecclesiasticall Exposition of the Holy Gospell After S. Mathewe*, 179*; quoting Mt 9:11; 11:19; Lk 7:34.

HAVE BEEN THE FIRST TO FOLLOW HIM.
JOHANN SPANGENBERG: What do the Pharisees and teachers of the law say about this high living? They complained to his disciples and said, "Why does your master eat and drink with the tax collectors and sinners?" With these words they brought to light the pride and conceit of their hearts: those are the fruits of disbelief, complaining against God and judging, sentencing and condemning other people. The high priests, Pharisees and teachers of the law should have been foremost in taking the lead to accept Christ with all reverence, to hear his word with all diligence and to follow his commands earnestly. But instead there were no people on earth who were more hostile to Christ, or strove against his word more strongly or were more wickedly opposed to his commands than these hypocrites. They did not want either to see or hear Christ and begrudged the others who did. They reproached Christ and his disciples because they were true blasphemers and slanderers. And how did Christ answer these complaining hypocrites? Although the high priests, Pharisees and teachers of the law were poisonous people, we still have much for which to thank them, for Christ our Savior responded to their reprimands and complaints from his divine heart and mouth with tremendously comforting words and salutary teaching. ON SAINT MATTHEW'S DAY.[6]

GOD DESIRES MERCY AND REPENTANCE, NOT SACRIFICE. RICHARD TAVERNER: Christ calls himself a physician, who by a wonderful kind of surgery was wounded for our iniquities, so that he might heal the wounds of our sins. He calls those "whole" or "well" who, deciding to establish their own justice, are not subject to the true justice of God. And he calls those "sick" and "diseased" who, being overcome in their conscience, acknowledge their frailty, and, seeing how they are not justified by the law, submit themselves through repentance to the grace of God. But go your way, Christ says,

and learn what this sentence of the prophet Hosea means, where God says, "I require mercy and not sacrifice." It is as if he should say, "Why do you accuse me, when I relieve and correct sinners? Why do you not rather accuse God the Father of heaven, who speaks this sentence by his prophet?" And so he admonishes us that it is by doing the works of mercy that we will receive the reward of heavenly mercy, and that we should not try to please God by the oblation of sacrifices, despising the difficulties of the poor and needy. Therefore, good people, let us follow this blessed apostle Saint Matthew—let us leave all filthy gains and come to Christ when he calls us by the preaching of his word. Let us be charitable and do the works of mercy as Christ teaches us, so that we will be among the number of those who shall inherit the kingdom of heaven, which is prepared from the beginning of the world by the Father of heaven, to whom be all praise, Amen. ON SAINT MATTHEW'S DAY.[7]

ONLY THE SELF-RIGHTEOUS THINK THEY DO NOT NEED CHRIST. HEINRICH BULLINGER: Now Christ, referring to what he had just said, that he came into the world as a physician, by a certain inference and exposition concludes the whole disputation, and those whom before he had called whole and strong he now calls righteous. He does not mean that they are righteous in deed, but he means that they boasted and thought themselves to be righteous, like the Pharisees. Because they thought themselves to be absolute, they persuaded themselves that the grace of God contributed nothing to their perfection, and for this reason they did not call for the mercy of the Lord. For what need have the righteous of mercy? Their offense was very great, as the Lord said in another place: "If you were blind, you would have no guilt; but now that you say, 'We see,' your guilt remains." And again, "You are those who justify yourselves before people, but God knows your hearts."

---

[6]Spangenberg, *Postilla Teütsch . . . von den fürnemsten Festen durch das gantze Jar*, LXXXVIr-v.

[7]Taverner, *On Saynt Andrewes Day*, 32v*; citing Is 53:5; Rom 4; Hos 6:6; Mt 24.

An Ecclesiasticall Exposition upon Saint Mathewe 9.[8]

5:33-35 Jesus' Critics Question Him About Fasting

The Pharisees Try to Use John's Authority Against Jesus. Philipp Melanchthon: We see by their questioning that the disciples of John were envious of Christ, through the zeal which they bore toward their master. This is evident in the Gospel of Saint John, where he said, "Now a discussion arose between some of John's disciples and a Jew over purification. And they came to John and said to him, 'Rabbi, he who was with you across the Jordan, to whom you bore witness—look, he is baptizing, and all are going to him.'" But here the Pharisees, who were the authors of this question, make the objection for John's disciples, and not for themselves alone, to the end that they might burden and discredit the cause of Christ with the authority of John. It is as if they were reproaching him by saying, "You bear an outward show of holiness, and you seem to sow the doctrine of a more perfect life; so how is it that you not only profane yourself with the company of sinners, but you also modify or refrain from the works of your own religion, such as fasting and prayers, with which we diligently exercise ourselves?" An Ecclesiasticall Exposition upon Saint Mathewe 9.[9]

A Fast Is Appropriate When the Wedding Is Over. The Book of Homilies: Their question was about fasting, but his answer is about mourning, which should have signified plainly to them that the outward fast of the body is not a fast before God unless it is accompanied by the inward fast. The inward fast is a mourning and a lamentation of the heart, as I said before. Concerning the time of fasting, Jesus said, "The day will come when the bridegroom will be taken from them; in those days they will fast." By these words it is manifest that as long as the wedding lasts and the bridegroom is present, it is not a time of fasting. But when the wedding is ended and the bridegroom is gone, then it is an appropriate time to fast. Now, let me make plain to you the the the sense and meaning of the words, "We are at the wedding," and "The bridegroom is taken from us." You should note that as long as God reveals his mercy to us and gives us his benefits, either spiritual or corporal, we are said to be with the bridegroom at the wedding. Thus good old father Jacob was at the wedding when he understood that his son Joseph was alive and ruled all Egypt under the king Pharoah. And David was at the wedding with the bridegroom when he achieved victory over the great Goliath and cut off his head. Judith and all the people of Bethulia were the children at the wedding and had the bridegroom with them when God, by the hand of a woman, slayed Holofernes, the grand captain of the Assyrian army, and embarrassed all their enemies. Thus the apostles were the children at the wedding while Christ was corporally present with them and defended them from all dangers, both spiritual and corporal. But the wedding is then said to be ended and the bridegroom gone when the almighty God strikes us with affliction and seems to leave us in the midst of a number of adversities. So God sometimes strikes us individually with sundry adversities, such as trouble of mind, loss of friends, loss of goods, long and dangerous sicknesses. That is a fit time for that person to humble himself to almighty God by fasting, and to mourn and bewail his sins with a sorrowful heart and to pray unfeignedly, saying with the prophet David, "Turn away your face, O Lord, from my sins, and blot out all my offenses." Again, when God afflicts a whole region or country with wars, famine, pestilence, strange diseases and unknown sicknesses, and other such calamities, then it is time for all sorts of people, high and low, men, women and children, to humble themselves by fasting, and bewail their sinful living before God and pray with one common voice. Homily 16: Of Good Works and First of Fasting.[10]

---

[8]Marlorat, ed., *Catholike and Ecclesiasticall Exposition of the Holy Gospell After S. Mathewe,* 181-82*; citing Jn 9:41; Lk 16:15.

[9]Marlorat, ed., *Catholike and Ecclesiasticall Exposition of the Holy Gospell After S. Mathewe,* 182-83*; citing Jn 3:25-26.

[10]*Certain Sermons or Homilies* (1852), 266-67*; citing Gen 45:27; 1 Sam 17:51; Jdt 13:8; Ps 51:9.

5:36-39 *The Parable of the New Wineskins*

THE PARABLES SHOWED THE DISCIPLES WERE STILL WEAK AND UNFORMED. MARTIN BUCER: He intended to declare by these parables that early on, great and intolerable burdens that were not necessary should not be laid on his disciples, because they were still weak and altogether unformed. These burdens included fasting and extraordinary prayers, which are such spiritual works that no one can be sufficiently prepared for them as soon as he enters into the faith. These works proceed from the Holy Spirit, which was the reason why Christ never commanded them. The diversity of abilities requires some moderation, that one way may apply to one, while another may apply to another. If a sick person is required to do some great and laborious work, he can faint, and because of his weakness and incapacity he will be unable to do it. If someone forces people to fast who cannot bear it, it is then a violent thing, done by compulsion. It does not make them better people but rather makes them into arrogant hypocrites, that is, just like the Pharisees. Therefore, if Christ had at their insistence burdened his disciples, who were still unformed and not at all spiritual, then he would have accomplished nothing but to make them more insolent and to make them into hypocrites. And so he compares them with a piece of old clothing, which when it is worn is soon torn and rent. If then someone sews a new and strong piece of cloth to it, it mars the seam and the tear is made worse. Then he compares them again with earthen vessels, which are not of sufficient strength to hold new wine that has not yet been aged and mellowed. By this he signifies that he bears with his disciples, who are still young scholars and not able yet to do what they desire because of their weakness. This similitude is therefore very apt, serving very well in this matter, although it might not seem at all points to agree. For Christ does not compare his disciples with old bottles and old clothing to imply that they had been worn before by long use; instead, he compares them with such things because they were weak and not strong. The sum of this doctrine, then, is that not all are to be brought to one form and manner and life, because the condition of all is not alike, neither do all things agree with all people. The weak must be spared, so that they do not sink under their burden and be overcome with violence. AN ECCLESIASTICALL EXPOSITION UPON SAINT MATHEWE 9.[11]

NO ONE WILLINGLY GIVES UP THE OLD WINE OR AN EASIER LIFE. HENRY HAMMOND: It is not best immediately to bring people to an austere course of life, but by degrees, lest they fall away because of the difficulties of it. For those who have tasted old wine, which is smoother, will not willingly leave it for the new, which is harsher (see Ecclesiasticus 9:10); the old is sweeter, easier, delightful and agreeable to the stomach. And thus it is fitting to condescend to human weaknesses and not presently to require of the disciples the austerities of fasting, especially while Christ is with them, which is rather a time of festivity to them. There will soon enough be a season for fasting (see Lk 5:35). PARAPHRASE ON LUKE 5.[12]

THE NEW WINE TASTES GOOD ONLY TO THOSE WHO ARE RENEWED. FRANÇOIS LAMBERT: The new wine is God's justice, which is only poured into new wineskins, because it is only given to those who are truly renewed and reformed by the Spirit of Christ, that is, the faithful. Of course, because the "old man" reigns in us, the new wine of divine justice is by no means well-received by us. . . . So for the one who drinks old wine, then tries the new, the new wine has a weak flavor. Of course that is the case, because the taste for the old is still in him. So the new wine of Christian justice does not please anyone who still has the taste for the old justice of the flesh. It would be foolish to think, then, that first the justice of the flesh is necessary and that then the pleasant justice of Christ will be most agreeable. COMMENTARY IN LUKE 5:37-38.[13]

---

[11]Marlorat, ed., *Catholike and Ecclesiasticall Exposition of the Holy Gospell After S. Mathewe*, 184-85*.
[12]Hammond, *Paraphrase and Annotations*, 205*.
[13]Lambert, *In Divi Lucae*, M7v-M8r.

6:1-11 THE FIRST SABBATH CONTROVERSY

On a Sabbath,^a while he was going through the grainfields, his disciples plucked and ate some heads of grain, rubbing them in their hands. ²But some of the Pharisees said, "Why are you doing what is not lawful to do on the Sabbath?" ³And Jesus answered them, "Have you not read what David did when he was hungry, he and those who were with him: ⁴how he entered the house of God and took and ate the bread of the Presence, which is not lawful for any but the priests to eat, and also gave it to those with him?" ⁵And he said to them, "The Son of Man is lord of the Sabbath."

⁶On another Sabbath, he entered the synagogue and was teaching, and a man was there whose right hand was withered. ⁷And the scribes and the Pharisees watched him, to see whether he would heal on the Sabbath, so that they might find a reason to accuse him. ⁸But he knew their thoughts, and he said to the man with the withered hand, "Come and stand here." And he rose and stood there. ⁹And Jesus said to them, "I ask you, is it lawful on the Sabbath to do good or to do harm, to save life or to destroy it?" ¹⁰And after looking around at them all he said to him, "Stretch out your hand." And he did so, and his hand was restored. ¹¹But they were filled with fury and discussed with one another what they might do to Jesus.

a Some manuscripts On the second first Sabbath (that is, on the second Sabbath after the first)

OVERVIEW: This passage brings up the difficult question of obedience to the law—when should the law be obeyed, and when is it acceptable to break it? In general, commentators prefer to stress that Jesus obeyed the law, even when he was exempt from it. But there are times when what is good for a person is more important than a customary restriction (notice that we are not talking about a law against stealing or murder, for example). Jesus wanted to make a point here to the Pharisees—he is the Lord of the sabbath, able to break those rules when necessary to do the right thing. His actions were an implicit condemnation of the Pharisees' dedication to excessive literalism and the absence of true charity in their hearts, and he explicitly condemned their hypocrisy at his sabbath healing. If it is acceptable, according to the law, to rescue an animal that falls into a pit on the sabbath, why is it not acceptable to do the work of healing a sick man on that same day? People who strictly adhere to the law without letting it reform their hearts are living by the letter but not the spirit of the law. Jesus concludes that it is not only lawful but also necessary to do good on the sabbath.

6:1-5 The Son of Man Is the Lord of the Sabbath

THEIR HUNGER WAS MEANT TO TEACH THE DISCIPLES A LESSON. PHILIPP MELANCHTHON: But it certainly came about by the special counsel and dispensation of God that the disciples of Christ on this holy day above all others should be so hungry and that they should pass through the fields of corn, especially while the Pharisees were present. It was necessary that the Lord should have an occasion offered to him to teach what they should think of the holy and sacred honoring of the sabbath. "And his disciples were hungry": Christ might easily have fed his disciples sufficiently, as he fed the five thousand with just a little bread. But he wanted rather that his disciples, in suffering this hunger, should be content with meager and simple fare. For it would happen, as it certainly did, that after his departing they would feel hunger. Therefore he thought it good, while he was still present, to let them have some experience of what they would afterward taste in his absence. AN ECCLESIASTICALL EXPOSITION UPON SAINT MATHEWE 12.[1]

CHRIST WILL NEVER PLEASE SOME PEOPLE.
JOHANNES BRENZ: There is a common proverb: He who pleases everyone must rise very early. This means that the judgments of people are so perverse and wayward that no one, no matter how righteous and godly, can thoroughly satisfy everyone. And it is no marvel that this is the fate of people who are conceived and born in sin, but it is quite remarkable that the same should happen to our Lord Jesus Christ, who never sinned, nor was there any guile found in his mouth. We have already read that the Pharisees and scribes murmured against Christ because he did not require ordinary fasts and prayers for his disciples. So Christ could never do anything so well or teach anything so properly, but there were some who would criticize him. But the slanders and complaints of the enemies of Christ are entirely vain, while the apologies and answers of Christ are so much more true and divine and are to be considered by us as heavenly oracles. AN ECCLESIASTICALL EXPOSITION UPON SAINT LUKE 6.[2]

DAVID'S HUNGER ALLOWED HIM TO EAT THE PRIESTS' BREAD. PHILIPP MELANCHTHON: Now when Christ says that it was only lawful for the priests to eat this bread, we must understand that he means according to the common law. For if David had done anything contrary to what is right, it would have been a waste of time for Christ to put forward his example. But necessity made lawful what otherwise was restricted to a certain end and purpose. According to the proverb, "Necessity has no law."[3] For extreme hunger always has a preroga-

tive, as the common proverb says, "Hunger breaks through stone walls." The Lord therefore answered the mean-spirited and full-bellied folks who will bear and consider nothing of their neighbor's necessity. For it commonly happens that a person who never feels the violence and necessity of hunger cannot take pity on those who are hungry—this fact is commonly observed among the rich. AN ECCLESIASTICALL EXPOSITION UPON SAINT MATHEWE 12.[4]

THIS PASSAGE PROVIDES COMFORT IN DIFFICULT TIMES. JOHANN AGRICOLA: This is a passage of faith, by which souls are encouraged, that they might hear it bravely. They will be strengthened if they are ever required, either through necessity or from charity, to offend against not only human law but also the divine law. Furthermore, the history of David and other common passages confirm this, namely, that the Son of Man is Lord of the sabbath. ANNOTATIONS IN THE GOSPEL OF LUKE 6.[5]

6:6-11 *Jesus Heals on a Sabbath*

TO NEGLECT YOUR NEIGHBOR IN NEED IS TO COMMIT MURDER IN YOUR HEART. JOHN CALVIN: Whoever destroys human life is guilty of crime. Whoever does not care about relieving those in distress differs very little from a murderer. Thus, Christ accuses them that under the pretext of holy rest they are willing to compel evil deeds. Not only does he sin, as was said, who does anything contrary to the law, but also who neglects his obligation. From this we see that Christ did not always use the same arguments to refute this false accusation. Here he does not argue about his divinity (as in John), nor was there any benefit to do so, because this one argument amply refuted the Pharisees. Surely nothing could be less consistent than to reckon a man who imitated God as a

---

[1]Marlorat, ed., *Catholike and Ecclesiasticall Exposition of the Holy Gospell After S. Mathewe*, 247*; alluding to Jn 6:1-14; 2 Cor 11:27.
[2]Marlorat, ed. *Catholike and Ecclesiasticall Exposition of the Holy Gospell After S. Marke and Luke*, 155-56*; alluding to 1 Pet 2:22.
[3]The quotation is attributed to William Langland (1332–1400), an English poet and author of *Piers Plowman* (1377).

[4]Marlorat, ed., *Catholike and Ecclesiasticall Exposition of the Holy Gospell After S. Mathewe*, 248*.
[5]Agricola, *In Evangelium Lucae Annotationes*, 78v.

transgressor of the sabbath. COMMENTARY ON A HARMONY OF THE GOSPELS.[6]

ENVY IS THE DISEASE OF THE PHARISEES.
HULDRYCH ZWINGLI: Both the words and the deeds of Christ were truly useful and salutary, and yet the Pharisees misrepresented them, even in death, out of hate and their bitter zeal. They could not be moved by any evidence or parable, through which Christ persuaded so many. Rejection of Christ today is also driven by hatred and jealousy; therefore it is very similar. Envy is the most harmful kind of witchcraft, bewitching the eye of the mind and binding it fast: just like when one views a white wall or green grass through a reddish glass, then they also appear to be reddish. Each person should therefore guard against feelings of this sort—they do not stop or decrease until they achieve what they desire. Each should consider himself diligently, to see whether he stands still, moves forward or diminishes in this by passions and diseases. Likewise, the doctor diligently observes and considers the condition of the disease, in order to be aware of diseases in the body. If the feeling is detected to be continuing, he is not free from danger, and it is judged to be increasing. But if it should abate every day, there is hope of good health. As long as the persecutors of the truth continue and move forward in their errors and persistence, as long as they do not yield, they are guarding against any hope of receiving correction. IN THE GOSPEL OF LUKE 6.[7]

JESUS HEALED THROUGH CHARITY BUT DID NOT WORK. MARTIN BUCER: When he had proved, both by reason and example, that it was not only lawful but also necessary to do good on the sabbath day (especially to people), he healed the man. In this situation we should note that he cured him with his word alone, not moving his hand or any external thing, as he commonly did at other times. The reason for this was that they would have less of an excuse to make false or petty objections against him. For how could he violate or break the sabbath with a word? Thereby he teaches us that it is not sufficient to do good, but we also must remove every stone or impediment, that our actions may have favor with every person. We can see here that this is how Christ behaved in this situation. He placed the man with the withered hand in the center, so that they might be able clearly to see his misery, and so count it a good and charitable deed to heal him, even though it was a sabbath day. And then, by skillful questioning, he admonished them that there is no time when it is unlawful to do good, much less on the sabbath. For to do a holy thing according to charity on the holy day follows the commandment of the Lord. AN ECCLESIASTICALL EXPOSITION UPON SAINT MATHEWE 12.[8]

THE HEIGHTS OF HUMAN WICKEDNESS. JOHN CALVIN: How obstinate is the rage which drives the wicked to oppose God! Even after having been proved wrong, they pour out their venom more and more. It is truly monstrous and abominable that the most distinguished teachers of the law, who were entrusted with the government of the church, prowl, like robbers, to plot murder. But this must happen whenever human malice reaches such a height that they want to destroy whatever is opposed to their desire, even if it might be from God. COMMENTARY ON A HARMONY OF THE GOSPELS.[9]

---

[6]CTS 32:54* (CO 45:328); citing Jn 5:18.
[7]D. Hvldrichi Zvinglii in Plerosqve Novi Testamenti Libros, 212.

[8]Marlorat, ed., Catholike and Ecclesiasticall Exposition of the Holy Gospell After S. Mathewe, 252-53*.
[9]CTS 32:55-56* (CO 45:329).

6:12-16 THE CALLING OF THE TWELVE

¹²In these days he went out to the mountain to pray, and all night he continued in prayer to God. ¹³And when day came, he called his disciples and chose from them twelve, whom he named apostles: ¹⁴Simon, whom he named Peter, and Andrew his brother, and James and John, and Philip, and Bartholomew, ¹⁵and Matthew, and Thomas, and James the son of Alphaeus, and Simon who was called the Zealot, ¹⁶and Judas the son of James, and Judas Iscariot, who became a traitor.

OVERVIEW: Like the twelve tribes of Israel, named for the twelve patriarchs or sons of Jacob, these twelve are the founding members of the church of Christ. Two points in particular relate to wider arguments in the Reformation: first, these apostles were chosen only after a period of following and learning from Jesus, and they continued to study, listen, discuss and pray for close to a year before being sent out to preach on their own. The implication is that training and study are needed before one is able or allowed to preach. The majority of Protestants did not accept the notion that the gifts of the Holy Spirit, given through sudden inspiration, were all one needed to preach—or that these gifts could be separated from the Word. The *Schwärmer* ("fanatics") of whom Luther was so dismissive thought that inspiration came apart from study, even apart from the biblical text itself, straight from the Holy Spirit, and that was all one needed to preach. But the example of the choosing of the apostles undergirded the more common opinion that training and study of the Word were essential.

The second point concerned Judas, the traitor, who is listed both as an apostle and as a traitor in all three Gospel versions of this story. Jesus, of course, knew at the choosing that Judas would be the one who would eventually betray him but chose him despite the role he would play—or was it perhaps because of it? Our commentators note that God's plan was unchanging, and Jesus came for the redemption of the world, which means that Judas's role was essential. He freely chose to do evil—he was not forced into it—but Jesus also did not avoid what was coming. Judas's inclusion in this group of the first leaders of the church also shows that the church in the world is always a mixture of good and bad, the faithful and hypocrites. Some Protestants—Anabaptists in particular—wanted to create a church community that included only the faithful, but most were practical enough to know that, as Augustine said, the church is a *corpus permixtum*, a mixed body. But the presence of Judas does not mean that all the work and teaching of the apostles are suspect, nor does the presence of evil people in the church mean that it is an infected or ruined body. God is the final judge of good and evil; we cannot make those decisions, and the goats will only be separated from the sheep at the Last Judgment.

6:12 Jesus Prays Alone on the Mountain

JESUS PRAYED BEFORE CHOOSING THE TWELVE. JOHN TRAPP: Jesus went out to pray before choosing the twelve. Likewise, Eleazar prayed when he was sent to seek a wife for Isaac. Solomon prayed for wisdom before he began building the temple. Ezra fasted and prayed before he committed the golden and silver vessels to those who kept them. So should there not be a prayer made for ministers before they are set over God's house and people? A COMMENTARY UPON THE GOSPEL ACCORDING TO SAINT LUKE 6.[10]

---

[10]Trapp, *Commentary or Exposition*, 387*; alluding to Gen

6:13-16 *Jesus Chooses the Twelve Apostles*

Even the Apostles Needed a Lot of Training. John Lightfoot: On a mountain near Capernaum he ordained a ministry for the church of the gospel and delivered the doctrine of the gospel, as Moses had likewise done at Sinai for the law. The number of the ministers which he here appointed and called apostles was twelve, parallel to the twelve tribes of Israel. These were the beginning of the church of the Jews; so also are these twelve the beginning for the Gentiles. And to both these numbers of twelve joined together, the number of the twenty-four elders, the representatives of the whole church. The text designates the following as the reasons for their appointment. First, so they might be with Christ to see his glory and be witnesses to all the things that he did. Second, so he might send them forth to preach. Third, to heal diseases and cast out devils.

But before they were complete in all their divine endowments, they progressed by degrees. They were auditors a good while, learning the doctrine of the gospel which they were to preach, before they embarked on that work. For although Christ chose them now, it was close to a year before he sent them abroad to preach, as will appear in the continuation of the story. So besides the time that they had spent before being chosen, they also spent that year in hearing and learning from the mouth of their Master, what they were to teach when he should employ them. So even the apostles themselves at their first setting forth into the ministry did not preach by the Spirit but rather what they had learned and gotten by hearing, study, conference and meditation. Harmony of the New Testament, Section 27.[11]

The Names of Those Who Do God's Work Are Important. Philipp Melanchthon: It is the manner and practice of Scripture not to allow the names of those whose work God uses in his ministry to lie hidden in oblivion but to make them known by their names. This happens partly so that we may know that those who serve him are not neglected by God and partly so that we, being mindful of their faith, should follow their godly example. It brings us great utility and profit to know the names of those whose ministry and service God has deigned to use, for our great good and salvation. Therefore Moses recorded the names of those whose industry and labor built the tabernacle, and in another place, the names of those who brought back the Ark of the Covenant again (which David made) to the tabernacle. An Ecclesiasticall Exposition upon Saint Mathewe 10.[12]

The Twelve Apostles Replace the Twelve Patriarchs. François Lambert: He names apostles, that perhaps by the name itself you might come to understand the ones to whom pertains the ministry of the Word—of course, it is to those who "are sent." Obviously, apostles are those who are sent out. Afterwards he also confirms the name of Peter, which he had previously established for him. Even Judas, the one who was identified as a traitor, is numbered with the holy apostles, so that both the unchanging plan of God and the redemption of the world (which was the highest thing he wished for) would be completed. To that purpose, therefore, he chooses twelve, for it is written in the psalms, "In place of your fathers, sons will be born to you." That is, in the place of the twelve patriarchs there will be twelve apostles. Commentary in Luke 6:13-16.[13]

The Wickedness of Judas Did Not Defile All the Apostles. Philipp Melanchthon: Judas is called Iscariot either because of the town where he was born or else because he belonged to the tribe of Issachar.... Here we also must note that there is no fellowship so holy, so pure and

24:12-14; 2 Chron 1:8-10; Ezra 8:21-30.
[11]Lightfoot, *Harmony, Chronicle and Order of the New Testament*, 24*; alluding to Rev 4; 5 (see also Rev 21:12, 14); Jn 1:14; Acts 10:39-41.

[12]Marlorat, ed., *Catholike and Ecclesiasticall Exposition of the Holy Gospell After S. Mathewe*, 201*; alluding to Ex 31:1-6; also see, for example, 2 Sam 15:27.
[13]Lambert, *In Divi Lucae*, N4r-v; citing Jn 1:42; Ps 44:17 Vg.

clean but that at the same time there may be found in it some evil person. Therefore, we must pay attention, so that for the sake of one evil person we do not reject all the good, and that for the sake of Judas we do not reject all the apostles. The church will also consist of both good and evil, of faithful folk and hypocrites, until the high Judge comes and separates the goats from the sheep. This lewd and filthy person, Judas, did not defile the integrity and ministry of saints, no matter how great his transgression was. And so let us note that godly,

virtuous and honest people are not always defiled by the company of the wicked and ungodly, especially if they are ignorant of their wickedness. Likewise, the doctrine of the truth and the administration of the sacraments is no worse on account of the unworthiness of the minister. AN ECCLESIASTICALL EXPOSITION UPON SAINT MATHEWE 10.[14]

---

[14]Marlorat, ed., *Catholike and Ecclesiasticall Exposition of the Holy Gospell After S. Mathewe*, 202*.

6:17-26 JESUS HEALS AND TEACHES: BLESSINGS AND WOES

[17]*And he came down with them and stood on a level place, with a great crowd of his disciples and a great multitude of people from all Judea and Jerusalem and the seacoast of Tyre and Sidon,* [18]*who came to hear him and to be healed of their diseases. And those who were troubled with unclean spirits were cured.* [19]*And all the crowd sought to touch him, for power came out from him and healed them all.*

[20]*And he lifted up his eyes on his disciples, and said:*

"Blessed are you who are poor, for yours is the kingdom of God.

[21]*"Blessed are you who are hungry now, for you shall be satisfied.*

"Blessed are you who weep now, for you shall laugh.

[22]*"Blessed are you when people hate you and when they exclude you and revile you and spurn your name as evil, on account of the Son of Man!* [23]*Rejoice in that day, and leap for joy, for behold, your reward is great in heaven; for so their fathers did to the prophets.*

[24]*"But woe to you who are rich, for you have received your consolation.*

[25]*"Woe to you who are full now, for you shall be hungry.*

"Woe to you who laugh now, for you shall mourn and weep.

[26]*"Woe to you, when all people speak well of you, for so their fathers did to the false prophets.*

OVERVIEW: Jesus' miracles are inseparable from his teaching. Without the Word these deeds are too ambiguous and too open to interpretation. Christ's words here in Luke's Gospel—which differ from the Matthaean record (Mt 5:1-12)—are deceptively simple. How is it that the poor are blessed? And why are the rich cursed? Most interpreters of the Reformation era did not understand these words as divine condemnation of the current state of economic affairs, but as divine insight into the human heart—material wealth or poverty in itself is not a blessing or a curse but our response to it can be. A few commentators—like Peter Walpot—see in Jesus' words a revolutionary approach to wealth distribution, but most could not even conceive of it; there must be a deeper meaning. Walpot argued that Jesus' words meant more or less what they said: it is the poor, that is, those who do not have their own possessions, who are blessed. According to Walpot and some other Anabaptists, the only truly Christian way of life required a communal rather than an individual ownership of goods. But others see in Jesus' words something spiritual rather than economic. The poor were not blessed because of their poverty (that is an affliction rather than a blessing) but because the kingdom of heaven would be given to them. Likewise, the rich are not cursed because of their wealth, but they are cursed only if they are devoted to their wealth, and they take their pleasure in the things of this world and ignore the world to come. There will be rich people in heaven—look at Abraham, after all—but only if they were more invested in the treasures there than here.

These commentators exhort us to hunger and thirst after Christ. Focus on him, not forgetting our duties to God and others. Of course, this does not earn our way to heaven; instead Christ freely rewards his people. Our good works are far too weak to earn any reward, and anyone would be simple enough to think anyone can ever deserve salvation from God. God gives us this reward freely and helps us to accomplish anything that he requires. Scripture calls this a reward only because no one receives it unless they suffer for Christ. It follows a faithful life but is not earned by such a life.

6:17-19 *Many Hear Jesus and Are Healed*

JESUS TAUGHT FIRST THE APOSTLES, THEN THE PEOPLE. THE ENGLISH ANNOTATIONS: What Luke records here seems to be part of what Christ taught in Matthew 5, although there it is said that he went up on the mountain, sat and taught. For he first went up and stood, and taught a smaller company (see Mark 3:13). But perceiving a greater gathering of people coming to hear him, he descended from the top so that they could hear him better. He sat down on the edge of some plain which was more spacious. ANNOTATIONS UPON THE GOSPEL ACCORDING TO SAINT LUKE 6:17.[1]

JESUS BROUGHT HEALING TO ALL AS THE SAVIOR. DESIDERIUS ERASMUS: Now many people from far away were drawn by the great desire to hear the words of the gospel, and not a few by the hope of being healed. And in fact he set everyone free from all the kinds of diseases which any of them had. All of those who were troubled by unclean spirits were made whole. And all of these things were accomplished so easily that he restored some to health by his command alone, and some suddenly if they simply touched his clothing. For there was in him the fountain and fullness of the power and virtue of God, which proceeded from him just as light comes from the sun and heat from a fire, and so he brought salvation to everyone. For he was the Savior, and he came into the world in order to heal everyone. PARAPHRASE ON THE GOSPEL OF LUKE 6:17-19.[2]

6:20-26 *Blessings and Woes*

RICH OR POOR, BY FAITH WE ARE MADE ACCEPTABLE TO GOD. PHILIPP MELANCHTHON: The text begins with poverty because it is the commonest misery of the pious. Another explanation should not be searched for; the text speaks about poverty—which we usually call "lack of necessities" when money and other necessities for living are absent. "The poor in spirit" . . . he says "are blessed." That is, they are not rejected by God, but have a favored status before God. Here "blessed" does not mean dead people who have eternal life—as we commonly say—or who merited eternal life, instead it means "good works" or a status not rejected by God. As if he were saying: "It is good to be among the poor, that is, they are not rejected by God."

It is also said about the church which first is made righteous by faith and then has many good works. . . . It should also be understood that poverty does not praise itself as the monks imagine who nevertheless do not lack any necessities! But it is said about obedience in poverty, that is, obedience to God.

Both wealth and poverty are ordained by God. Neither on account of wealth nor on account of poverty is a person accepted or rejected, but to use wealth correctly is a good work, to use poverty correctly is also a good work. . . . We see many such examples in daily life. Anyone of us is able to be a wealthy canon by means of impiety—better to be a poor deacon by means of piety. . . .

Do the poor by their poverty merit the kingdom of heaven? No! Instead because they have already been made sons and heirs, and the kingdom of heaven is also compensation for their poverty. What does the kingdom of heaven signify? Not only future glory but also universal divine defense in this life. ANNOTATIONS ON THE GOSPEL OF MATTHEW.[3]

THE POOR IN SPIRIT GIVE UP THEIR POSSESSIONS FOR CHRIST. PETER WALPOT: "Blessed are the poor in spirit," namely, those who withdraw themselves from temporal concerns by surrendering their possessions. For Christ's sake they forsake, give up and have no more possessions, but instead stand and persevere in community in the true Christian church. Therefore it follows that those who do the opposite do not stand in the blessed

[1]Downame, ed., *Annotations*, Tt2r*.
[2]Erasmus, *In Evangelivm Lvce Paraphrasis*, l4r-v (LB 7:345-46).
[3]MO 14:567-68.

estate. For by "the poor" here he does not mean those who have nothing on account of laziness, or those who have wasted, gambled or drunk up their wealth, or have gone astray, or even those who have nothing and yet are as corrupt as anyone else. Instead he is speaking of those whom the Spirit makes poor. For just as the Spirit drove Christ into the desert where the devil tempted him, so also the Spirit drives them into poverty, so they have nothing of their own, just like Christ, their master; those are the "poor in spirit." Therefore whoever fears this poverty should also be feared; whoever is afraid of living in community, of them we should also be afraid. The Great Article Book: On Peace and Joint Property.[4]

The Reward Is Freely Given, Not Deserved. Heinrich Bullinger: It is as if he said, "If it grieves you that your reputation suffers and that you are persecuted in this world, try to remember how greatly your glory shall increase in the world to come. For however great your affliction is here on earth, so much the brighter shall your glory be in heaven." Here the Catholics misinterpret the word *reward*, saying that there is a special relation between the reward and what one deserves. But they are mistaken; the promise of the reward is free. Furthermore, if we consider how mutilated, imperfect and weak all good works are (whatsoever they be) that come even from the very best, we shall then understand well that God shall at no time find any work worthy of reward. There is no one so simple that, when he hears mention made of the reward, will think that we deserve anything at the hands of God, just because we spend our lives for the gospel; that is, that we can do anything by

which God may become a debtor to us. We are all at the will and pleasure of God. And he made not only us but also all our possessions—out of nothing. It is he who works in us both the will and the deed, even of good will.

Now the Scriptures do call a reward what is given by God to those who do not and cannot deserve it, even though they work as hard as possible to attain it. Even as the father says to his son, "Go and read your book diligently, apply your mind to learning, and you will have a good reward from me, a new coat or something else just as good." Now this coat is a reward, and at the same time it is not, because the son obtained the coat not by his diligence but by the father's gift, even though he would not have received it without that diligence and studying which the father required. In the same way, there is no one who obtains this reward of which the Lord speaks here, unless he suffers for Christ, and for this reason it is called a reward. If it were possible that you could die a hundred times for the gospel, even for that you would not deserve the worth of a reward at the hands of God, that is, you cannot constrain and bind him to owe you anything at all; for as often as you receive life, so often you become a debtor to him again. And for this reason, those things which God gives to us are not rewards, but they are his free gifts freely given without any merit in us. An Ecclesiasticall Exposition upon Saint Mathewe 5.[5]

Those Who Seek Their Wealth Only in This World Are Condemned. John Calvin: Just as Luke recounts four points of such blessing, so now he opposes to them four curses, so that the phrases correspond to each other. But this antithesis is not only meant to inspire terror in the ungodly but also to rouse the faithful, so that they are not lulled to sleep by the vain and deceitful enticements of the world. We know indeed how inclined people are to be intoxicated by good fortune or to be entrapped by human flattery. Thus

---

[4] QGT 12:181; citing Mt 5:3. This section of *The Great Article Book* is *Von der waren Gelassenheit und christlichen Gmainschafft der Güetter*. *Gelassenheit*, also translated as "resignation," "letting go" or "releasement," is a common and complex term in Christian (and German intellectual) history. Often traced back to Meister Eckhart and German mysticism, the concept was important to Anabaptists in the sixteenth century and remains important to their religious heirs (for example, Mennonites and Hutterites). For more information, see the articles "Anabaptists" and "Mysticism," OER 1:31-35; 3:119-24, respectively.

[5] Marlorat, ed., *Catholike and Ecclesiasticall Exposition of the Holy Gospell After S. Mathewe*, 82-83*.

the children of God often envy the reprobate, when they see that their lives are prosperous and successful. But here he curses the rich, not each one, of course, but those who receive their comfort in this world; that is, those who find such pleasure in their fortune that they disregard the future life. Therefore it signifies that riches are so far from making a person happy, that they often turn into an occasion of destruction. Otherwise God does not prohibit the rich from his kingdom, if they do not become snares to themselves and do not fix their hopes on earth, thereby closing up the entrance of heaven to themselves. COMMENTARY ON A HARMONY OF THE GOSPELS.[6]

GOD HATES EXCESSIVE EATING AND DRINKING. THE BOOK OF HOMILIES: And first, so that you might perceive how detestable and hateful all excess in eating and drinking is before the almighty God, you should call to mind what is written by Saint Paul to the Galatians, where he numbers gluttony and drunkenness among those horrible crimes that will keep a person from inheriting the kingdom of heaven. He reckons them among the "desires of the flesh" and couples them with idolatry, whoredom and murder, which are the greatest offenses that can be named among us. For the first removes God's honor, the second defiles his holy temple (that is to say, our own bodies), and the third makes us companions of Cain in the slaughter of our brothers and sisters. Whoever commits these things, as Saint Paul says, "will not inherit the kingdom of God." Certainly that sin is very odious and loathsome before God if it causes him to turn his favorable countenance so far from us that he would entirely bar us outside the heavenly gates and disinherit us from his heavenly kingdom. But he so abhors all animalistic feasting that through his Son, our Savior Christ, in this Gospel he declares his terrible indignation against all belly-gods in that he pronounces them to be accursed, saying, "Woe to you who are full, for you shall be hungry." ...

Therefore those who either feed themselves like pigs, disrespecting the sanctification by the Word of God and prayer, or unthankfully abuse the good creatures of God by excessive eating and drunkenness, are without excuse before God, because God's ordinances relating to his creatures plainly forbid it. HOMILY 17: AGAINST GLUTTONY AND DRUNKENNESS.[7]

A GOOD REPUTATION DOES NOT GUARANTEE A JUST CAUSE. JOHANNES BRENZ: Christ does not condemn fame in this passage, but rather the vain belief that people have concerning praise and fame. For the common sort of people do not judge matters according to truth and their true nature, but rather according to public reputation. If someone is thought well of by everyone, people think he has a just cause and that he is righteous, but if a person is abject and disdained by most people, then they think that he is unjust and evil. So people do not usually try to investigate whether a person's cause is just or not, but rather whether he has a good reputation among the common folk and is well-thought of, and if he does, then they figure that he does good things, just because he pleases the greatest number of people.

But Christ condemns this way of proceeding, so that no one will depend on human judgment. "For that is how their ancestors treated the false prophets." That is, most of the ancestors of the Israelites praised the false prophets rather than true prophets. They persecuted and punished the true prophets, but they enriched and honored the false ones. AN ECCLESIASTICALL EXPOSITION UPON SAINT LUKE 6.[8]

---

[7]*Certain Sermons or Homilies* (1852), 271-72*; quoting 1 Cor 6:10; alluding to Gal 5:16-21; Is 5:11, 22.

[8]Marlorat, ed., *Catholike and Ecclesiasticall Exposition of the Holy Gospell After S. Marke and Luke*, 158*; alluding to Jn 15:18-19.

---

[6]CO 45:166 (cf. CTS 31:268-69).

6:27-36 JESUS TEACHES LOVE FOR ENEMIES

[27]"But I say to you who hear, Love your enemies, do good to those who hate you, [28]bless those who curse you, pray for those who abuse you. [29]To one who strikes you on the cheek, offer the other also, and from one who takes away your cloak do not withhold your tunic[a] either. [30]Give to everyone who begs from you, and from one who takes away your goods do not demand them back. [31]And as you wish that others would do to you, do so to them.

[32]"If you love those who love you, what benefit is that to you? For even sinners love those who love them. [33]And if you do good to those who do good to you, what benefit is that to you? For even sinners do the same. [34]And if you lend to those from whom you expect to receive, what credit is that to you? Even sinners lend to sinners, to get back the same amount. [35]But love your enemies, and do good, and lend, expecting nothing in return, and your reward will be great, and you will be sons of the Most High, for he is kind to the ungrateful and the evil. [36]Be merciful, even as your Father is merciful.

a Greek *chiton*, a long garment worn under the cloak next to the skin

---

OVERVIEW: Christian love is the subject of this pericope. What is special about love? How should it be applied in daily life? What does the gospel forbid or demand of us? Everyone, Christian or not, knows about love, so in itself love is not a particular invention of Jesus. But there is something different and unusual about love from his perspective. The commentators point out that Christ's version of love is, in fact, opposite to the normal version. While human nature and reason tell us that we should love those who love us and those who are worthy, Christ here tells us that his disciples must love those who are not lovable—those who hate us, those who are unkind, those who do not deserve it and will not repay us. In other words, we must love our enemies. We must go so far as to turn the other cheek when we are treated wrongly by anyone; we should even suffer further mistreatment rather than breaking charity by resisting and losing our patience. The golden rule should rule—how would we like people to treat us in similar circumstances? In essence, what Jesus requires is far more than what nature or reason suggests; he demands that we love where we will not be repaid.

This idea has several implications for the reformers. One is the simplest: If we love those who love us in return, then we are paid and should expect no praise. It is only if we love those who do not love us, in fact, those who hate or persecute us, that our love can rise to a higher level. This is the sort of love that God demands and is the sort of love that he showed us when he sent his Son to sacrifice himself for us while we were still his enemies. Another implication of this idea of love is that it should be given freely, which means it is most appropriately given to those of whom we expect no return. In particular, this means it should be given as charity to the poor (that is, the deserving poor, not lazy people who do not want to work for a living). The generosity that Christ demanded of his disciples was not a wastefulness— give until it is gone—but rather an attitude of always being willing to help, without any thought of return. The practical extension of this idea was controversial in the early modern period: giving in love with no thought of return meant that usury, the practice of receiving interest on a loan, was unacceptable. Several comments on this passage explicitly reject and condemn the idea of charging interest as counter to God's commands, making its practitioners the object of God's wrath and vengeance. The practice of usury was seen by some as the downfall of Christian Europe, despite (or perhaps because of) the fact that it was the basis for the nascent banking industry, trading and merchant activities, and the protocapitalist economy. Tirades against usury also undergirded the frequent expulsion of Jews from various parts of Europe, for, among other issues, Jews were frequently involved in moneylending activities.

6:27-34 Loving One's Enemies Is Greater Than Loving One's Friends

LOVE'S ABUNDANT GENEROSITY. WILLIAM TYNDALE: The office of love is to pour out again the same goodness that one has received from God on one's neighbor—to be to him as he experiences Christ is to him. The office of love is to have compassion and to bear with one's neighbor the burden of his infirmities. As it is written, love "covers a multitude of sins." That is to say, one considers infirmities and interprets everything for the best and considers a thousand things—of which the least would be enough, if one did not love, to go to court for, to trouble and unquiet a whole town, even a whole realm or two—as no sin at all. EXPOSITION OF SAINT MATTHEW'S GOSPEL 5:43-48.[1]

WORLDLY PEOPLE SEE THESE WORDS AS ABSURD. THE BOOK OF HOMILIES: These sentences, good people, seem to be mere absurdities to a natural person, and contrary to all reason. For "the natural person does not understand the things that belong to God, and he cannot do so as long as the old Adam dwells in him." Therefore Christ is saying that he wants his servants to be so far from vengeance and resisting wrong that he would rather have them ready to suffer another wrong than to break charity by resisting it and losing their patience. He wants our good deeds to be so far from anything carnal that he does not want even our closest friends to know of our good deeds, so that we might resist pride and vainglory.

And even though our friends and family are as dear to us as our right eyes and our right hands, if they draw us away from God, we ought to renounce and forsake them.

Thus if you want to be profitable hearers and readers of the holy Scriptures, you must first deny yourselves, repressing your carnal senses which are taken by the outward words, and instead search the inward meaning. Reason must give place to God's Holy Spirit. You must submit your worldly wisdom and judgment to his divine wisdom and judgment. Remember that the Scripture, no matter in what strange form it might be pronounced, is the Word of the living God. HOMILY 22: INFORMATION FOR THEM WHICH TAKE OFFENSE AT CERTAIN PLACES OF SCRIPTURE.[2]

CHARITY IS REQUIRED OF A CHRISTIAN, WITH NO USURY. HENRY HAMMOND: Everyone who is truly in need—this does not include the one who makes begging his trade and refuses to work to sustain himself or rescue himself from want—is the proper object of everyone's charity. Therefore no one who is thus qualified to receive, and by asking offers you an opportunity, is to be rejected by you. And because liberality consists of two branches, giving and lending freely without interest, you must exercise both parts of it toward the poor. Give to all distressed people who ask help of you, and from him who requests and receives any loan from you, exact no interest. PARAPHRASE ON LUKE 6.[3]

OUR LOVE MUST REFLECT GOD'S LOVE. WILLIAM TYNDALE: Wherever you see need . . . to the utmost of your power, there open your heart and be merciful. And of mercifulness, set God your Father and Christ your Lord and Master as an example. Be like them as much as you are able. If you are merciful, God has bound himself to be merciful to you again. Is this not an exceedingly great thing, that God who has no obligation to his creatures has nevertheless put it in your hands to

---

[1]Tyndale, *Expositions and Notes*, 14*; citing 1 Pet 4:8.

[2]*Certain Sermons or Homilies* (1852), 347*; quoting 1 Cor 2:14.
[3]Hammond, *Paraphrase and Annotations*, 207*.

bind him for the day of your tribulation, to show you mercy then?

Concerning lending, proceed by this rule of mercy. Many in extreme need still ashamed to beg will want you to lend. To such instead of lending give, or say: "Here is as much as you need. If you can pay it back, good, do so and you will find me ready another time to lend or give (if need be) as much or more. And if you will not be able to pay it back, do not trouble your conscience; I give it to you. We are all one man's children. One man has bought us all with his blood and bound us to help one another." And by doing so you will win his heart for your Father. EXPOSITION OF SAINT MATTHEW'S GOSPEL 5:43-48.[4]

NATURE LEADS PEOPLE TO LOVE THOSE WHO LOVE THEM. KONRAD PELLIKAN: If you love those who love you, what favor will you ask of God? Love is repaid by love. Whoever loves in return if he is loved, or whoever will not love unless he is loved in return, is far away from the charity of the gospel, which embraces friends and enemies equally. What in truth makes that person who loves in return because he is loved exempt and worthy of the loftiness of the gospel? Do not those who love the world, but in other respects are sinners, nevertheless by the guidance of nature love loving, and will they not turn away from one who does not respond to mutual love? If you will grant benefits to those who were of benefit to you, what favor is then owed to you? This is not the kindness of the gospel but an exchange of benefits. Because both sinners and those who are strangers to the loftiness of the profession of the gospel repay the benefits which they receive, cursing ingratitude by the guidance of nature, then not to do this is most shameful, but to do it deserves no great praise. COMMENTARY IN LUKE 6:27-28.[5]

WE ARE TO GIVE BUT TO EXPECT NOTHING IN RETURN. JOHN CALVIN: Although these words of Christ, which are related by Matthew, sound as if he is commanding that we have no choice but to give to everyone, we draw out a different sense from Luke, who more fully explains the matter. First, it is certain that the intention of Christ was to make his disciples more generous, but not wasteful. And it would be a foolish wastefulness to squander thoughtlessly what the Lord has given. In this we see that rule of liberality that the Spirit teaches in another place. Let us therefore hold first that Christ exhorts his disciples to be generous and kind. Next, they should not think that they have discharged this duty once they have helped a few people, but they should be eager to bestow his blessings on everyone and not to weary of it as long as the means are available. And so that no one might complain about Matthew's words, let us compare what is written by Luke. Christ denies that we perform our duties toward God, whether in lending or in some other service, if we hope for a reward in return; thus charity is distinguished from friendship of the flesh. Worldly people do not love each other freely but only have a self-interested affection. Thus, as Plato prudently suggests, everyone brings back the love which he gives to others. But Christ demands from his followers free beneficence, that they might be eager to help the poor, from whom nothing can be expected in return. Now we see what it means to have an open hand to those who ask: it is to be liberally disposed toward all who need our help and who are unable to repay the kindness. COMMENTARY ON A HARMONY OF THE GOSPELS.[6]

LIVE BY CHRIST'S ROYAL LAW! VALENTIN ICKELSHAMER:

What you don't like to experience here,
Don't do it to your neighbor, either early or late;
remember what love has to teach you,
and do to others
what you would wish to happen to you.
That's what the Law and the Prophets are all
about.

---

[4]Tyndale, *Expositions and Notes*, 68-69*.
[5]Pellikan, *In Sacrosancta Quatuor Evangelia*, 84 (cf. LB 7:347).

[6]CTS 31:301-2 (CO 45:186); quoting Mt 5:42.

Pray for your enemy when he is in need.
Repay evil with good. . . .
Take not of this, both poor and rich!
Let no one depend on his own delusion;
if you've done that, then quit it!
Confess it with remorse and sorrow,
and take up the cross with patience.
With Christ you'll find grace;
that's what the apostles clearly teach.
Christ led the way
so that we should follow him.
Patiently he spent his time here
and remained constant through all his suffering,
not like those pretending to be Christians,
who confuse law and gospel,
with the present as well as the former teachers,
trying to maintain their power with the sword.
In eternity that will not stand the test,
and it is truth I claim as my witness.
O God, come quickly; rescue us!
The godless ones are taking over,
and because of that the godly suffer.
As you yourself have said,
it is clearly revealed to many
that the final hour is at hand.
Let us not be put to shame;
help us grow in faith and love;
take us up into your eternal rest,
which we anticipate in Christ.
Let us die in peace.
Do not let the world terrify us,
that we might continue on your path until death
and comport ourselves nobly
by the power of the Holy Spirit.
Lord, make us victorious in our faith. Amen.

Kunstbuch: The Learned Ones,
The Wrongheaded Ones.[7]

Trust Your Conscience. William Tyndale:
And so, in all cases, examine your conscience. Ask
it what is to be done in all doubts between your

neighbor and you; it will teach you unless you are
filthier than a swine and altogether beastly. Exposition of Saint Matthew's Gospel 5:43-48.[8]

6:35-36 Loving One's Enemies Imitates God's Love

Usury Is Utterly Opposed to God's Command. Edwin Sandys: Every person is to
his neighbor a debtor, not only of what he himself
borrows but of whatever his neighbor needs. He is
a debtor not only to pay what he owes but also to
lend what he has and may conveniently spare, to
lend, I say, according to the rule of Christ. "Lend,
looking for nothing thereby, and your reward shall
be much, you shall be the children of the Most
High." So these overpayments, the usury which has
spoiled and eaten up many, the canker of the
commonwealth, is both utterly forbidden to people
and abhorred by God. To bargain for lead, grain or
leases with those who have neither lead, grain or
lease to pay. . . but only unlawful gain of money, the
borrower will then forfeit his obligation, because
he neither can nor means to make such a payment,
and the lender is not content to receive less
advantage than thirty percent: this is nothing but a
patched cloak with which to cover this vile sin. If
you ever receive anything on condition or you
receive more than was lent, you are a usurer toward
your brother, and God will revenge himself against
you. He whom you should obey, if you want to be
saved, has in express words commanded you not to
lend your money for usury. "If you lend money to
my people, to the poor among you, do not charge
him interest." This word of God people cannot
dispense with, and it shall not return in vain. . . .

The reasons of people for usury must give place
to the precept of God against it. Who are you to
think that you are wiser than your Maker? If God
has condemned it, will you dare to defend it? In his
judgment it is injurious, but your opinion finds it
acceptable? He has seen reason to prohibit it, and
now you see reason why you may use it? Such

---

[7]CRR 12:56-58 (QGT 17:125-26); citing Mt 7:12; Tob 4:16; Mt
5:44; Rom 12:17; Lk 6:27; 8:23; Acts 2:38; Mt 24:12; 1 Jn 2:18; Lk
17:5; Ps 25.

[8]Tyndale, *Expositions and Notes,* 119*.

reasons, with the makers and users of them, the Lord's justice shall destroy. And yet, in truth, all reason and the very law of nature is against it. All nations at all times have condemned it as the very bane and pestilence of a commonwealth, as we see a witness in both the old Roman history and practice. These secret shifts are seen by God and abhorred, and will be revenged. You may well escape the hands of people by your colored delusions, but you cannot escape the sharp and swift judgment of God. In accordance with what he has threatened, he will exclude you from his kingdom, ban you from his tabernacle and hurl you into hell, where your evil-gotten money can neither redeem nor help you. A just reward for your unjust usury! The Eleventh Sermon. A Sermon Made at York.[9]

Christ Reveals the Mercy of God in Coming to Us Sinners.

John Donne: Sin cannot be a way of honor. We do not dare to affirm our sins, but rather are ashamed of them after they are committed. They are fruitless—unprofitable before, shameful and dishonorable after—and for these we are enemies to God. Yet for all this, God still comes to us. The Lord of Hosts comes to naked and disarmed people, the God of peace to this enemy of God. Some people will continue to be kind when they find a thankful receiver, but God "is kind to the unthankful," says Christ himself. A person may be found who will die for his friend, he says, but God died for his enemies, so that when you were enemies, you were reconciled to God by the death of his Son. Our first disproportion and the first exaltation of his mercy is that he came so ingloriously, he who is infinitely more than all, to we who are infinitely less than nothing. He came, shall we venture to say, in a way so treacherous to himself as to betray himself and deliver himself to his enemies. Sermon 7, Preached on Christmas Day (1629).[10]

Mercy Is a Good Work That Will Be Required of Us.

Kaspar von Schwenckfeld: Our heavenly teacher Jesus Christ relates to us here five commandments, which he wants all Christians to keep. The first is that we should be merciful, we should have pity and show mercy. That is, give help to everyone, where need and occasion are before us. This virtue of mercy established by Christ in the heart stretches it wide, and all of the following commands flow out of it and will be kept through faith. The second is that we should not judge. The third is that we should not condemn anyone. The fourth is that we should forgive. The fifth is that we should give. The Lord Christ attaches his promise of reward to this good work, completely out of pure love and grace, for he carries us, worthless servants that we are, and makes us happy and eager to accomplish the purpose of his saints. First we want to talk about mercy. The mercy about which Christ teaches us here is one of the eight blessings from Matthew 5. The Lord orders that this be shown, as mentioned, not only to the thankful but also to the unthankful, following the example of the heavenly Father. God will require this work from every person at the Last Judgment.

The work of mercy is twofold, namely, corporal and spiritual. Corporal mercy is like what is described in the Gospel, such as feeding the hungry, giving drink to the thirsty, giving shelter to strangers, clothing the naked, visiting the sick, helping out those in prison or comforting them. However, the spiritual work of mercy is to teach those who lack understanding, train or give good advice to the needy, punish sinners, comfort the grieving, pray for the neighbor and forgive everyone for God's sake. For the word *mercy* means, as much as all sorts of good deeds, when a person comes to help another in love and helps him faithfully to carry his burden and pain—such things please God. Postil for the Fourth Sunday After Trinity.[11]

---

[9]Sandys, *Sermons*, 202-4*; quoting Ex 22:25; alluding to Is 55:11.
[10]Donne, *Works*, 1:133*; alluding to Rom 5:7-8.

[11]CS 10:449-50.

6:37-49 JESUS TEACHES JUDGMENT

[39]He also told them a parable: "Can a blind man lead a blind man? Will they not both fall into a pit? [40]A disciple is not above his teacher, but everyone when he is fully trained will be like his teacher. [41]Why do you see the speck that is in your brother's eye, but do not notice the log that is in your own eye? [42]How can you say to your brother, 'Brother, let me take out the speck that is in your eye,' when you yourself do not see the log that is in your own eye? You hypocrite, first take the log out of your own eye, and then you will see clearly to take out the speck that is in your brother's eye.

[43]"For no good tree bears bad fruit, nor again does a bad tree bear good fruit, [44]for each tree is known by its own fruit. For figs are not gathered from thornbushes, nor are grapes picked from a bramble bush.

[45]The good person out of the good treasure of his heart produces good, and the evil person out of his evil treasure produces evil, for out of the abundance of the heart his mouth speaks.

[46]"Why do you call me 'Lord, Lord,' and not do what I tell you? [47]Everyone who comes to me and hears my words and does them, I will show you what he is like: [48]he is like a man building a house, who dug deep and laid the foundation on the rock. And when a flood arose, the stream broke against that house and could not shake it, because it had been well built.[a] [49]But the one who hears and does not do them is like a man who built a house on the ground without a foundation. When the stream broke against it, immediately it fell, and the ruin of that house was great."

a Some manuscripts *founded upon the rock*

OVERVIEW: If love for enemies and charity to those who cannot repay is the positive requirement for the Christian life, then in this passage we see the negative realities that we should avoid: judgmentalism and hypocrisy. Both of these faults are common among religious people, as the example of the Pharisees makes clear. They constantly judge Christ and find him wanting, while at the same time seeing themselves as pious, just and righteous. Instead, Christ tells us we should not judge others but should rather forgive. Christ does not mean, our commentators tell us, that we are never to judge—for some people, such as pastors, rulers and magistrates, are authorized by their office to judge, and there are also forms of judgment appropriate to private individuals. But rather we must avoid uncharitable censuring of our brothers and sisters. We are to interpret people's words and actions with charity and look for the best in everyone.

The example of the log and the speck reveals the danger in being judgmental: in judging another for his minor faults, we most likely are missing the major sins and guilt in our own lives. Such judgmentalism, as we see it for example in the Pharisees, will lead us straight into hypocrisy—a common problem in the world and in the church. Hypocrites generally do not see the truth about themselves, or assume that others will not see it, but they are quick to criticize others for much smaller faults than those of which they are guilty. The danger of hypocrites is that they usually present such a holy face to the world—how are we to know who is truly good and pious, and who just appears to be so?

Christ uses the notion of the blind leading the blind to instruct us that anyone who interprets the law differently from him is blind to the truth, and when blind teachers lead equally blind students, they all end up in the ditch. Then, he turns to the example of the tree and its fruit to explain that it is only in the fruit that we can see the true nature of the tree. Good fruit is produced by a good tree, but that goodness has to come up from the roots; it is not merely in the appearance of the leaves. Likewise, one can tell the hypocrites from the faithful Christians only by the fruit they produce, that is, by their words and actions. Although the reformers affirm that people are not saved by their own works, they also argue that good Christians will produce good works, works that are according to God's command and are of benefit to the neighbor. But the evil hypocrites, no matter how good they may appear on the outside, will only produce evil fruit, works contrary to God's commands. These "holy hypocrites," who do not forgive others or look for the good in them, will not be forgiven by God and will not enter into the kingdom.

6:37-38 As We Judge Others, So Will We Be Judged

Christ Does Not Forbid All Judgment, Only Uncharitable Censoring. John Boys: He does not simply forbid us here to judge, but rather he instructs us how to judge. He does not infringe on the public judging of the pastor or prince. Nor of the pastor, for his apostle Paul excommunicated an incestuous Corinthian in Christ's name, and it was his own rule elsewhere for the church. And as for the civil magistrate's authority to judge, God commanded Moses to provide "men who fear God, who are trustworthy and hate a bribe," and place them as rulers and judges over his people. He also strictly charged all people under the gospel to submit themselves to governing authorities. He also does not condemn private judging of ourselves and others on sufficient ground. . . . Our Savior's meaning, then, is not (as interpreters generally note) to forbid all kinds of judging but only rash and uncharitable censuring of our brothers and sisters. It is our part to commend in another everything which is apparently good and to make the best of anything which is doubtful. As Christ himself said, we may not be curious in observing or critical in condemning a "speck" in another's eye, not seeing the "log" that is in our own. We may not be forward in finding peccadilloes in others while overlooking gross faults in ourselves. The Fourth Sunday After Trinity.[1]

We Must Forgive Others If We Want God to Forgive Us. Richard Taverner: Here, my friends, you see that unless we forgive others for the offenses which they have committed against us, our heavenly Father will surely not forgive us. And therefore we say in our Lord's Prayer, "Forgive us our debts, or sins, even as we forgive those who trespass against us." So if you cannot find it in your heart to forgive your neighbor his faults, you may be sure that God will not forgive you your faults. On the Fourth Sunday After Trinity.[2]

"Do Unto Others" Is Governed by God's Justice. Martin Bucer: Christ wants us to shun those things which contribute to the breaking of charity and to embrace those things which spring from it, such as to give and to do good. To one who gives shall be given, and that most abundantly. That is what he means by "a good measure, pressed down, shaken together and running over" (which is mentioned in the next verse). For these sentences are borrowed from the common way of speaking, the same as the words the Lord uses to exhort us to do to others as we would have them do to us. And throughout he also gives us to understand that it is ordained and appointed by God that however we have behaved toward others, we will find them behaving so toward us, according to this saying: "He who seeks good finds goodwill, but evil comes to him who searches for it." Not that no one will be ever treated ungratefully by someone whom they had treated well, but rather that by the goodness of God it will happen that even if one's good works are received ungratefully, the good works themselves will not be lacking in fruit, for others will supply it. . . . As

---

[1]Boys, *Exposition of the Dominical Epistles and Gospels*, 3:119-20*; citing 1 Cor 5:3-5; Mt 18:17; Ex 18:21; Rom 13:1.
[2]Taverner, *Epistles and Gospelles (Sommer Parte)*, 96r-v*; quoting Mt 6:23; Lk 11:4.

Solomon says, "One man gives freely yet gains even more; another withholds unduly but comes to poverty." And so likewise those who are malicious against others, those who seek revenge and remember how they were wronged in the past, those who are severe judges of others' faults, they will find that, by God's justice, they will be treated in a similar fashion. An Ecclesiasticall Exposition upon Saint Luke 6.[3]

6:39-40 *The Student Does Not Overtake the Teacher*

The Blind Teachers of the Law Mislead Their Hearers. Heinrich Bullinger: In order that he might more surely impress these things on the minds of his disciples, the Lord added this common example. In it he teaches that we should not follow along with the blind Pharisees and what they recommend for a way of life in following the letter of the law, but rather we should follow the one who gives a true interpretation of the law and gives the strength to fulfill it. It is as if he said, "By this sermon I have so clearly, perfectly and truly shown you the sense of the law that anyone who tries to interpret the law in another way must be an ignorant and blind interpreter. And how can the blind lead the blind? If the blind lead the blind, they will both fall into the ditch in the end. So whoever wants to have the true sense and meaning of the law, and does not want to fall into the deep ditch of blindness, needs to know that these scribes, Pharisees and false prophets are teaching a different sense of the law than the one which I have taught." An Ecclesiasticall Exposition upon Saint Luke 7.[4]

Do Not Be Impatient to Be Greater Than the Master. Johann Baumgart (Pomarius): He warns us against vexation and impatience in the presentation of his own examples, in which he says, "The disciple is not above his teacher. When he is like his teacher, then his training is complete." It is as if he were to say, "It will not fail. You will be judged and suffer condemnation with the tongue and fist. Do not let that annoy you. Do not become impatient, and do not think that you would be better than me, your master."

For the Scriptures testify that people judged him to be a friend to tax collectors and sinners and called him a glutton and drunkard or even a devil or partner to the devil. And finally they even cried out, "Crucify him, crucify him!" And now the Lord will finish, "I have not reproached anyone, although I was reproached. I have not paid back evil with evil but with good. Look at my example and do likewise. Do not let evil overcome you. Rather, overcome evil with good, and learn gentleness, humility and charity from me. Devote yourselves to the new commands of Christian and brotherly love, that people may recognize by it that you are my disciples." Gospel on the Fifth Sunday After Trinity.[5]

6:41-42 *Avoid Hypocrisy*

We Must Be Very Cautious in Judging Another. Caspar Huberinus: Christ our Lord chastises the false Christians and hypocrites explicitly and by name, and the Lord thus shows that such false judgments, opinion, and punishments are not only against his kingdom and teachings but also against all justice and order. He makes it quite clear for them to understand by the example of the splinter and the log in the eye that it is a completely turned-around and mixed-up practice for a brother or Christian to chastise another for some small mistake, when he himself is up to his ears in all kinds of sin and immorality. But this is the common practice in the world, even among those who call themselves Christian, because there is no end to all the sophistry, fault-finding, judgmentalism, chastising and condemna-

---

[3]Marlorat, ed., *Catholike and Ecclesiasticall Exposition of the Holy Gospell After S. Marke and Luke*, 160*; citing Jn 10:10; Prov 11:27, 24.
[4]Marlorat, ed., *Catholike and Ecclesiasticall Exposition of the Holy Gospell After S. Marke and Luke*, 160-61*.

[5]Baumgart, *Postilla*, 169r; citing Lk 15:1-2; Jn 8:48-52; Mt 11:19; Lk 7:34; 23:21; 1 Pet 3:9.

tions. And those who usually do it could use some chastisement themselves and could be charged in both important and evil matters. These same people attempt to take to task poor, weak and fragile Christians who have committed very minor infractions. They usurp the cases which God alone should judge, to whom alone it is fitting to chastise the secret sins of the heart and to find the appropriate means to punish ordinary bad habits.

Therefore a person should sweep first in front of his own door, and look into his own heart and only then go before his neighbor's door. But before he does that he should make everything clean, pure and clear at his own door and in his own person, for justice requires that he should be his own acccuser rather than that of another, as Solomon says in his Proverbs. And so Christ concludes this gospel here: he does not want to forbid everything to a Christian, that he should never chastise his neighbor. However, we should not do this out of evil habit, or worldly judgment or from a desire for vengeance against our neighbor but only out of Christian zeal, according to the law of Christ. ON THE FOURTH SUNDAY AFTER TRINITY.[6]

HYPOCRISY IS A TERRIBLE DISEASE FROM WHICH MANY SUFFER. PHILIPP MELANCHTHON: The person who is infected with this disease is at the point that he would seem to be a certain person to another which he actually is not. Hypocrisy so blinds a person that either he does not say what is true about himself, or at least he thinks that other people do not see or regard it. In the meantime he criticizes the faults of others, even if they are very small, to the end that he might seem to hate evil and to be a lover of righteousness and a follower of it.

Here we may note that it is not in vain that while Christ at other times was very meek and gentle toward the publicans and sinners, he does not stop from naming this kind of person (usually the Pharisees) by the reproachful name of "hypocrites." It is not in vain, I say, for he does it to show

that the whole and only destruction of these people comes about because they do not know themselves for what they are. Therefore it is quite necessary that people should be called what they are, so that they may amend themselves. That may be the reason why the Lord so named them in various places, such as when he said, "You hypocrites! Well did Isaiah prophesy of you." Often he very earnestly called them hypocrites, in fact.

So if we desire to eschew and avoid this terrible vice, each one of us should first search properly into our own faults and only then take it on ourselves to judge other people. Even then we should not judge others with a desire to defame and hurt them but only out of brotherly love and affection, linked with the bond of charity, to help bring back the one who has strayed. AN ECCLESIASTICALL EXPOSITION UPON SAINT MATHEWE 7.[7]

THE SPLINTER AND THE BEAM. JOHANN SPANGENBERG: What is the splinter? Nothing other than the small fault in our neighbor, into which he has fallen through weakness. And what is the beam? The opinion of and satisfaction in oneself, which so blinds a person that he only sees faults in other people, but he can neither see nor recognize his own sins and vices, which are great. For example, the Pharisees condemned Christ because he healed the sick on the sabbath, because his disciples did not fast as often as they did and because of handwashing. But they did not see the huge beam of unbelief and godless living in their own eyes, because they opposed the truth of God. . . .

So now Christ is also saying: "To judge and to pronounce sentence against others is an evil, shameful vice, a truly devilish pride, with which people accomplish nothing else than to bring God's judgment on themselves. And so, you who want to judge other people, to pass sentence and condemn them, reach down into your own heart and see what a villain lies hidden within you. First, work

---

[6]Huberinus, *Postilla Teütsch*, 2:b8r-cr; citing Prov 18 (perhaps Prov 18:17); Mt 18.

[7]Marlorat, ed., *Catholike and Ecclesiasticall Exposition of the Holy Gospell After S. Mathewe*, 137-38*; citing Mt 15:7; 22:18; 23:15; Lk 13:15.

on your own piety. Think back, read the daily record of your own life, and you will undoubtedly find such a story that will not be pleasing to you and that you would gladly keep secret. Well, others also do this, so you can relax." GOSPEL ON THE FOURTH SUNDAY AFTER TRINITY.[8]

6:43-45 *A Tree and Its Fruit*

GOOD AND BAD ARE WHAT GOD HAS COMMANDED OR FORBIDDEN. JOHANN SPANGENBERG: What is a good tree? It is a pious, faithful person who lives according to God's command. For example, it is a lord, ruler, mayor, preacher, head of a household, servant who lives in faith and does what is appropriate for him. Those are the same trees that bring forth fruit at the proper time and increase and prosper into eternal life.

What is a bad tree? It is a wicked, unbelieving person who lives outside of God's Word and command in all sin and vice. It is hypocrites who think they are holy because of their works, and false Christians who go about in their unbelief, building on and trusting in their own works and merit and thereby despising poor sinners, just like the proud Pharisees. These are the worthless, ruined trees that produce only worm-eaten fruit which belongs in the fires of hell.

What are the good fruits? They are the good works of Christians, which are done according to God's Word and command and benefit the neighbor.

What are the bad fruits? They are the works which are done outside of faith and God's command, no matter how pretty they may appear. For no work is good unless God has commanded it, and no work is bad unless God has forbidden it. Whoever wants to do a good work must look at God's commands: whatever he finds is commanded there is a good work, and whatever is forbidden there is a bad work. GOSPEL ON THE EIGHTH SUNDAY AFTER TRINITY.[9]

THE EVANGELICAL TREE BRINGS FORTH GOOD FRUIT. DESIDERIUS ERASMUS: Why do you claim praise of holiness for yourself from such things that can be common both to good people and to bad? Neither clothing, nor food, nor long prayers nor wearing phylacteries declare a person to be good.[10] For a tree is not valued for its leaves but for its fruit. But the fruit draws its sap from the root: if the root is bitter, the tree cannot bear sweet fruit. But if it is good, the tree cannot produce fruit but what corresponds to its sap. The leaves and the rind of the fruit are visible to the eye and can deceive, but the sap and the root are not visible. If the heart is corrupt, anything which arises from it is evil; if it is sincere, anything which it produces is sincere. Every tree produces its own kind of fruit, which it is unable to disguise. Figs cannot be gathered from the blackthorn tree, nor are grapes gathered from a bramble bush. . . .

And do you desire to know the fruits of the tree of the gospel, whose roots are filled with the sweetest sap of faith and charity? Such a one loves everyone and hates no one; he is so far from treating anyone badly that he wishes well even for his enemies. He prays for blessings on those who curse him, and he prays for the health of even those who would kill him; he earnestly tries to do good to everyone, hoping for a reward from God. He suspects evil of no one. Whatever is ambiguous, he interprets in the best light. He condemns no one but leaves all judgment to God, so much does he desire to be well-deserving. He is patient with the ungodly, in order that they might come to their senses. He admonishes his neighbor with affection when he does wrong. He freely forgives those who sin against him and does not remember the offense. If you should see these fruits anywhere, know that they come from an evangelical tree, because it has fruit worthy of the gospel. PARAPHRASE ON THE GOSPEL OF LUKE 6:43-45.[11]

---

[10]The phylactery, or *tefillin*, is one of two small black leather cases with Torah texts worn by Jewish men—one is worn on the left arm and the other on the forehead. They serve as reminders of God and the obligation to keep the law during daily life.
[11]Erasmus, *In Evangelivm Lvce Paraphrasis*, mr-v (LB 7:349).

---

[8]Spangenberg, *Postilla . . . von Ostern biß auffs Aduent*, LXXXVIIr.
[9]Spangenberg, *Postilla . . . von Ostern biß auffs Aduent*, CIIIIv-CVr.

6:46-49 *How Firm a Foundation*

THE "HOLY HYPOCRITES" WILL NOT INHERIT THE KINGDOM. RICHARD TAVERNER: Finally, Christ teaches us here that these glorious and holy hypocrites who in outward appearance and in name appear Christian, always speaking of God but doing nothing that God demands of them, shall not enter into the kingdom of heaven. Rather, those shall enter the kingdom who have Christ and the gospel not only in their mouths but also in their hearts, those who do the will of Christ and live as the gospel teaches them. These shall inherit the kingdom of heaven, where they will live eternally in joy with the Father, Son and Holy Spirit, to whom be all glory, Amen. ON THE EIGHTH SUNDAY AFTER TRINITY.[12]

HEARING THE WORD IS NOT ENOUGH. HEINRICH BULLINGER: By these words the Lord teaches that it is not enough to hear the Word of God, unless you also endeavor to do what the Word commands at the same time. According to this passage, those who hear the Word of God and keep it are blessed. And Saint James says, "But be doers of the word, and not hearers only, deceiving yourselves. For if anyone is a hearer of the word and not a doer, he is like a man who looks intently at his natural face in a mirror." For there are certain people today, and in fact there have always been, who think that religion consists in hearing the Word of God often, and then in disputing about it at community meetings. But our Lord Jesus announces here that true piety does not consist in knowledge and talking but in action and conversation. AN ECCLESIASTICALL EXPOSITION UPON SAINT MATHEWE 7.[13]

THE HOUSE STANDS ON FAITH, CHRIST'S WORDS AND DOING HIS WILL. JACQUES LEFÈVRE D'ÉTAPLES: This last one who hears Christ's teaching and does it, that is, lives according to it, is not only like the good fruit which is produced by the land but also a building which is built on top of a most solid foundation. And what will be more solid to Christ than that they were established on holy faith, his holy teachings and those works? And what is a more beautiful building than the temple of God which stands on them? IN THE GOSPEL OF LUKE 6.[14]

BUILD ON THE TRUE FOUNDATION, CHRIST THE ROCK. HEINRICH BULLINGER: To build means to make, to erect or to set up some spiritual workmanship. Peter uses the same allegory, saying, "If indeed you have tasted that the Lord is good, come to him, a living stone rejected by people but in the sight of God chosen and precious; then you yourselves like living stones are being built up as a spiritual house." . . . The rock is Christ, and true and perfect godliness—I mean faith, working through love. And so truth itself is the foundation, by the firm and immoveable power of Christ. The house is the work which is done, and all the conversation of the whole life. AN ECCLESIASTICALL EXPOSITION UPON SAINT MATHEWE 7.[15]

OUR WORK OF BUILDING MUST BE FOUNDED ON FAITH. FRANÇOIS LAMBERT: The one who does not build the foundation of his house on top of this rock is the one who does not sincerely believe. If he does not work from the standpoint of faith, he will not stand firm. Therefore, whoever builds, that is, works without the necessary foundation of faith, is helpless, for he is certainly false and a liar, worldly-minded, and for that reason he will surely fall into ruin. For although the house he builds would seem to be beautiful and elegant, he is a hypocrite whose works do not proceed from faith, and so the house will be overtaken by the

---

[12]Taverner, *Epistles and Gospelles (Sommer Parte)*, 116r*.
[13]Marlorat, ed., *Catholike and Ecclesiasticall Exposition of the Holy Gospell After S. Mathewe*, 149*; citing Jas 1:22.
[14]Lefèvre d'Étaples, *Commentarii Initiatorii in Quatuor Evangelia*, 2:38r.
[15]Marlorat, ed., *Catholike and Ecclesiasticall Exposition of the Holy Gospell After S. Mathewe*, 149*; citing 1 Pet 2:3-5.

violent river of adversity. When that river rushes in, it will show the fragility of the structure. Of course it will destroy that house, for whenever persecution comes, those who were not sincere in heart when they first built the house will abandon it. And we experience every day how much this is true in the false prophets and false Christians. COMMENTARY IN LUKE 6:46-49.[16]

---

[16]Lambert, *In Divi Lucae*, O6v.

7:1-10 THE FAITH OF THE CENTURION

After he had finished all his sayings in the hearing of the people, he entered Capernaum. ²Now a centurion had a servant^a who was sick and at the point of death, who was highly valued by him. ³When the centurion^b heard about Jesus, he sent to him elders of the Jews, asking him to come and heal his servant. ⁴And when they came to Jesus, they pleaded with him earnestly, saying, "He is worthy to have you do this for him, ⁵for he loves our nation, and he is the one who built us our synagogue." ⁶And Jesus went with them. When he was not far from the house, the centurion sent friends, saying to him, "Lord, do not trouble yourself, for I am not worthy to have you come under my roof. ⁷Therefore I did not presume to come to you. But say the word, and let my servant be healed. ⁸For I too am a man set under authority, with soldiers under me: and I say to one, 'Go,' and he goes; and to another, 'Come,' and he comes; and to my servant, 'Do this,' and he does it." ⁹When Jesus heard these things, he marveled at him, and turning to the crowd that followed him, said, "I tell you, not even in Israel have I found such faith." ¹⁰And when those who had been sent returned to the house, they found the servant well.

a Greek *bondservant*; also verses 3, 8, 10   b Greek *he*

OVERVIEW: In his actions and in the message he sends to Jesus, our commentators commend the centurion as an important role model: he is a heathen and yet is supportive of God's Word and work; he is a caring master, seeking healing for a valued servant; he comes to Christ with his troubles and request, showing that we should always turn in prayer to Christ; and although he is a relatively powerful and wealthy man, he shows a commendable humility in his words. This individual provides an important model not only for the people of Jesus' day, the reformers remind us, but also for us. We constantly need to be reminded of the importance of humility, the need to turn to Christ in difficult times and the demand to treat our subordinates with loyalty and consideration. But most importantly the centurion is an example of faith. He has a deep confidence in Christ despite not having been raised with the Law and the Prophets. He does not have the advantages of those to whom Christ was preaching, and yet he teaches them a lesson. However, these commentators contend, he does not receive what he requests as a reward for meritorious faith, but rather his faith gives glory to God, and his request is granted out of pure grace.

THERE IS BUT ONE GOSPEL; THEREFORE MATTHEW AND LUKE AGREE. JOHN CALVIN: Those who think that Matthew and Luke repeat different narratives are mistaken in the matter. This is the only difference in their words: Matthew says that the centurion came to Christ, while Luke says that he sent some of the Jews to speak on his behalf. But there is nothing inappropriate in Matthew granting that the centurion did what was accomplished in his name at his request. Otherwise the two Evangelists are in agreement in all circumstances, so it would be ridiculous to contrive two miracles where there is only one. COMMENTARY ON A HARMONY OF THE GOSPELS.[1]

7:1-2 The Centurion's Valued Servant Lies Ill

THE CENTURION IS AN EXAMPLE OF GOD'S SUBVERSIVE WAYS. JOHN CALVIN: While he discerned that the morals of the people in Capernaum were very depraved and sinful (for we know that because it was a maritime city it was full of more corruption than other places), nevertheless it

---

[1]CTS 31:378* (CO 45:234); alluding to Mt 8:5.

did not hinder him from condemning the superstitions of his own country and acquiring a taste for true and sincere piety. He did not construct a synagogue for the Jews there without being the target of some jealousy and danger, and he only loved that nation because he had embraced the worship of the one God. And so before Christ healed his servant, he himself was healed by the Lord. And this is certainly a miracle: that a man of the military, who had crossed the sea with a company of soldiers that he might accustom the Jews to carrying the yoke of Roman tyranny, of his own accord should submit himself and in obedience dedicate himself to the God of Israel. COMMENTARY ON A HARMONY OF THE GOSPELS.[2]

THIS IS A GOOD LESSON FOR MASTERS. JOHANN BAUMGART (POMARIUS): The centurion took care of his servant in his sickness. First he sent for Christ, and after that he went to Christ himself, which is an indication that this servant was pious and faithful. This example teaches those in authority that they should not abandon their servants in sickness or need. It is unfortunately all too common that many masters treat their domestics like donkeys—as long as they can keep going, they keep them. Later, when they are no longer able to work, they are put out to pasture like an old horse, or if they are stricken with a serious disease, they are cast out of the house or put into a hospital (which would be a bit better), but with all support entirely taken away. Those masters should remember that they also have a master over them, who can quickly make servants into masters and masters into servants. GOSPEL ON THE THIRD SUNDAY AFTER EPIPHANY.[3]

7:3-5 The Jewish Elders Request Jesus' Help for the Centurion

THE CENTURION WAS A WORTHY AND FAITHFUL MAN. HEINRICH BULLINGER: Now, let us learn from this man's example to come to Christ in all our troubles, and to open all the sorrows of our mind to him and to crave his sure and undoubted help. Luke adds that the messengers told Jesus, "He is worthy that you do this for him," or "he deserves this at your hands, for he loves our nation and has built us a synagogue." There is no doubt but that the Jews gave him a singular report and commendation of godliness with these words. In building a synagogue, he plainly declared himself to be someone who favored the law. And so it is not without cause that they pronounce him to be worthy, this one whom Christ himself offers to benefit and help, just as he would offer himself to a pious worshiper of the Lord. AN ECCLESIASTICALL EXPOSITION UPON SAINT MATHEWE 8.[4]

JESUS SHOWS BY HIS MERCY THAT HE RECOGNIZES THE MAN'S FAITH. MARTIN BUCER: Truly this centurion knew that the Jews were the people who had the Word of God and to whom God had committed his counsels; therefore the man loved them and sought to win them by giving them many benefits. For he was constrained with that same Spirit that also forced Cornelius to give himself to fasting and to prayer. The Holy Spirit also cannot choose but to offer himself to the elect, however ignorant and infirm and weak they may be. Nevertheless, we can see the great blindness of the Jewish leaders, because by their consent and assistance they would transport the grace of God (which they themselves disdainfully refused) to a Gentile. For if Christ were the minister and dispenser of the gifts of God to them, why did they not receive that proffered grace themselves, before they gave it away to strangers? Therefore in this action they condemn themselves. AN ECCLESIASTICALL EXPOSITION UPON SAINT MATHEWE 8.[5]

---

[2]CTS 31:378-79* (CO 45:234-35). For similar stereotypes about maritime cities, see RCS NT 6:251-52 and the prolegomenal material to 1 Corinthians in RCS NT 9.
[3]Baumgart, *Postilla*, 50r; alluding to Col 4:1.
[4]Marlorat, ed., *Catholike and Ecclesiasticall Exposition of the Holy Gospell After S. Mathewe*, 155*.
[5]Marlorat, ed., *Catholike and Ecclesiasticall Exposition of the Holy Gospell After S. Mathewe*, 155*; citing Acts 10.

7:6-10 *The Centurion Declares a True Faith*

"AND JESUS WENT WITH THEM." MARTIN BUCER: In this phrase we can see the incomparable goodness and submission of Christ. For although the centurion was a heathen man, and his messengers were also puffed up with a vain show of holiness, eventually Jesus of his own free will offered to go and see the servant of this foreigner. What deed can be more gentle and loving than this? And who is the one who will not look for help at his hands? AN ECCLESIASTICALL EXPOSITION UPON SAINT MATHEWE 8.[6]

THE CENTURION'S FAITH IMPRESSES JESUS. DESIDERIUS ERASMUS: Jesus was delighted with these words, which were full of affection for the man's servant, a modest opinion of himself and admirable faith and trust in the Lord. He came to a stop and displayed the appearance of wonder, not that what he heard was new to him, because he already knew the heart of the centurion before he even said these words. He did this, however, that his admiration would commend such a trust in God to the Jews. He also wanted to reproach them for their unbelief with this example of a person who was both a heathen and a soldier. PARAPHRASE ON THE GOSPEL OF LUKE 7:8-9.[7]

THE CENTURION'S POWER LED HIM TO RESPECT CHRIST'S POWER. PHILIPP MELANCHTHON: The centurion here confirms his confession of faith in the power of Christ by his example, bringing in an argument of the greater to the lesser. For he esteemed the divine power which is in Christ as greater than the rule and domination which he had over his soldiers and servants. All those who are magistrates and masters over households can find an example here of how they may learn by their power to acknowledge the power of God and to think about his divine word and commands. If our words can so prevail among people that they do and fulfill whatever we say and command, even though we are just poor and miserable beings and do not differ from others, how much more does the word of God have power to rule everyone universally? So let them understand their own obedience according to this example: Behold, you are a person, set under the power of another, and you say to this one, "Go," and he goes, to another, "Come," and he comes, and to a third, "Do this," and he does it; you require of them the obedience which they owe. Therefore, if such great obedience is shown to you, who are just a person subject to others, and also what you require is to be done as a duty, tell me how you will behave yourself if you are disobedient to your master (the one who gave you that power and in whose name that obedience is given to you), if he says to you, "Go," and you do not go, "Come" and you do not come, and "Do this," and you do not do it? AN ECCLESIASTICALL EXPOSITION UPON SAINT MATHEWE 8.[8]

THE SOLDIER, A GENTILE, HAS A REMARKABLE FAITH. JOHANN SPANGENBERG: How does Christ answer? This faith pleases Christ so well that he must praise and honor him before the whole world. He says to the people with great amazement: "Truly I say to you, I have never found such faith in Israel." It is as if he would say: "There is a soldier, born a Gentile, a guest and a stranger in Israel, and he has more faith than all of you! You no longer believe Moses or the prophets, and this Gentile soldier comes naked and bare, without either the Law or the prophets, and yet he believes so masterfully that it is a joy." GOSPEL ON THE THIRD SUNDAY AFTER EPIPHANY.[9]

---

[6]Marlorat, ed., *Catholike and Ecclesiasticall Exposition of the Holy Gospell After S. Mathewe*, 155*.
[7]Erasmus, *In Evangelivm Lvce Paraphrasis*, m3r-v (LB 7:351-52).
[8]Marlorat, ed., *Catholike and Ecclesiasticall Exposition of the Holy Gospell After S. Mathewe*, 156-57*.
[9]Spangenberg, *Postilla* (1582), LVv.

7:11-17 THE RAISING OF THE WIDOW'S SON

[11]*Soon afterward*[a] *he went to a town called Nain, and his disciples and a great crowd went with him.* [12]*As he drew near to the gate of the town, behold, a man who had died was being carried out, the only son of his mother, and she was a widow, and a considerable crowd from the town was with her.* [13]*And when the Lord saw her, he had compassion on her and said to her, "Do not weep."* [14]*Then he came up and* touched the bier, and the bearers stood still. And he said, "Young man, I say to you, arise."* [15]*And the dead man sat up and began to speak, and Jesus*[b] *gave him to his mother.* [16]*Fear seized them all, and they glorified God, saying, "A great prophet has arisen among us!" and "God has visited his people!"* [17]*And this report about him spread through the whole of Judea and all the surrounding country.*

a Some manuscripts *The next day*   b Greek *he*

OVERVIEW: These commentators note the widow's sorrow and plight in a general way (they do not describe the situation in which a widow who lost her husband *and* her son would find herself in this ancient culture); they focus on Jesus' compassion for her. What do we learn from the story? First, even rich, young people die every day—the world mourns them more than the elderly. Raising people from the dead is the sort of miracle that fully reveals Jesus' divinity along with his compassion and generosity—only God can bring the dead to life. This young man was raised as a benefit to his mother and as an example for all of us, but not so much as a benefit to the young man himself, for it meant that he would have to go back to work and eventually die a second time. Jesus told the widow, "Do not weep," because he was giving her son back to her alive. He did not mean that we should not mourn those who die, although we should continue to live in the hope of the resurrection. This young man, for the reformers, was raised to life especially to reveal the glory of God in Jesus.

7:11-12 *Jesus Encounters the Funeral Procession*

CHRIST CAME TO THE CITY GATE OF NAIN.
JOHANN BAUMGART (POMARIUS): The Evangelist writes here how the Lord Christ went to a town by the name of Nain shortly after he healed the servant of the centurion in Capernaum. . . . Nain is in Galilee, not far from Mount Tabor, and situated on the Kishon River. Jesus was attended by a large company, a crowd of his disciples and other listeners. When he came there to the city gate, a wonderful opportunity for an excellent and glorious miracle presented itself, which demonstrated his omnipotence, his good nature and his generosity, and that history is recorded with diligence in this Gospel. GOSPEL ON THE SIXTEENTH SUNDAY AFTER TRINITY.[1]

THE YOUNG AND WEALTHY CAN AND DO DIE.
JOHN BOYS: The word *behold* in the Scriptures is like a hand in the margin of a book, which always points out some remarkable thing.[2] Here it is like that hand that Belshazzar saw writing on the walls of his palace, for as that forewarned him of his utter ruin, so this admonishes us of our last end: "Behold a dead man carried out." This dead man was a young man, as it is expressed in the text, "Young man, I say to you, arise," and a rich and honorable man, which some gather out of this text, in that many people were with his mother.

---

[1]Baumgart, *Postilla*, 125r.
[2]That is, ☞. Thumbing through early modern books one often finds this symbol, called an *index* or *manicule*.

This teaches us that often those die who least expect death and who are most embraced by the world. Poor people or old people have their passport, as they begin to leave the world, so the world is content to part with them. At their carrying out to be buried usually there is less weeping, because their friends are comforted in that, departing in peace, they are now delivered from the burdens of the flesh and the infinite miseries of this life. But death is "the way of all flesh," and "all flesh is grass, and all its beauty is like the flower of the field." The Sixteenth Sunday After Trinity.[3]

Christ Is the Lord of the Wretched.
Martin Luther: This is not a sermon for the satisfied crowd, but it is delightful for the small and insignificant. The widow, whose only, beloved son has died, is set forth as an example for them. By this woman, the Gospel teaches us what we poor folks need to know: our Lord is a Lord of wretched, forsaken, dead and corrupt people. That is the content and text of the gospel. Paul also said, "Because the world in its wisdom does not recognize God, he turns everything around and becomes a God of foolishness and fools." Those who are well satisfied do not wish to have him for a God, but instead they trample him underfoot and do not notice him, as Moses said. Therefore it has pleased God to turn everything around and to be a God of those who are not full and satisfied but are rather poor and thin, those who suffer hunger, thirst and distress, who are imprisoned and who die.

This gospel belongs to those who discover how affectionately he takes care of the widow, even before he is asked to do anything. She has no hope at all that her tears could still be turned into the highest joy; she desires no blessing at all from him, but in a moment it is placed before her very eyes. The world does not want to learn it, but look here how it happens. Each person should accept this example as doctrine and think hard about it, so

that he learns it well. I have already said that Christ is the Lord of the wretched. A Sermon from September 24, 1531.[4]

7:13-15 Jesus Takes Compassion on the Widow and Raises Her Son

This Miracle Reveals Christ's Divinity.
Johannes Brenz: We see here in Christ the image of those affections which God the Father bears toward human beings. For no one, says Saint John, has seen God at any time, unless the only-begotten Son who is in the bosom of the Father has shown him. And the apostle Paul says, Christ is the image of the invisible God.

And so it is made clear in Christ that the Father is so full of pity and compassion that he will help the lowly, the afflicted and the oppressed even before they pray. For so he speaks through the mouth of the prophet, saying, "And it shall come to pass that before they cry I will hear them." Christ might have preserved the young man in health before he had died, but imagine that he makes the same answer to you which he made to those who questioned him concerning the man who was born blind. For this young man died so that the works of God might be seen in him, and the more impossible the raising up of a dead man seems to be to flesh and blood, the more the glory of Christ shines by the raising up of the dead. For this miracle is a heavenly seal which testifies that Christ is endowed with divine majesty and power and that he is by nature the true God, as we shall see further on. An Ecclesiasticall Exposition upon Saint Luke 7.[5]

It Is Acceptable to Mourn the Dead.
Philipp Melanchthon: Christ does not forbid all weeping with these words, "Weep not." He is comforting the mourning widow, which in itself is a godly duty, and forbids her to weep, not because

[3]Boys, *Exposition of the Dominical Epistles and Gospels*, 4:87-88*; citing Dan 5; Lk 8:41-42; Jn 11; Josh 23:14; Is 40:6.

[4]LEA 3:93-94 (cf. WA 34,2:206-7); citing 1 Cor 1:21; Lev 26:27-28.
[5]Marlorat, ed., *Catholike and Ecclesiasticall Exposition of the Holy Gospell After S. Marke and Luke*, 162-63*; citing Jn 1:18; Col 1:15; Is 65:24; Jn 9:3.

her son is dead but because he will live. It is, in fact, lawful for us to weep for our departed friends by the example of Christ, who wept when his friend Lazarus died, and is here moved with compassion. For whoever is not moved with compassion at the suffering of others, especially that of his own friends, is not worthy of the name of human being. And yet, we still should be different from others who mourn, in that we should moderate our sorrow, as Paul commands: "Do not grieve as some do, who have no hope."

He does not forbid mourning in the death of those who are dear to us. For although we hope that they are in a good situation after this life, still that sharpness which is the separation of life from the body has to move us. But because we have hope, our sorrow should not be excessive, as it might be in others. That is true fortitude: not that people remain unmoved at sorrowful sights but that they restrain themselves, so that they are not so moved by grief that, because of the corruption of human nature, they might commit some wickedness. AN ECCLESIASTICALL EXPOSITION UPON SAINT LUKE 7.[6]

RESTORING LIFE IS WITHIN CHRIST'S POWER, CONVEYED BY HIS WORD. EDWARD LEIGH: Christ really showed the efficacy of comfort, restoring the raised son to his mother. He uses two instruments, as it were, in the raising up of this dead person, for he touched the bier and spoke to the dead person. He did this, first, to show that the destruction of death, and restitution of life, is the power and work of his person, not in the divine nature only but also in what he, in assuming from us, enriched with the fulness of the divinity; and second to teach that the means or instrument by which those benefits of Christ are communicated

to us is his Word, by which he will destroy death and restore life in us. This is the first raising of the dead made by Christ in the New Testament. ANNOTATIONS UPON SAINT LUKE 7.[7]

7:16-17 The People Were Amazed and Spread the News

JESUS IS NOT JUST A PROPHET BUT THE TRUE SON OF GOD, OUR SAVIOR. JOHANN SPANGENBERG: What did the people do when they witnessed this miracle? They were overcome with fear, praised God and said: "A great prophet has arisen among us, and God has visited his people." And this talk of him spread forth throughout the whole land of Judah and to all the surrounding areas. You see, those are the fruits of the wonders and work of God, for where God's Word, wonders and works are joined with a true believing heart, there Christ will be rightly known. And where he is recognized, there pure thanks, praise and glory will follow. Then all people must say: "Well, God did not visit us in wrath but in grace. He has given us a great prophet—but no, not a prophet, but rather his own dear Son for our Savior, who will save us from the devil, death and hell. Why should we not rightly thank such a Savior, and for his sake suffer everything gladly? Where is another who has shown himself to be so friendly and charitable to us, yes, who has done us so much good, as this Savior Christ? Let the Jews hope in their Messiah and the Turks in their Muhammed: they will fail. But we hope in God's Son, our Lord Jesus Christ, who is the Way, the Truth and the Life. He will never fail us." GOSPEL ON THE SIXTEENTH SUNDAY AFTER TRINITY.[8]

---

[6]Marlorat, ed., *Catholike and Ecclesiasticall Exposition of the Holy Gospell After S. Marke and Luke*, 163*; citing Jn 11:35; 1 Thess 4:13.

[7]Leigh, *Annotations upon All the New Testament Philologicall and Theologicall*, 108*.
[8]Spangenberg, *Postilla . . . von Ostern biß auffs Aduent*, CXLIIr-v; alluding to Jn 14:6.

7:18-35 JESUS AND JOHN THE BAPTIST

¹⁸*The disciples of John reported all these things to him. And John,* ¹⁹*calling two of his disciples to him, sent them to the Lord, saying, "Are you the one who is to come, or shall we look for another?"* ²⁰*And when the men had come to him, they said, "John the Baptist has sent us to you, saying, 'Are you the one who is to come, or shall we look for another?'"* ²¹*In that hour he healed many people of diseases and plagues and evil spirits, and on many who were blind he bestowed sight.* ²²*And he answered them, "Go and tell John what you have seen and heard: the blind receive their sight, the lame walk, lepers*ᵃ *are cleansed, and the deaf hear, the dead are raised up, the poor have good news preached to them.* ²³*And blessed is the one who is not offended by me."*

²⁴*When John's messengers had gone, Jesus*ᵇ *began to speak to the crowds concerning John: "What did you go out into the wilderness to see? A reed shaken by the wind?* ²⁵*What then did you go out to see? A man dressed in soft clothing? Behold, those who are dressed in splendid clothing and live in luxury are in kings' courts.* ²⁶*What then did you go out to see? A prophet? Yes, I tell you, and more than a prophet.* ²⁷*This is he of whom it is written,*

"'Behold, I send my messenger before your face,
who will prepare your way before you.'

²⁸*I tell you, among those born of women none is greater than John. Yet the one who is least in the kingdom of God is greater than he."* ²⁹(*When all the people heard this, and the tax collectors too, they declared God just,*ᶜ *having been baptized with the baptism of John,* ³⁰*but the Pharisees and the lawyers rejected the purpose of God for themselves, not having been baptized by him.*)

³¹*"To what then shall I compare the people of this generation, and what are they like?* ³²*They are like children sitting in the marketplace and calling to one another,*

"'We played the flute for you, and you did not
dance;
we sang a dirge, and you did not weep.'

³³*For John the Baptist has come eating no bread and drinking no wine, and you say, 'He has a demon.'* ³⁴*The Son of Man has come eating and drinking, and you say, 'Look at him! A glutton and a drunkard, a friend of tax collectors and sinners!'* ³⁵*Yet wisdom is justified by all her children."*

a *Leprosy* was a term for several skin diseases; see Leviticus 13   b Greek *he*   c Greek *they justified God*

OVERVIEW: The reformers too were perplexed as to why John sent his disciples to Jesus to ask if he were "the one who is to come," that is, the Messiah. Rather than understand this as some redactional contradiction or John's growing doubt, our commentators suggest interpretations that take both the text and faith in Christ seriously. Why did John send his disciples to Jesus? It was not to determine if Jesus were "the one," because John already knew that he was. Nor was it to give his disciples—already somewhat jealous of Jesus and the attention he was receiving—the opportunity to criticize him. Instead he sent his disciples to Jesus for their benefit. They could be schooled by the master—a fine example for all pastors and parents. From Jesus they could learn humility to oppose their envy, hear words of wisdom to erase their ignorance and see works of wonder that would counter their inability to believe. The miracles, whatever private benefits they may have conferred, were designed to reveal Jesus as the true Messiah and the Son of God. These disciples of John should have been led by Jesus' words and works to realize who he was and then to follow him instead of John. However, some interpreters posit, they were offended by Jesus instead—

offended that he did not help to free John from prison (which Lightfoot speculates is the real reason that John sent his followers to Jesus) and that he did not live the same sort of ascetic lifestyle that John did. John sent his disciples to Jesus for improvement, but instead they turned out to be like the Pharisees, ready to be displeased with everything Jesus said or did. However, after they left, Jesus clarified for his listeners that John is the greatest of the prophets—the forerunner to the Messiah but not the Messiah himself. John's disciples were disappointed that Jesus was not more like John, but they failed to understand that all John's work, even his baptism, pointed to and in a sense belonged to Jesus as the Christ.

7:18-23 John Seeks Information about Jesus, and Jesus Responds

JOHN SENT HIS DISCIPLES TO CHRIST FOR CORRECTION. JOHN BOYS: The disciples of John had three faults, which we see in this Gospel. Envy: for they said to John, "Rabbi, he who was with you across the Jordan, to whom you bore witness— look, he is baptizing, and all are going to him." Ignorance: for they supposed that John was the Christ. And incredulity: for they joined with the Pharisees against Christ, saying, "Why do we and the Pharisees fast, but your disciples do not fast?"

Now in Christ's school there were three virtues to oppose to these defects. Against envy, there were examples of humility; against ignorance, there were words of wisdom; and against incredulity, there were works of wonder. Therefore, John sent his disciples to Christ, that in seeing his humility, their envy might be lessened; that in hearing his wisdom, their ignorance might be rectified; and that in wondering at his works, their incredulity might be confounded. Because faith is the mother of all virtues and infidelity the nurse of all wickedness, when John heard of the great works of Christ, he sent his disciples, so that in going, they might see; in seeing, they might wonder; in wondering, they might believe; and in believing, they might be saved.

This is a good example for all preachers to follow, that they take the occasion and best opportunity to benefit their listeners. Every pastor is a steward in God's house, and a steward must not only provide enough food but also prepare it in due season; otherwise, as Bernard says, it is not dispensation but dissipation.[1] This ought to be their first and last care, for even when he was in prison at death's door, John was most careful to commend his students to the best Tutor. This pattern also fits all parents, as well as preachers. In a word, all superiors should be watchful for the good of such as are under them. THE THIRD SUNDAY IN ADVENT.[2]

JOHN HOPED THAT JESUS MIGHT MIRACU- LOUSLY LIBERATE HIM. JOHN LIGHTFOOT: It is not that John was ignorant of who Jesus was, having had so many demonstrations of him as he had had, and having giving such ample testimony of him as he had done. And John's disciples also were not so willfully ignorant of him as not to be persuaded by their master that it was he. John's message to him appears to be to this purpose: John and his disciples had heard of the great and many miracles that Christ had done, healing the sick, raising the dead, and it may be that they thought it strange that Christ, among all his miraculous workings, would not work John's liberty from imprisonment, especially because he was a prisoner on Christ's behalf and for the gospel he had preached prior to him. And so perhaps at the bottom of their question, "Are you he who is to come, or shall we look for another?" we find that they expected somewhat more from the Messiah than they had yet obtained. They received a full answer to their question by the miracles that they witnessed, which abundantly proved that he was "he who was to come." But as to their expectation of his miraculous release of John from prison, his

---

[1]Bernard, *De Consideratione* 3. Bernard of Clairvaux, *Five Books on Consideration: Advice to a Pope*, trans. John Anderson and Elizabeth T. Kennan, Cistercian Fathers Series 37 (Kalamazoo, MI: Cistercian Publications, 1976).
[2]Boys, *Exposition of the Dominical Epistles and Gospels*, 1:50*; alluding to Jn 3:26, 28; Mt 9:14.

answer was that his work was to preach the gospel and that it was a blessed thing not to take any offense at him but to yield and submit to his wise dispensations. And accordingly when the messengers of John had departed, he gave a glorious testimony concerning John to the people but yet showed how far one truly and fully acquainted with and established in the kingdom of God went beyond him in judging of it who looked for temporal redemption by it. HARMONY OF THE NEW TESTAMENT, SECTION 31.[3]

CHRIST'S MIRACLES WERE INTENDED TO CONVINCE JOHN'S FOLLOWERS.

THE ENGLISH ANNOTATIONS: At the very time that these messengers of John came to Christ, the providence of God so disposed that they should see many cured of such various and desperate maladies that their incredulity might be convinced, not by John's words only but also by the divine works of Christ. It is also observable that by the same providence, John the Baptist, who was greater than any prophet, should be less than most of the prophets in that he did no miracle. Christ, however, and the apostles afterwards, did many, so that John's disciples might be more easily transmitted to Christ. Otherwise they might possibly have been too tenacious of that suspicion that John might be the Messiah which then amazed most people. ANNOTATIONS UPON THE GOSPEL ACCORDING TO SAINT LUKE 7:21.[4]

THE PURPOSE OF MIRACLES IS TO REVEAL JESUS AS THE CHRIST.

JOHANNES BRENZ: But we must diligently note Christ's entire answer, because he shows by it the reason for all the miracles he did. For although the miracles of Christ contained certain private benefits in them, they were done especially for this reason: to declare that this Jesus, Son of Mary, was the true Messiah and Son of God. AN ECCLESIASTICALL EXPOSITION UPON SAINT MATHEWE 11.[5]

JOHN KNOWS THAT CHRIST IS THE PROMISED SAVIOR.

JOHANN SPANGENBERG: What does it mean, that "the good news is preached to the poor"? Christ means to say: "Up until now, Moses terrified you with the law and threatened many troubles and vexations, where you cannot do this and that, but gave you no help in keeping it. Now, however," he says to John, "the poor, the shattered consciences who cannot find any help or comfort on their own have now been announced a joyous message. Namely, that through me they will receive a gracious and merciful God and Father and forgiveness of sins and will obtain eternal life out of pure grace. When John hears this, he will also certainly tell you whether or not I am the one, because he knows very well that he has prophesied such things of me." GOSPEL ON THE THIRD SUNDAY OF ADVENT.[6]

THEY WERE OFFENDED, THOUGH HE GAVE NO OFFENSE.

HUGH LATIMER: Now, after our Savior had told John's disciples about the works and miracles which he did, he added a nice little phrase and a sharp private rebuke, saying, "And blessed is he who is not offended by me." He scored a hit here and rankled them. He did not mean John, for John was not offended, but he meant them, for they were offended by his lowly and informal style of speaking. But you might say, "How can a person be hurt by someone who never hurts anyone?" I tell you, John's disciples were hurt by Christ, and yet the fault did not belong to Christ but rather to them. Christ lived a normal life—he was a good, everyday sort of man. He ate and drank like others did, eating in people's homes when he was invited—in fact, some even called him a sycophant.[7] So the disciples of John, seeing his relaxed lifestyle, were offended by him. But let me ask you, should Christ have given up his manner of living and followed John's lifestyle, just because some were offended with him? No, not at all! It was *scandalum*

---

[3]Lightfoot, *Harmony, Chronicle and Order of the New Testament*, 27*; alluding to Jn 1:34-36, 3:29-30.
[4]Downame, ed., *Annotations*, Tt2v*; alluding to Jn 10:41; Lk 3:15.
[5]Marlorat, ed., *Catholike and Ecclesiasticall Exposition of the Holy*

Gospell After S. Mathewe, 231*; alluding to Jn 5:36; 10:25, 37-38; 20:30.
[6]Spangenberg, *Postilla* (1582), XVIIIv.
[7]The word Latimer uses here is "glosser."

acceptum et non datum, that is, "They took offense at him, but he gave them none." He lived according to his calling, to which he was appointed by his Father. SERMON ON THE THIRD SUNDAY IN ADVENT (1552).[8]

THE DIFFICULTY OF JESUS' HUMBLE FORM.

JOHANN SPANGENBERG: What does it mean when he says, "Blessed is the one who is not offended by me"? Christ means to say: "Although I have certainly come in a humble form and figure, I am still the one of whom my Father said, 'This is my beloved Son.' Likewise, although my teaching is certainly simple and despised by the wise ones of the world, it is nevertheless such a teaching that all of those who believe in it will be saved." GOSPEL ON THE THIRD SUNDAY OF ADVENT.[9]

7:24-28 Jesus Affirms John's Status as the Forerunner

JESUS PROTECTS JOHN FROM SUSPICION THAT HE IS WAVERING IN HIS SUPPORT. DESID-

ERIUS ERASMUS: So Jesus removes from him the suspicion of inconstancy and claims faithfulness and weight for John's testimony concerning himself, thus extolling his special virtues. Nevertheless he did not give to him the title of Messiah, which for some time certain people had tried to ascribe to him. And this was the manner in which Jesus spoke: "If you suspect," he said, "that John, who has long testified about me, is now wavering in his heart, why then did you once run about, leaving the towns for the desert places, for the sight of this man? That you might see a reed which blows in the wind, not standing firm in himself? But come on, what did you go out there to see finally? A man dressed in soft garments, who might be corrupted by allurements or ambition? But this suspicion cannot fall on a man who dressed himself in camels' hair, who girded his loins with a belt of animal

hide and who lived on locusts and water; and while this diet sustained his life, he also fasted frequently. The one who is pleased by splendid attire and delighted by delicate foods eagerly seeks to be in the king's court. Of such people who have an affection for those sorts of things, suspicion of a corrupt intention, inconstancy or even flattery perhaps is suitable. But John preferred the desert to the courts of princes; he preferred the camel's hide to costly fabrics or clothing covered with gold or jewels. He preferred wild honey and locusts to the cakes and pastries of a king, and plain water to the sweet wine of the rich man. His prison cries out quite sufficiently that John is unable to flatter. Therefore there is no reason for anyone to suspect that he gave me such a high and wonderful testimony before on account of anyone's influence or favor, and now he has changed his opinion." PARAPHRASE ON THE GOSPEL OF LUKE 7:24-25.[10]

JOHN EXCELLED AS THE FORERUNNER OF

CHRIST. HEINRICH BULLINGER: John the Baptist was a messenger of very great things, which is witnessed by his father Zechariah in these words, "And you, child, will be called the prophet of the Most High; for you will go before the Lord to prepare his ways, to give knowledge of salvation to his people in the forgiveness of their sins, because of the tender mercy of our God." Not long after this preaching of John's, Christ came into his temple, that is, to his people who are the true temple of the living God, and so they are a holy temple. This therefore is the sum of this passage: John excelled in that he was the crier and forerunner of Christ. But although the prophets in former times spoke of the kingdom of Christ, nevertheless they were not, like John, placed directly before his face, that they might immediately show him and say, "Behold the Lamb of God, who takes away the sin of the world." AN ECCLESIASTICALL EXPOSITION UPON SAINT MATHEWE 11.[11]

---

[8]Latimer, *Sermons and Remains*, 76-77*; alluding to Mk 6:3; Mt 13:57.
[9]Spangenberg, *Postilla* (1582), XVIIIv; citing Mt 3:17; 17:5; Rom 1:16.

[10]Erasmus, *In Evangelivm Lvce Paraphrasis*, miɪ-v (LB 7:355).
[11]Marlorat, ed., *Catholike and Ecclesiasticall Exposition of the Holy Gospell After S. Mathewe*, 233*; quoting Lk 1:76-78; Jn 1:29.

JOHN IS THE GREATEST IN THE KINGDOM.
JOHANN AGRICOLA: In explaining the dignity and
office of John through his testimony, he directs
everything to himself and at the same time declares
how it could happen that they attend to him so
little despite hearing John's testimony. He explains
that John is "the least," remarkable for no merit
above other people, putting on no lofty behavior
before others or placing himself above others. John
did not claim to be the heir or cry out for himself,
but instead he served the needs of others, putting
their convenience over his inconvenience. He
presented this brief judgment properly by a certain
antithesis, that John is the greatest in his kingdom,
and he sketched the image of his teaching or gospel
for the future, so that no one would be confused
that his kingdom exists now in this dreadful
present age in which believers suffer, but that they
would know by the spirit to look forward to the
glory of the future life. ANNOTATIONS IN THE
GOSPEL OF LUKE 7.[12]

7:29-30 John's Baptism Brings the People to Faith

**THE BAPTISM "OF JOHN" IS STILL GOD'S
BAPTISM.** HULDRYCH ZWINGLI: Whether the
sacraments are administered by Moses, by John, by
the apostles or by some other person, nevertheless
they are not of a human being but of God himself
or Christ. Thus circumcision is not of Moses but
of God. This baptism is said to be of John, but it is
really of God. Saint Paul says "my gospel," when
nevertheless it is not really of Paul but of Christ. It
was his only in the sense that it was administered
and preached among the people through him.
(Thus the Gospel of Matthew is the one which
Matthew wrote.) Therefore what Christ says to the
Father in John 17 pertains here: "I do not ask for
these only, but also for those who will believe in me
through their word," when nevertheless a little
before he had said, "I have given them your word,"
and "Your word is truth." The word, therefore, is

both of God and of the disciples: it is God's as the
author, and it is theirs as the ministers of it. IN THE
GOSPEL OF LUKE 7.[13]

**JOHN PREPARED THE PEOPLE THROUGH
BAPTISM AND PREACHING.** KONRAD PELLIKAN:
The Pharisees, scribes and experts in the law were
ashamed to acknowledge their unfairness—they
preferred to make God into a liar rather than to
embrace the truth. They scorned those who were
baptized by John and rejected God's good counsel
in their ruin of themselves, for God had arranged
baptism as the easiest way to destroy mortal sins.
For what is easier than to confess and to bathe?
Not that innocence was granted through John, but
his baptism and preaching could have prepared
many, who would then have been led to salvation
through the preaching of the one for whom John
was the forerunner, because their souls would have
been prepared for him. None of this occurred by
chance, but divine providence managed all things
for the well-being and salvation of the human race.
The uneducated, the lowly and the sinners embraced the kindness of God, although they were
thought to be the furthest from true piety and far
removed from the knowledge of the law. By
contrast, those who quite properly knew and
understood well the oracles of the prophets, that is,
those seen as the leaders of religion, rejected the
offering of the benevolence of God, both in the
preaching of John and in his prodding to repentance. COMMENTARY IN LUKE 7:29-30.[14]

7:31-35 Neither John Nor Jesus Can Convince the Skeptics

**THESE PEOPLE ARE ENTIRELY CONTRARY AND
PUSH AWAY SALVATION.** HEINRICH BULLINGER:
He says that they are like willful children who are
pleased with no pleasant or musical noise, or even
more, they are like rebellious and obstinate people

---

[12]Agricola, *In Evangelium Lucae Annotationes*, 87r-v.

[13]D. *Hvldrichi Zvinglii in Plerosqve Novi Testamenti Libros*, 223;
alluding to Jn 7:22; Mt 21:25; 2 Tim 2:8 (cf. 1 Cor 1:10-17);
quoting Jn 17:20, 14, 17.
[14]Pellikan, *In Sacrosancta Quatuor Evangelia*, 94 (cf. LB 7:356).

to whom the diligence and devotion of their fellows is never acceptable, but only the contrary is allowed and pleasing to them. If someone is happy and makes merry or pleasant music, these people cry and say, "We want mourning!" If someone makes a sorrowful noise, right away they wish for pleasant tunes, because they are extremely inconstant and mutable. . . .

By an excellent antithesis, he shows all of them that the faith and diligence of God has omitted none of those things which pertain to the working of their salvation. Again, he proves that because they are in contention with God, they omit nothing which pertains to the hindrance of their salvation, for they constantly push away the care and benevolence of God. Therefore, it comes to pass that they perish, but it is through their own fault and malice. AN ECCLESIASTICALL EXPOSITION UPON SAINT MATHEWE 11.[15]

LIKE THE PHARISEES, THOSE WHO FLATTER EXCESSIVELY ALSO SLANDER. EDWIN SANDYS: Whatever the nature of the fountain, so is the river that runs from it. A double heart makes a double tongue. Those who think deceitfully "speak deceitfully and flatter with their lips." The disciples of the Pharisees and the Herodians, as they had double hearts, so they had double tongues. Before Christ's face they could say: "Master, we know that you are true and teach truly the way of God, not caring for any human beings nor respecting their persons," but behind his back they termed him a "seducer, a companion of publicans and sinners, a wine-bibber," and most spitefully railed against the righteous Lord of glory. All flatterers are double-tongued. Whomever they praise excessively when he is present, they will speak of him most slanderously and vilely when he is out of sight. In this way they are completely unlike our Savior Christ, who would not praise John to John's disciples but after their departure commended him to the people. It is Saint Augustine's judgment that "the tongue of a flatterer is more grievous than the hand of a murderer."[16] THE SEVENTH SERMON. A SERMON PREACHED BEFORE THE QUEEN (1585).[17]

GOD'S WISDOM IS JUSTIFIED BY THOSE WHO BELIEVE HIS TRUTH. FRANÇOIS LAMBERT: Surely this wisdom is the truth of God's Word, which was announced and justified through Christ and John, that is, it was held in the place of ceremonies by his children, those same ones who believed the truth. But it was not believed at all by others—those who instead contradicted it in every possible way. There is no doubt that they are the children not of the truth and wisdom of God but rather of folly, lies and ruin. And it is never possible for those ones to justify the wisdom of God through holding all of their ceremonies and rituals. COMMENTARY IN LUKE 7:31-35.[18]

---

[15]Marlorat, ed., *Catholike and Ecclesiasticall Exposition of the Holy Gospell After S. Mathewe*, 236*.

[16]*Plus persequitur lingua adulatoris, quam manus interfectoris. Enarratio in Psalmos* 69.5 (PL 30:4.714; NPNF 8:313).
[17]Sandys, *Sermons*, 132*; citing Ps 12:2; Mt 22:16; Lk 7:34.
[18]Lambert, *In Divi Lucae*, P5v.

7:36-50 JESUS IS ANOINTED BY A SINFUL WOMAN

[36]One of the Pharisees asked him to eat with him, and he went into the Pharisee's house and reclined at the table. [37]And behold, a woman of the city, who was a sinner, when she learned that he was reclining at table in the Pharisee's house, brought an alabaster flask of ointment, [38]and standing behind him at his feet, weeping, she began to wet his feet with her tears and wiped them with the hair of her head and kissed his feet and anointed them with the ointment. [39]Now when the Pharisee who had invited him saw this, he said to himself, "If this man were a prophet, he would have known who and what sort of woman this is who is touching him, for she is a sinner." [40]And Jesus answering said to him, "Simon, I have something to say to you." And he answered, "Say it, Teacher."

[41]"A certain moneylender had two debtors. One owed five hundred denarii, and the other fifty. [42]When they could not pay, he cancelled the debt of both. Now which of them will love him more?" [43]Simon answered, "The one, I suppose, for whom he cancelled the larger debt." And he said to him, "You have judged rightly." [44]Then turning toward the woman he said to Simon, "Do you see this woman? I entered your house; you gave me no water for my feet, but she has wet my feet with her tears and wiped them with her hair. [45]You gave me no kiss, but from the time I came in she has not ceased to kiss my feet. [46]You did not anoint my head with oil, but she has anointed my feet with ointment. [47]Therefore I tell you, her sins, which are many, are forgiven—for she loved much. But he who is forgiven little, loves little." [48]And he said to her, "Your sins are forgiven." [49]Then those who were at table with him began to say among[a] themselves, "Who is this, who even forgives sins?" [50]And he said to the woman, "Your faith has saved you; go in peace."

a Or to

OVERVIEW: For Reformation exegetes this passage presents two frameworks for a godly life: love and law. The woman in this passage knew she was sinful and would be ostracized by the host of this party, but she crashed the party anyway in repentance and love, seeking Jesus and his forgiveness.[1] Simon, however, is satisfied with himself but judgmental of others, of both Jesus (who consorted with sinners) and the sinful woman herself. As the commentators point out, we see in him all the ways we should not act, for we should not be presumptuous or judgmental (God can change anyone at anytime). We should not assume that we are pious or sinless simply because we follow the law—we might notice the speck in another's eye but miss the log in our own! We should not think that right actions, following the letter of the law, make up for the lack of love in our hearts. It is in love that the sinful woman far exceeds Simon. She knows that she needs forgiveness, and she comes to Christ in tears, kissing and anointing his feet in humility. We are, in fact, to imitate this humble and repentant sinner—she seeks out Christ, and her faith is poured out in love. She knew that she was condemned by the law, but she grasped in faith the gospel that she would be forgiven and was moved by love to action. What a wonderful example of conversion!

But if anyone should wonder whether it was her great love that somehow earned her forgiveness, we must turn to the story within the story, the parable that Jesus used to explain the situation to Simon. The two debtors are, as Jesus explained, Simon and the woman—for both were sinners

---

[1]There are competing strands of exegetical tradition concerning this woman's identity. Some have harmonized the Synoptic record of this event with John 12:1-8, thus identifying the woman as Mary Magdalene; many others have resisted this. Regardless, the majority have interpreted this woman as a fitting allegory for the church. See ACCS NT 3:125-30; ACCS NT 4b:42. Contemporary biblical scholars reject harmonizing these texts.

who owed a debt to God. The debts of one were lesser, while the debts of the other were greater, but both were forgiven—and Simon knew instinctively that the one who was forgiven the most would love the most. But, the reformers emphasize, the woman's great love did not earn her forgiveness. Jesus makes the process clear. First the woman was forgiven through pure grace, then she loved, and loved so ardently that she broke into action.

7:36-38 The Woman Anoints Jesus' Feet at the Pharisee's Table

CHRIST USED THE OPPORTUNITY TO TEACH THE PHARISEES. MARTIN BUCER: The Lord omitted no occasion to teach, and so whenever someone invited him (if there was hope of their conversion), he agreed to go and attended their feasts. And so, we ought to shun evil people and sinners, so that we do not seem to condone their sins but rather to reprove them severely. And yet, if there might be an occasion where we could join with them for their edification, we should not neglect that opportunity to win them. But only those who have no care for the glory of Christ will wink at what the wicked do for profit and for pleasure's sake and be their table companions.

To be sure, we should not deny the necessities of life even to the wicked and the reprobate, for we must feed our enemy. That is how Christ acted, and that is how all those who are blessed with Christ's Spirit must act. It is shown that Christ acted this way by the present history. It may be that this Simon and the other Pharisees who were also at the feast were swelled and puffed up with trust in their own righteousness. And so Christ's purpose was to cure this both by his words and by the example of the sinful woman. This is the reason why he did not refuse to come to their feasts, and not because he was trying to get any benefit from them or that he was just winking at their sins. AN ECCLESIASTICALL EXPOSITION UPON SAINT LUKE 7.[2]

RISKING GREAT CRITICISM, THE WOMAN CAME TO REPENT. THOMAS BASTARD: No doubt but this woman had intended to come to Christ, wherever he might have been, being so touched with repentance that she could no longer defer the remedy. She was so sin-sick, so soul-sick, how could she have known where Christ was dining, if she had not made inquiry about him? So when she knew, she made no delay, even though she had to come to the proud Pharisee's house, where she knew her work of repentance should be held in scorn. Even though she had to come at dinner time, a time unseasonable for tears and mourning. Even though she had to come into the presence of those who well knew her wicked life and, as might be supposed, would be offended at her action.

Alas, dear Christians, many places can witness our sins, but where is the place that can testify to our repentance? There is no time or place unseasonable for this. Here is a knowledge which brings good effect: the woman, knowing where Christ is, comes to him. We also know as much, and yet we do not seek Christ. We know where he is, yet we do not come to him. We shun repentance; we do not fear sin. What wicked shame! THE SINNER'S LOOKING-GLASS. THE FIRST SERMON.[3]

HE ACCEPTED GENTLE SERVICE FROM A WOMAN. CATHARINA REGINA VON GREIFFENBERG: It was precious [ointment] because it served, as a sign of his incorruptibility, to embalm the Most Precious One in heaven and to anoint the Immortal One since his death drew near. The salvific seed of woman did not reject women, refusing to be served by them. Since he dignified them by his own being made flesh of a woman, he therefore also found them worthy to witness his death. He wanted to begin his life emerging from this sex and to end it in their company. He knew that he had caressed and pressed the ardor of love into them and granted fidelity to them in particular. Thus he meant to enjoy the noble fruit of this tree that his right hand had planted and to receive the sweet perfume of the

---

[2]Marlorat, ed., *Catholike and Ecclesiasticall Exposition of the Holy Gospel After S. Marke and Luke*, 167-68*.

[3]Bastard, *Five Sermons*, 58*.

love of this true-hearted refresher before his suffering, bitter as gall. Thus he testified that he respected not strength but gentleness and that he cared more for the inward ardor of love than the outward pretense of holiness from good works. What can soften his heart is ardor that melts the heart together with the desire to do good, however feebly their manifestations reflect them. ON THE SUPREMELY HOLY AND THE SUPREMELY SALVIFIC SUFFERING OF JESUS: FIRST MEDITATION.[4]

THE SINFUL WOMAN IS A GREAT EXAMPLE OF REPENTANCE AND LOVE. JOHANN SPANGENBERG: She shows what sort of faith she had in Christ by her crying, her anointing, her washing and drying of his feet. By this example we can see how someone should behave who wants to receive forgiveness of sins from God. And how does she show this faith? With works of love and mercy, for she started to wet his feet with her tears and to dry them with the hair of her head. She kissed his feet and anointed them with ointment. Those are certain signs of her repentance, her faith and her love. You see, she had a heartfelt dislike for her sins, which urged her on to Christ with such an earnestness that she paid no attention to the Pharisee's insults and scolding. That is a great sign of her faith, of which Christ also gives witness to her. He said, "Your faith has helped you." Therefore such a faith is not idle or lazy but spreads itself out through love. Then, after the custom of the land, she anointed Christ's head with perfume, wet his feet with her tears and dried them with her hair. ON THE DAY OF MARY MAGDALENE.[5]

7:39 The Pharisee Judges Both Jesus and the Woman

THE PHARISEE MISTAKENLY JUDGES THAT CHRIST IS NOT A PROPHET. MARTIN BUCER: The Pharisee thinks to himself that Christ is not a prophet and that it is not in the office of a prophet to welcome just anyone. He thinks that Christ is polluted and dishonored by the woman's presence. But Simon is deceived, because he judges Christ by his own imagination. That is, because he is such a proud man, he judges according to what he thinks is appropriate for important people like himself. He is deceived also in judging the woman according to her former life. People are rather to be judged according to their present state; God can change a person at any time.

And this error caused another, which commonly happens, for Simon judged that Christ was not a prophet because he did not know (so he presumed) what kind of woman she was. Now although we sometimes see that something at sometime was hidden from the prophets, because the Lord only revealed as much to them as they needed to know, Christ is the true Prophet and so he knew well enough what she was. Not only did he know her, but he wanted her there especially so that by her example he could beat down the pride of the Pharisee. And so we see here how greatly we ought to beware of presumptuous opinions, because they bring us into other errors. We can easily avoid this evil if we judge only in matters in which we are completely certain. AN ECCLESIASTICALL EXPOSITION UPON SAINT LUKE 7.[6]

7:40-43 The Parable of the Two Debtors

JESUS TELLS THE TRUTH TO THE PHARISEE. JOHN TRAPP: Whoever receives a courtesy, we say, sells his liberty. But that was not the case with Christ at Simon's table, or at Martha's. His mouth was not stopped by good cheer. He entertains the Pharisees with as many annoyances as they do him with fine meals. . . . In this parable Christ tells the supercilious and self-conceited Pharisee that he is a sinner as well as the woman and, as a debtor to God's judgment, has just as much need of his grace in Christ for the remission of sin and the removal

---

[4]Greiffenberg, *Meditations on the Incarnation, Passion and Death of Jesus Christ*, 68-69* (*Zwölf andächtige Betrachtungen*, 12-13).
[5]Spangenberg, *Postilla Teütsch . . . von den fürnemsten Festen durch das gantze Jar* (Augsburg: Valentein Othmar, 1544), LXIIIr.

[6]Marlorat, ed., *Catholike and Ecclesiasticall Exposition of the Holy Gospell After S. Marke and Luke*, 169-70*.

of wrath. A COMMENTARY UPON THE GOSPEL ACCORDING TO SAINT LUKE 7.[7]

THE PARABLE EXPLAINED. JACQUES LEFÈVRE D'ÉTAPLES: On account of this situation, the Lord set forth a parable to Simon. Concerning the two debtors, one is Simon and the other is the sinful woman; the moneylender, that is, the creditor who gave them the loan, is Christ. The coins: the debts, the gifts of God paid out to evil through sin. The one who gives the coins is the one who pardons. She waters, that is, washes the feet, who banishes earthly affections. She anoints the feet, who honors God by works of piety through an active life. She kisses, who unites herself with God. The community in which the Pharisee and the sinful woman were, we can see to be the world. The home of the Pharisee is Judea, while the Pharisee represents the people who measure justice by works and neglect repentance. . . . The sinful woman is a type of the faithful people, who are the greatest part of the race, a type of those who repent, a type of those expecting justification by grace, not from works. It is therefore a truly penitent people, who, recovering the good works of faith, expect justification not through their works, although they are works of the divine law (and are therefore owed) but from grace. IN THE GOSPEL OF LUKE 7.[8]

7:44-50 *Jesus Forgives the Woman's Sins*

SHE REVEALED HER BURNING LOVE THROUGH LOVING DEEDS. WILLIAM TYNDALE: Simon believed and had faith, but only weakly. According to the proportion of his faith, he loved coldly, and his deeds were the same: he invited Christ only to a simple and bare feast and did not receive him with any great humanity. But Mary Magdalene had a strong faith and therefore had burning love and notable deeds, done with exceedingly profound and deep meekness. On the

one side, she saw herself clearly in the law, both in what danger she was in and her cruel bondage under sin, her horrible damnation and the fearful sentence and judgment of God on sinners. On the other side, she heard the gospel of Christ preached, and in its promises she saw with eagles' eyes the exceedingly abundant mercy of God that passes all utterance of speech. This is set forth in Christ for all meek sinners who acknowledge their sins. She believed the Word of God mightily and glorified God because of his mercy and truth; and being overcome and overwhelmed with the unspeakable, yes, and incomprehensible, abundant riches of the kindness of God, did inflame and burn in love. In fact, she was so overwhelmed with love that she could not abide or hold still but must break forth. She was so drunk in love that she regarded nothing but only to utter the fervent and burning love of her heart. She had no respect to herself, though she was ever so great and notable a sinner, or to the judgmental hypocrisy of the Pharisees, who always disdained weak sinners. She ignored the costliness of her ointment but with all humbleness ran to his feet, washed them with the tears of her eyes, wiped them with the hairs of her head and anointed them with her precious ointment. No doubt she would have run into the ground under his feet to have uttered her love toward him and even would have descended down into hell, if it had been possible. THE PARABLE OF THE WICKED MAMMON (1527).[9]

HER GREAT LOVE IS A RESULT OF HER EXTENSIVE FORGIVENESS. JOHN MAYER: As all of us are sinners, then like this sinner we should stand at the feet of Christ, that is, with true repentance turn to walk in his steps. We should anoint him with sweet ointment, which happens when the sweet odor of a good name is diffused throughout the church, his body. And we must wash his feet with tears by extending our compassion to the poor, who are, as it were, the extreme

---

[7]Trapp, *Commentary or Exposition*, 390*.
[8]Lefèvre d'Étaples, *Commentarii Initiatorii in Quatuor Evangelia*, 2:42r.

[9]Tyndale, *Doctrinal Treatises*, 57-58*.

parts of his body (as Gregory says at the end of this story).[10]

Now, because Christ says, "Many sins are forgiven her, because she has loved much," a doubt may arise, whether anything in a person may be the cause of the pardoning of his sins, as if he merited it. The answer can be found here, and the passage clearly disproves it. Before these words the Lord tells of a man who had two debtors, one of whom owed him more and the other less. The man forgave them both, and so out of the Pharisee's own mouth Christ draws his point: the person loves the most of whom the most is forgiven. Applying that point to this sinner, he said, "Many sins are forgiven her, because she has loved much." So the great debtor, when he is forgiven, then he loves much; likewise with this woman. If her love did not flow from the pardon of her sins but the pardon of her sins from her love, then the parable does not apply. In saying this, then, Christ did not mean anything else but that her great love showed that she had committed many and very great sins, but she believed through the mercy of God in Christ, and so they were pardoned, which made her profuse in her ointment, tears and kisses. And in order to show that she was delivered from her sins by faith, and not by her love, he adds, "Your faith has saved you." A COMMENTARY ON THE NEW TESTAMENT, LUKE 7:36.[11]

THE WOMAN CONFESSES AND SHOWS A NEW OBEDIENCE. PHILIPP MELANCHTHON: It can be proven from this passage that there was faith in this woman, because Christ said, "Your faith has saved you." Now how can a new obedience be demonstrated in her? Because confession is in her. She declares publicly that she recognizes Christ to be the Messiah, and certainly she understood many things that anyone might have known, having picked it up along the way, and not recognizing his character. But she gives him this honor: she comes to him, asking and expecting from him consolation

in her suffering, in her repentence. Afterwards she gives this loving service: she washes the feet of Christ with her tears and anoints them. And the Lord himself commends these sacred rites of a new obedience by a beautiful testimony.

Thus you can see in this woman these three things: contrition, faith and new obedience. It is proper that all conversions in the church should be like this one, everyone who might be called by name by the callings. It is proper to have produced this kind of mortification and this kind of making alive. These are two distinct motions, one making dead and the other making alive the heart to life eternal. THE GOSPEL ON THE DAY OF MARY MAGDALENE.[12]

CHRIST CAME TO SAVE SINNERS, NOT THE PIOUS. JOHANN BAUMGART (POMARIUS): It is also comforting that he so willingly and graciously accepts and receives into grace this great sinner, who was so infamous in her town, and he speaks on her behalf against the judge who was pointing out the splinter in her eye—the Pharisee. Christ takes her under his guard and protection, and all her works, as well as the works the Pharisees did for appearance's sake, she makes into nothing without being noticed by anyone. Yet this Simon, who is a living saint in his own and in others' eyes, is far removed by Christ, and instead he praises and extols her love as a sign of the great forgiveness which she received. He publicly absolves her and sends her from him in peace.

Therefore no poor sinner should despair in his sins, like Cain, Saul, Judas, no matter how great his sins might be. He should not be fearful like Cain and say, "My sins are greater than you can forgive." Rather he should speak with Saint Augustine and say, "Cain, you lie, for God's mercy is greater than all human need and misery."[13] Where sin has become powerful, there grace is even more powerful. And Saint Paul says, "I received mercy

---

[10]Gregory, *Homilarion in Evangelia* 11, Homily 33 (PL 76).
[11]Mayer, *Commentarie vpon the New Testament*, 369*.

[12]MO 25:194-95.
[13]Augustine discusses Cain and Abel in the *City of God*, especially in book 15.

for this reason, that in me, as the foremost sinner, Christ might display his perfect patience as an example to those who were to believe in him for eternal life." The Son of Man has come into the world to save sinners—to call sinners, and not the pious, to confession, and to save what was lost. GOSPEL ON THE DAY OF MARY MAGDALENE.[14]

HYPOCRITES ALWAYS MURMUR AT SOME-THING UNFAMILIAR. JOHN CALVIN: Here again we observe that out of their ignorance of Christ's office, people immediately produce new stumbling blocks. The root of the evil is that no one examines his own miseries, which undoubtedly would awaken everyone to seek a remedy. It is not at all surprising that real hypocrites, who grow careless with their own faults, should murmur about Christ forgiving sins, as if at a new and unfamiliar thing. COMMENTARY ON A HARMONY OF THE GOSPELS.[15]

FAITH PROVIDES PEACE. JOHN TRAPP: Faith has the virtue of peacefulness. It fills the conscience with a blessed calm and fortifies the heart against all discouragements. People may mutter, as they did here, but the answer, or rather the demand of faith is, "Who is to condemn? It is Christ Jesus who justifies." A COMMENTARY UPON THE GOSPEL ACCORDING TO SAINT LUKE 7.[16]

---

[14]Baumgart, *Postilla*, 433v-434r; citing Gen 4:13; 1 Tim 1:12-16; Mt 9:13; Mt 18:21-35; 1 Tim 1:16.

[15]CO 45:380 (cf. CTS 32:140).

[16]Trapp, *Commentary or Exposition*, 391*; citing Rom 5:1; 8:34.

8:1-18 THE PARABLES OF
THE SOWER AND THE LAMP

Soon afterward he went on through cities and villages, proclaiming and bringing the good news of the kingdom of God. And the twelve were with him, ²and also some women who had been healed of evil spirits and infirmities: Mary, called Magdalene, from whom seven demons had gone out, ³and Joanna, the wife of Chuza, Herod's household manager, and Susanna, and many others, who provided for them^a out of their means.

⁴And when a great crowd was gathering and people from town after town came to him, he said in a parable, ⁵"A sower went out to sow his seed. And as he sowed, some fell along the path and was trampled underfoot, and the birds of the air devoured it. ⁶And some fell on the rock, and as it grew up, it withered away, because it had no moisture. ⁷And some fell among thorns, and the thorns grew up with it and choked it. ⁸And some fell into good soil and grew and yielded a hundredfold." As he said these things, he called out, "He who has ears to hear, let him hear."

⁹And when his disciples asked him what this parable meant, ¹⁰he said, "To you it has been given to know the secrets of the kingdom of God, but for others they are in parables, so that 'seeing they may not see,

and hearing they may not understand.' ¹¹Now the parable is this: The seed is the word of God. ¹²The ones along the path are those who have heard; then the devil comes and takes away the word from their hearts, so that they may not believe and be saved. ¹³And the ones on the rock are those who, when they hear the word, receive it with joy. But these have no root; they believe for a while, and in time of testing fall away. ¹⁴And as for what fell among the thorns, they are those who hear, but as they go on their way they are choked by the cares and riches and pleasures of life, and their fruit does not mature. ¹⁵As for that in the good soil, they are those who, hearing the word, hold it fast in an honest and good heart, and bear fruit with patience.

¹⁶"No one after lighting a lamp covers it with a jar or puts it under a bed, but puts it on a stand, so that those who enter may see the light. ¹⁷For nothing is hidden that will not be made manifest, nor is anything secret that will not be known and come to light. ¹⁸Take care then how you hear, for to the one who has, more will be given, and from the one who has not, even what he thinks that he has will be taken away."

a Some manuscripts *him*

OVERVIEW: We learn here that parables were the common form of teaching story for the Hebrews, and people learned more easily and gladly through parables, because they explained sometimes complicated spiritual truths through common examples drawn from everyday life.

The fact that Jesus had some unusual disciples leads directly into the following parable of the sower, which addresses why some accept and believe the message of the gospel but others do not. If the Word is equally powerful in every instance, as these commentators believe, why is it not equally

effective in turning its auditors to Christ? Not all people are equally prepared to hear the message and incorporate it into their lives. The message for listeners is clear: bring your ears when you come to hear the gospel! Be ready to listen fully with both ears and heart, and let the gospel take root and bear fruit. God plays a role in this successful growth, for he prepares our hearts, but the emphasis of this parable and its interpretations is not on God's necessary work but ours.

The parable of the lamp is another quick and easy example that helps us understand a more difficult idea: How is it that God's Word acts in the world? God's Word is like the light of a lamp. It is not meant to be hidden but instead should shine brightly throughout the room. In fact, although people might want to hide this light or extinguish it if they are distracted or drawn away by the world, its pleasures and duties, the light will seek out dark corners and bring light to hidden spaces. God's Word, once it is unleashed in the world, will bring what is hidden in people's hearts and thoughts out into the light. Once it is heard, it will have its effect: the Word will enter the hearts of those who are prepared to hear it.

8:1-3 Jesus Is Followed by Both Male and Female Disciples

CHRIST TRAVELED TO FULFILL HIS MESSIANIC VOCATION. JOHANNES BRENZ: In this passage it is declared that Jesus Christ, when he had publicly begun his ministry as Messiah, did not live in one city, staying idle or slothful, but that he went through cities and towns. This declares the great love of God toward humanity. For Christ the Son of God did not stay in any one city, so that those who were sick and lived elsewhere had to come to him to be healed and be brought into the way of truth, but instead he walked through the whole country, and looked for the miserable people who were not even hoping to be healed and healed them. And by this traveling around, Christ teaches each one of us to follow his calling. For Christ was ordained by God the Father to this end and purpose: that he might be the public and general preacher to the Jews and to Galilee. If therefore Christ, the Son of God, does not avoid any labor, trouble or danger in order to pursue his calling, all of us miserable people should be stirred up by his example to do nothing else but, by any means possible and with all diligence, to follow our own calling. AN ECCLESIASTICALL EXPOSITION UPON SAINT LUKE 8.[1]

THE WOMEN FOLLOWED CHRIST AND WERE A SIGN OF HIS GREAT MERCY. AUGUSTIN MARLORAT: The women followed Jesus as a token of their thankfulness, because they had received both physical and spiritual benefits from him. They were taught the gospel of the kingdom of God, and they were delivered from evil spirits. . . . Now this fellowship may seem to bring small honor to Christ, for what would be more inappropriate than that the Son of God should travel around with women with poor reputations! But in fact this shows us that those vices with which we were burdened before we came to faith do not hinder the glory of Christ, but rather they increase it. He did not come to find the church which he had chosen without any wrinkle or spot, but rather he cleansed it with his blood so that he might make it pure and fair. And so after they were delivered from the evil spirits, the former miserable and shameful condition of these women added to the great glory of Christ in declaring the excellent signs of his power and grace. Their thankfulness is also commended by Luke because they followed the one who delivered them and condemned the shame which was heaped on them by the world. There is no doubt but that some people pointed at them and that Christ's presence put them on a public stage where they would be seen, but they refused to hide their shame, so that the grace of Christ might be made known. And there was a singular miracle of the unspeakable goodness of Christ in Mary, for she had been possessed by seven devils and was, as it were, the most vile habitation of Satan, and Christ not only made her his disciple but kept her in his company. AN ECCLESIASTICALL EXPOSITION UPON SAINT LUKE 8.[2]

"SEVEN DEMONS" MEANS MANY AND GREAT SINS. HULDRYCH ZWINGLI: I think that in the presence of all evils and all physical pain, the devil is admitted. However the number seven in

---

[1]Marlorat, ed., *Catholike and Ecclesiasticall Exposition of the Holy Gospell After S. Marke and Luke*, 174-75*. [2]Marlorat, ed., *Catholike and Ecclesiasticall Exposition of the Holy Gospell After S. Marke and Luke*, 175*.

Scripture is taken for a greater number, as in Ruth: "She is more to you than seven sons." Likewise in Proverbs: "Wisdom . . . has hewn her seven pillars"; that is, wisdom is enduring. Thus "seven demons" signifies great wickedness. The Lord set her free from many and great sins. Thus Matthew 12: "seven spirits even more evil," that is, it moves toward all his power and strength. IN THE GOSPEL OF LUKE 8.[3]

8:4-8 *The Parable of the Sower*

THIS PARABLE REQUIRES HEARING EARS AND QUICK MINDS. DESIDERIUS ERASMUS: He spoke many things to the crowd under the cover of parables, by which he excited in them a zeal for learning. The parables also occupied their minds and impressed his teaching on them by the mystery. Therefore he first offered a parable which reminded everyone to hear the words of the gospel with eager hearts and minds and not to feel they had listened sufficiently unless they also applied what they had learned in the practice of piety. . . . After the Lord had spoken these things, because he knew that not everyone understood what he had said, but desiring that they would keep this parable which pertained to the prosperity of everyone in mind afterwards, cried out in a loud voice, saying, "He who has ears suited to hear the wisdom of the gospel, let him hear those things which I have said. For they require a hearer who is neither dull-witted nor half-asleep. And they pertain to every single one of you. There are some who are like statues—they have ears, but they do not hear. They have ears enough for all the various little rules of the Pharisees, but they are totally deaf to the doctrine of true piety." PARAPHRASE ON THE GOSPEL OF LUKE 8:4-8.[4]

THE SEED ALWAYS HAS POWER BUT DOES NOT ALWAYS PRODUCE FRUIT. MARTIN BUCER: The occasion of this parable, as we just touched on,

seems to be the great multitude of people who came from diverse places with a desire to learn. Christ declared to them by this parable that it is not sufficient simply to hear the Word and that not everyone who hears it is made better by it, unless they bring forth its fruits. The similitude is very apt and fitting, for we are born anew by the teaching of the gospel, which is the incorruptible seed. As the seed by its own proper nature is fruitful, so is the gospel; if it does not profit those who hear it, we cannot therefore say that it is unfruitful, for it is always fruitful in power, even if not always in act or deed. Where the earth is lacking, there the seed does not by itself bring forth fruit. Therefore Christ professed himself here to be, as it were, a farmer who has come out to sow his seed but suggests that many of his listeners are like barren and untilled soil, or perhaps like the thorny and bushy ground, in which both the labor and the seed are wasted. . . .

The readers should be admonished that if those folks, who came from far away like hunger-starved people to hear Christ, are compared with barren and unfruitful land, it is no surprise that the gospel does not bring forth fruit in many today, of whom some are slothful, some slow, some negligent and some are such drones that they can scarcely be dragged to hear the Word of God. AN ECCLESIASTICALL EXPOSITION UPON SAINT MATHEWE 13.[5]

PREPARE YOUR EARS TO HEAR THE GOSPEL. JOHN BOYS: "A good ear," says the wise man, "will gladly listen to wisdom." From this we note two lessons concerning hearing. First, we should listen to nothing but what is good, that is, to wisdom. Second, we should listen to it gladly, with a great desire to learn. For we see in the Scripture that to hear is to obey, as Christ says in the Gospel: "He who hears you, hears me." That is, he who obeys you, obeys me, and he who despises you, despises me.[6] If

[3]*D. Hvldrichi Zvinglii in Plerosqve Novi Testamenti Libros*, 226; quoting Ruth 4:15; Prov 9:1; Mt 12:45.
[4]Erasmus, *In Evangelivm Lvce Paraphrasis*, n6r-n7r (LB 7:361).
[5]Marlorat, ed., *Catholike and Ecclesiasticall Exposition of the Holy Gospell After S. Mathewe*, 278*; citing 1 Pet 1:23.
[6]See Lk 10:16. *Obaudire* and *obedire* are different spellings of the same verb, which means both "to listen to" and "to obey." *Audire* means "to hear."

your brother hears you, then you have won your brother; that is, if your brother follows your counsel and will be content to be ruled by your opinion.

We read in the law that if a bondservant does not wish to be freed but will stay with his master, he shall be brought before the judges and set to the door or the post, and his master shall bore through his ear with an awl, and so he shall serve him forever. Every sinner is the devil's vassal, and therefore if he refuses to be freed when the liberty and free grace of the gospel is offered, before long the devil will so bore his ears that they will be unfit for hearing, and then he shall serve his old master forever. It is possible that he will come to church and hear the sermon, but he will be like the person who beholds his face in a mirror. When that person has considered himself, he goes on his way and immediately forgets what sort of person he was.

Therefore, when you come to Christ, bring your ears with you, ears to hear, so that hearing, you might understand; understanding, you might remember; remembering, you might practice; and practicing, you might continue. In this way, God's seed will be sown in good ground and bring forth fruit, in some thirtyfold, in some sixtyfold and in some a hundredfold. SEXAGESIMA SUNDAY.[7]

8:9-10 *The Meaning of Parables*

PARABLES HELP THE PEOPLE TO HEAR AND UNDERSTAND. JOHANN SPANGENBERG: Why does Christ use parables and allegories? Just as the Gentiles take care to teach their children through poetic fables, so the Jews take care to teach their children through parables and allegories. And because Christ was among the Jews, he teaches in their manner, using allegories drawn from the things that the people deal with every day, such as plants and seed, growing and harvesting, wheat and weeds, vines and vineyards. Because he speaks of these things, the listeners are able to understand his sermons so much more easily. Parables have a

certain style or art that allow people to accept them easily, and they can be understood quickly by those who hear them. And what does he want to show with this parable? He gives an example here of how things go in Christendom: when the gospel is preached, it is received in a variety of ways, and it brings forth fruit in only a few people. And how does that happen? All sorts of people find themselves brought to hear the Word of God. Some hear and accept it. Some, when they have heard it, forget it again. And others despise it entirely and completely. THE GOSPEL ON SEXAGESIMA SUNDAY.[8]

TODAY'S TRUE BELIEVERS CAN ALSO LEARN THE SPIRITUAL SENSE. RICHARD TAVERNER: After the disciples of our Lord Jesus Christ had heard these words, they desired that he would explain to them the spiritual sense and right meaning of the parable. The Lord answered them in the following way: "The Father of heaven has given you grace (by you I mean those who earnestly go about to hear and follow my teaching) so that you may know the mysteries of the kingdom of heaven, but to the rest of the people, that is to say, those who pay little attention to me, it has not been given to understand, except through parables and darkly. So those who esteem themselves as cunning and wise will see nothing at all, and those who repute themselves to have excellent understanding will have no knowledge, except according to their fleshly and worldly wisdom."

What should we understand by this, my friends? Surely we should understand that the heavenly Father gives grace to know his mysteries and godly will not only to those disciples who were then with Jesus Christ but also to all true believers who have steadfast faith and stable confidence in his mercy and infinite goodness. These persons, in whatever state or condition they might be, are truly disciples and students of Jesus Christ. But on the contrary part, to those who are unbelievers and infidels, that is to say, those who trust in them-

---

[7]Boys, *Exposition of the Dominical Epistles and Gospels*, 1:264-65*; citing Sir 3:28; Mt 18:15; Ex 21:5-6; Deut 15:16-17; Jas 1:23.

[8]Spangenberg, *Postilla* (1582), LXXIIIv.

selves or in any other thing rather than God, surely the Father of heaven will not disclose or open the mystery of his heavenly Word but rather will suffer them to fall in miserable blindness so that they will not see or understand except in a fleshly sort of way, and not at all according to the Spirit. THE GOSPEL ON THE SUNDAY OF SEXAGESIME.[9]

8:11-15 The Meaning of the Parable of the Sower

SOME ONLY SEEM TO HEAR THE WORD AND FOLLOW IT. MARTIN LUTHER: This Gospel speaks about the students and the fruit which the Word of God has in the world. It does not speak about the law or about human ordinances but, as he himself says, about the Word of God which he himself—Christ the sower—preaches. The law produces no fruit, just as little as human ordinances do. He establishes four groups of students of the Word of God.

The first group are those who hear but do not understand or pay attention to it. These are not the common people on earth but the greatest, wisest and holiest—in short they are the majority. He is not speaking here about those who persecute the Word or who do not listen to it but about those who hear it and are students of it, who even want to be called true Christians, who live with us in the Christian congregation and who participate in baptism and the sacrament with us. But they are and remain fleshly hearts who do not accept the Word. It goes in one ear and out the other. Similarly, the kernel fell on the path and not on the ground and remained lying out on the path, for the path is trodden hard by human and animal feet.

That is why he says that "the devil comes and takes away the Word from their hearts, so that may not believe and be saved." This power of the devil not only means that hearts which were hardened through a worldly mind and life lose and abandon the Word, so that they never understand or know it, but it also means that hearts which were hardened through a worldly mind and life lose and abandon the Word, so that they never understand or know it, but it also means that instead of God's Word the devil sends false teachers, who trample it down with human teaching. THE CHURCH POSTIL (1540): SEXAGISMA SUNDAY.[10]

THE ROCKY SOIL SIGNIFIES THOSE WHOSE FAITH DOES NOT LAST. HEINRICH BULLINGER: This is another type of the hearers. The rocky or stony ground signifies untimely hearers, that is, those whose minds are ripe too soon, who receive the Word of God as soon as it is preached and rejoice with great gladness for the revelation of the truth. They have some earth, although not very deep or sufficient enough; they have some goodness and integrity, and the seed can begin to sprout and shoot up. That is, they declare by a certain token that they are attracted to the gospel and that they like evangelical teaching and piety very well. But when they do not have a proper faith of the right proportion, and the root of charity and vital moisture from the watering of the Spirit of God in due time, their faith is only momentary and their religion is of short duration—it does not last until the end but only for a short time. AN ECCLESIASTICALL EXPOSITION UPON SAINT MATHEWE 13.[11]

THORNS PREVENT THE SEED FROM TAKING ROOT IN OUR HEARTS. PHILIPP MELANCHTHON: Some hear, understand and receive the Word but are prevented from producing fruit by the cares of the world, by the deceitfulness of riches, by the pleasures of this life, and so on, and the seed of the gospel is choked by these thorns. These are the folks who said, "I have bought five yoke of oxen, I have bought a farm, I have married a wife and therefore I cannot come." Christ therefore compares the pleasures of the world, or the evil desires of the flesh, covetousness and other worldly cares with thorns. Matthew places the cares of the world

---

[9]Taverner, Epistles and Gospelles (Wynter Parte), 68v-69r*.

[10]LW 76:331* (WA 17,2:154; E² 11:90-91).
[11]Marlorat, ed., Catholike and Ecclesiasticall Exposition of the Holy Gospell After S. Mathewe, 286*.

under "covetousness," but it means the same, because this word comprehends the entangling enticements of pleasures (which Luke mentions) and all kinds of desire.

The thorns and other hurtful impediments choke the pleasant and fruitful corn when it shoots up and becomes an ear, and likewise the vicious and wicked affections of the flesh prevail in human hearts and grow higher than their faith, that they might overthrow and press down the force of heavenly doctrine, which is not yet ripened and perfected. For although evil desires spring up and arise and possess the heart before the Word of the Lord is green and appears, nevertheless at first they seem not to possess it entirely but overcome it little by little, after the corn is sprung up and the ear is visible. Everyone therefore should endeavor to pluck out these thorns from his heart, unless they want to have the Word of God choked. There is no one who does not have these thorns, and in fact even a thick forest of thorns within him. We see truly how few people come into perfection and ripeness, because scarcely one in ten people occupies himself (I won't even say in plucking up the thorns) in cutting and knocking them down. AN ECCLESIASTICALL EXPOSITION UPON SAINT MATHEWE 13.[12]

GOD PREPARES OUR HEARTS, AND THE SEED PRODUCES GOOD FRUIT. AUGUSTIN MARLORAT: There is not one of us who is truly prepared to receive the seeds of the gospel or who is capable in and of ourselves. Therefore we would hear it in vain if God did not kill hearts who are sure of themselves with his holy and gracious Spirit. For otherwise many wicked weeds would spring up and choke the seed. This preparation comes about not by human nature but by the cultivation and workmanship of God. . . .

Wheat seed does not bring forth nor does it bear any other grain or corn than what is of the same nature and kind. It is contrary to nature for

wheat to bring forth rye, barley or peas. Likewise, when the gospel is preached, what else would it bring forth from a good heart than what it contains in itself, what it teaches and appoints? Faith in Christ is preached and sown, the repentance for our past life, knowledge of God, love toward God and our neighbor, and so on, which never bring forth contrary fruits. AN ECCLESIASTICALL EXPOSITION UPON SAINT MATHEWE 13.[13]

PATIENCE AND SUFFERING WILL YIELD THEIR FRUIT. THOMAS BECON: When the heart becomes studious, strong and religious with the fear and love of God, then it is pure and suitable for the purpose of yielding fruit in patience and long-suffering. The cross, tribulation and affliction will certainly not be lacking. For as Paul says, all who wish to live a godly life in Christ will suffer persecution. That is why patience is a necessary remedy in the Christian person, along with prayer. First of all, our greatest disadvantage is that we are so entangled and encumbered that we cannot, by reason of our natural inclination, neglect and despise worldly things. Besides this, the devil lets no occasion pass but devises all possible means to take the Word from us and put in its place covetousness, pride, wrath and other similar things. There are many examples we could show, for there would be many excellent people in every congregation if they were not hindered by avarice, ambition and lechery, which keep them from regarding God's Word. That is why it is very expedient to note our vicious nature diligently and not to live as carelessly as most people do, but rather to entreat God for the gift of the Holy Spirit. He promised us with a guarantee to give the Spirit to us, for the Father will "give the Holy Spirit to those who ask him," so that he may remove from us any barriers and cut down all those thorns and snares, so that we may hear and keep the Word of God and bring forth true fruit of faith in Christ. By this faith we will not only show obedience to God but we will

---

[12]Marlorat, ed., *Catholike and Ecclesiasticall Exposition of the Holy Gospell After S. Mathewe*, 287-88*; citing Lk 14:18-20.

[13]Marlorat, ed., *Catholike and Ecclesiasticall Exposition of the Holy Gospell After S. Mathewe*, 288-89*.

also become his children and heirs. For this is the chief cause why this seed is spread and the gospel preached throughout the whole world: so that such fruits may be yielded to everlasting life. THE SUNDAY CALLED SEXAGESIMA.[14]

8:16-18 The Parable of the Lamp and Its Application

THE FAITH OF BELIEVERS SHINES FORTH LIKE A LIGHTED CANDLE. JACQUES LEFÈVRE D'ÉTAPLES: The lamp is the faithful soul: its light is the doctrine of life, the Word of God, the law of grace. The one who lights it is our Lord Jesus Christ, who is the true light, which illumines every person who comes into this world. The one who hides the light is the one who keeps it idle without using it, or by neglect, as if, forgetting both God and his Word, he lets it slip away and vanish. He hides the object when the flesh suppresses the spirit. He puts it under a bed when pleasures and attractions of the flesh destroy the soul and extinguish the light of God. The candlestick is the holy congregation above which the divine light is placed. The house is the universal church. Those entering are those just coming to faith or those who are being illumined by faith only now. . . .

Matthew places before this parable the one about the city placed on a hill, which cannot be hidden: and it cannot be hidden to merit. For if this city is the church of Christ, the hill on which it is placed is Christ the Lord, for there can be no church unless it is built on him. And it is shown here how it might have been hidden, for without the hill, the church of Christ would not have been perceived to exist. But when it is built on Christ, then faith shines in it, and all trust and love in Christ. IN THE GOSPEL OF LUKE 8.[15]

GOD'S WORD MAKES KNOWN WHAT IS HIDDEN. FRANÇOIS LAMBERT: You see that the highest effectiveness of God's speech is from this place. It makes public what is hidden and buried, simply that it might be plain. That is, it would be announced most plainly and simply. It is because it is testimony by the Holy Spirit, and the same Spirit "searches everything, even the depths of God." Therefore, in the saints, true and sound judgment concerning everything works through it, as we see in Job 28: The depths of the rivers he searches out, and "the thing that is hidden he brings out into the light."

And finally Christ made himself known, and his words revealed what was secret in their hearts and thoughts, as we said above in chapter two. For it is revealed when people agree with the teachings of Christ, and when they disagree. For whoever is from God hears the words of God most faithfully and clings to Christ with all his heart. The rest who are not at all from God are not able to be content with his words. COMMENTARY IN LUKE 8:17.[16]

THE LORD GIVES INCREASE TO THOSE HE HAS CHOSEN. PHILIPP MELANCHTHON: By this saying, our Savior Christ wishes to signify that it would also be true in his kingdom that the knowledge of life would be communicated and given only to those who have the gift of election. Those who want this gift will have the divine knowledge which they seem to have by the preaching of the Word taken away. Through their contempt of the Word, which they cannot receive, the reprobate are blinded more and more, until at length we will seen them deprived even of their common sense. The Lord brought the disciples to him in order that they might profit more and more in his school, and because they were chosen, the Lord promoted them, as it were, by degrees. They were not made perfect the first day, but every day they learned new lessons, and so, increasing little by little, they grew greatly. AN ECCLESIASTICALL EXPOSITION UPON SAINT MATHEWE 13.[17]

---

[14]Becon, *New Postil*, 126 r-v*; citing 2 Tim 3:12; Lk 11:13.
[15]Lefèvre d'Étaples, *Commentarii Initiatorii in Quatuor Evangelia*, 2:45v.

[16]Lambert, *In Divi Lucae*, Q3v-Q4r; citing 1 Cor 2:10; Job 28:11.
[17]Marlorat, ed., *Catholike and Ecclesiasticall Exposition of the Holy Gospell after S. Mathewe*, 279-80*.

8:19-21 A NEW FAMILY
REPLACES THE OLD ONE

[19]*Then his mother and his brothers came to him, but they could not reach him because of the crowd.* [20]*And he was told, "Your mother and your brothers are standing outside, desiring to see you."* [21]*But he answered them, "My mother and my brothers are those who hear the word of God and do it."*

OVERVIEW: The "brothers of Christ" have challenged Christian interpreters since the early centuries of the church. Who are these brothers, and what sort of familial relationship did they have with Mary and Jesus? Actual, blood brothers of Christ would be problematic for the traditional belief in Mary as ever-virgin, a concept largely significant because of the long-held connection between sexuality and sin. In the early church, there were a number of treatises written for and against (mostly against) the possibility that Mary might have had other children, in the usual way, after Jesus. The opponents of this idea eventually established Mary's perpetual virginity as orthodox teaching and proposed a number of different options to explain who these brothers were. A common solution, that the brothers were cousins of Jesus, is the explanation given here. By the later medieval period, a wide-ranging kinship had been established for Jesus, which included all the apostles and their parents. Because the term "brother" was used for a variety of relationships in the Bible, these brothers could be explained as other relatives of Jesus and Mary.

But why did Jesus minimize the importance of his blood relatives? Although Protestant interpreters did not hold Mary in as high a regard as Catholics—a regard which they saw as excessive if not idolatrous—they still held a high opinion of Mary both as a role model and as a faithful believer. The fact that she was Jesus' physical mother was deemphasized, but she remained important as the model of humble faith. In this context, Mary could not be suspected of any sinful or doubting tendencies. She only wanted to see Jesus because she was concerned about him, or perhaps she was eager to learn from him. In either case, her only fault was in being overly emotional. She might not deserve special attention as Jesus' physical mother, but she was foremost among believers and a blessed member of his spiritual family.

8:19-21 Jesus' Family Is Tied by the Bonds of Faith, Not Kinship

THESE "BROTHERS" WERE JESUS' COUSINS.
HENRY SMITH: You must understand that those who are here called Christ's brothers were actually his cousins on his mother's side, that is, her sisters' children.[1] There were three Marys, and these three were sisters: Mary the virgin, Mary the mother of James and Mary the daughter of Cleophas, whose sons these were. The names of the sons were James, Joseph, Judas and Simon, and they are called the Lord's brothers because they were kin to him. Therefore note that in holy Scripture there are four sorts of brothers: brothers by nature, such as Esau and Jacob, who had one father and one mother; brothers by nation, so all the Jews are called brothers, because they were all from the same country; brothers by consanguinity, where every-

---

[1]Questions about the brothers of Jesus have been discussed from the early church through the present day; Smith presents here the common opinion in the medieval period. For a look at medieval views of the "holy kinship," see John Bossy, *Christianity in the West 1400–1700* (Oxford: Oxford University Press, 1985). For the reformers and their forebears the need to find another explanation for Jesus' "brothers" is predicated on the doctrine of Mary's perpetual virginity.

one in the same family is called a brother, as Abraham called Lot his brother and Sarah his sister, because they were from one familial line; and brothers by profession, so all Christians are called brothers, because they are of one religion. These were brothers of the third kind, that is, of consanguinity, because they were of one family. The Affinity of the Faithful.[2]

His Mother and Brothers Wanted to Join Him. John Calvin: All three Evangelists agree in this matter that Christ was speaking in the midst of a crowd of people when his mother and brothers came. There is no doubt that they came either because they were worried about him or because they were eager to learn. So it was not without a good reason that they attempted to draw near to him, nor is it probable that anyone accompanying the holy Mother would be an unbeliever. While Ambrose and Chrysostom accuse Mary of ambition, there is no cause for that.[3] What need is there for such a guess, when the testimony of the Spirit everywhere commends her high piety and modesty? Perhaps the strength of their human affection propelled them further than was right, giving them trouble—I do not deny this, but I have no doubt that they were led by pious zeal to join themselves to him. Commentary on a Harmony of the Gospels.[4]

Christ Gives Priority to His Spiritual Kin. Philipp Melanchthon: To believe in Christ the Son of God and to hear the word of Christ as the Word of God is to do the will of the Father who is in heaven. So whoever hears the Word of God and does it and believes in him is the brother or sister or mother of Christ. And therefore in place of what is writtten in Matthew and in Mark ("whoever does the will of my Father") is written in Luke, "Whoever hears the Word of God and does it." And in another passage he says, "Whoever is of God hears God's Word." Now, to be kin with God is to be of him, and to be of kin is to be of that spiritual consanguinity with him. As it is written, "But to all who did receive him, who believed in his name, he gave the right to become children of God, who were born not of blood or of the will of the flesh or of the will of man but of God." Now, what other thing did the disciples of Christ do, whom Jesus declared to be his brothers, sisters and mother by the stretching forth of his hand? Did they not believe what he said and abandoned everything and followed him? An Ecclesiasticall Exposition upon Saint Mathewe 12.[5]

The Veneration of Mary is Unscriptural. Philipp Melanchthon: By this passage we also see how preposterous the veneration of Mary is, when she is worshiped as a goddess just because she was the carnal mother of Christ. Here we see that Christ diminishes that relationship, preferring his spiritual kindred only, which pertains to all the children of God, far above any other relationship. An Ecclesiasticall Exposition upon Saint Mathewe 12.[6]

---

[2]Smith, *Affinitie of the Faithfull*, A4v*; alluding to Gen 27:30, Deut 15:12, Gen 13:8, Gen 12:13, Mt 23:8.
[3]See Chrysostom, Homily 54 on the Gospel of Matthew (NPNF 10:278-84).
[4]CO 45:350 (cf. CTS 32:90).
[5]Marlorat, ed., *Catholike and Ecclesiasticall Exposition of the Holy Gospell After S. Mathewe*, 276; citing Mt 17:5; Mk 3:35; Mt 12:50; Jn 8:47; Jn 1:12-13.
[6]Marlorat, ed., *Catholike and Ecclesiasticall Exposition of the Holy Gospell After S. Mathewe*, 276*.

8:22-25 THE CALMING OF THE STORM

²²One day he got into a boat with his disciples, and he said to them, "Let us go across to the other side of the lake." So they set out, ²³and as they sailed he fell asleep. And a windstorm came down on the lake, and they were filling with water and were in danger. ²⁴And they went and woke him, saying, "Master, Master, we are perishing!" And he awoke and rebuked the wind and the raging waves, and they ceased, and there was a calm. ²⁵He said to them, "Where is your faith?" And they were afraid, and they marveled, saying to one another, "Who then is this, that he commands even winds and water, and they obey him?"

OVERVIEW: Like other miracles, the reformers remind us, Jesus here intends to test his disciples' faith and to reveal his glory and power. Still we might wonder why any of his disciples, after all this time, question who Jesus is, but it is likely, Calvin notes, that those who questioned him were new and had not yet seen enough to establish their faith. But the others were being tested, and clearly they still had a way to go. The main import of the story for us, the reformers state, is that we are Jesus' disciples and are often tested by difficulties and calamities. The gospel raises a storm wherever it is preached (as Luther's example shows), so Christ's followers are inevitably going to experience trials. How should we respond? Not in utter fear and terror, as these disciples did, but rather with continued hope in Christ's help. Some fear is healthy, for it pushes us into prayer—in fact, no fear at all leaves us lazy and careless—but excessive fear shows our faith to be weak. Like the disciples in the boat, we must believe that Christ "neither slumbers nor sleeps" (Ps 121:4) but will always be there to support and care for us. We are and will be tried so that we learn not to trust in our own strength and abilities but instead to turn to him.

8:22-23 The Storm Threatens the Boat While Jesus Sleeps

THE DISCIPLES ARE QUITE EASY IN THEIR FAITH. JOHANN SPANGENBERG: Christ steps into a boat, and his disciples follow him, as is right, and the other people stay behind. Now Christ had preached the gospel to his disciples, and had taught on the mountain and had reinforced what he taught with many examples and miracles (such as with the leper, the centurion's servant and Peter's mother-in-law, and many other possessed and sick people). So now he wants to put them to the test, both on water and on land, to see whether they will be steadfast in their faith even in time of trial. And so he takes them onto the sea while it is perfectly calm. Because he was tired from much preaching and traveling, he lies down in the boat and sleeps on a pillow. Meanwhile, what are the disciples of Christ doing? They are easy and at peace. They think that because Christ is with them in the boat, no disaster can happen. There is no fear or alarm. If they had been asked at the time if they had faith and trusted in God, they would have answered quite easily: "Why not? Should we not believe?" But then what happened? While they are secure and do not expect any danger, and the weather is still calm, Jesus lies down in the boat and sleeps. But then the stormy and raging winds come along, and he acts as though he knows nothing about it. Then such fear and terror, such trembling and quaking comes over the apostles that they do not know how to continue. GOSPEL ON THE FOURTH SUNDAY AFTER EPIPHANY.[1]

---

[1]Spangenberg, *Postilla* (1582), LVIIIv; citing Lk 5:12-13; 7:10; 4:38-39.

GOD'S WORD RAISES THE STORM AS A TRIAL OF FAITH. JOHN BOYS: Until Christ was in the ship, there was no storm. While people have pillows sewn under their elbows, all is peace; but as soon as Christ rebukes the world of sin, the wicked are like the raging sea that cannot rest and whose waters cast up dirt and mire. John the Baptist raised such a storm by preaching against Herod that it cost him his head. When Paul preached at Athens, Corinth and Ephesus, storms and uproars always followed among the people. When Luther first preached the gospel, instantly there was a great thundering from Rome and a great tempest in Germany, France, England, Scotland, and in the whole Christian world, which all the papal bulls (and calves, too) could not appease. This storm was not by chance but was raised by God's providence, who brings the wind out of his storehouses; and the tempest was great, that the miracle might be great: the greater the tempest, the greater was the trial of the disciples' faith. THE FOURTH SUNDAY AFTER THE EPIPHANY.[2]

8:24-25 Jesus Calms the Storm, to the Disciples' Amazement

CHRIST FEIGNS SLEEP TO TEACH US TO TURN TO HIM. JOHANN BAUMGART (POMARIUS): And for our good, he will let it appear for a time that he is sleeping (although as the protector of Israel, he neither slumbers nor sleeps, but his heart always notices us and watches). Although without him we are capable of nothing, when we are not in danger or dire need we are vainglorious, foolish boasters and braggarts, and we presume a great deal, just like Saint Peter.[3] Then we want to walk across the water, until it comes to the actual event, and the Lord stands a little ways off, as if he were resting. Then we fall into fear and danger of death, and so we cry out with the disciples, "Lord, do you not notice that

we are perishing?" . . . This is how it usually goes with us, as David confessed for his own part, "I said in my prosperity, 'I shall never be moved.' But when you hid your face, I was dismayed."

Thus the Lord also sleeps sometimes to awaken faith, hope and prayers in us. He does it so that we will abandon our trust in our own strength and flee with the disciples to him, wake him up and cry to him for help. Then he will show that he is awake and powerful—he can calm the wind and the water, curb the devil, his helpers and their accomplices and smash his enemies like clay pots. GOSPEL ON THE FOURTH SUNDAY AFTER EPIPHANY.[4]

NOT ALL FEAR IS OPPOSED TO FAITH. HEINRICH BULLINGER: Now it follows how Christ behaved himself in this danger, and how he dealt with his disciples, who were almost past hope. First he criticizes the imbecility of their faith, in that he teaches that they ought not to be so terrified when they are in danger, but they should continue to hope constantly with minds free from doubt for present help from the hands of their Lord and Savior. Now, a question may be raised about Christ's criticism of them, whether all fear ought to be condemned and considered to be repugnant to faith. At first, he criticized them not simply because they were afraid but because they were full of fear, and it was out of all measure. Against their fear he opposes faith and declares that he speaks of their immoderate terror, which did not so much test their faith as it shook their minds. And so it appears that not all kinds of fear are opposed to faith, for if we are afraid of nothing, then a certain carelessness of the flesh arises, so that faith languishes, sin increases and the remembrance of God vanishes away. So we see that the fear that tests faith is not evil in itself, until it becomes excessive. This excess occurs when the tranquility of faith is troubled or disquieted,

---

[2]Boys, *Exposition of the Dominical Epistles and Gospels*, 1:190*; citing Ezek 13:18 (DV); Is 57:20; Ps 135:7.
[3]For "boasters," he uses the term *Thrasones*, from Thraso, a foolish captain who appears in Terence (*Eunuchus* 3:1). See Calvin's comment on 1 Cor 2:3 (CTS 37:98; CO 49:334).

[4]Baumgart, *Postilla*, 56r; alluding to Ps 121:3-4; Mt 14:28-30; Ps 30:6-7b.

when it ought to stop and rest in the Word of God. AN ECCLESIASTICALL EXPOSITION UPON SAINT MATHEWE 8.[5]

THE MIRACLE HELPS THE OBSERVERS TO DEVELOP FAITH. JOHN CALVIN: It seems that Mark and Luke ascribe this [amazement] to the disciples, for after they said that they were rebuked by Christ, they add that they exclaimed in fear, "Who is this?" Nevertheless it is more suitable that this was said by others to whom

Christ was not yet known. Whichever interpretation we follow, the fruit of the miracle emerges here, where the glory of Christ is made known. If anyone thinks it was spoken by the disciples, the sense of the words will be that his divine power is sufficiently proved in that the wind and the sea obey him. Because, however, it is more probable that these words were spoken by others, the Evangelists teach that this miracle frightened their minds and prepared a certain reverence for Christ which would help their faith. COMMENTARY ON A HARMONY OF THE GOSPELS.[6]

---

[5]Marlorat, ed., *Catholike and Ecclesiasticall Exposition of the Holy Gospell After S. Mathewe*, 166*.

[6]CO 45:266 (cf. CTS 31:426).

8:26-39 HEALING A GERASENE MAN
FROM DEMON POSSESSION

²⁶*Then they sailed to the country of the Gerasenes,ᵃ which is opposite Galilee. ²⁷When Jesusᵇ had stepped out on land, there met him a man from the city who had demons. For a long time he had worn no clothes, and he had not lived in a house but among the tombs. ²⁸When he saw Jesus, he cried out and fell down before him and said with a loud voice, "What have you to do with me, Jesus, Son of the Most High God? I beg you, do not torment me." ²⁹For he had commanded the unclean spirit to come out of the man. (For many a time it had seized him. He was kept under guard and bound with chains and shackles, but he would break the bonds and be driven by the demon into the desert.) ³⁰Jesus then asked him, "What is your name?" And he said, "Legion," for many demons had entered him. ³¹And they begged him not to command them to depart into the abyss. ³²Now a large herd of pigs was feeding there on the hillside, and they begged him to let them enter these. So he gave them permission. ³³Then the* demons came out of the man and entered the pigs, and the herd rushed down the steep bank into the lake and drowned.

³⁴*When the herdsmen saw what had happened, they fled and told it in the city and in the country. ³⁵Then people went out to see what had happened, and they came to Jesus and found the man from whom the demons had gone, sitting at the feet of Jesus, clothed and in his right mind, and they were afraid. ³⁶And those who had seen it told them how the demon-possessedᶜ man had been healed. ³⁷Then all the people of the surrounding country of the Gerasenes asked him to depart from them, for they were seized with great fear. So he got into the boat and returned. ³⁸The man from whom the demons had gone begged that he might be with him, but Jesus sent him away, saying, ³⁹"Return to your home, and declare how much God has done for you." And he went away, proclaiming throughout the whole city how much Jesus had done for him.*

a Some manuscripts *Gadarenes*; others *Gergesenes*; also verse 37   b Greek *he*; also verses 38, 42   c Greek *daimonizomai*; elsewhere rendered *oppressed by demons*

OVERVIEW: The story of the Gerasene man who was healed from demon possession serves largely to explain more about the devil and his power and how he can and cannot interact with human beings (and animals as well). The demons tormented this man among the tombs, reminding him constantly of death, but they could not destroy him. Our commentators emphasize that these demons even had to ask Jesus permission to enter the herd of pigs—that they wanted to enter pigs reveals their beastly and foul nature. Yes, the demons acknowledge that Jesus is the Son of God, but like all the reprobate they do not believe that he has come for their own salvation but rather to torment and bother them—they were terrified by the sight of him, because the knew what sort of punishment they deserved. The demons are not nearly as powerful as God, and they are under his authority—a comforting thought!

However, should Jesus not be criticized for allowing these pigs to be destroyed? What about the owner of the herd? Was it not wrong for Jesus to allow his property to be destroyed? Zwingli addresses this point, arguing that all property belongs, in the beginning and the end, to God, and thus private property is a result of sin and selfishness. Returning to communal ownership, however, is not possible, as human beings will always be selfish and want to own things for themselves. But we should recognize all our possessions as gifts of God and realize that if they are taken away from us, it is because of our own guilt. The fact that Jesus asked the Gerasene man to stay shows that if we bear witness to the gospel where we are, it will bear fruit, even if it is among people who are actively opposed to it.

8:26-27 Jesus Is Met by the Possessed and Outcast Man

THE DEMON KEPT THE MAN AMONG THE DEAD. JOHN CALVIN: Some think that the man lived among the graves because demons are delighted by the odor of dead bodies or soothed by the scent of offerings, or perhaps because they lie in wait for souls who approach their nearby bodies. But these are foolish and stupid attempts to divine the matter. Rather, an unclean spirit kept the miserable man among the graves, that he might squander his time by continuing to frighten the man with the sad sight of death, as if he were already removed from among the living and residing with the dead. From this we learn that the devil not only tortures people during their present life but pursues them continuously up to death, and that even in death his reign over them flourishes. COMMENTARY ON A HARMONY OF THE GOSPELS.[1]

8:28-31 The Demons, Though Powerful, Fear Jesus

THE DEVIL'S POWER IS LIMITED BY GOD. EDWARD LEIGH: We may find three pieces of notable evidence of Satan's limited power in this one history of the man possessed in the region of the Gerasenes. First, he begs leave to enter into the swine. The one who afterward boasts that all the world was his, and the kingdoms thereof, does not even have power over a vile pig. Second, as soon as he enters into the swine, he immediately carries them headlong into the sea. Why did he not do so to the man possessed? Not for any love he had for him greater than the pigs, but because he was limited by God. Third, his name was Legion.

There was a whole legion of devils in the man; even though such an army of them was in one poor man, they were not able to destroy and drown him as they did the swine. ANNOTATIONS UPON SAINT LUKE 8.[2]

THE DEVILS FEAR PUNISHMENT FROM CHRIST THEIR JUDGE. PHILIPP MELANCHTHON: The devils confess Jesus to be the Christ, just like all the reprobate, but they do not believe that they may be saved by this Jesus. On the contrary, they think that he has come to torment, trouble and taunt them. But the reason why Christ does not openly reject and refuse this confession of the devil (as he did in Luke 4) is because the discord was well enough known, and in order that all evil reports might be shut down. In reference to this present passage, this ought to be sufficient, because the devil—despite humbly beseeching him—outrageously fretted and fumed against him. They complain that they are tormented (as some say) because they were forced to set this man free and at liberty whom before they had abused and controlled. Others refer this torment which they complain about to the day of judgment. But we must rather understand this place, that the devils, being made afraid by the presence of their Judge, thought about their punishment. For although Christ held his peace, their own evil consciences accused them. For just as when thieves are brought to court or the place of judgment, they imagine in their own minds what punishment they deserve, so it is that the devils and all the wicked ones tremble and quake with fear at the sight of God, the celestial, mighty and terrible Judge, as if they were already feeling the pains and torments of hell fire. Because the devils knew that Christ will be the Judge of the whole world, it is no marvel that they were afraid of torment even at the very sight of him. AN ECCLESIASTICALL EXPOSITION UPON SAINT MATHEWE 8.[3]

---

[1]CO 45:268-69 (cf. CTS 31:429).

[2]Leigh, *Annotations upon All the New Testament Philologicall and Theologicall*, 111*.
[3]Marlorat, ed., *Catholike and Ecclesiasticall Exposition of the Holy Gospell After S. Mathewe*, 169*.

8:32-33 *The Exorcism*

The Devils Reveal Their True Character by Their Request. Heinrich Bullinger: Here this foul and ugly demon shows himself for what he truly is. He does not crave pardon or forgiveness at the hands of the Lord, or any other excellent gift, but rather a foul, unclean and abominable mansion—namely, that he might have license to enter into the herd of swine. Still today the children of the devil make such requests. They ask not for holy things which are suitable for human beings but filthy and unclean things, which prove that their affections are corrupt, beastly and abominable. And as their affections are brutish, so in all points they are to be compared with brute beasts, with filthy and unclean hogs. An Ecclesiasticall Exposition upon Saint Mathewe 8.[4]

The Pigs Belong to God, Their Creator. Huldrych Zwingli: He is able to destroy the pigs because they are his. He does no one an injury if he either ruins or fetches back what is his. The private ownership of goods has its origin in faithlessness and self-love. God first made creation so that all things might be held in common, but human wickedness and selfish desire made them individually owned property. Seeing that therefore self-love and selfish desire is a distortion in all people, there is nothing that I might say about the common ownership of goods. If we were to make all things to be held in common, from that moment each one would think about private property. An example can be found in Ananias and Sapphira: what they did, everyone does. With this knowledge, we should be even more on our guard so that our selfish desire does not spread more broadly. Let us not consider ourselves to be masters of our possessions, but rather only managers and administrators of what actually belongs to God. So although we may be surprised by the Lord's action, and perhaps see it as unworthy that Christ destroys so many pigs, causing such damage to the Gerasenes, it stems from this cause: while we might think that the pigs are ours, in fact they are God's. So if God ever takes away our goods, we should recognize that this has been done because of our guilt: if he gives something to us, we should receive it with joy, giving thanks to him, and we should recognize that it comes from God's goodness. Meanwhile we should continue to fear him, so that we will not throw away by our guilt what his grace has given to us. And if on the contrary he takes something away from us, we should realize that we have abused the gifts of God and have been poor managers. In the Gospel of Luke 8.[5]

8:34-37 *The Fearful Response of the People*

The Devils Did Not Achieve Their True Purpose. Philipp Melanchthon: We see, therefore, how little the devils prevailed in attaining their purpose, or rather how greatly they were deceived in their expectation. For there can be no doubt that they were attempting to hurt Christ and the people of that country who lost their hogs; but in the end, their malice only accomplished the loss of the hogs. By this we see how wisely the divine power of God works to confound the crafty devices of Satan and to make them foolish and impotent, so that his malice is constrained to serve contrary to his own opinion and will, to the glory of God and to the setting forth of his praise. An Ecclesiasticall Exposition upon Saint Mathewe 8.[6]

The People Were Disturbed by the Event. Konrad Pellikan: Those who believed what the herdsmen were reporting went out that they might see evidence of such an incredible thing. And now they see that the herd, which only a little before had been very numerous, had disappeared, and they found the man who earlier had been possessed by devils, and was known to all on account of his overt

---

[4]Marlorat, ed., *Catholike and Ecclesiasticall Exposition of the Holy Gospell After S. Mathewe*, 170*.

[5]*D. Hvldrichi Zvinglii in Plerosqve Novi Testamenti Libros*, 231; citing Acts 5:1-11.
[6]Marlorat, ed., *Catholike and Ecclesiasticall Exposition of the Holy Gospell After S. Mathewe*, 170*.

savagery, now calm and of sane mind, clothed and sitting at the feet of Jesus. He who before had committed crimes against everyone because of the evil spirits was now by a gift of the Lord transformed to an eager piety, sitting calmly and mildly with a most gentle spirit. . . . Then a certain fear seized them all, when it would instead have been proper for them to glorify God and embrace his power, who had restored to health one so deplorably wretched. . . .

They were eager for Jesus to leave their region, because they were afraid of his power but did not understand his goodness. They were more greatly shaken by the loss of the pigs than by the man restored to health. Nevertheless they did not dare to throw him out but made a public request that he would withdraw to their borders, they were all so seized by fear. And so Jesus, rather than throwing pearls before swine or giving dogs what is holy, returned to the ship. COMMENTARY IN LUKE 8:34-37.[7]

8:38-39 *The Joyful Response of the Man*

THE DEMONIAC PREACHES TO THOSE WHO REJECTED JESUS. DESIDERIUS ERASMUS: Jesus did not allow the demoniac to join him but said to him, "Return to your own house, that by the retelling of your story and by the sight of you, everyone may certainly recognize what you were before and what you are now through the kindness and favor of God. Your friends reject me, but at least you can testify to this among them, that they have hindered themselves by driving me out." The man obeyed the Lord's commands, and going into Decapolis and throughout every city, he announced to everyone what great benefits he had received from Jesus.

And this was the beginning of the preaching of the gospel among those rude and wicked people, who were very much like the pigs into which the demons fled. And this preaching of the demoniac was not completely unprofitable, for many did believe and were amazed. By this example the Lord Jesus taught us a great deal, especially that the grace of the gospel should be offered to everyone, no matter how impious they might be, although it should not be forced on those who are unwilling or who reject it. But on the contrary, if we leave them alone, we might leave behind in some degree a spark of true piety that some day perhaps might shine out at the right time. PARAPHRASE ON THE GOSPEL OF LUKE 8:39.[8]

---

[7]Pellikan, *In Sacrosancta Quatuor Evangelia*, 104 (cf. LB 7:364); alluding to Mt 7:6.

[8]Erasmus, *In Evangelivm Lvce Paraphrasis*, 04r (LB 7:364-65).

8:40-56 THE RAISING OF JAIRUS'S DAUGHTER AND THE HEALING OF THE BLEEDING WOMAN

⁴⁰Now when Jesus returned, the crowd welcomed him, for they were all waiting for him. ⁴¹And there came a man named Jairus, who was a ruler of the synagogue. And falling at Jesus' feet, he implored him to come to his house, ⁴²for he had an only daughter, about twelve years of age, and she was dying.

As Jesus went, the people pressed around him. ⁴³And there was a woman who had had a discharge of blood for twelve years, and though she had spent all her living on physicians,ᵃ she could not be healed by anyone. ⁴⁴She came up behind him and touched the fringe of his garment, and immediately her discharge of blood ceased. ⁴⁵And Jesus said, "Who was it that touched me?" When all denied it, Peterᵇ said, "Master, the crowds surround you and are pressing in on you!" ⁴⁶But Jesus said, "Someone touched me, for I perceive that power has gone out from me." ⁴⁷And when the woman saw that she was not hidden, she came trembling, and falling down before him declared in the presence of all the people why she had touched him, and how she had been immediately healed. ⁴⁸And he said to her, "Daughter, your faith has made you well; go in peace."

⁴⁹While he was still speaking, someone from the ruler's house came and said, "Your daughter is dead; do not trouble the Teacher any more." ⁵⁰But Jesus on hearing this answered him, "Do not fear; only believe, and she will be well." ⁵¹And when he came to the house, he allowed no one to enter with him, except Peter and John and James, and the father and mother of the child. ⁵²And all were weeping and mourning for her, but he said, "Do not weep, for she is not dead but sleeping." ⁵³And they laughed at him, knowing that she was dead. ⁵⁴But taking her by the hand he called, saying, "Child, arise." ⁵⁵And her spirit returned, and she got up at once. And he directed that something should be given her to eat. ⁵⁶And her parents were amazed, but he charged them to tell no one what had happened.

a Some manuscripts omit *and though she had spent all her living on physicians,* b Some manuscripts add *and those who were with him*

OVERVIEW: These two intertwined healing stories are about more than just Jesus' works, according to our commentators—they are about faith. Jesus' power in these miracles does offer proof that he is the Messiah and comfort that he is the Lord over all disease and even death. But faith is the center of these stories. Jairus has weak faith; the sick woman has strong faith. Jesus accommodates himself to both. The woman's faith precedes and makes possible her healing—according to Schwenckfeld, it is not a common human touch that does it, but only the "touch of faith" that can access Jesus' healing power. Jairus's faith is buoyed by this healing but falters again at the bad news from home. Jesus reminds him that he should just believe. The laughing mourners are expelled from the home because they have no faith. Likewise, all those in the world who see Jesus' words and actions as foolishness are expelled from the church and will be eternally lost and condemned. In raising the little girl from death to life, Jesus revealed his divine power to increase and confirm the faith of the parents and his disciples, but he also gives comfort to faithful hearts even now, for all Christians will carry the cross at some point. But we should know that such punishment is a "fatherly rod"—God always disciplines the children whom he loves (Heb 12:3-11).

8:40-42 Jairus's Daughter Is Near Death

HAVING ONLY ONE TEMPLE HELPED WITH UNIFORMITY OF RELIGION. JOHN BOYS: This Jairus was the ruler of a synagogue. In order that you might better understand what office this was, I must inform you that there was among all Jews only one temple, where the people were commanded to celebrate their solemn feasts and offer up their sacrifices to God. And there was only one temple for the purpose of the preservation of unity in piety, that there might be only one religion, of only one God, in only one temple. We should note here that uniformity in discipline is a hedge to unity in doctrine. Where laws and injunctions of order are despised and everyone is left to himself, many times there are as many sects as there are cities, and almost as many gospels as gossips. On the contrary, when all things in the church are done in an orderly fashion, when the Christian magistrate enjoins one kind of discipline in outward ceremonies for the public worship of God, there for the most part a union in law breeds a union in love, a conformity in fashion a uniformity in faith, endeavoring to keep the unity of the spirit in the bond of peace, following the truth in love. This I take to be the true reason why God's Israel had but one tabernacle and one temple. But there were synagogues in every town, where divine prayers were offered and God's holy Word was read and expounded every sabbath, as Saint Luke records in Acts 15:21. And for this purpose there was a convent or college of students and sons of the prophets, among whom Jairus was a ruler. THE TWENTY-FOURTH SUNDAY AFTER TRINITY.[1]

OUR LIVES CAN CHANGE IN AN INSTANT.

CASPAR HUBERINUS: Pay special attention here to the amazing way of this world, how momentary and fleeting are all joys, entertainments, pleasures of the flesh, amusements and luxury here on earth. In the first example, Jairus is leader of the school, held in great honor and esteem. He has happiness, money, advantages, property, spirit, wife, child, house, servants. Second, his young daughter also has joys, entertainments, health, life, advantages, love, a nurse and all sorts of amusements. And

third, the woman lived in happiness for a long time, possessing health, money and property. She was a fine and honorable matron, a distinguished woman of means.

Now all of these things are very fine and good gifts, very useful and essential, but uncertain and changeable for everyone, as we see here. Jairus, in his highest joy and dignity, becomes in a day, in one hour, so full of sadness, grief and sorrow on account of his only dear little daughter who is dying that he says goodbye to his courage, forgets all his happiness and considers as nothing all honor. The little girl also forgets all joys, and she is like a little rose that blooms in its lovely youth but then falls, like a flower in the field. That woman, who was in her best age and health, loses all her energy, beauty, strength, health, riches and charm. Our whole lives are fashioned in this way, and that is the wonderful course of our entire being. When everything is at its best, then we fall down quickly, and all lasting things with us, like a flower. And when we have lived a long time and our life was precious, so it was however only trouble and work. Therefore a true and pious Christian should learn from this that he should not place his hope in uncertain riches, nor should he be presumptuous because of his ability or rely on his strength and health, for all of it is changeable. ON THE TWENTY-FOURTH SUNDAY AFTER TRINITY.[2]

JAIRUS'S FAITH WAS WEAK, BUT CHRIST'S MERCY IS STRONG.

PHILIPP MELANCHTHON: Jairus believed that the physical presence of Christ, as of some holy man, might profit his daughter. Mary and Martha did as well, as they said to Christ, "Lord, if you had been here, our brother would not have died." Likewise, Naaman the Syrian despised the command of Elisha, because he did not come in person to him to touch the leprosy. So also another one of the rulers of the people said to Christ, "Sir, come down before my child dies." We see therefore that the faith of this

---

[1]Boys, *Exposition of the Dominical Epistles and Gospels*, 4:215-16*; citing Deut 16; 1 Cor 14:40; Eph 4:3, 15.

[2]Huberinus, *Postilla Teütsch*, 2:Ii3r-v; citing Ps 103:15-16; Is 40:6; Ps 90:10; 1 Tim 6; 1 Cor 7.

ruler was very weak, but despite this, as we shall soon hear, he was not forsaken. . . .

Now we see all the wonderful clemency and gentleness of Christ. The Jews excluded from the temple all those who confessed Christ, and yet for all that Christ does not cast this in the ruler's teeth, nor does he say to him, "Why do you come to me, whom you hate and abhor? Now that you are oppressed and grieved, you run to me for help!" Moreover, he did not bring up any objections to him about the weakness and imperfection of his faith, saying, "Do you think that I am not able to restore your daughter to you without the laying on of my hands? How should I deal with such a person?" But he did not say any of these things, but, rising quietly, he granted the asker his request. AN ECCLESIASTICALL EXPOSITION UPON SAINT MATHEWE 9.[3]

8:43-48 *The Healing of the Bleeding Woman*

THIS MIRACLE STRESSES THAT CHRIST IS LORD OVER DISEASES. HEINRICH BULLINGER: The story was begun but then broken off in the middle, and the miracle which happened along the way is introduced and, as it were, inserted. As the history of the leper and of Peter's wife's mother, sick with a fever, both teach and declare that Christ is the Physician and Lord over all diseases, so also this history of the woman troubled with an issue of blood for so many years teaches the same. It declares to us that there is nothing so incurable and far gone that cannot be healed by the virtue and power of Christ. The Evangelists expressly say that this flow of blood continued for twelve whole years, while all that time she was seeking a remedy, so much so that she spent all her wealth on medicines: by this circumstance, the glory of the miracle appears even greater. AN ECCLESIASTICALL EXPOSITION UPON SAINT MATHEWE 9.[4]

THE MIRACLE OFFERS DIVINE PROOF THAT CHRIST IS THE MESSIAH. AUGUSTIN MARLORAT: Mark says that when the woman heard of Jesus, she came into the pressing crowd behind him. There is mention made that she heard of Jesus, and no doubt she had heard of him from those who were talking about him, and so because of his fame she was moved to seek healing. Now it was necessary that those things which she had heard of Christ were not common or human, or such reports as are normally spread about physicians and their cures. For by these reports she could not have conceived any hope of health, having so often failed to find healing among physicians. . . . But what were those things that were so divine? Surely they were the same things that he did everywhere and by which he declared himself to be one for whom there was nothing too hard, who could heal all kinds of diseases, and brought the conclusion that he wanted to help the misery of humankind. Therefore they showed that he is the true Messiah, whom God promised through the prophets, to come in these later times, who received all with gentleness and good will, who despised no one, who offered himself to all; to be short, who was the saving health of all humankind. AN ECCLESIASTICALL EXPOSITION UPON SAINT MATHEWE 9.[5]

THE DISEASE HAD PLAGUED HER A LONG TIME. THOMAS BECON: She was afraid to make a direct intercession to Christ for her health, but instead, through humility and lowliness of mind she came behind, as though Christ would not know it, and touched his garment. And as soon as she believed, she immediately began to be better, and the issue of blood was stopped, whereas before she had tried everything and spent all her money, yet found no healing but grew daily worse and worse, as Mark also testifies in his Gospel. THE TWENTY-THIRD SUNDAY AFTER TRINITY SUNDAY.[6]

---

[3]Marlorat, ed., *Catholike and Ecclesiasticall Exposition of the Holy Gospell After S. Mathewe*, 186*; quoting Jn 11:21; 4:49; alluding to 2 Kings 5:10-12.
[4]Marlorat, ed., *Catholike and Ecclesiasticall Exposition of the Holy Gospell After S. Mathewe*, 187*.
[5]Marlorat, ed., *Catholike and Ecclesiasticall Exposition of the Holy Gospell After S. Mathewe*, 187*; citing Mk 5:27.
[6]Becon, *A new Postil (second parte)*, 182v.

HER FAITH HEALS HER MORE THAN THE TOUCH. KASPAR VON SCHWENCKFELD: This is the reason why Christ so severely questioned who had touched him, for he had felt the power go out from him. Namely, the Lord Jesus Christ perceives the grace with his outgoing power and wants it to be confessed before the whole world. Peter and the other disciples only thought that Christ was speaking of a common, simple, human touch, but he chiefly means the touch of faith, which comes from the faith of a believing heart. Only this kind of faith can draw the power of Christ to itself and bring Christ fully and completely into heart and soul.

The poor woman was afraid and trembled, for the Lord asked very formally and looked around him to see who had done it. She knew what had happened to her, and she came and announced before all of the people why she had touched him, and how as soon as she had done so she was healed. But she was afraid, because she was an unclean person and had touched the pure Lord Christ against the requirements of the law. But because she reached for him out of faith and the necessity of her body, the Lord comforted her and said, "Be comforted, my daughter, your faith has helped you." INTERPRETATION OF THE GOSPEL, MATTHEW 9, ON THE TWENTY-FOURTH SUNDAY AFTER TRINITY.[7]

8:49-56 The Death and Raising of Jairus's Daughter

THE RULER'S WEAK FAITH IS REVEALED. AUGUSTIN MARLORAT: Now let us return to the history of the ruler of the synagogue. Concerning that matter, Mark writes, "While he was still speaking, there came from the ruler's house some who said, 'Your daughter is dead. Why trouble the Teacher any further?'" We have already shown how small and weak a faith this ruler had, but how by the example of the woman healed previously his faith was greatly built up and confirmed. Now again by these messengers, he was made as weak

and feeble as before. By this example, the temptation of faith is exhibited to us, how faith is resisted by the judgment and sense of reason. We see it in that his faith is built and lifted up by the words of Christ which he spoke to the woman, "Go in peace, your faith has made you well," and so he conceived in his mind greater things of Christ than he did before. But then when this message was brought by his servants, his trust was laid in the dust, because he never managed to believe that Christ, by his power, was able to raise up the dead. But what did Christ say to this? Did he altogether reject the man for wavering in his faith? Not at all. For hearing the word that was brought, he said to the ruler of the synagogue, "Fear not, only believe." AN ECCLESIASTICALL EXPOSITION UPON SAINT MATHEWE 9.[8]

PEOPLE STILL LAUGH AT CHRIST, DISBELIEVING HIM. JOHANN SPANGENBERG: When he saw the tumult of the people and the pipers and their great moaning and crying, he said, "Why do you cry and make a scene? Calm down, for the girl is not dead but asleep." And they laughed at him, for they knew very well that she was dead. They thought, "What kind of doctor is this? Does he not know the difference between sleep and death?" But for Christ, she was asleep, because he could more easily awaken her from death than a person could wake someone up who was sleeping.

Do we still see such derision and mockery of the words and works of Christ in the world? Of course. The world today does not see the words and works of Christ as anything but pure folly and foolishness. It mocks and laughs at everything that Christ teaches and does. It is unbelievable for the world that a dead body, that lies there misshapen, cold, rigid and smelly, could be asleep. If it could believe the creed's article about creation, that God is almighty, then of course it could also believe the article about the resurrection of the dead.

What did the people achieve with their derision and mockery? Christ drove them all out

---

[7]CS 10:615.

[8]Marlorat, ed., *Catholike and Ecclesiasticall Exposition of the Holy Gospell After S. Mathewe*, 189-90*; citing Mk 5:35.

of the house and did not consider them worthy to see such a wonderful work of God with their own eyes. This is also how it will go with our adversaries, whose hearts laugh when they hear that anyone despises, rejects, profanes and slanders Christ in his holy Word. Christ will also drive these ones out of the house of the Christian community and will "give them up to a debased mind," blind and stubborn, so that they will never again participate in the secret of the suffering and dying of Christ, his blessed death and resurrection, but instead will be eternally lost and condemned. For the first psalm calls that person blessed "who does not walk in the counsel of the wicked, or stand in the way of sinners or sit in the seat of mockers." GOSPEL ON THE TWENTY-FOURTH SUNDAY AFTER TRINITY.[9]

GOD DISCIPLINES HIS CHILDREN. JOHANN BAUMGART (POMARIUS): When he reached the home, he found a sorrowful situation and an uproar with the funeral musicians. So he took the father and mother with him, grasped the girl by the hand and spoke a clear word to her in Syriac, which was the common dialect there, so that all suspicion of fraud would cease. He raised the girl and told them to give her something to eat, as proof that she was really alive.

With this the Lord comforts all faithful, hard-pressed and frightened hearts and consciences. He looks for a contrite heart and a humble spirit—he does not look down on them, but his eyes look at their faith. To those who believe in his name, he makes a gift that they become the children of God, to the comfort of all poor and miserable sinners. And they are God's sons and daughters even with the cross and with sorrow, for such punishment is a fatherly rod, for when he loves a person, he will discipline them. He corrects every child whom he adopts, and the dearer the child, the harsher the rod. Also the more pious the Christians, the heavier the crosses they

must bear, but those who endure this discipline are raised up by God as his children. GOSPEL ON THE TWENTY-FOURTH SUNDAY AFTER TRINITY.[10]

CHRIST RAISED THE GIRL WITH DIVINE POWER. PHILIPP MELANCHTHON: These words are spoken to amplify and set forth the power of Christ, for he raised one who was already dead, and contrary to the manner of the prophets, he raised her by commanding her with his word, not by prayer as they did, but he so raised her that she was suddenly alive, and not only alive but also walking, free from all sickness and disease. What physician can so raise up anybody that is sick, that he would get up and soon begin to walk? We do read that the prophet Elisha raised up one who was dead, but in a far different manner than Christ did here. Also we read how Peter raised up from death a woman who was a disciple, but not without prayer before. Moreover, the girl is said to be twelve years old, so that no one might think she was an infant and unable to walk. AN ECCLESIASTICALL EXPOSITION UPON SAINT MATHEWE 9.[11]

CAPERNAUM DID NOT DESERVE FURTHER REVELATIONS OF CHRIST. JOHN LIGHTFOOT: A good while ago, Jesus had proclaimed a sad doom against Capernaum: "And you, Capernaum, will you be lifted up to the skies? No, you will go down to the depths." This was spoken generally of the city inhabitants, who although they had seen and heard many things, because it was Christ's own city or the place of his habitation, yet they did not believe. And this may be partly the reason why, when he had raised this dead girl, he bids her parents keep the matter quiet; for that city had justly forfeited all such revelations of him. Yet for all his proclaiming that sad fate against the city, he returned there frequently and did not forsake his lodgings there; partly because there were some there who, for all the unbelief of the general

---

[9]Spangenberg, *Postilla . . . von Ostern biß auffs Aduent*, CLXX-VIIIr-v; citing Rom 1:28; Ps 1:1.

[10]Baumgart, *Postilla*, 268v; citing Is 66:2; Ps 51:17; Jn 1:12-13; Prov 1:29-33; Heb 12:5-11; Rev 3:19.
[11]Marlorat, ed., *Catholike and Ecclesiasticall Exposition of the Holy Gospell After S. Mathewe*, 189-90*; citing 2 Kings 4; Acts 9.

population, belonged to him and believed in him; and partly because he had no reason to remove his habitation on account of their unbelief or to give up his dwelling for the wickedness of others. For where could he go to reside, where he would not live among the same sort of people? THE HAR-MONY OF THE NEW TESTAMENT, SECTION 41.[12]

---

[12]Lightfoot, *Harmony, Chronicle and Order of the New Testament,* 34*; quoting Mt 11:23.

9:1-9 JESUS SENDS OUT THE TWELVE

And he called the twelve together and gave them power and authority over all demons and to cure diseases, ²and he sent them out to proclaim the kingdom of God and to heal. ³And he said to them, "Take nothing for your journey, no staff, nor bag, nor bread, nor money; and do not have two tunics.ᵃ ⁴And whatever house you enter, stay there, and from there depart. ⁵And wherever they do not receive you, when you leave that town shake off the dust from your feet as a testimony against them." ⁶And they departed and went through the villages, preaching the gospel and healing everywhere.

⁷Now Herod the tetrarch heard about all that was happening, and he was perplexed, because it was said by some that John had been raised from the dead, ⁸by some that Elijah had appeared, and by others that one of the prophets of old had risen. ⁹Herod said, "John I beheaded, but who is this about whom I hear such things?" And he sought to see him.

a Greek *chiton*, a long garment worn under the cloak next to the skin

OVERVIEW: For this trip, Jesus sent them out without any gear. So is the implication that the church's ministers should not be prepared with any possessions? Not at all, for this initial journey was a trial run. The twelve apostles were now distinguished from Jesus' other followers by the gifts of the Spirit and the ability to heal and cast out demons. They were sent to preach, but only what they had learned from Jesus. Jesus' intention with this test was that the apostles should learn to rely on God rather than on themselves, and so that they would start to become accustomed to some trials and tribulations. Once they placed their full reliance on God, then it would be acceptable, as Jesus allowed later, for them to be more fully outfitted for their journeys. People today have so many clothes and other rich possessions, these commentators lament, that they forget to be grateful to God for everything they have. But true Christians should be satisfied with simple clothes and food and not chase after worldly pleasure. Jesus also taught the apostles how they should behave along the way: they should stay at only one home, implying that they should move on quickly, so as not to burden their host; they should stay with worthy people, those who would receive them and gladly hear their message; and they should avoid those who reject them and give notice of God's vengeance against them by shaking the dust off their feet.

9:1-2 Jesus Imbues the Apostles with Power and Authority

THE APOSTLES NOW RECEIVE THE GIFTS OF THE SPIRIT. JOHN LIGHTFOOT: The Twelve had been ordained as apostles for a long while, and all that while had been with Christ as novices, to see his works and learn his doctrine. Since their selection as apostles it is observable how much Christ applied himself to teaching doctrine, that they might learn the gospel of the kingdom and have stored up what to preach when he should send them forth. Up to this point they had been learners, and as for the gifts of the Spirit they did not differ at all from the rest who followed Jesus. But now he gives them the power of healing and casting out devils, and now is the power of miracles restored. So they cured diseases by the Spirit, but they preached not by Spirit but taught only what they had learned from the mouth of Christ. THE HARMONY OF THE NEW TESTAMENT, SECTION 45.[1]

---

[1]Lightfoot, *Harmony, Chronicle and Order of the New Testament*, 35*.

9:3-5 Instructions for the Journey

THE APOSTLES NEEDED TO DO WITHOUT, FOR A WHILE. MARTIN BUCER: Christ wanted his disciples at least once to have trials and tough experiences, so that nothing should be lacking for them to be faithful ministers, and therefore he sent them forth naked, as it were, and destitute of these things, but not for a very long time. For we read that Paul took a cloak for his journey, and Peter was found to have a sword. And therefore we read, as it were, an exposition of this passage and of the mind of Christ when he said, "When I sent you out with no moneybag or knapsack or sandals, did you lack anything?" And they said, "Nothing." And so he said to them, "But now let the one who has a moneybag take it, and likewise a knapsack." And so, first, we understand that it was only commanded for a time, and second, it was commanded in order that the apostles (as it was said even then) might understand that nothing was lacking for the faithful ministers of Christ. AN ECCLESIASTICALL EXPOSITION UPON SAINT MATHEWE 10.[2]

ONE COAT IS ENOUGH. THE BOOK OF HOMILIES: Our Savior Christ directed his disciples that they should not have two coats. But unlike his disciples, most people have closets so full of clothing that they do not even know how many sorts they have. This caused Saint James to pronounce a terrible curse against such wealthy and worldly folks: "Come now, rich people, weep and wail for the wretchedness that will come to you. Your riches are corrupt and your garments are moth-eaten. . . . You have lived on the earth in luxury and in pleasure; you have nourished your hearts, as in the day of slaughter." Notice well that Saint James has called them miserable, despite all of their riches and plenty of apparel, because they pamper their bodies to their own destruction. How was the rich glutton better off for all his fine fare

and costly apparel? Did he not nourish himself only to be tormented later in hell fire? Therefore let us learn to content ourselves in having simple food and clothing, as Saint Paul teaches, because "those who want to be rich fall into temptation and are trapped by many senseless and harmful desires that drown people in ruin and destruction." HOMILY 18: AGAINST EXCESS OF APPAREL.[3]

THEY SHOULD STAY IN ONE HOUSE. JOHN CALVIN: This also is related to haste, for if they would have stayed for a longer time in a place, they would have had to change lodging, so as not to burden any host too much. And so, when Christ orders them to stay at their first lodging the whole time, it means that they should be quick, and when they make the gospel known in one town, they should soon run on to the next one. COMMENTARY ON A HARMONY OF THE GOSPELS.[4]

THE APOSTLES SHOULD AVOID THE UNWORTHY. PHILIPP MELANCHTHON: Before this, the Lord instructed his apostles how they should shun and avoid the unworthy and instead associate with those who are worthy. Now he teaches them what they should do if they chance to come to any who are unworthy and despisers of the grace of God. He had told them how they should behave toward the worthy, and now he speaks with them about the unworthy. First of all he sets before them a mark or token which they must respect, and according to which they must judge the worthy with whom they stay and the unworthy from whom they depart. Namely, if they are received and heard, or not received and not heard. By this means they may discover quite well who is worthy and who is not. And he not only commands his disciples to depart from those who with ingratitude reject the grace offered to them but also to shake the dust off their feet against them, and so to testify what horrible punishment will come in time

---

[2]Marlorat, ed., *Catholike and Ecclesiasticall Exposition of the Holy Gospell After S. Mathewe*, 205*; alluding to 2 Tim 4:13; Jn 18:10; quoting Lk 22:35.

[3]*Certain Sermons or Homilies* (1852), 285*; cf. Mt 10:10; quoting Jas 5:1, 2, 5; 1 Tim 6:9; alluding to Lk 16:19-25.
[4]CO 45:277-78 (cf. CTS 31:445).

on those who despise the gospel. By this severe announcement of the vengeance of God, Christ also wants to comfort his disciples, so that they will not be dismayed and discouraged by the contempt for his doctrine which they will encounter, and so that they will not be deterred from their mission by the ingratitude of the world. We see how Paul grasped this consolation firmly, and boldly despised the stubborn attitude against authority which people have, that he might go with constancy even through the midst of troubles. He boasts that he is a sweet aroma to Christ but the aroma of death to those who perish. Moreover, this place teaches how much the Lord esteems the gospel, and rightly so, for it is an excellent treasure, and those who reject it when it is offered to them are too unthankful. And inasmuch as it is the scepter of his kingdom, it cannot be despised and rejected without reproach to him. An Ecclesiasticall Exposition upon Saint Mathewe 10.[5]

9:6 The Twelve Depart to Spread the Good News

THIS WAS A TEMPORARY COMMISSION. JOHN CALVIN: Matthew silently passes over what the apostles did. Mark and Luke relate that they proceeded to execute the commission they had received. From their words it seems very clear—as I have said—that the office with which Christ then entrusted them was temporary. Indeed it lasted

only a few days. They tell us that the apostles went through the cities and villages. There is no doubt that they soon returned to their Master. COMMENTARY ON A HARMONY OF THE GOSPELS.[6]

9:7-9 Herod Is Confused About Jesus and His Power

HEROD WAS CURIOUS AND FEARFUL OF JESUS' POTENTIAL THREAT. DESIDERIUS ERASMUS: Herod was himself quite afraid—if John, whom he had killed, was now come back to life, and considering it incredible that a man once dead should now be restored to life, he said, "I beheaded John, and now that he is done away with, I thought no one would still live who would be bold enough to do such great things. And who is this man, of whom I have been hearing such great things, far greater things than even John could do?" Consequently he sought an opportunity to see him, not that he might be improved by it but that he might satisfy his curiosity, or to see if it might be good that he should do the same to him that he had done to John. However, because Jesus was not ignorant of his plans, he did not give an opportunity to him. For he did not come that he might gratify the eyes of an impious prince by his miracles but that he might lead simple folk to health, nor did it please him to be beheaded, because he had predestined himself to the exalted standard of the cross. PARAPHRASE ON THE GOSPEL OF LUKE 9:9.[7]

---

[5]Marlorat, ed., *Catholike and Ecclesiasticall Exposition of the Holy Gospell After S. Mathewe*, 207-8*; alluding to 2 Cor 2:15-16; Ps 45:6.

[6]CTS 32:5* (CO 45:297-98).
[7]Erasmus, *In Evangelivm Lvce Paraphrasis*, 07v (LB 7:367-68).

9:10-17 THE FEEDING OF THE FIVE THOUSAND

¹⁰*On their return the apostles told him all that they had done. And he took them and withdrew apart to a town called Bethsaida.* ¹¹*When the crowds learned it, they followed him, and he welcomed them and spoke to them of the kingdom of God and cured those who had need of healing.* ¹²*Now the day began to wear away, and the twelve came and said to him, "Send the crowd away to go into the surrounding villages and countryside to find lodging and get provisions, for we are here in a desolate place."* ¹³*But he said to them, "You give them something to eat." They said, "We have no more than five loaves and two fish—unless we are to go and buy food for all these people."* ¹⁴*For there were about five thousand men. And he said to his disciples, "Have them sit down in groups of about fifty each."* ¹⁵*And they did so, and had them all sit down.* ¹⁶*And taking the five loaves and the two fish, he looked up to heaven and said a blessing over them. Then he broke the loaves and gave them to the disciples to set before the crowd.* ¹⁷*And they all ate and were satisfied. And what was left over was picked up, twelve baskets of broken pieces.*

OVERVIEW: The feeding of the five thousand is one of the most recognizable miracle stories in the New Testament. It appears in all four Gospels—the only miracle (besides the resurrection) to do so. The story amazes in its staggering scope; it is not surprising that such a large crowd, five thousand and maybe more, would come to hear Jesus, but it is remarkable that sufficient food for such a crowd could be created out of little more than several loaves and a few dried fish. There are several central points in this story for our interpreters: the disciples' lack of faith and understanding; the miraculous expansion of a little food to a vast amount, even to the point of copious leftovers; and the breaking of the bread and the extension of this feeding miracle to the eucharistic feeding that we experience.

Most of the crowd came out of curiosity, for entertainment or to see what they might receive from Jesus, but very few out of real faith. While their hearts lacked spiritual hunger, their bellies did not lack physical hunger. The disciples thus advise Jesus to send the crowd to nearby towns for food. While they sounded wise, as Erasmus notes, they were quite weak in faith—was Jesus so absent-minded that he needed their advice? Did they not understand that Jesus could feed these people if he wanted to, after all the evidence they had seen of his divine power? They could not feed the people, but Jesus could. When Christ requires anything of us that we cannot perform, our commentators assert, it is meant to reveal to us our weakness and inability, and to push us to turn to him and to rely on him for everything. This was a law-gospel moment for the disciples.

For our interpreters, the breaking of the bread is a sacramental moment in this miracle and it brings to mind not only Jesus' mealtime habit but also the breaking of the bread in the Eucharist and the miraculous sharing of that bread, Christ's body given for us. Bread must be broken for it to be shared, and the participation of all the hungry people in this miraculous feeding represents how we are spiritually fed in the Lord's Supper.

9:10-11 *Jesus Preaches to and Heals the People*

THEY FOLLOWED HIM WITH THEIR FEET BUT NOT THEIR HEARTS. HULDRYCH ZWINGLI: And a great many of these followed him more based on emotion rather than on sound judgment. We are all eager and desirous of new things; we embrace shadows in the place of truth. Nothing is trustworthy or lasting in the world, and so the human mind is seized by weariness for this life. It was certainly part of God's creation that no creature is able to rest if he rejects his own Creator. If the human mind would have been steadfast in God, he would not have had to suffer that various things would lead him away from God. When we are accustomed to one way, we find that another is not good enough: whoever wanders through life in uncertainty shows the proof of a fickle and curious mind. Thus the people of Judea follow Christ with their feet, but they do not follow him with their hearts, for they soon desert him, crying out, "Lift him up! Crucify him!" So make your soul strong, so that it does not move in whichever direction the wind might blow. Those who follow Christ wherever he goes and hear his Word are not without merit. Therefore Christ takes them back, however imperfect and ignorant they may be. Anywhere people hear the Word of God, hope can be entertained for them. In the Gospel of Luke 9.[1]

The Gospel Kingdom. Huldrych Zwingli: "He spoke to them about the kingdom of God." That is, about the gospel. The kingdom of God is wherever God dwells in a person through grace and justice. Christ drew them out of the kingdom of Satan into his own kingdom, and he taught them the will of God. First he teaches, then he heals. The Word of God belongs to the care of souls, for faith comes from hearing, but nevertheless it is given within by the Spirit alone. In the Gospel of Luke 9.[2]

9:12-13 The Disciples Urge Jesus to Disperse the Crowd

The Disciples Seem Smart but Are Stupid. Johann Spangenberg: Here the disciples give proof of their intelligence, for there was a very large crowd of people here—around five thousand men, not counting women and children. Evening was coming, and they were out in the wilderness, far away from other people, because there were no towns or villages nearby. They did not have fire or water, no granary or bakery, and they had only five loaves of bread and two fish. And they would have naturally considered the way of the people, how the people acted in the desert with Moses, for when they had nothing to eat or drink, they often wanted to stone him. Therefore it seemed best to them that Christ send the people away from him. It is as if they should say, "We see that you have remarkable concern for the people, especially that their souls are fed, but you do not care at all if their stomachs are also fed. But what does it matter if the soul is fed, if the body dies of hunger? Do you think that if they stay with you in the wilderness for a long time and listen to you, that a roasted dove will just fly into their mouths? Look, it is already evening, and we are in the wilderness. The people will be hungry, and we have nothing to give them, and so you, along with us, will come into misery and distress. For the stomach is a peculiar guest: it does not let itself be fed with words, but it wants, in short, to be full. Therefore it is our advice that you would send the people away from you, so that they can go buy food in the nearest towns and markets. If they like you so well, they can come back another time."

See, when we look at the words so plainly, they appear to us to have been spoken very wisely. But if we consider them correctly, we will discover that they are empty words, flowing out of unbelieving hearts. They themselves bring to light their lack of faith, for they consider Christ to be a careless man who has absolutely no foresight for the poor people and has to be constantly reminded to do the right thing. That is nothing else than that they consider themselves to be wise and intelligent, but instead they bring their own stupidity and lack of faith to light. Despite the fact that they had seen so many miracles from him and heard so many beneficial sermons, clearly they could not adapt themselves to the situation. Gospel on the Fourth Sunday of Lent.[3]

---

[1] *D. Hvldrichi Zvinglii in Plerosqve Novi Testamenti Libros*, 233-34.
[2] *D. Hvldrichi Zvinglii in Plerosqve Novi Testamenti Libros*, 234; alluding to Rom 10:17.

[3] Spangenberg, *Postilla* (1582), XCVIv-XCVIIr.

JESUS WAS TESTING AND TRAINING THE DISCIPLES. AUGUSTIN MARLORAT: Our Savior Christ knew (as John says) what he would do, but he did not reveal his intent and purpose immediately to his disciples, in order that he might prepare the way little by little and ready their minds for the miracle which he had determined to do. . . . He commanded his disciples to do what he had decided to do himself, but which was impossible for them to do. He gives them this command so that, because they would know the impossibility of what he was asking (namely, to feed so many people with so little food), the miracle might be all the more wonderful to them. He knew that his disciples still had only a weak and imperfect faith, and they did not as of yet sufficiently consider and respect the power of God. Therefore he sought diligently that the miracle which he was about to show might be made very clear to them, so that seeing clearly the power of God in it, they might be more confirmed and strengthened in their faith, and so be more capable and prepared for all the work pertaining to the kingdom of God. Therefore Christ spoke these things to his disciples to try them. AN ECCLESIASTICALL EXPOSITION UPON SAINT MATHEWE 13.[4]

9:14-16 *Jesus Blesses the Loaves and Fishes and Provides for All*

THE BREAKING OF THE BREAD SHARES CHRIST WITH US. PHILIPP MELANCHTHON: The breaking of bread was so common and usual with Christ that he was recognized when he did it by the two disciples as they were going to Emmaus. This practice of breaking of bread was very father-like and well-respected among the elders of long ago, and it was done in many places in the same sort of way. It was certainly very seemly and appropriate for Christ, by whom we all are fed. Furthermore, this breaking of bread has in itself a sign or token of communication, or

participation, so that the word *breaking* often signifies to divide, as we can see by this passage in Isaiah: "Break your loaf with the hungry." A loaf of bread cannot refresh many people unless it is broken and divided. And therefore the word is appropriate and agreeable to the mystery of communicating the body of the Lord, as the apostle said, "The bread we break, is it not a participation in the body of the Lord?" Not that the body of Christ is therefore said to be broken, as if it had in it some cut, but because it is made communicable, that is, able and qualified to be participated in and received by many. The apostle Paul said in another passage, in the person of Christ, "This is my body, which is broken for you." Instead of "broken," Saint Luke has "which is given for you." AN ECCLESIASTICALL EXPOSITION UPON SAINT MATHEWE 13.[5]

9:17 *The Disciples Collect Twelve Baskets of Leftovers*

GOD'S RICHES FILL US UP AND SPILL OVER. PHILIPP MELANCHTHON: These things are spoken to commend the power of Christ and to set forth the miracle, so that no one might think that not everyone ate of these loaves, or that perhaps everyone ate, but not enough to be satisfied. . . . In this example we see the riches of the glory of God, by which he feeds those who are his, that they are not only satisfied with what he gives them but also have a great surplus remaining for them. We are also taught here to beware that we do not lose the remnant of those good things with which we are fed. AN ECCLESIASTICALL EXPOSITION UPON SAINT MATHEWE 13.[6]

CHRIST TEACHES US TO BE THRIFTY. THOMAS BECON: We must not forget the command that Christ gave his disciples concerning the gathering

---

[4]Marlorat, ed., *Catholike and Ecclesiasticall Exposition of the Holy Gospell After S. Mathewe*, 316*; alluding to Jn 6:6.
[5]Marlorat, ed., *Catholike and Ecclesiasticall Exposition of the Holy Gospell After S. Mathewe*, 317-18*; citing Lk 24:30-31; Is 58:7; 1 Cor 10:16; 11:24; Lk 22:19.
[6]Marlorat, ed., *Catholike and Ecclesiasticall Exposition of the Holy Gospell After S. Mathewe*, 318*.

up of the bread and fish that were left over so that nothing might be lost. In times of necessity, our reason can do nothing but reckon and figure how to arrange things to serve our needs and cannot rely on faith, constantly clinging to the promise of God. Likewise, when the blessings of God are plentiful, the world cannot and will not rightfully and thankfully use those blessings. For many abuse the blessings of God to excess. They spend them on frivolity, as experience teaches. If there is a good year for grapes, so that there is plenty of wine, then people will drink, gulp, chug, quaff and most unthankfully abuse that precious and good gift of God, as though God had only sent such an abundance of wine for the purpose of people getting drunk.

They ought to use but not abuse the blessings of God. If we have more than our present need requires, it ought to be diligently gathered and stored up so that it might supply that lack and necessity that is coming, as Joseph counseled Pharaoh, the king of Egypt. With the great and plentiful increase of the first seven years, he was able to provide for the seven lean years that followed, and by this means there would be stores of grain for all the land. In like manner, when God sends a good year to artisans and businessmen, so that their wares sell well and they receive a good income, they should not abuse this blessing of God and wastefully spend everything they gained, but rather they must keep them in store and carefully save, so that in the future they will weather the lean times that are likely to follow. But of course many do not do this, but spend as fast as they get and spare nothing for the necessity that is to come, and so in time of need they are in want, and God withdraws his blessing from them. THE FOURTH SUNDAY OF LENT.[7]

---

[7] Becon, *New Postil*, 180v-181r*; alluding to Gen 41.

9:18-27 PETER'S CONFESSION OF CHRIST

[18]Now it happened that as he was praying alone, the disciples were with him. And he asked them, "Who do the crowds say that I am?" [19]And they answered, "John the Baptist. But others say, Elijah, and others, that one of the prophets of old has risen." [20]Then he said to them, "But who do you say that I am?" And Peter answered, "The Christ of God."

[21]And he strictly charged and commanded them to tell this to no one, [22]saying, "The Son of Man must suffer many things and be rejected by the elders and chief priests and scribes, and be killed, and on the third day be raised."

[23]And he said to all, "If anyone would come after me, let him deny himself and take up his cross daily and follow me. [24]For whoever would save his life will lose it, but whoever loses his life for my sake will save it. [25]For what does it profit a man if he gains the whole world and loses or forfeits himself? [26]For whoever is ashamed of me and of my words, of him will the Son of Man be ashamed when he comes in his glory and the glory of the Father and of the holy angels. [27]But I tell you truly, there are some standing here who will not taste death until they see the kingdom of God."

OVERVIEW: There are two basic questions at the heart of this pericope: Who is Christ? And what does it mean to be his disciple? Christ himself sets up the first question by asking, "Who do people say that I am?" This question was not asked out of vanity or because Jesus did not already know the answer but to address this question with the disciples and to allow Peter to make a brilliant confession of faith. Peter's statement confirms that Jesus is the Christ—true God and true human being, in one person (in creedally correct formulation). We should not be misled by what the world thinks of Jesus, for Satan easily confuses people by disguising or dividing the true Jesus. Instead of following the world or inventing a Christ out of our own heads, we should hold on to Christ, the anointed King and High Priest who is both divine and human.

But Jesus' disciples were not quite ready for the full picture. Jesus did not want his glory to be revealed at this point. If the disciples focused only on the glory, they would be dismayed and their faith would be shaken by the cross. This cross that he mentions now is a great stumbling block for the disciples. They thought he would be a worldly king, honored by all, and could not fathom that he would be so scorned and rejected. That is why,

Calvin notes, Jesus follows the mention of the cross with his coming resurrection—the bitter pill is easier to swallow with the spoonful of sugar. Even now, these interpreters argue, preachers should not dwell on the cross without also emphasizing the resurrection; this allows hope and faith to be sustained.

Like Christ, all his followers, too, will experience a cross. They must deny themselves and give all glory instead to God; they must take up the cross and bear it with cheerfulness; and they must follow Christ by practicing the virtues of meekness, patience, love and obedience. Some followers of Christ quite literally have to take up the cross and suffer martyrdom for his sake. Dirk Philips, one of the early Anabaptist leaders, notes that Christ's disciples must be ready to give up everything, even their own lives, to follow him. Others are not so extreme—not all Christ's followers will be martyrs—but there are still consequences to following Jesus. Focusing on God rather than ourselves, turning our backs on the world to obey God's commands, living simply so that we can give to and do for others—all these things are required of us as disciples of Christ. The Last Day is coming soon, these commentators contend, when we will be judged according to our deeds, that is, according to whether we denied him or professed him, in order to enter into the kingdom.

9:18-20 Peter Confesses Faith in Jesus as the Messiah

MANY THOUGHT JESUS WAS ONE OF THE PROPHETS. PHILIPP MELANCHTHON: "Some say John the Baptist." This was the Herodians, who were mentioned in Matthew 14. "Others say Elijah." Those who thought him to be Elijah were moved to think so by the prophecy of Malachi concerning the coming of Elijah, whom they expected to appear in his body again. Many today are still blinded by this error, for they believe that Enoch and Elijah will appear again in their bodies, and be, as it were, forerunners to the second coming of Christ. However, Christ himself taught that this same prophecy of Elijah was fulfilled in John the Baptist. "Some say Jeremiah." Jeremiah was added to this opinion, because the mouth of the Lord said to him, "Behold, I have put my words in your mouth. See, I have set you this day over nations and over kingdoms, to pluck up and to break down, to destroy and to overthrow, to build and to plant." And a little later he said, "Behold, I make you this day a fortified city, an iron pillar and bronze walls, against the whole land, against the kings of Judah, its officials, its priests and the people of the land." They thought that all of these things would be fulfilled in Christ. "One of the prophets of long ago." The strangeness and unusual sight of Christ's miracles might have given them occasion to think that he was one of the dead prophets, for they believed that those who were restored from the dead to life were indued by God with far greater power and virtue than they had before, when they were alive. AN ECCLESIASTI-CALL EXPOSITION UPON SAINT MATHEWE 13.[1]

WE SHOULD BE UNITED IN FAITH BUT SEPA-RATED FROM THE WORLD. JOHN CALVIN: Here Christ distinguishes his disciples from the rest of the crowd, so that it might be better known that it is senseless for us to be separated from the unity of faith, however we might disagree with others. For those who devote themselves simply to Christ and are not tempted to invent the gospel out of their own heads will never be lacking the true light. But here attentive vigilance is necessary, that when all the world leans toward its own inventions, they may steadily hold on to Christ. Because Satan could not remove from the Jews the persuasion that they had about the coming of Christ from the law and the prophets, he dissected him, as it were, into various parts, transfiguring him. Then he forced these many fictitious Christs on them, so that the true Redeemer would be forgotten. In the same way, after this he did not stop from tearing Christ into pieces or disguising him as another person. Among the confused and dissonant voices of the world, nevertheless this voice of Christ should always resound in our ears, dividing us from inconstant and wandering people, so that we might be removed from the crowd and not have our faith thrown about among the turbulence of contrary opinions. COMMENTARY ON A HARMONY OF THE GOSPELS.[2]

PETER WITNESSES TO JESUS' DIVINE AND HUMAN NATURES. JOHANN BAUMGART (POMARIUS): We learn in this passage that it is not enough to know the various opinions about Christ that there are in the world. Instead, our blessedness and eternal life come from properly recognizing God and Christ, the one whom he sent. So we need to learn from Peter's confession here what to believe about Christ's person and office. He says, "You are the Christ, the Son of the living God," which agrees with what he says in John 6, where he also says in the name of all the apostles, "You are Christ, the Son of the living God," recognizing and acknowledging him as true God and the Son of Man. For Peter talks to Christ and says, "You," that is, "You, who now and

---

[1]Marlorat, ed., *Catholike and Ecclesiasticall Exposition of the Holy Gospell After S. Mathewe*, 356*; citing Mal 4:5; Mt 11:14; Jer 1:9-10, 18.

[2]CTS 32:288-89* (CO 45:472).

frequently call youself the Son of Man, because you have taken on a real human nature—you, Son of Man, are also a Son of the living God, and therefore are also true, essential, eternal, natural and living God."

He also acknowledges that in the one person of Christ there are two distinct natures, the divine and the human, just as in the ark of the covenant there was both gold and wood, but there was only one ark and mercy seat. Of his office, Peter says that Jesus is the Christ, that is, the promised Messiah, the anointed King and High Priest. GOSPEL ON THE DAY OF PETER AND PAUL.[3]

9:21-22 Jesus Foretells His Death and Resurrection

THE MYSTERY MUST BE REVEALED AT THE PROPER TIME. THE ENGLISH ANNOTATIONS: "Tell it to no one" until the appointed time, when it was to be divulged to the world. He did not say this as if it did not highly concern all the elect to know and confess it but because he did not want his glory to be manifested before he had accomplished the work of the cross, in suffering an ignominious death to redeem us from death and hell. He would yet leave the devil in suspense, but primarily it was lest the faith of the disciples in confessing this should be dangerously shaken in the sight of his bitter passion. Also, because neither the disciples nor the crowds yet fully understood the mystery of Christ's death, resurrection and ascension into heaven, the people listening might have doubted the truth that they preached if things had been revealed before the opportune time. Those who should have by degrees ascended to that great mystery of godliness and salvation by Christ would have had the proper steps removed. . . . But this present restraint is limited, for he said, "Tell the vision to no one until the Son of Man is risen from the dead," and this the following words declare, which

foretell of his passion. ANNOTATIONS UPON THE GOSPEL ACCORDING TO SAINT LUKE 9:21.[4]

THE DEATH AND THE RESURRECTION MUST BE TAUGHT TOGETHER. JOHN CALVIN: Having announced a sign of his future glory, Christ warns his disciples of what he would suffer, that they might also prepare themselves to carry the cross; for the time was at hand for the battle, to which he had long known they would be unequal, unless they were prepared by new fortitude. In the first place, it was necessary to do this so they would know that Christ's reign would begin not with splendid pomp, or with magnificent riches or with the joyful applause of the world but rather with a shameful death. But yet nothing was more difficult than to overcome such a stumbling block, especially if we reflect upon what they were now thoroughly persuaded of concerning their master: they imagined that he was the author of worldly happiness. Therefore they were kept in suspense by this vain hope, eagerly anticipating that moment in time when suddenly Christ would disclose the glory of his kingdom. They had not even considered in their minds the dishonor of the cross, and they believed that it was entirely unreasonable that anything should happen to him that was not honorable. It was a painful circumstance that he should be rejected by the elders and scribes, who held the highest places of authority in the church, and so we may easily conclude that this admonition was necessary. Because the cross could not be mentioned without throwing their weak minds into confusion, he also healed the wound at once, by saying that on the third day he would be resurrected from the dead. And certainly, in the cross nothing but infirmity of the flesh appears, so that until we come to his resurrection, in which the power of the Spirit shines forth, our faith will not meet with anything that might sustain it or by which it might raise itself up. Therefore it is always prudent for ministers of the Word who desire to be successful in teaching to join the glory of the

---

[3]Baumgart, *Postilla*, 417v; quoting Mt 15:16; alluding to Jn 6:69; Ex 25:17-22; Ps 2; 110.

[4]Downame, ed., *Annotations*, Tt4v*; citing Mt 10:27; 17:9.

resurrection together with the dishonor of his death. COMMENTARY ON A HARMONY OF THE GOSPELS.[5]

9:23-27 The Consequences of Discipleship

FOLLOWING CHRIST REQUIRES DENYING ONESELF. EDWARD LEIGH: Everyone who wants to become a student in the school of Christ and learn obedience to God must "deny himself." That is, he must in the first place exalt and magnify the grace of God and become nothing in himself, renouncing his own reason, will and affections and subjecting them to the wisdom and will of God in all things. Second, "take up his cross." That is, he ought always to make a prior reckoning, even of private crosses and particular afflictions, and when they come, to bear them with cheerfulness, for there is that emphasis in the phrase "take up." This done, he must "follow Christ" by practicing the virtues of meekness, patience, love and obedience and by conforming to Christ's death in crucifying the sin in his own body. ANNOTATIONS UPON SAINT LUKE 9.[6]

LOVE GIVES UP ALL FOR GOD. DIRK PHILIPS: This [Phinehas's zeal for Israel's purity] took place in figures according to the letter of the Old Testament—indeed as a witness to true faith and honest love of God and is written for our teaching and admonition that we should love God above all creatures, just as Christ also taught us in the gospel that one must for his sake forsake all things, that is, father, mother, brothers, sisters, wife and children, in addition to his own life, take his cross on him and follow after him. And whoever loves anything more than him is not worthy of him, namely, Christ and his gospel. For this is the first and highest commandment, both in the Old and New Testaments, that one must love God the Lord with the whole heart, with the whole soul, with all strength and all ability. And this love is confessed by keeping God's commandments, just as Christ himself said: "Whoever loves me keeps my commandments, but whoever does not love me does not keep my commandments."

Therefore the apostle says love does not rejoice at unrighteousness but rejoices with the truth. Therefore love does not act hypocritically and does not deal deceitfully. Love does not transgress the teaching and rule of Christ. It shuns all false worship, all idolatry, ceremonies and human institutions which are contrary to God. It does not seek the friendship of this world; it does not desire to please people. It knows well that all which is regarded as high among people is an abomination before God. It does not adorn the flesh; it does not seek what is temporal and perishable. It does not fear the cross of Jesus Christ, but it rejoices in the same. THE ENCHIRIDION: AN APOLOGY OR REPLY.[7]

CHARITABLE DEEDS PURGE THE SOUL FROM THE FILTH OF SIN. THE BOOK OF HOMILIES: I will show you how profitable it is for us to exercise charitable deeds and what fruit will thereby come to us if we do them faithfully. In the Gospel, our Savior Christ teaches us that it profits us nothing if we possess all the riches of the whole world and the wealth or glory of it, if in the meantime we lose our souls or do those things that would make them captive to death, sin and hell fire. By this saying he not only instructs us how much the soul's health is to be preferred above worldly possessions but also serves to stir up our minds and push us forward to seek diligently and to learn by what means we may always preserve and keep our souls in safety. That is, we must learn how we may recover our health, if it is lost or impaired, and how it may be defended and maintained, if we do have it. Likewise he also teaches us to esteem it as a precious medicine and inestimable jewel, because it has such strength and

---

[5]CO 45:479 (cf. CTS 32:299-300).
[6]Leigh, *Annotations upon All the New Testament Philologicall and Theologicall*, 112*.

[7]CRR 6:192-93* (BRN 10:199-200); alluding to Num 25:5-9; Rom 15:4; Mt 10:36; 16:24; Mk 8:34-35; Lk 14:27; 17:33; Jn 12:25; Deut 6:5 (cf. Mt 22:37-38); 1 Cor 13:6; Gal 6:16 quoting Jn 14:15, 24.

virtue in it that it can either procure or preserve so incomparable a treasure. For if we greatly regard that medicine or salve that is able to heal sundry, grievous diseases of the body, much more will we esteem what has a similar power over the soul. And because we might be better assured both to know and to have in readiness such a profitable remedy, Christ, as a most faithful and loving teacher, shows us what it is, where we may find it and how we may use and apply it. For when he and his disciples were sharply accused by the Pharisees of having defiled their souls by breaking the constitutions of the elders, because they went to the meal without washing their hands before, according to the custom of the Jews, Christ, answering their superstitious complaint, teaches them a special remedy for keeping their souls clean, despite disregarding the superstitious orders: "Give alms," he said, "and behold, all things are clean to you." He teaches them that the means of keeping the soul pure and clean in the sight of God is to be merciful and charitable in helping the poor. Therefore we are taught that merciful and charitable deeds are profitable for purging the soul from the infection and filthy spots of sin. HOMILY 23: OF ALMS DEEDS AND MERCIFULNESS TOWARD THE POOR AND NEEDY.[8]

WHOEVER SUFFERS WITH CHRIST WILL REIGN WITH HIM. MARTIN BUCER: When the Son of Man comes in judgment, he will give to everyone according to what he deserves. But Christ exhorts all those who desire to be followers of him and his disciples and gives them three reasons to deny themselves, to take up their crosses and to follow him. The first reason is that he who wants to save his life will lose it, and that he who loses it will save it. The second is that to him, who appeared for a time in the flesh as a mortal, all judgment is given, and that therefore he will come in the glory of his Father with his angels, that he may give to every person according to his deeds. To those who deny him, he will give hell fire, but to those who profess him, he will give the kingdom of his Father. . . . The third reason, which gives a wonderful consolation, is that he says that it will not be very long until he will come with great power and that some of those who were present at that time would see it. So who would not now follow him, and for his sake deny himself and take up his cross, when he knows that very shortly he will reign gloriously in divine power, and that he himself will reign along with Christ? For whoever suffers with Christ will reign with him. AN ECCLESIASTICALL EXPOSITION UPON SAINT MATHEWE 17.[9]

THE KINGDOM OF GOD WAS COME, BUT NOT YET IN GLORY. MARTIN BUCER: Therefore, to see Christ coming in his kingdom is nothing else than, as Mark and Luke have it, to see the kingdom of God. That is, the glory and good success of the kingdom of God. The Evangelist Mark expressly says, "until they see the kingdom of God after it has come with power." The kingdom of God had already come, which is why he preached at the beginning that the kingdom of heaven was at hand. . . . But because the kingdom of God was not yet glorious, as it would be in all the world after his resurrection, he said truly, "until they see the kingdom of God after it has come." . . .

The glorious power of the kingdom of Christ chiefly declared itself within twenty years or thereabouts after his passion, and until that time there is no doubt that many to whom the Lord spoke in this moment were still alive. But for what purpose did Christ say this? Surely for the purpose that he might give them some comfort against the time of cross and affliction, because shortly the kingdom and power of God would be declared and revealed. AN ECCLESIASTICALL EXPOSITION UPON SAINT MATHEWE 17.[10]

---

[8]*Certain Sermons or Homilies* (1852), 359-60*; citing Mt 16:26; Lk 11:41.

[9]Marlorat, ed., *Catholike and Ecclesiasticall Exposition of the Holy Gospell After S. Mathewe*, 372-73*.

[10]Marlorat, ed., *Catholike and Ecclesiasticall Exposition of the Holy Gospell After S. Mathewe*, 374-75*; quoting Mk 9:1; Mt 12:28; alluding to Mk 1:14-15.

9:28-36 THE TRANSFIGURATION

²⁸Now about eight days after these sayings he took with him Peter and John and James and went up on the mountain to pray. ²⁹And as he was praying, the appearance of his face was altered, and his clothing became dazzling white. ³⁰And behold, two men were talking with him, Moses and Elijah, ³¹who appeared in glory and spoke of his departure,ᵃ which he was about to accomplish at Jerusalem. ³²Now Peter and those who were with him were heavy with sleep, but when they became fully awake they saw his glory and the two men who stood with him. ³³And as the men were parting from him, Peter said to Jesus, "Master, it is good that we are here. Let us make three tents, one for you and one for Moses and one for Elijah"— not knowing what he said. ³⁴As he was saying these things, a cloud came and overshadowed them, and they were afraid as they entered the cloud. ³⁵And a voice came out of the cloud, saying, "This is my Son, my Chosen One;ᵇ listen to him!" ³⁶And when the voice had spoken, Jesus was found alone. And they kept silent and told no one in those days anything of what they had seen.

a Greek exodus   b Some manuscripts my Beloved

OVERVIEW: Like other miracle stories, the transfiguration reveals Jesus as the Son of God, and yet while it is even more obvious than a healing or an exorcism, it is at the same time more complicated. Why did he bring only three of the apostles with him? Would it not have made sense to make this revelation before the whole group, or perhaps even the greater crowd of people who followed him? And what was the point of bringing back Moses and Elijah? What is not surprising is that this was an overwhelming experience for Peter, James and John, just as coming face to face (in a way) with God was overwhelming for Moses. So the fact that Peter placed his foot in his mouth should not surprise anyone. But why have such a great show for only three people? We do not know why these particular apostles were chosen over others—as François Lambert makes clear, it is certainly not because Peter was preeminent among the disciples, John was a virgin and James was the first to be martyred. Rather, it was part of Jesus' plan, and therefore it was right. For our commentators, the experience was shared by only a few of Jesus' followers because the time was not yet right for the others to see such a clear revelation of Christ's divinity. First they had to experience the resurrection; then they would find out about earlier manifestations and come to understand them. Only in this way would their faith be strengthened. Moses and Elijah, most likely truly present in the flesh and not just visions, the reformers state, represent the Law and the Prophets and reveal that these come to an end in Christ—he is the fulfillment of all that came before. Jesus himself was not really changed in the transfiguration. His divinity was unveiled, but only his human frailty was changed, not the substance of his body. Likewise important for these interpreters was the fact that he was transformed during prayer, which emphasizes the significance of that act, even while the apostles slept, showing their weakness. Peter was so overwhelmed that he wanted this mountaintop experience to last forever, but in this life it cannot. However, the revelation does show to us that we, too, will be transformed in our bodies when we are in heaven. Christ assumed our body for suffering *and* glorification. In the end, then, this miraculous revelation of Christ's divinity is for us.

9:28-29 *Jesus Is Transfigured During Prayer*

GOD CHOSE THESE APOSTLES BY HIS OWN PLAN. FRANÇOIS LAMBERT: No one has recognized the plan of God as to why these ones were chosen before the rest, both for these events and for other things. Indeed, God's plan should be revered, and one should not thoughtlessly set limits on it. The reasons marked out by the sophists, however, are nothing at all. For they say that Peter was chosen because he held the first place among the apostles, but he did not have first place over the others but was rather a brother and co-bishop among them. Indeed, for all true believers, there is only one who has first place: Christ our Lord. They claim that James was chosen for the reason that he would be the first among the apostles to endure martyrdom, but they do not observe that for the Lord, the question of who was first or second was of little importance. If it had been the order of martyrdom that was really important, it would have been proper for Saint Stephen to have been chosen. Concerning John, they mention his virginity and his deep knowledge of mysteries. But although we certainly do not deny his virginity, nevertheless we say that it does not have authority from the holy Scriptures. And also the highest mysteries of God were revealed to others besides John, and it is not certain that Paul, Peter, or some of the others might not have known more. COMMENTARY IN LUKE 9:28-29.[1]

EARNEST PRAYER TRANSFORMS US AS WELL. PHILIPP MELANCHTHON: But because Christ was transformed from the form of humility into that heavenly and divine shape, it was a manifest token that the state in which he was then was not eternal but mutable and subject to change. However, it does not mean that the substance of his body was subject to transmutation and change, in so much that the truth of his human flesh was turned into the truth of the Spirit. God forbid! But there was a transmutation of his human condition and fragility, while his humanity remained the same. Because he was transformed while he was at prayer, it shows how we are transformed into God when we are praying, which should cause us to be that much

more earnest to pray. That is why it happened that the ancestors and holy people were so often rapt and carried into heaven during prayer: Peter, the apostle of Christ (in Acts 10); Daniel, to whom an angel appeared when he was in prayer, declaring to him things that were to come (in Daniel 9); Cornelius, who in prayer saw an angel (in Acts 10); and Paul, who as he prayed saw Ananias in a vision, laying his hand on him (in Acts 9). Also, the same Paul testifies of himself, "When I had returned to Jerusalem and was praying in the temple, I fell into a trance and saw him saying to me, 'Make haste and get out of Jerusalem quickly, because they will not accept your testimony about me.'" Hereby we gather that those who are never led by the fervency of mind to prayer are the farthest from the company and fellowship of God and of the heavenly spirits. AN ECCLESIASTICALL EXPOSITION UPON SAINT MATHEWE 17.[2]

9:30-31 *Jesus Talks with Moses and Elijah*

IN MOSES AND ELIJAH, THE LAW AND PROPHETS REACH THEIR END IN CHRIST. MARTIN BUCER: There is no doubt that this appearance and conversation with Moses and Elijah added a great deal to the declaration of the kingdom of Christ. However, some still question whether they were truly present or whether a mere figure or image of them was set before the disciples' eyes, even as visions of absent things were set before the prophets. Although either conclusion is probable and both sides might have a good reason to dispute, however it is more likely that they were truly brought to that place. It is also not at all absurd to say that the dead may be restored to life for a time, according to God's will, because he has both body and soul in his hand and power. Moses and Elijah did not rise by themselves at that time, but they rose at the will and command of God, to be present for that time with Christ.

---

[1]Lambert, *In Divi Lucae*, Sr-v.

[2]Marlorat, ed., *Catholike and Ecclesiasticall Exposition of the Holy Gospell After S. Mathewe*, 376-77*; quoting Acts 22:17-18.

Now, if anyone wants to know how it is that the apostles recognized Moses and Elijah, whom they had never seen, it may easily be answered that when God had set them in the midst of them, he gave them signs and tokens by which they might be recognized. This was done by a truly extraordinary manner of revelation, that they might be certain that it was Moses and Elijah. But why did these two rather than any of the other saints appear? This reason ought to satisfy us: to say that the Law and the Prophets had no other scope or end than Christ. For it was a great aid and help to our faith that Christ came forth with such authoritative testimony, even as he had been commended by God long before. Therefore in Moses the Law and in Elijah the Prophets are represented. AN ECCLESIASTICALL EXPOSITION UPON SAINT MATHEWE 17.[3]

CHRIST IS PREPARING FOR HIS EXODUS. JOHN TRAPP: In Greek, it says, "of his exodus," in reference to that expedition or departure of Israel out of Egypt. It signifies a transition from a condition and state of hardship. (We see it used thus by Saint Peter in 2 Peter 1:15.) Death to the saints is only a going out to heaven, a loosing from the shore of life and launching out into the ocean of immortality. A COMMENTARY UPON THE GOSPEL ACCORDING TO SAINT LUKE 9.[4]

CHRIST'S BETTER EXODUS FOR US. JOHN DONNE: That Moses and Elijah talked with Christ in the transfiguration both Saint Matthew and Saint Mark tell us, but what they talked of, only Saint Luke. They talked of his departure, he says, of his death, which was to be accomplished in Jerusalem. The word is of his exodus, the very word of our text, *exitus*, his issue by death. Moses, who in his exodus had prefigured this issue of our Lord, and in passing Israel out of Egypt through the Red Sea, had foretold in that actual prophecy Christ's

passing of humankind through the sea of his blood. Elijah, whose exodus and issue out of this world was a figure of Christ's ascension, had no doubt a great satisfaction in talking with our blessed Lord concerning his departure, of the full consummation of all this in his death which was to be accomplished in Jerusalem.

Our meditation of his death should be more visceral and affect us more, because it is something already completed. The ancient Romans had a certain tenderness and detestation of the name of death. They would not name death—no, not even in their wills! There they would not say "if or when I die," but instead "when the course of nature is accomplished in me." To us who speak daily of the death of Christ—he was crucified, dead and buried—can the memory or the mention of our death be irksome or bitter? There are in these latter times those among us who name death freely enough, and the death of God only in blasphemous oaths and curses.[5] Miserable people who shall therefore be said never to have named Jesus, because they have named him too often; and therefore hear Jesus say, "I never knew you," because they made themselves too familiar with him. Moses and Elijah talked with Christ of his death only in a holy and joyful sense of the benefit which they and all the world were to receive by it. Discourses of religion should not be out of curiosity but edification.

And then they talked with Christ of his death at that time when he was at the greatest height of glory that he ever admitted in this world—that is, his transfiguration. And we are afraid to speak to the important people of this world concerning their death but nourish in them a vain imagination of immortality and immutability. But "it is good for us to be" (as Saint Peter said there). It is good to dwell here in this consideration of his death. Therefore we transfer our tabernacle—our

---

[3]Marlorat, ed., *Catholike and Ecclesiasticall Exposition of the Holy Gospell After S. Mathewe*, 377*.
[4]Trapp, *Commentary or Exposition*, 393*; alluding to Phil 1:21.

[5]Donne refers not only to using the Lord's name in vain but also to more graphic swear words concerning his death, particularly "God's blood" and "God's wounds." See further Melissa Mohr, *Holy Sh*t: A Brief History of Swearing* (New York: Oxford University Press, 2013), esp. 88-172.

devotion—through some of these steps, which God the Lord made to his issue of death that day. SERMON 158, PREACHED AT WHITEHALL (1630).[6]

9:32-33 Peter Suggests Staying on the Mountaintop

THE APOSTLES ALMOST MISSED THE GLORIOUS SIGHT. JOHANN SPANGENBERG: What were the three apostles doing meanwhile? They were heavy with sleep, as Luke says, but when they woke up, they saw his brightness, and two men standing by him. Flesh and blood is so weak that while Christ prayed, they slept. This also relates to us, for when we should be praying, we are instead sleeping. On account of their laziness, they did not deserve to be admitted to this glorious sight, and so what happened to them was pure grace. Christ awoke them from their sleep, so that they might see the glory of God and receive a foretaste of eternal life. GOSPEL ON THE TWENTY-FIFTH SUNDAY AFTER TRINITY.[7]

PETER ERRED, FOR THE FLESH CANNOT CONTROL HEAVENLY THINGS. FRANÇOIS LAMBERT: Peter did not want them to go, and he rejoiced in their majesty, so he said, "Master," and so on. However, he made a mistake, and he was unaware of what he was saying. Indeed, he was still flesh. For although he was a servant of Christ, nevertheless judgment shows that these first words originated in the flesh. And really, who still bound in human flesh and weakness could clearly examine those things which relate to heavenly glory? On the contrary, those who are elect but are still living in the flesh do not yet have the authority to rule, so we are not able to reveal anything completely, unless the Spirit of Christ would have it revealed. For in fact those things are private of which a person is not allowed to speak, that is, of which he

is not able to speak. From this you can see the thoughtlessness and madness of the sophists, who presumed to set limits to the properties of the soul and the body, to the hidden future of God, and more. Therefore they are crushed by the majesty of their mysteries, while by the fairest judgment of God they are both blinded and made strangers to the truth. COMMENTARY IN LUKE 9:33.[8]

9:34-36 A Voice from Heaven and the Vision's End

IT WAS NOT YET TIME FOR CHRIST'S FULL DIVINITY TO BE REVEALED. JOHN CALVIN: When it is said that in the end they saw Christ "alone," this means that the Law and the Prophets had only a temporary glory, that Christ alone might remain in view. For although we should rightly make use of the services of Moses, we must not adhere to him, but rather, those services having been given, we should be led by his hand to Christ, whose minister he is, along with all the others. This passage can also be applied to condemning the superstitions of those who confuse Christ not only with the prophets and apostles but also with the most common saints, as if he were just one among that number. But yet the graces of God are superior in the saints for far different reasons than that they might seize for themselves any part of the honor that belongs to Christ. However, the source of the error is seen in the disciples themselves: as long as they were terrified by God's majesty, their minds were wandering in search of people, but when Christ gently raised them up, they saw him alone. Just so, if that consolation by which Christ remedies our fears should flourish in us, all those foolish affections that constantly distract us will disappear. . . .

We have said that the time was not yet ripe to make those visions known. And certainly the faith of the disciples would not have grasped it, if Christ had not given a more brilliant sign of his glory in his resurrection. But after he himself

---

[6]Donne, *Works*, 6:294-95*; citing Mt 17:3; Mk 9:4; Lk 9:31; 7:23. Donne is reliant on Calvin's terse comments here; see CTS 32:311 (CO 45:486).
[7]Spangenberg, *Postilla . . . von Ostern biß auffs Aduent*, CLXXXIr-v.

[8]Lambert, *In Divi Lucae*, S2r; citing 2 Cor 12:4.

openly revealed his divine power, that temporal glimpse of his glory began to be known, that it might be established that, even at the time when he "emptied himself," nevertheless his whole divinity remained intact, even though it was hidden by the veil of flesh. Therefore for good reason he ordered his disciples to be silent until he had risen from the dead. COMMENTARY ON A HARMONY OF THE GOSPELS.[9]

THE VEILED TRINITY OF THE OLD TESTAMENT IS REVEALED IN THE NEW. MARTIN LUTHER: Three persons and one God—they appeared as distinguishable. The figures are different from one another: there is the Father who speaks, the Son about whom the Father speaks and the Holy Spirit

. . . in the shining cloud. This we confess in the Symbol.[10] Since the gospel has been revealed, we should believe this. Before Christ's advent and nativity this teaching was not clear. That people God bore as a mother bears her child in her womb. They remained in the faith of the one God. Among us simple people we do not speculate but are taught. True faith is that the Father, Son and Holy Spirit are the one God. The Son became human, and he died and gave us the Holy Spirit who gives us the sacrament, consolation, strengthens us and leads us into eternal life. Otherwise no one's faith—not any single person's!—has endured for long. SERMON ON TRINITY SUNDAY (1538).[11]

---

[9]CTS 32:316, 317* (CO 45:489, 490); alluding to Phil 2:7.

[10]Luther means the Apostles' Creed. See further Rufinius, *A Commentary on the Apostles' Creed*, NPNF[2] 3:543.
[11]WA 46:433-34.

9:37-50 THE HEALING OF A BOY AND THE QUESTION OF THE GREATEST

³⁷On the next day, when they had come down from the mountain, a great crowd met him. ³⁸And behold, a man from the crowd cried out, "Teacher, I beg you to look at my son, for he is my only child. ³⁹And behold, a spirit seizes him, and he suddenly cries out. It convulses him so that he foams at the mouth, and shatters him, and will hardly leave him. ⁴⁰And I begged your disciples to cast it out, but they could not." ⁴¹Jesus answered, "O faithless and twisted generation, how long am I to be with you and bear with you? Bring your son here." ⁴²While he was coming, the demon threw him to the ground and convulsed him. But Jesus rebuked the unclean spirit and healed the boy, and gave him back to his father. ⁴³And all were astonished at the majesty of God.

But while they were all marveling at everything he was doing, Jesus*ᵃ* said to his disciples, ⁴⁴"Let these words sink into your ears: The Son of Man is about to be delivered into the hands of men." ⁴⁵But they did not understand this saying, and it was concealed from them, so that they might not perceive it. And they were afraid to ask him about this saying.

⁴⁶An argument arose among them as to which of them was the greatest. ⁴⁷But Jesus, knowing the reasoning of their hearts, took a child and put him by his side ⁴⁸and said to them, "Whoever receives this child in my name receives me, and whoever receives me receives him who sent me. For he who is least among you all is the one who is great."

⁴⁹John answered, "Master, we saw someone casting out demons in your name, and we tried to stop him, because he does not follow with us." ⁵⁰But Jesus said to him, "Do not stop him, for the one who is not against you is for you."

a Greek *he*

OVERVIEW: Clearly there was some confusion between what people expected of and believed about the Messiah, and the reality of the Messiah as embodied by Jesus. This pericope begins with another healing and exorcism, but in this case, the apostles (apart from Peter, James and John, who were with Jesus on the mountain) tried, and failed, to heal the child. They had healed people of illnesses and even demonic influence before, but this case was somehow especially difficult. It seems that the boy had epilepsy, which was interpreted as demonic possession. In any case, the disciples found it too challenging. They were disturbed by the raillery of the scribes and Pharisees, lacked confidence because their leaders were gone and generally did not have enough faith to be successful. Jesus was disappointed in them, calling them "a faithless and perverse generation," making a comparison between them and the people whom Moses had to lead. Why was it that the crowd was consistently amazed but not necessarily brought to a true faith? And why were the disciples dismayed by the mention of his passion, when he had already spoken of it to them before? Our commentators observe that while many believed Christ to be a prophet, and even the prophet promised by Moses who would be their Messiah, their preconceived notions of the Messiah did not allow them to see Jesus and hear his words clearly. They were convinced that the Messiah would be someone who would free them from Roman occupancy and restore Israel. The Messiah would be successful and respected by all. They could not comprehend that the Messiah would be despised and rejected (despite some of Isaiah's prophecies); that he might not be an earthly Savior but a spiritual one.

Just when the disciples seemed to be on the right path, they hit a roadblock caused by their human nature. In this case, envy and ambition overtook them, and they began to argue over who would be the greatest in the kingdom of heaven. The disciples were still confused over the truly spiritual nature of Jesus as the Messiah and his kingdom in heaven. They still believed that the kingdom of heaven would, like kingdoms on earth, have a variety of offices with varying degrees of authority and honor. They feared, based on recent examples of preference, that Peter would be placed in the highest authority, and they would have to suffer less glorious positions.

Jesus used a visual aid—a child—to help them understand the reality of the heavenly kingdom. One must be like a child—humble, innocent, not ambitious or political—in order to be great in heaven. The concepts of the least and the greatest in heaven are entirely opposite to the earthly concepts. The greatest in heaven will not be the most powerful ruler but the humblest servant—such a person should have contempt for glory and honor, instead humbly looking outward, desiring to serve everyone rather than himself. Not only did Jesus want the disciples to lay aside their pride and ambition, but also, as Melanchthon suggests, he meant to commend the faith of children. Although children tend to be undervalued as agents, even today, they can have a healthy and deep faith in Christ—they are role models (sometimes even martyrs) for the rest of us.

9:37-42 Jesus Heals a Boy Possessed by an Evil Spirit

A Case Too Difficult for the Apostles. John Lightfoot: Now in this child there were not only fits of convulsions or the falling sickness and the like, but he was really possessed with the devil indeed. So although the disciples had healed several persons of maladies which the Jews in their language called possessions by evil spirits, this subject was more difficult by far, as the devil was actually in the body of this child. Now granting, for we dare not deny, that they had cast out devils

before, yet this case carried some extraordinary matter in it above those other times. They were then preaching throughout the land, and their commission gave them power to cast out devils to confirm their doctrine, but now they were not in that employment. They were also now set on by the scribes and Pharisees with this extraordinary example of a possessed person, who had been possessed since infancy, on purpose that they might puzzle them, especially now because their master and three of the chief of their company, Peter, James and John, were absent. Therefore if by all these disadvantages together their faith was somewhat shaken, it is not to be wondered at so much, because the case was more strange and unusual to them, and they had not been put to such a trial before. The Harmony of the New Testament, Section 53.[1]

These People Were as Contrary as the People Moses Led. Desiderius Erasmus: "O unbelieving and perverse generation!" That is to say, perverse, contrary and always bending from the truth, and so obstinate that they could not be persuaded in the truth, nor could they abide or suffer themselves to be taught or persuaded to anything that was profitable for them. This was how the Israelites showed themselves to be in so often murmuring against God and in so often rebelling against Moses and Aaron. No matter what marvelous signs and wonders were done for their profit and health, no matter what horrible and fearful punishments were given for their rebellion, not even the remarkable clemency and gentleness of Moses and his infinite labor and daily care for them could make them do their duty toward him. Christ had to deal with people who showed no less obstinacy and crooked contrariness than those Israelites. An Ecclesiasticall Exposition upon Saint Mathewe 17.[2]

---

[1]Lightfoot, *Harmony, Chronicle and Order of the New Testament,* 41-42*.
[2]Marlorat, ed., *Catholike and Ecclesiasticall Exposition of the Holy Gospell After S. Mathewe,* 386*.

9:43-44 *While the Crowds Marvel, Jesus Reveals His Passion for the Second Time*

CHRIST HUMBLED HIMSELF AS THE SON OF MAN. FRANÇOIS LAMBERT: Why is it that Christ so often called himself the Son of Man? He said it to a great many people really so that we might pay attention to God's great love for us, who deigned to become the Son of Man on behalf of such impious, miserable worms. Hence Paul says in Philippians 2 that we should feel what Christ also felt, "who, though he was in the form of God, did not count equality with God a thing to be grasped, but emptied himself by taking the form of a servant, being born in the likeness of men. And being found in human form, he humbled himself by becoming obedient to the point of death, even death on a cross." Consequently in holy Scripture, no one else is so often called Son of Man.

Therefore when we hear of Christ, who as the Son of Man shows the extent of God's love and mercy as well as his own humility as the greatest Savior, it is proper for us to remember that we should put our trust in him, and we should hope in him, and by his example we should learn to bear patiently with adversity. And it certainly would not happen that he would ever abandon those who believed, when he loved them so much that he was willing to die for them. COMMENTARY IN LUKE 9:44.[3]

9:45 *The Disciples Do Not Understand*

THE DISCIPLES WERE MISLED BY THEIR OWN OPINIONS. JOHN CALVIN: Although by now the disciples had been warned several times about these things, they were nevertheless thrown into confusion as if they had never heard anything about it. A preconceived opinion is so effective that it brings a shadow over minds in the clearest light. The apostles imagined for themselves pleasant and delightful conditions in the reign of Christ and thought that, as soon as he became known, he

would receive the highest approval of everyone. It was unbelievable to them that the priests, scribes and leaders of the church would be against him. Therefore, this error having seized them, they did not admit anything that was contrary to it, for Mark says they did not understand what the Lord had in mind. But how could they be ignorant, when the words were so clear and distinct, unless that vain illusion had clouded their minds? The fact that they did not dare to question any further has been ascribed in part to their reverence for him. But there is no doubt that they were also kept silent by their grief and by foolishness that they themselves invented. This modesty was not totally laudable, for it helped to maintain both confused doubt and sinful sadness. COMMENTARY ON A HARMONY OF THE GOSPELS.[4]

9:46 *The Disciples Argue Among Themselves*

THE OTHERS WERE ENVIOUS OF PETER'S SUPPOSED AUTHORITY. RICHARD TAVERNER: You should first understand that an example of the natural ignorance, blindness and infirmity of humankind is here set forth in the disciples of Christ, who still measured the kingdom of heaven after the fashion of the kingdom of the world. The disciples come to Christ and ask him, "Who will be greater in the kingdom of heaven?" According to the mind of the ancient doctors, this was certainly a human affectation which crept into the apostles' minds and, as it were, pricked their envy and ambition. They had heard of the kingdom of heaven and had seen three apostles go off with Christ to the mountain—that is, Peter, James and John. They had heard how the keys of the kingdom were given to Peter and how it was said to him, "Blessed are you, Simon, son of Jonah," and "I say to you, you are Peter, and on this rock I will build my church." They noticed that Peter spoke more familiarly and boldly with the Lord, and lately they also saw him preferred before the rest of the

---

[3]Lambert, *In Divi Lucae*, S4v; citing Phil 2:5-8.

[4]CO 45:498 (cf. CTS 32:329); citing Mk 9:32.

apostles in the paying of the tribute, and treated similarly to Christ. They did not yet perfectly understand these and other such things, and so they had a small, private grudge against and envy of Peter, because they thought that he was appointed prince in the kingdom of heaven, even though he was younger in age than they. Therefore they came, as I said, to Jesus, and asked him who would have the chief authority in the kingdom of heaven. It had not yet been driven out of their heads that there would be similar dignities and powers in the heavenly and spiritual kingdom to what they saw in the princes' courts of this world. ON MICHEL-MAS DAY.[5]

9:47-48 The Least Shall Be the Greatest

DREAMS OF GREATNESS. DESIDERIUS ERAS-MUS: A certain worldly thought entered them; it broke out at last among them, and so they began to discuss and argue among themselves which of them should hold the highest place in the kingdom of God. For they dreamed that there would be a certain dignity in the heavenly kingdom, such as they saw in the court of worldly princes or in the houses of rich people, where he who is prouder and more presumptious is treated as greater. And although Jesus was not ignorant of what they were discussing, nevertheless when he had come into the house he questioned them about what they were arguing about with each other. PARAPHRASE ON THE GOSPEL OF LUKE 9:47.[6]

JESUS USED THE CHILD AS A VISUAL AID. HEINRICH BULLINGER: In order that he might make them hear in their minds what he was about to teach, the Lord used not only words but also a lively pattern and express example. The prophets often did the same thing, because it was profitable both to teach and also to demonstrate, to move and to imprint those things on the mind which they

wanted people to remember. The action sets the thing to be seen before our eyes, and the words declare to us what the action means. Therefore the prophet Jeremiah not only said that the city of Jerusalem would be destroyed; he also took an earthen pot and destroyed it in the presence of those to whom he was speaking, saying, "Even so will I destroy this city and this people, says the Lord." Also the same prophet made bonds and chains and showed them to everyone, and after-ward he explained the meaning of them. The Lord does something similar here, and therefore when he had called a little child to him, he set the child down in the midst of those who were contending and disputing. After he had their attention, he declared the meaning of the example by saying, "He who is least among you all—he is the greatest." AN ECCLESIASTICALL EXPOSITION UPON SAINT MATHEWE 17.[7]

THE INVERTED GREATNESS OF THE KINGDOM. DESIDERIUS ERASMUS: "The kingdom of faith and charity does not know ambition, it does not recognize lordly domination, nor does it suffer tyranny. . . . And whoever receives me, receives him who sent me. If I have exercised lordship over you, go ahead and dispute among yourselves about who is to be first; if however I have rather been a servant to what is advantageous to others, fleeing all the glory of this world, then you must know that he who will be greatest among all of you will be the least of all in his contempt for glory, in his humility and in his zeal to serve everyone." PARA-PHRASE ON THE GOSPEL OF LUKE 9:47-48.[8]

CHRIST HIGHLY VALUED CHILDREN AND THEIR FAITH. PHILIPP MELANCHTHON: Some understand this passage to be about children who reach a mature age and who already have a sure faith in Christ, such as those who cried out, "Hosanna to the Son of David." Concerning them,

[5]Taverner, *On Saynt Andrewes Day*, 37r-v*; alluding to Mt 17:1; Lk 9:28; Mt 17:24-27; quoting Mt 16:17-19 (cf. Mk 8:29-30; Lk 9:20). [6]Erasmus, *In Evangelivm Lvce Paraphrasis*, p 5 r-v (LB 7:372). [7]Marlorat, ed., *Catholike and Ecclesiasticall Exposition of the Holy Gospell After S. Mathewe*, 394*; citing Jer 19:10-11. [8]Erasmus, *In Evangelivm Lvce Paraphrasis*, p5r-v (LB 7:372).

Christ answered the chief priests from the psalm of David, saying, "Out of the mouth of infants and nursing babies you have prepared praise." These cries of the children declared a great faith toward Christ. And this also may be spoken of those children to whom John writes, saying, "I write to you, children, because you know the Father." They were the children of Christians, and therefore they were formed in faith in Christ and were such to whom he might take good occasion to write. And in another passage, the twelve-year-old girl who Christ raised from death is called *pais*, which sometimes signifies a child in the state of infancy. Therefore, so that no one might criticize the example of a little child, he wonderfully commends children, for Mark says that he took the child into his own arms, as a singular and most precious pledge. Likewise, Simeon was said to take up the Christ-child in his arms in the same way. There are others who think that Christ not only spoke of those who are children in age but also of those who are children in manners and simplicity, no matter what age they might be. Therefore Christ calls those children metaphorically who lay aside all pride and haughtiness of mind and instead focus themselves on modesty and submission. By this means, the faithful are taught how they should esteem one another, when every person submits himself. AN ECCLESIASTICALL EXPOSITION UPON SAINT MATHEWE 17.[9]

---

[9]Marlorat, ed., *Catholike and Ecclesiasticall Exposition of the Holy*

9:49-50 *"Whoever Is Not Against You Is for You"*

THOSE NOT WITH CHRIST ARE NOT NECESSARILY AGAINST HIM. HULDRYCH ZWINGLI: "Whoever is not against us is with us." These words are perceived to be inconsistent with those spoken in Matthew 12: "Whoever is not with me is against me." But in Matthew, these words are spoken against the Pharisees and the unbelievers, who, when they saw the miracles of Christ, despised them and attributed them to demons. Therefore this word that he then declared against them, "Whoever is not with me is against me," extends to those who are similar to them. Yet it is not the case that all of the time those who are not with Christ are opposed to Christ. There are those who are not with Christ now out of ignorance but are going to be with him someday, and they might be elect from all eternity. How would they be able to oppose Christ, when they did not know him? And so the words which he says here are true, and they relate to those people who out of ignorance are not yet with Christ, but they do not oppose him. Just as a lamp is used in dark places, so the circumstances must be used to understand the holy Scriptures. IN THE GOSPEL OF LUKE 9.[10]

Gospell After S. Mathewe, 396*; quoting Mt 21:15-16 (cf. Ps 8:2); 1 Jn 2:13; Lk 8:54; alluding to Mk 9:36; Lk 2:28.

[10]*D. Hvldrichi Zvinglii in Plerosqve Novi Testamenti Libros*, 240-41; quoting Mt 12:30.

9:51-62 SAMARITAN OPPOSITION AND THE COST OF FOLLOWING JESUS

[51]*When the days drew near for him to be taken up, he set his face to go to Jerusalem.* [52]*And he sent messengers ahead of him, who went and entered a village of the Samaritans, to make preparations for him.* [53]*But the people did not receive him, because his face was set toward Jerusalem.* [54]*And when his disciples James and John saw it, they said, "Lord, do you want us to tell fire to come down from heaven and consume them?"[a]* [55]*But he turned and rebuked them.[b]* [56]*And they went on to another village.*

[57]*As they were going along the road, someone said to him, "I will follow you wherever you go."* [58]*And Jesus said to him, "Foxes have holes, and birds of the air have nests, but the Son of Man has nowhere to lay his head."* [59]*To another he said, "Follow me." But he said, "Lord, let me first go and bury my father."* [60]*And Jesus[c] said to him, "Leave the dead to bury their own dead. But as for you, go and proclaim the kingdom of God."* [61]*Yet another said, "I will follow you, Lord, but let me first say farewell to those at my home."* [62]*Jesus said to him, "No one who puts his hand to the plow and looks back is fit for the kingdom of God."*

a Some manuscripts add *as Elijah did*   b Some manuscripts add *and he said, "You do not know what manner of spirit you are of; for the Son of Man came not to destroy people's lives but to save them"*   c Greek *he*

OVERVIEW: James and John's all-too-human desire for revenge, and Jesus' response to it, is the central theme of interpretations of this passage. As Brenz notes, when people disagree about religious beliefs, they easily fall into mutual dislike, even hatred and violence. The fact that Jesus' followers already considered the Samaritans heretics and schismatics made it easy to take serious and violent offense at their refusal to allow Jesus to enter. Not only did the disciples feel they were reacting against that offense, our commentators observe, but also they thought they were following the example of Elijah.[1] So how is it that Elijah could exact revenge, but Jesus did not allow his disciples to do so? Clearly there has to be a difference here, and our interpreters see the difference in the motivation, as well as the time. Elijah was acting under the guidance of the Holy Spirit and according to his office as a prophet. He was moved by God's will to his actions, but in the case of the disciples, they were moved by human emotions and personal desires. At a later point, when the disciples were more mature in the faith, they would be led by the Spirit to punish "notorious offenders" such as Ananias and Sapphira (Acts 5:1-11), but in those cases the point was not revenge but to deter others from sinning. Jesus came not for punishment and revenge but for patient correction of wrongs and the preservation of life.

Are the disciples ready to commit themselves to this weary and dangerous path of Jesus' passion and resurrection? Some who find the gospel appealing are not ready to commit wholly to Jesus and abandon the world's customs and comforts. Life in Christ, our commentators observe, is the way of the cross. Ministers of the gospel must keep their minds and hearts directed toward God's work, not entangling themselves with the affairs of this world unless necessity demands it. The true disciples of Christ will not defer the work or procrastinate but immediately place their hands on the plow and keep laboring until the

---

[1]See 2 Kings 1:10. The reformers, following Erasmus's *Novum Instrumentum,* here accept the variant ōs kai Ēlias epoiēsen according to the Majority text. Beza recognized that this clause is not preserved in some mss., including the Vulgate, but that it might have been expunged. See Theodore Beza, *Theodori Bezae Annotationes Majores in Novum Dn. Nostri Jesu Christi Testamentum,* 2 vols. (Geneva: Jeremie des Planches, 1594), 1:282.

day is done. Only such a one is fit to be a disciple of Christ.

9:51-53 The Samaritan Villagers Oppose Jesus

A LONG-STANDING CONFLICT EXISTED BETWEEN SAMARITANS AND JEWS. JOHANNES BRENZ: When the messengers entered into a certain Samaritan city to make the necessary preparations for the Lord and those who were with him, the citizens would not receive them and would not allow the Lord to enter into their gates, because they saw that he was heading toward Jerusalem. They believed that he was taking this journey in order to worship at the temple and attend the festival. The Samaritans did not like this, because they had their own temple at Mount Gerizim. (This temple is supposed to have been built by Sanballat, for the sake of his son-in-law Manasseh, who was expelled from the priesthood in Jerusalem [for marrying a Samaritan woman].) The Samaritans came so quickly to worship in this temple that sedition often arose and murders were committed between the Samaritans and the Jews, as we can read in Josephus.[2] The woman who disputed with our Lord by the well made mention of this hill.

And here we see again what we noted before, namely, that when people disagree among themselves about religious doctrines, they easily break out into mutual hatred. For example, it was a sign of cruel hatred to deny food to the hungry and lodging to the weary. But the Samaritans so hated and abhorred the Jewish religion that they thought no Jew was worthy of even these humanitarian gestures. They also were quite upset by the disagreements between them, because they knew that the Jews detested their temple as a profane place and counted the Samaritans as false worshipers of God. But once superstition has been planted it is hard to remove it, so they continued with tenacity and spite to defend it. The burning conten-

tion between the two groups at last went so far that it finally consumed both nations with one flame, for it was the occasion of the Jewish War, as we read in Josephus. AN ECCLESIASTICALL EXPOSITION UPON SAINT LUKE 9.[3]

9:54-56 Jesus Rejects the Punishment of the Samaritans

WE SHOULD NOT REVENGE OURSELVES BUT RATHER BE GOVERNED BY THE SPIRIT. JOHANNES BRENZ: If anyone is injured by another, he thinks it must be right and just to injure that person and be revenged. One curses his opponent, while another wishes not only death for his enemy but also an infinite number of devils and hell fire itself for him. And because these things are done, so sometimes they are thought to be justly done. And why should that be? Because, as they say, "He hurt me first. Why should he injure me, when I have done him no harm but only good? And why is it not lawful for me to do what the prophets did? When he was mocked by children, Elisha cursed them in the name of the Lord, and two bears came and tore forty of them into pieces. Also, Samson said about the Philistines, 'As they have done to me, so have I done to them.' So if it is lawful for holy men to curse and do evil to their adversaries, why may I not do it, because I have receieved so many and such great injuries?" This is how the desire for private revenge is not only counted as just but also as acceptable before God. But unless our zeal is governed by the Spirit of God, it will be of no benefit to us to make any excuse at all for what we have done. For the Spirit governs us with his counsel and wisdom, so that we will not begin any course of action unwisely, contrary to our office or our calling. Rather, the Spirit will endow our minds with right affections, putting away all the demands of the flesh, so that we may desire

---

[2]See Josephus, *Antiquities* 11-13.

[3]Marlorat, ed., *Catholike and Ecclesiasticall Exposition of the Holy Gospell After S. Marke and Luke*, 178-79*; alluding to Jn 4:20. According to Josephus, in A.D. 50 there was a conflict between Jews and Samaritans over the murder of a Galilean Jew on his way to Jerusalem. See Josephus, *Jewish War* 2.232-37.

nothing but what is according to God's will. An ECCLESIASTICALL EXPOSITION UPON SAINT LUKE 9.[4]

PREACHERS OF THE GOSPEL SHOULD NOT PUNISH FOR THE SAKE OF REVENGE. JOHN MAYER: But how is the Lord to be understood, because he reproved in his disciples what the holy man Elijah did after he was provoked? The answer is that they were not yet filled with such a spirit as Elijah, for they were moved by passion against the indignity and so would have done it out of revenge, but Elijah did it out of zeal for God's glory, that the power of his God (whom they insulted, preferring idols instead) might appear, and so that when others heard about it, they might be brought to fear the Lord. But the time would come when they would also be filled with the Holy Spirit like Elijah and so sometimes (although rarely) castigate notorious offenders, as Peter did to Ananias and Sapphira, to deter others from sinning in a similar way, and not through passion to be revenged. . . .

But there is also a further reason in this text: "The Son of Man came not to destroy but to save."[5] According to the earlier prophecies of him, he had great patience to bear wrongs, and not to revenge them. He was to do all things tending to the preservation of life, and nothing toward its destruction, reserving severity to the proper time, that is, when the gospel should be sufficiently taught and known, but people still would sin against it, and of course fully at the day of judgment. Note with what patience and lenity the preachers of the gospel should procede, even toward the most wicked, waiting to see if God would give them repentance to come out of the snare of the devil, even at the last moment. As Cyril said, the Lord taught them in preaching this

divine doctrine that they should be full of patience and mildness, and not angry or hostile, pushing cruelly back against those who wrong them. A COMMENTARY ON THE NEW TESTAMENT, LUKE 9:53.[6]

9:57-62 Few Can Commit to the Hardships of Discipleship

THE MAN WAS NOT READY TO BE A TRUE DISCIPLE. PHILIPP MELANCHTHON: What this man sought cannot be gathered from his words, but it is clear from Christ's words and his answer to the man. After a little taste of Christ's teaching, he seems ready to acknowledge the gospel to be the true doctrine of God, and he is moved with zeal and a certain affection to follow Christ. But he did not really consider what it would mean to follow Christ, so before long he wavered. There are many like him these days, who as soon as they hear the gospel give their names to Christ and profess that they believe in him. But if by chance any little persecution arises, before long they become just like this man and forget what they professed. This man wanted to follow Christ, but he wanted to be able to walk along a pleasant path and at his journey's end find a quiet inn or resting place and enjoy good cheer, whereas the disciples of Christ must pass through brambles and thorns and through many troubles to the cross. Therefore the more he hurried, the less he was ready; his heat was mere cold, and his diligence became negligence. He was like a man who wanted to be a warrior but who would not fight in the sun or in the dust; he also did not want the ordinary food, and he was not willing to be in danger of being shot.

It is no marvel if Christ rejects such soldiers, such disciples who, just as they rashly offer themselves, so they rashly and in shame pull back their foot. And so we should understand that all of

---

[4]Marlorat, ed., *Catholike and Ecclesiasticall Exposition of the Holy Gospell After S. Marke and Luke*, 180-81*; citing 2 Kings 2:23-24; Judg 15:11.

[5]In Lk 9:55 Erasmus's *Novum Instrumentum* included the variant "You do not know what manner of spirit you are of; for the Son of Man came not to destroy people's lives but to save them." Today only the KJV and NKJV include this rather late variant (mss. from the ninth and tenth centuries).

[6]Mayer, *Commentarie vpon the New Testament*, 373-74*; alluding to 2 Kings 1:9-12; Acts 5:1-10; citing Cyril of Alexandria, Sermon 56—see *Commentary upon the Gospel According to S. Luke*, 2 vols., trans. R. Payne Smith (Oxford: Oxford University Press, 1859), 1:253-57.

us are admonished in the person of this man, that we do not rashly or carelessly boast that we are the disciples of Christ, without any consideration of the cross or the trouble to come. Rather, let us consider beforehand what the condition of such a disciple must be. This ignorance calls us to his school and teaches us to deny ourselves, to take up the cross and follow him. AN ECCLESIASTICALL EXPOSITION UPON SAINT MATHEWE 8.[7]

SALVATION IS MORE PRESSING THAN ANY EARTHLY AFFAIR. KONRAD PELLIKAN: Hinting that he had placed human affairs before the business of salvation, Jesus said to him: "Allow the dead to bury their own dead." By this image, the Lord takes away any excuse that those might have who, on the pretext of human piety, postpone care and eagerness for eternal salvation. These awful people are those who under the pretext of domestic affairs prolong and procrastinate the business of salvation, which regularly from the first occasion should be accomplished. . . . The Lord said this, however, not to prevent us from taking care of our parents but to teach us that one should prefer piety to unbelieving parents, so that by it nothing should

be an obstacle to virtue and a cause to the despising of one's proper nature. Therefore, although this one was seeking to follow him, he first wanted to report this to those at home. But Jesus certainly did not allow him to go to his home and to report to his family. COMMENTARY IN LUKE 9:59-60.[8]

A TRUE CHRISTIAN WILL NOT REMOVE HIS HAND FROM THE PLOW. HENRY HAMMOND: He that holds the plow must follow it closely and not make errands home, or take up any other business until the day's work is done. If he does, he will not be fit for that employment. So you, if you will undertake Christ's service, must not defer or procrastinate but set to it now without any delay, and then follow it with the same diligence. And if you are not ready in this way to set out with Christ, if you either pretend to or really have such affection for your former way of life and what you have left at home, to cause you to take off even one day of his service, you are not worthy of the dignity and advantages of a Christian life, are not a competent judge of them and consequently are not fit to be a disciple of Christ. PARAPHRASE ON LUKE 9.[9]

---

[7]Marlorat, ed., *Catholike and Ecclesiasticall Exposition of the Holy Gospell After S. Mathewe*, 162-63*; alluding to Mk 8:34.

[8]Pellikan, *In Sacrosancta Quatuor Evangelia*, 118 (cf. LB 7:373-47). The comment about still needing to take care of one's parents here is Pellikan's sole contribution to Erasmus's *Paraphrase*.
[9]Hammond, *Paraphrase and Annotations*, 221*.

10:1-24 JESUS SENDS OUT THE SEVENTY

After this the Lord appointed seventy[a] others and sent them on ahead of him, two by two, into every town and place where he himself was about to go. [2]And he said to them, "The harvest is plentiful, but the laborers are few. Therefore pray earnestly to the Lord of the harvest to send out laborers into his harvest. [3]Go your way; behold, I am sending you out as lambs in the midst of wolves. [4]Carry no moneybag, no knapsack, no sandals, and greet no one on the road. [5]Whatever house you enter, first say, 'Peace be to this house!' [6]And if a son of peace is there, your peace will rest upon him. But if not, it will return to you. [7]And remain in the same house, eating and drinking what they provide, for the laborer deserves his wages. Do not go from house to house. [8]Whenever you enter a town and they receive you, eat what is set before you. [9]Heal the sick in it and say to them, 'The kingdom of God has come near to you.' [10]But whenever you enter a town and they do not receive you, go into its streets and say, [11]'Even the dust of your town that clings to our feet we wipe off against you. Nevertheless know this, that the kingdom of God has come near.' [12]I tell you, it will be more bearable on that day for Sodom than for that town.

[13]"Woe to you, Chorazin! Woe to you, Bethsaida! For if the mighty works done in you had been done in Tyre and Sidon, they would have repented long ago, sitting in sackcloth and ashes. [14]But it will be more bearable in the judgment for Tyre and Sidon than for

you. [15]And you, Capernaum, will you be exalted to heaven? You shall be brought down to Hades.

[16]"The one who hears you hears me, and the one who rejects you rejects me, and the one who rejects me rejects him who sent me."

[17]The seventy returned with joy, saying, "Lord, even the demons are subject to us in your name!" [18]And he said to them, "I saw Satan fall like lightning from heaven. [19]Behold, I have given you authority to tread on serpents and scorpions, and over all the power of the enemy, and nothing shall hurt you. [20]Nevertheless, do not rejoice in this, that the spirits are subject to you, but rejoice that your names are written in heaven."

[21]In that same hour he rejoiced in the Holy Spirit and said, "I thank you, Father, Lord of heaven and earth, that you have hidden these things from the wise and understanding and revealed them to little children; yes, Father, for such was your gracious will.[b] [22]All things have been handed over to me by my Father, and no one knows who the Son is except the Father, or who the Father is except the Son and anyone to whom the Son chooses to reveal him."

[23]Then turning to the disciples he said privately, "Blessed are the eyes that see what you see! [24]For I tell you that many prophets and kings desired to see what you see, and did not see it, and to hear what you hear, and did not hear it."

a Some manuscripts seventy-two; also verse 17   b Or for so it pleased you well

---

OVERVIEW: The sending of the seventy is an opportune passage for interpreters to find instructions for ministers.[1] New challenges faced Protes-

tant ministers in the Reformation, with fewer sources of income and often now with a wife and family for whom to care. Jesus' words to his disciples to set off "without bag or sack" struck a

---

[1]While the Lukan manuscript tradition is ambiguous concerning the precise number of disciples that Jesus sent out—seventy or seventy-two—most of the reformers follow Erasmus's *Novum Instrumentum* instead of the Vulgate, accepting seventy as authentic. Thus, we have amended the ESV text to fit the reformers' comment. Some contemporary scholars prefer

seventy-two based on discrepancies between the LXX and the Masoretic Text for the table of nations in Genesis 10, since Luke seems to prefer the LXX; but there is no scholarly agreement. See Bovon, *Luke 1*, 26.

chord, for these ministers had to trust that God would provide. But the "laborer is worthy of his hire." Ministers should not have to worry about their livelihood, these commentators argue, nor should they be distracted by worldly concerns or business unless it is of absolute necessity. Ministers should work for a living, but it is best if they can always be about God's work; Christ expects that the people who hear and receive the Word will take care of those who bring it to them. And preachers should accept the gifts as payment for their labor, rather than charity, for they have earned it, but they should be satisfied with simple fare and a humble lifestyle. Their bellies should not be their gods.

Other lessons that Jesus gave to his disciples could also be applied to present-day ministers, as the reformers assent. The world will not accept the gospel, and so its ministers will be despised and rejected and will suffer for it, but they are the representatives of Christ—whoever rejects them, rejects him. But such rejection should not deter those who are called to preach God's Word. In this case, Christ provided extra comfort and support to his ministers by sending them out in pairs, but no one should let fear of the world's reaction cause them to avoid ministry. Despite their lowly and humble lot, ministers have great responsibility and authority: by shaking off of their feet the dust of a town that rejects them, they are symbolically representing the judgment of God. The dust of the ministers' feet bears witness against those who rejected them, and this will be noted by God at the Last Judgment. Finally, Jesus notes that the harvest is plentiful—there is much work to be done to bring in the fruits of the gospel—but the laborers, those who are willing to dedicate their lives to the difficult task of working for the kingdom, are few.

10:1-2 Jesus Sends Out the Seventy

CHRIST SENDS HIS DISCIPLES IN LIGHT OF THE OLD TESTAMENT. EDWARD LEIGH: As there were twelve in the Old Testament, from which the twelve tribes were propagated and which the whole nation of the Jews acknowledged for their progenitors, so Christ also would have twelve apostles who should regenerate both the Jews and the Gentiles by the Word, and which the whole Christian nation should acknowledge for their patriarchs. As Jacob descended with seventy souls into Egypt, so Christ would have seventy disciples. But who these seventy disciples were, it is nowhere expressed in Scripture.

The sending of two together commends brotherly agreement and makes for consolation in adversity and for the greater confirmation of the truth. By this it is also signified that this business is such to which one will not suffice, for two sets of eyes always see more than one. Thus both Moses and Aaron were sent to Pharoah, and both Paul and Barnabas were sent by the church. ANNOTATIONS UPON SAINT LUKE 10.[2]

THE WORK OF THE GOSPEL IS COMPARED WITH A HARVEST. RICHARD TAVERNER: And he adds a reason why he sends forth so many, saying, "The harvest is great, but the laborers are few. Therefore ask the Lord of the harvest to send out laborers into his harvest." These are few words, but many things in them should be especially noted. First, the great number of those who desire the gospel is here expressed with a handsome analogy in calling it a "harvest." For in farming there are certain seasons and activities, until at last the grain is ripe and the harvest is at hand. First of all the ground is broken up with the plow; then it is sowed. After that the seeds spring up into grass, then shoot up into blades and stalks, and at last the grain ripens and is cut down and brought into the barn. Similarly the tilling of the Lord's ground has its certain times and proceeding. At the beginning, Moses broke up the Lord's ground with the plow of the law. Then the prophets came who sowed the seed. After that, in the time of John the Baptist appeared the blades. And at last, when Christ came and sent forth his apostles, the harvest came and

---

[2]Leigh, *Annotations upon All the New Testament Philologicall and Theologicall*, 113*; citing Gen 46:27; Ex 7; Acts 13:2-3.

the wheat began to be carried into God's barn. . . .

Therefore, because the time that the gospel of Jesus Christ is preached is the time of harvest, it must be seen what sort of grain is brought into God's barn. The grain is partly those who are gathered into the barn of Christ's church by the preaching of the gospel and partly the riches which people gather from the gospel by faith. These riches are not worldly goods but spiritual goods. They are, first of all, righteousness before God and others, the first of which comes through faith in Christ (for the righteous live by faith) and the second through obedience and the fruits of faith. Finally it is everlasting life and heavenly joy. These are the goods, riches and grain which are gathered from the spiritual harvest. But just as in a physical harvest the grain is not gathered into the barns without great sweat and labor, so whoever will gather the spiritual grain must deal with many adversities. ON SAINT LUKE'S DAY.[3]

10:3-12 *Instructions for the Mission*

THE WORLD WILL REJECT THEIR TEACHING. HULDRYCH ZWINGLI: "I am sending you out" not as princes of the world send out their ambassadors, with great and splendid pomp, of course: above all you will care for the people, and you should not be terrified but unshaken in your hearts and faithful in your souls. The treasure which you introduce to others was first produced in your hearts. Therefore you will be like lambs among wolves, for the world will not accept your teaching and admonition, which it opposes in all its ways. And so they will attack you by various means. Therefore dedicate your life to the truth. IN THE GOSPEL OF LUKE 10.[4]

THE PREACHERS OF THE WORD SHOULD NOT BE HINDERED BY EXTRAS. FRANÇOIS LAMBERT: Now you see that Christ intends that the holy preachers of the gospel come to the ministry of his Word unhampered and that nothing external

should hinder them from such necessary work. Therefore he forbids them to carry a bag and a sack, so that they might not rely on human providence. After that, he said, "Do not greet anyone on the way," but he did not mean that sort of greeting which is given in Christian moderation to those one meets, as Paul says in Romans 12, "Outdo one another in showing honor." Rather, he meant that sort of greeting which would hinder the spreading of the Word, especially by making it take longer, that is, visiting friends and relatives, which often takes all day. Therefore he says in the previous chapter that he does not want his disciples to return to bury their parents, but he commanded that they should immediately announce the kingdom of God, and those who first wanted to go home to say goodbye would not be chosen to be a disciple. COMMENTARY IN LUKE 10:4.[5]

WISH PEACE ON THOSE WHO RECEIVE YOU IN PEACE. PHILIPP MELANCHTHON: This salutation seems to be what Christ commanded to his disciples, saying, "When you enter a house, first say, 'Peace to this house.'" The Jews regularly greeted each other in this manner. Therefore Christ wanted his disciples to use this common and kind salutation, in order that they might win over the minds of those who, through the gospel, would be brought to the kingdom. . . . For a salutation is a sign of benevolence, friendship and love by which we wish well to those to whom we have come. Therefore Christ commands us to salute not only our friends, after the custom of the Gentiles, but also our enemies. AN ECCLESIASTICALL EXPOSITION UPON SAINT MATHEWE 10.[6]

MINISTERS SHOULD NOT BE WORRIED ABOUT THEIR FOOD AND DRINK. MARTIN BUCER: Christ prevents a possible objection that his disciples might make, where they might say, "You force us on strangers, destitute of everything,

---

[3]Taverner, *On Saynt Andrewes Day*, 40v-41r*; citing Rom 1:17.
[4]*D. Hvldrichi Zvinglii in Plerosqve Novi Testamenti Libros*, 243.

[5]Lambert, *In Divi Lucae*, Tr-v; citing Rom 12:10.
[6]Marlorat, ed., *Catholike and Ecclesiasticall Exposition of the Holy Gospell After S. Mathewe*, 207*.

saying that the worker is worthy of his food. But however 'worthy' we may be of our food, working in the harvest of the Father, who will give this food to us?" Christ makes a preemptive answer to this thought by saying, "I would not have you prepare to do anything but go and preach the kingdom of God. Just worry about that, and be assured that no one will harm you, and you will want for nothing. For (according to the proverb) the laborer is worthy of his food. Work for my Father, and he will provide meat for you without you having to get it yourself; it is not appropriate that the preachers of the kingdom of heaven should be troubled about these small matters. For who will not thankfully offer all things to them who preach everlasting life to all people and make them partakers of the kingdom of heaven? Therefore eat and drink what they set before you, and do it without shame, for this is not other people's meat but your own, as your pay and reward. For you will heal those who are sick among them, and will tell them that the kingdom of heaven is at hand and will provide heavenly doctrine to teach them."

All Christian preachers must learn from these words of Christ to make good choices about those with whom they will spend their lives, even as good farmers have to consider the ground before they break it up with the plow and sow good seed. The Word of God must not be set before reprobates or those who act like ignorant beasts. AN ECCLESIASTICALL EXPOSITION UPON SAINT LUKE 10.[7]

10:13-16 *Vengeance on Those Who Will Not Listen*

THE CITIES OF GALILEE REJECTED THEIR OPPORTUNITY TO ACCEPT CHRIST. PHILIPP MELANCHTHON: He notes that there is a remarkable obstinacy in those cities, in which he had often preached, because the idolatrous and corrupt cities of the Gentiles could sooner be converted to

repentance than they. But in order that no one should ask troublesome questions concerning the secret judgments of God, we must note that this saying of the Lord is applied to the weak and feeble capacity of the human mind, comparing the inhabitants of Bethsaida and that region with those of Tyre and Sidon. He does not dispute that what God had foreseen would come to pass concerning this one or that one, but rather what the other would have done, which may easily be perceived by what he said. For while the manners of these cities were very corrupt and disordered, that may be attributed to ignorance, because at no time was God's Word preached there, nor were there any miracles done that they might see, and to work repentance in them. But the people in the cities of Galilee that Christ rebuked showed great obstinacy in despising the miracles which he did many times among them through the power of God. In effect, the words of Christ are for no other purpose than to show that Chorazin and Bethsaida exceeded Tyre and Sidon in malice and in the incurable contempt of God. AN ECCLESIASTICALL EXPOSITION UPON SAINT MATHEWE 11.[8]

10:17-20 *The Seventy Return Full of Christ's Power*

TRUE BELIEVERS ARE GIVEN AUTHORITY OVER SATAN'S POISON. FRANÇOIS LAMBERT: Because as long as we live in the flesh, with the senses and emotions of the flesh, it is not fully extinguished. Therefore again and again the saints are moved by it, and they go astray in judging not according to the Spirit but according to the flesh. Truly the sense of the Spirit predominates in them, and so the sense or judgment of the flesh is not at all reckoned, but nonetheless that same sense is daily mortified. Therefore the disciples rejoiced that the demons submitted to them, but he forbade them to be joyful about it. Indeed, he wants them always to condemn the judgment of the flesh by

---

[7]Marlorat, ed., *Catholike and Ecclesiasticall Exposition of the Holy Gospell After S. Marke and Luke*, 184-85*; citing Mt 10:10; 1 Tim 5:18 (cf. Lev 19:13; Deut 24:14-15).

[8]Marlorat, ed., *Catholike and Ecclesiasticall Exposition of the Holy Gospell After S. Mathewe*, 238-39*.

the judgment of the Spirit. He also is teaching them where their true joy should come from by saying, "Rejoice that your names are written in heaven," that is, "that you are numbered among the elect and believers, and that you are part of the Lord's church."

Then, so that no one would be opposed to those believing, he shows all of them the power of Satan, saying, "I was watching Satan." That is, "he fell from the sky just like lightning during that amazing assault, and I perceived then the destruction of every strength and cunning of Satan, so he will be able to do nothing to those who would believe in me. No, on the contrary, every strength of theirs is thrown down, away from those who believe." For that reason he says to the faithful ones, "Behold, I have given you authority." They literally have authority over all the poisoning, as in the last chapter of Mark: "They will pick up serpents, and if they drink any deadly poison, it will not hurt them." Therefore in this passage it seems to have mentioned serpents and scorpions so that the poisonous cunning of the demons would be expressed more plainly and that the poisonous evil often done by Satan might be prevented. In addition to all these things, the fact that the faithful are receiving this authority is made clear by Psalm 91: "You will tread on the asp and the basilisk, and you will trample the lion and the serpent under foot." COMMENTARY IN LUKE 10:17-20.[9]

10:21-22 *Jesus Praises His Father*

CHRIST REJOICED WHEN HIS WORD WAS ACCEPTED. JOHANN SPANGENBERG: He rejoiced in his Spirit and spoke to the heavenly Father, thanking him and saying, "I praise you, Father, Lord of heaven and earth, because you have hidden these things from the wise and learned and revealed them to the little ones." People rejoice when things go well and are sad when things go badly, and because Christ was not only true God but also true man, he also found himself in such a

human state of emotion. He did not rejoice in the flesh, however, but in the Spirit, for if we look at the whole life of Christ, we do not find much externally expressed joy. His birth was poor and wretched, his life was filled with work and hardship, and his death was pitiful. But his greatest joy was when he saw that the poor sinners, the simple-hearted folk, heard and accepted his healing word so eagerly. He rejoiced so greatly in his heart over this that he forgot to eat and drink, and he was encouraged to preach even more.

Who does he call the "wise and learned"? Those who depend on their own wisdom and who wish to measure everything according to reason. The prophet Isaiah said of such people, "Woe to those who are wise in their own eyes and shrewd in their own sight." Such fleshly wisdom which despises the Word of God and the preaching of the cross cannot act in accordance with those things relating to justification. So we can see that such people rarely come to the recognition of God. ON SAINT MATTHEW'S DAY.[10]

THE SON REVEALS HIMSELF AND THE FATHER. RICHARD TAVERNER: Furthermore, in the interchangeable or mutual knowledge of the Father and the Son, we should learn that there is nothing in God the Son that is not in God the Father. For it follows in the text, "No one knows the Son except the Father, and no one knows the Father but the Son." For surely by saying that only he knows the Father, he means us to understand that he is of the self-same substance as the Father. It is as if he would say to us, "Who should marvel, I ask you, if I am true Lord of all, but there is yet a greater thing in me, that is, the knowledge of the Father in heaven, and that I am of the same substance as he?" Thus by these words Christ our Savior declares himself to be not only a human being but also God, and equal in power with his Father. And when he says that no one knows the Father but the Son, he does not mean that all people are utterly ignorant of him, but rather he means that

---

[9]Lambert, *In Divi Lucae*, T5r-v; citing Mk 16:18; Ps 91:13.

[10]Spangenberg, *Postilla Teütsch . . . von den fürnemsten Festen durch das gantze Jar*, XXXIIIIr-v; citing Is 5:21.

he knows his heavenly Father with a knowledge that no one else possesses. And it is true that any knowledge that we may have either of the Father or the Son comes from the Son's disclosure of it. So the Son discloses not only his Father but also himself to us. For as the holy doctor Saint Augustine said, "The Word not only opens that thing that is declared by the Word, but it also declares itself."[11] But how does the Son disclose his Father's will and pleasure to us? Surely by his most comforting Word, which is called his gospel. ON SAINT MATTHEW'S DAY.[12]

10:23-24 The Disciples Are Blessed in Faith

GOD REVEALED GREAT MYSTERIES TO THESE FISHERMEN. MARTIN BUCER: The Lord is not speaking here of physical seeing and hearing only, but also of that spiritual seeing and hearing which was withdrawn from the wise and revealed instead to these men, for which he gives thanks to his heavenly Father. He commented on this another time when he said, "To you it is given to know the mystery of the kingdom of God." And we must note that God observes an order and degree in revealing the knowledge of himself. For although those prophets and just men chosen by the Lord, and holy kings also, were the sons of God, yet he did not reveal to them the things which he revealed to these fishermen, who did not excel in dignity, or in wisdom or in righteousness. But the desire of the just to gain this knowledge is shown in the example of Simeon. Because they sought the glory of God and because a greater knowledge of God was still to be revealed, they wished and prayed for the coming of Christ most earnestly, as we can see in many passages of the prophets and Psalms. AN ECCLESIASTICALL EXPOSITION UPON SAINT LUKE 10.[13]

MANY DESIRED TO SEE THE MESSIAH BUT DID NOT RECEIVE THE OPPORTUNITY. JOHN BOYS: Those things which affect great and good people should be highly respected, but as Jesus said, "I tell you that many prophets and kings desired to see what you see, and did not see it, and to hear what you hear, and did not hear it." For holy Scripture calls the Messiah the "desire of nations" and says, "The prophets who prophesied about the grace that was to be yours searched and inquired carefully, inquiring what person or time the Spirit of Christ in them was indicating when he predicted the sufferings of Christ and the subsequent glories." When Balaam had prophesied of Christ, "a star shall come out of Jacob, and a scepter shall rise out of Israel," he broke forth into this lament, "Alas, who shall live when God does this?" It is as if he had said, "Happy are those who shall see that glorious star and sun of righteousness, coming out of his chamber as a bridegroom, giving light to those who sit in darkness and in the shadow of death."

"Oh, that you would rend the heavens and come down," said the prophet Isaiah. Good old Simeon waited for the consolation of Israel. Augustine wished he might have seen three things especially: Rome in its glory, Paul in the pulpit and Christ in the flesh. If the Queen of Sheba considered the servants of Solomon happy because while they were attending near his throne they could hear his wisdom, discoursing on trees—from the cedar that is in Lebanon to the hyssop that springs out of the wall—how blessed and happy were the disciples in hearing one who was greater than Solomon and in seeing him who was "the most handsome of the sons of men," "in whom are hidden all the treasures of wisdom and knowledge." THE THIRTEENTH SUNDAY AFTER TRINITY.[14]

---

[11]See Augustine, *On the Trinity* 7.3 (NPNF 3:107): "For if that word which we utter, and which is temporal and transitory, declares both itself and that of which it speaks, how much more the Word of God, by which all things are made?"
[12]Taverner, *On Saynt Andrewes Day*, 12r*.
[13]Marlorat, ed., *Catholike and Ecclesiasticall Exposition of the Holy Gospell After S. Marke and Luke*, 189*; citing Mt 13:11; Lk 2:25.
[14]Boys, *Exposition of the Dominical Epistles and Gospels*, 4:34-35*; quoting Hag 2:7; 1 Pet 1:10-11; Num 24:17, 23; Is 64:1; Col 2:3; alluding to Lk 2:25; 1 Kings 10:8; 4:33; Mt 12:42; Ps 45:2.

10:25-37 THE GOOD SAMARITAN

²⁵And behold, a lawyer stood up to put him to the test, saying, "Teacher, what shall I do to inherit eternal life?" ²⁶He said to him, "What is written in the Law? How do you read it?" ²⁷And he answered, "You shall love the Lord your God with all your heart and with all your soul and with all your strength and with all your mind, and your neighbor as yourself." ²⁸And he said to him, "You have answered correctly; do this, and you will live."

²⁹But he, desiring to justify himself, said to Jesus, "And who is my neighbor?" ³⁰Jesus replied, "A man was going down from Jerusalem to Jericho, and he fell among robbers, who stripped him and beat him and departed, leaving him half dead. ³¹Now by chance a priest was going down that road, and when he saw him he passed by on the other side. ³²So likewise a Levite, when he came to the place and saw him, passed by on the other side. ³³But a Samaritan, as he journeyed, came to where he was, and when he saw him, he had compassion. ³⁴He went to him and bound up his wounds, pouring on oil and wine. Then he set him on his own animal and brought him to an inn and took care of him. ³⁵And the next day he took out two denarii^a and gave them to the innkeeper, saying, 'Take care of him, and whatever more you spend, I will repay you when I come back.' ³⁶Which of these three, do you think, proved to be a neighbor to the man who fell among the robbers?" ³⁷He said, "The one who showed him mercy." And Jesus said to him, "You go, and do likewise."

a A *denarius* was a day's wage for a laborer

OVERVIEW: The question of "Who is our neighbor?" is one that continues to vex us. Like the pious lawyer in the story, religious people who revere God's commands and have great zeal to fulfill them may still have some confusion over what it means to do God's will. Jesus helpfully provides a summation of the law in two commandments: love God above all things, and love one's neighbor as oneself. However, these commands seem to take the requirements of the law to a new level. What does it mean to love God above all things, and is there any way we can even do so? For these Protestant commentators, the answer is difficult and easy at the same time. Loving God above all things means to place him before all others, all things, even oneself, and to devote all time and attention to doing God's will and giving him thanks and praise. This might be something we could strive for, but we will never achieve it on our own. Like the law, this "greatest commandment" remains a "word of wrath," teaching us that we always fall short. The pious lawyer thought he had completely kept the law because he had not broken any laws, but just because we do not worship idols does not mean that we love God above all things.

Likewise with loving our neighbors as ourselves: Good works and charity are wonderful but do not reach the level of Jesus' command, as he makes clear in the parable of the Good Samaritan. The lawyer asked Jesus, rather wisely, "Who is my neighbor?" The parable answers that question, for none of the characters in the story who might have been expected to help the injured man did so. The priest and the Levite passed him by, and only the Samaritan—considered unclean and an enemy by the Jews—stopped to help the wounded man. He not only helped him up but also tended his wounds, carried him to an inn and left money for the man's care and expenses until he could return. The Samaritan clearly treated the man as he would have hoped someone would have treated him—as we would all hope to be treated.

But for the reformers Jesus' point is not simply that the Samaritan was the good neighbor in this story. He also meant to show that the wounded man was the neighbor of the Samaritan, as well as the others who passed him by. The neighbor is not only someone like us, someone from our community, a friend, but also an enemy who might bring us into danger, expense or discomfort. Jesus' command is that we love such a neighbor as ourselves. Most interpreters found Jesus' second command as challenging as the first. How can either of these commands be kept to the fullest, in both exterior action and interior affection? It is clear that we cannot do it on our own.

10:25-28 The Greatest Commandments of the Law

KNOWING GOD'S LAW IS VITALLY IMPORTANT. CASPAR HUBERINUS: The next piece which we have here in this Gospel particularly concerns divine law, and we are shown our own arrogance, ignorance and inability through this lawyer as through a special and powerful example. He comes to Christ as such a learned and pious man, certainly a true paragon; he *should* be the best among all pious people, because this person has a great advantage over others. First he is learned—and to be learned and to know or to recognize the will of God from the law is truly a great thing. How many people are there who do not have God's law, or do not know what its contents are, but only have human statutes to go on? But if you do not know what God's law is, how can you know his will? If you do not know God's will from his commandments, how can you do or accomplish it, if you do not know what it is? Therefore this lawyer has a special, great advantage over those who do not know God's commands or will. Second, he also has a particular zeal, desire and intention to do God's commands, and so he comes here to Christ and desires to know how he may become pious and blessed. That is also something special and good to praise in this person, that he is not like other children of the world, nor does he behave like them, who do not ask about God but despise his commands, and do not profit from blessedness but

instead seek after the pleasures of the flesh and the joys of the world. Third, he desires only to test Christ alone, as one learned person perhaps desires to challenge another, and he wants to be praised over the other master and doctor.

However, we hear how Christ says to him that he has answered correctly, and such an answer pleases Christ greatly, just as he was pleased at the scribe's answer in Mark 12. For he saw that he answered wisely, and so he said, "You are not far from the kingdom of God," for that is the first level toward heaven, when we know God's law and recognize what we can learn from it for ourselves. However, if a person despises God's law and only worries about human commands, then that person will not know God's will but only human will. And so we will also not be able to learn to recognize it for ourselves and humble ourselves before God, but we will be haughty and presumptuous and will trust in false good works. Then we will be far from the kingdom of God, for recognition comes to the sinner through the law of God. ON THE THIRTEENTH SUNDAY AFTER TRINITY.[1]

ALL OF OUR BEING MUST LOVE GOD. JOHANN SPANGENBERG: There is much to be said here. Do not let any creature be so dear to you that you place it above God. Let all your thoughts, your words and works, your wit, reason and opinions be engaged in the things of God and give honor only to God. Focus everything you have toward God: body and soul, flesh and spirit, everything in your power, your members and more, your strength, your health, all your senses, externally and internally. In short, people should extend this love through their whole bodies and lives, through all their members, so that all parts of them from their head down to their feet, inside and out, move with delight and love toward God and the neighbor, without any annoyance, aversion or disgust. The eyes must not see anything obscene, the ears hear nothing wicked, the mouth speak nothing evil, and the hands and feet must be pure and innocent. In

---

[1]Huberinus, *Postilla Teütsch*, 2:p3r-v; citing Mk 12:34; Rom 3.

sum, a person must be pure in his thoughts, friendly in his words, blameless in his works, chaste in what he sees, upright in what he hears, honorable in what he says, and sincere in his heart. This person would rather die a thousand times than make God angry by any sins.

Now, that is a severe command. Who can fulfill it? No one should boast that he has fulfilled it. We have our whole lives to study it. It remains a command and a word of wrath, because it does not give the spirit to do what it commands. It will not be accomplished with words alone, but the heart, senses, courage, will, thoughts, words and works must agree together; otherwise it is pure hypocrisy. The decree is spiritual, and therefore it also wants to have the heart and the spirit. GOSPEL ON THE THIRTEENTH SUNDAY AFTER TRINITY.[2]

TRUE LOVE FOR THE NEIGHBOR MEANS HOLDING POSSESSIONS IN COMMON. PETER WALPOT: Those few words, "as yourself," comprise a true community and all works of love and mercy that a person can and would render to another. Yes, to love one's neighbor as oneself is the mother of true community and all good things. Wherever this love is poured out from God into our hearts, it teaches true community through the Holy Spirit and the bond of peace; here we do not desire to have an advantage over our neighbor, but equality and common concern for each other. But a person does not love his neighbor as himself when he desires out of self-interest to own, keep and hold possessions. For love is a bond of perfection—a golden chain that proceeds from the temple of God. Whoever has a link must throw everything into it. Loving one's neighbor as oneself means to hold not a part, not half, but everything in common, and to enjoy everything as an equal benefit. Otherwise it is only a pharisaical, heathen and false love, not a Christian one. THE GREAT ARTICLE BOOK: ON PEACE AND JOINT PROPERTY.[3]

CHRIST SIMPLY TELLS THE MAN TO "DO THIS." MARTIN LUTHER: But Christ says, "Do this and you will live." That was a thunderbolt! Christ says, "Well do I know that in the writings of the prophets it is written what one should do, but I say, 'Do it!' Where are the people who actually do it? Show me one!" Preaching the Ten Commandments is the highest office, for they contain the highest wisdom, which not even the wisest person could invent. Imperial law also states that a person should honor his parents and should not steal, but very weakly. For it does not say how far this honor of parents extends. However such is already the highest wisdom of the imperial law. But what does this law know about the first three commandments, and about Christ? But above all: to teach and to do, that is, to know and to be able to do are two different things. We see that the prophets and kings only grasped after these things. Therefore Christ says, "You have answered well, but now go and do it." He answers with just two little words: "Do it!" But it is impossible. He says, "I teach a different doctrine, which does not deal with what is lawful, but rather with how a person acts." You teach, indeed, that a person can keep these commandments with works. If you do not worship any idols, you think that means that you love God with your whole hearts. This is also what the pope says: "The holy Scriptures are true," but then he does not follow them. It is the doing that stops him short. We also are not able to act; another must act for us: Christ. SERMON ON THE THIRTEENTH SUNDAY AFTER TRINITY (1529).[4]

10:29-37 Who Is My Neighbor?

EVERYONE IS OUR NEIGHBOR, WHETHER WE LIKE IT OR NOT. JOHN LAWSON: The party to whom Christ related this parable would have been content to have received this kindness from a Samaritan, although he was a Jew, if he had been wounded and half dead as the wounded man was in the parable. However, he did not think himself

---

[2]Spangenberg, *Postilla . . . von Ostern biß auffs Aduent*, CXXVIIr.
[3]QGT 12:191; citing Mt 22:37-38.

[4]LEA 3:142 (cf. WA 29:525-26).

bound to show the same kindness to a Samaritan. Therefore Christ corrects him, teaching him to do to a Samaritan just as he would receive from a Samaritan.

Those who profess religion will be content to receive kindness where they will not bestow kindness, but it is a religion without a conscience to do so. Those who sequester themselves in narrow societies must examine whether they do not thereby also shut themselves off from the offices of love and charity to the bodies and souls of those who are not part of their fellowship, as if they were not bound to feed, clothe or minister a wholesome word of reproof or exhortation to help reduce the sin in another's soul, unless he is one of their group. The poor may fear that such communities will not receive them, as Nebuchadnezzar saved whom he chose, and that whomever they choose they will keep out. If they do this, their claims of religion are vain. This lawyer (for so he is said to be in Luke 10:25) would have been content that the Jew should be called his neighbor, but he did not want the Samaritans to be called his neighbors, or else he would be bound to do for them as he would want others to do for him. GLEANINGS AND EXPOSITIONS OF SOME PLACES OF SCRIPTURES.[5]

GOD'S WORD CREATES TRUE SAINTS, LIKE THIS SAMARITAN. THOMAS BECON: Here Christ puts forth the fruit of the gospel—that is, the good works that ought to ensue when God's Word is preached. He describes it with a plain example of a certain man who, as he came down from Jerusalem, chanced on some robbers, who beat him and left him half dead. Not long after, a priest went that way who saw him, but he passed by and was not moved to help him. Likewise the Levite who came after the priest had no regard for him. At last came the Samaritan, who had no holy name but was a Gentile, not related at all to the wretched man, who was a Jew. He did not come from the same stock, as did the priest and the Levite, but was a stranger.

He sees this miserable man and, grieved by his misfortune, gets down from his animal, pours oil and wine into his wounds, binds them up and puts him on his mount. He continues on foot and carries the wounded man to an inn. Because he could not stay long on account of his business, he commits the man to the innkeeper and gives money to care for him until he can return.

This is the second picture in which Christ paints the fruits of the word and Christian charity, that is, that the Word creates such people as this Samaritan: gentle, merciful, those who do not despise others in their calamity, but when they see them, bestow their goods on them and help them with all that they can. I speak of the poor and needy who are not wicked, as most beggars are, who on purpose seek this sort of gain and will not take money to serve, either to help the sick or to do any other thing that they can do; to such beggars nothing must be given. But where there are truly needy persons, a Christian must behave himself according to the example of this Samaritan and think: "This poor person is my neighbor and is made up of body and soul, just as I am. He has the same God that I have, which makes him closer in kinship to me than a dumb beast, or than the devil. Therefore I do not do well if I forsake him." He should embrace that person as a brother or sister and, in case he might die without help, should take compassion on him as a parent. And these are the true saints.

But other stone-hearted saints have no natural pity toward the wretched but are people of exceedingly great meanness. They seem to think that God is delighted to serve them, and therefore they think that they are not bound to serve others, as this priest does. He was a holy person for his office and his kin, but what does Christ say of him? That when he saw this miserable man, he passed him by. These "holy ones" are truly wicked when they see their neighbors in peril and might help them, but will not. Why, then, do they trust and maintain their pride? Because of their holiness, so they think that when they have said mass, made sacrifices and sung songs, they have done enough,

---

[5]Lawson, *Gleanings and Expositions*, 23-24*; citing 2 Kings 24.

and they do not need to do an inch more than their requirements. These are "stony" saints, even "devilish" saints, who seem to count God as their debtor and think they owe nothing to any person. THE FOURTEENTH SUNDAY AFTER TRINITY SUNDAY.[6]

THE NEIGHBOR IS THE ONE WHO NEEDS CHARITY AND THE ONE WHO PROVIDES IT. JOHANN SPANGENBERG: Now who is the "neighbor" of this wounded man? The one who showed mercy to him. The neighbor is not only the one who provides charity but the also the one in need of charity, whether he is friend or enemy. For we are all neighbors to each other. Now let us look at how it goes. The priest and the Levite in all fairness should have taken up this wounded man, a Jew, both because of their shared lineage and on account of their positions. But what did they do instead? They crossed over to the other side of the road and left him lying there. But the Samaritan, who was an enemy to the Jews, had mercy on him, walked over to him and bandaged up his wounds, pouring on oil and wine. He lifted him up onto his own animal, took him to the inn and cared for him. Christ directs the teacher of the law through this example and says, "Go and do likewise. Do good not only to your friend and benefactor but also to your enemy and to the one who does evil to you." GOSPEL ON THE THIRTEENTH SUNDAY AFTER TRINITY.[7]

---

[6]Becon, *New Postil (Second Parte)*, 105r-106r*.

[7]Spangenberg, *Postilla . . . von Ostern biß auffs Aduent*, CXXVIIIr.

10:38-42 MARY AND MARTHA

^{38}Now as they went on their way, Jesus^a entered a village. And a woman named Martha welcomed him into her house. ^{39}And she had a sister called Mary, who sat at the Lord's feet and listened to his teaching. ^{40}But Martha was distracted with much serving. And she went up to him and said, "Lord, do you not care that my sister has left me to serve alone? Tell her then to help me." ^{41}But the Lord answered her, "Martha, Martha, you are anxious and troubled about many things, ^{42}but one thing is necessary.^{b} Mary has chosen the good portion, which will not be taken away from her."

a Greek he   b Some manuscripts few things are necessary, or only one

OVERVIEW: Mary and Martha were close friends of Jesus and the sisters of Lazarus, whom he later raised from the dead. This is the more well-known story of the two sisters, and it offers a rather simple dichotomy: Martha represents the hardworking, careworn person who is so busy with chores that she is too distracted to listen to Jesus' message; Mary neglects the chores because she is enrapt in Jesus' words. In the standard course of things, Martha would be the more responsible and upright of the two, for she works hard to provide for her household and guests, while Mary seems a bit lazy and irresponsible, distracted by pleasure. But of course, this is the gospel, so spiritual matters outweigh worldly ones. In this case, Martha is in the wrong for wishing to censure her sister, for Mary has chosen the "one thing needful" in focusing wholly on Christ. But just how wrong was Martha? She and her sister both loved Jesus, and he had great affection for them—this was not a case of a wicked, faithless person who needed punishment. Martha even meant well, for her intentions were good, and she was serving Christ in her own way. But while Erasmus is unwilling to chastise Martha, saying only that Jesus saw Mary as more in the right, most of the commentators insist that Martha sinned. She let her worries overtake her and distract her; she criticized her sister and implicitly criticized Jesus as well. She wanted to have things her own way, rather than to follow his way. But as Luther points out, the best part of this gospel is how Jesus reacts to her. Martha is a beloved member of the family—a faithful follower who needs a little correction now and then, as we all do. He did not push her away or react angrily, but instead he corrected her gently, pointing out her fault so that she might correct her actions and attitude. Just so is he kind and gentle with us in correcting us, and we should respond as Martha did, with humility rather than anger and rejection.

But if we need to avoid Martha's worries and distractions, does that mean that instead we should be like Mary, forgetting all our responsibilities to sit at Jesus' feet? Not at all! Or at least, not very often. In fact, the world would fall apart if everyone followed Mary's example all the time. Each person must continue to follow his vocation and work (that is, in the Protestant viewpoint there was no calling to a completely contemplative life). The only time we should imitate Mary is when we are listening to sermons. That is when no worldly cares should distract, no matter how important they seem to be, but we should instead focus wholly on God's Word and message to us.

10:38-40 Martha Plays the Good Hostess

WHAT GOOD IS THE BELLY WITH FOOD IF THE MOUTH IS WITHOUT THE WORD? MARTIN LUTHER: This Gospel teaches a difference between the things that relate to the stomach and those which relate to the soul. Christ, although he is of course hungry, is also so desirous of the blessedness of the soul that he forgets the meal and only preaches to Mary. He is so attentive to the Word that he rebukes Martha, who wanted to go about the business over which she was troubled, neglecting the gospel. On the Day of Mary's Ascension.[1]

Martha Loved and Served the Lord, While Mary Loved and Listened. Desiderius Erasmus: Martha and Mary had equal devotion to the Lord, but their styles of life were quite different. Likewise the expression of their devotion was different, just as in one body there are different uses of the parts, and in the body of Christ, which is the church, there are various gifts of the Spirit. . . . They each had the same love toward the Lord, but Mary would not suffer being pulled away from his feet, while Martha, who was turned around all up and down, did not want to let her cling so closely to the Lord. Thus the same devotion led the two sisters to act in different ways, although they were in agreement in loving the Lord. Paraphrase on the Gospel of Luke 10:38-40.[2]

We Should Not Follow Mary's Example, Except During Sermons. John Mayer: Is it acceptable for any man or woman to do as Mary did, to focus wholly on the Word and not trouble themselves about any worldly thing? The answer is no, for everyone must continue in his calling, through which he is called to be a Christian. The time was then extraordinary: Christ was living on the earth, and the time that he would be with them was short. Likewise the knowledge of the divine mysteries was very little, and therefore it was necessary to make a choice in favor of listening to him. But now knowledge abounds and education is widely available, and therefore such examples are not to be imitated, lest we be categorized with the Eutychians, who only wanted to pray but were condemned as heretics rather than praised for

devotion.[3] But note that the hearing of the Word should be the only focus when it is preached—no worldly business, even if it seems quite necessary, should call us away from it. In this case, too much worldly employment, even if through it good is done for the commonwealth, can be criticized. Last, when we socialize with preachers, they should not regard it as feeding the soul, even at the time of feasting, as Christ did here. A Commentary on the New Testament, Luke 7:39.[4]

Martha Sinned Further in Criticizing Her Sister. Richard Baxter: There is one thing further which the text mentions about Martha which should be noted: because she is overcareful and troubled about many things which were not entirely necessary, she thinks her sister should also have been so concerned and should have acted as she did. So Martha resented Mary and complained about her to Christ, as if Mary's work was somehow less necessary than her own. This shows us that those who choose unnecessary or less necessary activities are likely to see religious exercises as less important and to censure those who choose them. The fact that Martha wrongly censured Mary for the work she chose to do was as much her sin as were her own poor choice and needless trouble. Those who sin despite what they know, and then confess that they have erred, are often desirous that their children and friends should avoid their mistakes. But those who think their sin is actually their duty will criticize those who do not sin along with them, as if it were a sin to fear and avoid sin. . . . The fact that she criticized her sister probably even affected Martha's love of Christ himself, because Mary did not serve him in the way that she thought was most necessary. The One Thing Necessary, or, Mary's Choice Justified.[5]

---

[3]The Eutychians followed the teaching of Eutyches of Constantinople, who taught a monophysite Christology. His teaching was condemned as heretical at Chalcedon in 451, although not for the reason Mayer lists here.
[4]Mayer, *Commentarie vpon the New Testament*, 373*.
[5]Baxter, *Christ's Justification of Mary's Choice*, 62-63*.

---

[1]WA 10,3:269-70.
[2]Erasmus, *In Evangelivm Lvce Paraphrasis*, q5r (LB 7:378-79).

10:41-42 *Mary Has Chosen the Better Portion*

WORK IS FINE SO LONG AS IT DOES NOT DIVIDE THE BODY FROM THE SOUL. DESIDERIUS ERASMUS: Now the Lord, moved by the affection of both women, did not condemn Martha's intention, nor did he rebuke her complaints against her sister, but he did support Mary, saying, "Martha, Martha, you are certainly churned up with anxiety in preparing the meal, and you are distracted and all in uproar about many things. Of all those things one is especially necessary, which should always be done, if one is able. Your work harasses you, but however the meal turns out, that's fine. Mary has chosen the far more important thing, which is forgetting those things having to do with the body and being completely wrapped up in those things having to do with the soul." PARAPHRASE ON THE GOSPEL OF LUKE 10:41-42.[6]

CHRIST CORRECTED MARTHA, AND SHE ACCEPTED IT HUMBLY. MARTIN LUTHER: This is the same as: "Martha, you have many worries. I have preached the gospel before which says that one should not worry: one should work but not worry, and especially when the Word is brought forward, then one should neglect his business—yes, not only his business but also wife and child, father and mother, friend and foe, honor and wealth, and only cling to the Word." Although Martha was a good child and meant well, still the Lord criticizes her intention and rebukes her work. This shows us that our good intention may be turned in whichever way we want, and so it is false, as Martha could very well have said, "I have taken a lot of trouble with the preparations, the washing, the setting up, so it should be my intention and not yours." But however a person reshapes his intention into whatever he likes, it is worth nothing with God, for God said, "You are not to do whatever you see fit."

You see here that Martha was rebuked for her intention, even though it was for good, and God rebukes her worry much more than her work. However, he rebukes her in a friendly way and does not push her away from him, and that is the best thing in this Gospel, for it paints a picture for us of what a gentle and friendly man he is, as he treats us gently even though from time to time we fail and do not do what is right. Despite this he can still approve of us. The Scripture shows us such a picture of the Lord that one must expect the very best, for the heart must have such an image before faith can be created, as we see here. Without a doubt, Martha sinned, because she was worried and tried to keep her sister from the true good work, and yet Christ rebuked her gently and did not repudiate her. Likewise God can approve of our infirmities, but only if we in turn close our eyes to them and gladly accept it when he rebukes and repudiates our work, as Martha does here. She was silent, allowed him to rebuke her work and accepted it well. We should do likewise; we should suffer when he rebukes and criticizes our things, we should remain silent and only say, "It is right, Lord." ON THE DAY OF MARY'S ASCENSION.[7]

MARTHA SINNED IN VALUING UNNECESSARY THINGS OVER A FOCUS ON CHRIST. RICHARD BAXTER: Here are some very important points to consider from this text. First, the author of this reproof was one who could not be suspected of making a mistake out of ignorance or of disliking Martha. And although he lived in a simple manner and not as rich people do, he did not blame her for focusing on unnecessary things because he desired such things. He was the Lord of all, and it was for our sake that he became poor, and yet he suffered as much as the rich are generally thought to do, because they are thought to be the greatest sinners: "And they made his grave with the wicked and with a rich man in his death." Second, his reproof was both very serious and very compassionate, as we can see in how he

---

[6]Erasmus, *In Evangelivm Lvce Paraphrasis*, q5v (LB 7:739).   [7]WA 10,3:270; citing Deut 12:8.

repeated her name, "Martha, Martha." Third, the one he reproved was not a wicked, fleshly, worldly person but one beloved by him, and a faithful believer. Fourth, the matter for which she is reproved is both positively expressed (that she is careful, and troubled about many things) and also seen as a lack, because she did not prefer the "one thing needful" at the time as much as she should have. This implies that the "many things" were not important, or at least were less important things; they took up too much of her time; and these cares weighed heavily on her mind, distracting her.

I should need no more words to convince you that Christ is teaching us this lesson here: care and trouble about many needless or less important things, which hinder a person from due attention to the "one thing needful," is a sin which Christ reproved in Martha, and therefore he considers it a sin in all others who are guilty of it. The One Thing Necessary, or, Mary's Choice Justified.[8]

---

[8]Baxter, *Christ's Justification of Mary's Choice*, 2-3*; citing Is 53:9.

11:1-13 THE LORD'S PRAYER

Now Jesus[a] was praying in a certain place, and when he finished, one of his disciples said to him, "Lord, teach us to pray, as John taught his disciples." [2]And he said to them, "When you pray, say:

"Father, hallowed be your name.
Your kingdom come.
[3]Give us each day our daily bread,[b]
[4]and forgive us our sins,
    for we ourselves forgive everyone who is
        indebted to us.
And lead us not into temptation."

[5]And he said to them, "Which of you who has a friend will go to him at midnight and say to him, 'Friend, lend me three loaves, [6]for a friend of mine has arrived on a journey, and I have nothing to set before him'; [7]and he will answer from within, 'Do not bother me; the door is now shut, and my children are with me in bed. I cannot get up and give you anything'? [8]I tell you, though he will not get up and give him anything because he is his friend, yet because of his impudence[c] he will rise and give him whatever he needs. [9]And I tell you, ask, and it will be given to you; seek, and you will find; knock, and it will be opened to you. [10]For everyone who asks receives, and the one who seeks finds, and to the one who knocks it will be opened. [11]What father among you, if his son asks for[d] a fish, will instead of a fish give him a serpent; [12]or if he asks for an egg, will give him a scorpion? [13]If you then, who are evil, know how to give good gifts to your children, how much more will the heavenly Father give the Holy Spirit to those who ask him!"

a Greek he b Or our bread for tomorrow c Or persistence d Some manuscripts insert bread, will give him a stone; or if he asks for

OVERVIEW: In this pericope, our commentators observe that Jesus not only teaches us to pray by providing us a model of prayer; he also encourages us to pray by insisting that our prayers will succeed in gaining what we need. Prayer is the dominant way in which we conduct our relationship with God, so Jesus teaches us to call him Father. It was common for Jews to refer to God as Father, and it teaches us what sort of relationship we have with him. While "lords of the earth" can be offended by and turn away from their subjects, requiring many intermediaries between them, a father does not act in such a way. As our Father, God is kind and indulgent, especially when we are at our most wretched and helpless. God loves sinners who recognize and confess their sins. He does not expect us to be perfect, and one does not need to be a great saint to call God Father. We should pray to him for everything we need: help in turning away from the devil and the world, our daily bread and all our needs, help in forgiving others (for we *must* forgive those who have offended us if we want God to forgive us) and help in turning away from sin. We might pray, "Lead us not into temptation," but the fault is ours, not God's. It is our guilt that leads God to punish us with darkness and temptations.

But what can we expect prayer to achieve? We have all experienced asking God for things that we do not receive or do not happen. It is easy to believe that God is the master of the house who is already asleep in bed when we come to knock on the door for help—he does not want to arise to help us. But for the reformers, Jesus' examples show that two factors must be met for prayer to be sincere and successful: we must pray for things that are good for us (and God, as our good Parent, will decide what is good for us), and we must continue to ask, seek and knock at the door—we must practice persistence in prayer. Like the master of the house already in bed, God will answer the door only if we keep on knocking, though unlike the sleeping master, God "neither slumbers nor sleeps." As our good Father he is always ready to help us in time of need, but he expects us to keep asking, to keep seeking and to keep knocking at the door. As Fenner notes, our prayer should be "restless"—we should not take no for an answer but should continue to ask, even to be impudent "in a holy way" until it succeeds. As Erasmus asks, if people, who are otherwise quite bad, are kind-hearted and giving to their children, how much more will our Father, who is good by nature, give to us what we need?

11:1-4 *Jesus Teaches His Disciples How to Pray*

THE LORD'S PRAYER REFLECTS COMMON USAGE. JOHN LIGHTFOOT: Christ had taught it almost a year and half before in his Sermon on the Mount, and now being desired to teach them to pray, he gives the same again. They who deny this for a form of prayer to be used either do not know or do not consider what kind of prayers the eminent men among the Jews taught. John had taught his disciples to pray after the same manner and use of the nation. Now that Christ's disciples desired him to teach them as John had taught his, he repeats this form which he had given before. They who again deny that this prayer is to be used by any but real saints, because, as they say, none but saints can call God our Father, either do not know or do not consider how usual this form of speech was among the nation in their devotions, and Christ speaks constantly according to the common and most usual language of the country. THE HARMONY OF THE NEW TESTAMENT, SECTION 60.[1]

GOD IS A LOVING FATHER, NOT AN OFFENDED PRINCE. HULDRYCH ZWINGLI: "Our Father who is in heaven." That is, "we recognize you as the Lord and Governor of heaven and earth," for if he governs the heavens, how much more must he govern the earth? "Who is in heaven" is, I think, periphrasis, and if we would have said "O heavenly Father," we would not be speaking there to a fleshly and earthly father.[2] He is glad to be called Father rather than Lord in prayers. The lords and princes of this earth, when they are offended, are quite indignant, and those who did them harm do not dare to approach them. These rulers turn away their faces; they shrink from the wretched. They do not allow entreaties except through many intermediaries. God, who is our Father, is not like this, for he is the kindest and most indulgent Father to us even when we are unclean, wretched and helpless. Earthly fathers often love and care more for those who are weaker and more helpless among their children; likewise the heavenly Father loves sinners more who plainly acknowledge themselves to be sinners, who recognize their sickness, who are displeased with themselves and who thirst for justice. The Father is compassionate, not cruel. He is rich, and he desires that we might enjoy his riches. He does not look down on us on account of our sins. Christ says, "Our Father," and so it is proper to speak to God, not to Gertrude, or Christopher or Erasmus.[3] Those who say Our Father to saints show themselves to be unfaithful. God alone is our Father—God, I say, who dwells in the heavens, who is Lord of heaven and earth. IN THE GOSPEL OF LUKE 11.[4]

THE NAME OF GOD IS HOLY AND UNIQUE, DESERVING OF HALLOWING. FRANÇOIS LAMBERT: This is the name that we explained extensively in chapter one above: "And you will call his name Jesus." This name is sanctified by everything, and we should always pray before it. That

---

[2]Periphrasis is indirect speech; in linguistics, it can also refer to terms that use more than one word to form a single concept. For example, "most beautiful" (two words) is periphrasis, while "prettiest" (one word) is not.

[3]Aside from Gertrude, Zwingli is referring to the Fourteen Holy Helpers—Agatha, Barbara, Blaise, Catherine of Alexandria, Christopher, Cyriacus, Denis, Erasmus, Eustace, George, Giles, Margaret of Antioch, Pantaleon and Vitus—saints venerated for their putative healing powers.

[4]*D. Hvldrichi Zvinglii in Plerosqve Novi Testamenti Libros*, 250.

---

[1]Lightfoot, *Harmony, Chronicle and Order of the New Testament*, 47*.

thing is holy which is not common and ordinary but rather singular and chosen out of all things, which we also taught in the first chapter above. Therefore it is prayed here that the name of God might be hallowed by everyone together; that is, that it might be recognized by everyone everywhere that it is most just and perfect, and that by virtue of such it might be held and announced. Its excellence is so lofty, superior and more than wonderful that nothing may be united to it. Therefore his name is holy because it is singularly glorious and the highest of all things whatsoever, having nothing in common with what is created and corruptible. COMMENTARY IN LUKE 11.[5]

BRING US TO YOUR KINGDOM, LORD! KATHARINA SCHÜTZ ZELL: O dear Father, grant that all that the enemy has in us may be killed and driven out. May we be the children of your kingdom and not cast out. May we not fail to hear because we do not pay attention, when today we hear your voice through Jesus Christ as he says, "Reform yourselves [*bessert eüch*], the kingdom of God has come near."[6] O God, help us to recognize and flee from the kingdom of the devil, to recognize and let go of the perishable kingdom of the world, for both are enemies that oppose you. But may we seek with seriousness and not hypocrisy and find your good, enduring, imperishable kingdom and its righteousness. May we be admitted to it and become citizens and receive wisdom and all that we need from you.

O dear God, help us: we are so far from your kingdom! Grant that we may not be so casual and stiff-necked toward you and your kingdom, so that when you come again you may not judge us to be your enemies who would not allow you to rule over us. But grant that we may receive and obey you from the heart and be the people of your kingdom. Through your Holy Spirit may you rule and be Lord in our hearts, souls, bodies and consciences. May your word and commandment live in us. For

you are the King of honored lords, and Lord of the true kingdom, whom we all must acknowledge, seek, honor, fear and love, to whom alone we should pray and to whom we should adhere as our true Lord, Ruler and King. OUR FATHER (1532).[7]

GOD PROVIDES OUR DAILY BREAD. PHILIPP MELANCHTHON: While we call it our bread, we should not think of it as if it were ours by right and as if it were owed to us like a debt, but rather that it is necessary for us and appointed to us by that providence of our life by which the Lord feeds all things out of his goodness. He gives it to us freely, because he does not want us to be in need. The fields must be tilled and plowed, we have to sweat in the gathering of the fruits of the earth, and everyone must labor according to his calling; but this does not change that we are fed by the free liberality and gift of God, without which a person cannot do anything but draw up water in a sieve—his labor would be in vain. But we are taught that whatsoever we seem to earn by our own labor and industry is acceptable to God. Now some who read this verse think that this bread is supersubstantial or superessential, as though Christ were not speaking of corporal food, but their reasoning is vain and repugnant to godliness. For we all know that it is the order of Scripture in many places to bring us by the taste of earthly things up to the knowledge of heavenly things. But here Christ speaks of corporal food, so if we were to assume otherwise, we would have to say that his words are mutilated and imperfect. In many places in Scripture we are commanded to cast all our cares on God, and he promises most liberally on his part that we shall want for nothing. Therefore in the exact rule for prayer, it was necessary that a request concerning the innumerable necessities of this present life should also be commanded. AN ECCLESIASTICALL EXPOSITION UPON SAINT MATHEWE 6.[8]

---

[5]Lambert, *In Divi Lucae*, V6r; citing Lk 1:31.
[6]As Elsie McKee points out, Schütz Zell here uses the translation of the Zurich Bible, *besserend euch* ("reform yourself"), rather than Luther's German translation, *thut busse*.

[7]Zell, *Church Mother*, 160-61*; citing Mt 4:17; Mt 6:33; Lk 19:27.
[8]Marlorat, ed., *Catholike and Ecclesiasticall Exposition of the Holy Gospell After S. Mathewe*, 121*.

WE MUST FORGIVE OTHERS' OFFENSES IF WE WANT GOD TO FORGIVE US. MARTIN BUCER: How can those who will not forgive their neighbors' offenses be excused? How can these folks then presume to ask God to forgive their sins? Is it a mere trifle to lie to the living God and to play the hypocrite? For when we say, "Forgive us, as we forgive others," what else are we doing but calling for vengeance on ourselves at the hands of God if we do not forgive those who offend us? And for this reason there are many people nowadays who, rather than forgiving and remitting offenses against them, will not say the Lord's Prayer. But these people do not escape the judgment of God, for what the Lord says abides forever. If you do not forgive other people's trespasses, your Father who is in heaven will not forgive you your trespasses. AN ECCLESIASTICALL EXPOSITION UPON SAINT MATHEWE 6.[9]

WE LEAD OURSELVES INTO TEMPTATION. KATHARINA SCHÜTZ ZELL: O righteous God and Father, save us from the temptation of becoming hardened in our hearts so that we come into your just judgment through our debt (as happened to Pharaoh)—hardened so that we do not want to forgive and let our debtors go free, as Pharaoh did to your people and as the servant in the Gospel strangled his fellow servant. You do not lead us into temptation; we do that ourselves! For you are not a tempter but the truth and the way through the revealed Word. Therefore without your will (for you desire that all people should be saved and do right), but through our own sufficient deserts and self-chosen blindness, we are led from one sin into another. As we do not forgive people their faults, so you do not forgive our faults and so you let us go to ruin because no sacrifice pleases you unless mercy and unity with the neighbor go before it.

Yes, dear Father, let us not because of our guilt be led by your wrath into darkness and the temptation of our flesh, but let us overcome them through the love of Jesus Christ. "Lead us also not into temptation." That is, do not let us relax into a false, wicked, hypocritical conscience by which we persuade ourselves that we have forgiven our debtors and that we wish them well and so we only cloak our hearts and consciences with a false show when there is actually nothing there—like the drunken gravedigger.[10] O Father, help us! Grant that such a counterfeit grave and the temptation of this severe affliction, this concealed jealousy and wrath, may fall away from us and that we may forgive our debtors from the heart. OUR FATHER (1532).[11]

11:5-8 The Friend Who Knocks at Midnight

KNOCK ON GOD'S DOOR WITH THE HAMMER OF PRAYER. JOHANN SPANGENBERG: Who is the traveling guest? The guest who comes at night and calls on us for hospitality is the various trials and temptations, adversities and afflictions, anxiety and sickness which can come on us suddenly and unforeseen. For we also take care to say, if one has a bad tooth, an ulcer or a pustule: "I have an evil guest who will not let me rest day or night." And who is the sleeping friend or neighbor? This sleeping friend is God our Lord, for when we call on him in times of trouble or danger and he does not answer us so quickly, he seems to us to be asleep. And so we continue to knock on the door of his fatherly heart with the hammer of prayer. For the prayer that flows from a faithful heart is such a hammer that it will be heard loud and clear in the highest heaven. The prayer of the distressed pierces the clouds and does not cease until it has come to God, and it does not stop until it reaches the highest places. But we go to him in the night, under our cross, in

---

[10]McKee clarifies this joke: the drunken gravedigger "thinks he has done his job but is too drunk to realize he has not buried the body."

[11]Zell, Church Mother, 168-69*; citing Ex 7:3; Mt 18:28-35; Jas 1:13-14; Jn 14:6; Mt 6:15; Ps 51:16; Mt 23:27; 18:35.

[9]Marlorat, ed., Catholike and Ecclesiasticall Exposition of the Holy Gospell After S. Mathewe, 123-24*.

fear and affliction, for the three loaves of bread, that is, help and comfort from God the Father, the Son and the Holy Spirit. But how does God, the heavenly master of the house, present himself? He lets us say many words and cry loudly, but he keeps silent and acts as if he were sleeping and does not hear us. And as the master of the house presents himself, so also do all his children and servants. And so he already gives us an answer, and he refuses us any help, saying, "Don't trouble me! The door is locked, and my children are with me in the chamber. It isn't right for me to disturb their sleep on your account. I cannot get up and give you the help that you want." That is a hard blow for a poor, troubled heart; yes, obviously a hard blow, but it is also at the same time a great comfort that Christ says, "I say to you, although he will not get up and give it to him because he is his friend, yet he will get up because of his shameless begging and give him what he needs." And even more, he says, "If one person can obtain something from another person through ill-timed knocking, begging and pleading, how much more will a person receive from God with his heartfelt prayer?" GOSPEL DURING ROGATION WEEK.[12]

GOD IS ALWAYS READY TO HEAR AND HELP US. THE ENGLISH ANNOTATIONS: Which of you will be so uncivil as to put off an importunate friend, saying, "Trouble me not"? But rather, as in Luke 11:8, he will rise and give him what he wants because of his importunity. How much more will the keeper of Israel, who neither slumbers nor sleeps, who is always ready to relieve our trouble, having in himself that eternal and unspeakable love for his elect, which can have no cause but itself and which needs no other solicitor or motive to entreat pity towards us, readily hear and relieve us? ANNOTATIONS UPON THE GOSPEL ACCORDING TO SAINT LUKE 11:7.[13]

11:9-13 *Ask, and It Shall Be Given to You*

THE SOUL MUST SEEK RESTLESSLY AND CONTINUALLY. WILLIAM FENNER: These words contain in them the main duty of persistent prayer. Ask; and if asking does not succeed, then seek. If seeking does not succeed, then knock. Try all means. . . . But someone may demand, what is persistent prayer? I would answer that is a restless prayer which will not take no or any scornful rejection for an answer, but it is impudent (in a holy way) until it succeeds. . . .

Whoever is persistent cannot rest until he succeeds in his suit before God, just as the poor woman of Canaan sought the Lord God of heaven and earth. She was of the cursed stock of Ham, whom the Lord had commanded to destroy, but she converted to the faith of Abraham. She wanted to see if the Lord would recognize and own her, but the Lord seemed to reject her and allowed the devil to possess her daughter. Now this woman might have thought that she had made a poor change of religion, seeing that God, the author of it, would not recognize her but allowed the devil to possess her daughter. But notice the importunity of this woman—she would not be quiet until she had found Christ. Christ could not hide. But really? Could he really not hide himself in some corner? "No, no," she thinks. "There is a Christ, and if he can be found anywhere under the sun, I will find him." Likewise the soul that is persistent in prayer is restless. What if Christ does hide himself in the Word and will not recognize a poor soul? But the poor soul knows there is a Christ, and if he can be found anywhere in the whole world, he will find him. "I will," he says, "turn over all obligations. I will go to all the ministers that are near. I will use all means." Christ cannot be hidden from a soul that is that persistent. THE EFFICACY OF IMPORTUNATE PRAYER.[14]

PRAY DILIGENTLY IN CHRIST. HEINRICH BULLINGER: By this eloquent sentence Christ exhorts us to diligent devotion in prayer, promising

---

[12]Spangenberg, *Postilla . . . von Ostern biß auffs Aduent*, XLIIIv; citing Sir 35:17.
[13]Downame, ed., *Annotations*, Uu3r*; citing Ps 121:4.

[14]Fenner, *Practicall Divinitie*, 58-60*; citing Mk 7:24-25.

that God will very graciously listen to our prayers of supplication and those which are beneficial for our salvation will be satisfied superabundantly. Likewise, he outlines how we should pray. What we want to obtain must be requested by faith, seeking by the light—which is Christ—what we desire to find. There is no other door than Christ on which we ought to knock. For through Christ all our prayers are accepted by God. COMMENTARY ON LUKE 11:9.[15]

THE HOLY SPIRIT SHARES NOTHING IN COMMON WITH THE SPIRITS OF THE WORLD. DESIDERIUS ERASMUS: But if, among human beings who are otherwise evil, natural devotion can do so much that they are generous with their children seeking necessities, how much more will your Father, who is the Father of spirits, who is by nature good, impart to you from heaven this good Spirit, which will bestow all good things if you ask for them from him? Satan also has his spirit, with which he inspires his followers, a tempter to everything evil; and the world has its own spirit, which lures to the love of transitory things. With this spirit the Spirit of the heavenly Father has nothing in common. The one must depart so that the other can make its dwelling in your breast. PARAPHRASE ON THE GOSPEL OF LUKE 11:13.[16]

---

[15]Bullinger, *In Luculentum et Sacrosanctum Euangelium Secundum Lucam Commentariorum*, 80r-v; citing Heb 13; Mt 7.

[16]CWE 48:9-10* (LB 7:381).

11:14-26 JESUS AND HIS POWER OVER DEMONS

¹⁴Now he was casting out a demon that was mute. When the demon had gone out, the mute man spoke, and the people marveled. ¹⁵But some of them said, "He casts out demons by Beelzebul, the prince of demons," ¹⁶while others, to test him, kept seeking from him a sign from heaven. ¹⁷But he, knowing their thoughts, said to them, "Every kingdom divided against itself is laid waste, and a divided household falls. ¹⁸And if Satan also is divided against himself, how will his kingdom stand? For you say that I cast out demons by Beelzebul. ¹⁹And if I cast out demons by Beelzebul, by whom do your sons cast them out? Therefore they will be your judges. ²⁰But if it is by the finger of God that I cast out demons, then the kingdom of God has come upon you. ²¹When a strong man, fully armed, guards his own palace, his goods are safe; ²²but when one stronger than he attacks him and overcomes him, he takes away his armor in which he trusted and divides his spoil. ²³Whoever is not with me is against me, and whoever does not gather with me scatters.

²⁴"When the unclean spirit has gone out of a person, it passes through waterless places seeking rest, and finding none it says, 'I will return to my house from which I came.' ²⁵And when it comes, it finds the house swept and put in order. ²⁶Then it goes and brings seven other spirits more evil than itself, and they enter and dwell there. And the last state of that person is worse than the first."

OVERVIEW: One of the big differences in worldview between people of the sixteenth century and people of today has to do with belief in the power, and even the existence, of spirits. Many people do not believe in God; even fewer believe that there is a devil, or, if there is, that he can physically attack or possess human beings. But commentators from the sixteenth century largely accepted as fact the idea that Jesus was exorcising demons from people, which then healed them from a variety of ills. But whether one believes demonic possession to be a physical possibility or simply acknowledges the existence of evil in the human heart, many of these comments are still applicable and wise.

Most commentators note that while the devil (or more than one demon) can live within a person, Jesus, as God, always has the power to drive him out. Boys notes that the devil usurps God's place in our hearts—the human soul is God's property in which the devil is illegally squatting, and so it is just for God to expel him. In this case, Jesus has both the justice and the power to drive the devil out. For these commentators, his power as the "seed of the woman" over the devil is foretold by Genesis 3:15, and his ability to exorcise demons reiterates his status as the Messiah and the Son of God. Not that everyone is convinced, for some still demand other miracles that might please them better, as do many today. The Pharisees suggest that his power over demons comes from being in league with them—it is the power of Beelzebub, they say. Spangenburg is so offended by this comment that he suggests it is blasphemy against the Holy Spirit, the "unforgiveable sin" (Mt 12:31; Mk 3:29); these people see a good and divine work and attribute it to the devil. But Christ knew their thoughts (again proving his divinity) and turned logic against these Pharisees: a kingdom divided against itself cannot stand, he argues. The power of the devil cannot be used to defeat the devil, for as Jesus notes, the only way to defeat a strong man is by taking away his weapons and tying him up. The only way to defeat Satan is by having a stronger power, and that can (quite logically) come only from God.

Jesus knows these Pharisees are hypocrites and make these claims because they hate him. Other exorcists (the "children" of Luke 11:19) also drive out demons, and the Pharisees approve of them—but do they use divine power? It is not likely, claim some commentators, but more likely that they are tools of the devil, or, like witches, have pacts with the devil that give them certain powers. Only Jesus, who is the God-man, uses his own divine power to defeat the devil and free us from the devil's control—a very comforting thought, whether one believes in physical demonic possession or not. But he goes on to note another danger: when the house is clean, the devil may return, bringing worse demons with him. Melanchthon warns that although Jesus heals us and drives the devil away, if we are lazy and do not keep watch, the devil and all his evils can return. Schwenckfeld suggests that these "seven devils" are the seven deadly sins, and those who do not keep the proper attitude and humility but instead are seduced by the world, will leave themselves open to these sins through Satan's "trickery." Evil continues to lurk and attack, and the human heart is the battleground.

11:14-16 The Crowd Doubts Jesus' Power Is Divine

IN SILENCE OR SPEECH CHRIST'S VICTORY IS WON. RICHARD CRASHAW:

> Two devils at one blow Thou hast laid flat,
> A speaking devil this, a dumb one that;
> Was't Thy full victory's fairer increase
> That th' one spake or that th' other held his
> peace?

STEPS TO THE TEMPLE.[1]

SATAN ILLEGALLY DWELLS IN GOD'S PROPERTY. JOHN BOYS: As Satan therefore plays the part of a murderer and destroyer, so Christ acts as a Redeemer and Savior; as the devil sows dissension between God and people, between one person and another, between a person and himself, so Christ on the contrary makes our peace with God,

exhorts us to peace with each other and grants us peace within ourselves. As the text tells us in brief, he "casts out the devil," that is, he cast the devil out of the poor sinner who was possessed by him, and he had four reasons which were especially justified by the law:

1. Because the devil does not pay the rent on God's house.

2. Because he allows God's property to decay.

3. Because he employs God's property for base uses.

4. Because God himself desires to dwell in it.

The almighty God, who is infinitely rich in mercy, lends to every person diverse possessions—in a sense, he rents them to us so that we may farm and cultivate them—such as the graces of the spirit, the virtues of the mind, the gifts of the body and the goods of the world. For all of these he requires no rent payment but only thanksgiving, that our souls may magnify the Lord and our mouths proclaim his praise. But as long as the devil is in any property, God cannot receive this little payment, this small crop. For the devil possesses the sinner's heart with such a numbness, and his tongue with such a dumbness, that he can neither think good things nor speak thankful things. THE THIRD SUNDAY IN LENT.[2]

CHRIST ALWAYS HAS POWER TO DEFEAT DEVILS. JOHANNES MATHESIUS: It is terrifying and dreadful to hear that not only one devil but often a whole regiment of devils will physically go into a person's heart and live there in peace, as Christ says, and will bewitch, blind, silence and cripple the person. But this is opposed to the full confidence that our Lord Christ is Lord over the devil and that our Lord Christ is stronger and greater than all devils and can drive them all out with his power, as all of these true miracles prove. We should learn from this that Christ is the true and accomplished "offspring of the woman." The evil enemy can take no part in him or his members. He

---

[1]Crashaw, *Complete Works of Richard Crashaw*, 24*.

[2]Boys, *Exposition of the Dominical Epistles and Gospels*, 2:90-91*; alluding to the Magnificat, Lk 1:46-47; see also Ps 51:15.

has conquered Satan, driven him out and stepped on his head and his work through his finger, that is, through his Word, and can disturb and undo him. GOSPEL ON OCULI SUNDAY, LUKE 11.[3]

ATTRIBUTING CHRIST'S WORK TO BEELZEBUB IS UNFORGIVEABLE. JOHANN SPANGENBERG:

We find in this Gospel that three types of people have different judgments on this miracle of Christ. The first sort were in awe and said, "Is this not David's son?" These were goodhearted people who were made better by this miracle and through it came to a recognition of Christ. All miracles should serve in this way. The second sort tempted him and desired a sign from heaven. To these ones he answers, "These evil and adulterous sort look for a sign, but no sign will be given to them except the sign of the prophet Jonah. For just as Jonah was in the belly of the whale for three days and three nights, so will the Son of Man be in the middle of the earth for three days and three nights." The third sort blaspheme and say, "He drives the devil out through Beelzebub, the chief of the devils." And what is Beelzebub? Beelzebub was an idol of the Philistines in Accaron.[4] Translated, the name means "fly-king," a great bumblebee. The Jews also call him a hornet, for the devil does nothing else but swarm around us and over us, just like the big bumblebees and meat flies in the summer.

Now see what godless people these were who were not pleased with Christ, who explained everything with malice. Christ did such a miracle here that the whole world had to recognize it. It is a glorious, great, divine work, namely, to drive out the devil and to restore a blind, deaf and dumb man so that he could again see, hear and speak. Certainly no living man has done such a thing from the beginning of the world. It might be tolerated, and, in a human way, one might even forgive if someone interprets something as evil that has an evil appearance. An example might be when the

Pharisees do not want to allow that Christ is the Messiah, because they do not see anything in him that agrees with their view of the Messiah or king of Israel. And although this is a great sin, nevertheless Christ calls it a "sin against the Son of Man," and he says that those will be forgiven and not condemned. But it is too much, and cannot be forgiven by God or by anyone, that someone should disgracefully and maliciously interpret and explain such a divine, good work of which there is none better, which Christ does here, and say, "He drives out the devil through Beelzebub, the chief of the devils." This is a sin which Christ calls a sin against the Holy Spirit and says, "Whoever blasphemes against the Holy Spirit can never receive any forgiveness. He will be guilty at the Last Judgment." GOSPEL ON THE THIRD SUNDAY IN LENT.[5]

SOME DEMANDED A MIRACLE OF THEIR OWN CHOOSING. THOMAS BECON:

They pretend that they would believe, if only Christ would work a miracle that pleased them, although they are not lacking in a miracle, because they see one plainly before their eyes. But they judge that one to be an earthly, base affair and not a true sign. If he was to have any authority with them, they wanted him to show them some heavenly sign; that is, they wanted him to make a new moon or stars, or something completely marvelous. And these are very wise people, who will take it on themselves to prescribe and appoint to God what signs, wonders and miracles he ought to do. They would prefer that he were like a juggler, to satisfy their fancy and to do such miracles as please them. As though God had nothing to do but to serve their lusts and foolish desires! One can also find this sort of people these days, especially among the kings, princes and other rulers of this world. For why else do the wise of this world talk like this? "How can I receive such a teaching when it is professed by a poor and beggarly sort of folk?". . . .

---

[3]Mathesius, *Postilla Symbolica*, 107r; citing Gen 3:15.
[4]Accaron was one of the five principal Philistine cities and had a famous altar to Beelzebub. See 2 Kings 1:2-3, 6, 16.

[5]Spangenberg, *Postilla* (1582), XCIIr-v; citing Lk 11:29-30; Lk 12:10; Mk 3:29.

The rulers of the world instruct God in how he should behave himself, and they set forth any doctrine which pleases them, any sort which they find to be good, so that God must do whatever it pleases them to appoint. Such are to be found even among those who profess the gospel. For in our days, many who would wish to be thought followers of the gospel may be found in the courts of princes, and also in cities, who are not ashamed to tell the preachers what they must preach and teach, and especially so that they may speak pleasant things that will delight and not offend. For when the preacher according to his office reproves sins and vices of which certain people are guilty, they immediately cry out, "These are matters of rebellion, and the magistrates won't put up with it! The gospel must be preached without such spiteful criticisms of anyone." And so when a preacher speaks the truth and rebukes sin, he is immediately accused of criticizing the government and promoting rebellion. These people are just as puffed up with pride as those who saw Christ's miracle and yet regarded it as nothing, because it was not a miracle which they themselves thought of and demanded of Christ. THE THIRD SUNDAY IN LENT.[6]

11:17-20 *How Can the Power of Beelzebub Work Against Itself?*

NATION WILL FIGHT AGAINST NATION AND WILL NOT STAND. MARTIN BUCER: The Lord means to admonish us here how great a mischief civil and mortal dissension is. It is so great that it destroys houses, cities and kingdoms. There are many examples of this both in the stories of the Gentiles and in sacred history. The saying of Sallust is not unknown to us: "By peace and concord small things grow and increase, but by discord and dissension great things are wasted, consumed and brought to confusion."[7] And the

prophet Isaiah, when he prophesied of the destruction of the kingdom of the Jews, said that there would be civil dissension among them. And before that terrible destruction of the city of Jerusalem there was great dissension and strife within it. It was divided into three pernicious sects which were headed by the chief leaders Symon, John and Eleazer.[8] . . . The kingdom of Rome was also brought to confusion by civil dissension and is likely to come to destruction again by that same problem. By the dissension between the two emperors of Constantinople, an opening was given to the empire of the Turks and to the destruction of the empire of Rome. . . . Christ did prophesy that before the destruction of the world, nation would rise up against nation and kingdom against kingdom. AN ECCLESIASTICALL EXPOSITION UPON SAINT MATHEWE 12.[9]

THE DEVILS ARE EVIL AND CANNOT CHANGE. PHILIPP MELANCHTHON: Just as the good spirits and heavenly angels cannot degenerate from their goodness and be contrary to themselves, so also the evil spirits cannot alter their malice and begin to do good to humankind, or disagree among themselves or degenerate from their own nature. That is why it is necessary that the kingdom of Satan will come to destruction only by the power of God. For Satan goes about to ratify, confirm and establish his kingdom as much as he can and to try to make it invincible.

And so Jesus takes the time here to show that the Pharisees, because they were hardened with hatred and envy against him, spread this criticism of him maliciously and even against their own consciences. Likewise this disease, or rather obstinate malice, is very much in evidence in our own days, so much so that we can be content to criticize a thing in one person and justify the same in another. And from what does this come? Merely from hatred—not that we hate the evil, for then we

---

[6]Becon, *New Postil*, 170v-171v*.
[7]Sallust, *Jugurtha* 10. This quotation is commonly rendered "By union the smallest states thrive. By discord the greatest are destroyed."

[8]Josephus, *Antiquities* 6.13.
[9]Marlorat, ed., *Catholike and Ecclesiasticall Exposition of the Holy Gospell After S. Mathewe*, 259-60*; citing Is 3:5; Mt 24:7.

would criticize justly and impartially, but because we hate the person. And so we note, pay close attention to and falsely interpret the sayings and doings of the one whom we hate, having no consideration as to whether what we are criticizing or contradicting is true or false. AN ECCLESIASTICALL EXPOSITION UPON SAINT MATHEWE 12.[10]

THE "FINGER OF GOD" IS THE HOLY SPIRIT.

MARTIN LUTHER: The enthymeme is this: "I drive out the devil through the finger of God, and so the kingdom of God is among you." That describes the gospel and the Christian church, for it is, of course, between the Holy Spirit and the evil spirit. So what does it mean when he says, "I drive out the devil through the finger of God"? In Exodus we read how Moses made the staff turn into a serpent in front of the pharoah, who did not want to let the people of Israel go, and likewise changed the water into blood, and caused the frogs to come out of the water and cover the land. The pharoah's magicians and conjurers also did these three things. But the fourth, that Moses made gnats come up out of the dust of the earth, this the magicians were not able to do, because gnats are themselves fertile creatures: God alone can create them. And so they said, "This is the finger of God." A little later in the same book, we see that the Lord gave to Moses "the two tablets of the testimony" that were made of stone and "written with the finger of God." From this we can see that the Holy Spirit is called the finger of God. For he writes living letters in the heart, creates a new will, heart and mind, creates all virtues and pours out grace. And so Christ says, "If I drive out the devil with the finger of God, the kingdom of God, grace and all good things come." It is as if he would say, "I write with the finger of God in your hearts, which pushes out the devil and brings in the kingdom of God"; therefore you see that you did not have the right idea. See how he deals with them in such a friendly manner; he

definitely wanted to dissuade them from that error. AFTERNOON SERMON ON THE THIRD SUNDAY IN LENT (1521).[11]

CHRIST'S DEFEAT OF SATAN SHOWS THAT THE KINGDOM IS HERE. JOHANNES BRENZ: In this passage, the kingdom of God is not understood to be that kingdom in which God, by his inscrutable and wonderful majesty, reigns in heaven and on earth, but rather that kingdom which was promised to be revealed and administered by the Messiah on earth, of which both Moses and the prophets have written much. For where it was said that the seed of the woman should tread on the head of the serpent, it was meant that the Messiah would tread on all the power of Satan and that he would also take away all his maledictions and curses. For now that Jesus, the Son of Mary, is come, he expels Satan by manifest miracles and treads his power under his feet. So now what remains but that the same time should come, of which the prophets had most plainly prophesied—this time when the Messiah is at hand and his kingdom is already here? AN ECCLESIASTICALL EXPOSITION UPON SAINT MATHEWE 12.[12]

11:21-23 The Stronger Power Will Conquer

CHRIST HAS NO NEED OF SATAN'S HELP BUT DEFEATS HIM. JOHANNES BRENZ: Christ's argument is basically this: "You slanderers say that I cast out devils with the help of Beelzebub, but I will prove that Beelzebub is made captive and bound by me, and is not my helper. For when I drive out the angels or ministers of Beelzebub, what else am I doing but raiding and ransacking his kingdom, taking away his ammunition and dividing the spoils? For people are the kingdom of Satan because of sin, and Satan reigns mightily because of the sin in human beings, whom he

---

[10]Marlorat, ed., *Catholike and Ecclesiasticall Exposition of the Holy Gospell After S. Mathewe*, 260-61*.

[11]*LEA* 3:166 (cf. WA 9:598-99); citing Ex 7:10–8:19; Ex 8:19; 31:18.
[12]Marlorat, ed., *Catholike and Ecclesiasticall Exposition of the Holy Gospell After S. Mathewe*, 261*; citing Gen 3:15.

keeps under duress and in bondage by his angels. But I deliver people from the angels of Satan and restore them to their former health, putting the devils to flight, which is to divide the spoils. But no one can take away a strong and armed man's armor and divide his spoils unless he first overcomes and binds him. Otherwise the strong, armed man will valiantly defend himself, and so all his possessions will be safe from his enemies. So because I take away the weapons and armor of Beelzebub, who is the prince of devils, and put his servants to flight (which is apparent by my miracles), it is quite clear that I have both overcome and bound Beelzebub himself. I clearly have no need of his help, and he would be of little help to me."

Thus we see that Christ teaches that the prince of devils is overcome by him. And if the prince is overcome, how is it possible that his ministers should be able to stand before him? If anyone has Christ, he should not be afraid of six hundred legions of devils. Therefore let us stand steadfast in our faith in Christ, and we shall be safe even amid all the machinations of Satan. An Ecclesiasticall Exposition upon Saint Luke ii.[13]

WE ARE CALLED TO PROMOTE THE KINGDOM AND BUILD UP CHRIST'S FLOCK. PHILIPP MELANCHTHON: To be with Christ is to gather along with him into the kingdom of God. Christ and his faithful servants gather when, with their doctrine and teaching, they reap the harvest and bring it into the barn of their Father, to everlasting life. This metaphor is taken from the time of harvest, when everyone makes all possible haste to gather and bring in the harvest, to avoid any sort of harm to it by storms or unseasonable weather. Satan, who is a true wolf, devours and disperses the flock of Christ from the sheepfold, and when any part of the gospel is sown in their hearts through preaching, he takes it away again, because he does not want them to believe, or they would be saved. Therefore by this sentence it plainly appears

that Christ now says truly that whoever does not gather with him scatters, because such is the promptness of our nature toward evil that the righteousness of God will not abide in those who apply themselves too late, and seek to get it after time is up. Also, this doctrine is greater, and spreads itself farther, because it teaches that those who do not bestow and refer all their studies and labors to him are unworthy to be counted in the flock of Christ. By their negligence and sloth it comes to pass that the kingdom of God moves backwards and does not prosper, when in fact we are all called to promote it. AN ECCLESIASTICALL EXPOSITION UPON SAINT MATHEWE 12.[14]

11:24-26 *The Power of Evil Constantly Attacks*

IF WE DENY CHRIST, THE EVIL SPIRITS WILL RETURN IN GREATER NUMBERS. PHILIPP MELANCHTHON: The way in which these words pertain to the present matter can be gathered from Matthew 12, where it is said, "Even so shall it happen to this perverse nation." He was speaking of the same nation when he said earlier, "The evil and adulterous generation seeks for a sign." These things therefore pertain to the Jewish people, which will be clearer if you read it in this manner: "It will happen to this generation just as if an unclean spirit, on leaving a person, wanders through dry places and, finding no rest, says, 'I will return to my house,'" and so on. The comparison is made with a person who is subject to an evil spirit or devil, but when he is delivered, he leaves open a gap for the devil to enter again through his sloth and negligence, and so he is in a far worse situation than he was before. It made good sense for Jesus to bring in this comparison, as he just a little before had driven the devil out of a demoniac, and prior to that he had disputed concerning the kingdoms of Christ and of Satan. And so the Lord says this, "I came to drive out Satan from among you, that I

---

[13]Marlorat, ed., *Catholike and Ecclesiasticall Exposition of the Holy Gospell After S. Marke and Luke*, 197*.

[14]Marlorat, ed., *Catholike and Ecclesiasticall Exposition of the Holy Gospell After S. Mathewe*, 263*; citing Jn 4:31-38; Lk 8:12.

myself might reign with you. But you will not allow me to reign in you or among you, and so you despise the grace which I offer to you. And so it will happen that the evil spirits will return again, greater in number than before, and things will be much worse, for you will become the most wicked person in the world, the most obstinate, the most blind, and subject in the end to horrible destruction." AN ECCLESIASTICALL EXPOSITION UPON SAINT MATHEWE 12.[15]

HYPOCRITES LEAVE THE DOOR OPEN TO MORE EVIL SPIRITS. KASPAR VON SCHWENCKFELD: This happens when people become too pleased with themselves. That is, the evil spirit returns if they have a fleshly confidence and say, "Christ has accomplished it, I can do nothing." Satan finds such a house that is not adorned by God in its conscience but is rather full of hypocrisy and duplicity. He finds the house and goes inside, taking seven evil spirits with him, and comes and lives within it. That is terrifying, when their depravity is not obvious outwardly, but rather they believe that they are pious. And so Christ says that the tax collectors and public sinners will go before these into the heavenly kingdom. They do penance, but the hypocrites do not. They only praise themselves, as we see with the Pharisee in the temple. These now become wicked, standing in fleshly security and arrogance, believing that they are not required to do anything good, for Christ has done it all.

By the seven evil spirits we are to understand the seven deadly sins. The world today glosses over them and gives them other names, so that no one may recognize them. The first evil spirit is pride, which the world calls an honorable estate. One must behave in a way that befits his honor. God the Lord hates a proud disposition and lofty eyes. It is a mortal sin, and in contrast Christ teaches humility and says you should be "humble of heart." The second evil spirit is greed, which the world calls thriftiness. Paul calls it idolatry, for greed does nothing good for one's neighbor. It is constantly worried about whether there will be enough for itself. It economizes and holds back. It is a mistrust of God. Our hearts should not be so invested in things, but we should possess temporal things as though we had nothing. The third evil spirit is unchastity, which the world calls love. The fourth evil spirit is anger, which the world calls seriousness and courage, and one has to show courage. The fifth evil spirit is envy. It is an old-fashioned rage and is a mortal sin, as John says. And the world calls this resentment, if you carry it in your heart. The sixth evil spirit is gluttony, or to overeat and carouse. The world calls this human nature, that people are happy and friendly with each other, and so under a figure of speech they call evil good. The seventh evil spirit is the spirit of laziness, where a person is lazy in the service of God. The world says, "Those things are for monks and priests to do. I have enough faith." We see how the evil spirit brings seven evils with him. The evil spirit has accomplished all of this through trickery, that the last is more evil than the first. God protect us, that Satan will not also get us by trickery, and the last become more evil than the first. Christ Jesus, protect us from this, Amen. ON THE THIRD SUNDAY IN LENT (OCULI).[16]

---

[15]Marlorat, ed., *Catholike and Ecclesiasticall Exposition of the Holy Gospell After S. Mathewe*, 272*; citing Mt 12:45; Lk 11:29.

[16]CS 10:254-55; citing Lk 18:10-13; Mt 11:29; 1 Jn 3:12; Is 5:20.

11:27-36 THE BLESSEDNESS OF FAITH AND WARNINGS ABOUT DISBELIEF

²⁷As he said these things, a woman in the crowd raised her voice and said to him, "Blessed is the womb that bore you, and the breasts at which you nursed!" ²⁸But he said, "Blessed rather are those who hear the word of God and keep it!"

²⁹When the crowds were increasing, he began to say, "This generation is an evil generation. It seeks for a sign, but no sign will be given to it except the sign of Jonah. ³⁰For as Jonah became a sign to the people of Nineveh, so will the Son of Man be to this generation. ³¹The queen of the South will rise up at the judgment with the men of this generation and condemn them, for she came from the ends of the earth to hear the wisdom of Solomon, and behold, something greater than Solomon is here. ³²The men of Nineveh will rise up at the judgment with this generation and condemn it, for they repented at the preaching of Jonah, and behold, something greater than Jonah is here.

³³"No one after lighting a lamp puts it in a cellar or under a basket, but on a stand, so that those who enter may see the light. ³⁴Your eye is the lamp of your body. When your eye is healthy, your whole body is full of light, but when it is bad, your body is full of darkness. ³⁵Therefore be careful lest the light in you be darkness. ³⁶If then your whole body is full of light, having no part dark, it will be wholly bright, as when a lamp with its rays gives you light."

OVERVIEW: Protestants often tried to dance delicately around Mary. It was difficult to maintain a proper, scripturally-based honor for her and yet reject and disdain the excesses they saw in Catholic devotion. Passages such as these, where Jesus downplays her blessedness as his mother, were quite useful in the war against Marian idolatry. Jesus himself notes that a physical connection to him did not convey blessings, at least not in the way that a spiritual connection did. Luther criticizes this unnamed woman for suggesting that Mary is blessed because of her physical, motherly connection—it is a "womanish," useless thought that nurturing a child from her own body would somehow translate to a special blessedness for Mary. Those who are truly, eternally blessed are those who listen to God's Word diligently and embrace it in their hearts. Fortunately, as Bucer points out, Mary is also included in that group; she is part of the elect and reveals her "lively faith" on more than one occasion. He is willing to accept that bearing Christ was indeed a blessing, but it was a minor one, and it should not be a matter on which we focus.

The sign of Jonah, that is, that Jesus would spend three days in the tomb before his resurrection, is the only sign that will be given to those who do not believe in him before their own destruction. This reference to Jonah is, for the reformers, also a reminder that foreigners, even if they are believed to be unsaveable barbarians, are often the first to repent and believe in the gospel. When Jonah went to Nineveh, he met unexpected and widespread acceptance, fasting and repentance. Likewise, the Gospel implies, while many of Jesus' own people reject him, he will be welcomed by Gentiles and foreigners. Thus the people of Nineveh at the Last Day will accuse the scribes, Pharisees and others who did not believe in Jesus although he preached and performed miracles among them and fulfilled all the messianic prophecies. Likewise, our commentators note, we will be judged, for we also have the Word preached and the good news placed before us. Here is one who is greater than Solomon but we do not always pay attention. Although it is this Word that will transform our hearts and change our lives, bringing us to true repentance, we would often rather fill our bellies and enjoy ourselves. But the kingdom of heaven is at hand, and the acceptable hour for repentance is now.

Jesus frequently uses metaphors to explain religious ideas, and in this case he turns to the example of a lamp or candle, suggesting that no one would hide a lamp under a bushel but would instead leave it on a table to lighten a whole room. This lamp is the Word of God, which should not be hidden away and which reveals things that previously were in the dark. Jesus then moves on to a comparison of the lamp with the eye. Our commentators understand this comparison to provide an analogy between the physical and the spiritual: what the eye is to the body, the soul and mind are to the whole person. By understanding how the eye functions within the body, we can have a better sense of the role of the mind and spirit within the person. A healthy eye allows light in the body and sees clearly, allowing us to move and act, but if it is diseased, then we will be hindered in many ways—darkness rather than light will enter the body. Likewise, if the soul and our judgment are healthy and can understand and accept God's Word, then God's light will enter in, but if our judgment is darkened, we will not know how to act or think correctly. Calvin notes that darkness takes over when we allow the "depraved desires of the flesh" to overwhelm what little reason we sinful human beings have. But if we live in hope and faith with sincere hearts, Erasmus suggests, the light will fill us.

11:27-28 Blessed Are Those Who Hear the Word of God and Obey

MARY'S PHYSICAL MOTHERHOOD IS NOT THE GREATEST BLESSING. MARTIN BUCER: Not that his holy Mother was not blessed, but she was not blessed because she physically bore Christ in her womb (as this woman thought). Rather, she was blessed by her lively faith, as all the elect are blessed. Christ will not be acknowledged carnally but spiritually. We do not behold any external glory in him, but rather the grace of redemption by which we are regenerated. The woman thought that Mary carrying him in her womb was the greatest blessedness, but what she thought was the greatest was actually the least. We certainly ought to praise that, but there are greater things to focus on. All the benefits of God, no matter how small, are to be praised, but not so that we make them equal to the greatest. So, for example, we ought to praise and give thanks to God for giving us our physical food and drink, but if we so focus on that that we forget the benefit of our illumination, of our redemption and of the gift of everlasting life, we are very foolish. AN ECCLESIASTICALL EXPOSITION UPON SAINT LUKE 11.[1]

TRUE BLESSEDNESS COMES FROM FAITH. MARTIN LUTHER: [It is] as if the Lord would say, "I do not like to have any carnal praise, and it is not a blessing to my mother. Your praise is in error, for you do not yet understand the things which are God's. You seek the benefit and desire of the flesh and please yourself with such womanish shameful thoughts, so that your soul does not achieve salvation and blessedness. So turn yourself from such useless, idle and vain thoughts and learn that those who are eternally blessed are those who diligently listen to God's Word and embrace it in their hearts, placing all their comfort and confidence in it, for it can never deceive you. Those are the ones who build their house on the rock, which the violence of the water and wind can never overpower. Therefore, believe in the Son of God, and you will be blessed." ROTH'S FESTPOSTILLE (1527): MARY'S CONCEPTION.[2]

THE DEVIL TRIES TO STOP US FROM KEEPING GOD'S WORD. JOHANN SPANGENBERG: What does it mean that he says *custodiant*, "and keep it"? He wants to say as much as: "It is not enough to hear God's Word. One must also grasp it and keep it as a valuable treasure, and not just let it go by.

---

[1]Marlorat, ed., *Catholike and Ecclesiasticall Exposition of the Holy Gospell After S. Marke and Luke*, 198*.
[2]WA 17,2:281; alluding to Mt 7:24. For more on Stephen Roth's postils and Luther's opinion of them, see LW 75:xvii-xxii.

The devil also hears it but does not obey it." What does it mean to say "to keep"? Keeping it means believing God's Word, always reflecting on it in faith, training oneself in it and guiding one's whole life by it. It is an art. The devil is very troublesome here, for he turns people away from God's Word, so that they do not hear God's Word, or if they hear it, they do not keep it. He uses many tricks and hellish traps, as he knows how to do quite masterfully, for he is a true doctor of wickedness. CONCERNING THE WORD OF GOD, A SERMON ON LUKE 11.[3]

11:29-32 *Jesus Is Greater Than Jonah, and Yet the People Do Not Repent*

THE SIGN OF JONAH WILL CONDEMN THE PEOPLE. DESIDERIUS ERASMUS: Now the people said this by no means with honest intentions but testing him, so that if he did not show them a sign they would allege that the other things had been done with Beelzebub's help; if he did show them a sign, then they would find something else in him to criticize. So he said, "This is an evil nation and not at all honest. It has seen so many wonders. Yet it will not get what it is fraudulently seeking but will receive the sign that it deserves; there will be given not what it can criticize but what can prove its guilt. For it will be given the sign of the prophet Jonah. The people of Ninevah did penance for their sins in response to Jonah's preaching, though he had done no miracles among them. This nation cannot be softened to penitence by any miracles, by any good deeds; yet there is one here who is greater than Jonah the prophet, at whom they marvel because he was taken by a whale, lived in its belly for three days and three nights and then, given up for dead, suddenly reappeared alive. There will be something like this but more marvelous: the Son of Man will be buried in the core of the earth for three days, but contrary to the expectation of all evil people, on the third day the earth will give back

alive the dead man it received." PARAPHRASE ON THE GOSPEL OF LUKE 11:29-32.[4]

THE WISDOM OF CHRIST IS EVEN GREATER THAN THAT OF SOLOMON. EDWIN SANDYS: But the world seems to be glutted with the Word: there are many stomachs that cannot digest it and many that loathe it. I stand in fear that God in his justice will give us, instead of plenty of this bread, a famine, and for wholesome food, meat that shall rot between our teeth. There is not that desire in us to know the wisdom of Christ, which was in the Queen of Saba [the South] to hear the wisdom of Solomon. There were of the Jews no small numbers that heard Christ three days together in the wilderness, and that while fasting: but he has fed us so full that we care not for him. The servants of Solomon were thought happy, that they might stand daily to hear his wisdom. Happy it were both for the servants of Solomon, and for Solomon, too, if every sabbath they would hear him who is far greater and wiser than Solomon. There is nothing wanting except for willingness only, for we have both leisure enough to hear and a great store of those whom God has enabled to speak well. No time can be better spent; nothing is more necessary for a Christian court. What is more prince-like than to honor the Prince of all princes with that service in which he is so highly delighted? The belly is daily and daintily fed: O suffer not the soul to want that food which abides forever! They are not blessed who feed and pamper the flesh, but rather those who "hear the Word and keep it." This Word, attentively and carefully heard, would convert our souls, correct our lives, soften our hearts, inflame our minds with the love of God. It would root out vice and ingraft virtue, banish vain and cherish good desires in us. It would lay our sins before our faces, humble our proud and haughty looks, bring us into true and hearty repentance, throw us down with godly sorrow and raise us up again with heavenly comfort in the merits and mercies of Christ Jesus. It would perfect us perfectly to every

---

[3]Spangenberg, *Postilla Teütsch . . . von den fürnemsten Festen durch das gantze Jar*, CXXXVIIv.

[4]CWE 48:16-17* (LB 7:384).

good work. THE SIXTH SERMON: A SERMON
PREACHED BEFORE THE QUEEN (1585).[5]

11:33-36 Let Your Body Be Full of Light Rather Than Darkness

THE CANDLE IS THE WORD OF GOD. EDWARD
LEIGH: Christ with the word *candle* understands
the Word of God, according to Psalm 119:105,
2 Peter 1:19 and Proverbs 6:23. The Word of God is
compared with a candle in many respects.

1. For the author, who is God, kindled this candle
   from the beginning by his Son (who is the light
   of the world), that is to say, he revealed his
   Word, and by it his will to us.

2. For its nature, because as there is nothing purer
   than light in all the world, with which no filth
   can be mingled, so the words of the Lord are
   pure words.

3. For its effects, which are manifold, the candle
   reveals those things (the darkness being expelled) which at first lay hidden; so the Word of
   God reveals many things, which are otherwise
   unknown. The candle directs the steps and actions of the body; the Word of the Lord shines
   in all spiritual actions. Light also expels the
   darkness of the mind, sadness and fear; so the
   Word of God first enlightens the consciences of
   people and afterward frees them from the terrors
   of sin and eternal damnation.

ANNOTATIONS UPON SAINT LUKE 11.[6]

TAKE CARE THAT YOUR MIND DOES NOT
DESTROY YOU. JOHN CALVIN: "Light" signifies
reason, the little that remains in people after the
fall of Adam; "darkness," however signifies crude
and monstrous affections. The meaning is that it is
not astonishing if people roll themselves about so
much in the mud of vices after the manner of cattle,
seeing that reason is not able to control the blind

and dark desires of the flesh. The "light" is truly
said to be turned into "darkness" not only when
people allow the judgment of their mind to be
overwhelmed by the depraved desires of the flesh
but also when they give up their nature to perverse
thoughts and degenerate into beasts. We see that
people indeed spitefully bend whatever wisdom
they were given into mere shrewdness, that as the
prophet says, they "hide their thoughts too deep for
the Lord," relying on themselves and scoffing boldly
at God. Finally, they strive in innumerable ways to
be clever, thereby destroying themselves. It is
because of this that Christ announces that this
horrible and deepest darkness must rule in life
when people go out of their way to become blind.
The sense of the words as we find them in Luke are
the same, except that Christ there connects the
sentence to what was previously explained in
Matthew 5, that no one lights a candle and then
hides it, and in the place of this clause, "if the light
which is in you is darkness," places the exhortation,
"See that the light which is in you does not become
darkness." It is as if he would say, "See that your
mind, which should have gleamed like a candle to
guide your actions, does not darken and destroy
your whole life." COMMENTARY ON A HARMONY
OF THE GOSPELS.[7]

THE LIGHT WILL DISPEL ALL DARKNESS
WITHIN US. DESIDERIUS ERASMUS: It is as if he
said, "If your eye, that is to say, your mind and
heart, is simple and sincere, defiled with no desires,
it will give its light to all the members, so that there
shall be no darkness in any part of the body. The
whole body shall be subject to no darkness, but it
shall be light, even as a whole house is alight when
the candle shines generally overall."

By the word *light* we understand good success
and happiness, rather than piety and righteousness
in the Scriptures. But we should not understand
this passage to mean that no sin or error would
ever affect those who live godly lives, but that none
of these things shall reign over them and that they

---

[5]Sandys, *Sermons*, 113-14*; citing 2 Tim 3:17.
[6]Leigh, *Annotations upon All the New Testament Philologicall and Theologicall*, 116-17*; alluding to Ps 12:6.
[7]CO 45:207 (cf. CTS 31:336-37); citing Is 29:15; Mt 5:15.

shall do nothing evil. But having regard in all things to the glory of the Lord, they shall become thoroughly light, and free from darkness in every point. By faith and hope we are already nothing but light, according to this saying: "For you were once darkness, but now you are light in the Lord."

And if God does not impute any sins to us now, who will dare to do it? An ECCLESIASTICALL EXPOSITION UPON SAINT LUKE 11.[8]

---

[8]Marlorat, ed., *Catholike and Ecclesiasticall Exposition of the Holy Gospell After S. Marke and Luke*, 199-200*; citing Eph 5:8.

11:37-54 WOE TO THE SCRIBES AND PHARISEES

[37]While Jesus[a] was speaking, a Pharisee asked him to dine with him, so he went in and reclined at table. [38]The Pharisee was astonished to see that he did not first wash before dinner. [39]And the Lord said to him, "Now you Pharisees cleanse the outside of the cup and of the dish, but inside you are full of greed and wickedness. [40]You fools! Did not he who made the outside make the inside also? [41]But give as alms those things that are within, and behold, everything is clean for you.

[42]"But woe to you Pharisees! For you tithe mint and rue and every herb, and neglect justice and the love of God. These you ought to have done, without neglecting the others. [43]Woe to you Pharisees! For you love the best seat in the synagogues and greetings in the marketplaces. [44]Woe to you! For you are like unmarked graves, and people walk over them without knowing it."

[45]One of the lawyers answered him, "Teacher, in saying these things you insult us also." [46]And he said, "Woe to you lawyers also! For you load people with burdens hard to bear, and you yourselves do not touch the burdens with one of your fingers. [47]Woe to you! For you build the tombs of the prophets whom your fathers killed. [48]So you are witnesses and you consent to the deeds of your fathers, for they killed them, and you build their tombs. [49]Therefore also the Wisdom of God said, 'I will send them prophets and apostles, some of whom they will kill and persecute,' [50]so that the blood of all the prophets, shed from the foundation of the world, may be charged against this generation, [51]from the blood of Abel to the blood of Zechariah, who perished between the altar and the sanctuary. Yes, I tell you, it will be required of this generation. [52]Woe to you lawyers! For you have taken away the key of knowledge. You did not enter yourselves, and you hindered those who were entering."

[53]As he went away from there, the scribes and the Pharisees began to press him hard and to provoke him to speak about many things, [54]lying in wait for him, to catch him in something he might say.

[a] Greek he

OVERVIEW: This passage clarifies the target of the previous comments on light—the Pharisees and the scribes are good examples of those who see darkness rather than light through their diseased eyes. The Pharisee who invited Jesus to dinner was critical of him because he did not wash his hands before dinner, which was a regular ritual of the Pharisees. However, rather than following modern-day concepts of cleanliness to avoid disease, their hand washing was a religious ritual with a moral dimension. But while the Pharisees assumed that washing hands before a meal made one a good, law-abiding person, our commentators insist that washing hands (or not) is not a moral act—the Pharisees once again mistook a minor point for a central element. They saw guilt in Christ where there was none and missed the major guilt within themselves. Their superstitions and hypocrisy impeded their sight; they saw only darkness because their eyes were blinded by their vices.

The remainder of Jesus' comments were directed toward criticism of the scribes and Pharisees and those like them: they were like cups scrubbed clean only on the outside, because all they cared about was external purity and the appearance of goodness. They tried to show their piety in small matters, like carefully tithing herbs, but they ignored the large requirements of the law. They wanted people to see their piety and be honored for it, seeking out the seats and titles of honor. Like their ancestors, they persecuted and killed the prophets for speaking the truth about them.

But these people were dangerous not only because of their power to persecute but also because of their influence over others. They were seen as good and pious, and so the "simple folk" wanted to imitate them. Because they misused their power to keep others from the kingdom of heaven, they are doubly condemned. True servants of God recognize their sinfulness and are patient under correction. But the scribes and Pharisees, the reformers note—like wicked people today—are servants of Satan and part of his body (rather than the body of Christ), and they will all receive the same punishment.

The scribes and Pharisees were Christ's constant enemies, and he frequently criticized them as hypocrites who were more interested in an external show of piety than in true interior faith. But Jesus also said to give alms so that "all things will be clean to you"—a curious and challenging statement for these Protestants to understand. Luther applies the hermeneutic of justification by faith to this comment, suggesting that it must be read through the lens of Hebrews 11. If giving alms is to help us be clean, then the alms must be given in faith—the righteousness that is then present is the same that would be present even without the works. For Luther, faith is necessary before any good works can be practiced, and when we are justified through faith, then we will do the works of faith. Only in this way can giving alms make us clean.

11:37-38 Jesus Is Invited to Eat with a Pharisee

THE PHARISEES SAW THROUGH CORRUPT EYES. KONRAD PELLIKAN: What the Lord taught, he would also have explained. Because the Pharisees had corrupt eyes and saw justice constituted in earthly ceremonies, they neglected those things which were not easily discernible, except by the pure eyes to whom the lamp of gospel truth shines forth. What they thought to be the light was really darkness, but nevertheless they pressed forward, going where it seemed to them beautiful to enter.

They condemned him as guilty for what they thought a grave fault, but there was really none, and yet where they could not see any was where the weighty fault really was. To be sure, their eyes could see, but only through superstition of the law, through ignorance, disdain, jealousy, avarice, hypocrisy, and through the rest of their evil vices.

Thus a certain Pharisee asked Jesus to dine with him. Jesus did not refuse, for he was willing to reach out to everyone, that all might be led to him. But when the Lord went, unwashed, to recline at the dinner table, contrary to the habit of the Pharisees, this Pharisee began to think silently to himself and to wonder why the Lord did not wash himself before being seated. And so immediately from something that does not make people either good or evil, something entirely evil is born. And likewise many people innately have their own pharisaical ceremonies which correspond to bodily matters that can give rise to disparagements, evil suspicions, perverse justice, disagreements, hatred and strife. COMMENTARY IN LUKE 11:37-38.[1]

11:39-41 The Hypocrisy of the Pharisees

GIVING ALMS PURGES ONE'S WEALTH OF POLLUTION. HENRY HAMMOND: The [Syriac and] Arabic word for alms, *zakat*, has a double meaning, they say, either of increasing or cleansing. The first because the giving of alms obtains a blessing on the wealth and increases it; the second because it purges the riches from the pollution and filthiness that adheres to them, as well as the mind from the sullies of covetousness. . . . In reference to this notion of the word in Syriac and Arabic, this seems to be spoken here by our Savior, "give alms," which comes from a word that signifies "to cleanse," and "all shall be clean to you"; your wealth shall be purged and blessed, and your mind cleansed also. ANNOTATIONS ON LUKE 11:40.[2]

---

[1]Pellikan, *In Sacrosancta Quatuor Evangelia*, 133 (cf. CWE 48:19-20; LB 7:385).
[2]Hammond, *Paraphrase and Annotations*, 229*.

JUSTIFICATION STILL COMES THROUGH FAITH, NOT WORKS. MARTIN LUTHER: For all the passages of Scripture on which the righteousness of works apparently rests, Hebrews 11 answers with these words: "through faith." For example: "Give alms," you see, "so that everything is clean for you." It answers, "Give in faith!" It says there concerning all the works of the saints: "through faith." And it provides this reason: "For without faith, it is impossible to please God." For if faith is present in each work, you have within it at the same time the righteousness without works, and also if the works are present. For faith must necessarily be before the works. But it is faith that justifies, yes, in fact, faith itself is righteousness. And whoever is justified through faith also does the works of faith. Giving alms makes one free from sins, it forgives, and so you will be forgiven—all comments of this kind, which our opponents use to show that righteousness comes from works and not from faith, do not change any of that. The difference is this: giving alms, forgiving debts, and similar works are works that we ourselves can do, but giving eternal life and forgiving sins are works that we cannot perform—they only happen through Christ. For he has freed us from sin and the devil through his incarnation, his suffering and his resurrection, and has reconciled us with the Father. Therefore it is not true, as our opponents would like to prove through such passages, that righteousness does not come from faith but rather from works. RHAPSODY OR OUTLINE FOR A BOOK ON THE DOCTRINE OF JUSTIFICATION (1530).[3]

11:42-44 Woe to the Pharisees as Hypocrites

THE SCRIBES SHOWED GREAT PIETY IN SMALL MATTERS. PHILIPP MELANCHTHON: Now he teaches another part of their hypocrisy, namely, the feigning and outward appearance of keeping the law in those things which are of less weight. All hypocrites have this fault, being very diligent and careful in trifling things but neglecting the principal parts of the law. This disease has reigned in all ages and among all nations; in fact, the greater part of humanity has studiously sought to please God with easy observances. Because they cannot exempt themselves from all obedience to God, they flee to this second remedy, namely, to redeeming great offenses for nothing, by "satisfactions." So we see that the papists, to this day, when they transgress the chief commandments of God, fervently busy themselves in cold ceremonies. Such feigning and outward show of holiness is what Christ here criticizes in the scribes, who were very diligent and scrupulous in the paying of tithes but paid little attention to the principal parts of the law. And in order that he might better point out their ridiculous ostentation and excessive show, he does not say in a general way, "They paid their tithes," but instead says, "They tithed anise, mint, cumin and all manner of herbs," that with the least expense they might show a rare and singular study of godliness. AN ECCLESIASTICALL EXPOSITION UPON SAINT MATHEWE 23.[4]

MINISTERS SHOULD NOT SEEK THEIR OWN GLORY BUT REPRESENT CHRIST. JOHN CALVIN: He shows by clear signs that no zeal for piety flourishes in the scribes [and Pharisees], but that they are absolutely dedicated to ambition. For those who seek the "seat of honor" and the first places are those who out of pride choose rather to be raised up among people than to be approved by God. What Christ chiefly condemns in them is that they strive to be called "master." Although the name "rabbi" certainly designates excellence, at that time among the Jews the name was commonly used for masters and teachers of the law. But Christ denies that this honor is suitable for anyone other than himself alone. It follows then that it cannot be transferred to any other person without doing injury to him. But this seems to be too hard and even absurd, for now Christ does not

---

[3]LEA 3:184 (cf. WA 30,2:660); citing Heb 11:6.

[4]Marlorat, ed., Catholike and Ecclesiasticall Exposition of the Holy Gospell After S. Mathewe, 535*.

teach us in person but ordains and appoints masters for us. It is ridiculous to take away the title from those to whom this duty has been given. Indeed, when he was active on earth, he appointed the apostles who undertook the teaching office in his name. But if the title is at stake, Paul certainly did not desire to do injury to Christ by wickedly stealing his glory when he claimed to be a master and "teacher of the Gentiles." But because Christ had no other intention than to gather together in order everyone from the least to the greatest so that his authority would be entirely preserved, there is no reason for the expression to trouble us. Christ does not care by what title those might be called who are engaged in the duty of teaching, but he restrains them within fair limits so that they will not lord it over others who are their brothers and sisters in the faith. There was always this distinction, that Christ alone should be obeyed, because of him alone the Father's voice called from heaven, "Hear him." Teachers are truly his ministers in that he should be heard in them and that they might be masters under him, insofar as they represent his person. COMMENTARY ON A HARMONY OF THE GOSPELS.[5]

11:45-52 Woe to the Teachers of the Law

THE HYPOCRITES INVENT THEIR OWN LAWS, WHICH OTHERS CANNOT BEAR. FRANÇOIS LAMBERT: Because the servants of God recognize themselves as sinners ("If we say that we have no sin, we deceive ourselves, and the truth is not in us"), once they are rebuked, they are converted. Thus accordingly they endure the criticism patiently, and even have disgust toward their own sins. But hypocrites are enraged by the truth. For while they do not wish to seem to be unjust, they hate nothing more than those who would uncover their sins. Truly following the example of Christ, the holy Evangelists never abandon the truth because of such hypocrites but instead more ardently criticize their misguided justice, and they act, so

that when they are confused and humbled, the lovely justice of God might be introduced. . . .

This is a very important passage against impious human inventions, and these burdens are indeed said to be so great that there is no one who is able to bear them, which is certainly quite different from the law. For "through the law comes the knowledge of sin." The law humbles the conscience most beneficially, so that it might seek the Savior and his gospel, for no one is able either to seek or to follow that word of the remission of sins unless the law first terrifies and humbles him. Therefore the law that cannot be borne is spoken to the flesh and not to the spirit, for those who are spiritual serve the Spirit through Christ: opposed to this, through the dung of human invention, a person is made into a hypocrite and completely blinded. Therefore he does not search for the Savior and his gospel, except falsely. And these are the sort of inventions that are the most insupportable and hateful to the Spirit (concerning human precepts, you must understand), that is, the ones that are so much from those who devised them, which are not able to be carried by the rest. But still the inventors of those things are criticized, for it is certain that they would not be able to invent them, if it were not for the diabolical "wisdom" of the flesh. COMMENTARY IN LUKE 11:45-46.[6]

YOU PERSECUTE THE PROPHETS SENT TO CALL YOU TO REPENTANCE. DESIDERIUS ERASMUS: Woe to you who in order to show off your own integrity and innocence build the tombs of the prophets, most of whom your ancestors killed! Thus it happens that this same thing with which you are eager to disguise your maliciousness reveals it quite clearly. For while you decorate the tombs of the prophets, you acknowledge that those who killed them were detestable, but whose memory is held to be holy by you who are their descendents. Furthermore, when you yourselves treat the prophets of this age much worse than your ancestors did the ancient prophets, even though

---

[5]CO 45:624-25 (cf. CTS 33:78-79); citing 1 Tim 2:7; Mt 17:5.

[6]Lambert, *In Divi Lucae*, X8r-v; citing 1 Jn 1:8; Rom 3:20.

they are far superior, do you not declare that, being blinded by profit, ambition, envy and hatred, you knowingly approve the impious and wicked things done by your ancestors, which you not only imitate but are even eager to surpass? The goodness of God has often called you to come to your senses, but you have always been cruel and violent in your wickedness to those who pour out the truth on you. This truth was hateful to you for no other reason than that it was directed against your perverse desires and passions. PARAPHRASE ON THE GOSPEL OF LUKE 11:47-48.[7]

THIS CRUELTY AGAINST THE PROPHETS WILL BE REVEALED. PHILIPP MELANCHTHON: Here the terrible malice of the scribes and Pharisees is described. It is a small matter not to receive a minister of grace, if it is compared with the cruelty by which the prophets (including Christ) are scornfully handled, afflicted, scourged and killed. This cruelty pertains to those who are swelled and puffed up by the name of holiness and righteousness. They cannot abide the preaching of the truth but resist it as much as they can with fire and sword, and they persecute it as though it were heresy. But those who are killed do not perish to the Lord, but the found sheep are brought to the Shepherd, and all excuse is taken away from the wicked when their malice (which otherwise would be hidden) is made manifest to everyone. AN ECCLESIASTICALL EXPOSITION UPON SAINT MATHEWE 23.[8]

PUNISHMENT FOR KILLING THE PROPHETS IS VISITED ON THE DESCENDANTS. HEINRICH BULLINGER: The Lord threatens revenge not only for those whom they kill but also for those whom their ancestors had killed. This signified the besieging and utter destruction of this people. For these people killed Christ, the head of all saints, and his apostles, who were also greater than all the saints (because they brought the more perfect knowledge of God to the world), and therefore they not only finished but also exceeded the cruelty of all their ancestors, who had shed the innocent blood of the prophets. Even as they brought this cruelty to fulfillment, they also made themselves guilty of the innocent blood which they at any time had shed. All the saints, from the first to the last, are one body, with Christ as their head, and all the benefits which the Lord gives to their posterity, he says that he also gives to their ancestors. Likewise, all the wicked are one body, with Satan as their head, and we say that vengeance is their reward and that they are punished with such punishments that are not felt in this life—although they are indeed inflicted on them, but first of all they are visited on their posterity. . . .

He added this earnest affirmation to terrify the people. It is as if he said, "There is no reason for any person to think that he may escape the judgment of God. For certainly all those punishments which the Lord threatens to pour out on those horrible murderers will come down from heaven onto their viperous progeny." And let all those who think it is a godly thing these days to persecute the truth of the gospel and those who profess it realize that these sayings also pertain to them. For the blood which cries out to God for vengeance will not go unrevenged. AN ECCLESIASTICALL EXPOSITION UPON SAINT MATHEWE 23.[9]

THE RULERS KEPT OTHERS FROM ENTERING THE KINGDOM. PHILIPP MELANCHTHON: There were two ways in which they shut up the kingdom of heaven for others. First, they themselves would not enter in, and the simple folk were greatly impressed with their authority, which can be seen in their saying, "Can it be that the authorities really know that this is the Christ?" This crowd which does not know the law is cursed; therefore to believe in Christ means to enter into the kingdom of heaven. Second, they stopped those who wanted

[7]Erasmus, *In Evangelivm Lvce Paraphrasis*, r6v-r7r (LB 7:386; CWE 48:24).

[8]Marlorat, ed., *Catholike and Ecclesiasticall Exposition of the Holy Gospel After S. Mathewe*, 544*.

[9]Marlorat, ed., *Catholike and Ecclesiasticall Exposition of the Holy Gospel After S. Mathewe*, 546-47*; citing Gen 4:10-11.

to enter, both by the wrong interpretation of the law, keeping to themselves the key of knowledge, and not allowing any opinion or understanding of the law which they themselves had not taught; and by the terrible threats of divine vengeance and excommunication. For they had already conspired in how they would cast those who confessed Christ out of the temple. This threat not only brought physical grief, but it was also a heavy and grievous burden to the consciences of the faithful people of God. AN ECCLESIASTICALL EXPOSITION UPON SAINT MATHEWE 23.[10]

11:53-54 The Scribes and Pharisees Plot Against Jesus

THROUGH INCESSANT QUESTIONS THEY STRUGGLED TO TRAP JESUS. HEINRICH BULLINGER: This is proof of their impious and stubborn obstinance. The Lord had rebuked them so as to correct them and lead them to better fruit. But, in fact, those men, having turned away from God, are all the more hardened and now attempt even to crush their benefactor with plots and to catch him with deceitful questions, and once he

was arrested to accuse and destroy him—this man whom they judged as unjust and abusive against the holy order of the priesthood. And today, the greater part of those who belong to the party of the papists are fixed on this same goal as they establish arguments against the preachers of the gospel of Jesus Christ.

What the translator rendered as "to question slyly" is the Greek word apostomatizein.[11] Explaining this word Theophylact said, "They began apostomatizein him, that is, they began to question him frequently and to try to confuse him. For apostomatizein happens when many people interrogate one person with one question after another. And when a person is not able to answer, he seems foolish because he hesitates. Of course, those wicked men back then were also endeavoring to do this against Christ. For because many people were interrogating a single person, they seemed to apostomatizein him and to lure him into hesitation so that he could not respond to what would probably happen to him. For how could one person be able to respond to many people asking one question after another?" COMMENTARY ON LUKE 11:53-54.[12]

---

[10]Marlorat, ed., Catholike and Ecclesiasticall Exposition of the Holy Gospell After S. Mathewe, 530*; citing Jn 7:26; Jn 9:22.

[11]Bullinger is referring to the Vulgate.
[12]Bullinger, In Luculentum et Sacrosanctum Euangelium Secundum Lucam Commentariorum, 84r-v; citing Theophlyact, Enarratio in Evangelium S. Lucae (PG 123:873-76).

12:1-12 JESUS TEACHES THAT ONLY GOD HAS POWER OVER LIFE AND DEATH

In the meantime, when so many thousands of the people had gathered together that they were trampling one another, he began to say to his disciples first, "Beware of the leaven of the Pharisees, which is hypocrisy. ²Nothing is covered up that will not be revealed, or hidden that will not be known. ³Therefore whatever you have said in the dark shall be heard in the light, and what you have whispered in private rooms shall be proclaimed on the housetops.

⁴"I tell you, my friends, do not fear those who kill the body, and after that have nothing more that they can do. ⁵But I will warn you whom to fear: fear him who, after he has killed, has authority to cast into hell.ᵃ Yes, I tell you, fear him! ⁶Are not five sparrows sold for two pennies?ᵇ And not one of them is forgotten before God. ⁷Why, even the hairs of your head are all numbered. Fear not; you are of more value than many sparrows.

⁸ "And I tell you, everyone who acknowledges me before men, the Son of Man also will acknowledge before the angels of God, ⁹but the one who denies me before men will be denied before the angels of God. ¹⁰And everyone who speaks a word against the Son of Man will be forgiven, but the one who blasphemes against the Holy Spirit will not be forgiven. ¹¹And when they bring you before the synagogues and the rulers and the authorities, do not be anxious about how you should defend yourself or what you should say, ¹²for the Holy Spirit will teach you in that very hour what you ought to say."

a Greek *Gehenna*   b Greek *two assaria*; an *assarion* was a Roman copper coin worth about 1/16 of a denarius (which was a day's wage for a laborer)

OVERVIEW: In this passage, Jesus warns his followers and prepares them for the days ahead. The times that were coming would be difficult: persecution would be intermittent but occasionally widespread and severe; with Jesus' death, his followers were terrified and at great risk; families and friends would turn over Christians for prosecution; and "worldly tyrants" would arrest, torture and even kill those who followed Christ. Jesus knew that the difficult times to come would challenge even his staunchest disciples, and he wanted to confirm their faith and provide them comfort and support for the challenges that lay ahead. He reminded them that the God they served is the ultimate judge for everyone. A time was coming when all that was secret would be revealed and when the innocence of those falsely accused would be manifest and acknowledged by all. Such a judge was not only all-knowing but also all-powerful, far more powerful than earthly rulers and tyrants. They can kill only the body but cannot harm the soul. But our heavenly Father so cares for us and values us that he even knows the number of the hairs on our heads.

Though it often resulted from Christians attacking Christians (whether verbally or physically), persecution was a reality during the Reformation. In that context the reformers echo Jesus' words by affirming that God will not leave us unprotected or unguided in times of trial and persecution. Any and all Christians may be called on to testify to their faith and the gospel, and we must trust that in that situation God will give us confidence and the Spirit will give us the words to witness to our faith. There will be a reward for those who proclaim him and suffer for his sake—he will accept those witnesses as his own—but those who deny him, whether out of fear or hope of gain or for any other reason, he will punish at the Last Judgment. The notion of election is a further assurance here, for the elect will not, in the end, deny Christ but will persevere in their faith.

A good example is Peter, who famously denied Christ but then tearfully repented. From that day he constantly and publicly proclaimed Christ, and was eventually martyred for his faith. Peter's example shows the difficulty and challenges for the followers of Christ but also God's continued grace and mercy for his chosen ones.

12:1-3 Beware the Hypocrisy of the Pharisees

ALL HYPOCRISY AND DECEIT SHALL SOON BE REVEALED. DESIDERIUS ERASMUS: And because the Lord Jesus knew the malice of the Pharisees, the scribes and the lawyers to be incurable, he wanted to proclaim their hypocrisy openly, so that no incautious or naive person might be deceived by their pretense. And so with a great number of people standing around—so many that they were trampling each other under foot—he began to say to his disciples, "Beware of the yeast of the Pharisees, which is hypocrisy. Strive to be the kind of person which you desire people to see you as. In the future, nothing artificial or false shall be able to escape notice for long. A time shall come when both your innocence and their malice shall be plainly revealed." PARAPHRASE ON THE GOSPEL OF LUKE 12:1.[1]

THE INNOCENCE OF THE INNOCENT WHO SUFFER WILL BE REVEALED. PHILIPP MELANCHTHON: There seems to be another use of this proverb, which may be taken in two different ways. The first provides great consolation for those who suffer injury, by letting them know that a day will come which shall manifest and declare their innocence to the whole world, which had been hidden for a long time. Examples of this aspect are Joseph, David, Susanna, and others. The other use of this proverb serves to make us shun and avoid all those things that are evil. Now because God is a just judge, he will not suffer that the impiety of the wicked will lie in secret, as Saint Paul says: "Therefore do not pronounce judgment before the time, before the Lord comes, who will bring to light the things now hidden in darkness and will disclose the purposes of the heart. Then each one will receive his commendation from God." But the first exposition agrees very well with the meaning of Christ. AN ECCLESIASTICALL EXPOSITION UPON SAINT MATHEWE 10.[2]

WHAT HAS BEEN SECRET WILL BE OPENLY PROCLAIMED. MARTIN BUCER: He sets here light against darkness, he joins hearing to the ear and preaching to the rooftops. He means by "speaking in darkness," committing something to the mind by secret talk. Therefore those who speak "in the light" tell openly and plainly what they have heard. Also, to hear or tell "in the ear" is to receive or commit something by a private meeting together. For people commonly whisper something in the ear which they do not want to be overheard by others. Therefore, to preach "from the roofs" is to disclose to everyone what was committed to them, and openly, manifestly and plainly to utter what was given to them before in secret. This is spoken according to the manner of that region, where their houses are built so that a person may stand or walk on the roofs of them, because they are flat and leaded, similar to a gallery. AN ECCLESIASTICALL EXPOSITION UPON SAINT MATHEWE 10.[3]

12:4-7 Fear God Who Alone Has Power over Your Life and Death

GOD, YOUR MAKER, IS THE ONLY ONE WHOM YOU SHOULD FEAR. PHILIPP MELANCHTHON: Now by gathering together the evidence of the divine power of God, he proves plainly that human cruelty ought to be despised. It is as if he should say, "If you fear those who by some means might hurt or punish you, why do you not fear him who

---

[1]Erasmus, *In Evangelivm Lvce Paraphrasis*, r8r (LB 7:387; CWE 48:26-27).

[2]Marlorat, ed., *Catholike and Ecclesiasticall Exposition of the Holy Gospell After S. Mathewe*, 218*; citing 1 Cor 4:5.

[3]Marlorat, ed., *Catholike and Ecclesiasticall Exposition of the Holy Gospell After S. Mathewe*, 218*; citing Deut 22:8; Judg 16:27.

is able to hurt you in every respect, and not simply with the power to kill your body, because your body will be restored again? A tyrant has not destroyed a person when he has killed the body. He who has taken away someone's life has not diminished that person's salvation at all, and the body is something we must all give up eventually, whether we want to or not, on God's timeline. Only he who has made both body and soul can kill both body and soul and throw it into everlasting hell. Therefore, if you are wise, he is the only one you will fear, and if you indeed fear him, you will despise and also set at naught all worldly tyrants." AN ECCLESIASTICALL EXPOSITION UPON SAINT MATHEWE 10.[4]

EVEN THE LEAST IMPORTANT PARTS OF YOU ARE IMPORTANT TO GOD. PHILIPP MELANCH-THON: All of the things which he had spoken of before have a marvelous emphasis and force. For when he might have added, "How much more will you not be killed without your Father's will?"—that one care might have answered another—he did not do so. Instead, he wanted to show them that not only their lives but also other things are of small importance and should be counted as superfluous, but all these things are likewise under the Father's providence. And so he said, "All the hairs of your head are numbered." It was as if he should say, "Not only your life, your bodies, and other things that are dear to you, but also even your hairs, however little they may be esteemed, are of care and charge to your heavenly Father, in so much that he knows their number. So there is nothing in you to which he does not pay some attention." For he does not say in vain that they "are numbered," but so that he may make known his singular and special care. For all things that are numbered and recorded are numbered so that none of them should at any time be lost. That is why he uses the word in the preterite tense, or time which is already past, for he does not say that they will be numbered sometime in the future but that they are already numbered. It is as if he should say, "Even from the time of your creation, the Lord has taken and does take charge of you." AN ECCLESIASTICALL EXPOSITION UPON SAINT MATHEWE 10.[5]

12:8-10 Confess the Son of Man, and He Will Confess You in Heaven

WE MUST CONFESS CHRIST WITH BOLDNESS, EVEN BEFORE TYRANTS. HEINRICH BULLINGER: To profess Christ in this passage is truly to publish the truth of the gospel, that is, constantly to acknowledge Christ to be perfect God and man and to be the only salvation and righteousness of the world, by whom the faithful are justified. And so we see that it is not enough for a Christian to have Christ in his heart, unless he will also profess him openly before others, according to the measure of the faith that is given to him—as we already said, according to his office and calling, and as the opportunity arises. If anyone therefore is called to confess his faith before tyrants, then he should openly and plainly confess Christ, even as if God himself were requiring testimony of him. Whatever he may actually have to do, he ought to pray to God that God will give him a sure trust and confidence with the spirit of boldness. AN ECCLESIASTICALL EXPOSITION UPON SAINT MATHEWE 10.[6]

THOSE WHO DENY CHRIST WILL BE DENIED BY HIM. THE ENGLISH ANNOTATIONS: To the previous argument he adds the mention of a reward: Christ will accept as his own those who suffer for his sake. To confess him relates either to all Christians, as in 1 Peter 3:15, or to those who are called out before persecutors to give testimony to the truth of Christ. But those who deny him before others for any reason, whether for fear, for human favor or to gain any worldly benefit, he will punish before the holy angels who will attend him

---

[4]Marlorat, ed., *Catholike and Ecclesiasticall Exposition of the Holy Gospell After S. Mathewe*, 219-20*.

[5]Marlorat, ed., *Catholike and Ecclesiasticall Exposition of the Holy Gospell After S. Mathewe*, 221*.
[6]Marlorat, ed., *Catholike and Ecclesiasticall Exposition of the Holy Gospell After S. Mathewe*, 223*.

when he judges the living and the dead. If any deny him to be true God and true man, our savior, justifier, redeemer or sole mediator; if any deny the gospel, or any part thereof, to be the truth; if any out of malice oppose the gospel, or out of fear of others are ashamed of it or by an impious silence betray the truth of it; all these who have denied him he will deny and cast off. This should, however, be understood as relating to cases of final impenitence. Peter's denial of Christ (through a deeply upset mind and sudden fear), then his bitter tears of repentance which followed, show how far the elect can sometimes be overcome by temptation or a terrible situation and yet by God's mercy be recovered again. ANNOTATIONS UPON THE GOSPEL ACCORDING TO SAINT LUKE 12:9.[7]

THOSE WHO BELIEVE CHRIST IS IN THE DEVIL'S SERVICE WILL BE GIVEN NO MERCY.

HENRY HAMMOND: Those who by the lowliness of Christ's human appearance are tempted to deny him to be the Messiah, and do accordingly oppose him, may have some place for pardon and be to some degree excuseable. However, those who attribute his works of power (his miracles done visibly by the finger of God) to the working of the devil in him—there is no place of excuse and mercy for them if they do not, on the resurrection of Christ and the apostles preaching it to them, return and repent, and effectually receive Christ. PARAPHRASE ON LUKE 12.[8]

ONLY THE REPROBATE BLASPHEME AGAINST THE SPIRIT.

FRANÇOIS LAMBERT: This sin is the most grave in the judgment of God, and those who blaspheme the Holy Spirit are hardened and blinded by him most justly. Indeed, those who reject the light of truth are justly humbled by God. Moreover, unless the reprobate are cut off in this judgment, the elect themselves might not be saved. Therefore, although the elect may go astray and, like Paul, blaspheme against Christ and his word

sometimes through ignorance, they will never blaspheme against the Holy Spirit, either in their spirits or in their hearts. Indeed, they are saved by God, who loved them from eternity. For according to election they are most dear to him, and the gifts and the calling of God are of such a sort that they would not be able to offend him. On the other hand, the reprobate, even if they were at some point beloved by God, they are now seen as foreign, and although they might be adorned by his Spirit, they never have his grace. He has condemned them from eternity. Therefore, although they might some day be illuminated, and they might taste those things which are of God, they will never truly worship his Spirit or hear his calling with their whole hearts, because they are not Christ's sheep. And the Father certainly did not give them to his Son, for if the Father had given them to him, he would never have thrown them out, that is, made them blind and hardened them forever. As Jesus said, "Everything that the Father gives me will come to me, and anyone who comes to me I will never drive away." Briefly, even if in the name of God the reprobate would drive out demons, and prophesy, and do other miraculous things, they would never hasten after the Spirit of God with their whole hearts through everything. COMMENTARY IN LUKE 12:10.[9]

12:11-12 Be a Witness Through the Power of the Spirit

JESUS WANTS TO INOCULATE THE DISCIPLES AGAINST FEAR.

KONRAD PELLIKAN: Although you all are uneducated, poor and lowly, you should not be afraid of the uproar of the world against you. The good and simple Spirit of God is sufficient against all the cheaters and violent people of this world. Therefore, when you are led into their synagogues, accused of great crimes, and when you are led before the magistrates and civic leaders, do not follow the usual practice of the common people when they are accused. They are anxious

---

[7]Downame, ed., *Annotations*, Uu4v*; citing Mk 8:38.
[8]Hammond, *Paraphrase and Annotations*, 231*.
[9]Lambert, *In Divi Lucae*, Y4r-v; citing Jn 10:26-30; 6:37.

when they make their response or when they speak to someone who might be able to help them escape the charge. You will hand this over to the power of the state, that, being called, you might be present. As for the rest, you should not be afraid of the sight of them, nor should you be anxious in worrying about how you will have to defend yourselves by your own eloquence. The simple language of truth will always be ready. As much as you need, the Holy Spirit will freely supply. And your speech will be appropriate to whatever sort of life you have. Nothing is more effective, however, than the simple truth. Just as through terror of the courts some are led astray from the sincerity of the profession of the gospel, so also many are ruined by eagerness for wealth. So that the Lord might thus take away this inward state from the souls of the disciples, having undertaken spiritual matters as humble and unworthy people, the argument is therefore presented through what would happen. COMMENTARY IN LUKE 12:11-12.[10]

---

[10]Pellikan, *In Sacrosancta Quatuor Evangelia*, 138-39 (cf. CWE 48:30; LB 7:389).

12:13-21 THE PARABLE OF THE RICH FOOL

[13]*Someone in the crowd said to him, "Teacher, tell my brother to divide the inheritance with me."* [14]*But he said to him, "Man, who made me a judge or arbitrator over you?"* [15]*And he said to them, "Take care, and be on your guard against all covetousness, for one's life does not consist in the abundance of his possessions."* [16]*And he told them a parable, saying, "The land of a rich man produced plentifully,* [17]*and he thought to himself, 'What shall I do, for I have* nowhere to store my crops?'* [18]*And he said, 'I will do this: I will tear down my barns and build larger ones, and there I will store all my grain and my goods.* [19]*And I will say to my soul, "Soul, you have ample goods laid up for many years; relax, eat, drink, be merry."'* [20]*But God said to him, 'Fool! This night your soul is required of you, and the things you have prepared, whose will they be?'* [21]*So is the one who lays up treasure for himself and is not rich toward God."*

OVERVIEW: Separating orthopraxy and orthodoxy was unthinkable for the reformers. These theologians and clerics often emphasized the need to reform our morals and live out our faith.

Covetousness, they teach, is a misdirection of desire and a misunderstanding of what is truly important. The rich man in the parable did not gain his wealth unjustly, but his grasping after wealth is already a problem. His attention is taken up with his plans to increase and store his wealth; he has forgotten that human life is not extended by wealth. God, not the rich man, is in charge; the rich man is God's steward, using the good gifts he was given, which he would have to return someday. But he selfishly thought he had created his own wealth, and had no gratitude toward God. He forgot about an essential element of life—death— and desired to build up more and more earthly treasures, more than he could ever use or enjoy. Worldly treasures have no value in themselves, except insofar as we use and enjoy them. The best use for worldly goods is whatever promotes love of God and neighbor.

12:13-15 Possessions Are Not the Center of One's Life

THE DESIRE FOR INHERITANCE SHOWS THE MAN IS TIED TO THIS WORLD. AUGUSTIN MARLORAT: So this man calls on Christ to proceed against his brother with his authority. "Speak to my brother," he says, "to divide the inheritance with me." As if he should say, "Because you seem to be the Messiah, and you teach brotherly love so often, make it happen that my brother will show to me in his action what you teach in word and which the office of the Messiah requires." By this comment he betrays his own covetousness. For while Christ called his disciples to the confession of his name and commanded them to prepare themselves against the persecution to come, this man ignored all the dangers that were at hand. Instead, he was so tied to his inheritance that he did not seek for anything else except for the riches and pleasures of this world. He did not seek to follow Christ but only to gather as much wealth as possible, as we can see by the words which Christ speaks to him. This is why Christ criticizes both his ignorance and his coveteousness. AN ECCLESIASTICALL EXPOSITION UPON SAINT LUKE 12.[1]

CHRIST IS NOT CONCERNED WITH TEMPORAL RICHES. PETER RIEDEMANN: In effect, Jesus said, "What is your quarrel to me, the quarrel between yourselves over what is temporal? I have not been sent by God to judge such matters. I have come to

---

[1]Marlorat, ed., *Catholike and Ecclesiasticall Exposition of the Holy Gospell After S. Marke and Luke*, 203*.

implant what is of God, so that whoever desires may find it in me and receive it. You, however, do not search for what is divine but for what is earthly and worldly. Therefore, go and let those in authority decide for you." Whoever seeks the things of this world does not seek what is in Christ and therefore cannot have such matters decided by Christ. As with Christ, so with his followers; they have not been appointed to judge over what is temporal. CONFESSION OF FAITH.[2]

CHRIST HAS GRANTED THE OFFICE OF THE SWORD TO TEMPORAL GOVERNMENT.

BALTHASAR HUBMAIER: "I am not here to interfere in the office and mandate of others. On the contrary, the office and orderly mandate has been given by God to the government to protect and guard the godly and to punish and kill the evil ones. For this he hung the sword on its side. For what reason should it hang there if one were not permitted to use it?" Now sometimes God punishes the evil ones by hail, floods and illnesses, also by special people who are chosen and elected for that end. For that reason Paul calls the government a servant of God. What God wants to do himself he often wants to do through creatures as his tools. ON THE SWORD.[3]

ONLY A LITTLE WILL MEET YOUR PHYSICAL NEEDS.

DESIDERIUS ERASMUS: Be continually on guard . . . against everything that borders on greed, for often under the pretext of need and prudence the gloomy vice creeps up, which once let in leads a person astray into every sort of disgrace. And it can scarcely be avoided unless we possess lightly and disdainfully even the things that we possess in our own right. But those who trust in their wealth so as to place some considerable assurance of human happiness in it deceive themselves greatly. For plenty does not make for happiness but for worry, and for neglect of the thing that ought to be sought for even apart from all else. Nature's needs are in fact satisfied with a little. PARAPHRASE ON THE GOSPEL OF LUKE 12:15.[4]

DO NOT SEEK COMMODITIES BUT THE KINGDOM.

ANDREAS BODENSTEIN VON KARLSTADT: The circus of lawyers is troublesome. In short, money and possessions cannot either give or take away life. There are thousands who live quite well who carry their possessions with them, while other thousands who have many possessions live poorly and miserably. The moment they have filled up their cellars and barns, they die. Therefore, if we wish to be yielded Christians, we must not be anxious to acquire goods and preserve wagonloads full of food. Neither must we be shocked when the goods we have already acquired vanish in an instant. Neither should the goods we now have either comfort or console us; nor should we fear or worry if we lose them. Instead, we ought to accept with love and delight the kingdom of God, that is, his eternal will. THE MEANING OF THE TERM GELASSEN AND WHERE IN HOLY SCRIPTURE IT IS FOUND.[5]

12:16-21 *The Rich Man Does Not Have the Power over His Own Death*

FOLLY GUIDED THE RICH MAN. DESIDERIUS ERASMUS: If the rich man had let himself be guided by love when he was in such mental turmoil, love would have said to him: "Look around at how many are in need of what you have in excess. Acknowledge to whom you owe even a year's productivity. God has favored you with capital from which you may garner the interest of heavenly deeds. Exchange transitory goods for permanent ones, earthly for heavenly, human for divine. Thus, your generosity will have been your gain." But

---

[2]CRR 9:139*; citing Is 61:1-2; Lk 4:16-19; Jn 7:38; Sir 7:17. The opposition of Christ and Mammon is fundamental to Hutterite theology concerning the community of goods; true Christians must imitate the Father-Son relationship. See Thomas N. Finger, *A Contemporary Anabaptist Theology: Biblical, Historical, Constructive* (Downers Grove, IL: InterVarsity Press, 2004), 235-43, esp. 237-39.
[3]CRR 5:500* (QGT 9:438-39); citing Rom 13:4.

[4]CWE 48:31-32* (LB 7:390).
[5]CRR 8:152*.

because he preferred to be guided by folly and thoughtlessness, at their urging he said to himself: "I will tear down my old barns and build bigger ones, and put all this year's yield and the rest of my goods in them, so that nothing is lost." PARAPHRASE ON THE GOSPEL OF LUKE 12:16-19.[6]

WE RARELY REALIZE THAT ALL OUR GOODS ARE GOD'S. HULDRYCH ZWINGLI: With these words he expresses an eagerness for riches, for riches are not content with older, little buildings, but they must build new ones which are much more magnificent. Riches add to the soul, but they add arrogance, not humility or modesty, for they also revile what came before. But people do not make these brilliant things; only virtue gives back brilliant things. How can their strength truly store up wealth, so that it will always last? Christ does not forbid us from storing up our little harvest, but we should not focus our minds on this, so that we do not become prideful. God hates an arrogant and ungrateful mind, whether one is poor or rich. We are stewards, put in place by God to take care of his goods—why do we so rarely realize that we will have to pay the account back to him? If you had a farmer or steward who perhaps had cheated you by the scales, would you not have said that he was worthless and laid the heavy punishment on him that he deserved? Or would you not have thought of firing him? So what do you think that God will do with you, who conduct your business so faithlessly? All of us certainly say, "I have this from God, God gave this to me," but in our hearts we deny God when we misuse his goods so arrogantly and faithlessly. IN THE GOSPEL OF LUKE 12.[7]

THE RICH MAN THINKS HE WILL NOT DIE, BUT GOD DECIDES. JOHANNES BRENZ: Here we see quite clearly the carefulness of the rich man. There is certainly nothing said here that we do not see daily in rich people, who are so drunk with their abundance that they are persuaded that they

shall have immortality. However, they shall die in this flourishing state, because they are their own executioners and are worse to themselves than anyone else is. God takes away their lives just when they might enjoy their abundance. Others he takes away in the middle of their race for gain, when they have a burning desire for those things which they think so necessary to them. Some he allows to come so far that they have gotten a great heap of goods, and then he removes them, even as someone might take away a person from a table loaded with tasty dishes and fabulous desserts. Everyone knows that this is true, but it is not imprinted on their minds, because they clearly do not fear something which is so common. And this fault is in all of us, that we know neither ourselves nor our condition. AN ECCLESIASTICALL EXPOSITION UPON SAINT LUKE 12.[8]

BETTER TO BE RICH TOWARD GOD THAN IN EARTHLY POSSESSIONS. ERASMUS SARCERIUS: This is the application of that parable, by which Christ declares that the riches of this world cannot save. It is as if he said, "You have the example and the condition of the man who laid up for himself the riches of this world and was only rich to himself and not toward God, who desires to be refreshed by those to whom temporal things are given." AN ECCLESIASTICALL EXPOSITION UPON SAINT LUKE 12.[9]

GRAMMATICAL DETAILS ASIDE, THE MEANING IS THE SAME. ERASMUS SARCERIUS: Even those who have only a minimal knowledge of the Scriptures know that the Greek word *eis*, which means "toward," is often taken for *en*, which means "in." But whether we say "toward God" or "in God" does not make any difference. This is the point: those people are rich toward God who do not trust in earthly things but only depend on his provi-

---

[6]CWE 48:33* (LB 7:390).
[7]*D. Hvldrichi Zvinglii in Plerosqve Novi Testamenti Libros*, 262-63.

[8]Marlorat, ed., *Catholike and Ecclesiasticall Exposition of the Holy Gospell After S. Marke and Luke*, 206*.
[9]Marlorat, ed., *Catholike and Ecclesiasticall Exposition of the Holy Gospell After S. Marke and Luke*, 207* (cf. CWE 48:34; LB 7:390).

dence. It makes no difference whether they have plenty or very little, as long as they desire their daily bread from the Lord. AN ECCLESIASTICALL EXPOSITION UPON SAINT LUKE 12.[10]

STORE RICHES, REAP NOTHING. MARTIN LUTHER: Whoever refuses to stick to the Word of Christ and to be guided by the invisible treasure, let him go his way. We will not drag anyone in by the hair. But wait and see when it comes time for you to depart. Then summon the treasure you have laid up, the one you have made your reliance. Just see what you have in it then and what help it can give you! . . .

---

[10]Marlorat, ed., *Catholike and Ecclesiasticall Exposition of the Holy Gospell After S. Marke and Luke*, 207*.

It really is terrible that those who have served Mammon all their life and who have wronged and harmed many other people on its account and who have despised the Word of God should be unable to make use of it in time of need. Then their eyes are opened for the first time. They catch sight of another world, and they go groping around for the supplies they have stored up. But they cannot find a thing, and their passing is ignominious and empty. In their anxiety and fear they forget about what they have laid up, and they do not find anything in heaven either. COMMENTARY ON THE SERMON ON THE MOUNT.[11]

---

[11]LW 21:174* (WA 32:443).

12:22-34 DO NOT BE AFRAID

22And he said to his disciples, "Therefore I tell you, do not be anxious about your life, what you will eat, nor about your body, what you will put on. 23For life is more than food, and the body more than clothing. 24Consider the ravens: they neither sow nor reap, they have neither storehouse nor barn, and yet God feeds them. Of how much more value are you than the birds! 25And which of you by being anxious can add a single hour to his span of life?*a* 26If then you are not able to do as small a thing as that, why are you anxious about the rest? 27Consider the lilies, how they grow: they neither toil nor spin,*b* yet I tell you, even Solomon in all his glory was not arrayed like one of these. 28But if God so clothes the grass, which is alive in the field today, and tomorrow is thrown into the oven, how much more will he clothe you, O you of little faith! 29And do not seek what you are to eat and what you are to drink, nor be worried. 30For all the nations of the world seek after these things, and your Father knows that you need them. 31Instead, seek his*c* kingdom, and these things will be added to you.

32"Fear not, little flock, for it is your Father's good pleasure to give you the kingdom. 33Sell your possessions, and give to the needy. Provide yourselves with moneybags that do not grow old, with a treasure in the heavens that does not fail, where no thief approaches and no moth destroys. 34For where your treasure is, there will your heart be also.

a Or *a single cubit to his stature; a cubit* was about 18 inches or 45 centimeters   b Some manuscripts *Consider the lilies; they neither spin nor weave*   c Some manuscripts *God's*

OVERVIEW: Clearly, the apostles were worried. They were preparing to go out to preach, and they were not sure where their next meals were coming from. Perhaps they were reconsidering—maybe life as fishermen would be the practical and better way to go. Or perhaps they were simply worried and asking questions. In any case, Jesus preaches here about God's providence. Although it is quite natural to be worried about the necessities of life and how we will procure them, anxiety about such things means that we do not trust God. Jesus notes the examples of the birds and the flowers—they "neither sow nor reap," but God's providence gives them what they need, and even adorns with great beauty the flowers that will wither and die tomorrow. If God cares for these insignificant creatures, how much more will he care for us as our Father? But, our commentators note, people often do not trust in God's providence. They pridefully trust in their own strength, thinking that they can and must support themselves. But such misplaced confidence is sacrilege, for can we cause the sun to rise or plants to grow? No, our commentators affirm, only God can do those things, and Jesus reminds us that everything we receive comes from God. If we worry about what we will eat and what we will wear, then we are holding on to the world's perspective and despising God's Word, and thus God himself, doubting his promises and denying his power and authority.

Instead, we should be confident in God, the same way children are confident that their parents will care for them and they go to sleep at night without worries. But trusting that God will provide and that his will will be done does not then excuse us from working—a true and faithful Christian will not be careless or idle. Those who seek the kingdom, our commentators remind us, will treat people justly and charitably, will work hard in their vocations to care for themselves and their families and will try to follow God's commands. They will work, but they will not be anxious about their work, because their treasure does not lie here on earth, and storing up riches here is not their goal. Rather, their highest treasure is found in heaven, and thus their hearts have found true and lasting happiness.

12:22-30 *Consider the Lilies, for Which God Provides*

THE APOSTLES WERE UNNECESSARILY CONCERNED ABOUT MAKING A LIVING. JOHANNES BRENZ: Although these words of Christ pertain to all believers, they were really most necessary for the apostles to hear. For because the time had arrived when they must be sent, not only into Galilee and Judah but also into the whole world to preach the gospel of Christ, first of all they were called away from their regular occupations, by which they had formerly earned their living. Second, public parishes and stipends were not yet appointed for the ministers of the gospel. People were very selfish, and no one could hope for much charitable giving. Finally, Christ was so poor in this world (which he was so that we might be rich) that he could not give his apostles sufficient provision. And so it is no surprise that they were so careful about food and clothing and thought they should probably go back to their original occupations, rather than follow the calling of the preaching of the gospel.

With these words, Christ comforts them with all their concerns and exhorts them to set aside this carefulness. And to this exhortation he added very strong arguments by which he showed that it is not only superfluous but also great unbelief to be so concerned about food and clothing, that one would forsake God's calling and follow instead the desires of the flesh. AN ECCLESIASTICALL EXPOSITION UPON SAINT LUKE 12.[1]

ANXIETY OVER THINGS MEANS WE DOUBT GOD'S PROVIDENCE. JACQUES LEFÈVRE D'ÉTAPLES: The rich, the ambitious and the pleasure seekers of this age are worried because of anxiety, not only about necessities but even more about what is extra and unnecessary. And thus, worst of all, they live as if there were no divine providence. Truly, those who are good should not be anxious about necessities, for they should perceive that divine providence is so good, so lavish, so abundant, that even to evil people it bestows not only the necessary things but also what is superfluous; although these things might not be superfluous if people knew how to make use of them according to the will and knowledge of God. Therefore, why would he refuse the necessities to good people who are rarely idle but are covered by his providence? Consequently, you must consider the necessities which you have not to be from yourself but from God's providence. And if you have more than the mere necessities, you must attribute it to the providence of God, so that by accomplishing the responsibilities of the good housekeeper, you might obtain even greater favor from your Lord. And why should one be worried about the providence of God? Will your anxiety be able to make the sun rise in the morning, or the evening star pass away? Will it make the cornfields spring up, the vines to put forth buds or the rain showers to burst out and come down from the sky? Reasonably, whoever is troubled is blind and stupid, as if he would attribute to himself what is of God: a person does not live by his own but by God's providence. Nevertheless he trusts in himself, when he ought to trust in God alone. Therefore the trouble, the uneasiness and the anxiety of the world are bad and do not come from the Spirit of God but rather from the flesh: they originate from the flesh and from concupiscence, or perhaps they are instigated by an evil spirit. But truly, no one who lives by the Spirit of Christ is all twisted up by anxiety about those things. IN THE GOSPEL OF LUKE 12.[2]

THE BIRDS ARE OUR EXAMPLE OF GOD'S PROVIDENTIAL CARE. PHILIPP MELANCHTHON: That he might set before our eyes the providence of

---

[1]Marlorat, ed., *Catholike and Ecclesiasticall Exposition of the Holy Gospell After S. Marke and Luke*, 208*. [2]Lefèvre d'Étaples, *Commentarii Initiatorii in Quatuor Evangelia*, 2:66v.

our heavenly Father more plainly, he brings in the brute beasts as examples, which are fed and nourished by the power of God without any care. This is so that we might learn from them the riches of his goodness and the ampleness of his divine providence, in which we ought to quiet ourselves. He names the birds of the air to make clear the difference between them and those which are brought up in houses, that is, those which are not fed by their own care or by human industry but by the providence of God. Luke names ravens particularly, perhaps wanting to allude to the psalm, "He provides food for the cattle and for the young ravens when they call." . . .

These words do not give us the liberty to be idle. But Christ means that, although we are not able to help ourselves, we shall find help in our heavenly Father, and so his providence should be sufficient to us. "And your heavenly Father feeds them"—he does not say "and their heavenly Father feeds them," but "your heavenly Father." It is as if he should have said, "What imbecillity and weakness of faith is this, that when you have a heavenly Father who feeds such an innumerable multitude of birds, you are still so careful about your food and clothing, as if he who feeds little birds would forsake you!" AN ECCLESIASTICALL EXPOSITION UPON SAINT MATHEWE 6.[3]

WE WORRY, BECAUSE WE THINK WE CAN ACCOMPLISH SOMETHING. JOHN CALVIN: Christ here condemns another offense, which is almost always mixed together with immoderate concern about the means of livelihood; that is, when a mortal person, usurping to himself more than is permitted, does not hesitate to overstep his limits by sacrilegious thoughtlessness. "I know," says Jeremiah, "that the way of a person is not his own, nor is it for a person to direct his own steps." But yet it would be difficult to find one person out of a hundred who does not dare to promise something from his own industry

and strength. What happens then is that those who claim their good fortune rests on themselves do not hesitate to think that God is less important in making things happen. That Christ might restrain this crazy boldness, he says that whatever pertains to the support of our lives depends on the blessings of God alone. It is as if he would have said: "People foolishly weary themselves, when all our labors are needless and futile and none of our worries leads to success, unless and insofar as God blesses them." This is more clearly expressed by Luke, for Christ adds, "If you are not able to do what is least, why are you anxious about the rest?" These words agree with the point: Christ finds fault not only with distrust but also with pride, when people claim more for their skill than is right. COMMENTARY ON A HARMONY OF THE GOSPELS.[4]

WILD FLOWERS ARE BEAUTIFULLY CLOTHED BY GOD. HEINRICH BULLINGER: From food he now comes to apparel, about which he also reasons quite particularly. And as he did before, so now he also brings in an example of natural things, which he plainly and manifestly declares, saying, "Consider the lilies of the field." He does not here speak of lilies that grow in gardens, which are planted with great care and diligence, but of those which grow in the field, whose colors all the painters in the world are not able to imitate. (Here he makes a distinction between the lilies of the field and those of the garden, as he said before, "the birds of the air," so as to make a difference between them and those that are brought up in houses.) . . . And truly, what silk, what purple, what shining tinsel, may be compared to flowers? What is so red as the rose? What is so white as the lily? What has such a purple color as the violet? Surely nothing. AN ECCLESIASTICALL EXPOSITION UPON SAINT MATHEWE 6.[5]

---

[3]Marlorat, ed., *Catholike and Ecclesiasticall Exposition of the Holy Gospell After S. Mathewe*, 132-33*; citing Ps 147:9 (cf. Job 38:41).

[4]CO 45:210-11 (cf. CTS 31:341-42); citing Jer 10:23.
[5]Marlorat, ed., *Catholike and Ecclesiasticall Exposition of the Holy Gospell After S. Mathewe*, 133*.

BEAUTY IN NATURE REMINDS US NOT TO WORRY ABOUT OUR CLOTHES. JOHANN BAUMGART (POMARIUS): As he provides comfort against the worries about food by his disclosure of his Father's workshop and pantry, he likewise comforts us so that we do not worry about clothing by revealing the dressing room and silk warehouse of the heavenly Father. He shows all the various and glorious ornaments he has therein with which he decorates and clothes his creation. Once again he does not present to us a miracle as an example, as when the clothes and shoes of the Israelites were not tattered or threadbare even after forty years. Instead, he mentions little plants, blossoms and lilies—and not the sort that we have to raise up with effort, care and caution (although all our work and care cannot give them either color or decoration). Instead, he describes those which grow wild in the fields through God's provision alone, that neither work nor spin but stand today, and tomorrow will be thrown in the oven. Nevertheless they are clothed and adorned by God their Creator. And even Solomon in all his glory was not bedecked as beautifully as one of these. "So how much more," Christ concludes, "will God clothe you, O you of little faith!"

So when we catch sight of a beautiful little herb or flower, we should take comfort against the worries about our clothing and remember that our faithful God is so good, kind and benevolent that he beautifully and richly clothes and ornaments such a poor little herb or flower from his grand dressing room and silk warehouse so that no artist could paint it better. And he does this even though it is so momentary and fleeting that it stands only for today, and tomorrow it will be used for the fire. Yes, and he will much less forget those who belong to him, leaving us in threadbare clothing, for that is why he creates us and why he saves us through his Son and heals us through the Holy Spirit—so that we might live with him eternally. And though certainly because of our sins, we will be taken out by the scythe of death just like the grass and flowers of the field, according to his promise, our bones will flourish and prosper again on that day.

CARES AND WORRIES SHOW A LACK OF TRUST IN GOD. THOMAS BECON: Therefore Christ forbids this, saying, "Do not be full of care, but labor only, for of this you have a commandment. But leave the worry to me, for that is mine, that I may be your Father. And I can somewhat prevail over it, but you cannot, so do not attempt a thing in vain. Or, if you are not content to be ruled by my counsel, know that you are not my worshipers but worshipers of Mammon: you love him, but you hate me; you cleave to him and despise me, following the example of the world." And if there were any occasion for opportunity at this time, you would find many who would rather let this sermon pass than to disregard the opportunity, or at least they would defer the sermon until afterwards. Mammon moves them so much that they fear that the opportunity may never return again, but they are not worried about the sermon. Now it is quite plain that whatever is done to the Word of God is done to God. One who despises the Word and prefers money in fact despises and and holds God in contempt. There is no room for interpretation, for the word and speech are too evident: no other thing can be understood from them.

Therefore, this sermon belongs to all Christians. They should not be pensive or say, "What shall we eat or drink, or what clothing shall we wear?" "The Gentiles," Christ says, "inquire about these things, for they do not know or believe that they have a Father in heaven. But you have a Father in heaven who gave you a body and soul, yes, and even his Son. He knows what your needs are, and, concerning him, how can you do him such an injury as to think him hard and unmerciful to you, as though he would deny you a livelihood and sustenance, so that you would die of hunger? Therefore, behave yourselves according to the example of your children. In the evening they go to bed without any worries and do not think about tomorrow, for they

---

[6]Baumgart, *Postilla*, 222v; citing Deut 2:7; Ps 103:15-17; Is 66:14.

know that their parents will provide for it—do this also. My children," Christ says, "pay attention to your Father in heaven, and all other things will be given to you—just beware of anxiety. For this is a sign that you have no trust in the heavenly Father; otherwise you would cast away all worries and would be of good hope." THE FIFTEENTH SUNDAY AFTER TRINITY SUNDAY.[7]

IF YOU WORK HARD AND FAITHFULLY, GOD WILL PROVIDE. HEINRICH BULLINGER: Someone might say, "If I must put away all care, what will I do then? Does a careless and idle mind please God?" The Lord answers, "See that you honor God above all things, that you submit yourself to him, walk in his laws and do those things which he has prescribed for you. Then he will nourish you, and you will not need to fear necessity or want of food." AN ECCLESIASTI-CALL EXPOSITION UPON SAINT MATHEWE 6.[8]

12:31-34 *The Kingdom Is the Greatest Treasure*

HOW DO WE SEEK THE KINGDOM OF GOD? HEINRICH BULLINGER: Those who seek the kingdom of God and the righteousness of it are those who, with all their mind and a sure faith, give themselves wholly to pure religion and so organize their whole life that God may dwell in them, that they may be just and deal justly with everyone, hurt no one and defraud no one. They must work hard to earn a living in their vocation, so that they and their family may have what is sufficient for themselves and that they may give of what they have extra to others in need. Whoever does these things will be sure not to perish from hunger but shall be someone who receives sufficiently from the liberality of God. Paul shows this throughout his epistles. AN ECCLESIASTICALL EXPOSITION UPON SAINT MATHEWE 6.[9]

CHRIST IS THE GOOD SHEPHERD. JOHANNES BRENZ: He calls them a little flock because there were only twelve apostles, seventy disciples, and a few others who followed Jesus out of all Galilee and Judea. It can also refer to those who believed in Christ by the preaching of the apostles, whose numbers were always small. As the Lord says, many are called, but few are chosen. He calls them a flock, and he is the shepherd who feeds them. "I am the good Shepherd," he said. "A good shepherd gives his life for his sheep." If we weighed this diligently in our hearts and were entirely persuaded that he is our Shepherd, it would take away all our fear of hunger, and our fear of all other perils as well. AN ECCLESIASTICALL EXPOSITION UPON SAINT LUKE 12.[10]

THE LORD LOVES HIS DEAR CHILDREN. JOHANNES BRENZ: Here he shows that we have eternal life only by the free mercy of God. Each word of this phrase has its own emphasis or force. If it pleases God, what can hurt us, even if it is disliked by all people and even all devils? Who can alter the pleasure and will of God? And who can withstand it? Again, if God is a Father, why do you doubt his will? He who is a father cannot put aside his affection for his children, but he must do good for them, especially when they are in danger. It is possible that among human beings there are some unnatural fathers who do not love their children. But God, who is by nature unchangeable, when he acknowledges some to be his children, preserves and keeps them so that they cannot perish in any adversity. And so he says through the prophet: "Will a woman forget her own infant and not pity the son of her womb? And though they do forget, I will not forget you." And again, "The mountains shall be removed, and the hills shall fall down, but my lovingkindness shall not move, and the bond of my peace shall not fall away from you." And he is not only the Father of the patriarchs, of the prophets and of David and Ezekiel, but he is also

[7]Becon, *New Postil (Second Parte)*, 122v-123r*.
[8]Marlorat, ed., *Catholike and Ecclesiasticall Exposition of the Holy Gospell After S. Mathewe*, 135*.
[9]Marlorat, ed., *Catholike and Ecclesiasticall Exposition of the Holy Gospell After S. Mathewe*, 135*.
[10]Marlorat, ed., *Catholike and Ecclesiasticall Exposition of the Holy Gospell After S. Marke and Luke*, 209*; citing Mt 22:14; Jn 10:11.

your Father, even if you are poor and not quite so famous. In fact, the poorer you are, so much the more is he your Father, if only you will attach yourself to his Son by faith. AN ECCLESIASTICALL EXPOSITION UPON SAINT LUKE 12.[11]

THE PURSES OF HEAVEN RATHER THAN THOSE OF EARTH MUST BE SOUGHT. FRANÇOIS LAMBERT: If you are not lacking these purses and you love the treasure in heaven, then your heart will always sigh for these things, and you will advance in the way by which you can pursue them. And this way is Christ, for if you live and work by trusting in him, you will be able to receive these things. But if these are purses of the flesh, you are able to love and to gain only useless and pernicious treasures. For if you have been affected by the vanishing purses and treasures of the flesh, soon you will proceed by the way of the flesh, by the foolish wisdom of the world and by confidence in your own works and responsibility. Observe briefly how one can gain heavenly treasures: first, it is necessary to believe; second, the love and desire for these same treasures will follow; third, one will carefully seek the way to reach these treasures until it is found; fourth, once the way is found, one will follow it diligently. COMMENTARY IN LUKE 12:34.[12]

OUR HEARTS ARE BOUND WHERE OUR TREASURE IS. JOHN CALVIN: Christ demonstrates that those people who have their treasures stored on earth are miserable, and that is because their happiness is transitory and vanishing. Those greedy people deny that they are hindered and that they do not aspire in their hearts to heaven, but Christ opposes to them a principle: wherever people imagine their highest good to be, there they are entangled and attached. Thus it follows that those who try to reach happiness in this world renounce heaven. We know how carefully the philosophers examined the [notion of the] highest good; indeed, this was the chief point to them, and the one over which they sweated the most, and quite rightly, for on this matter the shaping of our entire lives depends, and all our senses are focused there. If it is necessary that honor is esteemed the highest good, then ambition will thoroughly occupy human minds; if it is money, then avarice will immediately seize the kingdom; if pleasure, it must happen that people will degenerate into thoughtless indulgence. Indeed, by nature we are all led to strive for the good, and thus it happens that false imaginations carry us off in all directions. But if we would be uprightly and earnestly persuaded that our happiness is in heaven, it would be easy to despise the world and trample on its blessings (and it is by these deceitful enticements that the greater part of people are bewitched), in order to climb up to heaven. For this reason, Paul, because he wants to lift up the faithful and encourage them in zeal for the heavenly life, offers Christ to them, in whom alone one is able to seek genuine happiness. It is as if he would say, "It is absurd and unworthy for those souls whose treasure is in heaven to sink down to earth." COMMENTARY ON A HARMONY OF THE GOSPELS.[13]

---

[11]Marlorat, ed., *Catholike and Ecclesiasticall Exposition of the Holy Gospell After S. Marke and Luke*, 209*; citing Is 49:15; 54:10.
[12]Lambert, *In Divi Lucae*, Y7v-Y8r.

[13]CO 45:205 (cf. CTS 31:333-34); citing Col 3:1.

12:35-48 BE READY FOR THE COMING OF THE SON OF MAN

35"Stay dressed for action[a] and keep your lamps burning, 36and be like men who are waiting for their master to come home from the wedding feast, so that they may open the door to him at once when he comes and knocks. 37Blessed are those servants[b] whom the master finds awake when he comes. Truly, I say to you, he will dress himself for service and have them recline at table, and he will come and serve them. 38If he comes in the second watch, or in the third, and finds them awake, blessed are those servants! 39But know this, that if the master of the house had known at what hour the thief was coming, he[c] would not have left his house to be broken into. 40You also must be ready, for the Son of Man is coming at an hour you do not expect."

41Peter said, "Lord, are you telling this parable for us or for all?" 42And the Lord said, "Who then is the faithful and wise manager, whom his master will set over his household, to give them their portion of food at the proper time? 43Blessed is that servant[d] whom his master will find so doing when he comes. 44Truly, I say to you, he will set him over all his possessions. 45But if that servant says to himself, 'My master is delayed in coming,' and begins to beat the male and female servants, and to eat and drink and get drunk, 46the master of that servant will come on a day when he does not expect him and at an hour he does not know, and will cut him in pieces and put him with the unfaithful. 47And that servant who knew his master's will but did not get ready or act according to his will, will receive a severe beating. 48But the one who did not know, and did what deserved a beating, will receive a light beating. Everyone to whom much was given, of him much will be required, and from him to whom they entrusted much, they will demand the more.

a Greek *let your loins stay girded*; compare Exodus 12:11   b Greek *bondservants*   c Some manuscripts add *would have stayed awake and*   d Greek *bondservant*; also verses 45, 46, 47

OVERVIEW: Jesus follows his comments regarding the focus of our hearts by letting us know that the time for preparation is short. The master may return at any time, and the servants must watch and be ready—watchfulness is the theme of this pericope. The reference is, these commentators assume, to Christ's second coming, when he will return in judgment. The parables instruct us, along with his disciples, that we do not know when Christ, our Lord and Master, will return, and so we must watch and keep ready, so that we can greet him when he comes again. Jesus lays out some of the benefits of keeping watch: the servants will be rewarded, even served at table by the master himself; and those who are ready will be invited in, not thrown out and punished. Christ's return will be as unexpected as a thief in the night, so we must always keep watch.

But what does "watchfulness" mean? These parables must be metaphors, our commentators argue, because we could hardly remain physically awake for the second coming. Watchfulness is rather a spiritual awakeness, a focus on Christ and his kingdom, while guarding against sleep means guarding against sin, particularly the lusts and desires of the flesh. While we all should keep watch and be on our guard, those who are assigned as shepherds (that is, those in leadership positions, especially in ministry) will be held to especially high standards. Those who guard over the rest of us not only must never sleep but also must be examples for us of self-control and zeal for service. The lazy servant who treats his fellows cruelly and wastes his master's goods will be punished when the master returns, but "of those who have more, more will be expected." Ministers who do not serve the people or God well but focus on their own pleasure and "sleep" in sin will be punished even more severely. Those with greater gifts of "knowledge of the gospel" who fail to keep watch will be more severely punished than those who sin out of ignorance.

12:35-38 Good Servants Are Ready for the Master No Matter the Hour

PREPARE AS LOYAL SERVANTS FOR CHRIST'S COMING. JOHANN SPANGENBERG: What does Christ say in his warning? He says, "Keep your loins girded and your lamps burning, and be like the servants who wait for their lord to return from a wedding feast, so that when he comes and knocks, they can quickly open it." What does it mean to "gird one's loins"? "Loins" in Scripture means the beginning of natural birth, as in Genesis 35: "Kings will come from your loins." This first birth is impure on account of original sin and brings with it great guilt that without a doubt brings condemnation and hinders blessedness, if the new birth does not also come, as Christ said to Nicodemus. So Christ does not unreasonably warn us to keep our loins girded, that is, that we should not let all sins, evil lusts and desires back in, once we have gotten rid of them, but we should wait on the Lord with new behavior and a new life, because we do not know when the Lord is coming.... And what did Christ mean by "keep your lamps burning"? By this simple parable which he takes from the office and occupation of the loyal servant, he wanted to warn Christians, especially those who lead, so that they would diligently and loyally tend to their offices and occupations until he comes again. ON SAINT MARTIN'S DAY.[1]

12:39-40 The Son of Man Comes When He Is Least Expected

THE LAST DAY WILL COME ON US UNEXPECTEDLY. PHILIPP MELANCHTHON: By this similitude we are taught how sudden and unexpected the coming of Christ will be. For the special desire of thieves is that they may steal from those who are not on the lookout for them, and therefore they execute their schemes in the night, when they think that the whole household is in deep sleep. By the owner of the house, he means each one of us, and by the thief, he means the Last Day. Therefore, seeing that it will come as unexpectedly as a thief in the night, at a time which we do not know, it behooves us to watch continually, so that it does not sneak up on us while we are sleeping. AN ECCLESIASTICALL EXPOSITION UPON SAINT MATHEWE 24.[2]

12:41-48 The Servants Must Always Remain Ready

PETER'S QUESTION BETRAYED A DESIRE TO BE SPECIAL. JOHN TRAPP: The disciples always dreamed of some singular happiness, some immunity and privilege that they would be granted over others. That is the cause of the question that gave occasion to the ensuing parables. A COMMENTARY UPON THE GOSPEL ACCORDING TO SAINT LUKE 12.[3]

THE PASTOR IS HELD TO A HIGHER STANDARD. JOHN CALVIN: This passage is explained more distinctly by Luke, where Peter's question is inserted, which gives occasion to a new parable. For when Christ had denied that there would be any opportunity for laziness because of the danger of the unknown time of his coming, Peter asked whether this teaching was for everyone, or if it applied alone to the Twelve. For, as we saw elsewhere, the disciples always seemed to think that they were treated unfairly, unless they were exempt from the common lot and greatly surpassed all others. Now, when he lays before them a condition not at all desirable or cheerful, they look

---

[1]Spangenberg, *Postilla Teütsch . . . von den fürnemsten Festen durch das gantze Jar*, CIIv-CIIIr; citing Gen 35:11; Jn 3:3-8.

[2]Marlorat, ed., *Catholike and Ecclesiasticall Exposition of the Holy Gospell After S. Mathewe*, 588*.
[3]Trapp, *Commentary or Exposition*, 400*.

all around them in amazement. Indeed, Christ's response shows that if every one of the common folk ought to stay awake, it is not at all acceptable that the apostles should be asleep. As Christ was first exhorting the whole family in general to be alert for his coming, now he requires a particular care from the principal servants. They are supervisors over the rest, that by their example they might show the way of sober attentiveness and worthy self-control. With these words he warns that they were not equipped with a leisurely authority, that they might have freedom for delights and ease; rather, the higher the level of honor to which they had arrived, the heavier the burden. Therefore, he teaches that they must especially excel in faith and wisdom. Those who are called to higher office should learn from this that they are more greatly obligated; not only must they avoid working with only minimal effort, but also they must exert themselves with all zeal and industry to exceptional service. For while it is enough for the common servants to discharge the obligation of private service, it is right for the steward, whose office comprises care for the whole family, to go further. Otherwise Christ charges them with ingratitude, because although they were chosen before others, they are not equal to their honor: why, indeed, did the Lord prefer them to the rest, except that they might outdo all others by a singular faith and wisdom? It is true that soberness and diligent attention are imposed on everyone, but in pastors, sleepiness is even more disgraceful and less excusable. COMMENTARY ON A HARMONY OF THE GOSPELS.[4]

THE LORD WILL BLESS HIS FAITHFUL SERVANT BUT PUNISH THE EVIL SERVANT. PHILIPP MELANCHTHON: He shows in these words that ministers who wisely govern that family of the Lord will not be faithful and wise in vain. For although a faithful steward is not greatly accepted by the family, because they have only a very small consideration of the lord, yet the lord to whom he is a faithful

servant will bless him. The happiness of the minister of Christ does not consist in that he appear faithful to human eyes but in that he is found faithful by Christ. So Paul says that he does not care about human judgment, but his only care is to be found faithful to the Lord. These things may be more clearly understood if they are considered with what follows concerning the evil servant. "I tell you the truth, he will put him in charge of all of his possessions." Now he goes on to show by this part of the similitude that the minister of Christ who is faithful will have great honor and will be made almost equal with his Lord. For when Joseph was made ruler over all the king's treasure in Egypt, he was reverenced above everyone except the king. And the Lord himself said, "And I assign to you, as my Father assigned to me, a kingdom, that you may eat and drink at my table in my kingdom and sit on thrones judging the twelve tribes of Israel." And the apostle Paul says of himself, "I have fought the good fight, I have finished the race, I have kept the faith. Henceforth there is laid up for me the crown of righteousness, which the Lord, the righteous Judge, will award to me on that day." And what the happiness of that faithful servant will be, "no eye has seen, nor ear heard, nor the heart of a human imagined." ...

When the evil servant is falsely convinced that his Lord will be a long time coming, this is the fruit that he produces: he does anything that he feels like doing without any fear. By this example, Christ shows how easy a thing it is for boldness to increase when a person, having once let loose the reins, gives himself over to sin. Christ not only makes mention here of a dissolute and wicked servant, but such a one who obstinately seeks to disturb the whole house, perversely abuses the power committed to him, exercises cruelty toward his fellow servants and carelessly spends his master's goods, to his reproach. This is the image and picture of a secure and careless servant. Now, if you will compare this image with the pope, the cardinals, the bishops, abbots, priors, clerks, the rest of the clergy, and the laity also, who serve the antichrist, you will say that they are all very much

---

[4]CO 45:679-80 (cf. CTS 33:165-66).

like that sluggish and careless servant. They would rather sit to eat and drink with those who are drunk than to repent at the preaching of the gospel. But do you think that they will do this and remain unpunished? Not at all. AN ECCLESIASTICALL EXPOSITION UPON SAINT MATHEWE 24.[5]

FROM ONE WHO HAS MORE, MORE SHALL BE REQUIRED.

JOHANNES BRENZ: Because those things which were spoken earlier in this sermon especially applied to the apostles, so also this verse ought to be referred especially to them. For the apostles were chosen to be the light of the world, the salt of the earth and the firstfruits of the Christian church. And so Christ required them above all others to watch. He wanted to make sure that it would not happen that after these had preached so often to others, they themselves should be castaways.

And in these words Christ also admonishes all the servants of God, because since we are all his children, we ought even more diligently to work toward godliness. Those who have received the most plentiful gifts of knowledge of the gospel commit the worse offense when they sin. Those who have received the most, from them the most is required. Therefore let those who have received more knowledge of the truth than others live more diligently according to the truth than others. The one who is best able to help and support his brothers and sisters should be the most liberal. Otherwise he makes himself like that vile and unfaithful servant who willingly disobeyed his master's will, and likewise he will receive the greater punishment of his Lord. AN ECCLESIASTICALL EXPOSITION UPON SAINT LUKE 12.[6]

CHRIST DISMANTLES AND DISHONORS THE DEVIL.

MARTIN LUTHER: Our Savior does not beat his servants with a club, but as it was said to Adam, he will act on my behalf. And Christ will say to my murderer, deceiver and seducer [that is, the devil]: "You have captured someone who belongs to me. Give him back to me!" Then he punches him in the mouth scattering his teeth to the earth, and rips open his stomach. "I am the Lord—true God from true God—and not you." SERMON ON THE FEAST OF SAINT STEPHEN (1532).[7]

DO NOT WASTE THE MASTER'S GOODS; FULFILL YOUR VOCATION FAITHFULLY.

DESIDERIUS ERASMUS: There is no reason why the stewardship of the gospel speech [sermo] entrusted to you should make you more arrogant; rather, it should make you more anxious. Whoever undertakes an ecclesiastical office undertakes a burden more truly than an honor. What is entrusted to him is unearned, and it is entrusted for the purpose of being brought out for the common good of the entire household. As masters require a more exact accounting from the one to whom they have entrusted more, so from the one to whom a more bountiful gift of knowledge and authority has been given by God more will be asked than from others; and one to whose faithfulness a broader and greater office has been committed will have more required of him inasmuch as he was obliged to benefit more people. The more learned you are, the more willingly shall you teach; the richer you are, the more willingly shall you assist the poor; the more powerful you are, the more people shall your authority draw to the gospel. What you have belongs to another; its master wishes what he has entrusted to you to be disbursed. PARAPHRASE ON THE GOSPEL OF LUKE 12:48.[8]

---

[5]Marlorat, ed., *Catholike and Ecclesiasticall Exposition of the Holy Gospell After S. Mathewe*, 589-90*; alluding to 1 Cor 4:3-4; Gen 41:40; quoting Lk 22:29-30; 2 Tim 4:7-8; 1 Cor 2:9 (cf. Is 64:4).
[6]Marlorat, ed., *Catholike and Ecclesiasticall Exposition of the Holy Gospell After S. Marke and Luke*, 213*.

---

[7]WA 36:402.
[8]CWE 48:42* (LB 7:393-94).

12:49-59 CHRIST CHALLENGES THE CROWDS

[49]"I came to cast fire on the earth, and would that it were already kindled! [50]I have a baptism to be baptized with, and how great is my distress until it is accomplished! [51]Do you think that I have come to give peace on earth? No, I tell you, but rather division. [52]For from now on in one house there will be five divided, three against two and two against three. [53]They will be divided, father against son and son against father, mother against daughter and daughter against mother, mother-in-law against her daughter-in-law and daughter-in-law against mother-in-law."

[54]He also said to the crowds, "When you see a cloud rising in the west, you say at once, 'A shower is coming.' And so it happens. [55]And when you see the south wind blowing, you say, 'There will be scorching heat,' and it happens. [56]You hypocrites! You know how to interpret the appearance of earth and sky, but why do you not know how to interpret the present time?

[57]"And why do you not judge for yourselves what is right? [58]As you go with your accuser before the magistrate, make an effort to settle with him on the way, lest he drag you to the judge, and the judge hand you over to the officer, and the officer put you in prison. [59]I tell you, you will never get out until you have paid the very last penny."[a]

a Greek *lepton*, a Jewish bronze or copper coin worth about 1/128 of a *denarius* (which was a day's wage for a laborer)

OVERVIEW: In this passage, Jesus confronts those who are listening to him. First, he points to the division that he will bring within families; second, he emphasizes the crowd's rejection of him and their failure to interpret the signs about him correctly. The difficulty in understanding verses such as these is how to explain them in light of other comments that Jesus makes, such as "Peace I leave with you; my peace I give to you" (Jn 14:27). How does Jesus bring and give peace, but then not bring peace, but rather division and the sword? Calvin suggests that the fire Jesus is bringing to the earth refers metaphorically to the effect of the gospel. Like a fire, the gospel will violently change things, burning away the chaff and purifying gold and silver. Jesus speaks of such destruction here to warn and instruct his disciples, who have not yet realized the difficulties, divisions and afflictions that are to come. His own baptism—that is, his passion—is coming, and it will kindle that great fire that will destroy but also purify. Brenz and Bullinger make a distinction between Christ's peace and the peace of the world, a "voluptuous, luxurious peace"—they are entirely different from each other.

The prophets foretold a time of great peace and joy in the reign of the Messiah, but Jesus' words make clear that such peace and happiness will come only in his heavenly kingdom, not here on earth. The world hates the peace that Christ brings, which is the peace that reunites God and humanity through his self-sacrifice. Such peace, the peace of the gospel, will serve to break apart and destroy families, rather than bring them happily together, Erasmus and Melanchthon note. For the gospel requires acceptance and dedication, and "the bonds of the Spirit are stronger" than those between families. When not everyone in a family accepts the gospel, as happened often among the early Christians (and during the Reformation as well), then dedication to the gospel meant division and disagreement among families—not because it is the nature of gospel, but because it is human nature.

Although the end times are coming and we must keep watch, for we do not know when the master is returning, there are still many who cannot read the signs of the times. They do not want to probe too far into their consciences and see that the good news that Jesus preaches is right, while their own hypocrisy is wrong. But because the end times are quickly approaching, it is essential, Jesus states, that we forgive those who have offended us while there is still time. If we do not reconcile now, we may be locked away without a key, "until we pay the very last penny." But, for some commentators, while the scene clearly refers to the ultimate judgment, that little word *until* remains problematic—could "until" imply that at some point the judgment might be reversed? Once we are judged and sent for punishment, these commentators insist, there is no return; hence the pressure to reconcile now, while there is still time. While some have used this passage to support the Catholic doctrine of purgatory—that place of purification and punishment that eventually leads to heaven—Schwenckfeld notes that none of the "ancient teachers" of the church interpreted this passage so; rather, it indicates a place of "eternal and everlasting pain." "Until" in the Scripture does not always mean that some event will eventually happen, and Jesus includes this metaphor to encourage us to make amends now and not to wait until it is too late.

12:49-51 *The Baptism by Fire Is Coming*

THE GOSPEL IS THE FIRE THAT THROWS ALL INTO CONFUSION. JOHN CALVIN: These words were from the last discourses of Christ, not from the time in which Luke narrates it. However, the sense is that the world has been thrown into the highest confusion by Christ, as if he wanted to mix up heaven and earth. For metaphorically the gospel is compared with fire, because it violently changes the shape of things. While the disciples falsely imagined that the kingdom of God was coming to the idle and the sleeping, Christ instead presents a terrible fire, by which it was necessary to burn the earth. And because the beginnings of this were appearing just then, Christ encourages the disciples in that they feel the power of the gospel in person. "Now," he says, "when great commotions begin to rage, you should not panic, but it should rather be the occasion of faithful trust; indeed, I rejoice that

this fruit of my labor is visible." Similarly, it is proper that all ministers of the gospel transfer this to themselves, that when there is confusion in the world, they apply themselves to their office more eagerly. In turn, it is noteworthy that this same fire of doctrine (when it burns freely) consumes chaff and straw but purifies silver and gold. COMMENTARY ON A HARMONY OF THE GOSPELS.[1]

THE SPIRIT MUST COMPLETE AND PERFECT WATER BAPTISM. DAVID JORIS: Few come to this baptism of truth, for it is that baptism of the Spirit which comes through the same person who comes after John (who nevertheless had been before him) who must also baptize, as it is written. This is what is meant by "through the water" and what its function and ministry is at present in its righteousness and true substance. But when this is fulfilled, the image, figure, shadow and letter will cease, just as the child is superseded by the adult, John by Jesus and Christ after the flesh by the spiritual, just as the light of mortals is superseded by the sun, which for the present must shine before that other may cease. Otherwise, the baptism of water would be able to make each person's conscience pure, holy and righteous. Otherwise, Simon Magus and everyone who is baptized in the world would have been Christ's. But it is otherwise and is not so. THE APOLOGY TO COUNTESS ANNA OF OLDENBURG.[2]

THE TIME OF HAPPINESS WILL COME IN HEAVEN, NOT ON EARTH. JOHANNES BRENZ: Christ here declares what the coming day will bring, according to the outward continuation of time which would endure from his coming in the flesh until his second and last coming in majesty. He takes away the offense which might discourage the faithful from the true faith in the gospel because of the troubles and calamities which arise when the gospel is revealed. The prophets had promised all kinds of joyful and happy things at the coming of Christ, such as "of the greatness of his government

---

[1]CO 45:681 (cf. CTS 33:168-69).
[2]CRR 7:278-79.

and peace there will be no end," and "nation will not take up sword against nation, nor will they train for war anymore." Also, "The wolf shall dwell with the lamb, and the leopard shall lie down with the goat." Furthermore we read, "Violence and robbery will never be heard of in the land, nor harm and destruction within its borders; your walls will be called 'health' and your gates 'the praise of God.'"

In short, there is no happiness which the prophets do not ascribe to the time in which the patriarchs were promised that Christ would come. Therefore Christ teaches that his kingdom is not of this world and that those things which were spoken by the prophets concerning the happiness of his time should not be expected to be realized in the external happiness of this world. For hatreds, debates and murders were to follow the preaching of the gospel. AN ECCLESIASTICALL EXPOSITION UPON SAINT LUKE 12.[3]

CHRIST'S PEACE IS WHAT THE WORLD HATES.
HEINRICH BULLINGER: As if Christ should say, "I would not have any of my disciples think that I came into the world to bring such peace as the world looks for and desires, namely, secure, voluptuous, luxurious peace." For Christ is not the author of sin or a patron or maintainer of vice and wickedness. He said, "I came not to bring peace." Christ truly is the Prince of Peace, and his kingdom is the kingdom of peace. He gives peace to those who are his, and he leaves peace with them, but it is a peace which the world cannot give; in fact, it is that peace which the world cannot stand but hates. For the peace of Christ passes all understanding, and it is the peace of consciences that agree with God, whose wrath we believe is appeased for Christ's sake. Therefore we walk in his commandments, and we avoid the concupiscence of the flesh; we agree with all good people, and we contend against all those who are evil and perverse. The peace of the world does not have to do with anything except what pertains to the world.

AN ECCLESIASTICALL EXPOSITION UPON SAINT MATHEWE 10.[4]

12:52-53 Families Will Be Divided Against Each Other

THE GOSPEL WILL DIVIDE FAMILIES WHEN SOME ACCEPT IT. PHILIPP MELANCHTHON: In order that Christ might express and make clear that this discord would not be the usual manner or sort, he brings in the degrees of consanguinity and nature, affirming that he will separate them with the sword, which was his purpose in coming into the world. For among those people, bitter and cruel contentions frequently arose on account of the Word. For the more people by nature are joined together, the greater and sharper is the contention between them. When the gospel is preached and received by the son but rejected by the father, eventually mutual discord will arise, which springs properly from the dissimilitude and variety of the minds, not from the gospel or the Lord himself. For this happens through the fault of the wicked, as we just said, contrary to the nature of the gospel. What the prophet Malachi teaches about John the Baptist is applicable to all the ministers of Christ, namely, that they are sent for this purpose: to turn the hearts of the parents toward their children and the hearts of the children toward their parents.[5] And truly the malice of the wicked brings about that those who before were joined together are separated and divided into contrary parties as soon as they hear the voice of Christ. AN ECCLESIASTICALL EXPOSITION UPON SAINT MATHEWE 10.[6]

12:54-56 Reading the Signs of the Times

DILIGENTLY INTERPRET THE PROOF OF THE GOSPEL. DESIDERIUS ERASMUS: Why are you

---

[3]Marlorat, ed., *Catholike and Ecclesiasticall Exposition of the Holy Gospell After S. Marke and Luke,* 214-15*; citing Is 9:7; 2:4; 11:6; 60:18.

[4]Marlorat, ed., *Catholike and Ecclesiasticall Exposition of the Holy Gospell After S. Mathewe,* 224*.
[5]Mal 4:6. Malachi names Elijah as the prophet who would be sent to accomplish this task.
[6]Marlorat, ed., *Catholike and Ecclesiasticall Exposition of the Holy Gospell After S. Mathewe,* 225*; citing Mt 10:34.

not preparing your hearts for the kingdom of God, because it is at hand? Or don't you realize its closeness from all the proofs of these things? Why are you so poor at drawing conclusions in this when you draw conclusions so shrewdly in matters of much less importance? . . . You hypocrites, how counterfeit are all your actions! Your wisdom is just like your sanctimony. In the things of this life you are wise; in eternal matters you see nothing. You observe the appearance of sky and land and from them you deduce forecasts of future events. Yet how is it that you do not notice from the appearance of so many signs that the time is near that brings salvation to all if it is accepted or eternal destruction if it is neglected? You know what the prophets promised, you see and hear so many things that are being said and done among you, you see that the world is being renewed, and do you still not conclude on your own that the promised time is at hand? This alone is what you ought to have done with all zeal, and no material thing should be so valuable to you that for its sake you take the loss of your gospel profits. PARAPHRASE ON THE GOSPEL OF LUKE 12:54-56.[7]

12:57-59 Last Chances to Repent Before Judgment

THEY IGNORED THEIR CONSCIENCES. JOHN CALVIN: Here Christ reveals the source of evil, and, as it were, places the knife at the ulcer. He says that they do not penetrate into their consciences or examine there within themselves, in the presence of God, what might be right. Indeed, the hypocrites are so led by impudence to criticize that they quite securely throw their pretentious words into the air. They do not place any check on their inclinations, nor do they bring themselves to God's tribunal, where the truth, once it was recognized, would gain the victory. Next, when Luke relates that this was spoken to the crowds, he does not contradict the narratives of Matthew and Mark, because it is probable that Christ

generally adapted his style of speaking to the hangers-on and disciples of the scribes, and other despisers of God similar to them, of whom he discerned there were too many. This complaint or rebuke was suitable to that whole lot. COMMENTARY ON A HARMONY OF THE GOSPELS.[8]

IF WE FORGIVE, WE WILL BE BLESSED BOTH NOW AND HEREAFTER. JOHANN SPANGENBERG: What is he saying with these words? This is what he wants to say: If you have been offended by someone and you are asked for forgiveness, it is your duty to forgive. This is what Christ did when he said, "Father, forgive them, for they know not what they do." If you are not asked, be ready and willing anyway to forgive, and quickly, while the wrath is still fresh and new, so that no long-lasting hate will come out of it: "Do not let the sun set on your anger." For we are uncertain of our lives, and so we should not put off our reconciliation until tomorrow, or next year, but instead we should reconcile and settle our differences as soon as possible. If you do not want to be reconciled, then on the Last Day you will be accused and convicted, and you will be delivered up to the judge, then to the jailor, and will not come out of prison until you pay the last coin; that is, never for eternity, for there is no salvation from hell. So think now about a person who allows himself to live forever in Christian righteousness, that is, in a true faith and brotherly love, not angry, nor cursing, not wishing any evil on any person in their body, their wife or child, their servants, cattle or possessions, offending their honor or reputation, but who lives in peace with everyone, has everything worked out with his enemies and opponents, is reconciled with them and has all differences settled. His prayer and worship are pleasing to God because of it, and he will benefit by receiving God's grace here, and eternal life hereafter, Amen. GOSPEL ON THE SIXTH SUNDAY AFTER TRINITY.[9]

---

[7]CWE 48:44* (LB 7:394).

[8]CO 45:466 (cf. CTS 32:278).
[9]Spangenberg, *Postilla . . . von Ostern biß auffs Aduent*, XCVIIv; citing Lk 23:24; Eph 4:26.

"UNTIL" DOES NOT MEAN YOU WILL EVER ESCAPE THIS PRISON. KASPAR VON SCHWENCKFELD: Some have wanted to prove or introduce purgatory by means of this text, as if there were a time of satisfaction or reconciliation represented there, as if the words "until you paid everything" made that possible. But the ancient teachers of the Christian church did not interpret this aforementioned place as referring to purgatory.[10] Rather, they suggested that the Lord wanted to frighten his listeners through the uncertain outcome of the court and wanted to show and exhort them to peace and reconciliation. If we do not reconcile ourselves here in the time of grace, then we must burn there eternally and never be able to come out of that prison, into which the severe judge will throw us. And also that little word *until*—"until you also pay that last penny"

does not necessarily indicate that the pain there will have an end. Anyone there can pay so little, but there is a worm there that never dies and a fire that never goes out. There are many examples of this use of "until" in the sacred Scriptures, such as when the prophet David said of Christ: "The Lord says to my Lord, 'Sit at my right hand, until I make your enemies your footstool.'" From this it does not follow that the Lord Christ on Judgment Day will be removed from his seat at the right hand of God or that he will have to give up his kingdom, for that should be eternal. Augustine also gives us an example and interprets this place as one of eternal and everlasting pain. INTERPRETATION OF THE GOSPEL, MATTHEW 5, ON THE SIXTH SUNDAY AFTER TRINITY.[11]

---

[10]See Hilary (PL 9:938); Bede (PL 92:27); Jerome (PL 26:38).

[11]CS 10:529-530; citing Mk 9:44 (or Mk 9:48); citing Ps 110:1; citing Augustine, *De Sermone Domini in Monte Secundum Matthaeum* (PL 34:1243-44; NPNF 6:13-14).

13:1-9 SUFFERING, REPENTANCE AND THE PARABLE OF THE FIG TREE

There were some present at that very time who told him about the Galileans whose blood Pilate had mingled with their sacrifices. ²And he answered them, "Do you think that these Galileans were worse sinners than all the other Galileans, because they suffered in this way? ³No, I tell you; but unless you repent, you will all likewise perish. ⁴Or those eighteen on whom the tower in Siloam fell and killed them: do you think that they were worse offenders than all the others who lived in Jerusalem? ⁵No, I tell you; but unless you repent, you will all likewise perish."

⁶And he told this parable: "A man had a fig tree planted in his vineyard, and he came seeking fruit on it and found none. ⁷And he said to the vinedresser, 'Look, for three years now I have come seeking fruit on this fig tree, and I find none. Cut it down. Why should it use up the ground?' ⁸And he answered him, 'Sir, let it alone this year also, until I dig around it and put on manure. ⁹Then if it should bear fruit next year, well and good; but if not, you can cut it down.'"

OVERVIEW: It is a frequent human desire to find meaning in suffering—a reality the reformers knew very well. Some of them were excommunicated from their church, exiled from their home; their spouses or children died; they were persecuted—even martyred—for their faith. We often judge that people must deserve what happens to them, whether bad or good. But this story reminds us, our commentators affirm, that God does not judge in the same way that we do and that people who are visited with afflictions are not necessarily bad (other than that they are sinners, as we all are). In fact, as Lambert notes, God's chastisement goes even to those who willingly carry their cross daily. Those who escape punishment do not do so because they are better than others but because God is being patient with them. The parable that Jesus tells makes this message clear: bear fruit—repent and return to God—or your destruction is coming. The reformers note that God expects every tree in his garden to bear good fruit, and that he will be patient for a time, but eventually an unfruitful tree will be chopped down and burned. The destruction of others around us, like those who inspired this parable, should remind us that we are sinners and must repent—God will not be patient forever.

But fortunately there is another character in the story—the gardener. The job of the gardener is to till the soil and prune the plant, to work hard to coax the tree to be fruitful. For the reformers, the gardeners of God's people are pastors. Their job is to work hard at training and correcting the people, lovingly guiding them like a shepherd. And like the gardener, pastors must also advocate for their flock; if they are not showing improvement, they must pray to God for more time, so that he might postpone the coming punishment.

13:1-5 Not Only the Guilty Suffer

OUR DAMNATION OF OTHERS AND DELUSION ABOUT OURSELVES. JOHN CALVIN: This passage is extremely useful, if for no other reason than that this disease is almost natural to us: to be too rigorous and severe in judging others and too disposed to delude ourselves about our own faults. The consequence is that we not only censure with excessive severity the offenses of our brothers, but also whenever they experience any calamity, we condemn them as wicked and reprobate people. But anyone who is not spurred on by the hand of God slumbers at ease in the midst of his sins, as if God were favorable and reconciled to him. This involves a double fault. For when God chastises anyone before our eyes, he warns us of his judgments, so that each may examine himself and consider what he deserves. If he spares us for a time, by this kindness and mercy he is inviting us to repentance; it should absolutely not be considered a chance for us to slumber. COMMENTARY ON A HARMONY OF THE GOSPELS.[1]

THE PUNISHMENT OF SINNERS ENCOURAGES US TO REPENT. JOHANNES BRENZ: It is as if Christ had said that Pilate punished these Galileans to discharge his office and to pacify the revolution ready to arise. But the Lord our God allowed this thing to happen, not that you should judge them alone to be sinners but that by their punishment you might be reminded of your own sins and so repent. Likewise, although God has ordained that those who are known and open sinners should be openly punished, this did not happen because these people were the greatest sinners above all others but that the lion (to speak proverbially) might be chastised with the dog's punishment. Those who want to tame a lion usually take a young dog and beat him with a club in the sight of the lion. The lion is supposed to be so terrified by the crying and howling of the dog that it is made gentle. Likewise, God sets the open punishments of the wicked before our eyes, that by their example all of us might be admonished for our sins and repent. AN ECCLESIASTICALL EXPOSITION UPON SAINT LUKE 12.[2]

GOD AND HUMAN BEINGS JUDGE DIFFERENTLY. FRANÇOIS LAMBERT: The judgments of God are something quite different from the judgments of people. For the flesh says that those who do not suffer any misfortune are better, and those who are tormented and struck down in various ways are worse. Conversely the Spirit of God judges those ones to be evil who do not

experience the suffering of other people and who are not scourged along with others. But those are truly happy who carry their cross daily and who are scourged and chastised "in the early morning," that is, those who are justified by faith from the beginning. Consequently now Jesus says, "Do you think," and so on. Every day many of you do inoffensive things which before God are worse than these things. Therefore, unless you repent, the same will happen; that is, "you will perish." COMMENTARY IN LUKE 13:2.[3]

13:6-9 *The Parable of the Fig Tree*

PARABLES HAD GREAT POWER OVER THE PEOPLE. NEHEMIAH ROGERS: The reason why our Savior so frequently used this kind of teaching is (in general) this: there is no kind of speech that more cunningly creeps by an insinuating way into the understanding and has greater command over the affections than a parable. It commands attention powerfully and moves devotion effectively. Of all ways of teaching this was esteemed by the Jews to be the most powerful, and they called parables and comparisons *potestates* or "powers," powerful insinuations. They had an order of doctors among them called Moselin who used this parabolical way of teaching with the people, and they had great power and dominion over the affections of their disciples. By teaching them in an obscure way, they created an admiration and a reverence among their hearers and laid a kind of necessity on them to return again to them for the interpretation and signification of those obscure and dark sayings which they delivered. In reference to this manner of teaching, it is certainly true that the Evangelists tell us that Christ "taught as one having authority" and that "his word had power." But he undoubtedly also gained a reverend esteem among the people by this manner of preaching, and because of it they held him to be at least some great and excellent prophet. THE FIGLESS FIG TREE.[4]

---

[1]CTS 32:151-52* (CO 45:386-87).
[2]Marlorat, ed., *Catholike and Ecclesiasticall Exposition of the Holy Gospell After S. Marke and Luke*, 217-18*.

[3]Lambert, *In Divi Lucae*, Z4r; citing Ps 62, esp. v. 6.
[4]Rogers, *Figg-less Figg-Tree*, 29-30*; citing Mt 7:29; Lk 4:32.

God Is Patient with Sinners but Will Not Let Sin Continue Forever. The

English Annotations: Our Savior told this parable in order to counter a possible objection which a secure sinner might make against what he said. The scope of the story is to show that many impenitent sinners, who are worthy of destruction, are spared for a time. Yet this will add to their final ruin, unless they truly repent in time. Continuing in sin is a great abuse of God's long-suffering attitude; his justice does not sleep, nor is he lazy but rather patient (see 2 Pet 3:9; Rom 2:5). The planter will try all possible means to make the barren tree fruitful. Likewise, our good God will not quickly cut down and destroy people but will use all means to improve them. If nothing works, then finally he will lay the ax to the root. Annotations upon the Gospel According to Saint Luke 13:6.[5]

Without Fruit, We Too Will Be Cut Out of the Garden. John Fary: This fig tree is every

person who, if after three years (that is, after an appointed time) does not bring forth good fruit, if after he is dug about and pruned, tilled and manured by the powerful instruments of God's husbandry, his Word and sacrament and holy orders, if after all these helps he still remains sterile and unfruitful, there is nothing to be looked for but judgment, nothing to be expected but the sharp ax of God's wrath to hew him down and make him fuel fit for the fire, according to Christ's own saying: "Every tree that does not bear good fruit is cut down and cast into the fire."

So although the parable was spoken to the Jews, yet as the apostle says, it was written for our sakes and uttered by Christ for our instruction. It teaches us three plain and wholesome doctrines. First, the thing which God expects from every tree that he has planted in his vineyard, what he looks for in a Christian, in every Christian, is that the person should bring forth good fruit.... Second, although the Lord may for a time bear with our

not bearing fruit, and may for a while leave us alone and suffer us to go on in our unfruitfulness, yet if we persist in that sterility, if we still continue to be unprofitable, he will not suffer us to take up space in his garden, but he will come with his ax and cut us down. Perhaps he may wait for three years for us to bear fruit, but if none comes by then, "Cut it down! Why should it be wasting the soil?" Third, it is the duty of the gardeners of the Lord's vineyard not only to intercede for the preservation of every plant committed to their charge but also to endeavor carefully to use every means possible to help their barreness and make them fruitful. God's Severity on Man's Sterility.[6]

Pastors Are the Ones Who Care for the Vine. Martin Bucer: In the example of the

caretaker of the vineyard who entreats the Lord on behalf of the fig tree, Jesus foreshadows and signifies himself, who is, as it were, the caretaker of his Father's vine, and especially at that time of the people of the Jews, that he might make them fruitful by both teaching and miracles. And also by this example he gives us to understand the office of those whom the Lord has appointed to trim and care for his vine. These are the pastors, and they ought to call on the Lord so that he does not eventually destroy those who are unfruitful. There ought to be a fatherly love in the shepherd toward the church. The example of Moses, who openly set himself against the wrath of God and tried to mitigate it, teaches us this. And so when pastors see that their teaching is not received the way it should be, they should flee to the Lord, so that he might be stopped from pouring forth his wrath on the people. An Ecclesiasticall Exposition upon Saint Luke 13.[7]

The Lord's Patience Saves and Sweetens the Fruit. John Calvin: The substance of this

parable is that for a time many are tolerated who

---

[5]Downame, ed., *Annotations*, XXiv*.

[6]Fary, *God's Severity on Man's Sterility*, 4-5*; citing Mt 7:19; 1 Cor 9:10.

[7]Marlorat, ed., *Catholike and Ecclesiasticall Exposition of the Holy Gospell After S. Marke and Luke*, 220*; alluding to Ex 32:31.

deserve to be cut off; but they gain nothing by the delay, if they persist in their obstinacy. The wicked flattery, by which hypocrites are hardened and become more obstinate, arises from this cause: they do not think of their sins until they are compelled. Therefore, so long as God overlooks these and delays his punishment, they imagine that he is well-pleased with them. Thus they indulge themselves more freely, as if, to use the words of Isaiah, they "had made a covenant with death and were in friendship with the grave." And this is the reason why Paul denounces them in such earnestness of language for treasuring up to themselves the wrath of God against the Last Day.

It is well known that trees are sometimes preserved, not because their owners find them to be useful and productive but because the careful and industrious farmer makes every possible trial and experiment before he determines to remove them out of the field or vineyard. This teaches us that when the Lord does not immediately take vengeance on the reprobate but delays to punish them, there are the best reasons for his forbearance. Such considerations serve to restrain human rashness, that no one may dare to murmur against the supreme Judge of all, if he does not always execute his judgments in one uniform manner. Here a comparison is made between the owner and the vine dresser. God's ministers are not able to outdo him in gentleness and forbearance. For the Lord not only prolongs the life of sinners but also cultivates them in many ways, so that they may yield better fruit. COMMENTARY ON A HARMONY OF THE GOSPELS.[8]

THE VINE DRESSER WINS A REPRIEVE FOR THE VINE. JOHN MAYER: Calvin understands this similitude as only in general serving to push people to the speedy repentance to which he had admonished them before. The Lord deals with us as the farmer with his trees, seeking first by every means to make them fruitful, but if he does not prevail, he will cut them down. And this is a true exposition, but it does not cover everything which this story intends, because it seems to me that the three years signifies the time of Christ's ministry and preaching. And because in that time many of the people remained unconverted, Christ the vine dresser prays, and obtains, that they should be spared another year, that is, a certain time longer, so that he could labor among them through his apostles. But after that extra time, they were still hardened, and so they were cut down by the Romans. And it is not outside the scope of the parable to apply it to all sinful states and people, with whom God is very forebearing for a long time, because of the intervention of his vine dressers. A COMMENTARY ON THE NEW TESTAMENT, LUKE 13:8-9.[9]

---

[8]CTS 32:153-54* (CO 45:387-88); citing Is 28:15; Rom 2:5.
[9]Mayer, *Commentarie vpon the New Testament*, 376*.

13:10-21 KINGDOM HEALING AND PARABLES

[10]Now he was teaching in one of the synagogues on the Sabbath. [11]And behold, there was a woman who had had a disabling spirit for eighteen years. She was bent over and could not fully straighten herself. [12]When Jesus saw her, he called her over and said to her, "Woman, you are freed from your disability." [13]And he laid his hands on her, and immediately she was made straight, and she glorified God. [14]But the ruler of the synagogue, indignant because Jesus had healed on the Sabbath, said to the people, "There are six days in which work ought to be done. Come on those days and be healed, and not on the Sabbath day." [15]Then the Lord answered him, "You hypocrites! Does not each of you on the Sabbath untie his ox or his donkey from the manger and lead it away to water it? [16]And ought not this woman, a daughter of Abraham whom Satan bound for eighteen years, be loosed from this bond on the Sabbath day?" [17]As he said these things, all his adversaries were put to shame, and all the people rejoiced at all the glorious things that were done by him.

[18]He said therefore, "What is the kingdom of God like? And to what shall I compare it? [19]It is like a grain of mustard seed that a man took and sowed in his garden, and it grew and became a tree, and the birds of the air made nests in its branches."

[20]And again he said, "To what shall I compare the kingdom of God? [21]It is like leaven that a woman took and hid in three measures of flour, until it was all leavened."

OVERVIEW: Through both his healing of a woman on the sabbath and his teaching through parables, Jesus reveals something about God's kingdom. Some might wonder why Jesus would continue to frequent synagogues, if more often than not the visits ended in confrontations, or at least bad feelings. Was he purposefully provoking the synagogue leaders? Marlorat insists that Jesus was always interested in sharing God's Word; he attended the gatherings at the synagogues because that was the most opportune time and place to do so. It was not the only time or place where Jesus taught and preached, but when people were already gathered to hear God's Word, it was a wonderful opportunity for the Word to bear fruit. Jesus did not attend services only to teach but also to heal, and in doing so he fell afoul of the synagogue leaders. In healing the woman who had been crippled for eighteen years, Jesus offended the leaders who saw his actions—which revealed both God's mercy and his own divine power—as work, inappropriate for the sabbath. Why should that be? Calvin wonders. Is God also not allowed to work on the sabbath? What else should we do on the sabbath but call on God for his help and support and hope for his blessings?

As in many other passages, Jesus speaks in parables, Erasmus notes, to bring the people to a deeper understanding of the kingdom of God by providing a comparison to something with which they are already familiar. The people may well have been expecting him to mention something great and powerful, but instead he compares God's kingdom with a mustard seed and yeast. Both these things seem tiny and insignificant at first, but the mustard seed grows into a mighty tree and a tiny bit of yeast leavens many measures of flour. Likewise, the kingdom of God might seem impotent and irrelevant, but it will expand and spread around the world—beginning with a small group of men from Galilee. Contrary to human wisdom, these interpreters observe, the wisdom of God has made such insignificant people capable and strong enough to leaven and season the whole world.

13:10-13 Jesus Heals the Crippled Woman

CHRIST IS AN EXAMPLE OF FREQUENT TEACHING AND PREACHING. AUGUSTIN MARLORAT: The Evangelists continually testify to how diligently and painstakingly the Lord taught the people. He was sent by his Father to preach the kingdom of God, and he discharges this office boldly, as he says, "I have declared your name to those whom you have given me in this world." He taught both privately and publicly, but especially in the synagogues of the Jews, where a great company of people gathered to hear the Word of God. The specifics of the time are noted when Christ is said to teach on the sabbaths. This was the most convenient time to teach doctrine, as we have noted out of various passages. Therefore, although the Word of God is not tied to a particular place or circumstance or time, yet, at the wisdom and discretion of the teacher, the Word ought to be taught when there is the greatest hope of it bearing fruit. An Ecclesiasticall Exposition upon Saint Luke 13.[1]

Satan Is the Origin of Disease, but God Can Use It to Our Good. Johannes Brenz:

Is Satan then the author of disease? Is everyone who has a disease bound by Satan? Shall we say that one who is sick in his body is captive with the bonds of Satan, or is it not the Lord our God who is said to send diseases and afflictions to us?

To answer this, we must first note who God is by his own nature. For God, if you consider his true and proper nature carefully, is nothing else but the chief and most excellent fountain of goodness and health. There is nothing in the nature of God which is evil or diseased. So by his own nature, God neither makes nor sends diseases to us. For how should he who is health itself create disease? And how should the most excellent joy make sorrow and grief? So then, you might ask, where do diseases come from? They come from sin. For just as death entered the world with sin, so diseases also entered with death and are its forerunners. And Satan is the author of sin. As Christ says, he was a murderer from the beginning and did not abide in the truth, because there is no truth in him. When he speaks a lie he speaks of his own, because he is a liar and the father of liars. And so it is the case that Satan is also the author of diseases, and diseases are rightly called the bonds of Satan. However, we must also understand that God himself sends diseases and other sorts of afflictions to us. First, because God gives liberty to Satan to annoy us with diseases. For so he said to Satan, concerning Job, "Behold, he is in your hands, but only spare his life." Second, we see that after Satan sends diseases by the permission of God, God takes them into his own hands and uses them as an instrument for our salvation. For even as the wicked act that the sons of Jacob committed against their brother Joseph, and by which they sold him to strangers, was the work of Satan, God took it into his own hands and used it as an instrument to work the salvation of the house of Israel. An Ecclesiasticall Exposition upon Saint Luke 13.[2]

13:14-17 Controversy with the Leaders of the Synagogue

God's Work Is Most Active on the Sabbath. John Calvin: This critic does not dare to rebuke Christ publicly but instead directs the poison of his crabbiness on others, condeming Christ indirectly by rebuking the crowd. The senselessness of his malice is really amazing. "Six days are appointed for labor," he admonishes, but he foolishly and incorrectly defines that work which is only permitted on six days. Why does he not also prevent them from entering the synagogue, just in case they might violate the sabbath? Why does he not order them to cease from all pious activities? But even if people perhaps should be prohibited from their work on the sabbath day, it is a great offense that the grace of God should also be so hindered. He orders them to come on other days to seek a cure, as if the power of God lay sleeping on the sabbath and was not rather most extended on that day for the salvation of his people. What other reason is there for holy gatherings,

---

[1]Marlorat, ed., *Catholike and Ecclesiasticall Exposition of the Holy Gospell After S. Marke and Luke*, 220*; quoting Jn 17:6.

[2]Marlorat, ed., *Catholike and Ecclesiasticall Exposition of the Holy Gospell After S. Marke and Luke*, 223*; citing Jn 8:44; Job 1:12.

than that the faithful might call on God for his help and support? That impious hypocrite therefore speaks just as if this legitimate observance of the sabbath interrupted the flow of God's blessings, hindered people from calling on him and deprived them of the sense of God's grace. COMMENTARY ON A HARMONY OF THE GOSPELS.[3]

SATAN USED EVERY OPPORTUNITY TO WORK AGAINST CHRIST. JOHN CALVIN: Now, although this impious critic was silenced by shame, we see nevertheless that no work was ever performed by Christ, no matter how excellent, that the wicked did not use as an opportunity to make false accusations. Nor is it surprising that Satan exerted himself with all zeal and effort to destroy the glory of Christ; he does not cease from spreading his darkness but incessantly works to suppress the holy works of the faithful. COMMENTARY ON A HARMONY OF THE GOSPELS.[4]

13:18-19 The Mustard Seed

THE DESPISED MUSTARD SEED GROWS TO TREMENDOUS HEIGHTS. DESIDERIUS ERASMUS: Jesus, however, wanted to testify against all that foolish boasting of the Pharisees, which had the appearance of great holiness, that it might quickly vanish. And against that he desired that the power of the gospel might advance from its humble beginnings to such greatness that the whole world might be drawn to it, even though it came through death and through humble and uneducated apostles. And so he offered two parables which have the same meaning. "You see," he said, "that the kingdom of the synagogue fights against the kingdom of God. Nevertheless, the one that is more powerful will conquer."

Thus the Lord, as if inspired by a new spirit, by which he might restore the attention of the crowd, said, "What shall I say is like the kingdom of God, or to what shall I compare it, that from a thing which is well known to all of you, you might understand what sort of a thing it is?" And when all the people expected some great and high comparison, such as with the sun or with lightning, he preferred to lead them by a parable of a most disregarded and ignored little bean. "It is like," he said, "a little mustard grain, which while it is whole is the smallest and most worthless thing. It is not at all pleasing to the eye either in its color or in its scent. If it has any strength at all, it is within. A certain wise man chancing on such a seed did not despise it but planted it in his garden. And then that most despised little seed sprouted up and grew into a mighty tree, so that the birds were able to make their nests in its branches, and from that one little grain many thousands were produced. Thus the kingdom of God, precisely when it shall seem to be entirely extinct, that is when it shall extend itself most broadly." PARAPHRASE ON THE GOSPEL OF LUKE 13:18-19.[5]

13:20-21 Yeast in the Dough

THE APOSTLES' YEAST LEAVENS THE WHOLE WORLD. PHILIPP MELANCHTHON: This parable of the yeast has the same meaning as the parable that immediately precedes it. The word *yeast* sometimes signifies what is evil, as when Christ warned his disciples to beware the "yeast of the Pharisees and Sadducees." Also, Paul teaches that a "little yeast sours the whole lump of dough." But here the application must be taken simply and to the present cause. The apostles were a little yeast—because they were taken out of Galilee, by the wisdom of God, they were made capable and of strong enough force to leaven and season. They were sent out into the whole world for that same purpose, until all points everywhere were leavened. AN ECCLESIASTICALL EXPOSITION UPON SAINT MATHEWE 13.[6]

---

[3]CO 45:389 (cf. CTS 32:155-56).
[4]CO 45:390 (cf. CTS 32:156).

[5]Erasmus, *In Evangelivm Lvce Paraphrasis*, t4v (LB 7:397-98; CWE 48:51-52).
[6]Marlorat, ed., *Catholike and Ecclesiasticall Exposition of the Holy Gospell after S. Mathewe*, 292*; citing Mt 16:6; Gal 5:9.

13:22-30 THE NARROW DOOR

²²He went on his way through towns and villages, teaching and journeying toward Jerusalem. ²³And someone said to him, "Lord, will those who are saved be few?" And he said to them, ²⁴"Strive to enter through the narrow door. For many, I tell you, will seek to enter and will not be able. ²⁵When once the master of the house has risen and shut the door, and you begin to stand outside and to knock at the door, saying, 'Lord, open to us,' then he will answer you, 'I do not know where you come from.' ²⁶Then you will begin to say, 'We ate and drank in your presence, and you taught in our streets.' ²⁷But he will say, 'I tell you, I do not know where you come from. Depart from me, all you workers of evil!' ²⁸In that place there will be weeping and gnashing of teeth, when you see Abraham and Isaac and Jacob and all the prophets in the kingdom of God but you yourselves cast out. ²⁹And people will come from east and west, and from north and south, and recline at table in the kingdom of God. ³⁰And behold, some are last who will be first, and some are first who will be last."

OVERVIEW: Concern, even fear, over one's own salvation has been a part of Christian life as long as the hope of it has. In this passage, Jesus is asked, "Lord, will only a few be saved?" Although our commentators do not explicitly address predestination here, it is an underlying assumption of the discussion. While all these interpreters affirmed that the elect would be saved, the real concern is closer to home: Am I one of those elect? Mayer notes that Jesus does not specifically answer the question. He does not state the number that will be saved, because such information does not help us. No, instead we must enter through the narrow door: faith in Christ.

The reformers stress that some who saw themselves as pillars of the church and those who relied on seeing and socializing with Jesus but did not change their lives or fully commit to him are not going to enter the kingdom. But while some commentators emphasize how many who assume they will be admitted will not, Brenz prioritizes the good news of the message—Jesus talks about how many people from all parts of the earth (that is, even Gentiles) will enter in. In Jesus, heaven's gates are open and inviting. Christ perfectly fulfilled the law for us because we could not do it ourselves. If anyone is shut out, it is not because the gate is so narrow; rather, it is through their own fault.

13:22-27 Enter in Time at the Narrow Door

IT DOES NOT PROFIT US TO KNOW IF MANY WILL BE SAVED. JOHN MAYER: For Luke 13:23, the question of whether there are many that will be saved seems to be grounded on the earlier parable of the mustard seed, which was said to grow to such a height that the birds of the heavens could come and make nests in its branches. And because there are so many, it may justly be asked whether then there will be many that will be saved and so come to rest in the kingdom of heaven.... But why does Christ not answer this question? Because knowing whether there will be many or few who will be saved is a thing that does not profit us very much, but setting out the difficulty of entering into that life, and how few shall enter, satisfies the question indirectly and edifies the hearer by encouraging him to take the right path. And to this he adds, "Once the owner of the house gets up and closes the door," that is, Christ will enter into heaven and take all the elect with him, which is what he will do on the Last Day. When he says that they will say, "We ate and drank with you," that is to be taken literally, because he lived among them. And in saying that they will "come from east and west," he speaks prophetically of the calling of the Gentiles. A COMMENTARY ON THE NEW TESTAMENT, LUKE 13:23.[1]

CHRIST IS THE GATE WHO WILL ADMIT THE ELECT TO HEAVEN. JOHANNES BRENZ: By these words, Christ seems to affirm that the number who shall be saved is small, but he speaks more plainly in Matthew, when he says, "Wide and broad is the way that leads to destruction, and there are many who enter it, but the way is narrow and the gate is small which leads to life, and there are few who find it." And so because the gate to life is small, there are few who attain salvation. Yet in another passage of Matthew we read, "Many shall come from the east and from the west and shall rest with Abraham, Isaac and Jacob in the kingdom of heaven." And the prophet Isaiah, speaking of the heavenly Jerusalem, says, "Your gates shall stand open both night and day and never be shut, so that the host of the Gentiles may come and their kings may be brought to you."

These words teach us not only that many will be saved but also that the gate of heaven will be set wide open. But here we must make a distinction. If we consider Christ, we must confess that the gate of heaven is broad and wide. For Christ is the true Gate of heaven, who ascended into heaven and is revealed to the whole world by the preaching of the gospel. He set the gates of heaven wide open for us and has consecrated the earth itself by his gospel, so that people from all corners of the earth may ascend into the kingdom of heaven. And although the commandments of the law are heavy and grievous on account of the infirmity of our flesh and are really impossible for us to accomplish, nevertheless Christ has perfectly fulfilled the law. He has made it so that those who believe in him shall be judged to be righteous, just as if by their own righteousness they had perfectly fulfilled the law. Christ gives the Holy Spirit to those who believe in him through faith, that by the power of the Spirit they may walk in the obedience of God's law with ease and with pleasure, as much as is possible in the flesh. And so, as far as this portion of the divine teaching goes, the gate of the kingdom of heaven must not be said to be small. Even if you consider the church of Christ in itself, we have to confess that many are elected and that an innumerable multitude are and shall be saved. . . .

Those who are shut out of the gate of heaven are shut out through their own fault and not by the smallness of the gate. And although the number of the elect is great, if you consider the church of Christ in itself, nevertheless if you compare this number with the church of the wicked, you will find that the number of those who are elected to the inheritance of the kingdom is the smaller. AN ECCLESIASTICALL EPOSITION UPON SAINT LUKE 13.[2]

THEY HAVE A CERTAIN FAITH BUT ARE ROOTED IN THE WORLD. JOHN TRAPP: These pretenders to Christ perish by catching their own catch, hanging on their own fancy, making a bridge of their own shadow. They truly believe that Christ is their own dear Savior, when it is not a matter of life or death. They trust in Christ just as the apricot tree leans against the wall but is still rooted fast in the earth. And these remain rooted in the world. "We have eaten and drunk in your presence," even at his very table, but it became a snare to them. A COMMENTARY UPON THE GOSPEL ACCORDING TO SAINT LUKE 13.[3]

PEOPLE MIGHT THINK THEY ARE GREAT, BUT CHRIST DID NOT KNOW THEM. JOHN CALVIN: And what is contained in Christ's response? That he never counted them among his own, even at the time when they boasted that they were the pillars of the church. Therefore he orders those to go away from him who stole by a false title of honor an unjust possession of his house for that time. Paul seems to have borrowed from these words of Christ when he says, "The Lord knows who are his;

---

[1]Mayer, *Commentarie vpon the New Testament*, 379*.

[2]Marlorat, ed., *Catholike and Ecclesiasticall Exposition of the Holy Gospell After S. Marke and Luke*, 225-27*; citing Mt 7:14; 8:11; Is 60:11.

[3]Trapp, *Commentary or Exposition*, 402*.

let him who calls on the name of the Lord turn away from wickedness." The first phrase is intended to keep the weak from being thrown into confusion or wavering by the desertion of any who might be famous or with a well-known name: he denies that they were known at all by God, even if they might have had an unfounded greatness in the eyes of others. Then he exhorts all those who want to be counted as disciples of Christ to withdraw quickly from sinfulness, so that Christ does not banish them from his sight when he separates the sheep from the goats. COMMENTARY ON A HARMONY OF THE GOSPELS.[4]

13:28-30 The First Shall Be Last and the Last Shall Be First

A PLACE IN THE KINGDOM COMES ONLY THROUGH FAITH. KONRAD PELLIKAN: Because my servants have suffered on account of me and my cause, they will delight with me in enjoyment of the eternal banquet. But you who put the pleasures of this age before eternal happiness—depart to that place where there will be weeping and gnashing of teeth! The happiness of those you had persecuted here will be increased by the sight of your misfortune. You will see your ancestors, Abraham, Isaac and Jacob, and all the prophets whom your elders either struck down or killed taking their place at the table in the kingdom of God. They will rule with me in heavenly joy, and, in fact, having been soldiers until now in the church of the faithful, they will be stationed in the highest glory. The faithful of the whole world will admire them and will recognize them as masters of faith and piety and as examples of holiness and all virtues. And yet you despised them, and despised the sacrifice of that one for all the world, and so it will return to you accursed in this life. They will take their place at the table in the kingdom of God, but you who are descended from them are expelled outside. Nothing will be any good to you here, not prerogative of lineage and kinship, not the observance of the law, not even hearing me or performing miracles: only through faith can one enter into this happiness. Yes, and that other will come who will burn your souls most piercingly—he will come to you who have rejected those who believed what you alone received. They will come from all the nations of the world, indiscriminately, chosen by none, not related by birth to Abraham, Isaac and Jacob, with no acquaintance with the law, with no fellowship through a covenant, with no familiarity with me, but unexpectedly, through faith adopted as children of Abraham they will take their place in the kingdom of God.

Thus, contrary to your expectations, the matter will turn in the opposite direction: those who had been seen to be nearest to salvation are thrown back far from salvation; and those who by your judgment were most foreign to God—the idolaters, centurions, tax collectors, soldiers and prostitutes—they will have the place of highest honor in the kingdom of God. COMMENTARY IN LUKE 13:28-30.[5]

---

[4]CTS 31:368-69* (CO 45:228); citing 2 Tim 2:19; Mt 25:33.

[5]Pellikan, *In Sacrosancta Quatuor Evangelia*, 151-52 (cf. CWE 48:54-55; LB 7:398-99).

13:31-35 JESUS' PROPHETIC DESTINY IS JERUSALEM

[31]*At that very hour some Pharisees came and said to him, "Get away from here, for Herod wants to kill you."* [32]*And he said to them, "Go and tell that fox, 'Behold, I cast out demons and perform cures today and tomorrow, and the third day I finish my course.* [33]*Nevertheless, I must go on my way today and tomorrow and the day following, for it cannot be that a prophet should perish away from Jerusalem.'* [34]*O Jerusalem, Jerusalem, the city that kills the prophets and stones those who are sent to it! How often would I have gathered your children together as a hen gathers her brood under her wings, and you were not willing!* [35]*Behold, your house is forsaken. And I tell you, you will not see me until you say, 'Blessed is he who comes in the name of the Lord!'"*

OVERVIEW: Neither the threats of the Pharisees nor those of Herod—which most of these interpreters see as more falsehoods of the Pharisees—can keep Jesus from his determined goal. Nor should we be deterred by any threats from preaching or following the gospel, our commentators exhort, for Christ protects us and keeps us safe from those who would harm us as a mother hen cares for her chicks. He desires to gather everyone under his wings, but especially his own people, many of whom reject him as they rejected and killed the prophets. We know that what God wills happens, the reformers state, and yet God wills all to come to him, and they do not. This is not easy to understand, the reformers admit, but we must respect the secret judgment of God and not seek to understand these mysteries. However confusing it may be, Jesus calls everyone and hopes for the salvation of all, but he effects salvation only in the elect.

13:31 The Warning of the Pharisees

THE LEADERS TRY TO FRIGHTEN JESUS. HULD-RYCH ZWINGLI: Just as all herbs always hold and preserve their fragrance, nature, and properties, so also with virtue and vice. Malice always seeks to kill Christ, but meanwhile it also advises him of it, as if it might suffer from his death. No doubt it does this so that it might frighten Christ off from the truth through flattery and fear. Thus first they tried this through the flattery of the high priest, then by terror of death threats, so that they might have diverted the pious people from confession and preaching of the truth. But we are not afraid of those who can only strike down the body, for they are not able to harm us. Although they might be able to wound us gravely, they are not able to take away eternal life. But why do they first frighten the prophets? Because it is the obligation of prophets especially to promote glory and truth, but they are not satisfied only to terrify them, so that they no longer address all the rest who hear the word of God. Let us therefore all be faithful to the example of Christ, and not endure that anyone might deter us from beginning a journey. The notion that Herod had been seeking to murder him was a fiction of the Jewish leaders, for Herod was not greatly persecuting Christ, but rather greatly desired to see and speak to him. This is clear from the fact that, having brought Christ up from Pilate to himself, in turn he sent him away unhurt. IN THE GOSPEL OF LUKE 13.[1]

13:32-33 Jesus' Response to Herod

THE PHARISEES TRIED TO DRIVE JESUS OUT OF THE COUNTRY. JOHN MAYER: I think that it

---

[1]*D. Hvldrichi Zvinglii in Plerosqve Novi Testamenti Libros,* 275.

was not Herod whom he meant when he said "that fox," but rather the person who sent these Pharisees to come and speak to him. For although Herod acted like a fox in the killing of John the Baptist, pretending sorrow for his death but really being glad about it, he was not the fox now. Rather, it was some subtle Pharisee who wanted Jesus to be told this, as though they were solicitous for him, when indeed they hated him to death and intended nothing else but to drive him away by any means they could, because his teaching was still against them. But it was not their desire to drive him out of Galilee to Jerusalem, which is how it may seem, because Herod was the tetrarch of Galilee, and that was where Jesus now was (although it may be that he was not there by Luke 13:22, where he is said to have been going toward Jerusalem, for Luke keeps no order in setting things down). But they thought that becase he was in danger in Judea from the high priests, and now in Galilee, that this would force him to leave the country altogether, not daring to stay there any longer. A COMMENTARY ON THE NEW TESTAMENT, LUKE 13:32.[2]

HEROD HAS NO AUTHORITY OVER JESUS' CONCERNS. DESIDERIUS ERASMUS: But Jesus, declaring that there could be no danger to himself from any person, unless he should desire it, or that he would die, unless it was at the time that he had decreed, or any sort of death or in any other place than as it was arranged, said to them: "Go, and say to that fox, who by his human cleverness believes himself able to do something against the wisdom of God, 'Behold, it is not human works that I accomplish, nor is it permitted that they come to an end before the time prescribed by God.' Herod has no authority in this matter. Just as his authority cannot give to anyone the ability to perform the deeds which I do, likewise it is not able to prevent anyone from completing what he would do. And why should he prevent it, if the things which I do are good? I expel demons and drive away diseases. I do these things freely but will not do them for long.

The time is short, although many desire that it should be longer, but it has been decreed by myself and my Father that I should do these things for the health of the people today and tomorrow, and on the third day I establish the highest and final work of all my deeds. Thus it is not right in this short time remaining to cease from my assigned office but with much greater effort to do what has been assigned, now when the period is short." PARAPHRASE ON THE GOSPEL OF LUKE 13:32-33.[3]

THE MESSIAH MUST DIE IN JERUSALEM. FRANÇOIS LAMBERT: "It will not be by the decision of Herod or any other person, but I will be killed only when I will it and when the time decreed from all eternity should come." This is a certain manner of speaking, whereby someone denies what others are claiming will soon happen. And then he adds, "Yet it is right for me today, tomorrow and the next day—that is, for some days—to be on my way before I should be killed. However, I will be killed in Jerusalem, because it is impossible for a prophet—much less the Messiah— to perish anywhere but in Jerusalem, that is, to be struck down." Doubtlessly, therefore, he understood himself to be that prophet of whom the Lord said to Moses, "I will raise up for them a prophet like you from among their brothers. And I will put my words into his mouth, and he shall speak to them all that I command him. And to whomever will not listen to his words that he shall speak in my name, I will be an avenger." But truly they could not have understood his words to be about other prophets, because it was well known that many of them were killed outside of Jerusalem. COMMENTARY IN LUKE 13:32-33.[4]

13:34-35 Jesus' Sorrow for Jerusalem

HIS CRY IS A SIGN OF GREAT AFFECTION. MARTIN BUCER: This bewailing of Christ was a

---

[2]Mayer, *Commentarie vpon the New Testament*, 378*.

[3]Erasmus, *In Evangelivm Lvce Paraphrasis*, t6v-t7r (LB 7:399; cf. CWE 48:56-57).
[4]Lambert, *In Divi Lucae*, Z7r; citing Deut 18:18-19.

token of his great and exceeding love toward this people. It is a sign of his great affection that he names the city itself, and especially that he says its name twice, repeating "Jerusalem, Jerusalem." Now, because the Evangelist uses the participle of the present tense, "you who kill the prophets," and the words of Christ seem to be about both times, past and present, the deed may be taken or understood without any certain limit of time. It is as if he should have said, "You killer of the prophets, which has killed, does kill and will kill them." AN ECCLESIASTICALL EXPOSITION UPON SAINT MATHEWE 23.[5]

CHRIST IS THE MOTHER HEN, AND WE ARE THE CHICKS. HEINRICH BULLINGER: He compares Jerusalem with a mother, according to the manner of the Scriptures, which commonly call the citizens "children." . . . Consider and weigh these words and this similitude diligently, and how he propounds it with earnest affection and a burning heart, and you shall know and see in his example how you should behave toward Christ, how you may employ him and what profit he can bring you. But now pay attention to the hen and her chicks. You see that Christ is here quite ingeniously depicted and more expressly conveyed than any painter could bring about by his art. There is scarcely any other creature that could be found that is so careful, diligent and loving to her little ones and that seeks with such industry and constancy to defend them when they are in danger. It is most certain that our souls are the little chicks that belong to Christ; the hawks in the air that seek to snatch them away are the devils, who are much more crafty at trying to catch our souls than even hawks are trying to steal the young chicks from the hen. We are under the wings and protection of Christ, when with true faith we cleave not to ourselves or to any other thing but only to Christ, when we commit ourselves wholly to him and abide under his righteousness, which we count as our

protection and safeguard. This is just like the chicks, who are not defended by their own strength or by running away but by hiding themselves under the body and wings of the hen. AN ECCLESIASTICALL EXPOSITION UPON SAINT MATHEWE 23.[6]

IT IS GOD'S WILL THAT WE BE GATHERED. HEINRICH BULLINGER: He casts their ingratitude back at them, as if he had said, "You cannot blame me because you will perish, for I would gather you together, but you are so obstinate that you will not be gathered." Some misguided people make an objection very wickedly at this place, saying, "Why does he say here that he *would* do it? For if God wills it, why does he not do it? For all things that he willed, he did. And further, we can be gathered together only by his Spirit, and when the Spirit is present, it effects movement in people's minds." Again, we answer that the secret judgment of God is not to be sought out or curiously searched into, but rather his work is to be considered. He would have us gathered together as often as he displays his banner, as the captain of the battle: let us respect that, and not attempt to enter into his secret judgment. He works effectually by his Spirit only in the elect, yet nevertheless he calls everyone generally. Also, he does not say that he did what he could, but rather he did whatever was necessary and as much as was needed. AN ECCLESIASTICALL EXPOSITION UPON SAINT MATHEWE 23.[7]

GOD TOOK HIS PROPHETS AND HIS WORD AWAY. PHILIPP MELANCHTHON: They killed so many prophets, and for such a long time, that God did not send them any more. The Lord had allowed them to be without prophet or preacher already for one thousand and fifty years. He took his Word away from them; therefore, their house remained desolate to them, because there was no one to edify their souls: God no longer dwelled among them. Now what they wanted was coming

---

[5]Marlorat, ed., *Catholike and Ecclesiasticall Exposition of the Holy Gospell After S. Mathewe*, 547*.

[6]Marlorat, ed., *Catholike and Ecclesiasticall Exposition of the Holy Gospell After S. Mathewe*, 549*.
[7]Marlorat, ed., *Catholike and Ecclesiasticall Exposition of the Holy Gospell After S. Mathewe*, 550-51*; citing Ps 135:6.

to pass, as the prophet David said: "He loved to curse; let curses come on him! He did not delight in blessing; may it be far from him!" We also read something like this in the prophet Isaiah, where the Lord of Hosts says, "And now I will tell you what I will do to my vineyard. I will remove its hedge, and it shall be devoured; I will break down its wall, and it shall be trampled down. I will make it a waste; it shall not be pruned or hoed, and briars and thorns shall grow up; I will also command the clouds that they rain no rain on it." An Ecclesiasticall Exposition upon Saint Mathewe 23.[8]

---

[8]Marlorat, ed., *Catholike and Ecclesiasticall Exposition of the Holy Gospell After S. Mathewe*, 551-52*; citing Ps 109:17; Is 5:5-6.

14:1-14 JESUS AT THE
FEAST OF THE PHARISEE

One Sabbath, when he went to dine at the house of a ruler of the Pharisees, they were watching him carefully. ²And behold, there was a man before him who had dropsy. ³And Jesus responded to the lawyers and Pharisees, saying, "Is it lawful to heal on the Sabbath, or not?" ⁴But they remained silent. Then he took him and healed him and sent him away. ⁵And he said to them, "Which of you, having a sonᵃ or an ox that has fallen into a well on a Sabbath day, will not immediately pull him out?" ⁶And they could not reply to these things.

⁷Now he told a parable to those who were invited, when he noticed how they chose the places of honor, saying to them, ⁸"When you are invited by someone to a wedding feast, do not sit down in a place of honor, lest someone more distinguished than you be invited by him, ⁹and he who invited you both will come and say to you, 'Give your place to this person,' and then you will begin with shame to take the lowest place. ¹⁰But when you are invited, go and sit in the lowest place, so that when your host comes he may say to you, 'Friend, move up higher.' Then you will be honored in the presence of all who sit at table with you. ¹¹For everyone who exalts himself will be humbled, and he who humbles himself will be exalted."

¹²He said also to the man who had invited him, "When you give a dinner or a banquet, do not invite your friends or your brothersᵇ or your relatives or rich neighbors, lest they also invite you in return and you be repaid. ¹³But when you give a feast, invite the poor, the crippled, the lame, the blind, ¹⁴and you will be blessed, because they cannot repay you. For you will be repaid at the resurrection of the just."

a Some manuscripts *a donkey*   b Or *your brothers and sisters.* The plural Greek word *adelphoi* (translated "brothers") refers to siblings in a family. In New Testament usage, depending on the context, *adelphoi* may refer either to *brothers* or to *brothers and sisters*

OVERVIEW: This passage, according to our commentators, clarifies the Pharisees' three basic flaws. First, they are full of malice, particularly toward Christ. Second, they are hypocrites, ambitious and self-serving, even while pretending to be holy and God-fearing. Finally they are proud, believing that they are holy in their keeping of the law, although it is a law largely of their own invention. The initial healing of the man with dropsy reveals their bad character, and with his parable of the wedding banquet Jesus continues to point out their shortcomings and to teach how we and the Pharisees should act instead. Christ came to save all people, including the Pharisees, not just those who were friendly to him. But the Pharisees could act only in malice toward Christ, using the feast (normally a time to bind friends and family together) as an opportunity to criticize Christ and to try to catch him in error: would he heal on the sabbath (against the law) or refuse to do so (against love)? But Christ's words and actions reveal God's true desire for keeping the sabbath. As Becon explains, God did not command this sabbath observance so we could appear holy, but so that we could love our neighbor.

After Jesus cured the man of his physical illness, he turns to cure the Pharisees of their spiritual illness: their pride. According to Calvin, the person who sees himself as superior will be thrown down by God into disgrace. The issue is not an exterior show of modesty, for often the proudest hypocrites appear to be humble and holy. Rather, it is in our hearts where we should have a sense of our own lowliness. This will be difficult, Luther reminds us; pride comes easily to us. Instead, we should follow

Christ's humble example, who placed himself on the same level with the sick man and did not raise his eyes up to the saints, although he himself was higher than them all. God will decide when to raise us up, but we must always keep in mind our own sin and lowliness.

14:1-6 *The Sabbath Healing*

CHRIST CAME TO SAVE THE PHARISEE AS WELL AS THE PUBLICAN. JOHN BOYS: Christ conversed with people of all sorts and both sexes, sometimes blessing little children, sometimes conferring with silly women, sometimes eating with the publicans who were considered the greatest sinners and here dining with the Pharisees who were accounted the greatest saints—he who came to save everyone despised no one. He cried out in the streets among the crowd, pouring out his thoughts and saying, "Come to me, all who labor and are heavy laden, and I will give you rest." And at his death, his hands on the cross were stretched out, his head bowed down, his breast open, ready to redeem and receive all those who would believe in him. . . .

It is apparent in the Gospels' history that the Pharisees were the greatest enemies of Christ, and therefore, because this was a chief Pharisee, he was certainly one of Christ's chief enemies. Yet, because Christ was formally invited to his house, it seems, he came in a friendly manner, without any further examination of his intent, and because he came, he benefitted the man and his friends in uttering a parable and performing a miracle, seeking to win them all to the truth. This example teaches us to bless those who hate us, embracing all occasions of love by which we may be reconciled with our mortal enemies. There is nothing but misery in malice, whereas a common union begets a communion of all good things. "Does your neighbor have a special gift? Love him, and it is yours. Do you have any notable gift? If he loves you, then it is his." And therefore Christ, although he did hate the pride, yet he loved the person of this Pharisee, and so he said and did good to him

and all his company. THE SEVENTEENTH SUNDAY AFTER TRINITY.[1]

THE PHARISEES' INTENTIONS ARE WICKED AND INHUMANE. JOHANNES BRENZ: We see here the various dispositions and personalities of these guests. Christ takes every occasion to bless and to do good, but the Pharisees take every occasion to curse and to do evil. They watch Christ in order to catch him in some word or deed, that they might have something which they can lie about and with which they can condemn him.

What greater discourtesy can there be? In terms of civility, the point of having a feast is to make friendship, or to confirm friendship, with free and merry cheer. And so feasts have a certain privilege of liberty, that if any excessive or inappropriate speech is used, it is ascribed to the effects of the wine. But the Pharisees forget all humanity and change the whole point of a feast: they rather abuse it to stir up enmity and to betray a friend, and they do not preserve friendship and keep a friend. Wicked hypocrisy is the mother of great inhumanity and cruelty, and so it should be shunned no less than the very image of Satan. AN ECCLESIASTICALL EXPOSITION UPON SAINT LUKE 14.[2]

THE SICK MAN SOUGHT OUT CHRIST IN FAITH. JOHANN SPANGENBERG: How did the man with dropsy come to be in the Pharisee's house? Necessity drove him there. When he heard that Jesus was in the Pharisee's house, he entered uninvited, and he did not ask permission, in case they would look askance at him. From this act one can also perceive his faith. How did he come to such faith? From all the positive talk he had heard about Christ, how he was such a pious and charitable man who would gladly help anyone who desired his assistance. The man took such faith from this news that he entered the Pharisee's house

---

[1]Boys, *Exposition of the Dominical Epistles and Gospels*, 4:113-14*; citing Mk 10:13-16; Jn 4:1-42; Mt 9:10; Lk 19:1-10; Prov 1:21; quoting Mt 11:28.
[2]Marlorat, ed., *Catholike and Ecclesiasticall Exposition of the Holy Gospell After S. Marke and Luke*, 232*.

and stood there. He would not let their grumbling against him deter him, for he thought, "The pious Jesus, who has helped so many suffering people, the blind, the lame, the deaf and mute, even lepers, will not let you leave him without any comfort." And see, through such faith he received what he desired.

And what did Christ do? Before he healed the man, he held a disputation and discussion with the Pharisees and scribes, who laid in wait for him there, trying to grasp and hold him. And why did they lie in wait for Christ? If he healed the man with dropsy on the sabbath, then they would accuse him and proclaim him as a destroyer of the law. But if he did not heal the man, they would charge him as an uncharitable and unmerciful man who would not help such a poor, suffering person, although he well could have. GOSPEL ON THE SEVENTEENTH SUNDAY AFTER TRINITY.[3]

THE PHARISEES COULD NOT SPEAK, BUT CHRIST IN HIS GOODNESS HEALED THE MAN. HULDRYCH ZWINGLI: If the Pharisees had answered that the diseased man ought to be healed, then they would have accused themselves; but if they said that he should not be healed, then they would have spoken both against the law and against reason. Therefore they held their peace, so that their answer would not be held against them. A liar is often ashamed or brought to shame; but this is not true shame, which rises at the amendment and grief of the fault, but only hypocrisy, which pretends to be sorry for a time and then returns eventually to its true form. Once the Pharisees determined to kill Christ, they spent all their time seeking to bring it about by any means possible. Sometimes they used fair, flattering words, while at other times they used cruel outrage. On this occasion they held their peace, but once they had the opportunity before Pilate, they cried out, "Crucify him, crucify him!" They even encouraged the people to cry out against him. . . .

Here we see that the Lord in every place and on

all occasions did good. He entered into the house of one of the chief Pharisees in order to take a meal, and when the man with dropsy brought himself before Christ, he did not disdainfully command the miserable man to depart.[4] Rather, he brought the man close to him, touched him and sent him away whole and happy. AN ECCLESIASTICALL EXPOSITION UPON SAINT LUKE 14.[5]

GOD EXPECTS WORKS OF CHARITY ON THE SABBATH. THOMAS BECON: So Christ reproves these perverse "saints" who deprave and corrupt the word of God, boasting that they keep the sabbath while they are really so far from charity that they will not bestow a worn garment to cover a poor, naked person. They are false writers who invert and change the Word of God. The Word of God commands: "Love your neighbor and do the best for him that you can," but they answer, "We will not do this, just in case we might violate the sabbath." But Christ confutes them with the fact that God commands it to be preached on the sabbath that we should love our neighbor, care for him and help him all we can. It is plain in this example that no one thinks it breaks the sabbath to deliver that person by all means possible. However, it is incredibly unreasonable to excuse action when it is done for a mute beast who is in danger but to affirm that it is a grave offense to do the like when a person is in peril, and therefore no work of charity should be done toward a person on the sabbath. Thus it is appropriate that those who take on themselves to judge and give sentence to God's actions should stumble, that they might entangle themselves and so betray their foolishness. For that is what the Pharisees do here, and presume against Christ, that they might catch him and trip him up, so that if he helps the man, he would seem to violate the sabbath, and if he does not help, he might be reproved for neglecting

---

[3]Spangenberg, *Postilla . . . von Ostern biß auffs Aduent*, CXLVv-CXLVIr.

[4]Dropsy, or edema, is the abnormal accumulation of fluid under the skin or in body cavities.
[5]Marlorat, ed., *Catholike and Ecclesiasticall Exposition of the Holy Gospell After S. Marke and Luke*, 234*.

charity. But Christ not only defends and maintains his actions against them; he also charges them with the same crime. For the way to sanctify the sabbath is to hear God's Word, to do holy works, to love one's neighbor, to help a neighbor in need, to show obedience, to be merciful, to help, to give counsel, to comfort, to share bread with the hungry. THE SEVENTEENTH SUNDAY AFTER TRINITY SUNDAY.[6]

EVEN CHRIST COULD NOT CONVERT THE OBSTINATE PHARISEES. JOHANNES BRENZ: Christ so convincingly refuted the trifling tricks of the Pharisees that they were not able even to mutter against him. But did they then repent of their impiety? Did they stay silent after this experience? Truly, they did not. Although in this moment they held their peace in shame, afterward, having found another occasion, they cried out even more strongly among their own followers, "He is worthy to be stoned," they said, "because he breaks the sabbath!" This is written for us, so that we might not be so surprised today, when we see so many people remaining so obstinate in their errors that we cannot bring them to the way of salvation. For if Christ, by so many miracles and by such clear arguments, could not bring the obstinate Pharisees out of their impiety, who are we that we should be able to bring those to health who are so clearly overwhelmed with errors? For even if you plainly contradict all the arguments of your adversaries, impiety still has many ways to disguise itself and to escape—only in the end will it come to utter destruction.

Therefore, you should work as hard as possible by all lawful means to convert the wicked to the Lord, but if they continue to persist in their impiety, let them die in their wickedness—you will have delivered your own soul. AN ECCLESIASTICALL EXPOSITION UPON SAINT LUKE 14.[7]

14:7-11 *How to Behave at a Wedding Feast*

THOSE WHO SEEK THE HIGHEST PLACE WILL BE DISGRACED. JOHN CALVIN: We know how much ambition reigned among all the scribes and Pharisees. While their pride made them eager to be masters over everyone, even among themselves there was also a dispute concerning the foremost place. Indeed, people who desire worthless glory will always envy each other, while each one tries to acquire for himself what the others believe should be their own. Thus the Pharisees and the scribes, who all equally ingratiated themselves with the people by the title of a holy order, now contend among themselves about the degree of honor, because each claims for himself the first place. Christ humorously derides their ambition with a suitable parable. If anyone coming to the table of another seats himself in the highest place, then is compelled to give it up to someone more important, it will be with shame and disgrace that he is removed by the lord of the feast to another place. But it is necessary that the same thing will happen to everyone who foolishly presents himself as superior to others, because God will throw him down in disgrace. It should be noted that Christ is not making a statement here about external and public modesty, for those who are most proud often excel in this aspect and carry themselves in public, as many note, with great modesty. But by a true comparison taken from people's lives, he wants to teach how we should be on the inside before God. It is as if he would say, "When a guest foolishly usurps for himself the highest place, and then he is removed to the back of the line, he will be ashamed and will wish that he had never tried to go higher than he should. To avoid having the same thing happen to you and having God reproach your arrogance with extreme dishonor, choose on your own to be humble and modest." COMMENTARY ON A HARMONY OF THE GOSPELS.[8]

---

[6]Becon, *New Postil (Second Parte)*, 130v-131v*; citing Mk 12:31; Mt 22:39.

[7]Marlorat, ed., *Catholike and Ecclesiasticall Exposition of the Holy Gospell After S. Marke and Luke*, 234-35*; citing Jn 9:16.

[8]CO 45:395 (cf. CTS 32:164-65).

WE MUST HUMBLE OURSELVES TO BE SAVED.
MARTIN LUTHER: Christ mentions an example
and intends it as a common teaching for [people
of] all walks of life and spiritual gifts. He does not
say, "Sit in the middle," but, "Sit below or behind."
He does not yield even two or three places. But
how is our nature capable of doing that? Just take a
look at sick people or criminals! How can I soften
this? It is too hard, and where can one find such
people? How can a person put himself on the same
level as such good-for-nothing people? Well, I can
do it easily if I just remind myself that I am Adam.
We all carry that ass [*Esel*] around our necks, and
we should not presume good things about ourselves. We should rather say: "I will not presume
too much of myself, but I will be patient with that
other fellow for a while, until he improves himself."
When we act in such a way, then peace and unity
follow, while strife and discord decrease. However,
such pride can come when we believe that the gifts
of God are grown in our own garden.

But Christ says: "If you will not humble
yourselves here, then you will have to do it there,
that is, before my court," as it is written in 2
Corinthians, "We must all be revealed before the
judgment seat of Christ." Do not think so much
of the higher things, but rather focus on the lesser
things to which you can show love. Wherever
there are poor and weak people, put yourself
there likewise. When one sees what another lacks,
and acts, that is love and a true Christian life.
Christ did this here and everywhere throughout
the Gospel, placing himself down with the poor
and in this passage with the man with dropsy. He
did not raise his eyes up to the saints, but he
looked at that man and ignored the higher things.
He was indeed holy, rich, wise and just—more
than all other people—however, he placed
himself lower. He wanted it to be this way, as
Paul says, "He emptied himself, taking on the
form of a servant and humbled himself." Job also
says this: "He lifts up those who humble themselves, and he will save those who cast down their
eyes." . . . If you want to be raised up, you must
first become humble. For only what is cast down

will be raised up. SERMON ON THE SEVEN-
TEENTH SUNDAY AFTER TRINITY (1523).[9]

**GOD DESPISES PRIDE BUT LIFTS UP THE
HUMBLE.** JOHANN BAUMGART (POMARIUS): Of
what is this gospel warning us? Of all kinds of
pride, because the Lord himself says, "Those who
exalt themselves will be humbled, and those who
humble themselves will be exalted." For pride and
presumption do nothing good, but rather throw
all social classes into confusion. Therefore God
cannot suffer them, either in heaven or in
Paradise, and will not endure them on earth either.
For "pride annoys me," says the Lord God of
Sabaoth. . . . The proud Lucifer was thrown like a
lightning bolt from heaven. Adam raised himself
up, but was brought to ruin, and kicked out of
Paradise. . . .

Opposed to this, those who humble themselves
are often lifted up and brought to honor, like
Esther, David, Daniel, Mordecai, Jacob, Joseph,
Mary, and the like. And we should especially
follow the example of Christ, and recognize our
unworthiness with Abraham, Jacob, and the
Prodigal Son, and humble ourselves under the
powerful hand of God, for he knows the right
time to lift us up. We should recognize and
confess with Peter and Paul that we have received
everything, and should not boast or become proud,
as if we had not received it but had everything
from ourselves. For God opposes the proud, but
gives grace to the humble. GOSPEL ON THE
SEVENTEENTH SUNDAY AFTER TRINITY.[10]

14:12-14 How to Host a Feast Pleasing to God

**IF OUR GUESTS CANNOT REPAY US, GOD
WILL.** JACQUES LEFÈVRE D'ÉTAPLES: These things
are said about a physical banquet or dinner, and

---

[9]*LEA* 3:200 (cf. WA 11:186-87); citing 2 Cor 5:10; Phil 2:7-8; Job
22:29.
[10]Baumgart, *Postilla*, 234r-v; citing Sir 10:11, 13-14; Judg 9:11; Prov
16:28; 17:11; Sir 3:28; Lk 1:52; 10:18; Is 14:12; Gen 3:23-24; 18; 32;
Lk 15:11-24; 1 Pet 5:6; 1 Cor 4:8-13.

these can indeed be made into a work of charity, although that should be done because of God alone. And certainly, when opportunities are present, our banquets should be superior to the normal sort, and we should not invite friends, siblings, relatives or wealthy neighbors. For if we invite friends, or siblings and family, then we will share the usual affection. If we invite wealthy neighbors, then there is a mutual exchange. However, if we invite the poor, the handicapped and the blind, it is not so. For inviting these folks can provide nothing for us but the regard of God, for they do not have any favor produced by themselves which they might exchange. However,

God, by whose grace that work was made pure, is the one who repays—he who is able to understand this will be greater in eternity. Therefore God is the Father of the poor and the bestower of eternal goods, which is the inheritance of those who are poor in spirit and who bear patiently the tribulations of the world. Thus he will repay them abundantly in the "resurrection of the just," that is, when the reign of God will be fulfilled and the universal judgment of good and evil will be made. IN THE GOSPEL OF LUKE 14.[11]

---

[11]Lefèvre d'Étaples, *Commentarii Initiatorii in Quatuor Evangelia*, 2:74v-75r.

14:15-24 THE PARABLE OF THE GREAT BANQUET

¹⁵*When one of those who reclined at table with him heard these things, he said to him, "Blessed is everyone who will eat bread in the kingdom of God!"* ¹⁶*But he said to him, "A man once gave a great banquet and invited many.* ¹⁷*And at the time for the banquet he sent his servant*ᵃ *to say to those who had been invited, 'Come, for everything is now ready.'* ¹⁸*But they all alike began to make excuses. The first said to him, 'I have bought a field, and I must go out and see it. Please have me excused.'* ¹⁹*And another said, 'I have bought five yoke of oxen, and I go to examine them. Please have me excused.'* ²⁰*And*

another said, 'I have married a wife, and therefore I cannot come.' ²¹*So the servant came and reported these things to his master. Then the master of the house became angry and said to his servant, 'Go out quickly to the streets and lanes of the city, and bring in the poor and crippled and blind and lame.'* ²²*And the servant said, 'Sir, what you commanded has been done, and still there is room.'* ²³*And the master said to the servant, 'Go out to the highways and hedges and compel people to come in, that my house may be filled.* ²⁴*For I tell you,*ᵇ *none of those men who were invited shall taste my banquet.'"*

a Greek bondservant; also verses 21, 22, 23   b The Greek word for *you* here is plural

---

OVERVIEW: How difficult it is, especially for the rich and powerful, to turn away from the charms of the world and to give ourselves fully to God! But God commands that first we seek his kingdom—nothing must cause us to neglect God's Word. The rich and important, the reformers argue, are content with the world and think they do not need Christ or his grace; they can make it on their own, and so it is the spiritually poor who are brought in to the banquet. Yet after all the poor, weak and humble are invited and welcomed to the banquet, there is still room left. Some note that this means that the work of the gospel continues, and we must continue to invite people to the banquet.

Our commentators discuss "holy compulsion" or coercion and insist that God does in fact push people along. People must be repeatedly shown heaven and hell, life and death, grace and wrath, so that they will be converted. The work of the gospel is constant and requires that people be followed, hounded and berated to repent and to walk the narrow path. Likewise, God applies various temptations and adversities to work on people, putting "dogs on the necks" of those who would

prefer to focus on the things of the world. But this is not a matter of forcing people against their will. The elect will come to repentance and will enjoy the banquet, while the reprobate will continue to refuse the gospel. All are invited, but not all participate in the festivities.

14:15-20 *Those Invited Will Not Attend*

THE SUPPER IS A GREAT HEAVENLY BANQUET. JOHN BOYS: Let us examine now why this supper is called great, and that is for four reasons: the maker of the feast, the cheer, the company and the place. The maker of the feast is so great that all the tongues of people and angels cannot explain how great, and therefore they tell of his greatness not in the positive degree but in the comparative or in the superlative: "A great king above all gods," and "that God may be all in all." . . .

Second, the supper is great in respect to the great cheer which exceeds all sense and all science, for as our eye cannot see, so our heart cannot conceive what delicious fare "God has prepared for those who love him." If the transfiguration of

Christ on the mount accompanied by only two saints, Elijah and Moses, amazed Peter so much that he cried out, "Lord, it is good that we are here," then how good will it be for us to rest on God's holy hill, where we shall ever enjoy the company of all the patriarchs, the prophets, the saints, the glorious angels, and even the presence of God himself, face to face?

Third, this supper is great in respect to the company, which is not only good, as I have said, but also great: many will come to this feast, but there are even more who are invited earnestly but will not come. God's elect compared with the reprobate are but a "little flock," but consider them in themselves and you shall find them many, for all the "poor and crippled and blind and lame" come to this feast. Our Savior expressly says that "many will come from east and west and recline at table with Abraham, Isaac and Jacob in the kingdom of heaven." Indeed, the number of those who eat at the Lamb's supper is without number.

Fourth, this supper is great in respect to the place, for the finest things are situated in the highest places. For example, because the earth is the coarsest, it is put in the lowest room, then the water above the earth, the air above the water, the fire above the air, the spheres of heaven above any of them, and the palace where this feast is held is above them all, in the heaven of heavens. THE SECOND SUNDAY AFTER TRINITY.[1]

THE FAITHFUL SERVANT BRINGS THE LORD'S WORD TO THOSE WHO WILL HEAR. CASPAR HUBERINUS: Christ says that this king sent out his servant at the hour of the evening meal. This servant is first of all John the Baptist, who invited the Jews to this costly banquet through baptism, his preaching on repentance and informing them of the present coming of Christ. But the Pharisees despised the counsel of God against them and refused to accept Christ for their Messiah; instead

it was the tax collectors and poor crowds who believed.

Christ himself is also this servant, for he is called a servant of God on account of his vocation and orders. He was sent by the Father in the form of a servant, that he might call the Jews, the chosen people of God, to the gospel. Now because the powerful coalitions [*die grossen Hannsen*]—the Pharisees, high priests, the teachers of the law, the elders and the wise men of the people—did not want to come and believe the gospel, by which Jesus called the sinful woman, the wicked Zacchaeus, the tax collector Matthew, the thief, Saul, the fishermen, and other unimportant and disregarded people among the Jews.

Third, this servant is also the beloved apostles, who went out on the highways and among the villages to the Gentiles, when the Jews did not want to come. This servant accomplishes the command of the Lord and King in the whole world. And all true servants of Christ still do this forever and ever, who invite and call the whole world through God's Word and desire to bring them to the gospel. THE THIRD SUNDAY AFTER TRINITY.[2]

WE PREFER THE THINGS OF THE WORLD BEFORE THE THINGS OF HEAVEN. FRANÇOIS LAMBERT: In this parable, Christ teaches the kinds of excuses people make when they do not want to receive the preaching of the gospel and be saved. He sets before us three types of people, which include all those who fall short of true salvation. All people generally prefer earthly things to heavenly ones and are addicted to the things of this present world. But these impediments are the sort that would easily be excused by the wise people of the world and would be justified by them, because they seem to be so legitimate. Seeking after honor, promotion and riches, providing for one's children and family, and so on, seem to be so honest and dignified. These things certainly deserve to be

---

[1]Boys, *Exposition of the Dominical Epistles and Gospels*, 3:87-88*; quoting Ps 95:3; 1 Cor 15:28; 1 Cor 2:9; Is 64:4; Mt 17:4; Ps 15:1; Lk 12:32; Mt 8:11; alluding to Rev 7:9.

[2]Huberinus, *Postilla Teütsch*, 2:Vr-v; citing Lk 7; Mt 21; Is 53; Phil 2; Is 61; Lk 4; Acts 13.

excused by the world but not by God, who commands us first and before all other things to seek the kingdom of God and its righteousness and to prefer the first table [of the commandments] before the second. Buying a farm or a yoke of oxen or marrying a wife is not evil in itself, but neglecting the Word of God in order to do these things is a great sin. "I have bought a farm . . ." This phrase shows that the man is too busy with increasing his honors, dignity, power, possessions and goods to worry about receiving the gospel. "Allow me to go and see it." These are words of love and affection, which signify that his heart was set on the farm. For Christ said, "Where your treasure is, there your heart will be also." "I pray you would excuse me . . ." This request is nothing but hypocrisy. But note here what a deep love we have of riches, honors and possessions. AN ECCLESIASTICALL EXPOSITION UPON SAINT LUKE 14.[3]

FOCUS ON THE CARES OF THIS LIFE DISTRACT US FROM THE HEAVENLY FEAST. ERASMUS SARCERIUS: This man [who recently had married] is held back by the care of his household. Christ sets before us diverse kinds of lives—not that we are supposed to live this way, but rather that they might be exercises for us that will make us more desirous of the feast in the kingdom of heaven. He does not condemn the lawful and ordinary way of living (such as buying possessions or farms, running a business, getting married, and so on), but rather he condemns human impiety, by which people make themselves captive to these kinds of lives and neglect the happiness of the heavenly banquet. The farmers say, "We have to work! We don't have the leisure time to listen very often to the preaching of the gospel." The merchants say, "We have to travel by sea and land, so that we may pursue our business." The newly married men say, "We must work hard to provide for our household, to get wealth, both for our future children and also for our old age. We don't have much leisure to

listen to the preaching of the gospel." What they are saying is, "I would rather die on earth than enter into the kingdom of heaven." This is nothing but wicked contempt for the Word of God and the kingdom of heaven and is worthy to be punished with everlasting fire. AN ECCLESIASTICALL EXPOSITION UPON SAINT LUKE 14.[4]

14:21-24 The Humble Are Welcomed to the Feast

THE HEAVENLY SUPPER IS FOR THE POOR IN SPIRIT. KASPAR VON SCHWENCKFELD: The Lord Jesus calls [us] out of the wide streets and ways of damnation, to the narrow, cramped way which leads to life. After the rich are restored to health, they selfishly and greedily take care of the sensual pleasures of their bodies. They despise the meal of heavenly bread and spiritual well-being, for they reject the Lord's Supper, and at the same time they misuse the gifts of God to their own condemnation. The Lord orders his servant and sends him out to invite the poor, crippled, blind and lame to the heavenly supper, that he might lead the sick to healing, the hungry to food and the blind to the light of the sun. As it is written, not many of those who are wise after the flesh, or many who are powerful or many who are noble are called, but God has chosen what is foolish and weak before the world, and what is ignoble and scorned by the world, so that no flesh can boast before him. This saying also belongs quite well to the interpretation of this Gospel.

The poor are set here in comparison against the rich, and the lowly against the proud. Not that worldly poverty or physical illness and frailty make one holy, or that riches well-employed in God's work condemn, but the Lord Christ sees the causes and spiritual condition and knows the spiritually

---

[3]Marlorat, ed., *Catholike and Ecclesiasticall Exposition of the Holy Gospell After S. Marke and Luke*, 238*; citing Lk 12:34.

[4]Marlorat, ed., *Catholike and Ecclesiasticall Exposition of the Holy Gospell After S. Marke and Luke*, 238-39*. Sarcerius carefully defends against using this passage to denigrate lay life or to condemn clerical marriage. The reformers believed that the pursuit of a godly life should never be divorced from life's practical matters.

poor, lowly, humble hearts who recognize themselves, punish themselves, deny themselves and don't think much of themselves. These are the true poor of whom Christ is speaking here, who are set in opposition to the rich, who trust so much in their own works and who build on an external, human justice, as if they didn't need Christ or his grace. Of these poor he says in Matthew: "Blessed are those who are poor in spirit, for theirs is the kingdom of heaven." And we must all become poor, that is, keep ourselves humble and lowly, so that we should be worthy and qualified for the supper of the Lord. Christ himself, the rich King and Lord of heaven and earth, became poor for our sakes, so that we might become rich through his poverty. The gospel, that happy message of invitation to the riches of heaven, is announced to all such poor people, and for them alone the supper of the heavenly good life is prepared. INTERPRETATION OF THE GOSPEL, LUKE 14, ON THE SECOND SUNDAY AFTER TRINITY.[5]

GOD USES HOLY COMPULSION. JOHANN SPANGENBERG: What does "make them come in" mean? This is what it means: Hold up before them heaven and hell, life and death, grace and wrath, salvation and damnation, so that they might be converted and do penance. Pull them off of the country lanes, grab them up out of the thorn hedges, drive them from their sinful lives, so that they will say, "Stop! Take it easy! We will gladly follow." So do not cease but keep on constraining, obliging, driving forever. And as Saint Paul said, "Preach the word; be ready in season and out of season; reprove, rebuke and exhort, with complete patience and teaching." It is necessary that they also overcome Satan according to the flesh, so that the spirit may be received. Therefore if they do not want to follow, fine, I will make a "holy compulsion" out of it, which will grieve them.[6] I will hunt them down with so many dogs on their necks, bring them so many troubles, send them so many disasters, they should be completely happy to follow.

Does God also use such coercion? Of course. He coerces and pulls us both internally and externally so that we come to this supper, to the recognition of Christ. Internally he accomplishes this through the law and gospel, externally through various temptations, adversities, persecution, sorrow, sickness, pestilence, famine, war, and other disasters. Those who follow him will do well, but those who despise it and stay away will grieve. GOSPEL ON THE SECOND SUNDAY AFTER TRINITY.[7]

---

[6]*Compelle intrare* is Latin for "make them come in" and was a frequently discussed principle of the early, medieval and even early modern church. See, for example, Edward Peters, ed., *Heresy and Authority in Medieval Europe* (Philadelphia: University of Pennsylvania Press, 1980), esp. pp. 42-47.
[7]Spangenberg, *Postilla . . . von Ostern biß auffs Aduent*, LXXVIIv; citing 1 Tim 4:2.

---

[5]CS 10:390-91; alluding to Mt 7:13-14; 1 Cor 1:26-29; 2 Cor 8:9; quoting Mt 5:3.

14:25-35 THE COST OF FOLLOWING JESUS

²⁵Now great crowds accompanied him, and he turned and said to them, ²⁶"If anyone comes to me and does not hate his own father and mother and wife and children and brothers and sisters, yes, and even his own life, he cannot be my disciple. ²⁷Whoever does not bear his own cross and come after me cannot be my disciple. ²⁸For which of you, desiring to build a tower, does not first sit down and count the cost, whether he has enough to complete it? ²⁹Otherwise, when he has laid a foundation and is not able to finish, all who see it begin to mock him, ³⁰saying, 'This man began to build and was not able to finish.' ³¹Or what king, going out to encounter another king in war, will not sit down first and deliberate whether he is able with ten thousand to meet him who comes against him with twenty thousand? ³²And if not, while the other is yet a great way off, he sends a delegation and asks for terms of peace. ³³So therefore, any one of you who does not renounce all that he has cannot be my disciple.

³⁴"Salt is good, but if salt has lost its taste, how shall its saltiness be restored? ³⁵It is of no use either for the soil or for the manure pile. It is thrown away. He who has ears to hear, let him hear."

OVERVIEW: In beginning his journey to the cross, Jesus takes time to instruct and admonish those who traveled with him but did not fully understand or consider what would be coming. As Brenz notes, many people who traveled with Jesus had their own agenda. They believed he was the Messiah but expected him to set up an earthly kingdom in Jerusalem, and they wanted to be a part of it. Jesus addresses their expectations and explains that rather than participating in an earthly kingdom with many blessings, those who followed him need to be prepared to carry the cross. The parables he tells in this passage are designed to convey that message. It takes resolve and preparation to be a disciple of Christ. Erasmus maintains that superficial or thoughtless followers will eventually lose their identity as disciples—they will become salt that has lost its saltiness, now good for nothing, and even destructive.

The most poignant and radical comments on these words come unsurprisingly from Anabaptists Walpot and Riedemann. Walpot insists that Jesus' words here, as in other passages in the Gospels, mean that his followers must renounce all their family and possessions. In order to have the kingdom of heaven we must flee the kingdom of earth. Riedemann asserts that we must be prepared to suffer persecution and even death for our faith. For many Anabaptist communities, martyrdom and persecution were the greatest signs of discipleship. They may have been turning a necessity into a virtue, but carrying the cross and suffering for Christ were quite real in their communities, and members needed to understand that from the beginning.

14:25-27 Disciples Carry the Cross

DESPITE EXPECTATIONS, JESUS' KINGDOM WOULD NOT BRING EARTHLY PLEASURES. JOHANNES BRENZ: When the days of Christ's ministry were coming to an end, and because he had testified that a prophet must die and that it must happen in Jerusalem, he thought it best to obey his Father's calling and to make satisfaction for our sins at Jerusalem through his cross and death, to save us from destruction and give us everlasting happiness. Therefore he moved forward on his journey to Jerusalem, which he had already begun. And because he had already gained great authority through his teaching and miracles, so that many secretly believed him to be the Messiah and thought that he was heading to Jerusalem to set up his kingdom there, he went forward with a great company of people following him. Some had various afflictions, others were oppressed with need, some were escaping bad reputations or the tyranny of the magistrates or trouble at home. They all thought that the kingdom of Christ would be a carnal and earthly kingdom and should bring with it earthly happiness, and so everyone hoped that if he followed Christ, he would not only be delivered from his affliction but also might obtain some kingdom or principality of his own. Christ was content that they should follow him and hear the teaching of the gospel, but he could not stand that they should promise themselves external and bodily happiness through him and his kingdom and should seek after nothing but the benefits of this world. And so he turned to them and explained to them that his kingdom was a different sort of kingdom than they had ever imagined. He set before them the laws that they would need to observe and keep if they wanted to follow him and be his disciples. AN ECCLESIASTICALL EXPOSITION UPON SAINT LUKE 14.[1]

POSSESSIONS INTERFERE WITH CHRISTIAN DISCIPLESHIP. PETER WALPOT: For each person cannot and should not keep and hold what is his and abide by it, to be himself the lord, the steward and the one in authority, for that one does not renounce [possessions]. Therefore we cannot have two kingdoms or inherit two estates. If we want to receive the one, we must flee from the other. If we want to grasp the one, we must put the other aside. If we want to focus on the eternal, we must scorn the temporal. If we want to accept the one, we must renounce the other. Whoever wants to have one thing must let the other go. For just as with illnesses and malignant ulcers, if one does not mitigate the discharge and the dirtiness of the wound with medicine and bandaging, the cause of the problem will not be taken away, and all treatment is for naught and of no avail. Likewise it

is the same with us: if we do not prepare our hearts to be free and transparent and do not restrain our hand and wash all greediness from it, we will not become healed and whole, as a disciple of Christ should be. THE GREAT ARTICLE BOOK: ON PEACE AND JOINT PROPERTY.[2]

14:28-33 The Parables of the Tower and the King Preparing for War

PREPARATION WILL HELP US BE READY TO BEAR THE CROSS. THE ENGLISH ANNOTATIONS: This shows us how to bear the cross patiently and constantly; that is, by resolving beforehand to do it. What causes people to give up in time of afflictions is principally their unpreparedness for the situation and their vain hope of having prosperity in this world. Concerning preparation, he proposes two comparisons: first, of the careless builder, who because he did not adequately prepare, loses much of his investment on what he is not able to build properly. This is what happens to those who follow Christ but never count on having to carry a cross; and second, of the ignorant soldier, who does not consider properly the might of those against whom he has to fight. This life is filled with never-ending warfare; it is great foolishness ever to be secure. ANNOTATIONS UPON THE GOSPEL ACCORDING TO SAINT LUKE 14:28.[3]

CHRIST IS THE FOUNDATION OF THE HOUSE WE WILL BUILD. PETER RIEDEMANN: And so, if we want to begin a building to eternal life, we must count the cost ahead of time, to see whether we will be able to bear everything that will come to us and whether we will be disposed toward the will of our loving God and Christ. We must ascertain whether we would be able to endure and suffer persecution and scorn on account of his merits, to tame and slay the flesh with all of its lusts, to abandon the world with all its sensual pleasures

---

[1]Marlorat, ed., *Catholike and Ecclesiasticall Exposition of the Holy Gospell After S. Marke and Luke*, 239*.

[2]QGT 12:194-95. Elsewhere Walpot explains that this passage also requires a Christian to give up his marriage for Christ, at least when it involves an unbelieving spouse; see pp. 308, 314-15.
[3]Downame, ed., *Annotations*, XX3r*.

and splendors and to oppose the devil with all his evilness, in order to gain the noble treasure of Christ. If we find such a will within us now, we should gladly begin to build on the foundation of all the apostles, where Christ is the cornerstone, as Paul said: "For no one can lay a foundation other than what is laid, which is Jesus Christ." THE FIRST CONFESSION: ON THE HOUSE OF GOD.[4]

14:34-35 The Parable of the Salt

A GOOD DISCIPLE IS LIKE SALTY SALT. DESIDERIUS ERASMUS: By these words the Lord Jesus admonished the thoughtlessness of certain folks who wanted to be seen as the disciples of Christ, while he was not ignorant that even those few whom he had selected out of everyone would abandon him at the horror of the cross. But so that these words might be impressed on their hearts, that they might be understood later, he added, "He who has ears capable of such things, let him hear." For not everyone's ears are able to endure such talk. PARAPHRASE ON THE GOSPEL OF LUKE 14:35.[5]

CHRISTIANS AS LIGHT AND SALT ARE FOR THE COMMON BENEFIT OF ALL. PETER WALPOT: Therefore he says to his disciples, "You are the light of the world—not a light thrown under a bushel, which is only useful to and lights up itself, but a light on the lampstand, which is a common benefit to the whole house." Likewise, they do the same with their good works. Therefore he calls them "salt," for they have a communal use and should show in everything how they have received good things from God. In itself neither the light, nor the salt nor the yeast are useful, but their usefulness applies to others. Likewise it will also be required of us that we be of benefit to others, rather than [just] to ourselves. If the salt does not give the taste of salt, it is not salt but something else. Likewise if we are good and loving, so we will also be an example to others of doing good. THE GREAT ARTICLE BOOK: ON PEACE AND JOINT PROPERTY.[6]

WE WERE NOT GIVEN EARS FOR NOTHING. NEHEMIAH ROGERS: Opportunities offered for hearing of the Word are to be taken. This is a duty enjoined on us by Christ himself. . . . "He who has ears to hear, let him hear." Not "let him if he pleases," as if he were being permissive, but "let him not dare to neglect hearing, and let him take heed if he dares to do otherwise." If he has ears, he must hear, for God has not given him ears for nothing. Christ often says this, and in fact, he commonly utters it as a cry, for we read, "Jesus cried, 'He who has ears to hear, let him hear.'" Therefore we can be sure that it is a duty with great importance, or else he would not have uttered it with a cry. For whenever he taught in such a manner, which only happened about four other times in his life (that we read of), he delivered a message of great consequence. Therefore we can conclude that it is a duty that concerns us quite closely. Such an action has been urged on us in all ages by God's servants, both prophets and apostles, still calling on all to hear what the Lord says. AN EXPOSITION OF THE PARABLE OF THE LOST SHEEP.[7]

---

[4]QGT 12:39; citing 1 Cor 3:11.
[5]Erasmus, *In Evangelivm Lvce Paraphrasis*, u3v (LB 7:404; cf. CWE 48:69).

[6]QGT 12:181; citing Mt 5:14-15; Mt 5:13; Lk 13:34.
[7]Rogers, *True Convert*, 4*; citing Lk 8:8; Jn 9:28; 11:43; 12:44; Mt 27:46.

15:1-10 THE PARABLES OF THE LOST SHEEP AND THE LOST COIN

Now the tax collectors and sinners were all drawing near to hear him. ²And the Pharisees and the scribes grumbled, saying, "This man receives sinners and eats with them."

³So he told them this parable: ⁴"What man of you, having a hundred sheep, if he has lost one of them, does not leave the ninety-nine in the open country, and go after the one that is lost, until he finds it? ⁵And when he has found it, he lays it on his shoulders, rejoicing. ⁶And when he comes home, he calls together his friends and his neighbors, saying to them, 'Rejoice with me, for I have found my sheep that was lost.'

⁷Just so, I tell you, there will be more joy in heaven over one sinner who repents than over ninety-nine righteous persons who need no repentance.

⁸"Or what woman, having ten silver coins,ᵃ if she loses one coin, does not light a lamp and sweep the house and seek diligently until she finds it? ⁹And when she has found it, she calls together her friends and neighbors, saying, 'Rejoice with me, for I have found the coin that I had lost.' ¹⁰Just so, I tell you, there is joy before the angels of God over one sinner who repents."

a Greek *ten drachmas*; a *drachma* was a Greek coin approximately equal in value to a Roman *denarius*, worth about a day's wage for a laborer

---

OVERVIEW: Why is it that Jesus spent so much time with sinners? These sinners, as in many other Gospel passages, were notorious sinners like tax collectors—people whom the scribes and Pharisees completely avoided. Our commentators note, however, that Jesus did not associate with these people because he was one of them but because they needed him, like sick people need a doctor. Jesus spent time with sinners to lead them to righteousness and salvation. Of course, the scribes and Pharisees were just as much sinners, and just as much in need of forgiveness, as any of the other public or notorious sinners, but they did not recognize or admit that they needed Jesus' help or forgiveness. Jesus graciously tried to explain the situation to them through the following parables.

The shepherd who leaves the ninety-nine sheep to seek the one who is lost is Jesus himself, the commentators agree. The irony is that, while the scribes and Pharisees would have seen themselves as the ninety-nine already safely in the sheepfold, they are just like the one lost sheep. The Good Shepherd cares deeply for all, Bucer reminds us. The parable of the lost coin reveals the same

pattern, for each coin is precious to this woman, so when one is lost she seeks diligently through her house until she finds it. Whether the woman represents Christ or the church, she seeks—through the preaching of the gospel and by the power of the Holy Spirit—to find the lost soul and bring it to repentance.

15:1-2 Jesus Welcomes Sinners

REPENTANT SINNERS CAME TO HEAR HIM.
THE ENGLISH ANNOTATIONS: Tax collectors were hated by the Jews because they gathered up the fees and taxes for Caesar. By "all" he means many, or all that came to him to be converted. There were (and are) two sorts of sinners: some acknowledged or were ashamed of their sin and misery; others were righteous in their own eyes. The first sort were the ones who came to hear Christ preaching mercy to those who repented and believed in him. The scribes and Pharisees were the second sort, for they valued their own merits highly and pretended to be righteous through the works of the law. They did not embrace faith in Christ for their justification.

So Christ came not to call them but those other sinners (see Mt 9:13); by sinners we should understand here "notorious sinners," for everyone is a sinner. . . .

They did not come to make their freedom from the curse of the law into a disguise for sin, but rather to hear his teaching and to convert. They came as the sick come to a physician, to be healed and saved. Feeling the restless stinging of their own consciences, against which the rigors of the law could afford them no ease or relief but rather caused greater terror and unrest, they came to Christ, who preached to them the comforting doctrine of justification by faith, repentance and remission of sins, with deliverance from the severe curse and rigor of the law. That is why this teaching is called "glad tidings." ANNOTATIONS UPON THE GOSPEL ACCORDING TO SAINT LUKE 15:1.[1]

MURMURING CAN BE CAUSED BY ENVY. JOHN BOYS: Murmuring is somewhere between secret backbiting and open railing; they could not utterly conceal their hatred, and they dared not openly vent it; therefore they murmured. Now there may be many causes of this murmuring: the first is envy, by which a person, who in creation is only a little less than an angel, is in this respect made a great deal worse than a devil. For one devil does not envy another, and yet the proud Pharisees envy the poor publicans in their coming to Christ. It is truly observed that we may save ourselves from the liar by not speaking with him, from the proud by not accompanying him, from the slothful by not troubling him, from the glutton by not eating with him and from the contentious by not disputing with him, but from the spiteful it is not sufficient either to flee or to flatter him, for he cannot be well if another is better. Therefore God, as it may seem, should wrong him exceedingly to send him to heaven, where one excels another in glory, and God above all; he must instead be cast into the pit of hell, where he will find nothing of which he may be

envious, but only objects of extreme misery. THE THIRD SUNDAY AFTER TRINITY.[2]

"LIKE WILL TO LIKE" IS NOT ALWAYS THE CASE. JOHANNES BRENZ: As they say, "like will to like." And because this fellow is so friendly with tax collectors and sinners, it is a great argument that not only is he no prophet as he boasted and taught of himself, but he is not even a man of honest life.

This is a false complaint, but the Pharisees do show some wisdom here. It is easy to judge persons' character and manners by the company and the fellowship they keep. But the Pharisees abuse this common judgment to obscure and discredit Christ's reputation. The proverb, "like will to like," is true enough, but if it is always true, then we have to say that the physician is sick, because he keeps company with sick people, and that all preachers of God's Word are ignorant, because they spend time in instructing the unlearned. There was a good reason for Christ to spend time with tax collectors and sinners, namely, that he might, as it were, lead them by the hand from their sins to righteousness. And this was so obvious that no one could deny it. But the Pharisees were so envious of Christ that they misconstrued and disliked everything he did well. And although they were not worthy to receive an answer, because their murmurings came from malicious minds, nevertheless the most gracious Lord through his mercy gave them a reason related to his office, so that if any among them were curable, they might be influenced by him, and if not, then they would be without any excuse. AN ECCLESIASTICALL EXPOSITION UPON SAINT LUKE 15.[3]

15:3-7 The Lost Sheep

CHRIST IS THE SHEPHERD WHO SEEKS THE SINFUL SHEEP. PHILIPP MELANCHTHON: The shepherd is the Son of God, who takes on

---

[1]Downame, ed., *Annotations*, XX3r*.

[2]Boys, *Exposition of the Dominical Epistles and Gospels*, 3:103-4*.
[3]Marlorat, ed., *Catholike and Ecclesiasticall Exposition of the Holy Gospell After S. Marke and Luke*, 242-43*.

himself the punishment of our sins and carries us. A similar image is most beautifully described in Isaiah: "I will carry you like a shepherd gathers up a lamb newly born." And Christ himself said, "No one will snatch my sheep out of my hand." Not only did he take the punishment of our sins on himself and by his merit reconcile us to God, but also by his efficacy he still keeps us safe. We consider this image often, when we see that we are in misery, and we experience the fury of the devil and his instruments every day, and how they bring ruin to everything in the world. But even in these things God will preserve the remnants, and by this faith we cry out to him that he might keep others safe.

What does it mean when he talks about the ninety-nine just ones who do not need repentance? These words allude to the analogy of the hundred sheep, and they praise the compassion of the Son of God, who still seeks one other sinner who wanders away from the flock, just as a shepherd leaves a great multitude who already are safe and seeks after one little lone missing sheep. However, at the same time the irony is quite harsh in opposition to the Pharisees, whom he criticizes and reproaches in their security of worldly things, in which they are persuaded and believe that they themselves are justified. For the rest, all people need repentance in this life, as it is said elsewhere: "That all the world be made subject to God and that every mouth may be stopped." THIRD SUNDAY AFTER TRINITY.[4]

CHRIST KEEPS COMPANY WITH SINNERS TO BRING THE LOST SHEEP BACK TO THE FOLD. MARTIN BUCER: The lost sheep is sought while the ninety-nine are left in the wilderness, and the shepherd rejoices more when he finds that one than over the ninety-nine who never went astray. Likewise, in God's heavenly kingdom the angels take more joy over one sinner who repents than in the many people who are righteous. The Lord tells these stories in order that we might understand

that, by the will of his Father and the consent of the angels, he had a great care for those who, although chosen for the fellowship of the saints, had gone astray. And so he kept company with tax collectors and sinners, so that he might bring these strays back onto the right path. We cannot sufficiently comprehend this unspeakable mercy of God toward sinners, nor can we think of anything more profitable for us to do. And so when the frivolous imaginations of people are left behind and we consider this unspeakable goodness of God toward us, we may grow in faith toward him and in love toward our neighbor.[5] We ourselves need to work hard to bring the straying sheep of Christ back to their Shepherd and Savior, and this is a very good reason for us also to keep company with sinners. AN ECCLESIASTICALL EXPOSITION UPON SAINT LUKE 15.[6]

15:8-10 *The Lost Coin*

THE CHURCH SEARCHES FOR THE LOST CHRISTIAN. CASPAR HUBERINUS: The love of God is so great that it covers up everything and forgives everything and allows you to be his beloved child for eternity. And the woman does that also, for she is the bride of this Shepherd. First she allows you to be her coin and especially her beloved treasure (for women especially love money). But because you have become lost to her through sin and an unrepentant life, this woman, who is the church, does not value the other nine coins nearly as highly as the one which she has lost. Therefore she turns on a light through the minis-

---

[4]MO 25:68-69*; citing Is 40:11; Jn 10:28; Rom 3:19.

[5]This language is reminiscent of the prayer of thanksgiving after the Eucharist. Bucer rephrased and revised the traditional Latin post-Communion prayer (perhaps reflecting Luther's; cf. LW 54:137-38 [WA 19:102]; Bard Thompson, *Liturgies of the Western Church* [Minneapolis: Fortress, 1980], 161, 178-79). Bucer's liturgy strongly influenced Reformed liturgies, especially the Book of Common Prayer. See Thompson, *Liturgies of the Western Church*, 159-66; and further G. J. van de Poll, *Martin Bucer's Liturgical Ideas: The Strasburg Reformer and His Connection with the Liturgies of the Sixteenth Century* (Assen: Van Gorcum, 1954). [6]Marlorat, ed., *Catholike and Ecclesiasticall Exposition of the Holy Gospell After S. Marke and Luke*, 243*.

ters of the church and searches with the evangelical light, which is God's Word and even Christ himself. She sweeps through the whole house, looking for you with the law, to comfort you and to scare you away from sin. She searches with diligence, praying for you that you will turn back again. When she finds you through absolution, she calls her friends and neighbors and shows you to these other Christians and the faithful church, who are thrilled and praise God. They give thanks that God the Lord, through his grace, calls the poor lost sinners to repentance and wins and enlightens them. This happens every day, especially and completely. In a unique way, however, the beginning Christian comes from sin to repentance and grace. ON THE THIRD SUNDAY AFTER TRINITY.[7]

CHRIST SWEEPS OUT THE HOUSE TO FIND THE CHOSEN SOUL. KASPAR VON SCHWENCK-FELD: The Lord compared his office with a shepherd who seeks his lost sheep, and in the following he also compares it with a woman or housewife who seeks her lost coin, for through this woman the wisdom, grace and power of God are signified. The ten coins represent all people,

originally created in the image or imprint of God. The coin, lost but then found again, is the sought-after soul chosen by Christ for everlasting life. The burning candle is the gospel and the enlightening grace of God. Sweeping out the house means to purify the heart through faith and to throw out the old yeast, for the house here means the inside of a person, as in Luke 11. . . .

Through the gospel of grace and the Holy Spirit, Christ seeks in the world among the children of humankind for the chosen ones. When he finds them, he lights up their hearts with the enlightenment of the recognition of the glory of God. This recognition does properly have to do with the matter, for sin is found internally within the flesh in all its corners, curves and edges. There is not only the external evil of works but also the internal roots and inborn evil of the heart, with its evil affections and desires. The house of the heart with its habitual sins is swept by the grace of God, until the rusty penny, that is, the chosen soul, purely formed, is discovered in it. This discovery is followed by boundless joy and peace. INTERPRE-TATION OF THE GOSPEL, LUKE 15, ON THE THIRD SUNDAY AFTER TRINITY.[8]

---

[7]Huberinus, *Postilla Teütsch*, 2:a4r-v; citing Eph 5; Ps 119; Jn 8.

[8]CS 10:437-38; citing Rom 5:11.

15:11-32 THE PARABLE OF THE LOST SON

¹¹And he said, "There was a man who had two sons. ¹²And the younger of them said to his father, 'Father, give me the share of property that is coming to me.' And he divided his property between them. ¹³Not many days later, the younger son gathered all he had and took a journey into a far country, and there he squandered his property in reckless living. ¹⁴And when he had spent everything, a severe famine arose in that country, and he began to be in need. ¹⁵So he went and hired himself out to^a one of the citizens of that country, who sent him into his fields to feed pigs. ¹⁶And he was longing to be fed with the pods that the pigs ate, and no one gave him anything.

¹⁷"But when he came to himself, he said, 'How many of my father's hired servants have more than enough bread, but I perish here with hunger! ¹⁸I will arise and go to my father, and I will say to him, "Father, I have sinned against heaven and before you. ¹⁹I am no longer worthy to be called your son. Treat me as one of your hired servants."' ²⁰And he arose and came to his father. But while he was still a long way off, his father saw him and felt compassion, and ran and embraced him and kissed him. ²¹And the son said to him, 'Father, I have sinned against heaven and before you. I am no longer worthy to be called your son.'^b ²²But the father said to his servants,^c 'Bring quickly the best robe, and put it on him, and put a ring on his hand, and shoes on his feet. ²³And bring the fattened calf and kill it, and let us eat and celebrate. ²⁴For this my son was dead, and is alive again; he was lost, and is found.' And they began to celebrate.

²⁵"Now his older son was in the field, and as he came and drew near to the house, he heard music and dancing. ²⁶And he called one of the servants and asked what these things meant. ²⁷And he said to him, 'Your brother has come, and your father has killed the fattened calf, because he has received him back safe and sound.' ²⁸But he was angry and refused to go in. His father came out and entreated him, ²⁹but he answered his father, 'Look, these many years I have served you, and I never disobeyed your command, yet you never gave me a young goat, that I might celebrate with my friends. ³⁰But when this son of yours came, who has devoured your property with prostitutes, you killed the fattened calf for him!' ³¹And he said to him, 'Son, you are always with me, and all that is mine is yours. ³²It was fitting to celebrate and be glad, for this your brother was dead, and is alive; he was lost, and is found.'"

a Greek *joined himself to*   b Some manuscripts add *treat me as one of your hired servants*   c Greek *bondservants*

OVERVIEW: The parable of the lost son is the longest and most involved of the parables addressing the nature of those who will be saved, as well as the nature of the God who saves those who are lost. While a few commentators mention that the elder brother can be associated with the Jews and the younger with Gentiles, in general, most agree that the elder son represents the confident and hypocritical scribes and Pharisees who initially murmured against Jesus, while the younger son stands for those public sinners of whom they were so critical. The reformers explain that Christ wanted to show the scribes and Pharisees that he had come to call sinners and that God would be merciful, even indulgent, to those sinners who were repentant.

The scribes and the Pharisees felt their own heavenly reward would be minimized if "undesirables" were also admitted into heaven. But although the elder son appears to be pious and obedient, his response to the event and to his father reveal his true nature: he is angry and petulant, accusing his father of unjust and even unrighteous behavior (something that Stifel suggests even the devil would not do to God). Calvin reminds us that despite the elder son's fears, it takes nothing away from us if others, even horrible sinners, are given God's grace. In fact, as in the parable, these sinners are our brothers and sisters—our family through faith and baptism—and it is inhuman and cruel to reject them, judge them harshly and insist that God keep them out. Our response should be to celebrate that our brothers and sisters who were dead are now returned to life.

Our commentators also suggest that we can also learn a great deal from looking carefully at the younger son. The younger son is indeed a sinner, but he uncovers the nature of sin in all of us. This son wanted to control his own life, make his own decisions and live according to his own pleasure rather than God's will. It required extreme misfortune—a "happy misfortune," as Erasmus terms it—to bring the son to his senses; he recognized his own sin, which is the first step toward salvation. The father draws the prodigal to himself, seeing not an enemy who no longer deserves to be called a son but instead someone who is miserable and in need of forgiveness. The Father will not reject his children.

The loving father, who symbolizes God, is the "good news" of the story, for he had the right to be distant and offended, but instead he ran to his son and embraced him in full forgiveness. The gifts of God—forgiveness, peace and happiness—are given to his repentant children, given in full measure without any condemnation or rebuke. The son who was dead, like our souls in sin, is now brought back to life.

15:11-24 The Lost Son and the Merciful Father

THE PARABLE TEACHES OF REPENTANCE AND FORGIVENESS. OBADIAH SEDGWICK: Concerning the parable . . . there are several conjectures about its sense and intention. Concering the father of the two sons, everyone is in agreement, but about the two sons they differ. Some understand by these two sons angels and human beings: the angels were the elder son, while human beings were the younger,

because they were created after them. . . . Others understand the two sons as the Jews and the Gentiles: the Jews were the elder, the Gentiles were the younger. The Jews stayed home, as it were: of all the nations of the earth, they seemed to be the home for God and his service. But the Gentiles were, as it were, the excluded, rejected, wandering sheep, a lost people; yet at length God through Christ looks after these lost sheep. . . .

But the third and general opinion is that the elder son represents the scribes and Pharisees (and under them any ministers), people who were too conceited and confident of their own works, service and righteousness, as was this elder son, who had been, as he said, "all these years in his father's house, and never disobeyed any of his commandments but served him carefully." This was indeed the opinion of the scribes and Pharisees, who trusted in and boasted of their own righteousness. The younger son represents the publicans and sinners, people more notoriously uncontrolled and infamous in sinning, utterly forsaking God, as it were, and living without him. And the point of this parable was to convince the proud and envious scribes and Pharisees . . . that, as Christ tells them, although they despised these notorious sinners, yet he had come to call them to repentance, and God would be most indulgent and gracious to them. Although they had been great transgressors, yet now that they were repentant, God would receive them with singular mercy and favor, and with much joy. Therefore they had little reason to snarl at his respect for and desire to be with publicans and great sinners. Thus the scope of this parable is to declare the singular readiness of God in and through Christ to receive even the most notorious sinners when they prove to be penitent. THE SCOPE OF THE PARABLE.[1]

SELF-LOVE LEADS THE SON AWAY. ANONYMOUS: It is as if he had said, "Father, give me leave to live as I please and to do as I think good." From this comes all the evils and inconveniences in the world—either because people desire to do what

---

[1]Sedgwick, *Parable of the Prodigal*, 2-3*.

they please, or else because they do not think to live according to God's will and in obedience to him. People want to be like God and to order all things according to their own pleasure. This pride and self-will is the beginning of all sin in the world, and it makes those cursed who are addicted to it. The son shakes off his father's government and makes his own will into his law. Self-love overthrows judgment, darkens sense and reason, poisons the will and hinders the course of salvation, shutting up all the passages toward it. For the people who are so entangled with love of themselves neither know God, nor love their neighbor nor seek after virtue but only pay attention to those things by which they may advance themselves, grasping for honor and hunting after promotion.

Free will props up this self-love, but by itself it is a weak support. For although our free will is not utterly taken away by sin in natural and moral actions, yet nevertheless it remains so weak and unable, and so defaced in spiritual matters, that it cannot resist any temptations. But just as a ship at sea, having lost her rudder, is tossed to and fro with the least blast of wind, so this free will of ours, unless it is conformed by repentance and humility and framed anew by yielding ourselves to God's gracious direction (for of ourselves we are not able even to think a good thought), is so crazed and so wavering that it is easily overthrown by every temptation of the flesh, the world, and the devil. . . . This made the prodigal son foolish, and like a child who lacks discretion, he desired to live according to his own liberty. God does not draw anyone against his will to salvation but allows the wicked to take their own course. The prodigal son's father did not hold him, because he wanted to leave; but neither would he force him to leave, if he were willing to stay. The portion of goods which God gives to everyone is, to some, eloquence, to others, wisdom, or riches, or strength, or knowledge or place of honor—all of which we are likely to abuse, just as this prodigal son spent his portion wastefully. THE PARABLE OF THE PRODIGAL SON.[2]

OUR CORRUPT NATURE IS UNTHANKFUL FOR ALL GOD'S BENEFITS. WILLIAM COWPER: This younger son, as you see, being left to himself, manifests his own weaknesses because he lacked self-control. All of us may see in him what a fearful thing it is to be forsaken by God and left to ourselves, for then we quickly become a prey to our enemy. Just as when someone lets go of a staff, it falls with no control to the ground, likewise if a person is not sustained by grace, he cannot stand in a good position. All the benefits which God created for Adam in six days he lost in six hours. . . .

This also reveals the cursed corruption of our nature, that when God is best to us, then we are the worst and most unthankful to God. This is why the Lord complained of the Israelites, "The more they increased, the more they sinned against me." And so the pharaoh, when the plague was on him, spoke and looked somewhat like a penitent man, but when he was relieved of it, he returned to his usual hardness like iron taken out of the fire. Just so, when natural people are pinched and troubled by poverty, sickness, or any other sort of affliction they make a show of godliness, but when God changes their situation and gives them prosperity and health, it becomes their ruin: "the complacency of fools destroys them," and "their table becomes a snare for them." This is seen daily in our unfortunate experience, for human hearts are most empty of thankfulness and their mouths are most filled with the blasphemies of God's name when their tables and their stomachs are most filled with God's benefits. Thus this forlorn son went away from his father just when his father was most beneficial to him and had given him his portion. A MIRROR OF MERCY.[3]

HE WASTED EVERYTHING AND HAD NOTHING LEFT. JOHN TRAPP: "And when he had spent everything," and left himself nothing at all except for air to breathe and earth on which to tread, he made his own hands his executors and his own

---

[2]*Certaine Godlie and Learned Sermons,* 39-41*.

[3]Cowper, *Mirrour of Mercie,* 129-34*; citing Hos 4:7; Prov 1:32; Ps 69:22.

eyes his overseers, swallowing much of his patrimony through his throat and spending the rest on harlots, who left him as bare as crows leave a dead carcass. Ruin follows riot at the heels. A COMMENTARY UPON THE GOSPEL ACCORDING TO SAINT LUKE 15.[4]

THE FATHER INFLUENCES THE SON TO COME TO HIS SENSES. DESIDERIUS ERASMUS: Thus he had now come into extreme misfortune, but it is a happy misfortune which forces a person to come to his senses. And this is the first step to salvation: to remember where one has fallen and to recognize where one has fallen short. And this was by the drawing of the Father. For that son had certainly gone away from the Father, but the Father is present everywhere.

Formerly the young man had been crazy, distracted by the illusions of this world, fleeing those things which alone one should wish for and wishing for those things which alone should be avoided. But it is well when the sinner, having been secretly inspired by the kind-hearted Father, returns to his heart. The young man, having finally come back to himself, as it were, spoke to himself: "Where did I come from, and how does it compare with where I am now, a miserable man? Out of my own country into exile, from a wealthy home into a place of poverty and hunger, from freedom into servitude, from a most loving father to a most cruel master, from the dignity of a son of the family to the foulest condition and from the fellowship of my brother and the servants to that of pigs. How many hired hands are there in my father's house, who have abundant food available to them through the liberality of my father? And I am a son of the family, and here I am dying of hunger."

Many of the Jews are hired hands who observe the commands of the law after a manner, not out of pious affection but out of fear or for the reward of temporal things. And nevertheless it is something important to work as a hired servant for a householder at the same time so wealthy and so generous, and not to be sent away from such a happy house. For a hired servant might be made into a son, if he grows to have the affection of a son. And so it was a sort of holy envy which provoked the young man to the hope of forgiveness. PARA-PHRASE ON THE GOSPEL OF LUKE 15:17.[5]

SIN TAKES US AWAY FROM GOD, BUT REPENTANCE RETURNS US TO HIM. WILLIAM COWPER: He sinned by going away from his father, and now when he repents he returns to his father again. Repentance takes the opposite course from what people keep when they walk in their sins. Thus Chrysostom alludes to the actions of wise people, who went home a different way from the way they came to the field. It can be observed in all penitent people that they come home to the Lord another way than they left him. If you have gone from the Lord by the way of anger or hatred, return again by the way of meekness and love. If you have sinned by intemperance, return by continence. If you have sinned by covetousness, taking from your neighbor what you should not, make restitution with Zacchaeus. . . .

Penitent sinners illuminate their sins with the light of faith and clarify them in two ways: first, their sins are committed against God; and second, they are committed before God. In his confession, David, like the prodigal here, joins these two together. Every sin is against God, but not every sin is done in the sight of God (I mean in respect to the sinner), for there are many who sin and yet do not know that they sin. . . . But those who have the light shining on them, who know the will of God and still act against it, they sin not only against God but also before him and in his sight. A MIRROR OF MERCY.[6]

LIKE THE FATHER, GOD IS MERCIFUL TO THE TRUE PENITENT. EDWARD LEIGH: Among all the parables of Christ, this one is most excellent, full of

---

[4]Trapp, *Commentary or Exposition*, 405*.

[5]Erasmus, *In Evangelivm Lvce Paraphrasis*, xr-v (LB 7:407-8; cf. CWE 48:79-80).
[6]Cowper, *Mirrour of Mercie*, 219-21, 236-38*; citing Lk 19:8; Ps 51.

affection and set forth in lively colors. The old father sees a long way off, for dim eyes can see a long distance when the son is the object. His heart moves within him, and he has compassion on him. "He runs." It would have been sufficient for him to have stood, because he was old, and a father, and even more so an offended father. But love descends rather than ascends: the son goes to the father, the father runs to the son. Then, he does not stop and embrace him or take him by the hand, but rather he falls on him and incorporates himself into him. He speaks not a single word—his joy was too great to be uttered—but he puts his whole mouth forward and kisses him, giving him the badge of peace, love and reconciliation. Through this example is declared the great goodness of God, who most mercifully pardons the sins of the truly penitent. ANNOTATIONS UPON SAINT LUKE 15.[7]

THE SON SINS AGAINST THE ORDER OF CREATION. HULDRYCH ZWINGLI: "I have sinned against heaven." This is hyperbole and an exaggeration of the deed. Sinning against one's father and mother is a very serious sin, and in it the order of heaven and earth is violated. For all creatures keep this order, except the person who sins against his father and mother. And if he disturbs the order of the universe, how much more will the one who offends the Creator of everything disturb it? Therefore, whenever someone offends God and disturbs the order of all things, whatever is in heaven and on earth would also be offended. David expresses the same sentiment with different words: "Against you only have I sinned." True contrition is true suffering, and when we see how we offended the highest good and threw away God's grace, our sins then give us great pain on his account. When the Father has been offended, the whole family is offended. When the Creator is offended, who does not see that the whole creation is also offended? And therefore, when we are truly turned back toward the Father, we are made right

with and reconciled to all creatures. IN THE GOSPEL OF LUKE 15.[8]

WE MUST RECOGNIZE AND CONFESS OUR SINS IN ORDER TO REPENT. JOHANNES BRENZ: It is not enough just to acknowledge sin, but we must also have such a recognition of sin in our consciences that we judge ourselves to be not only unworthy of being called the sons and daughters of God but also that we have deserved death and damnation. David acknowledged his sin when he said, "For your arrows have sunk into me, and your hand has come down on me. . . . There is no health in my bones because of my sin." Daniel likewise acknowledged his sins and the sins of the Israelites when he said, "We have sinned and done wrong and acted wickedly and rebelled." All those who seek to attain true salvation need to confess their sins. Now, perfect repentance does not exist, and righteousness does not automatically follow, but we must progress to further degrees of repentance. That is to say, we must conceive a good hope that the Father will not reject us, even though we are not worthy of pardon. AN ECCLESIASTICALL EXPOSITION UPON SAINT LUKE 15.[9]

GOD STILL SEES OUR SIN BUT DOES NOT HOLD IT AGAINST US. OBADIAH SEDGWICK: There is another implicit observation we can discover in the father's action toward this penitential prodigal on his confession. It is this: as there is nothing in the son's thoughts and expressions but his sins, so there is nothing in the father's intentions and expressions but kindness. The son thinks of his sins, intends to leave his sins and to confess them, and that is what he does. The father thinks of mercy and compassion and intends to accept and pardon him. When the son comes, he does not speak a word of his sins, but every expression is mercy, peace and kindness: "Fetch the best robe, put on

---

[7]Leigh, *Annotations upon All the New Testament Philologicall and Theologicall*, 125*.

[8]*D. Hvldrichi Zvinglii in Plerosqve Novi Testamenti Libros*, 279; citing Ps 51:4.

[9]Marlorat, ed., *Catholike and Ecclesiasticall Exposition of the Holy Gospell After S. Marke and Luke*, 248*; citing Ps 38:2-3; Dan 9:5.

the ring." Therefore I believe that this statement can be proposed: God takes no notice of our sins on our true repentance but wholly expresses himself in love and kindness.

There are two parts to this assertion. The first is that God takes no notice of former sins on our true repentance. There are three ways in which God notices sins. First, *notitia intuitiva*: which is his all-observing eye of omniscience, from which nothing can be hidden. Every creature and its every movement, whether open or secret, is visible and manifest to that God. The distinction between known and unknown, between secret and open, has no place with God, to whose eye all things are naked. In this respect the former sins of a penitent fall within God's notice, for the goodness of divine mercy does not blindfold the eye of divine omniscience. Second, *notitia charitativa*: which is a noticing of sins as a kind creditor takes notice of debts owed to him and which are set down in his book, for his eye is on them, and his pen is ready to cross and mark them out. In this respect also God takes notice of former sins, so that from his rich love and gracious favor he may cross them out and forgive them—unless, of course, we foolishly imagine that God forgives sins by chance, as a lark, never seeing and considering what he does. Third, *notitia vindictiva*: which is a juridical notice, as a judge takes notice of the evil deeds of a malefactor to condemn him or to trouble and vex him. In this respect, then, on true repentance, God takes no notice of former sins, either to condemn the penitent person for them or to upbraid and dishearten him by casting them into his teeth (as we say proverbially). . . .

The second part is that God expresses himself wholly in love and kindness, which is most evident in Jeremiah 31, for when Ephraim repented and confessed his sin, God's expressions were full of tender love: "Is Ephraim my dear son? Is he my darling child? For as often as I speak against him, I do remember him still." GOD'S GRACIOUS ACCEPTANCE OF THE RETURNING PRODIGAL.[10]

15:25-32 *The Resentful Elder Son*

THE SCRIBES NEED TO CONSIDER THESE SINNERS AS THEIR FAMILY. JOHN CALVIN: This latter part of the parable accuses those people of inhumanity who maliciously desire to restrain the grace of God, as if they begrudged salvation to miserable sinners. We understand that this is pointed at the arrogance of the scribes, who did not think that they were being rewarded properly for their merits if Christ also admitted the publicans and the common crowd to the hope of the eternal inheritance. The main point, therefore, is that if we desire to be counted as the children of God, we must forgive like family the faults of our brothers and sisters, which he forgives as a Father.

Some think that the Jewish people are described by the figure of the firstborn son, but although there are grounds for this assumption, it does not seem to me to attend enough to the whole context. For this speech was brought about by the murmuring of the scribes, who were annoyed by the kindness of Christ toward miserable people whose lives were not very good. He therefore compares the scribes, who were puffed up with arrogance, with worthy and modest people who had always lived honestly and attended to their household affairs, yes, even to obedient children who patiently bore their father's authority for their whole lives. And although they were not at all worthy of this praise, yet Christ, speaking according to their understanding, as a concession considers their false sanctity as a virtue. It is as if he had said, "Even if I were to concede to you what you falsely boast, that you were always obedient children of God, still you should not proudly and cruelly slight your brothers and sisters, when they repent of their wasted lives." COMMENTARY ON A HARMONY OF THE GOSPELS.[11]

WE SHOULD ALWAYS BE CONTENT WITH GOD'S WILL. MICHAEL STIFEL: God does all things according to his pleasure, and each person should be content with that. The will of God

---

[10]Sedgwick, *Parable of the Prodigal*, 199-200*; citing Jer 31:20.

[11]CO 45:510 (cf. CTS 32:349-50).

should please him in all things, without asking why God does those things. But here the old Adam makes himself felt, and the devil's poison, too, which he poured out as he questioned Eve, "And why has God forbidden this for you?" Now this "holy" son wants to argue. He wants to know the cause of the celebration and is not happy about what is pleasing to his father. It almost astonishes him, so he becomes neglectful here and ruins his great holiness. He asks, "Why has my father prepared such an event without me?" Just so did the "spiritual" Pharisees in Matthew 9 ask the disciples of Christ, "Why does your master eat with such people and sinners?"

God must teach the heart inwardly; otherwise everything, even he, is lost to the evil of the human heart. This holy son hears what should inspire him to run in eagerness to his father and brother but instead so angers him that it makes him murmur and makes him unwilling. Fatherly kindness makes him spiteful, and brotherly grace distresses him. Then he flies into a temper (as follows subsequently). He is of the same opinion as the Pharisees, that Christ should stick with them, and not with such dissolute people (as Saint Matthew was, along with his community). It would have been just for the father to give him such a life of luxury, and not the prodigal son, because he was righteous, although he does not want to control his will and thoughts. So now likewise the one who stays is righteous, and not the unjust one with his free will, which is what the teachers of the antichrist say to us. Truly the human will is just like a ball which children throw back and forth. If a person is now living in grace, so he must and will be moved by the Holy Spirit and should do the right thing. But if a person is not in grace, his will is nothing but a plaything of the devil, tossed to all the desires of evil. THE GOSPEL OF THE LOST SON.[12]

THE ELDEST SON IS AN EXAMPLE OF A HYPOCRITE. ERASMUS SARCERIUS: Hypocrites cannot stand that such great mercy is offered to

the people of God. Christ assigned this character to the firstborn, that the goodness of God might be better expressed. For if the eldest son had sinned, it is possible that someone might have thought that God does not forgive others as he does the firstborn. So in this story the goodness of God is quite clearly expressed. Often times in Scripture we see that the elder are forsaken and the younger are chosen. The purpose of Christ was to reject the judgment of the flesh. But it commonly happens that, as the eldest brothers have preeminence, so then hypocrites have most authority in the church. In regards to external duties, they are obedient to their parents, as in the example of Esau. However, they cannot stand that the mercy of God should be extended to sinners, and they throw their duties back into God's face: "We are always with you, we serve you, and yet you give us no more than you give to sinners!" If they could, they would call God to an account!

If anyone wants to know why he compares hypocrites with the firstborn who will not be heirs, we answer that although hypocrites are the sons of the bondwoman Hagar, yet despite this they hold a prominent position for a time, so that they seem to be heirs, even as Ishmael boasted of being the eldest and scorned his brother Isaac. AN ECCLESIASTICALL EXPOSITION UPON SAINT LUKE 15.[13]

THE ELDER SON IS JUST AS WICKED AS HIS BROTHER. MICHAEL STIFEL: In his own mind, this elder son is better than the other, who is a public sinner. Likewise, he was not abandoned by God as the younger son was in his opinion. And so we see here why Paul says to the Romans, "Therefore you have no excuse, O man, every one of you who judges. For in passing judgment on another you condemn yourself, because you, the judge, practice the very same things." And the elder son judges the younger son here and so separates himself from his father, but he is not any better than the younger son had been. But now the

---

[12]Stifel, *Dz Euangelium von dem verlornen Son*, G4v-Hr; citing Gen 3:1; Mt 9:11.

[13]Marlorat, ed., *Catholike and Ecclesiasticall Exposition of the Holy Gospell After S. Marke and Luke*, 250*.

younger son is saved from that evil and made righteous. Likewise, the Pharisee despised the public sinner who was really righteous before God, while he was unrighteous. . . .

Now the son reveals his nature to be like the devil, for the devil also accuses the children of God "day and night," and he is also called "the accuser of our brothers." . . . His wickedness has come to the highest point, for he accuses God of being unrighteous, which is beyond even the devil. "Yes," he said, "you have killed the fattened calf for him," just as if he would say, "Is that right? Or is it fair?" Just like all of our righteousness, so this should also be judged or rewarded by God according to its merit (for behind it sits God's mercy), and therefore likewise the holy Son of God was sent. THE GOSPEL OF THE LOST SON.[14]

WE LOSE NOTHING WHEN GOD RECEIVES BACK A SINNER. JOHN CALVIN: In this response there are two parts: the first is that there is no cause for the firstborn to become angry when he sees his brother kindly welcomed with no penalty; and the second is that, with no consideration of the welfare of his brother, he is distressed because this celebration happened on his brother's return. "All that I have," the father says, "is yours"; that is, "Even if you have not taken anything away from this house thus far, there is no loss to you, because everything remains here unharmed for you. Why does our joyfulness offend you, when you should have been a participant in it? For it was just that your brother, who we thought was lost, should now be congratulated on his safe return." These two reasons are noteworthy for us, because, first, nothing is taken away from us if God kindly receives into grace those who had been separated from him because of their sins; and second, it is impious hardness of heart not to rejoice when we see our brothers and sisters returned to life from death. COMMENTARY ON A HARMONY OF THE GOSPELS.[15]

THOSE SEPARATED FROM GOD ARE DEAD, BUT GOD'S MERCY BRINGS LIFE. ANONYMOUS: Note that he did not say, "My son," but "This your brother," to entice him to mutual concord, love and good will. This gives us a warning to show compassion to one another and to rejoice when good things happen to another, seeing that we are the same people and nation, with one God, one Redeemer and one baptism. When the people had offended the Lord, he said to Moses, "Go down at once! Your people have committed a great sin." And Moses said to the Lord, "O Lord, do not let your wrath break forth against your people to consume them utterly. If you pardon their sin now, your mercy will appear, but if you will not, I pray that you will blot me out of the book that you have written." . . .

It is the condition of those who depart from God that they are counted as dead and lost, but when they return to God, they live again. For it is repentance that makes the way to God's mercy; and we take hold of this mercy by faith, but we are not capable of that mercy until we displease ourselves. Through sin comes death, for "the wages of sin is death." It is God's mercy that we are recovered from sin and death, as the prophet Hosea says: "O Israel, one has destroyed you, but in me is your help." Where was Jonah, and what would have happened to him if God had not thought of him in mercy and brought him again to safety? The benefits that God pours down on us daily show us that our destruction does not come from him, but we ourselves are the workers of our own overthrowing. And when we are restored, we are to rejoice in God's mercy and goodness and to accuse and condemn our own willfulness, our contrary and stubborn nature, which is set so rebelliously against God's commandments, holy will and law. THE PARABLE OF THE PRODIGAL SON.[16]

---

[14]Stifel, *Dz Euangelium von dem verlornen Son*, H3r-v; quoting Rom 2:1-2; Rev 12:10; allduing to Lk 18:14.
[15]CO 45:511 (cf. CTS 32:350-51).

[16]*Certaine Godlie and Learned Sermons*, 109*; citing Eph 4:4-6; quoting Ex 32:7, 11, 32; Rom 6:23; Hos 13:9 (the ESV reads, "He destroys you, O Israel, for you are against me, against your helper").

16:1-18 SHREWD MANAGING:
PARABLES AND THE SCRIPTURES

He also said to the disciples, "There was a rich man who had a manager, and charges were brought to him that this man was wasting his possessions. ²And he called him and said to him, 'What is this that I hear about you? Turn in the account of your management, for you can no longer be manager.' ³And the manager said to himself, 'What shall I do, since my master is taking the management away from me? I am not strong enough to dig, and I am ashamed to beg. ⁴I have decided what to do, so that when I am removed from management, people may receive me into their houses.' ⁵So, summoning his master's debtors one by one, he said to the first, 'How much do you owe my master?' ⁶He said, 'A hundred measures^a of oil.' He said to him, 'Take your bill, and sit down quickly and write fifty.' ⁷Then he said to another, 'And how much do you owe?' He said, 'A hundred measures^b of wheat.' He said to him, 'Take your bill, and write eighty.' ⁸The master commended the dishonest manager for his shrewdness. For the sons of this world^c are more shrewd in dealing with their own generation than the sons of light. ⁹And I tell you, make friends for yourselves by means of unrighteous wealth,^d so that when it fails they may receive you into the eternal dwellings.

¹⁰"One who is faithful in a very little is also faithful in much, and one who is dishonest in a very little is also dishonest in much. ¹¹If then you have not been faithful in the unrighteous wealth, who will entrust to you the true riches? ¹²And if you have not been faithful in that which is another's, who will give you that which is your own? ¹³No servant can serve two masters, for either he will hate the one and love the other, or he will be devoted to the one and despise the other. You cannot serve God and money."

¹⁴The Pharisees, who were lovers of money, heard all these things, and they ridiculed him. ¹⁵And he said to them, "You are those who justify yourselves before men, but God knows your hearts. For what is exalted among men is an abomination in the sight of God.

¹⁶"The Law and the Prophets were until John; since then the good news of the kingdom of God is preached, and everyone forces his way into it.^e ¹⁷But it is easier for heaven and earth to pass away than for one dot of the Law to become void.

¹⁸"Everyone who divorces his wife and marries another commits adultery, and he who marries a woman divorced from her husband commits adultery.

a About 875 gallons   b Between 1,000 and 1,200 bushels   c Greek *age*   d Greek *mammon*, a Semitic word for money or possessions; also verse 11; rendered *money* in verse 13   e Or *everyone is forcefully urged into it*

OVERVIEW: The parable of the dishonest steward is confusing. Jesus recommends that his followers should make friends for themselves "by means of dishonest wealth," or "unrighteous mammon." So how is it that this clearly underhanded servant should be a role model? The Reformation commentators all agree that the steward is not someone whom we should imitate—as a child of the world he is selfish and deceitful. He would rather live off the work and wealth of others and does not care if it injures them. He defrauds his master and then blatantly alters his debtors' accounts in order to make friends for himself. It is in this one point alone, all the reformers agree, that the steward should be a model for us: we should use our resources for the benefit of the life to come. If we use our worldly goods in proper ways, on Judgment Day, the poor and those we have helped will testify for us.

The children of the light should share their

wealth, or give it all away to serve the community, as Walpot insists, without being attached to it. No person can serve two masters, at least not if they oppose each other, Brenz adds. Thus no one can be dedicated to earthly gain and to God at the same time. We can use God's gifts in service of him and to help others, but they are not ours to keep.

Jesus turned the tables on the Pharisees after this parable, remarking that although they prided themselves on knowing God's will and following the law, in fact they were far from living out what God commanded. The laws that Moses gave to the people were already weakened (hence his comments on divorce and adultery), and external adherence to the law without a concomitant engagement of the heart is not truly keeping the law. God's Word—whether law or gospel—has always suffered dishonor, our commentators note, but its truth will never be destroyed. Jesus himself came to fulfill and perfect the law, not abrogate it. Erasmus declares that the Pharisees needed to start looking beyond the Law and the Prophets, for these spoke God's truth in figures and in promises, to their true substance now revealed in Christ.

16:1-8 *The Dishonest but Shrewd Steward*

WE ARE THE STEWARDS OF GOD'S GOOD GIFTS. EDWARD LEIGH: Christ puts forward two persons in this parable, a rich man and his steward. The rich man is God, whose stewards are all human beings, because he gives their good things to them, although he gives more to one and less to another. Those good things are (1) the goods of the world, or fortune, as some call them, such as gold, silver, fields, cattle, livings and dominions; (2) the goods of the body, such as health, beauty, strength and all the senses; and (3) the goods of the mind, or spiritual goods, such as wit, wisdom, prudence, memory, eloquence, peace, the word of salvation, the promise of grace, righteousness and life eternal.

God has bestowed his gifts on us, so that we may use them moderately and in the fear of him, serve our neighbors with them and improve them

for the Lord, because we shall be expected to give an account of them. To show ourselves to be good stewards, we should use our goods in two ways: (1) for God, we must serve him with all of our goods; and (2) for our neighbor, if we have more than he, we should share freely with him, as in Proverbs 5:16. ANNOTATIONS UPON SAINT LUKE 16.[1]

THE SERVANT PRACTICES THE WAYS OF THE WORLD. CASPAR HUBERINUS: Let's take another look at this villainous and crafty servant, and the way of the world and all Adam's children. They are very quick and crafty in all their doings and business, as they so masterfully are able to use their reason, understanding, wit, cleverness and so forth, to turn everything to their own advantage. For this servant not only is quick to make friendships and patronage for himself through the injuries to his own master but also works hard to avoid becoming a beggar, Lord willing, whether he ruins his master or not in the process. He would prefer to work much less, but he sees that he either must burden other people and be discreet or celebrate over their misfortunes and enjoy himself. That is how it goes in the world, and that is the common habit of the world's children, so it is more than just the Roman practice. The world's practice follows these three rules, learned from the old Adam: first, a child of the world supports himself and becomes rich off of other people's injuries, through various kinds of deceit, money matters, tricks, evil whims and intrigues; second, a child of the world is ashamed of poverty and flees from the beggar, therefore he robs, steals, commits adultery and treachery, and all other evil things, but he is not at all ashamed of these things, although they are very serious sins before God and also very shameful before those who understand; third, a child of the world does not like to work but is lazy, gluttonous, idle and useless, prevailing over other people and living off of their blood and sweat. That is the way of the world, and the children of this world behave

---

[1]Leigh, *Annotations upon All the New Testament Philologicall and Theologicall*, 125-26*; citing Gen 9:2.

according to these three rules of proportion, or should I say, "of the world" or "of the devil."[2] On the Ninth Sunday After Trinity.[3]

The Master, Who Is God, Sees All Our Deeds.

Robert Bagnall: These words (as I said before), if they are taken allegorically, contain *aliud verbis, aliud sensu*,[4] speaking of a rich man, and yet meaning God, and speaking of a rich man's steward, and yet understanding all humankind (a large collective or noun of multitude). These words should cause us to note two things: first, that our faults are not hidden from the Lord; and second, that the Lord is displeased with them.

Human faults are not hidden from the Lord: no matter how we may work to keep them so secret and quiet, which wicked people still attempt (for this reason their works are called the "works of darkness," because they proceed from the darkness of human understanding, are done in darkness and lead people into extreme darkness), yet they are all known to the omniscient God, the all-seeing God, the searcher of the heart and affections, who is *totus animi, totus animæ*, knowing, seeing and foreseeing all things.[5] Who would be so crazy as to deny it? The psalmist truly and reverently speaks to God, "O Lord, you have searched me out and known me; you know my sitting down and my rising up; you understand my thoughts long before." The wicked steward, then, cannot flee from the Lord. His case must come before his Master—he must endure a sharp reprimand and strict examination and must come to an account, as we see afterwards. The Steward's Last Account.[6]

The Steward Reveals the Vice of Laziness.

Johann Baumgart (Pomarius): This vice is laziness and a certain low-class pride, of which the steward is guilty when he takes counsel with himself and says, "I do not want to dig, and I am ashamed to beg." He is too lazy to work and too proud to beg, and in this he once again shows a serious vice to unjust stewards of all levels of society.

It sometimes happens that when a person is dismissed from his position, he will be driven to reflection and to take counsel with himself. He does not know where to begin, or how he will support himself. He may realize that he does not want to work, but people were created to work, just as birds were created to fly, and he must earn his bread by the sweat of his brow. That is why people may devote themselves to evil tricks and schemes, as we see here with the steward. Gospel on the Ninth Sunday After Trinity.[7]

The Steward Is Prudent in Making Friends with Money.

Thomas Becon: The steward perceived beforehand that if he must give up his stewardship, he would need the help of other people. Therefore while still in a time of wealth he provided for himself. He forgave half the debt of one person and a quarter of another, so that when he would be in need, he might find kindness and liberality again from them. Christ did not mean that we should study to be unrighteous and to deceive one another, and so give alms, but he meant that we should follow the steward's foresight or providence, his circumspection, prudence and wisdom, and bestow our riches in such a way that the fruit of them might benefit us in another life. He meant that we should make friends for ourselves through our "wicked mammon," as the steward made friends for himself by wicked mammon. . . .

Therefore the doctrine of this Gospel points especially to the idea that covetousness may be repressed and the true use of worldly goods promoted, and that friends may be made with what God gives us, so that when we die and have nothing left, but leave all things behind us, we may find friends to receive us into the everlasting tabernacles. For whatever benefit we bestow here

---

[2]The *regel detri*—"rule of three" or "rule of proportion"—is a mathematical concept.

[3]Huberinus, *Postilla Teütsch*, 2:i7v-i8r.

[4]This explanation of allegory—"one word, but with another meaning"—comes from Quintilian, *De Institutione Oratoria* 8.6.

[5]"Wholly of soul, wholly of mind," from Pliny's discussion of the nature of God (*Natural History* 2.7).

[6]Bagnall, *Stewards Last Account*, 58-60*; citing Ps 139:1-2.

[7]Baumgart, *Postilla*, 191r; citing Gen 3:17-19; Job 5:7.

on the poor will on our final day bear record for us that we have shown Christian charity, but it will also be recompensed abundantly, for the poor will come forward as witnesses for us. THE NINTH SUNDAY AFTER TRINITY SUNDAY.[8]

THE STEWARD IS A CHILD OF THE WORLD. JOHANN SPANGENBERG: So what did he do? He did not think about it too long but quickly called on all those who were in debt to his master. To the first, who owed a hundred barrels of oil, he said, "Take your bill, sit down, and quickly write fifty." To the second, who owed a hundred measures of wheat, he said, "Take your bill, and write eighty." Therefore he allowed them to reduce their debt.

And what does the master say to this unfaithful steward? He praised the unjust steward because he had been clever. For the children of this world are a more clever sort of people than the children of light. So is such an act praiseworthy? He does not praise him on account of his craftiness and disloyalty, but that as a child of the world, he dealt with the situation with cleverness and care. And who are the "children of the world"? They are those who look for their own profit in all things and take precautions with all care so that they will always have enough, God grant it, justly or unjustly, and let the poor and needy take care of themselves.

So does Christ want us also to do this to the people? Not at all. Rather, he wants us to seek after the heavenly, eternal treasures with as much earnestness and diligence as we see that the children of the world seek after their temporal, transitory treasures and lie in wait for them. We should seek after eternal treasures as industriously as the children of the world seek their worldly treasures. And it should not hinder us if they ridicule and deride these eternal treasures. Let them store up their treasures on earth, and you store up your treasures in heaven, and afterward let us see who employed their time in searching and storing most wisely. GOSPEL ON THE NINTH SUNDAY AFTER TRINITY.[9]

THE DEVIL IS THE FATHER OF THE CHILDREN OF THIS WORLD. RICHARD TAVERNER: My friends, you should understand that in this comment, our Savior Christ touched on the steward's sloth and sluggishness, not on his fraud and subtlety. Indeed, he was not glad that it was as he said, but rather he complained that it should be so, just as many people say things, not because they ought to be so but because they frequently are so. In fact, it grieved Christ that the children of the world should be more politic than the children of light, which was certainly true in Christ's time, and now in our time is definitely true. Who is so blind that he cannot see this clearly, unless perchance there is someone who cannot distinguish the children of the world from the children of light? The children of the world conceive and bring forth things more prudently, and nourish and observe these things with more political sense than do the children of the light. This fact is as sorrowful to be said as it seems strange to be heard. When you hear the term "children of the world," you must understand the world as a father. For the world is the father of many children, not by first creation and work but by imitation and love. He is not only a father but also the son of another father. And if you know the father, by and by you will also know the children. For whoever has the devil for his father must necessarily have devilish children. Now, the devil is taken not only as the father but also as the prince of the world—that is, of worldly people. It is all one thing, or at least not much different to say "children of the world" and "children of the devil." ON THE NINTH SUNDAY AFTER TRINITY.[10]

16:9-13 *The Message About Wealth*

GIVE AWAY YOUR WEALTH, SO THAT FRIENDS WILL TESTIFY TO YOUR FAITH. WILLIAM TYNDALE: This is what James means in his epistle where he says, "Faith without works is dead." That is, if works do not follow, it is a sure and evident sign that there is no faith in the heart but only a

---

[8]Becon, *New Postil*, 72r-73r*.
[9]Spangenberg, *Postilla . . . von Ostern biß auffs Aduent*, CVIIIv.

[10]Taverner, *Epistles and Gospelles (Sommer Parte)*, 122v-123r*.

dead imagination and dream which they falsely call faith.

This saying of Christ is to be understood in the same manner: "Make friends with the unrighteous mammon." That is, show your faith openly, and what you are within your heart, with outward giving and by bestowing your goods on the poor, that you may obtain friends, that is, that the poor, on whom you have shown mercy, may at the day of judgment testify and witness to your good works; that your faith and what you are within your heart before God may appear by your fruits openly to all people. For to those who believe rightly, all things will be comforting and consoling on that terrible day. And contrariwise, to the unbelieving all things will serve for desperation and confusion; and every person shall be judged openly and outwardly, in the presence of all people, according to his deeds and works. So not without cause you may call those your friends who testify on that day about you, that you lived as a true and right Christian person and followed the steps of Christ in showing mercy, as no doubt that one does who feels God's mercy in his heart. And by the works is the faith known, that it was right and perfect. For the outward works can never please God or make friends unless they spring from faith. . . . Now without faith there is no true heart or healthy eye, so that we are compelled to confess that the works do not make a person righteous or good but that the heart must first be righteous and good before any good work can proceed from it. The Parable of the Wicked Mammon.[11]

Things in This World Are Uncertain, but Our Eternal Reward Is a Firm Promise. The English Annotations: That is, when you die, or when your interest in or further use of these things (of which you are presently the appointed stewards) shall fail you, which may be in this life, and certainly will be in death, the short time of this life, and the uncertainty of our possession in this world of those things which God's providence has allotted to us, should teach us to hold all that we have here with a loose hand. We should not be foolishly tenacious of what may suddenly, and certainly will be in the end, taken from us. . . .

The meaning of this passage is not that we could merit to find favor with God by our alms, for he was our friend when we were his enemies and had no strength to do any good. Also, merit is between those where there is no debt or grace, but here, where a person can never pay his own debt of sin, all our merit is God's mercy. The meaning is, therefore, if the unjust steward was not lacking in friends to whom he could give his master's goods, how much less shall we lack, if we give our goods to relieve the poor, for which God has promised repayment? Works of mercy testify to the giver's conscience, that he is the elect of God, who has given him such a happy use of those secular riches which he gave him. It shall also be rewarded in the everlasting life to come. Annotations upon the Gospel According to Saint Luke 16:9.[12]

The Little Things Are the Things of the World. John Mayer: The "little" here, also called "unjust" and "another's," is worldly wealth, and the "great," called also "true" and "our own," is grace and glory, because heavenly things are peculiar to the faithful, but worldly things are common to others, and indeed in respect to the power of possession are the Lord's only and not any person's. This relates to the prior parable in the first section, where the steward is said to have been accused to his lord for wasting his goods, and the lord then threatens to remove him from his position. Likewise, the Christian who is unjust about worldly things will never rise higher to partake of heavenly things, that is, grace here and glory hereafter, but on the contrary, will eventually also be stripped of all these worldly things and so be buried under woe and misery. Injustice is such a bar to grace and the gifts of the Holy Spirit that one who sins in this way will never partake of them,

---

[11]Tyndale, *Doctrinal Treatises*, 61-62*; citing Jas 2:17.

[12]Downame, ed., *Annotations*, XX4r*; citing Rom 5:10; Mt 25; 2 Pet 1:10; Jas 2:22-23.

for he cannot have true faith or knowledge of the mysteries of godliness by which his soul might be saved. This injustice is not only in those who steal, deceive or do any sort of wrong, but also in the prodigal, who lives on his abundance in pleasure, never thinking of the poor and needy or giving them their due portion. It also is in those who are covetous, for they turn their goods to another use by hoarding them up to satisfy their avaricious minds and withholding them from the poor. That is what it means to be a steward who wastes his master's goods and therefore is worthy to be censured by him. A COMMENTARY ON THE NEW TESTAMENT, LUKE 16:10-12.[13]

BE FAITHFUL IN SMALL, THAT IS, EARTHLY THINGS. PETER WALPOT: If one is righteous in what is his to offer, even if it is small and poor—that is, in temporal things—he will also be righteous and faithful in great things—that is, in what is spiritual. For faithfulness in great things, namely, in what is spiritual, is the tree out of which flows faithfulness in small things, namely, in what is temporal. For if the little brook does not flow, how will it go with the fountain? For these two stand together. If one is not willing to serve the community in temporal things, how can he live according to Christ's commands and will? Instead he is an Ananias, who was also unfaithful in the great and spiritual things—he will become nothing before God.

So if you were not faithful in unrighteous mammon, who will consider you to be trustworthy? And because you were not faithful in those particular matters, who will even give you what is called yours, things particular to this world? Therefore whoever presumes to possess it for his own and keep it for himself is unrighteous and deals unfaithfully, just like the unjust steward. And who will now give to him the heavenly treasure, namely, the real one? If one wants to serve God, he must leave behind his own mammon; and if one wants to serve mammon and hold on to it, he must leave God behind. For whoever

holds on to what is earthly gives witness that he still does not know any better; he neither seeks nor desires nor inquires after more. For normally one turns toward what is better and more useful, and gladly lets go of what is bad, so as better to hinder it. It is great insanity that we do not want to give up those things voluntarily that we will receive again later in great abundance, and that otherwise will be taken away from us entirely, to our resentment. Then we will be forced to leave those things behind with great difficulty, whether we want to or not. THE GREAT ARTICLE BOOK: ON PEACE AND JOINT PROPERTY.[14]

ALL RICHES BELONG TO GOD. JOHN TRAPP: Riches are not properly ours but are God's, and he has entrusted them to us. He usually assigns them to the wicked, those people of "his hand," for their portion, for that is all the heaven they are ever to expect. Better things await the saints, who are only foreigners here and have to catch as catch can. A COMMENTARY UPON THE GOSPEL ACCORDING TO SAINT LUKE 16.[15]

GOD AND MONEY ARE CONTRARY MASTERS. JOHANNES BRENZ: What Christ says here is taken from common speech and experience. The matter itself declares that no one can serve two masters. A person can only serve two masters if they agree with each other, or if one submits to the other. That is why Paul remarks, "Servants, obey your earthly masters as you would Christ." In obeying his earthly master, the servant also obeys Christ, the Lord of heaven. For in this matter, these two masters agree and require the same thing. Christ commands that the servant should serve faithfully according to his calling, and this is the same thing that the earthly master requires. Christ commands servants to obey their earthly master willingly, and the master requires the same. Christ forbids servants to give only lip service, and the earthly master forbids this also, and requires from

---

[13]Mayer, *Commentarie vpon the New Testament*, 391*.

[14]QGT 12:195-96.
[15]Trapp, *Commentary or Exposition*, 407*; citing Ps 17:14.

the servant sincere and faithful service. For example, Joseph served both God and the king of Egypt, who required nothing to be done which was against God. But, if two masters command contrary things and disagree with each other, there is no one who can serve them both at once.

Now the Lord our God and money are two masters who are contrary to each other. They do not disagree as to their basic nature, because riches are of themselves the good creatures of God, but because of the corruption of human beings, riches have become contrary to God. For example, God and money command contrary things: God commands us to help the poor with our riches, but money, being moved with the desire of the flesh, commands us to hold fast to our riches, so that we do not part with even a penny to help the poor. God commands us to store up for ourselves treasures in heaven, where rust and moths will not corrupt them, and which thieves cannot steal; but money commands us to store up our treasure here on earth. And if we consider the works of both masters, they are definitely contrary to each other. God works in us the love of our neighbor, but money works hatred and envy. God works peace and tranquility in our consciences, but money stirs up great debate and disquiet. God increases the hearing of the Word of God, but money chokes the hearing of the Word of God. So how could it be that anyone could serve them both? An Ecclesiasti-call Exposition upon Saint Luke 16.[16]

16:14-15 The Pharisees Reject Jesus' Message

The Pharisees Find Christ's Teaching False and Dangerous. Johannes Brenz: We have already made it clear that these Pharisees were hypocrites and covetous people. When they deride Christ because he taught that no one could serve both God and money, they show that they judge the teaching of Christ to be not only false and vain but also dangerous for common folk. For

if this were the case, that no one could be godly unless he condemned and refused riches, then how could the common good be maintained? And who could be saved? And so we have here the judgment of all the Pharisees and the judgment of all hypocrites and covetous people, who here reveal their own lack of honesty and what they see as the vanity of the Word of God. Because they believe themselves to be just and godly, they judge the teaching of the Word of God to be false as well as dangerous to the common salvation of the people. This is a great impiety, and that is why Christ goes on to condemn it sharply. An Ecclesiasticall Exposition upon Saint Luke 16.[17]

Friendship with the World Is Enmity with God. Dirk Philips: It is impossible for one to observe simultaneously the commandments of God and human beings. For God and the world are opposed to each other. Christ and Belial are not in accord. Therefore, if anyone wishes to serve God, he must forsake the world. If anyone wishes to follow Christ, he must despise Satan. For this reason Paul says that he would not be Christ's servant if he pleased people. For the friendship of this world is enmity with God, and whoever would be a friend of the world must become God's enemy, as the apostle James says. Christ also says the same in the Gospel, that is, what "is exalted among human beings is an abomination before God." That is the reason we are not inclined to observe all human institutions of the world, all false worship and ceremonies of the Roman Church which are opposed to Christ. Rather, we desire in our simplicity to remain and abide—for better or for worse—in the teaching and example of Jesus Christ and to allow ourselves to be guided by the first apostolic congregation insofar as the Lord gives us grace. The Enchiridion: Our Confession Concerning the Creation, Redemption and Salvation of Humanity.[18]

---

[17]Marlorat, ed., *Catholike and Ecclesiasticall Exposition of the Holy Gospell After S. Marke and Luke*, 258*.

[18]CRR 6:70-71* (BRN 10:67-68); alluding to Mt 15:1-6; 2 Cor 6:15; Mt 6:24; Gal 1:10; 1 Jn 2:15; Jas 4:4; 1 Cor 10:14; Eph 2:19-20; 1 Pet 2:21; quoting Lk 16:15.

[16]Marlorat, ed., *Catholike and Ecclesiasticall Exposition of the Holy Gospell After S. Marke and Luke*, 256-57*; citing Eph 6:5.

16:16-18 *Jesus Teaches About the Law and Prophets*

THE GOSPEL IS THE TRUTH THAT THE PROPHETS FORETOLD. DESIDERIUS ERASMUS: You still doggedly hold the rind of the law in your teeth and boast of shadows: but now that the kernel is revealed, the rising light of evangelical truth dispels all the shadows. You should become unaccustomed to the sour wine of the Mosaic law and drink in the fresh must of firmer doctrine.[19] The figures of the law had their time: people expected and awaited those things which the sayings of the prophets promised. But figures cease after the truth appears, and prophetic promises are now no longer expected, because what they promised is clearly shown. It is right that one should advance out of the shadows toward the truth. From faith in the promises, one should move forward toward love of the truth which is now shown. John was the boundary separating the law with its figures, and the prophets with their promises, from the gospel. The gospel presents the reality itself which the law had only signified with its shadows and that the prophets, being inspired by God, had promised should come. John prophesied that the kingdom of God was at hand, and it is indeed this which the law foreshadowed and the prophets predicted. But you should understand that the truth agrees with John's proclamation. For ever since his time, the kingdom of God has been preached to everyone, and many grasp at the happy news with glad hearts. They drink the new must, they consume the heavenly teaching; they despise earthly things and grow rich with heavenly goods. PARAPHRASE ON THE GOSPEL OF LUKE 16:16.[20]

THE WORD OF THE LORD REMAINS FOREVER. FRANÇOIS LAMBERT: He said these things because of the Pharisees and because of those who rejected and scoffed at such truth. For even before John, these impious people themselves contradicted the law of God and the prophets, which we discover all over the ancient Scriptures. Similarly the gospel of the kingdom of God, and all those who are from that same kingdom, have suffered force, persecution, contempt and derision from the impious—no matter where they are—from the time of John, by whom Christ was first preached. Nevertheless, the truth of the Law, the Prophets and the gospel of Christ will never be wiped away because of that persecution. Therefore he said, "But it is easier." That is, it is more likely that heaven and earth will fall and be annihilated than that even the least iota of the Word of God will not be fulfilled. In short, heaven and earth will pass away, until they are altered—that is, they will be restored and perfected—but the Word of the Lord remains forever.[21] For however much it is attacked by the enemies of truth, it will be fulfilled in the Lord's time. Therefore it is always proclaimed when the Lord commands that it should be. COMMENTARY IN LUKE 16:17.[22]

THE GOSPEL PERFECTS THE LAW. KONRAD PELLIKAN: The perspective of nature and the integrity of the gospel both demand perpetual friendship and inseparable union, not only in marriage but truly also in all friendship. It is not that anyone might plead the evangelical doctrine to fight against the prescriptions of Moses. . . . The one who requires what is more perfect does not abrogate the law but completes and perfects it. Just as a father will hardly fight against the son whom he indulged long ago when he was young, but now that he is grown up he will expect more of him than he had required before. COMMENTARY IN LUKE 16:18.[23]

---

[19]Must, from the Latin *vinum mustum*, or "young wine," is freshly pressed grape or other fruit juice that contains the seeds, skins and stems of the fruit. It is the first step in wine making.
[20]Erasmus, *In Evangelivm Lvce Paraphrasis*, yr-v (LB 7:413-14; cf. CWE 48:96).

[21]*Verbum domini manet in aeternum* (VDMA) was one of the catchphrases and symbols of the Lutheran reform (cf. 1 Pet 1:25; Is 40:8).
[22]Lambert, *In Divi Lucae*, Bb5v-Bb6r.
[23]Pellikan, *In Sacrosancta Quatuor Evangelia*, 172 (cf. CWE 48:97-98; LB 7:414).

16:19-31 THE RICH MAN AND LAZARUS

¹⁹"There was a rich man who was clothed in purple and fine linen and who feasted sumptuously every day. ²⁰And at his gate was laid a poor man named Lazarus, covered with sores, ²¹who desired to be fed with what fell from the rich man's table. Moreover, even the dogs came and licked his sores. ²²The poor man died and was carried by the angels to Abraham's side.ᵃ The rich man also died and was buried, ²³and in Hades, being in torment, he lifted up his eyes and saw Abraham far off and Lazarus at his side. ²⁴And he called out, 'Father Abraham, have mercy on me, and send Lazarus to dip the end of his finger in water and cool my tongue, for I am in anguish in this flame.' ²⁵But Abraham said, 'Child, remember that you in your lifetime received your good things, and Lazarus in like manner bad things; but now he is comforted here, and you are in anguish. ²⁶And besides all this, between us and you a great chasm has been fixed, in order that those who would pass from here to you may not be able, and none may cross from there to us.' ²⁷And he said, 'Then I beg you, father, to send him to my father's house— ²⁸for I have five brothersᵇ—so that he may warn them, lest they also come into this place of torment.' ²⁹But Abraham said, 'They have Moses and the Prophets; let them hear them.' ³⁰And he said, 'No, father Abraham, but if someone goes to them from the dead, they will repent.' ³¹He said to him, 'If they do not hear Moses and the Prophets, neither will they be convinced if someone should rise from the dead.'"

a Greek bosom; also verse 23   b Or brothers and sisters

OVERVIEW: Unlike the usual way of the world, Jesus gives us the name of the beggar but not the wealthy man, indicating for our interpreters that the end of the story will also not follow worldly expectations. While in the world's eyes Lazarus was poor and wretched, when he died, he was carried to heaven and comforted in the bosom of Abraham. While the rich man had many blessings of wealth and pleasure in his life, on his death his body was placed in the ground and his soul immediately found its way to hell. It was not that he needed to be poor to be blessed, the reformers note; it is not wealth that is the problem. (In fact, the reformers observe that we need wealth in order for governments, the church, its ministers, and even our own bodies to thrive. Wealth may create disparities, but it is a necessity.) Unfortunately, the rich man was dedicated to his wealth and its enjoyment and he let it possess him; he chose to serve wicked mammon as his master rather than God.

The afterlife is a focus of intense interest among the commentators. What will heaven be like? Still greater attention is given to hell and its torments. The pain and torment of hell are vividly conveyed through the picture of unquenchable fire and burning heat. The man begs for a little water to cool his tongue. Yet the man's anguish is increased by psychological pressures—the fear and worry for his brothers, the knowledge that it was his own poor choices and behavior that led to his punishment, but especially the vision of Lazarus, happy and well cared for in the bosom of Abraham. Many commentators note that seeing the happy Lazarus was part of his punishment. The pains and torments of hell are made real by this story and serve as a severe reminder of the necessity of repentance now, before it is too late.

Thankfully we have Moses and the Prophets! Everything that anyone needs to know about God's will and about what we should do and believe is already recorded in Scripture, these commentators remind us. The brothers do not need and will not receive a special message; they already have the neccessary and precious Word. Everything they need to know is already available to them; God's Word will not change, nor will it pass away.

16:19-22 *The Life and Death of the Beggar and the Rich Man*

JESUS OMITS THE RICH MAN'S NAME ON PURPOSE. JOHN BOYS: The poor man's name is mentioned here—"There was a beggar named Lazarus"—but the name of the rich man is omitted. He is styled "a certain man," which our blessed Savior did for a number of reasons, as many interpreters have observed. First, he wanted to show that his ways are not our ways, for we scorn the poor and take notice of the rich only. Genealogies of princes and pedigrees of nobles are as well known to us as our fingers, but if anyone should ask the name of a certain beggar, it will be "a certain man," "old father" or "old what's-his-name." It is clear that the wretch has no name, for only a few specific ones have names, like "blind Bartimaeus" or "lame Giles."[1] Therefore Christ, quite contrary to the world's attitude, acknowledged the poor man but not the rich one.

Second, Christ omitted this epicure's name because he does not recognize the wicked: "I never knew you." God knows his own children by name, for their names are written in heaven, and because they are in his book, he recognizes them as his own sheep: "I am the good shepherd. I know my own and my own know me." This is a great comfort to the godly, because they are in the book of life, not only *secundum eorum opinionem*, as the wicked are, but *secundum rei veritatem*, as Augustine writes in his explanation of that psalm.[2] Third, Christ omitted the glutton's name to signify that "the memory of the righteous is a blessing, but the name of the wicked will rot." THE FIRST SUNDAY AFTER TRINITY.[3]

THE WORLD EQUATES POVERTY WITH SINFULNESS. JOHANN SPANGENBERG: How does Luke describe the poor Lazarus? As a good and fruitful tree, as a pious, godly person who bore his poverty, hunger and affliction with patience and committed himself to God. But by the judgment of the world, he was not a blessed person. For as you see, he was poor and wretched—that is a heavy burden. Poverty is always despised and rejected. And along with that, he is not only miserably poor, but he is also a beggar, which is a great disgrace for the world. For the world soon passes through and says, "That one is a beggar. And why? His sins make him guilty before God; therefore God is punishing him." This is just the sort of judgment which Job's friends spoke over him. Therefore he has heavy burdens and is so hungry that he begs for the scraps which fall from the rich man's table. But no one gives them to him, no one comforts him, he is entirely forsaken. He has nothing to eat or drink, neither food nor shelter, neither house nor yard, no money, no possessions, no friends, no comforter. No one takes care of him. Only the dogs take pity on him and lick his wounds. GOSPEL ON THE FIRST SUNDAY AFTER TRINITY.[4]

THE RICH MAN HAD NO EXCUSE NOT TO HELP LAZARUS. CASPAR HUBERINUS: Here we should especially note the great unrighteousness and injustice of the rich man, who will be able to give no excuse for himself on Judgment Day or show himself in a favorable light. For he had every opportunity, and room, time, cause, reason and justice enough, and had it in plenty, to do something good for this poor Lazarus and to show him some compassion. First, the beggar sat not far from his door, so he must have had to look for an excuse why he could not help a poor beggar, because the poor Lazarus was available and God had so especially blessed him. Second, Lazarus is poor, thirsty and suffering—he has nothing on which to live—therefore the rich man cannot excuse himself

---

[1]In one of the legends of Saint Giles, he was wounded by an arrow meant to kill a deer, and he became a patron saint of those who are lame.
[2]See Augustine, *Enarrationes in Psalmos* 69.29; NPNF 8:310. These technical phrases translate as "according to their opinion," and "according to the truth of the matter."
[3]Boys, *Exposition of the Dominical Epistles and Gospels*, 3:60-61*; alluding to Is 45:8; Mk 10:46-51; Mt 7:23; Ps 69:28; quoting

Jn 10:14 (cf. Ex 33:12; Is 43:1; Lk 10:20); Prov 10:7 (cf. Sir 49:1).
[4]Spangenberg, *Postilla . . . von Ostern biß auffs Aduent*, LXXIIr.

by arguing that Lazarus had enough and did not need his help, so it was unnecessary for him to give help. Third, because he recognizes Lazarus, then the rich man is familiar with him and knows who he is; he was close by, and so the rich man cannot claim that he did not know him or was not familiar with whether he was rich or poor. Fourth, the poor man lay so close to his door, it is not like he was a mile away, so that the rich man could complain about the distance, and how he couldn't go running off to take care of some beggar and see what he needed. Fifth, Lazarus had so many difficulties, was so sick and full of pain, that the rich man could not use the excuse that the beggar did not work and support himself with his own hands but was burdensome and a nuisance, as the strong and healthy vagrants and beggars who make their living off of the blood and sweat of the poor people do. The rich man cannot make these charges, because Lazarus is sick and cannot work, as Paul commanded, that each one should work for his own keep, and should produce what he needs. But he is poor and sick; therefore, the rich man is responsible for helping him, according to the commands in Deuteronomy 15 and Leviticus 19. ON THE SECOND SUNDAY AFTER TRINITY.[5]

THE DEATH OF THE SAINTS IS PRECIOUS TO GOD. JOHN BUNYAN: Again, it is said that when the rich man died he was buried, or put into the earth, but when the beggar died, he was carried by the angels to Abraham's bosom. It is in a very excellent style, when he says, "he was carried by the angels to Abraham's bosom," for it denotes the excellent condition of the saints of God, as I said before. And not only does it denote their condition, but also the preciousness of the death of the saints in the eyes of the Lord; later generations may see how precious the death of the saints is in the sight of the Lord, when he says that they are carried by the angels to Abraham's bosom. Therefore the Lord often adorns the death and departure of his saints to show later generations how excellent they are in

his eyes. It is said of Enoch that God took him; of Abraham, that he died in a good old age; of Moses, that the Lord buried him; of Elijah, that he was taken up into heaven; that the saints sleep in Jesus; that they "die in the Lord"; that they rest from their labor; that their works follow them; that they are under the altar; that they are with Christ; that they are in light; that they will come with the Lord Jesus to judge the world. All of these sayings signify that dying a saint is a very great honor and dignity. But the ungodly have a very different experience. A FEW SIGHS FROM HELL: OR, THE GROANS OF A DAMNED SOUL.[6]

THE RICH MAN DESERVED CONDEMNATION FOR HIS LACK OF CHARITY. KASPAR VON SCHWENCKFELD: So you see, what remains of all the wealth of the lordly rich man? Money, possessions, clothes, jewels, luxury and close associates—he has to leave everything behind him. Greedy people should make fair note of the fact that this man who never gave anything of his to the poor is tortured in hell. How much more pain will that one suffer who extorts the rightful possessions from others with wickedness, force and injustice; who not only robs and unjustly seizes possessions but also is guilty of greed and ruthlessness, excessive stinginess, and so deserves the pain of hell? Therefore the prophet David taught in the psalm that when a person comes into riches, he should not throw his heart after them. A person can have a more peaceful and free life, and a death that is quieter with fewer pains, if he is dead before that in his heart to all his possessions, money and riches, as well all other creatures, in the words of the cross. He should also remain unaffected by the things of the world, as Saint Paul teaches, and hold everything as if he did not possess it. INTERPRETATION OF THE GOSPEL, LUKE 16: ON THE FIRST SUNDAY AFTER TRINITY.[7]

---

[5]Huberinus, *Postilla Teütsch*, 2:Yr; citing 1 Thess 5.

[6]Bunyan, *Few Sighs from Hell*, 30-31*; citing Ps 116:15; Gen 5:24; 25:8; Deut 34:6; 2 Kings 2:11; Rev 14:13; 6:9; Col 1:12; 1 Cor 6:2.
[7]CS 10:350; citing Ps 62:10; 1 Cor 7:30-31.

16:23-26 *Heaven and Hell*

**Lazarus Is Blessed for His Life and
Faith.** Johann Spangenberg: This Lazarus
believes in the blessed seed, promised to Abraham;
therefore the angels carry him to the bosom of
Abraham. He also demonstrates this faith with
good works. For you can see that there is a fine,
quiet heart, a patient and willing poor man. He lies
there before the door of the rich man, full of
burdens. Everyone walks over him and turns their
eyes away from him, turning up their noses at him,
wiping their shoes on him. He was a despised
mirror for the whole world. But he is still patient
and does not grumble against God. He does not
complain about the rich man, nor does he wish
him any harm, but he stays meekly silent and is at
peace, no matter what God does with him. He says
with Job, "God gave, God took, blessed be the name
of the Lord." And that is the fine fruit of a pious
heart, that he does not demand delicious meals,
but he desires only to be filled with the crumbs. He
does not act like the thankless beggar, who, if
someone does not give him something that he likes,
mutters oaths against him, scolds and curses, but
Lazarus does not do this.

And what sort of end did these two have? How
did they die? Just as their lives were entirely unlike,
so were their deaths. Everyone in the world saw the
rich man as the friend of God, but before one could
even look around, he lay in the pit of hell. Lazarus
was a despised mirror for all the world, but in the
twinkling of an eye, he was resting in the bosom of
Abraham, in eternal peace and blessedness, where
no disaster or misery could ever touch him but
where he would live in eternal happiness. Gospel
on the First Sunday After Trinity.[8]

The Point of Funerals. Edwin Sandys:
Saint Augustine suggests three reasons for funerals.
First, it is a human responsibility—the duty of
charity—decently to commit the dead to the earth,

out of which they came. This charitable duty is
commended by Tobit and others, whose names I
mentioned before, and was very religiously
observed even by the heathen. Second, it is a very
appropriate and convenient thing to lay a corpse in
a grave with reverence, because our bodies are
temples of the Holy Spirit, in whom and by whom
through these living instruments God has been
glorified and his people have received good things.
"Do you not know that your body is a temple of the
Holy Spirit within you?" And so what has been
such an important instrument should still be
reverently treated, although it is dead. Third, by
this action our faith concerning the article of the
resurrection is confirmed. For we lay down the
body in the earth in the hope that "this mortal
body must put on immortality," and we confess
with Job, "I know that my Redeemer lives . . . and
that I shall see God in my flesh, whom I shall see
for myself, and my eyes shall behold him, and none
other." But the Christian church does not and
should not use funerals to relieve or benefit the
dead. "All these last offices," says Saint Augustine,
"and ceremonies that concern the dead, the careful
funeral arrangements, and the equipment of the
tomb and the pomp of funeral rites, are rather the
solace of the living than the comfort of the dead."[9]
The glutton of whom Saint Luke speaks in the
Gospel was buried with pomp enough, no doubt,
and yet his wicked soul was plunged into hell. So
we see that no blessedness comes to the dead by
funerals, but rather "blessed are the dead who die
in the Lord." Lazarus wanted a funeral, so we
should think, but the lack of one did not bereave
him of his happy estate: he died in the Lord, and
so he was blessed.

Therefore, because death brings with it our
particular judgment, and because "whoever believes
in the Son has eternal life, and whoever does not
obey the Son shall not see life but the wrath of
God remains on him," so let us live as we will die,
and die as those who hope to rise again and live
with Christ hereafter. A Sermon Made in Saint

[8]Spangenberg, *Postilla . . . on Ostern biß auffs Aduent*, LXXIIr-v;
citing Job 1:21.

[9]Augustine, *City of God* 1.12 (NPNF 2:9).

PAUL'S AT THE SOLEMNIZATION OF CHARLES THE NINTH, THE FRENCH KING'S FUNERAL (1574).[10]

IT IS NOT HIS WEALTH THAT CONDEMNS THE RICH MAN BUT HIS MISUSE OF IT.

PHILIPP MELANCHTHON: Is it permitted for a Christian to have wealth, when this rich man is condemned? I respond: it is allowed, because wealth is necessary to preseve the body, likewise for economic needs, and to preserve the church or its ministers, and in order that the state might be preserved. Scripture approves wealth in these words: "Your springs shall overflow in the streets, but in the Lord you shall remain by them. Rich and poor live as one; the Lord made them both." If everyone were equally poor, they could not preserve governments. Money has the power of sustaining things. But if everyone were equally wealthy, no one would serve anyone else.

The rich man is not condemned because of his wealth but because of its abuse. The true enjoyment of wealth is pleasing to God, but this man is condemned. He squandered his wealth and did not contribute to any necessary uses of it, and he neglected Lazarus: just as now many people sin who, when they are able, do not offer aid to those in distress. Afterwards, many other faults were condemned in this rich man: he did not listen to Moses and the prophets, and he was without both repentance and faith. THE FIRST SUNDAY AFTER TRINITY.[11]

THE WICKED ARE FURTHER PUNISHED BY THE SIGHT OF BLESSEDNESS.

MARTIN BUCER: The reprobate are tormented with the knowledge of the happiness of the good, and this same knowledge increases their sorrow. This is how the wicked are tormented: here they see their own pain, there they see the happy situation and condition of those who are blessed. The physical things which are recorded here, such as the distant sign, the burning heat of the tongue, the cooling, the dipping of the finger in water, the gulf, and so on, should be understood in an altogether spiritual way. For the wicked, rich man saw high above him Abraham, with Lazarus in his bosom, and then he knew that Lazarus, whom he had so wickedly condemned, now enjoyed blessed rest with the father of the faithful, while he himself was tormented with cruel flames, that is to say, with unspeakable torment (because nothing is more burning than fire). And finally, he desired to have his tongue cooled by Lazarus's finger, a wish which was entirely vain, as was his hope for any of the comfort which Lazarus enjoyed. AN ECCLESIASTICALL EXPOSITION UPON SAINT LUKE 16.[12]

SOME REPENT TOO LATE.

JOHN JEWEL: Thus, dear brothers and sisters, a wicked conscience always carries shame around with it, always carries a heavy burden, is always poked and tormented and is never at peace. And although there are some people who are so given over to sin that they feel no shame in this life and are never disturbed in their conscience in this world, yet they should be aware that they will feel bitter torments in the world to come, and eternal shame that will never end. And there may be some who will say, like the people of Daniel's day, "No matter what we do, God will not look at us; he pays no attention to our actions, whether we do good or evil, for he doesn't care about it."[13] Their consciences are not affected by their sinful living, but some day they will be cast into utter darkness, where there will be weeping and gnashing of teeth, and then their consciences will be moved to repentance, and they will be ashamed—but then it will be too late. Remember the glutton—the rich glutton—who in his lifetime had nothing but pleasure, never felt adversity and was never pricked in his conscience about his thoughtless living. After he fell into hell fire and was tormented there, then the worm of his

---

[10]Sandys, *Sermons*, 161-62*; citing Tob 2:3-9; 1 Cor 6:19; 15:53; Job 19:25-27; Rev 14:13; Jn 3:36.
[11]MO 25:30; citing Prov 5:16; 22:2.
[12]Marlorat, ed., *Catholike and Ecclesiasticall Exposition of the Holy Gospell After S. Marke and Luke*, 262-63*.
[13]Such a passage is not in the book of Daniel.

conscience began to gnaw him, then he cried out to Abraham, then he was ashamed, but then it was too late. And this is what the wicked people will do on the Last Day—the wicked people, I say, who will then be alive and will see the great terror of that day: "They will say to the hills, 'Fall on us,' and to the mountains, 'Come, cover us.'" Then their own wicked consciences will accuse them—then they will be ashamed, but it will be too late. SERMON 9, ON ROMANS 6:19.[14]

THE CHASM IS A PERMANENT SEPARATION.
MARTIN LUTHER: Christ is sharp and severe in this parable, for he is an enemy to foul avarice; that is why he presents for us the man in hell, who would gladly have had a little drop of water. The man received a twofold answer. First he mocks the rich man: "You have received your good things in life; you wanted to have your heaven on earth. Money was your salvation and your paradise—let the gold, silver, and purple robes help you now! Why should Lazarus help you? He only had evil, and now he is comforted, but you will now be tormented," that is, the rich man in hell and the poor man in heaven. The second answer is: "Even if we should really want this thing, it cannot be; we do not act according to *your* will, for we are responsible to comply with God's wishes and to do what he wants; and even if we should also want to [help], we cannot, for there is a great chasm between us, and it separates us. While you were both alive and were neighbors, you and Lazarus, you did not need to step over a chasm. You could have easily placed him even in a stable, but now he is too far from you and the chasm too broad. You cannot come to us, therefore he will not help you." People say that it would be the greatest torment for the rich to see the poor, whom they had so despised in life, sitting in heaven. That would also have caused this rich man heartfelt pain—the fire would have burned even hotter, since he saw Lazarus in such a place of honor. But Abraham does this to him for punishment, and shows him

nothing else but Lazarus. In whatever way a person sins, that is how he will be punished. And this man is punished with [the sight of] Lazarus. Likewise, on Judgment Day our Lord God will show the misers the poor orphans whom they oppressed: the sight of them will cause them great pain. This is the sentence. They say, "We do not desire it, and we are unable to do it." And so [the rich man] must despair. SERMON ON THE SECOND SUNDAY AFTER TRINITY (1535).[15]

16:27-31 *Moses and the Prophets Speak the Right Words*

SOULS IN HELL CRY OUT TO KEEP THEIR COMPANIONS AWAY. JOHN BUNYAN: You can see here the lamentable state of those who go to hell and leave behind their fathers, mothers, sisters, brothers. While they are in the world, people delight to set their children bad examples, and children also love to follow in the wicked steps of their ungodly parents, but when they depart from this life, drop down into hell and find themselves in unrecoverable misery, then they cry, "Send somebody to my father's house, to my brother's house; O, tell them that my state is miserable, tell them I am undone forever; and tell them also that if they continue walking in the ungodly path where I left them, they will assuredly fall into this place of torments." Ah, friends and neighbors, it is likely that you rarely think that some of your friends and relations are crying out in hell, "Lord, send somebody to my father's house, to preach the gospel to them so that they will avoid coming to this torment!" While they live, people can willingly walk together in the way of sin, and when they are parted by death, those who are living seldom or never consider the sad condition into which those who died descended. But, you ungodly parents, how are your ungodly children now crying out in hell? And you ungodly children, how are your ungodly parents who lived and died ungodly now also in the pains of hell? . . .

---

[14]Jewel, *Works*, 2:1063-64*; citing Mt 8:12; Lk 23:30.

[15]*LEA* 3:266-67 (cf. WA 41:298-99).

Here you can see that there may be, and in fact are, whole households in a damnable state and condition, which our Lord Jesus signifies here. "Send him to my father's house, for they are all in the same state—I left all my brothers in pitiful shape." While they live here, people cannot endure to hear that they will all be in a miserable condition, but when they are under the wrath of God, they see it, they know it, and they are very sure of it, for when they were in the world they themselves lived as these others do. But they fell short of heaven, and therefore they know that if these others continue along the same path, so shall they. "Oh, please send him quickly to my father's house, for the whole house is in terrible condition, and if they continue so, they will all be damned." What we can observe in this is that those who are in hell do not desire that their companions come there. A FEW SIGHS FROM HELL: OR, THE GROANS OF A DAMNED SOUL.[16]

THE WORD IS SUFFICIENT FOR ALL OF US.
RICHARD TAVERNER: But how was he answered? "They have Moses and the Prophets—let them hear them," as if he would say, "They have God's Word among them, which teaches them how to avoid everlasting punishment and how to be saved, and if they will not pay attention to it, there is no recovery for them." Undoubtedly this answer teaches us two things. First, it teaches us that the will of God should not be learned from the dead, as Moses also forbids in Deuteronomy, saying, "Let no one search the truth from the dead, for God abhors it." And this is surely not without cause, for whoever seeks the truth from dead people shows himself to be discontented with God's Word, which is a sin against the second commandment. Also, to seek the truth from dead people is to choose other means over preachers, by whom God wants his Word known and spread abroad. The example of Saul teaches us this, for after he was cast off by the Lord and utterly wicked in his heart, he raised up the prophet Samuel from the dead

with the help of a witch, or at least a certain person resembling Samuel in voice and conduct.

Second, this answer of Abraham teaches us that besides the written Word, none other is to be looked for or heard, even if an angel should come from heaven or a ghost rise from death to life. Wherefore, good Christian brothers and sisters, in the Lord's name I exhort those of you who are rich that you make yourselves friends with your wicked mammon, that is to say, with your worldly goods, so that when you die, they may receive you into everlasting tabernacles and so that you can escape the fate of this rich man. And again, I exhort those of you who are poor to have sure faith in the Lord and patience in your adversity and poverty. Do not doubt but that, on your departure out of this transitory world, according to the example of this poor Lazarus, you will be carried by angels to the bosom of Abraham, that is to say, to everlasting life in which, according to the example of the father Abraham, who is the father of all believing children, the godly are received as into the bosom of the heavenly Father. ON THE FIRST SUNDAY AFTER TRINITY.[17]

THE RICH MAN RECOGNIZES THAT REPENTANCE WOULD HAVE SAVED HIM. KASPAR VON SCHWENCKFELD: Once more we see how the soul of the rich man is open to memory and recognition there in hell, as well as to the increase of his pain. He sees that his brothers must behave differently, must become pious and repent, if they want to escape such a heavy sentence and the pain of hell. We should also especially notice here that the damned rich man even thought of repentance and that his brothers should need it more than anybody else. Therefore also the Lord Christ began to preach of the kingdom of God and on repentance, which the rich man was lacking. Now the man could well see that if he had produced repentance here on earth, that is, improved his sinful life and changed it in all godliness, then he would not have come to that place of torment and

---

[16]Bunyan, *Few Sighs from Hell*, 104-5, 110-11*.

[17]Taverner, *Epistles and Gospelles (Sommer Parte)*, 80r-v*; citing Deut 18:11-12; 1 Sam 28; Lk 16:9.

pain. And as we can see, not only the blessed but also the damned know and recognize such a thing. Therefore we should not take it lightly, that without prior, thorough repentance, no one can enter into heaven or become blessed in the kingdom of God. INTERPRETATION OF THE GOSPEL, LUKE 16: ON THE FIRST SUNDAY AFTER TRINITY.[18]

GOD'S WORD IS ALREADY KNOWN AND WILL NOT CHANGE. JOHN BUNYAN: [God said:] "I myself sent the prophets—they did not run out according to their own plans. I gave them a commission, I thrust them out and told them what they should say. In a word, they have told the world what my plan is for both sinners and for saints. 'They have Moses and the Prophets—let them hear them.' Therefore he who rejects and turns his back on the threats, counsels, admonitions, invitations, promises, or whatever else I have commanded them to speak concerning salvation and life, and any directions about them, will be sure to have a share in the many curses that they have spoken and the destruction that they have pronounced." . . .

It is as if God had said, "You would have me send someone from the dead to them? Why is that necessary? They already know my mind: I have declared to them what my plan is, both for saving those who believe and damning those who do not. Whatever I have said, I will do, whether they hear or hold themselves back. And as for this desire of yours, you might as well ask that I make a whole new Bible, and so revoke everything I said before by the mouths of the prophets. But I am God, not a human being, and my word is immutable, unchangeable, and will stand as firm as my decrees can make it: Heaven and earth will pass away, but my words will not pass away. If you had ten thousand brothers, and every one of them were in danger of losing his soul if he did not come to follow what is contained and recorded in the Scriptures of truth, then each one of them would perish and be damned in hell, for the Scriptures cannot be broken." A FEW SIGHS FROM HELL: OR, THE GROANS OF A DAMNED SOUL.[19]

---

[18]CS 10:357-58.

[19]Bunyan, *Few Sighs from Hell*, 186-87*; citing Lk 21:33.

17:1-10 SIN, FAITH AND DUTY

And he said to his disciples, "Temptations to sin[a] are sure to come, but woe to the one through whom they come! [2]It would be better for him if a millstone were hung around his neck and he were cast into the sea than that he should cause one of these little ones to sin.[b] [3]Pay attention to yourselves! If your brother sins, rebuke him, and if he repents, forgive him, [4]and if he sins against you seven times in the day, and turns to you seven times, saying, 'I repent,' you must forgive him."

[5]The apostles said to the Lord, "Increase our faith!" [6]And the Lord said, "If you had faith like a grain of mustard seed, you could say to this mulberry tree, 'Be uprooted and planted in the sea,' and it would obey you.

[7]"Will any one of you who has a servant[c] plowing or keeping sheep say to him when he has come in from the field, 'Come at once and recline at table'? [8]Will he not rather say to him, 'Prepare supper for me, and dress properly,[d] and serve me while I eat and drink, and afterward you will eat and drink'? [9]Does he thank the servant because he did what was commanded? [10]So you also, when you have done all that you were commanded, say, 'We are unworthy servants;[e] we have only done what was our duty.'"

a Greek Stumbling blocks   b Greek stumble   c Greek bondservant; also verse 9   d Greek gird yourself   e Greek bondservants

OVERVIEW: Early modern commentators tended to connect these seemingly unrelated verses. It is the duty of the servants of God to live a life of repentance and forgiveness by faith. Some might think that because offenses or occasions of sin are necessarily going to come, God might somehow be blamed as the cause of sin and evil, but God is just and can never be unjust. His loving providence guides our lives; still we do not always understand his plans. Yes, we must accept that sin and offense are going to happen. Still we are guilty, particularly if we lead others to sin. We are also responsible for forgiving those who sin against us. This is God's will. It leads to peace and unity, while seeking vengeance causes division.

And yet it is difficult to forgive those who have offended us, which is why, the reformers argue, the apostles respond to Jesus by asking him to increase their faith. Their request shows that the faith is God's gift, not our own doing. Even if our faith is as tiny as a mustard seed, because it is God working in us, it is capable of great feats. God can accomplish all that he has promised and more. Whatever God requires of us is nothing for which we should be praised and rewarded if we accomplish it. It is, in fact, just our duty. Whether we avoid sin, manage to forgive those who offend us or increase in faith, we are incapable of completing all of our required tasks on our own, and the fact that our Master accepts our labor and gives us a reward is due only to his grace and mercy.

17:1-2 Do Not Provide Occasion for Others to Sin

THE OFFENSES ARE GOING TO COME. PHILIPP MELANCHTHON: When our Savior Christ says that it is necessary that offenses will come, no one should be troubled, because it reveals to us the providence of God. The ancient writers subtly disputed and wrote about this word *necessary*, because they wanted to avoid what might have been said, namely, that God is the author of evil. We say that the judgments of God are unsearchable, and that this necessity is one of the judgments of God. So just because we can find no reason for it, we still must not seek to deny it. This necessity comes from the providence of God, and yet for all that, he is not the author of evil or the cause of the fault. Other punishments, by which the rebellions and blindness of infidels are punished, proceed from God. When he allows the wicked to fall and gives them over to filthy desires and shameful filthiness, we see that he is a just judge and cannot be said to be the author of evil, for the wicked cannot be excused from their sin. Likewise, we must remember about these offenses that the judgments of God are certain and pure, by which he revenges the contempt of his Word and other rebellions. And when he lays this vengeance on the wicked, he cannot be blamed. And it should not seem like a new thing to us, when we see so many offenses today. Those things which Christ foresaw are now fulfilled, and the devil (although God also lays stumbling blocks) does his duty and tries to draw us away from Christ. AN ECCLESIASTICALL EXPOSITION UPON SAINT MATHEWE 18.[1]

AVOID SCANDALIZING THE WEAK. THE ENGLISH ANNOTATIONS: Christ is pointing out the sin of those times, which was to think it little or no sin, by one's pride and demanding insistence, to scandalize an infirm, poor or lower-class brother or sister. Here he also tells of the punishment, speaking of scandals given by heretics, schismatics, apostates, and the like, whether in word or deed (see Rom 16:13; Tit 1:16). Otherwise offense may be taken by perverse and ignorant people from good and laudable things done or spoken, if they do not agree with their own blind and corrupt opinions. The scribes and Pharisees were often scandalized and offended by Christ's teaching and works of mercy. But blessed are those who are not offended in Christ (see Mt 11:6). It would be better (or more tolerable, as in the Syriac translation) for someone who has scandalized the humblest of God's children to be cast into the most desperate or helpless condition of this life than to endure the eternal torments which await him in hell. ANNOTATIONS UPON THE GOSPEL ACCORDING TO SAINT LUKE 17:2.[2]

17:3-4 Forgive Your Brother

REPROACH YOUR BROTHER, BUT WITH KINDNESS. DESIDERIUS ERASMUS: Therefore, if it should

by chance happen that your brother has committed anything against you, do not ignore his fault, or else freedom from punishment might encourage him to greater sins. Rather, play the part of the faithful doctor and reveal his disease to him in secret with a small reproach, that through a sense of shame he might be corrected. He will more readily hear a friendly counselor than a raging accuser, whom he is going to regard as an enemy. For, as a rule, it is the human inclination to be more agreeable to advice than to submit to harshness and insult. It will certainly be perceived as a great favor, when you point out the sin in secret. He who openly announces someone's fault and calls for punishment does not seem to want to heal a brother's badness but to make a show of it. But if your brother should come to his senses through a warning from you and recognize his fault, let your forgiveness be ready, and receive him kindly and gently after his reform; do not think about avenging yourself but consider as much as possible his own sense of shame and honor. If he should fall back again into the fault, through human infirmity, even if he should sin against you seven times in the same day and then repent seven times in a day, if he shall earnestly try to appease you and say, "I have sinned, I am sorry, please forgive me," then forgive him his fault from your heart. The good-natured quality of these pardons will promote peace and concord among you much better than mutual retaliation for offenses. PARAPHRASE ON THE GOSPEL OF LUKE 17:3-4.[3]

17:5-6 The Power of Faith

WE SHOULD ALSO PRAY THAT GOD INCREASE OUR FAITH. JOHANNES BRENZ: There is a question on what occasion the apostles made this request, but it is most likely that it happened after Christ had preached concerning the suffering of injuries and the forgiving of one's neighbor. The apostles, considering that no one could follow this doctrine of charity without faith (for charity is the fruit of faith), then prayed that their faith might be

---

[1]Marlorat, ed., *Catholike and Ecclesiasticall Exposition of the Holy Gospell After S. Mathewe*, 399*.
[2]Downame, ed., *Annotations*, Yy1r*.

[3]Erasmus, *In Evangelivm Lvce Paraphrasis*, y5v-y6r (LB 7:417-18; cf. CWE 48:106-7).

increased. That way they might, although not perfectly, yet to the utmost of their power follow Christ's teaching and forgive their neighbors their offenses from their heart.

We also see in Matthew 17, that the apostles desired to have their faith increased because they were not able to cast the devil out of the afflicted child, and because Christ had said that they could not cast out the devil because of their unbelief. But no matter on what occasion it was which they prayed, it is such a prayer that we should always use. For faith does not spring from our flesh, because by nature we desire the Holy Spirit; rather, the beginning of faith is the gift of God in us, and so also is the increase of faith. Therefore we must by necessity always pray that God in his goodness would make strong and increase true faith in us. AN ECCLESIASTICALL EXPOSITION UPON SAINT LUKE 17.[4]

THERE ARE DIFFERENT KINDS OF FAITH.

PHILIPP MELANCHTHON: He shows the liveliness and efficacy of faith by the similitude which he uses of the grain of mustard seed. For although that is the smallest of all seeds, in a short time it springs and shoots up above all other plants; likewise, if faith is lively, it earnestly shows itself forth, and nothing is impossible for it, because it overcomes every obstacle. It only seeks to do what pertains to the glory of God, and whatever it undertakes, it is convinced that the Lord will finish it, for which it praises God continually. But some people might think (and certain perverse people do this) that whoever has faith like a grain of mustard seed can move mountains and do all other things, and they say, "We believe, therefore we are able to do everything, even, if need be, to move mountains, and to cast out evil spirits." But we should note what sort of faith the Lord is talking about here. We should understand that there are three kinds of faith. The first is what believes that certain things are indeed what they are declared to be in the Scriptures: for example, in Scripture we hear that there is one God, who is omnipotent and the creator of all things, and if

we believe it for that reason, then we believe with a historical faith. The second sort of faith is what believes in the promises of God and apprehends the mercy and grace of God in Christ Jesus. This faith is called a justifying faith. The third sort is what believes that there is nothing impossible for God; with this faith, the mind can be carried by a certain inspiration of the Spirit to do marvelous things. This is called a miraculous faith. AN ECCLESIASTICALL EXPOSITION UPON SAINT MATHEWE 17.[5]

17:7-10 *The Followers of Christ Are Servants*

WE ARE UNWORTHY SERVANTS, ACCEPTED BY GRACE.

KONRAD PELLIKAN: Nevertheless that servant performed his job in the field in good faith. But why would the master feel grateful to him, when he was doing what he was commanded to do? I do not doubt but that he would have punished him if it would not have been done. And for what reason? Simply because they are servants, and they owe all their work to their master—indeed it belongs to him. However the master takes to himself the glory of all which they do—a person does this whenever he accomplishes deeds through those who are able to do nothing good at all without him. Therefore, so that you will not claim for yourselves the glory of having done well—go out and perform such faithful work. And when you will have completed all which you were prescribed (which you will never be able to do), say nevertheless: "We are unworthy servants, and we only did what we were already required to do." This will preserve the treasure of faith in you by a worthy modesty. Meanwhile you will remember that you are nothing other than servants who are in debt for all your labor, and it is worthless to the master: he accepts and recognizes it only by grace, and awards by a proportion above your merits. COMMENTARY IN LUKE 17:7-10.[6]

---

[4]Marlorat, ed., *Catholike and Ecclesiasticall Exposition of the Holy Gospell After S. Marke and Luke*, 267-68*.

[5]Marlorat, ed., *Catholike and Ecclesiasticall Exposition of the Holy Gospell After S. Mathewe*, 387*.
[6]Pellikan, *In Sacrosancta Quatuor Evangelia*, 177-78 (cf. CWE 48:109-10; LB 7:418).

17:11-19 TEN MEN ARE HEALED OF LEPROSY

[11]On the way to Jerusalem he was passing along between Samaria and Galilee. [12]And as he entered a village, he was met by ten lepers,[a] who stood at a distance [13]and lifted up their voices, saying, "Jesus, Master, have mercy on us." [14]When he saw them he said to them, "Go and show yourselves to the priests." And as they went they were cleansed. [15]Then one of them, when he saw that he was healed, turned back, praising God with a loud voice; [16]and he fell on his face at Jesus' feet, giving him thanks. Now he was a Samaritan. [17]Then Jesus answered, "Were not ten cleansed? Where are the nine? [18]Was no one found to return and give praise to God except this foreigner?" [19]And he said to him, "Rise and go your way; your faith has made you well."[b]

a *Leprosy was a term for several skin diseases; see Leviticus 13*   b *Or has saved you*

OVERVIEW: The healing of the ten lepers affirms, our commentators argue, that Jesus came to clean and purify us, so that, like these lepers, we too might be able to rejoin our communities, that is, our fellowship in the kingdom of heaven. The lepers, separated and unclean, are a symbol of all of us, who are separated from God by our sin. How are the lepers cleansed? By faith. Does this mean that we have power over God or that our faith is somehow a meritorious work that deserves a reward? No, instead it means that God is so good and gracious that he rouses faith in us and leads us to expect all good things from him.

The reformers also focus on this passage's lesson of thanksgiving. Prayer is required of us, but so is giving thanks after we have received our request. That only one leper, a Samaritan, returns to thank Jesus leads Brenz to be critical of the "remarkable ingratitude" of the Jews, but Boys intimates that ironically it is the priests to whom Jesus directed these men who in turn direct them away from Jesus of Nazareth to his shadow, the law. True faith consists in prayer and gratitude to the triune God who so richly blesses his creation.

17:11-14 *Jesus Heals the Lepers*

WE ARE LIKE THE TEN LEPERS, CAST OUT OF THE HEAVENLY KINGDOM. JOHANNES BRENZ: By this clear and certain miracle, Christ confirms as by a heavenly seal the truth of the teaching of his gospel, which is that he came into the world to purge us from all uncleanness of sins and to restore us to the fellowship of the heavenly kingdom. For as the lepers are cast out from the company of humanity because of their leprosy, so we are cast out of Paradise and the kingdom of heaven because of sin. But Christ came to make satisfaction for our sins and to give us the cleanliness of his righteousness. He came therefore to reconcile us and to bring us into the kingdom of true and everlasting happiness. And Christ confirmed the truth of this teaching by the miracle which he did for the ten lepers. Matthew and the other two Evangelists show that one leper was cleansed by Christ, but Luke shows that the same miracle of healing was given to ten lepers. However, this history has another purpose: it shows the remarkable ingratitude of the Jews, so that no one will marvel that so many of the benefits of Christ were suppressed among them. The circumstance which makes this fact even more infamous is that when the Lord had healed nine Jews, not one of them gave him thanks but stole away so that they might extinguish any remembrance of their disease. But the one Samaritan alone came and gave thanks to Christ, as was his duty....

Christ desired that his gospel be made known among the Jews, and he had forbidden his apostles to go into Gentile areas or to enter into the cities of the Samaritans. But he also declared by many arguments that his gospel also applied to the Gentiles and the Samaritans and that it should be revealed and preached to them in due time, which afterward came to pass. An Ecclesiasticall Exposition upon Saint Luke 17.[1]

They Ran and Cried Out to Him in Faith.
Johann Spangenberg: What do the lepers do? They stand a ways off, raise their voices and say: "Jesus, dear master, have mercy on us!" They believe that because of his graciousness, he will certainly heal them and make them well. How does a person seek out such faith? Out of their own action: they meet Christ, stand at a distance and cry out. Where there is a true faith, there is a running, standing and crying. All those things are signs of a great faith, for if they had doubted, they would not have gone toward him, nor would they have stood there and cried out. Whence comes such faith to them? They had heard that Jesus of Nazareth was a friendly fellow and how gracious he was to everyone, so they desired his help and sought out his grace and aid. From all the shouting, they drew good confidence and trust, thinking: "If this Jesus is so gracious, why would we want to just lie here and waste away?" And so they set off in faith. And as it now happens that Jesus meets them in the market town, they stop with the greatest joy, according to the form of true faith, standing still, as if they would say, "Look, there is the one who can and will help us—why would we want to go farther? Let us show our affliction to the gracious Christ. He will not let us go away from him hopeless." Gospel on the Fourteenth Sunday After Trinity.[2]

Faith Receives What It Seeks Before We Can Even Ask. Martin Luther: In this example, the Lord attracts all hearts to himself with his friendliness and pleasantness and rouses them to believe in him. For there is no doubt: what he does for these lepers he will do for anyone, if we only freely expect all goodness and grace from him, which a true Christian faith and a true Christian heart should do and certainly does. For he is very glad when a person freely and happily ventures to build on his goodness, before he even experiences or feels it. He testified to that well enough here, because he so willingly answers them without delay. He does not say that he wanted to do it, but rather he did for them what they wanted—it already happened. For he does not say, "Yes, I want to take pity on you, so you shall be clean," but simply, "Go and show yourselves to the priests." As if he would say, "It requires no asking—your faith has already achieved and gained it, before you even began to ask. You were already clean before me, just as you began to hope for such a thing from me. It is no longer necessary to ask; just go and show your cleanliness to the priests. As I consider you and as you believe, so you are and should become." For he would not have sent them to the priests if he had not regarded them as clean, and wanted to treat them so that they became clean. You see, faith is so powerful that it gains everything from God that he wants, and your request will be considered by God as if it were already accomplished, even before you ask it. That is why Isaiah says, "It will happen that before they call, I will answer them, and before they speak, I will hear them." Not that we or our faith would be worthy of it, but he shows his inexpressible goodness and willing grace, with which he rouses us to believe in him and, comforted, to expect everything good from him with happy and unwavering confidence, which does not clutch at him or put him on trial. So you also see here that he hears these lepers before they call and is ready to do everything that their hearts desire before they even speak. "Go," he says, "I do not need to make any promises to you, for you have already come so far that you need no promises. You have what you prayed for, so go." Are those not strong enticements, which can make a heart happy and brave? You see, then let yourself grasp and feel his grace—yes, it grasps and touches us! The Gospel on the Ten Lepers (1521).[3]

[1]Marlorat, ed., *Catholike and Ecclesiasticall Exposition of the Holy Gospell After S. Marke and Luke*, 270-71*; citing Mt 10:5; Acts 8:4-5. [2]Spangenberg, *Postilla . . . von Ostern biß auffs Aduent*, CXXXIr-v. [3]*LEA* 3:281-82 (cf. *WA* 8:359); citing Is 65:24.

17:15-19 *The Samaritan Returns to Praise and Give Thanks*

BY GOD'S COMMAND, PRAYER IS JOINED WITH THANKSGIVING. MATHEW CAYLIE: From the practice of this Samaritan we may learn our duty, which is this: to glorify God and give him thanks for favors and benefits received from him. This is the express commandment of God: "Call on me in the day of trouble; I will deliver you, and you shall glorify me." Just as prayer is required, so also praise is required for deliverance, even as the apostle Paul would also have thanksgiving joined with "prayer and supplication." Thus there is a necessary coherence between prayer and thanksgiving: just as prayer is the sending out for those things we need, so thanksgiving is for when we receive them, for having received the things which we desired of God through prayer, we must then give him thanks for them. The first thing which we ask in the Lord's Prayer is to have grace to glorify God's name, and the last thing we are to perform in the same prayer is to ascribe all glory to that same sacred name. THE CLEANSING OF THE TEN LEPERS.[4]

THE SAMARITAN DISPLAYED FAITH AND VIRTUE. JOHN BOYS: The thankfulness of the Samaritan is accompanied by many notable virtues, such as obedience, for although he knew that he was cleansed from his leprosy as he went away, yet according to Christ's express commandment he showed himself to the priests. And when he was with them he was not seduced by them as were the rest of his company. For whereas the priests (as it is thought) corrupted and persuaded those other nine that they were cured by observance of the laws and not by Christ's might or miracle, the Samaritan believed without hesitation that Christ was "a priest forever after the order of Melchizedek," even a high priest who is "able to sympathize with our weaknesses." Therefore leaving the priests of the law, he was eager to be with Jesus his Savior. Everyone goes astray, but the good person goes

back, returning again to Christ, who is the way. When he came back to Christ, he performed his duties to God and to humanity. He performed his duty to God in "praising him with a loud voice," which argues for his devotion, and "in falling on his face at Christ's feet," which argues for his humility. He performed his duty to humanity, for when Christ said to him, "Were not ten cleansed? Where are the nine?" the man made no reply but held his peace. This signifies that he came back to remember and offer his own thanks, not to tell tales of the ingratitude of others. These good things, which arise from a lively faith, are well pleasing to God. Therefore Christ dismissed him accordingly, "Rise and go your way, your faith has made you well." THE FOURTEENTH SUNDAY AFTER TRINITY.[5]

THE EXAMPLE ENCOURAGES BOLD BELIEF AND THANKSGIVING. THOMAS BECON: You hear how in the gospel of the day, Christ sets forth a notable example of faith. "Your faith," he says, "has saved you." By this he ascribes all the glory of the saving of the Samaritan not to himself (which he would have done if he had said, "I restore you to health") but to faith. Christ does this with the intent that we should also be encouraged by this example and believe boldly, and be sure in thinking that through Christ we will obtain whatever we believe. If we believe in the remission of sin and everlasting life, our faith will not deceive us. If we believe that God is favorable and merciful, then he cannot be anything but favorable and merciful. Thus all things are in this way referred to faith and not to God, who indeed works all things, so that we may all learn that whenever we lack anything that we would have or that we need, the fault is not in God but in ourselves, because we do not believe. For if we believed, we would surely have it. . . .

In the other part is a terrible example that shows ten who believe and are healed, but nine abandon their faith and do not give thanks to Christ for his benefit. We ought to consider that

---

[4]Caylie, *Cleansing of the Ten Lepers*, 39-41*; citing Ps 50:15; Phil 4:6.

[5]Boys, *Exposition of the Dominical Epistles and Gospels*, 4:56*; citing Heb 7:17 (cf. Ps 110:4); 4:15.

this example is for the purpose that we learn from it to be thankful and to avoid the wicked sin of unkindness. For God worthily focused this glory on himself so that we would render him thanks—and we should do it gladly and willingly, for it is a thing of no great labor or difficulty. For what labor is required of you to turn to God and say, "Lord, you have given me healthy eyes, hands, feet. I thank you heartily for your gift!" Likewise, how hard is it to give thanks to your parents, teachers, bosses and neighbors when they do good to you? It should be done if only that they may understand that their benefit is well bestowed. The Samaritan also does this: he returns to the Lord and gives him thanks. This required no cost or charge but just a few words, and yet it pleased Christ marvelously. Other people also find this acceptable, and they take great pleasure in it, and they are encouraged by it afterwards to do good for such a person again. THE ELEVENTH SUNDAY AFTER TRINITY SUNDAY.[6]

---

[6]Becon, *New Postil (Second Parte)*, 111v-112v*.

17:20-37 THE COMING OF THE KINGDOM OF GOD

[20]*Being asked by the Pharisees when the kingdom of God would come, he answered them, "The kingdom of God is not coming in ways that can be observed,* [21]*nor will they say, 'Look, here it is!' or 'There!' for behold, the kingdom of God is in the midst of you."*[a]

[22]*And he said to the disciples, "The days are coming when you will desire to see one of the days of the Son of Man, and you will not see it.* [23]*And they will say to you, 'Look, there!' or 'Look, here!' Do not go out or follow them.* [24]*For as the lightning flashes and lights up the sky from one side to the other, so will the Son of Man be in his day.*[b] [25]*But first he must suffer many things and be rejected by this generation.* [26]*Just as it was in the days of Noah, so will it be in the days of the Son of Man.* [27]*They were eating and drinking and marrying and being given in marriage, until the day when Noah entered the ark, and the flood came and destroyed them all.* [28]*Likewise, just as it was in the days of Lot—they were eating and drinking, buying and selling, planting and building,* [29]*but on the day when Lot went out from Sodom, fire and sulfur rained from heaven and destroyed them all—*[30]*so will it be on the day when the Son of Man is revealed.* [31]*On that day, let the one who is on the housetop, with his goods in the house, not come down to take them away, and likewise let the one who is in the field not turn back.* [32]*Remember Lot's wife.* [33]*Whoever seeks to preserve his life will lose it, but whoever loses his life will keep it.* [34]*I tell you, in that night there will be two in one bed. One will be taken and the other left.* [35]*There will be two women grinding together. One will be taken and the other left."*[c] [37]*And they said to him, "Where, Lord?" He said to them, "Where the corpse*[d] *is, there the vultures*[e] *will gather."*

a Or *within you,* or *within your grasp* b Some manuscripts omit *in his day* c Some manuscripts add verse 36: *Two men will be in the field; one will be taken and the other left* d Greek *body* e Or *eagles*

OVERVIEW: Is the kingdom of God coming, or is it already here? Both—as Lefèvre d'Étaples notes, "the kingdom of God is twofold: it is present and future." The kingdom is present because Christ is present. This does not mean what many people want to believe; we should not expect a crown, but a cross. Jesus would be rejected and persecuted rather than create an earthly kingdom. Jesus' words make a distinction between the present, when he was physically present, the future when he would not be present and his disciples would experience many challenges, and then a time when the kingdom would come in full force unexpectedly. The time when Christ was present was difficult and ended in a shameful death, but at least he was there to lead and speak clearly to them. After his death, troubles, false prophets and persecution would come to his followers, so they would wish again for the presence of Christ.

As Bucer remarks, Jesus wants to be sure that his disciples would not receive any false messiahs after his death. He wants to prepare them for the future, so that difficult times and false leaders would not derail their faith. His vision of the future recalls historical events of cataclysmic proportions: Noah and the flood, Lot and the destruction of Sodom and Gomorrah. Like the difficult times after Jesus' death, people in Noah's and Lot's time were not faithful—they were corrupt, focused on their present life, comforts and concerns. But as Calvin remarks, no one knew that the flood was coming—it came suddenly, like lightning streaking across the sky. Even Lot's wife, one of those faithful, was not ready to give up her former comforts. Many commentators note that she ended up lacking faith in God's prophecy—she did not persevere. But when the flood and the fire came—suddenly, destructively—only those few chosen ones were saved, while the others were left to suffer their punishment. Likewise, these commentators note, the second coming of Christ will be sudden and unexpected.

17:20-21 The Kingdom of God Is Present Within You

THE KINGDOM OF GOD IS PRESENT AND FUTURE. JACQUES LEFÈVRE D'ÉTAPLES: The kingdom of God is twofold: it is present and future, and the kingdom of Christ is the same. Christ began the first in his first coming, and in a way he came with an outward show: for an outward appearance was able to be grasped, both from the seventy weeks of Daniel and from the failure of the kingdom and the priesthood of the Jews and its transference to other people. According to these things, it is from the signs by the appointed prophets and by many others. But the following kingdom of God, which is to come, is not able to be grasped by an outward show or to be perceived. Of this the Lord says, both to the Pharisees and to the disciples: "It will not come with outward show, and it will be neither in this nor in that region of the earth, because it will not be earthly but heavenly." Concerning that reality, he also said to the Pharisees who believed in him (that is to say, some believed) and to his disciples: "For behold, the kingdom of God is in the midst of you." And what is the kingdom of God if not faith in Christ, the teaching of the Spirit and a new creation by him? And he, who is the greatest, was already dwelling in them by faith. IN THE GOSPEL OF LUKE 17.[1]

17:22-25 The Son of Man Must Suffer

CHRIST'S DAYS ARE FOR HIS TRUE BELIEVERS. FRANÇOIS LAMBERT: You can see this quite plain teaching which Christ preached clearly but which has blinded everyone, even to this day so

many centuries later. For if you see what Christ did in his days, then you will recognize the desire for even one such day in his disciples, that is, in those who believe. He preached most sincerely and announced most openly the truth and the kingdom of God. But the days came which were nothing like this, but instead the proud and lying ministers of the kingdom of the antichrist put forward their vain human teachings, and we heard only their foolish talk of wicked falsehoods. These teachers say that the kingdom of God and the church of Christ are only those which are subject to the pope and the pseudo-bishops. And they say, "Behold! This, or that, is Christ." They invent and claim temples, monasteries, vows and privileges of the sleeping saints, and vain indulgences, trying to look for Christ there, but he seeks nothing less from them than to be worshiped truly, for he desires that they should worship him "in spirit and in truth." The seducers have also preached and done mischief to all the Scriptures of God and have obscured by their inventions what he revealed by his judgment. Thus it happens that all the faithful have long desired greatly for one of Christ's days. The believer who hears Christ in the preaching of the faithful Evangelists sees one of Christ's days; Christ the greatest and best would bring about that his days, which are able to be seen by individual believers, might be seen in all the world.[2] COMMENTARY IN LUKE 17:22.[3]

CHRIST REMINDS HIS DISCIPLES THAT HE IS THE ONLY MESSIAH. MARTIN BUCER: Christ wants his disciples to depend wholly on him, even after his departure, even though he would no longer be present in the flesh, and not to receive any other earthly messiahs, for whom the Jews were still waiting. When there would be dissension between the disciples and the rulers of the people concerning their opinions and beliefs, when many would fall away from the faith and all places

---

[1]Lefèvre d'Étaples, *Commentarii Initiatorii in Quatuor Evangelia*, 2:87v; citing Dan 9:24.

[2]Lambert refers to *Christus optimus maximus*, which seems to be a clear reference to Jupiter Optimus Maximus—the temple to Jupiter under this title was the most important temple in ancient Rome. [3]Lambert, *In Divi Lucae*, Cc3v-Cc4r; citing Jn 4:23.

would be full of false prophets, when there would be perseuction in every corner and when tribulation would be at hand, then many who were full of care would wish for the presence of Christ, even if it would only be for an hour, so that they might receive consolation and strength of mind. Therefore, seeing that human beings require a Christ and Savior in the flesh, and that the disciples should feel all adversity and trouble and they might follow some false Christ or deceiver who would promise to his followers earthly liberty and happiness, he admonishes them here to acknowledge no other Christ beside him. He will reign, not in the flesh but in the spirit, until that time when he should come like lightning from heaven, to be seen by all people with glorious majesty to judge the whole world. Those who understand this passage to refer to the time of the Last Judgment are deceived. AN ECCLESIASTICALL EXPOSITION UPON SAINT LUKE 17.[4]

WHEN THE GLORY OF CHRIST COMES, IT WILL BE SUDDEN AND UNEXPECTED. DESIDERIUS ERASMUS: There is nothing speedier and swifter than lightning, and although it does not actually reach from the east to the west, nevertheless it often seems like it does to us. It certainly comes a long way in a very short time. The lightning comes not out of the heavens but out of the cloudy region. Now, the Lord does not say that the lightning reaches from the east to the west, but he says that it appears in the east and then suddenly shines in the west. . . . But if anyone should be critical and say that it is inappropriate for Christ to allege things that only seem to be, for things that are actually true, we may answer that it is sufficient to apply the way things seem to our eyes to the expression of the sudden and unlooked-for glory of Christ, which is how it will appear to everyone. As soon as we see lightning, we listen for thunder, but when the lightning bursts forth, it is not preceded by any sign: before you can even look for it, it

appears and then is gone. Likewise, the doctrine of the gospel appeared, unlooked-for and beyond all human reason, and was made manifest to the world. AN ECCLESIASTICALL EXPOSITION UPON SAINT MATHEWE 23.[5]

17:26-33 *The Examples of Noah, Lot and Lot's Wife*

THIS EXAMPLE FROM THE PAST IS MEANT TO CONVINCE US. PHILIPP MELANCHTHON: And we should note also how the Lord, in confirming this, does not bring in a similitude but rather a plain example (and such a one which happened to the whole world in the past but was not believed until it actually happened), so that those who will not believe things that will happen in the future may at least be moved by this example which is from the past. The apostle Peter also makes mention of these examples, showing that God made them an example to those who were tempted to live wicked lives. Moses showed sufficiently in Genesis how greatly all things were corrupted in the time of Noah. By this we are taught that the faithful who will lift up their minds to Christ and the hope of his coming will be a very small number. AN ECCLESIASTICALL EXPOSITION UPON SAINT MATHEWE 23.[6]

THE PEOPLE OF THE WORLD SCORN THESE EXAMPLES. THE BOOK OF HOMILIES: The wicked people in the days of Noah only made a mockery of the word of God when Noah told them that God would take vengeance on them for their sins. Therefore the flood came suddenly on them and drowned them, along with the whole world. Lot preached to the Sodomites that unless they repented, both they and their city would be destroyed. They thought his sayings could not possibly be true, so they scorned and mocked his admonition and considered him to be an old,

---

[4]Marlorat, ed., *Catholike and Ecclesiasticall Exposition of the Holy Gospell After S. Marke and Luke*, 275*.

[5]Marlorat, ed., *Catholike and Ecclesiasticall Exposition of the Holy Gospell After S. Mathewe*, 575*.
[6]Marlorat, ed., *Catholike and Ecclesiasticall Exposition of the Holy Gospell After S. Mathewe*, 585*; citing 2 Pet 2:4-10.

doddering fool. But when God had taken Lot, his wife and two daughters from among them by his holy angels, he rained down fire and brimstone from heaven and burned up those scorners and mockers of his holy word. And what respect did Christ's doctrine gain among the scribes and Pharisees? What reward did they give him? The Gospel reports, "the Pharisees, who were lovers of money, scorned him and his teachings." By these examples you see that worldly people scorn the doctrine of their salvation. The wise of the world scorn the doctrine of Christ, because it appears foolish to their understanding. There have always been those who scorn, and there will always be, even to the end of the world, as Saint Peter prophesied: "Scorners will come in the Last Days." Therefore, take heed, my brothers and sisters, take heed that you are not scorners of God's most holy Word: do not provoke him to pour out his wrath on you now, as he did on those scornful and mocking folks. Do not be wilful murderers of your own souls. Turn to God while there is still time for mercy, or else you will repent it in the world to come, when it will be too late, for then there will be judgment without mercy.

This might suffice to admonish us and cause us to revere God's holy Scriptures from now on, but "not everyone has faith." So this will not satisfy and content everyone's mind, but as some people are carnal, they will still continue to abuse the Word carnally to their greater damnation. HOMILY 22: INFORMATION FOR THEM WHICH TAKE OFFENSE AT CERTAIN PLACES OF SCRIPTURE.[7]

WE MUST BE READY, FOR THE END WILL COME UNEXPECTEDLY.

JOHN CALVIN: And now we have the counsel of Christ: the faithful, to avoid being suddenly overwhelmed, should always keep watch, because the day of the Last Judgment will come unexpectedly. Luke alone mentions Sodom, here in the seventeenth chapter, where he takes the occasion, neglecting the calculation of

time, to recite these words of Christ. . . . Thus, now Christ teaches that the last age of the world will certainly be a stupid one, and the people will think of nothing besides their present life and will extend their concerns for a long time, following their usual course of life, as if the world would always remain in that state. The comparisons are most appropriate, because if what then happened was put forward to us, we would no longer be deceived by the view that the same series of events in the world, that we believe perpetually established, would continue uninterrupted. For after three days, when everyone was conducting his usual business in the height of tranquility, the world was drowned by a flood, and five cities were consumed by fire. . . .

Before Luke mentions this, he inserts certain sentences, the first of which, according to Matthew, pertains to the destruction of Jerusalem: "Whoever will be on the rooftop should not go down into his house to remove the possessions." But it is possible that Christ applied the same words to different things. And according to Luke, a warning follows that the disciples should "remember Lot's wife," that is, forgetting those things that are behind, they should strive for the goal of the heavenly calling. For Lot's wife was changed into a pillar of salt because, doubting whether there really was a good reason to leave the city, she looked behind her; this showed that she did not have faith in the prophecy of God. It is also likely that a desire for her home, in which she had rested quietly, made her reluctant. Therefore, because God wanted her to stand as an eternal example, our minds should be strengthened by the steadfastness of faith, so that they will not wither away because of hesitation in the middle of the course. Likewise, they should be formed in perseverance, so that, bidding good-bye to the attractions of this transitory life, they might desire freely and cheerfully to reach heaven. COMMENTARY ON A HARMONY OF THE GOSPELS.[8]

---

[7]*Certain Sermons or Homilies* (1852), 349-50*; alluding to Gen 6–7; 19; 2 Pet 2:6-8; 2 Thess 3:2; quoting Lk 16:14; 2 Pet 3:3.

[8]CO 45:673-74, 675 (cf. CTS 33:156-57, 158-59); citing Phil 3:13; Gen 19:26.

THE WORLD, LIKE SODOM, MUST BE LEFT BEHIND. DIRK PHILIPS: The action of God with Sodom, with the angels and with Lot and his wife is repeated here. For the spiritual Sodom whereby the Lord was crucified is the evil world, full of all haughtiness, all abominations and inhuman uncleanliness. Out of this Sodom will be led and guided by the angels of God all those who with Lot fear God, who are pleasing to him and who are ordained to eternal life. But the world shall pass away with its evil lusts, desires and works, just as Sodom and Gomorrah have passed away. And the unbelievers who with Lot's wife looked back and therefore are not fit for God's kingdom, they remain standing, they will be blinded and hardened by God, and in their perverse mind they will be delivered over so that they shall not escape the punishment of God. THE ENCHIRIDION: CONCERNING SPIRITUAL RESTITUTION.[9]

17:34-37 *Some Will Be Taken, Others Will Be Left*

THE SUDDEN DIVISION OF THE ELECT AND THE DAMNED WILL OCCUR. MARTIN BUCER: He shows here that there will be an amazing choice and that few will be saved at his coming. By these words he thereby admonishes us to watch carefully, that we may be in the number of those who will be received into eternal life. It is as if he should say, "Just as during the time of the flood, only a few were taken up in the ark and saved, and the rest were shut out of the doors and perished, so at the coming of the Son of Man, those who will perish will be divided suddenly from those who will be saved." God will not spare anyone, from the highest to the lowest, for the elect will be taken up and the damned shut into prison. At night, two will be sleeping in bed, and one will be taken for a reward, but the other one will be forsaken. AN ECCLESIASTICALL EXPOSITION UPON SAINT MATHEWE 23.[10]

---

[9]CRR 6:324* (BRN 10:349); citing Gen 19; Rev 11:8; 16:8-9; 1 Jn 2:15-17; 2 Esdr 2:36; 2 Pet 2:6; Acts 28:27; Rom 1:28.

[10]Marlorat, ed., *Catholike and Ecclesiasticall Exposition of the Holy Gospell After S. Mathewe*, 587*.

18:1-14 THE PARABLES OF THE PERSISTENT WIDOW AND HUMBLE TAX COLLECTOR

And he told them a parable to the effect that they ought always to pray and not lose heart. ²He said, "In a certain city there was a judge who neither feared God nor respected man. ³And there was a widow in that city who kept coming to him and saying, 'Give me justice against my adversary.' ⁴For a while he refused, but afterward he said to himself, 'Though I neither fear God nor respect man, ⁵yet because this widow keeps bothering me, I will give her justice, so that she will not beat me down by her continual coming.'" ⁶And the Lord said, "Hear what the unrighteous judge says. ⁷And will not God give justice to his elect, who cry to him day and night? Will he delay long over them? ⁸I tell you, he will give justice to them speedily. Nevertheless, when the Son of Man comes, will he find faith on earth?"

⁹He also told this parable to some who trusted in themselves that they were righteous, and treated others with contempt: ¹⁰"Two men went up into the temple to pray, one a Pharisee and the other a tax collector. ¹¹The Pharisee, standing by himself, prayedᵃ thus: 'God, I thank you that I am not like other men, extortioners, unjust, adulterers, or even like this tax collector. ¹²I fast twice a week; I give tithes of all that I get.' ¹³But the tax collector, standing far off, would not even lift up his eyes to heaven, but beat his breast, saying, 'God, be merciful to me, a sinner!' ¹⁴I tell you, this man went down to his house justified, rather than the other. For everyone who exalts himself will be humbled, but the one who humbles himself will be exalted."

a Or *standing, prayed to himself*

OVERVIEW: The parable of the persistent widow continues the theme of the Last Days. But, these commentators argue, the example of the widow is perhaps even more important in showing Christians how to behave every day, especially in times of adversity. According to Pellikan (following Erasmus), the point of the story is to encourage us in persistent prayer—whether the Last Days are here or not, we should keep on praying to God, even when he does not seem to be listening. After all, if even an unjust judge is eventually "beaten" into helping the woman, as Leigh suggests, how much more is the good and merciful God going to help us? But we must continue to pray no matter how difficult the circumstances or how long it takes God to respond. Nevertheless very few will be like this widow, persevering in prayer and true faith. Sarcerius suggests that many of the faithful will follow false prophets and fake messiahs, while others will not be able to withstand the great suffering. Only those with strong perseverance will

be able to stand fast, like the widow, until Christ comes in glory and justice.

Although the second parable was inspired by the proud and hypocritical Pharisees he saw around him, Jesus also intended this story to offer a lesson on true repentance for all of us. It was, according to our commentators, an opportune time to encourage humility, a chance to remind us not to judge as the world judges. The Pharisees knew their own worth and virtue and took every opportunity to show it to others. But Christ can see into the heart and can recognize both hypocrisy and true repentance. While people could see that the Pharisees were good and that tax collectors were greedy people, Jesus judged the two men in his story in quite the opposite manner. The sinful but repentant tax collector went home justified, but the Pharisee, who thought he had reason to give thanks but not to repent, did not.

But what was the problem here? Why would the Pharisee, who obeyed the law and acted well towards others, need to repent? The English Annotations names the problem "spiritual pride" and insists that it is very dangerous. The Pharisee thanked God for many blessings but still had confidence in his own worth and goodness. He felt that he deserved God's blessings because he was so good on his own. Luther notes that the Pharisee was most likely utterly sincere—Jesus may have portrayed him as a hypocrite, but that does not mean that he was aware of his own hypocrisy, any more than he was aware of his sinful pride. This insight adds another layer to the story—the Pharisee is proud and sinful, but the real problem for him is his inability to see it. That is really the difference between him and the sinful tax collector (nobody is good in this story): the tax collector recognizes and admits his sin. He gives us an example of true confession which requires, as many commentators note, true humility. For only the truly humble will see that they can do nothing for themselves and will instead place all their hope and confidence in God.

18:1-8 Jesus Teaches About Persistent Prayer

CHRISTIANS SHOULD ALWAYS ASK GOD FOR HELP. KONRAD PELLIKAN: In this world saints are always going to have pressure, and so at some time a heavy burden will arise and faith will desert us, therefore it might be possible that the elect could fall away. The Lord Jesus teaches his disciples that in bad times they should not ask another for help but should turn to God and should not try to get revenge or to avoid injury by causing injuries. But if God does not immediately set us free from our affliction, we should not therefore leave off from praying: he will without a doubt hear the prayers of his children and will answer when the time is right—and a delay may result in a greater and holier good! But the wicked will be more heavily oppressed, the more they had convinced themselves that they had the impunity to do whatever they had done. The Lord implanted this precept in their souls by an excellent parable. COMMENTARY IN LUKE 18:1.[1]

LIKE THE WIDOW, WE MUST CONTINUALLY PRAY FOR HELP. JACQUES LEFÈVRE D'ÉTAPLES: This parable proceeds from the one who appears to be lesser to the one who is greater. The city is this world. The judge of injustice is each judge of the world, one who walks according to the flesh, neither honoring God nor attending to the people. The widow is any person who is deprived of her rights. She seeks to be defended from her adversary, fleeing for help to the judge, and now she demands that justice be done for her. She will persevere in entreating that justice be done for her, even by an unjust judge. And because he is annoyed by her and fears that she might insult, blame or say bad things about him, he will protect her and free her from her adversary, providing justice. Now, if the unjust judges are willing to help those who, suffering unjustly, persevere in entreating them, how much more will the highest judge, who is the best and most just, do it? Truly without comparison, he defends and protects those most diligently who are struck down unjustly but who pray day and night to be defended and protected by him, that is, those who persevere in prayer. Therefore they should always be affirming the good and never doing evil or destroying. But are those things not adversaries to us which keep us praying to God continually, that he might defend, protect and rescue us? Why not? For our perpetual adversaries are the flesh, the world and evil spirits, who always fight, press against and strike us—they continually work at taking away all spiritual and eternal goods from us. Therefore, we should always entreat the highest judge, who is able to free us, and not resign our souls, for it says here, "Do not lose heart." IN THE GOSPEL OF LUKE 18.[2]

---

[1]Pellikan, *In Sacrosancta Quatuor Evangelia*, 182-83 (cf. CWE 48:116; LB 7:421).
[2]Lefèvre d'Étaples, *Commentarii Initiatorii in Quatuor Evangelia*, 2:89v.

BY HER CONTINUAL PESTERING, THE WIDOW RECEIVED JUSTICE. EDWARD LEIGH: The judge hears the widow, not out of the fear of God, or in commiseration with her afflictions or even because she had a just cause, which a just judge ought to regard. Instead he was motivated by other reasons: first, because she was troublesome to him, as if he should say, "I would be freed from the clamoring of that importunate woman!" and second, in order that she not weary him by continually pestering him. "Weary me" is literally "beat me down with her blows," and it is a metaphor taken from fighters, who beat their adversaries with their fists or clubs. Likewise, those who are importunate beat the judge's ears with their crying out, as if it were with blows.[3] If the unwearied prayer of a widow leads to a just sentence from an unjust judge, what may the godly not hope from God? ANNOTATIONS UPON SAINT LUKE 18.[4]

FEW WILL REMAIN FAITHFUL IN THE LAST DAYS. ERASMUS SARCERIUS: Christ told his disciples that a little before his coming there would be a great security in the world. Now he tells them that at the same time there will be a great scarcity of faith. . . . God suspends his help for a time, so that of that small group only a few will stand strong in the great affliction. Many false Christs and prophets will lead the holy and faithful into error by accomplishing mighty signs and wonders. No one will escape, except for those who with great patience and long-suffering stand fast looking for the coming of the Lord. And so it is no surprise that Jesus inquires about the number of the faithful that there will be in that day, when he shall not find faith on the earth. For no one will be saved who does not continually pray to the Lord, following the example of the widow, constantly bearing evil in the meantime, until he answers their cry by his coming and ends their calamity and affliction. AN ECCLESIASTICALL EXPOSITION UPON SAINT LUKE 18.[5]

18:9-14 Jesus Tells a Story for the Overconfident

CHRIST USES THIS OPPORTUNITY TO TEACH HUMILITY. JOHN BOYS: There are four kinds of proud people:

1. Arrogant people, who attribute every good thing in themselves to themselves, and not to God.

2. Presumptuous people, who acknowledge that God is the giver of their grace, but because of their own merit.

3. Those who boast of their own eminence, which indeed they do not have.

4. Those who despise others and portray themselves as singular and unique in what they have.

To all these generally but to the last three more principally Christ told this parable. Bad lives occasion good laws, and he that extracted "honey out of the rock" and "oil out of the flinty rock," when he saw some that trusted in themselves as if they were perfect and despised others, gained a good opportunity to commend humility. Humility is such an excellent virtue that all other gifts of grace contend for it, as all the cities of Greece strived for Homer. Temperance makes a challenge to own it, because there is *arduum* and *bonum* in every virtue: the one requires magnanimity and the other humility.[6] Fortitude makes a challenge to own it, because humility overcomes prosperity, which assaults us on the right, and adversity, which fights against us on the left hand. Justice makes a challenge to own it, in that humility gives to God, ourselves and our neighbor whatever is due. Therefore Christ termed humility justice: "it is fitting for us to fulfill all

---

[3]Leigh suggests here to see the writing of Paul of Burgos (1351–1435), a Spanish archbishop and famous convert from Judaism. It is most likely that Leigh means Paul's *Additiones* to the *Postilla* of Nicholas of Lyra.
[4]Leigh, *Annotations upon All the New Testament Philologicall and Theologicall*, 128*.

[5]Marlorat, ed., *Catholike and Ecclesiasticall Exposition of the Holy Gospell After S. Marke and Luke*, 279*; citing Lk 17:26-27; Mt 24:12-13, 22.
[6]Thomas Aquinas, *Summa Theologica* 2.2æ, q. 161, art. 1.

righteousness." That is humility. THE ELEVENTH SUNDAY AFTER TRINITY.[7]

A PHARISEE SEES AND PROCLAIMS HIS OWN GREATNESS. KASPAR VON SCHWENCKFELD: The Pharisees were particular people, as Paul says: "I was a Pharisee." They suppose that no one else is equal to them. It is also the Pharisees who wanted their cleverness, their skill and their philosophy to be seen and to give themselves airs about it. They do not deal in humility, but in everything they seek their own glory, fame and praise in the flesh; however, those things belong only to Christ and are his property. They also contrive, when they deal with something good and right (as they believe), that it is well-known and evident to everyone. But the Lord knows the heart of every person. He perceives or sees deep into the heart. He also recognizes the art of hypocrisy as the inclination of our hearts. But the Lord Christ came only for the sake of sinner, and not for the sake of the righteous. Those who recognize their sins, who repent and cry over them and beat their breasts, like this tax collector, move forward in the improvement of their lives. They do not maliciously persist in their sin. ON THE ELEVENTH SUNDAY AFTER TRINITY, LUKE 18.[8]

THE PUBLICAN HERE, MOST UNUSUALLY, IS RIGHTEOUS. THOMAS BECON: The publicans were just what tax officials are to us—they gather taxes, tolls, customs from the people. But they purchased the office for a certain sum of money, and afterward by robbery, extortion, and other crafty and injurious ways, they made the most money from these means to the great grievance of other people. And therefore of all people they were considered to be the most covetous and thought to be great sinners and wicked, because those who were in those offices robbed and extorted for all they could get and wrongfully

harassed the people by taking from them more than they were due. Therefore it was not very likely that any of them were righteous, and likewise it was also commonly judged that among the Pharisees there were none who were evil. But Christ judges here quite otherwise, pronouncing the publican righteous and the Pharisee a sinner—yes, and in fact a grievous sinner. THE ELEVENTH SUNDAY AFTER TRINITY SUNDAY.[9]

SPIRITUAL PRIDE LEADS TO BLINDNESS. THE ENGLISH ANNOTATIONS: Although he attributed to God's grace all the good he speaks of himself, yet he was not justified. He did not place all his confidence in the free mercy of God through Christ and in humility consider all that he had as a "loss for the sake of Christ," that he might not be found in his pretended righteousness, which was of the law, but rather in what is through faith in Christ. Although he did not proclaim his merit before others but spoke only to God, yet the searcher of hearts condemned that secret pride and confidence in his own merit, which showed itself first in contempt of others (whom he counted as ungodly) and second in magnifying himself as free from the sins of others, and just in doing those things which he claimed. He probably did do those things, and possibly he had done nothing for which he might be reproved before the people, but spiritual pride is very dangerous, even in the most glorious and greatest excellence of human beings. Humility is a safe virtue: leave everything to God, who rewards the holy with plenty and will abundantly crown his own gifts. Be assured that you will lose nothing by this exchange. . . .

He says this as if the vices of others were his virtues. To justify himself, he condemns others and treats them with contempt. And yet he is so much worse than others by how much prouder he is than them. He confesses no faults, but because he thinks of himself as without fault, he casts stones at others. It is as if a sick man would only talk about the parts of his body which were healthy. It

---

[7] Boys, *Exposition of the Dominical Epistles and Gospels*, 3:236-37*; citing Deut 32:13; Mt 3:15.
[8] CS 10:569; citing Acts 23:6; Phil 3:5.

[9] Becon, *New Postill*, 90r-v*.

seems that he praises God, as hypocrites do, only to enhance his view of himself. Hypocrisy is blind at home and too quick-sighted abroad. It is natural for the malicious to judge everyone to be evil whom they hate. But when proud hypocrites criticize the just, God still sees how much more damnable the judge is than those he has condemned. ANNOTATIONS ON THE GOSPEL ACCORDING TO SAINT LUKE 18:11.[10]

THE HYPOCRITE IS FULL OF BEAUTIFUL WORKS. MARTIN LUTHER: Now let's take a look at the other person. He exemplifies the most beautiful works of all. First he thanks God, and he fasts twice a week to honor God. He gives a tenth of all his goods, is upright in his marriage, has never committed adultery, has never done violence against another person or taken what belongs to someone else. If that is not an honorable life, I don't know what is! According to the world's ideals, one could not find fault with him but must rather praise him. Yes, in fact, he does it himself! Then God comes along and says, first, that all this work is nothing but blasphemy. O Lord almighty, what a verdict that is! Nuns and monks would have been shaking in their boots, even though none of them are half as pious as he. Would to God that we had more such hypocrites! So what is he lacking? He does not really know his own heart. So, as you can see, we are our own worst enemies, in that we close our own eyes and hearts. For he tells us how he truly feels. If someone would have asked him, "My dear fellow, do you believe in your heart what you are saying?" he would have sworn that it was entirely true. Now you can see how deeply God's sword cuts, and how it cleaves to the very foundation of the soul. Therefore everything must go to pieces and fall to the ground, and each person must humble himself; otherwise no one can stand before God. SERMON ON THE ELEVENTH SUNDAY AFTER TRINITY (1522).[11]

THE SINNER RECEIVES TRUE ABSOLUTION FROM GOD. CASPAR HUBERINUS: Here we learn about true confession and absolution, namely, that a poor sinner recognizes his sin from his heart, before God, and confesses or laments to God, his Lord in heaven. As David said in the psalm: "I acknowledge my sin and do not cover my iniquity. I say, 'I will confess my transgressions to the Lord'" (he says "the Lord" expressly). Then the proper absolution is when the Lord himself, out of grace, absolves your sins and says that you are free. The holy David also shows this and says, "You, O Lord, forgave me the iniquity of my sins." I say this for the sake of the strong Christians and for the sake of those who are attacked suddenly and distressed in the greatest need, and cannot receive absolution from their priest but are stuck alone in some unhappiness or in their final misery. Now with this I do not want in any way to say that the gracious, comforting absolution of the church's minister is unimportant or means nothing, when it is especially useful and helpful to those with weaker faith. Do not forget that Christ entrusted the apostles with the key to unbind. ON THE ELEVENTH SUNDAY AFTER TRINITY.[12]

THIS EXAMPLE TEACHES US TO HUMBLE OURSELVES BEFORE GOD. RICHARD TAVERNER: My friends, you know well the conclusion and end of this various and diverse prayer: that same publican who came into the church a sinner, by Christ's own sentence and determination went home in the sight of God more just and righteous than the Pharisee who thought himself most righteous. For assuredly whoever advances himself by putting himself forward will be cast down and lowly in the eyes of God. And whoever casts himself down and lowers himself will be high in the eyes of God. And so, good people, let us learn from this parable to humble ourselves and present ourselves as lowly. Let us learn, when we are out of God's favor because of the heinous nature of our sins, to reconcile ourselves again to God through

---

[10]Downame, ed., *Annotations*, Yy2r*; citing Phil 3:6-8; Mt 25:34; Heb 6:10; 10:35; 11:26; 2 Jn 8; Rev 22:12.
[11]*LEA* 3:314 (cf. WA 10,3:300).

---

[12]Huberinus, *Postilla Teütsch*, 2: m7v-m8r; citing Ps 32:5; Jn 21.

appropriate penance and to seek remission through that repentance. ON THE ELEVENTH SUNDAY AFTER TRINITY.[13]

THOSE WHO EXALT THEMSELVES WILL FALL, WHILE THE HUMBLE WILL BE LIFTED UP.
JOHANNES BRENZ: This sentence agrees with the saying of the Virgin Mary: "He has put down the mighty from their thrones and has exalted the humble and meek." And the more general and common this sentence, the more it should be weighed and kept always before our eyes, that in prosperity we may learn to fear God and in adversity to trust in him alone. For what is spoken here is commonly seen to be true, both among people and before God, even from the very definitions of the words, if we properly consider what it means to exalt and what it means to humble ourselves. A person exalts himself before others when he condemns others to make himself look better, criticizes the works of others and only praises and boasts of his own actions. This person is cast down and condemned along with the same sort of people, by God's command. A person humbles himself when in following his calling, he shows himself to be dutiful and lowly before

everyone. Whoever behaves in this way toward others will find himself exalted. Now, a person exalts himself before God when he thinks he can get righteousness by his own power, and not only that, but also all the gifts of God. This is how the Pharisee in the parable exalted himself. This is how Nebuchadnezzar, the king of Babylon, exalted himself. Absalom also exalted himself in this way, by thinking that he was more worthy of the kingdom than his father. Herod also exalted himself when he heard the people shout, "The voice of a God, and not of a man!" But what happened to these men? The same thing that is pronounced in this general sentence: the more highly they exalted themselves, the greater was their fall. And those humble themselves before God who feel their sins, and have a humble spirit and contrite heart for their sins and judge themselves worthy of eternal death. This is not a feigned but a true humility; this is not hypocrisy but true confession. This is how the tax collector humbled himself, when he acknowledged himself to be a sinner and unworthy to lift his eyes up to heaven. AN ECCLESIASTICALL EXPOSITION UPON SAINT LUKE 18.[14]

---

[13]Taverner, *Epistles and Gospelles (Sommer Parte)*, 135r-v*.

[14]Marlorat, ed., *Catholike and Ecclesiasticall Exposition of the Holy Gospell After S. Marke and Luke*, 284*; citing Lk 1:52; Dan 3–4; 2 Sam 15; Acts 12:22.

18:15-17 JESUS AND THE LITTLE CHILDREN

[15]*Now they were bringing even infants to him that he might touch them. And when the disciples saw it, they rebuked them.* [16]*But Jesus called them to him, saying, "Let the children come to me, and do not hinder them, for to such belongs the kingdom of God.* [17]*Truly, I say to you, whoever does not receive the kingdom of God like a child shall not enter it."*

OVERVIEW: This short passage had deep significance in an era when baptism—in particular, whether infants should be baptized—was an important topic of debate. While both Radical and magisterial reformers agree that this is an authoritative and powerful passage, they disagree about its application to children. The magisterial reformers, who had further disputes among themselves about the precise nature and significance of the sacraments, see this passage as clear support of—even a command for—paedobaptism. If our Lord grants his grace to infants, this group would argue, who are we to rob them of the sign and seal of his grace? The Radical reformers see paedobaptism as unwarranted by—even contrary to—Scripture. Yes, Jesus cherishes children, but that does not overturn his command in Matthew 28—as they interpreted it—to teach and *then* baptize. If this passage in Luke means children should be baptized, the Radicals would claim, then we should baptize all things that are brought to the Lord—donkeys, coins, myrrh. These baptismal disputes proved fruitless, since both sides generally argued from predetermined baptismal commitments rather than toward such commitments.

Schwenckfeld, an anomalous reformer, insists that both the magisterial and Radical reformers are wrong; these words about children must be understood spiritually. We become heirs and children of the kingdom through a spiritual rebirth; therefore water baptism is not necessary. Still, very few people accepted Schwenckfeld's doctrine of the internal word, which led him to abandon church assemblies and the use of the sacraments.

18:15-17 Receive the Kingdom Like a Little Child

WE NEED TO LEARN TO JUDGE CHRIST CORRECTLY. MARTIN BUCER: They rebuked the parents who brought the children, as the Evangelist Mark testifies. The apostles were angry and disdainful that Christ should be forced to have dealings with infants—they considered it a reproach to his person that these children were brought forward. And they did not feel that they needed to disguise their attitude (which was in error), for what did this excellent prophet and Son of God have to do with infants? But here we can see that those who esteem and judge Christ according to their carnal reason are perverse judges: by doing so they rob him of his own proper virtues, and under a show of honor they ascribe to him those things which do not after all belong to him. In this way, a great heap of superstitions brought into the world a pretend Christ. Therefore let us learn to judge and esteem him in no other way than he himself has taught and to put no other person on him than his heavenly Father has already done. AN ECCLESIASTICALL EXPOSITION UPON SAINT MATHEWE 19.[1]

CHRIST ADMITS CHILDREN TO HIS PRESENCE AND SALVATION. PHILIPP MELANCHTHON: And Luke says, "By these words our Savior Christ testified that he wanted to have children admitted, and taking them in his arms, he not only embraced

---

[1]Marlorat, ed., *Catholike and Ecclesiasticall Exposition of the Holy Gospell After S. Mathewe*, 425-26*; citing Mk 10:13.

them but also laid his hands on them and blessed them." From this example we may gather that his grace was extended even to infants, and it is no marvel, for because all of the posterity and offspring of Adam were included under the condemnation of death, it is the case that everyone, from the highest to the lowest, would perish, except those whom the Redeemer would deliver. Therefore that embracing which Mark mentions shows us that not only are little ones relevant to Christ but they are also dear to him. For what does it mean to come to Christ, except only to come to life in Christ? AN ECCLESIASTICALL EXPOSITION UPON SAINT MATHEWE 19.[2]

IF JESUS' WORDS SUPPORT PAEDOBAPTISM, THEN EVERYTHING BROUGHT TO CHRIST MUST BE BAPTIZED. PETER WALPOT: The

infant baptizers claim that infant baptism is from Christ. But how can Christ be reconciled with infant baptism, because he indeed knew nothing of such infant baptism? If that were the case, then the desolate abomination and Pharisees would be from Christ, witchcraft would be blessed, and the poor creatures would have been taken in his arms and terrified with cold water. Yes, whoever baptizes a child and says that he stands in God's place and does not obey the command of the Lord, does indeed stand in God's place, but not as Christ, instead as a desolate abomination.

So then, if *come* means "baptize," it is a new German word. And Christ must baptize the donkey in the same manner, too, because he asked for it to be brought, to come to him. He must have also baptized the two blind men who sat by the road and shouted, "Have mercy on us!" For he said, "Bring them here." . . . Yes, everything that was brought to Christ should have been baptized. That would have become a strange spectacle, we would have to let the stone jars, the coin for taxes, gold, frankincense and myrrh be presented for baptism and be baptized. For we find that all these things

and even more were brought to him as well as children. Or if the laying on of hands is supposed to mean "baptize," then he must have baptized the sick, on whom he laid his hands and healed them, and the deaf, too.

But Christ did not baptize children. Nor did his disciples baptize them. There is not even one letter here that could be understood about baptism. Thus, they simply remained unbaptized until they came to [the age] of understanding. What does Christ do to them instead? He wishes them well, embraces them and lays his hands on them. We should leave it at that. We should not be proud and concoct something from our own minds. So it is a false cover. If the children had been brought forward to be baptized—and it was Christ's custom to baptize children—then the disciples would not have objected to it. But whoever brings the children of the flesh to Christ in this way, so that he would obey the children of the rebirth and not come to Christ, is opposed to Christ and is antichrist.

Christ therefore does not say in this passage "to these" but instead "to such" belongs the kingdom of heaven. By this he affirms what he said . . . when he explained and said, "Unless you turn and become like children, you will not enter the kingdom of heaven." Still, we admit that the kingdom of heaven also belongs to infants. But that we should therefore baptize them before they are taught and instructed or inclined to learn—this does not follow. So, let them come when they are grown up, and before that, if they come they should be taught. They may become Christians, once they learn to know Christ. Prior to that they should know how they ought to long for salvation, so that we may give it to those who long for it. THE GREAT ARTICLE BOOK: ON BAPTISM.[3]

JESUS' WORDS ARE A SHIELD AGAINST ANABAPTISTS. JOHN CALVIN: Jesus declares that he wishes to receive children. Indeed, taking them

---

[2]Marlorat, ed., *Catholike and Ecclesiasticall Exposition of the Holy Gospell After S. Mathewe*, 426*.

[3]QGT 12:78-79; citing Mt 21:5; 20:30; Jn 2:8; Mt 22:19; 2:11; Lk 4:40; Mt 9:27; 18:3.

in his arms, he not only embraces but also blesses them by the laying on of hands; from which we infer that his grace is extended even to those who are of that age. And no wonder, because the whole race of Adam is shut up under the sentence of death, all from the least even to the greatest must perish, except those who are rescued by the only Redeemer. To exclude from the grace of redemption those who are of that age would be too cruel; and therefore it is not without reason that we employ this passage as a shield against the Anabaptists.

They refuse baptism to infants, because infants are incapable of understanding that mystery which is sealed by it. We . . . maintain that, because baptism is the pledge and figure of the forgiveness of sins, and likewise of adoption by God, it ought not to be denied to infants, whom God adopts and washes with the blood of his Son. Their objection, that repentance and newness of life are also figured by it, is easily answered. Infants are renewed by the Spirit of God, according to the capacity of their age, until that power which was concealed within them grows by degrees and becomes fully manifest at the proper time. Again, when they argue that there is no other way in which we are reconciled to God and become heirs of adoption than by faith, we admit this concerning adults, but, with respect to infants, this passage demonstrates it to be false. Certainly, the laying on of hands was not a trifling or empty sign, and the prayers of Christ were not idly cast into the breeze. But he could not present the infants solemnly to God without giving them purity. And for what did he pray for them, but that they might be received among children of God? From this it follows that they were renewed by the Spirit to the hope of salvation.

In short, by embracing them, he testified that they were reckoned by Christ among his flock. And if they were partakers of the spiritual gifts, which baptism figures, it is unreasonable that they should be deprived of the outward sign. It is presumption and sacrilege to drive far from the fold of Christ those whom he cherishes in his bosom, and to shut the door and exclude as strangers those whom he does not wish to be forbidden to come to him. COMMENTARY ON A HARMONY OF THE GOSPELS.[4]

THE CHILDREN ARE ONLY THE SPIRITUAL CHILDREN.

KASPAR VON SCHWENCKFELD: First: the words of Christ, "to such belong the kingdom of heaven," are not alphabet letters but are spirit and life. Therefore they explain to us spiritual business through a material image. We see this in John 6: "The word which I speak to you is spirit and life, but there are some among you who do not believe," says the Lord. Therefore then such words of Christ about the children require not a material judgment but a spiritual one. And while the kingdom of God is not material but spiritual, so it follows that likewise the children of the kingdom are spiritual, and so the Scripture speaks of them—the spiritual must become righteous. Thus the saying, "to such belong the kingdom of heaven," must be understood not of the children of the flesh but of the children of rebirth, who also can alone understand properly the secrets of the kingdom of God. As we read in Matthew 13, "To you has been given that you perceive the secrets of the heavenly kingdom, but to those who are on the outside it has not been given."

Second: These words of Christ were written for the good of those who belong. They are not for the small children, who can neither read nor understand them, but they are written down for the comfort of the faithful. What is written down for us is written to teach us. We are given hope through the patience and comfort of the writing; therefore, it should also be interpreted and understood alone as referring to the children of faith. A CHRISTIAN REFLECTION UPON THE SAYING: "LET THE CHILDREN COME TO ME."[5]

THE CHILDREN ARE NATURAL CHILDREN.

MARTIN LUTHER: Without a doubt this was written about natural children, and it is wrong

---

[4]CTS 32:390-91* (CO 45:535-36).
[5]CS 10:937; quoting Jn 6:63-64; Mt 13:11; alluding to Rom 15:4.

when people want to explain Christ's word as if he had meant spiritual children, who are small because of their humility. These were bodily small children, whom Luke calls "infants."[6] On them his blessing was placed, and about them he says that the kingdom of heaven is theirs. What do we want to say here? Do we want to say that they were without their own faith and that the other passage is false: "Whoever does not believe will be condemned"? Then Christ is also lying or shadowboxing when he says that the kingdom of heaven is theirs, and is not speaking seriously about the true kingdom of heaven. Interpet these words of Christ as you please, we have [to conclude] that children are to be brought to Christ and are not to be hindered; when they are brought to him, he compels us to believe that he blesses them and gives them the kingdom of heaven, as he does for these children. THE CHURCH POSTIL (1540): THIRD SUNDAY AFTER EPIPHANY.[7]

BE LIKE CHILDREN! DESIDERIUS ERASMUS: Let this example be offered to all, so they may know how progress is to be made. Children know no deceit, they know no contempt, they know no striking back, they know no repaying of insults, they know no greed, they know no self-seeking; their innocence is uncompromised, their simplicity is uncompromised. I tell you, the kingdom of God welcomes only those transformed to this image. PARAPHRASE ON THE GOSPEL OF LUKE 18:17.[8]

---

[6]*Infantes*; the Greek is *ta brephe*

[7]LW 76:262* (WA 17,2:83; E2 11:66-67); citing Lk 18:15; Mk 16:16.
[8]CWE 48:121 (LB 7:423).

18:18-30 THE RICH RULER

¹⁸And a ruler asked him, "Good Teacher, what must I do to inherit eternal life?" ¹⁹And Jesus said to him, "Why do you call me good? No one is good except God alone. ²⁰You know the commandments: 'Do not commit adultery, Do not murder, Do not steal, Do not bear false witness, Honor your father and mother.'" ²¹And he said, "All these I have kept from my youth." ²²When Jesus heard this, he said to him, "One thing you still lack. Sell all that you have and distribute to the poor, and you will have treasure in heaven; and come, follow me." ²³But when he heard these things, he became very sad, for he was extremely rich. ²⁴Jesus, seeing that he had become sad, said, "How difficult it is for those who have wealth to enter the kingdom of God! ²⁵For it is easier for a camel to go through the eye of a needle than for a rich person to enter the kingdom of God." ²⁶Those who heard it said, "Then who can be saved?" ²⁷But he said, "What is impossible with man is possible with God." ²⁸And Peter said, "See, we have left our homes and followed you." ²⁹And he said to them, "Truly, I say to you, there is no one who has left house or wife or brothers[a] or parents or children, for the sake of the kingdom of God, ³⁰who will not receive many times more in this time, and in the age to come eternal life."

a Or wife or brothers and sisters

OVERVIEW: In this passage Jesus clearly addresses money and material wealth, but what does it mean for us? Our commentators disagree. The Hutterite bishop Peter Walpot takes Jesus' words literally and insists that Christ means that we should turn away from our possessions, which are a barrier to Christian discipleship. The other (magisterial) commentators, however, agree that the statement needs further interpretation. Melanchthon notes that "perfection" consists of not only supporting the poor, but more importantly imitating Christ's example—no easy task. He and other magisterial reformers suggest that Christ did not really condemn riches or rich people. After all, God created riches, so they are good in themselves. (In fact, many of the important men of the Bible— Abraham, Isaac, Jacob, David, Solomon—were wealthy.) The real problem here, for them, is love of and attachment to riches or possessions, or, even more generally, all worldly things. Riches can give pleasure, allow us to indulge ourselves and generally distract us from other realities, especially God's will. They can blind people into thinking that everything we need is here and that we can create our own happiness. As the authors of the Book of Homilies suggest, we need to set our heart and desire on Christ and our hope of everlasting life, rather than on material things. Attachment to this world and its things is a danger for all of us, not just the rich, which is why the people worried that Christ's words meant that no one could be saved. While Walpot demands that we need to rid ourselves of all private possessions, others suggest that we need to rest in God's grace. Only then will we be able to refocus our hearts and love God and his will, not the enticements of the world.

18:18-23 How Can a Rich Person Inherit Eternal Life?

THE MAN WAS STOPPED BY HIS TRUST IN WORKS. AUGUSTIN MARLORAT: Just like before, our Savior provides an example of simplicity and modesty to his disciples. In the young man who desires perfect godliness but is laden with riches, he sets before their eyes how difficult it is for those who give themselves to riches to come to the true and everlasting life. . . . Luke says that he was a ruler, that is, one set over the people in authority, and not one of the common sort. It is true that riches bring honor, but he also seems to have been considered a grave and honest man. For if one weighs and considers the circumstances, although he was called a young man, it is likely that he was of the number of those who led a godly and honest life. He did not come craftily and deceitfully, which was the manner of the scribes, but rather with a mind desirous to learn. He declares this by both his words and by the bowing of his knee, reverencing Christ as a faithful teacher. But again, a blind trust in works stopped him, so that he could not profit from Christ, at whose hands he was so desirous to learn. Similarly, we see various people today who do not have evil intentions, but although they may have an outward show of godliness, they do not have the sweet taste of the gospel. AN ECCLESIASTICALL EXPOSITION UPON SAINT MATHEWE 19.[1]

GOD IS THE AUTHOR OF ALL TRUE GOODNESS. JOHN DONNE: Our Savior Christ here undertakes the further improvement of this disciple who is disposed to learn, and by a fair method leads him to the true end, the good end, and by good ways, to consummate goodness. . . . When this man called him "good master," Christ said, "No one is good but God," and when this man asked him, "What good thing should I do?" then Christ said, "Why do you ask me, whom you think to be a mere man, what is goodness? There is no one good but God." If you seek to understand goodness from a human being, you must look out for a person who is also God. So that was Christ's method: to bring this man by these holy insinuations, by these approaches and degrees to a knowledge that he was true God and so was the Messiah who was expected. *Nihil est falsitas, nisi cum esse putatur, quod non est*: There is no falsehood unless what does not exist is thought to exist.[2] All error consists in taking things to be

less or more than they really are. Christ was pleased to save this man from this error and bring him to know what he truly was—that he was God. Therefore Christ does not rebuke this man by any sort of denial that he was good, for Christ also makes that addition to himself, "I am the good Shepherd." God also does not forbid that those good parts which are in human beings can be celebrated with appropriate praise. We see that when God saw that anything was good, he said so—he uttered it, he declared it, first of the light, and then of other creatures. God did not want to be the origin or example of smothering the due praise of good actions. Surely a person has no good in himself if he cannot praise the goodness in other people.

But Christ's purpose was also that this praise, this recognition, this testimony of his goodness might be carried higher and referred to the only true author of it, that is, to God. SERMON 14, PREACHED AT WHITEHALL, MARCH 4, 1624.[3]

WORKS OF CHARITY REVEAL WHETHER OR NOT ONE IS RIGHTEOUS. PHILIPP MELANCHTHON: Now one might ask why Christ did not mention the commandments of the first table and only brought in those things which are in the second table. We answer that it was done because every person's mind may be discerned better by the duties of charity. For the truth of the first table is not so easily perceived in a person, because obedience to it was for the most part either in the affection of the heart or in ceremonies. The affection of the heart does not appear externally, and every day hypocrites give themselves over to ceremonies, but the works of charity are such that thereby we testify and declare true and perfect righteousness. No one should think, however, that because Christ answered out of the second table that it is somehow more excellent than the first. He is not speaking here of its estimation or excellence but rather of the knowledge of a person's righteousness, which can be more clearly seen by an observa-

---

[1]Marlorat, ed., *Catholike and Ecclesiasticall Exposition of the Holy Gospell After S. Mathewe*, 427*.
[2]Augustine, *Confessions* 7.15 (NPNF 1:111).

[3]Donne, *Works*, 1:280-81*; citing Jn 10:11, 14.

tion of how one follows the second table rather than the first. An Ecclesiasticall Exposition upon Saint Mathewe 19.[4]

Our Treasure Comes from Bearing Christ's Cross. Philipp Melanchthon: That is to say: "Then you will receive eternal life, which you declare that you so greatly desire to have." In order that the young man might not think that he would be deprived of goods if he would give them to the poor, our Savior Christ adjoins this utility and profit to the commandment. But he speaks by imitation, as if he should say: "You think that you have treasure because you are rich, and you covetously embrace it, not intending to give it up lightly; but if you would listen to me, you would rather seek to have treasure in heaven and to be rich in heavenly things rather than earthly things." . . . Therefore perfection consists not only in selling all that we have and giving to the poor but also in following Christ in bearing his cross and in mortifying the perverse and crooked disposition of the flesh. An Ecclesiasticall Exposition upon Saint Mathewe 19.[5]

The Christian Life Requires Denying Worldly Desires. Edwin Sandys: It is not enough to deny impiety, unless we also deny our fleshly lusts. If we look into our evil and corrupt nature, we will find nothing but what leads us away from Christ, nothing but rebellion against the Spirit, distrust in the providence of almighty God, joy and delight in earthly things, blindness of mind and hardness of heart. We must mortify all of this and shake it off; we must entirely relinquish our own wills and submit ourselves wholly to the will of God. . . . But this is only the entrance to Christianity, and yet how few will there be who even come this far! The rich young man in the Gospel seemed to be very far along in this way, but Christ discovered his true affection and showed

that he had not denied himself, and therefore was not a fit disciple for him. It made him pensive and heavy-hearted to think of leaving such great possessions and of weaning his heart so soon from the world. He would have been content to deny impiety, but Christ also wanted him to deny worldly concupiscence. "For the grace of God has appeared," says the apostle, "bringing salvation for all people, teaching us to deny impiety and worldly desires and to live self-controlled, upright and godly lives in the present age."

This is the way in which all those who desire to travel along with Christ and be numbered among his people must follow him. This is the door of entrance into the church. After we have entered and been received as his traveling companions, just as we followed him thus far by believing the gospel and by "denying impiety and worldly lusts," so we must continue to follow him by walking with him as our example. We must purge ourselves even "as he is pure" and show forth "the virtues of him who called [us] out of darkness into his marvelous light." A Sermon Preached at Paul's Cross.[6]

18:24-30 *All Things Are Possible with God*

We Are All Chained to Earthly Desires. Desiderius Erasmus: By these words of Christ, the hearers understood generally that no one could be saved, although he spoke specifically only of a rich man. And they did well, for they perceived that the same thing which would hinder a rich person from entering into the kingdom of heaven would also be a barrier to all mortals, no matter how poor they might be. All people, whether poor or rich, have one disease of mind, namely, to be willing to forsake those things which are present and to desire those things which they do not have. The hearts of both rich and poor depend on creatures who have no intelligence or affection in heavenly things. They knew, therefore, by the aid of the Spirit that they themselves had not as of yet put

---

[4]Marlorat, ed., *Catholike and Ecclesiasticall Exposition of the Holy Gospell After S. Mathewe*, 429-30*.
[5]Marlorat, ed., *Catholike and Ecclesiasticall Exposition of the Holy Gospell After S. Mathewe*, 431-32*.

[6]Sandys, *Sermons*, 374-75*; citing Tit 2:11-12; 1 Jn 3:3; 1 Pet 2:9.

away these affections entirely, and that they themselves were tied with the same chain and fetters with which that rich man was tied, except that the Lord lifted them up from earthly cares which freed them. An Ecclesiasticall Exposition upon Saint Mathewe 19.[7]

Do Not Doubt the Truth of God's Word or Sacraments. The Book of Homilies: If you doubt that there is such great wealth and happiness made for you, call to your mind that that is why you have received into your own possession the everlasting Truth, our Savior Jesus Christ, to confirm for your conscience the truth of this whole matter. You have received him if in true faith and repentance of heart you have received him, and if for the purpose of amendment you have received him as an everlasting gauge or pledge of your salvation. You have received his body which was once broken and his blood which was shed for the remission of your sin. You have received his body so that you might have within you the Father, the Son and the Holy Spirit—to dwell within you, to endow you with grace, to strengthen you against your enemies and to comfort you with their presence. You have received his body to endow you with everlasting righteousness and to assure you of the everlasting bliss and life of your soul. For "together with Christ" by true faith you are made alive again, Saint Paul says, from the death of sin to the life of grace, and in hope translated from corporal and everlasting death to the everlasting life of glory in heaven, on which your thoughts should now focus and where you should set your heart and desire. Doubt not of the truth of this matter, no matter how great and high these things might be. It is appropriate for God to do no little deeds, however impossible they may seem to you. Pray to God that you may have faith to perceive this great mystery of Christ's resurrection, and that by faith you may certainly believe that nothing is impossible with God. Only bring faith to Christ's holy Word

and sacrament. Let your repentance show your faith, and let the amendment and the obedience of your heart to God's law hereafter declare your true belief. Homily 26: Of the Resurrection of Our Savior Jesus Christ for Easter Day.[8]

Give Up Earthly Possessions to Gain Heavenly Rewards. Peter Walpot: Peter said, "See, we have left everything behind and followed you." Likewise, a disciple of the Lord can say the same today. The Lord said, "Anyone who has left behind their house, brothers, sisters, father or mother, spouse or children, or fields for the sake of my name, will receive it a hundredfold and will gain eternal life." Adam's fall was that he wanted something different from what God wanted, and he inclined his heart toward what is created and thereby scorned his creator. Likewise, all people fall along with Adam in loving what is created. But Christ wants us to turn away from this creaturely love back toward his Father; he comes, calls for repentence and says, "You should give up everything that people have loved more than God, and surrender it for God's sake—turn your heart from what is created and fasten it again on God."

You may see here that he does not say, "Stay attached to your home, your farm and your possessions." Those things really get in the way of Christian discipleship and can also prevent the word from remaining active and being fruitful. So someone might say that he wants to teach you a good method or way by which you might keep the fruits of the earth for a long time, but more importantly, what will you give up so that you can enjoy these fruits uninjured for many years? But here Christ teaches how you may keep everything that you have into eternity well-received as a heavenly treasure, not merely the outward goods, but also rather how your body and soul might be received in eternity. The Great Article Book: On Peace and Joint Property.[9]

---

[7]Marlorat, ed., *Catholike and Ecclesiasticall Exposition of the Holy Gospell After S. Mathewe*, 435*.

[8]*Certain Sermons or Homilies* (1852), 406-7*; citing Eph 2:1-2, 5-6.
[9]QGT 12:190.

CHRISTIANS ARE HAPPIER, EVEN WITH FEWER THINGS. MARTIN BUCER: When he says "a hundredfold," he means that we shall have an infinite amount of pleasure in using that small quantity which the Lord has given us for this present life, even while being persecuted—much more than we had with the abundance of those things which we enjoyed before we knew the gospel. For the children of God esteem the knowledge of the gospel so much that they would not change it for the whole world. Furthermore, because those who fear the Lord will want for nothing that is good, and all things needful will be given to those who seek the kingdom of God and its righteousness, even if Christians are banished from their homes and are left destitute of necessary things, even then they will lack nothing which they might need or which might be profitable to them. In the meantime, they have learned from Saint Paul to be content with those things that they have: they know how to be low and how to be raised up, they know how to be full and they know how to be hungry, both how to have plenty and how to suffer need. AN ECCLESIASTICALL EXPOSITION UPON SAINT MATHEWE 19.[10]

---

[10]Marlorat, ed., *Catholike and Ecclesiasticall Exposition of the Holy Gospell After S. Mathewe*, 439-40*; citing Ps 33; Mt 6:19-21, 33; Phil 4:10-12.

18:31-43 SPIRITUAL AND PHYSICAL BLINDNESS

³¹And taking the twelve, he said to them, "See, we are going up to Jerusalem, and everything that is written about the Son of Man by the prophets will be accomplished. ³²For he will be delivered over to the Gentiles and will be mocked and shamefully treated and spit upon. ³³And after flogging him, they will kill him, and on the third day he will rise." ³⁴But they understood none of these things. This saying was hidden from them, and they did not grasp what was said.

³⁵As he drew near to Jericho, a blind man was sitting by the roadside begging. ³⁶And hearing a crowd going by, he inquired what this meant. ³⁷They told him, "Jesus of Nazareth is passing by." ³⁸And he cried out, "Jesus, Son of David, have mercy on me!" ³⁹And those who were in front rebuked him, telling him to be silent. But he cried out all the more, "Son of David, have mercy on me!" ⁴⁰And Jesus stopped and commanded him to be brought to him. And when he came near, he asked him, ⁴¹"What do you want me to do for you?" He said, "Lord, let me recover my sight." ⁴²And Jesus said to him, "Recover your sight; your faith has made you well." ⁴³And immediately he recovered his sight and followed him, glorifying God. And all the people, when they saw it, gave praise to God.

OVERVIEW: It is a challenge to people who believe that Jesus is the Son of God, whether in the sixteenth or the twenty-first century, to understand how people who walked and talked with him every day could not easily see that he was divine. It is especially difficult to fathom how his disciples, who had chosen to follow him, could have such a hard time understanding and accepting the repeated explanations that Jesus gave of his upcoming suffering and death. Of course, many people kept company with him because they had great expectations of his soon-to-be-established earthly kingdom, but even his closest associates, the Twelve, were unable to understand what he said to them regarding his persecution and death. Our commentators remind us that Jesus wanted to explain things to them clearly so that they would be prepared for the events that would begin in Jerusalem and not be overwhelmed by fear, but he also wanted to confirm by his prophetic knowledge that he was God, so that their faith in him as the Messiah would not be diminished by his dishonorable death. But the Twelve did not understand him. They were, first, blinded by human reason, which could not understand how the Son of God should be ridiculed, abused and killed, and that his suffering and death should somehow obtain for us glory and life—it was too illogical. Only those who are spiritually minded can understand such things. Second, the disciples were too wedded to a wrong opinion—that Jesus would begin an earthly kingdom—to understand and accept this quite different portrayal of events. Brenz notes that along with being misled by their wrong opinions, their ignorance could also be explained by fear, which made them incapable of understanding, at least at that time. But finally, the reformers suggest, they did not understand because their faith was not strong enough; they simply did not believe what he told them. Their spiritual blindness led Jesus to attempt to establish for them yet again who he was by miraculously healing the man's physical blindness.

In so many ways, these interpreters affirm, this blind man is a good example for us all—his solid faith in Jesus as the Messiah, his prayer, his joy and alacrity when he is called and particularly in his response after he is healed, for he followed Jesus, praising God. Significantly, all those who witnessed the miracle also praised God, which shows that our lives are mirrors for others, as Spangenberg remarks. The man who was blind is shown to have deeper, clearer vision than most of us, who, Marlorat suggests, prefer to remain among worldly filth instead of Jesus' friendship. The man was truly saved by his faith—despite not having been a follower of Jesus, nor having heard him preach—for he could see by the Spirit long before the sight was restored to his eyes.

18:31-33 *Jesus Predicts His Death and Resurrection*

JESUS TRIES AGAIN TO EXPLAIN HIS DEATH. PHILIPP MELANCHTHON: Now the time of his passion was at hand, the time of darkness and offense, and this was the last journey that he made to Jerusalem. But the disciples who followed him were astonished and afraid, for they were "going up to Jerusalem, and Jesus was walking ahead of them." Therefore, although earlier they had been admonished and told what the Lord's end should be, what he had often spoken and explained to them did not profit them at all, and so he now repeated the whole summary again from the beginning to the end. He also exhorted them to constancy, so that they would not fall away as soon as they were tempted. He confirmed them in two different ways: first, he showed them clearly what was to come, in order to guard and fortify them, so that a sudden or unlooked for challenge might not cause them to faint; second, by the essence of the cross, he set before them a show of his deity, so that they would be persuaded that he was the Son of God, and therefore the conquerer of death, and that they might not become discouraged by the upcoming events. Finally, he confirmed them by explaining to them the resurrection, which would shortly follow his death. AN ECCLESIASTICALL EXPOSITION UPON SAINT MATHEWE 20.[1]

THE GOSPEL SHOWS CLEARLY WHAT THE PROPHETS FORETOLD. JOHN BOYS: As the painter at the beginning draws his picture roughly with a coal, then accurately with a pencil and then exactly with radiant colors, so the Holy Spirit in the prophets and Old Testament shadowed Christ's passion obscurely, but in the New, paints it, as it were, plainly to life. The two Testaments are two coins bearing the same king's image, although not of the same stamp; for because all things written by the prophets of the Son of Man are now fulfilled, our Savior's picture which is engraven in the Gospel is more full and clear than that imprinted in the law. Now God has shown us the light of his face. Therefore let us search the Scripture, for that is the way to Christ, and Christ is the way to God....

Jesus foretold the manner of his suffering particularly, so that his disciples might see that as God he did foresee these things and that they might be strengthened at his cross, when they would finally understand all things to be fulfilled which they had been told by Christ and which were foretold by the prophets. For it was foretold that he should be betrayed, mocked, spat on, scourged and put to death. QUINQUAGESIMA SUNDAY.[2]

18:34 *The Disciples Do Not Understand*

THE DISCIPLES DID NOT UNDERSTAND THAT LIFE WOULD COME THROUGH DEATH. JOHANN BAUMGART (POMARIUS): Therefore we should not become fixed like Lot's wife or stay behind in the valley like Abraham's donkey, becoming rooted in the earthly. Rather, our hearts and souls should be lifted up to the mountains of Israel, and our thoughts, desires and senses should spring up in the heights to heaven. However, this is heavy and bitter for the old Adam, with his fear and lack of understanding, as we see here with the disciples. For the disciples could hardly understand how it would all happen, how the Son of God would be ridiculed, abused, crucified and killed, and that through such suffering and humiliation, honor should be received, and that through his death, life would be given. Likewise our blind reason can

---

[1] Marlorat, ed., *Catholike and Ecclesiasticall Exposition of the Holy Gospell After S. Mathewe*, 443-44*; citing Mk 10:32.

[2] Boys, *Exposition of the Dominical Epistles and Gospels*, 1:293-94*; citing Lk 10:35; Ps 67:1; 41:9; 69:7, 12, 22; Is 50:6; 53:5; Ps 22:17.

hardly understand that it will also come to pass that those who are the children of God, his sons and daughters who are praised as "blessed," endure the most abuse, ridicule and crosses and must come through dishonor to honor, through suffering to glory, through death to life. Therefore, just as God announced his Son's suffering through the holy Scripture, so he also warned us, his sons and daughters, that everyone who would live a blessed life must suffer persecution, must carry a cross and must enter the kingdom of God through great affliction. GOSPEL ON QUINQUAGESIMA.[3]

THE DISCIPLES WERE WEAK AND COULD NOT UNDERSTAND. JOHANNES BRENZ: This dullness and this ignorance were caused by the fact that the disciples were blinded by the idea of the carnal kingdom of Christ, and so they could not understand any of these things which were prophesied about Christ, his sufferings and afflictions. This shows us the weakness of the human intellect when it is infected with a wrongheaded opinion. Some argue that the disciples were made so afraid by the preaching about afflictions that they went out of their minds and understood nothing for a little while. This shows us how weak human nature is. The Lord is never absent; he reaches out his hand to us, but we will not accept it. Nevertheless, we can see that this warning was of benefit to the disciples. Even if at first it did not benefit them, later they began to remember what Jesus had said, so it was not entirely unprofitable. Therefore we should not be discouraged if at first we do not receive any benefit from the Word of God, for in time it will have its effect on us. AN ECCLESIASTICALL EXPOSITION UPON SAINT LUKE 18.[4]

THE APOSTLES WERE LACKING IN FAITH. RICHARD TAVERNER: Truly, good people, these words were marvelous and very strange to the disciples, that is, that the true Son of God would suffer so many torments, horrors and shame, and at the hands of his own people. But surely it was also a marvel that the apostles could not understand any of it, and the words were hidden from them. And now, why did the apostles understand nothing of what he said? What was the cause of their ignorance and blindness? No doubt it was lack of faith. They were not yet rooted and confirmed in faith, and for that reason they could not perceive how he, who was the true Son of the everlasting Father, should suffer death so shamefully and be treated so spitefully by the people. Therefore, considering their weakness and lack of faith, and in order that he might confirm and strengthen them in faith, our Lord decided to show them a useful token and miracle as he approached the city of Jericho. THE GOSPEL ON QUINQUAGESIME.[5]

18:35-39 The Blind Beggar Shouts to Jesus for Help

THE BLIND MAN CONFIDENTLY CALLS ON JESUS. JOHANN SPANGENBERG: That is a fine example of faith. And how did he come to such faith? Without a doubt he must have heard how Christ was a very friendly person who would not refuse his help to anyone. From such reports he draws a strong confidence in Christ and believes that Christ will not leave him without hope. Therefore he calls on the heavenly Doctor: "Jesus, Son of David, have mercy on me." What is he doing with these words? He teaches us how we should pray properly in faith and who we should call on in our need. And with his words he confesses that Christ is true God and true man. GOSPEL ON QUINQUAGESIMA.[6]

SPIRITUAL INTERPRETATION OF THE BLIND MAN. MARTIN LUTHER: This blind man signifies the spiritually blind, which is each person born from Adam who does not see or know the kingdom

---

[3]Baumgart, *Postilla*, 74r-v, citing Gen 19:26; 22:5; Ezek 36, esp. Ezek 36:1, 4, 8; Mk 10:32; Mt 5:11-12; 2 Tim 3:12. Quinquagesima Sunday, or *Esto Mihi* (Ps 30 Vg), is the last Sunday before Lent.
[4]Marlorat, ed., *Catholike and Ecclesiasticall Exposition of the Holy Gospell After S. Marke and Luke*, 285-86*.

[5]Taverner, *Epistles and Gospelles (Wynter Parte)*, 81r-82v*.
[6]Spangenberg, *Postilla* (1582), LXXIIIv.

of God. It is grace that he feels and knows his blindness and desires to be freed from it. They are holy sinners who sense their faults and sigh for grace.

He sits along the road and begs; that is, he sits among the teachers of the law and desires help. Begging means that he must struggle with works alone and have recourse only to them. The people pass by and leave him sitting there; that is, the people of the law are noisy and make themselves heard with their doctrine of works; they tromp before Christ and make Christ follow them.

He hears Christ; that is, when a heart hears about the gospel and faith, it calls and cries and has no rest until it comes to Christ. Those who would silence and scold him are the teachers of works who want to suffocate and quiet the doctrine and reputation of faith, but they stir up hearts all the more. The gospel is such that the more it is restrained, the more it increases. The Church Postil (1540): Quinquagesima Sunday.[7]

18:40-43 Jesus Heals Him, and the People Rejoice

The Blind Man's Joy Is an Example for Us.

Augustin Marlorat: With these words, the blind man conceived such a hope that, casting aside his cloak which protected him from the cold, he ran to Jesus. In this action we should consider the cheerfulness of the blind man, and diligently note it. Whenever we are called to Christ, we do not cast off our cloak, we do not leap for joy, nor do we run to him, but rather we turn our backs, suggest a different time, stand still, make excuses, wallow along in the darkness. We would rather keep our filthy cloak and beg alms from this world than receive the blessed light of Jesus, which includes the whole state of felicity. If this man cast away his cloak for the joy of his corporal sight, what should we not cast off to receive and possess.Christ, the most comfortable and blessed light? An Ecclesiasticall Exposition upon Saint Mathewe 20.[8]

The Blind Man Revealed His Great Faith.

Philipp Melanchthon: Christ was not ignorant of what the man wanted, but the crowd did not yet know that he desired so great a thing, something which so greatly excelled human power. They thought rather that he was just asking Jesus for alms, and so Christ asked the man what he wanted, that he might make an open declaration of it, that is, that he might show what a great faith and trust he had in him, whose help he requested with such a great cry. For in the quality and largeness of the petition, the quality and largeness of his faith also appeared. An Ecclesiasticall Exposition upon Saint Mathewe 20.[9]

The Blind Man Was Justified by Faith.

John Calvin: By the word *faith* we should understand not so much a confidence in the recovering of his sight but a higher conviction, that is, that the blind man here acknowledged Jesus to be the Messiah who was promised by God. Nor should we suppose that this was just some confused notion, for we have seen from the first that his confession was taken from the law and the prophets. It was not at all by chance that the blind man bestowed on Christ the name of the Son of David, but rather he esteemed him as the one who was to come, having been taught by the divine prophecies. Now Christ ascribes it to faith that the blind man receives sight, because although the power and grace of God sometimes also come to unbelievers, nevertheless no one rightly and profitably enjoys his benefits unless he receives them through faith. On the contrary, for unbelievers, the use of the gifts of God is truly not beneficial, but is rather even harmful. That is why this "wellness" that Christ mentions does not mean the external health alone but also includes the health and welfare of the soul. It is as if Christ had said that it was by faith that the blind man achieved that God was well-disposed

---

[7]LW 76:355* (WA 17,2:178; E² 11:107).
[8]Marlorat, ed., *Catholike and Ecclesiasticall Exposition of the Holy*

Gospell After S. Mathewe, 455-56*.
[9]Marlorat, ed., *Catholike and Ecclesiasticall Exposition of the Holy Gospell After S. Mathewe*, 456*.

to him, and his prayer was answered. And if it was in regard to his faith that God thought the blind man worthy of his grace, it follows that he was justified by faith. COMMENTARY ON A HARMONY OF THE GOSPELS.[10]

THE FORMERLY BLIND MAN PRAISES GOD.
JOHANN SPANGENBERG: And what does the blind man do after he can see? He follows after Christ and praises God, and all the people who saw it happen also glorify God. As soon as the blind man realizes the goodness of God, he cannot contain himself but breaks forth, with words and actions, following Christ and praising God. And because

the other people also saw and heard what happened, they did the same. And so we can see that a Christian life should be a mirror for all other people, to show them true Christian conduct and life, as Christ said in Matthew 5: "And let your light shine before the people, that they may see your good deeds and praise your Father in heaven." And God also looks out for this: that we praise him for his benefits and thank him without ceasing, as this blind man and the rest of the people did here. And who is the blind man? We poor people are the blind man—may God also allow us to be enlightened with his divine Word and Spirit! GOSPEL ON QUINQUAGESIMA SUNDAY.[11]

---

[10]CTS 32:432* (CO 45:562).

[11]Spangenberg, *Postilla* (1582), LXXIXr; quoting Mt 5:16.

19:1-10 ZACCHAEUS THE TAX COLLECTOR

He entered Jericho and was passing through.
²And behold, there was a man named Zacchaeus.
He was a chief tax collector and was rich. ³And he
was seeking to see who Jesus was, but on account of
the crowd he could not, because he was small in
stature. ⁴So he ran on ahead and climbed up into a
sycamore tree to see him, for he was about to pass
that way. ⁵And when Jesus came to the place, he
looked up and said to him, "Zacchaeus, hurry and
come down, for I must stay at your house today."

⁶So he hurried and came down and received him
joyfully. ⁷And when they saw it, they all grumbled,
"He has gone in to be the guest of a man who is a sin-
ner." ⁸And Zacchaeus stood and said to the Lord,
"Behold, Lord, the half of my goods I give to the poor.
And if I have defrauded anyone of anything, I
restore it fourfold." ⁹And Jesus said to him, "Today
salvation has come to this house, since he also is a
son of Abraham. ¹⁰For the Son of Man came to seek
and to save the lost."

OVERVIEW: The case of Zacchaeus the tax collector appears to affirm what Jesus said earlier, that it is difficult if not impossible for a rich person to enter the kingdom of heaven, but nothing is impossible with God. But this wealthy official—in a shameless show of childlike fervor—climbed a tree to see Jesus. For the reformers, it is this great desire, emphasized by the fact that he did not care that people would laugh at him, that shows us that something deep and important was happening with Zacchaeus. Brenz notes that he had come to a knowledge of his own sin and a realization that God would not suffer it for too long, which helped him (along with hearing about Jesus and the salvation he offered) want to have his sins forgiven and to change his life. This nascent faith was recognized by Jesus, who saw with spiritual insight rather than physical sight, as Leigh suggests, and Jesus then spoke to him, called him by name and even (very unusually) invited himself to the man's house. The murmurers in the crowd—those who saw Zacchaeus as he had always been—could not see the changes, but he was ready to repent. Jewel notes that Zacchaeus was turned into a new person, one like other early Christians who wholly surrendered themselves to Christ. He was, in fact, a model of conversion, because he repented and showed it to be true repentance by immediately

rejecting his former life and turning to good works of repayment.

But his story also shows how this repentance and conversion only come about through God's mercy—it was Jesus' presence in his life that led to this change from sinner to saint, as the English Annotations describe it. This is the good news of the gospel in one short story, these interpreters note. Sinners and those who suffer should not despair but should rejoice, for Jesus did not come because we were looking for him. Rather, he came to seek us and to save us.

19:1-4 Zacchaeus Is Desperate to See Jesus

ZACCHAEUS WAS READY TO REPENT OF HIS SINS. JOHANNES BRENZ: Luke implies here that Zacchaeus had the knowledge and feeling of his sin and thought to himself that God would not allow his wickedness and deceit always to remain unpunished. He heard about a certain man named Jesus, whom people reported to be the Christ, who forgave sins and promised the kingdom of God to those who were willing to repent. Then he was inflamed with a desire to have remission of his sins and wanted to see who Jesus was. When he could not see because of the press of people, he ran ahead and climbed up to the top of a wild fig tree. This made his great desire to see Christ apparent. An ECCLESI-ASTICALL EXPOSITION UPON SAINT LUKE 19.[1]

THIS RICH MAN WAS WILLING TO EMBARRASS HIMSELF TO SEE JESUS. MARTIN BUCER: For the most part, rich people are proud and full of disdain and love to show themselves as quite serious, especially before a large crowd of people. But this man, although he was quite rich and in his estate was equal to a prince, was not ashamed to be seen by the crowd of people to climb up into a tree like a boy. It is quite possible that he would not have done this if any prince of this world had passed by! But now he ignored the scoffing and the scorn of people, so that he might see Christ. Therefore we may understand that Zacchaeus was looking for more in Jesus than simply a glimpse of his outward form. An ECCLESI-ASTICALL EXPOSITION UPON SAINT LUKE 19.[2]

19:5-8 Jesus Effects a Change in Zacchaeus

BECAUSE OF HIS EXCITEMENT TO SEE CHRIST, ZACCHAEUS IS BLESSED. EDWARD LEIGH: Jesus saw him not only in his physical aspect but also by a spiritual and saving insight. He did not only see him but chose to speak to him, calling him by his proper name, because it was known to him. . . . For Christ calls his own sheep by name. . . .

What a wonderful thing! We read in the Gospels that the Lord visited people when he was invited by them, but we never read that he came to a feast at someone's house by his own accord, as he did with this prince of the tax collectors. Faith always obtains more than it wishes: Zacchaeus desired to see Jesus, and now he has Jesus for his guest. Christ requires haste, that his readiness to bestow faith may appear to everyone. ANNOTATIONS UPON SAINT LUKE 19.[3]

ZACCHAEUS COULD SEE JESUS ONLY FROM THE TREE. JOHANN SPANGENBERG: What did Zacchaeus do in response to this summons of Christ? He quickly came down and took Jesus with him with joy. Now look: while Zacchaeus was on the ground, among the people, he could not see Christ. He climbs up a tree because he wants to see him, and Christ anticipates him and sees him. He does not want to leave him in the tree, but he must come down and take Christ into his home.

What should this example teach us? As long as we are in the crowd of evil company, evil thoughts, words and works, we cannot see Christ, as Christ says in Matthew: "Blessed are the pure in heart, for they shall see God." We must go up, climb up the tree, lift up our hearts to God. We must look up to Christ on the cross, ponder his bitter sufferings and death and carry the cross which God sends to us with patience and thankfulness. Then he will not be away for long but will graciously regard us and seek us out. He will prepare a room for us with the Father and help us in body and soul. ON THE DAY OF DEDICATION.[4]

JESUS' EFFECT ON ZACCHAEUS WAS IMMEDIATE. JOHN JEWEL: And so, good brothers and sisters, such was the life of all Christian people in the beginning of God's church: such was, I say, their life and living. They subdued their flesh, mortified their members and gave them wholly over to Christ, and so made them members for righteousness. When Christ walked here on this earth and spoke in our flesh and in our nature, at that time he entered into the house of Zacchaeus, who was a ruler of the publicans who desired to see Jesus. And then Zacchaeus was turned into a new man, and he stood up and said to the Lord, "Behold, Lord, half of my goods I will give to the poor, and if I have defrauded anyone, I will restore it to him fourfold." It was only by the presence of Christ that he was turned into a new man, and from an uncircumcized publican he was made into a child of Abraham, and from a sinful and wretched

---

[1]Marlorat, ed., *Catholike and Ecclesiasticall Exposition of the Holy Gospell After S. Marke and Luke*, 287*.
[2]Marlorat, ed., *Catholike and Ecclesiasticall Exposition of the Holy Gospell After S. Marke and Luke*, 287*.
[3]Leigh, *Annotations upon All the New Testament Philologicall and Theologicall*, 132*.

[4]Spangenberg, *Postilla Teütsch . . . von den fürnemsten Festen durch das gantze Jar*, CXVv-CXVIr; citing Mt 5:8.

creature he immediately became a Christian. Likewise, when Christ had called to Matthew only once and requested that he follow him, Matthew immediately left off gathering tolls and receiving taxes, left his own proper gain and profit and ran after Christ. The presence of Christ was an effective force to Zacchaeus, and the commandment of Christ had a powerful effect on Matthew the toll collector. SERMON 9, ON ROMANS 6:19.[5]

19:9-10 *The Son of Man Came to Seek the Lost*

SALVATION AND PEACE ARE BROUGHT TO ZACCHAEUS THIS DAY. THE ENGLISH ANNOTATIONS: "This day is salvation come to this house," in his conversion and doing the works of holy Abraham, by God's mercy shown to him and his family. It is as if Christ had said, "Before this, Zacchaeus went along with the perishing world in the broad way of destruction. His main care, study and endeavor was to get wealth, whether by right or wrong. But this day God showed mercy to him in his conversion, so that now he loathes his former life and conversation. Now he has chosen the better part, restoring what he had unfairly gained by any means, that it may be clear that his repentance is true, so that it may be acceptable to the God of mercy. He gives so largely to the poor that he may lay up treasure in heaven and lay down a good foundation in store against the time to come, that he may receive eternal life by faith (in Christ the only Savior), which works by love. Salvation is come to this house wherein the Savior of the elect, Christ, is entertained, heard and believed this day; this house whose master is changed from a tax collector to a convert, from a

sinner to a saint. Salvation, the means to and assurance of eternal life and true blessedness, along with his sins' free remission, his peace with God and his justification, is sealed to him this day by the Spirit of regeneration." ANNOTATIONS ON THE GOSPEL ACCORDING TO SAINT LUKE 19:9.[6]

CHRIST'S FIRST PRIORITY IS TO SAVE THOSE WHO ARE LOST. JOHANNES BRENZ: In these words Christ makes a response to those who murmured against him and said that he was going to the home of a man who was a sinner. He answered them by reference to his office, which is to seek and to save sinners. For those who are strong have no need of a physician, but rather those who are sick. This sentence of Christ is truly a golden sentence, instructing us in the chief and proper office of Christ, for which he came into the world. Those who are afflicted and at the brink of destruction think that because of their miseries they are forgotten by Christ and that there is no way for them to attain salvation. But it was for this reason that Christ came into the world, that is, to seek and to save what was lost. One perishes with sins, another with sickness, another with poverty, another with infamy and another with the horror of death and hell. What then? Should we despair? God forbid. Rather, we must then especially be of good cheer and hope and trust for the best. For Christ came, not because we first sought him out but rather to seek for us, and not only to seek for us but also to save us. He came, not to save what was whole and in good condition but what was lost. AN ECCLESIASTICALL EXPOSITION UPON SAINT LUKE 19.[7]

---

[6]Downame, ed., *Annotations*, Yy3r*; citing Mt 6:19; 1 Tim 6:19; Gal 5:6.
[7]Marlorat, ed., *Catholike and Ecclesiasticall Exposition of the Holy Gospell After S. Marke and Luke*, 291*; citing Mt 9:12.

---

[5]Jewel, *Works*, 2:1062*; citing Mt 9:9.

19:11-27 THE PARABLE OF THE TEN MINAS

[11]As they heard these things, he proceeded to tell a parable, because he was near to Jerusalem, and because they supposed that the kingdom of God was to appear immediately. [12]He said therefore, "A nobleman went into a far country to receive for himself a kingdom and then return. [13]Calling ten of his servants,[a] he gave them ten minas,[b] and said to them, 'Engage in business until I come.' [14]But his citizens hated him and sent a delegation after him, saying, 'We do not want this man to reign over us.' [15]When he returned, having received the kingdom, he ordered these servants to whom he had given the money to be called to him, that he might know what they had gained by doing business. [16]The first came before him, saying, 'Lord, your mina has made ten minas more.' [17]And he said to him, 'Well done, good servant![c] Because you have been faithful in a very little, you shall have authority over ten cities.' [18]And the second came, saying, 'Lord, your mina has made five minas.' [19]And he said to him, 'And you are to be over five cities.' [20]Then another came, saying, 'Lord, here is your mina, which I kept laid away in a handkerchief; [21]for I was afraid of you, because you are a severe man. You take what you did not deposit, and reap what you did not sow.' [22]He said to him, 'I will condemn you with your own words, you wicked servant! You knew that I was a severe man, taking what I did not deposit and reaping what I did not sow? [23]Why then did you not put my money in the bank, and at my coming I might have collected it with interest?' [24]And he said to those who stood by, 'Take the mina from him, and give it to the one who has the ten minas.' [25]And they said to him, 'Lord, he has ten minas!' [26]'I tell you that to everyone who has, more will be given, but from the one who has not, even what he has will be taken away. [27]But as for these enemies of mine, who did not want me to reign over them, bring them here and slaughter them before me.'"

a Greek *bondservants*; also verse 15   b A *mina* was about three months' wages for a laborer   c Greek *bondservant*; also verse 22

OVERVIEW: Jesus emphasizes here, Calvin reminds us, that he is not headed to Jerusalem to set up his earthly kingdom, and anyone who thinks that is mistaken. Still he wanted them to continue to hope for the future coming of a more glorious kingdom, despite whatever suffering they might have to endure in the meanwhile and however long it might take. The servants in this parable, according to several commentators, are the apostles and other preachers of the gospel, who are given gifts and are then responsible to use those gifts to build up the church. In the unity of the Holy Spirit each person is given different gifts, but all will be held accountable for how faithfully and diligently they wield those gifts. Bullinger comments that those who are like the lazy and wicked servant twist the doctrine of predestination as an excuse to do nothing, saying, "I cannot change either my election or my condemnation." While only through God's grace are we able to carry out his commands, still hypocrites are condemned by their own words. Even if we cannot fulfill the requirements of the law or please God on our own, we can always live in faith in Jesus Christ, which is the best way to be counted as righteous and to be reconciled with God.

Several other questions arise at the end of this pericope. Why will those who have been given more, while those who have nothing, even what little they have will be taken away? Despite the difficulty of the statement, Calvin suggests that it means that God gives more and more benefits to his own, especially grace, which contribute to our salvation. While the reprobate, those who have nothing, may now appear to have the gifts of the Spirit, even this pretense will be stripped away.

19:11-15 *The Parable Teaches About the Kingdom*

THE KINGDOM WILL BE RULED WITH THE ROD OF IRON. FRANÇOIS LAMBERT: The Savior was heading towards Jerusalem, where he would be killed for the salvation of the elect, and those who were with him were thinking that the kingdom of God was coming soon. So he told them the most suitable parable about that same kingdom, where he showed it to be that one which is spoken of by the Father on high: "Ask of me, and I will make the nations your heritage and the ends of the earth your possession. You will rule them with a rod of iron, and you will break them like a potter's vessel." And again, "The Lord said to my lord, sit at my right hand, until I make your enemies your footstool." COMMENTARY IN LUKE 19:11-27.[1]

THE SERVANTS OF THE LORD WORK TO INCREASE HIS RICHES. JOHANNES BRENZ: When Christ took this journey, he called his ten servants and gave ten minas to them, one mina to each, so that they might be occupied while he was absent.[2] These "servants" are the apostles and preachers of the word to whom Christ committed the office and ministry of the preaching of the gospel. As the church is built, the riches of Christ are increased by the gospel, and these "riches" are people obtaining salvation by faith in Christ. As Saint Paul says, "Grace was given to each one of us according to the measure of Christ's gift. Therefore it says, 'When he ascended on high he led a host of captives, and he gave gifts to human beings.'" And right after this the same apostle says, "He gave the apostles, the prophets, the evangelists, the shepherds and teachers, to equip the saints for the work of ministry, for building up the body of Christ." We understand this to mean all those who are called by the gospel to the faith of Jesus Christ. God has given proper and special gifts to every one of these, spiritual as well as corporal. There

are diversities of gifts but only one Spirit, and there are differences of administration and yet but one Lord, and there are diverse manners of operations, and yet God is one who works all in all. Therefore the gifts of God (whether they belong to the mind, like knowledge and wisdom, or to the body, like health, beauty, fortitude, riches) are given for this purpose of God: that until Christ comes to judge the living and the dead, everyone may be occupied in increasing the riches of our Lord and to exercise faith and charity in themselves. For when the Lord gave these minas to his servants, he commanded them, saying, "Engage in business until I come." AN ECCLESIASTICALL EXPOSITION UPON SAINT LUKE 19.[3]

THE PARABLE WAS TO TEACH THEM THE TRUTH ABOUT THE KINGDOM. JOHN CALVIN: Matthew interweaves this parable with others, neglecting the order of time. But it was his plan in Matthew 25 to collect a large number of Christ's last words, so readers should not be troubled about which were spoken on the first, the second or the third day of that brief period. Now, it is worthwhile to note how Matthew and Luke differ from each other, for while the one touches on only one part, the other later includes two. What is common to them both is that Christ is compared with a ruler who, in order to acquire a kingdom, undertakes a long journey, commits his money to his servants to be managed, and so on. Another point is peculiar to Luke, that the subjects abused the absence of the prince by beginning a rebellion, so that they might throw off his yoke. In both parts Christ wished to point out that the disciples who thought that his ruling position was now established and that he was coming to Jerusalem to set up that happy state right then were greatly in error. Thus, having taken away the hope of a present kingdom, he exhorts them to hope and endurance. He tells them that they would have to

---

[1] Lambert, *In Divi Lucae*, Dd5r; citing Ps 2:8-9; 110:1.
[2] A mina is about three months' wages for a laborer.

[3] Marlorat, ed., *Catholike and Ecclesiasticall Exposition of the Holy Gospell After S. Marke and Luke*, 293*; citing Eph 4:7-8 (cf. Ps 68:18); 4:11-12.

engage in many labors diligently and for a long time, before they enjoy that glory which they so greatly covet. COMMENTARY ON A HARMONY OF THE GOSPELS.[4]

19:16-27 The Faithful Servants Use the Gifts Wisely

THE GIFTS WE ARE GIVEN ARE NOT REALLY OURS. PHILIPP MELANCHTHON: Although it may be a long time before Christ comes, yet he will come eventually to judge, so no one should be negligent or misbehave just because it may take a long time. . . . He shows that whatever we have received from the Lord is not simply given to us but is given on the condition that we must give an account of it, as we have said before. But often we are not careful enough and do not show ourselves to be very diligent in obeying God, because we think that the things we have received are our own. And so a person who has possessions may lose some part of his possessions, and he will think that he has not lost anything except what was his own and does not consider that he will have to make an account of what he has lost. Instead, a person who cares for and has oversight over the possessions of someone else pays attention to the smallest penny, because he knows that he will have to give an account. AN ECCLESIASTICALL EXPOSITION UPON SAINT MATHEWE 25.[5]

THE GOOD SERVANTS SERVE GOD AND THEIR NEIGHBORS. JOHANN SPANGENBERG: What will he say to the first servant? To the first servant, who gained ten minas with one mina, he will say, "Okay, you loyal servant, because you were faithful in a small matter, you shall have charge over ten cities." This means those who use God's blessings, grace and gifts, in the highest level of faith and love (as much as is possible for a mortal person), for God's honor and for the use and improvement of the

neighbor. Moses and Paul were such people, who would much rather have been erased from the book of the living than that they should see their people, the Jews, destroyed. The prophets, the apostles and the martyrs were also such people, who sacrificed their bodies and lives in their vocations and who sealed their teaching and sermons with their blood.

What will he say to the second servant? To the second servant, who gained five minas with one mina, he will say, "Okay, you pious servant, you will be over five cities." This means all the pious Christians who fulfill their vocation with a righteous faith and in true brotherly love, who live blameless lives and who are a good example to everyone. The dear old bishops were such people: Ambrose, Augustine, Basil, Cyril, Eusebius, Hilary, Martin, Nicolaus, Tertullian, and now we also include all loyal preachers of the gospel. CONCERNING THE CONFESSORS.[6]

THE LAZY SERVANT GIVES A HYPOCRITE'S EXCUSES. HEINRICH BULLINGER: Now we are shown the very wicked and corrupt disposition of this slothful and lazy servant, far worse than the others. And the fellow uses quite well all the blasphemous words of the wicked and the ungodly and vain excuses of all hypocrites. The wicked cry, "It is a hard and dangerous thing to serve the Lord! He requires great things of us, but he has only given us small ability to perform them. I don't want to ruin any of his gifts with my lack of wisdom, so I won't do any work and will leave them untouched." Another one says: "Why should I worry about righteousness and holiness? If I am one of the elect, I will without a doubt be saved no matter how sinful I am, and again, if I am one of the reprobate, I will undoubtedly be damned no matter how hard I try, and how I afflict my body with discipline and how I pray for faith. I would pray in vain, because election is not obtained by prayer. Therefore, in order not to offend God, I will be content and will

---

[4]CTS 32:439-40* (CO 45:567).
[5]Marlorat, ed., Catholike and Ecclesiasticall Exposition of the Holy Gospell After S. Mathewe, 598*.

[6]Spangenberg, Postilla Teütsch . . . von den fürnemsten Festen durch das gantze Jar, CXXIXr-v.

leave my election to him, that I may be saved not through any merits of my own but by the free election and grace of God." AN ECCLESIASTICALL EXPOSITION UPON SAINT MATHEWE 25.[7]

ONLY FAITH IN CHRIST FULFILLS THE LAW. JOHANNES BRENZ: First of all, hypocrites are reprehended and condemned by their own words. For if they find God to be a cruel tyrant, why do they not follow that way by which God may be made into a favorable and merciful Father? And if they believe through experience that no one can fulfill the law with his whole strength, why do they not seek another way by which the righteousness of the law may be fulfilled in them? This other way is a true and lively faith in Jesus Christ. After Christ is received by faith, God, who is otherwise a severe judge according to his law, is instead reconciled to him who believes and forgives his sins. He also imputes to the believer all the righteousness of Christ and imbues him with his Holy Spirit. That way he will not only have the perfect fulfillment of the law in Christ through faith but may also follow the law of God himself in his own works, as far as may be done in this flesh. This returns to the Lord what is his, with interest. For Jesus Christ is our portion; when he is received by faith, he brings with him the gift of the fulfillment of the whole law. AN ECCLESIASTICALL EXPOSITION UPON SAINT LUKE 19.[8]

A GOOD SERVANT WORKS TOWARD THE COMMON GOOD. HEINRICH BULLINGER: Luke's Gospel adds at the beginning of the master's reply, "I will judge you by your own words." He is condemned by his own words in that his excuse can be turned against him. It is as if the Lord should say, "You knew that I was very focused on gain. Why then did you not give my money to the exchangers out of fear of me? And since I look for gain where I have no cost, I could at least go there and get my money back with interest; that is to say,

I would reap where I did not sow. That investment and its risk were mine and not yours, and you owed the duty of a servant to your master." He goes on to say, "Take his mina away from him." Some may ask what sort of saying this is. Does this mean that no one should work? The answer is that we must remember that those are mistaken who scrupulously stand on every word of parables. The true and natural sense of the phrase is this: although currently slothful and unprofitable servants have the gifts of the Spirit, they will eventually be stripped of everything, that their nakedness and reproachful need may turn to the glory of the good. Christ says that these people are slothful and that they bury their mina or dollar under the earth, because they seek for ease and pleasure, and so they do not want to be bothered at all. There are many who are wholly addicted to their private possessions and business, ignoring all the duties of charity and with no regard for the common good. From this parable we learn quickly that there is no kind of life more acceptable before God than the one that makes a contribution to human society. AN ECCLESIASTICALL EXPOSITION UPON SAINT MATHEWE 25.[9]

GOD GIVES GOOD THINGS TO THE ELECT, BUT THE REPROBATE ARE EMPTY. JOHN CALVIN: Christ continues on with what I just mentioned, for he reminds his disciples how liberally God deals with them, so that they might value his grace so much more and might recognize that they are even more greatly obliged to him for his help than they thought. These same words he repeats elsewhere but in a different sense, for there the discussion concerns the proper use of gifts. But here he simply teaches that more is given to the apostles than to people generally, because his Father in heaven desires to supply his benefits to the highest level for them. Because "he does not forsake the work of his hands," as it is said in the Psalms. Those whom he once begins to form, he

---

[7]Marlorat, ed., *Catholike and Ecclesiasticall Exposition of the Holy Gospell After S. Mathewe*, 600*.
[8]Marlorat, ed., *Catholike and Ecclesiasticall Exposition of the Holy Gospell After S. Marke and Luke*, 296*.

[9]Marlorat, ed., *Catholike and Ecclesiasticall Exposition of the Holy Gospell After S. Mathewe*, 600-601*.

continually embellishes more and more, until in the end he polishes them to the highest perfection. From this many graces flow from him immediately to us, and we make such happy progress, because God's consideration of his own liberality inspires him to a continued flow of generosity. And just as his riches are inexhaustible, so he is never tired of enriching his children. Therefore, as often as he leads us on higher, let us remember that whatever is daily added to these benefits to us flows from that fountain of his desire to complete this unfinished work of our salvation.

On the other hand, however, Christ says that the reprobate always rush on from bad to worse, until, in short, they are completely emptied and begin to decay in their own helplessness. This expression is indeed hard in appearance, that even what the impious do not have will be taken away from them, but Luke mitigates the harshness and removes the ambiguity by a small change in words, saying "what he seems to have" is taken away. And certainly it often happens that the reprobate excel in noble gifts and share a certain likeness with the children of God. However, nothing in them is genuine, because their minds are empty of piety, and it is clear that their splendor is worthless. That is why Matthew denies that they have any

worth, for what they have is reputed as worthless before God and has no inner permanency. Luke, however, aptly points out that the gifts with which they are furnished are corrupted by them, so that although they are magnificent in the eyes of people, they have nothing more than an ostentatious and empty display. Here we should also learn that we should aspire to progress throughout our lives, seeing that by this principle God offers to us a taste of his heavenly doctrine, that we might feast on it abundantly every day until we come to full satiety. . . .

In this second part . . . he includes all who in the absence of their master raise themselves up to revolt. It was, however, Christ's purpose not only to terrify such people by warning of a horrible revenge but also to keep his own people in faithful subjection. Indeed, it is no small temptation to see the kingdom of God overthrown by the falseness and rebellion of many. Therefore, that we might remain calm among turmoil, Christ advises us that he will return, and that at his coming he will punish such wicked rebellion. COMMENTARY ON A HARMONY OF THE GOSPELS.[10]

---

[10]CTS 32:104-5, 445* (CO 45:358-59; 570); citing Mt 25:29; Ps 138:8.

19:28-44 THE TRIUMPHAL ENTRY INTO JERUSALEM

²⁸And when he had said these things, he went on ahead, going up to Jerusalem. ²⁹When he drew near to Bethphage and Bethany, at the mount that is called Olivet, he sent two of the disciples, ³⁰saying, "Go into the village in front of you, where on entering you will find a colt tied, on which no one has ever yet sat. Untie it and bring it here. ³¹If anyone asks you, 'Why are you untying it?' you shall say this: 'The Lord has need of it.'" ³²So those who were sent went away and found it just as he had told them. ³³And as they were untying the colt, its owners said to them, "Why are you untying the colt?" ³⁴And they said, "The Lord has need of it." ³⁵And they brought it to Jesus, and throwing their cloaks on the colt, they set Jesus on it. ³⁶And as he rode along, they spread their cloaks on the road. ³⁷As he was drawing near—already on the way down the Mount of Olives—the whole multitude of his disciples began to rejoice and praise God with a loud voice for all the mighty works that they had seen, ³⁸saying, "Blessed is the King who comes in the name of the Lord! Peace in heaven and glory in the highest!" ³⁹And some of the Pharisees in the crowd said to him, "Teacher, rebuke your disciples." ⁴⁰He answered, "I tell you, if these were silent, the very stones would cry out."

⁴¹And when he drew near and saw the city, he wept over it, ⁴²saying, "Would that you, even you, had known on this day the things that make for peace! But now they are hidden from your eyes. ⁴³For the days will come upon you, when your enemies will set up a barricade around you and surround you and hem you in on every side ⁴⁴and tear you down to the ground, you and your children within you. And they will not leave one stone upon another in you, because you did not know the time of your visitation."

OVERVIEW: Jesus' triumphal entry was layered by the reality that these joyous songs of praise would soon change to cries of "Crucify him!" Erasmus notes that Jesus traveled to Jerusalem not for this show of honor but rather to ascend the cross and complete his work—his public entry into the city affirms that he was following his own plans and came willingly to suffer and die. But why, then, would he choose to enter the city in such a way? Yes, it was public and the whole city likely knew very quickly that he had arrived. But why such an upside-down type of procession, almost comical in its humble imitation of a grand king's entry? Erasmus suggests that Jesus "amused himself" by allowing such a show, taking delight in the people's affections but laughing "at the glory of this world," which would shortly be revealed to be utterly hollow. The strange dichotomy of the events—the royal approach on a humble donkey, the cheering crowds of humble visitors (Melachthon suggests they were not even citizens of Jerusalem), the palm branches and rough clothes strewn along the way—might suggest that this was all in jest, but it was not. Rather, it revealed both the superficiality of worldly splendor and fame, as Erasmus notes, and the role of Jesus as the Messiah promised by the prophets, who would come in humility to suffer, not in glory to rule.

For the reformers, each element of the story has at least a double significance—one for Jesus and his followers, and another for us. For example, by sending two disciples to retrieve the donkey and her colt, Jesus was revealing his divine knowledge to the disciples, but choosing a humble mount for his royal entry into the city. Taverner suggests that the church fathers saw the donkey and her colt as symbols of the two peoples that Jesus came to save, the Jews (on whom God had long rested through the law) and the Gentiles (who had not yet been "ridden"). Those who were sent to lead the two animals to Christ are the apostles and ministers of the Word, according to Schwenckfeld, for their office is to serve and point to Christ and not to ride along with him in princely show. That the owners of these animals were so easily pacified would again have been a sign to Jesus' disciples of his divine knowledge and prophetic nature, but for us, according to Brenz, it is a sign that the kingdom of God is to be "defended and preserved in this world" not by force or abuse but through "the preaching of the gospel." Magistrates may use the sword to defend the state, but ministers of the church have only the Word of God as their sword.

In the final part of this section, as Jesus' procession neared the city, he wept for the city and its people—a prophetic mourning for a city that would soon be destroyed. Boys notes that the celebratory atmosphere for the procession "turned into mourning," which reveals Jesus' own humanity, for it is the human lot to suffer as "pilgrims in a strange land." Jesus wept, Bucer suggests, because although he came to save the people of Jerusalem, they rejected him—he was humble and poor, not at all what they expected of a Messiah. So they condemned the only one who could bring them peace and instead headed down the path of destruction. The coming destruction of the city which Jesus here prophesied should be seen, Becon argues, as "a monument to God's anger." For this city was the holiest place on earth, most beloved to God, and yet when the people rejected God's Word, he was willing to punish them severely—a lesson we should all learn! But if we accept the grace offered to us and come to repentance, as Brenz notes, this coming "visitation from God" will be a time of mercy and redemption, not one of wrath.

19:28-36 *Preparations for the Entry*

THE LORD CHOSE TO GO TO HIS OWN SUFFERING AND SACRIFICE. DESIDERIUS ERASMUS: The Lord went on toward Jerusalem, where he would accomplish that special sacrifice for the salvation of the human race, and from the summit of the cross, draw in all things to himself like a greedy and ambitious king. And while there have been many people in every place, and will continue to be, who will cry out by their deeds,

"We do not want him to be king over us!" yet there is no nation so far removed from the Jews that he would not be able to draw many to himself from there. . . .

The Lord takes care of those things that before he also often took care of, so that it might be clear to everyone that whatever he might have suffered, he did so willingly and knowingly of his own accord, and in any case he had the power to do whatever he desired. However, he had resolved to claim for himself the highest glory among humankind through the highest disgrace and fall, but his disciples were not yet capable of understanding the fullness of this mystery, and in their ignorance they expected something magnificent and brilliant in a worldly sense from the Lord. Before his death, he wanted for a time to flatter, or rather to amuse himself better by their affections, and to laugh at the glory of this world, showing how empty and untrustworthy it is, for so much applause and honor, so many loud acclamations and so much affection from the people were followed so quickly by the cross. PARAPHRASE ON THE GOSPEL OF LUKE 19:28-29.[1]

THE DONKEY AND ITS FOAL ARE THE JEWS AND THE GENTILES. RICHARD TAVERNER: Now when he came into Bethphage, to the Mount of Olives, he sent two of his disciples to bring the donkey and the donkey's foal to him. The holy doctors suggest that this means that when he came down for our sakes into this vale of misery and drew near to the hill where he would show his great mercy (which he did for us through his glorious passion), he sent two of his disciples, who are the holy ones who reveal his coming both through the Old Testament and the New, to bring to him two peoples by faith. These two peoples are the Jews, on whom God had long before sat and rested himself by the law, who are signified by the donkey, and the Gentiles, on whom God had not rested or sat himself but who were outside of the law and were unbelievers, who are signified by the donkey's foal. For through his

[1]Erasmus, *In Evangelivm Lvce Paraphrasis*, A8v-B1r (LB 7:432-33; cf. CWE 48:145).

goodness and mercy, the Lord Jesus Christ wanted that the Gentiles should also be brought to him, so that he might sit and rest on them by faith and grace. And so now the disciples and the holy messengers of the coming of the Son of God have done the thing which he commanded them. They have brought the two peoples to him, and now he sits and rests on them both: on the one by the law and the grace of faith and on the other by the grace of faith and by his mercy. THE GOSPEL ON THE FIRST SUNDAY IN ADVENT.[2]

OUR SPIRIT—THE COLT—CARRIES CHRIST.

MARTIN LUTHER: The question arises here whether Christ rode on both donkeys. Matthew reads as if the disciples put him on both donkeys, while Mark, Luke and John speak only of the colt. Some think he sat first on the colt, but because it was too wild and untamed he then sat on the donkey. These are fables and dreams. We should take it that he rode only on the colt and not on the donkey. . . . Now consider the spiritual riding. Christ rides on the colt; the donkey follows. That is, when Christ dwells through faith in our inner person, then we are under him in his government. But the outer person, the donkey, goes alone. Christ does not ride on it, though it follows after. That is, as Saint Paul says, the outer person is unwilling, he does not yet carry Christ—indeed, he struggles against the inner person, as he says: "The flesh craves what is contrary to the spirit, and the spirit craves what is contrary to the flesh. For these two are opposed to each other, to keep you from doing the thing you want to do." Yet because the colt carries Christ and the spirit is willing by grace, the donkey (that is, the flesh) must be led after by the reins, for the spirit crucifies and chastises the flesh, so that it must be subject.

See, this is the reason Christ rides on the colt and not on the donkey, and yet he wants to have both for his entrance, for body and soul must be saved. Although here on earth the body is unwilling,

incapable of grace and of carrying Christ, it must endure the spirit on which Christ rides. The spirit pulls the body and leads it along by the power of grace received through Christ. THE CHURCH POSTIL (1540): FIRST SUNDAY OF ADVENT.[3]

THE DISCIPLES' OBEDIENCE IS OUR EXAMPLE.

KASPAR VON SCHWENCKFELD: Here one can see the obedience of the disciples of the Lord Christ, for they execute the command of the Lord without delay and without human fear. That is what Peter did in the great catch of fish, when the Lord told him to cast out the nets on the sea of Gennesaret and make an effort, although he had already been fishing all night. All of this is given to us as an example, that we should live according to the will and Word of God without anxiety and human fear, that we should pay no attention to attempts to prohibit Christian truth or to use force or necessity against it. Instead we should do what is godly, right and worthy of Christ, so that we will be considered true Christians and disciples of the Lord Christ.

We see here also again from this example of the disciples what is the proper office of the apostles and all genuine preachers and ministers of the Holy Spirit; namely, that they lead the donkey and its colt to Christ. They do not ride alongside of Christ, but they only serve Christ in his triumphal procession, leading and pointing to Christ, praising and glorifying him, making the Lord Christ known (as is here provided) with his grace, benefits and truth. FOUR SERMONS ON THE GOSPEL OF THE ENTRANCE OF CHRIST INTO JERUSALEM, MATTHEW 21.[4]

THE SWORD OF GOD'S WORD IS THE CHRISTIAN'S WEAPON.

JOHANNES BRENZ: We see here another miracle, in that the owners of the donkey and the colt are so quickly pacified with one word, and in that they allow these strange and unknown men to carry away the colt. This passage shows with

---

[2]Taverner, *Epistles and Gospelles (Wynter Parte)*, 7r*. Erasmus interprets the colt similarly; see CWE 48:149-51 (LB 7:434-35).

[3]LW 75:57-58* (WA 10,1.2:55-57; E² 10:44-45); citing Gal 5:17. Before this section Luther allegorizes the donkey and colt as a person's conscience; see LW 75:53-56 (WA 10,1.2:50-53; E² 10:38-43).
[4]CS 10:654-55; citing Lk 5:1-11.

what power and weapons the kingdom of Christ is to be defended and preserved in this world. When Christ commanded the disciples to bring the donkey, he did not tell them to berate the owners, to beat them or by force of arms to take the animal away, but only to answer them with his word, and by his word to do what they were commanded. For the Word, that is to say, the preaching of the gospel (which is the commandment of Christ), is that instrument by which the kingdom of God is set up and preserved. This sword and these weapons are ours to use. We are not speaking now of the office of the civil magistrate, who has to use the sword according to the laws of the state and to defend his subjects, so that they may lead a quiet life with all godliness and honesty. Now we are speaking of the office of the apostles and ministers of the church, whose sword is the Word of God. This sword not only preserves the external face of the church but also protects the conscience from the invasion of Satan, and through it we may be brought to everlasting salvation. AN ECCLESIASTICALL EXPOSITION UPON SAINT LUKE 19.[5]

AN ALLEGORICAL INTERPRETATION OF THE TRIUMPHAL ENTRY. DESIDERIUS ERASMUS:

There is . . . salvific meaning in the fact that there is a descent from the mountain, then a journey through the plain, then again an ascent up from Mount Zion, for the temple of the Lord had been erected on this latter mountain. Unless the mountain had the oil on which the lamp of faith is fed, there would be no descent from trust in the law, in which the Jews swell with pride, or from trust in philosophy, in which the Gentiles take smug pleasure. For the journey starts from faith. Moreover, it is necessary to approach the house of the mouth—for that is what Bethphage means in Syrian.[6] This is not the mouth that swells with scorn but the one that gives birth to the confession of sins. And it ought to be not far from Bethany,

which means the house of obedience. Now not everyone obeys the gospel. Yet from it is the beginning of salvation. After the descent the journey is through the plain, everywhere strewn with the palm branches of good examples until the route goes uphill again onto Mount Zion, which means watchtower. This is surely that peak of virtue from which, as from a lofty watchtower, there is a view down to all the things below that this world boasts of as lofty. And now near to heaven the heart contemplates the things that are eternal and that surpass every human sense. PARAPHRASE ON THE GOSPEL OF LUKE 19:28-40.[7]

AS THE PROPHET SAID, THE CHRIST COMES ON A DONKEY. THOMAS BECON:

This act of Christ was not done in a private and solitary place, but he came in broad daylight to his people, as a beggar, riding on another man's donkey, which was not prepared or ready for this purpose, to such an extent that his disciples wanted to help their poor king by casting their clothing on it, so that there might be more pomp. Therefore no one has any excuse. The prophecy is quite clear, that when Christ would come into his kingdom at Jerusalem, he would not come in the manner of other kings, with a great show of horses and an army, but meekly, as the Gospel says, and poor, according to the prophet [Zechariah]. The prophet spoke it to admonish them in this way: Note diligently the donkey, and know that it is truly the Christ who sits on it. Therefore, be wise and do not look for scepter, diadem or king's robes. For the Christ shall come poor, meek and humble, riding on a donkey. This will be the only magnificence and glory which he will show before the world, in the pomp of his coming to Jerusalem.

And this is the reason why Christ used this pomp before he suffered, and the matter was done with such circumspection, as Christ declared here sufficiently when he commanded all things to be done with such diligence; and he came, not in the night or privately, but openly in the day, and he did not enter into Jerusalem alone, but with a great

---

[5]Marlorat, ed., *Catholike and Ecclesiasticall Exposition of the Holy Gospell After S. Marke and Luke*, 298*.
[6]That is, Aramaic.

[7]CWE 48:151-52* (LB 7:435); citing Rom 10:16.

multitude of people who went both before him and after him, and preceeded him with praises to the true Son of David, and with wishes that his kingdom might be prosperous. The matter was done so openly that his coming must have been known throughout the whole city. Let them behold the donkey, the poor king of whom Zechariah prophesied and concerning whom he warned them that they should not be offended by the poor show and the humble and lowly coming of Christ, but instead they should condemn their own imaginations, because they thought that Christ should come gloriously in the sight of the world. The First Sunday of Advent.[8]

Christ Chooses the Lowly to Announce His Kingdom. Philipp Melanchthon: Surely the counsel and purpose of God is wonderful in that he uses rude, simple and abject sort of people, not the great citizens of Jerusalem, the scribes, Pharisees and high priests, to receive his Son and to set forth the beginning of his kingdom. He so stirs up their minds and makes them so joyful that, setting aside all fear of higher powers and of being excommunicated, they proclaim him with loud cries to be their king and the Lord's anointed, and by doing so they condemn their elders. These people were clearly not citizens of Jerusalem but had come there from far away on account of the festival. . . .

It might appear to be a May game or jesting matter when the rude crowd cut down boughs, spread their garments on the road and gave Christ the vain title of king, but they did this in good earnest and faithfully declared their minds. Christ clearly thought them to be appropriate and worthy proclaimers of his kingdom. There is certainly no cause for us to marvel at such a beginning, for even today when he sits at the right hand of his Father, he sends obscure and lowly people from his heavenly throne, by whom his majesty is celebrated in a most contemptible manner. An Ecclesiasticall Exposition upon Saint Mathewe 21.[9]

19:37-38 The Disciples and the People Praise Jesus

Likewise We Must Lay Everything Under Him. Johann Baumgart (Pomarius): The example of these people who spread their clothing and branches along the way and sing praises from the beautiful *Confitemini* of David should remind us what we owe. It should remind us how we should gladly receive, prepare for and submit to Advent and to our Lord and King, as we constantly and readily follow him—the old the forerunners of the young, and the young the successors of the old. We should maintain Christian conduct and honor the Lord with all our possessions and income. We must take off the clothes of the old Adam and the old snakeskin to throw it under Christ and dare to lay on him everything that we have and hold, our lives and property, even our miserable bodies. We should also furnish the Lord with twigs and branches, to be ourselves good trunks and trees of a good variety and fruit and to carry and spread our young sprouts and twigs (not wild weeds or runners) under Christ in season, so that they may be grafted as little plants of honor into his kingdom. Afterwards, when he comes again, we must desire as the true evergreen and undecaying trunks and trees to be transplanted into eternal life. So we should also, both old and young, ring out the glad Hosanna, and let praise for the Lord be always in our mouths, and wish from our hearts for happiness and success to his kingdom and ask that he would come soon and would lead us with him into the eternal and heavenly Jerusalem. The Gospel on the First Sunday of Advent.[10]

The Gospel Has Many Fair-Weather Friends. Edwin Sandys: At first, when he came toward Jerusalem, Christ was highly magnified and received with applause by the people, who cried, "Hosanna! Blessed is he who comes as king in the name of the Lord; peace in heaven and glory on high!" But this fair weather did not continue long. As soon as he entered the city and taught, the chief

---

[8]Becon, *New Postil*, f3r-v*; citing Zech 9:9.
[9]Marlorat, ed., *Catholike and Ecclesiasticall Exposition of the Holy Gospell After S. Mathewe*, 464*; citing Jn 12:12-13.

[10]Baumgart, *Postilla*, 4v; citing Ps 118:1.

priests, scribes and princes of the people sought to destroy him. And even the people, who before gave him great applause, crying, "Hosanna," soon after cried with a loud voice, "Crucify him." In times of prosperity, the gospel has many supposed friends and flatterers, but when it is persecuted by the wise and mighty of the world, then these counterfeit friends show themselves in their true colors, and the hollowness of their hearts becomes apparent. And so let the minister, who indeed minds the glory of God, beware that he never depend on people, whose minds are changeable and always wavering, but instead let him rest on God and rely wholly on his providence. Let us all faithfully and painfully work in our vocation, making ourselves ready for the cross, to suffer patiently with Christ Jesus. A SERMON MADE IN YORK, AT A VISITATION.[11]

19:39-40 *The Pharisees Complain*

THEIR COMPLAINTS AND THE SHOUTS OF THE SIMPLE SHAME THE PHARISEES. JOHN CALVIN: What vexed the Pharisees so greatly? Now we know how eagerly they contended for their authority. Their zeal brought them to this point, so that the tyranny which they had once usurped would remain unharmed for them. And it was no slight reduction of their power, if the people were free to grant Christ the title of king. Even in trifling matters they wanted their decisions to be regarded as oracles, so that nothing would be approved or rejected except according to their pleasure. They therefore reckon it to be foolish and unreasonable that the people would honor someone with the title of Messiah whom they themselves do not respect. Now certainly it was right—if they had performed their office—for them to go before the whole people as their authorities and leaders. For the priests had been appointed, so that from their lips everyone would desire the knowledge of the law, in short, so that they might be the messengers and interpreters of the Lord of hosts. But because they had treacherously extinguished the

light of truth, Christ appropriately replies that they gain nothing by trying to suppress the doctrine of salvation—it will instead erupt from the stones.

There is also an implied admission. Christ does not deny that this is an upside-down arrangement when uneducated common people and children are the first to celebrate loudly the Messiah's arrival. But because those who should be the rightful witnesses wickedly strangle the truth, it is no surprise that God stirs up others and to their shame chooses children instead. From this we receive no small consolation. Even though the wicked leave absolutely no stone unturned to hide Christ's kingdom, in this passage we hear how their works are mocked. Out of those in the crowd who are promoting the kingdom of Christ they hope to destroy some and to silence others by fear; in this way they will accomplish their goal. But the Lord will disappoint them. Because he will fashion mouths and tongues from stones rather than allow his Son's kingdom to be without witnesses. COMMENTARY ON A HARMONY OF THE GOSPELS.[12]

THE VANITY OF THE PHARISEES' REQUEST. THE ENGLISH ANNOTATIONS: "The stones would immediately cry out," meaning that the Pharisees labored in vain to suppress his testimony. For God would rather cause the senseless creatures to testify for him—as in the rending of the temple veil in his passion and of the rocks—than that his will should not be done by him. And indeed Christ's person, doctrine and miracles were so evident that they could not be concealed. ANNOTATIONS ON THE GOSPEL ACCORDING TO SAINT LUKE 19:40.[13]

19:41-44 *Jesus Prophesies About Jerusalem*

JESUS MOURNS, FEELING HUMAN EMOTION. JOHN BOYS: In his progress to Jerusalem, our blessed Savior was greatly honored by the multitude, as Saint Matthew reports [Mt 21:8-9]: some spread their garments in the passages, others cut

---

[11]Sandys, *Sermons*, 236-37*.

[12]CTS 33:15-16* (CO 45:583); citing Mal 2:7.
[13]Downame, ed., *Annotations*, Yy3v*; citing Mt 27:51.

down branches from the trees and strew them in the way. The whole company coming before him and going after him cried, "Hosanna, blessed be he who comes in the name of the Lord." And yet in the midst of all this jollity, when he beheld Jerusalem, he wept. This implies that all the pomp and delights of the present world are soon turned into mourning: "Even in laughter the heart may ache, and the end of joy may be grief." In heaven there is nothing but pure joy, in hell nothing but mere misery, but on earth are both, one mingled with another. Our life resembles a river, for as all rivers come from the sea and return there again, so the beginning and ending of our days are full of salt water, our first voice being a cry and the last a groan. There is happily some sweet and fair water in the middle of our age, but it passes away so swiftly that it is no sooner seen than it is gone. . . . Christ is often said in the Gospels' history to weep, but not once to laugh. This teaches us that, as long as we are pilgrims in a strange land outside of our own country, we must sit down by the waters of Babylon and weep. As for our harps, we must hang them up until we come to the Jerusalem above.

This weeping of Christ concerns all people, especially the clergy. It concerns us all as a demonstration of his humanity, for hereby we know that our high priest is touched with the feeling of our infirmities. It is an instruction for the clergy more particularly because in it he confirmed his own precept with his own practice. He said elsewhere, "Blessed are they who mourn," and behold, he himself weeps here. THE TENTH SUNDAY AFTER TRINITY.[14]

JESUS MOURNS FOR THE LOST OPPORTUNITIES OF JERUSALEM. MARTIN BUCER: It is likely that these thoughts disquieted the Lord's mind: "Behold, I come to you, O daughter of Zion, O Jerusalem, your King and Savior, even as the prophets have promised you, only poor and humble. Therefore you condemn me, the one from whose hands alone you might receive righteousness

and life. If only you had known those things which would bring peace to you and had not been so blind about your own evil, especially in these days when so many wonderful things should have made this knowledge abundantly clear! I have been preaching the kingdom of heaven to you, and the day of salvation and visitation is on you, which you ought to have known by my life, by my teaching and by the many miracles which I have lately shown you. But (and this makes me so unhappy!) now these things are hidden from your eyes. Therefore you are outraged and set against me, and you seek my blood, when instead you ought to receive your Savior and King with most ardent affection, as this crowd does. And so it shall come to pass that you shall be besieged by your enemies and laid flat on the ground. Your children will be slain, and your houses and expensive buildings will be knocked down, so that one stone will not be left on another. These unspeakable evils shall come on you because you did not recognize this present time of your visitation, in which my Father's grace has visited you through me and has gently called you to salvation, which he never did before, nor shall he ever do again." AN ECCLESIASTICALL EXPOSITION UPON SAINT LUKE 19.[15]

EVEN TODAY MANY DO NOT RECEIVE HIM, AND SUFFER DESTRUCTION. RICHARD TAVERNER: Now, my friends, we see in this description of the desolation and temporal confusion of those in Jerusalem who would not believe or receive Jesus Christ a figure of the spiritual confusion which will come on those who even now will not receive him or follow him and who make a resistance against him and his gospel—and the number of these is great. And knowing their destruction which was to come, Jesus also wept for them. Those who think they will be saved by any other means than by him and who have their faith and hope in any other than in him and by him, surely they have not yet received him, and evil will come to them. For God alone is the

---

[14]Boys, *Exposition of the Dominical Epistles and Gospels*, 3:217-18*; citing Prov 14:13; Eccl 1:7; Ps 137; Heb 4:15; Mt 5:4.

[15]Marlorat, ed., *Catholike and Ecclesiasticall Exposition of the Holy Gospell After S. Marke and Luke*, 300*.

object of the faith, hope and charity of Christian people. ON THE TENTH SUNDAY AFTER TRINITY.[16]

GOD LOVED JERUSALEM BUT PUNISHED IT.
THOMAS BECON: This city was the house and dwelling place of God, and the people in it were his own family and household. Next to heaven, Jerusalem was the holiest place—it was where God and his angels dwelled, where all the service of God was appointed to be done, where almost all the patriarchs lived and were buried. It is also where Christ the Son of God was and walked in the flesh, died and was buried, rose again and sent the Holy Spirit. This city surpassed all other cities in the world in holiness, and its equal was never found on the earth, nor will it be until the world's end. And yet for all that, with none of these things regarded at all, seeing that it did not receive or obey the Word of God, God severely punished that offense against the honor of his word. He would rather have that city, once so tenderly loved, extirpated and plucked up by the roots than suffer his Word to be so dishonored and the glory of it defaced. If God dealt thus with his best beloved city, is it to be thought that he will spare other cities, kingdoms and nations, where he has not dwelled and where the people are not so close to him as the citizens of this kingdom were?

Therefore this example ought to be a monument to God's anger, so that we do not despise the Word of God. Let us not use this language, "Peace, peace," as we were wont to do, saying, "There is no jeopardy, everything is well. The anger of God will never be so strong against us. Silence! He will never punish us as he did the city of Jerusalem and its inhabitants!" But brothers and sisters, let us not deceive ourselves. For if he allowed this holy city, in which he had such great delight here on the earth, to be so utterly destroyed and subverted, so that one stone was not left on another because of their wickedness, because although they heard his Word they did not repent or amend themselves, truly we

ought not to think that he will spare us if we offend him as the inhabitants of that city did. Like sin brings like punishment. And this city was so destroyed that not so much as a footprint or a token of a house remained. THE TENTH SUNDAY AFTER TRINITY SUNDAY.[17]

THIS TIME OF VISITATION IS A TIME OF MERCY AND GRACE. JOHANNES BRENZ: The "time of visitation" can mean two different things in the Scriptures. One example is when the Lord said, "In the day when I visit, I will visit their sin on them." Also it is said, "I will visit (or bring) four plagues on them: The sword shall slay them. The dogs shall tear them in pieces, the birds of the air and beasts of the earth shall eat them up." It can also mean when he delivers them from evil and blesses them, as in "When you have fulfilled seventy years in Babylon, I will visit you. I will bring you home, and out of my own goodness I will carry you again to this place." And again, the Lord says, "Behold, I will look for my sheep myself and visit them. Like the shepherd who has been among the flock searches for the sheep who are scattered about, even so will I seek after my sheep." Seeing that Christ came not to destroy but to save us and that he calls the time of his coming the time of his visitation, it is quite clear that he means by "time of visitation" in this passage not the time of wrath but the time of mercy; not the time of punishment but the time of deliverance; not the time of slaughter but the time of salvation. And the time of mercy and salvation is when the Word of God is revealed, by which the clemency of God is offered to us and by which we are called to repentance and admonished to receive the grace offered to us. AN ECCLESIASTICALL EXPOSITION UPON SAINT LUKE 19.[18]

---

[16]Taverner, *Epistles and Gospelles (Sommer Parte)*, 131v*.

[17]Becon, *New Postil (Second Parte)*, 80v-81r*; citing Jer 6:14; 8:11; Rom 11.
[18]Marlorat, ed., *Catholike and Ecclesiasticall Exposition of the Holy Gospell After S. Marke and Luke*, 302*; citing Ex 32:34 (cf. Lev 26:16); Jer 15:3; 29:10; Ezek 34:11.

19:45-48 JESUS CLEARS THE TEMPLE

[45]And he entered the temple and began to drive out those who sold, [46]saying to them, "It is written, 'My house shall be a house of prayer,' but you have made it a den of robbers."

[47]And he was teaching daily in the temple. The chief priests and the scribes and the principal men of the people were seeking to destroy him, [48]but they did not find anything they could do, for all the people were hanging on his words.

OVERVIEW: When Jesus entered Jerusalem, his first order of business was to go to the temple. He had, of course, frequently spent time in the temple in the past, but on this visit he was seemingly overwhelmed—with anger or perhaps the same sadness he had just expressed on seeing the city—and decided to drive out the people who were selling things there. This episode receives greater attention in the other Gospels (Mt 21:12-17; Mk 11:15-19; Jn 2:12-25)—in Luke only two verses are devoted to the cleansing of the temple. But the longer versions of this episode are kept in mind by those commenting on it. Huberinus, for example, discusses Christ's whip, which appears in John's Gospel but not in Luke's. The physical whip was used by Christ to kick the "soul murderers" out of the temple, but Christ still uses a "spiritual whip" to cleanse the church and rid it of "unconverted" clergy—that is, those who do not accept the evangelical perspective. In fact, the notion of purging or cleansing the church was quite popular for reforming commentators. Melanchthon notes that as Jesus cleansed the temple of those using piety to cover over what was a desire for gain, those who are empowered by God today should both by word and deed "purge the congregations of Christ," even though such cleansing will not rid the church of all idolatry and superstition. Those sins remain in the hearts of the reprobate and cannot be eradicated. Jesus cleansed the temple of its marketplace to show us that one's salvation is not a matter of external sacrifice but rather of internal transformation.

19:45-46 Jesus Clears the Temple

THE KING RESTORES WHAT HAS BEEN CORRUPTED. HEINRICH BULLINGER: It was the practice of kings in olden times, once they were received by the people, to restore and amend those things which were depraved and corrupted, either by the negligence or else by the malice of other princes. For example, once David was settled and established in the kingdom, he exercised and restored judgment and righteousness, which had been neglected in the time of Saul's government. Likewise our King and Lord Jesus Christ, being received by the people and acknowledged to be their king, went straight away into the temple. AN ECCLESIASTICALL EXPOSITION UPON SAINT MATHEWE 21.[1]

ABUSES AGAINST THE GLORY OF GOD MUST BE ABOLISHED. PHILIPP MELANCHTHON: It is true that God commanded the people to make offerings, but he did not want his institution to serve for the maintenance of human covetousness. He could not stand for his holy temple to be so profaned. For in what light did this show the temple? Therefore, when Christ entered into the temple, he first purged it of all foul spots and blemishes, and declared how greatly they displeased him and how intolerable those were in the church who, under the show and pretense of piety, sought after nothing but gain. There were many

---

[1]Marlorat, ed., *Catholike and Ecclesiasticall Exposition of the Holy Gospell After S. Mathewe*, 464*.

other wicked abuses in the temple which he left untouched, to teach us that those evils which most closely concern the glory of God are the first which must be purged. He also teaches that there is wickedness which is more abominable in God's sight than hypocrisy. And he abolished those things from the temple which displeased him not only by his word but also by his deed, although he knew that in a short time both the city and the temple would be destroyed. Through his example, those who have received power from God in the church are taught that they should, not only by their word but also by their deed, purge the congregations of Christ, even though they will know that corruption, superstition and idolatry will still be firmly embedded in the hearts of the reprobate. AN ECCLESIASTICALL EXPOSITION UPON SAINT MATHEWE 21.[2]

CHRIST'S WHIP PUNISHES THE CLERGY WHO DO NOT CONVERT. CASPAR HUBERINUS: We need to know what the scourge or whip of Christ is, for we already saw in John 2 how Christ made and used a real whip, and showed a great zeal in using it through his almighty power and eternal divinity and kicked the "soul murderers" out of the temple. Even today Christ still uses his spiritual whip, although through physical means and instruments. First, it is the true whip of Christ that through the preaching of the law, he allows the clergy who do not want to convert to make it apparent through their supposed worship services and their troublesome sinful lives. This switch bites them so hard and strikes them so powerfully that they can never fully recover! Then they raise such a howling and wailing and grumbling that each one feels that he has been thoroughly cut to the quick. Second, this whip has very hard knots and sharp prongs, which are the city councils who accept the gospel, and then through God's command, throw these fellows so hard off their shoulders that it makes their whole bodies want to shake. Now we

come to the third, the thorny prongs, such as pestilence, war, death and contempt. This happened not only through God's Word in Christ's edict, by which they were often admonished and required to confess, but they also were dismissed by the city council, rejected through war, removed from their office through temporal death and kicked out of the church of Christ through various other kinds of punishment. So now this is what the whip of Christ does, the hand of God, the power of the almighty Lord. Whoever will fight against his almighty power, it will be hard for him to kick against the goads, for no one can hinder what comes from God. All plants which have not been planted by the heavenly Father must be pulled out. And now in the ministerial office, so much garbage, so many weeds and so many human plants have gained the upper hand. So now the angel of God comes, almost at the end of the harvest, and collects the pious teachers and preachers together with the weeds and throws all the causes of offense out of the church, as Christ said. Therefore no one should place himself against such godly work, or it will lead to his ruin. ON THE TENTH SUNDAY AFTER TRINITY.[3]

THE PRIESTS WERE MURDERERS OF PEOPLE'S SOULS. MARTIN LUTHER: That is a severe statement, that the house of prayer was now a den [of murderers]. How can he venture to call it that, when there had been no murder committed there, but there was only buying and selling, and an office of exchange, so that people could buy the animals for sacrifice? Those are good works meant to honor God, so how can he call it a den [of murderers]? His statement is appropriate because the petty trading and sacrifices led the people astray into arrogance. Through them the people became hardened against the gospel—they leveled a reproach against it with their sacrifices and called them the righteousness through which Jerusalem would be preserved, and without which it would be ruined. These activities led the people to believe

---

[2]Marlorat, ed., *Catholike and Ecclesiasticall Exposition of the Holy Gospell After S. Mathewe*, 469*.

[3]Huberinus, *Postilla Teütsch*, 2:l3r-v; citing Acts 5; 9:5 (cf. 26:14); Mt 13.

that these offerings were righteous, and whatever sort of evil deed they might do afterward, it did not matter anymore if they just provided a sacrifice. Whenever that happens, it kills a person's soul. And so the priests of Jerusalem were guilty of their destruction. For they killed the souls of the people, and by doing this they had also made them responsible for and deserving of their physical deaths on account of their sins. SERMON ON THE TENTH SUNDAY AFTER TRINITY (1529).[4]

19:47-48 The Authorities Plot to Kill Jesus

THE PEOPLE CAME TO THE MESSIAH FOR HEALING AND WORSHIP. MELCHIOR NEUKIRCH: After he had punished the misuse of God's house, he began to preach and teach the people. By these actions, he wanted to bring us to understand what is the proper worship that we should perform toward God: prayer and hearing God's Word. He is also recommending the office of preacher to the people and teaching them to submit themselves faithfully to the Word of God.

Many ailing and sick people found their way to Christ in the temple, the blind, the lame, and so forth, and the Lord healed them and made them well. There were also children who followed Christ in the temple. Because they had been taught that their ancestors had received the Lord with song, they began to confess him as the Messiah and to sing Psalm 118 to honor the Lord. For they were taught by their parents that, if they should live to see the day when the Messiah would come, they should receive him with this psalm. THE FIRST PART OF THE PASSION.[5]

THE PRIESTS AND SCRIBES WERE HARDENED IN IMPIETY. JOHANNES BRENZ: We see here in the priests and scribes the image of true impiety. Christ was doing the work of the Holy Spirit, and the priests and scribes ought to have admired his work and imitated it, because they had the lawful administration of ecclesiastical matters. But they were so far from acknowledging the work of God and repenting that they were instead provoked to cruelty and conspired to bring about the death of Christ. They display obstinate wickedness—it will not be brought to godliness by doctrine, by miracles or even by example. They are like Pharoah and Judas the traitor, who were made worse by miracles and admonitions. So whoever is obdurate and hardened in impiety continues in his filthiness, no matter what anyone else may do. We should learn from this to take care that we not fall from piety into impiety, and in case we should fall into impiety through some weakness of the flesh, we should come quickly to repentance, so that impiety will not take root in us and bring us to everlasting destruction. AN ECCLESIASTICALL EXPOSITION UPON SAINT LUKE 19.[6]

THE PEOPLE WERE ATTACHED TO HIM FOR HIS WORDS. JOHN TRAPP: In Greek, the word is "hung on him," as the bee hangs on the flower, the baby on the breast or the little bird on its mother's bill. Christ drew the people after him, as it were, by the golden chain of his heavenly eloquence. A COMMENTARY UPON THE GOSPEL ACCORDING TO SAINT LUKE 19.[7]

---

[4]*LEA* 3:352 (cf. WA 29:509-10). *Spelunca* ("cave" or "den") is used here in the sense of *Mördergrube* ("murderers' pit"), which is how Luther renders "den of robbers" in his Bible translation.
[5]Neukirch, *Historia der Passion*, 67v-68r.

[6]Marlorat, ed., *Catholike and Ecclesiasticall Exposition of the Holy Gospell After S. Marke and Luke*, 305*.
[7]Trapp, *Commentary or Exposition*, 415*.

20:1-8 THE AUTHORITY OF JESUS IS QUESTIONED

One day, as Jesus[a] was teaching the people in the temple and preaching the gospel, the chief priests and the scribes with the elders came up [2]and said to him, "Tell us by what authority you do these things, or who it is that gave you this authority." [3]He answered them, "I also will ask you a question. Now tell me, [4]was the baptism of John from heaven or from man?" [5]And they discussed it with one another, saying, "If we say, 'From heaven,' he will say, 'Why did you not believe him?' [6]But if we say, 'From man,' all the people will stone us to death, for they are convinced that John was a prophet." [7]So they answered that they did not know where it came from. [8]And Jesus said to them, "Neither will I tell you by what authority I do these things."

a Greek he

OVERVIEW: The chief priests, scribes and elders of whom we read in the previous passage decided to take a direct approach to frighten Jesus with their authority. However, once again the Gospel shows us that Jesus had the upper hand. He turned the tables on the leaders to ask what was the source of John's baptism, and they knew they were in trouble, whatever their answer. This text was only infrequently preached by reformers, but those who did comment on it generally note that these authorities truly took the wrong approach. They are trying to trap Jesus, so they should not expect a direct answer, and Jesus' question ties his own mission and authority to John's—if John was truly a prophet from God, then how could Jesus' own miracles and preaching be taken in any other way?

20:1-2 The Authorities Question Jesus' Authority

THE AUTHORITIES SOUGHT THE SOURCE OF JESUS' POWER. PHILIPP MELANCHTHON: These men saw the great glory of his miracles and the fervent affection of the people toward Christ. They felt and perceived a certain authority in the teacher and in him who purged the temple. And yet all they looked for was contempt for his authority and power, and they tried to obscure his desired glory. They saw that he who accomplished these great miracles and took on these weighty matters did not have any principle or priestly form or show of power, at least not according to this world. If anyone should try to conduct himself this way without proper authority, he would rightly be considered rash and seditious. And so they come with a great appearance and show of power, demanding by what authority he does what he does. They thought that by this question they might convict him either as a blasphemer, if he said that he did these things by the power of God, seeing that he was a man, or else as a seditious person, if he answered that he used his own authority. They were not disputing about his doctrine (as we have just said) but concerning formalities, as if they had said, "Although your doctrine is true, nevertheless you should not presume to teach unless you are licensed to teach by our authority." AN ECCLESIASTICALL EXPOSITION UPON SAINT MATHEWE 21.[1]

UNDER A CLEVER PRETEXT THE AUTHORITIES TRY TO EXCUSE THEIR STUBBORNNESS. JOHN CALVIN: Indeed, this was an attractive pretext. For no one should—of his own accord—meddle with either the priesthood's honor or the prophet's office but instead should wait for God's calling. How much less is someone able to seize for himself the

---

[1]Marlorat, ed., *Catholike and Ecclesiasticall Exposition of the Holy Gospell After S. Mathewe*, 476*.

title Messiah, unless it is evident that he has been chosen by God. For he must have been appointed not only by the voice of God but also by an oath, as it is written.

But they act wickedly and impiously—because Christ's divine majesty had been attested by so many miracles—when they ask from where he came, as if ignorant of all that he had done. What is more absurd? After they see the hand of God openly stretched out—because the lame and blind are cured—they wonder whether he is a private individual who had rashly assumed this authority. Besides, more than enough evidence had already demonstrated that Christ was sent from heaven, so that nothing was farther from their minds than to accept Christ's acts, even after having learned that God was their author. They therefore insist on this: there is no legitimate minister of God whom they did not choose with their own votes—as if this power belonged only to them. And although they had been legitimate guardians of the church still it was monstrous to rise up against God. Now we understand why Christ did not answer them directly. Certainly it was because they wickedly and shamelessly interrogated him about a matter clear in itself. COMMENTARY ON A HARMONY OF THE GOSPELS.[2]

20:3-8 Conflict over John's Baptism

JESUS CONQUERS GUILE WITH GUILE.
DESIDERIUS ERASMUS: Now Jesus understood that this interrogation came from godless scheming, that is, so that they could make their false charge, not so that they could learn. He did not attempt to instruct them but blunted their malice as if driving out one nail with another.[3] For they had esteemed John the Baptist highly and had streamed to his baptism. . . . Indeed, the loaded question of the leading men had this aim: if Christ answered that authority had been given to him by God, they would accuse him of

blasphemy, because he—a human being—claimed for himself an intimate connection or relationship with God. PARAPHRASE ON THE GOSPEL OF LUKE 20:3.[4]

THE PHARISEES SHOULD HAVE LEARNED FROM JOHN WHO JESUS WAS.
PHILIPP MELANCHTHON: Our Savior Christ might seem here to give a poor example in refusing to give a reason for his calling. But it is not so: in his question was contained a full and perfect answer by which he satisfied his adversaries. For when Saint John had witnessed that Jesus was the Son of God, the Pharisees were no doubt taught by him, and so they ought to have acknowledged that Jesus was the messenger of God, and they could not have doubted by what authority he preached and performed miracles. They held Saint John to be the prophet of God, sent by God, and they gave him great credit. But the Lord by his question was also evidently declaring how wicked and malicious the high priests and Pharisees were, not only for resisting him but also because they had shown that same malice toward others, namely, toward John the Baptist. Although they could find no fault in him, they still rejected his doctrine and his administration of baptism; and so it would certainly be no surprise if they did the same here to Jesus. AN ECCLESIASTICALL EXPOSITION UPON SAINT MATHEWE 21.[5]

THE AUTHORITIES' BLIND HYPOCRISY.
DESIDERIUS ERASMUS: It did not even occur to them that God had long ago handed over his power when he spoke through his prophets. They accepted the authority of the prophets, and they rejected the reality the prophets had foretold. So, wanting to mock their wicked wisdom and stupid cunning, the Lord replied in this way. PARAPHRASE ON THE GOSPEL OF LUKE 20:1-8.[6]

[2]CTS 33:21-22* (CO 45:587); citing Ps 110:4; Heb 7:21.
[3]Adages 1.2.4 (CWE 32:47; LB 2:70).
[4]CWE 48:157 (LB 7:437).
[5]Marlorat, ed., Catholike and Ecclesiasticall Exposition of the Holy Gospell After S. Mathewe, 477*.
[6]CWE 48:158 (LB 7:437).

CHRIST'S EXAMPLE IS SIMPLE AND SKILLFUL.
JOHN CALVIN: Christ employed no cunning trick
in order to escape but thoroughly and firmly
answered the question which had been raised. It
was impossible to acknowledge John as God's
servant without acknowledging the Lord himself.
Thus, he did not strengthen impudent human
beings who without any mandate but out of their
own audacity usurp a public office. Nor by his
example did he encourage the sophists' art of
passing over the truth—as many crafty people do,
falsely using his authority as a pretext. I do indeed
admit that we should not always respond in the
same way, if impious people set snares for us;
instead we should be prudently on guard against
their malice, so that truth is not deprived of a
proper defense. COMMENTARY ON A HARMONY OF
THE GOSPELS.[7]

---

[7]CTS 33:22-23* (CO 45:588); citing Ps 110:4; Heb 7:21.

20:9-19 THE PARABLE OF
THE TENANTS IN THE VINEYARD

⁹And he began to tell the people this parable: "A man planted a vineyard and let it out to tenants and went into another country for a long while. ¹⁰When the time came, he sent a servant[a] to the tenants, so that they would give him some of the fruit of the vineyard. But the tenants beat him and sent him away empty-handed. ¹¹And he sent another servant. But they also beat and treated him shamefully, and sent him away empty-handed. ¹²And he sent yet a third. This one also they wounded and cast out. ¹³Then the owner of the vineyard said, 'What shall I do? I will send my beloved son; perhaps they will respect him.' ¹⁴But when the tenants saw him, they said to themselves, 'This is the heir. Let us kill him, so that the inheritance may be ours.' ¹⁵And they threw him out of the vineyard and killed him. What then will the owner of the vineyard do to them? ¹⁶He will come and destroy those tenants and give the vineyard to others." When they heard this, they said, "Surely not!" ¹⁷But he looked directly at them and said, "What then is this that is written:

"'The stone that the builders rejected
has become the cornerstone'?[b]

¹⁸Everyone who falls on that stone will be broken to pieces, and when it falls on anyone, it will crush him." ¹⁹The scribes and the chief priests sought to lay hands on him at that very hour, for they perceived that he had told this parable against them, but they feared the people.

a Greek *bondservant*; also verse 11   b Greek *the head of the corner*

OVERVIEW: After the conflict with the priests, scribes and elders recorded in the previous passage, Jesus told a parable which confirmed his perspective on that group of leaders. Sometimes called the parable of the wicked tenants, the story quite obviously faults the Jewish authorities for their poor leadership of the people, their mistreatment of God's servants and especially for their final insult: the killing of the king's son and heir. Erasmus notes that the beloved vineyard is the people whom the Lord brought up out of Egypt. He built a temple for them and established priests and leaders to keep them safe and to produce a good harvest. But these laborers degenerated, rejecting their Master's law, messengers and ultimately his Son. Because the vineyard only produced inedible fruit—the fault, of course, of the laborers—the Lord sent his servants, the prophets, to bring his word to the people and the leaders. But, as Sarcerius asserts, the priests killed the true prophets of God, despising them and their messages.

Calvin notes here that parables, as metaphors and stories, often attribute human emotions and comments to God. Unlike the vineyard owner, however, God knew what would happen when he sent his Son, and it was part of his providential plan. In the story, the laborers decide to kill the son, so that they can keep the inheritance. Bullinger explains that the priests and leaders, like these laborers, convinced themselves that Jesus was blasphemous for claiming divine authority for himself, "making himself equal with the Father." But in reality they wanted to kill him because they were jealous and threatened by him—they hoped by killing him to retain their power and authority over the people. They would not, however, accept the conclusion of the parable—that these wicked tenants would be destroyed—so Jesus turned to the passage about the rejected cornerstone to make his point even clearer. The leaders could no longer escape the implications of the story, and it made them even angrier than before. But, as Bullinger comments, this should provide us great comfort, because no matter how much they wanted to kill Jesus, they were not able to act before the proper time—and his power will deliver us from our enemies, as well.

20:9-16 *The Parable of the Tenants*

THE VINEYARD IS ESTABLISHED BY THE LORD. DESIDERIUS ERASMUS: And so having silenced to an extent the priests, Pharisees, scribes and the leaders among the people, the Lord added a parable that placed before their eyes their incurable malice, which was worthy of damnation. They had been encouraged by God to amend in many ways but were always becoming progressively worse, disdaining the law, striking down and killing the prophets, and after this they would kill the Son of God, the final remedy of evils, and frequently strike him down in the apostles and martyrs. . . .

Now, this certainly is the vineyard of the Lord of the sabbath, which he brought up out of Egypt and established in the promised land. He separated it by the border of the law and protected it by watching over it. He provided a temple and added priests, judges, leaders and doctors: He omitted nothing that pertained to their care. But this well-tended and cared for vineyard, which was long expected to produce good grapes, in the end produced wild grapes through the fault of the laborers. Meanwhile, the Lord, who was never far away, seemed to them to be far away, because he conducted his administration from heaven. PARAPHRASE ON THE GOSPEL OF LUKE 20:9.[1]

THE SERVANTS ARE GOD'S PROPHETS. HEINRICH BULLINGER: Before this, he had mentioned the benefits given to the people; note in the following how unjustly they recompensed such a loving and beneficial Father. . . . His servants were the prophets, by whom the Lord urged the priests to offer fruit to God. But it is somewhat surprising

that Christ compared the prophets with the servants who are sent to require fruit, now that the harvest time was past. For we know that the prophets were also vine dressers and that the same office that was enjoined on the priests also belonged to them. However, it was not necessary that Christ should exactly or scrupulously express what was like or unlike between these two orders. Certainly in the beginning the priests were ordained so that they might perfectly and truly till and instruct the church with sound doctrine. But when they neglected the work committed to them through their slothful negligence, the prophets were sent as extraordinary helpers to purge and take away all the weeds that were hurtful to the vine and to supply what the priests were lacking. But in the process they also sharply reprimanded the people, they restored godliness which was quite decayed, they wakened sleepy minds, they renewed the worship of God and brought a new life. And what is this but to require the yearly profit due to God from the vine? And so Christ aptly and truly applied this example to his purpose. AN ECCLESIASTICALL EXPOSITION UPON SAINT MATHEWE 21.[2]

THE PEOPLE ALWAYS ATTACK OR KILL THE LORD'S PROPHETS. ERASMUS SARCERIUS: The priests who allowed and upheld the false prophets, who prophesied lies (as the prophet Jeremiah said), killed the true prophets of God. Some of the prophets, like Jeremiah and Micaiah, they beat; some they killed, such as Isaiah and Amos; some they stoned in the temple, like Zechariah and Barachiah.[3] "He sent still a third." They also killed the prophets who came in later days, including Saint John the Baptist. Concerning these we read: "All the officers of the priests and the people

---

[1] Erasmus, *In Evangelivm Lvce Paraphrasis*, B7v-B8r (LB 7:438; cf. CWE 48:159-60).

[2] Marlorat, ed., *Catholike and Ecclesiasticall Exposition of the Holy Gospell After S. Mathewe*, 484*.

[3] Jer 37:15; 1 Kings 22:24. Isaiah is traditionally thought to have been sawn in half by the evil king Manasseh (see the apocryphal *Ascension of Isaiah*); Amos is traditionally thought to have died violently at the hands of Jeroboam II. Zechariah was stoned in the porch of the temple (2 Chron 24:20-22). For "the blood of Zechariah the son of Barachiah, whom you murdered between the sanctuary and the altar" see Mt 23:35; Zech 1:1, 7.

likewise were exceedingly unfaithful, following all the abominations of the nations. And they polluted the house of the Lord that he had made holy in Jerusalem. The Lord, the God of their ancestors, sent persistently to them by his messengers, because he had compassion on his people and on his dwelling place. But they kept mocking the messengers of God, despising his words and scoffing at his prophets, until the wrath of the Lord rose against his people, until there was no remedy." And Christ himself said, "Therefore I send you prophets and wise men and scribes, some of whom you will kill and crucify, and some you will flog in your synagogues and persecute from town to town." And again he said, "O Jerusalem, Jerusalem, the city that kills the prophets and stones those who are sent to it!" AN ECCLESIASTICALL EXPOSITION UPON SAINT MATHEWE 21.[4]

CHRIST WAS THE PROMISED SACRIFICE AND HEIR. AUGUSTIN MARLORAT: The goodness of God, as we said before, contends with the malice of the priests. For although certain Jews did not believe, yet nevertheless their unbelief could not make faith in God of no effect. Christ was that immaculate lamb who was ordained by God to be a sacrifice before the foundation of the world. Therfore it was necessary that he should be made manifest in these later days and that he should be sent into this world in order that the truth of God could confirm the promises made to the ancestors. Moreover, in times past, God spoke to the people diversely and in many ways by the prophets, but in these Last Days he has spoken to us by his own Son, whom he made heir of all things. AN ECCLESIASTICALL EXPOSITION UPON SAINT MATHEWE 21.[5]

THE PRIESTS WANTED THE LORD'S INHERITANCE FOR THEMSELVES. HEINRICH BULLINGER: It is as if they might have said, "This man challenges

that the vineyard should be his inheritance, making himself the king of the people of God. He arrogates to himself divine majesty, making himself equal with the Father. Therefore come, let us kill this blasphemous person, so that we might enjoy his inheritance in safety. The inheritance of the Lord is the power over all things, the people of God, the holy city, the dignity of the priesthood and the government among saints. And so therefore," they say, "it may be lawful for us to retain and keep the dignity of the priesthood and the government over the people. So let us kill him, or else there is a chance that the Romans might hear that a king and savior has come to us. Then they will attack us in a battle, spoil our city, lead our people into captivity and burn our temple!" AN ECCLESIASTICALL EXPOSITION UPON SAINT MATHEWE 21.[6]

THEY REJECTED THE AUTHORITY OF THE SON. JOHN CALVIN: Strictly speaking, this thought would certainly not be applicable to God, for he knew what would happen, nor was he deceived by the hope of a better outcome. But it is customary, especially in parables, to ascribe human feelings to God. And it was not without reason that this was added, because Christ wanted to show, as if in a mirror, that their impiety was deplorable; and this consideration was quite certain, because they had risen up in diabolical madness against the Son of God, who had come to bring them back to a sound mind. Just as they had earlier driven God away from his inheritance, as much as they could, by the cruel murder of the prophets, thus here it was the high point of all their wicked deeds to murder the Son, that they might reign, as it were, in a childless house. For certainly the reason why the priests were raging against Christ was so that they might not have to part with their tyranny, or, one might say, their plunder. For it is he indeed whom God chooses to govern and to whom he has granted all sovereignty. COMMENTARY ON A HARMONY OF THE GOSPELS.[7]

---

[4]Marlorat, ed., *Catholike and Ecclesiasticall Exposition of the Holy Gospell After S. Mathewe*, 484-85*; citing Jer 5:31; 2 Chron 36:14-16; Mt 23:34; Lk 13:34.
[5]Marlorat, ed., *Catholike and Ecclesiasticall Exposition of the Holy Gospell After S. Mathewe*, 485*; citing Rom 3:23-26; 15:8; Heb 1:1-2.

[6]Marlorat, ed., *Catholike and Ecclesiasticall Exposition of the Holy Gospell After S. Mathewe*, 485-86*.
[7]CTS 33:31* (CO 45:593-94); citing Mt 21:37.

20:17-18 *Jesus Interprets the Parable*

DESPITE DIFFERENCES THE SYNOPTICS AGREE. JOHN CALVIN: The Evangelists also differ slightly in the end of the story. For instance, Matthew reports that the confession was wrenched from them, by which they condemned themselves, while Mark simply notes that Christ announced what punishment would come to servants who were so worthless and rebellious. Luke differs more openly in outward appearance, saying that they were repulsed by Christ's warning of punishment. But if we truly weigh the particular sense, there is no contradiction: concerning the punishment which such servants merit, there is no doubt that they gave assent to Christ; but when they discerned that the wicked deeds and the judgment were joined together in applying to themselves, they sought to avoid it. COMMENTARY ON A HARMONY OF THE GOSPELS.[8]

CHRIST WOULD BE REJECTED BY HIS OWN PEOPLE. PHILIPP MELANCHTHON: But the leaders would not accept the parable, which showed that the wicked tenants would be destroyed and that the Son of God, the Lord of the vineyard, would be destroyed by them (for they did not want to be known as the ones who would kill the Christ, promised by the prophets, when he was coming into his vineyard). And so he brings in this very clear passage of Scripture out of the prophet, which evidently teaches that the Christ would be rejected by his own, and that when he was rejected, he would be by the wonderful counsel and power of the Lord the prince and head of the house of God and receive the great admiration of all people.

Whereas before the church was compared with a vineyard, now it is also compared with a building. Christ is the stone; the priests, magistrates and elders of the people are the builders. As the apostle Peter said, "This Jesus is the stone that was rejected by you, the builders, which has become the cornerstone." "To build" in the Scripture is some-

times used in place of "to teach." But this passage to which our Savior Christ here refers is taken from the same psalm as that rousing cry which the people made to Christ, when they shouted "Hosanna," was taken. And it is quite evident that it was a prophecy of the kingdom of the Messiah, for David was made king on this condition, that his seat would stand forever, as long as the sun and moon endured, and that the decayed kingdom would come again, by the grace of God, into its former state. Therefore, seeing that the psalm contains a description of David's kingdom, there is a perpetuity and a restitution also connected to it. AN ECCLESIASTICALL EXPOSITION UPON SAINT MATHEWE 21.[9]

THE FAITHFUL WILL BE CRUSHED BY THE ROCK. FRANÇOIS LAMBERT: Those who believe in him fall on this stone, all who trust that their foundation is laid and that they are built on him alone, not on themselves or on any other person. These ones are severely shaken, for all who piously desire to live in Christ will have to suffer adversities. This stone will fall on them, his feet treading on them, and he will condemn them to a perpetual fire. At the last, he will break them into pieces, while all who are faithful he will separate out, and the rest in the end will perish in eternity. As we see in Psalm 2: "You will reign with a rod of iron and break them in pieces like a potter's vessel." COMMENTARY IN LUKE 20:18.[10]

20:19 *The Authorities Intensify Their Plotting*

THE ENEMIES OF CHRIST CAN DO NOTHING UNTIL HIS HOUR COMES. HEINRICH BULLINGER: Although they were overcome by Scripture and perfect reason, they would give no place to the truth. And although they had heard the divine judgment of God, nevertheless they were afraid of

---

[8]CTS 33:31-32* (CO 45:594); citing Mt 21:41-46; Mk 12:9-12.

[9]Marlorat, ed., *Catholike and Ecclesiasticall Exposition of the Holy Gospell After S. Mathewe*, 487*; citing Ps 118:22; Acts 4:11.
[10]Lambert, *In Divi Lucae*, Ee6r; citing Ps 2:9.

nothing, but, going forward in their usual malice and envy, they plotted and took counsel about how they might destroy the Lord Jesus. . . . Here the scribes and the Pharisees, according to their manner, grew more and more inflamed against Christ. But because his hour was not yet come, they were able to do nothing and were stricken once again with useless fear. In this example we find a singular comfort and consolation, namely, that the Lord will take and deliver those who are his, even from the jaws of the lions. For he restrains his enemies, even as it were with a bridle, in so much that they are able to do nothing unless he gives them leave, in order that he might test their patience. AN ECCLESIASTICALL EXPOSITION UPON SAINT MATHEWE 21.[11]

[11]Marlorat, ed., *Catholike and Ecclesiasticall Exposition of the Holy Gospell After S. Mathewe*, 492-93*.

20:20-47 JESUS' DISCUSSIONS WITH THE PHARISEES AND SADDUCEES

²⁰So they watched him and sent spies, who pretended to be sincere, that they might catch him in something he said, so as to deliver him up to the authority and jurisdiction of the governor. ²¹So they asked him, "Teacher, we know that you speak and teach rightly, and show no partiality,ᵃ but truly teach the way of God. ²²Is it lawful for us to give tribute to Caesar, or not?" ²³But he perceived their craftiness, and said to them, ²⁴"Show me a denarius.ᵇ Whose likeness and inscription does it have?" They said, "Caesar's." ²⁵He said to them, "Then render to Caesar the things that are Caesar's, and to God the things that are God's." ²⁶And they were not able in the presence of the people to catch him in what he said, but marveling at his answer they became silent.

²⁷There came to him some Sadducees, those who deny that there is a resurrection, ²⁸and they asked him a question, saying, "Teacher, Moses wrote for us that if a man's brother dies, having a wife but no children, the manᶜ must take the widow and raise up offspring for his brother. ²⁹Now there were seven brothers. The first took a wife, and died without children. ³⁰And the second ³¹and the third took her, and likewise all seven left no children and died. ³²Afterward the woman also died. ³³In the resurrection, therefore, whose wife will the woman be? For the seven had her as wife."

³⁴And Jesus said to them, "The sons of this age marry and are given in marriage, ³⁵but those who are considered worthy to attain to that age and to the resurrection from the dead neither marry nor are given in marriage, ³⁶for they cannot die anymore, because they are equal to angels and are sons of God, being sonsᵈ of the resurrection. ³⁷But that the dead are raised, even Moses showed, in the passage about the bush, where he calls the Lord the God of Abraham and the God of Isaac and the God of Jacob. ³⁸Now he is not God of the dead, but of the living, for all live to him." ³⁹Then some of the scribes answered, "Teacher, you have spoken well." ⁴⁰For they no longer dared to ask him any question.

⁴¹But he said to them, "How can they say that the Christ is David's son? ⁴²For David himself says in the Book of Psalms,

"'The Lord said to my Lord,
   Sit at my right hand,
   ⁴³until I make your enemies your footstool.'
⁴⁴David thus calls him Lord, so how is he his son?"

⁴⁵And in the hearing of all the people he said to his disciples, ⁴⁶"Beware of the scribes, who like to walk around in long robes, and love greetings in the marketplaces and the best seats in the synagogues and the places of honor at feasts, ⁴⁷who devour widows' houses and for a pretense make long prayers. They will receive the greater condemnation."

a Greek *and do not receive a face*   b A *denarius* was a day's wage for a laborer   c Greek *his brother*   d Greek *huioi*

OVERVIEW: One of Jesus' many talents was bringing his enemies together—the Pharisees and Sadducees, especially, who were regularly in opposition to each other but found common ground in their hatred and envy of Jesus. In this passage, Jesus was attacked by his enemies in a variety of ways—all attempts to trick him, to undermine his popularity with the people and to bring him to the attention of the Romans as a troublemaker. Instead Jesus reveals his opponents' own ignorance of the Scriptures and of God's power, schooling them and the crowd in God's Word. First, Jesus' response to the trick question about taxes, for Melanchthon, suggests that we should obey governing authorities as God's ministers—at least in the Lutheran two-kingdom sense. God established governments in the world to rule and keep the peace. We should give civil obedience and pay taxes to Caesar but remember that our heart belongs to God. Second, Jesus teaches that the afterlife is not like this one; we will not have the same sorts of relationships. We will, instead, be like the angels. As children of the resurrection, our interpreters remind us, we can live in assured hope of that future life because of God's promise to us through the Holy Spirit.

Finally, Jesus poses a riddle about Psalm 110 to his critics. The Pharisees in particular, the reformers assert, were to blame for the fact that the people believed that the Messiah was coming to be an earthly king, like David, who would restore the glory of Israel. But Jesus intimates, these interpreters claim, that David himself had witnessed that the Messiah would be his Lord, that is, not only a human son but also the Son of God—someone greater than David, who would govern in God's name. The fact that the Pharisees did not understand this showed that they did not understand the Scripture and helped to explain why they had no faith in Christ or his gospel.

20:20-26 *Paying Taxes to Caesar*

THE RULERS SET OUT TO CATCH HIM WITH DECEIT. MELCHIOR NEUKIRCH: Because they were not able to move against him with any public show of power, they thought of this trick: they would come to him with fair words and see if they could somehow catch him in his speech, so they could show the secular government that he was a revolutionary and it was too dangerous to allow him to live. So they attacked him with the question of whether it was right and justifiable before God that the people should give the tribute payment to Caesar, who was a pagan ruler. And indeed, God's law decreed that the money should be used to support the temple and divine worship. They undertook this questioning so slyly that they thought they would not fail to catch the Lord with this question, no matter how carefully he answered. THE FIRST PART OF THE PASSION.[1]

THE SPIES ACTED AS IF THEY BELIEVED IN CHRIST. PHILIPP MELANCHTHON: They praise him for his truthfulness; because he was free from all dissimulation, he gave special regard to no person, and he made no pretense about himself. . . . By these words they declare what they meant when they said, "You are true," that is to say, "You teach the will of God faithfully and truly, teaching only what is acceptable to him, and not just what people want to hear." These men were pretending and acting as if they sought God and that they were not just like the Pharisees, who had asked him, "By what authority are you doing these things?" They pretended to be truly persuaded by the teaching of Christ and to believe that he was a teacher of the truth sent by God. They said, "You do not show partiality," as if they should have said, "In your dealings with the scribes, priests and elders of the people, you have declared and thoroughly persuaded us that you are no respecter of persons,and that you care for no person, or for the people or for the nobles or those in high position, not even for Caesar or Herod, but you only have regard for God." AN ECCLESIASTICALL EXPOSITION UPON SAINT MATHEWE 22.[2]

THE QUESTION PRESENTED A DANGEROUS DILEMMA. JOHN BOYS: God ordained in his law that every man of twenty years old and above should give half a shekel yearly as an offering to the Lord, toward the reparation of his house and for other pious uses. And this collection, as conjectured by Melanchthon, amounted every year to three tons of gold.[3] Now when the Romans conquered the Jews and made them tributary, as we read in Luke 2, the money which was given to the temple was paid into Caesar's treasury. When this occurred, there was immediately a great dispute among the chief priests and Pharisees about whether it was lawful to pay this tribute to Caesar or not. Shortly afterwards, open rebellion

---

[1]Neukirch, *Historia der Passion*, 84v.

[2]Marlorat, ed., *Catholike and Ecclesiasticall Exposition of the Holy Gospell After S. Mathewe*, 502*; citing Mt 21:23.
[3]MO 14:953.

broke out among the people, with Judas of Galilee as their captain, as Saint Luke mentions in Acts 5:37. For this Judas Galileus, conspiring with a Pharisee named Sadducus, drew away many people with him, openly maintaining against the faction of Herod that this tax by the Roman emperor was intolerable and contrary to the laws of God and the immunity of the Jews, his free people.[4] With this background, it appears that the question concerning Caesar's tribute was exceedingly captious and provided Christ an uncomfortable dilemma. For if Christ had answered, "It is lawful," then the Pharisees would have accused him to the chief priests as being opposed to the temple, but if he had said, "It is unlawful," the servants of Herod would have delivered him to the secular power of the governor, as a seditious fellow perverting the people and forbidding them to pay tribute to Caesar. If he had disputed against the tribute, he would have offended Caesar; if in favor of the tribute, he would have displeased the people, who bore this burden against their wills. And so the Pharisees might have found a gap opened up to destroy him if the people abandoned him. From both options, he appeared to be in imminent danger, perhaps even of death. THE TWENTY-THIRD SUNDAY AFTER TRINITY.[5]

THE SPIES THOUGHT THEY HAD CAUGHT HIM, BUT HE ESCAPED THE TRAP. JOHANN SPAN-GENBERG: They think that they have already caught Christ between their spears and pitchforks. But Christ turns around and hits them with their own weapons, saying, "Show me the denarius." They offer him a coin, and Christ says, "Whose are the picture and inscription?" He acted as if he were unfamiliar with money and as if he could not read. Now they must have thought, "Oh, he is caught! He is afraid. He will dissemble for the government. He dares not say what he really thinks. What are you asking about? Can't you see whose image and inscription are there? It's Caesar's!" Therefore Christ says, "Then give to Caesar what is Caesar's, and to God what is God's." And so the matter is closed, as if he would say, "If it has come about that Caesar has minted coins among you, why are you asking me about it? Give to Caesar what is Caesar's, and to God what is God's."

What does Christ mean by this saying? He wants to say, "Up until now, you leaders of the Jews have stolen and robbed God's honor from him, like true committers of sacrilege, and you have falsified God's Word like the blasphemers. Now you also want to take away from Caesar what is his, like true rebels. That falls under the judgment of God and of Caesar, and so you should be justly punished both in body and in possessions." GOSPEL ON THE TWENTY-THIRD SUNDAY AFTER TRINITY.[6]

SOME THINGS ARE OWED TO GOD, OTHERS TO CAESAR. PHILIPP MELANCHTHON: Here also we can see how far we ought to obey magistrates and how we must also make a difference between God and Caesar. For although Caesar is the minister of God, nevertheless it is one sort of thing that belongs to God and another sort of thing that belongs to him. Therefore, what pertains to the world belongs as a right to Caesar, and what pertains to religion belongs to God. In the world we have the image of Caesar on our money, which teaches us what we owe to Caesar. But in our mind we bear the seal of Christ and of the Holy Spirit, because we are sealed by baptism and engraved with the name of Christ: this teaches us what we owe to God. God does not command us to withhold from Caesar those things that are due to Caesar. Likewise, it would be a wicked and ungodly act if Caesar would not allow those things to be given to God which are due to him but instead to keep them for himself. AN ECCLESIASTICALL EXPOSITION UPON SAINT MATHEWE 22.[7]

---

[4]Josephus, *Antiquities* 18.1.
[5]Boys, *Exposition of the Dominical Epistles and Gospels*, 4:196-97*; citing Ex 30:11-16; Lk 23:2.
[6]Spangenberg, *Postilla . . . von Ostern biß auffs Aduent*, CLXXIIIv.
[7]Marlorat, ed., *Catholike and Ecclesiasticall Exposition of the Holy Gospell After S. Mathewe*, 505-6*.

THE PHARISEES TRY TO TRIP UP JESUS. THE
ENGLISH ANNOTATIONS: Their purpose was to
render him hateful to the people, and so they
hoped by this question to ensnare him, no matter
what he answered. If he had said, "It is not lawful,"
then they could have possibly cried, "Behold, a seditious man, who (like that former Galilean) would
have us rise up in rebellions against Caesar and so
bring the Roman sword on us!" If he had said, "It is
lawful," they would have murmured among the
people that he was a flatterer of Caesar, trying to
confirm the servitude and oppression of God's
people. If they could have brought about a negative
opinion of him among the people, they could have
destroyed him without much hullabaloo. Their
chief aim was that they might find some occasion
to hand him over to the authorities in power and
to destroy him whom they themselves dared not
destroy for fear of the people and for fear of the
Romans, who did not permit them to judge in
capital matters, that is, concerning life and death.
ANNOTATIONS ON THE GOSPEL ACCORDING TO
SAINT LUKE 20:26.[8]

20:27-40 *The Resurrection and Marriage*

**GOD'S LAW OF INHERITANCE ENSURES PUBLIC
TRANQUILITY.** MARTIN BUCER: This law was
made for the same reason that all other political
laws are made: for the sake of public tranquility,
which is much better established if inheritances are
maintained without mixture and every member of
a lineage and kindred has his own inheritance.
Therefore the Lord provided diligently by this law
(to which the Sadducees objected) as well as by
others for the continuance and perpetuation of the
various lines within kindreds, and for a lawful
succession of inheritances. The law provides that if
one brother dies with no heir, the other brother, by
marrying his wife, should provide him with
posterity and provides that the first begotten son of
his brother's wife will possess the name and

inheritance, just as if he were adopted by the dead
brother. AN ECCLESIASTICALL EXPOSITION UPON
SAINT MATHEWE 22.[9]

**THE RESURRECTION BRINGS ONLY HAPPINESS
IN THE LIFE TO COME.** PHILIPP MELANCHTHON:
He shows us the state of those who will be happy
and blessed after the resurrection and rejects the
absurd opinion concerning the world to come. He
uses a distinction between the times present and to
come, which is plentifully and plainly expressed by
the Evangelist Luke. He calls all those who live in
the world children of this world. But he calls those
worthy of the world to come who understand the
happiness that is to come.... We should therefore
note how great the happiness of the life to come
shall be. What is now full of infirmity, mortality and
corruption, what is now heavy, troublesome, slow,
miserable and base shall be made strong, immortal,
incorruptible, light, pleasant, quick, happy and
glorious by the resurrection. The soul shall be freed
from ignorance, blindness, false opinions, wicked
affections, anger, envy, fear, pride, and so on. So
whoever is oppressed and afflicted in this present
life by the wicked affections of the mind, or by
corruption or trouble, should pay attention to this
angelical state of the life to come and find solace in
it. AN ECCLESIASTICALL EXPOSITION UPON
SAINT MATHEWE 22.[10]

**THE ELECT ARE THE CHILDREN OF GOD BY
ADOPTION.** JOHN CALVIN: He does not mean that
the children of God, after they have risen, are going
to be like the angels in every way, but they will be
totally free from every infirmity of the present life,
thereby denying that they would be subject to the
necessities of a fallen and corruptible life. Luke
more clearly expresses the matter of the similarity,
that then they will not be able to die, and therefore
there will be no perpetuation of their lineage, as on
earth. However, he is speaking only of the faithful,

---

[8]Downame, ed., *Annotations*, Yy4v*.

[9]Marlorat, ed., *Catholike and Ecclesiasticall Exposition of the Holy Gospell After S. Mathewe*, 508*.
[10]Marlorat, ed., *Catholike and Ecclesiasticall Exposition of the Holy Gospell After S. Mathewe*, 509-10*.

because they had not been discussing the reprobate.

But one might ask, why does he say they will then be the children of God, because they will be children of the resurrection, since the Lord thinks the faithful are worthy of this honor, even though they are confined in the fragile prison of the body? And how would we be heirs of eternal life after death, unless God already now recognized us as his children? I answer, by the faith through which we are joined into the body of Christ, we are adopted by God as his children, and the Spirit is the "witness," seal, earnest money and pledge of this adoption, so that with this assurance we may freely cry, "Abba, Father!" Finally, although we know ourselves to be the children of God, what we will be is not yet apparent, until, transformed into his glory, we will see him in his true form. So we are not yet counted as children, because it is not yet finished. And although we are renewed by the Spirit of God, our life is nevertheless still hidden, so its manifestation will truly and completely set us apart from strangers. In this sense our adoption is said by Paul to be deferred until the Last Day. . . .

After Christ refuted the absurd objection against him, now he confirms the doctrine of the final resurrection by the testimony of Scripture. And this is the order that we must always keep: once the false accusations of the enemies of God are removed, they should come to understand that they oppose the Word of God. Indeed, until they are convicted by the testimony of Scripture, they will always be free to shout against it. To continue, Christ cites the passage from Moses because he was dealing with the Sadducees, who did not have much faith in the prophets, or at least they view them similarly to how we view the book of Ecclesiasticus or the history of the Maccabees. Next, because they had brought up Moses, he chose to make his retort to them with the same rather than to use one of the other prophets. Besides, he did not intend here to collect all the passages of Scripture, as we see that the apostles do not always make use of the same passages in the same case. Nevertheless, it was not by chance that Christ seized on this passage before others. He

chose it with the best judgment (although it might seem to be more obscure in appearance), because it was fitting that it would be especially well-known and remembered by the Jews, since it would prove that they were redeemed by the Lord because they were the children of Abraham. There, indeed, God announces that in coming to them, he comes to help an afflicted people, but at the same time adds that he recognizes that people as his own, with respect to adoption, on account of the covenant made with Abraham. COMMENTARY ON A HARMONY OF THE GOSPELS.[11]

GOD IS THE GOD OF THE LIVING, NOT THE DEAD. MARTIN BUCER: Now we see how wisely our Savior Christ has put this all together: to whomever the Lord is a God, he is also a savior and lifegiver forever. But he cannot be a lifegiver to the dead, that is, to those for whom all hope of life is taken away. Whoever believes that God is God is blessed, that is, to that person he declares himself to be God. But if the dead were wholly void of life, as the Sadducees thought, and would never return to it, how would God bless them or bestow any benefits on them? The saints, therefore, are not void of participation in life. And just in case the Sadducees might have said, "No one denies that God is the God of Abraham, Isaac and Jacob," he adds, "God is not the God of the dead." But Abraham, Isaac and Jacob were and are dead—that is true! But to God they are not dead; they are only dead to the world and to the flesh, but they live to God. For "to him all are alive," as the Evangelist Luke says. AN ECCLESIASTICALL EXPOSITION UPON SAINT MATHEWE 22.[12]

20:41-44 Whose Son Is the Christ?

JESUS IS DAVID'S SON AND DAVID'S LORD. PHILIPP MELANCHTHON: Christ our Savior did not reprimand the Pharisees because they confessed

---

[11]CTS 33:50-52* (CO 45:606-7); citing Rom 8:15-16; Gal 4:6; 1 Jn 3:2; Rom 8:23; Ex 3:6; 2 Sam 22:28; Ps 18:27.
[12]Marlorat, ed., *Catholike and Ecclesiasticall Exposition of the Holy Gospell After S. Mathewe*, 511*.

him to be the Son of David but because people commonly said that the one who was to be the Messiah would be nothing else but an earthly king, who would bring the people of God into a certain earthly liberty. He was to be of the tribe of David, and he should so enlarge the earthly, transitory kingdom that it should extend itself even to the ends of the world. It was for this reason that he thought it would be good to provide a further consideration of his glory and majesty in their presence; namely, that he was not the son of David according to the flesh, but at the same time the Son of David and David's Lord. For in the sense that he took flesh from the Virgin Mary, he is the son of David, but in the sense that he was conceived by the Holy Spirit, he is the Son of God and David's Lord. This is no new or recently invented error: this impiety reigned among the Pharisees long before he came into the world. The devil had clearly sought from the beginning to take away the deity and godhead from Christ, so that by this means all the salvation of humankind might be utterly and entirely overthrown. AN ECCLESIASTICALL EXPOSITION UPON SAINT MATHEWE 22.[13]

THE PSALM REVEALS CHRIST'S POWER.

MARTIN BUCER: The Hebrew word for the first "Lord" is *Yahweh*, and for the second "Lord" is *Adonai*. It could be translated as something like "the eternal God said to my Christ." Our Savior Christ would be known as more excellent than David in that David himself called him his Lord. For the father would not have called his son Lord unless he knew him to be greater than himself.... To "sit at the right hand of God" means to reign in his name, so that he might justly be thought to hold the same power—wherever he reigned he can be understood to sustain the power of God. Just as the legate and the ambassador represent and sustain the person of the king, so God governs all things by the hands of Christ.... We should also note that Christ uses the testimony of this psalm to declare that not only

is he David's Lord but also to set forth the invincible power and victory of his kingdom against his enemies. It is as if he had said, "You will be so far from resisting me that before long, my Father will set me at his right hand and give me full possession of all power. And I will exercise this power until such time as you and all my enemies are made into my footstool." AN ECCLESIASTICALL EXPOSITION UPON SAINT MATHEWE 22.[14]

THEY MUST LEARN WITH DAVID TO CALL HIM LORD.

MELCHIOR NEUKIRCH: They knew from the Scripture that it was promised to David that the Messiah would be born from his lineage. But it was not enough that the Jews should know that their Messiah was to be David's son—that is, a true man. That is why Christ asked them further, "Is he David's son? Then why is it that David, who is a great and powerful king, should call the Christ his Lord in the Spirit, if he is to be his son?" It is as if he would say, "David will understand by the Spirit that the Christ will be a much greater Lord than himself. That is why he calls him his son according to his human nature but his Lord according to his divine nature." Through this the Lord shows them that it would be much better if they were not only burdened by the law but also that they should not completely forget the teaching of the gospel of Christ. They should learn with David to call him their brother and Lord in true faith and believe in him, so that they might be saved through such faith. THE FIRST PART OF THE PASSION.[15]

20:45-47 *Beware of the Scribes*

CHRIST REPROVES THOSE WHO LOVE THE HIGHEST SEATS.

PHILIPP MELANCHTHON: These things declare what the hypocrites seek by their ostentation and bragging. The purpose of their bragging is to obtain glory and human praise, for it is a glorious thing to have the place of superiority at all

---

[13]Marlorat, ed., *Catholike and Ecclesiasticall Exposition of the Holy Gospell After S. Mathewe*, 516-17*.

[14]Marlorat, ed., *Catholike and Ecclesiasticall Exposition of the Holy Gospell After S. Mathewe*, 518*; citing Ps 110.
[15]Neukirch, *Historia der Passion*, 86r-v.

times, "and have the most important seats in the councils," or synagogues (which is how the Latin translation reads); that is to say, in ecclesiastical meetings. But what about this? Is it not lawful for some to sit in the highest seats at feasts and councils? Is it not appropriate that those who excel others in virtue should also be honored by others? Yes, certainly, for Christ is not trying to take away the honor and reverence due to elders and superiors, but he is only reproving ambition and an attitude of excessive vanity. Therefore he does not say, "They are placed in the highest seats at feasts and councils," but he says, "They love to sit in the highest seats," which only pertains to those who are proud. We should also understand the admonition which Christ gave in Luke 14 in this same manner, for he reproves them there in the same way that he does here. Now, just as it is not evil in itself to sit in the highest place, so it is not good in itself to sit in the lowest seat. For it may be that the person who is sitting in the highest spot has a modest and humble mind, while the person in the lowest seat may have a proud and lofty attitude. "They love to be greeted in the marketplace." The scribes and Pharisees not only loved to be greeted but to be greeted in front of others, and especially in the marketplace, that is, in a public place where many people would see it. AN ECCLESIASTICALL EXPOSITION UPON SAINT MATHEWE 23.[16]

THEY MAKE THE TEMPLE INTO A MARKETPLACE. MARTIN BUCER: Our Savior Christ mentions houses here because they represent one's goods and possessions. By the name of widows he signifies those who are poor and needy, and so they become easy prey, good and simple folk, and those in the lowest condition who need patrons and defenders. But certainly he especially means widows here, who are more inclined toward superstition and may more easily be deceived by the pretense of sanctimony and holiness. Prayer is a holy thing which they defiled, abusing it for filthy gain. For it is the duty of every person to pray for one another and not to make merchandise out of prayer. For what else do those do who sell prayers but buy and sell, making a market and exercising sacrilege in the temple of God? Therefore Christ criticized the Pharisees, because under the pretense and cover of long prayers, they allured and enticed widows and other simple people to bring their houses, or else really the price of their houses, to *corban*, an offering reserved to God.[17] And because a false persuasion had already entered into the hearts of the common people, our Savior Christ more sharply threatens the scribes and Pharisees, saying, "Such people will be punished most severely." AN ECCLESIASTICALL EXPOSITION UPON SAINT MATHEWE 23.[18]

---

[16]Marlorat, ed., *Catholike and Ecclesiasticall Exposition of the Holy Gospell After S. Mathewe*, 525*.

[17]For Jesus' criticism of the practice of *corban*, see Mk 7:9-13.
[18]Marlorat, ed., *Catholike and Ecclesiasticall Exposition of the Holy Gospell After S. Mathewe*, 531*.

21:1-4 THE WIDOW'S MITE

Jesus[a] looked up and saw the rich putting their gifts into the offering box, ²and he saw a poor widow put in two small copper coins.[b] ³And he said, "Truly, I tell you, this poor widow has put in more than all of them. ⁴For they all contributed out of their abundance, but she out of her poverty put in all she had to live on."

a Greek *He*   b Greek *two lepta*; a *lepton* was a Jewish bronze or copper coin worth about 1/128 of a *denarius* (which was a day's wage for a laborer)

OVERVIEW: God knows and cares about our charitable giving. Jesus is impressed that this woman with so little should give so generously. This demonstrates to the reformers that the Lord is not concerned with how much or even what is given, but with how and why we give. What is the state of our heart? Do we seek approval before human beings or God? Nestled in this passage for the reformers is the reminder that we human beings are unable to judge others, because we judge by appearances while the triune God judges by the heart. Therefore, knowing who we are and who God is, our commentators encourage us to embrace humility and consider others as more significant than ourselves (Phil 2:3).

Peter Walpot is the only commentator who understands this text to prohibit any personal property. For him the community of goods is at the heart of the gospel message. Maintaining our own possessions keeps us from being truly Christian, and God requires of us, he argues, that we do not hold anything back but, like this widow, give all we have to God. While all the reformers would agree with Walpot that our possessions are not our own and that we only give to God what he has first given us, still most of them, including other Radicals, do not accept the Hutterite teaching but rather understand tithing and sharing our wealth to be voluntary, not compulsory.

21:1-4 The Widow Gave All That She Had

WHAT OFFERING BOX? THE ENGLISH ANNO-TATIONS: There were other treasuries about the temple, but this was a chest set at the eastern door through which all the people passed in and out, so that everyone with his own hand might cast into it either what was taxed from him or what he voluntarily offered or gave to the poor. ANNOTATIONS ON THE GOSPEL ACCORDING TO SAINT LUKE 21:1.[1]

THE LORD JESUS WANTS OUR HEART, NOT THINGS. JOHN CALVIN: Christ's reply contains a teaching of no little use: whatever human beings offer to God is not to be assessed by its external value but only by the heart's condition. Indeed, his piety is far greater who according to his small measure offers to God whatever little he has than whoever gives a hundred times more from his abundance. This doctrine is useful in two ways. The Lord animates the poor who seem absolutely unable to do good, so that they do not hesitate to testify to their zeal cheerfully even in their feeble status. Because if they consecrate themselves, their offering which in appearance is common and worthless will be no less costly than if they had presented all the treasures of Croesus.[2] In turn those whose wealth is more than sufficient for them and who overflow with many gifts are warned that it is not enough if they lavishly outdo commoners and the weak. Before God it is worth less for a rich person to offer out of a huge heap a mediocre sum than for a pauper by giving

---

[1]Downame, ed., *Annotations*, Yy4v*; citing 2 Kings 12:9; 2 Chron 24:8; Neh 10:38.

[2]Croesus was a king of Lydia whose wealth was proverbial among the ancients.

an insignificant sum to empty himself. . . . The chief sacrifice which God requires from us is self-denial. COMMENTARY ON A HARMONY OF THE GOSPELS.[3]

OUTDO ONE ANOTHER IN PRAISE AND HONOR. MARTIN LUTHER: Thus it is simply not possible for us human beings to know or to discover the verdict on and distinction of persons and their works. Instead we should praise everyone and honor them equally, not prefer one person above another, humble ourselves accordingly and always exalt our neighbors above ourselves. Then let God alone judge who is the greatest. THE CHURCH POSTIL (1540): THIRD SUNDAY IN ADVENT.[4]

THE GOSPEL IS THE VISIBLE REALITY. DESIDERIUS ERASMUS: In this way Jesus everywhere and at every opportunity called his followers from reliance on visible things, to which the Jews ascribed much, toward zeal for gospel godliness, which is rooted in the honest feelings of the heart. PARAPHRASE ON THE GOSPEL OF LUKE 21:1-4.[5]

THE WIDOW IS THE TRUE CHRISTIAN, FOR SHE GAVE UP ALL HER WEALTH. PETER WALPOT: Notice, all her nourishment. Therefore the Lord requires that all our wealth and all our heart be given to the Christian community, however much or little it might be. And how could

Christ have proven, taught and indicated what is true resignation and true community more amply than he did? He tells his disciples how they should present [this teaching] to the rich, and here, he shows how the poor do not say, "I have little," and he teaches them to do exactly the same. Therefore we should all practice the Christian community [of goods], for there is no one at all who gives more than this evangelical widow, who offered up two small coins in God's temple. She surpassed all the others, for she placed her entire wealth there. For God does not examine what we offer, but rather the heart and the will of the one who gives is on display. THE GREAT ARTICLE BOOK: ON PEACE AND JOINT PROPERTY.[6]

THE COMMUNITY OF GOODS IS VOLUNTARY. LEUPOLD SCHARNSCHLAGER: The example of the primitive church . . . is misunderstood by some, giving rise to error and contempt. Special sects and the like arise; some of them have made of this example a law, a requirement, a fetter—even almost a carnal righteousness, demand and the like. Therefore let us recognize that in the early church . . . the sharing of goods was a voluntary matter. . . . Even Paul wrote about sharing material possessions and community of goods, and we likewise in true apostolic character are to pay heed that the bride and flock of Christ be not forced but led and fed voluntarily. KUNSTBUCH: ARTICLE 5, CONGREGATIONAL ORDER FOR CHRIST'S MEMBERS.[7]

---

[3]CTS 33:113-14* (CO 45:646-47).
[4]WA 10,1.2:142 (cf. E² 7:108; LW 75:131).
[5]CWE 48:173 (LB 7:444).

[6]QGT 12:196-97; citing Mt 19:16-21.
[7]CRR 12:408 (QGT 17:444); citing Acts 4:34-35; 5:1-13; Rom 15:26-27; 1 Cor 16:1-2; 2 Cor 9:1-2; 1 Pet 5:2.

21:5-38 PERSECUTION AND THE END TIMES

⁵And while some were speaking of the temple, how it was adorned with noble stones and offerings, he said, ⁶"As for these things that you see, the days will come when there will not be left here one stone upon another that will not be thrown down." ⁷And they asked him, "Teacher, when will these things be, and what will be the sign when these things are about to take place?" ⁸And he said, "See that you are not led astray. For many will come in my name, saying, 'I am he!' and, 'The time is at hand!' Do not go after them. ⁹And when you hear of wars and tumults, do not be terrified, for these things must first take place, but the end will not be at once."

¹⁰Then he said to them, "Nation will rise against nation, and kingdom against kingdom. ¹¹There will be great earthquakes, and in various places famines and pestilences. And there will be terrors and great signs from heaven. ¹²But before all this they will lay their hands on you and persecute you, delivering you up to the synagogues and prisons, and you will be brought before kings and governors for my name's sake. ¹³This will be your opportunity to bear witness. ¹⁴Settle it therefore in your minds not to meditate beforehand how to answer, ¹⁵for I will give you a mouth and wisdom, which none of your adversaries will be able to withstand or contradict. ¹⁶You will be delivered up even by parents and brothersᵃ and relatives and friends, and some of you they will put to death. ¹⁷You will be hated by all for my name's sake. ¹⁸But not a hair of your head will perish. ¹⁹By your endurance you will gain your lives.

²⁰"But when you see Jerusalem surrounded by armies, then know that its desolation has come near. ²¹Then let those who are in Judea flee to the mountains, and let those who are inside the city depart, and let not those who are out in the country enter it, ²²for these are days of vengeance, to fulfill all that is written. ²³Alas for women who are pregnant and for those who are nursing infants in those days! For there will be great distress upon the earth and wrath against this people. ²⁴They will fall by the edge of the sword and be led captive among all nations, and Jerusalem will be trampled underfoot by the Gentiles, until the times of the Gentiles are fulfilled.

²⁵"And there will be signs in sun and moon and stars, and on the earth distress of nations in perplexity because of the roaring of the sea and the waves, ²⁶people fainting with fear and with foreboding of what is coming on the world. For the powers of the heavens will be shaken. ²⁷And then they will see the Son of Man coming in a cloud with power and great glory. ²⁸Now when these things begin to take place, straighten up and raise your heads, because your redemption is drawing near."

²⁹And he told them a parable: "Look at the fig tree, and all the trees. ³⁰As soon as they come out in leaf, you see for yourselves and know that the summer is already near. ³¹So also, when you see these things taking place, you know that the kingdom of God is near. ³²Truly, I say to you, this generation will not pass away until all has taken place. ³³Heaven and earth will pass away, but my words will not pass away.

³⁴"But watch yourselves lest your hearts be weighed down with dissipation and drunkenness and cares of this life, and that day come upon you suddenly like a trap. ³⁵For it will come upon all who dwell on the face of the whole earth. ³⁶But stay awake at all times, praying that you may have strength to escape all these things that are going to take place, and to stand before the Son of Man."

³⁷And every day he was teaching in the temple, but at night he went out and lodged on the mount called Olivet. ³⁸And early in the morning all the people came to him in the temple to hear him.

a Or parents and brothers and sisters

OVERVIEW: In this last long speech before the Passover festival and his arrest, Jesus spoke at length about the times that were coming, and how difficult they would be for the disciples. He spoke of destruction, of wars and earthquakes, of armies and heavenly signs. He spoke quite specifically of both the coming destruction of Jerusalem and his own second coming in glory. Because Jesus spoke of historical events that came to pass, some commentators assumed that the whole passage reports verifiable (if future) history as well as spiritual realities. The destruction of Jerusalem and the temple by the Romans in and around the year 70 is a focus, not only because at least some of the people to whom Jesus was speaking would still have been alive at that time, but also because Jerusalem and the temple within it were such important symbols—of God's love and faithfulness, or God's presence in the world and among his people. Why should such a beautiful, sacred place be destroyed, it seems, by God's will? The English Annotations suggest that the temple would be destroyed after Christ's death and resurrection to let the people know their law and ceremonies were now at an end. Jesus himself was sad about the coming destruction but knew that it was deserved, because they had rejected him and his teaching. Those who followed Christ should flee the city, for despite what some believed, God would not in this case come to save it—Melanchthon notes that this shows us that it is appropriate to flee when God visits destruction and punishment on a place. But unfortunately for the followers of Christ, the suffering and difficulties would not rain down only on those who rejected him. Instead, Christians would also suffer in the wars, earthquakes, famines and plagues, and even more, they would also suffer persecution for his sake, legal persecution by governments, by religious councils, even by members of their families. Satan will always work against Christ's kingdom, but Jesus' message was that while the terrible signs would confirm the coming destruction, they would also confirm that it is God's will in action.

Likewise, Jesus spoke specifically of his second coming and the signs that would precede it. It may be that Jesus' initial audience associated these two events—the destruction of Jerusalem and the coming of the Son of Man in glory—closely together, but early modern commentators knew that long centuries, if not millennia, would separate the two. So the challenge was not so much believing that it would come (with these miraculous signs preceding it) but remaining watchful and prepared. Psychologically it is very difficult to stay on high alert for an event that may be generations away. These interpreters remind us to prepare ourselves so that we are not found dozing off; we must keep our hearts free from the cares of life and live as if that day is coming very soon. The things of which Christ spoke will not come at once but gradually and sequentially. Though we do not know when, we know it is coming. Once the day is here, it will be too late to beg for mercy. We cannot wait until the last minute to repent but must work throughout our lives to do God's will. That way, when we do begin to see and recognize the signs, even if they are painful and frightening, we can be glad because we will know that the kingdom will be here soon and the long winter and reign of the devil will soon be over.

21:5-6 The Destruction of the Temple

A PURE SOUL IS A GREATER TEMPLE. KONRAD PELLIKAN: The Jews had held a particular pride in the temple at Jerusalem, which was built with the greatest effort and enriched with magnificent altars. It was viewed with the greatest reverence, not only by all of the Jews but also by all those born in foreign lands. Now, however, a time had come when the religious practices of that temple with its sacrifices might have ceased, and instead the temple of the soul, consecrated by the Holy Spirit, would have been prepared for God, in which every day the most pleasing sacrifices would have been offered, not of animals but of vows and expressions of gladness. Therefore the pure soul of anyone at all, even the poorest person, would be a holier and more magnificent temple to God than that most splendid temple built over so many years. Chastity, modesty and charity are ornaments much more valuable in the eyes of God than the marble, ivory, cedar, gold, silver and gems in which the priests and Pharisees took such pride. Commentary in Luke 21:5.[1]

The Disciples Could Not Believe That the Temple Would Be Destroyed. Philipp Melanchthon:

The noble sights of the temple astonished the disciples of Christ, and they thought it was impossible, because the temple was so grand and sumptuous, that it should be destroyed, as Christ had said. He was so far from pleasing them and changing their minds that he went on to exaggerate and earnestly inveigh against that in which they seemed so invested. He confirmed this coming destruction with an earnest affirmation, saying that it should certainly come to pass. He said, "As for what you see here," as if he should say, "Behold all these things diligently and wonder at them, but all these things shall fade away, no matter how sumptuous and beautiful they might be." An Ecclesiasticall Exposition upon Saint Mathewe 23.[2]

The Destruction of Jerusalem Showed That the Levitical Law Was Abolished. The English Annotations:

God would have Jerusalem, the place which he had chosen for himself (he had for a long time restrained the public rituals and sacrifices to that place, prefiguring that Christ the Savior would come and suffer there) be utterly destroyed, with the temple in which the Jews so gloried. He wanted this to happen after Christ had come and suffered there and had accomplished the work of our redemption, to let the Jews know that now all their ceremonies were ended. The one who was prefigured and expected had now come and finished all necessary things, and they should no longer stick to the dead and antiquated letter of the Levitical law, circumcision and sacrifices but should come to Christ, the end of the law to every believer. God well knew how unwillingly they would part from the rites in which they had previously been instructed and in which they esteemed themselves to be more excellent and holy than any other nation in the world, and how unwillingly they would join the faith of Christ and be made equal with the Gentiles whom they despised. Therefore, as Chrysostom says, God, who is present everywhere and fills every place, reduced his worship to sacrifices, then all the sacrifices to only a certain kind of sacrifice, then that kind only to a certain time, then to a certain city, then he overthrew that city, to declare the utter destruction and abolition of that law and ceremonies, which were tied to that place and were not to be used anywhere else in the world but there.[3] Annotations on the Gospel According to Saint Luke 21:6.[4]

21:7-11 Fearful Events and Great Signs

These Are Sure Signs of the End. Melchior Neukirch:

Because they had the beautiful temple right there before them, and they were looking at it, they asked when it would happen that the splendid city and the beautiful temple would be torn down. Then the Lord showed them some assured signs by which they would be able to see and know ahead of time when the final destruction by the rod was coming. He also informed them of the signs that would precede the Judgment Day. And he admonished his apostles and all Christians through certain parables and examples to be prepared and to resign themselves so that they could endure it. He informed them that the Judgment Day would come swiftly, suddenly and unexpectedly, so that they might be resigned to it, and so always be prepared. The First Part of the Passion.[5]

---

[1]Pellikan, *In Sacrosancta Quatuor Evangelia*, 210 (cf. CWE 48:173; LB 7:444).
[2]Marlorat, ed., *Catholike and Ecclesiasticall Exposition of the Holy Gospell After S. Mathewe*, 553*.
[3]John Chrysostom, *Discourses Against Judaizing Christians* oration 1 (FC 68:1-34).
[4]Downame, ed., *Annotations*, Zz1r*; citing Lk 19:44.
[5]Neukirch, *Historia der Passion*, 88r-v.

TWO COMMANDS FOR THE AGE BETWEEN THE FIRST AND SECOND ADVENTS. JOHN CALVIN: Christ explicitly gives two commands to his disciples: to beware of false teaching and not to be thrown into confusion by scandals. By these words he indicates that his church—as long as it sojourns in the world—will be subject to these evils. This might seem to be inconsistent, because long ago the prophets described the future Christ's kingdom differently. Isaiah promises that all will be taught by God. . . . An even greater light of understanding is promised by Jeremiah. "After this each person will no longer teach his neighbor, or a man his brother, saying 'Know the Lord.' Everyone will know me, from the least to the greatest." Therefore, after the Sun of righteousness had arisen, as it was foretold by Malachi, it is no wonder if the Jews hoped that they would be pure and entirely free from every cloud of error. That is why the Samaritan woman said, "When the Messiah comes, he will teach us everything." Truly we know what magnificent promises of peace, righteousness, joy and abundance of every good thing there are everywhere in Scripture. It is therefore no surprise if after Christ's advent they believed that they would be delivered from the tumults of war, from financial woes and every injustice, in short from famine and pestilence.

But Christ warns them that in the future false teachers will trouble the godly no less than false prophets did the ancient people. Nor will the disturbances under the gospel be inferior to those formerly under the law. This is not because these prophecies which I have just mentioned will fail to be accomplished, but because their full completion does not emerge immediately in one day. It is enough to give the faithful a taste of those good things, so that they cherish the hope of their full enjoyment that is yet to come. Therefore, they were greatly mistaken who at the beginning of the gospel wanted to produce immediately and perfectly those things which we see accomplished over time. COMMENTARY ON A HARMONY OF THE GOSPELS.[6]

THE LORD DOES NOT WANT US TO BE DISTRESSED ABOUT WHAT MUST BE. MARTIN BUCER: Now, in case they might be greatly troubled by the manifold and horrible tumults of wars and revolutions with which the Jewish nation would be afflicted before their destruction, he forewarns them of those events, so that they would not be hurt by them. In order that he might also disabuse them of the notion that they were going to have a quiet kingdom, in which everything would flourish, he gives them this admonition. . . . Then he tells them, "Do not be frightened." This happens today with some who at any happenstance begin to doubt the gospel, or hold it in suspicion or else altogether to condemn it. . . . This word *must* contains within it no small consolation. For what wise person will be afflicted by something which must be, and cannot be otherwise? There is no person who trusts in God who will be troubled when that thing which must happen by the ordinance of God comes to pass, because he knows that it must be the best and most wholesome thing for the saints of God. God truly does not want those who are his to be troubled in these necessary and continual turmoils, but he rather wants them to be of stout mind, like those who know it to be the decree and ordinance of God. He says that it must be, and yet nevertheless he does not show the cause but declares that none of these things happen by chance, without the providence of God, in order that we should not struggle in vain against the goad. AN ECCLESIASTICALL EXPOSITION UPON SAINT MATHEWE 23.[7]

THE INCREASING TERROR OF THESE SIGNS AS HISTORY PROGRESSES. MARTIN LUTHER: We have seen much of these signs, even though they also happened previously; but they are not for that reason any less sure of signs, especially because they occur at the same time as the others. And everyone acknowledges that today's wars are of such a character as to make former wars appear as mere child's play—so very horrible and devastating is what comes with

---

[6]CTS 33:119* (CO 45:650); citing Is 54:13; Jer 31:34; Mal 4:2; Jn 4:25.

[7]Marlorat, ed., *Catholike and Ecclesiasticall Exposition of the Holy Gospell After S. Mathewe*, 558-59*.

guns, armor and munitions. . . . Let these signs be signs, great signs, signifying great things; but they are already forgotten and despised. The Church Postil (1540): Second Sunday in Advent.[8]

21:12-19 Prior Persecution

The Apostles Will Suffer by Legal Authority. Philipp Melanchthon: Now he shows the reason why his apostles should take heed of others: because they will suffer much evil at their hands. He does not say, "They will go about to deliver you, or beat you or betray you," but he certainly affirms that they will indeed deliver them up to the councils and scourge them. Hereby we may truly note that the adversaries of Christ, although they show themselves to be wolves and brute beasts rather than human beings, yet they seem to condemn the ministers of Christ as schismatics and seditious people. They do not condemn them by violence but by just judgment, by law, by consent of the people and by public authority. But really these kind of people do not have regard either for others or for the authorities; rather, they only seek, with earnest study, to school their emotions, so that nothing might seem to be done out of hatred or sinister feelings but by law and conscience. After this manner, when they had taken Christ himself by their soldiers and might have slain him right away without any more fuss, instead they sought first to bring him before the council of elders and high priests, and there to condemn him. Once he was condemned by the authority and consent of the council, he was delivered to the deputy to be punished, who then brought him to the people to be condemned, and afterwards to be scourged and delivered again to the people to be put to death. The Evangelists Mark and Luke write at length about this. In this same manner, Peter and John were violently treated, and all the rest of the apostles. An Ecclesiasticall Exposition upon Saint Mathewe 10.[9]

Truth Is Never Separated from the Cross. François Lambert: What this Lord wants, if not the fulfillment of the prophecies, is the most faithful testimony which will itself fortell the truth. And consequently, when someone sees that a person is afflicted on account of the testimony to the truth, he recognizes the truth of Christ's words. In the end, persecution itself is a great testimony of the truth, for the truth is never able to be separated from the cross itself. Commentary in Luke 21:13.[10]

The Enemies of the Truth Cannot Overcome It. Johannes Brenz: The enemies of the truth shall speak many vain words and reason sophistically with worldly arguments, but they shall not be able to contradict the arguments of truth. They shall vehemently resist the truth, but they shall not be able to overthrow it—they will keep working at it, but without success. They are like beasts who are enemies to human beings: when they are shut up in cages, they rage and behave fiercely, which shows their cruel and wild natures, and yet despite this they are unable to act on their outraged wildness. Likewise, the enemies of truth, being shut up and restrained with the invincible arguments of truth, roar and rage against it but cannot overcome it.

Peter and John answered to the council concerning the man who was healed, saying, "Let it be known to all of you and to all the people of Israel that by the name of Jesus Christ of Nazareth, whom you crucified, whom God raised from the dead—by him this man is standing before you well." Did the high priests then hold their peace? Not at all, but rather they forbade them and threatened them never to speak again to anyone in that same name. They tried to resist the truth, but they were unable and could not contradict it even with their words and threats. For Luke writes, "Now when they saw the boldness of Peter and John and perceived that they were uneducated, common men, they were astonished. And they recognized

[8]LW 75:102* (WA 10,1.2:108; E² 10:70).
[9]Marlorat, ed., *Catholike and Ecclesasticall Exposition of the Holy Gospell After S. Mathewe,* 211-12*; citing Mk 14; Lk 22.

[10]Lambert, *In Divi Lucae,* Ff4r.

that they had been with Jesus. But seeing the man who was healed standing beside them, they had nothing to say in opposition." Likewise, when Stephen said that God did not dwell in temples made with hands, the enemies of truth were so crazed and outraged against him that they gnashed on him with their teeth, but yet they were not able to resist the truth which this blessed martyr uttered. AN ECCLESIASTICALL EXPOSITION UPON SAINT LUKE 21.[11]

THE APOSTLES' WORDS ARE THE WORDS OF GOD. PHILIPP MELANCHTHON: This place teaches us what authority, credit and estimation the writings of the apostles ought to have among us. For if the Spirit of God spoke through the apostles, why should we not esteem their words as words that proceed out of the mouth of God? Seeing they have this testimony of Christ, we cannot be deceived in obeying their godly doctrine. But we might err if we follow and credit those who boast of the succession to the apostles but in whom no spark of the Spirit of God appears, either in life or in doctrine. We should lament that gross dullness and obstinate blindness of the world, by which it was brought to pass that those in whom the Spirit of God spoke have been slain. The prophets and apostles spoke boldly and constantly preached the gospel with the ferventness of the Spirit of God, and yet despite this they were counted as seducers of the people of God and thus were put to death. Therefore this great obstinacy of the world is to be left to the just judgment of God. AN ECCLESIASTICALL EXPOSITION UPON SAINT MATHEWE 10.[12]

SATAN STIRS UP PEOPLE AGAINST EACH OTHER. MARTIN BUCER: He expresses the danger strongly, in order that he might give them a forewarning and strengthen and comfort them. For nothing in the whole world can be safe, sure and certain for those who will preach and set forth the gospel. In this case, they can hardly trust their own brothers or sisters, or children, or even their parents. For the Word of Christ abides forever, when he says, "Whoever is not with me is against me, and whoever does not gather with me scatters." Satan, with all his kingdom and his power, wages continual war against Christ and his kingdom, and no force of nature is able to withstand this furor and outrageous rebellion. For he holds the wicked as bond and captives, at his will and pleasure. Therefore it is in his hand to stir and set brother against brother, the children against the parents and the parents against the children—truly, to set all people against each other. AN ECCLESIASTICALL EXPOSITION UPON SAINT MATHEWE 10.[13]

CHRIST WARNS THE FAITHFUL OF COMING PERSECUTION. JOHN CALVIN: Christ now forewarns his disciples of another type of temptation by which, besides ordinary afflictions, their faith would be tried, which is that without a doubt they would be hated and detested by the whole world. It is sad and difficult in itself for the children of God to be thrown together indiscriminately with the reprobate and those who despise God, and to be subject to the same punishment that they bear on account of their sins. And it seems to be even more unfair that they are heavily oppressed by burdensome evils from which the ungodly are exempt. Just as the wheat, after it is beaten together with the chaff by the threshing flail, is ground and bruised by the grindstone, so God not only afflicts his children together with the ungodly but also disciplines them even more than others by the cross, so that they seem to be even more miserable than the rest of humankind. But Christ here strictly discusses the afflictions by which the disciples were attacked on account of the gospel. Even if it is indeed true what Paul says, that those whom God elects are also destined to bear the cross, that they might be "conformed to the image

---

[11]Marlorat, ed., *Catholike and Ecclesiasticall Exposition of the Holy Gospell After S. Marke and Luke*, 307-8*; citing Acts 4:10, 13-14; 6–7.

[12]Marlorat, ed., *Catholike and Ecclesiasticall Exposition of the Holy Gospell After S. Mathewe*, 214*.

[13]Marlorat, ed., *Catholike and Ecclesiasticall Exposition of the Holy Gospell After S. Mathewe*, 214*; citing Mt 12:30; 2 Tim 2:26.

of his Son," nevertheless he does not distinguish them by the unique sign that they would suffer persecution from the enemies of the gospel. It is of that type of cross that Christ now makes a statement, that it is necessary that the faithful will suffer hatred, expose themselves to disgrace and provoke the fury of the ungodly because of the testimony of the gospel. For he desired to warn the disciples that the teaching of the gospel (of which they were to be witnesses and messengers) would not be at all welcomed or appreciated by the world, just as he had formerly explained to them. He foretells that they will be in battle not only with a few enemies but that, wherever they might come, all peoples will be hostile to them. COMMENTARY ON A HARMONY OF THE GOSPELS.[14]

WE SHOULD LIVE BY BEING PREPARED TO DIE.

JOHN CALVIN: Here, at greater length, Christ prescribes to his disciples another way of guarding their life than that dictated by fleshly reason. It is quite natural that each person desires to place his life in safety; from every place we collect all the protections that we think are in our best interest, and we run away from all danger—in short, we do not consider ourselves really living unless we are properly protected. But Christ commands that we instead pursue this care of our lives—that we should always walk exposed to death "through fire and water" and sword. And certainly, no one will really place his soul in God's hand except for one who has learned to live in the moment, always prepared to die. In sum, Christ orders us to possess our lives both under the cross and among the continual terrors of death. COMMENTARY ON A HARMONY OF THE GOSPELS.[15]

21:20-24 The Destruction of Jerusalem

WE SHOULD FLEE TO ESCAPE DANGER.

PHILIPP MELANCHTHON: He means that there will be no cities in all of Judea void of fear or existing in safety. Likewise, the angel commanded

Lot to flee into the mountains, that he might reach safety there. Jesus said this to the disciples, so that later he might admonish those who were faithful among them. Eusebius writes that the Christians who still remained in Jerusalem when it was besieged by the Roman armies were commanded by the oracle and Word of God to flee to a certain city called Pella, beyond the Jordan.[16] We are admonished by this information not to trust too much in ourselves, as though by our own strength and wisdom or by a miracle of God we should be delivered. Rather, if we are able, we should try to escape by flight. AN ECCLESIASTICALL EXPOSITION UPON SAINT MATHEWE 23.[17]

EVEN THE UNBORN CHILDREN WILL NOT BE SPARED.

JAKOB ANDREAE: But Christ is mercy itself, and he took no enjoyment in their downfall and ruin. Rather, it brought him heartfelt pain, despite the fact that they had only themselves to blame and deserved such sorrow for rejecting him and his teaching. He especially shows his compassion toward that weak instrument, the pregnant or nursing woman, and says, "Woe to those who are pregnant and those who are nursing in those days." Even the children still in their mothers' wombs would not be spared, and women take this more to heart than men. Therefore the experience will be much more difficult and unbearable for them. SERMON ON THE TWENTY-FIFTH SUNDAY AFTER TRINITY.[18]

GOD SENDS TROUBLES TO PUNISH THE PEOPLE.

PHILIPP MELANCHTHON: He now shows the reason why there will be such an urgent necessity to flee.... He means here in the land of Judea. By the word *wrath* he signifies the vengeance of God from heaven, that is to say, great afflictions and calamities sent by God from heaven, which declare that God is angry. He joined wrath and distress together, because when God is angry he sends trouble and distress. It is as if he should say,

---

[14]CTS 33:123-24* (CO 45:653); citing Rom 8:29.
[15]CTS 33:126-27* (CO 45:655); citing Ps 66:12.

[16]Eusebius, *The History of the Church* 3.5 (NPNF[2] 1:138).
[17]Marlorat, ed., *Catholike and Ecclesiasticall Exposition of the Holy Gospell After S. Mathewe*, 567*; citing Gen 19:17.
[18]Andreae, *Ein Christliche Predigt*, B4v.

"By this great trouble the Lord declares that he is angry against the people dwelling in the land of Judea." And afterward he declares what this trouble will be when he says, "They will fall by the sword." An Ecclesiasticall Exposition upon Saint Mathewe 23.[19]

JERUSALEM WOULD BE UTTERLY DESTROYED. JOHN CALVIN: "Abomination" means the same as "profanation," for this word denotes an uncleanness which corrupts or overthrows the pure worship of God. It is called desolation, however, because it drew along with it the destruction of the temple and the government; likewise, in Daniel 9 he said that the pollution introduced by Antiochus was, as it were, the standard of temporary desolation, which is how I interpret the word *wing*, or "spreading out." However, those who interpret this to mean the siege of Jerusalem are confused, and the words of Luke do not support that error, who did not intend to indicate that but something different. For although that city was once delivered in the midst of its destruction, believers should not hope for such a thing in the future, when it will also be surrounded by enemies, for Christ announces that it will be sacrificed, because it would be absolutely divested of God's help. The sense is, therefore, that the success of war will not be in doubt, because that city is addicted to destruction, which it will not be able to escape any more than it could abrogate the decree of heaven. For that reason, a little later it is added that "Jerusalem will be trampled on by the Gentiles," and that saying means its final ruin. But, because it appeared absurd that the holy city would be so exposed to dishonor at the pleasure of the Gentiles, he adds the consolation that the Gentiles would be permitted such license only for a time, until their iniquity had come to its fullness, and the vengeance which was set aside for them would be clearly seen. COMMENTARY ON A HARMONY OF THE GOSPELS.[20]

21:25-28 *Signs in Heaven and Earth*

THE SIGNS OF DESTRUCTION GIVE COMFORT TO THE FAITHFUL. JOHN BOYS: When Christ comes in judgment, it shall be shown here by wonders in the heavens, the earth and the sea, which shall be like harbingers of that dreadful and terrible day. . . . Everyone desires to buy an almanac, so that at the beginning of the year he may know what will happen in the end. Merchants and farmers especially desire to know this year what failures or death or accidents are likely to occur the next year. So here we have Christ's prophecy, foretelling by signs in the sun, the moon and the stars what will come to pass at the end of our years, and what will happen in the new year, in the world to come. The scientists of the world never mentioned or dreamed of a universal eclipse of the sun and moon together—only Christ's almanac reports this. I do not plan to discuss in particular any questions of curiosity but only to note in general that these wonders in the heavens and extraordinary troubles on earth are clear forerunners of the world's ruin; just as we know that summer is near when the trees bud, so when we see these things come to pass, we may be sure that the kingdom of God is close. For as one who is dying has many dreams or fantasies, even so, says Chrysostom, when the world is in decline it will have many errors, so many in fact that if it were possible, even God's elect should be deceived. . . .[21]

These signs give comfort to God's elect, for when these things begin to happen, Christ says in Luke 21:28, "Lift up your heads, for your redemption draws near." Now you are prosecuted and persecuted, delivered up to the synagogues and cast into prison, but at that great Judgment Day there shall be a general sentencing of everyone. You that have done good shall go into everlasting joy, but your enemies who have done evil shall be cast into everlasting fire. Here you mourn, but hereafter all tears shall be wiped from your eyes; here you sow

---

[19]Marlorat, ed., *Catholike and Ecclesiasticall Exposition of the Holy Gospell After S. Mathewe*, 568*.

[20]CTS 33:134-35* (CO 45:660); citing Mt 24:15; Lk 21:20; Dan 9:27.

[21]See Chrysostom, *Homilies on the Gospel of Saint Matthew*, Homily 77 (NPNF 10:444-51).

in hope, but then you shall reap with joy, when you see the Son of Man coming in the clouds. THE SECOND SUNDAY IN ADVENT.[22]

THE SIGNS ARE GOD'S JUDGMENT ON THE WICKED. MARTIN BUCER: These words of Luke are not to be taken as though these signs must occur before the Day of the Lord, but "signs" here mean miracles and things not commonly seen, which will not so much signify the Day of the Lord as they shall bring the mighty wrath of God on the wicked. Concerning the darkening of the sun and all the rest, there are diverse opinions among the interpreters, especially the older ones, but it seems that the simplicity and plainness of Christ's words ought to be retained and kept. He says that the sun will be darkened, the moon will lose its light, and the stars will fall from heaven, and so on: we should certainly believe that it will happen just so. But how the sun will be darkened, that to this day we still do not know, and we cannot guess, but when it happens, then we will know. And when he says "the stars shall fall," he does not mean that the stars will actually fall but that people will think that they are falling. And that is why Luke only indicates that there will be signs in the sun, moon and stars. The meaning of his words is that the striking and shaking of the foundation of the heavens will be so great that people will believe that the very stars are falling. Luke also speaks about the terrible motion of the sea, that people "will faint from terror" and sorrow. But the sum of the whole is that all creatures, both above and below, will be, as it were, criers or accusers who will bring evidence against people at the horrible tribunal seat of judgment, but these will wickedly continue to despise it even until the very Last Day. AN ECCLESIASTICALL EXPOSITION UPON SAINT MATHEWE 23.[23]

IS JESUS TALKING ABOUT A PLANETARY ALIGNMENT? MARTIN LUTHER: I still do not know what is meant by the shaking of the heavenly hosts, unless it is the great conjunction of the planets which happened in 1524. For the planets are certainly the chief of the powers and hosts of heaven, and their strange gathering is a definite sign for the world. Christ does not say that all the hosts of heaven will be shaken, but some of them. For not all stars are shaken, just as it was said . . . that not all people endure difficulty and fear, not all waters always roar and rumble, sun and moon are not dark every day; for these are all to be only signs, which can only occur in some few places, so that they may be something special compared with the other places which are not signs. Therefore, I am convinced that this shaking of the heavenly host is the conjunction of the planets. THE CHURCH POSTIL (1540): SECOND SUNDAY OF ADVENT.[24]

CHRIST WILL RETURN IN THE SAME FORM IN WHICH HE ASCENDED. PHILIPP MELANCHTHON: There is an emphasis or force in the fact that he does not say "and they will come," but "they will see." It is as if he had said, "They will see with great terror and fear the one whom they reviled and persecuted coming in power and great glory to judge." When they brought him before the high priests, he spoke in this manner, saying, "From now on you will see the Son of Man seated at the right hand of power and coming on the clouds of heaven." And in John 19 it says, "They will look on him whom they have pierced," that is, they shall see the Son of Man. For when he ascended into heaven, he left his human nature, but he also clarified it, so he means that when he descends he will come in the same form and substance in which he ascended. . . . He ascended into the clouds. . . . And as he ascended, so will he again descend. The angels said, "This Jesus, who was taken up from you into heaven, will come in the same way as you saw him go into heaven." AN ECCLESIASTICALL EXPOSITION UPON SAINT MATHEWE 23.[25]

---

[22]Boys, *Exposition of the Dominical Epistles and Gospels*, 1:32-33*; citing Mt 24:24.

[23]Marlorat, ed., *Catholike and Ecclesiasticall Exposition of the Holy Gospell After S. Mathewe*, 577*.

[24]LW 75:101-2* (WA 10,1.2:107-8; E² 10:69).

[25]Marlorat, ed., *Catholike and Ecclesiasticall Exposition of the Holy Gospell After S. Mathewe*, 579-80*; citing Mt 26:64; Jn 19:37 (cf. Zech 12:10); Acts 1:9, 11.

THE RAPTURE AND HELL. HUGH LATIMER: It is certain that he will come to judge, but we cannot tell the time when he will come. Therefore, seeing that he will come, let us make ready so that he will not find us unprepared. We should take it as a rule that however he finds us, that is how he will judge us. Saint Paul says to the Thessalonians, when he speaks of the resurrection of the good, "With the sound of God's trumpet, the Lord will descend from heaven, and the dead in Christ will rise first. Then we who are alive, who are left, will be caught up in the clouds together with them to meet the Lord in the air." All those, I say, who are content to strive and fight against sin, who will not be ruled by sin, will be taken in this way up into the air and will meet with Christ and so will come down with him again. But as for the other sort, who are wicked, who take delight in wickedness and will not leave it but will rather go forward in all wickedness—they will be left on the earth with the devils until they are judged. And after they have received their sentence, they will go to hell with the devil and all his minions, and there will be punished for their sins in hellish fire for ever and ever. For so it is written: *Vermis eorum non moritur*, that is, "Their worm shall not die." THE SECOND SUNDAY IN ADVENT (1552).[26]

THAT WILL BE A HAPPY DAY OF SALVATION. JOHANN SPANGENBERG: How does he want the pious and faithful to be? Cheerful, for they will be saved on that day from all evil. And where is that written? Christ therefore said, "When these things begin to take place, stand up and lift up your heads, because your redemption is drawing near." What is he saying with these words? He is showing how we should prepare ourselves for his future, as if he should say, "You poor little band has had to suffer greatly in this world for my sake. Now look at the one whom you trusted. And where are those now who persecuted you? Where is all their great pomp and pride now? Have they not been brought altogether in body and soul into disgrace? Look,

now your cross and sorrow will have an end, and their eternal unhappiness and damnation will begin. Do not be afraid of my power and majesty. It is not against you, but rather it is for you." And he told them a sweet and happy parable. THE GOSPEL ON THE SECOND SUNDAY OF ADVENT, LUKE 21.[27]

21:29-31 *The Parable of the Fig Tree*

SUMMERTIME BRINGS MANY PLEASURES, JUST LIKE THE KINGDOM OF GOD. JOHANN BAUMGART (POMARIUS): The winter has very short days, but for many poor people it is much too long, on account of its unfriendly, rough and difficult weather: frost, cold, rain, wind, snow, and one hardship after another. Winter requires many provisions, and people suffer many losses. All creatures mourn, the leaves, grass, trees and flowers wither away, happy birds are silent, and people have little lasting pleasure or joy in the winter.

On the contrary, summer brings with it longer days, happier times and pleasant refreshment, pleasure and joy, for the days are lengthened, all creatures are renewed, and the swallows, insects and worms that had vanished or died out over the winter are brought to life again by the warm shining of the sun. The birds sing and hop, leaves and grass, trees and everything that grows sprout and all creatures are glad because of the happy summertime. . . .

So when the buds on the trees begin to sprout in the spring, we should remember the signs of the Last Days already mentioned. Just as such buds frighten no one but rather give them joy on account of the pleasant summertime to come, and the bigger the buds become and the more abundantly they appear, the gladder people are to see them, and they rejoice over the summer which is coming soon; just so should we also think when more and more signs occur, that the kingdom of God is that much closer, which is the eternal spring and summer, and should be even dearer to us than

---

[26]Latimer, *Sermons and Remains*, 53*; citing 1 Thess 4:16-17; Is 66:24.   [27]Spangenberg, *Postilla* (1582), XIIIr.

those seasons. The Gospel on the Second Sunday of Advent.[28]

The Signs of the End Will Come in Order.
Heinrich Bullinger: Just as summer has not arrived immediately when we see the buds of the fig tree, but first the bud comes, then the blossom, then the leaf, then the fig, and last of all the fig ripens; even so we should understand that all those things of which Christ spoke will not come at once but by degrees and in order. When we see the beginning, we should not doubt that the middle will come shortly after, and when the middle is come, we will know that it will not be long until the end is finished. Likewise, when the disciples of Christ saw that many were exalting themselves as Christs and seducing many, they knew straight away that wars and rumors of wars would follow. And yet they knew that Jerusalem would not be destroyed right away, but that first they would suffer many persecutions, and the gospel must be preached everywhere. Then they looked for the desolation of the holy city, and after that, that many false prophets and false Christs would prevail, and so in this order they knew that the end of the world would come. In like manner, when we know that many of those things of which the Lord has spoken come to pass, we ought to acknowledge that the kingdom of God and the Day of the Lord is already at the door and that therefore we should look for it by diligently working to form ourselves in godliness and virtue. For if we follow the estimation of God—as in these things we must—a thousand years for us are but a day for him, or even as a watch in the night. An Ecclesiasticall Exposition upon Saint Mathewe 23.[29]

The Terrible Signs Mean That Paradise Is Coming. Johann Spangenberg: What does Christ want to tell us with this parable? This is what he is saying: When you see that the sun and the moon are darkened, the stars fall, comets appear, pestilence and unheard-of illnesses come, fire and water wreak havoc, the wind rages, mountains and valleys, lands and islands, towns and villages all fall, heaven and earth crash, the people tremble and shake, all elements change themselves, all creatures surrender, as if everything would perish, war is heard and the cries of war, riots, false teaching, lies and errors, then you should say with joy: "God be praised, it will be summer again!" The blossoms and leaves burst out, the beautiful lilies and roses break forth. It was winter for long enough. The devil and his servants have delighted themselves long enough. Once again a beautiful summer will come that will never come to an end, and all the angels and all creatures will rejoice that they are free from the evil world, and the children of God will be called to everlasting life. The Gospel on the Second Sunday of Advent, Luke 21.[30]

21:32-36 Be Ready for the Coming of the Son of Man

The Signs Will Be Hard to Believe.
Martin Luther: Why does the Lord make his words so firm and precious and sternly confirm them beyond measure with comparisons, oaths and tokens of the generation that shall remain with them, that heaven and earth shall pass away sooner? This all happens, as was said above, so that all the world would become so secure and with open eyes despise the signs to such a degree that no words of God have been so despised as these which proclaim and characterize the Last Day.[31] It will appear to the world that there are no signs; and even though they see them, they will not believe them. Even the elect of God might doubt such words of God and signs, in order that the day may come at a time when the world has never before been so secure and be suddenly assaulted in the greatest security, as we heard from Saint Paul above.

[28]Baumgart, *Postilla*, 8v-9v.
[29]Marlorat, ed., *Catholike and Ecclesiasticall Exposition of the Holy Gospell After S. Mathewe*, 581*; citing Ps 90:4; 2 Pet 3:8.
[30]Spangenberg, *Postilla* (1582), XIIIv.
[31]See LW 75:92-93 (WA 10,1.2:95-97; E² 10:55-58).

Therefore, Christ wants to make us certain and wake us up so that we await the day when the signs appear with certainty. In fact, even if the signs were uncertain, those are not in danger who regard them as certain, while those are in danger who despise them. Therefore, let us deal with certainties and consider the above-named signs as correct, so that we do not run with the unspiritual. If we are mistaken, we have at least hit the mark; if they are mistaken, they will remain mistaken. THE CHURCH POSTIL (1540): SECOND SUNDAY OF ADVENT.[32]

JESUS WARNS AGAINST WICKED BEHAVIOR.
JOHANNES MATHESIUS: In this passage we hear how Christ, the true savior and gracious judge, so sincerely warns and affectionately admonishes. For he knew it at the time, as God's Son before whose eyes everything is present, and he saw that shortly before Judgment Day the godless people of the world would become gluttons and drunkards, living in anxiety and avarice, running rampant and pawing the ground, doing violence and weighing down and burdening their hearts with their laziness and lack of desire to hear and to pray God's Word. In those days, people will carouse all night long, then in the morning sleep through the sermon and prayers, or they might just go to church out of habit but stand out in front of the church, neglect the prayer, sleep or gossip through the sermon and not notice one word of it, not even saying the Our Father. Such people will not escape punishment, as the experience these days gives evidence, and in addition they will appear before the Lord Jesus Christ dishonorably and with shame, as the kingly prophet David also says, and will receive a severe and speedy dismissal, when Christ says, "Get away from me, you accursed people; while you were on earth you gorged yourselves, got drunk, caroused, scoffed at my Word and did not pray; go now into hell fire with the gluttonous and drunken devils." O God, that

will be a difficult position! It is a great shame and evil when drunken people stand before a sober judge. How, O God, can people be so sick that they will stand drunk before our sober emperor? GOSPEL FOR THE SECOND SUNDAY IN ADVENT, LUKE 21.[33]

THOSE DREADFUL TIMES ARE COMING AT AN UNKNOWN HOUR. DESIDERIUS ERASMUS: Therefore, because it is certain that this terrible time is going to come, prepare yourselves for its coming, so that it does not catch you yawning. You will accomplish this if you take care that your hearts are not weighed down by excess and drunkenness and by the rest of the cares of this present life. Rather, you should live as if that day might come very soon, loving nothing in this world, with your entire hearts and minds focused on heaven. That is how we can ensure that the day does not catch us unawares. The rest, however, who are living as if that time will never come, will find that day will spring on them like a snare placed stealthily in an ambush. It will overwhelm everyone who does not have heart or eyes raised up to heaven but who instead lives focused on this life on earth. But this is not our fixed home—instead, we should make haste to our eternal home. And it is certain that while they are busy with other matters, they will find themselves caught before they even notice the trap.

Flee sleepiness, so that the same does not happen to you through habit! Push aside the desire to sink down into the pleasures and cares of this world, but instead keep awake eagerly in constant consideration of heavenly things, continually praying that God might find you worthy to be counted in the number of those who are able to escape the times of such danger and are able to stand before the unavoidable judge, the Son of Man. He now summons all people to repentance with great gentleness, but then he will judge the living and the dead with great severity. No one

---

[32]LW 75:107-8* (WA 10,1.2:115; E² 10:78-79); citing 2 Tim 4:8; Tit 2:13; 1 Thess 5:2-3.

[33]Mathesius, *Postilla Symbolica*, 22r-v; citing Ps 1; 25; 34; Is 49; Jer 17; Mt 25.

should trust in his own defenses, for no one will endure this judgment unless he has been protected by divine favor. But this favor will not be present except to those who endeavor in the meantime with the highest zeal to show themselves worthy of it. Therefore, when that time comes, it will be too late for those who abuse his gentleness to beg for his mercy. Paraphrase on the Gospel of Luke 21:32-36.[34]

21:37-38 Jesus Teaches in the Temple

In Preparation for Death, He Prayed and Taught Without Ceasing. Konrad Pellikan: When the time of his death was drawing near, the Lord Jesus instructed his disciples by his example, that one should be even more alert in pious zeal at the time when the last moments and days of life are at hand. But now that it is the final day of the earth, which many had already predicted, it is each person's own day of death. Consequently, during the day the Lord taught the people in the temple, not ceasing to benefit even those whom he recognized would kill him. At night, he moved up to the Mount of Olives to pray, because it would have been unoccupied, so that he could pray without interruption, pleading with the Father on behalf of the salvation of the world and spending the least time in sleep. But the people rose at dawn (this is a Hebrew figure of speech meaning *manicare*, that is, "to rise and set off in the morning") and kept coming to him in the temple in order to hear his teaching. Commentary in Luke 21:37-38.[35]

[34]Erasmus, *In Evangelivm Lvce Paraphrasis*, D3v-D4r (LB 7:448; cf. CWE 48:181-82).

[35]Pellikan, *In Sacrosancta Quatuor Evangelia*, 215 (cf. CWE 48:182-83; LB 7:448).

22:1-6 JUDAS AGREES TO BETRAY JESUS

Now the Feast of Unleavened Bread drew near, which is called the Passover. ²And the chief priests and the scribes were seeking how to put him to death, for they feared the people.

³Then Satan entered into Judas called Iscariot, who was of the number of the twelve. ⁴He went away and conferred with the chief priests and officers how he might betray him to them. ⁵And they were glad, and agreed to give him money. ⁶So he consented and sought an opportunity to betray him to them in the absence of a crowd.

OVERVIEW: There is very little disagreement over the character of Judas, no matter the stripe of reformer: everyone agrees that Judas is moved by his vicious nature to betray Jesus. It is especially his love of money—the root of all kinds of evil (1 Tim 6:10)—that leads Judas, a member of Jesus' innermost circle, to hand Jesus over to his enemies. Satan found easy and ready servants in all these men. The religious establishment are solely interested in preserving their own authority, their priestly kingdom, and Judas complied all the more willingly because of the promise of money. These leaders of God's people were supposed to safeguard God's will and the gospel, but instead they were influenced by Satan to serve his evil plans and their own selfishness.

22:1-2 The Enemies of Jesus Prepare to Capture Him

THE PASSOVER FEAST IS COMMANDED BY GOD. THOMAS MORE: To understand the words of the Gospel, "Now the Feast of the Unleavened Bread drew near, which is called the Passover," you should understand that the Jews, among all their feasts and holy days throughout the year, had one feast which was the most solemn called Passover, and the Feast of Unleavened Bread, which God had commanded them to celebrate every year forever, as appears in [Exodus 12]. For after that, the proud, stiff-necked pharaoh, although he was commanded by Moses in God's name to allow the children of Israel to depart from his land into the desert with

all their wives, children and cattle, would not allow it. Certainly he was forced and constrained by many blows and plagues from God to grant their delivery when he stood in dread of the rod of God which lashed him, but as soon as that rod was removed, his stubborn pride sprang into his hard heart and made him forbid their passage again, in order to keep them in servitude. At last the Lord commanded Moses that on the tenth day of that month, every household should take a lamb without any spot, and on the fourteenth day of the same month, they should in that evening offer it and eat it all together. . . .

But now, this feast of the unleavened bread was kept holy every year for the seven days required by the special commandment of God; it was called . . . the days of the unleavened bread. The first of these days was the great, solemn day [of the festival], and it always began the night before in the evening feast of Passover, when the unspotted lamb was offered in sacrifice and cooked. For as I have shown, they were commanded to eat this lamb with unleavened bread, and from that day to continue only to eat unleavened bread for the following seven days. Therefore this feast of the sacrifice of the unspotted lamb is the feast that is called "Passover," of which the Evangelists speak here. And they also call it the Feast of the Unleavened Bread, because that feast began the same night in which the lamb was sacrificed. NAMES OF THE PASCHAL FEAST.[1]

---

[1]CWM 13:59, 61*.

THE RELIGIOUS LEADERS DEFENDED THEIR OWN AUTHORITY. PHILIPP MELANCHTHON: Although the death of Christ was ordained by God and depended only on the secret counsel and purpose of God and not that of human beings, nonetheless the narration of the story required a description of how and by whom these events came about. It is important that the history be told so that we may know that there is no one more destructive toward the kingdom of God than those who reign and exercise tyranny against the people of God under the show of godliness. And we should note who the passage says joins here together: they are truly the leaders of the religious establishment, and what innocent person would have been afraid of this assembly of men? They were the leaders of the priestly kingdom, and so this matter was now about their authority. They had one goal and purpose: to defend and preserve that priestly kingdom. AN ECCLESIASTICALL EXPOSITION UPON SAINT MATHEWE 25.[2]

22:3-6 Judas Offers to Betray Jesus

JUDAS WAS INSPIRED BY GREED AND THE DEVIL. THOMAS MORE: Good Christian people, with these words we are given the occasion to speak now of the third cause of Christ's passion, that is, the moment when the false traitor Judas was first moved to descend toward this wicked treason. In order to show it, we must repeat something that happened a few days before. As Saint Matthew in [Matthew 26], Saint Mark in [Mark 14] and Saint John in [John 12] write, six days before the feast of Passover, our Savior went to Bethany where he had earlier raised Lazarus from death to life. There he had a supper prepared for him in the house of Simon the leper, whom Christ had cured. Martha served them, and Lazarus was one of the guests who attended the supper. Then Mary Magdalene came, the sister of Lazarus and Martha, and took a pound of nard

ointment, which was pure and quite expensive, and anointed Christ's feet with it, wiping them with her hair.[3] Then she broke the alabaster jar which held the ointment and poured the rest onto his head. . . . But when Judas, that wretched, covetous fellow, saw that the ointment was not sold, so that he could steal some of the money it was worth, and when he saw that our Savior allowed her devotion through this deed but did not allow Judas to find fault with her (even though Jesus was very mild with him), the proud beast could not bear it, and along with his covetousness, he fell into malice as well. The devil then saw his opportunity and entered into Judas's heart, planting in it the suggestion of his horrible treason, and brought him to devise and determine that the money that he had lost through the anointing of his master, he would regain by betraying his master. That is why he came to this assembly of which we are now speaking and presented himself to them, although he was not sent for, to help forward their wicked plans. JUDAS AND MARY MAGDALENE.[4]

THEY CHANGED THEIR PLANS AT JUDAS'S SUGGESTION. MELCHIOR NEUKIRCH: The enemies of Christ now heard that one from among the Twelve wanted to betray him and would reveal an opportunity for them to set about the business without danger to themselves. When they heard this, they were pleased, for they thought, "If his own disciples and apostles even start to desert him, there will be no difficulty. We will soon be able to persuade the people that they should also desert him, if they see that his own close and trusted friends no longer have confidence in the cause." The high priests and leaders of the people conferred with each other, for they did not want to disregard this long-desired opportunity but rather to use it soon, because it was just handed to them. They

---

[2]Marlorat, ed., *Catholike and Ecclesiasticall Exposition of the Holy Gospell After S. Mathewe*, 617-18*.

[3]More repeats a common perception, now discounted by biblical scholars, that Mary the sister of Lazarus and Martha was also Mary of Magdalene. Prior to the modern era of biblical study, many biblical commentators collapsed the various women named Mary in the New Testament into only one or two figures. [4]CWM 13:76-77*.

took the occasion to change their counsel and result, for previously they had come to an agreement and conclusion that they did not want in any way to deal with the Lord Christ prior to the Passover festival, but rather their bloodthirsty consultations placed it after the festival. But now they changed their minds and consented to the plan in agreement with Judas, that he should seek for an opportunity for him to surrender Jesus to them, and the sooner the better. And so that it would happen without any uproar, they wanted to do it farther from the event. They hoped that things would go their way, if they had one of the Twelve on their side. They wanted to make a quick end to Jesus of Nazareth, if they could just get their hands on him. If anyone among the people would be ready to take up his cause themselves in the beginning, they would quiet that down quickly, because they could show that his own apostles themselves deserted him. THE SECOND PART OF THE PASSION.[5]

---

[5]Neukirch, *Historia der Passion*, 203v-204v.

BETRAYAL WILL COME FROM LEADERS OF THE CHURCH. HEINRICH BULLINGER: So after Judas had accepted the most unhappy money ever received, he sought with great diligence a convenient time in which he might deliver Jesus over to them without any trouble from the people. So bribes make their receivers nimble, diligent and quick. By this image, Christ meant to declare that some will come who, for the love of money, will betray the doctrine of the gospel. He also meant to show that this betrayal would especially come from those who, being the heads and pillars of the church, seem to know the secrets of their Lord, with which they are so familiar that they betray his doctrine to the wicked and to heathen magistrates by false interpretation of it. They are seeking for nothing less than the destruction of the truth of the gospel. AN ECCLESIASTICALL EXPOSITION UPON SAINT MATHEWE 26.[6]

---

[6]Marlorat, ed., *Catholike and Ecclesiasticall Exposition of the Holy Gospell After S. Mathewe*, 627*.

22:7-23 THE LAST SUPPER

⁷*Then came the day of Unleavened Bread, on which the Passover lamb had to be sacrificed.* ⁸*So Jesusᵃ sent Peter and John, saying, "Go and prepare the Passover for us, that we may eat it."* ⁹*They said to him, "Where will you have us prepare it?"* ¹⁰*He said to them, "Behold, when you have entered the city, a man carrying a jar of water will meet you. Follow him into the house that he enters* ¹¹*and tell the master of the house, 'The Teacher says to you, Where is the guest room, where I may eat the Passover with my disciples?'* ¹²*And he will show you a large upper room furnished; prepare it there."* ¹³*And they went and found it just as he had told them, and they prepared the Passover.*

¹⁴*And when the hour came, he reclined at table, and the apostles with him.* ¹⁵*And he said to them, "I have earnestly desired to eat this Passover with you before I suffer.* ¹⁶*For I tell you I will not eat itᵇ until it is fulfilled in the kingdom of God."* ¹⁷*And he took a cup, and when he had given thanks he said, "Take this, and divide it among yourselves.* ¹⁸*For I tell you that from now on I will not drink of the fruit of the vine until the kingdom of God comes."* ¹⁹*And he took bread, and when he had given thanks, he broke it and gave it to them, saying, "This is my body, which is given for you. Do this in remembrance of me."* ²⁰*And likewise the cup after they had eaten, saying, "This cup that is poured out for you is the new covenant in my blood.ᶜ* ²¹*But behold, the hand of him who betrays me is with me on the table.* ²²*For the Son of Man goes as it has been determined, but woe to that man by whom he is betrayed!"* ²³*And they began to question one another, which of them it could be who was going to do this.*

a Greek *he*   b Some manuscripts *never eat it again*   c Some manuscripts omit, in whole or in part, verses 19b-20 (*which is given. . .in my blood*)

OVERVIEW: The Lord's Supper engendered perhaps the most significant and heated debate that can be found in the context of sixteenth-century biblical interpretation and theology. The controversy focused on how to interpret the words "This is my body" (Mt 26:26; Mk 14:22; Lk 22:19) and what this means concerning Christ's presence in the church's celebration of the sacrament. The variety of Reformation opinions are not fully represented here, but the included comments give a sense of the main areas of disagreement.

Although various Protestants quarreled among themselves about eucharistic theology, still each group agreed about rejecting medieval Catholic eucharistic dogma, particularly transubstantiation. According to this doctrine, Catholic theologians—following the Fourth Lateran Council (1215) and Thomas Aquinas—interpreted these words of Christ literally and affirmed that in the celebration of the Mass, the substance of the bread and wine becomes the substance of Christ's body and blood, while the external accidents remain.

Protestant eucharistic theology can be loosely grouped into three categories: real presence, spiritual presence and memorialism.[1] Luther, like the Catholics, read Jesus' words literally. However, contrary to transubstantiation, he insisted that Christ's body and blood are really and truly present in, with and under the bread and wine. For Luther, Christ is ubiquitous according to his humanity *and* divinity, which means that his body and blood are truly present in the Eucharist. According to

---

[1] For a more detailed treatment of sixteenth-century views, see "Eucharist," OER 2:71-81; Lee Palmer Wandel, *The Eucharist in the Reformation: Incarnation and Liturgy* (Cambridge: Cambridge University Press, 2006); Amy Nelson Burnett, *Karlstadt and the Origins of the Eucharistic Controversy: A Study in the Circulation of Ideas* (Oxford: Oxford University Press, 2011). Real presence is often mischaracterized as consubstantiation, see "Consubstantiation," OER 1:418-19; Richard A. Muller, *Dictionary of Latin and Greek Theological Terms* (Baker Academic: Grand Rapids, 1995), 80-81.

Reformed theologians, because Christ has ascended into heaven, his body and blood cannot be present in the sacrament itself. Zwingli argued that "is" should here be understood figuratively (as we interpret phrases like "I am the true vine"). Although he is often misrepresented as strictly memorialist, Zwingli affirmed that Christ's spiritual presence in the Supper not only reminds believing participants of Christ's sacrifice, but also nourishes them.[2] Calvin agreed that Christ could not be corporeally present in the sacrament because of his ascension, however, he believed that when believers celebrate the Lord's Supper, by the Holy Spirit's mediation they ascend to heaven to feed spiritually on Christ's true body and blood. Finally, most Anabaptists understood the Supper as a memorial to Christ's sacrifice. Although many Radicals stated that the bread and wine are just bread and wine, the meal was still a communal event with important spiritual implications and benefits.[3]

Another element of the eucharistic debates is the *manducatio infidelium*, the eating by the unfaithful. Judas's presence at the table is an important locus for this problem: did he in fact receive the benefit of them, even though he was clearly a wicked reprobate? The general consensus is no, Judas did not receive Christ through the bread and wine, for no spiritual benefit could be gained by someone who had no faith. However, Luther suggests that the unfaithful *do* receive Christ, because he is present when the words are joined to the elements; however, it is only the faithful who receive what the words promise, that is, the forgiveness of sins. The unfaithful will instead condemn themselves by consuming the eucharistic meal but not believing in its benefits. The reformers note that although Judas's betrayal was part of God's plan, it was his own choice to commit that betrayal. God brought about good through these evil machinations.

22:7-13 *Preparations for the Passover*

THE PASSOVER LAMB IS A SYMBOL OF CHRIST, THE LAMB OF GOD. HEINRICH SALMUTH: Therefore the Passover feast was instituted for the Jews so that it would serve as a reminder of the miraculous liberation of the people of Israel from Egypt, and so that on account of that liberation, the people of Israel should heartily rejoice and give thanks to God for it. The Passover lamb was also intended to be a symbol of the future Passover Lamb, the Lord Christ, who was to accomplish for us the eternal liberation from the kingdom of the devil. For just as the people of Israel were subject to oppressive slavery by the pharaoh in Egypt, so also the whole human race is stuck in this oppressive bondage and prison of the devil, who rules over us and holds us fast in his kingdom through sin and death.

But when God wanted to lead the people out of Egypt and liberate them, they had to slaughter a lamb, which must be an unblemished yearling, separated out from the rest of the herd. Likewise, our Lord Jesus Christ has freed us from the kingdom of the devil, in that he became a Lamb of God and was unblemished, that is, without all sin and impurity. And he was a "yearling," that is, very delicate, weak and wretched, albeit without sin. Like any other person, he was tried, so that he could come to help our weakness and have a heartfelt sympathy with us. He is also separated out from all other people in that he alone was without sin and that he decided in the counsel of divine majesty that he would obtain for us an eternal liberation, a benefit for all other people. THE THIRD SERMON ON THE PASSION AND DEATH OF JESUS CHRIST.[4]

THEY DID NOT KNOW WHERE TO PREPARE THE PASSOVER. AUGUSTIN MARLORAT: The fact that Peter and John asked Jesus where he would eat the Passover is a sign that they were wandering and unstable, having no certain place, and their

[2]See W. P. Stephens, *The Theology of Huldrych Zwingli* (Oxford: Clarendon Press, 1986), 218-59, esp. 250-55.

[3]See Thomas N. Finger, *A Contemporary Anabaptist Theology: Biblical, Historical, Constructive* (Downers Grove, IL: InterVarsity Press, 2004), 184-97.

[4]Salmuth, *Passional*, 143-44.

entrance into the city could not be without great danger. For they had mortal enemies there, who were looking for an occasion to take them. But pay attention to how Christ neglected nothing which pertained to the common rule of the godly. He wanted to be subject to the law, so that he might redeem us from the curse of that law, to which Saint Paul witnesses, and therefore he would not omit the observance of the Passover any more than he would of any other rites. AN ECCLESIASTICALL EXPOSITION UPON SAINT MATHEWE 26.[5]

CHRIST'S POVERTY TEACHES US TO VALUE OUR BLESSINGS. HEINRICH SALMUTH: Now we see that our Lord Jesus Christ did not have his own house in which he could celebrate Passover with his disciples, but instead he had to look for a room in an inn. From this we can see the great poverty of our Lord—he had nothing of his own, and nowhere he might have laid his head. He testifies thereby that he is not a king of this world, but rather that he serves a spiritual kingdom. And we should take him as an example and model, that we should be obedient to God, even in poverty, and we should discipline our wills to be more in accord with his. We should always remember that he became poor so that we might be made rich in heavenly and spiritual blessings through him. Therefore we should always have a heartfelt longing and desire toward those blessings. THE THIRD SERMON ON THE PASSION AND DEATH OF JESUS CHRIST.[6]

CHRIST'S RESPONSE WAS WISE AND A SIGN OF HIS POWER. THOMAS MORE: It is clear in these words that our Lord, when he sent Saint Peter and Saint John to the house where they would prepare the Last Supper, would not name the man who lived in the house, nor would he give them any address or description of the house.[7]

The old doctors of the church discussed this point and put forth diverse reasons for it. Some say that Jesus sent them to an unnamed man as a sign that God will come not only to those who are famous and whose names are well-known but also to those whom the world thinks unimportant and whose names are not recognized. Some others say (and both may well be true) that because our Savior (to whom nothing was unknown) knew of the promise that Judas, that false traitor, made to the Jewish leaders the day before to betray him, and that he was looking for a fit time to betray him to them out of the sight of the people, then if Jesus had named the man or the place, the traitor might have caused him and his disciples to be taken before his Last Supper and before he consecrated his body in the blessed sacrament. And even if the traitor had come and brought the whole town with him, our Savior could have stopped them all with one word from his mouth, yet in his great wisdom he decided on this way as the most appropriate and convenient by which he would keep the traitor from accomplishing his traitorous purpose until the time should come when he had determined that he should suffer it. And in this matter our Savior acted rightly and wonderfully. For although the two disciples whom he sent were of all his apostles the ones most especially chosen, and most in trust and favor with him, for Saint Peter (as it appears in Scripture and as the Fathers say) especially loved him, and Saint John (as Scriptures say and the doctors also) was especially beloved of him, yet he did not take them aside and tell them the name of the man. For by doing so he might have given occasion for envy or suspicion to Judas, or perhaps grief to the rest, if Christ had seemed to trust them with that errand secretly, with which he would not trust the rest. And so he gave them their errand in such a strange fashion that neither they nor any of the other ten could know what to think about it, for he answered them as if he would say, "I will not tell you where you should prepare it, nor

---

[5]Marlorat, ed., *Catholike and Ecclesiasticall Exposition of the Holy Gospell After S. Mathewe*, 627*; citing Gal 5:1-6.
[6]Salmuth, *Passional*, 136.
[7]Rather than the phrase "Last Supper," More used the term "maundy." The origins of the term are disputed—likely from the

---

Latin word for "commandment," based on John 13:34—but many Christians still use the name Maundy Thursday for this feast.

will I tell you who will bring you there. But in order to show you what I can do when I so desire, I will give you a sign to bring you there which no person knows nor could know, except myself, because at that time I am able to make it happen." A PROOF OF CHRIST'S GODHEAD.[8]

CHRIST'S DETAILS SOOTHE THE APOSTLES' FEARS. MELCHIOR NEUKIRCH: As if he would say: "I know well that the Pharisees will not eat their Passover lamb today but will delay it to the next day after. But this is my time. I act according to God's will, which commands that the Passover lamb should be eaten on this evening. Say to him: 'Show us a place where we may prepare it.' And he will not show you to a little nook but to a large, beautiful, grand, painted room, which he will lend to you. Prepare the Passover lamb there." This is supposed to be the same room, so people say, where the apostles later went into hiding out of fear of the Jews, and where on Pentecost the 120 people were converted. The Lord said this to them clearly, on account of everything that would happen to them. He also did this on Palm Sunday, with the donkey and her colt, where they would find it, and what the person would say if they would dare to untie it. This was so that they might take some courage and not be quite so afraid of the violence of the Jews, if they heard how the Lord knew everything ahead of time which would befall them. THE SECOND PART OF THE PASSION.[9]

22:14-16 *Jesus' Last Passover Meal*

THE DINNER WAS SEPARATE FROM THE PASSOVER RITUAL. JOHN CALVIN: "When the evening came, he took his place at the table" is not to eat the Passover feast. That they must do while standing (as travelers, when they move quickly, hastily eat their food with their shoes on and holding their staff). Rather, I understand it to be that having completed the solemn ceremony, he took

his place at the table to eat dinner. Therefore the Evangelists say, "When the evening came," because at the beginning of the evening they sacrificed the lamb and then ate its roasted meat. COMMENTARY ON A HARMONY OF THE GOSPELS.[10]

CHRIST HAS A GREAT DESIRE TO SAVE US. JOHANNES BRENZ: Here we should note the desire which Christ has to provide our salvation. During this feast of Passover, Christ was to suffer a most shameful and cruel death. Another person would have desired by any means possible to shun and escape so horrible a death. But Christ instead desires to suffer it. Not that death itself was so pleasant, but because he so earnestly thirsted for our salvation, which we were to receive by his death. Therefore this desire of Christ ought to stir up every careless and slothful person to repent in time. If Christ had called us to something that would have brought danger instead of profit, then we might have made an excuse and turned ourselves away, but now he has called us to those labors, or rather to those happinesses, which will always bring salvation with them. For no one who believes in him will ever be condemned. Why then do we delay to take them in hand and to follow them? This desire of Christ also ought to strengthen the minds of those who fear that Christ does not accept or receive them on account of their sins. Why are you afraid to come to Christ? He desires your salvation more earnestly than you ever could. He is more ready to offer his benefits to you than you are to receive them. AN ECCLESIASTICALL EXPOSITION UPON SAINT LUKE 22.[11]

CHRIST REPLACED THE OLD FIGURE WITH THE NEW TRUTH. THOMAS MORE: The fulfilling, or performing, of the sacrifice of the paschal lamb was a figure [or symbol] of the offering of his own blessed body in sacrifice, which would restore human nature to the kingdom of heaven. And by that new offering

---

[8]CWM 13:93-94*.
[9]Neukirch, *Historia der Passion*, 108v-109r.

[10]CTS 33:197* (CO 45:700); alluding to Ex 12:11.
[11]Marlorat, ed., *Catholike and Ecclesiasticall Exposition of the Holy Gospell After S. Marke and Luke*, 311*.

of the innocent lamb, which is the offering in truth, the old offering of the paschal lamb in Jerusalem (which was a figure of it) was fully performed and was given its full perfection in the kingdom of heaven.

But here we should consider that our Savior, in saying that he would eat the old paschal lamb no more until it was performed in the kingdom of heaven, did not mean that after the figure was performed and had its perfection in heaven, he would then use or have used it again on earth. He meant that he would never again eat it. For the word *donec* in Latin, which is "until" in English, when it limits a time before which it denies a certain thing to be done, does not always mean or imply (although sometimes it does) that the thing will be done after that time. . . . And therefore regarding the paschal lamb, when our Savior said, "I will not eat it until it is fulfilled in the kingdom of God," he meant to say, "I will never eat it again." In such a way, someone whose death is approaching, or is preparing to enter into the Carthusian order, might say, "I will never again eat meat in this world," or "I will be in heaven before I eat any meat," or something like that.[12] He would not mean that he would be eating meat in another world but that he would eat none here, and consequently would never again eat meat.

The other factor, by which it plainly appears that our Savior did not intend that the figurative old paschal lamb should continue, is that he went on to institute the true offering—the new sacrifice of his blessed body and blood, the blessed sacrament of the altar. The Old and the New Sacrifices.[13]

22:17-20 *The New Covenant of Body and Blood*

Christ Twice Observed Ritual Tasting of the Cup. John Calvin: Because Luke recounts that the cup was offered by Christ twice, it must first be asked if it might be the author's repetition (because on occasion the Evangelists will often say the same thing twice), or if, after Christ took a sip from the cup, he might have done the same thing a second time. This latter option seems more probable to me. We know, indeed, that during the sacrifices, the holy fathers had observed this solemn rite of tasting the cup. As we see in Psalm 116, "I will take the cup of salvation and will call on the name of the Lord." And thus I do not doubt that Christ tasted the cup, following the ancient custom in the holy feast, which otherwise would not have been properly completed; Luke reports this clearly before turning to the narration of the new mystery, whose order is distinct from the paschal lamb. It was also because of received and usual practice that he is expressly said to have given thanks when he took the cup. For I do not doubt that at the beginning of the supper he had prayed, for he was accustomed never to go to the table without calling on God. But now he wanted to perform that duty once more, so that he might not omit a ceremony which I just pointed out was connected with the sacred taking of the cup. Commentary on a Harmony of the Gospels.[14]

The Bread and Wine Are a Shared Sacramental Communion. Anne Askew (John Bale): I perceive, dear friend in the Lord, that you are not yet thoroughly persuaded of the truth concerning the Lord's Supper. Christ said to his apostles, "Take, eat. This is my body which is given for you." In giving the bread as an outward sign or token to be received by the mouth, he indicated to them to receive his body which would die for the people in perfect faith and to realize that the death of his body was the only health and salvation for their souls. The bread and wine were given to us as a sacramental communion, or a mutual participation in the inestimable benefits of his most precious death and the shedding of his blood, so that at the end we should be thankful all together for that grace so necessary for our redemption. For

---

[12]More uses the phrase "entering into the charter house," which is the English name for the monastic house of the Carthusians, an order founded in the eleventh century. A combination of eremitical (hermits) and cenobitical (living together in community) monasticism, Carthusians were known for their strict diet, which included no meat.
[13]CWM 13:121-22*.

[14]CTS 33:203* (CO 45:704); citing Ps 116:13.

in his closing, he said, "Do this in remembrance of me, as often as you shall eat or drink it." He said this so that we would not be forgetful of what we should rather keep in our minds every day and that we should not be unthankful for it. THE LATTER EXAMINATION OF ANNE ASKEW (1547).[15]

CHRIST ADDED SIGNS TO WORDS IN THIS WEIGHTY MATTER. MARTIN BUCER: It was the practice in times past among religious and godly Jews that when they sat down at the table, the man of the house or the person who sat in the highest seat would take bread in his hands and give thanks to the Lord, and after that, he would break the bread in pieces and distribute it to the guests, as out of the hand of the Lord, and before they had tasted any of the other food. At the end of the feast they carried the cup around in the same manner. This practice was committed to the Jews by their holy ancestors before the incarnation of Christ, that they might always take food and drink before the Lord and, as it were, from his hand, and might thereby be reminded to live wholly for God, by whom they acknowledged themselves to be so lovingly fed and nourished. . . .

It is a solemn and usual custom for people in matters of great weight between them to deal not by words only but also to join to their words external signs relating to those matters, that by those signs they might deliver with their hand what they offer in their mind. This is especially true when spiritual things must be delivered, or else physical things which either are not present or cannot simply be handed over. When people give their word to another, they do it not only with words but also by shaking hands, just as we often do when we promise to perform some thing which is required of us. When people swear, they do it not only with words but also by lifting up their hands toward heaven, and the kissing of a book is required.[16] Those who

receive a kingdom are consecrated not only by words but also by the reaching forth of the scepter and other ceremonies. . . . After this manner, therefore, the Lord thought it good to commend his oblation and exhibition to us—this sum of our entire salvation—not only by words, or by baptism only (which is the sign that he has washed away our sins), but by the added signs of food and drink; that is to say, by himself, who is the true and heavenly living bread, the food of eternal life which sustains us and which he gives to us as long as he is and lives in us. AN ECCLESIASTICALL EXPOSITION UPON SAINT MATHEWE 26.[17]

THE BODY AND BLOOD ARE TRULY PRESENT IN BREAD AND WINE. MARTIN LUTHER: What is the Sacrament of the Altar? Answer: It is the true body and blood of our Lord Jesus Christ under the bread and wine, instituted by Christ himself for us Christians to eat and to drink. . . .

What is the benefit of such eating and drinking? Answer: The words "given for you" and "shed for you for the forgiveness of sins" show us that forgiveness of sin, life and salvation are given to us in the sacrament through these words, because where there is forgiveness of sin, there is also life and salvation.

How can bodily eating and drinking do such a great thing? Answer: Eating and drinking certainly do not do it, but rather the words that are recorded: "given for you" and "shed for you for the forgiveness of sins." These words, when accompanied by the physical eating and drinking, are the essential thing in the sacrament, and whoever believes these very words has what they declare and state, namely, "forgiveness of sins."

Who then receives this sacrament worthily? Answer: Fasting and bodily preparation are in fact

---

[15]*Examinations of Anne Askew*, 88-89; citing 1 Cor 11:24-26. Askew recorded her own trial examinations, and this text, including some letters and supporting documents, was first edited and published by the clergyman John Bale in 1547.

[16]Kissing the book (usually the Gospels) was commonly required in oath taking, at least since the medieval period, and continued

in the United States until at least 1875. In H. C. Ulman, *Trow's Legal Directory and Lawyer's Record of the United States* (New York: John F. Trow, 1875), the instructions for taking depositions in the state of New York include: "The oath shall be administered (except in the cases hereinafter mentioned), by the witness laying his hand upon and kissing the Gospels" (p. 276).

[17]Marlorat, ed., *Catholike and Ecclesiasticall Exposition of the Holy Gospell After S. Mathewe*, 635-36*; citing Deut 8:3.

a fine external discipline, but a person who has faith in these words "given for you" and "shed for you for the forgiveness of sins" is really worthy and well prepared. However, a person who does not believe these words or doubts them is unworthy and unprepared, because the words "for you" require truly believing hearts. THE SMALL CATECHISM (1529).[18]

A SACRAMENT MUST BE ORDAINED BY CHRIST. JOHN JEWEL: What then? Do we refuse confirmation, penance, holy orders and matrimony? Do we not use these things? Do we not allow them? Yes, for we do confirm, and teach repentance, and administer holy orders and consider matrimony and use it as an honorable state of life. We visit the sick among us and anoint them with the precious oil of the mercy of God. But we do not call these things sacraments, because they do not have the same institution. Confirmation was not ordained by Christ; penance does not have any outward element joined to the Word; the same may be said of holy orders. And matrimony was not first instituted by Christ, for God had ordained it in Paradise long before. But in two we have both the element and the institution: in baptism, the element is water; in the Lord's Supper, bread and wine. Baptism has this word of institution: "Teach all nations, baptizing them in the name of the Father, and the Son and the Holy Spirit." Likewise, the Lord's Supper has this word of institution: "Do this in remembrance of me." Therefore these two are properly and truly called the sacraments of the church, because in them the element is joined to the Word, and they take their ordinance from Christ. They are visible signs of invisible grace. A TREATISE ON THE SACRAMENTS (1583).[19]

WE DRINK TO REMEMBER THE NEW COVENANT. PETER WALPOT: And these few words, "This is my body," do not have such strength that we would therefore understand that the material body

with flesh and bone, skin and hair, hands and feet, is in the bread, and the material blood is in the wine. No, but we certainly should not consider and use it as other visible food and drink, for it has a great significance and points to him and is dedicated to the holiest use—to remind us of the Lord and to announce his death. Another supper will be needed for the maintenance of one's natural life, but the supper of Lord [is needed] for the remembrance of Christ. Therefore it will be called his "body and blood" through figurative and changeable speech, and thereby distinguished from other sorts of suppers. "In the same way, he took the cup": this signifies his new covenant, share, decree and testament of his last, real will, which the suffering of Christ both alludes to and produces. And he says, "Drink from it, all of you," that is, "Drink, and use this product of the grapevine for a true remembrance and a way to meet this wonderful grace, which I have given you all to drink with my spirit from the promised rock, and, just as the grapes give their juice to all to drink, I have brought and instituted for you the true communion of saints in the grapevine of Christ." We do not need the propitiation of the blood of oxen, goats and calves, as in the Old Testament, where forgiveness was not given unless blood was poured out. For Jesus said, "This is my blood of the new testament, which will be poured out for many for the forgiveness of sins," that is, "My last will was established on the trunk of the cross, for on account of that payment and reconciliation, your sins will be poured out, that you may enjoy it to your salvation." THE GREAT ARTICLE BOOK: ON THE EUCHARIST.[20]

22:21-23 *One of You Will Betray Me*

JUDAS DID NOT RECEIVE CHRIST'S BODY AND BLOOD. DIRK PHILIPS: Judas also ate of the bread and drank the wine, but nevertheless he did not receive the flesh and blood of Christ. For all that God gives us in the use of the sacraments faith receives; God works in his elect alone through his

---

[18]BoC 362-63* (WA 30,1:315-19).
[19]Jewel, *Works*, 2:1103*; citing Mt 28:19.

[20]QGT 12:126-27.

Spirit what the sacraments signify externally. Therefore, it is impossible without faith to become partakers of Christ and his gifts. It is even more impossible that the unbelieving and evil ones (in whom Satan dwells) may receive the pure unblemished and holy flesh and the precious blood of Jesus Christ. But a hungering and thirsting soul (for righteousness) is fed with it and refreshed (as with spiritual food and with spiritual drink), yes, is established and maintained through this in the fellowship of Christ Jesus as he himself said: "Whoever eats me shall live because of my will." Again, "whoever eats my flesh and drinks my blood abides in me and I in him." From this it follows incontrovertibly that the unbelieving and evil ones have no part in the flesh and blood of Christ, so little as they are and abide in Christ and Christ in them. Though they may eat the bread with Judas, they do not through this partake of the body and blood of Christ but much more become guilty because of it. THE ENCHIRIDION: THE SUPPER OF OUR LORD JESUS CHRIST—OUR CONFESSION.[21]

GOD'S PROVIDENCE BRINGS SALVATION OUT OF EVIL PURPOSES. THE ENGLISH ANNOTATIONS: God did not determine sin, but he determined the salvation of humankind by Christ being betrayed and crucified. That is how he draws good out of evil. God gave Christ into the hands and power of sinners, so that he might satisfy God's justice for us, and we might be saved. God used to good purpose what impious people designed for evil and in which they acted most sinfully. Take a look at the different ends which motivated the different actors: Judas betrayed Christ for gain; the devil put the thought into Judas's heart, in the hope of taking away the one who destroyed his works; the priests were encouraged to this action by their malice and envy, because their honor and gains were lessened by Christ's preaching and miracles; Pilate pronounced sentence in order to please the people; the people cried, "Crucify him!" to ingratiate themselves with their rulers; and the soldiers acted as the priests, people and the devil moved them. But God, out of his unspeakable love and mercy, permitted all of these voluntary agents to act as each one desired in this situation and yet brought everything to the determination of his will and counsel for human salvation. None of the actors knew or would even know, but it is not the least of the beneficial effects of God's providence that some of those who were to be saved by the death of Christ should be actors in and promoters of this chain of events. (This is evident especially in Acts 2:36-41.) ANNOTATIONS ON THE GOSPEL ACCORDING TO SAINT LUKE 22:22.[22]

THE WICKED SERVE GOD'S PURPOSE AND YET ARE JUSTLY CONDEMNED. HULDRYCH ZWINGLI: And so we see that the wicked who are the persecutors of the faithful are not excused. When Judas betrayed Christ, he did not consider or know the will of God but rather the wickedness of his own heart, that he might receive money. According to the same wickedness, therefore, he is justly condemned. And so at a glance, the wicked seem to have some fellowship with God, yet for all that we must look at them more narrowly, and then we will see that they are as far from him as heaven is from earth. They are not excusable but rather deserve woe. We should note these things diligently, because many frenzied and headstrong people confuse and confound things, not in disputing but with controlling and reproaching God. They do not seek for anything but to defame the whole doctrine of God, that by hate of religion, contempt for God and brutish boldness may arise, and people will be no different from beasts. Let us then learn to make a distinction, the way Christ did here. And yet for all that we must not deny that God uses the works of the wicked, that they may serve his providence (although against their wills) and do what he has decreed. AN ECCLESIASTICALL EXPOSITION UPON SAINT MATHEWE 26.[23]

---

[21]CRR 6:116* (BRN 10:115-16); citing Jn 6:56; 1 Cor 11:27.

[22]Downame, ed., *Annotations*, Zz2r*; citing Acts 4:28; Rev 13:8.
[23]Marlorat, ed., *Catholike and Ecclesiasticall Exposition of the Holy Gospell After S. Mathewe*, 632*.

THE APOSTLES WERE DISTRAUGHT ABOUT THE COMING BETRAYAL. PHILIPP MELANCHTHON: Three things caused the sorrow of the apostles. The first is that Jesus said he would be betrayed and delivered up to the hands of his enemies. Then they would be like orphans, which is why the Lord comforted them in John 14. The second is because it was one of them who would commit such a horrible deed. For what godly person would not be sorry that an enemy of Christ would come out of that congregation which was joined together in the faith of Christ? When Paul said to the Ephesian bishops, "Even from your own number men will arise and distort the truth in order to draw away disciples after them," how could any of them who were godly be free from trouble? The third is because they did not know who the traitor would be. Moreover, Christ, when he had testified these things, was troubled in spirit, as John says, and so how could the apostles not also be troubled when they saw it? Therefore, the disciples were not afraid as people who are disquieted and afraid without cause, but they abhorred the wicked event that was going to happen, and they desired to be freed from any suspicion of it. It is truly a sign of reverence that, although they were touched and stricken by what he said, they did not churlishly or unthinkingly respond to their master, but rather each one considered his own judgment. Nevertheless, they were bold in their good consciences and freely testified how far they were from doing such a deed. That is why each one questioned, "Is it I?" AN ECCLESIASTICALL EXPOSITION UPON SAINT MATHEWE 26.[24]

---

[24]Marlorat, ed., *Catholike and Ecclesiasticall Exposition of the Holy Gospell After S. Mathewe*, 630*; citing Acts 20:30; Jn 13:21.

22:24-38 THE APOSTLES FACE THE END

²⁴*A dispute also arose among them, as to which of them was to be regarded as the greatest.* ²⁵*And he said to them, "The kings of the Gentiles exercise lordship over them, and those in authority over them are called benefactors.* ²⁶*But not so with you. Rather, let the greatest among you become as the youngest, and the leader as one who serves.* ²⁷*For who is the greater, one who reclines at table or one who serves? Is it not the one who reclines at table? But I am among you as the one who serves.*

²⁸*"You are those who have stayed with me in my trials,* ²⁹*and I assign to you, as my Father assigned to me, a kingdom,* ³⁰*that you may eat and drink at my table in my kingdom and sit on thrones judging the twelve tribes of Israel.*

³¹*"Simon, Simon, behold, Satan demanded to have you,ᵃ that he might sift you like wheat,* ³²*but I have prayed for you that your faith may not fail. And when you have turned again, strengthen your brothers."* ³³*Peterᵇ said to him, "Lord, I am ready to go with you both to prison and to death."* ³⁴*Jesusᶜ said, "I tell you, Peter, the rooster will not crow this day, until you deny three times that you know me."*

³⁵*And he said to them, "When I sent you out with no moneybag or knapsack or sandals, did you lack anything?" They said, "Nothing."* ³⁶*He said to them, "But now let the one who has a moneybag take it, and likewise a knapsack. And let the one who has no sword sell his cloak and buy one.* ³⁷*For I tell you that this Scripture must be fulfilled in me: 'And he was numbered with the transgressors.' For what is written about me has its fulfillment."* ³⁸*And they said, "Look, Lord, here are two swords." And he said to them, "It is enough."*

a The Greek word for *you* (twice in this verse) is plural; in verse 32, all four instances are singular   b Greek *He*   c Greek *He*

OVERVIEW: Even in these final hours before Jesus' death, his disciples showed quite clearly their own limitations. Jesus recognized that they still had a "fleshly understanding" and spoke to them to correct them and to encourage their faith in the face of the trials that were shortly to begin. Spangenberg notes that the argument over who would be the greatest in the kingdom also shows us that we need not only the gospel but also the Holy Spirit so that we can have a proper understanding of it. Those who work to establish the kingdom of heaven here (especially ministers and bishops) should know that the point of Christian leadership is not to lord it over others or to rule, but rather it is to serve, like Jesus himself. Walpot understands Jesus' words even more literally and argues that not only can ministers not be "lordly benefactors" but also anyone who is a lord or a ruler—anyone who works in the government—cannot be a Christian. The use of the sword is "pagan" and incompatible with Christianity. Many Anabaptists—but generally not other Protestants—accepted this pacifist position.

Jesus then turned to a brief description of the kingdom of heaven. Although his disciples were not to expect an earthly kingdom where they could hold high position, he did indicate that in heaven they would "rule." He praised their constancy, although Neukirch notes that in fact even the apostles were not all that constant but were "easily impatient and faint-hearted" at the slightest danger. But he wisely gave them more praise than they deserved to help increase their confidence. By saying that they would rule heaven, Bulinger argues, Jesus meant to retrain their thoughts away from the hoped-for earthly kingdom to the yet-to-come heavenly kingdom. But Lambert suggests that their rule over the twelve tribes (that is, "all the churches of believers") was in fact the same kind of servant leadership that Jesus had already discussed. Jesus did not mean that they would be able to lord it over others in heaven. In fact, he went on to prophesy to Peter that even he, Jesus' staunchest supporter, would deny him and that his faith would fail him that very night. The apostles wanted positions of power and glory but would not be able even to withstand the challenges that would come over the next few days. However, although Peter and the others would fall, their faith would not die altogether, and the experience not only would teach them humility and patience with others but also would give them strength for their own future trials.

22:24-27 A Call to Humble Service

THE APOSTLES ACT LIKE THEY HAD NEVER HEARD CHRIST BEFORE. JOHANN SPANGENBERG: Why did the apostles lack this understanding? They had often heard from Christ that his kingdom was not of this world but that it was instead a spiritual kingdom. He had also told them that it had no external lordship but that it was an office of service. Afterwards, when he mentioned his kingdom during the Last Supper, they believed that it was a worldly kingdom and thought that they would be great and powerful princes and rulers in it. But that is of course a fleshly, crude perception. But one sees that there was a fleshly understanding in the apostles, even though they had listened to Christ for more than three years. One would presume a greater understanding among those who had heard even only one or two sermons. But we can learn something important here concerning faith and the gospel: we must not only hear the gospel but also pray to God, that he would give us the Holy Spirit, who will teach us the proper understanding. That way we will not only hear but will also spend our time fruitfully. And did the apostles sin by this? Yes, with two noticeable sins: with ambition and with quarreling. ON SAINT BARTHOLOMEW'S DAY.[1]

WORLDLY RULERS CANNOT BE CHRISTIANS. PETER WALPOT: You see, he makes a tight knot with this that will not be easily undone or reversed. For he introduces the authorities and the lords of the world and says drily, "But it should not be so among you, who are mine." The princes "proceed by force, but it should not be so among you, but whoever among you wants to be thought powerful should be your servant, and whoever wants to be foremost should be your slave. Likewise the Son of Man did not come in order to be served but to serve." That would be a bad sort of worldly glory, and it would not be at all right if Christ led a poor, slavish life and we disciples would want to be lordly benefactors instead. Therefore it should not be among Christians as it is among the princes of this world, who have power on earth and even over each other. One is the chief general of the cavalry, while another is the undergeneral; this one is the chamberlain, that one the chancellor, and so on, and so on. "But it should not be so among you," he says. Christ does not remove the power of the worldly government with this comment, but he does leave it in the world. He takes it away from his disciples and Christians—they should not proceed by force or reek of blood, which will not be allowed here any more than it is in heaven. Likewise, there should be no worldly rulers at all among the Christians on earth. For Lucifer must have been cast out because, more than the others, he also wanted to sit in heaven, but even more will those who burden themselves on earth with such pagan business be cast out, so that they cannot be Christians. Luke said, "Those in authority are called benefactors, but not so with you." For nothing leads to pride so much as the desire to rule and have a seat in government, and this is the origin of great crimes. For human honor and dignity lead into many harmful things, and lavish honors make them into self-important, immoral blasphemers and hypocrites. THE GREAT ARTICLE BOOK: ON THE SWORD.[2]

---

[1]Spangenberg, *Postilla Teütsch . . . von den fürnemsten Festen durch das gantze Jar*, LXXXr.

[2]QGT 12:255-56; citing Mt 20:25-28; Mk 10:43-45.

A PASTOR OR BISHOP IS A SERVANT, NOT A LORD. PHILIPP MELANCHTHON: The greatest honor in the church of Christ is to be a minister and to serve. Therefore the person who is called to be a pastor and a governor in the church should know that he has not obtained a lordship but the office of a minister or servant. The apostle Peter, when he prescribed the duties of a minister's life, said, "Do not reign as lords over the parishes, but see that you are an example to the flock." And the apostle Paul wrote, "This is how one should regard us, as servants of Christ and stewards of the mysteries of God." The person who is chosen to be a bishop, therefore, has been given the ministry and office of a servant, not one of lordship, or of superiority or of a principality. Therefore Peter, speaking of Judas, said, "For he was numbered among us and was allotted his share in this ministry." AN ECCLESIASTICALL EXPOSITION UPON SAINT MATHEWE 20.[3]

CHRIST HIMSELF WAS A MINISTER AND SERVANT. HEINRICH BULLINGER: The Lord adds to his command his own example, in order that he might persuade his disciples even more strongly. We must always remember that the servant is not greater than his master, nor is the disciple above his teacher. Christ is speaking here of the time of his abasement, of which Saint Paul writes: "Christ Jesus, who, though he was in the form of God, did not count equality with God a thing to be grasped, but made himself nothing, taking the form of a servant, being born in the likeness of men. And being found in human form, he humbled himself by becoming obedient to the point of death, even death on a cross." Who will refuse this condition, seeing that we have the example of our Lord and Master? He behaved himself in a manner appropriate to a servant, a servant of humanity: "Christ became a servant to the circumcised to show God's truthfulness, in order to confirm the promises." And he did not only declare himself to be a

minister and servant in his death but also in the whole course of his life. AN ECCLESIASTICALL EXPOSITION UPON SAINT MATHEWE 20.[4]

22:28-30 *The Apostles Receive a Kingdom*

CHRIST PRAISES THE APOSTLES TO ENCOURAGE THEM. MELCHIOR NEUKIRCH: But the steadfastnest of the apostles was hardly so valuable, for the gospel history testifies that their constancy and perseverance were often quite pitiful, and in fact they were frequently and easily impatient and faint-hearted, even if something happened to them that was only a little bit dangerous. In addition, the Lord knew well what more was going to happen with them shortly, for soon after this he also said to them that they would all be upset concerning him even that very evening. And that is why the Lord praised their constancy to him and their perseverance so highly. God also does the same thing with us today—he praises as a great delight to himself whatever we do that is good, even if it is very small, and he promises us a great reward even though our accomplishment is minimal and not worth any praise. We also read in Matthew 25 how he will praise our good works on Judgment Day—whatever we have done that is good—however meager and imperfect those things are in his sight. THE SECOND PART OF THE PASSION.[5]

GREATNESS IN THIS LIFE CONSISTS OF SERVICE, NOT RULING. HEINRICH BULLINGER: This is the sense: "Why do you contend among yourselves who shall be the greatest? Instead, learn from me to serve, for the more someone serves, the greater he will be. But be of good cheer—every one of you will be great. For you have walked with me in humility, remaining with me in my temptations which I have suffered on account of the Jews, and for which my brothers have also forsaken me. Therefore

---

[3]Marlorat, ed., *Catholike and Ecclesiasticall Exposition of the Holy Gospell After S. Mathewe*, 452*; citing 1 Pet 5:3; 1 Cor 4:1; Acts 1:17.

[4]Marlorat, ed., *Catholike and Ecclesiasticall Exposition of the Holy Gospell After S. Mathewe*, 452*; citing Mt 10:24; Phil 2:6-8; Rom 15:8.
[5]Neukirch, *Historia der Passion*, 140v-141v.

you will reign with me. Already I am giving to you the kingdom of heaven, even as my Father has given it to me, that you may also enjoy it with me and that you may eat and drink with me at my table, that is to say, that you may enjoy the glory and pleasures of the life to come with me. And so lift up your minds to those things which are to come, and put away your dreams about this present happiness and earthly kingdom. Here we must serve, but there we will reign." An Ecclesiasticall Exposition upon Saint Luke 22.[6]

They Will Be Princes in the Heavenly Kingdom. Johann Spangenberg: The dear apostles must have thought, "If we are then subject to everyone, where are those lovely promises that the prophets prophesied concerning the kingdom of Christ? But we also believed that we were going to be somebody in the kingdom of Christ." Christ addressed their thoughts with these words, as if he would say: "Be comforted, my disciples: although the world has persecuted me, you have remained with me the whole time, throughout all of my challenges. And therefore I am now going there to prepare the kingdom for you, as my Father has prepared it for me—not an earthly but a heavenly one, not a physical but a spiritual one. I will not make you into princes of the world but princes of heaven. The kings and princes of this world will not invite you to the table, but they will instead persecute you and torment you with hunger and thirst. But I will supply you with food and drink on my table in my kingdom. The kings and princes of this world will not permit you to exercise worldly justice or to pass judgment, but I will provide you with thrones on which you can sit and judge the twelve tribes of Israel." On Saint Bartholomew's Day.[7]

These Elected Ones Are Leaders and Judges in the Church. François Lambert:

These thrones are the ability to judge through the Spirit of God, in whom those sit who have the spirit of true judgment, and that is, of course, believers. They are made into spiritual people, and of all people, they are able to judge rightly. Therefore they judge the twelve tribes of Israel, that is, all the churches of believers, who are the true seed of Abraham and the true Israelites. These children of God are not children of the flesh (of Abraham, of course) but are children of the promise and are counted among his seed. They are also believers in the church, judges, princes and kings, among whom they hold the first place (although you must understand primacy not as lording over others but in teaching and administering the Word of God). They are elected to that same ministry of the Word by God, as we see in Psalm 45: he will "make them princes over all the earth." Commentary in Luke 22:28-29.[8]

22:31-34 Peter and His Faith

Satan Will Attack Peter and the Apostles. Melchior Neukirch: By saying this, he would give him to understand: "Peter, you mean well, but you do not know how hard the devil will plague you and the other apostles, and if I do not maintain my intercession for you, there is no way that you will all make it! O, how Satan will plague you and test you! But I will support you, Peter, so that although you will fall very hard, nevertheless your faith will not be completely removed from your heart. And because you will have to turn back again and repent after your heavy fall, so you should also remember that, and treat your neighbor who has fallen very gently, and deal with him in a friendly way, that he also might again be converted." The Second Part of the Passion.[9]

Our Own Flaws Should Make Us More Merciful to Others. Heinrich Bullinger: Faith in the elect is like the sun in the heavens,

---

[6]Marlorat, ed., *Catholike and Ecclesiasticall Exposition of the Holy Gospell After S. Marke and Luke*, 312*.
[7]Spangenberg, *Postilla Teütsch . . . von den fürnemsten Festen durch das gantze Jar*, LXXXIIv.

[8]Lambert, *In Divi Lucae*, Gg3v; citing 1 Cor 2:13-15; Rom 9:6-8; Ps 45:16.
[9]Neukirch, *Historia der Passion*, 144r-v.

which is hidden and darkened for a time with clouds but not actually extinguished. For affections, errors and sins are like black clouds bringing darkness, but the sun of our faith is confirmed and inflamed again by the merit of our intercessor in such a way that with firm and bright beams it eventually puts away those clouds and brings a clear conscience. And we should not think that this prayer of Christ applies only to Peter, as though he prayed for him alone. Christ prayed also for the rest of the apostles and for those who should believe their preaching. For he said, "I do not pray for them alone but for all who should believe in me by their preaching." . . . It is as if he should say, "When you are converted, strengthen your brothers and sisters by your example, that they do not despair. Consider how great your fall was when you see others fall, so that you do not condemn or reject them but rather lift them up and comfort them."

We ought not to think that strength is given to us to overthrow others. Everyone should bear with his brother's infirmities, but those who have fallen once should be most ready to bear with the weak, because they have been taught by their own experience. The experience of evils ought to make us even more merciful. And so the apostle says, "We do not have a high priest who cannot be touched with sympathy for our infirmities; he was tempted in all ways, just as we are, only without sin." Therefore we should not be too severe but always keep this admonition in mind. AN ECCLESIASTICALL EXPOSITION UPON SAINT LUKE 22.[10]

CHRIST'S FORETELLING TEACHES PETER. ERASMUS SARCERIUS: It is remarkable that Peter brags so willfully that he will not be overcome. . . . He had felt nothing before, nor had he weighed his own strength. And whatever experience he had had of the danger of death, and however strong and stout he may have been, nevertheless he was also

not lacking in presumption and amazing rashness, in that he strove against the words of Christ, which were so manifest and confirmed by the testimony of the prophet. This teaches us that we cannot learn true humility unless we have experience of our own infirmity. And so we should not find it remarkable that we fall so often, for otherwise we could not profit in the doctrine of humility. But as often as we fall, we should remember that we are being admonished for our infirmity by the Lord. . . .

Christ swears here in a sure matter, and he shows that it is not in human power not to be offended at this cross. . . . He sets a very short time against a very large promise: "before the rooster crows." . . . For the house rooster begins to crow around midnight, and before the break of day. Therefore he makes mention of the rooster crowing, in order to give Peter a token and to print that certain sign in his mind, which would bring to mind that his denial was foretold to him. AN ECCLESIASTICALL EXPOSITION UPON SAINT MATHEWE 25.[11]

22:35-38 The Time for Fulfillment Is at Hand

THE TIME OF REST IS OVER. JOHN CALVIN: The whole object of Christ's speech here is to show that until this time he spared his disciples— he placed no burden on them greater than the small measure they could bear. He commends the earlier leniency so that now they can prepare themselves more courageously for harsher warfare. Why did he keep these untrained men—still beginners—in the shade and at rest away from hurled darts, unless during this quiet they gradually developed courage and strength to fight? Therefore, it is as if he had said: "Until now your situation has been easy and cheerful, because I wanted to treat you gently like children. Now the right time has come when I must

---

[10]Marlorat, ed., *Catholike and Ecclesiasticall Exposition of the Holy Gospell After S. Marke and Luke*, 314*; citing Jn 17:20; Heb 4:15.

[11]Marlorat, ed., *Catholike and Ecclesiasticall Exposition of the Holy Gospell After S. Mathewe*, 648-49*; citing Mk 14:30-31; Mt 26:74-75; Lk 22:60-61.

occupy you with labor like men." The comparison which he makes between the two periods is still more extensive. For if they lacked nothing when they proceeded to discharge their office without taking with them a stock of provisions, when a state of peace allowed them leisure to provide for their necessities, much more now in the midst of tumult and excitement should they lay aside anxiety about the present life and run wherever necessity calls them. Even though Christ specifically remembers what he had done with the twelve apostles, he also teaches us too that while we are still novices and weak in faith, a time of grace is given until we mature into men [*viros*]. Thus they act incorrectly who use their peace for delights which weaken faith's vigor. And let us not doubt that today also Christ has regard for us, because he does not throw us novices unpracticed into battle but first fits us with arms and courage. COMMENTARY ON A HARMONY OF THE GOSPELS.[12]

BE FREE FROM EARTHLY HINDRANCES.

DESIDERIUS ERASMUS: After he had taken away their confidence in themselves, he impressed on them again what he had often taught, that they should not fortify themselves against necessity on their travels or arm themselves with human defenses against the violence of evil people. It is proper that a minister of the heavenly gospel be free from the sordid cares of this life and only be armed against the impiety and dangers of the world with the sword of the Spirit, which is the divine Word. . . .

Then Jesus, so that going forward he might pluck out of their souls all desire for revenge, beguiled them for a time with the obscurity of his speech, but in this he let them be mistaken, so that he would more certainly and powerfully remove all feelings of vengeance. For he knew that they would be enkindled with the zeal of defending him when they saw their Lord, whom they loved with earnest, if quite human affection,

seized by armed guards during such an uproar. If he had not plainly chastised it, we would have thought it lawful to defend ourselves with weapons against the violence of wicked people and to drive back violence by violence. But because Peter was rebuked for drawing his sword against ungodly and wicked people on behalf of the Lord, who was most innocent, why might a Christian ever think that it is acceptable to push against violence with violence?

Thus the Lord said, "At the first preaching of the gospel, you went about unburdened, with nothing provided for the journey. Nevertheless, through my protection, you lacked for nothing. And that was enough, when there was no heavy storm threatening you. But from now on, your souls must be prepared for tougher times. For the greater and more ferocious the storm of persecution will be, so much more must you be free from earthly hindrances." PARAPHRASE ON THE GOSPEL OF LUKE 22:35-36.[13]

THE DISCIPLES' DULLNESS AND THE CANONISTS' CONTEMPT.

JOHN CALVIN: It was truly shameful and brute ignorance that the disciples, after having been warned so often about bearing the cross, imagine that they must fight with iron swords. By "here are two swords" it is uncertain whether they proclaim that they are well-equipped against their enemies or complain that they lack sufficient arms. However, this is indeed clear: they were so stupid that they did not consider the spiritual enemy. As to what the Canonists coax from this passage—that their mitered bishops have a double jurisdiction—not only is it foul allegory but also an impudent mockery by which they insult God's Word. But the antichrist's slaves had to sink into such madness that openly with sacrilegious contempt they trampled God's sacred oracles. COMMENTARY ON A HARMONY OF THE GOSPELS.[14]

---

[13]Erasmus, *In Evangelivm Lvce Paraphrasis*, E2r-v (LB 7:453; cf. CWE 48:195-96).
[14]CTS 33:224* (CO 45:717). Calvin is referring to the bull *Unam Sanctam* (1302) promulgated by Boniface VIII (1235–1303) as

---

[12]CTS 33:221-22* (CO 45:716).

THE TWO SWORDS ARE THE WORD OF GOD.
PETER WALPOT: They say in their blindness:
"But Christ certainly said to his disciples, 'Whoever has a moneybag take it, and so also the
knapsack, but whoever has nothing should sell
his cloak and buy a sword.'" Yes, dear friend, but
not an external one, not a sword of blood with
which we should strike others. Otherwise, Paul
would not have been correct when he said, "We
are not fighting in a human fashion, and the
weapons of our warfare are not fleshly." Christ
also says, "If your hand or your foot causes you to
sin, then cut it off!" So, here too it is not to be
understood literally but spiritually. For concerning the external sword of blood there is nothing
that needs to be commanded by Christ; the flesh
itself is already predisposed to that. Jews, Gentiles and Turks have swords; God has no
pleasure in that.

Thus, Christ himself did not intend or want
[to say anything about the external sword];
instead, by this Christ wants to depict for them
the coming opposition and struggle against sin
and the godlessness of the world—into which he
will send them—so that they can prepare
themselves with the sword of the Spirit, with
the Christian sword which is the Word of God.
Therefore, Christ adds to this and says, "For I
say to you, it still must be fulfilled in me what
stands written, 'He was numbered under the
evildoers.'" As if he wants to say, "Such will also
happen with you. Therefore, go forth with the
weapon of the Spirit!"

Now that it is true that he did not mean the
sword of blood he proves clearly when the
disciples said, "Lord, here are two swords," to
which he responded, "It is enough." That is, it is no
longer acceptable to fight with the physical sword,
but instead from now on it is necessary to suffer
on account of the gospel and to bear the cross. So
it is necessary to grasp the spiritual sword, the
Word of God now. If he had meant to talk about
buying an external sword, he would not have said
that two were enough. There were twelve of them,
and many more besides them, and they continued
to multiply daily, so that obviously two swords
would be insufficient.

But each person should have one; thus it is
imperative that he must sell his cloak. So, if by
this he meant that they should carry and use the
sword, they did not keep this command well. For
we find nowhere that they defended themselves or
the gospel against their enemies with the sword.
And when Peter wanted to do it, the Lord
chastised him, saying, "It is not acceptable to fight
with this sword." Peter must put it back in its
place. Or Christ must be against himself. For
Christ said, "If someone hits you on the right
cheek, then turn the other to him also." Again, we
should not strive against evil people. Also, the
apostles must be against Christ, because they
forbid revenge—"not to repay evil for evil, insult
for insult." . . . Also, the prophets must be against
Christ, because they prophesy how in the Last
Days "the people of the church will beat their
swords into plowshares and their spears into
pruning hooks, sickles and scythes and will raise
no weapon against one another." All this and
much more would be false and surrendered, if
Christ had meant "buy external swords."

Therefore, it is not that. He means no other
sword than what he himself had, namely, the
double-edged sword that came out of his mouth.
With *that* he wants his disciples to be armed,
because he will be taken from them through
suffering. Then it will be very necessary for each
of them. For that reason we should let the two
swords be enough, namely, the sword of government, which is and must be in the world, and the
sword of the Spirit and the Word of God, which
is only in the church of Christ. That is enough,

part of a controversy over temporal power with Philip IV of
France (1268–1314). *Unam Sanctam* claims papal authority over
both spiritual and secular realms: "And we learn from the words
of the Gospel that in this Church and in her power are two
swords, the spiritual and the temporal. For when the apostles
said, 'Behold, here' (that is, in the Church, since it was the
apostles who spoke) 'are two swords'—the Lord did not reply, 'It
is too much,' but 'It is enough'" (Henry Bettenson and Chris
Maunder, eds., *Documents of the Christian Church*, 3rd ed.
[Oxford: Oxford University Press, 1999], 126).

and anything further is too much and comes from evil. Or we might understand the two swords to be the Word of God, the divine teaching contained in the Scripture—the Old and New Testaments.... Indeed, they come from the one Spirit with whom we should be armed. The Great Article Book: On the Sword.[15]

---

[15]QGT 12:279-81; citing Lk 22:36; 2 Cor 10:3; Eph 6:12; Mt 5:30; Eph 6:17; Lk 22:37, 38; Mt 26:51; Mt 5:39; Rom 12:17; Heb 10:30; 1 Pet 3:9; Is 2:4; Mic 4:3; Rev 1:16; 19:15; Heb 4:12; Mt 5:37. For a similar allegorization of the two swords as the Testaments see Erasmus's paraphrase on this passage, CWE 48:197 (LB 7:454).

Jesus Is Irritated with the Disciples.
Cardinal Cajetan: He does not say "they are enough," because he means to show that the disciples' response was inappropriate. Therefore, Jesus neglected their question, saying, "It is enough." That is, the conversation about this teaching is sufficient for now. According to human custom to halt a conversation about something we say "it is enough"; according to this usage Jesus says "it is enough." Commentary on Luke 22:38.[16]

---

[16]Cajetan, *Evangelia*, 131r.

22:39-46 JESUS PRAYS ON THE MOUNT OF OLIVES

³⁹And he came out and went, as was his custom, to the Mount of Olives, and the disciples followed him. ⁴⁰And when he came to the place, he said to them, "Pray that you may not enter into temptation." ⁴¹And he withdrew from them about a stone's throw, and knelt down and prayed, ⁴²saying, "Father, if you are willing, remove this cup from me. Nevertheless, not my will, but yours, be done." ⁴³And there appeared to

him an angel from heaven, strengthening him. ⁴⁴And being in an agony he prayed more earnestly; and his sweat became like great drops of blood falling down to the ground.ª ⁴⁵And when he rose from prayer, he came to the disciples and found them sleeping for sorrow, ⁴⁶and he said to them, "Why are you sleeping? Rise and pray that you may not enter into temptation."

a Some manuscripts omit verses 43 and 44

OVERVIEW: As Jesus prepared to face his suffering and death, he offered a valuable lesson in how to face difficult times and even death—he prayed to God. In fact, he prayed earnestly and long, and so diligently that he sweated his own blood. Now, it is no surprise that Christians should be exhorted to pray in times of adversity or that Jesus himself prayed to the Father, as he had done many times before. What is somewhat unusual in this passage is that Jesus prayed that he might avoid the suffering and painful death that he knew was coming. He struggled in this prayer and wrestled with his own fears and worry—perhaps he doubted his strength and ability to face the coming trials. He showed clearly, as our commentators note, that he was a real human being, with a real body and heart, for none of us die gladly. In fact, he suffered more than any of us ever will when facing our own death, because he also carried everyone's sin. Any other person would have been crushed under this weight. It was only because he was also God (and could turn to his Father in prayer) that he was able to bear it. So in times of great trial and fear, suffering and death, our best option is to turn to God, even if our best effort is only to beg to be spared. Melanchthon writes that, as Jesus did, we also can pray that troubles may be avoided, as long as we remember to accept that it is God's will that will be done.

Jesus himself told his disciples to pray—to keep watch and to pray especially that they should avoid temptation, for he knew the challenges that were coming their way. Like us, the disciples would not be able to make it through their difficulties on their own, so instead of relying on their own strength in pride, he teaches us both by word and example to turn in humility and faith to God.

22:39-40 Jesus Tells His Disciples to Pray

CHRIST WAS WILLINGLY CAPTURED ON THE MOUNT OF OLIVES. MARTIN BUCER: This was not the first time that the Lord went out to the Mount of Olives, but (as Luke says) he went there often. For, as Luke also says, in those days, from the time he entered Jerusalem in such a king-like manner, he would usually teach in the temple during the day and then retire to the Mount of Olives for the night. On this night, Judas took the occasion and opportunity to betray him without any tumult, and the Lord, knowing what he was doing and where he went, willingly gave him the opportunity. Often before he had fled from the danger of capture, because his hour was not yet come. So, seeing that he went as usual to the accustomed place well known to Judas the traitor, it is a manifest token that he did not suffer his passion against his will. AN ECCLESIASTICALL EXPOSITION UPON SAINT MATHEWE 26.[1]

CHRIST'S FEAR SHOWS HIS TRUE HUMANITY.

MILES COVERDALE: By going forth to meet death, Christ declares that he will suffer not by compulsion but willingly; by this he gives us comfort. But in that he is troubled, and shows his worry to his disciples and confesses how he fears death, he reveals for our benefit that same weakness and feebleness that we experience at the sight of adversity: for in all things except sin he deigned to become like us, his brothers and sisters. He took true humanity on himself and felt our adversity in his own flesh, so that he could have compassion on us. And besides this, he also shows to whom we should turn in our weakness for comfort and help in adversity, namely, to our Father in heaven, before whom we must fall down in devout and fervent prayer and to whom we should disclose and open up our anguish and trouble. FRUITFUL LESSONS UPON THE PASSION, BURIAL, RESURRECTION, ASCENSION AND OF THE SENDING OF THE HOLY SPIRIT (1593).[2]

WE SHOULD PRAY TO AVOID TEMPTATION.

THOMAS MORE: [Christ] tells us to pray not occasionally but constantly. "Pray," he says, "unceasingly." He tells us to pray not only during the day (for it is hardly necessary to command anyone to stay awake during the day) but rather he exhorts us to devote to intense prayer a large part of that very time which most of us usually devote entirely to sleep. How much more, then, should we be ashamed of our miserable performance and recognize the enormous guilt we incur by saying no more than a short prayer or two, perhaps, during the day, and even those said as we doze and yawn. Finally our Savior tells us to pray, not that we may roll in wealth, not that we may live in a continuous round of pleasures, not that something

awful may happen to our enemies, not that we may receive honor in this world, but rather that we may not enter into temptation. In fact, he wishes us to understand that all those worldly goods are either downright harmful, or else, by comparison with that one benefit, the merest trifles; and hence in his wisdom he placed this one petition at the end of the prayer which he had previously taught his disciples, as if it were a summary, in a way, of all the rest: "And lead us not into temptation, but deliver us from evil." THE SADNESS OF CHRIST.[3]

22:41-44 *Jesus Prays to the Father*

CHRIST TEACHES US TO PRAY IN OUR DARK MOMENTS.

VEIT DIETRICH: But this story of Jesus on the Mount of Olives is also very useful, for we learn from the example of our Lord Christ how we should behave when fear, trials and affliction are at hand. It was at the time that Judas would betray him, the Jews would arrest him and the pagans would nail him to the cross, and what did he do? He was grieved and worried, but he did not simply dwell on his problems. Instead he went out, fell on his face and prayed. You should learn from this, and do not let affliction bother you so much that you forget to pray. For when we are facing fear and affliction, it is very pleasing to God if we do not give up hope but rather turn our hearts toward him and seek for help from him. Psalm 91 testifies to this, for God says, "When he calls to me, I will answer him; I will be with him in trouble; I will rescue him and honor him." THE FIRST PASSION SERMON, ON THE MOUNT OF OLIVES.[4]

JESUS PRAYED HUMBLY TO THE FATHER TO AVOID THE PASSION.

PHILIPP MELANCHTHON: Such gestures belong to a troubled and disquieted mind. They also have an argument for and an element of humility, which is always joined to the prayers of the godly. Thus we see that the truly

---

[1]Marlorat, ed., *Catholike and Ecclesiasticall Exposition of the Holy Gospell After S. Mathewe*, 646*.
[2]*Writings and Translations of Myles Coverdale*, 257*; citing Heb 2:17.

[3]CWM 14,1:171-75*; citing 1 Thess 5:17 (cf. Lk 18:1); Mt 6:13.
[4]Dietrich, *Passio oder Histori vom leiden Christi Jesus vnsers Heylands*, ciij r-v; citing Ps 91:15.

holy and godly sort of people usually either kneel or prostrate themselves on their faces to declare a humble mind before the majesty of God. "Father": Mark recorded the Chaldee word, adjoining it to the Greek word, expounding, as it were, the other, as "Abba, Father." By this he taught us that these two things are required in prayer, namely, the ardent affection of the mind and the faithful trust of children toward God: these two words testify that both of these aspects were present in Christ.

"Remove this cup from me" . . . is a Hebrew phrase of speech and is as much to say, "Let me be delivered from this cruel kind of death, I pray you: Take away this cup from me." This prayer brings much consolation to the afflicted minds among the godly. In this matter, Christ knew the will of his Father, and he knew that all these things would certainly happen to him; nevertheless he seeks through prayer to avoid his passion yet to come— not lightly but earnestly, not once but twice, even three times, as the Evangelist notes. Therefore, it is not inappropriate or disagreeing with their affection for the godly, when they are in danger, to seek to avoid the cross and other troubles through prayer, but always adding, "Nevertheless, not my will, but yours, be done." An Ecclesiasticall Exposition upon Saint Mathewe 26.[5]

Christ's Weakness Conquers Our Own. Desiderius Erasmus: The Lord knew what his Father wanted, and he himself desired to drink the cup of death for the salvation of the world, but he took into himself his body's emotional state and was eager to set down for his followers a form of prayer. This prayer indeed would suit a martyr at the time of execution excellently: "Your will, not mine, be done, whether you wish me to live or to die." What is more, Christ took this trembling of our nature into himself in order to take it away from his followers. But to teach us that after we have entirely surrendered ourselves to God's will, whether for life or for death, then

heavenly help will be with us from the Lord, an angel from heaven appeared to him and strengthened him. Paraphrase on the Gospel of Luke 22:40-43.[6]

Christ's Suffering Was Great in Body and in Mind. Thomas Becon: Of the inward passion and suffering that Christ had in his heart and mind when he had to strive with death right before his eyes, with hell and devil, Luke writes in his Gospel in this manner: "He was in agony and prayed even longer, and his sweat was like drops of blood trickling down to the ground." From these words the exceedingly great horror and torment that Christ suffered in mind and body may be esteemed and judged, and how horrible was the sight of death, of the sin which he took on himself, of hell and of the devil which was before him, seeing that his sweat contrary to all reason and nature was bloody. We can also judge that it was horrible in that the comforter and creator of all the world was cast into such necessity and fear that his Father sent an angel to him to comfort him, as Luke also testifies. The strife of death is fearful beyond all measure and takes away all our natural strength, as we see in condemned people who are suddenly taken away to be put to death. A terrible torment and anger appears in them then, until nature has made itself captive to death, so that the pain and death itself may justly seem to be nothing in comparison with that great agony, trouble and fear. The bloody sweat that came from him, which was a thing never heard of in any other person, manifestly declares how exceedingly great and immeasurable this agony was in Christ. The Last Sunday Before Easter.[7]

His Suffering Shows He Is Both Man and God. Martin Luther: But what should we learn from our Lord's anguish and sorrow? What do we learn from this situation, where he presents himself as so distressed and dejected, and

---

[5]Marlorat, ed., *Catholike and Ecclesiasticall Exposition of the Holy Gospell After S. Mathewe*, 652-653*; citing Mk 14:35.

[6]CWE 48:198-99 (LB 7:454-55).
[7]Becon, *New Postil*, 199r*.

freely admits that the anguish and sorrow in his heart is so great that he could almost die from the pain? I reported above that it serves us in that we note from it how he is a true, natural person, who had a true human body and a real human heart, because death also terrifies him. For it is the way of our inborn nature and our real bodies to be horrified by death, and not to die gladly. But the fear and distress was greater in our Lord Jesus Christ—more than is possible for a human heart otherwise to bear—and the reason is that he bore the sins of all people, and he was going to suffer the death which all people had earned with all their sins. Here he proves himself quite powerfully, for he did not sink under such a weight but carried it without prejudice, showing that he is more than just a person but is also God. Therefore even this agony of death helps us greatly and serves against the heretics who teach that Christ was neither a true person nor true God. For we must acknowledge that both can be seen powerfully here: on account of his fear, he is a true human being; but in that he gives himself up to God's will and triumphs even in such sorrow, we see his divine power. House Postil (1544): The Passion, On the Mount of Olives.[8]

22:45-46 The Disciples Are Sleeping

The Disciples Were Exhausted by Sorrow. Philipp Melanchthon: This sleepiness of the disciples came not from security of mind, by which they would not have cared what was happening. Instead it was grief that brought this slothfulness on them, as Luke suggests, saying, "He found them asleep, exhausted from sorrow." And earlier after supper, Christ had said to them, "But now I am going to him who sent me, and none of you asks me, 'Where are you going?' But because I have said these things to you, sorrow has filled your heart." And because we see all these things that happened to the disciples, we should learn that human nature is full of great infirmity and

weakness. Unless Christ will be present in us by his Holy Spirit, what will we do? An Ecclesiastical Exposition upon Mathewe 26.[9]

We Must Stay Awake to Fight Against Temptation. Miles Coverdale: The love of Christ toward us is fervent, earnest and great, but our flesh is so weak that we do not think of it, and we are also so slow that we sleep and do not realize that it is for our sake that Christ has suffered such great things. Oftentimes we are ready and willing to take important matters onto ourselves, as Peter and the other disciples did, but in the end we fail and take a painful fall. Therefore Christ, who knows us better than we know ourselves, because he wants to expel all pride and presumption from us, teaches us to be lowly-minded and humble, to be constantly watching and to cleave to him alone with continual prayer. For without him we are able to do nothing, but in him we may do all things. So for this purpose he shows us his own feebleness, which assaulted him as a true human being, with the intent that we, always remembering our own weakness, might understand how to tame the rebellious flesh and not to trust it in any situation. We must also be careful and vigilant, so that the subtle enemy might not come up behind us, fall on us and oppress us with temptations. It is no time to sleep: the battle is still being fought, the enemy is still alive, and he besieges our castle, which Christ holds. There are snares and dangers everywhere which no person is able to escape, except for the one who watches earnestly and fights stoutly in fervent prayer and belief and continues faithfully until the end. Fruitful Lessons on the Passion, Burial, Resurrection, Ascension and of the Sending of the Holy Spirit (1593).[10]

Pray to Avoid Temptation. Philipp Melanchthon: He is not a sharp and severe master, and he does not immediately cease to care for us,

---

[8]WA 52:735.

[9]Marlorat, ed., *Catholike and Ecclesiasticall Exposition of the Holy Gospell After S. Mathewe,* 655*; citing Jn 16:5-6.
[10]*Writings and Translations of Myles Coverdale,* 259*.

but instead he repeats what he taught us before. Likewise, for our part we should not reject the commandments of the Lord. If we think it is sufficient to have a thing told to us one time, we are deceived: we can see how easily we fall unless he confirms us with his doctrine. Getting up pertains to the busying and lifting up of the mind to God, but prayer serves to call on God for his help. These two things must be joined together, namely, getting up and prayer. He declares by this that we have need of the help and sustaining that comes from God. This place should be especially noted, for we must fight daily by diverse means against temptations. . . .

This was the danger that the disciples should have feared: the temptation had come of which the Lord said: "Simon, Simon, behold, Satan demanded to have you, that he might sift you like wheat." And Peter in a sense expounded on this, saying, "Be sober-minded; be watchful. Your adversary the devil prowls around like a roaring lion, seeking someone to devour." Christ does not say here: "So that you will not be tempted," but "so that you will not fall into temptation," that is, so that you will not be vanquished with the temptation to come and be in a sense swallowed up by it. AN ECCLESIASTICALL EXPOSITION UPON SAINT MATHEWE 26.[11]

---

[11]Marlorat, ed., *Catholike and Ecclesiasticall Exposition of the Holy Gospell After S. Mathewe*, 656*; citing Lk 22:31; 1 Pet 5:8.

22:47-53 JESUS IS BETRAYED AND ARRESTED

⁴⁷*While he was still speaking, there came a crowd, and the man called Judas, one of the twelve, was leading them. He drew near to Jesus to kiss him,* ⁴⁸*but Jesus said to him, "Judas, would you betray the Son of Man with a kiss?"* ⁴⁹*And when those who were around him saw what would follow, they said, "Lord, shall we strike with the sword?"* ⁵⁰*And one of them struck the servantᵃ of the high priest and cut off his right ear.* ⁵¹*But Jesus said, "No more of this!" And he touched his ear and healed him.* ⁵²*Then Jesus said to the chief priests and officers of the temple and elders, who had come out against him, "Have you come out as against a robber, with swords and clubs?* ⁵³*When I was with you day after day in the temple, you did not lay hands on me. But this is your hour, and the power of darkness."*

a Greek *bondservant*

OVERVIEW: The scene of chaotic confusion at Jesus' arrest is muted by Luke. We hear only hints of the shouting and fear, the clash of swords and confusion. Three scenes are highlighted in Luke's Gospel: the kiss of betrayal, the severing and subsequent healing of the slave's ear and finally Jesus' accusatory words to his captors. Judas had shifted from Jesus' trusted inner circle—those called to do miracles and preach the gospel—to become a traitor whose pretended respect and friendship marked him as a great hypocrite. But Jesus does not react angrily but rather speaks to him with patience and gentleness, as Coverdale notes. Likewise, these interpreters exhort us, we should love and treat kindly those who hate us, in hopes of turning them away from their wickedness.

When Jesus is seized, the disciples are confused as to what they should do—should they defend themselves, or perhaps run away? Peter did not wait for direction but struck out with his sword—perhaps still confused by Jesus' previous statement that "it is enough." This brief mention of Peter's sword leads to a heated debate among our commentators over the proper or improper use of force by Christians. If Peter carried a sword, was it not allowed?

But because Jesus chastised him, certainly that must have meant that it was forbidden? Some interpreters suggest that the apostles themselves did not know whether it was allowed or not. Others, like Walpot, insist that Peter here is not a positive example for Christians, rather Jesus denies any use of force. (For many Anabaptists, especially after the fall of the Münster kingdom in 1535, there was no compatibility at all between Christianity and the sword.) Zwingli suggests that Peter was rebelling against proper authority, and thus his attack was against God. If Jesus had wanted to avoid the arrest, he could have easily done so—he did not need Peter's intervention.

And yet the final focus of this passage—Jesus' accusatory words to the officials who had come to arrest him—shows that it was Jesus' own free decision, in conjunction with the proper time, that led to their success in arresting him. They may have congratulated themselves, as More notes, on their great strength or wily strategy, but it was only through God's will that they were able to seize Jesus. In that "short hour" they were able to achieve their purpose, but the "power of darkness" would reign only for a time and would be forced to serve the larger purpose of salvation.

22:47-48 *Judas Betrays Jesus with a Kiss*

THE WICKED ARE DILIGENT IN THEIR EVIL PLANS. PHILIPP MELANCHTHON: The weapons mentioned by John are called swords and clubs by Matthew, Mark and Luke. . . . The disciples Peter, James and John were asleep, but Judas did not sleep. Instead he watched diligently that he might bring the work of his treason to completion. This is a very good example of the wicked human disposition, by which it comes to pass that the reprobate are more vigilant to do evil than the elect are to do good. AN ECCLESIASTICALL EXPOSITION UPON SAINT MATHEWE 26.[1]

JUDAS WAS ONE OF THE TWELVE. MARTIN LUTHER: Here you should see yourself as the scoundrel Judas, who is neither a pagan nor a Turk. He is also not a Jew with whom the Lord Christ is an enemy, and who had not heard God's Word. He is "one of the twelve," as Matthew [and Luke] say, whom Christ called to preach, to baptize in his name, to drive out the devil and to do all sorts of glorious miracles. And there is no doubt that, because the Lord foreknew this downfall from the beginning, he would have instructed Judas more than the others, and he would have always known not to give him opportunity to sin and temptation. Thus the Evangelists report, especially at the Last Supper, that the Lord always made certain comments as to whether Judas would turn away from such sins. And finally he gives him the memorial bread, probably along with a sad look, as if he would say, "Oh, you wretched man, how can you be an enemy to me? What did I do to you, that you should take such a dislike to me?" But nothing would help it, and he had given himself up completely to the temptation and had given it free reign, so the Lord said to him, "Do what you desire, but do it quickly," as if he would say, "I see

that no warning or sermon will help, so go on, after all—no more counsel or help is possible." HOUSE POSTIL (1544): THE PASSION, CHRIST IS ARRESTED IN THE GARDEN.[2]

JESUS' WORDS MELT STONE. DESIDERIUS ERASMUS: Judas understood that he was not escaping notice; he knew the Lord's innocence; he was invited so often by unheard-of mildness to change his plans—even a stone could have been softened, if Satan had not now occupied his whole breast with the disease of greed. PARAPHRASE ON THE GOSPEL OF LUKE 22:48.[3]

JUDAS IS AN IMPIOUS HYPOCRITE. HEINRICH BULLINGER: Judas made a pretense of these two things: the existence of friendship and the show of godliness. He was an open enemy, and yet he still called Christ his master; he even repeated it, thinking that he might thereby deceive the minds of Christ and the disciples. Similarly Joab was going to kill Amasa, and he kissed him and flattered him in this way, saying, "Is it well with you, my brother?" And so we should learn from this example how great the force of impiety is, and where it will eventually take us, if we do not resist its beginning and origins. This Judas is not afraid on account of money, envy and impiety to salute his Savior and to give his master a kiss. But he acknowledged him to be his master and he kissed him, not for any love or friendship but only to give him a deadly wound. This is how Cain treated Abel, when he killed him under the pretense of a friendly meal. It should be no surprise that today those who seek for nothing else than to overthrow Christ and his gospel also use fair promises, oaths, words and signs. Anyone who does not understand that Judas is the father of these people, because they are wicked hypocrites just as he was, will believe their false interpretations and painted promises.

---

[1]Marlorat, ed., *Catholike and Ecclesiasticall Exposition of the Holy Gospell After S. Mathewe*, 660*; citing Jn 18:2-3; Lk 16:9.

[2]WA 52:743-44; citing Mt 26:50.
[3]CWE 48:201 (LB 7:455).

An Ecclesiasticall Exposition upon Saint Mathewe 26.[4]

Christ Treated His Traitor with Love and Patience. Miles Coverdale: At this time, Christ withdrew his high power. In the weakness of the flesh and in wonderful, great patience, he stepped forward to suffer. We must learn from his example not to demand all of our privileges but to meet the enemy with patience and humbleness of mind.

He also used such patience and gentleness toward his traitor, whom he went out to meet. He did not speak rough words to him, or fight with him or even berate him, although he certainly deserved it. Instead, Christ received him with a soft heart and gentleness, even though he came to deliver and betray Christ into the hands of the wicked and to death. The Lord did not even deny a kiss to him, the token of friendship, and he spoke with him lovingly, although he did mention his feigned and dissembling friendship, telling him of it and admonishing him to cease from his conceived plan of treason. But his heart was hardened. From this example we should also learn from Christ, as far as it concerns our own person and estimation, that we should meet those who hate and betray us with all mildness, heartfelt gentleness, patience and the greatest love. And perhaps with such love and gentleness we may turn them away from their malice and wickedness. Fruitful Lessons upon the Passion, Burial, Resurrection, Ascension and of the Sending of the Holy Spirit (1593).[5]

22:49-51 Jesus Allows No Rebellion

The Apostles Did Not Understand What Christ Wanted. François Lambert: Whatever the Lord had said about acquiring a sword, he was speaking in his usual manner and not commanding them. And because he usually spoke to them in parables, the apostles were not sure if he really wanted them to use force to drive away the tyrants. Consequently they said, "Should we strike with the sword?" What they meant by this was, "We do not know what you want, because we do not understand your words." One of them—no doubt it was Peter—did not expect a response, so he struck. It shows that first he was filled with ardor, although soon he would be an apostate from Christ. Because he was not on fire through the Holy Spirit, his fervor quickly faded to lukewarm. Of course it must be that all strength of the flesh collapses. You see that we are not able to do anything successfully without the working of the Spirit of God, even if by Peter's example, because of Christ, we believe him to do what apart from his Spirit is not able to be done. Commentary in Luke 22:49-50.[6]

Holy Ears Hear Christ's Yes, Not His No. Desiderius Erasmus: Blessed are they whose ear, which till now has heeded godless priests and unspiritual law, is cut off; and when the ear is restored by Christ it gives heed to the things that cause eternal salvation! Paraphrase on the Gospel of Luke 22:50-51.[7]

Peter Wielded the Sword Against Christ's Will. Peter Walpot: We see that Peter carried a sword at his side, for according to the Jewish custom, they had just killed and eaten the Passover lamb, and because he clearly understood from the Lord that soon, and even that very night, he would be betrayed and captured. They still followed much of Jewish practice, but it does not follow that we should also do it. And they did not all carry swords. They still observed the Jewish Passover at that time, but it does not make it fitting for us to do

---

[4]Marlorat, ed., *Catholike and Ecclesiasticall Exposition of the Holy Gospell After S. Mathewe*, 662*; citing 2 Sam 20:9; Gen 4:8.
[5]*Writings and Translations of Myles Coverdale*, 265-66*.

[6]Lambert, *In Divi Lucae*, Gg8v-Hhr.
[7]CWE 48:202* (LB 7:455).

it. Christ celebrated the Jewish Passover with them at that time, using the opportunity to perfect and institute his Supper, which would be continued afterwards.

We also see that, although Peter wanted to fight with the sword, Christ puts an end to that plan and rebukes him: "Put your sword in its place. For all who take up the sword will die by the sword." With these words he completely cuts off this option and wants it put away from those who are his (because the proper "place" of the sword is not with them, as he clearly says). And so Peter puts the sword in its place and leaves it there. He puts it where it cannot be found, so that no other disciple would take out or wield the sword again. Therefore we in the community of Christ should also never take it out, for the worldly sword and the spiritual one cannot be placed next to each other in a scabbard; each has its own special sheath. The spiritual [sword] belongs in the community of Christ, the worldly one in the world among those who are evil, who use it to strike. Therefore Christ announces that misfortune and punishment cling to it, for the one who fights with the sword will also be overcome by it. THE GREAT ARTICLE BOOK: ON THE SWORD.[8]

PETER'S ZEAL WAS MISPLACED AND REBELLIOUS. HULDRYCH ZWINGLI: This is a heavy rebuke, and with it Christ teaches that the deed or zeal of Peter was nothing other than rash rebellion against authority, an insult against God the Father, arrogance against the majesty of God and a violation of the whole of Scripture. It was the farthest thing from true fortitude or godliness. Therefore, we should understand that in the person of Peter, Christ condemns whatever people presume to attempt out of their own brain. This teaching is particularly important and should be noted, for there is nothing more common these days than to defend our actions under the pretense of zeal, as if it did not matter

that those things which people believe to be right and good also must be allowed by God. It is as if God's wisdom is nothing else but mere vanity. Even if we could see nothing wrong with this zeal of Peter, we should still be content with the fact that Christ announced that it did not please him. In fact, it appears that Peter did everything he could to stop Christ from going to his death, and that his own name might be subject to perpetual infamy. Because he resisted the Roman captain and the soldiers violently, he played the part of a rebel: he resisted the power ordained by God. Christ was already so hated by the world that this event might have given them the opportunity to lay on him justly all those condemnations with which he was falsely oppressed. It was out of order that Peter should try to prove his faith with his sword, because he could not do it by his word. AN ECCLESIASTICALL EXPOSITION UPON SAINT MATHEWE 26.[9]

JESUS HEALS THE SLAVE TO REMIND THEM OF HIS POWER. MELCHIOR NEUKIRCH: He heals Malchus, the slave of the high priest who was his enemy and who acted with maliciousness toward him. He places the ear which Peter had hacked off back on his head. In so doing, he reminds the high priests, the temple officials and the elders who were ganging up against him and who were depending on their power and their weapons that they should not think that they were too strong and powerful for the Lord and that he was therefore forced to yield to their might. Rather, he says, "You would not be able to accomplish it with these weapons. You would be able to accomplish only as little as before, when you often tried to catch me in vain. But this is the hour which God ordained for this—the hour in which the power of darkness shall fall on me, and everything which belongs to the sin of the whole world will come on me." THE THIRD PART OF THE PASSION.[10]

---

[8]QGT 12:273.

[9]Marlorat, ed., *Catholike and Ecclesiasticall Exposition of the Holy Gospell After S. Mathewe*, 664*.
[10]Neukirch, *Historia der Passion*, 254r-v.

22:52-53 Jesus Questions His Captors

THEIR CAPTURE OF JESUS WAS NOT DUE TO THEIR OWN SKILL. THOMAS MORE: Addressing, therefore, the princes of the priests, the Pharisees and the elders of the people, Christ implicitly reminds them that they should not attribute his capture to their own strength or adroitness and should not foolishly boast of it as a clever and ingenious achievement (according to that unfortunate tendency of those who are fortunate in evil). He lets them know that the foolish contrivances and maneuvers by which they labored to suppress the truth were powerless to accomplish anything against him, but rather the profound wisdom of God had foreseen and set the time when the prince of this world would be justly tricked into losing his ill-gotten prey, the human race, even as he strove by unjust means to keep it. If this were not the case, Christ explains to them, there would have been no need at all for them to pay for the services of the betrayer, to come at night with lanterns and torches, to make their approach surrounded by the dense ranks of the cohort and armed with swords and clubs, because they had previously had many opportunities to arrest him as he sat teaching in the temple, and then they could have done it without expense, without any special effort, without spending a sleepless night, without any saber rattling at all.

But if they should take special credit for their prudent foresight and say that the arrest of Christ was no easy matter, as he claimed, but rather quite difficult because it necessarily brought with it the great danger of a popular uprising, this difficulty, for the most part, had arisen only recently, after the resurrection of Lazarus. Before that event, it had happened more than once that, in spite of the people's great love of his virtues and their profound respect for him, he had had to use his own power to escape from their midst. On those occasions anyone attempting to capture and kill him would not have been in the least danger from the crowd but would have found them to be willing accomplices in crime. THE SADNESS OF CHRIST.[11]

THEY DID NOT DARE TO ARREST HIM IN THE TEMPLE. PHILIPP MELANCHTHON: With this example we see that it is the duty of a Christian, no matter how well-prepared he may be for the cross, to declare his innocence when he sees that he is craftily accused. Jesus said, "Every day I was with you in the temple courts," and so we see that they used to sit and teach in those days. "I was," he said, "conversing daily in the temple, not with a host or band of men, but teaching. I have given you no occasion for this behavior." Note this word *daily* and consider that he was always occupied in teaching his Father's will. In the daytime he taught in the temple, and at night he went up to the Mount of Olives. . . . Christ did not say "you did not try to take me," but "you did not lay a hand on me." For they had often tried to take him, but his hour had not yet come. Notice how he secretly reminded them of that event which John mentions in John 7: the servants of the high priest were sent to take the Lord in the temple. They found him teaching, they listened to him and were amazed, so they went on their way. When the priests asked them why they had not brought him, they answered, "No one ever spoke like this man!" It was the same people who were sent to arrest Christ this time, so they were well reminded of this deed. It is as if he should say, "Why did you not take me in the temple? You heard me and were amazed, so much so that you thought it was not right to lay hands on me. Don't you think I could escape now, if I wanted to?" AN ECCLESIASTICALL EXPOSITION UPON SAINT MATHEWE 26.[12]

THEIR POWER IS PART OF GOD'S UNSEARCHABLE PLAN. THOMAS MORE: And so Christ said

---

[11]CWM 14,1:523-27*; citing Jn 12:31; 14:30; 16:11; Mt 21:46; Lk 20:19; Jn 11:45-48; Lk 4:28-30.
[12]Marlorat, ed., *Catholike and Ecclesiasticall Exposition of the Holy Gospell After S. Mathewe*, 669*; citing Jn 7:45-46.

to them, "This is your hour and the power of darkness." In the past, although you hated me intensely, although you longed to destroy me, although you could have done so at that time with less trouble (except that heavenly power prevented it), yet you did not detain me in the temple—you did not even make a single move to lay hands on me. Why was this? It was because the time and the hour had not yet come, the hour fixed not by the heavenly bodies, not by your cleverness, but rather by the unsearchable plan of my Father, to which I too had given my consent. Would you like to know when he did this? Not only as long ago as the times of Abraham, but from all eternity. For from all eternity, together with the Father, before Abraham came to be, I am.

And so this is your hour and the power of darkness. This is the short hour allowed to you and the power granted to darkness, so that now in the dark you might do what you were not permitted to do in the daylight, flying in my face like winged creatures from the Stygian marsh, like harpies, like horned owls and screech owls, like night ravens and bats and night owls, futilely swarming in a shrill uproar of beaks, talons and teeth.[13] You are in the dark when you ascribe my death to your strength. So too the governor Pilate will be in the dark when he takes pride in possessing the power to free me or to crucify me. For, even though my people and my high priests are about to hand me over to him, he would not have any power over me if it were not given to him from above. THE SADNESS OF CHRIST.[14]

---

[13] The Stygian marsh is a part of the river Styx, the border between earth and the underworld in Greek mythology. In Dante's *Inferno*, the Stygian marsh was the fifth circle of hell, where the wrathful and sullen were eternally punished by being drowned in the mud. Owls appear to have been revered by the Greeks, but to the Romans they were connected to the underworld and impending death. These negative ideas appear to have influenced the development of English folklore. There is a Stygian owl, native to South America.

[14] CWM 14,1:537-41*; citing Jn 8:58.

22:54-62 PETER DENIES JESUS

[54] Then they seized him and led him away, bringing him into the high priest's house, and Peter was following at a distance. [55] And when they had kindled a fire in the middle of the courtyard and sat down together, Peter sat down among them. [56] Then a servant girl, seeing him as he sat in the light and looking closely at him, said, "This man also was with him." [57] But he denied it, saying, "Woman, I do not know him." [58] And a little later someone else saw him and said, "You also are one of them." But Peter said, "Man, I am not." [59] And after an interval of about an hour still another insisted, saying, "Certainly this man also was with him, for he too is a Galilean." [60] But Peter said, "Man, I do not know what you are talking about." And immediately, while he was still speaking, the rooster crowed. [61] And the Lord turned and looked at Peter. And Peter remembered the saying of the Lord, how he had said to him, "Before the rooster crows today, you will deny me three times." [62] And he went out and wept bitterly.

OVERVIEW: Peter, for the reformers, is a complex figure who believes and doubts. He was a loyal and convinced follower of Jesus. However, this situation was more terrifying than anything Peter could have imagined. He had been convinced that he was ready to follow Jesus even to death, but when the moment came, the fear was too overwhelming. When the servants in the courtyard recognized him as a follower of Jesus, the only thing he could think of at that moment was self-preservation through denial. He denied knowing Christ, he cursed and swore, even renounced his heavenly inheritance if he was lying, as Neukirch recounts.

What happened to that confident Peter who had spoken of following Jesus even to death? Still when the cock crows and Jesus looks at Peter, the difference between Judas, one of the reprobate, and Peter, one of the elect, becomes clear. They had both denied and betrayed their Lord, but while Judas despaired and killed himself (Mt 27:5), Peter broke down in tears and repented. For our interpreters, Peter shows that anyone, even the strongest and most faithful Christian, can fall, but more importantly he shows how one should act when the realization of sin sets in. Repentance is painful, the reformers remind us, for when we recognize our sin and realize what sort of punishment we deserve, our hearts tremble. But the gospel promises of forgiveness and salvation in which we can find comfort are always there, and we should rely on those promises when we pray to God for mercy.

22:54-55 Peter Follows Jesus

JESUS WAS TAKEN, BUT THE WORD OF GOD IS NOT BOUND. DESIDERIUS ERASMUS: The wicked crowd observed the traitorous sign which they were given, laid hands on Jesus and took him. But it was for this reason that he was arrested and for this reason that he was taken: that he might deliver us from the bondage of sin and the thralldom of Satan into the glorious liberty of the children of God, and that he might teach patience to his worshipers, if they should be taken with violence at any time or should be arrested. There is no danger that the Word would be put into bondage with us, for Saint Paul says that the Word of God is not bound. The Son of Man was overcome and taken, but nevertheless the eternal truth of God abides free and invincible. AN ECCLESI-ASTICALL EXPOSITION UPON SAINT MATHEWE 26.[1]

THIS CORRUPT HIGH PRIEST WAS THE LEADER OF GOD'S CHURCH. PHILIPP MELANCH-THON: Caiaphas was no true high priest, of course,

---

[1] Marlorat, ed., *Catholike and Ecclesiasticall Exposition of the Holy Gospell After S. Mathewe*, 663*; citing 2 Tim 2:9.

because he had bought his office for money, against the law of God, and yet nevertheless, because like will to like, he was accepted and respected by the scribes and elders of the people, by whom he should have been rejected. The high priest was a mortal enemy to Christ, because he feared the loss of his office, which had cost him a great deal of money. The rest of them were also recipients of the high priest's gains. Therefore, things within the priesthood were entirely corrupt, and they all conspired against Christ and gathered a council to discuss how they might destroy him—and all this to preserve their priestly kingdom! And so once Christ was taken, they all came to the high priest. Truly this sets before our eyes a horrible and fearful spectacle: because at the time, the temple of God, the lawful worship, the face and image of the church was nowhere else but in Jerusalem, the high priest was a type and figure of the only mediator between God and humanity. Those who gathered together at this council represented the whole church of God, and yet nevertheless they conspired together to destroy Christ, the only hope of salvation. AN ECCLESIASTICALL EXPOSITION UPON SAINT MATHEWE 26.[2]

PETER WAS STRONG IN FAITH BUT WEAK IN HIS NATURE. HEINRICH SALMUTH: Saint Peter had been requested and called to the office of apostle by Jesus Christ himself. He had heard the teaching and sermons of Christ and seen his miracles. He lived in him, and God the Holy Spirit was strong in him, for he believed in Jesus as the Christ and gave a beautiful confession of him: "You are the Christ, the Son of the living God." Peter had seen Christ's transfiguration on the mountain. He had walked on the water and had greatly loved his master. Therefore he also gave this answer to his question, "Lord, where should we go? You have the word of eternal life." He was very sure that he would go to prison with him and even die with him. But as soon as a lowly maid spoke to him out

of sympathy, he disavowed his Lord and master, and he swore that God would curse him if he knew this man.

This and other examples testify to how poor, weak and miserable our corrupt nature is. And we should pay attention to such examples, so that we might be reminded of our weakness and not be secure or overconfident, trusting too much in ourselves. But instead we should fear God the Lord, and call on him and ask him for help and support. THE FIFTH SERMON ON THE PASSION AND DEATH OF JESUS CHRIST.[3]

22:56-62 *Jesus' Prophecy Is Fulfilled*

PETER'S FEAR AND WEAKNESS LEAD HIM INTO SIN. THE ENGLISH ANNOTATIONS: Fear is a dangerous temptation. It was undoubtedly because of love that Peter followed Christ into that danger, and certainly also because of a violent disturbance of his mind by fear that he denied him. Those who truly love God (by the grace of God) are still weak in themselves, because they are still partly flesh. Here are three immediate causes of Peter's failure: first, too much confidence in himself; second, the company of Christ's enemies, it is very difficult not to fail with them, . . . third, the wisdom of the flesh, which suggests to him what he once said to Christ when he was speaking of his passion, "Far be it from you, Lord!" . . .

Once he fell, he could not recover quickly: the falls of a sinner take away the present sense of sin and affect the mind with such a stupor that it cannot understand the evil it has just done. It is so easy for the best of us to fall, and so hard for us to rise again. ANNOTATIONS ON THE GOSPEL ACCORDING TO SAINT LUKE 22:57-58.[4]

PETER CURSES HIMSELF AND CHRIST. MELCHIOR NEUKIRCH: The man could hear this in his speech, for there was a distinction among the Jews in their speech, as there are distinctions within the

---

[2]Marlorat, ed., *Catholike and Ecclesiasticall Exposition of the Holy Gospell After S. Mathewe*, 671-72*.

[3]Salmuth, *Passional*, 235; citing Mt 16:16; Jn 6:68.
[4]Downame, ed., *Annotations*, Zz3r*; citing Mt 16:22.

German speech among High German, Saxon German, Westphalian German, Netherlandish. And as he was speaking with Peter, one of the high priest's slaves stepped up to him—it was a friend of Malchus, whose ear Peter had hacked off in the garden. This slave spoke to him directly in the courtyard, "What are you saying? Why are you denying that you are his disciple? Didn't I see you in the garden with him? Aren't you the one who drew his sword and cut off the ear of my cousin?" Then Peter thought, "If you can't answer and make excuses for yourself quite seriously, you will give it away. Then they will grab you and deliver you up to the hands of the high priest." So he began to curse and swear. He did not just stick to the denials, and did not only swear but also said, as thoughtless people are used to saying, "If that is so, then I'll be damned, and in the next world I will have no part in the kingdom of God." That is what Peter does here—he renounces his portion in the kingdom of heaven, where he would know the people, and moreover he curses himself in the extreme, and, as this word can also be understood in the speech of the Evangelists, he also cursed Christ himself: "What do I have to do with that accursed man? What concern is he of mine?" And moreover, this is quite diligently described, for it comes after Peter wanted to have all the glory alone because he did not want to abandon his Lord and master and thoroughly intended that it should never happen. Now it not only happened that he abandoned him, but he also denied him so vigorously as to blaspheme and dishonor him. From this we learn about what Jeremiah says: the human heart is so malicious and corrupt, the person himself cannot know every sort of evil that hides in his heart, as we see here with Peter. THE THIRD PART OF THE PASSION.[5]

GOD USES THE COCK'S CROWING TO ADMONISH PETER. HULDRYCH ZWINGLI: The Lord knows how to use the failings of his own to his own glory. If we have sinned with Peter, let us repent with Peter and weep bitterly, for the elect who have fallen arise again once they are admonished. They do not boast in their sins, nor do they rejoice when they have done evil, nor despise God's admonition. The fact that Christ looks on Peter in the midst of his sins teaches us that God does not forget his children but admonishes them both internally and externally. . . . Christ uses the crowing of the cock, which is a natural event, not only as a sign of Peter's denial but also to admonish Peter to repent. We see that even in such a little thing God's providence does not cease, and it declares that creatures are the instruments of God's power and grace. The cock knew nothing of Peter but was moved and crowed by his own nature, but God knew and appointed him for this purpose. Let us also note that there is a great difference between those who sin out of weakness and fear and those who sin on purpose out of malice. The sin of the weak ones does not bring death, but the sin of the ungodly is committed against the Holy Spirit, and that means it will never be forgiven. Those who fall or slip, even if it is very grievous, but then rise up again from their fall after being admonished and emerge from their sins, forsaking their ungodliness, and if the ungodly weep and show signs of true repentance, it is manifest that those people are elect and godly and that they sinned only from weakness. They no longer abide in the filth of sins, but as soon as they come to themselves, they place their feet on the way of righteousness, they run to God's mercy for forgiveness, and they become more humble, wary and diligent. ON THE PASSION AND DEATH OF CHRIST.[6]

PETER REVEALS TRUE REPENTANCE TO US. MARTIN LUTHER: We can learn from this what true repentance is. The beginning of repentance comes when the heart truly recognizes sin and allows itself to be in sorrow. It comes when a person no longer desires or loves the sin, or continues in it, but concerns himself from his heart

[5]Neukirch, *Historia der Passion*, 292v-293v; citing Jer 17:9.

[6]Zwingli, *A Briefe Rehersal of the Death, Resurrection and Ascension of Christ*, 83-85*; citing Mk 3:28-29; Mt 12:32; Lk 12:10; Prov 8:20.

as to whether he has followed God's will or transgressed it. But we can't do this from our own impulse—the Lord must regard us, just as he regarded Peter here. For our nature loves sin, and we are always continuing in it with great desire, just as we observe here with Peter. Once he denied Christ, he just continues on and does not pay attention. But then the rooster crows, and the Lord looks back at Peter, then it hits him for the first time, and he thinks about what he did.

Now according to his (and our) nature, sin cannot do anything but frighten us, threatening us with God's wrath and making the heart full of anxiety, as we can see in the examples of both Judas and Peter. We see it in Judas, because as soon as he realized his sin, he became so afraid that he did not know where he should stay. Peter also became so frightened that he needed to get away from other people—his sin alarmed him so much that he could not cry enough. It is best, when you find yourself in such anxiety and grief, that you first humble yourself toward God and freely confess your sins: "Oh, God, I am a miserable sinner and can do nothing more than sin, if you take your grace away from me." Afterwards, hold on tight to God's word and promises and say, "Be merciful to me, for the sake of your Son, Jesus Christ." If the heart then takes comfort in God's Word and has hope that God will be merciful for the sake of his Son, then fear must decrease, and comfort will certainly follow. When our sins have humbled us, and the Lord Jesus Christ and his sufferings give comfort, that is true and complete repentance. House Postil (1544): The Passion, How Peter Denied the Lord in Caiaphas's House for the Third Time.[7]

---

[7]WA 52:768.

22:63-71 JESUS IS MOCKED AND TRIED

⁶³*Now the men who were holding Jesus in custody were mocking him as they beat him.* ⁶⁴*They also blindfolded him and kept asking him, "Prophesy! Who is it that struck you?"* ⁶⁵*And they said many other things against him, blaspheming him.*

⁶⁶*When day came, the assembly of the elders of the people gathered together, both chief priests and scribes. And they led him away to their council, and they said,* ⁶⁷*"If you are the Christ, tell us." But he said to them, "If I tell you, you will not believe,* ⁶⁸*and if I ask you, you will not answer.* ⁶⁹*But from now on the Son of Man shall be seated at the right hand of the power of God."* ⁷⁰*So they all said, "Are you the Son of God, then?" And he said to them, "You say that I am."* ⁷¹*Then they said, "What further testimony do we need? We have heard it ourselves from his own lips."*

Overview: The treatment that Jesus suffered at the soldiers' hands only increases the pain that Christians feel when they reflect on the fact the Jesus himself was innocent, and it was only for the sake of our sins that he was so abused. Our commentators suggest that, in fact, Jesus was the only one who would have borne such abuse for all of us unworthy human beings. The Lord transfigured this abuse, so that through Jesus' marred and bloodied face we would be brought back into fellowship with our Creator.

Jesus' initial trial before the council of leaders and priests was a solemn affair, too. Despite the show of legality and uprightness, these interpreters assert, the outcome was already fixed, and they were determined ahead of time to send him to death. Such a miscarriage of justice was a sign of the devil's involvement. But, according to our commentators, the trial did produce at least two important results. When the council pressed Jesus to tell them whether or not he was the Messiah, he replied to them quite openly that he was, although he noted that they would not believe his statement. Yet, Neukirch suggests, their own question (asking whether he was the "Son of God") as well as his answer, "You say that I am," reveal that these leaders in their consciences and in their hearts believed that Jesus was the Messiah and the Son of God. Second, in confessing that he was the Christ, Jesus became the first martyr for the gospel, for he was condemned solely for that statement. Melanchthon argues that we do not always have to answer the wicked when they unjustly press us, but if a witness is required, then like Jesus, we, too, must witness to the truth of the gospel.

22:63-65 The Soldiers Mock and Beat Jesus

Jesus Suffered on Our Behalf. Konrad Pellikan: That entire night was spent in the mocking of Jesus. . . . No one else would bear this for us who are so unworthy, if he would be attacked and abused because of the word of the gospel and wickedly struck down by those who serve the desire of the wickedness of the high priest, the falsity of the Pharisees and the foolishness of the leaders. Commentary in Luke 22:63-65.[1]

The Lord Transformed This Disgrace. John Calvin: Either Luke has inverted the history's order or our Lord twice endured this great indignity. To me the latter seems to be likely. Nor do I doubt that the ministers decided to spit on and strike Christ more insolently after they saw that the council had condemned him to death. All this mockery was to show that nothing was less fitting than that he be the Prince of prophets who

---

[1]Pellikan, *In Sacrosancta Quatuor Evangelia*, 227-28 (cf. CWE 48:205; LB 7:457).

was unable to ward off their punches because he was blindfolded. But God's providence transformed this insolence into something very different: Christ's face—disgraced by spit and punches—has restored in us that image which had been corrupted, indeed erased by sin. COMMENTARY ON A HARMONY OF THE GOSPELS.[2]

WHAT BLASPHEMIES THEY UTTERED. THE ENGLISH ANNOTATIONS: Perhaps some were saying that he was a glutton, wine drinker and friend of tax collectors and sinners; others that he had formerly cast out devils by Beelzebub who now failed him, so that he could not deliver himself from punishment. . . . Others were saying that he was no prophet who would not foresee his own dangers and deliver himself from them; that he had deceived foolish people. Satan was witty to invent blasphemous suggestions; they were malicious to seize and utter them. All this Jesus heard and patiently endured in his suffering for our sins. ANNOTATIONS UPON THE GOSPEL ACCORDING TO SAINT LUKE 22:65.[3]

22:66-69 *Jesus Is Questioned Before the Sanhedrin*

SATAN MANIPULATES OUR RISING AND SETTING FOR HIS PURPOSES. THE ENGLISH ANNOTATIONS: So industrious is his malice that Satan will not let the wicked—his servants—sleep when any mischief is to be done but sits heavy on their eyes at church or when they should rise to go to it. For he fears that they might be moved to faith and repentance; thus he would lose them and their service. ANNOTATIONS UPON THE GOSPEL ACCORDING TO SAINT LUKE 22:66.[4]

JESUS WAS CONDEMNED BEFORE HE WAS EVEN TRIED. JOHN CROMPE: But there was an artificial show and pretext, I must confess, of much sincerity and uprightness in their proceedings

against him. This was a solemnly called and gathered council, as you see, and it had the greatest and gravest, the most learned and wisest men among them, such as the high priests, scribes and elders, besides the spectators and bystanders. Among such members it could not be thought, or even imagined, that all things would not be fairly and uprightly conducted by such an assembly. . . . Who could expect anything but good from such a famous and illustrious convention and meeting, with such a great crowd of noble men who had such reverence and appearance of honesty? Here we see gathered together so many fair but empty excuses of nothing less than sincere and upright dealings, as a congregation and gathering together of the most renowned and famous men of the city, an orderly and solemn sort of legal proceeding, a production of several witnesses, and the like. But all these are but masked and dissembling appearances, a disguise only and not a true face of justice. For the text tells us that for all their fair appearance, their intent was foul, even to put him to death, so that he had his doom before his day of hearing and his judgment before his trial. All things were determined and decreed concerning him before the group even came together, which is a piece of the greatest injustice and the vilest and most obscene mischief that either the devil can invent or his instruments actuate. When a person has his case sentenced before it is heard and himself condemned before he is legally convicted—that is proper devilry indeed. THE GREAT WEEK OF CHRIST'S PASSION.[5]

WHATEVER HIS ANSWER THEY WOULD NOT HAVE LISTENED. JOHN CALVIN: By these words he means that even if he were to prove to them a hundred times that he is the Christ, it would be of no use with obstinate people. They had not only heard about his miracles, but with their own eyes they had witnessed them—which, despite Christ's silence, confirmed his heavenly and divine power. In fact they cried out that he was the formerly

---

[2]CTS 33:259* (CO 45:740).
[3]Downame, ed., *Annotations*, Zz3r*; citing Lk 7:35; 11:15.
[4]Downame, ed., *Annotations*, Zz3r-v*.

[5]Crompe, *Hebdomada Magna*, 60*.

promised Redeemer! COMMENTARY ON A HAR-MONY OF THE GOSPELS.[6]

JESUS ANSWERED TO SHOW RESPECT TO GOD. PHILIPP MELANCHTHON: Christ no longer held his peace, but out of reverence for the name of God, he told the truth, because that is what he was asked and charged to tell (although he knew that they sought something other than the truth). He did not want to seem like he did not respect God or the people, or that he was lacking in zeal, by treating this request with contempt. It is important to note that the wicked do not always need to be answered, although they might charge us a thousand times by the name of the living God, but we must pay careful attention so that we do not damage the glory of God if we hold our peace, but rather we should give some sign of respect, so that no one thinks we are separated from God.

And he did not simply state, "from now on the Son of Man will be seated," but he said, "If I tell you, you will not believe me," then continued. It is as if he should have said, "You do not now believe me, but I will tell you (because you have adjured me by the living God to tell whether or not I am the Christ) that hereafter you will see the Son of Man, whom you now despise as a lowly figure, sitting at the right hand of power, endued with divine majesty to reign forever, and you will see him come at length in the clouds of heaven to judge the reprobate. No matter what you judge of me now, you will see those things in the future." AN ECCLESIASTICALL EXPOSITION UPON SAINT MATHEWE 26.[7]

WHAT DOES "AT THE RIGHT HAND OF THE POWER OF GOD" MEAN? JOHN CALVIN: The metaphor of the phrase "right hand" should be recognized well enough; it frequently occurs in Scripture. It states that Christ is seated at the right

hand of the Father, because ordained as the Most High King—who governs the world by his name—he occupies the seat of honor and authority next to the Father. Therefore, Christ sits at the Father's right hand, because he is the Father's vicar. And thus it is called "the right hand of power" because only through the hand of his Son does God now display his power—only through him will he execute judgment on the Last Day. COMMENTARY ON A HARMONY OF THE GOSPELS.[8]

22:70-71 Jesus Is Condemned as the Son of Man

THE COUNCIL HAD PROPERLY UNDERSTOOD BUT NOT ACCEPTED CHRIST'S PREACHING. MELCHIOR NEUKIRCH: It is as if the high priest were saying, "You have declared about yourself in your sermons that you are the Messiah and the promised Christ, God's Son." (In fact, the Lord did preach this in John 5, where he said he was God's Son.) Therefore the high priest debated with him and said, "You have persuaded the people that you are God's Son. You have publicly testified to your disciples that you are the Christ, the Son of the living God, and allowed the hosanna to be sung for you, which gave everyone to understand that you were our Messiah. So now I ask of you, as the high priest, that you make a statement before this consistory, as to whether or not you are the Messiah." THE THIRD PART OF THE PASSION.[9]

THE SANHEDRIN SPOKE SARCASTICALLY. THE ENGLISH ANNOTATIONS: It is as if in blasphemous scorn they said, "You, the carpenter's son? You, friend of tax collectors and sinners? You, profaner of sabbaths? You, the Son of God?" ANNOTATIONS UPON THE GOSPEL ACCORDING TO SAINT LUKE 22:70.[10]

---

[6]CTS 33:257* (CO 45:739).
[7]Marlorat, ed., Catholike and Ecclesiasticall Exposition of the Holy Gospell After S. Mathewe, 676*.

[8]CTS 33:258* (CO 45:739-40).
[9]Neukirch, Historia der Passion, 323r-324v; citing Jn 5:18-29; Mt 16:13-20.
[10]Downame, ed., Annotations, Zz3v*.

JESUS' MODEST AND MEASURED ANSWER.
DESIDERIUS ERASMUS: Jesus so framed his
answer that he neither denied that he was what he
was nor provided them with an opening for an
accusation nor gave the appearance of arrogance
about himself. The Lord indeed everywhere
preferred to make his divine nature known in
deeds rather than proclaim it in words. So he
replied, "You say that I am," modestly implying
that what they were asking as an uncertainty could
be asserted in the same words if one only changed
the intonation. PARAPHRASE ON THE GOSPEL OF
LUKE 22:70.[11]

**JESUS IS THE PROMISED MESSIAH, EVEN IF
SCORNED.** MELCHIOR NEUKIRCH: It is as if Jesus
were saying, "Your own conscience convinces you
that I am the Messiah, and your own heart
promises it to you. Therefore, you should also
know that I am the only true Messiah, which God
has promised to the world and now has finally sent."
He says further, "Do not take exception to the fact
that I go on my way in this poor, despised form as
a person—a humble, common man. I do not stand
here as a hero or as a Son of Man but as poor and
pitiful, under the most extreme contempt." THE
THIRD PART OF THE PASSION.[12]

---

[11]CWE 48:206* (LB 7:457-58).

[12]Neukirch, *Historia der Passion*, 323r-324v; citing Jn 5:18-29; Mt 16:13-20.

23:1-25 JESUS IS BROUGHT BEFORE PILATE AND HEROD

Then the whole company of them arose and brought him before Pilate. ²And they began to accuse him, saying, "We found this man misleading our nation and forbidding us to give tribute to Caesar, and saying that he himself is Christ, a king." ³And Pilate asked him, "Are you the King of the Jews?" And he answered him, "You have said so." ⁴Then Pilate said to the chief priests and the crowds, "I find no guilt in this man." ⁵But they were urgent, saying, "He stirs up the people, teaching throughout all Judea, from Galilee even to this place."

⁶When Pilate heard this, he asked whether the man was a Galilean. ⁷And when he learned that he belonged to Herod's jurisdiction, he sent him over to Herod, who was himself in Jerusalem at that time. ⁸When Herod saw Jesus, he was very glad, for he had long desired to see him, because he had heard about him, and he was hoping to see some sign done by him. ⁹So he questioned him at some length, but he made no answer. ¹⁰The chief priests and the scribes stood by, vehemently accusing him. ¹¹And Herod with his soldiers treated him with contempt and mocked him. Then, arraying him in splendid clothing, he sent him back to Pilate. ¹²And Herod and Pilate became friends with each other that very day, for before this they had been at enmity with each other.

¹³Pilate then called together the chief priests and the rulers and the people, ¹⁴and said to them, "You brought me this man as one who was misleading the people. And after examining him before you, behold, I did not find this man guilty of any of your charges against him. ¹⁵Neither did Herod, for he sent him back to us. Look, nothing deserving death has been done by him. ¹⁶I will therefore punish and release him." ᵃ

¹⁸But they all cried out together, "Away with this man, and release to us Barabbas"— ¹⁹a man who had been thrown into prison for an insurrection started in the city and for murder. ²⁰Pilate addressed them once more, desiring to release Jesus, ²¹but they kept shouting, "Crucify, crucify him!" ²²A third time he said to them, "Why, what evil has he done? I have found in him no guilt deserving death. I will therefore punish and release him." ²³But they were urgent, demanding with loud cries that he should be crucified. And their voices prevailed. ²⁴So Pilate decided that their demand should be granted. ²⁵He released the man who had been thrown into prison for insurrection and murder, for whom they asked, but he delivered Jesus over to their will.

a Here, or after verse 19, some manuscripts add verse 17: *Now he was obliged to release one man to them at the festival*

OVERVIEW: Despite the false accusations before Pilate and Herod, the commentators argue, Jesus offers an example of faithfulness to God's will in the midst of suffering while his innocence and identity are declared. The first trial before Pilate was a disaster for Jesus' enemies. They accused him of actions that could not fail—so they thought— to elicit a reaction from Pilate. They were crafty, Melanchthon notes, for instead of bringing Jesus to Pilate for blasphemy or some religious infraction, they accused him of perverting the nation—that is, stirring up the people to rebellion—and forbidding the people to pay taxes to the emperor. If these charges of rebellion had been true, they would have been quite serious, for other leaders of insurrection had already been imprisoned and executed for such acts. But the best (or worst) charge was designed to make Pilate particularly envious of Jesus—that he claimed to be a king, which Calvin agrees is the most serious charge against him. But Pilate, while "wicked and unjust," as Marlorat notes, would not sentence an innocent man to death, unless there was some sort of threat to himself. The council and the false witnesses were not able to convince anyone of Jesus' guilt, least of all Pilate, who himself announced Jesus' innocence. His clear and uncontested innocence underlined that his trials, all his suffering and his eventual death—while freely undertaken—were not for any guilt of his own but instead were only for us.

Jesus' next legal proceeding was a trial before Herod the tetrarch, ruler of Galilee. Pilate seemed quite happy to transfer Jesus to Herod, both to avoid judging him when he knew him to be innocent and to avoid offending the Jews if he should let him go. Herod was also pleased, for he had been wanting to meet Jesus and witness some wonder working. But, as Lambert notes, Jesus was not willing to waste his time with someone interested only in entertainment. Jesus' teaching was reserved for those seeking the truth. It was only with such people that Jesus would share the mysteries of his kingdom, and that did not include either Pilate or Herod. Herod further revealed his bad character by mocking and abusing Jesus before returning him to Pilate. In what might seem an unusual side note, this sending of Jesus back and forth led to rapprochement between Herod and Pilate, who had hitherto not been friends. But Calvin remarks that it is not too surprising, for while before they had clashed over matters of importance—probably challenges to their authority—now they bonded over what was worthless to them, that is, Christ.

Pilate's second trial of Jesus is a despicable miscarriage of justice in a variety of ways, even if it was part of God's plan and necessary for our salvation. Pilate knows, and declares openly, that Jesus is innocent. But, the reformers argue, because Pilate cared more about keeping the peace and mollifying the people, he agreed to condemn Jesus to death. The high priests and other leaders believed that this hoped-for result was in keeping with law and justice because Jesus had claimed falsely, in their opinion, to be divine. However, what they fail to consider, according to Marlorat, is that Jesus *is* the Messiah—it would have been a

punishable offense in anyone else, but not in him. The entire affair is unjust, from beginning to end; yet according to his divine wisdom God allowed the condemnation of his innocent Son.

23:1-5 *The First Trial Before Pilate*

THE LEADERS COULD NOT CONDEMN CHRIST THEMSELVES. HEINRICH SALMUTH: The Romans had seized the kingdom of the Jews and their land, and the Roman emperor, as their feudal lord, had placed Herod as king in Galilee and had established Pilate as the procurator in the Judean region.

Then, because the Jews had lost sovereign authority and the right to adjudicate capital punishment, and their royal prerogatives and privileges were lost, they could not sentence the Lord Jesus Christ to death, although they had captured and bound him, nor could they actually put him to death. Instead, they had to present him to the chief procurator, and so they led the captured Lord Christ into the judgment hall before Pilate and accused him themselves, to show why he should deserve the death penalty. THE SIXTH SERMON ON THE PASSION AND DEATH OF JESUS CHRIST.[1]

THE LEADERS CHARGE JESUS WITH SERIOUS CRIMES. PHILIPP MELANCHTHON: This is the accusation by which they desired to stir up the mind of Pilate against the Lord, and they did it very craftily. For although they tried to overthrow Christ by accusing him of many and sundry things, it is certain that this accusation, that he desired the name of a king, was very wickedly put up against him so that it would cause Pilate to envy him. That is why they expressly said that they found him altering the state of things, subverting the people and forbidding the payment of tribute to Caesar. Of all the faults this one was most odious to Pilate, as he cared for nothing more than to defend and maintain the quiet state of the people and the government. The Jewish leaders knew that a

---

[1]Salmuth, *Passional*, 253-54.

profane man would not be very moved if they said, "We found this man speaking blasphemy against God and despising our temple." But they knew that Pilate and men like him counted rebelliousness as a serious crime, and it was not tolerable for anyone to forbid tribute being paid to Caesar. And if anyone should make himself out to be a king, it would be seen as serious hatred of the Roman Empire. AN ECCLESIASTICALL EXPOSITION UPON SAINT MATHEWE 27.[2]

PILATE FOUND CHRIST TO BE INNOCENT.

AUGUSTIN MARLORAT: Although Pilate was a wicked and unjust man, nevertheless he would not condemn an innocent person to death, as long as neither his reputation nor his office was in danger. Moreover, as the Evangelists diligently describe, Christ did not go to his death constrained by external forces but by his own free will, that he might fulfill his Father's commandment. Therefore, they show that all sorts of people gave evidence of his innocence. First, the whole council, in seeking out false witnesses, proves him to be innocent. Next, Judas the traitor openly confessed him to be innocent. And now Pilate also comes forth before all the people and declares him to be innocent, besides many other testimonies of Christ's innocence which follow. "Why is everyone in such an uproar?" asks Pilate. "Even though you have accused this man of being a seducer, a seditious person and rebel, and an ambitious seeker after the kingdom, I find nothing in the man worthy of such accusations." Therefore, Pilate excused Christ openly after he was openly accused, because he had no one to defend him. AN ECCLESIASTICALL EXPOSITION UPON SAINT MATHEWE 27.[3]

CHRIST IS SEEN AS A RIVAL BY THE RULERS OF THE WORLD.

JOHN CALVIN: Although they tried to overthrow Christ with many and various charges, nevertheless it is likely that they maliciously seized

on the name of king in order to kindle the greatest animosity of Pilate against him. Therefore Luke describes that they said, "We caught this man subverting the people and prohibiting the tribute from being given to Caesar, saying that he himself is the Messiah, a king." There was truly no crime more hateful to Pilate than this, because his greatest concern was to maintain the kingdom in a state of calm. From John's Gospel we know that Christ was pursued on various grounds, but clearly from the whole context it appears that this accusation was the principal charge. Likewise today Satan also endeavors to render the gospel hateful or suspect by this pretext, as if Christ, in setting up his kingdom, might cause all the realms of the world to crumble, and tear down the authority of kings and magistrates. In terms of kings, so many of them are so blind and arrogant that they reckon that Christ is not able to rule without diminishing their power. Thus the sort of accusation by which Christ was once unjustly oppressed is always plausible to them. COMMENTARY ON A HARMONY OF THE GOSPELS.[4]

23:6-10 The Trial Before Herod, Who Wanted to be Entertained

PILATE WANTED TO AVOID PASSING SENTENCE ON JESUS.

MELCHIOR NEUKIRCH: But when Pilate heard that they called him a Galilean and indicated that he had lived most of his life in Galilee, he thought that he would use this opportunity and would try to see whether he could be free from this man and get away from him, so that he would not have to pass judgment on him, or, if he were to set him free, that he would not earn the ingratitude of the Jews. Therefore he said to the Jews, "What do I understand about this business? Your complaint about this man is primarily that he is a false teacher, he undermines your faith, and he seduces the people away from your old religion. So I do not know about passing judgment or giving an opinion." So he protested to them that while Jesus had dared to

[2]Marlorat, ed., *Catholike and Ecclesiasticall Exposition of the Holy Gospell After S. Mathewe*, 692*.
[3]Marlorat, ed., *Catholike and Ecclesiasticall Exposition of the Holy Gospell After S. Mathewe*, 696*.
[4]CTS 33:275-76* (CO 45:751).

organize an uprising in the region, he had mostly worked and tempted the people in Galilee, which was a country under the jurisdiction of Herod. "So I know of no better way to treat him than to send him to Herod at his court. Herod is even now in the city to eat the Passover lamb with you. He is of your religion and understands about this business better. So let it be judged: the prisoner is a Galilean, which I understand from you, and I do not want to violate the law, and I am ready to do without the animosity and strife with Herod at this time." Therefore he called the prisoner, sent him off to Herod and accused him of those things, so that Herod would judge him and set a sentence. THE FOURTH PART OF THE PASSION.[5]

HEROD IS GUILTY OF IMPIOUS CURIOSITY.

FRANÇOIS LAMBERT: Herod is pleased at the sight of Jesus, not because he is the Savior but because of his impious curiosity, and he hoped that the Lord would do some miraculous sign in his presence. The Lord did not respond to him, to show that one should not respond to the prying, impious questions of someone who is not seeking after the truth out of zeal for the truth but only out of curiosity. Of course this produces no satisfaction for them. Without a doubt, when they hear the truth, they become quite haughty, which makes them much worse. These ones are the swine before whom the pearls should not be cast. COMMENTARY IN LUKE 23:8.[6]

CHRIST WOULD NOT ANSWER HEROD.

NEHEMIAH ROGERS: Christ chooses only tractable spirits to instruct and teach in the ways of piety. Those who are of tractable dispositions and willing to be instructed in the ways of salvation are the ones whom Christ will teach. Christ chooses to instruct in holy duties and to reveal the mysteries of his kingdom to these, and only these. So when the high priest questioned our Savior about destroying the temple and rebuilding it in three days, he would not answer him at all. And when Herod questioned him about many things, our Savior would not make him any answer. When Pilate asked him what was truth, our Savior (although he did not usually smother or suppress the truth) would not instruct him in it, as we see in John 18:38. He knew that these were not fit auditors to hear of such matters. However, when his disciples came to him and asked him questions about religion, he instructed them and satisfied them in all their doubts, for he knew that they were people of tractable minds and spirits. A FRIEND AT MIDNIGHT.[7]

CHRIST IS TREATED AS A FOOL AND AN EVILDOER.

MILES COVERDALE: The everlasting Wisdom of God is mocked and jested at, as if he were a foolish idiot; the Truth is contradicted. Therefore it should not grieve us to be reviled for God's sake, because we are by nature fools and liars. Christ gives no answer to the ungodly, voluptuous king who, out of curious desire, wants to see or hear some new thing of Christ—it could not be edifying for him to answer at that time. At that time, it pleased him to suffer, not to do miracles. Thus the innocent Lord Jesus, guilty on our behalf, is dragged around from one unrighteous judge to another. He takes on himself all reproach, shame, dishonor and derision for our sakes; he is grievously accused everywhere, is attacked in every place, and after many questions and examinations, they hang him on a cross. Thus the high God is brought low, as if he were the vilest thing; the Almighty is defaced, as if he were the weakest of all; the wisest of all is laughed to scorn, as if he were a natural fool; the least guilty one is treated as an evildoer.

We ought to behold this spectacle very diligently, for we are loaded down with heavy burdens of all wickedness and have deserved so much for our iniquity that we are worthy of all rebuke, shame and confusion. And yet we are impatient when we are despised! Nevertheless,

---

[5]Neukirch, *Historia der Passion*, 58r-v.
[6]Lambert, *In Divi Lucae*, Hh5v.

[7]Rogers, *The Fast Friend*, 13*; citing Mk 14:60; Mt 13:11-12, 36, 51.

Christ suffers all such vile treatment for our sakes, to deliver us from the eternal shame and confusion which we have justly deserved. FRUITFUL LESSONS UPON THE PASSION, BURIAL, RESURRECTION, ASCENSION AND OF THE SENDING OF THE HOLY SPIRIT (1593).[8]

23:11-12 Herod Returns Jesus to Pilate, and They Are Reconciled

CHRIST BROUGHT PEACE TO TWO WICKED MEN. JOHN CALVIN: As Christ was the surety for the restoring of a friendship between wicked men, let us learn here how the children of God, and religion itself, are contemptible to the world. It is probable that because both these men were driven by their ambition, they came into some conflict over sovereignty. But whatever was the origin of their disagreement, neither would have given even the smallest place to the other concerning his authority in worldly matters; however, because Christ is brought to nothing, Pilate easily hands him over to Herod, and Herod in his turn sends him back to Pilate. Thus we see today that when judges dispute among themselves on account of thieves and other criminals, the children of God are thrown aside scornfully as so much rubbish. Indeed, hatred of piety often leads to mutual reconciliation among the wicked, that those who at first had nothing in common now plot together to extinguish the name of God. But when the wicked mutually consign the children of God to death, it is not by an expensive payment that they purchase mutual friendship, but what is most worthless to themselves they are willing to toss out, just as someone would throw a crust of bread to a dog. But indeed, among us, Christ should contrive a different kind of peace by destroying discord. Having first been reconciled to God, of course, we should then support each other by a pious and holy agreement to cultivate righteousness and to work toward brotherly kindness and

mutual compassion. COMMENTARY ON A HARMONY OF THE GOSPELS.[9]

23:13-16 The Second Trial Before Pilate

PILATE DEFENDS JESUS. DESIDERIUS ERASMUS: When Pilate saw that the prisoner was sent back to him and that his attempt had not succeeded, instead of Jesus' judge he began to be his advocate. PARAPHRASE ON THE GOSPEL OF LUKE 23:13-16.[10]

WHY DOES PILATE FLOG CHRIST? JOHN CALVIN: Pilate not only declares that he has found no crime in Christ worthy of death but also asserts his innocence in the most unqualified manner. Why, then, does he flog him? Even though they want to maintain justice, worldly people—whom God's Spirit does not continually strengthen with zeal for virtue—are accustomed to commit minor offenses under pressure. Not only do they consider it a valid excuse, so that they have not sinned in the least, but also they even claim to be worthy of praise for their mercy, because to some extent they have spared the innocent. Meanwhile they do not realize . . . that with rods, no less than with an ax, they have violated justice, which is more precious than human life. Concerning the Son of God, had he been released in this manner, he would have borne the shame of being flogged without accomplishing our salvation. But on the cross, no differently than in a magnificent chariot, he triumphed over his enemies and ours. COMMENTARY ON A HARMONY OF THE GOSPELS.[11]

PILATE HOPED THE PEOPLE WOULD PITY JESUS. JOHN TRAPP: And Pilate did this on purpose to move the people to pity, but it was all in vain, even though he afterward presented him as a pitiful spectacle, saying, "Behold the man!" A COMMENTARY UPON THE GOSPEL ACCORDING TO SAINT LUKE 23.[12]

---

[8]*Writings and Translations of Myles Coverdale*, 284-85*.

[9]CO 45:753-54 (cf. CTS 33:279-80).
[10]CWE 48:211-12 (LB 7:460).
[11]CTS 33:285* (CO 45:757).
[12]Trapp, *Commentary or Exposition*, 420*; citing Jn 19:1, 5.

23:17-25 The People Insist on Jesus' Crucifixion

FREEING CRIMINALS IS A GODLESS CUSTOM.
JOHANNES BRENZ: It appears that this custom of releasing a prisoner at the Passover feast grew out of ambition and superstition among the people rather than out of any lawful cause or true godliness. If the heathen rulers brought in this custom themselves, they seem not to have done it for any other purpose than to use it to gain the favor of the Jewish people, that they might seem to reverence the law of Moses as concerning the celebration of Passover. However, it is the responsibility of a good magistrate to get and keep the love of subjects, not by neglecting their office but by diligent administration of public and common laws. One of these laws is that malefactors should be severely punished, so that others might fear and so that honest people might live in safety. The reverence for Moses' law should have been declared in another way than by the freeing of those who were openly known to be criminals, and whom the very law of Moses commanded should be put to death. But if this custom was brought in by the Jews themselves, which seems most likely, it appears that it was used especially for the reason that it might be a monument to the deliverance out of Egypt. People commonly worship God with evil deeds, and we see what came about through this vain custom, namely, that Christ, although an innocent man, was condemned to death. AN ECCLESIASTICALL EXPOSITION UPON SAINT MATHEWE 27.[13]

THE CROWD DEMANDS BARABBAS'S RELEASE AND JESUS' DEATH. MILES COVERDALE: Here likewise we learn the weak and changeable nature of the world. Those who earlier ran after Christ, wanting to make him king, crying joyfully, "Hosanna to the Lord!" now cry, "Crucify him, crucify him!" And so the praise and commendation of the world should be little regarded. Those who before said, "Praise to him who comes in the name of the Lord," now cry, "Away with him, crucify him," and so they chose a murderer instead of the Savior. Their request is that the murderer might live; as for the Savior and Well of life, they desire to put him to death. If we pondered this thoroughly in our hearts, that our Savior, our Jesus, was less esteemed and thought more vile than a murderer, we should be glad to suffer anything for his sake.

Now when the world is against us and casts many scornful words on us, we must not be overcome with impatience; the false accusations and threats of wicked people should not make us shrink. If we love Christ with our hearts, we must remember his patience when he was falsely accused and reviled for our sakes. Then, with stopped-up ears, we should let all sharp words pass us by, and we should even pray for those who speak evil of, or to, us. FRUITFUL LESSONS UPON THE PASSION, BURIAL, RESURRECTION, ASCENSION AND OF THE SENDING OF THE HOLY SPIRIT (1593).[14]

HOW COULD ANYONE CHOOSE BARABBAS OVER CHRIST? JOHN CROMPE: O, sweet Jesus! Now there is hope and comfort near! After your many tortures and troubles, here recounted, which you have so quietly and patiently put up with and borne at the hands of your malicious and unkind fellow countryfolk, even your relatives according to the flesh, your life notwithstanding shall be spared, and your person set free and at liberty again at the last. For seeing that you are balanced in the scales with Barabbas, the worst malefactor of your time, and the people have to choose to release either him or you, it cannot possibly be imagined that they will choose him and cast you away, save him and condemn you. For he has been a thief and has taken away by violence the bread of the poor and needy, but you

---

[13]Marlorat, ed., *Catholike and Ecclesiasticall Exposition of the Holy Gospell After S. Mathewe*, 700*. Verse 17 is excluded from modern translations (except for the KJV and NKJV) on the basis of P[75], Codex Alexandrinus and other early uncial witnesses, despite the early witness of Codex Sinaiticus.

[14]*Writings and Translations of Myles Coverdale*, 287-88*.

have been a feeder of them and a supplier of their wants and needs on all occasions. He has been an attacker and robber on the highways, and by that means wounded and manhandled the peaceable travelers going between Jerusalem and Jericho. But you, as the good Samaritan, have healed them again by binding up their wounds and pouring wine and oil into them. He has been a murderer (see Mk 15:7) and slain the living, but you have been a reviver and restorer of life to those who were dead. Therefore, all those to whom you have been helpful and beneficial in one way or another—and thousands more—will call and cry aloud, "Set free and at liberty for us, not Barabbas, our cruel enemy, but Christ, our considerate friend, yes, our kind and universal benefactor."

It is impossible, even in the judgment of Pilate himself, that anyone would be so ungrateful as to do the contrary. That is what caused him to offer up the most notorious criminal who was then in custody—he would be in competition with Christ, and Pilate might be sure (as he conceived and imagined on good ground and reason) not to fail to achieve the freedom and release of Jesus. And yet, for all this, they cry out with one voice and unanimous consent, "Not this man, but Barabbas!" as you see in the text. THE GREAT WEEK OF CHRIST'S PASSION.[15]

PILATE AGAIN PRONOUNCES HIM INNOCENT. AUGUSTIN MARLORAT: Again, he openly pronounces Christ to be innocent. It is as if he should say, "If it is right to put a man to death before a just cause is known or discovered, take him yourselves, for I find nothing in him worthy of death." The Jews answered him, "We have a law, and according to that law he ought to die, because he made himself out to be the Son of God." They declare that they persecute Christ lawfully, not out of malice or to

satisfy their wills, for they perceived that Pilate thwarted and crossed them. But they speak as people ignorant of the law, as if they should say, "We must live and conduct ourselves according to our custom, but our religion does not allow anyone to boast that he is the Son of God." While their accusation was not altogether lacking in justice, yet they made a grave mistake in their hypothesis. For the general doctrine is true: it is not appropriate for anyone to take to themselves any part of the honor that is due to God, and those who take to themselves something that is only proper to God are indeed worthy of death. But the cause of the error was in the person of Christ, because they did not consider what titles the Scripture gave to Christ, nor did they try to discover whether Jesus was that Messiah which was promised by God long before. AN ECCLESIASTICALL EXPOSITION UPON SAINT MATHEWE 27.[16]

PILATE WAS CONSTRAINED BY THE PEOPLE TO CONDEMN CHRIST. PHILIPP MELANCHTHON: Thus we read this passage out of all four Evangelists. And so Pilate, in order to pacify the people, gave sentence that it should be as they required. He set Barabbas free for them, as they desired, although he had been imprisoned for insurrection and murder. And he delivered Jesus to them to do with him what they wanted and to be crucified. Their persistent arguments truly constrained Pilate to deliver up Christ, and yet for all that it was not done as by a raging mob, but rather he was condemned in a solemn manner, because everyone knew that two theives were also being condemned to the cross. AN ECCLESIASTICALL EXPOSITION UPON SAINT MATHEWE 27.[17]

[15]Crompe, *Hebdomada Magna*, 90-91*.

[16]Marlorat, ed., *Catholike and Ecclesiasticall Exposition of the Holy Gospell After S. Mathewe*, 704*.
[17]Marlorat, ed., *Catholike and Ecclesiasticall Exposition of the Holy Gospell After S. Mathewe*, 710-11*; citing Mt 27:26; Mk 15:15; Lk 23:25; Jn 19:16.

23:26-43 THE CRUCIFIXION

²⁶And as they led him away, they seized one Simon of Cyrene, who was coming in from the country, and laid on him the cross, to carry it behind Jesus. ²⁷And there followed him a great multitude of the people and of women who were mourning and lamenting for him. ²⁸But turning to them Jesus said, "Daughters of Jerusalem, do not weep for me, but weep for yourselves and for your children. ²⁹For behold, the days are coming when they will say, 'Blessed are the barren and the wombs that never bore and the breasts that never nursed!' ³⁰Then they will begin to say to the mountains, 'Fall on us,' and to the hills, 'Cover us.' ³¹For if they do these things when the wood is green, what will happen when it is dry?"

³²Two others, who were criminals, were led away to be put to death with him. ³³And when they came to the place that is called The Skull, there they crucified him, and the criminals, one on his right and one on his left. ³⁴And Jesus said, "Father, forgive them, for they know not what they do."ᵃ And they cast lots to divide his garments. ³⁵And the people stood by, watching, but the rulers scoffed at him, saying, "He saved others; let him save himself, if he is the Christ of God, his Chosen One!" ³⁶The soldiers also mocked him, coming up and offering him sour wine ³⁷and saying, "If you are the King of the Jews, save yourself!" ³⁸There was also an inscription over him,ᵇ "This is the King of the Jews."

³⁹One of the criminals who were hanged railed at him,ᶜ saying, "Are you not the Christ? Save yourself and us!" ⁴⁰But the other rebuked him, saying, "Do you not fear God, since you are under the same sentence of condemnation? ⁴¹And we indeed justly, for we are receiving the due reward of our deeds; but this man has done nothing wrong." ⁴²And he said, "Jesus, remember me when you come into your kingdom." ⁴³And he said to him, "Truly, I say to you, today you will be with me in Paradise."

a Some manuscripts omit the sentence *And Jesus. . .what they do*   b Some manuscripts add *in letters of Greek and Latin and Hebrew*   c Or *blasphemed him*

OVERVIEW: In Luke's account of Jesus' final walk to the cross and the time he spent upon it before dying, the reformers focus on the witnesses of the crucifixion, the proper response to Jesus' death and the repentant thief. Simon of Cyrene stands in for all of us, Bullinger posits, because we also do not want to carry the cross but are forced to do so. Many others followed Jesus to the execution area, but not his own disciples. Most of the people in the crowd were simply curious, or perhaps bloodthirsty. But those who came out of love and sympathy were taking a risk by publicly mourning Jesus because it was forbidden by the priests. Here the women showed more courage and devotion than Jesus' male disciples.

Jesus does not want us to weep for him, Luther asserts, but rather we should rejoice. He sacrificed himself and suffered great pain for us not so that we should constantly mourn for him but so that we should be glad and give thanks because his painful sacrifice reunites us with God. However, we *should* mourn our own sins and the judgment they will bring on us. Still, once on the cross, Jesus' first act (in Luke's account) is to ask the Father to forgive those who had hung him there. Here he showed love even to his worst enemies and revealed to us, Coverdale writes, that none of us should despair of God's mercy and forgiveness, no matter how much we have sinned—even those who crucified the Son of God were forgiven. This forgiveness was also extended to the thieves who were hung with him.

The repentant thief is a special example of God's grace, Bullinger reminds us, for the man converted quite suddenly but is granted remission of the sins of his wicked life just before his death—even entering into the kingdom of heaven before any of the apostles. The man worked to convert the other criminal hanging with him, defending Jesus' innocence, and prayed to be with Jesus in heaven. He showed a rare faith and is an example to all of us not to judge by appearances, for many looked at Christ and saw a God-forsaken man, but the thief looked and saw his Savior.

23:26 Simon of Cyrene Carries the Cross

SIMON WAS FORCED TO BEAR THE CROSS FOR THE WEAKENED CHRIST. PHILIPP MELANCH-THON: And as they came out, they found a man of Cyrene named Simon. Saint John says in this passage that Christ carried his own cross. The other three say that Simon of Cyrene was forced to carry the cross, and in this we can see the extreme cruelty both of the people present and the soldiers. There is no doubt but that those who were criminals condemned to die usually carried their own crosses to the place of punishment, but the only ones able to carry such a heavy burden were thieves who were very strong in body. The weakness of Christ's body which was not able to bear such a heavy cross plainly declared that a lamb should be offered. It may well be that the fact that they whipped him and oppressed him with injury caused him to faint under the burden of the cross. And so that they would not have to stay there and linger on the road, they constrained Simon, who had come up from the country and was passing by, to carry his cross after him. There were no men there who would so much as touch the cross, because the death to be suffered on it was so shameful to them. AN ECCLESIASTICALL EXPOSITION UPON SAINT MATHEWE 27.[1]

LIKE ALL OF US, SIMON IS FORCED TO CARRY THE CROSS. HEINRICH BULLINGER: So Simon came behind and, bearing the burden with Christ (as some argue), helped the Lord who was walking in

the front. Now in the way that Simon does not carry the cross of his own free will but is constrained to do it, he bears the image of all human flesh, which never submits itself willingly to the cross of Christ but continually strives against it. Saint Luke also says that many people and many women followed him as he went by the way, and they cried and lamented for him. AN ECCLESIASTICALL EXPOSITION UPON SAINT MATHEWE 27.[2]

23:27-31 Jesus Speaks to the Women

THE WOMEN FOLLOW HIM IN PRAISEWORTHY LOVE. CATHARINA REGINA VON GREIFFENBERG: Common people are wont to accompany poor sinners [to the place of execution]. This is an evil practice (though certainly not a forbidden one) and [a matter of] cruel curiosity; for their tumult only increases the agony of these poor sinners, which is, moreover, completely unnecessary. People are supposed to rejoice in the carrying out of justice, but many a person (who should see himself reflected in the mirror there and mend his ways) derides it, since he finds in himself many greater crimes than in the condemned person and secretly triumphs that he himself gets off scot free. There is a thirst for blood in the hastening to the execution of these miserable people: their punishment alone is [agonizing] enough without all those eyes witnessing it. It is inhumane to relish the sight of another person's agony. It is more Christian meanwhile to bestir our lips at home to pray for his soul than to open our eyes wide to view his torment. . . .

When, however, it is done (as with these women) out of love and sympathy, the circumstances change the matter, and what was otherwise reprehensible becomes praiseworthy. Love, like the philosopher's stone, makes everything it touches golden and good. It brings about the deftest changes of form: from evil, it makes goodness; from cruelty, sympathy; from inhumanity, ardor. What those people do out of evil curiosity, it does

---

[1]Marlorat, ed., *Catholike and Ecclesiasticall Exposition of the Holy Gospell After S. Mathewe*, 713*; citing Jn 19:17.

[2]Marlorat, ed., *Catholike and Ecclesiasticall Exposition of the Holy Gospell After S. Mathewe*, 713*.

out of loving care. Even if both do the same thing [outwardly], [the latter] stems from different origins and aims at a completely different goal. The rabble follows in its fury; the sympathetic women in their ardor: they were much more ardent and constant in their love of and loyalty to Jesus, because they did not hesitate, despite the strict prohibition of their high priests, to bewail him publicly. In contrast, almost none of his disciples, not to mention others from the rabble, bestirred themselves to open their mouths. On the Supremely Holy and Supremely Salvific Suffering of Jesus: Ninth Meditation.[3]

We Should Rejoice over Christ's Suffering. Martin Luther: But the Lord teaches us here one final point: we should weep over ourselves and our children, but we should not weep over him but should rather laugh, be happy and of good cheer. For why did he suffer? He is a true, good and fruitful tree and did not deserve such a severe sentence—rather, he suffers on our behalf. And now it is up to him to walk this path, to carry out his priestly office, and not only to intercede for sinners but also be willing to offer up his body and life on the altar of the cross. In this way, God will be appeased through such a sacrifice, and poor, miserable sinners will be freed from God's wrath and become heirs of eternal life. Therefore it grieves the Lord when we weep, because his suffering is ordered toward [our happiness]. He wants us to be happy, to glorify God and to give him thanks for his grace. We should praise, glorify and confess him, because we come in this way to the grace of God, freed from sin and death, and thus we become God's beloved children.

But one thing will please us just as little as the other. We follow the way of the world more than the warning and exhortation of our Lord. We should weep for ourselves, that we are ruined to such a degree through sin and have received such a severe sentence and judgment for ourselves. But no one sheds a tear for such things, and in fact, the deeper that people are stuck in the mire of sin, the more secure and happy they are. As I said before, their joy, desire and whole life is that they have so many occasions to sin. House Postil (1544): The Passion, How the Lord Was Led Out, Simon Carried the Cross and the Women Who Were Present Wept.[4]

The People Should Weep for Their Own Punishment. Augustin Marlorat: By this sentence Christ confirms and proves that his death will not go unpunished and that the people would not stand or continue long, because their wickedness was already fully ripe, or even half rotten. And by a common similitude he proves that the fire of God's wrath will soon consume them. We do know that people normally cast the dry wood on the fire first. So if the moist and green wood is being burned, it is not likely that the dry wood will be spared. And this is how we will explain it: if the green wood is brought to the fire before its time, what do you think will become of what is dry? It is as if Christ had said, "The wicked (who are like the dry wood), when they have destroyed the godly, will also be destroyed themselves by God. For how will those who take such freedom for themselves for a time to destroy the good and innocent escape the hands of the heavenly judge, especially because they were ordained long ago to destruction? But the sum of his words is that the women uselessly shed their tears, because the horrible judgment of God to punish the wickedness of the people was far more sorrowful for them, and this event was now at hand. An Ecclesiasticall Exposition upon Saint Mathewe 27.[5]

23:32-33 Jesus Is Crucified with Two Criminals

Christ Appeared to Be the Chief Criminal on the Cross. Augustin Marlorat:

---

[3]Greiffenberg, *Meditations on the Incarnation, Passion and Death of Jesus Christ*, 83-84* (*Zwölf andächtige Betrachtungen*, 578-80).

[4]WA 52:799.
[5]Marlorat, ed., *Catholike and Ecclesiasticall Exposition of the Holy Gospell After S. Mathewe*, 714*.

There were two thieves crucified along with him. But the Greek word signifies murderers rather than thieves, those who lurk in dens along the highways, waiting to kill people. It was not a usual practice for thieves to be crucified. And so in order that Christ might experience even greater public humiliation, he is placed in the middle, as though he had been the chief murderer. If he had been nailed to the cross alone, separated from other criminals, his cause might have seemed better. But now he was not only placed with murderers, but in the chief spot among them, as though he were the worst of all of them. It was necessary that he be placed in this horrible position, so that we might know what great punishment was due for our sins. There would be no punishment cruel enough that could be invented for our wickedness, if Christ had not died for us. So in order that he might deliver us from the pain due for sin, this kind of satisfaction was necessary, so that he might put himself into our place. And here we may perceive how terrible the wrath of God is against sins, for in order to pacify it, it was necessary that Christ, who is the eternal righteousness, should be counted as unrighteous and placed in the category of murderers. AN ECCLESIASTICALL EXPOSITION UPON SAINT MATHEWE 27.[6]

THE SAVIOR OF ALL EXPERIENCED HORRIBLE PAIN. CATHARINA REGINA VON GREIFFENBERG: Now, dearest Lord Jesus, you will experience terrible agony, and I will agonize in my heart. Oh! It is a cross for me to bear to name your crucifixion and agony for me to imagine it. How can my hands describe the pain of you without trembling and shaking with pain? How can I recall the stripping of you without dying of sheer horror? O Jesus! You who surround all of creation and Creator of all surroundings except for yourself! Why must your noble body be robbed of even the smallest part of it? You who are beautifully and magnificently adorned with immortal glory and splender suffer yourself to be most miserably and lamentably stripped. You,

whose clothes are the blinding radiance of God and the most divine beam of light, stand now completely naked, covered with bloody welts and cuts. You who spread out heaven like a carpet hast on earth not a scrap in which to wrap yourself. The raw, sharp air of the wind that is yet cold must cut through your body, which is covered with wounds, blood and bruises. O, what agony must this alone have caused you? What lesions, traumatic fever and horror of nature must have arisen from this?

But what is all that compared with the violent hurling of your holy body onto the unplaned, rough and splintery wooden cross? There they must have renewed and broken open and made bloody the wounds of lashing, torn open the cuts again and pulled the weals wide apart so that a mortal pain arose. O you who embrace the entire globe, you who stretch out heaven! How will you be stretched out on the cross! ON THE SUPREMELY HOLY AND SUPREMELY SALVIFIC SUFFERING OF JESUS: NINTH MEDITATION.[7]

23:34-35 Jesus Asks the Father to Forgive, but the People Scorn Him

HIS LAST WORDS GIVE BLESSED FORGIVENESS. MILES COVERDALE: The last words which Jesus spoke on the cross should be written by all faithful believers in their hearts, and they should diligently keep them there. First, he spoke a loving, friendly word, a word full of grace and sweet comfort to all sinners, sufficient and enough to break all hardness of heart and to provoke fruitful repentance: "Father, forgive them." What great goodness and loving kindness this is! And how ready is Jesus to have mercy! And he is very willing to forgive those who love him, because he shows himself so mild and gracious even to his enemies. He pours out no angry word, no displeasure against those who crucified him; he desires no vengeance or plague to fall on those ungracious people, but he speaks the sweetest words, full of ardent love: "O Father, forgive them."

---

[6]Marlorat, ed., *Catholike and Ecclesiasticall Exposition of the Holy Gospell After S. Mathewe*, 719*.

[7]Greiffenberg, *Meditations on the Incarnation, Passion and Death of Jesus Christ*, 91* (*Zwölf andächtige Betrachtungen*, 596-97).

In these words we can see his exceedingly great love and his unspeakable gentleness of heart, which cannot be overcome by any malice. Like crazed, bloodthirsty people they cried, "Away with him; crucify him, crucify him!" O, the wonderful and great lenience of our Lord Jesus Christ! They revile and mistreat him completely; he prays for them, so that they, being converted from their wickedness, might acknowledge him to be the true Son of God now appearing in the flesh. Here we see fulfilled the prophecy of Isaiah: "Yet he bore the sin of many and makes intercession for the transgressors," that they should not perish. Who will despair of God's mercy, even if they are now in sin, when the great offenders who crucified and killed the giver of all remission found such great grace and goodness? FRUITFUL LESSONS UPON THE PASSION, BURIAL, RESURRECTION, ASCENSION AND OF THE SENDING OF THE HOLY SPIRIT (1593).[8]

HE LOST HIS CLOTHING BUT GAINED IMMORTALITY. HEINRICH SALMUTH: The Evangelist reports that after they had crucified the Lord Jesus, the soldiers divided his clothes among themselves and cast lots for them. This was prophesied in Psalm 22, and it was certainly a great affliction for the Lord Jesus.

It also relates to and would be dealt with by the Christian church: that faithful Christians should also not have their lives or bodies endangered and be killed or slaughtered by the godless tyrants and those who murdered Christ. But they would be robbed of all their property—their enemies would snatch it and divide it up among themselves, just as happened with the Lord's clothing.

But the suffering of the Lord Jesus was very beneficial and honorable, even though he certainly lost the perishable clothing and had to leave it behind. Someone took the clothes from him, and the soldiers cast lots for them and divided them up. But in spite of this, he took on a glorious body and became clothed with an immortal, transfigured body. And through this suffering he gained

us back again and attained the beautiful, glorious ornament that we had lost in Paradise, namely, righteousness, holiness, peace, joy and blessedness. THE SEVENTH SERMON ON THE PASSION AND DEATH OF JESUS CHRIST.[9]

THE CROWD WATCHES CURIOUSLY. CATHARINA REGINA VON GREIFFENBERG: Here again the Scripture was fulfilled that says, "I can count all my bones—they stare and gloat over me." O! The godless rabble is permitted to behold with their curious eyes the torture that saved many among them from debilities of the eye and other things. They regard him without feeling sympathy, him who, filled with compassion, turned around their suffering and transformed it into joy. They nurse their cruel curiosity in beholding the agony of him who so faithfully alleviated their agony and who made it so Satan's cruelty ceased with them. O, ingratitude that seeks delight in the torment of the Savior. ON THE SUPREMELY HOLY AND SUPREMELY SALVIFIC SUFFERING OF JESUS: TENTH MEDITATION.[10]

HE SHOWED US THE HIGHEST EXAMPLE OF SUFFERING. HULDRYCH ZWINGLI: A most absolute example of all virtues is set forth to the faithful in Christ, and this example should never be taken from their sight, for it is also the price of our redemption. He took on himself all manner of reproach for our sake: he is reviled from the lowest to the highest, no one pities him, no one has compassion on him for his afflictions, no one comforts him. Instead they rage against him most cruelly without mercy, and yet his goodness could not be overcome by their malice. Nothing could hold him back from the work of our salvation which he had begun—nothing could withdraw him from his office. Let us follow our head and despise whatever is delightful and glorious in the world. Let us also willingly suffer reproach, following in the footsteps of his humility

---

[8]*Writings and Translations of Myles Coverdale*, 298*; citing Is 53:12.

[9]Salmuth, *Passional*, 311-12.

[10]Greiffenberg, *Meditations on the Incarnation, Passion and Death of Jesus Christ*, 99* (*Zwölf andächtige Betrachtungen*, 736-37); citing Ps 22:17.

and patience. Let there be nothing so hard or so painful as to tear us away from our vocation. For in patience we shall possess our souls, and he who abides to the end will be saved. Let us not be ashamed to be spoken of evilly for Christ. Let us not be ashamed of the witness of our Lord Jesus Christ, and let us not be embarrassed if any afflictions must be suffered for his sake. For if we have been partakers of his cross, we will also be partners in his glory. OF THE PASSION AND DEATH OF CHRIST.[11]

CHRIST COULD HAVE SAVED HIMSELF, BUT HE WOULD NOT. AUGUSTIN MARLORAT: As if they should say, "Finally we see what those great benefits bestowed on the blind profit you: you healed the lame and all the others that were troubled with diseases, but now you are not able to help yourself. Where is your power now?" This is always the way of the wicked—they measure the power of God by the present situation, and so whatever he does not do, they think that he cannot do, and therefore they condemn him for weakness, as often as he will not satisfy their wicked desire. But we should note that although Christ was easily able to deliver himself from death, he did not do it, because he would not do it. And there is no other reason why for a time he had so little care about his own salvation, than that our salvation was more dear to him. And he would not deliver himself, only because he wanted to save us all. This temptation is like those that had happened before. AN ECCLESIASTICALL EXPOSITION UPON SAINT MATHEWE 27.[12]

23:36-39 Many People Mock Him

JESUS IS THE MESSIAH PROMISED BY THE PROPHETS, BUT THE PEOPLE DO NOT RECOGNIZE IT. JOHN CALVIN: Indeed it was not proper for them to embrace a king, unless he was of the sort described by the prophets. But Isaiah and Zechariah expressly present the Christ as misshapen, afflicted, condemned and abused, almost lifeless, poor and despised, before he ascends the royal throne. It is therefore absurd for the people to seek for someone different who they can recognize as a king, because that testifies that they are not interested in having the king that God has promised to give to them. But we should, in contrast, seek support in his cross, so that our faith might rest solidly in Christ, and indeed, no one could be counted the legitimate king of Israel unless he fulfilled the part of redeemer. And hence we gather how deadly it would be to depart from God's Word and go wandering about after our own speculations. For because the people had imagined a king who was suggested to them by their own senses, they rejected Christ crucified, because they thought it was absurd to believe in him. But for us, the best and highest reason for believing in him is that he subjected himself for our sake to the dishonor of the cross. COMMENTARY ON A HARMONY OF THE GOSPELS.[13]

JESUS IS KING TO ALL PEOPLES OF THE WORLD. EDWARD LEIGH: We read in the original, "Jesus that Nazarene, that King of the Jews." The use of the three languages shows first, that he is a Savior of all sorts of people; second, they are prayers in a known language; third, nothing can hinder Christ's kingdom. Pilate's purpose was that the sign might be read and understood by everyone, both inhabitants and strangers who were now gathered together from all over the world. But we should pay attention to the counsel of God in this matter, who would with this usage consecrate these three languages for the propagation of his kingdom. The Scripture of the Old Testament was written in Hebrew, that of the New in Greek, and both were translated into Latin, and that version was the most common and usual one in the church up until now. Also, the most excellent commentaries on the Scriptures were written in one of these three languages.

In terms of the words, we find in them first an exact description of the substance of our faith. Second, Jesus acknowledges his name on the cross. Third, he is the king and able to save; he has lost no

---

[11]Zwingli, *A Briefe Rehersal of the Death, Resurrection and Ascension of Christ*, 129-30*; citing Lk 21:12-19.
[12]Marlorat, ed., *Catholike and Ecclesiasticall Exposition of the Holy Gospell After S. Mathewe*, 722*.

[13]CTS 33:305-6* (CO 45:770-71); citing Is 52:14; 53:2; Zech 13:7.

power through his abasement. ANNOTATIONS UPON SAINT LUKE 23.[14]

THE REPROBATE THIEF BLASPHEMED CHRIST.
HEINRICH BULLINGER: This criminal's reproach was not insignificant to Christ. For what innocent person can bear being insulted and criticized by a wicked person, a thief and a reprobate? And yet the Lord did suffer it, and he did so with great patience. By his great suffering he achieved honor for us among the angels, so they could acknowledge us to be their brothers and sisters. Along with that, we see here a notable example of obstinacy in this reprobate man, who even in the middle of his own torment did not cease to spew out horrible blasphemy with great rage. Desperate people often behave this way, for when they cannot escape their own torment, they seek to be revenged by stubborn refusal to obey. AN ECCLESIASTICALL EXPOSITION UPON SAINT MATHEWE 27.[15]

23:40-43 The Second Thief Confesses and Is Forgiven

THE HOLY EXAMPLE OF THE THIEF. JOHN DONNE: The text itself is a christening sermon and a funeral sermon and a sermon at a consecration and a sermon at the canonization of himself who makes it. This thief whose words they are, is baptized in blood; there is his christening. He dies in that profession; there is his funeral. His diocese is his cross, and he takes care of his soul, who is crucified with him, and to him he is a bishop; there is his consecration. And he is translated to heaven; there is his canonization. . . .

This condemned person who had been a thief, execrable among human beings, and a blasphemer, execrating God, was suddenly a convert, suddenly a confessor, suddenly a martyr, suddenly a doctor to preach to others. . . . We shall see what doctrine he preaches; not curiosities, not unrevealed mysteries, not matter of state, nor of wit, nor of carnal delight,

but only the fear of God: *Do you not fear God?"* SERMON 132, LENTEN SERMON PREACHED AT WHITEHALL (1617).[16]

THE SECOND THIEF TEACHES US OF REPENTANCE AND CONFESSION. HEINRICH BULLINGER: But the other answered and rebuked him. We see in this miserable man a singular spectacle of the wonderful and unspeakable grace of God, both because he was suddenly changed a little before death into a new man and brought from hell to heaven, but also because he obtained remission of all the sins and wickedness with which his whole life was overwhelmed, in that he was received up into heaven even before the apostles and the firstfruits of the new church. First of all, therefore, in the conversion of this man we have a singular example and proof of God's grace, for he did not put off the beastly cruelty and proud contempt of God by the proper instinct and motion of the flesh in order to come to his repentance, but rather he was brought to it by the hand of God, just as the whole Scripture teaches that repentance is the work of God. And this grace excelled so much the more because it happened contrary to all human expectation. For who would ever have thought that a thief, being now at his last breath, would be not only a true worshiper of God but also an excellent master of faith and godliness to the whole world, so that we might also be glad to catch the rule of true and lawful confession from his mouth? AN ECCLESIASTICALL EXPOSITION UPON SAINT MATHEWE 27.[17]

THE THIEF SEEKS HIS FELLOW THIEF'S REPENTANCE. WILLIAM FENNER: Here is the thief's penitential satisfaction: as he had been partner with the other thief in sin, so now he labors to provide satisfaction in turning him to God. As he says in Luke 23:40, "Do you not fear God, seeing that you have received the same condemnation? Unfortunately you and I have been villains against God and are justly damned.

---

[14]Leigh, *Annotations upon All the New Testament Philologicall and Theologicall*, 137*.
[15]Marlorat, ed., *Catholike and Ecclesiasticall Exposition of the Holy Gospell After S. Mathewe*, 723*.
[16]Donne, *Works*, 5:361-62, 363-64*; citing Lk 23:40.
[17]Marlorat, ed., *Catholike and Ecclesiasticall Exposition of the Holy Gospell After S. Mathewe*, 723*.

But as we have been thieves together, let us now repent together, and call on God together. Do you not fear God, seeing that you have received the same condemnation?" And thus he labors to convert his fellow thief.

And here is his penitential self-denial: he denies himself and loves the glory of God more than his own soul or salvation. Note here how he labors to convert his fellow thief and to make him give all the glory to God. He was so wounded to his soul that his fellow thief should dishonor God that he worked to convert him before he prayed for his own soul. "Do you not fear God?" He said this before he said, "Lord, remember me." He lets his own soul lie at the stake while he labors to glorify God, so that it is plain that he loves God more than his own soul. A Caveat Against Late Repentance.[18]

True Faith Can Recognize the Savior Despite the Cross. The English Annotations: "'Lord, remember me' when you come into your glory, and receive me into mercy as one of your own. Do not remember my sin (as in Ps 25:7), but accomplish your mercy, which you have now begun to show me in my conversion. Remember me when you come into that state of blessedness which you have purchased and to which you are going from the cross, that I may follow you into that blessedness." Here was a rare and excellent faith, which apprehended the merit of Christ for his salvation! He believed this one to be the Savior, whom people condemned as a criminal, whom the tormenters crucified, whom the impious crowds derided, now dying, and to people's eyes forsaken by God. In this pitiful state and posture, he believed him to be the holy Son of God, able to save him even in death. The disciples forsook him, Peter forswore all acquaintance with him, but this poor convert acknowledged him to be the Lord of life even as he was dying. True faith has piercing eyes, seeing the glory and kingdom of Christ through the dark despair of the cross. Annotations on the Gospel According to Saint Luke 23:42.[19]

The Thief Who Called on Christ Was Saved. Augustin Marlorat: It should also be noted that he did not only believe in Christ, but he also called on him, for wherever there is faith, there is usually invocation also. And Jesus said to him, "Truly I say to you, today you will be with me in Paradise." And so we see that the thief did not pray in vain, for he was heard; neither did Christ only notice him, but he also performed what he promised. If Christ could draw the thief to him while he was on the cross, how much more now will he hear us from his heavenly throne, where he sits now that his enemies have been overcome? Therefore, whoever commits the custody of his soul to Christ with a true faith when he is dying will not be left to languish in extremity but will have his desire and the same mercy granted to him which Christ granted to the thief on the cross. An Ecclesiasticall Exposition upon Saint Mathewe 27.[20]

The Life Is in the Blood for Me. John Donne:

By miracles exceeding power of man,
Hee faith in some, envie in some begat,
For, what weake spirits admire ambitious hate;
In both affections many to him ran,
But Oh! the worst are most, they will and can,
Alas, and do, unto the immaculate,
Whose creature Fate is, now prescribe a Fate,
Measuring selfe-lifes infinity to'a span,
Nay to an inch. Loe, where condemned hee
Beares his owne crosse, with paine, yet by and by
When it beares him, he must beare more and die.
Now thou art lifted up, draw mee to thee,
And at thy death giving such liberall dole,
Moyst with one drop of thy blood my dry soule.
La Corona.[21]

[18]Fenner, *Practicall Divinitie*, 168-69*.

[19]Downame, ed., *Annotations*, Zz4r*.
[20]Marlorat, ed., *Catholike and Ecclesiasticall Exposition of the Holy Gospell After S. Mathewe*, 725*.
[21]Donne, *Poems of John Donne*, 320.

23:44-56 JESUS' DEATH AND BURIAL

⁴⁴It was now about the sixth hour,ᵃ and there was darkness over the whole land until the ninth hour,ᵇ ⁴⁵while the sun's light failed. And the curtain of the temple was torn in two. ⁴⁶Then Jesus, calling out with a loud voice, said, "Father, into your hands I commit my spirit!" And having said this he breathed his last. ⁴⁷Now when the centurion saw what had taken place, he praised God, saying, "Certainly this man was innocent!" ⁴⁸And all the crowds that had assembled for this spectacle, when they saw what had taken place, returned home beating their breasts. ⁴⁹And all his acquaintances and the women who had followed him from Galilee stood at a distance watching these things.

⁵⁰Now there was a man named Joseph, from the Jewish town of Arimathea. He was a member of the council, a good and righteous man, ⁵¹who had not consented to their decision and action; and he was looking for the kingdom of God. ⁵²This man went to Pilate and asked for the body of Jesus. ⁵³Then he took it down and wrapped it in a linen shroud and laid him in a tomb cut in stone, where no one had ever yet been laid. ⁵⁴It was the day of Preparation, and the Sabbath was beginning.ᶜ ⁵⁵The women who had come with him from Galilee followed and saw the tomb and how his body was laid. ⁵⁶Then they returned and prepared spices and ointments.

On the Sabbath they rested according to the commandment.

a That is, noon   b That is, 3 p.m.   c Greek *was dawning*

OVERVIEW: At the death of Jesus, all heaven and earth reacted—earthquakes, a solar eclipse and the tearing of the curtain veil were all recorded. Erasmus notes that these were signs from God of Jesus' heavenly glory and divine nature, meant to console the godly. Jesus might have been dying a painful and ignominious death, but he was still the Son of God, and his death had reverberations throughout nature and human history. Salmuth suggests that the tearing of the temple curtain meant not only that the temple priesthood should (and had) come to an end but also that Paradise has now been opened to us. It was only when Jesus entered those holy spaces, through the sacrifice of his own blood as the precious Lamb, that he earned salvation for us. We now have a clear passage to our loving God and can enter the gates of heaven. For the reformers, reflecting on Jesus' death also has application to our own deaths, for we can remember his suffering, and—however much we may suffer at the moment of death—we know that through his death we have life, through his death we are freed from death's grip. The people who witnessed Jesus' death, including the centurion on guard at the cross, also knew that something special and terrible had happened. They went home beating their breasts, which Melanchthon suggests is a sign of grief but also a sign that they were afraid that God would now visit vengeance on them for killing an innocent man.

The final act of Jesus' death, as far as anyone knew, had to do with the preparation and burial of his body. At great danger to himself, Joseph of Arimathea approached Pilate to ask for Jesus' body and gave him an appropriate albeit quick burial, prior to the beginning of the sabbath. For the reformers Joseph was a great example of constancy and faith. He placed himself in danger first by not consenting to the plot against Jesus and then by publicly asking for and burying Jesus' body. Joseph's actions would have let everyone know that he thought Jesus had been treated unjustly, both by the council and by Pilate himself. So why did he risk it? Because he was waiting for the kingdom of God; despite the fact that Jesus had died, Joseph still had faith that the kingdom would be coming through him because he was the Messiah. Joseph buried Jesus' body in an unused tomb without knowing what would happen next or that it was God's will, but still waiting for the kingdom. And he was not the only one who continued to serve Jesus in death, for the women who had been present all along prepared to return after the sabbath to anoint and care for the body as was their custom. Many commentators emphasize the women's example, which they suggest instructs us to love Christ devoutly, especially because they were jeopardizing themselves by their actions. While we cannot express our love in caring physically for Christ's body because he is now in his kingdom, we can and should serve the poor, the needy and the oppressed among us. We can serve Christ in his members.

23:44-46 Jesus Gives Up His Spirit

SIGNS AT CHRIST'S DEATH REVEAL HIS DIVINITY. DESIDERIUS ERASMUS: By this passage we see that Christ hung on the cross for almost three hours, for Mark declares that he was crucified at the third hour. "Darkness came over the whole land." Although in Christ's death the infirmity of the flesh hid the glory of the deity for a time, and although the Son of God lay deformed under reproach and contempt, nevertheless the Father of heaven did not cease to adorn him with heavenly tokens and figures. And even in his final moment, God set forth certain offerings and signs of his heavenly glory, which might reassure and comfort the minds of the godly against the offense or stumbling block of the cross. The majesty of Christ was wonderfully declared by the darkness of the sun, by the earthquake, by the cleaving of the rocks and by the tearing of the veil, as if heaven and earth should show forth their due reverence for their workmaster and maker. But, first of all, it may be demanded why there was an eclipse of the sun. Some interpreters think that God sent darkness at the death of Christ as a sign of disgust, as if God hid his face and the sun was darkened from the abominable wickedness of all humanity. Others say that when the visible sun was extinguished, it

declared the destruction of the Son of righteousness. Others suggest that it referred to the blinding of the nation, which followed not long after this. AN ECCLESIASTICALL EXPOSITION UPON SAINT MATHEWE 27.[1]

CHRIST TORE OPEN THE CURTAIN TO BRING US INSIDE. HEINRICH SALMUTH: The second miracle is that the curtain in the temple was torn in two. This curtain hid the Holy of Holies where the Ark of the Covenant was kept, and which the high priest had to enter once a year and bring in the blood of animals with him. Now this curtain was torn in two, which not only meant that the Levitical and Mosaic priesthood should come to an end, but this event also testifies that it was first on account of our sins that the Holy of Holies and Paradise itself were closed, and we were not allowed to enter in. But now the Lord has entered into the Holy of Holies through his own blood and achieved for us eternal salvation. And he went to heaven, sat himself down at the right hand of the heavenly Father and opened heaven for us; he mediated for us with his Father and prepared the way for us. Now that the curtain is torn in two, we have a clear passage and a joyful entrance to our loving God, so that we may call on him in certain and cheerful confidence that our prayer will be truly answered.

And so we should be consoled from our hearts, because we know that the curtain is torn, heaven is opened and the Holy of Holies also stands open, so that we may appear before our loving God and call on him with childlike trust. Therefore we should come before God in every need, asking for help and deliverance from him, and we should expect it with certainty. THE SEVENTH SERMON ON THE PASSION AND DEATH OF JESUS CHRIST.[2]

CHRIST'S DEATH GIVES US EVERLASTING LIFE. MILES COVERDALE: All living things die according to the flesh; Jesus also departed through

---

[1]Marlorat, ed., *Catholike and Ecclesiasticall Exposition of the Holy Gospell After S. Mathewe*, 726*; citing Mk 15:25.
[2]Salmuth, *Passional*, 331-32*.

the painful torment of death. But by his death he opened up to us the way of life and took everlasting death away from us. This is a precious, dear and victorious death, which has destroyed our death and conquered life again for us. Let this death continue forever in our hearts, and let our own deaths be considered when we consider his death. This will bring us a comforting trust and hope when our own death is battling within us. We will not be afraid, nor will we despair, if we steadfastly believe that Christ died for us and that through his death he has opened to us everlasting life.

So let us with devout hearts consider his death, which has redeemed us and restored us again. The gracious, innocent Lord Jesus dies miserable and naked, poorer and more destitute than anyone else; yet there is no one else so dear to God, although he is so vilely treated by all people. This is always the reward that the world gives, for they despise the children of God and pay back evil for good. If it should happen to us, we must not think that it is strange, for the servant is not above the lord. The Lord hangs on the cross, pierced through not only with nails but also with ardent love toward us, sorely beaten and hurting all over, with no succor or help or comfort, even as a dead man who is forgotten and put out of people's minds. Ponder well, good servant of Christ, who and how great he is, even while crying out with a loud voice and giving up his spirit: truly, even the Son of God, as the centurion testifies! FRUITFUL LESSONS UPON THE PASSION, BURIAL, RESURRECTION, ASCENSION AND OF THE SENDING OF THE HOLY SPIRIT (1593).[3]

REST IN CHRIST'S DEATH WAITING FOR YOUR FUTURE RESURRECTION AND ASCENSION. JOHN DONNE: And as God breathed a soul into the first Adam, so this second Adam breathed his soul into God, into the hands of God. There we leave you, in that blessed dependency to hang on him who hangs on the cross. There bathe in his tears, there suck at his wounds, and lie down in peace in his grave till he vouchsafe you a resurrec-

tion and an ascension into that kingdom which he has purchased for you with the inestimable price of his incorruptible blood. Amen. SERMON 158, PREACHED AT WHITEHALL (1630).[4]

23:47 The Declaration of the Centurion

THE CENTURION PRONOUNCES THE INJUSTICE OF CHRIST'S DEATH. KONRAD PELLIKAN: The centurion had paid attention to whoever made any movements here around Christ. He stood below the cross at this time, to make sure that no one would try to steal anyone alive off the crosses. From this position, he also bore witness to the innocence of Jesus. In declaring him to have so much virtue, he also glorified God in saying, "Truly this was a righteous man." In saying this he clearly condemned the injustice of Christ's accusers. When he pronounces this man to be innocent who was condemned, he insists that those who condemned him inflicted an injury. And through this centurion the faith of the church is represented; the veil of the heavenly mysteries was opened through the death of the Lord, and soon the righteousness of the Son of God was confirmed through the silence of his opponents. COMMENTARY IN LUKE 23:47.[5]

23:48-49 The Women Stayed

THE PEOPLE SHOWED SIGNS OF GRIEF AND REPENTANCE. PHILIPP MELANCHTHON: After these things, Saint Luke adds, "When all the people who had gathered to witness this sight saw what took place, they beat their breasts and went away." The striking of the breasts was a sign of grief, and they did so because they feared that the Lord would take vengeance on them for the blood of an innocent man. For we tend to use that gesture either when we repent of our sin or when we fear some calamity that is hanging over our heads. And it is certainly true that when innocent blood is shed,

---

[3]*Writings and Translations of Myles Coverdale*, 308-9*; citing Mt 27:54.

[4]Donne, *Works*, 6:298*.
[5]Pellikan, *In Sacrosancta Quatuor Evangelia*, 237 (cf. CWE 48:222-23; LB 7:464). The centurion as a representative of the church's faith is Pellikan's own addition to Erasmus's *Paraphrase*.

the whole region is polluted. AN ECCLESIASTICALL EXPOSITION UPON SAINT MATHEWE 27.[6]

LIKE THESE WOMEN, WE MUST CHOOSE CHRIST OVER EVERYTHING ELSE. CATHARINA REGINA VON GREIFFENBERG: Not merely a few, but many women were standing with these intimates afar off. The female sex has always been devoted and attached to our dear Lord Jesus. The fear (and love) of God dwells only with women who are chosen. Their simplicity and tenderness made them capable of loving Jesus; for he chose what is paltry and despised in the eyes of the world. What is, however, more despised than woman who is not regarded by some as capable of salvation? To be sure, many women make themselves despicable through their frivolity or stubborn stupidity—I too utterly despise and exclude them from those who love Christ. But in general the fear of God has always found more of a place with women's simplicity than with men's cunning, and they have always followed Christ in greater numbers and more frequently, as did then these women from Galilee. . . . To follow Jesus, many [of these women] must have abandoned their husbands, children, friends and relatives, and also their household and housekeeping for a few days and perhaps did not leave them all that well provided for and instead in danger of unpleasant occurrences. The heavenly bridegroom must be given precedence not merely for a few short days but always over all earthly things, the Son of God over the children of man, the Eternal One over all temporal friends, even though they would jeer at it. One has to persevere in one's intentions with heroic courage and to think of Christ's words: "He who does not love me more than his own family is not worthy of me." ON THE SUPREMELY HOLY AND SUPREMELY SALVIFIC SUFFERING OF JESUS: ELEVENTH MEDITATION.[7]

23:50-53 Joseph of Arimathea Prepares His Body

JOSEPH WAS JUST, FAITHFUL AND BRAVE. HULDRYCH ZWINGLI: Joseph was called just, not that he was without sin but because he abhorred the decision of the council of the ungodly and did not consent to the death of Christ. He also waited for the kingdom of heaven. So we are also just if we receive by faith the Christ whom they awaited and if we keep ourselves unspotted from this world, for Christ is our righteousness. This man sets forth an example both of great constancy and of faith. For he put himself into great danger when he did not consent to or else withstood the plans of the malicious: who cannot see that it would be a real danger for any person to ask for the body of Jesus where there was so much hatred and cruelty, and to bury it honorably? Faith, if it is a true faith, attempts great and perilous things with an invincible courage. So when the Evangelist says that he was a noble and rich man, we must not only respect those things but also pay attention to his courageous mind and great faith, which the Evangelist also notes. It is as though he would say, "Although Joseph was a rich man, neither favor, nor fear nor riches make him decline from the truth to consent to the endeavor of the wicked." Along with that he was quite brave, for after Jesus' death, when others blasphemed and ridiculed him, Joseph was not ashamed to go to the judge, nor did he fear to bury him, whom all others had condemned. OF THE PASSION AND DEATH OF CHRIST.[8]

JOSEPH LOOKED FORWARD TO THE COMING OF CHRIST. AUGUSTIN MARLORAT: Joseph is praised here for waiting for the kingdom of God, and he is praised for his righteousness. But the fact that he was waiting for the kingdom of God was the root and origin of his righteousness. By the "kingdom of God" we must understand the promised renewal in Christ. For the integrity of order cannot stand

---

[6]Marlorat, ed., *Catholike and Ecclesiasticall Exposition of the Holy Gospell After S. Mathewe*, 733*.
[7]Greiffenberg, *Meditations on the Incarnation, Passion and Death of Jesus Christ*, 110-11 (*Zwölf andächtige Betrachtungen*, 897-98); citing Sir 1:13; Mt 10:37.

---

[8]Zwingli, *Briefe Rehersal of the Death, Resurrection and Ascension of Christ*, 145-46*; citing Mt 27:57.

(which the prophets said would happen at the coming of Christ), except when God gathers together all those people who are under his rule. Therefore Joseph is commended in that although he was in a miserable state and subject to destruction, he kept the hope of redemption which was promised by God. From this hope springs fear and respect of God and a desire to lead a godly life. For no one will serve God unless he has assured himself that God will be his deliverer. Let us also note that salvation in Christ was offered to all the Jews alike and was common to everyone, but the Holy Spirit witnesses that it was only received by a few, as we can see here in the example of Joseph. And so it appears that the unspeakable grace of God was wickedly despised by everyone for the most part through forgetfulness. Everyone could boast about the coming of Christ, but the covenant of God was fixed in the hearts of only a few, that they might rise by faith to the spiritual renovation. AN ECCLESIASTICALL EXPOSITION UPON SAINT MATHEWE 27.[9]

JOSEPH STILL HOPED FOR THE KINGDOM.

MARTIN LUTHER: Luke and Mark now report especially about Joseph. He was a disciple of the Lord: that is, he listened diligently to his preaching, approved of it and was waiting for the kingdom of God. We should consider such little passages well, for here we can see what moved him to risk this and go to Pilate. For it was not a simple affair. The high priests and the entire council in Jerusalem had accused the Lord Jesus of being an insurgent, a seducer [of the people] and a blasphemer. Pilate had delivered his verdict based on such accusations, and now Joseph has to approach the one who had already made up his mind against Jesus before all these events, who had expressed that he wanted nothing to do with it. Now Joseph asks about the body of Christ, that he might bury it honorably in the ground. But this was a risky move, for by doing so he brought down on himself the entire council

as well as Pilate himself, who had condemned the Lord, and gave them to understand that he considered Jesus to have been a pious, upright man, who was unjustly treated before God and the whole world.

But what moved Joseph to risk this so openly? Quite simply, that he was waiting for the kingdom of God. That is, he still had hope that, although Christ had been hung and had died so miserably on the cross, the kingdom of God would not fail to appear but would indeed come. He still hoped that God would accomplish and fulfill everything through this Christ, even though he was dead, which had been promised through the prophets about the Messiah and his kingdom. HOUSE POSTIL (1544): THE PASSION, HOW THE LORD WAS TAKEN FROM THE CROSS AND LAID IN A NEW TOMB.[10]

CHRIST'S BURIAL WAS A PREPARATION FOR THE RESURRECTION. AUGUSTIN MARLORAT:

God truly wanted to bury his Christ with a glorious burial, although his death had nothing but public disgrace. But his burial was sumptuous and done with great cost, because it was a certain preparation for the glory of the resurrection. And therefore the dead ought to be buried with some honest preparation to cover their bodies, for that is how they are kept until the day of resurrection. Although a great light did not shine among them, the Jews had many ceremonies for burying their dead. We share one practice in common with them: we do not leave the dead carcasses on the ground for birds and beasts to consume, but we bury them in the earth, where they may be kept until the day of Christ's coming. Joseph "wrapped it in linen cloth": Christ's body was wrapped in a clean linen cloth and laid in a new sepulcher, which declares that some new thing had been done which was never heard of before. It was right that Christ was not buried with other dead people, because he went to open the way to a new life. The burial of Christ also admonishes us about our duty, about which the apostle writes: "Do you

---

[9]Marlorat, ed., *Catholike and Ecclesiasticall Exposition of the Holy Gospell After S. Mathewe*, 736*.

[10]WA 52:821.

not know that all of us who have been baptized into Christ Jesus were baptized into his death?" He teaches here more generally what it means to be buried with Christ and to rise with him again. An Ecclesiasticall Exposition upon Saint Mathewe 27.[11]

23:54-56 The Women Prepare to Return After the Sabbath

Their Service Points Us to Service to Others. Huldrych Zwingli: We see in these women an example of godliness and diligent love, for as they had followed the Lord in his lifetime, so they do not forsake him when he is dead. They run and watch with a pious thoughtfulness, having an earnest care to anoint his body. This is an example we ought to follow, for we may yet bestow these pious attentions on Christ, but through his members, because after this he is no more with us in his body. Let us not be ashamed to serve Christ and to be liberal to the poor. Let it not dismay us to give over some of our goods, when we can see that he has given his life for us. And seeing these women and honest men have spared no cost in burying the body of Christ most honorably, this commends the poor to us highly. For we learn here what grief and sorrow they had even though they did not dare to confess Christ openly for fear, and nevertheless they did not cease to run secretly, to watch, to admonish and to help so that they might at least do Christ some service in some way. Because we may profess the doctrine of Christ freely and without danger, we ought to pray for the poor and needy, to help them with our service, to succor them with our benefits, to cherish them by comforting and exhorting them. Of the Passion and Death of Christ.[12]

The Women Prepared Perfumes After the Sabbath. Desiderius Erasmus: At his burial they noted the place and saw how the Lord was put into the tomb, but then the sabbath came on them, and so they rested according to the commandment. Once the sabbath day was past, they prepared their sweet perfumes and ointments to anoint the body. But the words of Luke seem to be placed out of order, for they should read: "But they rested on the sabbath day in obedience to the commandment, and once it was past they prepared sweet perfumes and ointments." An Ecclesiasticall Exposition upon Saint Mathewe 27.[13]

Their Service to Christ Shows Us What We Should Do. Miles Coverdale: When we hear with what zeal and fervency the devout women clung to him and served him in life and death, their example teaches us to have an earnest, diligent and fervent love toward Christ. They will not forsake in death the one whom they loved in life, but cheerfully, with constant minds, they jeopardize their own lives and goods. But what can we do, because we cannot show friendship, love and service to Christ as well as these women did? Because we do not always have Christ physically with us, for he is in his kingdom and does not need any corporal ministration or service, we ought instead to bestow such service on his poor ones, whom we always have with us. We should spare neither goods nor money in this service, in order to serve and please Christ, who endangered and gave his body and life to death for us. Fruitful Lessons upon the Passion, Burial, Resurrection, Ascension and of the Sending of the Holy Spirit (1593).[14]

The Blessed Quiet of the Sabbath Is Usually Disturbed. Catharina Regina von Greiffenberg: Quiet generally comes with godliness. A soul that loves God also loves the quiet in which God is wont to reveal himself, particularly over the sabbath. What is sweeter and

---

[11]Marlorat, ed., *Catholike and Ecclesiasticall Exposition of the Holy Gospell After S. Mathewe*, 737*; citing Rom 6:3.

[12]Zwingli, *Briefe Rehersal of the Death, Resurrection and Ascension of Christ*, 149-50*.

[13]Marlorat, ed., *Catholike and Ecclesiasticall Exposition of the Holy Gospell After S. Mathewe*, 738*; citing Mk 16:1.

[14]*Writings and Translations of Myles Coverdale*, 320-21*.

more delightful than being quiet and being spared all vanity and emptiness on the sabbath so that eternity and spirit do their work in us; celebrating so that God works in our hearts; being quiet so that we can listen to the music of the Holy Spirit and the angels and can hear what Jesus says in and to our souls. O, blessed quiet of the sea that makes us hatch this heavenly halcyon in us![15] But oh! how Satan and the wicked world oppose this quiet! Unfortunately the sabbath of all days never allows for quiet. All of the meetings, visits, trips and

festivities take place then. One is supposed to leave God behind and attend to the world, to set knocking on the door of heaven at naught and dance to the tune of vanity, to push away the Bible and take up cards. If one does not do it, one is considered a foolish woman or what is worse a pious hypocrite. One does not have a choice; rather, one is disturbed against one's will in one's peace and quiet in God, for one is flushed out everywhere like a solitary little bird. ON THE SUPREMELY HOLY AND SUPREMELY SALVIFIC SUFFERING OF JESUS: TWELFTH MEDITATION.[16]

---

[15]Tatlock notes, "The halcyon (Greek for kingfisher), a mythological bird, is said to breed in the winter when the sea is calm and the weather fine, laying and sitting on its eggs on the surface of the water" (p. 131 n. 159).

[16]Greiffenberg, *Meditations on the Incarnation, Passion and Death of Jesus Christ*, 131-32* (*Zwölf andächtige Betrachtungen*, 980-81).

24:1-12 THE RESURRECTION

But on the first day of the week, at early dawn, they went to the tomb, taking the spices they had prepared. ²And they found the stone rolled away from the tomb, ³but when they went in they did not find the body of the Lord Jesus. ⁴While they were perplexed about this, behold, two men stood by them in dazzling apparel. ⁵And as they were frightened and bowed their faces to the ground, the men said to them, "Why do you seek the living among the dead? ⁶He is not here, but has risen. Remember how he told you, while he was still in Galilee, ⁷that the Son of Man must be delivered into the hands of sinful men and be crucified and on the third day rise." ⁸And they remembered his words, ⁹and returning from the tomb they told all these things to the eleven and to all the rest. ¹⁰Now it was Mary Magdalene and Joanna and Mary the mother of James and the other women with them who told these things to the apostles, ¹¹but these words seemed to them an idle tale, and they did not believe them. ¹²But Peter rose and ran to the tomb; stooping and looking in, he saw the linen cloths by themselves; and he went home marveling at what had happened.

OVERVIEW: Several commentators note that the fact the women came to find and prepare the body, however courageous and devoted they may have been, shows that they did not really have faith in Jesus' words about his own resurrection. Donne seems to have accepted the notion that women were weaker not only in strength but also in intellect, for although they had seen the initial burial preparations and the stone in front of the tomb, they still came expecting to be able to anoint the body. But while it may have been foolish to forget about the boulder, they went there to serve Christ and were then chosen to be the first witnesses of the resurrection. The angels who brought this news to the women had two messages for them, Luther suggests: first, they told the women they should not be frightened but instead should rejoice because Christ had risen; second, they insisted that the women not keep this message a secret but that they should go quickly and tell the other disciples.

Why is it, some wonder, that the women were chosen to be the first to preach the good news? It could be that they were the first to venture to the tomb, and thus the first to discover that the body was missing, although Leigh suggests that Christ was rewarding their piety and courage in coming to the tomb while the men were hiding out in fear. However, he also notes a number of other reasons for this choice, including that Christ often chose those seen as weak or lowly in the world. These women were not only of the supposedly weaker sex, but they were also from Galilee, so choosing them to be "apostles to the apostles" contradicted any worldly expectations. He also suggests that as women they were more emotionally affected by Jesus' death, so this news would give them great comfort. Because women, through Eve, were responsible for introducing death into the world, it would be appropriate for women to bring the message of the defeat of death in a sort of recapitulation. In general, as female preachers were highly unusual in this period (if not utterly forbidden), the commentators see the charge given to these women to bring the good news to the others as unique to this moment, and not a sign that women should be ordained to preach.

24:1-8 The Angels' Announcement to the Women

LIKE THE WOMEN, SEEK JESUS EARLY. JOHN BOYS: Mary and the other women sought Christ on the first day of the week, and in the first hour of the day, but many put off seeking the Lord until the last week of their life, the last day of the week, the last hour of the day, the last minute of the hour. While the ship is sound, the tackle sure, the pilot well, the sailors strong, the wind favorable and the sea calm, it is a risky course to lie idle at anchor, playing cards and dice, drinking and wasting the seasonable weather, and only launch forth and hoist up sail for a voyage to a distant country when the ship leaks, the pilot is sick, the mariners faint, the storms boisterous and the sea full of raging surges. Yet these "evening repenters," when they are in the morning of youth, with soundness of health and the perfect use of their reason, cannot resolve to weigh the anchor and cut the cable that holds them back from seeking Christ. Nevertheless they convince themselves with a strong persuasion that when their wits are distracted, their senses dazed and all the powers of their mind and parts of their body are disordered, they will suddenly be able to become saints on their death, no matter how much they may have demeaned themselves as devils all of their life. EASTER DAY.[1]

THE WOMEN BROUGHT SPICES TO PRESERVE THE BODY. RICHARD TAVERNER: At the beginning, then, of our Gospel, it is said that after the sabbath feast had passed, the good women who had followed our Lord from the city of Galilee out of fervent devotion—that is, Mary Magdalene, Mary the mother of James, and Salome—brought sweet and precious ointments and came together to the sepulcher or grave, where they thought they would find the body of our Lord Jesus Christ, so that they might anoint him with the ointments, according to the custom of the Jews. They did this in order to preserve the body from putrefaction and corruption. But in doing this, these women surely showed that they did not yet have entire and full faith in the resurrection and that they were not fully assured that he was the holy man of whom it was written that he should "see no corruption." . . . By this we are taught, good brothers and sisters, that we ought to take great pains and with great diligence to seek the

Lord in our hearts by the faith and trust in his passion, carrying with us ointments of grace to mortify and purge our bodies, and to flee the vermin and contagion of the flesh, and so to preserve it from all putrefaction and corruption— that is to say, from worldly things, from infidelity and from sin. THE GOSPEL ON EASTER DAY.[2]

THE WOMEN ATTEMPT AN IMPOSSIBLE AND REDUNDANT TASK. JOHN DONNE: Even to see the sepulcher was an act of love, and every act of love to Christ is devotion. There is a love that will make one kiss the frame of a picture, even if it is covered over; there is a love that will melt one's heart if he only passes over or passes by the grave of a dear friend. But their purpose was not only to see the sepulcher but to see whether the sepulcher were in such a state that they might achieve their purpose, which was to embalm their master's body. But this had already been done, and they knew about it, as all the Evangelists testify, particularly Saint Luke, who wrote, "The women followed, and beheld the sepulcher and how the body was laid." "How," that is, how abundantly it was embalmed by Nicodemus, and "how," that is, how decently and orderly it was wound and bound up, according to the manner of the Jews' funerals. What more, then, did these women intend to do than had already been done?

Truly, I have often wondered why, among all our many expositors of the Gospels (I can tell you of scores of them myself), none have touched on this doubt. They all make good use of their piety and devout service toward their dead master but make no mention of the impossibility of coming to that body and of the irregularity and impertinence in undertaking and proceeding so far in what could not possibly be done. What should be said of this? What Chrysologus says on another occasion could also be said here: *Sæva passionis procella turbaverat*, "A bitter storm of passion and consternation had put them in such disarray that no faculty of theirs

---

[1]Boys, *Exposition of the Dominical Epistles and Gospels*, 2:158*.

[2]Taverner, *Epistles and Gospelles (Wynter Parte)*, 126r-127r*; citing Ps 16:10.

performed its proper function."[3] Vehemence and earnestness had discomposed and amazed them, had flustered them so that they discerned nothing clearly, did nothing orderly. Some of the authors say these things of the women's inconsideration of how, in particular, they were going to remove the stone from the sepulcher. For they had prepared their ointments and come on their way before they ever thought of that. Then they stopped and said to each other, "Who will roll away for us the stone from the door of the sepulcher? We never thought of that." Likewise, they also were given a rebuke by the angel for another thoughtless move: "Why do you seek the living among the dead? Why do you seek him who is the Son of the living God?" SERMON 23, PREACHED AT SAINT PAUL'S ON EASTER DAY (1630).[4]

THE ANGELS ANNOUNCE THAT THE RESURREC-TION IS FOR OUR BENEFIT. MARTIN LUTHER: You have heard about Christ's resurrection, how it happened and why, and how we ourselves should benefit from it. This Gospel also teaches about such an application of the resurrection. For in the first place it is a great thing that the beloved angels are the first messengers who bring the good news that Christ has arisen and is no longer in the grave. They remind the women that Christ had earlier told them about these events, but they did not believe or understand him. Such a message is certain proof that, although the angels are totally pure and holy spirits and we are only poor sinners, nevertheless they do not shun or despise us but rather want to be good friends with us, because Christ died for our benefit and is risen again. . . .

Along with this work, one also hears in these words what sort of meaning is in the resurrection of Christ. For the angels come with two commands: the first is to the women, that they should not be frightened by their appearance, but they should rejoice that Christ is risen; the other

command is that they should not keep the resurrection a secret, but they should quickly go forth and announce it to the disciples. We should be very glad in both of these parts, for the angel says first, "Do not be afraid. I know that you seek Jesus who was crucified. He is not here, but has risen from the dead." It was as if he should have said, "But what sort of silly, simple people are you, that you prefer to be shocked and terrified? However, Christ is alive and has risen from the dead. Therefore it is fitting that you should be happy and that you should not be frightened by anything. For Christ lives that he might live for your good, that you will benefit from him and that you will be protected by him and kept safe from all affliction." HOUSE POSTIL (1544): EASTER, THE FRUIT OF CHRIST'S RESURRECTION.[5]

THEY HAD FORGOTTEN CHRIST'S WORDS. JOHN CALVIN: The angel affirms that what he said was true. However, he did not invent this himself, as if he was the true author, but he assents to the promise made by Christ. Therefore in Mark's Gospel he only reminds them of Christ's words themselves. Luke continues the words farther and says that the disciples were admonished by Christ that "he must be crucified, and on the third day rise again." Nevertheless the sense is the same, because along with his death he also foretold his resurrection. He even added there, "they remembered the words of the Lord," by which we are taught that although they had made poor progress in the teaching of Christ, nevertheless it was not destroyed but was merely choked, until at the right time it produced a sprout. COMMENTARY ON A HARMONY OF THE GOSPELS.[6]

24:9-11 The Women Run to Tell the Disbelieving Others

THE WOMEN PREACHED THE FRUITS OF THE RESURRECTION. JOHANN BAUMGART (POMAR-

---

[3]See Peter Chrysologus, "Sermon 79, On the Lord's Resurrection," FC 110:35-38.
[4]Donne, *Works*, 1:455-57*; citing Mk 16:3; Mt 16:16.

[5]WA 52:253-54; citing Mt 28:5-6.
[6]CTS 33:345* (CO 45:796-97); citing Mt 28:7.

IUS): It is also very comforting that the angels prove themselves to be so friendly toward these women and are pleasant to them, for it shows that through Christ's resurrection, God's wrath and aversion toward the human race is lifted. Therefore, here the angels act in this positive way toward the people, and not as in Paradise when they drove them out and blocked them from the garden. But here in this garden they draw the poor women to them and comfort them. And the angels even send the women out to preach, that they might bring the good news to the poor, distressed disciples, and especially to the perjured and faithless Peter, that the Lord is risen. They were sent to report that the Lord Jesus arose to comfort all poor sinners and that a person can participate in his resurrection and its fruits through the office of preaching.

The Lord himself shows the extremely glorious comfort and fruit of his resurrection that he gained for us, which is to be elected the children of God, for he also dispatched the women to his disciples to announce his resurrection to them. He told them to tell the disciples, "I am going now to my Father and your Father, to my God and your God." He calls us all his brothers and sisters, and the children of God, which is our greatest happiness, for we are born in the flesh children of flesh and wrath. But God has brought us to be reborn through his great mercy in the resurrection of Jesus Christ from the dead, to a permanent, spotless, unfading inheritance, that we are and are called the children of God. THE GOSPEL ON HOLY EASTER DAY.[7]

THE WOMEN WERE CHOSEN BY GOD TO ANNOUNCE THE RESURRECTION. EDWARD LEIGH: God chose these women, to whom the resurrection of Christ should be first manifested, for several reasons:

1. That he might observe his ancient custom, by which he generally chooses things which are viewed with contempt, or seen as ignoble or low in this world. The women were viewed with contempt not only on account of the weakness of their sex but also for their country of origin, because they were from Galilee. But God exalted them by manifesting to them the resurrection of his Son, which is a principle article of our faith, and afterwards by sending them to the apostles, that they might be *apostolorum apostolae*, as the ancients would say, or "apostles to the apostles."

2. The women, who are weaker by nature, were struck with the most vehement grief of mind because of the public disgrace and torments of Christ, which they saw on the day before Passover while standing under the cross. Therefore, the most joyful resurrection of Christ is told to them first of all, as Christ also afterwards appeared several times to Peter, because as he committed a more serious offense than the other disciples, so he was more grievously troubled. And so it appears that the resurrection of Christ brings consolation to troubled consciences and contrite hearts.

3. By this means, God planned to prevent the lies of the priests, who spread the rumor that the disciples stole away the body of Christ from the grave. In order to reprove the impudence and absurdity of this lie, it happened by the wonderful providence of God that the women should come to the grave before the apostles. It is hardly likely that women, and so few of them, should steal his body out of a sepulcher guarded by armed men and shut up with a great stone.

4. The death of all humankind came about through Eve, a woman, and therefore Christ wanted his resurrection, through which righteousness and life are restored to us, to be told about by women.

5. These women went with a great deal of courage early in the morning to Christ's tomb, while the apostles were still hiding out in fear. Christ therefore wanted to reward this great piety of theirs with the most joyful tidings of the resurrection.

ANNOTATIONS UPON SAINT LUKE 24.[8]

---

[7]Baumgart, *Postilla*, 106v-107r; quoting Jn 20:17.

[8]Leigh, *Annotations upon All the New Testament Philologicall and Theologicall*, 139*; citing 1 Cor 1: 27-29; Jn 1:46.

THE APOSTLES WERE TOO DIMWITTED TO BELIEVE THE WOMEN. AUGUSTIN MARLORAT: The women, having received the commandment of Christ, went to tell the apostles. . . . "But their words seemed to them to be nonsense, and they did not believe them." The blindness in which the apostles were mired was foul, because they could not call to mind that what they had earlier heard from their master had now been fulfilled. If the women had spoken anything to them which they had not heard before, then it would have been more excuseable that they did not believe such an incredible story. But they had heard it declared and promised many times by the Son of God, so they must have been remarkably dull to consider the news a fable or a dream, especially because it was now reported to them by eyewitnesses. And so it appears that they were so overthrown by temptation that all their remembrance and understanding of Christ's words had completely fled their minds. AN ECCLESIASTICALL EXPOSITION UPON SAINT MATHEWE 28.[9]

---

[9]Marlorat, ed., *Catholike and Ecclesiasticall Exposition of the Holy Gospell After S. Mathewe,* 747*.

24:12 Peter Investigates the Empty Tomb

PETER KNEW OF THE EMPTY GRAVE, AND YET THEY STILL DID NOT BELIEVE. JOHN CALVIN: I have no doubt that Luke inverts the order of the account here, which is easily drawn out from the words of John; it would not be wrong, in my opinion, to take the word *currendi,* or "running," in the pluperfect tense, as "had run." Those who have reflected on Scripture even slightly know that it is usual with the Hebrews to refer later to those things which were omitted in the proper place. And by mentioning this circumstance, Luke greatly magnifies the insensibility of the apostles in rejecting the words of the women, even though Peter had already seen the empty grave and would have been compelled to wonder at a manifest sign of the resurrection. COMMENTARY ON A HARMONY OF THE GOSPELS.[10]

---

[10]CTS 33:350* (CO 45:800); citing Jn 20:3.

24:13-35 THE ROAD TO EMMAUS

¹³That very day two of them were going to a village named Emmaus, about seven miles^a from Jerusalem, ¹⁴and they were talking with each other about all these things that had happened. ¹⁵While they were talking and discussing together, Jesus himself drew near and went with them. ¹⁶But their eyes were kept from recognizing him. ¹⁷And he said to them, "What is this conversation that you are holding with each other as you walk?" And they stood still, looking sad. ¹⁸Then one of them, named Cleopas, answered him, "Are you the only visitor to Jerusalem who does not know the things that have happened there in these days?" ¹⁹And he said to them, "What things?" And they said to him, "Concerning Jesus of Nazareth, a man who was a prophet mighty in deed and word before God and all the people, ²⁰and how our chief priests and rulers delivered him up to be condemned to death, and crucified him. ²¹But we had hoped that he was the one to redeem Israel. Yes, and besides all this, it is now the third day since these things happened. ²²Moreover, some women of our company amazed us. They were at the tomb early in the morning, ²³and when they did not find his body, they came back saying that they had even seen a vision of angels, who said that he was alive. ²⁴Some of those who were with us went to the tomb and found it just as the women had said, but him they did not see." ²⁵And he said to them, "O foolish ones, and slow of heart to believe all that the prophets have spoken! ²⁶Was it not necessary that the Christ should suffer these things and enter into his glory?" ²⁷And beginning with Moses and all the Prophets, he interpreted to them in all the Scriptures the things concerning himself.

²⁸So they drew near to the village to which they were going. He acted as if he were going farther, ²⁹but they urged him strongly, saying, "Stay with us, for it is toward evening and the day is now far spent." So he went in to stay with them. ³⁰When he was at table with them, he took the bread and blessed and broke it and gave it to them. ³¹And their eyes were opened, and they recognized him. And he vanished from their sight. ³²They said to each other, "Did not our hearts burn within us while he talked to us on the road, while he opened to us the Scriptures?" ³³And they rose that same hour and returned to Jerusalem. And they found the eleven and those who were with them gathered together, ³⁴saying, "The Lord has risen indeed, and has appeared to Simon!" ³⁵Then they told what had happened on the road, and how he was known to them in the breaking of the bread.

a Greek *sixty stadia*; a *stadion* was about 607 feet or 185 meters

OVERVIEW: One result of the male disciples not believing the women when they reported that Jesus had arisen was that two of the disciples—Cleopas and an unnamed disciple, who some assume to be Luke—decided to leave town. There is no explanation in the Gospel for their trip to Emmaus and perhaps beyond. The two were brotherly companions for each other, our commentators state, but clearly they were sorrowful and still focused on what had been happening in Jerusalem with Jesus' arrest and execution.

However, as many commentators note, because two were gathered in his name, Jesus was there. He appeared to them simply as a fellow traveler, and they fell into conversation. One important aspect of Jesus' appearance on the road to Emmaus is that it shows, according to Bullinger, that Jesus had a true physical body after his resurrection. His body had been raised from the dead—it was a glorified body, free from all infirmities and corruption, but it was still a physical body, and he was not merely a ghost, although he could appear and disappear, a fact which Bullinger does not address. The fact that they did not recognize him had more to do with God's power than with any sort of shape shifting or ghostly talent. Calvin also remarks that it was not an immoral deception—Jesus cannot be used here as an excuse to lie or deceive others. He was keeping his plans to himself and holding them in suspense until the time was right. Clearly, as Jesus—and the reformers— could see, they still needed instruction and help to understand what had happened. Jesus sharply criticized them—he had spent so much time with them and had taught them so frequently of his coming death and new life that he was disappointed in them for not remembering or understanding. His own teaching, as well as that of the prophets, was so clear that they should have understood. So Jesus began again with the Scripture, explaining everything to them again. He demonstrates for these two disciples and for us that Scripture only opens itself to its hearers and readers when approached as pointing to Christ.

After they reached Emmaus, the disciples were moved to ask Jesus to stay with them, although they still did not know who he was. Luther notes that they prayed the prayer of the pious, asking Jesus to enter in, although they did not understand fully and were not necessarily asking for the right thing. We do this as well, but even when we do not understand, God often comes to help us through different, even better ways than we ask. In this case, Baumgart suggests, Jesus was testing them by appearing under another form, but then he allows himself to be seen again, proving to be both friendly and comforting to them. The two disciples were comforted without understanding why, but their hearts were truly set on fire when Jesus revealed himself in the breaking of the bread. They had never expected that such grace would come to them, but they were made so happy by Christ's presence, our commentators suggest, that they could not stay where they were but hurried to reunite with their friends and share the good news.

24:13-18 Two Disciples Are Travelling Together

GOD IS PRESENT WHERE TWO ARE GATHERED. HULDRYCH ZWINGLI: That same day on

which the Lord had risen, two of those seventy disciples whom the Lord had chosen while he was living went forth. It appears that these disciples fled out of fear of the persecution which they believed to be at hand. This history also teaches that what Christ promised was true, namely, that he would be present even if there were only two gathered together in his name. God is always present with his children, even when they think he is the least there. That is when he reminds them of himself, telling them what counsel is the best to take and manifesting himself to them. Moreover, he speaks externally by his Word, by his sacraments and finally by all his creatures, to stir up and provoke us to praise him. God therefore is always and everywhere present with us, a judge and an observer not only of all our deeds but also of our thoughts. This teaches us to live honestly with fear and great reverence before him. For if we are ashamed to commit vile deeds when people can see us, how much more ought we to be ashamed to commit any such thing in God's sight? OF THE RESURRECTION OF CHRIST.[1]

WE SHOULD JOURNEY WITH OUR COMPANIONS TO EMMAUS. JOHANN BAUMGART (POMARIUS): Emmaus is a town in the Jewish countryside, situated about two miles from Jerusalem. It is also known as Nicopolis, that is, Victory City, for it was near this city that Judah Maccabee defeated the powerful military leader of Antioch. Near this little town, at the fork in the road, were situated the warm baths from the fountain or spring called Calliroe, which had been especially beneficial and healing for many injuries and illnesses. Some write that the fountain and these warm baths were on the way that Jesus traveled that Easter day with his disciples.[2] Once before, while traveling through this region with his disciples, Jesus washed his own feet in this same fountain and received for himself its healing power. . . .

---

[1]Zwingli, *Briefe Rehersal of the Death, Resurrection and Ascention of Christ*, 169*; citing Mt 18:20.
[2]Baumgart cites Josephus as his source for these comments. See Josephus, *Antiquities* 12.21; 18.3.

Cleophas, who is called a worthy father, and Luke, who is called an associate and companion, traveled in their sorrow to Emmaus, keeping each other company in a brotherly fashion and keeping Christ close to themselves. They remind us that preachers and teachers, as worthy spiritual parents, pious rulers, as parents of the country, pious fathers and mothers, as parents of the home, pious teachers, as parents of the school, with their companions of listeners, subjects, children, servants and students, should always keep each other company in a brotherly and harmonious way, especially in all sorrow and misery, in times of persecution and adversity. They should travel together to Emmaus to the house and church of the Lord, just as to the mother of comfort, counsel, light and strength, to support each other with comfort and counsel, enlightenment and strength, and to speak with each other of Christ, his suffering, death and resurrection. Then Christ will be in the midst of them and their faithful fellow pilgrims and companions and will be everything that is necessary for them. GOSPEL ON EASTER MONDAY.[3]

CHRIST COMES TO BE WITH THOSE WHO LOVE HIM. HEINRICH BULLINGER: As these two disciples communed and talked together, the Lord at last overtook them and went forward with them on their journey. We should note two things here especially. First, the Lord rushes to be with them, when their thoughts and words were all of him. And second, the truth that his very body was raised from death is shown, in that he came near to them and overtook them, walking with them. The Lord is not moved and carried like a spirit from place to place. Although his body was now glorified and free from corruption, infirmity and grief, yet it retained the substance and properties of a true human body. In the glorification, his body did not lose its substance and nature but only the defect of nature and its infirmity. In respect to this, Saint Augustine said, "He shall come to judgment even as he was

seen to ascend into heaven; that is to say, in the same form and substance of flesh, for the Father did not take away his nature from him to whom he gave immortality."[4] And so these two disciples had various conversations as they went, as it usually happens when one's mind is sorrowful. They were very troubled by the Lord's death and were very close to being completely discouraged. Their whole conversation concerned Jesus and all those things which they had heard and seen only a little while before, for they loved him as a unique and wonderful man. And although they had no hope concerning the restoration of the kingdom of Israel, still it helped them to call to mind through their conversation the one who was only a little earlier put to death. Their minds were confused, as if they had been asleep, for they loved him whom they could not forget, as if it were all a dream. And finally, as they discussed many things concerning Jesus, behold, Jesus himself quite unexpectedly came and joined them. Here in the body he fulfilled what he had promised to perform in spirit up to the end of the word: namely, where two or three are gathered in his name, there he will be among them. He joined with them as if he were just another traveler, a companion on their journey still unrecognized by them. And it was not that he had a different body than the one he had before his death, but only because it pleased him to leave them in the dark a little longer. AN ECCLESIASTICALL EXPOSITION UPON SAINT LUKE 24.[5]

24:19-24 They Recount Recent Events for the Newcomer

WITHOUT THE SCRIPTURES PROPERLY PREACHED THE DISCIPLES WAVERED IN THEIR FAITH. MARTIN LUTHER: It is as if they wanted to say, "It is finished with our hope. He is now dead; we do not believe." They staggered here and there, saying neither no nor yes. There is something in

---

[3]Baumgart, *Postilla*, 371v-372v.

[4]See Augustine, Sermon 77 on John 5:25 (NPNF 6:489-90).
[5]Marlorat, ed., *Catholike and Ecclesiasticall Exposition of the Holy Gospell After S. Marke and Luke*, 318-19*; citing Mt 18:20.

their heart which they do not hold to. For they had heard that he lives, and they disputed whether it were true or not. Because he was in their hearts, thus he came to them also before their eyes. He is really present; however, he looks strange to them. He did not introduce himself but continued on as if he were someone else. The text emphasizes this; it says "their eyes were shut, so that they did not recognize him."

It was his natural form, but the brokenness in them caused them not to recognize him—even though they looked him in the face. They would have seen him as he naturally was; however, they pictured him before their eyes in a different form. It is like when someone holds colored glass before his eyes: everything that he looks at seems to be colored accordingly. Each object still retains all its natural color and does not change at all; however, he does not see the natural color, but instead he sees the color of the glass. Or like when someone has a fever, he thinks everything is bitter, because the tongue's ability is altered; nothing tastes like its natural taste—as it is in itself. Thus, here too the condition of their heart is indicated: in their hearts they were not correctly oriented. In their hearts they did not have faith that he was their Redeemer; as was said, they still staggered, not standing firm in Christian faith.

From this follows this lesson: how we consider Christ, so he is. Christ and his divine truth—what he is, does or preaches—is grasped and accepted according to the character of those who hear it.... "With the saints he will be saintly, and with the perverse he will be perverse."... How you consider God and the Scriptures and God's works, so you have it. If you consider him to be angry, he is angry; if you consider him to be merciful, he is merciful. In order to institute such a light, God ignited a true light, Christ, who must open our eyes as he does here, turning to and preaching the Scriptures—in this way he opens their eyes so they finally recognize him. In order for our heart to be illuminated and to learn to see God correctly, we must preach Christ alone and no other thing! SERMON ON EASTER MONDAY (1521).[6]

CLEOPAS FELT BOTH FEAR AND FAITH. JOHN CALVIN: From the context it is clear that the hope that they had conceived about Christ was not destroyed, although at first it might seem that their words give an indication of this. But because a person who had never been introduced to the gospel could have been alienated by his inserted narrative of the condemnation of Christ—that he had been condemned by the rulers of the church—Cleopas opposes the hope of the redemption to this scandal. And although afterwards he shows his nervousness and the appearance of wavering in this hope, he continues in it and diligently collects whatever he can that will aid in its support. For it is probable that he had mentioned the third day only because the Lord had promised his own resurrection after three days. After this he relates that the women had not found the body but had seen a vision of angels, and that what the women had said about the empty grave was also confirmed by the testimony of the men. This all refers to the main point: that Christ had risen. Thus, the pious man, between faith and fear, applies a bandage to his wavering faith and struggles against fear to the best of his ability. COMMENTARY ON A HARMONY OF THE GOSPELS.[7]

YOU OF LITTLE FAITH. DESIDERIUS ERASMUS: They explained the gist of the matter to Jesus simply, as if he were a visitor and unaware of what had happened, unselfconsciously disclosing how they still understood nothing about Jesus worthy of his true status and how they had cast off almost all hope of the resurrection.... The disciples had guilelessly made clear in this account how they wavered in their heart, how small a hope they had in the Lord's promises. Jesus did not yet allow himself to be recognized, but like some more learned disciple of Jesus he scolded their slowness and rebuked their unbelief. PARAPHRASE ON THE GOSPEL OF LUKE 22:19-24.[8]

---

[6]WA 9:666-67, 668; citing Tit 1:15; Ps 18:26.

[7]CTS 33:357-58* (CO 45:805).
[8]CWE 48:232, 233* (LB 7:468).

24:25-27 Jesus Explains Moses and the Prophets to Them

JESUS CRITICIZES THE DISCIPLES FOR FAILING TO UNDERSTAND. JOHN CALVIN: This reproof appears to be too harsh and severe considering this person's weakness; but whoever considers all the circumstances will easily understand that the Lord had good reason for rebuking so sharply those on whom he had long bestowed labor to little purpose, and almost without any fruit. It should be noted that what is said here is not confined to these two, but, as a reproof of a common fault, the rest of their companions should hear it immediately from their mouths. So frequently had Christ forewarned them of his death—so frequently had he discussed the new and spiritual life and confirmed his teaching by prophets' oracles—it is as if he had spoken among the deaf—rather to sticks and stones! Overpowered with dread at his death they did not know where to turn. This hesitation, therefore, he justly attributes to folly, and he identifies its cause as their torpor that they were not more ready to believe. And he does not only reprove them because they had the best Teacher, were sluggish and slow to learn, but also because they had not listened to the prophets' words. It is as if he had said that their stupidity is without excuse. It was their own fault—in and of themselves the prophets' teaching shines radiantly and was correctly explained to them. Similarly today, most people sustain their ignorance through their own fault, because they are unteachable and rigid. But let us note when Christ sees that his disciples are exceedingly sluggish, in order to stir them he begins to scold. Thus we must compel those whom we have found to be stubborn or sluggish. COMMENTARY ON A HARMONY OF THE GOSPELS.[9]

CHRIST IS THE SUBSTANCE OF SCRIPTURE. MARTIN LUTHER: It is sin and shame that with us Christians it has come to the point that we are so torpid in the gospel that not only do we not understand it but also first need someone to show us with other books and explanations what is to be sought and expected in it. The Gospels and the Epistles of the apostles were written so that they themselves would be such pointers and lead us into the writings of the prophets and Moses—the Old Testament—so that there we ourselves could read and see that Christ was wrapped in swaddling cloths and laid in the manger, that is, that he is contained in the writings of the prophets. Then our studying and our reading should lead us to see who Christ is, why he was given, how he was promised and how all Scripture points to him, as he himself says, "If you believed Moses, you would believe me; for he wrote about me."...

Therefore, Luke says that Christ opened the understanding of the apostles so that they understood Scripture. Christ says that he is the door through whom people must enter; and whoever enters through him, the gatekeeper—the Holy Spirit—grants him entry so that he finds pasture and salvation. Finally, it is true that the gospel itself is the pointer and instructor in the Scriptures....

But look at what "fine, tender, godly children" we are! So that we might not need to study the Scriptures and learn Christ there, we regard the whole Old Testament as nothing, as something expired and of no value. Nevertheless, it alone should be called holy Scripture. The gospel should not be written but instead should be spoken Word which produces Scripture, as Christ and the apostles did. Thus, even Christ himself wrote nothing, but only spoke. And he called his teaching not Scripture but gospel, that is, a good message or proclamation which is to be promoted not with the pen but with the mouth. Then we go ahead and make out of the gospel a law book—a doctrine of commandments—out of Christ a Moses, out of the Helper[10] only a teacher. What punishment should God not impose on such stupid, perverse people? SHORT INSTRUCTION: WHAT SHOULD BE SOUGHT AND EXPECTED IN THE GOSPELS.[11]

---

[9]CTS 33:358-59* (CO 45:805-6).

[10]Luther means the Holy Spirit, the Paraclete (see Jn 14:16, 26; 15:26; 16:7).

[11]LW 75:10-12* (WA 10,1.1:14-18; E² 7:10-13; cf. LW 35:122-23); citing Jn 5:46, 39; Lk 24:27; Jn 10:9.

Why Did Luke Not Narrate Christ's Words Here? Johann Eck: O Luke, you holy Evangelist of God! You chancellor of Mary! Why did you not describe for us Christ's reading of the Scriptures—how he drew together the Scriptures, and which ones, concerning himself? With such knowledge we could better answer the heretics and Jews. But it pleased the divine Majesty that in this way we must steep ourselves in Scripture to experience it. Second Sermon on Easter Monday.[12]

This Is What Christ Said. Desiderius Erasmus: The Jews honor Moses almost as a god because he led the people of Israel out of Egypt, and in the desert he gave the law for them to observe and thus obtain salvation and come into a land flowing with milk and honey. Yet what else was that Moses than a foreshadowing of the Christ to come? He was not the Son of God; he was a slave. . . . But Christ is the true Moses, who by means of his own power frees not only the Hebrews but also all the nations who trust in him. He frees them from the vengeance of God, he frees them from the tyranny of the devil, he frees them from the darkness of error, he frees them from shameful enslavement to sin. And when they have been washed in his blood, he leads them forth into the freedom of the Spirit, himself being their constant leader and companion, until he leads them through all the changes and chances of this life to the heavenly land, overflowing with every sort of blessedness. He brought the law of the Spirit and the gospel, a law that would not deliver physical righteousness by ceremonies and animal sacrifices but would bestow true and perfect righteousness through faith and love. . . .

Hence in the spiritual temple, under Christ the high priest, no longer will a public distribution be put on of flesh from calves, goats or sheep but of the precious body and blood of Jesus Christ, which he sacrificed once and for all, so that it could thereafter be consumed spiritually by his anointed,

who through their thankful commemoration in a way renew for themselves the death of their high priest. This surely is the sacrifice that soon will be offered all over the world by new priests whom God has anointed, a sacrifice about which Malachi prophesied. . . . This is the sacrifice that Christ gave to his disciples at the paschal meal, offering them bread that he said was his body and a cup that he said was the cup of his blood, by which he consecrated for them a new covenant, that is, a bond of undying friendship. If you yourselves did not see these things, you certainly should have heard them from the Twelve, through whom he desired that what has taken place would reach everyone. As Christ, coming from heaven, turned all fleshly things into spiritual things—the city, the temple, the priesthood, the sacrifices—so he also desired the kingdom to be new, and therefore he regularly called it the kingdom of heaven, so that you would not look for something like what you see in a worldly kingdom. . . .

Do you want to understand this sort of kingdom? See what kind of servants and extenders of his sway he chose: insignificant, lowly, uneducated, equipped with neither wealth nor weapons nor provisions nor any of the resources of this world against the treacherous malice of the Pharisees, against the power of princes, against the arrogance of philosophers. And with these commanders he is going to defeat all the kingdoms of the world, with no other equipment than the helmet of salvation, which is a right understanding of holy Scripture; the shield of faith, by which—with God as their protector—they will be safe from all assaults of the ungodly; with the breastplate of righteousness, woven of all the gospel virtues; with the swordbelt of chastity and the gospel footgear, which is a heart cleansed from all earthly affections. But above all with the sword of the Spirit, which is the divine Word.

So it seemed best to God to show his power through the weakness of his Son, to declare his wisdom through the foolishness of preaching, to make his glory illustrious through the shame of the cross. For the present time the gospel kingdom is

---

[12]Eck, *Christenliche Predigen*, 2:12v-13r.

situated in these, until at the end of the world the majesty of Christ, all lowliness put aside, and the bliss of the godly, unstained by any afflictions, come forth. And yet this lowliness has spiritual strength, powerful and fit to cast down all the foundations that raise themselves against the glory of God. Or have you ever seen anything gentler than Christ, lowlier, poorer, milder, more in favor with the people and further removed from every appearance of kingship? And yet what is more regal than with a word to cast out evil spirits, with a command to quell the winds and waves, with a touch to heal lepers, with a single order to dispel every kind of disease? How often did he escape through the midst of Jews plotting death for him? He let himself be taken, but at the sound of his voice armed guards fell to the ground. He died on the cross, but what is mightier than his death, which shattered the elements of the universe, which darkened the sun, split rocks, opened tombs, roused the dead? Nothing was more lowly than his birth, but here too evidence of his concealed sublimity flashed instantly forth. He is born of a mere girl, but by the operation of the divine Spirit. He is laid in a manger, but angels sing glory to God in the highest. A baby cries in his cradle, but Herod the king trembles and the magi adore him. These things, still not known to very many, will someday be preached throughout the whole world. With resources of this kind he will equip his apostles also.

But if you read the Scriptures closely and compare with them what you have seen and heard, you cannot doubt that he is the Christ who was promised, Priest, King and Savior of the whole world, after whom no other is to be looked for. Review, please, in your minds his whole life, which in part you saw with your own eyes, in part you were able to learn of from relatives and friends. You will find nothing that was not both prefigured in the Old Testament and predicted by the prophets. PARAPHRASE ON THE GOSPEL OF LUKE 24:27.[13]

CHRIST ALONE AUTHORIZES CHRISTOCENTRIC READINGS OF THE OLD TESTAMENT.

MARTIN BUCER: Now where in Moses can you read anything like this? That Christ the only-begotten of God must be born as a human being, and die, and then in three days rise from the dead? And in his name repentance and the remission of sins is to be preached to all the nations? But there in Luke Christ said that thus it was written. Therefore, this is not without veil of types, as I have said. Undoubtedly the story of Jonah was one of these passages. Still, where in all of Jonah is it written that Christ, the Son of God, will die and will be shut in a tomb for three whole days and then after this rise? Nevertheless, Christ himself derived that from it. The prophecy of the salvation that will be accomplished through the cross of Christ is nowhere clearer than when Moses narrated the lifting up of the serpent in the desert. COMMENTARY ON EPHESIANS.[14]

MUTUAL AND INSEPARABLE NATURE OF THE WORD AND SPIRIT.

JOHN CALVIN: By a kind of mutual bond the Lord has joined together the certainty of his Word and Spirit so that the perfect religion of the Word may abide in our minds when the Spirit, who causes us to contemplate God's face, shines; and that we in turn may embrace the Spirit with no fear of being deceived when we recognize him in his own image, namely, in the Word. So indeed it is. God did not bring forth his Word among human beings for the sake of a momentary display, intending at the coming of his Spirit to abolish it. Rather, he sent down the same Spirit by whose power he had dispensed the Word, to complete his work by the efficacious confirmation of the Word.

In this manner Christ opened the minds of the two disciples not so that they would cast away the Scriptures and become wise of themselves but so that they should know the Scriptures. Similarly Paul, while he urges the Thessalonians not to

---

[13]CWE 48:235, 236, 247-48, 250-51* (LB 7:469, 474-75, 476); citing Mal 1:10-11; Eph 6:10-20; 1 Cor 1:21-25; 2 Cor 10:4. For the complete paraphrase on Luke 24:27, see CWE 48:235-70 (LB 7:469-84).

[14]Bucer, *Epistola D. Pauli ad Ephesios*, 102v (cf. David F. Wright, "Bucer, Martin," in *DMBI*, 251); citing Num 21:8-9; Jn 3:14-15.

"quench the Spirit," does not loftily tie them up in empty speculations without the Word but immediately adds that prophecies are not to be despised. By this, no doubt, he intimates that the light of the Spirit is put out as soon as prophecies fall into contempt. What say these fanatics, swollen with pride, who consider this the one excellent illumination when, carelessly forsaking and bidding farewell to God's Word, they, no less confidently than boldly, seize on whatever they may have conceived while snoring? Certainly a far different sobriety befits the children of God, bereft of the whole light of truth, who thus are not unaware that the Word is the instrument by which the Lord dispenses the illumination of his Spirit to believers. For they know no other Spirit than him who dwelled and spoke in the apostles and by whose oracles they are continually recalled to the hearing of the Word. INSTITUTES 1.9.3.[15]

ONLY THE SCRIPTURES GIVE COMFORT.

CASPAR HUBERINUS: Christ shows us here very nicely how one should instruct and comfort the unfaithful, fearful, mistaken, miserable conscience: namely, with the Word of God, and not with human teaching. That is why Christ begins here with Moses and the prophets, and not with councils and papal decrees. Preachers should take this heavenly teaching as an example, that they should take up the prophets and search for Christ in them, and also open up the Gospels. This is how the hearts of their listeners will be set afire and alight and become devout, so that they may be able to endure all danger and distress and believe that their crucified Christ rose again from the dead, and became a Lord on heaven and on earth. Therefore, all righteous followers and disciples of Christ should take hold of, hear and have faith only in the holy Scriptures alone, as God our Lord also demands of us. ON THE MONDAY AFTER EASTER.[16]

24:28-32 Jesus Opens Their Eyes at the Breaking of the Bread

CHRIST DID NOT LIE TO HIS DISCIPLES. JOHN

CALVIN: Although some interpreters suggest that this is a different place than Emmaus, there is no reason for that, for the journey was not so long that they needed to stop to rest at a nearer inn. We know that seven thousand steps—even if a person walks slowly just for pleasure—would take only four hours at the most. Therefore I do not doubt that Christ had traveled all the way to Emmaus. Now, one might ask whether pretense is suitable in him who is the eternal truth of God. I answer that the Son of God is not bound by the law to make his plans public to everyone. But, because some forms of pretense are in fact lying, the difficulty is not yet cleared up, especially because this example leads many people to believe that they have license to lie. However, I answer that Christ might quite equally have pretended what is here mentioned without lying, just as he manifested himself as a traveler to them—there was the same reason for both. A somewhat more subtle solution is found in Augustine (To Consentius, bk. 2, chap. 13, and in Questions on the Gospels, chap. 51), for he wants to judge this sort of fiction among tropes and figures, then next among parables and fables. For me, this one explanation suffices: just as Christ for a time veiled the eyes of those with whom he was speaking, so that, having assumed a different persona, they would think him a common stranger, so when he revealed his plan to continue on his journey at that time, it was not that he pretended that what he had decided to do was something different than it was, but only that he wished to conceal from them the mode of his departure. None will deny that he had "gone farther," because then he was separated from human fellowship. So by this pretense he did not deceive his disciples but held them in suspense for a little while, until the right time had come for him to make himself known. Therefore, those who call him a patron of lying make themselves ridiculous; we would never be allowed to use his example as an excuse to lie, any more than we could emulate his divine power in closing anyone's

---

[15]LCC 20:95-96* (CO 2:71-72); citing Lk 24:27, 45; 1 Thess 5:19-20.
[16]Huberinus, Postilla Teütsch, 2:B7r-v; citing Is 8; Jn 5, 8.

eyes to sight. It is safest to hold as a rule what was written before—we should speak with truth and simplicity. It is not that the Lord himself ever departed from the law of his Father, but rather than worrying about the letter of the commandments, he held to the true heart of the law; but because of the weakness of our senses, we need another bridle. COMMENTARY ON A HARMONY OF THE GOSPELS.[17]

GOD INSPIRED THEIR PRAYER TO CHRIST. MARTIN LUTHER: God inspired [these pious people] to invite Christ, but they did not yet know that this would be salvation. The prayer is good, but God rejects the means that we suggest to him. Likewise it also happens with us; God comes to help us sometimes through another way or a better way. AFTERNOON SERMON ON EASTER MONDAY (1524).[18]

JESUS FINALLY REVEALS HIMSELF TO THE DISCIPLES. JOHANN BAUMGART (POMARIUS): It is also comforting that he portrayed himself as a stranger at the beginning but finally allowed himself to be seen and recognized for who he really was. He does this often with us, for if we are distressed and forsaken by everyone in our life as pilgrims, he often shows himself to us as a stranger. We imagine that he will always be charming and friendly to us, as if he were completely meek and gentle, as if he never wanted to abandon us but always wanted to glorify and bless us, so that we would never lack for anything. But when we fall into trouble and need, and death approaches, then he often appears in an unfamiliar form and shows himself to us as a stranger and a pilgrim, who would join his path to ours and stop with us to refresh himself. Then we begin to complain and hesitate and to think that the Lord has turned his face away from us, abandoning us and forgetting his own. Then along with Gideon we would hardly believe that the Lord was with us and among us, because things were going so badly. And we would often ask along with Saint Anthony, "O Lord, where were you when I was miserably and wretchedly beaten and tormented?"[19] But that is only an unfamiliar image with which the Lord tests us, as his Father tested him in the desert, as Joseph tested his brothers and as he himself tested Jacob and the Canaanite women. But finally he allows himself to be seen again in his happy, loving form and proves himelf to be friendly and comforting, just as he did to Jacob, the Canaanite mother and these disciples, so that we long for his presence more and more. THE GOSPEL ON EASTER MONDAY.[20]

THE EYES OF FAITH SEE BECAUSE THEY BELIEVE. DESIDERIUS ERASMUS: After his death Jesus made his body available gradually and sparingly, either because human weakness would not bear the majesty of the resurrected body or to accustom them slowly to being without the sight of his body; it was going to be taken away soon so that they would then love him in spirit. . . . When Jesus was taken away in body they now saw him better than when he was with them in body. Their eyes had been held fast because they did not believe. Now, though he was not there, they saw him with the eyes of faith. PARAPHRASE ON THE GOSPEL OF LUKE 24:31-32.[21]

JESUS' HABIT OF BREAKING BREAD. CARDINAL CAJETAN: Four actions of Jesus are described concerning the bread: taking, blessing, breaking and offering. And only after the breaking of the bread did the two disciples recognize him, so that we understand there to have been a miracle in the breaking of the bread. That is, he broke the bread with his hands as others cut it with a knife, this, we believe, was Jesus' customary way of breaking the bread. Thus the disciples from this custom of Jesus recognized him. COMMENTARY ON LUKE 24:30.[22]

---

[17]CTS 33:361-63* (CO 45:807-8).
[18]LEA 5:283 (cf. WA 15:528).
[19]See Athanasius, *Life of St. Anthony* (or Antony), para. 10.
[20]Baumgart, *Postilla*, 370v-371r; citing Ps 34; Mt 11:28-30; 28:20; Jn 14:18-21; Ps 31; Is 49; Judg 8; Mt 4:1-11; Gen 44; 32:22-32; Mt 15:21-28.
[21]CWE 48:271, 272 (LB 7:485).
[22]Cajetan, *Evangelia*, 153v.

WE MUST FOLLOW CHRIST'S EXAMPLE IN CELEBRATING HIS SUPPER. BALTHASAR
HUBMAIER: Now let the priest sit down with the people and open his mouth, explaining the Scriptures concerning Christ, so that the eyes of those who are gathered together may be opened, which were still somewhat darkened or closed, so that they may recognize Christ, who was a man, a prophet, mighty in works and teaching before God and all the people, and how the highest bishops among the priests and princes gave him over to condemnation to death and how they crucified him, and how he has redeemed Israel, that is, all believers. The priest shall also rebuke those who are foolish and slow to believe all the things that Moses and the prophets have spoken, that he may kindle and make fervent and warm the hearts of those at the table, that they may be afire in fervent meditation of his bitter suffering and death in contemplation, love and thanksgiving, so that the congregation with its whole heart, soul and strength calls out to him: "Stay with us, O Christ! It is toward evening, and the day is now far spent. Abide with us, O Jesus, abide with us. For where you are not, there everything is darkness, night and shadow, but you are the true Sun, light and shining brightness. The one whose way you illuminate cannot go astray." A FORM FOR CHRIST'S SUPPER (1527).[23]

PEACE WITH GOD IGNITES OUR HEART.
MARTIN LUTHER: I want to dismiss the question whether he gave them the sacrament or not. Now the breaking of the bread means that the apostles distributed the Word among the people. He himself blessed it, and immediately they acknowledged Christ—with this it certainly follows that we should know who he is and how to see him correctly. *Then* we can know why our heart burned within us. The heart says, "Hey! This is a merciful God!" And love and desire follow, burning in our heart. This light lets us see God in no other way than as pure sweetness. When it sees grace and lovingkindness abundantly, it knows that God did this and sees that he loves us with a perfect love. This is pure grace and kindness. Once the heart seizes him in this way, it cannot see anything terrifying in him. It is not even possible! Instead the heart must be joyous and gain peace, as Paul says: "Therefore, having been justified by faith we have peace with God." Otherwise there is never any peace or joy in our heart.

This is how everything is to be understood that stands in Scripture concerning the cleansing of sin, baptism—in everything like this we must see Christ in this way: faith is in our heart, and it recognizes what Christ is. This is the washing and the bath through which we become pure, get a good conscience and whatever else is like that. The Scriptures give him more than a hundred thousand names to this one acknowledgment, and God always lets this be preached in various ways. Nevertheless it is no more than this recognition; God cannot suffer that we preach anything else. When it happens that we have this confession or faith in our heart it is pure and lovely splendor. Thus, God and the holy Scriptures cannot suffer when we lead people to another path; he cannot suffer when we add something in addition to this. SERMON ON EASTER MONDAY (1521).[24]

COMMUNION IS A MEMORIAL. PETER WALPOT:
This is a symbol: a feast of thanksgiving, that the body of Christ was sacrificed for us. Thus, the bread that is offered, broken, taken and eaten is only the body of Christ as memorial or exhortation. Likewise the cup that is taken, distributed and drunk is the blood of Christ as memorial and remembrance. Now that this is true, we see in the two disciples to whom Christ appeared on the road to Emmaus after his resurrection. And even though he explained the Scriptures to them and their hearts were aflame, still they did not recognize him. Only in the breaking of the bread ... did they finally recognize him, preparing themselves quickly and proclaiming it to the other disciples—

---

[23]CRR 5:394-95* (QGT 9:355-56); citing Lk 24:31; Jn 8:12.　　[24]WA 9:669-70; citing Rom 5:1.

how they saw the Lord and how they recognized him in breaking of the bread. THE GREAT ARTICLE BOOK: ON THE EUCHARIST.[25]

BREAK OPEN THE SCRIPTURES TO LEARN THAT CHRIST IS LORD. MARTIN LUTHER: Why did he disappear? When through the gospel Christ's goodness and God's is revealed to us and our conscience is comforted, we are directed to and strengthened in the cross. These two disciples do not lose Christ's knowledge or presence. His presence is sweet to them, as his Word is sweet to us, but when he disappeared, then crossbearing begins and he allows us to be tested as if he were very, very distant. Because he does not allow his Word to be threatened, his disappearance follows after the breaking of the bread. No one knows Christ without breaking bread; therefore, whoever does not break bread does not know Christ—even if the entire Scriptures were kept in mind, nothing would help you. . . . Christ is not known through carrying bread, but by its breaking—when he distributed and blessed it. When we want to help, we carry bread; we have the Scriptures in a basket, but we do not learn that Christ is Lord. AFTERNOON SERMON ON EASTER MONDAY (1524).[26]

THE WORD INFLAMES AND COMFORTS THEM. JOHANN SPANGENBERG: What do the disciples do after they recognized Christ? They spoke to each other: "Were not our hearts burning within us as he spoke to us along the way and opened the Scriptures to us?" Here we can see what the holy Scripture is capable of doing: it can take listeners who are weak in faith, cold in love and fainthearted in hope, and wonderfully inflame, comfort and strengthen them. For that is the way and the capacity of the divine Word: it strengthens foolish, discouraged hearts and consciences, it comforts miserable, lamenting hearts and sets them aflame

in faith, love and hope, so that they cannot keep silent but must announce to all the world all the blessings of God which they have experienced. And that is what these disciples do. Before, they were leaving Jerusalem and were so afraid that they knew of nowhere to stay. Now, because they had seen that Christ was again alive and they recognized him, they took heart again, and in that same hour they got up and turned back toward Jerusalem. GOSPEL ON EASTER MONDAY.[27]

24:33-35 They Return to Jerusalem to Tell the Others

THOSE IN EMMAUS HURRY TO BRING COMFORT TO THE REST. THE ENGLISH ANNOTATIONS: Considering the sorrow into which the disciples were now plunged, these two thought they would bring comfort to them by assuring them that Christ was risen from the dead. Therefore they left their own present affairs and rest and set off for what was far more necessary. They had such joy that they greatly desired to communicate it to the others. All private interest must give way to God's honor and the comfort and salvation of souls. And in these matters, we cannot put off until tomorrow what we can do today. . . .

It must have been very late when these two arrived back after supper, returning from Emmaus to Jerusalem back to the disciples. Yet they found them still up and conferring together about the passion and resurrection of Christ. Those who came to bring comfort found it here as well: that is how God rewarded their mutual concern to confirm the faith of each other. The disciples relate how Christ was risen and how he appeared to Peter. What we read in Mark 16:13, "they did not believe them," is to be understood distributively, as if he had said, some (like Thomas, see Jn 20:25) did not yet believe, but some of them believed. ANNOTATIONS UPON THE GOSPEL ACCORDING TO SAINT LUKE 24:33-34.[28]

[25]QGT 12:130.
[26]WA 15:529. Before this Luther, interpreting allegorically, states that "the bread is the gospel."
[27]Spangenberg, *Postilla . . . von Ostern biß auffs Aduent*, Xr.
[28]Downame, ed., *Annotations*, Aaa1r*; citing 1 Cor 15:5.

God Sees More Deeply into Our Hearts Than We Do. Martin Luther: It is not enough that you come so far, that you have God's Word, that it calls you and to that end you feel your misfortune, for it pulls you in. But Christ is there and he waits for you, so that he might help you, and what more should he do? But he excludes no one except for the rude jerks and dirtbags who do not believe it earnestly. Therefore you should go toward him and hold onto him, because Christ sees much deeper into your heart than you can, as we can see here in this Gospel. These two poor men would not have dared to hope that Christ would meet them there, nor did they ever expect such grace that Christ himself would come to them while they were talking about him, [but he came] and opened their hearts so that they recognized him. When this happened, their hearts were made so happy that they could not stay in this place, but instead they ran back to the other disciples and told them how the Lord revealed himself to them. Then they were filled with a joy which none of them had even expected, because it lay so deep in the bottom of their hearts that they did not themelves see that they longed for such a thing, although they knew in their hearts that there was nothing they would rather see in the world than that the Lord Christ would rise again and become king. Therefore God sees more deeply into the bottom of our hearts than we ourselves, and gives us more than we desire. Sermon on Easter Monday (1523).[29]

---

[29]WA 12:501-2.

24:36-49 JESUS APPEARS TO THE DISCIPLES

³⁶As they were talking about these things, Jesus himself stood among them, and said to them, "Peace to you!" ³⁷But they were startled and frightened and thought they saw a spirit. ³⁸And he said to them, "Why are you troubled, and why do doubts arise in your hearts? ³⁹See my hands and my feet, that it is I myself. Touch me, and see. For a spirit does not have flesh and bones as you see that I have." ⁴⁰And when he had said this, he showed them his hands and his feet. ⁴¹And while they still disbelieved for joy and were marveling, he said to them, "Have you anything here to eat?" ⁴²They gave him a piece of broiled fish,ᵃ ⁴³and he took it and ate before them.

⁴⁴Then he said to them, "These are my words that I spoke to you while I was still with you, that everything written about me in the Law of Moses and the Prophets and the Psalms must be fulfilled." ⁴⁵Then he opened their minds to understand the Scriptures, ⁴⁶and said to them, "Thus it is written, that the Christ should suffer and on the third day rise from the dead, ⁴⁷and that repentance and forgiveness of sins should be proclaimed in his name to all nations, beginning from Jerusalem. ⁴⁸You are witnesses of these things.⁴⁹And behold, I am sending the promise of my Father upon you. But stay in the city until you are clothed with power from on high."

a Some manuscripts add *and some honeycomb*

OVERVIEW: After the return of the two men who had gone to Emmaus, the disciples were gathered together eagerly discussing what they knew and hoped regarding Jesus. It was into that context of hope and fear that Jesus made his appearance. He came into their midst and offered them peace, but they were "startled and terrified," as if they had seen a ghost. Although this was not too surprising, considering that they had seen Jesus die and knew he had been buried, it showed a consistent lack of faith both in what they had been taught about the resurrection and what the various followers of Jesus had witnessed. So Jesus chastised and corrected them and then turned to instruct them about his resurrection so that he could lead, strengthen and renew their faith. He went about instructing and confirming them in two ways: first, by showing them the reality of his body; and second, by showing them the truth through the Scriptures. He brought their attention to his flesh and bones, the wounds in his hands, feet and side, allowing them to touch him and confirm that he had a true body. For those who still were not sure, he also ate some fish, which gave some difficulty to commentators on this text, for how could Jesus eat and have his body process the food in the usual way? How could such a conversation even be broached appropriately? This was a topic over which people must have argued, because several writers note the dilemma, but they insist there is no real problem here. Because elimination of waste was a bodily process to which Jesus' glorified body must no longer be subject, God could make that bit of food "vanish away into nothing" quite easily, Mayer suggests. After all, the angels who visited Abraham ate with him, and their bodies (and presumably the food they had eaten) vanished afterward. If God could raise a body from death to life, it would hardly be a problem for him to deal appropriately with any food that Jesus ate. After proving the reality of his body through eating, Jesus again turned to the Scriptures and opened their minds to understand the truth—his suffering and death, and his resurrection as well, were prophesied throughout Scripture and had been predestined by God. But now it was time for his disciples to grow the kingdom, as Brenz writes, and teach others through the preaching of the gospel. Despite the fact that his followers had been afraid and doubtful, lacking in both faith and understanding, Jesus wanted them to bring this message of salvation to others. They were to begin in Jerusalem, waiting for the gift of the Spirit, but then they should proclaim it to all nations, bringing its benefits to all people.

24:36-43 Jesus Appears and Eats with the Disciples

CHRIST COMES IN OUR MIDST AND BRINGS INTERNAL PEACE. JOHANN SPANGENBERG: Why does Christ enter into the midst of them? Christ always held the middle place. In the cradle, he lay in the midst of the animals, oxen and donkeys. In the temple, he sat in the middle among the teachers. On the cross, he hung in the middle between the murderers. And here in the house, he stands in the midst of his disciples. What he wants to show by this is that he is the true mediator between God and human beings. He is the proper nourishment and leader for our souls, the true doctor and teacher and the only comfort in trouble and mortal danger.

And what does Christ say to them? He says, "Peace be with you." Here we must know that because the kingdom of Christ is not of this world, he does not bring us worldly peace, for he says, "In the world you will have tribulation" and difficulties, but he brings the divine, inner, spiritual peace, the peace of hearts and consciences that comes from faith. . . . And what is this inner peace? It is when a person is at peace with God in his heart and in his conscience. This peace comes from faith and God's Word. Christ wishes this peace for his disciples and all the faithful. We cannot find any external, worldly peace now, for it is not at all possible in the kingdom of Satan, so we should rather seek after this internal peace which we are able to receive. GOSPEL ON EASTER TUESDAY.[1]

CHRIST CHASTISES THE DISCIPLES FOR THEIR ERROR. CASPAR HUBERINUS: We see here how Christ corrects and chastises his followers, although he is very patient with their weakness and frailty. He does not approve of it, however, and say that it is acceptable, but rather he chastises and improves what is not right. That is a special aspect of love, that a stronger Christ tolerates his weaker brothers and bears with them for a while. But nevertheless, he chastises them all the same, both earnestly and with brotherly love, so that he should not make a right or custom out of such weakness. Therefore those people make a mistake when out of love they do not chastise the wrong in another but allow him to become corrupt. In fact, through their hypocrisy and coddling, they accept as good and right what they see and hear to be wrong. This is especially the case with very important people, for people have to be careful about ill will, damages, danger, anger and punishments. So people keep quiet, because no one wants to hang the bell on the cat. But one should chastise what needs to be chastised with God's Word. However, it must be done out of love, and not out of jealousy, or to take revenge or in bitterness. We should never upset, hinder or do damage through unnecessary, untimely or needless chastisement. Rather, we should encourage and help the situation, the person and the right thing. ON EASTER TUESDAY.[2]

CHRIST'S APPEARANCES AND BODY CONFIRM THEIR FAITH. MILES COVERDALE: And this is the reason that Christ appears so often to his disciples, instructing them so fully and so perfectly of his resurrection: so that he could make them steadfast in their faith, and to assure them of this joy. That is why he shows them his body and allows them to touch him. A body that could be touched proves to them that it is a true body: the immortal body shows that it is glorified and of highest honor; meanwhile the prints of his wounds declare that it is the same body that it was before. He shows them the tokens of victory, as a mighty

---

[1]Spangenberg, Postilla . . . von Ostern biß auffs Aduent, XIr-v; citing 1 Tim 2:5; Jn 16:33.

[2]Huberinus, Postilla Teütsch, 2:Dr.

vanquisher of death; he shows the wounds he received for them in battle, and likewise his side that was opened, declaring his great love. He showed his wounds to them to heal the wounds of their unbelief, as if he would say: "Look at me, and fight valiantly; no one shall be crowned without first fighting the battle. But to the one who overcomes in the conflict, I will grant to eat of the bread of heaven, and will crown him forever." FRUITFUL LESSONS UPON THE PASSION, BURIAL, RESURRECTION, ASCENSION AND OF THE SENDING OF THE HOLY SPIRIT (1593).[3]

CHRIST ATE TO AFFIRM HIS HUMANITY. JOHN MAYER: The mystery of this place is quite diverse according to those who find different allegories here, and so I think it is the safest thing to hold nothing else but that such meat that they had, they offered to him, and he ate it to prove that his body was a true body. . . . Therefore, along with Calvin, let us shun curiosity and hold this to be the true and pious meditation on this place: Christ ate for our confirmation, just as in the beginning he took on a nature which needed the support of meat and drink for us, that in all things he might become wholly ours. If there seems to be any difficulty arising from the various bodily processes that would go along with eating this meat, we must know that as he made all things originally out of nothing, so he could make a little meat vanish away again into nothing. When the angels appeared to Abraham, they were endued with true bodies, and so they truly ate. They did not eat out of infirmity, but because it was granted to them to assume bodies for Abraham's sake, it was also granted to him that they should take a meal in his tent. And once their message was ended, we believe that their bodies vanished, so why should we deny that the same thing happened to their food? A COMMENTARY ON THE NEW TESTAMENT, LUKE 24:42.[4]

24:44-49 *Jesus Explains the Meaning of the Scriptures*

GOD'S WORD IS THE BASIS OF OUR FAITH AND COMFORT. JOHANN BAUMGART (POMARIUS): In addition, he reinforces his speech, "I am he," from the Scriptures—the Law, Prophets and Psalms. By this he teaches us that we should learn the truth not from the dead but from the Scriptures. We should not believe in any apparition without God's Word. Also, his suffering, death and resurrection did not occur by chance but happened only through God's predestination, and through them he has gained for us every fruit and benefit. And through the preaching of grace and repentance and the office of the Word, these benefits will be offered to all. He also teaches us that sorrowful and fearful hearts should not only follow what they can see with their eyes or what is manifested to their senses, or look for the strengthening of their faith through those things which one can see and grasp through the five senses. But rather they should rely for all things on God's Word and should draw comfort and strength from it. THE GOSPEL ON EASTER TUESDAY.[5]

CHRIST'S RESURRECTION MUST BE PREACHED FOR THE BENEFIT OF ALL. JOHANNES BRENZ: After our Savior Christ had proved by clear and evident signs to his disciples that he was risen from death to life, he proceeded to set forth what would be necessary in order to expand the borders of his kingdom and to set forth that glory of his majesty on earth. For Christ came into the world not only to benefit the nation of the Jews but also that he might be salvation to the whole world. Christ rose again from death, not that this person or that one might have life but that the happiness of everlasting life might be offered to all nations. And there is no better and convenient instrument through which these things might be revealed to the whole world and to all nations than the preaching of the gospel concerning Christ. And that is why Christ

---

[3]*Writings and Translations of Myles Coverdale*, 343*; citing 2 Tim 2:3-5; Rev 2:10-11.
[4]Mayer, *Commentarie vpon the New Testament*, 376*; citing Gen 18:1-8.

[5]Baumgart, *Postilla*, 374v-375r; citing Deut 18:11.

did not only prove his resurrection before his disciples but also ordained that open preaching of the gospel which would bring the benefit of his resurrection to all of us. An Ecclesiasticall Exposition upon Saint Luke 24.[6]

Preach Repentance, Then Faith in Christ.

Dirk Philips: Now the law teaches the knowledge of sin, and the fear of the Lord comes out of such knowledge—that beginning of all wisdom without which no one can be justified. And out of the fear of the Lord comes a broken, defeated and humbled heart which is well-pleasing to God. Therefore the law serves partly for the new birth. Because no one can be born or made alive and no one can believe the gospel unless he first genuinely repents, just as the Lord Christ himself testifies. He taught the people repentance first and after that faith; he has also commanded his apostles to do so.

But the gospel is the word of grace, the joyful message of Christ Jesus, the only born Son of God, the only Redeemer and Savior, who has given himself for us, so that he would redeem us from the power of Satan, sin and eternal death, making us children and heirs of our heavenly Father—a royal priesthood, a holy people, a chosen lineage belonging to God in the Spirit. . . . That is the true gospel, the pure teaching of our God, full of grace and mercy, full of comfort, salvation and eternal life. It was given to us from God out of his grace—without our merit and works of the law—on account of the will of the only and precious Savior Jesus Christ who submitted himself under the law for us and has become for all believers the fulfillment of the law for eternal salvation, provided we accept it with true faith. The Enchiridion: The Congregation of God.[7]

Christ's Death and Resurrection Fulfill the Prophecies. Johannes Brenz:

As if he should say that the Scripture concerning the majesty of the kingdom of Christ must be so understood that it teaches this kingdom is not of a physical sort here on earth. Rather, it teaches that Christ must suffer the cross and death in this world and through these experiences enter into the spiritual majesty of his kingdom. For the very first promise we have concerning Christ brings us to understand that he must suffer in this world: "The seed of the woman shall tread on your head, and you shall tread on his heel." To tread on Christ's heel is to cast him into various afflictions and into corporal death. The sacrifices which the patriarchs offered also signified that Christ would shed his blood, that is to say, that he would die. "And to rise again from death." The Scripture does not only make mention of the passion and death of Christ but also adds his resurrection. It makes no sense to omit those places of Scripture that plainly prophesy that Christ will rise again—in fact, there was never any prophet who wrote that Christ should suffer and die, without also testifying plainly that he would rise again and reign forever. And when he would rise again, what should become of his kingdom? Would he then gather together an army of soldiers and invade the kingdoms of this world with external violence? Of course not. But it was written that Christ should suffer and that he would rise again from death on the third day. An Ecclesiasticall Exposition upon Saint Luke 24.[8]

They Were to Preach First in Jerusalem.

John Bunyan: These words were spoken by Christ after he rose from the dead, and they are spoken here in a historical manner, but they also contain in them a formal commission, along with a special clause. The commission is, as you see, for the preaching of the gospel and is very distinctly inserted in the holy record by Matthew and Mark: "Go therefore and make disciples of all nations," and "Go into the world and preach the gospel to

---

[6]Marlorat, ed., *Catholike and Ecclesiasticall Exposition of the Holy Gospell After S. Marke and Luke*, 334-35*; citing Is 49:6.
[7]CRR 6:359-60* (BRN 10:389-90); citing Rom 7:7; Sir 1:16-17; Ps 51:17; Mt 3:2; Lk 24:46-47; 1 Tim 2:3-4; Tit 2:13; Gal 1:4; Heb 2:15; 1 Pet 2:9.

[8]Marlorat, ed., *Catholike and Ecclesiasticall Exposition of the Holy Gospell After S. Marke and Luke*, 337*; citing Gen 3:15.

every creature." The special clause is only mentioned by Luke, who says that, while Christ wanted to have the doctrine of repentance and remission of sins preached in his name among all nations, he wanted it to be offered first to the people of Jerusalem. "Preach it," says Christ, "in all nations, but begin in Jerusalem."

So although the apostles had a commission so large as to give them warrant to go and preach the gospel in all the world, yet this clause limited them in the beginning of their ministry: they were to begin this work in Jerusalem. . . .

Second, I now come to the point of what it meant to preach the gospel to them. It was, Luke says, to preach to them repentance and remission of sins in Christ's name. Or, as Mark has it, to "bid them repent and believe the gospel." It is not that repentance is a cause of remission, but rather it is a sign of our hearty reception of it. Therefore repentance is included here to indicate that no pretended faith in the gospel is any good without it.

And he does this on purpose, for he would not have them deceive themselves. For what kind of faith does a person have if he expects the remission of sins in the name of Christ, but is not heartily sorry for them? Or how can a person give to others a satisfactory account of his true subjection to the gospel, if he continues to be impenitent? GOOD NEWS FOR THE VILEST OF HUMAN BEINGS.[9]

JESUS WILL STILL USE THE DISCIPLES IN HIS MINISTRY. JOHN TRAPP: Prepare to preach the gospel to every creature. And take it for a singular seal of my love that, despite your recent and shameful defection and desertion of me, I will still employ you as my witnesses and make use of your ministry. A COMMENTARY UPON THE GOSPEL ACCORDING TO SAINT LUKE 24.[10]

[9]Bunyan, *Jerusalem-Sinner Saved*, 1-2, 6-7*; citing Mt 28:19; Mk 16:15; 1:15.
[10]Trapp, *Commentary or Exposition*, 425*; citing Mk 16:15.

24:50-53 THE ASCENSION

⁵⁰Then he led them out as far as Bethany, and lifting up his hands he blessed them. ⁵¹While he blessed them, he parted from them and was carried up into heaven. ⁵²And they worshiped him and returned to Jerusalem with great joy, ⁵³and were continually in the temple blessing God.

OVERVIEW: In Luke's Gospel narrative, Jesus and the disciples move immediately from his appearance to them to an area outside the city where he blessed them, and then ascended into heaven. The blessing, Becon notes, was especially for the ministry in which they were now to be engaged, that is, the preaching of the gospel. Likewise, this blessing rests on everyone with the vocation to preach and teach the gospel, and it is a blessing that brings its fruit to all of us. Then Jesus—at least in his physical, visible nature—went to heaven to be with the Father, but he promised that his Spirit would be present with his disciples. This heaven was seen by some as not so much a place as a state of being.[1] The disciples' response to the ascension is the opposite of what we might imagine—they were energized by it and filled with joy. They chose to stay in Jerusalem as he had commanded, despite the great danger to themselves, and to worship publicly in the temple with greater reverence to him than ever before. Calvin suggests that while they had revered him as the Messiah, now they worshiped him as the "King of glory and Judge of the world." Now the resurrection was confirmed for them, and they were free from doubt, so despite the constant danger in which they lived, they felt free to praise and glorify God's name for the salvation offered through his Son, Jesus Christ.

THE GOSPELS SHOULD NOT BE SEPARATED.
DESIDERIUS ERASMUS: This passage is added to the Acts of the Apostles, too. For Luke wrote this history to Theophilus. Now he himself joins it with the first. Acts is clearly part of the evangelical history. Yes, it did not seem good to us to separate John from the Evangelists. We divided the two books of Luke and placed Acts as near as possible. ANNOTATIONS ON LUKE 24:52-53.[2]

24:50-51 Jesus Ascends into Heaven

CHRIST BLESSES US AND THE WORK OF THE GOSPEL. THOMAS BECON: Luke very appropriately signifies in his evangelical history that when Christ was ready to ascend into heaven, he lifted up his hands and blessed his disciples, not as the papist bishops are wont to do by wagging their fingers over the people who kneel down before them, but rather he prayed and blessed the ministries which he enjoined on them, that is, that they should preach the gospel to every creature—that is to say, to every sort of person, to all nations, to all people. . . .

Therefore, wherever the gospel is taught, Christ lifts up his hands and brings forth his blessing, that it may bring forth fruit and not return in vain. And it is without doubt a great comfort that Christ, at the very time when he was going to ascend, lifted up his hands and blessed his disciples. For by this he declares most evidently that his ascension brings to us sweet consolation and comfort, great help

---

[1]Because of the Christological implications—especially for Christ's presence in the Eucharist—the reformers disagreed about how to understand the ascension. See the above overview for 22:7-23, see further "Christology," OER 1:314-22; Jill Raitt, *The Colloquy of Montbéliard: Religion and Politics in the Sixteenth Century* (New York: Oxford University Press, 1993), esp. 73-109, 110-23.

[2]LB 6:332; Pellikan, however, changed the order of the Gospels and Acts so that Luke's twofold work could be uninterrupted: Matthew, John, Mark, Luke and Acts.

against sin, devil, death and hell, and diverse noble gifts for the edification of God's church, and finally his blessing, good will and favor. And after this transitory life, it also brings us everlasting life, with immortal glory and unspeakable joy. For why would Christ have given so loving and gentle a token of his loving and gentle good will toward us by lifting up his hands and blessing us, if he did not have good will toward us? He would also not have suffered us to join with him in his kingdom. Seeing then that he lifted up his hands and wished well to the disciples and their newly enjoined ministry, we see a most evident argument, a sure sign and manifest token that he bears a singular good will toward us and that his desire is that we should always be partakers of this blessing and receive from it great consolation and comfort through the preaching of the gospel, which is the power of God to salvation for as many as believe it. ASCENSION DAY.[3]

CHRIST DWELLS WITH GOD IN GLORIOUS LIGHT. MILES COVERDALE: By "heaven" we understand the incomprehensible light in which God dwells and to which no mortal can attain. Christ came to us from this place, and he returns there again, into the invisible glory and clarity of God. For the eternal Word and Power of God, dwelling in God's incomprehensible light from everlasting, became a human being and had his conversation on earth in all parts, except for sin, as an entirely true human being. But when he had fully finished and thoroughly ended the word that was given to him by commission of his heavenly Father and had obeyed him even to death, as he had honored and glorified his Father in all things on earth, so it was appropriate that the Father should also glorify his Son. And therefore he raised him from the dead and took him up into heaven—not in the sense of his Godhead, for in that sense he was always in heaven, but in the sense of his humanity. For his true human nature, which he took on himself for our sakes, is carried and taken up out of this world

into the invisible honor and glory, in the highest incomprehensibility and into the perfect fruition of the Godhead.

In this honor and glory, Christ dwells and reigns, and yet among those who are his, he finishes and performs all things by his Spirit. He governs in the hearts of the faithful through belief, through love, through patience and through innocence of life. FRUITFUL LESSONS UPON THE PASSION, BURIAL, RESURRECTION, ASCENSION AND OF THE SENDING OF THE HOLY SPIRIT (1593).[4]

WHAT IS THE DIFFERENCE BETWEEN THE RESURRECTION AND ASCENSION? MARTIN LUTHER: Through the resurrection Christ became Lord; through the ascension he accepts his rule and administration. These two things are different. My Hans[5] is also lord of my goods; still I do not allow him to rule immediately. To ascend to heaven and sit at the right hand is truly the same as to administer the kingdom. TABLE TALK (1532).[6]

THE BENEFITS OF CHRIST'S ASCENSION. JOHN CALVIN: From this our faith receives many benefits. First it understands that the Lord by his ascent to heaven opened the way into the heavenly kingdom, which had been closed through Adam. Because he entered heaven in our flesh, as if in our name, it follows, as the apostle says, that in a sense we already "sit with God in the heavenly places in him," so that we do not await heaven with a bare hope but in our Head already possess it.

Second, as faith recognizes, it is to our great benefit that Christ resides with the Father. For, having entered a sanctuary not made with hands, he appears before the Father's face as our constant advocate and intercessor. Thus he turns the Father's eyes to his own righteousness to avert his gaze from our sins. He so reconciles the Father's heart to us that by his intercession he prepares a way and access to the Father's throne. He fills

---

[3]Becon, *New Postil*, 263v-264v*; citing Rom 3:22.

[4]*Writings and Translations of Myles Coverdale*, 382-83*.
[5]Luther's oldest son, Johannes (1526–1575).
[6]WATR 1:111-12 no. 267*.

with grace and kindness the throne that for miserable sinners would otherwise have been filled with dread.

Third, faith comprehends his might, in which reposes our strength, power, wealth and glorying against hell. "When he ascended into heaven he took captivity captive," and despoiling his enemies, he enriches his own people and daily lavishes spiritual riches on them. He therefore sits on high, transfusing us with his power, that he may vivify us to spiritual life, sanctify us by his Spirit, adorn his church with diverse gifts of his grace, keep it safe from all harm by his protection, restrain the raging enemies of his cross and of our salvation by the strength of his hand and finally hold all power in heaven and earth. All this he does until he shall lay low his enemies (who are our enemies too) and complete the building of his church. This is the true state of his kingdom; this is the power that the Father has conferred on him, until, in coming to judge the living and the dead, he accomplishes his final act. INSTITUTES 2.16.16.[7]

CHRIST'S INCARNATION AND ASCENSION ARE FOR US. MARTIN LUTHER: Christ became human, not like Adam and Eve—he from earth, she from her husband's rib. Christ is much more closely related to us. . . . He really is the son of a true natural woman. But Adam and Eve weren't born but created; Adam was made from earth, Eve from a rib. Therefore he is much closer to us than Eve and Adam, her husband. For here is flesh and blood; we should cherish this honor. . . .

He became a human being, now he is in heaven. . . . He proved what love he had for us, so that we can say, "We have a brother in heaven." We can and should accept what is his as ours. Damned is the one who does not accept what is his and who does not receive this joy in his heart. Every disciple should picture this favor in his heart, thank God for this. . . .

Why did he come? I say, he surely came to free us from sin and death. But I can hardly say anything about the honor of the entire human race. But for us Christians there is something else, something even greater that happened, here below we have honor. . . . Christ humbles himself in this way, so that he transferred all his honor—*all his honor*—in this poor flesh, and then ascends to majesty that causes angels to tremble. He humbled himself as a poor beggar. Up above the angels pray to him; here he serves us—he clothes himself in our muck. . . . If someone were an angel, he would choose instead to be a human being, so that he could say, "My flesh and blood sits over all the angels. Blessed is that creature called human being." SERMON AT HOME ON CHRISTMAS (1533).[8]

IN AND THROUGH US MAY YOUR KINGDOM COME. VALENTIN WEIGEL: Christ has come and has erected a new eternal temple through himself, that is, through his flesh and blood which he gives to us so that we would grow out of him, as if taken from his side like the woman from the man, and not he out of us—that is, not his flesh from our flesh, but rather we from his flesh. Thus, when Christ dwells and rules in faith, then his advent has happened to us—or his future coming, so we can correctly pray, "Your kingdom come." That is, God's kingdom not only is wherever Christ dwells in us with all his peace which overcomes the world, but also God extends or reigns through Christ in us. O blessed and forever blessed are they who find this advent of Christ in themselves. Only such people receive the benefit that Christ was born a human being. To them is the benefit that on a donkey Christ entered the earthly city Jerusalem. To them is the benefit of his suffering, death and resurrection. To them is the benefit that he will come again on the Last Day to judge the living and the dead.

If we are to enjoy God, it cannot happen from the outside; he must be in us, as he is in us through his Spirit whom he gave us. If we are to enjoy the kingdom of God, it must not be external to us, but

---

[7]LCC 20:524-25* (CO 2:383); citing Jn 14:3; Eph 2:6; Heb 7:25; 9:11-12; Rom 8:34; Eph 4:8 (cf. Vg; Ps 68:18); 1 Cor 15:25 (cf. Ps 110:1).

[8]WA 37:231-32.

in us, as it is in us. Therefore we pray "your kingdom come." If Christ is to be beneficial to us, then he must not remain external to us but must be in us and we in him, as it is written. "I am in you, and you are in me. Yes, on the Last Day you will recognize that I am in the Father and the Father is in me and I am in you." Never will we enter the kingdom of God if it is not also in us. Christ cannot make me holy if he remains outside me. I would have no fruit in me for eternal life, so little as a branch without the vine—how could the severed branch have energy and life if it does not remain in the vine?! In the same way, how could a person become holy if Christ is not in him and he also in Christ? For that reason everything is placed on this unseen advent of Christ to and in us. Otherwise, everything else would be forfeited and for nothing; his incarnation, birth, cross, death, resurrection and final coming would be absolutely worthless to us, because this unseen and yet discernable coming would not be in us. Our conscience testifies to this in the Holy Spirit. GOSPEL FOR THE FIRST SUNDAY IN ADVENT.[9]

THROUGH YOUR SPIRIT DRAW US INTO YOUR PRESENCE. BOOK OF COMMON PRAYER (1549): Grant, we beseech you, almighty God, that just as we believe your only begotten Son our Lord to have ascended into the heavens, so may we also in heart and mind ascend there and dwell with him continually. THE COLLECT FOR THE ASCENSION.[10]

24:52-53 The Disciples Returned to the Temple to Praise God

CHRIST DEPARTED IN THE FLESH BUT REMAINED IN THE SPIRIT. JOHANNES BRENZ: Although the disciples had lost sight of the Lord, they returned to Jerusalem with great joy. They felt then that what the Lord said to them was true,

namely, that it was good for them that he departed from them in the flesh. While he was with them in the flesh, they were altogether carnal and did not appreciate anything but what was fleshly. But when he departed according to the flesh and was present with them in the Spirit, they were wonderfully filled with joy and began to extol and magnify the name of the God. They obeyed the command which Christ had given them before to go to Jerusalem: "Stay in the city until you have been clothed with power from on high." It was very dangerous for them to be in Jerusalem in the midst of Christ's enemies, but they obeyed. If we fully weigh the circumstances, we will see that they returned almost to certain death. For why would those who put Christ to death so cruelly spare his disciples? But the power of the Spirit of Christ filled them with incredible joy and made them obedient to the work of their office. AN ECCLESIASTICALL EXPOSITION UPON SAINT MATHEWE 28.[11]

THEY WORSHIPED CHRIST AS THE KING OF GLORY. JOHN CALVIN: By the word *worshiping* Luke means, first, that the apostles were freed from doubt because now the majesty of Christ shone in all respects, so that there could be no doubt of the resurrection; second, for this same reason, they began to worship him with greater reverence than they had when they enjoyed his society on earth. Indeed, the worship which is here performed was given to him not so much as a master, or prophet or even the Messiah, for that part had only been half understood, but as the King of glory and Judge of the world. Because, however, Luke intended to compose a longer account, he only says here briefly what the apostles did in those ten days. The summary is that, through the passion of their joy, they burst out publicly into praises of God and were continually in the temple—not that they spent night and day there, but that they attended all the gatherings and were present at the fixed and

---

[9]Weigel, *Sämtliche Schriften*, 12,1:10-11; citing Jn 19:34; Gen 2:21-22; Mt 6:10 (cf. Lk 11:2); Jn 16:25-33; Phil 4:7; Mt 21:1-11; Acts 10:42; 1 Pet 4:5; 2 Tim 4:1; Rom 5:5; 1 Cor 6:11, 19-20; Lk 17:20-21; Jn 14:15-21; 15:1-11. [10]BCP 1549, 57*.

[11]Marlorat, ed., *Catholike and Ecclesiasticall Exposition of the Holy Gospell After S. Mathewe*, 758*.

usual hours to give thanks to God. Furthermore, this eagerness is opposed to the fear which earlier kept them hidden and shut up at home. COMMENTARY ON A HARMONY OF THE GOSPELS.[12]

LIFT UP YOUR HEARTS TO THE LORD! HEINRICH BULLINGER: Now all these things are written for our instruction and benefit. So certainly we understand the mystery of Christ from this gospel proclamation, and we see that he now reigns in heaven at the right hand of the Father. We adore the King of kings, our Lord and the life of all the saints—our head—by lifting our faces, hands and hearts to heaven. . . .

We should adore the ascended Lord by lifting up our minds. We also should recognize because of the Lord's resurrection and ascension that our Lord Jesus Christ is truly God and by faith we eat this life-giving food of our souls. So then, we should obey the divine precepts, doing what God commands us to do and avoiding what he prohibits us to do. And we should do it voluntarily, not resentfully and unenthusiastically but with joy. Again we should rejoice in him alone who has redeemed us; by grace we have been made his children and therefore also co-heirs. Finally we should be constantly in the temple, not in the corruptible Jerusalem temple but surely the temple of our hearts, that is, in the communion of saints. In him we should pray steadfastly. We should bless the Lord. We should praise his goodness and give thanks for the abundance of his benefits, anticipating his promise of life never-ending for us which he will undoubtedly give to us who believe that he is truthful and that he died for us. To him be thanks and praise forever and ever. Amen. COMMENTARY ON LUKE 24:50-53.[13]

---

[12]CO 45:827-28 (cf. CTS 33:392-93).

[13]Bullinger, *In Luculentum et Sacrosanctum Euangelium Secundum Lucam Commentariorum*, 147r-v.

Map of Europe at the Time of the Reformation

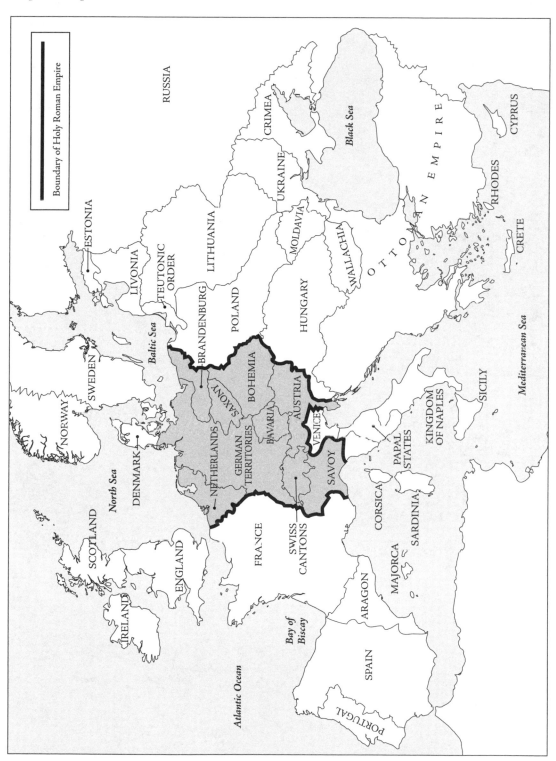

Timeline of the Reformation

	German Territories	France	Spain	Italy	Switzerland	Netherlands	British Isles
1337-1453		Hundred Years' War					Hundred Years' War
1378-1415		Western Schism (Avignon Papacy)		Western Schism			
1384							d. John Wycliffe
1414-1418							
1415				Council of Constance; d. Jan Huss			
1450	Invention of printing press						
1452				b. Leonardo da Vinci (d. 1519)			
1453				Fall of Constantinople			
1455-1485							War of Roses; Rise of House of Tudor
1456	Gutenberg Bible						
1460							
1466		b. Jacques Lafèvres d'Étaples (d. 1536)					
1467						b. Desiderius Erasmus (d. 1536)	b. John Colet (d. 1519)
1469	b. Antoius Broickwy von Königstein (d. 541)						
1470							b. John (Mair) Major (d. 1550)
1475				b. Michelangelo (d. 1564)			
1478	b. Wolfgang Capito (d. 1541)		Ferdinand and Isabella				b. Thomas More (d. 1535)
1480	b. Balthasar Hubmaier (d. 1528); b. Andreas Bodenstein von Karlstadt (d. 1541)						
1481-1530			Spanish Inquisition				
1482					b. Johannes Oecolampadius (d. 1531)		
1483	b. Martin Luther (d. 1546)						

	German Territories	France	Spain	Italy	Switzerland	Netherlands	British Isles
1484	b. Johann Spangenberg (d. 1550)				b. Huldrych Zwingli (d. 1531)		
1485	b. Johannes Bugenhagen (d. 1554)						b. Hugh Latimer (d. 1555)
1486	r. Frederick the Wise, Elector (d. 1525); b. Johann Eck (d. 1543)						
1488	b. Otto Brunfels (d. 1534)						b. Miles Coverdale (d. 1568)
1489	b. Thomas Müntzer (d. 1525); b. Kaspar von Schwenckfeld (d. 1561)						b. Thomas Cranmer (d. 1556)
1491	b. Martin Bucer (d. 1551)		b. Ignatius Loyola (d. 1556)				
1492			Defeat of Moors in Grenada; Columbus discovers America; Explusion of Jews from Spain				
1493	b. Justus Jonas (d. 1555)						
1494							b. William Tyndale (d. 1536)
1496	b. Andreas Osiander (d. 1552)					b. Menno Simons (d. 1561)	
1497	b. Philipp Melanchthon (d. 1560); b. Wolfgang Musculus (d. 1563) b. Johannes (Ferus) Wild (d. 1554)						
1498				d. Girolamo Savonarola	b. Conrad Grebel (d. 1526)		
1499	b. Johannes Brenz (d. 1570)			b. Peter Martyr Vermigli (d. 1562)			
1500			b. Charles V (-1558)				
1501	b. Erasmus Sarcerius (d. 1559)						
1502	Founding of University of Wittenberg					b. Frans Titelmans (d. 1537)	
1504					b. Heinrich Bullinger (d. 1575)		

	German Territories	France	Spain	Italy	Switzerland	Netherlands	British Isles
1505	Luther joins Augustinian Order			b. Benedict Aretius (d. 1574)			
1506		b. Augustin Marlorat (d. 1562)		Restoration to St. Peter's begins			
1507				Sale of indulgences approved to fund building			
1508	b. Lucas Lossius (d. 1582)						
1509		b. John Calvin (d. 1564)					r. Henry VIII (-1547)
1510	Luther moves to Rome						b. Nicholas Ridley (d. 1555)
1511	Luther moves to Wittenberg						
1512				Sistene Chapel completed			
1512-1517				Fifth Lateran Council; rejection of conciliarism			
1513	Luther lectures on Psalms			r. Pope Leo X (-1521)			b. John Knox (d. 1572)
1515	Luther lectures on Romans	r. Francis I (-1547); b. Peter Ramus (d. 1572)					
1516		Est. French National Church (via Concordat of Bologna)		Concordat of Bologna		publication of Erasmus's Greek New Testament	
1517	Tetzel sells indulgences in Saxony; Luther's Ninety-five Theses						
1518	Heidelberg Disputation; Luther examined by Eck at Diet of Augsburg			Diet of Augsburg			
1519	Leipzig Disputation	b. Theodore Beza (d. 1605)	Cortés conquers Aztecs; Portuguese sailor Magellan circumnavigates the globe		Zwingli appointed pastor of Grossmünster in Zurich; b. Rudolf Gwalther (d. 1586)		
1520	Publication of Luther's "Three Treatises"; Burning of papal bull in Wittenberg		Coronation of Charles V	Papal Bull v. Luther: *Exsurge Domine*			

	German Territories	France	Spain	Italy	Switzerland	Netherlands	British Isles
1521	Luther excommunicated; Diet/Edict of Worms—Luther condemned; Luther in hiding; Melanchthon's *Loci Communes*	French-Spanish War (-1526)	French-Spanish War; Loyola converts	Papal excommunication of Luther			Henry VIII publishes *Affirmation of the Seven Sacraments* against Luther; awarded title "Defender of the Faith" by Pope
1521-1522	Disorder in Wittenberg; Luther translates New Testament						
1521-1525		First and Second Habsburg–Valois War					
1522	Luther returns to Wittenberg; Luther's NT published; criticizes Zwickau prophets; b. Martin Chemnitz (d. 1586)		Publication of Complutensian Polyglot Bible under Cisneros		Sausage Affair & reform begins in Zurich under Zwingli		
1523	Knight's Revolt	Bucer begins ministry in Strasbourg	Loyola writes Spiritual Exercises	r. Pope Clement VII (-1534)	Iconoclasm in Zurich		
1524-1526	Peasants' War						
1524	Luther criticizes peasants					Erasmus's disputation on free will	
1525	Luther marries; execution of Thomas Müntzer				Abolition of mass in Zurich; disputation on baptism; first believers' baptism performed in Zurich		
1526					Zurich council mandates capital punishment of Anabaptists	Publication of Tyndale's English translation of NT	
1527	d. Hans Denck (b. c. 1500) d. Hans Hut (b. 1490)			Sack of Rome by mutinous troops of Charles V	First Anabaptist executed in Zurich; drafting of Schleitheim Confession		
1528	Execution of Hubmaier						

	German Territories	France	Spain	Italy	Switzerland	Netherlands	British Isles
1529	Second Diet of Speyer; evangelical "protest"; publication of Luther's catechisms; Marburg Colloquy; siege of Vienna by Turkish forces	Abolition of mass in Strasbourg			d. Georg Blaurock (b. 1492)		Thomas More appointed chancellor to Henry VIII
1530	Diet of Augsburg; Confession of Augsburg	d. Francois Lambert (Lambert of Avignon) (b. 1487)	Charles V crowned Holy Roman Emperor				
1531	Formation of Schmalkaldic League				d. H. Zwingli; succeeded by H. Bullinger		
1532		Publication of Calvin's commentary on Seneca; conversion of Calvin	b. Francisco de Toledo (d. 1596)				
1533	b. Valentein Weigel (d. 1588)	Nicholas Cop addresses University of Paris; Cop and Calvin implicated as "Lutheran" sympathizers	b. Juan de Maldonado (d. 1583)				Thomas Cranmer appointed as Archbishop of Canterbury; Henry VIII divorces
1534	First edition of Luther's Bible published	Affair of the Placards; Calvin flees d. Guillame Briçonnet (b. 1470)		Jesuits founded; d. Cardinal Cajetan (Thomas de Vio) (b. 1469)			Act of Supremacy; English church breaks with Rome
1535	Bohemian Confession of 1535; Anabaptist theocracy at Münster collapses after eighteen months						d. Thomas More; d. John Fisher
1536	Wittenberg Concord; b. Kaspar Olevianus (d. 1587)				First edition of Calvin's *Institutes* published; Calvin arrives in Geneva (-1538); First Helvetic Confession	Publication of Tyndale's translation of NT; d. W. Tyndale	d. A. Boleyn; Henry VIII dissolves monasteries (-1541)
1537					Calvin presents ecclesiastical ordinances to Genevan Council		

	German Territories	France	Spain	Italy	Switzerland	Netherlands	British Isles
1538					Calvin exiled from Geneva; arrives in Strasbourg (-1541)		
1539		Calvin publishes second edition of *Institutes* in Strasbourg					Statute of Six Articles; publication of Coverdale's Wheat Bible
1540				Papal approval of Jesuit order			d. Thomas Cromwell
1541	Colloquy of Regensberg	French translation of Calvin's *Institutes* published	d. Juan de Valdés (b. 1500/1510)		d. A. Karlstadt; Calvin returns to Geneva (-1564)		
1542	d. Sebastian Franck (b. 1499)			Institution of Roman Inquisition			War between England and Scotland; James V of Scotland defeated; Ireland declared sovereign kingdom
1543	Copernicus publishes *On the Revolutions of the Heavenly Spheres*; d. Johann Eck (Johann Maier of Eck) (b. 1486)						
1545-1547	Schmalkaldic Wars; d. Martin Luther			First session of Council of Trent			
1546	b. Johannes Piscator (d. 1625)						
1547	Defeat of Protestants at Mühlberg	d. Francis I; r. Henri II (-1559)					d. Henry VIII; r. Edward VI (-1553)
1548	Augsburg Interim (-1552) d. Caspar Cruciger (b. 1504)						
1549	d. Paul Fagius (b. 1504)				Consensus Tigurinus between Calvin and Bullinger		First Book of Common Prayer published
1550	b. Aegidius Hunnius (d. 1603)						
1551-1552				Second session of Council of Trent			Cranmer's Forty-Two Articles
1552	d. Sebastian Münster (b. 1488) d. Friedrich Nausea (b. c. 1496)						

	German Territories	France	Spain	Italy	Switzerland	Netherlands	British Isles
1553	d. Johannes Aepinus (b. 1449)						Book of Common Prayer revised; d. Edward VI; r. Mary I (1558)
1554							Richard Hooker (d. 1600)
1555	Diet of Augsburg; Peace of Augsburg; establishes legal territorial existence of Lutheranism and Catholicism	First mission of French; pastors trained in Geneva				b. Sibbrandus Lubbertus (d. 1625)	b. Robert Rollock (d. 1599); d. Hugh Latimer; d. Nicholas Ridley
1556	d. Pilgram Marpeck (b. 1495) d. Konrad Pellikan (b. 1478) d. Peter Riedemann (b. 1506)		Charles V resigns			d. David Joris (b. c. 1501)	d. Thomas Cranmer
1557					Michael Servetus executed in Geneva		Alliance with Spain in war against France
1558			d. Charles V				b. William Perkins (d. 1602); d. Mary I; r. Elizabeth I (-1603)
1559		d. Henry II; r. Francis II (-1560); first national synod of French reformed churches (1559) in Paris; Gallic Confession		First index of prohibited books issued	Final edition of Calvin's *Institutes*; founding of Genevan Academy	b. Jacobus Arminius (d. 1609)	Elizabethan Settlement
1560	d. P. Melanchthon	d. Francis II; r. Charles IX (1574); Edict of Toleration created peace with Huguenots			Geneva Bible		Kirk of Scotland established; Scottish Confession
1561-1563				Third session of Council of Trent			
1561						Belgic Confession	
1562	d. Katharina Schütz Zell (b. 1497/98)	Massacre of Huguenots begins French Wars of Religion (-1598)					The Articles of Religion—in Elizabethan "final" form (1562/71)
1563	Heidelberg Catechism						
1564				b. Galileo (d. 1642)	d. J. Calvin		b. William Shakespeare (d. 1616)

	German Territories	France	Spain	Italy	Switzerland	Netherlands	British Isles
1566	d. Johann Agricola (b. 1494)			Roman Catechism	Second Helvetic Confession		
1567						Spanish occupation	Abdication of Scottish throne by Mary Stuart; r. James VI (-1603)
1568						d. Dirk Phillips (b. 1504) Dutch movement for liberation (-1645)	
1570		d. Johannes Mercerus (Jean Mercier)		Papal Bull *Regnans in Excelsis* excommunicates Elizabeth I			Elizabeth I excommunicated
1571	b. Johannes Kepler (d. 1630)		Spain defeats Ottoman navy at Battle of Lepanto				b. John Downame (d. 1652)
1572		Massacre of Huguenots on St. Bartholomew's Day		r. Pope Gregory XIII (-1583)		William of Orange invades	b. John Donne (d. 1631)
1574		d. Charles IX; r. Henri III (d. 1589)					
1575	d. Georg Major (b. 1502); Bohemian Confession of 1575						
1576		Declaration of Toleration, formation of Catholic League		b. Giovanni Diodati (d. 1649)		Sack of Antwerp; Pacification of Ghent	
1577	Lutheran Formula of Concord						England allies with Netherlands against Spain
1578	Swiss Brethren Confession of Hesse d. Peter Walpot		Truce with Ottomans				Sir Francis Drake circumnavigates the globe
1579			Expeditions to Ireland			Division of Dutch provinces	
1580	Lutheran Book of Concord						
1581			d. Teresa of Avila				Anti-Catholic statutes passed
1582				Gregorian Reform of calendar			
1583							b. David Dickson (d. 1663)

	German Territories	France	Spain	Italy	Switzerland	Netherlands	British Isles
1584		Treaty of Joinville with Spain	Treaty of Joinville; Spain inducted into Catholic League; defeats Dutch at Antwerp			Fall of Antwerp; d. William of Orange	
1585	d. Josua Opitz (b. c. 1542)	Henri of Navarre excommunicated		r. Pope Sixtus V (-1590)			
1586							Sir Francis Drake's expedition to West Indies; Sir Walter Raleigh in Roanoke
1587	d. Johann Wigand (b. 1523)	Henri of Navarre defeats royal army					d. Mary Stuart of Scotland
1588		Henri of Navarre drives Henri III from Paris; assassination of Catholic League Leaders	Armada destroyed				English Mary defeats Spanish Armada
1589		d. Henri III; r. Henri (of Navarre) IV (-1610)	Victory over England at Lisbon				Defeated by Spain in Lisbon
1590		Henri IV's siege of Paris		d. Girolamo Zanchi (b. 1516)			Alliance with Henri IV
1592	d. Nikolaus Selnecker (b. 1530)						
1593		Henri IV converts to Catholicism					
1594		Henri grants toleration to Huguenots					
1595		Henri IV declares war on Spain; received into Catholic Church		Pope Sixtus accepts Henri IV into Church			Alliance with France
1596		b. René Descartes (d. 1650) b. Moïse Amyraut (d. 1664)					
1598		Edict of Nantes; toleration of Huguenots; peace with Spain	Treaty of Vervins; peace with France				
1600	d. David Chytraeus (b. 1531)						
1601							b. John Trapp (d. 1669)
1602				d. Daniel Toussain (b. 1541)			

	German Territories	France	Spain	Italy	Switzerland	Netherlands	British Isles
1603							d. Elizabeth I; r. James I (James VI of Scotland) (-1625)
1604	d. Cyriacus Spangenberg (b. 1528)						d. John Whitgift (b. 1530)
1605						b. Rembrandt (d. 1669)	Guy Fawkes and gunpowder plot
1606							Jamestown Settlement
1607							b. John Milton (d. 1674)
1608							
1610		d. Henri IV; r. Louis XIII (-1643)	d. Benedict Pererius (b. 1535)			The Remonstrance; Short Confession	
1611							Publication of Authorized English Translation of Bible (AV/KJV)
1612							b. Richard Crashaw (d. 1649)
1616							b. John Owen (d. 1683)
1617							b. Ralph Cudworth (d. 1689)
1618-1648	Thirty Years' War						
1618-1619						Synod of Dordrecht	
1620							English Puritans land in Massachusetts
1621							d. Andrew Willet (b. 1562)
1633	d. Christoph Pelargus (b. 1565)						Laud becomes Archbishop of Canterbury
1637	d. Johann Gerhard (b. 1582)						
1638							d. Joseph Mede (b. 1638)
1640				Diodati's Italian translation of Bible published			
1642-1649							English civil wars; d. Charles I; r. Oliver Cromwell (1660)
1643-1649							Westminster Assembly

	German Territories	France	Spain	Italy	Switzerland	Netherlands	British Isles
1643		d. Louis XIII; r. Louis XIV (-1715)					
1645							d. William Laud (b. 1573)
1648		Treaty of Westphalia ends Thirty Years' War					
1656	d. Georg Calixtus (b. 1586)						
1660							English Restoration; d. Oliver Cromwell; r. Charles II (-1685)
1662							Act of Uniformity
1664						d. Thieleman Jans van Braght (b. 1625)	d. John Mayer (b. 1583)
1671							d. William Greenhill (b. 1591)
1677							d. Thomas Manton (b. 1620)
1678						d. Anna Maria von Schurman (b. 1607)	
1688							Glorious Revolution; r. William and Mary (-1702); d. John Bunyan (b. 1628)
1691							d. Richard Baxter (b. 1615)

BIOGRAPHICAL SKETCHES OF
REFORMATION-ERA FIGURES AND WORKS

For works consulted, see "Sources for Biographical Sketches," p. 547.

Johannes Aepinus (1499–1553). German Lutheran preacher and theologian. Aepinus studied under Martin Luther,* Philipp Melanchthon* and Johannes Bugenhagen* in Wittenberg. Because of his Lutheran beliefs, Aepinus lost his first teaching position in Brandenburg. He fled north to Stralsund and became a preacher and superintendent at Saint Peter's Church in Hamburg. In 1534, he made a diplomatic visit to England but could not convince Henry VIII to embrace the Augsburg Confession.* His works include sermons and theological writings. Aepinus became best known as leader of the Infernalists, who believed that Christ underwent torment in hell after his crucifixion.

Johann Agricola (c. 1494–1566). German Lutheran pastor and theologian. An early student of Martin Luther,* Agricola eventually began a controversy over the role of the law, first with Melanchthon* and then with Luther himself. Agricola claimed to defend Luther's true position, asserting that only the gospel of the crucified Christ calls Christians to truly good works, not the fear of the law. After this first controversy, Agricola seems to have radicalized his views to the point that he eliminated Luther's *simul iustus et peccator* ("at the same time righteous and sinful") paradox of the Christian life, emphasizing instead that believers have no need for the law once they are united with Christ through faith. Luther

responded by writing anonymous pamphlets against antinomianism. Agricola later published a recantation of his views, hoping to assuage relations with Luther, although they were never personally reconciled. He published a commentary on Luke, a series of sermons on Colossians, and a massive collection of German proverbs.

Henry Airay (c. 1560–1616). English Puritan professor and pastor. He was especially noted for his preaching, a blend of hostility toward Catholicism and articulate exposition of English Calvinism. He was promoted to provost of Queen's College Oxford (1598) and then to vice chancellor of the university in 1606. He disputed with William Laud* concerning Laud's putative Catholicization of the Church of England, particularly over the practice of genuflection, which Airay vehemently opposed. He also opposed fellow Puritans who wished to separate from the Church of England. His lectures on Philippians were his only work published during his lifetime.

Moïse Amyraut (1596–1664). French Reformed pastor and professor. Originally intending to be a lawyer, Amyraut turned to theology after an encounter with several Huguenot pastors and having read Calvin's* *Institutes*. After a brief stint as a parish pastor, Amyraut spent the majority of his career at the Saumur Academy. He was well known for his irenicism and ecumenism (for example, in advocating intercommunion with Lutherans). Certain aspects of his writings on justification, faith, the covenants and especially predestination proved controversial among the Reformed. His doctrine of election is often called hypothetical universalism or Amyraldianism, stating that Christ's atoning work was intended by God for all human beings indiscriminately, although its effectiveness for salvation depends on faith, which is a free gift of God given only to those whom God has chosen from eternity. Amyraut was charged with grave doctrinal error three times before the National Synod but was acquitted each time. Aside from his theological treatises, Amyraut published paraphrases of almost the entire New Testament and the Psalms, as well as many sermons.

Jakob Andreae (1528–1590). German Lutheran theologian. Andreae studied at the University of Tübingen before being called to the diaconate in Stuttgart in 1546. He was appointed ecclesiastical superintendent of Göppingen in 1553 and supported Johannes Brenz's* proposal to place the church under civil administrative control. An ecclesial diplomat for the duke of Württemberg, Andreae debated eucharistic theology, the use of images and predestination with Theodore Beza* at the Colloquy of Montbéliard (1586) to determine whether French Reformed exiles would be required to submit to the Formula of Concord.* Andreae coauthored the Formula of Concord. He and his wife had eighteen children.

Benedict Aretius (d. 1574). Swiss Reformed professor. Trained at the universities of Bern, Strasbourg and Marburg, Aretius taught logic and philosophy as well as the biblical languages and theology. He advocated for stronger unity and peace between the Lutheran and Reformed churches. Aretius joined others in denouncing the antitrinitarian Giovanni Valentino Gentile (d. 1566). He published commentaries on the New Testament, as well as various works on astronomy, botany and medicine.

Jacobus Arminius (1559–1609). Dutch Remonstrant pastor and theologian. Arminius was a vocal critic of high Calvinist scholasticism, whose views were repudiated by the synod of Dordrecht. Arminius was a student of Theodore Beza* at the academy of Geneva. He served as a pastor in Amsterdam and later joined the faculty of theology at the university in Leiden, where his lectures on predestination were popular and controversial. Predestination, as Arminius understood it, was the decree of God determined on the basis of divine foreknowledge of faith or rejection by humans who are the recipients of prevenient, but resistible, grace.

Articles of Religion (1562; revised 1571). The Articles underwent a long editorial process that drew from the influence of Continental confessions in England, resulting in a uniquely Anglican blend of Protestantism and Catholicism. In their final form, they were reduced from Thomas Cranmer's* Forty-two Articles (1539) to the Elizabethan Thirty-nine Articles (1571), excising polemical articles against the Anabaptists and Millenarians as well as adding articles on the Holy Spirit, good works and Communion. Originating in a 1535 meeting with Lutherans, the Articles retained a minor influence from the Augsburg Confession* and Württemberg Confession (1552), but showed significant revision in accordance with Genevan theology, as well as the Second Helvetic Confession.*

Anne Askew (1521–1546). English Protestant martyr. Askew was forced to marry her deceased sister's intended husband, who later expelled Askew from his house—after the birth of two children—on account of her religious views. After unsuccessfully seeking a divorce in Lincoln, Askew moved to London, where she met other Protestants and began to preach. In 1546, she was arrested, imprisoned and convicted of heresy for denying the doctrine of transubstantiation. Under torture in the Tower of London she refused to name any other Protestants. On July 16, 1546, she was burned at the stake. Askew is best known through her accounts of her arrests and examinations. John Bale (1495–1563), a bishop, historian and playwright, published these manuscripts. Later John Foxe (1516–1587) included them in his

Acts and Monuments, presenting her as a role model for other pious Protestant women.

Augsburg Confession (1530). In the wake of Luther's* stand against ecclesial authorities at the Diet of Worms (1521), the Holy Roman Empire splintered along theological lines. Emperor Charles V sought to ameliorate this—while also hoping to secure a united European front against Turkish invasion—by calling together another imperial diet in Augsburg in 1530. The Evangelical party was cast in a strongly heretical light at the diet by Johann Eck.* For this reason, Philipp Melanchthon* and Justus Jonas* thought it best to strike a conciliatory tone (Luther, as an official outlaw, did not attend), submitting a confession rather than a defense. The resulting Augsburg Confession was approved by many of the rulers of the northeastern Empire; however, due to differences in eucharistic theology, Martin Bucer* and the representatives of Strasbourg, Constance, Lindau and Memmingen drafted a separate confession (the Tetrapolitan Confession). Charles V accepted neither confession, demanding that the Evangelicals accept the Catholic rebuttal instead. In 1531, along with the publication of the Augsburg Confession itself, Melanchthon released a defense of the confession that responded to the Catholic confutation and expanded on the original articles. Most subsequent Protestant confessions followed the general structure of the Augsburg Confession.

Robert Bagnall (b. 1559 or 1560). English Protestant minister. Bagnall authored *The Steward's Last Account* (1622), a collection of five sermons on Luke 16.

Thomas Bastard (c. 1565–1618). English Protestant minister and poet. Educated at Winchester and New College, Oxford, Bastard published numerous works, including collections of poems and sermons; his most famous title is *Chrestoleros* (1598), a collection of epigrams. Bastard was alleged to be the author of an anonymous work, *An Admonition to the City of Oxford*, which revealed the carnal vices of many clergy and scholars in Oxford; despite denying authorship, he was dismissed from Oxford in

1591. Bastard was recognized as a skilled classical scholar and preacher. He died impoverished in a debtor's prison in Dorchester.

Johann (Pomarius) Baumgart (1514–1578). Lutheran pastor and amateur playwright. Baumgart studied under Georg Major,* Martin Luther* and Philipp Melanchthon* at the University of Wittenberg. Before becoming pastor of the Church of the Holy Spirit in 1540, Baumgart taught secondary school. He authored catechetical and polemical works, a postil for the Gospel readings throughout the church year, numerous hymns and a didactic play (*Juditium Salomonis*).

Richard Baxter (1615–1691). English Puritan minister. Baxter was a leading Puritan pastor, evangelist and theologian, known throughout England for his landmark ministry in Kidderminster and a prodigious literary output, producing 135 books in just over forty years. Baxter came to faith through reading William Perkins,* Richard Sibbes* and other early Puritan writers and was the first cleric to decline the terms of ministry in the national English church imposed by the 1662 Act of Uniformity; Baxter wrote on behalf of the more than 1700 who shared ejection from the national church. He hoped for restoration to national church ministry, or toleration, that would allow lawful preaching and pastoring. Baxter sought unity in theological, ecclesiastical, sociopolitical and personal terms and is regarded as a forerunner of Noncomformist ecumenicity, though he was defeated in his efforts at the 1661 Savoy Conference to take seriously Puritan objections to the revision of the 1604 Prayer Book. Baxter's views on church ministry were considerably hybrid: he was a paedo-baptist, Nonconformist minister who approved of synodical Episcopal government and fixed liturgy. He is most known for his classic writings on the Christian life, such as *The Saints' Everlasting Rest* and *A Christian Directory*, and pastoral ministry, such as *The Reformed Pastor*. He also produced *Catholick Theology*, a large volume squaring current Reformed, Lutheran, Arminian and Roman Catholic systems with each other.

Thomas Becon (1511/1512–1567). English Puritan preacher. Becon was a friend of Hugh Latimer,* and for several years chaplain to Archbishop Thomas Cranmer.* Becon was sent to the Tower of London by Mary I and then exiled for his controversial preaching at the English royal court. He returned to England upon Elizabeth I's accession. Becon was one of the most widely read popular preachers in England during the Reformation. He published many of his sermons, including a postil, or collection of sermon helps for undertrained or inexperienced preachers.

Belgic Confession (1561). Written by Guy de Brès (1523–1567), this statement of Dutch Reformed faith was heavily reliant on the Gallic Confession,* although more detailed, especially in how strongly it distances the Reformed from Roman Catholics and Anabaptists. The Confession first appeared in French in 1561 and was translated to Dutch in 1562. It was presented to Philip II (1527–1598) in the hope that he would grant toleration to the Reformed, to no avail. At the Synod of Dordrecht* the Confession was revised, clarifying and strengthening the article on election as well as sharpening the distinctives of Reformed theology against the Anabaptists, thus situating the Dutch Reformed more closely to the international Calvinist movement. The Belgic Confession in conjunction with the Heidelberg Catechism* and the Canons of Dordrecht were granted official status as the confessional standards (the Three Forms of Unity) of the Dutch Reformed Church.

Theodore Beza (1519–1605). French pastor and professor. Beza was compatriot and successor to John Calvin* as moderator of the Company of Pastors in Geneva during the second half of the sixteenth century. He was a noteworthy New Testament scholar whose *Codex Bezae* formed the basis of the New Testament section of later English translations. A leader in the academy and the church, Beza served as professor of Greek at the Lausanne Academy until 1558, at which time he moved to Geneva to become the rector of the newly founded Genevan Academy. He enjoyed an international reputation through his correspondence with key European leaders. Beza developed and extended Calvin's doctrinal thought on several important themes such as the nature of predestination and the real spiritual presence of Christ in the Eucharist.

Georg Blaurock (1492–1529). Swiss Anabaptist. Blaurock (a nickname meaning "blue coat," because of his preference for this garment) was one of the first leaders of Switzerland's radical reform movement. In the first public disputations on baptism in Zurich, he argued for believer's baptism and was the first person to receive adult believers' baptism there, having been baptized by Conrad Grebel* in 1525. Blaurock was arrested several times for performing mass adult baptisms and engaging in social disobedience by disrupting worship services. He was eventually expelled from Zurich but continued preaching and baptizing in various Swiss cantons until his execution.

Bohemian Confession (1535). Bohemian Christianity was subdivided between traditional Catholics, Utraquists (who demanded Communion in both kinds) and the *Unitas Fratrum*, who were not Protestants but whose theology bore strong affinities to the Waldensians and the Reformed. The 1535 Latin edition of this confession—an earlier Czech edition had already been drafted—was an attempt to clarify and redefine the beliefs of the *Unitas Fratrum*. This confession purged all earlier openness to rebaptism and inched toward Luther's* eucharistic theology. Jan Augusta (c. 1500–1572) and Jan Roh (also Johannes Horn; c. 1490–1547) presented the confession to King Ferdinand I (1503–1564) in Vienna, but the king would not print it. The *Unitas Fratrum* sought, and with slight amendments eventually obtained, Luther's advocacy of the confession. It generally follows the structure of the Augsburg Confession.*

Bohemian Confession (1575). This confession was an attempt to shield Bohemian Christian minorities—the Utraquists and the *Unitas Fratrum*—from the Counter-Reformation and Habsburg insistence on uniformity. The hope was that this umbrella consensus would ensure peace in the midst of Christian diversity; anyone who affirmed the 1575 Confession, passed by the Bohemian legislature, would be tolerated. This confession was, like the Bohemian Confession of 1535, patterned after the Augsburg Confession.* It emphasizes both justification by faith alone and good works as the fruit of salvation. Baptism and the Eucharist are the focus of the sacramental section, although the five traditional Catholic sacraments are also listed for the Utraquists. Though it was eventually accepted in 1609 by Rudolf II (1552–1612), the Thirty Years' War (1618–1648) rendered the confession moot.

Book of Common Prayer (1549; 1552). After the Church of England's break with Rome, it needed a liturgical manual to distinguish its theology and practice from that of Catholicism. Thomas Cranmer* drafted the Book of Common Prayer based on the medieval Roman Missal, under the dual influence of the revised Lutheran Mass and the reforms of the Spanish Cardinal Quiñones. This manual details the eucharistic service, as well as services for rites such as baptism, confirmation, marriage and funerals. It includes a matrix of the epistle and Gospel readings and the appropriate collect for each Sunday and feast day of the church year. The 1548 Act of Uniformity established the Book of Common Prayer as *the* authoritative liturgical manual for the Church of England, to be implemented everywhere by Pentecost 1549. After its 1552 revision, Queen Mary I banned it; Elizabeth reestablished it in 1559, although it was rejected by Puritans and Catholics alike.

The Book of Homilies (1547; 1563; 1570). This collection of approved sermons, published in three parts during the reigns of Edward VI and Elizabeth I, was intended to inculcate Anglican theological distinctives and mitigate the problems raised by the lack of educated preachers. Addressing doctrinal and practical topics, Thomas Cranmer* likely wrote the majority of the first twelve sermons, published in 1547; John Jewel* added another twenty sermons in 1563. A final sermon, *A Homily against Disobedience*, was appended to the canon in 1570. Reprinted regularly, the *Book of Homilies* was an important resource in Anglican preaching until at least the end of the seventeenth century.

John Boys (1571–1625). Anglican priest and theologian. Before doctoral work at Cambridge, Boys pastored several parishes in Kent; after completing his studies he was appointed to more prominent positions, culminating in his 1619 appointment as the Dean of Canterbury by James I. Boys published a popular four-volume postil of the Gospel and epistle readings for the church year, as well as a companion volume for the Psalms.

Thieleman Jans van Braght (1625–1664). Dutch Radical preacher. After demonstrating great ability with languages, this cloth merchant was made preacher in his hometown of Dordrecht in 1648. He served in this office for the next sixteen years, until his death. This celebrated preacher had a reputation for engaging in debate wherever an opportunity presented itself, particularly concerning infant baptism. The publication of his book of martyrs, *Het Bloedigh Tooneel of Martelaersspiegel* (1660; *Martyrs' Mirror*), proved to be his lasting contribution to the Mennonite tradition. *Martyrs' Mirror* is heavily indebted to the earlier martyr book *Offer des Heeren* (1562), to which Braght added many early church martyrs who rejected infant baptism, as well as over 800 contemporary martyrs.

Johannes Brenz (1499–1570). German Lutheran theologian and pastor. Brenz was converted to the reformation cause after hearing Martin Luther* speak; later, Brenz became a student of Johannes Oecolampadius.* His central achievement lay in his talent for organization. As city preacher in Schwäbisch-Hall and afterward in Württemberg and Tübingen, he oversaw the introduction of reform measures and doctrines and new governing structures for ecclesial and educational communities. Brenz also helped establish Lutheran orthodoxy through treatises, commentaries and catechisms. He defended Luther's position on eucharistic presence against Huldrych Zwingli* and opposed the death penalty for religious dissenters.

Guillaume Briçonnet (1470–1534). French Catholic abbot and bishop. Briçonnet created a short-lived circle of reformist-minded humanists in his diocese under the sponsorship of Marguerite d'Angoulême. His desire for ecclesial reform developed throughout his prestigious career (including positions as royal chaplain to the queen, abbot at Saint-Germain-des-Prés and bishop of Meaux), influenced by Jacques Lefèvre d'Étaples.* Briçonnet encouraged reform through ministerial visitation, Scripture and preaching in the vernacular and active study of the Bible. When this triggered the ire of the theology faculty at the Sorbonne in Paris, Briçonnet quelled the activity and departed, envisioning an ecclesial reform that proceeded hierarchically.

Otto Brunfels (c. 1488–1534). German Lutheran botanist, teacher and physician. Brunfels joined the Carthusian order, where he developed interests in the natural sciences and became involved with a humanist circle associated with Ulrich von Hutten and Wolfgang Capito.* In 1521, after coming into contact with Luther's* teaching, Brunfels abandoned the monastic life, traveling and spending time in botanical research and pastoral care. He received a medical degree in Basel and was appointed city physician of Bern in 1534. Brunfels penned defenses of Luther and Hutten, devotional biographies of biblical figures, a prayer book, and annotations on the Gospels and the Acts of the Apostles. His most influential contribution, however, is as a Renaissance botanist.

Martin Bucer (1491–1551). German Reformed theologian and pastor. A Dominican friar, Bucer was influenced by Desiderius Erasmus* during his doctoral studies at the University of Heidelberg, where he began corresponding with Martin Luther.* After advocating reform in Alsace, Bucer was excommunicated and fled to Strasbourg, where he became a leader in the city's Reformed ecclesial and educational communities. Bucer sought concord between Lutherans and Zwinglians and Protestants and Catholics. He emigrated to England, becoming a professor at Cambridge. Bucer's greatest theological concern was the centrality of Christ's sacrificial death, which achieved justification and sanctification and orients Christian community.

Johannes Bugenhagen (1485–1558). German Lutheran pastor and professor. Bugenhagen, a priest and lecturer at a Premonstratensian monastery, became a city preacher in Wittenberg during the reform efforts of Martin Luther* and Philipp Melanchthon.* Initially influenced by his reading of Desiderius Erasmus,* Bugenhagen grew in evangelical orientation through Luther's works; later, he studied under Melanchthon at the University of Wittenberg, eventually serving as rector and faculty member there. Bugenhagen was a versatile commentator, exegete and lecturer on Scripture. Through these roles and his development of lectionary and devotional material, Bugenhagen facilitated rapid establishment of church order throughout many German provinces.

Heinrich Bullinger (1504–1575). Swiss Reformed pastor and theologian. Bullinger succeeded Huldrych Zwingli* as minister and leader in Zurich. The primary author of the First and Second Helvetic Confessions,* Bullinger was drawn toward reform through the works of Martin Luther* and Philipp Melanchthon.* After Zwingli died, Bullinger was vital in maintaining adherence to the cause of reform; he oversaw the expansion of the Zurich synodal system while preaching, teaching and writing extensively. One of Bullinger's lasting legacies was the development of a federal view of the divine covenant with humanity, making baptism and the Eucharist covenantal signs.

John Bunyan (1628–1688). English Puritan preacher and writer. His *Pilgrim's Progress* is one of the best-selling English-language titles in history. Born to a working-class family, Bunyan was largely unschooled, gaining literacy (and entering the faith) through reading the Bible and such early Puritan devotional works as *The Plain Man's Pathway to Heaven* and *The Practice of Piety*. Following a short stint in Oliver Cromwell's parliamentary army, in which Bunyan narrowly escaped death in combat, he turned to a preaching ministry, succeeding John Gifford as pastor at the Congregational church in Bedford. A noted preacher, Bunyan drew large crowds in itinerant appearances and it was in the sermonic form that Bunyan developed his theological outlook, which was an Augustinian-inflected Calvinism. Bunyan's opposition to the Book of Common Prayer and refusal of official ecclesiastical licensure led to multiple imprisonments, where he wrote many of his famous allegorical works, including *Pilgrim's Progress*, *The Holy City*, *Prison Meditations* and *Holy War*.

Jeremiah Burroughs (c. 1600–1646). English Puritan pastor and delegate to the Westminster Assembly. Burroughs left Cambridge, as well as a rectorate in Norfolk, because of his nonconformity. After returning to England from pastoring an English congregation in Rotterdam for several years (1637–1641), he became one of only a few dissenters from the official presbyterianism of the Assembly in favor of a congregationalist polity. Nevertheless, he was well known and respected by presbyterian colleagues such as Richard Baxter* for his irenic tone and conciliatory manner. The vast majority of Burroughs's corpus was published posthumously, although during his lifetime he published annotations on Hosea and several polemical works.

Cardinal Cajetan (Thomas de Vio) (1469–1534). Italian Catholic cardinal, professor, theologian and biblical exegete. This Dominican monk was the leading Thomist theologian and one of the most important Catholic exegetes of the sixteenth century. Cajetan is best-known for his interview with Martin Luther* at the Diet of Augsburg (1518). Among his many works are polemical treatises, extensive biblical commentaries and most importantly a four-volume commentary (1508–1523) on the *Summa Theologiae* of Thomas Aquinas.

Georg Calixtus (1586–1656). German Lutheran theologian. Calixtus studied at the University of Helmstedt where he developed regard for Philipp Melanchthon.* Between his time as a student and later as a professor at Helmstedt, Calixtus traveled through Europe seeking a way to unite and reconcile Lutherans, Calvinists and Catholics. He attempted to fuse these denominations through use of the Scriptures, the Apostles' Creed, and the first five centuries, interpreted by the Vincentian canon. Calixtus's position was stamped as syncretist and yielded further debate even after his death.

John Calvin (1509–1564). French Reformed pastor and theologian. In his *Institutes of the Christian Religion*, Calvin provided a theological dogmatics for the Reformed churches. Calvin's gradual conversion to the cause of reform occurred through his study with chief humanist scholars in Paris, but he spent most of his career in Geneva (excepting a three-year exile in Strasbourg with Martin Bucer*). In Geneva, Calvin reorganized the structure and governance of the church and established an academy that became an international center for theological education. He was a tireless writer, producing his *Institutes*, theological treatises and Scripture commentaries.

Wolfgang Capito (1478?–1541). German Reformed humanist and theologian. Capito, a Hebrew scholar, produced a Hebrew grammar and published several Latin commentaries on books of the Hebrew Scriptures. He corresponded with Desiderius Erasmus* and fellow humanists. Capito translated Martin Luther's* early works into Latin for the printer Johann Froben. On meeting Luther, Capito was converted to Luther's vision, left Mainz and settled in Strasbourg, where he lectured on Luther's theology to the city clergy. With Martin Bucer,* Capito reformed liturgy, ecclesial life and teachings, education, welfare and government. Capito worked for the theological unification of the Swiss cantons with Strasbourg.

Thomas Cartwright (1535–1606). English Puritan preacher and professor. Cartwright was educated at St. John's College, Cambridge, although as an influential leader of the Presbyterian party in the Church of England he was continually at odds with the Anglican party, especially John Whitgift.* Cartwright spent some time as an exile in Geneva and Heidelberg as well as in Antwerp, where he pastored an English church. In 1585, Cartwright was arrested and eventually jailed for trying to return to England despite Elizabeth I's refusal of his request. Many acknowledged him to be learned but also quite cantankerous. His publications include commentaries on Colossians, Ecclesiastes, Proverbs and the Gospels, as well as a dispute against Whitgift on church discipline.

Mathew Caylie (unknown). English Protestant minister. Caylie authored *The Cleansing of the Ten Lepers* (1623), an exposition of Luke 17:14-18.

John Chardon (d. 1601). Irish Anglican bishop. Chardon was educated at Oxford. He advocated Reformed doctrine in his preaching, yet opposed those Puritans who rejected Anglican church order. He published several sermons.

Martin Chemnitz (1522–1586). German Lutheran theologian. A leading figure in establishing Lutheran orthodoxy, Chemnitz studied theology and patristics at the University of Wittenburg, later becoming a defender of Philipp Melanchthon's* interpretation of the doctrine of justification. Chemnitz drafted a compendium of doctrine and reorganized the structure of the church in Wolfenbüttel; later, he led efforts to reconcile divisions within Lutheranism, culminating in the Formula of Concord*. One of his chief theological accomplishments was a modification of the christological doctrine of the *communicatio idiomatium*, which provided a Lutheran platform for understanding the sacramental presence of Christ's humanity in the Eucharist.

David Chytraeus (1531–1600). German Lutheran professor, theologian and biblical exegete. At the age of eight Chytraeus was admitted to the University of Tübingen. There he studied law, philology, philosophy, and theology, finally receiving his master's degree in 1546. Chytraeus befriended Philipp Melanchthon* while sojourning in Wittenberg, where he taught the *Loci communes*. While teaching exegesis at the University of Rostock Chytraeus became acquainted with Tilemann Heshusius,* who strongly influenced Chytraeus away from Philippist theology. As a defender of Gnesio-Lutheran theology Chytraeus helped organize churches throughout Austria in accordance with the Augsburg Confession.* Chytraeus coauthored the Formula of Concord* with Martin Chemnitz,* Andreas Musculus (1514–1581), Nikolaus Selnecker* and Jakob Andreae.* He wrote commentaries on most of the Bible, as well as a devotional work titled *Regula vitae* (1555) that described the Christian virtues.

John Colet (1467–1519). English Catholic priest, preacher and educator. Colet, appointed dean of Saint Paul's Cathedral by Henry VII, was a friend of Desiderius Erasmus,* on whose classical ideals Colet reconstructed the curriculum of Saint Paul's school. Colet was convinced that the foundation of moral reform lay in the education of children. Though an ardent advocate of reform, Colet, like Erasmus, remained loyal to the Catholic Church throughout his life. Colet's agenda of reform was oriented around spiritual and ethical themes, demonstrated in his commentaries on select books of the New Testament and the writings of Pseudo-Dionysius the Areopagite.

Gasparo Contarini (1483–1542). Italian statesman, theologian and reform-minded cardinal. Contarini was an able negotiator and graceful compromiser. Charles V requested Contarini as the papal legate for the Colloquy of Regensburg (1541), where Contarini reached agreement with Melanchthon* on the doctrine of justification (although neither the pope nor Luther* ratified the agreement). He had come to a similar belief in the priority of faith in the work of Christ rather than works as the basis for Christian life in 1511, though unlike Luther, he never left the papal church over the issue; instead he remainied within it to try to seek gentle reform, and he adhered to papal sacramental teaching. Contarini was an important voice for reform within the Catholic Church, always seeking reconciliation rather than confrontation with Protestant reformers. He wrote many works, including a treatise detailing the ideal bishop, a manual for lay church leaders, a political text on right governance, and brief commentaries on the Pauline letters.

John Cosin (1594–1672). Anglican preacher and bishop. Early in his career Cosin was the vice chancellor of Cambridge and canon at the Durham cathedral. But as a friend of William Laud* and an advocate for "Laudian" changes, he was suspected of being a crypto-Catholic. In 1640 during the Long Parliament a Puritan lodged a complaint with the House of Commons concerning Cosin's "popish innovations." Cosin was promptly removed from office. During the turmoil of the English Civil Wars, Cosin sojourned in Paris among English nobility but struggled financially. Cosin returned to England after the Restoration in 1660 to be consecrated as the bishop of Durham. He published annotations on the Book of Common Prayer* and a history of the canon.

Miles Coverdale (1488–1568). Anglican bishop. Coverdale is known for his translations of the Bible into English, completing William Tyndale's* efforts and later producing the Great Bible commissioned by Henry VIII (1539). A former friar, Coverdale was among the Cambridge scholars who met at the White Horse Tavern to discuss Martin Luther's* ideas. During Coverdale's three terms of exile in Europe, he undertook various translations, including the Geneva Bible*. He was appointed bishop of Exeter by Thomas Cranmer* and served as chaplain to Edward VI. Coverdale contributed to Cranmer's first edition of the Book of Common Prayer.*

William Cowper (Couper) (1568–1619). Scottish Puritan bishop. After graduating from the University of St. Andrews, Cowper worked in parish ministry for twenty-five years before becoming bishop. As a zealous Puritan and advocate of regular preaching and rigorous discipline, Cowper championed Presbyterian polity and lay participation in church government. Cowper published devotional works, sermon collections and a commentary on Revelation.

Thomas Cranmer (1489–1556). Anglican archbishop and theologian. Cranmer supervised church reform and produced the first two editions of the Book of Common Prayer.* As a doctoral student at Cambridge, he was involved in the discussions at the White Horse Tavern. Cranmer contributed to a religious defense of Henry VIII's divorce; Henry then appointed him Archbishop of Canterbury. Cranmer cautiously steered the course of reform, accelerating under Edward VI. After supporting the attempted coup to prevent Mary's assuming the throne, Cranmer was convicted of treason and burned at the stake. Cranmer's legacy is the splendid English of his liturgy and prayer books.

Richard Crashaw (1612–1649). English Catholic poet. Educated at Cambridge, Crashaw was fluent in Hebrew, Greek and Latin. His first volume of poetry was *Epigrammatum sacrorum liber* (1634). Despite being born into a Puritan family, Crashaw was attracted to Catholicism, finally converting in 1644 after he was forced to resign his fellowship for not signing the Solemn League and Covenant (1643). In 1649, he was made a subcanon of Our Lady of Loretto by Cardinal Palotta.

John Crompe (d. 1661). Anglican priest. Educated at Cambridge, Crompe published a commentary on the Apostles' Creed, a sermon on Psalm 21:3 and an exposition of Christ's passion.

Caspar Cruciger (1504–1548). German Lutheran theologian. Recognized for his alignment with the theological views of Philipp Melanchthon,* Cruciger was a scholar respected among both Protestants and Catholics. In 1521, Cruciger came Wittenberg to study Hebrew and remained there most of his life. He became a valuable partner for Martin Luther* in translating the Old Testament and served as teacher, delegate to major theological colloquies and rector. Cruciger was an agent of reform in his birthplace of Leipzig, where at the age of fifteen he had observed the disputation between Luther and Johann Eck.*

Jean Daillé (1594–1670). French Reformed pastor. Born into a devout Reformed family, Daillé studied theology and philosophy at Saumur under the most influential contemporary lay leader in French Protestantism, Philippe Duplessis-Mornay (1549–1623). Daillé held to Amyraldianism—the belief that Christ died for all humanity inclusively, not particularly for the elect who would inherit salvation (though only the elect are in fact saved). He wrote a controversial treatise on the church fathers that aggravated many Catholic and Anglican scholars because of Daillé's apparent demotion of patristic authority in matters of faith.

John Davenant (1576–1641). Anglican bishop and professor. Davenant attended Queen's College, Cambridge, where he received his doctorate and was appointed professor of divinity. During the Remonstrant controversy, James I sent Davenant as one of the four representatives for the Church of England to the Synod of Dordrecht.* Following James's instructions, Davenant advocated a *via media* between the Calvinists and the Remonstrants, although in later years he defended against the rise of Arminianism in England. In 1621, Davenant was promoted to the bishopric of Salisbury, where he was generally receptive to Laudian reforms. Davenant's lectures on Colossians are his best-known work.

Defense of the Augsburg Confession (1531). See *Augsburg Confession*.

Hans Denck (c. 1500–1527). German Radical theologian. Denck, a crucial early figure of the German Anabaptist movement, combined medieval German mysticism with the radical sacramental theology of Andreas Bodenstein von Karlstadt* and Thomas Müntzer.* Denck argued that the exterior forms of Scripture and sacrament are symbolic witnesses secondary to the internally revealed truth of the Sprit in the human soul. This view led to his expulsion from Nuremberg in 1525; he spent the next two years in various centers of reform in the German territories. At the time of his death, violent persecution against Anabaptists was on the rise throughout northern Europe.

Stephen Denison (unknown). English Puritan pastor. Denison received the post of curate at St. Katherine Cree in London sometime in the 1610s, where he ministered until his ejection from office in 1635. During his career at St. Katherine Cree, Denison waded into controversy with both Puritans (over the doctrine of predestination) and Anglicans (over concerns about liturgical ceremonies). He approached both altercations with rancor and rigidity, although he seems to have been quite popular and beloved by most of his congregation. In 1631, William Laud* consecrated the newly renovated St. Katherine Cree, and as part of the festivities Denison offered a sermon on Luke 19:27 in which he publicly rebuked Laud for fashioning the Lord's house into a "den of robbers." Aside from the record of his quarrels, very little is known about Denison. In addition to *The White Wolf* (a 1627 sermon against another opponent), he published a catechism for children (1621), a treatise on the sacraments (1621) and a commentary on 2 Peter 1 (1622).

David Dickson (1583?–1663). Scottish Reformed pastor, preacher, professor and theologian. Dickson defended the Presbyterian form of ecclesial reformation in Scotland and was recognized for his iteration of Calvinist federal theology and expository biblical commentaries. Dickson served for over twenty years as professor of philosophy at the University of Glasgow before being appointed professor of divinity. He opposed the imposition of Episcopalian measures on the church in Scotland and was active in political and ecclesial venues to protest and prohibit such influences. Dickson was removed from his academic post following his refusal of the oath of supremacy during the Restoration era.

Veit Dietrich (1506–1549). German Lutheran preacher and theologian. Dietrich intended to study medicine at the University of Wittenberg, but Martin Luther* and Philipp Melanchthon* convinced him to study theology instead. Dietrich developed a strong relationship with Luther, accompanying him to the Marburg Colloquy (1529) and to Coburg Castle during the Diet of Augsburg (1530). After graduating, Dietrich taught on the arts faculty, eventually becoming dean. In 1535 he returned to his hometown, Nuremberg, to pastor. Later in life, Dietrich worked with Melanchthon to reform the church in Regensburg. In 1547, when Charles V arrived in Nuremberg, Dietrich was suspended from the pastorate; he resisted the imposition of the Augsburg Interim to no avail. In addition to transcribing some of Luther's lectures, portions of the Table Talk and the very popular *Hauspostille* (1544), Dietrich published his own sermons for children, a manual for pastors and a summary of the Bible.

Giovanni Diodati (1576–1649). Italian Reformed theologian. Diodati was from an Italian banking family who fled for religious reasons to Geneva. There he trained under Theodore Beza;* on completion of his doctoral degree, Diodati became professor of Hebrew at the academy. He was an ecclesiastical representative of the church in Geneva (for whom he was a delegate at the Synod of Dordrecht*) and an advocate for reform in Venice. Diodati's chief contribution to the Italian reform movement was a translation of the Bible into Italian (1640–1641), which remains the standard translation in Italian Protestantism.

John Donne (1572–1631). Anglican poet and preacher. Donne was born into a strong Catholic family. However, sometime between his brother's death from the plague while in prison in 1593 and the publication of his *Pseudo-Martyr* in 1610, Donne joined the Church of England. Ordained to the Anglican priesthood in 1615 and already widely recognized for his verse, Donne quickly rose to prominence as a preacher—some have deemed him the best of his era. His textual corpus is an amalgam of erotic *and* divine poetry (e.g., "Batter My Heart"), as well as a great number of sermons.

John Downame (c. 1571–1652). English Puritan pastor and theologian. See *English Annotations.*

Daniel Dyke (d. 1614). English Puritan preacher. Born of nonconformist stock, Dyke championed a more thorough reformation of church practice in England. After the promulgation of John Whitgift's* articles in 1583, Dyke refused to accept what he saw as remnants of Catholicism, bringing him into conflict with the bishop of London. Despite the petitions of his congregation and some politicians, the bishop of London suspended Dyke from his ministry for refusing priestly ordination and conformity to the Book of Common Prayer.* All of his work was published posthumously; it is mostly focused on biblical interpretation.

Johann Eck (Johann Maier of Eck) (1486–1543). German Catholic theologian. Though Eck was not an antagonist of Martin Luther* until the dispute over indulgences, Luther's Ninety-five Theses (1517) sealed the two as adversaries. After their debate at the Leipzig Disputation (1519), Eck participated in the writing of the papal bull that led to Luther's excommunication. Much of Eck's work was written to oppose Protestantism or to defend Catholic doctrine and the papacy; his *Enchiridion* was a manual written to counter Protestant doctrine. However, Eck was also deeply invested in the status of parish preaching, publishing a five-volume set of postils. He participated in the assemblies at Regensburg and Augsburg and led the Catholics in their rejection of the Augsburg Confession.

English Annotations (1645; 1651; 1657). Under a commission from the Westminster Assembly, the editors of the English Annotations—John Downame* along with unnamed colleagues—translated, collated and digested in a compact and accessible format several significant Continental biblical resources, including Calvin's* commentaries, Beza's* *Annotationes majores* and Diodati's* *Annotations.*

Desiderius Erasmus (1466–1536). Dutch Catholic humanist and pedagogue. Erasmus, a celebrated humanist scholar, was recognized for translations of ancient texts, reform of education according to classical studies, moral and spiritual writings and the first printed edition of the Greek New Testament. A former Augustinian who never left the Catholic Church, Erasmus addressed deficiencies he saw in the church and society, challenging numerous prevailing doctrines but advocating reform. He envisioned a simple, spiritual Christian life shaped by the teachings of Jesus and ancient wisdom. He was often accused of collusion with Martin Luther* on account of some resonance of their ideas but hotly debated Luther on human will.

Paul Fagius (1504–1549). German Reformed Hebraist and pastor. After studying at the University of Heidelberg, Fagius went to Strasbourg where he perfected his Hebrew under Wolfgang Capito.* In Isny im Allgäu (Baden-Württemberg) he met the great Jewish grammarian Elias Levita (1469–1549), with whom he established a Hebrew printing press. In 1544 Fagius returned to Strasbourg, succeeding Capito as preacher and Old Testament lecturer. During the Augsburg Interim, Fagius (with Martin Bucer*) accepted Thomas Cranmer's* invitation to translate and interpret the Bible at Cambridge. However, Fagius died before he could begin any of the work. Fagius wrote commentaries on the first four chapters of Genesis and the deutero-canonical books of Sirach and Tobit.

John Fary (unknown). English Puritan pastor. Fary authored *God's Severity on Man's Sterility* (1645), a sermon on the fruitless fig tree in Luke 13:6-9.

William Fenner (1600–1640). English Puritan pastor. After studying at Cambridge and Oxford, Fenner ministered at Sedgley and Rochford. Fenner's extant writings, which primarily deal with practical and devotional topics, demonstrate a zealous Puritan piety and a keen interest in Scripture and theology.

First Helvetic Confession (1536). Anticipating the planned church council at Mantua (1537, but delayed until 1545 at Trent), Reformed theologians of the Swiss cantons drafted a confession to distinguish themselves from both Catholics and the churches of the Augsburg Confession.* Heinrich Bullinger* led the discussion and wrote the confession itself; Leo Jud, Oswald Myconius, Simon Grynaeus and others were part of the assembly. Martin Bucer* and Wolfgang Capito* had desired to draw the Lutheran and Reformed communions closer together through this document, but Luther* proved unwilling after Bullinger refused to accept the Wittenberg Concord (1536). This confession was largely eclipsed by Bullinger's Second Helvetic Confession.*

John Flavel (c. 1630–1691). English Puritan pastor. Trained at Oxford, Flavel ministered in southwest England from 1650 until the Act of Uniformity in 1662, which reaffirmed the compulsory use of the Book of Common Prayer. Flavel preached unofficially for many years, until his congregation was eventually allowed to build a meeting place in 1687. His works were numerous, varied and popular.

Formula of Concord (1577). After Luther's* death, intra-Lutheran controversies between the Gnesio-Lutherans (partisans of Luther) and the Philippists (partisans of Melanchthon*) threatened to cause a split among those who had subscribed to the Augsburg Confession.* In 1576, Jakob Andreae,* Martin Chemnitz,* Nikolaus Selnecker,* David Chytraeus* and Andreas Musculus (1514–1581) met with the intent of resolving the controversies, which mainly regarded the relationship between good works and salvation, the third use of the law, and the role of the human will in accepting God's grace. In 1580, celebrating the fiftieth anniversary of the presentation of the Augsburg Confession to Charles V (1500–1558), the *Book of Concord* was printed as the authoritative interpretation of the Augsburg Confession; it included the three ancient creeds, the Augsburg Confession, its Apology (1531), the Schmalkald Articles,* Luther's *Treatise on the Power and Primacy of the Pope* (1537) and both his Small and Large Catechisms (1529).

Sebastian Franck (1499–1542). German Radical theologian. Franck became a Lutheran in 1525, but by 1529 he began to develop ideas that distanced him from Protestants and Catholics. Expelled from Strasbourg and later Ulm due to his controversial writings, Franck spent the end of his life in Basel. Franck emphasized God's word as a divine internal spark that cannot be adequately expressed in outward forms. Thus he criticized religious institutions and dogmas. His work consists mostly of commentaries, compilations and translations. In his sweeping historical *Chronica* (1531), Franck supported numerous heretics condemned by the Catholic Church and criticized political and church authorities.

Leonhard Frick (d. 1528). Austrian Radical martyr. See *Kunstbuch*.

Gallic Confession (1559). This confession was accepted at the first National Synod of the Reformed Churches of France (1559). It was intended to be a touchstone of Reformed faith but also to show to the people of France that the Huguenots—who faced persecution—were not seditious. The French Reformed Church presented this confession to Francis II (1544–1560) in 1560, and to his successor, Charles IX (1550–1574), in 1561. The later Genevan draft, likely written by Calvin,* Beza,* and Pierre Viret (1511–1571), was received as the true Reformed confession at the seventh National Synod in La Rochelle (1571).

Geneva Bible (originally printed 1560). During Mary I's reign many English Protestants sought safety abroad in Reformed territories of the Empire and the Swiss Cantons, especially in Calvin's* Geneva. A team of English exiles in Geneva led by William Whittingham (c. 1524–1579) brought this complete translation to press in the course of two years. Notable for several innovations—Roman type, verse numbers, italics indicating English idiom and not literal phrasing of the original languages, even variant readings in the Gospels and Acts—this translation is most well known for its marginal notes, which reflect a strongly Calvinist theology. The notes explained Scripture in an accessible way for the laity, also giving unlearned clergy a new sermon resource. Although controversial because of its implicit critique of royal power, this translation was wildly popular; even after the publication of the Authorized Version (1611) and James I's 1616 ban on its printing, the Geneva Bible continued to be the most popular English translation until after the English Civil Wars.

Johann Gerhard (1582–1637). German Lutheran theologian, professor and superintendent. Gerhard is considered one of the most eminent Lutheran theologians, after Martin Luther* and Martin Chemnitz.* After studying patristics and Hebrew at Wittenberg, Jena and Marburg, Gerhard was appointed superintendent at the age of twenty-four. In 1616 he was appointed to a post at the University of Jena, where he reintroduced Aristotelian metaphysics to theology and gained widespread fame. His most important work was the nine-volume *Loci Theologici* (1610–1625). He also expanded Chemnitz's harmony of the Gospels (*Harmonia Evangelicae*), which was finally published by Polykarp Leyser (1552–1610) in 1593. Gerhard was well-known for an irenic spirit and an ability to communicate clearly.

Bernard Gilpin (1517–1583). Anglican theologian and priest. In public disputations, Gilpin defended Roman Catholic theology against John Hooper (c. 1495-1555) and Peter Martyr Vermigli.* These debates caused Gilpin to reexamine his faith. Upon Mary I's accession, Gilpin resigned his benefice. He sojourned in Belgium and France, returning to pastoral ministry in England in 1556. Gilpin dedicated himself to a preaching circuit in northern England, thus earning the moniker "the Apostle to the North." His zealous preaching and almsgiving roused royal opposition and a warrant for his arrest. On his way to the queen's commission, Gilpin fractured his leg, delaying his arrival in London until after Mary's death and thus likely saving his life. His only extant writing is a sermon on Luke 2 confronting clerical abuses.

Conrad Grebel (c. 1498–1526). Swiss Radical theologian. Grebel, considered the father of the Anabaptist movement, was one of the first defenders and performers of believers' baptism, for which he was eventually imprisoned in Zurich. One of Huldrych Zwingli's* early compatriots, Grebel advocated rapid, radical reform, clashing publicly with the civil authorities and Zwingli. Grebel's views, particularly on baptism, were influenced by Andreas Bodenstein von Karlstadt* and Thomas Müntzer.* Grebel advocated elimination of magisterial involvement in governing the church; instead, he envisioned the church as lay Christians determining their own affairs with strict adherence to the biblical text, and unified in volitional baptism.

William Greenhill (1591–1671). English Puritan pastor. Greenhill attended and worked at Magdalen College. He ministered in the diocese of Norwich but soon left for London, where he preached at Stepney. Greenhill was a member of the Westminster Assembly of Divines and was appointed the parliament chaplain by the children of Charles I. Oliver Cromwell included him among the preachers who helped draw up the Savoy Declaration. Greenhill was evicted from his post following the Restoration, after which he pastored independently. Among Greenhill's most significant contributions to church history was his *Exposition of the Prophet of Ezekiel.*

Catharina Regina von Greiffenberg (1633–1694). Austrian Lutheran poet. Upon her adulthood her guardian (and half uncle) sought to marry her; despite her protests of their consanguinity and her desire to remain celibate, she relented in 1664. After the deaths of her mother and husband, Greiffenberg abandoned her home to debtors and joined her friends Susanne Popp (d. 1683) and Sigmund von Birken (1626–1681) in Nuremberg. During her final years she dedicated herself to studying the biblical languages and to writing meditations on Jesus' death and resurrection, which she never completed. One of the most important and learned Austrian poets of the Baroque period, Greiffenberg published a collection of sonnets, songs and poems (1662) as well as three sets of mystical meditations on Jesus' life, suffering and death (1672; 1683; 1693). She participated in a society of poets called the Ister Gesellschaft.

Rudolf Gwalther (1519–1586). Swiss Reformed preacher. Gwalther was a consummate servant of the Reformed church in Zurich, its chief religious officer and preacher, a responsibility fulfilled previously by Huldrych Zwingli* and Heinrich Bullinger.* Gwalther provided sermons and commentaries and translated the works of Zwingli into Latin. He worked for many years alongside Bullinger in structuring and governing the church in Zurich. Gwalther also strove to strengthen the connections to the Reformed churches on the Continent and England: he was a participant in the Colloquy of Regensburg (1541) and an opponent of the Formula of Concord.*

Hans Has von Hallstatt (d. 1527). Austrian Reformed pastor. See *Kunstbuch.*

Henry Hammond (1605–1660). Anglican priest. After completing his studies at Oxford, Hammond was ordained in 1629. A Royalist, Hammond helped recruit soldiers for the king; he was chaplain to Charles I. During the king's captivity, Hammond was imprisoned for not submitting to Parliament. Later he was allowed to pastor again, until his death. Hammond published a catechism, numerous polemical sermons and treatises as well as his *Paraphrase and Annotations on the New Testament* (1653).

Peter Hausted (d. 1645). Anglican priest and playwright. Educated at Cambridge and Oxford, Hausted ministered in a number of parishes and preached adamantly and vehemently against Puritanism. He is best known for his play *The Rival Friends*, which is filled with invective against the Puritans; during a performance before the king and queen, a riot nearly broke out. Haustead died during the siege of Banbury Castle.

Heidelberg Catechism (1563). This German Reformed catechism was commissioned by the elector of the Palatinate, Frederick III (1515–1576) for pastors and teachers in his territories to use in instructing children and new believers in the faith. It was written by theologian Zacharias Ursinus (1534–1583) in consultation with Frederick's court preacher Kaspar Olevianus* and the entire theology faculty at the University of Heidelberg. The Heidelberg Catechism was accepted as one of the Dutch Reformed Church's Three Forms of Unity—along with the Belgic Confession* and the Canons of Dordrecht—at the Synod of Dordrecht,* and became widely popular among other Reformed confessional traditions throughout Europe.

Niels Hemmingsen (1513–1600). Danish Lutheran theologian. Hemmingsen studied at the University of Wittenberg, where he befriended Philipp Melanchthon.* In 1542, Hemmingsen returned to Denmark to pastor and to teach Greek, dialectics and theology at the University of Copenhagen. Foremost of the Danish theologians, Hemmingsen oversaw the preparation and publication of the first Danish Bible (1550). Later in his career he became embroiled in controversies because of his Philippist theology, especially regarding the Eucharist. Due to rising tensions with Lutheran nobles outside of Denmark, King Frederick II (1534–1588) dismissed Hemmingsen from his university post in 1579, transferring him to a prominent but less internationally visible Cathedral outside of Copenhagen. Hemmingsen was a prolific author, writing commentaries on the New Testament and Psalms, sermon collections and several methodological, theological and pastoral handbooks.

Christopher Hooke (unknown). English Puritan physician and pastor. Hooke published a treatise promoting the joys and blessings of childbirth (1590) and a sermon on Hebrews 12:11-12. To support the poor, Hooke proposed a bank funded by voluntary investment of wealthy households.

Richard Hooker (c. 1553–1600). Anglican priest. Shortly after graduating from Corpus Christi College Oxford, Hooker took holy orders as a priest in 1581. After his marriage, he struggled to find work and temporarily tended sheep until Archbishop John Whitgift* appointed him to the Temple Church in London. Hooker's primary work is *The Laws of Ecclesiastical Polity* (1593), in which he sought to establish a philosophical and logical foundation for the highly controversial Elizabethan Religious Settlement (1559). The Elizabethan Settlement, through the Act of Supremacy, reasserted the Church of England's independence from the Church of Rome, and, through the Act of Uniformity, constructed a common church structure based on the reinstitution of the Book of Common Prayer.* Hooker's argumentation strongly emphasizes natural law and anticipates the social contract theory of John Locke (1632–1704).

Rudolf Hospinian (Wirth) (1547–1626). Swiss Reformed theologian and minister. After studying

theology at Marburg and Heidelberg, Hospinian pastored in rural parishes around Zurich and taught secondary school. In 1588, he transferred to Zurich, ministering at Grossmünster and Fraumünster. A keen student of church history, Hospinian wanted to show the differences between early church doctrine and contemporary Catholic teaching, particularly with regard to sacramental theology. He also criticized Lutheran dogma and the Formula of Concord*. Most of Hospinian's corpus consists of polemical treatises; he also published a series of sermons on the Magnificat.

Caspar Huberinus (1500–1553). German Lutheran theologian and pastor. After studying theology at Wittenberg, Huberinus moved to Augsburg to serve as Urbanus Rhegius's* assistant. Huberinus represented Augsburg at the Bern Disputation (1528) on the Eucharist and images. In 1551, along with the nobility, Huberinus supported the Augsburg Interim, so long as communion of both kinds and regular preaching were allowed. Nevertheless the people viewed him as a traitor because of his official participation in the Interim, nicknaming him "Buberinus" (i.e. scoundrel). He wrote a number of popular devotional works as well as tracts defending Lutheran eucharistic theology against Zwinglian and Anabaptist detractions.

Balthasar Hubmaier (1480/5–1528). German Radical theologian. Hubmaier, a former priest who studied under Johann Eck,* is identified with his leadership in the peasants' uprising at Waldshut. Hubmaier served as the cathedral preacher in Regensberg, where he became involved in a series of anti-Semitic attacks. He was drawn to reform through the early works of Martin Luther*; his contact with Huldrych Zwingli* made Hubmaier a defender of more radical reform, including believers' baptism and a memorialist account of the Eucharist. His involvement in the Peasants' War led to his extradition and execution by the Austrians.

Aegidius Hunnius (1550–1603). German Lutheran theologian and preacher. Educated at Tübingen by Jakob Andreae (1528–1590) and

Johannes Brenz,* Hunnius bolstered and advanced early Lutheran orthodoxy. After his crusade to root out all "crypto-Calvinism" divided Hesse into Lutheran and Reformed regions, Hunnius joined the Wittenberg theological faculty, where with Polykarp Leyser (1552–1610) he helped shape the university into an orthodox stronghold. Passionately confessional, Hunnius developed and nuanced the orthodox doctrines of predestination, Scripture, the church and Christology (more explicitly Chalcedonian), reflecting their codification in the Formula of Concord.* He was unafraid to engage in confessional polemics from the pulpit. In addition to his many treatises (most notably *De persona Christi*, in which he defended Christ's ubiquity), Hunnius published commentaries on Matthew, John, Ephesians and Colossians; his notes on Galatians, Philemon and 1 Corinthians were published posthumously.

Hans Hut (1490–1527). German Radical leader. Hut was an early leader of a mystical, apocalyptic strand of Anabaptist radical reform. His theological views were shaped by Andreas Bodenstein von Karlstadt,* Thomas Müntzer* and Hans Denck,* by whom Hut had been baptized. Hut rejected society and the established church and heralded the imminent end of days, which he perceived in the Peasants' War. Eventually arrested for practicing believers' baptism and participating in the Peasants' War, Hut was tortured and died accidentally in a fire in the Augsburg prison. The next day, the authorities sentenced his corpse to death and burned him.

George Hutcheson (1615–1674). Scottish Puritan pastor. Hutcheson, a pastor in Edinburgh, published commentaries on Job, John and the Minor Prophets, as well as sermons on Psalm 130.

Valentin Ickelshamer (c. 1500–1547). German Radical teacher. After time at Erfurt, he studied under Luther,* Melanchthon,* Bugenhagen* and Karlstadt* in Wittenberg. He sided with Karlstadt against Luther, writing a treatise in Karlstadt's defense. Ickelshamer also represented the Wittenberg guilds in opposition to the city council. This guild committee allied with the peasants in 1525, leading to Ickelshamer's eventual exile. His poem in the Marpeck Circle's *Kunstbuch** is an expansion of a similar poem by Sebastian Franck.*

John Jewel (1522–1571). Anglican theologian and bishop. Jewel studied at Oxford where he met Peter Martyr Vermigli.* After graduating in 1552, Jewel was appointed to his first vicarage and became the orator for the university. Upon Mary I's accession, Jewel lost his post as orator because of his Protestant views. After the trials of Thomas Cranmer* and Nicholas Ridley,* Jewel affirmed Catholic teaching to avoid their fate. Still he had to flee to the continent. Confronted by John Knox,* Jewel publicly repented of his cowardice before the English congregation in Frankfurt, then reunited with Vermigli in Strasbourg. After Mary I's death, Jewel returned to England and was consecrated bishop in 1560. He advocated low-church ecclesiology, but supported the Elizabethan Settlement against Catholics and Puritans. In response to the Council of Trent, he published the *Apoligia ecclesiae Anglicanae* (1562), which established him as the apostle for Anglicanism and incited numerous controversies.

Justus Jonas (1493–1555). German Lutheran theologian, pastor and administrator. Jonas studied law at Erfurt, where he befriended the poet Eobanus Hessus (1488–1540), whom Luther* dubbed "king of the poets"; later, under the influence of the humanist Konrad Muth, Jonas focused on theology. In 1516 he was ordained as a priest, and in 1518 he became a doctor of theology and law. After witnessing the Leipzig Disputation, Jonas was converted to Luther's* cause. While traveling with Luther to the Diet of Worms, Jonas was appointed professor of canon law at Wittenberg. Later he became its dean of theology, lecturing on Romans, Acts and the Psalms. Jonas was also instrumental for reform in Halle. He preached Luther's funeral sermon but had a falling-out with Melanchthon* over the Leipzig Interim. Jonas's most influential contribution was translating Luther's *The Bondage of the Will* and Melanchthon's *Loci communes* into German.

David Joris (c. 1501–1556). Dutch Radical pastor and hymnist. This former glass painter was one of the leading Dutch Anabaptist leaders after the fall of Münster (1535), although due to his increasingly radical ideas his influence waned in the early 1540s. Joris came to see himself as a "third David," a Spirit-anointed prophet ordained to proclaim the coming third kingdom of God, which would be established in the Netherlands with Dutch as its *lingua franca*. Joris's interpretation of Scripture, with his heavy emphasis on personal mystical experience, led to a very public dispute with Menno Simons* whom Joris considered a teacher of the "dead letter." In 1544 Joris and about one hundred followers moved to Basel, conforming outwardly to the teaching of the Reformed church there. Today 240 of Joris's books are extant, the most important of which is his *Twonder Boek* (1542/43).

Andreas Bodenstein von Karlstadt (Carlstadt) (1486–1541). German Radical theologian. Karlstadt, an early associate of Martin Luther* and Philipp Melanchthon* at the University of Wittenberg, participated alongside Luther in the dispute at Leipzig with Johann Eck.* He also influenced the configuration of the Old Testament canon in Protestantism. During Luther's captivity in Wartburg Castle in Eisenach, Karlstadt oversaw reform in Wittenberg. His acceleration of the pace of reform brought conflict with Luther, so Karlstadt left Wittenberg, eventually settling at the University of Basel as professor of Old Testament (after a sojourn in Zurich with Huldrych Zwingli*). During his time in Switzerland, Karlstadt opposed infant baptism and repudiated Luther's doctrine of Christ's real presence in the Eucharist.

John Knox (1513–1572). Scottish Reformed preacher. Knox, a fiery preacher to monarchs and zealous defender of high Calvinism, was a leading figure of reform in Scotland. Following imprisonment in the French galleys, Knox went to England, where he became a royal chaplain to Edward VI. At the accession of Mary, Knox fled to Geneva, studying under John Calvin* and serving as a pastor. Knox returned to Scotland after Mary's death and became a chief architect of the reform of the Scottish church (Presbyterian), serving as one of the authors of the Book of Discipline and writing many pamphlets and sermons.

Antonius Broickwy von Königstein (1470–1541). German Catholic preacher. Very little is known about this important cathedral preacher in Cologne. Strongly opposed to evangelicals, he sought to develop robust resources for Catholic homilies. His postils were bestsellers, and his biblical concordance helped Catholic preachers to construct doctrinal loci from Scripture itself.

Kunstbuch. In 1956, two German students rediscovered this unique collection of Anabaptist works. Four hundred years earlier, a friend of the recently deceased Pilgram Marpeck*—the painter Jörg Probst—had entrusted this collection of letters, tracts and poetry to a Zurich bindery; today only half of it remains. Probst's redaction arranges various compositions from the Marpeck Circle into a devotional anthology focused on the theme of the church as Christ incarnate (cf. Gal 2:20).

François Lambert (Lambert of Avignon) (1487–1530). French Reformed theologian. In 1522, after becoming drawn to the writings of Martin Luther* and meeting Huldrych Zwingli,* Lambert left the Franciscan order. He spent time in Wittenberg, Strasbourg, and Hesse, where Lambert took a leading role at the Homberg Synod (1526) and in creating a biblically based plan for church reform. He served as professor of theology at Marburg University from 1527 to his death. After the Marburg Colloquy (1529), Lambert accepted Zwingli's symbolic view of the Eucharist. Lambert produced nineteen books, mostly biblical commentaries that favored spiritual interpretations; his unfinished work of comprehensive theology was published posthumously.

Hugh Latimer (c. 1485–1555). Anglican bishop and preacher. Latimer was celebrated for his sermons critiquing the idolatrous nature of Catholic practices and the social injustices visited on the underclass by the aristocracy and the individualism of Protestant government. After his support for Henry's petition of divorce he served as a court preacher under Henry VIII and Edward VI. Latimer became a proponent of reform following his education at Cambridge University and received license as a preacher. Following Edward's death, Latimer was tried for heresy, perishing at the stake with Nicholas Ridley* and Thomas Cranmer.*

William Laud (1573–1645). Anglican archbishop, one of the most pivotal and controversial figures in Anglican church history. Early in his career, Laud offended many with his highly traditional, anti-Puritan approach to ecclesial policies. After his election as Archbishop of Canterbury in 1633, Laud continued to strive against the Puritans, demanding the eastward placement of the Communion altar (affirming the religious centrality of the Eucharist), the use of clerical garments, the reintroduction of stained-glass windows, and the uniform use of the Book of Common Prayer.* Laud was accused of being a crypto-Catholic—an ominous accusation during the protracted threat of invasion by the Spanish Armada. In 1640 the Long Parliament met, quickly impeached Laud on charges of treason, and placed him in jail for several years before his execution.

John Lawson (unknown). Seventeenth-century English Puritan. Lawson wrote *Gleanings and Expositions of Some of Scripture* (1646) and a treatise on the sabbath in the New Testament.

Jacques Lefèvre d'Étaples (Faber Stapulensis) (1460?–1536). French Catholic humanist, publisher and translator. Lefèvre d'Étaples studied classical literature and philosophy, as well as patristic and medieval mysticism. He advocated the principle of *ad fontes*, issuing a full-scale annotation on the corpus of Aristotle, publishing the writings of key Christian mystics, and contributing to efforts at biblical translation and commentary. Although he never broke with the Catholic Church, his views prefigured those of Martin Luther,* for which he was condemned by

the University of Sorbonne in Paris. He then found refuge in the court of Marguerite d'Angoulême, where he met John Calvin* and Martin Bucer.*

Edward Leigh (1602–1671). English Puritan biblical critic, historian and politician. Educated at Oxford, Leigh's public career included appointments as a Justice of the Peace, an officer in the parliamentary army during the English Civil Wars and a member of Parliament. Although never ordained, Leigh devoted himself to the study of theology and Scripture; he participated in the Westminster Assembly. Leigh published a diverse corpus, including lexicons of Greek, Hebrew and juristic terms, and histories of Roman, Greek and English rulers. His most important theological work is *A Systeme or Body of Divinity* (1662).

John Lightfoot (1602–1675). Anglican priest and biblical scholar. After graduating from Cambridge, Lightfoot was ordained and pastored at several small parishes. He continued to study classics under the support of the politician Rowland Cotton (1581–1634). Siding with the Parliamentarians during the English Civil Wars, Lightfoot relocated to London in 1643. He was one of the original members of the Westminster Assembly, where he defended a moderate Presbyterianism. His best-known work is the six-volume *Horae Hebraicae et Talmudicae* (1658–1677), a verse-by-verse commentary illumined by Hebrew customs, language and the Jewish interpretive tradition.

Lucas Lossius (1508–1582). German Lutheran teacher and musician. While a student at Leipzig and Wittenberg, Lossius was deeply influenced by Melanchthon* and Luther,* who found work for him as Urbanus Rhegius's* secretary. Soon after going to work for Rhegius, Lossius began teaching at a local gymnasium (or secondary school), *Das Johanneum*, eventually becoming its headmaster. Lossius remained at *Das Johanneum* until his death, even turning down appointments to university professorships. A man of varied interests, he wrote on dialectics, music and church history, as well as publishing a postil and a five-volume set of annotations on the New Testament.

Sibrandus Lubbertus (c. 1555–1625). Dutch Reformed theologian. Lubbertis, a key figure in the establishment of orthodox Calvinism in Frisia, studied theology at Wittenburg and Geneva (under Theodore Beza*) before his appointment as professor of theology at the University of Franeker. Throughout his career, Lubbertis advocated for high Calvinist theology, defending it in disputes with representatives of Socinianism, Arminianism and Roman Catholicism. Lubbertis criticized the Catholic theologian Robert Bellarmine and fellow Dutch reformer Jacobus Arminius*; the views of the latter he opposed as a prominent participant in the Synod of Dordrecht.*

Martin Luther (1483–1546). German Lutheran priest, professor and theologian. While a professor in Wittenberg, Luther reinterpreted the doctrine of justification. Convinced that righteousness comes only from God's grace, he disputed the sale of indulgences with the Ninety-five Theses. Luther's positions brought conflict with Rome; his denial of papal authority led to excommunication. He also challenged the Mass, transubstantiation and communion under one kind. Though Luther was condemned by the Diet of Worms, the Elector of Saxony provided him safe haven. Luther returned to Wittenberg with public order collapsing under Andreas Bodenstein von Karlstadt;* Luther steered a more cautious path of reform. His rendering of the Bible and liturgy in the vernacular, as well as his hymns and sermons, proved extensively influential.

Georg Major (1502–1574). German Lutheran theologian. Major was on the theological faculty of the University of Wittenberg, succeeding as dean Johannes Bugenhagen* and Philipp Melanchthon.* One of the chief editors on the Wittenberg edition of Luther's works, Major is most identified with the controversy bearing his name, in which he stated that good works are necessary to salvation. Major qualified his statement, which was in reference to the totality of the Christian life. The Formula of Concord* rejected the statement, ending the controversy. As a theologian, Major further refined Lutheran

views of the inspiration of Scripture and the doctrine of the Trinity.

John (Mair) Major (1467–1550). Scottish Catholic philosopher. Major taught logic and theology at the universities of Paris (his alma mater), Glasgow and St Andrews. His broad interests and impressive work drew students from all over Europe. While disapproving of evangelicals (though he did teach John Knox*), Major advocated reform programs for Rome. He supported collegial episcopacy and even challenged the curia's teaching on sexuality. Still he was a nominalist who was critical of humanist approaches to biblical exegesis. His best-known publication is *A History of Greater Britain, Both England and Scotland* (1521), which promoted the union of the kingdoms. He also published a commentary on Peter Lombard's *Sentences* and the Gospel of John.

Juan de Maldonado (1533–1583). Spanish Catholic biblical scholar. A student of Francisco de Toledo,* Maldonado taught philosophy and theology at the universities of Paris and Salamanca. Ordained to the priesthood in Rome, he revised the Septuagint under papal appointment. While Maldonado vehemently criticized Protestants, he asserted that Reformed baptism was valid and that mixed confessional marriages were acceptable. His views on Mary's immaculate conception proved controversial among many Catholics who conflated his statement that it was not an article of faith with its denial. He was intrigued by demonology (blaming demonic influence for the Reformation). All his work was published posthumously; his Gospel commentaries were highly valued and important.

Thomas Manton (1620–1677). English Puritan minister. Manton, educated at Oxford, served for a time as lecturer at Westminster Abbey and rector of St. Paul's, Covent Garden, and was a strong advocate of Presbyterianism. He was known as a rigorous evangelical Calvinist who preached long expository sermons. At different times in his ecclesial career he worked side-by-side with Richard Baxter* and John Owen.* In his later life, Manton's Nonconformist position led to his ejection as a clergyman from the Church of England (1662) and eventual imprisonment (1670). Although a voluminous writer, Manton was best known for his preaching. At his funeral in 1677, he was dubbed "the king of preachers."

Augustin Marlorat (c. 1506–1562). French Reformed pastor. Committed by his family to a monastery at the age of eight, Marlorat was also ordained into the priesthood at an early age in 1524. He fled to Geneva in 1535, where he pastored until the Genevan Company of Pastors sent him to France to shepherd the nascent evangelical congregations. His petition to the young Charles IX (1550–1574) for the right to public evangelical worship was denied. In response to a massacre of evangelicals in Vassy (over sixty dead, many more wounded), Marlorat's congregation planned to overtake Rouen. After the crown captured Rouen, Marlorat was arrested and executed three days later for treason. His principle published work was an anthology of New Testament comment modeled after Thomas Aquinas's *Catena aurea in quatuor Evangelia*. Marlorat harmonized Reformed and Lutheran comment with the church fathers, interspersed with his own brief comments. He also wrote such anthologies for Genesis, Job, the Psalms, Song of Songs and Isaiah.

Pilgram Marpeck (c. 1495–1556). Austrian Radical elder and theologian. During a brief sojourn in Strasbourg, Marpeck debated with Martin Bucer* before the city council; Bucer was declared the winner, and Marpeck was asked to leave Strasbourg for his views concerning paedobaptism (which he compared to a sacrifice to Moloch). After his time in Strasbourg, Marpeck travelled throughout southern Germany and western Austria, planting Anabaptist congregations. Marpeck criticized the strict use of the ban, however, particularly among the Swiss brethren. He also engaged in a Christological controversy with Kaspar von Schwenckfeld.*

Johannes Mathesius (1504–1565). German Lutheran theologian and pastor. After reading Martin Luther's* *On Good Works*, Mathesius left his teaching post in Ingolstadt and traveled to Wittenberg to study theology. Mathesius was an important agent of reform in the Bohemian town of Jáchymov, where he pastored, preached and taught. Over one thousand of Mathesius's sermons are extant, including numerous wedding and funeral sermons as well as a series on Luther's life. Mathesius also transcribed portions of Luther's Table Talk.

John Mayer (1583–1664). Anglican priest and biblical exegete. Mayer dedicated much of his life to biblical exegesis, writing a seven-volume commentary on the entire Bible (1627–1653). Styled after Philipp Melanchthon's* *locus* method, Mayer's work avoided running commentary, focusing instead on textual and theological problems. He was a parish priest for fifty-five years. In the office of priest Mayer also wrote a popular catechism, *The English Catechisme, or a Commentarie on the Short Catechisme* (1621), which went through twelve editions in his lifetime.

Joseph Mede (1586–1638). Anglican biblical scholar, Hebraist and Greek lecturer. A man of encyclopedic knowledge, Mede was interested in numerous fields, varying from philology and history to mathematics and physics, although millennial thought and apocalyptic prophesy were clearly his chief interests. Mede's most important work was his *Clavis Apocalyptica* (1627, later translated into English as *The Key of the Revelation*). This work examined the structure of Revelation as the key to its interpretation. Mede saw the visions as a connected and chronological sequence hinging around Revelation 17:18. He is remembered as an important figure in the history of millenarian theology. He was respected as a mild-mannered and generous scholar who avoided controversy and debate, but who had many original thoughts.

Philipp Melanchthon (1497–1560). German Lutheran educator, reformer and theologian. Melanchthon is known as the partner and successor to Martin Luther* in reform in Germany and for his pioneering *Loci Communes*, which served as a theological textbook. Melanchthon participated with Luther in the Leipzig disputation, helped implement reform in Wittenberg and was a chief architect of the Augsburg Confession.* Later, Melanchthon and Martin Bucer* worked for union between the reformed and Catholic churches. On account of Melanchthon's more ecumenical disposition and his modification of several of Luther's doctrines, he was held in suspicion by some.

Johannes Mercerus (Jean Mercier) (d. 1570). French Hebraist. Mercerus studied under the first Hebrew chair at the Collège Royal de Paris, François Vatable (d. 1547), whom he succeeded in 1546. John Calvin* tried to recruit Mercerus to the Genevan Academy as professor of Hebrew, once in 1558 and again in 1563; he refused both times. During his lifetime Mercerus published grammatical helps for Hebrew and Chaldean, an aid to the Masoretic symbols in the Hebrew text, and translated the commentaries and grammars of several medieval rabbis. He himself wrote commentaries on Genesis, the wisdom books, and most of the Minor Prophets. These commentaries—most of them only published after his death—were philologically focused and interacted with the work of Jerome, Nicholas of Lyra,* notable rabbis and Johannes Oecolampadius.*

Thomas More (1478–1535). English Catholic lawyer, politician, humanist and martyr. More briefly studied at Oxford, but completed his legal studies in London. After contemplating the priesthood for four years, he opted for politics and was elected a member of Parliament in 1504. A devout Catholic, More worked with church leaders in England to root out heresy while he also confronted Lutheran teachings in writing. After four years as Lord Chancellor, More resigned due to heightened tensions with Henry VIII over papal supremacy (which More supported and Henry did not). Tensions did not abate. More's steadfast refusal to accept the Act of Supremacy (1534)—which declared the King of England to be the supreme ecclesial primate not the pope—resulted in his arrest and trial for high treason. He

was found guilty and beheaded with John Fisher (1469–1535). Friends with John Colet* and Desiderius Erasmus,* More was a widely respected humanist in England as well as on the continent. Well-known for his novel *Utopia* (1516), More also penned several religious treatises on Christ's passion and suffering during his imprisonment in the Tower of London, which were published posthumously.

Sebastian Münster (1488–1552). German Reformed Hebraist, exegete, printer, and geographer. After converting to the Reformation in 1524, Münster taught Hebrew at the universities of Heidelberg and Basel. During his lengthy tenure in Basel he published more than 70 books, including Hebrew dictionaries and rabbinic commentaries. He also produced an evangelistic work for Jews titled *Vikuach* (1539). Münster's *Torat ha-Maschiach* (1537), the Gospel of Matthew, was the first published Hebrew translation of any portion of the New Testament. Despite his massive contribution to contemporary understanding of the Hebrew language, Münster was criticized by many of the reformers as a Judaizer.

Thomas Müntzer (c. 1489–1525). German Radical preacher. As a preacher in the town of Zwickau, Müntzer was influenced by German mysticism and, growing convinced that Martin Luther* had not carried through reform properly, sought to restore the pure apostolic church of the New Testament. Müntzer's radical ideas led to expulsions from various cities; he developed a highly apocalyptic theology, in which he heralded the last days that would establish the pure community out of suffering, prompting Müntzer's proactive role in the Peasants' War, which he perceived as a crucial apocalyptic event. Six thousand of Müntzer's followers were annihilated by magisterial troops; Müntzer was executed.

John Murcot (1625–1654). English Puritan pastor. After completing his bachelor's at Oxford in 1647, Murcot was ordained as a pastor, transferring to several parishes until in 1651 he moved to Dublin. All his works were published posthumously.

Simon Musaeus (1521–1582). German Lutheran theologian. After studying at the universities of Frankfurt an der Oder and Wittenberg, Musaeus began teaching Greek at the Cathedral school in Nuremberg and was ordained. Having returned to Wittenberg to complete a doctoral degree, Musaeus spent the rest of his career in numerous ecclesial and academic administrative posts. He opposed Matthias Flacius's (1505–1575) view of original sin—that the formal essence of human beings is marred by original sin—even calling the pro-Flacian faculty at Wittenberg "the devil's latrine." Musaeus published a disputation on original sin and a postil.

Wolfgang Musculus (1497–1563). German Reformed pastor and theologian. Musculus produced translations, biblical commentaries and an influential theological text, *Loci Communes Sacrae Theologiae* (*Commonplaces of Sacred Theology*), outlining a Zwinglian theology. Musculus began to study theology while at a Benedictine monastery; he departed in 1527 and became secretary to Martin Bucer* in Strasbourg. He was later installed as a pastor in Augsburg, eventually performing the first evangelical liturgy in the city's cathedral. Though Musculus was active in the pursuit of the reform agenda, he was also concerned for ecumenism, participating in the Wittenberg Concord (1536) and discussions between Lutherans and Catholics.

Friedrich Nausea (c. 1496–1552). German Catholic bishop and preacher. After completing his studies at Leipzig, this famed preacher was appointed priest in Frankfurt but was run out of town by his congregants during his first sermon. He transferred to Mainz as cathedral preacher. Nausea was well connected through the German papal hierarchy and traveled widely to preach to influential ecclesial and secular courts. Court preacher for Ferdinand I (1503–1564), his reform tendencies fit well with royal Austrian theological leanings, and he was enthroned as the bishop of Vienna. Nausea thought that rather than endless colloquies only a council could settle reform. Unfortunately he could not participate in the first session of Trent due to insufficient funding, but he arrived for the second session. Nausea defended the laity's reception of the cup and stressed the importance of promulgating official Catholic teaching in the vernacular.

Melchior Neukirch (1540–1597). German Lutheran pastor and playwright. Neukirch's pastoral career spanned more than thirty years in several northern German parishes. Neukirch published a history of the Braunschweig church since the Reformation and a dramatization of Acts 4–7. He died of the plague.

Nicholas of Lyra (1270–1349). French Catholic biblical exegete. Very little is known about this influential medieval theologian of the Sorbonne aside from the works he published, particularly the *Postilla litteralis super totam Bibliam* (1322–1333). With the advent of the printing press this work was regularly published alongside the Latin Vulgate and the *Glossa ordinaria*. In this running commentary on the Bible Nicholas promoted literal interpretation as the basis for theology. Despite his preference for literal interpretation, Nicholas also published a companion volume, the *Postilla moralis super totam Bibliam* (1339), a commentary on the spiritual meaning of the biblical text. Nicholas was a major conversation partner for many reformers though many of them rejected his exegesis as too literal and too "Jewish" (not concerned enough with the Bible's fulfillment in Jesus Christ).

Johannes Oecolampadius (Johannes Huszgen) (1482–1531). Swiss-German Reformed humanist, reformer and theologian. Oecolampadius (an assumed name meaning "house light") assisted with Desiderius Erasmus's* Greek New Testament, lectured on biblical languages and exegesis and completed an influential Greek grammar. After joining the evangelical cause through studying patristics and the work of Martin Luther,* Oecolampadius went to Basel, where he lectured on biblical exegesis and participated in ecclesial reform. On account of Oecolampadius's effort, the city council passed legislation restricting preaching to the gospel and releasing the city from compulsory Mass. Oecolampadius was a chief ally of Huldrych Zwingli,* whom he supported at the Marburg Colloquy (1529).

Kaspar Olevianus (1536–1587). German Reformed theologian. Olevianus is celebrated for composing the Heidelberg Catechism and producing a critical edition of Calvin's *Institutes* in German. Olevianus studied theology with many, including John Calvin,* Theodore Beza,* Heinrich Bullinger* and Peter Martyr Vermigli.* As an advocate of Reformed doctrine, Olevianus oversaw the shift from Lutheranism to Calvinism throughout Heidelberg, organizing the city's churches after Calvin's Geneva. The Calvinist ecclesial vision of Olevianus entangled him in a dispute with another Heidelberg reformer over the rights of ecclesiastical discipline, which Olevianus felt belonged to the council of clergy and elders rather than civil magistrates.

Josua Opitz (c. 1542–1585). German Lutheran pastor. After a brief stint as superintendent in Regensburg, Opitz, a longtime preacher, was dismissed for his support of Matthias Flacius's (1520–1575) view of original sin. (Using Aristotelian categories, Flacius argued that the formal essence of human beings is marred by original sin, forming sinners into the image of Satan; his views were officially rejected in Article 1 of the Formula of Concord.*) Hans Wilhelm Roggendorf (1533–1591) invited Opitz to lower Austria as part of his Lutheranizing program. Unfortunately Roggendorf and Opitz never succeed in getting Lutheranism legal recognition, perhaps in large part due to Opitz's staunch criticism of Catholics, which resulted in his exile. He died of plague.

John Owen (1616–1683). English Puritan theologian. Owen trained at Oxford University, where he was later appointed dean of Christ Church and vice chancellor of the university, following his service as chaplain to Oliver Cromwell. Although Owen began his career as a Presbyterian minister, he eventually departed to the party of Independents. Owen composed many sermons, biblical commentaries (including seven volumes on the book of Hebrews), theological treatises and controversial monographs (including disputations with Arminians, Anglicans, Catholics and Socinians).

Christoph Pelargus (1565–1633). German Lutheran pastor, theologian, professor and superintendent. Pelargus studied philosophy and theology at the University of Frankfurt an der Oder, in Brandenburg. This irenic Philippist was appointed as the superintendent of Brandenburg and later became a pastor in Frankfurt, although the local authorities first required him to condemn Calvinist theology, because several years earlier he had been called before the consistory in Berlin under suspicion of being a crypto-Calvinist. Among his most important works were a four-volume commentary on *De orthodoxa fide* by John of Damascus (d. 749), a treatise defending the breaking of the bread during communion, and a volume of funeral sermons. He also published commentaries on the Pentateuch, the Psalms, Matthew, John and Acts.

Konrad Pellikan (1478–1556). German Reformed Hebraist and theologian. Pellikan attended the University of Heidelberg, where he mastered Hebrew under Johannes Reuchlin. In 1504 Pellikan published one of the first Hebrew grammars that was not merely a translation of the work of medieval rabbis. While living in Basel, Pellikan assisted the printer Johannes Amerbach, with whom he published some of Luther's* early writings. He also worked with Sebastian Münster* and Wolfgang Capito* on a Hebrew Psalter (1516). In 1526, after teaching theology for three years at the University of Basel, Huldrych Zwingli* brought Pellikan to Zurich to chair the faculty of Old Testament. Pellikan's magnum opus is a seven-volume commentary on the entire Bible (except Revelation) and the Apocrypha; it is often heavily dependent upon the work of others (esp. Desiderius Erasmus* and Johannes Oecolampadius*).

Benedict Pererius (1535–1610). Spanish Catholic theologian, philosopher and exegete. Pererius entered the Society of Jesus in 1552. He taught philosophy, theology, and exegesis at the Roman College of the Jesuits. Early in his career he warned against neo-Platonism and astrology in his *De principiis* (1576). Pererius wrote a lengthy commentary on Daniel, and five volumes of exegetical theses on Exodus, Romans, Revelation and part of the Gospel of John (chs. 1–14). His four-volume commentary on Genesis (1591–1599) was lauded by Protestants and Catholics alike.

William Perkins (1558–1602). English Puritan preacher and theologian. Perkins was a highly regarded Puritan Presbyterian preacher and biblical commentator in the Elizabethan era. He studied at Cambridge University and later became a fellow of Christ's Church college as a preacher and professor, receiving acclaim for his sermons and lectures. Even more, Perkins gained an esteemed reputation for his ardent exposition of Calvinist reformed doctrine in the style of Petrus Ramus,* becoming one of the first English reformed theologians to achieve international recognition. Perkins influenced the federal Calvinist shape of Puritan theology and the vision of logical, practical expository preaching.

Dirk Philips (1504–1568). Dutch Radical elder and theologian. This former Franciscan monk, known for being severe and obstinate, was a leading theologian of the sixteenth-century Anabaptist movement. Despite the fame of Menno Simons* and his own older brother Obbe, Philips wielded great influence over Anabaptists in the Netherlands and northern Germany where he ministered. As a result of Philips's understanding of the apostolic church as radically separated from the children of the world, he advocated a very strict interpretation of the ban, including formal shunning. His writings were collected and published near the end of his life as *Enchiridion oft Hantboecxken van de Christelijcke Leere* (1564).

Johannes Piscator (1546–1625). German Reformed theologian. Educated at Tübingen (though he wanted to study at Wittenberg), Piscator taught at the universities of Strasbourg and Heidelberg, as well as academies in Neustadt and Herborn. His commentaries on both the Old and New Testaments involve a tripartite analysis

of a given passage's argument, of scholia on the text and of doctrinal loci. Some consider Piscator's method to be a full flowering of Beza's* "logical" scriptural analysis, focused on the text's meaning and its relationship to the pericopes around it.

Petrus Ramus (1515–1572). French Reformed humanist philosopher. Ramus was an influential professor of philosophy and logic at the French royal college in Paris; he converted to Protestantism and left France for Germany, where he came under the influence of Calvinist thought. Ramus was a trenchant critic of Aristotle and noted for his method of classification based on a deductive movement from universals to particulars, the latter becoming branching divisions that provided a visual chart of the parts to the whole. His system profoundly influenced Puritan theology and preaching. After returning to Paris, Ramus died in the Saint Bartholomew's Day Massacre.

Remonstrance (1610). See *Synod of Dordrecht*.

Urbanus Rhegius (1489–1541). German Lutheran pastor. Rhegius, who was likely the son of a priest, studied under the humanists at Freiburg and Ingolstadt. After a brief stint as a foot soldier, he received ordination in 1519 and was made cathedral preacher in Augsburg. During his time in Augsburg he closely read Luther's* works, becoming an enthusiastic follower. Despite his close friendship with Zwingli* and Oecolampadius,* Rhegius supported Luther in the eucharistic debates, later playing a major role in the Wittenberg Concord (1536). He advocated for peace during the Peasants' War and had extended interactions with the Anabaptists in Augsburg. Later in his career he concerned himself with the training of pastors, writing a pastoral guide and two catechisms. About one hundred of his writings were published posthumously.

Lancelot Ridley (d. 1576). Anglican preacher. Ridley was the first cousin of Nicholas Ridley,* the bishop of London who was martyred during the Marian persecutions. By Cranmer's* recommendation, Ridley became one of the six Canterbury Cathedral preachers. Upon Mary I's accession in 1553, Ridley was defrocked (as a married priest). Ridley returned to Canterbury Cathedral after Mary's death. He wrote commentaries on Jude, Ephesians, Philippians and Colossians.

Nicholas Ridley (c. 1502–1555). Anglican bishop. Ridley was a student and fellow at Cambridge University who was appointed chaplain to Archbishop Thomas Cranmer* and is thought to be partially responsible for Cranmer's shift to a symbolic view of the Eucharist. Cranmer promoted Ridley twice: as bishop of Rochester, where he openly advocated Reformed theological views, and, later, as bishop of London. Ridley assisted Cranmer in the revisions of the Book of Common Prayer.* Ridley's support of Lady Jane Grey against the claims of Mary to the throne led to his arrest; he was tried for heresy and burned at the stake with Hugh Latimer.*

Peter Riedemann (1506–1556). German Radical elder, theologian and hymnist. While traveling as a Silesian cobbler, Riedemann came into contact with Anabaptist teachings and joined a congregation in Linz. In 1529 he was called to be a minister, only to be imprisoned soon after as part of Archduke Ferdinand's efforts to suppress heterodoxy in his realm. Once he was released, he moved to Moravia in 1532 where he was elected as a minister and missionary of the Hutterite community there. His *Account of Our Religion, Doctrine and Faith* (1542), with its more than two thousand biblical references, is Riedemann's most important work and is still used by Hutterites today.

Nehemiah Rogers (1593–1660). Anglican priest. After studying at Cambridge, Rogers ministered at numerous parishes during his more than forty-year career. In 1643, he seems to have been forced out of a parish on account of being a Royalist and friend of William Laud.* Rogers published a number of sermons and tracts, including a series of expositions on Jesus' parables in the Gospels.

Robert Rollock (c. 1555–1599). Scottish Reformed pastor, educator and theologian. Rollock was deeply influenced by Petrus Ramus's* system of logic, which he implemented as a tutor and (later) principal of Edinburgh University and

in his expositions of the Bible. Rollock, as a divinity professor and theologian, was instrumental in diffusing a federalist Calvinism in the Scottish church; he lectured on theology using the texts of Theodore Beza* and articulated a highly covenantal interpretation of the biblical narratives. He was a prolific writer of sermons, expositions, commentaries, lectures and occasional treatises.

Heinrich Salmuth (1522–1576). German Lutheran theologian. After earning his doctorate from the University of Leipzig, Salmuth served in several coterminous pastoral and academic positions. He was integral to the reorganization of the University of Jena. Except for a few disputations, all of Salmuth's works—mostly sermons— were published posthumously by his son.

Edwin Sandys (1519–1588). Anglican bishop. During his doctoral studies at Cambridge, Sandys befriended Martin Bucer.* Having supported the Protestant Lady Jane Grey's claim to the throne, Sandys resigned his post at Cambridge upon Mary I's accession. He was then arrested and imprisoned in the Tower of London. Released in 1554, he sojourned on the continent until Mary's death. On his return to England he was appointed to revise the liturgy and was consecrated bishop. Many of his sermons were published, but his most significant literary legacy is his work as a translator of the Bishop's Bible (1568), which served as the foundational English text for the translators of the King James Bible (1611).

Erasmus Sarcerius (1501–1559). German Lutheran superintendent, educator and pastor. Sarcerius served as educational superintendent, court preacher and pastor in Nassau and, later, in Leipzig. The hallmark of Sarcerius's reputation was his ethical emphasis as exercised through ecclesial oversight and family structure; he also drafted disciplinary codes for regional churches in Germany. Sarcerius served with Philipp Melanchthon* as Protestant delegates at the Council of Trent, though both withdrew prior to the dismissal of the session; he eventually became an opponent of Melanchthon, contesting the latter's understanding of the Eucharist at a colloquy in Worms in 1557.

Michael Sattler (c. 1490–1527). Swiss Radical leader. Sattler was a Benedictine monk who abandoned the monastic life during the upheavals of the Peasants' War. He took up the trade of weaving under the guidance of an outspoken Anabaptist. It seems that Sattler did not openly join the Anabaptist movement until after the suppression of the Peasants' War in 1526. Sattler interceded with Martin Bucer* and Wolfgang Capito* for imprisoned Anabaptists in Strasbourg. Shortly before he was convicted of heresy and executed, he wrote the definitive expression of Anabaptist theology, the Schleitheim Articles.*

Leupold Scharnschlager (d. 1563). Austrian Radical elder. See *Kunstbuch*.

Leonhard Schiemer (d. 1528). Austrian Radical martyr. See *Kunstbuch*.

Hans Schlaffer (c. 1490–1528). Austrian Radical martyr. See *Kunstbuch*.

Schleitheim Articles (1527). After the death of Conrad Grebel* in 1526 and the execution of Felix Manz (born c. 1498) in early 1527, the young Swiss Anabaptist movement was in need of unity and direction. A synod convened at Schleitheim under the chairmanship of Michael Sattler,* which passed seven articles of Anabaptist distinctives—likely defined against both magisterial reformers and other Anabaptists with less orthodox and more militant views (e.g., Balthasar Hubmaier*). Unlike most confessions, these articles do not explicitly address traditional creedal interests; they explicate instead the Anabaptist view of the sacraments, church discipline, separatism, the role of ministers, pacifism and oaths. Throughout the document there is a resolute focus on Christ's example. The Schleitheim Articles are considered the definitive statement of Anabaptist theology, particularly regarding separatism.

Schmalkald Articles (1537). In response to Pope Paul III's (1468–1549) 1536 decree ordering a general church council to solve the Protestant crisis, Elector John Frederick (1503–1554) commissioned Martin Luther* to draft the sum of his teaching. Intended by Luther as a last will and testament—and composed with advice from well-known colleagues Justus Jonas,* Johann Bugenhagen,* Caspar Cruciger,* Nikolaus von Amsdorf (1483–1565), Georg Spalatin (1484–1545), Philipp Melanchthon* and Johann Agricola*—these articles provide perhaps the briefest and most systematic summary of Luther's teaching. The document was not adopted formally by the Lutheran Schmalkald League, as was hoped, and the general church council was postponed for several years (until convening at Trent in 1545). Only in 1580 were the articles officially received, by being incorporated into the *Book of Concord* defining orthodox Lutheranism.

Anna Maria van Schurman (1607–1678). Dutch Reformed polymath. Van Schurman cultivated talents in art, poetry, botany, linguistics and theology. She mastered most contemporary European languages, in addition to Latin, Greek, Hebrew, Arabic, Farsi and Ethiopian. With the encouragement of leading Reformed theologian Gisbertus Voetius (1589–1676), van Schurman attended lectures at the University of Utrecht—although she was required to sit behind a wooden screen so that the male students could not see her. In 1638 van Schurman published her famous treatise advocating female scholarship, *Amica dissertatio . . . de capacitate ingenii muliebris ad scientias*. In addition to these more polemical works, van Schurman also wrote hymns and poems, including a paraphrase of Genesis 1–3. Later in life she became a devotee of Jean de Labadie (1610–1674), a former Jesuit who was also expelled from the Reformed church for his separatist leanings. Her *Eucleria* (1673) is the most well known defense of Labadie's theology.

Kaspar von Schwenckfeld (1489–1561). German Radical reformer. Schwenckfeld was a Silesian nobleman who encountered Luther's* works in 1521. He traveled to Wittenberg twice: first to meet Luther and Karlstadt,* and a second time to convince Luther of his doctrine of the "internal word"—emphasizing inner revelation so strongly that he did not see church meetings or the sacraments as necessary—after which Luther considered him heterodox. Schwenckfeld won his native territory to the Reformation in 1524 and later lived in Strasbourg for five years until Bucer* sought to purify the city of less traditional theologies. Schwenckfeld wrote numerous polemical and exegetical tracts.

Scots Confession (1560). In 1560, the Scottish Parliament undertook to reform the Church of Scotland and to commission a Reformed confession of faith. In the course of four days, a committee—which included John Knox*—wrote this confession, largely based on Calvin's* work, the Confession of the English Congregation in Geneva (1556) and the Gallic Confession.* The articles were not ratified until 1567 and were displaced by the Westminster Confession (1646), adopted by the Scottish in 1647.

Second Helvetic Confession (1566). Believing he would soon die, Heinrich Bullinger* penned a personal statement of his Reformed faith in 1561 as a theological will. In 1563, Bullinger sent a copy of this confession, which blended Zwingli's and Calvin's theology, to the elector of the Palatinate, Frederick III (1515–1576), who had asked for a complete explication of the Reformed faith in order to defend himself against aggressive Lutheran attacks after printing the Heidelberg Confession.* Although not published until 1566, the Second Helvetic Confession became the definitive sixteenth-century Reformed statement of faith. Theodore Beza* used it as the organizing confession for his *Harmonia Confessionum* (1581), which sought to emphasize the unity of the Reformed churches. Bullinger's personal confession was adopted by the Reformed churches of Scotland (1566), Hungary (1567), France (1571) and Poland (1571).

Obadiah Sedgwick (c. 1600–1658). English Puritan minister. Educated at Oxford, Sedgwick pastored in London and participated in the Westminster Assembly. An ardent Puritan, Sedgwick was appointed by Oliver Cromwell (1599–1658) to examine clerical candidates. Sedgwick published a catechism, several sermons and a treatise on how to deal with doubt.

Nikolaus Selnecker (1530–1592). German Lutheran theologian, preacher, pastor and hymnist. Selnecker taught in Wittenberg, Jena and Leipzig, preached in Dresden and Wolfenbüttel, and pastored in Leipzig. He was forced out of his post at Jena because of suspicions that he was a crypto-Calvinist. He sought refuge in Wolfenbüttel, where he met Martin Chemnitz* and Jakob Andreae.* Under their influence Selnecker was drawn away from Philippist theology. Selnecker's shift in theology can be seen in his *Institutio religionis christianae* (1573). Selnecker coauthored the Formula of Concord* with Chemnitz, Andreae, Andreas Musculus (1514–1581), and David Chytraeus.* Selnecker also published lectures on Genesis, the Psalms, and the New Testament epistles, as well as composing over a hundred hymn tunes and texts.

Short Confession (1610). In response to some of William Laud's* reforms in the Church of England—particularly a law stating that ministers who refused to comply with the Book of Common Prayer* would lose their ordination—a group of English Puritans immigrated to the Netherlands in protest, where they eventually embraced the practice of believer's baptism. The resulting Short Confession was an attempt at union between these Puritans and local Dutch Anabaptists ("Waterlanders"). The document highlights the importance of love in the church and reflects optimism regarding the freedom of the will while explicitly rejecting double predestination.

Richard Sibbes (1577–1635). English Puritan preacher. Sibbes was educated at St. John's College, Cambridge, where he was converted to reforming views and became a popular preacher. As a moderate Puritan emphasizing interior piety and brotherly love, Sibbes always remained within the established Church of England, though opposed to some of its liturgical ceremonies. His collected sermons constitute his main literary legacy.

Menno Simons (c. 1496–1561). Dutch Radical leader. Simons led a separatist Anabaptist group in the Netherlands that would later be called Mennonites, known for nonviolence and renunciation of the world. A former priest, Simons rejected Catholicism through the influence of Anabaptist disciples of Melchior Hoffmann and based on his study of Scripture, in which he found no support for transubstantiation or infant baptism. Following the sack of Anabaptists at Münster, Simons committed to a nonviolent way of life. Simons proclaimed a message of radical discipleship of obedience and inner purity, marked by voluntary adult baptism and communal discipline.

Henry Smith (c. 1550–1591). English Puritan minister. Smith stridently opposed the Book of Common Prayer* and refused to subscribe to the Articles of Religion,* thus limiting his pastoral opportunities. Nevertheless he gained a reputation as an eloquent preacher in London. He published sermon collections as well as several treatises.

Cyriacus Spangenberg (1528–1604). German Lutheran pastor, preacher and theologian. Spangenberg was a staunch, often acerbic, Gnesio-Lutheran. He rejected the Formula of Concord* because of concerns about the princely control of the church, as well as its rejection of Flacian language of original sin (as constituting the "substance" of human nature after the fall). He published many commentaries and sermons, most famously seventy wedding sermons (*Ehespiegel* [1561]), his sermons on Luther* (*Theander Luther* [1562–1571]) and Luther's hymns (*Cithara Lutheri* [1569–1570]). He also published an analysis of the Old Testament (though he only got as far as Job), based on a methodology that anticipated the logical bifurcations of Peter Ramus.*

Johann Spangenberg (1484–1550). German Lutheran pastor and catechist. Spangenberg studied at the University of Erfurt, where he was welcomed into a group of humanists associated with Konrad Muth (1470–1526). There he met the reformer Justus Jonas,* and Eobanus Hessius (1488–1540), whom Luther* dubbed "king of the poets." Spangenberg served at parishes in Stolberg (1520–1524), Nordhausen (1524–1546) and, by Luther's recommendation, Eisleben (1546–1550). Spangenberg published one of the best-selling postils of the sixteenth century, the *Postilla*

Teütsch, a six-volume work meant to prepare children to understand the lectionary readings. It borrowed the question-answer form of Luther's *Small Catechism* and was so popular that a monk, Johannes Craendonch, purged overt anti-Catholic statements from it and republished it under his own name. Among Spangenberg's other pastoral works are *ars moriendi* ("the art of dying") booklets, a postil for the Acts of the Apostles and a question-answer version of Luther's *Large Catechism*. In addition to preaching and pastoring, Spangenberg wrote pamphlets on controversial topics such as purgatory, as well as textbooks on music, mathematics and grammar.

Georg Spindler (1525–1605). German Reformed theologian and pastor. After studying theology under Caspar Cruciger* and Philipp Melanchthon,* Spindler accepted a pastorate in Bohemia. A well-respected preacher, Spindler published postils in 1576 which some of his peers viewed as crypto-Calvinist. To investigate this allegation Spindler read John Calvin's* *Institutes*, and subsequently converted to the Reformed faith. After years of travel, he settled in the Palatinate and pastored there until his death. In addition to his Lutheran postils, Spindler also published Reformed postils in 1594 as well as several treatises on the Lord's Supper and predestination.

Michael Stifel (1486–1567). German Lutheran mathematician, theologian and pastor. An Augustinian monk, Stifel's interest in mysticism, apocalypticism and numerology led him to identify Pope Leo X as the antichrist. Stifel soon joined the reform movement, writing a 1522 pamphlet in support of Martin Luther's* theology. After Luther quelled the fallout of Stifel's failed prediction of the Apocalypse—October 19, 1533 at 8AM—Stifel focused more on mathematics and his pastoral duties. He was the first professor of mathematics at the University of Jena. He published several numerological interpretations of texts from the Gospels, Daniel and Revelation. However, Stifel's most important work is his *Arithmetica Integra* (1544), in which he standardized the approach to quadratic equations. He also developed notations for exponents and radicals.

Johann Sutell (1504–1575). German Lutheran pastor. After studying at the University of Wittenberg, Sutell received a call to a pastorate in Göttingen, where he eventually became superintendent. He wrote new church orders for Göttingen (1531) and Schweinfurt (1543), and expanded two sermons for publication, *The Dreadful Destruction of Jerusalem* (1539) and *History of Lazarus* (1543).

Swiss Brethren Confession of Hesse (1578). Anabaptist leader Hans Pauly Kuchenbecker penned this confession after a 1577 interrogation by Lutheran authorities. This confession was unusually amenable to Lutheran views—there is no mention of pacifism or rejection of oath taking.

Synod of Dordrecht (1618–1619). This large Dutch Reformed Church council—also attended by English, German and Swiss delegates—met to settle the theological issues raised by the followers of Jacobus Arminius.* Arminius's theological disagreements with mainstream Reformed teaching erupted into open conflict with the publication of the *Remonstrance* (1610). This "protest" was based on five points: that election is based on foreseen faith or unbelief; that Christ died indiscriminately for all people (although only believers receive salvation); that people are thoroughly sinful by nature apart from the prevenient grace of God that enables their free will to embrace or reject the gospel; that humans are able to resist the working of God's grace; and that it is possible for true believers to fall away from faith completely. The Synod ruled in favor of the Contra-Remonstrants, its Canons often remembered with a TULIP acrostic—total depravity, unconditional election, limited atonement, irresistible grace, perseverance of the saints—each letter countering one of the five Remonstrant articles. The Synod also officially accepted the Belgic Confession,* Heidelberg Catechism* and the Canons of Dordrecht as standards of the Dutch Reformed Church.

Richard Taverner (1505–1575). English Puritan humanist and translator. After graduating from Oxford, Taverner briefly studied abroad. When he returned to England, he joined Thomas Cromwell's (1485–1540) circle. After Cromwell's beheading, Taverner escaped severe punishment and retired from public life during Mary I's reign. Under Elizabeth I, Taverner served as justice of the peace, sheriff and a licensed lay preacher. Taverner translated many important continental Reformation works into English, most notably the Augsburg Confession* and several of Desiderius Erasmus's* works. Some of these translations—John Calvin's* 1536 catechism, Wolfgang Capito's* work on the Psalms and probably Erasmus Sarcerius's* postils—he presented as his own work. Underwritten by Cromwell, Taverner also published an edited version of the Matthew Bible (1537).

Thomas Thorowgood (1595–1669). English Puritan pastor. Thorowgood was a Puritan minister in Norfolk and the chief financier of John Eliot (1604–1690), a Puritan missionary among the Native American tribes in Massachusetts. In 1650, under the title *Jews in America, or, Probabilities that Americans be of that Race*, Thorowgood became one of the first to put forward the thesis that Native Americans were actually the ten lost tribes of Israel.

Frans Titelmans (1502–1537). Belgian Catholic philosopher. Titelmans studied at the University of Leuven, where he was influenced by Petrus Ramus.* After first joining a Franciscan monastery, Titelmans realigned with the stricter Capuchins and moved to Italy. He is best known for his advocacy for the Vulgate and his debates with Desiderius Erasmus* over Pauline theology (1527–1530)—he was deeply suspicious of the fruits of humanism, especially regarding biblical studies. His work was published posthumously by his brother, Pieter Titelmans (1501–1572).

Francisco de Toledo (1532–1596). Spanish Catholic theologian. This important Jesuit taught philosophy at the universities of Salamanca and Rome. He published works on Aristotelian philosophy and a commentary on Thomas Aquinas's work, as well as biblical commentaries on John,

Romans and the first half of Luke. He was also the general editor for the Clementine Vulgate (1598).

Daniel Toussain (1541–1602). Swiss Reformed pastor and professor. Toussain became pastor at Orléans after attending college in Basel. After the third War of Religion, Toussain was exiled, eventually returning to Montbéliard, his birthplace. In 1571, he faced opposition there from the strict Lutheran rulers and was eventually exiled due to his influence over the clergy. He returned to Orléans but fled following the Saint Bartholomew's Day Massacre (1572), eventually becoming pastor in Basel. He relocated to Heidelberg in 1583 as pastor to the new regent, becoming professor of theology at the university, and he remained there until his death.

John Trapp (1601–1669). Anglican biblical exegete. After studying at Oxford, Trapp entered the pastorate in 1636. During the English Civil Wars he sided with Parliament, which later made it difficult for him to collect tithes from a congregation whose royalist pastor had been evicted. Trapp published commentaries on all the books of the Bible from 1646 to 1656.

William Tyndale (Hychyns) (1494–1536). English reformer, theologian and translator. Tyndale was educated at Oxford University, where he was influenced by the writings of humanist thinkers. Believing that piety is fostered through personal encounter with the Bible, he asked to translate the Bible into English; denied permission, Tyndale left for the Continent to complete the task. His New Testament was the equivalent of a modern-day bestseller in England but was banned and ordered burned. Tyndale's theology was oriented around justification, the authority of Scripture and Christian obedience; Tyndale emphasized the ethical as a concomitant reality of justification. He was martyred in Brussels before completing his English translation of the Old Testament, which Miles Coverdale* finished.

Juan de Valdés (1500/10–1541). Spanish Catholic theologian and writer. Although Valdés adopted an evangelical doctrine, had Erasmian affiliations and published works that were listed on the Index of Prohibited Books, Valdés rebuked the reformers for creating disunity and never left the Catholic Church. His writings included translations of the Hebrew Psalter and various biblical books, a work on the Spanish language and several commentaries. Valdés fled to Rome in 1531 to escape the Spanish Inquisition and worked in the court of Clement VII in Bologna until the pope's death in 1534. Valdés subsequently returned to Naples, where he led the reform- and revival-minded Valdesian circle.

Peter Martyr Vermigli (1499–1562). Italian Reformed humanist and theologian. Vermigli was one of the most influential theologians of the era, held in common regard with such figures as Martin Luther* and John Calvin.* In Italy, Vermigli was a distinguished theologian, preacher and advocate for moral reform; however, during the reinstitution of the Roman Inquisition Vermigli fled to Protestant regions in northern Europe. He was eventually appointed professor of divinity at Oxford University, where Vermigli delivered acclaimed disputations on the Eucharist. Vermigli was widely noted for his deeply integrated biblical commentaries and theological treatises.

Peter Walpot (d. 1578). Moravian Radical pastor and bishop. Walpot was a bishop of the Hutterite community after Jakob Hutter, Peter Riedemann* and Leonhard Lanzenstiel. Riedemann's *Confession of Faith* (1545; 1565) became a vital authority for Hutterite exegesis, theology and morals. Walpot added his own *Great Article Book* (1577), which collates primary biblical passages on baptism, communion, the community of goods, the sword and divorce. In keeping with Hutterite theology, Walpot defended the community of goods as a mark of the true church.

Valentin Weigel (1533–1588). German Lutheran pastor. Weigel studied at Leipzig and Wittenberg, entering the pastorate in 1567. Despite a strong anti-institutional bias, he was recognized by the church hierarchy as a talented preacher and compassionate minister of mercy to the poor. Although he signed the Formula of Concord,* Weigel's orthodoxy was questioned so openly that he had to publish a defense. He appears to have tried to synthesize several medieval mystics with the ideas of Sebastian Franck,* Thomas Müntzer* and others. His posthumously published works have led some recent scholars to suggest that Weigel's works may have deeply influenced later Pietism.

John Whitgift (1530–1604). Anglican archbishop. Though Whitgift shared much theological common ground with Puritans, after his election as Archbishop of Canterbury (1583) he moved decisively to squelch the political and ecclesiastical threat they posed during Elizabeth's reign. Whitgift enforced strict compliance to the Book of Common Prayer,* the Act of Uniformity (1559) and the Articles of Religion.* Whitgift's policies led to a large migration of Puritans to Holland. The bulk of Whitgift's published corpus is the fruit of a lengthy public disputation with Thomas Cartwright,* in which Whitgift defines Anglican doctrine against Cartwright's staunch Puritanism.

Johann Wigand (1523–1587). German Lutheran theologian. Wigand is most noted as one of the compilers of the *Magdeburg Centuries*, a German ecclesiastical history of the first thirteen centuries of the church. He was a student of Philipp Melanchthon* at the University of Wittenburg and became a significant figure in the controversies dividing Lutheranism. Strongly opposed to Roman Catholicism, Wigand lobbied against innovations in Lutheran theology that appeared sympathetic to Catholic thought. In the later debates, Wigand's support for Gnesio-Lutheranism established his role in the development of confessional Lutheranism. Wigand was appointed bishop of Pomerania after serving academic posts at the universities in Jena and Königsburg.

Johann (Ferus) Wild (1495–1554). German Catholic pastor. After studying at Heidelberg and teaching at Tübingen, this Franciscan was appointed as lector in the Mainz cathedral, eventually being promoted to cathedral preacher—a post for which he became widely popular but also controversial. Wild strongly identified as Catholic but was not unwilling to criticize the curia. Known for an irenic spirit—criticized in fact as *too* kind—he was troubled by the polemics between all parties of the Reformation. He preached with great lucidity, integrating the liturgy, Scripture and doctrine to exposit Catholic worship and teaching for common people. His sermons on John were pirated for publication without his knowledge; the Sorbonne banned them as heretical. Despite his popularity among clergy, the majority of his works were on the Roman Index until 1900.

Andrew Willet (1562–1621). Anglican priest, professor, and biblical expositor. Willet was a gifted biblical expositor and powerful preacher. He walked away from a promising university career in 1588 when he was ordained a priest in the Church of England. For the next thirty-three years he served as a parish priest. Willet's commentaries summarized the present state of discussion while also offering practical applications for preachers. They have been cited as some of the most technical commentaries of the early seventeenth century. His most important publication was *Synopsis Papismi, or a General View of Papistrie* (1594), in which he responded to many of Robert Bellarmine's critiques. After years of royal favor, Willet was imprisoned in 1618 for a month after presenting to King James I his opposition to the "Spanish Match" of Prince Charles to the Infanta Maria. While serving as a parish priest, he wrote forty-two works, most of which were either commentaries on books of the Bible or controversial works against Catholics.

John Woolton (c. 1535–1594). Anglican bishop. After graduating from Oxford, Woolton lived in Germany until the accession of Elizabeth I. He was ordained as a priest in 1560 and as a bishop in 1578. Woolton published many theological, devotional and practical works, including a treatise on the immortality of the soul, a discourse on conscience and a manual for Christian living.

Girolamo Zanchi (1516–1590). Italian Reformed theologian and pastor. Zanchi joined an Augustinian monastery at the age of fifteen, where he studied Greek and Latin, the church fathers and the works of Aristotle and Thomas Aquinas. Under the influence of his prior, Peter Martyr Vermigli,* Zanchi also imbibed the writings of the Swiss and German reformers. To avoid the Inquisition, Zanchi fled to Geneva where he was strongly attracted to the preaching and teaching of John Calvin.* Zanchi taught biblical theology and the *locus* method at academies in Strasbourg, Heidelberg, and Neustadt. He also served as pastor of an Italian refugee congregation. Zanchi's theological works, *De tribus Elohim* (1572) and *De natura Dei* (1577), have received more attention than his commentaries. His commentaries comprise about a quarter of his literary output, however, and display a strong typological and Christological interpretation in conversation with the church fathers, medieval exegetes, and other reformers.

Katharina Schütz Zell (1497/98–1562). German Reformed writer. Zell became infamous in Strasbourg and the Empire when in 1523 she married the priest Matthias Zell, and then published an apology defending her husband against charges of impiety and libertinism. Longing for a united church, she called for toleration of Catholics and Anabaptists, famously writing to Martin Luther* after the failed Marburg Colloquy of 1529 to exhort him to check his hostility and to be ruled instead by Christian charity. Much to the chagrin of her contemporaries, Zell published diverse works, ranging from polemical treatises on marriage to letters of consolation, as well as editing a hymnal and penning an exposition of Psalm 51.

Huldrych Zwingli (1484–1531). Swiss Reformed humanist, preacher and theologian. Zwingli, a parish priest, was influenced by the writings of Desiderius Erasmus* and taught himself Greek. While a preacher to the city cathedral in Zurich, Zwingli enacted reform through sermons, public disputations and conciliation with the town council, abolishing the Mass and images in the church. Zwingli broke with the lectionary preaching tradition, instead preaching serial expository biblical sermons. He later was embroiled in controversy with Anabaptists over infant baptism and with Martin Luther* at the Marburg Colloquy (1529) over their differing views of the Eucharist. Zwingli, serving as chaplain to Zurich's military, was killed in battle.

SOURCES FOR
BIOGRAPHICAL SKETCHES

General Reference Works

Allgemeine Deutsche Biographie. 56 vols. Leipzig: Duncker & Humblot, 1875–1912; reprint, 1967–1971. Accessible online via deutsche-biographie.de/index.html.

Haag, Eugene and Émile Haag. *La France protestante ou vies des protestants français*. 2nd ed. 6 vols. Paris: Sandoz & Fischbacher, 1877–1888.

Hillerbrand, Hans J., ed. *Oxford Encyclopedia of the Reformation*. 4 vols. New York: Oxford University Press, 1996.

Kolb, Robert, and Timothy J. Wengert, eds. *The Book of Concord: The Confessions of the Evangelical Lutheran Church*. Translated by Charles Arand et al. Minneapolis: Fortress, 2000.

McKim, Donald K., ed. *Dictionary of Major Biblical Interpreters*. Downers Grove, IL: InterVarsity Press, 2007.

Müller, Gerhard, et al., ed. *Theologische Realenzyklopadie*. Berlin: Walter de Gruyter, 1994.

Neue Deutsche Biographie. 28 vols. projected. Berlin: Duncker & Humblot, 1953–. Accessible online via deutsche-biographie.de/index.html.

New Catholic Encyclopedia. 15 vols. New York: McGraw-Hill, 1967; 2nd ed., Detroit: Thomson-Gale, 2002.

Oxford Dictionary of National Biography. 60 vols. Oxford: Oxford University Press, 2004.

Stephen, Leslie, and Sidney Lee, eds. *Dictionary of National Biography*. 63 vols. London: Smith, Elder and Co., 1885–1900.

Wordsworth, Christopher, ed. *Lives of Eminent Men connected with the History of Religion in England*. 4 vols. London: J. G. & F. Rivington, 1839.

Additional Works for Individual Sketches

Akin, Daniel L. "An Expositional Analysis of the Schleitheim Confession." *Criswell Theological Review* 2 (1988): 345-70.

Bald, R. C. *John Donne: A Life*. Oxford: Oxford University Press, 1970.

Doornkaat Koolman, J ten. "The First Edition of Peter Riedemann's 'Rechenschaft.'" *Mennonite Quarterly Review* 36, no. 2 (1962): 169-70.

Friedmann, Robert. "Second Generation Anabaptism as Illustrated by the Walpot Era of the Hutterites." *Mennonite Quarterly* 44, no. 4 (1970): 390-93.

Frymire, John M. *The Primacy of the Postils: Catholics, Protestants, and the Dissemination of Ideas in Early Modern Germany*. Leiden: Brill, 2010.

Furcha, Edward J. "Key Concepts in Caspar von Schwenckfeld's Thought, Regeneration and the New Life." *Church History* 37, no. 2 (1968): 160-73.

Greaves, Richard L. *Society and Religion in Elizabethan England*. Minneapolis: University of Minnesota, 1981.

Greiffenberg, Catharina Regina von. *Meditations on the Incarnation, Passion and Death of Jesus Christ*. Edited and translated by Lynne Tatlock. The Other Voice in Early Modern Europe. Chicago: University of Chicago Press, 2009.

Hendrix, Scott H., ed. and trans. *Early Protestant Spirituality*. New York: Paulist Press, 2009.

Hvolbek, Russell H. "Being and Knowing: Spiritualist Epistelmology and Anthropology from Schwenckfeld to Böhme." *Sixteenth Century Journal* 22, no. 1 (1991): 97-110.

Lake, Peter. *The Boxmaker's Revenge: 'Orthodoxy', 'Heterodox' and the Politics of the Parish in Early Stuart London*. Stanford, CA: Stanford University Press, 2001.

Lockhart, Paul Douglas. *Frederick II and the Protestant Cause: Denmark's Role in the Wars of Religion, 1559–1596*. Leiden: Brill, 2004.

Packull, Werner O. "The Origins of Peter Riedemann's Account of Our Faith." *Sixteenth Century Journal* 30, no. 1 (1999): 61-69.

Papazian, Mary Arshagouni, ed. *John Donne and the Protestant Reformation: New Perspectives*. Detroit: Wayne State University Press, 2003.

Pragman, James H. "The Augsburg Confession in the English Reformation: Richard Taverner's Contribution." *Sixteenth Century Journal* 11, no. 3 (1980): 75-85.

Synder, C. Arnold. "The Schleitheim Articles in Light of the Revolution of the Common Man: Continuation or Departure?" *Sixteenth Century Journal* 16, no. 4 (1985): 419-30.

———. "The Confession of the Swiss Brethren in Hesse, 1578." In *Anabaptism Revisited: Essays on Anabaptist/Mennonite Studies in Honor of C. J. Dyck.* Edited by Walter Klaassen, 29-49. Waterloo, ON; Scottdale, PA: Herald Press, 1992.

Todd, Margo. "Bishops in the Kirk: William Cowper of Galloway and the Puritan Episcopacy of Scotland." *Scottish Journal of Theology,* 57 (2004): 300-312.

Wengert, Timothy J. "'Fear and Love' in the Ten Commandments." *Concordia Journal* 21, no. 1 (1995): 14-27.

Voogt, Gerrit. "Remonstrant-Counter-Remonstrant Debates: Crafting a Principled Defense of Toleration after the Synod of Dordrecht (1619–1650)." *Church History and Religious Culture* 89, no. 4 (2009): 489-524.

BIBLIOGRAPHY

Primary Sources and Translations Used in the Volume

Agricola, Johannes. *In Evangelium Lucae Annotationes Ioannis Agricolae Islebii, Iam per Authorem Ipsum et Locupletatae, et Recognitae.* Hagenau: Farcallius, 1526. Digital copy online at www.gateway-bayern.de.

Andreae, Jakob. *Ein Christliche Predigt Vber das Euangelium auff den xxv. Sontag nach Trinitatis Matthei am 24.* Leipzig: Hanß Steinman, 1578. Digital copy online at www.gateway-bayern.de.

Anonymous. *Certaine Godlie and Learned Sermons; Made vpon These Six Following Parables of Our Sauiour Christ, Declared in the Gospell.* London: R. Bankworth, 1601. Accessed digitally via EEBO.

Bagnall, Robert. *The Stewards Last Account: Delivered in Five Sermons upon the Sixteenth Chapter of the Gospell by Saint Luke, the First and Second Verses.* London: Iohn Clarke, 1622. Accessed digitally via EEBO.

Bastard, Thomas. *Five Sermons: The Three Former, On Luke Chap. 1. Verse 76. Called, The Marigold and the Sunne; The Two Latter, on Luke Chap. 7. Verse 37.38. Called, The Sinners Looking-glasse.* London: Mathew Lownes, 1615. Accessed digitally via EEBO.

Baumgart (Pomarius), Johann. *Postilla: In welcher was aus einem jeden Sontags vnd Fests Euangelio benebenst desselbigen Occasion vnd Summa furnemlich fur Lehren Trost Erinnerungen vnd Warnungen zu mercken auffs kurtzte angezeigt vnd in gewisse Fragen vnd Antwort gefasset ist.* Magdeburg: Andreas Gene, 1587. Digital copy online at www.gateway-bayern.de.

Baxter, Richard. *The One Thing Necessary: Or Christ's Justification of Mary's Choice; and of His Servants Wrongfully Accused.* London: F. Salusbury, 1685. Accessed digitally via EEBO.

Becon, Thomas. *A New Postil Conteinyng Most Godly and Learned Sermons upon All the Sonday Gospelles, That Be Redde in the Church Thorowout the Yeare.* London: Thomas Marshe, 1566. The postil is divided into two parts: winter (Advent to Trinity Sunday) and summer (Trinity Sunday to Advent); pagination begins anew after the postil for Trinity Sunday. Accessed digitally via EEBO.

———. *The Catechism of Thomas Becon, with Other Pieces Written by Him in the Reign of King Edward VI.* Edited by John Ayre. Cambridge: Cambridge University Press, 1844. Digital copy online at archive.org.

Beilin, Elaine V., ed. *The Examinations of Anne Askew.* New York: Oxford University Press, 1996.

Bibliotheca Reformatoria Neederlandica. 10 vols. Edited by S. Cramer and F. Pijper. The Hague: Martinus Nijhoff, 1903–1914. Digital copies online at babel.hathitrust.org.

The Book of Common Prayer (1549). In *The Two Liturgies,* A.D. 1549 and A.D. 1552. Edited by Joseph Ketley, 9-158. Cambridge: Cambridge University Press, 1844. Digital copy online at books.google.com.

Boys, John. *An Exposition of the Dominical Epistles and Gospels Vsed in Our English Liturgie Through the Whole Yeare.* 4 vols. London: Felix Kyngston, for William Aspley, 1610–1612. The individual volumes are *The Winter Part from the First Aduentuall Sunday to Lent,* An Exposition of the

Dominical Epistles and Gospels 1 (1610); *The Spring-part from the First in Lent to Whitsunday*, An Exposition of the Dominical Epistles and Gospels 2 (1610); *The Summer-part from Whitsunday to the Twelfth After Trinitie*, An Exposition of the Dominical Epistles and Gospels 3 (1611); *The Autumne Part from the Twelfth Sunday after Trinitie, to the Last in the Whole Yeere*, An Exposition of the Dominical Epistles and Gospels 4 (1612). Accessed digitally via EEBO.

Bucer, Martin. *Epistola D. Pauli ad Ephesios*. Strasbourg: Johann Herwagen, 1527. Digital copy online at www.gateway-bayern.de.

———. *In Sacra Quatuor Evangelia, Enarrationes Perpetuae*. Basel: Johann Herwagen, 1536. Digital copy online at www.gateway-bayern.de.

Bullinger, Heinrich. *The Decades of Henry Bullinger*. 5 vols. Translated by H. I. Edited by Thomas Harding. Cambridge: Cambridge University Press, 1849–1852. Volumes 1 and 2 are bound as one. Digital copies online at archive.org.

———. *In Luculentum et Sacrosanctum Euangelium Domini Nostri Iesu Christi Secundum Lucam, Commentariorum*. Zurich: Christoph Froschauer, 1546. Digital copy online at www.e-rara.ch.

Bunyan, John. *A Few Sighs from Hell, or, The Groans of a Damned Soul; Or, An Exposition of Those Words in the Sixteenth of Luke, Concerning the Rich Man and the Beggar*. London: Ralph Wood, for M. Wright, 1658. Accessed digitally via EEBO.

———. *The Jerusalem-Sinner Saved: or, Good News for the Vilest of Men, Being a Help for Despairing Souls; Shewing That Jesus Christ Would Have Mercy in the First Place Offered to the Biggest Sinners*. 3rd ed. London: John Gwillim, 1697. Accessed digitally via EEBO.

Cajetan, Cardinal (Thomas de Vio). *Evangelia cum Commentariis*. Venice: Luccantonii, 1530. Digital copy online at www.gateway-bayern.de and books.google.com.

Calvin, John. *Commentarius in Harmoniam Evangelicam*. Ioannis Calvini Opera quae supersunt omnia 45. Edited by G. Baum, E. Cunitz and E. Reuss. Brunswick: C. A. Schwetschke, 1891. Digital copies online at archive-ouverte.unige.ch/unige:650.

———. *Commentary on a Harmony of the Evangelists*. 3 vols. Calvin Translation Society 31-33. Translated by William Pringle. Edinburgh: Calvin Translation Society, 1845–1846. Digital copies online at archive.org.

———. *Institutes of the Christian Religion* (1559). Edited by John T. McNeill. Translated by Ford Lewis Battles. Library of Christian Classics 20-21. Philadelphia: Westminster Press, 1960. Latin text availble in CO 2 (1864); digital copy online at archive-ouverte.unige.ch/unige:650.

Caylie, Mathew. *The Cleansing of the Ten Lepers: or, Briefe Notes on Luke 17. vers. 14, 15, 16, 17, 18*. London: William Sheffard, 1623. Accessed digitally via EEBO.

Certain Sermons or Homilies Appointed to be Read in Churches, in the Time of the Late Queen Elizabeth. London: Prayer-Book and Homily Society, 1852. Digital copy online at books.google.com.

Coverdale, Miles. *Writings and Translations of Myles Coverdale, Bishop of Exeter*. Edited by George Pearson. Cambridge: Cambridge University Press, 1844. Digital copy online at archive.org.

Cowper, William. *Three Heavenly Treatises Concerning Christ: His Genealogie; His Baptisme; His Combat with Sathan*. London: Iohn Budge, 1612. Accessed digitally via EEBO.

———. *A Mirrour of Mercie: Or The Prodigals Conuersion, Briefely and Learnedly Expounded, and Full of Comfortable Consolations for All Repentant Sinners*. London: Edward Griffin, for Iohn Budge, 1614. Accessed digitally via EEBO.

Crashaw, Richard. *The Complete Works of Richard Crashaw, Canon of Loretto*. Edited by William B. Turnbull. London: John Russell Smith, 1858. Digital copy online at books.google.com.

Crompe, John. *Hebdomada Magna: or the Great Weeke of Christs Passion; Handled by Way of Exposition upon the Fourth Article of the Apostles Creed; He Suffered Under Pontius Pilate; Was Crucified, Dead, Buried*. London: Henry Twyford, 1641. Accessed digitally via EEBO.

Denck, Hans. *The Spiritual Legacy of Hans Denck: Interpretation and Translation of Key Texts*. Edited by Clarence Bauman. Leiden: Brill, 1991.

Dietrich, Veit. *Passio oder Histori vom leiden Christi Jesus vnsers Heylands*. Nuremberg: Johann von Berg & Ulrich Neuber, 1545. Digital copy online at www.gateway-bayern.de.

Donne, John. *The Works of John Donne*. 6 vols. Edited by Henry Alford. London: John Parker, 1839. Digital copy online at books.google.com.

———. *The Poems of John Donne*. Edited by Herbert J. C. Grierson. Oxford: The Clarendon Press, 1912. Digital copy online at books.google.com.

Downame, John, ed. *Annotations upon All the Books of the Old and Nevv Testament*. London: Evan Tyler, 1657. Accessed digitally via EEBO.

Eck, Johann. *Christenliche Predigen*. 5 vols. Ingolstadt: Apian, 1530–1539. Digital copy online at www.gateway-bayern.de.

Erasmus, Desiderius. *Desderii Erasmi Roterodami Opera Omnia*. 10 vols. Edited by Jean LeClerc. Leiden: Van der Aa, 1704–1706; reprint, Hildesheim: Georg Olms, 1961–1962. Digital copies online at babel.hathitrust.org.

———. *In Evangelivm Lvcae Paraphrasis Erasmi Roterodami, per Aautorem Recognitu*. Basel: J. Froben, 1523. Digital copy online at www.gateway-bayern.de.

———. *Paraphrase on Luke 11–24. Collected Works of Erasmus 48*. Translated and annotated by Jane E. Phillips. Toronto: University of Toronto Press, 2003.

Fary, John. *God's Severity on Man's Sterility: Taken from the Parable of the Fruitlesse Fig-Tree, and Delivered in a Sermon*. London: Andrew Crook, 1645. Accessed digitally via EEBO.

Fast, Heinold, and Gottfried Seebaß, eds. *Briefe und Schriften oberdeutscher Täufer 1527–1555: Das 'Kunstbuch' des Jörg Probst Rotenfelder gen. Maler (Burgerbibliothek Bern, Cod. 464)*. Quellen zur Geschichte der Täufer 17. Gütersloh: Gütersloher Verlagshaus, 2007.

Fenner, William. *Practicall Divinitie: or, Gospel-Light Shining Forth in Severall Choyce Sermons, on Divers Texts of Scripture*. London: John Stafford, 1647. Accessed digitally via EEBO.

Gilpin, Bernard. *A Godly Sermon Preached in the Court at Greenwich the Firste Sonday After the Epiphanie, Anno Domini 1552*. London: Henrie Middleton, for Thomas Man, 1581. Accessed digitally via EEBO.

Greiffenberg, Catharina Regina von. *Des Allerheiligst- und Allerheilsamsten Leidens und Sterbens Jesu Christi Zwölf andächtige Betrachtungen*. Nuremberg: Johann Hofmann, 1762. Digital copy online at www.gateway-bayern.de.

———. *Meditations on the Incarnation, Passion and Death of Jesus Christ*. Edited and translated by Lynne Tatlock. The Other Voice in Early Modern Europe. Chicago: University of Chicago Press, 2009.

Hammond, Henry. *A Paraphrase and Annotations upon All the Books of the New Testament, Briefly Explaining All the Difficult Places Thereof*. 4th ed. London: Richard Davis, 1675. Accessed digitally via EEBO.

Hausted, Peter. *Ten Sermons Preached vpon Severall Svndayes and Saints Dayes*. London: John Clark, 1636. Accessed digitally via EEBO.

Hemmingsen, Niels. *Postilla oder Auslegung der Euangelien welche man auff die Sontage vnd andere Feste in der Kirchen Gottes pfleget zu verlesen*. Wittenberg: Hans Krafft, 1571.

Hooke, Christopher. *The Child-birth or Womans Lecture, That Is: A Lecture upon Chap. 1. ver. 57, 58, of the Holie Gospell According to Luke; Very Necessaries to Bee Read and Knowne of All Young Mar-*

ried and Teeming Women, and Not Vnprofitable for Men of All Sortes. London: Thomas Orwin, for Henry Hooke, 1590. Accessed digitally via EEBO.

Hospinian, Rudolf. *Lobgesang der Heiligen Hochgelobten Reinen Jungfrauwen Maria vnnd Mutter vnsers Herren Jesu Christi auß dem Ersten Capitel Luce.* Zurich: Hans Rudolf Wyssenbach, 1600. Digital copy online at www.gateway-bayern.de.

Huberinus, Caspar. *Postilla Teütsch Uber alle Sontägliche Euangelien.* 2 vols. Augsburg: Philipp Ulhart, 1545. *Advent biß auf Ostern,* Postilla Teütsch 1; *Ostern biß aufs Advent,* Postilla Teütsch 2. Digital copies online at www.gateway-bayern.de.

Hubmaier, Balthasar. *Schriften.* Edited by Gunnar Westin and Torsten Bergsten. Quellen zur Geschichte der Täufer 9. Gütersloh: Gerd Mohn, 1962.

———. *Balthasar Hubmaier: Theologian of Anabaptism.* Translated and edited by H. Wayne Pipkin and John H. Yoder. Classics of the Radical Reformation 5. Scottdale, PA: Herald Press, 1989.

Jewel, John. *The Works of John Jewel, Bishop of Salisbury.* 4 vols. Edited by John Ayre. Cambridge: Cambridge University Press, 1845–1850. Digital copies online at archive.org.

Joris, David. *The Anabaptist Writings of David Joris, 1535–1543.* Edited and translated by Gary K. Waite. Classics of the Radical Reformation 7. Scottdale, PA: Herald Press, 1993.

Karlstadt, Andreas Bodenstein von. *The Essential Carlstadt: Fifteen Tracts by Andreas Bodenstein (Carlstadt) from Karlstadt.* Edited and translated by E. J. Furcha. Classics of the Radical Reformation 8. Scottdale, PA: Herald Press, 1995.

Lambert, François. *In Divi Lucae Evangelium Commentarii.* Nuremberg: Johann Petreius, 1524. Digital copy online at www.gateway-bayern.de.

Latimer, Hugh. *Sermons and Remains of Hugh Latimer.* Edited by George E. Corrie. Cambridge: Cambridge University Press, 1845. Digital copy online at archive.org.

Lawson, John. *Gleanings and Expositions of Some, and But Some of the More Difficult Places of Scriptures: Perhaps, But the First-Fruits unto a More Plentifull Harvest.* London: Nathan Webb and Will Grantham, 1646. Accessed digitally via EEBO.

Lefèvre d'Etaples, Jacques. *Commentarii Initiatorii in Quatuor Evangelia.* 2 vols. Cologne: Hittorp, 1521. Digital copies online at www.gateway-bayern.de.

Leigh, Edward. *Annotations upon All the New Testatment Philologicall and Theologicall.* London: William Lee, 1650. Accessed digitally via EEBO.

Lightfoot, John. *The Harmony, Chronicle and Order of the New Testament.* London: Simon Miller, 1655. Accessed digitally via EEBO.

Lossius, Lucas. *Novum Testamentum de Jesu Christo Nazreno . . . Annotationibus Eruditis & Pijs Iam Primum Explicati & Illustrati.* Tomus Secundus, Lucas & Ioannes. Frankfurt: Christian Egenolff, 1554. Digital copy online at www.gateway-bayern.de.

Luther, Martin. *D. Martin Luthers Werke, Kritische Gesamtausgabe: [Schriften].* 73 vols. Weimar: Hermann Böhlaus Nachfolger, 1883–2009. Digital copies online at archive.org.

———. *D. Martin Luthers Werke, Kritische Gesamtausgabe: Tischreden.* 6 vols. Weimar: Hermann Böhlaus Nachfolger, 1912–1921. Digital copies online at archive.org.

———. *Dr. Martin Luther's sämmtliche Werke.* 2nd ed. 26 vols. Frankfurt and Erlangen: Heyder & Zimmer, 1862–1885. Digital copies online at babel.hathitrust.org.

———. *D. Martin Luthers Evangelien-Auslegung.* 5 vols. Edited by Erwin Mülhaupt. Göttingen: Vandenhoeck & Ruprecht, 1961. Digital copies online at digi20.digitale-sammlungen.de.

———. *Luther's Works [American edition].* 82 vols. projected. St. Louis: Concordia; Philadelphia: Fortress, 1955–1986; 2009–.

Marlorat, Augustin, ed. *A Catholike and Ecclesiasticall Exposition of the Holy Gospell After S. Marke and Luke: Gathered Out of All the Singular and Approved Devines (Which the Lorde Hath Geven to Hys Church)*. Translated by Thomas Timme. London: Thomas March, 1583. Accessed digitally via EEBO.

———. *A Catholike and Ecclesiasticall Exposition of the Holy Gospell After S. Mathewe: Gathered Out of All the Singular and Aproved Deuines (Which the Lorde Hath Geven to Hys Church)*. Translated by Thomas Timme. London: Thomas Marshe, 1570. Accessed digitally via EEBO.

Mathesius, Johannes. *Postilla Symbolica, Oder Spruchpostill, Das ist: Auslegung vnd Erklerung der fûrnembsten Sprûche des Newen Testaments aus der Euangelisten vnd Apostel Historien vnd Schrifften genommen vnnd auff die Sontags vnnd Fest Euangelien durchs gantze Jahr gezogen vnd accommodiret*. Leipzig: Johannes Beyer, 1588. Digital copy online at www.gateway-bayern.de.

Mayer, John. *A Commentarie vpon the New Testament: Representing the Divers Expositions Thereof, Out of the Workes of the Most Learned, Both Ancient Fathers, and Moderne Writers*. 3 vols. London: Thomas Cotes for John Bellamie, 1631.

———. *The First Volumne upon the Foure Evangelists and the Acts of the Apostles; The Second Volumne upon All the Epistles of the Apostle Saint Pavl, Being Fourteene; The Third Volumne Containing the Seuen Smaller Epistles, Called Catholike, and the Book of the Revelation*. Accessed digitally via EEBO.

Melanchthon, Philipp. *Philippi Melanthonis Opera Quae Supersunt Omnia*. 28 vols. Corpus Reformatorum 1-28. Edited by C. G. Bretschneider. Halle: C. A. Schwetschke, 1834–1860. Digital copies online at archive.org and books.google.com.

———. *Annotationes in Evangelia*. Philippi Melanthonis Opera Quae Supersunt Omnia 14. Edited by C. Bretschneider. Saxon Hall: C. A. Schwetschke and Sons, 1847. Digital copies online at archive.org and books.google.com.

———. *Postillae Melanthonianae, Partes I et II*. Philippi Melanthonis Opera Quae Supersunt Omnia 24. Edited by C. Bretschneider and H. Bindseil. Braunschweig: C. A. Schwetschke and Sons, 1856. Digital copies online at archive.org and books.google.com.

———. *Postillae Melanthonianae, Partes III et IV atque Appendix*. Philippi Melanthonis Opera Quae Supersunt Omnia 25. Edited by C. Bretschneider and H. Bindseil. Braunschweig: C. A. Schwetschke and Sons, 1856. Digital copies online at archive.org and books.google.com.

More, Thomas. *The Complete Works of St. Thomas More*. 15 vols. New Haven, CT: Yale University Press, 1963–1997.

———. "A Treatice vpon the Passion of Chryste" (1534). The Complete Works of St. Thomas More 13. Edited by Garry E. Haupt, 1-188. New Haven, CT: Yale University Press, 1976.

———. *De Tristitia Christi*. The Complete Works of St. Thomas More 14,1. Edited and translated by Clarence H. Miller. New Haven, CT: Yale University Press, 1976.

Musaeus, Simon. *Außlegung der Episteln vnd Euangelien uber die gewônliche namhatte Feste der heyligen Apostel Mârtyrer vnd Zeugen Christi durchs gantze Jar*. Frankfurt am Main: Nicolaus Bassæus, 1590. Digital copy online at www.gateway-bayern.de.

Neukirch, Melchior. *Historia der Passion Unseres Herrn Jesus Christus*. Wölfenbüttel: Horn, 1590. Digital copy online at www.gateway-bayern.de.

Pellikan, Konrad. *In Sacrosancta Quatuor Evangelia Et Apostolorum Acta*. Zurich: Christoph Froschauer, 1537. Digital copy online at e-rara.ch.

Perkins, William. *The Workes of That Famous and Worthy Minister of Christ, in the Universitie of Cambridge, Mr. William Perkins*. London: John Legatt, 1616. Accessed digitally via EEBO.

———. *The Whole Treatise of the Cases of Conscience, Distinguished into Three Bookes*. London: John Legatt, 1617. Accessed digitally via EEBO.

Philips, Dirk. *The Writings of Dirk Philips 1504–1568*. Edited by Cornelius J. Dyck, William E. Keeney and Alvin J. Beachy. Classics of the Radical Reformation 6. Scottdale, PA: Herald Press, 1992.

Plass, Ewald, ed. *What Luther Says: An Anthology*. 3 vols. St. Louis: Concordia, 1959.

Rempel, John D., ed. *Jörg Maler's Kunstbuch: Writings of the Pilgram Marpeck Circle*. Classics of the Radical Reformation 12. Kitchener, ON: Pandora, 2012.

Riedemann, Peter. "Die erste Rechenschaft (1529–1532)." In *Glaubenszeugnisse oberdeutscher Taufgesinnter II*. Edited by Robert Friedmann and Lydia Müller, 4-47. Quellen zur Geschichte der Täufer 12. Gütersloh: Gerd Mohn, 1967.

———. *Peter Riedemann's Hutterite Confession of Faith: Translation of the 1565 German Edition of Confession of Our Religion, Teaching and Faith by the Brothers Who Are Known as the Hutterites*. Edited and translated by John J. Friesen. Classics of the Radical Reformation 9. Scottdale, PA: Herald Press, 1999.

Rogers, Nehemiah. *The Fast Friend: or A Friend at Mid-Night; Set Forth in an Exposition on That Parable Luke 11.5.-11*. London: George Sawbridge, 1658. Accessed digitally via EEBO.

———. *The Figg-less Figg-Tree: or, the Doome of a Barren and Unfruitful Profession Lay'd Open; In an Exposition upon That Parable a Certain Man Had a Figg-Tree Planted in His Vineyard, &c. Luke 13.6, 7, 8, 9, 10*. London: George Sawbridge, 1658. Accessed digitally via EEBO.

———. *The True Convert: or, An Exposition vpon the XV. Chapter of St. Lukes Gospell, Containing Three Parables; The Lost Sheepe; The Lost Groat; The Lost Sonne*. London: George Miller for Edward Brewster, 1632. Accessed digitally via EEBO.

Salmuth, Heinrich. *Passional . . . Das ist: Christliche Erklerung Der gnadenreichen Historien von dem bittern vnd thewren leiden, sterben vnd Begrebnis unsers lieben Herrn vnd Heylandes Jhesu Christi*. Leipzig: Georg Oefner, 1583. Digital copy online at www.gateway-bayern.de.

Salmuth, Heinrich. *Weihenacht Predigten: Darinnen von der Person vnnd Ampt des Herren Jesu Christi gehandelt wird*. Edited by Johan Salmuth. Leipzig: Georg Deffner, 1582. Digital copy online at www.gateway-bayern.de.

Sandys, Edwin. *The Sermons of Edwin Sandys (1585)*. Edited by John Ayre. Cambridge: Cambridge University Press, 1841. Digital copy online at archive.org.

Schütz Zell, Katharina. *Church Mother: The Writings of a Protestant Reformer in Sixteenth-Century Germany*. Edited and translated by Elsie McKee. Chicago: University of Chicago Press, 2006.

Schwenckfeld, Caspar [Kaspar]. *Corpus Schwenckfeldianorum*. 19 vols. Edited by Chester David Hartranft. Leipzig: Breitkopf and Härtel, 1907–1961. Digital copies online at babel.hathitrust.org.

———. *Letters and Treatises 1540–1541*. Corpus Schwenckfeldianorum 7. Edited by C. D. Hartranft and E. E. S. Johnson. Leipzig: Breitkopf and Härtel, 1926.

———. *Letters and Treatises 1546–1547*. Corpus Schwenckfeldianorum 10. Edited by C. D. Hartranft and E. E. S. Johnson. Leipzig: Breitkopf and Härtel, 1929.

Sedgwick, Obadiah. *The Parable of the Prodigal; Containing, The Riotous Prodigal, or the Sinners Aversion from God; The Returning Prodigal, or the Penitents Conversion to God; The Prodigals Acceptation, or Favourable Entertainment from God*. London: D. Maxwel, for S. Gellibrand, 1659. Accessed digitally via EEBO.

Smith, Henry. *The Affinitie of the Faithfull: Being a Very Godly and Fruitfull Sermon, Made vpon a Parte of the Eyght Chapter of Sainct Luke*. 2nd ed. London: Nicholas Ling and Iohn Busbie, 1591. Accessed digitally via EEBO.

Spangenberg, Johann. *Postilla, Das ist Auszlegung der Episteln vnd Euangelien auff alle Sontag vnd fürnembsten Fest durchs gantze Jar. Für die jungen Christen Knaben vnd Megdlein in Fragstück verfasset*.

Nuremberg: Leonhardt Heußler, 1582. Digital copy online at www.gateway-bayern.de.

———. *Postilla, Das ist Auzslegung der Episteln vnd Euangelien von Ostern biß auffs Aduent.* Nuremberg: Leonhard Heußler, 1582. Digital copy online at www.gateway-bayern.de.

———. *Postilla Teütsch, für die jungen Christen, Knaben vnd Meidlin, in Fragstuck verfasset, von den fürnemsten Festen durch das gantze Jar.* Augsburg: Valentein Othmar, 1544. Digital copy online at www.gateway-bayern.de.

Spindler, Georg. *Postilla: Außlegung der Euangelien von den fürnemsten Festen durch das gantze Jar; Der dritte Theil.* Leipzig: Hans Steinman, 1576.

Stifel, Michael. *Dz Euangelium von dem verlornen Son Luce xv.* Augsburg: Melchior Ramminger, 1524. Digital copy online at www.gateway-bayern.de.

Taverner, Richard. *The Epistles and Gospelles wyth a Brief Postil vpon the Same from Aduent tyll Lowe Sondaye Whiche Is the (Wynter Parte) Drawen Forth by Diuerse Learned Men for the Singuler Commoditie of All Good Christen Persons and Namely of Prestes and Curates Newly Recognized.* London: Rycharde Bankes, 1540. Accessed digitally via EEBO.

———. *The Epistles and Gospelles with a Brief Postyll vpon the Same from Trinitie Sonday tyll Aduent, [Which Is the (Sommer Parte)] Drawen Forth by Dyuerse Learned Men for the Singuler Commoditie of Al Good Christians and Namely of Prestes and Curates.* London: Richarde Bankes, 1540. Accessed digitally via EEBO.

———. *On Saynt Andrewes Day the Gospels with Brief Sermons vpon Them for Al the Holy Dayes in the Yere.* London: Rycharde Bankes, 1542. Accessed digitally via EEBO.

Trapp, John. *A Commentary or Exposition upon All the Books of the New Testament: Wherein the Text Is Explained, Some Controversies Are Discussed, Divers Common Places Are Handled and Many Remarkable Matters Hinted, That Had by Former Interpreters Been Pretermitted.* 2nd ed. London: Nathan Ekins, 1656. Accessed digitally via EEBO.

Tyndale, William. *Doctrinal Treatises and Introductions to Different Portion of the Holy Scriptures.* Edited by Henry Walker. Cambridge: Cambridge University Press, 1848. Digital copy online at archive.org.

———. *Expositions and Notes on Sundry Portions of the Holy Scriptures, Together with The Practice of Prelates.* Edited by Henry Walter. Cambridge: Cambridge University Press, 1849. Digital copy online at archive.org.

Walpot, Peter. "Das Grosse Artikelbuch (1577)." In *Glaubenszeugnisse oberdeutscher Taufgesinnter II.* Edited by Robert Friedmann and Lydia Müller, 59-317. Quellen zur Geschichte der Täufer 12. Gütersloh: Gerd Mohn, 1967.

Weigel, Valentin. *Valentin Weigel Sämtliche Schriften.* 14 vols. Stuttgart-Bad Cannstatt: Frommann-Holzboog, 1996–.

Wigand, Johannes. *Postilla: Ausslegung der Euangelien, soll man durch das gantze Jar auff einen jeden Sontag vnd fürnemste Fest in der Kirchen pfleget für zutragen.* Translated by Christopher Obenhin. Ursel: Nikolaus Henricus, 1569. Digital copy online at www.gateway-bayern.de.

Williams, George H., and Angel M. Mergal, eds. *Spiritual and Anabaptist Writers.* Library of Christian Classics 25. Philadelphia: Westminster Press, 1957.

Woolton, John. *The Christian Manual; or, of the Life and Manners of True Christians (1576).* Cambridge: Cambridge University Press, 1851. Digital copy online at archive.org.

Zwingli, Huldrych. *Huldrici Zuinglii Opera.* 8 vols. Edited by Johann Melchior Schuler and Johannes Schulthess. Zurich: F. Schulthess, 1828–1842. The first two volumes are German works. Digital copies online at babel.hathitrust.org.

————. *D. Hvldrichi Zvinglii in Plerosqve Novi Testamenti Libros Qvorvm Elenchum Post Praefationem & Indicem Reperies, Annotationes ex Ipsius Ore Exceptae per Leonem Ivdae. Adiecta Est Epistola Pavli ad Hebraeos, & Ioannis Apostoli Epistola per Gasparem Megandrum.* Edited by Leo Jud and Kaspar Megander Zurich: Christoph Froschauer, 1581. Digital copy online at www.gateway-bayern. de.

————. *A Briefe Rehersal of the Death, Resurrection and Ascension of Christ, Gathered Together Oute of the Foure Euangelistes and Acts of the Apostles by the Most Godly and Great Learned Man Huldriche Zuinglius.* London: John Daye, 1560. Accessed digitally via EEBO.

Other Works Consulted

Bernard of Clairvaux. *Sermons for Lent and the Easter Season.* Translated by Irene Edmonds. Edited by Mark A. Scott. Cistercian Fathers Series 52. Collegeville, MN: Liturgical Press, 2013.

Bettenson, Henry, and Chris Maunder, eds. *Documents of the Christian Church.* 3rd ed. Oxford: Oxford University Press, 1999.

Beza, Theodore. *Theodori Bezae Annotationes Majores in Novum Dn. Nostri Jesu Christi Testamentum.* 2 vols. Geneva: Jeremie des Planches, 1594. Digital copy online at www.e-rara.ch.

Biblia Sacra: Cum Glossa Oridinaria et Nicolai Lyrani Expositionibus, Literali et Morali. 6 vols. Lyon: Vincent, 1545.

Bovon, François. *Luke: A Commentary.* 3 vols. Translated by Christine M. Thomas, Donald S. Deer and James Crouch. Edited by Helmut Koester. Minneapolis: Fortress, 2002–2013.

Burnett, Amy Nelson. *Karlstadt and the Origins of the Eucharistic Controversy: A Study in the Circulation of Ideas.* Oxford: Oxford University Press, 2011.

Chung-Kim, Esther, and Todd R. Hains, eds. *Acts.* Reformation Commentary on Scripture New Testament 6. Downers Grove, IL: IVP Academic, 2014.

Chrysologus, Peter. *Selected Sermons Volume 3.* Translated by William B. Palardy. Fathers of the Church 110. Washington, DC: Catholic University of America Press, 2005.

Elowsky, Joel C., ed. *John 11–21.* Ancient Christian Commentary on Scripture New Testament 4b. Downers Grove, IL: InterVarsity Press, 2007.

Finger, Thomas N. *A Contemporary Anabaptist Theology: Biblical, Historical, Constructive.* Downers Grove, IL: InterVarsity Press, 2004.

Just, Arthur A., ed. *Luke.* Ancient Christian Commentary on Scripture New Testament 3. Downers Grove, IL: InterVarsity Press, 2003.

Malina, Bruce J., and Richard L. Rohrbaugh. *Social-Science Commentary on the Synoptic Gospels.* Minneapolis: Fortress, 1992.

Manetsch, Scott M., ed. *1-2 Corinthians.* Reformation Commentary on Scripture New Testament 9. Downers Grove, IL: IVP Academic, forthcoming.

McKim, Donald K., ed. *Dictionary of Major Biblical Interpreters.* Downers Grove, IL: InterVarsity Press, 2007.

Mohr, Melissa. *Holy Sh*t: A Brief History of Swearing.* New York: Oxford University Press, 2013.

Muller, Richard A. *Dictionary of Latin and Greek Theological Terms.* Grand Rapids: Baker Academic, 1995.

Peters, Edward, ed. *Heresy and Authority in Medieval Europe.* Philadelphia: University of Pennsylvania Press, 1980.

Poll, G. J. van de. *Martin Bucer's Liturgical Ideas: The Strasburg Reformer and His Connection with the Liturgies of the Sixteenth Century.* Assen: Van Gorcum, 1954.

Raitt, Jill. *The Colloquy of Montbéliard: Religion and Politics in the Sixteenth Century*. New York: Oxford University Press, 1993.

Stephens, W. P. *The Theology of Huldrych Zwingli*. Oxford: Clarendon Press, 1986.

Strauss, Emmauel. *Dictionary of European Proverbs*. 3 vols. London: Routledge, 1994.

Thompson, Bard. *Liturgies of the Western Church*. Minneapolis: Fortress, 1980.

Thompson, John L. "'So Ridiculous a Sign': Men, Women, and the Lessons of Circumcision in Sixteenth-Century Exegesis." *Archiv für Reformationsgeschichte* 86 (1995): 236-56.

Tomlin, Graham, ed. *Philippians, Colossians*. Reformation Commentary on Scripture New Testament 11. Downers Grove, IL: IVP Academic, 2012.

Wandel, Lee Palmer. *The Eucharist in the Reformation: Incarnation and Liturgy*. Cambridge: Cambridge University Press, 2006.

Winston-Allen, Anne. *Stories of the Rose: The Making of the Rosary in the Middle Ages*. University Park: Pennsylvania State University Press, 1997.

Author and Writings Index

Subject Index

Scripture Index